# A CASEBOOK ON SCOTTISH CRIMINAL LAW

AUSTRALIA
LBC Information Services—Sydney

CANADA and USA
Carswell—Toronto

NEW ZEALAND
Brooker's—Auckland

SINGAPORE and MALAYSIA
Sweet & Maxwell Asia
Singapore and Kuala Lumpur

# A CASEBOOK ON SCOTTISH CRIMINAL LAW
# (3rd EDITION)

Christopher H.W. Gane, LL.B.,
*Professor of Scots Law, University of Aberdeen*

Charles N. Stoddart, LL.B., LL.M. (McGill), Ph.D., S.S.C.,
*Sheriff of Lothian and Borders at Edinburgh*
and
James Chalmers, LL.B., LL.M., Dip.L.P.,
*Lecturer in Law, University of Aberdeen*

EDINBURGH
W. GREEN/Sweet & Maxwell
2001

Published in 2001 by W. Green & Son Ltd
21 Alva Street
Edinburgh EH2 4PS

Reprinted 2007

*Typeset by Mendip Communications Ltd*
*Printed and bound in Great Britain by MPG Books Ltd, Bodmin, Cornwall*

No natural forests were destroyed to make this product;
only farmed timber was used and replanted

A CIP catalogue record for this book is available from
the British Library

ISBN 978 0 414 01050 5

# PREFACE TO THIRD EDITION

Since the last edition of this work was published in 1988, the criminal law of Scotland has developed at a fast pace. A number of old uncertainties have been removed, only to be replaced by new points of difficulty, not least of all in relation to the impact of the Human Rights Act 1998 and the human rights provisions of the Scotland Act 1998. The workload of the courts has increased greatly, leading to an increased number of appeals, in some of which a Full Bench has been convened to review and clarify the principles of the law. Hardly any area has escaped some scrutiny, leading us firmly to the view that we too needed to revisit our earlier work.

This new edition has been fully revised. We have not hesitated to increase in depth our examination of some of the basic concepts of our law, nor to jettison some of the material which has been overtaken by events. We have noted with interest the greater use by the High Court of comparative material from other jurisdictions (not just England) and have included excerpts of decisions where this is appropriate. But many old friends will still be found in their accustomed places.

We have, once again, tried to meet the needs of the student and practitioner market by the increased coverage we have attempted to provide. In making our selections we acknowledge the helpful suggestions we have received from many quarters. We are especially pleased to acknowledge the contribution of James Chalmers in the task of selecting, editing and commenting upon the material in this edition. Special thanks are also due to Frazer McCallum, formerly of the University of Aberdeen and to Christine Gane who prepared the Index and Tables.

As usual, the staff of W. Green & Son., including Karen Taylor, Neil McKinlay and Carole McMurray, have been very supportive throughout. We are indebted to them all.

We have included cases decided up to May 1, 2001.

Aberdeen and Edinburgh
June 2001

CHRISTOPHER GANE
CHARLES N. STODDART

# PREFACE TO SECOND EDITION

Eight years have elapsed since publication of the first edition of this book. During that time there has been a considerable increase in the number of crimes, criminal cases decided and criminal cases reported. We are of course concerned with the latter, which explains the somewhat larger size of this volume compared to the earlier version. Indeed, the reporting of criminal cases has been greatly improved by one event above all others: the publication of the series of *Scottish Criminal Case Reports* under the auspices of the Law Society of Scotland. This series began in 1981, so we have been fortunate enough to be able to draw upon the considerable range of reported material contained therein, as well as tapping the longer-established books of authority.

In this edition we have permitted ourselves the indulgence of somewhat longer notes on the decisions, and we have rearranged the order of some of the chapters. We had added a chapter on malicious mischief, in view of the decision in *H.M. Advocate v. Wilson*, 1984 S.L.T. 117, and we have not shirked from the regular use of comparative material and excerpts from relevant statutes. We have again deliberately ignored matters of procedure and evidence, and the entire topic of road traffic law.

We are glad to acknowledge the permission we received from the Scottish Council for Law Reporting to reproduce excerpts from judgments contained in **Justiciary Cases** and **Session Cases**; and from Her Majesty's Stationery Office to reproduce extracts from Lord Cooper's evidence to the Royal Commission on Capital Punishment and the Scottish Law Commission's report on the Mental Element in Crime. We are also indebted to our many friends and colleagues who have encouraged us to complete this edition. That it has been completed at all is a tribute to the forebearance particularly of our respective families, who have had to suffer our many late nights of research.

We have included cases decided up to 29 February 1988.

Edinburgh
June 1988

C. H. W. GANE
C. N. STODDART

# PREFACE TO FIRST EDITION

It is often said that Scots law is a system based on principle, rather than precedent. But with regard to Scots criminal law, this shibboleth becomes harder to justify as the years pass; indeed it is doubtful whether it ever applied even at the time of Hume, who is generally regarded as the father of our criminal law.

The primary sources for Hume's *Commentaries* were the Books of Adjournal for the previous century, in which there were recorded the actual decisions of the Court of Justiciary from its inception in 1672. In the late eighteenth century two selections of criminal cases, by Maclaurin and Arnot respectively, were published in an attempt to illustrate the then practice of the court; the strong influence of the case law on crimes has persisted ever since. In the twentieth century the publication of textbooks on criminal law was intermittent and unsatisfactory until the first edition of Gordon's *Criminal Law* appeared in 1967, to be followed by a second edition 11 years later. However no modern collection of Scottish criminal cases has been compiled, and so we decided to attempt the task.

The present work is intended primarily for students of criminal law in Scottish universities, although we hope it will appeal to a wider readership. The experience of teaching the subject which each of us has gained over the past few years has convinced us of the need for such a volume, as an aid to study and as a supplement to other teaching materials. As will be seen from the table of contents, we cover both the general theory and the law relating to those crimes commonly encountered in practice. For many of these topics Scottish authority abounds, but where none is available we have not hesitated to include materials drawn from other jurisdictions.

Two matters are however outwith the scope of the work. First, we have dealt only in passing with criminal procedure, because the system seems likely to be altered in a number of material respects by the Criminal Justice (Scotland) Bill which is presently before Parliament. Although the basic division into solemn and summary cases will continue, the mechanics of trials and appeals under both will be affected by the new provisions to such a marked extent that a sizeable body of case law will be rendered obsolete, doubtless to be succeeded by new and, as yet, unforeseen problems. Secondly, we have deliberately excluded road traffic law from our collection. Many of the points which have arisen recently before the Scots courts on this subject have related to procedure and sentence, not least of all in connection with the breathalyser provisions of the Road Traffic Act 1972. These too are to be made the subject of legislation in the near future, and so it seemed singularly inapt to include cases thereon on this work.

We have however managed to assemble a certain amount of unreported material including a Full Bench decision in 1949 on the question of automatism which graces the pages of neither the *Justiciary Cases* nor the *Scots Law Times*. Where appropriate, we have also included excerpts from the Institutional writers and references to other cases and statutes.

We are pleased to acknowledge here the assistance given to us by Mr W. Howard and the staff of the Justiciary Office in making much material available to us and for their patience in dealing with our repeated requests. We are also obliged to the publishers for the assistance at every turn in the preparation of the work. Each of us has been responsible for different sections of this volume but we have each read and commented on the work of the other; we hereby accept "art and part" liability for the contents.

The cases included are those decided up to 31 May 1980.

Edinburgh  
June 1980

C. H. W. GANE  
C. N. STODDART

# TABLE OF CONTENTS

## PART I—GENERAL PRINCIPLES OF CRIMINAL RESPONSIBILITY

### CHAPTER 1

### GENERAL CHARACTERISTICS AND SOURCES OF SCOTTISH CRIMINAL LAW

### CHAPTER 2

### *ACTUS REUS AND MENS REA*

## CHAPTER 3

# STRICT LIABILITY, VICARIOUS LIABILITY AND CORPORATE LIABILITY

## CHAPTER 4

# CAUSATION

## PART II—OFFENCES AGAINST PERSONAL INTEGRITY

### CHAPTER 8

### NON-FATAL OFFENCES AGAINST THE PERSON

Chapter 9

# SEXUAL OFFENCES

Chapter 10

# HOMICIDE AND RELATED MATTERS

# PART III

## OFFENCES AGAINST PROPERTY INTERESTS

CHAPTER 11

### THEFT, EMBEZZLEMENT AND RELATED OFFENCES

CHAPTER 12

### ROBBERY AND EXTORTION

CHAPTER 13

### FRAUD, FORGERY AND UTTERING

## CHAPTER 14

## **RESET**

## CHAPTER 15

## **DAMAGING AND DESTROYING PROPERTY**

## **PART IV**

## **OFFENCES AGAINST COMMUNITY INTERESTS**

## CHAPTER 16

## **OFFENCES AGAINST PUBLIC ORDER AND DECENCY**

## CHAPTER 17

## **OFFENCES AGAINST THE COURSE OF JUSTICE**

# TABLE OF CASES

Location references are to paragraph numbers. **Bold** paragraph numbering refers to extracts of cases.

## Table of Cases before the European Court / Commission of Human Rights

# TABLE OF CONVENTIONS

Location references are to paragraph numbers. The paragraph reference is in **bold** where the legislation is reproduced in full.

# TABLE OF STATUTES

References are to paragraph numbers. The paragraph numbers in **bold** refer to legislation reproduced in full.

# TABLE OF STATUTORY INSTRUMENTS

Location references are to paragraph numbers.

# Chapter 1

# General Characteristics and Sources of Scottish Criminal Law

## 1. General characteristics of the criminal law of Scotland

Nearly fifty years ago, in a memorandum submitted to the Royal Commission on Capital Punishment, **1.01** the Lord Justice-General (Cooper) described the substantive criminal law in the following terms (*Royal Commission on Capital Punishment,* Minutes of Evidence, p. 428):

> "The Scottish law of crime is not statutory but almost exclusively common law, which has been and is still being evolved by judicial decisions applied with anxious care to the precise facts of actual cases. It is contrary to the tradition and genius of our criminal law to deal with its basic conceptions *in vacuo.* No two cases are exactly alike, and very slight distinctions in the circumstances may tilt the balance as between murder and culpable homicide, and even as between innocence and guilt. By the application of our native methods to our native principles, it has proved possible (within the limits of human fallibility) to keep the law sufficiently flexible and elastic to enable a just discrimination to be applied to the ascertained facts of each case, and sufficiently rigid to prevent proved guilt from escaping the just consequences on any mere technicality ..."

Although Lord Cooper was principally concerned with the law of homicide, his remarks concerning the importance of the common law are as true today as they were in the 1950s. Thus, most offences against the person (such as murder, assault and rape), property interests (such as theft, fraud, and malicious mischief), most offences against public order and decency (breach of the peace, mobbing and shameless indecency), offences against the course of justice, inchoate offences and the general principles of criminal responsibility, are all dependent upon the common law.

But it is important to remember that, while large areas of the substantive criminal law are not governed by statute, this is not the same thing as saying that legislation has had very little impact on the bulk of cases handled by the Scottish courts. The criminal courts deal with many thousands of statutory offences every year—particularly in the area of road traffic—so that it would be fair to say that although the "criminal code" is very largely based on the common law, in practice statutory crimes make up a substantial proportion of the business of the courts.

Lord Cooper's remarks concerning the flexibility of the common law, are, if anything, even more true today than they were when he made them. The period since Lord Cooper wrote, and in particular the period spanning the mid-1970s to the present day, have demonstrated beyond any argument the willingness of public prosecutors to take advantage of this flexibility, and the largely uncritical acceptance by the courts of the virtue of judicial development of the criminal law. The chapters which follow provide many examples of reliance upon the criminal law to meet new forms of behaviour which has been perceived as anti-social and deserving of criminal sanctions. The classic example of this is perhaps to be found in the case of *Khaliq v. H.M. Advocate,* 1984 S.L.T 137 (*post,* Chapter 4) in which it was held that persons who supplied what could be described as "glue-sniffing kits" to children and young persons could be held guilty of a crime at common law. That decision was taken to its logical conclusion in the *Lord Advocate's Reference (No. 1 of 1994)* 1995 S.L.T. 248, in which it was held that where a person used a controlled drug unlawfully supplied to her by a drug-pusher and died as a result of that use, the supplier could properly be convicted of culpable homicide. While most people would agree that the conduct of the offenders in these cases was reprehensible, and deserving of punishment, the manner in which this was achieved is open to criticism. And the chapters which follow provide examples of cases in which reliance upon the criminal law is much more questionable, cases in which the conduct of the accused is not self-evidently deserving of criminal sanctions, or at least cases in which the use of the criminal law is much less well-supported by a broad consensus of public opinion. See, in this respect, the cases on "shameless indecency" (*post*, Chapter 17). The flexibility of the criminal law, and the willingness of prosecutors and courts to use this flexibility to develop the criminal law is, of course, a matter which will now have to be addressed in light of the Human Rights Act 1998, and in particular in the light of the principle of legality as it is expressed in Article 7 of the European Convention on Human Rights (as to which, see *post*, pp. 7 to 8).

## 2. SOURCES OF THE CRIMINAL LAW

### A. Domestic legislation

**1.02** As a source of criminal law, legislation performs three functions in the criminal law of Scotland. In the first place, it provides a regulatory framework for a wide range of modern technological, economic and social phenomena. So, for example, most of the criminal law relating to the use of motor vehicles is statutory. So too are many "economic" offences such as insider dealing and other offences regulating corporate and financial affairs. Offences intended for the promotion of public safety (such as firearms regulation, food hygiene regulations and health and safety laws) are likewise statute-based. Offences directed towards regulating the use of drugs and preventing their misuse are also creations of statute. There are two reasons why legislation predominates in these areas. The first is, simply, that the common law provides few appropriate rules to govern the activities in question. There is, for example, no common law rule which prohibits a motor vehicle being driven at a speed of more than thirty miles an hour in a built-up area. There is a common law rule which prohibits the reckless driving of vehicles, but it is felt that the demands of public safety require stricter regulation than is provided by the common law, hence the statutory regulation of speed limits. The second reason is that legislation provides a legal device which, it is believed, promotes the ends of the criminal law in many of these areas. This is the doctrine of "strict liability" which allows the imposition of criminal responsibility without proof of intention, recklessness or any other degree of fault on the part of the offender. (It is thus no defence to a charge of exceeding a statutory speed limit that the driver was unaware of the limit in question.) This is a device which is not recognised by the common law, and, to the extent that strict liability is seen as an important element of criminal policy, places a limitation on the use of the common law as a regulatory device.

The second, and much less frequent, role for legislation is to supplement the criminal law in areas where there already exists some relevant common law rule. An example of this is to be found in the legislation regulating sexual relations with girls under sixteen. Prior to the end of the nineteenth century, the common law prohibited sexual relations with girls under the age of puberty (for these purposes, the age of twelve). Thus it was (and remains) rape for a man to have sexual intercourse with a girl under the age of 12. However, it was not an offence for a man to engage in any form of sexual activity with a girl who had reached the age of puberty provided that the girl consented. Various statutory offences dating from the end of the nineteenth century (and now contained in the Criminal Law (Consolidation) (Scotland) Act 1995 (see, *post*, Chapter 9) have extended the protection of the criminal law to girls above that age. Thus section 5(1) of that Act makes it an offence (punishable with up to life imprisonment) for a man to have unlawful sexual intercourse with a girl under the age of 13. Section 5(3) similarly makes it an offence (punishable with up to ten years' imprisonment) for a man to have unlawful sexual intercourse with a girl aged between 13 and sixteen.

The third role for legislation—and one which again is only infrequently encountered—is to abolish offences, or to de-criminalise conduct which has hitherto been regarded as criminal.

As a general rule, legislation emanates either from the domestic legislature, or, in certain areas, from the European Community. The competence of the European Community in criminal matters is very restricted, and in general one can say that community law is not a direct source of criminal offences. However, as in all other areas of the law, it is not possible completely to ignore community law, and its significance as a source of criminal law is discussed below. This section concentrates on domestic legislation as a source of criminal law.

Four types of such legislation can be identified: (a) Acts of the United Kingdom Parliament; (b) Acts of the Scottish Parliament; (c) Acts of the Parliaments of Scotland; (d) Subordinate legislation.

## (a) Acts of the United Kingdom Parliament

As the supreme legislature for the United Kingdom, the Westminster parliament may create criminal **1.03** offences which apply throughout the United Kingdom, or which apply only to designated parts of that state. Modern legislation generally contains a section stating explicitly the extent of application of the Act's provisions. Where an Act is silent as to its application, it has traditionally been presumed to extend throughout the United Kingdom. With the creation of the Scottish Parliament, however, and the division of legislative competence between the latter and Westminster, any such presumption must be read subject to the proviso that that the legislation does not concern matters which fall within the devolved competence of the Scottish Parliament.

Where legislation creating a criminal offence applies throughout the United Kingdom the Scottish courts will pay particular attention to the construction placed upon those provisions by the courts in other parts of the United Kingdom. They are not, however, obliged to follow the decisions of courts in England or Northern Ireland. In *Keane v. Gallacher*, 1980 J.C. 77, the accused was found to be in possession of two minute quantities of cannabis resin, and was charged with possession of the drug, contrary to section 5(2) of the Misuse of Drugs Act 1971. The sheriff, following the decision of the Court of Appeal (Criminal Division) in *R. v. Carver* [1978] 2 W.L.R. 872, held that the quantities of cannabis involved were so small that they could not be used for any purpose struck at by the Act, and acquitted the accused. The prosecutor's appeal against acquittal was upheld by the High Court. In its opinion the Court while paying "proper regard" to the decision of the Court of Appeal in the case of *R. v. Carver*, and stating that it would "not lightly differ from it" preferred to examine the question afresh for itself, since the matter had never before come before the High Court. Having examined the case of *Carver* and other English authorities, the Court concluded that it preferred a test of 'measurability' as opposed to the test of 'usability' adopted in *Carver*. See also, in this context, the decision of the High Court in *Ritchie v. Pirie*, 1972 J.C. 7.

## (b) Acts of the Scottish Parliament

## (i) The legislative powers of the Parliament

The Scottish Parliament was created by section 1(1) of the Scotland Act 1998 which, with historic **1.04** simplicity, states: "There shall be a Scottish Parliament." Following elections in May of 1999, the Parliament assumed its legislative functions on July 1, 1999. The Parliament has the power, within its legislative competence, to make laws, known as Acts of the Scottish Parliament: Scotland Act 1998, s.28(1). An Act of the Scottish Parliament is not law "so far as any provision of the Act is outside the legislative competence of the Parliament": s.29(1). A provision is outside that competence if, amongst other considerations:

— it relates to a 'reserved matter', *i.e.*, a matter reserved to the Westminster Parliament: s.29(1)(b) and Schedule 5;
— it is in breach of restrictions set out in Schedule 4 to the Scotland Act (which, amongst other things, prevents the Parliament from modifying the law on reserved matters, provides that the Parliament cannot modify the Scotland Act itself, and protects the Human Rights Act 1998 from modification by the Scottish Parliament): s.29(1)(c) and Schedule 4;
— it is in breach of or it is incompatible with any of the Convention Rights contained in the Human Rights Act 1998 or with Community Law: s.29(1)(d) and s.126(1).

## (ii) Criminal law and reserved matters

**1.05**   The "reserved matters"—those matters on which the Scottish Parliament cannot legislate—are set out in Schedule 5 to the Act. For the most part, "Scots criminal law" is not a reserved matter. The Parliament may therefore create offences, abolish or modify existing offences, and legislate on matters of criminal procedure and criminal penalties. To the extent that this may be necessary, it may also pass criminal legislation relating to other devolved matters.

There are, however, some significant qualifications to this general principle. These arise because Scots criminal law touches upon a great many "reserved matters" as these are defined by Schedule 5 to the Act. Within the broad range of reserved matters, many areas in which the criminal law plays a particularly important role, are beyond the general legislative competence of the Scottish Parliament. These include taxes and excise duties, currency (coinage, legal tender and bank notes), financial services and the regulation of financial markets, money laundering, misuse of drugs, data protection, firearms, immigration and nationality, national security, interception of communications, official secrets and terrorism, import and export controls, consumer protection and road transport. One reserved area over which there has been particular controversy is that of abortion.

Suppose, now, that the Scottish Parliament were to pass legislation enacting, for example, general principles of criminal responsibility, which were to be applied by the Scottish criminal courts. These principles would be capable of application not only to the general criminal law, but also to the criminal law as it relates to reserved matters. In so far as the legislation does not relate to a reserved matter (the criminal law) it would be within the legislative competence of the Parliament. But in so far as it relates, for example, to the law on misuse of drugs, it would relate to a reserved matter and be outwith the Parliament's legislative competence.

This general problem is addressed in section 29(4) of the Scotland Act. This section states that a legislative provision of the Parliament which would not otherwise relate to reserved matters but which makes modifications to Scots private law or Scots criminal law as it applies to reserved matters, is to be treated as if it related to a reserved matter. The effect of this is, in the example given above, to place the provision concerning general principles of criminal responsibility outwith the legislative competence of the Parliament. However, if the purpose of the provision is to "make the law in question apply consistently to reserved matters and otherwise" then, according to section 29(4), it will not be treated as relating to reserved matters and will therefore be within the legislative competence of the Parliament.

## (iii) Legislative competence and Human Rights

**1.06**   A legislative provision of the Parliament which is incompatible with any of the "Convention Rights" is outside the legislative competence of the Parliament, and therefore not law: section 29(1) and 29(2)(d). For these purposes "Convention Rights" are the rights set out in the Human Rights Act 1998: Scotland Act, section 126(1). The scope of these rights and the impact of the Human Rights Act on the criminal law of Scotland are discussed later in this chapter.

## (iii) Legislative competence and the power of the courts

**1.07**   While in most respects the Acts of the Scottish Parliament will be indistinguishable in their effect from Acts of the Westminster Parliament, there is one critical difference between them. No court has the power to declare an Act of the Westminster Parliament to be invalid. Acts of the Westminster Parliament, once passed, cannot be challenged on the ground that they are outwith the legislative competence of that Parliament. It is true that directly applicable and directly effective rules of European law prevail over inconsistent domestic law, but even this does not give the courts the power to strike down Acts of the Westminster Parliament. (See *R. v. Secretary of State for Transport ex parte Factortame Ltd (No. 3)* [1992] Q.B. 680.)

Matters are entirely otherwise in the case of Acts of the Scottish Parliament. Since an Act of the Scottish Parliament "is not law" (section 29(1)) so far as it is outside the legislative competence of the Parliament, the courts (both in Scotland and elsewhere in the United Kingdom) will have the power to hold that an Act of the Scottish Parliament is invalid on the ground that it was not within the legislative competence of the Parliament to pass the measure in question. If an Act is held to be invalid, then it cannot be applied as law.

It is important to notice, furthermore, that the power to hold that a legislative provision is outside the competence of the Parliament is not restricted to the higher courts (as it is in some other jurisdictions). Any court—from the district court upwards—is entitled to consider and determine questions of legislative competence. However, the lower courts are not obliged to resolve such issues, and section 98 and Schedule 6 of the Scotland Act makes provision for such questions to be referred to higher courts for resolution.

## (c) Acts of the Parliaments of Scotland

Prior to 1707, the Scottish Parliament legislated frequently in the field of criminal law. Most of this **1.08** legislation is now repealed, either expressly or by virtue of the doctrine of desuetude. According to the latter doctrine, an Act of the Scottish Parliament may be held to have been impliedly repealed on proof of long established practice contrary to the legislation or where the legislation is accepted as being out of line with modern conditions. (See *McAra v. Magistrates of Edinburgh*, 1913 S.C. 1059; *Brown v. Magistrates of Edinburgh*, 1931 S.L.T. 456.) A few examples, however, remain in force. One such example is the Theft Act 1607, which provides a particular statutory example of the crime of theft of "Beis and fisches in propir stankis and loches". For cases discussing the terms of this Act, see *Pollok v. McCabe and Another* (1909) 6 Adam 139 and *Valentine v. Kennedy*, 1985 S.C.C.R. 89.

## (d) Subordinate legislation

Subordinate legislation is legislation passed by a body other than the Westminster Parliament or the **1.09** Scottish Parliament by virtue of powers delegated to it by one or other of those bodies. Legislation of this kind may be made by a variety of bodies, but it is most frequently made by Ministers of the Crown (*i.e.* Ministers at Westminster) or Scottish Ministers (*i.e.* members of the Scottish Executive: Scotland Act, section 44(1) and (2)). Such legislation is to be found in measures known as "statutory instruments" (see Scotland Act, 1998, section 112(5)). Local government bodies may also pass subordinate legislation in the shape of byelaws. A body of subordinate legislation particular to the Scottish criminal justice system is know as "Acts of Adjournal". These are subordinate rules of criminal procedure drawn up by the High Court of Justiciary to regulate criminal practice, and are supplementary to the rules of procedure contained in legislation such as the Criminal Procedure (Scotland) Act 1995.

Like legislation of the Scottish Parliament, subordinate legislation is subject to judicial review, and a court may strike down a piece of subordinate legislation on the ground that it is *"ultra vires"*—outside the legislative competence of the body which purported to draw it up. There is, however, a presumption in favour of the validity of subordinate legislation. See *Aldred v. Miller*, 1925 J.C. 21; *McCallum v. Brown*, 2000 S.L.T. 97.

By a convenient fiction, the judges in all courts are presumed to know the terms of all Acts of Parliament, and such legislation is produced in court merely to 'remind' the court of the precise terms of the law. (See, for example, *Herkes v. Dickie*, 1959 S.L.T. 74, *per* Lord Patrick at p. 76.) In contrast to Acts of the Westminster Parliament and the Scottish Parliament, the terms of subordinate legislation, which does not have the force of a statute, must be proved in court if challenged. (See, *inter alia, Todd v. Anderson*, 1912 S.C. (J.) 105; *Brander v. Mackenzie*, 1915 S.C. (J.) 47; *MacMillan v. McConnell*, 1917 J.C. 43; *Herkes v. Dickie*, 1958 J.C. 51; *Knox v. Lockhart*, 1985 S.L.T. 248; *Donnelly v. Carmichael*, 1996 S.L.T. 153.

Under section 279A(3) of the Criminal Procedure (Scotland) Act 1995, "any order made by any of the departments of state or government or any local authority or public body made under powers conferred by any statute or a print or a copy of such order, shall when produced in a prosecution be received as evidence of the due making, confirmation, and existence of the order without being sworn to by any witness and without any further or other proof". This provision is without prejudice to the accused's right to challenge any order as being *ultra vires* of the authority making it or any other competent ground: Criminal Procedure (Scotland) Act 1995, s.279A(4).

## *(e) Interpreting criminal statutes*

**1.10**  In construing legislation in the criminal sphere the courts apply the general principles of statutory interpretation. These include the rule that the words of a statute are to be given their ordinary meaning, unless that results in a manifestly absurd result, and, most significantly, the rule, contained in section 3 of the Human Rights Act 1998 that, so far as it is possible to do so, primary legislation and subordinate legislation must be read and given effect in a way which is compatible with the Convention rights (see below, at p. 11).

There are, in addition, certain guidelines which are of particular importance in relation to criminal statutes. The most important of these is said to be the rule that statutes which impose criminal penalties are to be construed narrowly, so that criminal liability is not imposed unless the court is satisfied that this was clearly the intention of the legislature in creating the offence. In *H.M. Advocate v. Mackenzie*, 1970 S.L.T. 81, the Lord Justice-Clerk (Grant) stated in relation to the statute which created the offence of incest, which dated from 1567, that "clear language is required for the creation of a criminal offence", particularly where the offence could carry a substantial penalty such as a lengthy period of imprisonment. Similarly, in *Friel v. Initial Contract Services Ltd*, 1994 S.L.T. 1216, it was stated (by Lord McCluskey at p. 1221H–I) that there is "a well understood principle in relation to the interpretation of statutes that in cases of doubt and ambiguity the statute should be construed in favour of the liberty of the subject". See also *Barty v. Hill*, 1907 S.C. (J.) 36 and *Perry v. West*, 2000 S.L.T. 363. In the latter case the Lord Justice Clerk observed that "penal provisions should not be read as creating a wider scope by implication unless the implication is clear".

This approach to the construction of criminal statutes is in marked contrast to the manner in which the Courts have been prepared to develop the common law. Here, as is discussed below, the Courts have shown no reluctance to extend the criminal law by a process of interpretation which permits the extension of criminal liability by analogy, and by frequently expansive interpretation of the definition of existing offences.

## B. The Common Law

### *(a) Judicial development of the Common law*

**1.11**  We have already noted that Scottish criminal law is very substantially based on the common law. This means that the courts play a central role in the development of the law, and it is fundamental to the understanding of the Scottish approach to criminal law to recognise that the common law is not regarded as inflexible and unchanging. As the Lord Justice-General (Clyde) stated in *McLaughlan v. Boyd*, 1933 S.L.T. 629, at p. 631:

> "It would be a mistake to imagine that the criminal law of Scotland countenances any precise and exact categorisation of the forms of conduct which amount to crime. It has been pointed out many times in this Court that such is not the nature or quality of the criminal law of Scotland."

The courts have from time to time taken advantage of this flexibility to create new defences to criminal charges. For example, the case of *Alexander Dingwall* (1867) 5 Irvine 466, saw the judicial creation of the defence of diminished responsibility (see below, Chapter 10). In most instances, however, the flexibility of the criminal law has been used for the purpose of extending the criminal law. This is typically done where some new or previously unencountered form of anti-social behaviour is encountered. The courts have also justified extending the scope of criminal offences where they consider that the existing law is out of keeping with contemporary attitudes, as the following case illustrates.

### S. v. H.M. Advocate
#### 1989 S.L.T. 469

The appellant was charged, *inter alia*, with raping his wife. An objection to the relevancy of the charge was repelled by the trial judge. The appellant's objection was based on the rule, dating from Hume's time (Hume, i, 306) that a husband could not be guilty of raping his wife. This rule was, according to Hume, based on a presumption of consent on the part of the wife arising from the fact of marriage.

OPINION OF THE COURT: "... By the second half of the twentieth century, however, the status of women, and the status of a married woman, in our law have changed quite dramatically. A husband and wife are now for all practical purposes equal partners in marriage and both husband and wife are tutors and curators of their children. A wife is not obliged to obey her husband in all things nor to suffer excessive sexual demands on the part of her husband. She may rely on such demands as evidence of unreasonable behaviour for the purposes of divorce. A live system of law will always have regard to changing circumstances to test the justification for any exception to the application of a general rule. Nowadays it cannot seriously be maintained that by marriage a wife submits herself irrevocably to sexual intercourse in all circumstances. It cannot be affirmed nowadays, whatever the position may have been in earlier centuries, that it is an incident of modern marriage that a wife consents to intercourse in all circumstances, including sexual intercourse obtained only by force. There is no doubt that a wife does not consent to assault upon her person and there is no plausible justification for saying today that she nevertheless is to be taken to consent to intercourse by assault.... The fiction of implied consent has no useful purpose to serve today in the law of rape in Scotland. The reason given by Hume for the husband's immunity from prosecution upon a charge of rape of his wife, if it ever was a good reason, no longer applies today. There is now, accordingly, no justification for the supposed immunity of a husband. Logically the only question is whether or not as matter of fact the wife consented to the acts complained of."

Appeal refused.

NOTES

1. A similar issue subsequently arose in the English case of *R. v. R.* [1992] 1 A.C. 599, in which the House of Lords reached a similar conclusion on English law. The decision in that case was subsequently challenged by the accused before the European Court of Human Rights on the ground that it violated Article 7 of the European Convention on Human Rights (which prohibits the retrospective imposition of criminal liability). See *post*, p. 14. **1.12**

2. Judicial extension of the criminal law is a controversial matter. On the one hand, it can be argued that a measure of flexibility in the criminal law is both inevitable and desirable. (See, in this regard, S. C. Styles, "Something to Declare: A Defence of the Declaratory Power of the High Court of Justiciary" in *Justice and Crime—Essays in Honour of the Rt Hon., The Lord Emslie* (R. F. Hunter ed., T. and T. Clark, Edinburgh, 1993)). A body of criminal law which cannot respond to new forms of anti-social behaviour, it is argued, would be impractical and undesirable, requiring frequent recourse to the legislature, which cannot always respond quickly enough or in terms which are appropriate to the perceived social threat.

3. On the other hand, judicial law-making is undemocratic and subject to inadequate external scrutiny. In its most extreme form, it confuses the judicial and legislative functions of government. The advent of the Human Rights Act 1998 may mean that for the future the extent of judicial creativity may be curbed since, although judicial development of the law is not contrary to the Convention Rights, the principle of legality, as reflected in those rights, means such development of the law must be kept within reasonable limits. This issue is further discussed below in the context of the Human Rights Act.

## (b) The declaratory power of the High Court

The most extreme example of the power of the courts to develop the criminal law is to be found in the so-called "declaratory power" of the High Court. In his *Commentaries* on the criminal law, Baron Hume (see *post*, p. 9) argued (Hume, i, 12) that the High Court of Justiciary had the power to declare criminal conduct which had not previously been regarded as a crime. Shortly afterwards, the High Court itself, in the case of *Bernard Greenhuff* (1838) 2 Swin. 236, held that it did indeed have such a power. (In that case it held that it was a crime to keep a public gaming house for profit.) That was the only case in which this power (which came to be known as the "declaratory power" of the High Court) was expressly **1.13** relied upon by the Court. It is, however, possible to point to cases in which this power, or something very close to it, was used to extend the criminal law in quite novel directions.

In *William Fraser* (1848) Arkley 280, the accused was charged with raping a woman by having intercourse with her while inducing her to believe that he was her husband, and, alternatively, with "fraudulently and deceitfully obtaining access to and having carnal knowledge of a married woman" by pretending to be her husband, or otherwise by deceiving her into believing that he was her husband. An objection to the relevancy of the charge of rape was upheld, but the alternative, innominate, charge was held relevant. A few years later, in the case of *Charles Sweenie* (1858) 3 Irvine 109, the court held that while a man could not be guilty of rape by having sexual intercourse with a woman while she was asleep, it was nonetheless an offence at common law "wickedly and feloniously" to have intercourse with a sleeping woman. In neither of the cases was the declaratory power invoked, but there is little doubt that the innominate charge in both cases was a complete novelty.

One of the clearest examples of the unacknowledged use of a declaratory power is to be found in the case of *Strathern v. Seaforth*, 1926 J.C. 100, *post*, p. 483, in which it was held to be a crime "clandestinely" to take possession of a motor car, and drive around without the permission of the owner, and knowing that such permission would not have been granted.

The most recent cases in which the High Court has been prepared to recognise the continued existence of the declaratory power are the cases of *Khaliq v. H.M. Advocate*, 1983 S.C.C.R. 483, 1984 S.C.C.R. 212 (*post*, p. 117) and *Grant v. Allan*, 1987 S.C.C.R. 402 (*post*, p. 451), although it should again be emphasised that the power was not in fact used in either case. In both of these cases the Crown demonstrated a willingness to rely on the declaratory power. In the first of these, the Court held that it was not necessary to do so, since the conduct in question (supplying "glue sniffing kits" to children and young persons) was already criminal. In the second, the court, although invited to apply the power to make it an offence dishonestly to "appropriate" commercially sensitive confidential information, declined to do so.

In practice, it has not proved necessary for the courts to rely on the declaratory power in order to develop the criminal law. They have been able to rely on the inherent flexibility of the common law, and the vagueness with which many offences are described ("defined" gives too great an air of precision). A common device (suggested by the opinion of Lord Cockburn in *Greenhuff*) is for the court to state, when extending the boundaries of the criminal law, that they are simply responding to new ways of committing established crimes.

The advent of the Human Rights Act 1998 and the Scotland Act 1998 should ensure that the declaratory power will not be invoked in the future. By virtue of these statutes, the European Convention on Human Rights is made enforceable in the Scottish courts. Article 7(1) of the Convention provides that "No one shall be held guilty of any criminal offence on account of any act or omission which did not constitute a criminal offence . . . at the time it was committed." While this provision does not prohibit the extension of the law by reasonable and foreseeable interpretation, it does prohibit the retrospective creation of new criminal offences. See, in this respect, *Kokkinakis v. Greece* (1994) 17 E.H.R.R. 297 and *SW v. United Kingdom, CR v. United Kingdom* (1995) 21 E.H.R.R. 363.

## (c) Judicial precedent and criminal law

**1.14**   Although Scots lawyers like to boast that our system is based on principle rather than precedent, the reality is rather different. Subject to what is said later about the interpretative duty on courts under section 3(1) of the Human Rights Act 1998, it is clear that in applying and developing the law, the courts have in practice observed a system of judicial precedent. Decisions of the High Court, when sitting as a court of appeal or review, on points of law, are binding on the High Court itself, and a quorum of the court is bound by a previous decision of a court of equal number: *Stair Encyclopaedia of the Laws of Scotland*, Vol. 22, para. 308l; *McAvoy v. Cameron*, 1917 J.C., p. 3; *Ritchie v. Pirie*, 1972 J.C., p. 14; *Elliott v. H.M. Advocate*, 1995 S.L.T. 612. The Court may be free to depart from an earlier decision which would otherwise be binding upon it if, for example, "the earlier case was decided on the basis of legislation which is no longer in force, or if in the earlier case the court's attention was not drawn to the existence of some relevant authority or no argument was addressed to the court on the subject being considered in the later case" (*Elliott v. H.M. Advocate, supra, per* the Lord Justice-Clerk (Ross) at pp. 615–616).

It is, however, possible for a binding decision of the High Court to be overturned by the High Court. This is done by convening a court consisting of a greater number of judges than were involved in taking the decision which is to be reviewed. Courts of five judges (see, for example, *Mcfadyen v. Stewart*, 1951 J.C. 164; *Brennan v. H.M. Advocate*; 1977 J.C. 38; *Elliott v. H.M. Advocate, supra*), seven judges (*Mitchell v. Morrison*, 1938 J.C. 64; *Todd v. H.M. Advocate*; 1983 S.C.C.R. 472), eleven judges (*Kirkwood v. H.M. Advocate*, 1939 J.C. 36) and twelve judges (*Sugden v. H.M. Advocate*, 1934 J.C. 103) have been convened to deal with difficult precedents.

It has been stated that in modern practice the purpose of convening a larger court is to obtain an authoritative statement of the law where it is in need of clarification or where there is a dispute about it in the existing authorities: *Lindsay v. H.M. Advocate*, 1997 S.L.T. 67, 1996 S.C.C.R. 870. Where the law has been clearly and consistently stated over a period of time, and no doubts have been cast upon the accuracy of that statement, reform of the law is a matter which should be left to Parliament, and should not be attempted by convening a larger court: *Lindsay v. H.M. Advocate, supra*.

Single judges of the High Court are bound by the decisions of the High Court sitting as a court of appeal or review, but they are not bound by decisions of other single judges in that court: *H.M. Advocate v. Higgins* (1914) 7 Adam 229. Judges in the sheriff and district courts are likewise bound to follow the rulings of the High Court sitting as a court of appeal or review (*Ritchie v. Pirie*, 1972 J.C. 7), but they are not bound to follow the decisions of other sheriffs or justices.

It has been held that a decision of a single judge of the High Court is a decision of the whole court itself and is thus binding on a sheriff (*Jessop v. Stevenson*, 1987 S.C.C.R. 655) but that case contains no extended discussion of the system of precedent in the context of the concurrent jurisdiction enjoyed (in many cases) by the High Court and the Sheriff court.

Section 3(1) of the Human Rights Act 1998, which provides that so far as it is possible to do so, legislation must be read and given effect in a way that is compatible with Convention rights, may alter the position, at least as regards statutory offences. It may not now be the case that decisions on appeal bind a lower court where to hold that they do would prevent the latter from complying with their duty (as public authorities under section 6(1) of the Act) to act in compliance with Convention rights. The first hint of this approach appeared in *O'Hagan v. Rea*, 2001 S.L.T. (Sh. Ct) 30, in which Sheriff Simpson dealt with the prosecution of a parent for her failure to secure the regular attendance by her child at school, contrary to section 35(1) of the Education (Scotland) Act 1980. That section provides the parent with a defence of "reasonable excuse", which term is further defined in section 42(1) and which was interpreted in two High Court decision (*Kiely v. Lunn*, 1982 S.C.C.R. 465 and *MacIntyre v. Annan*, 1991 S.C.C.R. 465) so as to confine it to circumstances affecting the child. The sheriff took the view that the current interpretation of section 35(1) was contrary to Article 6 of the European Convention on Human Rights, and applied section 3(1) of the Human Rights Act (which he described as "relentless" and preventing the maintenance of the doctrine of *stare decisis*) so as to include within section 42(1) of the 1980 Act circumstances relating to the parent as well as those relating to the child, a construction of the section which would be compatible with Article 6. In doing so, the sheriff declined to follow the two earlier High Court decisions which he described as no longer accurately expressing the law of Scotland. (*Cf. Maan v. H.M. Advocate*, 2001 S.L.T. 408.)

## C. Legal writings

It is a feature of Scots law in general that the works of certain writers, known as "Institutional writers", **1.15** occupy a particular status as sources of the law. In the field of criminal law, Baron David Hume's *Commentaries on the Law of Scotland Respecting Crimes* (commonly known as "Hume on Crimes", or often simply as "Hume") enjoy a pre-eminent position as a source of modern Scottish criminal law, despite the fact that the first edition was published in 1797–1800, and the standard edition (containing supplementary notes by Benjamin Bell) in 1844. If anything, Hume's significance is greater today than it was 20 years ago, and arguably Hume's status as an "Institutional writer" on criminal law has greater practical significance than "Institutional writings" in other areas of the law. Certainly the High Court relies to a much greater extent on Hume than does the Court of Session on Stair or Erskine. To a certain extent, this is simply a reflection of the fact that neither Parliament nor the English courts have been particularly influential in the development of modern Scots criminal law. But given that the High Court has never taken the view that it is *obliged* to adopt the views of Hume, and indeed from time to time disregards them, it is clear that the reliance upon Hume is to a large degree a matter of choice. This may in many cases be unobjectionable, but there are occasions when Hume's views, by virtue of changed social conditions, will be quite inappropriate (see, for example, the rejection of Hume's views on rape in marriage—*ante*, p. 7).

Certain other writings are regularly referred to by the courts, in particular, Macdonald's *Practical*

*Treatise on the Criminal Law of Scotland* (1st ed., 1867; 5th and standard ed., J. Walker and D. J. Stevenson, ed., 1948). Macdonald is basically a student text, which receives varying degrees of respect from the courts. In *Brown v. Macpherson*, 1918 J.C. 3, Lord Strathclyde referred to Macdonald as a "well-known textbook", a description which was critically received by Lord Carmont in *Dow v. Macknight*, 1949 J.C. 38, who suggested that Lord Strathclyde, in using that description, had not meant "to disparage the authority of Lord Justice-Clerk Macdonald's great work on the criminal law of Scotland". More recently, in *Raffaelli v. Heatly*, 1949 J.C. 101, Lord Mackay also referred to Macdonald as a "textbook" (although in this case as the "leading" textbook on criminal law). It is clear, however, that Macdonald has no authority in the "Institutional" sense.

Sir Archibald Alison's *Principles and Practice of the Criminal Law of Scotland* (1832–33) is also frequently encountered, but it should be said that volume i dealing with *Principles* (in particular) is heavily dependent upon Hume.

## D. European Law

**1.16** In general terms, the institutions of the European Community do not have a criminal competence. Consequently, European Community law has not been a significant direct source of criminal offences, although it has been an indirect source in the sense that the United Kingdom has adopted criminal measures designed to enforce community law. At the same time, it is clear that community law may provide a defence to a criminal charge in certain circumstances. If, for example, an accused is prosecuted under domestic law for engaging in conduct which he or she has a right to pursue under Community law, then the fact that he or she is acting in compliance with Community law may be pleaded as a defence to the domestic criminal charge. So, for example, where an accused was charged with unlawfully importing obscene articles into the United Kingdom, it was argued that the domestic law which forbade such importation was a "quantitative restriction" on imports, which was contrary to community law. The argument was unsuccessful since, in the circumstances, there was an equivalent ban on the domestic production and marketing of such goods. But had it been the case that the ban had operated solely to exclude such goods produced in another Member State, then arguably the accused would have been entitled to plead community law as a defence. See *R. v. Henn and Darby* [1981] 2 All E.R. 166, and *Conegate Ltd v. Customs and Excise Commissioners* [1986] 2 All E.R. 688.

## E. Human Rights

**1.17** The European Convention on Human Rights was adopted for signature by the Council of Europe in 1950, and entered into force in 1953. Although the United Kingdom was one of the first states to ratify the Convention, it did not take any steps to incorporate the Convention into domestic law, or otherwise make the Convention enforceable in the courts in any part of the United Kingdom.

Unlike the English courts, which took the view that the terms of the Convention could be relied upon as an aid to the interpretation of legislation and the development of the common law (see, generally, *R. v. Secretary of State for the Home Department, ex parte Brind* [1991] 1 A.C. 696) reliance on the Convention was for many years not permitted in the Scottish courts. In *Surjit Kaur v. Lord Advocate*, 1981 S.L.T. 322, it was held that the Convention, not being part of the domestic law of Scotland, could not be invoked, even as an aid to the construction of a United Kingdom statute. The decision in *Surjit Kaur* was confirmed by the decision of the Inner House of Court of Session in *Moore v. Secretary of State for Scotland*, 1985 S.L.T. 38. See also *Montes and Others v. H.M. Advocate*, 1990 S.C.C.R 645. However, in *T., Petitioner*, 1997 S.L.T. 724, Lord Hope expressed the opinion that this approach was outdated, and went on to state that the Scottish Courts should adopt the same approach as the English courts. This approach was endorsed by the High Court in *McLeod, Petitioner*, 1998 S.L.T. 233 in which the court relied upon Article 6 of the Convention, and the case law of the European Court of Human Rights, in considering the extent to which the Crown is under a legal obligation to disclose to the defence material which it has in its possession which may have a bearing upon the guilt or innocence of the accused.

Most of the rights set out in the European Convention are now given domestic effect by the Human Rights Act 1998, and the Scotland Act 1998.

## Human Rights Act 1998

An Act to give further effect to rights and freedoms guaranteed under the European Convention on **1.18** Human Rights; to make provision with respect to holders of certain judicial offices who become judges of the European Court of Human Rights; and for connected purposes.

### *Introduction*

**The Convention Rights**

**1.**—(1) In this Act "the Convention rights" means the rights and fundamental freedoms set **1.19** out in—

(a) Articles 2 to 12 and 14 of the Convention,
(b) Articles 1 to 3 of the First Protocol, and
(c) Articles 1 and 2 of the Sixth Protocol,

as read with Articles 16 to 18 of the Convention.

(2) Those Articles are to have effect for the purposes of this Act subject to any designated derogation or reservation (as to which see sections 14 and 15).

(3) The Articles are set out in Schedule 1 . . . .

**2.**—(1) A court or tribunal determining a question which has arisen in connection with a **1.20** Convention right must take into account any—

(a) judgment, decision, declaration or advisory opinion of the European Court of Human Rights,
(b) opinion of the Commission given in a report adopted under Article 31 of the Convention,
(c) decision of the Commission in connection with Article 26 or 27(2) of the Convention, or
(d) decision of the Committee of Ministers taken under Article 46 of the Convention,

whenever made or given, so far as, in the opinion of the court or tribunal, it is relevant to the proceedings in which that question has arisen . . . .

### *Legislation*

**Interpretation of legislation**

**3.**—(1) So far as it is possible to do so, primary legislation and subordinate legislation must **1.21** be read and given effect in a way which is compatible with the Convention rights.

(2) This section—

(a) applies to primary legislation and subordinate legislation whenever enacted;
(b) does not affect the validity, continuing operation or enforcement of any incompatible primary legislation; and
(c) does not affect the validity, continuing operation or enforcement of any incompatible subordinate legislation if (disregarding any possibility of revocation) primary legislation prevents removal of the incompatibility.

**Declaration of incompatibility**

**4.**—(1) Subsection (2) applies in any proceedings in which a court determines whether a **1.22** provision of primary legislation is compatible with a Convention right.

(2) If the court is satisfied that the provision is incompatible with a Convention right, it may make a declaration of that incompatibility.

(3) Subsection (4) applies in any proceedings in which a court determines whether a provision of subordinate legislation, made in the exercise of a power conferred by primary legislation, is compatible with a Convention right.

(4) If the court is satisfied—

(a) that the provision is incompatible with a Convention right, and

(b) that (disregarding any possibility of revocation) the primary legislation concerned prevents removal of the incompatibility,

it may make a declaration of that incompatibility.

    (5) In this section "court" means—

        (a) the House of Lords;

        (b) the Judicial Committee of the Privy Council;

        (c) the Courts-Martial Appeal Court;

        (d) in Scotland, the High Court of Justiciary sitting otherwise than as a trial court or the Court of Session;

        (e) in England and Wales or Northern Ireland, the High Court or the Court of Appeal.

    (6) A declaration under this section ("a declaration of incompatibility")—

        (a) does not affect the validity, continuing operation or enforcement of the provision in respect of which it is given; and

        (b) is not binding on the parties to the proceedings in which it is made ....

*Public authorities*

**Acts of public authorities**

**1.23**    **6.**—(1) It is unlawful for a public authority to act in a way which is incompatible with a Convention right.

    (2) Subsection (1) does not apply to an act if—

        (a) as the result of one or more provisions of primary legislation, the authority could not have acted differently; or

        (b) in the case of one or more provisions of, or made under, primary legislation which cannot be read or given effect in a way which is compatible with the Convention rights, the authority was acting so as to give effect to or enforce those provisions.

    (3) In this section "public authority" includes—

        (a) a court or tribunal, ...

SCHEDULE 1

THE ARTICLES

PART I

THE CONVENTION RIGHTS AND FREEDOMS

Article 2
**Right to life**

**1.24**    1. Everyone's right to life shall be protected by law. No one shall be deprived of his life intentionally save in the execution of a sentence of a court following his conviction of a crime for which this penalty is provided by law.

    2. Deprivation of life shall not be regarded as inflicted in contravention of this Article when it results from the use of force which is no more than absolutely necessary:

        (a) in defence of any person from unlawful violence;

        (b) in order to effect a lawful arrest or to prevent the escape of a person lawfully detained;

        (c) in action lawfully taken for the purpose of quelling a riot or insurrection.

Article 3
**Prohibition of torture**

No one shall be subjected to torture or to inhuman or degrading treatment or punishment.

## Article 4
### Prohibition of slavery and forced labour

1. No one shall be held in slavery or servitude.
2. No one shall be required to perform forced or compulsory labour.
3. For the purpose of this Article the term "forced or compulsory labour" shall not include:
   (a) any work required to be done in the ordinary course of detention imposed according to the provisions of Article 5 of this Convention or during conditional release from such detention;
   (b) any service of a military character or, in case of conscientious objectors in countries where they are recognised, service exacted instead of compulsory military service;
   (c) any service exacted in case of an emergency or calamity threatening the life or well-being of the community;
   (d) any work or service which forms part of normal civic obligations.

## Article 5
### Right to liberty and security

1. Everyone has the right to liberty and security of person. No one shall be deprived of his liberty save in the following cases and in accordance with a procedure prescribed by law:
   (a) the lawful detention of a person after conviction by a competent court;
   (b) the lawful arrest or detention of a person for non-compliance with the lawful order of a court or in order to secure the fulfilment of any obligation prescribed by law;
   (c) the lawful arrest or detention of a person effected for the purpose of bringing him before the competent legal authority on reasonable suspicion of having committed an offence or when it is reasonably considered necessary to prevent his committing an offence or fleeing after having done so;
   (d) the detention of a minor by lawful order for the purpose of educational supervision or his lawful detention for the purpose of bringing him before the competent legal authority;
   (e) the lawful detention of persons for the prevention of the spreading of infectious diseases, of persons of unsound mind, alcoholics or drug addicts or vagrants;
   (f) the lawful arrest or detention of a person to prevent his effecting an unauthorised entry into the country or of a person against whom action is being taken with a view to deportation or extradition.
2. Everyone who is arrested shall be informed promptly, in a language which he understands, of the reasons for his arrest and of any charge against him.
3. Everyone arrested or detained in accordance with the provisions of paragraph 1(c) of this Article shall be brought promptly before a judge or other officer authorised by law to exercise judicial power and shall be entitled to trial within a reasonable time or to release pending trial. Release may be conditioned by guarantees to appear for trial.
4. Everyone who is deprived of his liberty by arrest or detention shall be entitled to take proceedings by which the lawfulness of his detention shall be decided speedily by a court and his release ordered if the detention is not lawful.
5. Everyone who has been the victim of arrest or detention in contravention of the provisions of this Article shall have an enforceable right to compensation.

## Article 6
### Right to a fair trial

1. In the determination of his civil rights and obligations or of any criminal charge against him, everyone is entitled to a fair and public hearing within a reasonable time by an

independent and impartial tribunal established by law. Judgment shall be pronounced publicly but the press and public may be excluded from all or part of the trial in the interest of morals, public order or national security in a democratic society, where the interests of juveniles or the protection of the private life of the parties so require, or to the extent strictly necessary in the opinion of the court in special circumstances where publicity would prejudice the interests of justice.

2. Everyone charged with a criminal offence shall be presumed innocent until proved guilty according to law.

3. Everyone charged with a criminal offence has the following minimum rights:

(a) to be informed promptly, in a language which he understands and in detail, of the nature and cause of the accusation against him;

(b) to have adequate time and facilities for the preparation of his defence;

(c) to defend himself in person or through legal assistance of his own choosing or, if he has not sufficient means to pay for legal assistance, to be given it free when the interests of justice so require;

(d) to examine or have examined witnesses against him and to obtain the attendance and examination of witnesses on his behalf under the same conditions as witnesses against him;

(e) to have the free assistance of an interpreter if he cannot understand or speak the language used in court.

## Article 7
### No punishment without law

1. No one shall be held guilty of any criminal offence on account of any act or omission which did not constitute a criminal offence under national or international law at the time when it was committed. Nor shall a heavier penalty be imposed than the one that was applicable at the time the criminal offence was committed.

2. This Article shall not prejudice the trial and punishment of any person for any act or omission which, at the time when it was committed, was criminal according to the general principles of law recognised by civilised nations.

## Article 8
### Right to respect for private and family life

1. Everyone has the right to respect for his private and family life, his home and his correspondence.

2. There shall be no interference by a public authority with the exercise of this right except such as is in accordance with the law and is necessary in a democratic society in the interests of national security, public safety or the economic well-being of the country, for the prevention of disorder or crime, for the protection of health or morals, or for the protection of the rights and freedoms of others.

## Article 9
### Freedom of thought, conscience and religion

1. Everyone has the right to freedom of thought, conscience and religion; this right includes freedom to change his religion or belief and freedom, either alone or in community with others and in public or private, to manifest his religion or belief, in worship, teaching, practice and observance.

2. Freedom to manifest one's religion or beliefs shall be subject only to such limitations as are prescribed by law and are necessary in a democratic society in the interests of public

safety, for the protection of public order, health or morals, or for the protection of the rights and freedoms of others.

## Article 10
### Freedom of expression

1. Everyone has the right to freedom of expression. This right shall include freedom to hold opinions and to receive and impart information and ideas without interference by public authority and regardless of frontiers. This Article shall not prevent States from requiring the licensing of broadcasting, television or cinema enterprises.

2. The exercise of these freedoms, since it carries with it duties and responsibilities, may be subject to such formalities, conditions, restrictions or penalties as are prescribed by law and are necessary in a democratic society, in the interests of national security, territorial integrity or public safety, for the prevention of disorder or crime, for the protection of health or morals, for the protection of the reputation or rights of others, for preventing the disclosure of information received in confidence, or for maintaining the authority and impartiality of the judiciary.

## Article 11
### Freedom of assembly and association

1. Everyone has the right to freedom of peaceful assembly and to freedom of association with others, including the right to form and to join trade unions for the protection of his interests.

2. No restrictions shall be placed on the exercise of these rights other than such as are prescribed by law and are necessary in a democratic society in the interests of national security or public safety, for the prevention of disorder or crime, for the protection of health or morals or for the protection of the rights and freedoms of others. This Article shall not prevent the imposition of lawful restrictions on the exercise of these rights by members of the armed forces, of the police or of the administration of the State.

## Article 12
### Right to marry

Men and women of marriageable age have the right to marry and to found a family, according to the national laws governing the exercise of this right.

## Article 14
### Prohibition of discrimination

The enjoyment of the rights and freedoms set forth in this Convention shall be secured without discrimination on any ground such as sex, race, colour, language, religion, political or other opinion, national or social origin, association with a national minority, property, birth or other status.

## Article 16
### Restrictions on political activity of aliens

Nothing in Articles 10, 11 and 14 shall be regarded as preventing the High Contracting Parties from imposing restrictions on the political activity of aliens.

## Article 17
### Prohibition of abuse of rights

Nothing in this Convention may be interpreted as implying for any State, group or person any right to engage in any activity or perform any act aimed at the destruction of any of the rights and freedoms set forth herein or at their limitation to a greater extent than is provided for in the Convention.

## Article 18
### Limitation on use of restrictions on rights

The restrictions permitted under this Convention to the said rights and freedoms shall not be applied for any purpose other than those for which they have been prescribed.

## PART II

### THE FIRST PROTOCOL

## Article 1
### Protection of property

**1.25**    Every natural or legal person is entitled to the peaceful enjoyment of his possessions. No one shall be deprived of his possessions except in the public interest and subject to the conditions provided for by law and by the general principles of international law.

The preceding provisions shall not, however, in any way impair the right of a State to enforce such laws as it deems necessary to control the use of property in accordance with the general interest or to secure the payment of taxes or other contributions or penalties.

## Article 2
### Right to education

No person shall be denied the right to education. In the exercise of any functions which it assumes in relation to education and to teaching, the State shall respect the right of parents to ensure such education and teaching in conformity with their own religious and philosophical convictions.

## Article 3
### Right to free elections

The High Contracting Parties undertake to hold free elections at reasonable intervals by secret ballot, under conditions which will ensure the free expression of the opinion of the people in the choice of the legislature.

## PART III

### THE SIXTH PROTOCOL

## Article 1
### Abolition of the death penalty

**1.26**    The death penalty shall be abolished. No one shall be condemned to such penalty or executed.

## Article 2
### Death penalty in time of war

A State may make provision in its law for the death penalty in respect of acts committed in time of war or of imminent threat of war; such penalty shall be applied only in the instances laid down in the law and in accordance with its provisions. The State shall communicate to the Secretary General of the Council of Europe the relevant provisions of that law.

## Scotland Act 1998

### PART I
### THE SCOTTISH PARLIAMENT

#### *The Scottish Parliament*

**The Scottish Parliament**
1.—(1) There shall be a Scottish Parliament ...                        **1.27**

#### *Legislation*

**Acts of the Scottish Parliament**
28.—(1) Subject to section 29, the Parliament may make laws, to be known as Acts of the **1.28** Scottish Parliament. ...
(6) Every Act of the Scottish Parliament shall be judicially noticed.
(7) This section does not affect the power of the Parliament of the United Kingdom to make laws for Scotland.

**Legislative competence**
29.—(1) An Act of the Scottish Parliament is not law so far as any provision of the Act is **1.29** outside the legislative competence of the Parliament.
(2) A provision is outside that competence so far as any of the following paragraphs apply—
   ...
   (d) it is incompatible with any of the Convention rights or with Community law...

**The Scottish Executive**
44.—(1) There shall be a Scottish Executive, whose members shall be—                **1.30**
   (a) the First Minister,
   (b) such Ministers as the First Minister may appoint under section 47, and
   (c) the Lord Advocate and the Solicitor General for Scotland.
57.— ... (2) A member of the Scottish Executive has no power to make any subordinate **1.31** legislation, or to do any other act, so far as the legislation or act is incompatible with any of the Convention rights or with Community law.
(3) Subsection (2) does not apply to an act of the Lord Advocate—
   (a) in prosecuting any offence, or
   (b) in his capacity as head of the systems of criminal prosecution and investigation of deaths in Scotland,
which, because of subsection (2) of section 6 of the Human Rights Act 1998, is not unlawful under subsection (1) of that section.

**Interpretation.**
126.—(1) In this Act— ...                                            **1.32**
   "the Convention rights" has the same meaning as in the Human Rights Act 1998.

NOTES

1. Prior to the Human Rights Act and the Scotland Act, the European Convention on Human Rights **1.33** did not, in general, have a significant effect on the substantive criminal law of Scotland. There are, however, several areas of the criminal law in which the Convention has been influential. The right to privacy has had a direct impact on the extent to which the criminal law may interfere with private consensual sexual relations, although almost entirely in relation to homosexual offences. See *Dudgeon v. United Kingdom* (1981) 4 E.H.R.R. 149; *Norris v. Ireland* (1988) 13 E.H.R.R. 186; *Sutherland v. United Kingdom*, Application No. 25186/94, March 27, 2001; *Lustig-Prean and Beckett v. United Kingdom*,

European Court of Human Rights, 27 September 1999 and *A. D. T. v. The United Kingdom*, 9 B.H.R.C. 112. The use of consensual violence (in the context of sado-masochistic practices) was also considered in the light of article 8: *Laskey, Jaggard and Brown v. United Kingdom* (1997) 24 E.H.R.R. 39. The right not to be subjected to inhumane or degrading treatment under Article 3 has had a direct impact on the rights of parents and teachers to administer corporal punishment to children (and hence on the defence of "lawful chastisement", see *post*, p. 299): *Costello-Roberts v. United Kingdom* (1995) 19 E.H.R.R. 112 and *A v. United Kingdom* (1999) 27 E.H.R.R. 611 (and see also *Campbell and Cosans v. United Kingdom* (1982) 4 E.H.R.R. 293). The English law relating to obscenity was discussed in *Handyside v. United Kingdom* (1976) 1 E.H.R.R. 737 (and see also *Müller v. Switzerland* (1988) 13 E.H.R.R. 212). The legality under Article 2 of taking human life was discussed in *McCann v. United Kingdom*, Series A, No. 324 (1996) 21 E.H.R.R. 97. In *T v. United Kingdom*, December 16, 1999, the Court considered the age of criminal responsibility in the context of Article 3. In *SW v. United Kingdom*, *CR v. United Kingdom*, Series A, No. 335-C and Series A, No. 335-B (1995) 21 E.H.R.R. 363, the Court considered the decision of the English courts to abolish the rule that a husband could not be found guilty of rape (*cf. S. v. H.M. Advocate, ante,* p. 6). In *Ahmed Sadik v. Greece* (1995) 24 E.H.R.R. 323; *Otto Preminger Institut v. Austria* (1994) 19 E.H.R.R. 34; *Wingrove v. United Kingdom*, RJD, 1996-V, No. 23 (1996) 24 E.H.R.R. 1; *Worm v. Austria* (1997) 25 E.H.R.R. 454, Application No. 24770/94; *Associated Newspapers Ltd and Others v. United Kingdom*, November 30, 1994 (Commission), criminal restraints on freedom of expression were considered. *Christians against Racism and Fascism v. United Kingdom*, Application No. 8440/78, 21 DR 148 (Commission); *Steel and Others v. United Kingdom* (1999) 28 E.H.R.R. 603 discussed restrictions imposed through the criminal law on freedom of expression and freedom of assembly.

2. There is a conflict of opinion on the likely impact of the Convention on the substantive criminal law. (Compare R. Buxton (Buxton L.J.), "The Human Rights Act and the Substantive Criminal Law" [2000] Crim. L.R. 331–340. For contrary views, see A. Ashworth, "The Human Rights Act and the Substantive Criminal Law: A Non-Minimalist View" [2000] Crim.L.R. 564–567, A. Ashworth, "The European Convention and the Criminal Law", in *The Human Rights Act and the Criminal Justice and Regulatory Process* (Hart Publishing for the Cambridge Centre for Public Law, 1999), pp. 39–42 and C. Gane, "The Substantive Criminal Law" in The Hon. Lord Reed (ed.), *A Practical Guide to Human Rights Law in Scotland* (W. Green, 2001), pp. 61 *et seq.*

3. In *Salabiaku v. France* (1991) 13 E.H.R.R. 363, the Court observed that "in principle the Contracting States remain free to apply the criminal law to an act where it is not carried out in the normal exercise of one of the rights protected under the Convention" (at para. 27). In other words, states are not free to apply the criminal law to an act which *is* carried out in the normal exercise of a Convention rights. So, any criminal offence which infringes the exercise of a Convention right can only be enforced to the extent that that is justified under the Convention.

4. In terms of section 3 of the Act, all statutory provisions (including those which create criminal offences) must be read and applied "so far as it is possible to do so" in such a way as to render the legislation compatible with the Convention rights. If the Court is unable to do so then it may, if it is one of the courts enumerated in section 4(5) of the Act, make a "declaration of incompatibility" which, while having no effect on the proceedings in which the issue has arisen, may have the effect of triggering remedial measures in Parliament, under section 10 of the Act, to bring the legislation into line with the Convention rights.

5. Where a court is faced with an incompatibility between the common law and Convention rights, the court is bound to apply the common law in such a way as to conform to the Convention rights. If the court fails to uphold the Convention right, then the court will be in breach of section 6(1) of the Act which makes it unlawful for any "public authority" (which, in terms of section 6(3)(a) includes a court) to act in a way which is incompatible with a Convention right. The Act is, therefore, likely to have a much greater impact on the common law of crimes than on statutory offences—which is, of course, of particular significance given the importance of the common law in Scottish criminal law.

6. The scheme of devolved competence set out in the Scotland Act makes it clear that the Scottish Parliament has no power to pass laws which are incompatible with the Convention rights. Any provision in a Scottish Act which is incompatible with a Convention right is not law, and cannot be enforced (section 29). Under sections 52 *et seq.* of the Scotland Act, the Scottish Executive exercises powers conferred upon it under the Act only to the extent that those powers, and the manner in which they are exercised, are compatible with Convention rights. Section 57(2) reinforces this rule, by expressly providing that a member of the Scottish Executive, which includes the Lord Advocate, has no power to act in a way that is incompatible with a Convention right.

So far as concerns the criminal law, the effect of section 57(2) (and section 6 of the Human Rights Act) is to ensure that all criminal prosecutions in Scotland must be conducted in a manner compatible with Convention rights, both in terms of the procedures adopted by the prosecutor, and also in terms of the substantive law. Section 57(2) applies in terms only the "acts" of the Lord Advocate, but the view was expressed in *Clancy v. Caird*, 2000 S.L.T. 546 that that section applies also to the "omissions" of the Executive. So far as concerns criminal proceedings, it might have been argued that section 57(2) only applies to criminal proceedings conducted in the name of the Lord Advocate, *i.e.*, proceedings on indictment, but it has been a matter of concession that section 57(2) applies to the acts and omissions of all prosecutors, including those at the instance of procurators fiscal in the sheriff and district courts.

## F. Other Aspects of International Law

In certain areas, international law has made a direct contribution to the substantive law. The United **1.34** Kingdom is a party to a number of international treaties which provide for the criminalisation of certain conduct. Examples of this include the Genocide Convention 1948, Article 5 of which requires parties to the Convention to take effective measures to punish acts of genocide as defined by the Convention. The Genocide Act 1969 gives effect to the Convention by making genocide an offence punishable by up to 14 years imprisonment, or, where the offence involves the killing of any person, punishable by life imprisonment. Similar provisions are to be found in the Geneva Conventions Act 1957 and the Geneva Conventions (Amendment) Act 1995 which give effect to the United Kingdom's obligations under the 1949 Geneva Conventions and the 1977 Protocols to those Conventions. Section 134 of the Criminal Justice Act 1988 makes it an offence for a public official or any person acting in an official capacity to commit torture, whether in the United Kingdom or elsewhere. This legislation was passed so that the United Kingdom could ratify the United Nations Convention Against Torture and other Cruel Inhuman or Degrading Treatment or Punishment (1984). Interestingly, while Article 4 of the Convention requires states to criminalise torture, and Article 5 requires them to establish extra-territorial jurisdiction over acts of torture committed by their own nations, the United Kingdom has gone further than this, and by section 135 makes torture punishable in the United Kingdom, even if committed outside the United Kingdom by non-nationals.

In 2001 legislation was introduced into the United Kingdom and Scottish Parliaments to enable ratification by the United Kingdom of the Rome Statute establishing a permanent International Criminal Court for the prosecution and punishment of Genocide, War Crimes, Crimes against Humanity and the Crime of Aggression. (See the International Criminal Court (Scotland) Bill 2001, the International Criminal Court Act 2001 and *International Criminal Court: Consultation on Draft Legislation*, Cm 4847 (2000).) This legislation will incorporate into the domestic law of Scotland the crimes set out in the Statute of the Court.

Outside these areas, the impact of international law on the criminal law has been less significant. For a recent case on the scope of customary international law and the defence of necessity, see *Lord Advocate's Reference (No. 1 of 2000)*, High Court, March 30, 2001, *post*, p. 217.

## C. THE SCOTTISH CRIMINAL JUSTICE SYSTEM

## A. Solemn and Summary Procedure

Criminal proceedings in Scotland may be conducted under "solemn" or "summary" procedure. Solemn **1.35** procedure is reserved for more serious cases, and the majority of criminal prosecutions are conducted under summary procedure. Perhaps the most obvious difference between the two forms of procedure can be seen in the trial. In solemn proceedings trial takes place before a judge and jury whereas in summary proceedings trial takes place before a judge sitting alone. As one might expect, the punitive powers of the court are significantly less in summary proceedings than in solemn proceedings. Pre-trial procedures also differ between the two forms of procedure. In solemn proceedings, for example, the arrest of the accused will be followed by judicial examination; in summary proceedings there is no such pre-trial judicial examination.

## B. The Criminal Courts

**1.36** Three courts exercise criminal jurisdiction in Scotland—the High Court of Justiciary (commonly referred to as the High Court), the sheriff court and the district court. The High Court may sit as a trial court, or as a court of appeal. The sheriff and district courts sit only as trial courts.

### (a) The High Court

**1.37** The jurisdiction of the High Court to try crimes committed within its territorial jurisdiction is almost universal. It may be excluded where jurisdiction is reserved by statute to some other court, but this must be done expressly or by necessary implication. The High Court exercises exclusive jurisdiction in cases of treason, murder, rape, deforcement of court messengers, breach of duty by magistrates and in any other case where exclusive jurisdiction is conferred on the court by statute. Trials before the High Court are always conducted according to the rules of solemn procedure before a judge and a jury. The High Court has no summary trial jurisdiction. Judges in the High Court enjoy a full range of sentencing powers. The maximum penalty that may be imposed in the High Court (where this is permitted) is life imprisonment.

### (b) The sheriff court

**1.38** Like the High Court, the competence of the sheriff court is virtually universal. The jurisdiction of the sheriff court may be excluded—as, for example, in the case of those offences reserved to the exclusive jurisdiction of the High Court—but otherwise any statutory or common law crime may be tried in the sheriff court.

   Trials before the sheriff court may be conducted according to the rules of solemn or summary procedure. In solemn proceedings, the sheriff sits with a jury and the maximum penalty he or she may impose is a sentence of three years' imprisonment. If the sheriff considers his sentencing powers to be inadequate in a particular case, he may remit that case to the High Court for sentence under section 195 of the Criminal Procedure (Scotland) Act 1995.

   In summary proceedings, the sheriff sits alone. Normally, the maximum punishment which the sheriff may impose in summary proceedings for a common law offence is three months' imprisonment, or a fine of five thousand pounds: Criminal Procedure (Scotland) Act 1995, ss.5(2) and 225(8). Where an offender has been convicted of a second or subsequent offence inferring dishonesty or violence the sheriff may impose imprisonment for up to six months: Criminal Procedure (Scotland) Act 1995, s.5(3). The penalties applicable in the case of statutory offences depend on the terms of the provision creating the offence.

### (c) The district court

**1.39** The district court was established by the District Courts (Scotland) Act 1975. District courts are presided over either by lay justices or by legally qualified judges known as stipendiary magistrates. When the district court is presided over by a stipendiary magistrate, it has the same criminal jurisdiction as the sheriff court in summary proceedings. When the district court is presided over by lay justices it has a more limited competence and it usually deals with minor assaults, thefts and breaches of the peace. Many offences are expressly excluded from the jurisdiction of the district court by section 7 of the Criminal Procedure (Scotland) Act 1995. These include offences reserved to the jurisdiction of other courts and serious examples of offences of a type which the district court is competent to try, such as theft when committed by housebreaking or where the value of the property stolen exceeds £2,500.

   Trials in the District court are always conducted according to summary procedure. Where the court is presided over by one or more lay justices, the court is assisted by a legally qualified clerk.

   The powers of the justices in terms of sentencing are limited. Section 7 of the Criminal Procedure

(Scotland) Act provides that generally the district court may not impose a sentence of imprisonment of more than sixty days, nor may it impose a fine exceeding £2,500.

## (d) The Judicial Committee of the Privy Council: "Devolution Issues"

We have noted (*ante*, p. 18) that under the Scotland Act, actions taken by the Lord Advocate in respect **1.40** of criminal proceedings may be challenged as being *ultra vires*. Such a challenge, under the Scotland Act, is known as a "devolution issue", in terms of paragraph 1(d) of Schedule 6 to that Act. A "devolution issue" of this type may be raised before any criminal court in Scotland, and where it is raised before a court other than a court consisting of two or more judges of the High Court of Justiciary, the issue may be referred to the High Court of Justiciary. A Court consisting of two or more judges of the High Court may refer a devolution issue to the Judicial Committee of the Privy Council (except where it arises before that court on a referral from another court). Where a devolution issue has been determined a court of two or more judges of the High Court of Justiciary (whether in the ordinary course of proceedings or on a reference from another court), an appeal may be taken against that determination to the Judicial Committee, but only with leave of the High Court or special leave of the Judicial Committee.

## (e) Criminal appeals

Appeals against conviction, conviction and sentence, or sentence alone, in solemn proceedings are **1.41** heard by the High Court, sitting as a court of criminal appeal, under Part VIII of the Criminal Procedure (Scotland) Act 1995. The sole ground of appeal is that there has been a miscarriage of justice. If an appeal against conviction is upheld, the Court may quash the conviction, or quash the conviction and substitute a conviction on any other charge which it would have been open to the jury to return on the indictment faced by the accused at the trial. The Court may, alternatively, grant authority to the Crown to bring a fresh prosecution: 1995 Act, s.118. If an appeal against sentence is upheld, the court may substitute the disposal which it thinks more appropriate. An appeal against sentence alone may, however, be unsuccessful, and in such a case the court will leave the sentence unaltered, unless it decides that the sentence was too lenient, in which case it may increase the sentence imposed upon the appellant: 1995 Act, s.118(4) and ss.108 and 108A.

The Crown has no right to appeal against an acquittal in solemn proceedings. The Lord Advocate may, however, appeal against the sentence imposed by the court, and certain forms of disposal, on the ground that the sentence or disposal was "unduly lenient": 1995 Act, ss.108 and 108(A).

Appeals in summary proceedings lie to the High Court, under Part X of the Criminal Procedure (Scotland) Act 1995. Under section 175(2) of that Act the accused may appeal against conviction, or conviction and sentence, or against sentence alone. In contrast to solemn proceedings the prosecutor may, in summary proceedings, appeal against an acquittal or sentence under section 175 of the 1995 Act. In disposing of an appeal, the High Court may, *inter alia*, affirm the verdict of the lower court, set aside the verdict and quash the conviction or substitute an amended verdict of guilty, or grant authority to bring a fresh prosecution: 1995 Act, s.183. The prosecutor also enjoys an additional right of appeal against a sentence or disposal on the ground that it was unduly lenient: 1995 Act, s.175(4).

In summary proceedings, it is also possible for an application to be made to the High Court for the setting aside of an illegal or improper warrant, conviction or judgment by an inferior court by presenting to the High Court a Bill of Suspension.

Subject to the exceptions introduced by the Scotland Act 1998, the High Court is the final court of appeal in criminal proceedings. Unlike civil proceedings, there is no appeal to the House of Lords in Scottish criminal proceedings: *Mackintosh v. Lord Advocate* (1876) 3 R. (H.L.) 34.

## C. The presumption of innocence and the burden of proof

The presumption of innocence is fundamental to the whole system of criminal prosecution and applies **1.42** to every person charged with a criminal offence. It is specifically referred to and guaranteed by Article 6 of the European Convention on Human Rights, but was well-established in Scotland long before the Convention.

**Slater v. H.M. Advocate**
1928 J.C. 94

**1.43** The appellant was charged with the murder of an old woman by striking her on the head with a hammer. The alleged motive for the killing was theft, the old lady having in her home a large quantity of jewellery. Evidence was led that the appellant lived by gambling and dealing in jewels. There was also evidence that he was supported by the earnings of a prostitute. These circumstances were remarked upon by the Lord Advocate in his speech to the jury as indicating a character depraved enough to commit the crime in question. In his charge to the jury, the presiding judge (Lord Guthrie) made the following remarks (*inter alia*):

"That is the kind of man, and you will see at once that his character is double-edged. The Lord Advocate takes it in his own favour, and he may quite fairly do so because, in the first place, a man of that kind has not the presumption of innocence in his favour which is not only a form in the case of every man but is a reality in the case of the ordinary man. Not only is every man presumed to be innocent, but the ordinary man has a strong presumption in his favour. Such a man may be capable of having committed this offence, and that man also may be capable from his previous character of exhibiting a callous behaviour after the offence. That was founded upon by Mr McClure. A man of such a character does not exhibit the symptoms that a respectable man who has been goaded into some serious crime of violence does after the crime is over, and so you will consider that matter from both points of view, telling in favour of the prisoner and telling against him. [After dealing with the pursuer's financial circumstances his Lordship continued]—Gentlemen, all these circumstances are relevant to the case, but I think if you make up your minds to convict the prisoner you will be wise to be in this position; to be able to say to yourselves, 'we have disregarded his character, we have disregarded his financial circumstances, we have convicted him without regard to these'. Having reached that conclusion, it might very well strengthen the conclusion to reflect on the two elements that I have mentioned, but I do not think they should be factors in enabling you to reach a conclusion, although they might support it after the conclusion had been reached."

The jury returned a verdict of guilty of murder. The appellant appealed on the ground, *inter alia*, of misdirection by the trial judge:

LORD JUSTICE-GENERAL (CLYDE): "It would be absurd to hold that a miscarriage of justice occurs whenever, in the report of a speech by counsel to the jury, anything is found which can be read as involving either a misstatement of some fact, or as presenting a wrong view of the relevancy of some piece of evidence; and there are many other passages in the prosecutor's speech which put the case against the appellant independently of any reference to any of the points in the evidence which were other than strictly relevant. But the specialty in this trial was that some of the aspects of the life which the appellant lived were relevant, while others were irrelevant, to the question of his guilt. Thus, the circumstance that the appellant never had a dentistry practice in Glasgow, but dealt in some way in articles of jewellery, was relevant to the motive which, according to the prosecution, drew the appellant to Miss Gilchrist's house in search of the valuables she kept there. But that other aspect of his life, with its peculiarly heinous implications, in which he was shown to be partly dependent on the proceeds of prostitution, was as remote from any bearing on the question of his guilt as it was suggestive against his case. Both the former aspects of the appellant's mode of life, and the latter aspect, unavoidably came—together and immixed—to the knowledge of the jury; and this made the possibility of misunderstanding on the jury's part the more likely if the odious (and irrelevant) aspect was referred to in the prosecutor's address to the jury for any other purpose than to distinguish it from the others as one which was irrelevant, and which must be put entirely out of their consideration. So far from this, it was unfortunately made the point of the opening passage of the presentation of the case for the prosecution.

We have already indicated our view that the decision of the case—particularly with regard to the vital point of satisfactory proof of identity—presented an unusually difficult and narrow issue, upon which the balance of judgment might easily be influenced in one direction or the other. It follows that the danger of allowing the minds of the jury to be distracted by considerations which were at once so irrelevant and so prejudicial as those connected with the relations of the appellant to his female associates was real and great; and in these circumstances we are of opinion that the clearest and most unambiguous instruction by the presiding judge was imperatively demanded, to prevent the possibility of any misunderstanding on the part of the jury with regard to so important a matter. As appears from the shorthand report of the judge's charge, however, the matter in question was the only one on which the directions given to the jury were open to serious criticism. They did nothing to remove the erroneous impression which the opening passages of the speech for the prosecution might so easily have produced in the minds of the jury. On the contrary, they were calculated to confirm them. No distinction was made between those aspects of the appellant's life which were relevant to the charge of murdering Miss Gilchrist, and those which were not. It was pointed out—quite justly—that the considerations arising out of the appellant's mode of life, as exhibited at the trial, were double-edged, and were founded on (for different purposes) by the prosecution and the defence alike. But the jury were told that what is familiarly known as the presumption of innocence in criminal cases applied to the appellant (in the light of his ambiguous character) with less effect than it would have applied to a man whose character was not open to suspicion. This amounted, in our opinion, to a clear misdirection in law. The presumption of innocence applies to every person charged with a criminal offence in precisely the same way, and it can be overcome only by evidence relevant to prove the crime with the commission of which he is charged. The presumption of innocence is fundamental to the whole system of criminal prosecution, and it was a radical error to suggest that the appellant did not have the benefit of it to the same effect as any other accused person. It is true that an accused person of evil repute has not the advantage, enjoyed by an accused person of proved good character, of being able to urge on the jury in his defence the improbability that a person of good character would commit the crime charged. The passage in the charge at present under discussion is suggestive that this was what was in the judge's mind. But, however that may be, he put the appellant's bad character as a consideration upon which the prosecution was entitled to found as qualifying the ordinary presumption of innocence . . . That a man should support himself on the proceeds of prostitution is regarded by all men as blackguardism, but by many people as a sign of almost inhuman depravity. It cannot be affirmed that any members of the jury were misled by feelings of this kind in weighing the question of the appellant's guilt, but neither can it be affirmed that none of them was. What is certain is that the judge's charge entirely failed to give the jury the essential warning against allowing themselves to be misled by any feelings of the kind referred to. It is manifestly possible that, but for the prejudicial effect of denying to the appellant the full benefit of the presumption of innocence, and of allowing the point of his dependence on the immoral earnings of his partner to go to the jury as a point not irrelevant to his guilt of Miss Gilchrist's murder, the proportion of nine to five, for 'guilty' and 'not proven' respectively, might have been reversed."

Appeal allowed: conviction quashed.

## NOTES

1. Slater's case is one of the most notorious in Scottish criminal law. After his conviction (in 1909) **1.44** Slater received a conditional pardon and his death sentence was commuted to life imprisonment. Disquiet over his trial and ultimate disposal contributed to the setting up of a criminal appeal court (under the Criminal Appeal (Scotland) Act 1926) to hear appeals from conviction on indictment. Slater's was one of the first cases to be dealt with by the new court.

2. In general, there is no onus on an accused person to prove his innocence. Certain defences must be

established on a balance of probabilities (for example, the defence of insanity) but this is exceptional. (See *Lambie v. H.M. Advocate*, 1973 S.L.T. 219.)

3. The presumption of innocence is protected by Article 6(2) of the European Convention on Human Rights. The European Court of Human Rights has, however, held that this provision does not prohibit states relying upon presumptions in order to assist the prosecutor to establish guilt, nor does it prohibit reliance upon offences which place upon the accused an obligation to rebut such presumptions or to establish a defence. See *Salabiaku v. France* (1991) 13 E.H.R.R. 379; *Pham Hoang v. France*, Series A, No. 243. In *H. v. United Kingdom*, Application No. 15023/89, April 4, 1990, the Commission expressed the view that placing upon an accused the onus of establishing the defence of insanity was not incompatible with Article 6(2). Such presumptions and reverse onus provisions must, however, be kept within "reasonable limits" which "which take into account the importance of what is at stake and maintain the rights of the defence". (*Salabiaku*, at para. 28.)

## D. Investigation and Prosecution of Offences

**1.45** Responsibility for the investigation of crime rests, at least in theory, with the local public prosecutor, the procurator fiscal. In practice, much of the day-to-day responsibility for the investigation of crime is delegated to the police who conduct the investigation under the general supervision of the procurator fiscal. Section 17(2) of the Police (Scotland) Act 1967 provides that in relation to the investigation of offences the chief constable of a police force shall comply with such lawful instructions as he may receive from the appropriate prosecutor.

The responsibilities of the police are limited to investigation. It is for the prosecutor and not the police to decide whether or not the results of the investigation justify a prosecution, and the police must put the result of their investigations fairly before the prosecutor so that he has a proper basis on which to decide whether or not to prosecute: *Smith v. H.M. Advocate*, 1952 J.C. 66. In practice prosecutors rely heavily on the reports submitted by the police, and in the vast majority of cases the prosecutor's decision is based entirely on these reports without further or additional investigation.

Scots law regards the prosecution of crime as primarily a public function, to be performed in the public interest by an official appointed for that purpose. The public prosecutor does not have an exclusive title to prosecute and in certain circumstances it is possible for a private citizen to initiate a prosecution. But for most practical purposes, responsibility for the prosecution of crime rests with a public official.

In Scotland, that official is the Lord Advocate who is a member of the Scottish Executive. The Lord Advocate is appointed by the Queen on the recommendation of the First Minister, who may only make such a recommendation with the consent of the Scottish Parliament. Although he is a member of the Executive, any decision of the Lord Advocate in his capacity as head of the systems of criminal prosecution is taken by him independently of any other person. (See, generally, Scotland Act, section 48.)

The Lord Advocate is assisted by the Solicitor-General for Scotland (also a member of the Executive), and a permanent staff of officials in the Crown Office in Edinburgh headed by the Crown Agent.

All prosecutions on indictment, whether in the High Court or the sheriff court, are conducted in the name of the Lord Advocate. While the Lord Advocate may appear personally to prosecute, and occasionally does so in cases of particular difficulty or public importance, it is customary today for him to be represented by Crown counsel appointed largely from members of the Scottish bar by the Lord Advocate and known as advocates-depute. Prosecutions on indictment in the sheriff court are conducted on behalf of the Lord Advocate by the procurator fiscal of the court.

Summary prosecutions are conducted in the sheriff courts and the district courts by the procurator fiscal of the appropriate court. In such cases the procurator fiscal does not prosecute in the name of the Lord Advocate but in a personal capacity as fiscal of the court. However, he remains responsible to the Lord Advocate and acts under his general supervision and guidance.

In Scottish criminal procedure the public prosecutor is "master of the instance". This means that it is for him to decide when and against whom to initiate criminal proceedings and upon what charges. Unless the mode of trial for a particular offence is fixed by statute, or the offence is one which is reserved to the exclusive jurisdiction of the High Court, the public prosecutor determines the mode of trial, and the court in which proceedings are to be taken. It is for the public prosecutor (and not the court) to decide what pleas of guilt to accept and it is for him to decide when to withdraw or abandon proceedings. At the end of the trial, even if a verdict of guilty has been returned, the court cannot impose any sentence on the accused unless the prosecutor moves the court to pronounce sentence: *Boyle v. H.M. Advocate*, 1976 J.C. 32.

It is possible, in exceptional circumstances, for the victim of a crime, or a person closely connected with the victim, to bring a private prosecution. This is, however, very rare. There have only been two such prosecutions on indictment this century. The first of these was in 1909, in *J. & P. Coats Ltd v. Brown*, 1909 S.C. (J.) 29. The second was in *H. v. Sweeney and Others,* 1983 S.L.T. 48, and in that case the Lord Advocate did not oppose the private prosecutor's application to bring criminal proceedings. For other, less successful attempts to bring a private prosecution on indictment, see *McBain v. Crichton*, 1961 J.C. 25; *Trapp v. M., Trapp v. Y.*, 1971 S.L.T. (Notes) 30, and *Meehan v. Inglis and Others*, 1974 S.L.T. (Notes) 61; *C. v. Forsyth* 1995 S.C.C.R 553.

# Chapter 2

# *ACTUS REUS* AND *MENS REA*

## 1. THE ANATOMY OF A CRIME: *ACTUS REUS, MENS REA* AND DEFENCES

**2.01**  It is common practice today to analyse crimes in the following way: in general, crimes consist of conduct (an "external" element), accompanied by a legally blameworthy state of mind (a "mental" element), and unless the prosecutor proves that both elements are present, there can be no criminal liability. Suppose, for example, that A, walking through a department store, accidentally knocks over a crystal vase which falls to the floor and is smashed to pieces. The "external" element of the crime of malicious mischief is satisfied: A has damaged or destroyed property belonging to another. But before A can be guilty of malicious mischief it must be shown that she did this intentionally, or recklessly, and since in these circumstances neither of those states of mind is present A is not criminally responsible for the damage. This general approach is often expressed in the Latin phrase *actus non facit reum nisi mens sit rea*. This phrase may be translated loosely as meaning that "no act is punishable unless it is performed with a criminal mind, *i.e.* by a person whose state of mind is such that it makes his actings criminal" (Gordon, 3rd ed., para. 7–01). Reliance upon this Latin phrase has led, in turn, to the use of the terms *actus reus* and *mens rea* as convenient labels for the conduct element in crimes and the mental element, respectively.

There are exceptions to this general rule. Thus, for example, in cases of *strict liability,* it is not necessary for the prosecutor to prove any mental element in respect of some, or perhaps any, of the external elements of the offence. (See Chapter 3.)

According to this analysis, crimes consist of two "definitional" elements—the *actus reus* and the *mens rea*. This analysis does not, however, deal very satisfactorily with the question of "defences" to crime. Simply put, the problem is whether to treat defences as an additional factor in the attribution of criminal responsibility, or somehow to incorporate them into the *actus reus* and *mens rea* analysis.

Take, for example, the crime of rape. This may be defined in the following way: A man is guilty of rape if he has sexual intercourse with a woman, by overcoming her will, knowing that she does not consent, or not believing that she is consenting. (See Chapter 9, and in particular the case of *Jamieson v. H.M. Advocate,* 1994 J.C. 88.) It is often said, rather loosely, that consent is a "defence" to a charge of rape. But it is clear from this definition that "absence of consent" is part of the definition of the offence, an element of the *actus reus*. The onus is on the prosecutor to prove not only that intercourse took place, but that it took place without the consent of the woman. In other words, a man accused of rape who argues in his defence that the woman consented, is simply denying the presence of one of the necessary elements of the offence.

Is this a generally applicable rule, or is it limited to certain offences and certain "defences"? What is the position, for example, of self-defence in a case of assault? How does self-defence function in determining the criminal responsibility of the accused? Is the accused merely denying that an essential element of the offence was present, or is the argument rather different? Suppose, for example, that the accused in a case of assault accepts (a) that she struck the victim, (b) that she did so intentionally but (c) that it was necessary for her to act in this way in order to protect herself from a lethal attack at the hands of the victim. The accused is certainly denying her guilt, but is she doing so because she denies a necessary element of the crime, or for some other reason?

Assault can be defined as a deliberate attack on the person of another. A person who accepts that she has struck someone, intending to do so, would seem, therefore, to be admitting to the conduct element of the offence (killing another human being) with the state of mind for the crime of assault. And yet, if she acted in self-defence, she would be entitled to an acquittal, since it is undoubtedly the case that striking someone in self-defence is regarded as justifiable.

Does this mean that the analysis of crimes in terms of *actus reus* and *mens rea* is inadequate since it makes no mention of defences (except, impliedly, those which are intrinsic to the definitional elements of the offence)? It is possible to bring the example of self-defence within the *actus reus–mens rea* analysis by defining the *actus reus* of assault as an "unlawful" attack on another. By defining assault in this way one brings within the definition of the *actus reus* any matter which might affect the lawfulness of the attack—such as whether it was done in self-defence. This approach does not appear to have been adopted in Scotland (although it has found approval with both the Privy Council and with the English Court of Appeal, see *Beckford v. R.* [1987] 3 All E.R. 425 and *Gladstone Williams* [1987] 3 All E.R. 411).

An alternative method is to regard the defence as affecting the *mens rea* of the crime. This approach has recently been adopted by the High Court in the case of *Drury v. H.M. Advocate*, High Court, February 2, 2001, *unreported, post*, p. 407, in a case of murder, where the court suggested that, properly defined, murder required proof of a "wicked" intent to kill and that certain "defences" may have the effect of removing that element of "wickedness".

There is a superficial attractiveness to this approach—all elements required for the attribution of criminal responsibility are incorporated into the two, traditionally recognised, elements. There are, however, difficulties. Suppose, for example, that A is forced at gun-point to drive at 90 miles an hour along a motorway. He claims, when charged with the offence of exceeding the speed limit, that he acted under duress (which would provide a defence in such circumstances). Exceeding the speed limit in this way is an offence of strict liability, so that any analysis which gives effect to his defence by excluding the mental element would mean that he had no defence. To attribute the defence to the conduct element of the crime would require writing in to the statutory provisions creating the offence some such word as "unlawfully" to qualify exceeding the speed limit.

Conceptually, it is simpler to accept that factors which might excuse or justify conduct that would otherwise be criminal do not form part of the definition of the offence, but that they are relvant to the attribution of responsibility, and for that reason form part of the general analysis of criminal responsibility. (*Cf.* Lord Advocate's Reference No. 1 of 2000, High Court, March 30, 2001, *unreported, post*, p. 217.) A comprehensive analysis of crimes must take account not only of the external and mental elements required by the definition of the crime, but also of the possibility of defences which are not merely denials of those elements. Such a definition would read something like this: "A person is guilty of a crime if, without justification or excuse, he or she carries out the *actus reus* of that crime with the *mens rea* required for that crime." Issues of justification and excuse are discussed *post* in Chapter 7. This chapter is concerned with the *actus reus* and *mens rea* of crimes.

## 2. THE CONDUCT ELEMENT IN CRIME: *ACTUS REUS*

As was noted above, the concept of the *actus reus* of crimes is not limited to "acts" but, depending upon **2.02** the definition of the offence, may include acts, omissions and even states of affairs, as well as the consequences of acts and omissions, and any surrounding circumstances necessary to establish the offence.

The question of whether the accused is responsible for the acts and consequences, or the state of affairs, required to establish the *actus reus* of an offence is logically prior to the question whether the *mens rea* is made out. In *Kilbride v. Lake* [1962] N.Z.L.R. 590 the appellant was convicted on a charge of operating a motor vehicle on which there was no current warrant of fitness carried, contrary to regulation 52(1) of the Traffic Regulations 1956. The appellant had left the car parked in the street. When he returned to the vehicle he found, stuck to the inside of the windscreen, a traffic offence notice drawing his attention to the fact that a current warrant of fitness was not displayed. It was accepted that there had been a current warrant of fitness displayed at the time when he left the car, but that it had become detached in some way for which the appellant was not responsible. Much of the debate surrounding the case centred on whether this was an offence of strict liability, but in upholding the appeal, Woodhouse J. noted that before the question of *mens rea* was addressed it was necessary to determine whether there was an *actus reas*:

> "It is fundamental that quite apart from any need there might be to prove *mens rea*, 'a person cannot be convicted for any crime unless she has committed an overt act prohibited by law, or has made default in doing some act which there was a legal obligation upon him to do. The act or omission must be voluntary': *10 Halsbury's Laws of England*, 3rd ed., 272. He must be shown to be responsible for the physical ingredient of the offence. This elementary principle obviously involves the proof of something which goes behind any subsequent and additional inquiry that might become necessary as to whether the *mens rea* must be proved as well. Until that initial proof exists arguments concerning *mens rea* are premature. If the first decision to be made is that the offence excludes *mens rea*, then that finding is likely to disguise the fact that there is an absence of proof showing that the accused has done all that is charged against him, should this in fact be the case."

## A. Criminal acts

**2.03** The external element(s) of an offence will most frequently consist in someone doing something, or "acting". Generally speaking it is rare for an "act" in isolation to constitute a criminal offence. It is much more likely that the definition of an offence will require proof of an act which has certain consequences, or which takes place against a background of particular circumstances. If, for example, an accused is charged with murdering someone by shooting them, the *actus reus* consists not in the act of pulling the trigger, but in the combination of that act and its result, the death of the victim.

Most of the difficulties surrounding criminal "acts" relate to the question of what constitutes an "act" for these purposes and in particular the requirement that criminal acts be "voluntary". A particularly difficult question is whether conduct which is unconscious (such as sleepwalking, or actions under the influence of certain drugs or reflex actions) can be said to be "voluntary". In Scotland these issues tend to be treated not as matters affecting the *actus reus* of offences, but as going to the presence or absence of *mens rea*, or the existence of some excusing factor. They are discussed below in Chapter 7. The material which follows concentrates on two important exceptions to the requirement of an "act".

## B. Criminal omissions

**2.04** Criminal omissions may be divided into two broad categories. The first, which may be termed "pure" omissions, is comprised of offences which consist simply in a failure to do something which one is required (generally by statute) to do. The law looks only at the failure to act, and is not concerned about the consequences (if any) of such failure.

The second category of criminal omissions consists of what are often termed "crimes of commission by omission". In these cases, the omission to act replaces positive conduct as the external element of the offence. The offence, however, consists not in the failure to act, but in the consequences of such failure. It may be that the definition of some offences precludes their commission by omission. It is not entirely clear, for example, how one could commit an assault by omission (although see the case of *Fagan v. Commissioner of Metropolitan Police* [1968] 3 W.L.R. 1120, *post*, p. 61).

All examples of criminal omissions are controversial, since they impose liability for doing nothing. Crimes of commission by omission are particularly controversial because they impose liability for causing harm by doing nothing. They are made even more problematic because of issues of causation. How can it be said, for example, in a case of homicide, that a person can be guilty of causing the death of another by doing nothing? If A sees B drowning in a river, and refrains from assisting B, how can A be said to have "caused" B's death?

This section is concerned with the general principles concerning crimes of commission by omission. Consideration of this topic is not made easier by the dearth of Scottish authorities, but the general principles governing liability for omissions are not difficult to state: in general, there is no criminal liability for failing to act unless there is in the circumstances a positive duty to act which is recognised by the criminal law. So, for example, if one comes across a child drowning in a river and does nothing to help him or her, normally one will incur no criminal liability if the child drowns. If, however, the onlooker in such a case is the child's parent, then the situation may be different since the parent may be under a duty to protect the child. The question of liability for omissions thus becomes: "When is one under a duty to act such that failure to do so will result in criminal liability?" It is worth noting that that question in turn conceals two distinct (but related) issues: (i) in what circumstances a duty will arise; and (ii) what constitutes a failure to discharge that duty.

## (a) Breach of a duty imposed by law

## (i) Duty arising from relationship between the accused and the "victim"

### R. v. Gibbins and Proctor
### (1918) 13 Cr.App.R. 134

Gibbins and Proctor were convicted of the murder of Gibbins's seven-year-old daughter **2.05** Nelly, by starving her to death. The relevant facts are outlined in the judgment of Darling J. on appeal.

DARLING J.: "It has been said that there ought not to have been a finding of guilty of murder against Gibbins. The Court agrees that the evidence was less against Gibbins than Proctor; Gibbins gave her money, and as far as we can see it was sufficient to provide for the wants of themselves and all the children. But he lived in the house and the child was his own, a little girl of seven, and he grossly neglected the child. He must have known what her condition was if he saw her, for she was little more than a skeleton. He is in this dilemma; if he did not see her the jury might well infer that he did not care if she died; if he did he must have known what was going on. The question is whether there was evidence that he so conducted himself as to shew that he desired that grievous bodily injury should be done to the child. He cannot pretend that he shewed any solicitude for her. He knew that Proctor hated her, knew that she was ill and that no doctor had been called in, and the jury may have come to the conclusion that he was so infatuated with Proctor, and so afraid of offending her, that he preferred that the child should starve to death rather than that he should be exposed to any injury or unpleasantness from Proctor. It is unnecessary to say more than that there was evidence that Gibbins did desire that grievous bodily harm should be done to the child; he did not interfere in what was being done, and he comes within the definition which I have read, and is therefore guilty of murder.

The case of Proctor is plainer. She had charge of the child. She was under no obligation to do so or to live with Gibbins, but she did so, and receiving money, as it is admitted she did, for the purpose of supplying food, her duty was to see that the child was properly fed and looked after, and to see that she had medical attention if necessary. We agree with what Lord Coleridge C.J. said in *Instan* [1893] 1 Q.B. 450 [see *post*]: 'There is no case directly in point, but it would be a slur upon, and a discredit to the administration of, justice in this country if there were any doubt as to the legal principle, or as to the present case being within it. The prisoner was under a moral obligation to the deceased from which arose a legal duty towards her; that legal duty the prisoner has wilfully and deliberately left unperformed, with the consequence that there has been an acceleration of the death of the deceased owing to the non-performance of that legal duty.' Here Proctor took upon herself the moral obligation of looking after the children; she was *de facto*, though not *de jure*, the wife of Gibbins and had excluded the child's own mother. She neglected the child undoubtedly, and the evidence shews that as a result the child died. So a verdict of manslaughter at least was inevitable."

Appeals dismissed.

NOTES

The case of the father was quite clear, that of the woman less so. In the end the court chose to rely on **2.06** the notion of implied parental duty. Was it necessary to do so? Could this situation have been analysed as involving a course of positive conduct on the part of Proctor, designed to bring about the death of the child? Assuming that the "omission" analysis is correct, would it have been possible for Proctor to have avoided liability by refusing to have anything to do with the children from the outset?

### R. v. Russell
### [1933] V.L.R. 59

**2.07**     The appellant was charged with the murder of his wife and two young children by drowning them in a swimming pool. Evidence was given by the appellant to the effect that his wife had jumped into the pool herself, taking the children with her, and that he had made four unsuccessful attempts to save them, and that he had only given up when he realised that the children were dead. The jury were directed that the appellant would be guilty of murder if he drowned his wife and children, and (in response to a question from the jury) that he would be guilty of manslaughter if he merely stood by and did nothing while his wife drowned herself and the children. If, however, he had encouraged his wife's suicide and murder of the children he would be guilty of murder as an aider and abettor. The jury returned a verdict of manslaughter on all three counts. On appeal:

MANN J. (the trial judge): "The question of the jury was: 'Assuming that the woman took the children into the water without the assistance of putting them in the water by the man, but that he stood by, conniving to the act, what is the position from the standpoint of the law?' This question, heard with knowledge of the course of the trial, including the addresses of counsel and my own charge to the jury, was clearly directed, as I thought and still think, to the second and third counts only, which charged the accused with murder of his two children.

Upon the further consideration given to the matter upon this appeal, I am of opinion that the proper answer for me to have given to the question was that in the case supposed the accused would be guilty of murder.

But apart altogether from the question of murder or manslaughter, it is important that a decision as to the criminal liability of the accused in given circumstances should be referred to the right legal principles. I rested my answer to the jury in effect upon the principles of such cases as *R. v. Instan* [*post*]; *R.v. Gibbins and Proctor* [*ante*] and *R. v. Bubb* (1850) 4 Cox C.C. 455. These cases may be regarded as defining the legal sanctions which the law attaches to the moral duty of a parent to protect his children of tender years from physical harm. If applicable to the present case, those authorities would point to the accused's being guilty of what I may call an independent crime of murder. The outstanding difference between the facts of such cases as I have cited and the facts of the present case is the interposition in the latter of a criminal act of a third person which is the immediate cause of death; and the difficulty in such a case is in saying, in the absence of express authority, that the inaction of the accused has caused the death of the children, within the meaning of the criminal law.

I think the more correct view in the present case is that the prisoner on the facts supposed, while perhaps guilty of an independent crime, was certainly guilty as participator in the murder committed by his wife. The moral duty of the accused to save his children, the control which by law he has over his wife, and his moral duty to exercise that control, do not in this view cease to be elements in his crime. On the contrary, it is these elements which as a matter of law give to the acquiescence of the father in the acts of the mother committed in his presence the quality of participation. The control which the law recognises as exercisable by a husband over his wife is well illustrated in the doctrine that the mere presence of the husband at the commission by his wife of a felony, other than murder, is generally enough to exempt the wife altogether from criminal liability. The physical presence and the 'connivance' of a parent in the position of the accused has in law, in my opinion, a criminal significance not attaching to the presence and connivance of the mere 'passer-by' referred to in some of the cases.

It follows that the case put by me to the jury by way of contrast, though based upon a sound theoretical distinction, was not applicable to the special facts. The facts necessary to constitute aiding and abetting were too narrowly conceived, since no legal distinction can be made between tacit and oral concurrence, and a correct direction would be that not only was the accused morally bound to take active steps to save his children from destruction, but by his deliberate abstention from so doing, and by giving the encouragement and authority of his presence and approval to his wife's act, he became an aider and abettor and liable as a principal offender in the second degree.

I agree therefore with the view expressed by the Acting Chief Justice that upon the case put by the jury the accused was properly convicted, and that it is not necessary to determine finally whether the verdict can also be justified upon those different principles to which I referred in what I said to the jury. I also agree with him in thinking that the two views as to the foundation of liability did not in this case involve any different findings of fact, and that upon any view of the law no injustice can arise from the direction given at the trial."

MCARTHUR J.: "The question whether the verdict of manslaughter can stand depends, in my opinion, upon whether the learned Judge's charge to the jury on that subject was correct in law, and whether, having regard to His Honour's charge, the jury were justified in finding that the death of the prisoner's wife and children or any of them was caused by the prisoner's gross culpable neglect.

Leaving over for the moment the question of the prisoner's responsibility for the death of his wife, I am of opinion that the learned Judge's charge with regard to the prisoner's responsibility for the death of the children was correct, and that the conviction on the second and third counts should stand. The learned Judge bases the responsibility primarily upon the duty of the father, by reason of his parenthood, of caring for the safety of his children, who were in his charge and power. So far that is quite correct; and his direction that neglect of that duty would constitute manslaughter and not murder is also, in my opinion, correct....

In describing the duty of the prisoner it would perhaps have been more accurate to have said that he came under a duty to take all *reasonable* steps to prevent the commission of the crime. A man is not bound to take steps which in the circumstances no reasonable man would take in an attempt to save the life of his child. But it is clear that the learned Judge's charge would convey nothing more than that to the jury, because he almost immediately pointed out that it was only where he had 'power to interfere' and 'could have saved them', and 'refrained from interfering', that he was criminally responsible; and moreover, on the facts and in the circumstances of the case, and having regard to the view which the jury were taking—as indicated by the question they asked—it was obvious that the steps which the prisoner might have taken in order to have prevented his wife from drowning the children were such as any reasonable man would have taken, and could have taken, without risk or serious trouble to himself....

I think the conviction on the first count, manslaughter of the wife, cannot stand. Having regard to the questions asked by the jury and to the whole conduct of the case, we must assume, I think, that the jury were of opinion that the wife committed suicide. For the reasons already given I am of opinion that the jury have either found that the prisoner was not a participator in that crime committed by the wife, or they have, at least, not found that he was. And I am not prepared to say that the rules applicable to persons having the care and control of young and helpless children or of helpless adults can be applied to persons having the care of, or having under their protection adults who are not helpless, but are quite capable mentally and physically of looking after themselves. I am therefore of opinion that the prisoner cannot be convicted of the manslaughter of his wife merely because he stood by and did nothing while she committed suicide.

For these reasons I am of opinion that the conviction on the first count should be quashed, and that the convictions on the second and third counts should stand."

Appeal dismissed.

NOTES

**2.08**     1. This and the previous case are clear authority for the view that the parents of a child are under a duty to protect the child which itself will encompass the duty to rescue him or her from danger. In addition, Mann J. suggests in *Russell* that where one parent stands by and allows the other to harm their child there may be liability for aiding and abetting the principal offender. (*Cf.* in this respect, the situation where there is no relationship between the accused and the victim such as would impose a duty to act: *H.M. Advocate v. Kerr and Others* (1871) 2 Coup. 334, *post*, p. 149.) If this is correct, is it possible to convict either parent (or both) in the following situation? A and B are the parents of C. C is found to have been killed by being placed in a bath of scalding water. It is proved that A and B were both present at the time, that one of them only placed the child in the water, but there is no evidence as to which parent put the child in the water, *cf. H.M. Advocate v. Robertson* (1896) 2 Adam 92.

2. There is no doubt a duty on parents to ensure that their children do not come to harm. But the Scottish courts have shown a reluctance to extend the scope of any such duty. In *Paterson v. Lees*, 1999 S.C.C.R. 231 *post*, p. 574 the accused was convicted of conducting himself in a shamelessly indecent manner by allowing two young children whom he was baby-sitting to watch a pornographic video. He did not show the video to the children, but took no steps to prevent them watching it. On appeal the High Court held that there was no basis in law for holding that the accused was under a duty to prevent the children from watching the video, even assuming that he could be regarded as being *in loco parentis* at the time.

3. *Russell* raises the question of the husband's liability for the death of his wife. McArthur J. states that the husband owed no duty to his wife in the circumstances of this case. Whether or not there is a duty between spouses as such is uncertain. *Russell* suggests not. A different conclusion may, however, be inferred from *People v. Beardsley*, 150 Mich. 206, 113 N.W. 1128 (1907).

In that case the accused, in the absence of his wife, spent the weekend drinking with a woman (Blanche Burns). Towards the end of the weekend, and when the accused's wife was due to return, Blanche Burns bought and began to consume morphine tablets. The accused prevented her from taking some of the tablets, although she managed to consume a significant quantity. He took no steps to ensure that she was not in danger, but left her in the care of an associate. She died and the accused was convicted of manslaughter. On appeal, the Supreme Court of Michigan set aside the conviction. In delivering an opinion with which the other members of the court agreed, McAlvay C.J. observed:

> "... In the brief of the prosecutor his position is stated as follows:
>> 'It is the theory of the prosecution that the facts and circumstances attending the death of Blanche Burns in the house of respondent were such as to lay upon him a duty to care for her, and the duty to take steps for her protection, the failure to take which, was sufficient to constitute such an omission as would render him legally responsible for her death.... There is no claim on the part of the people that the respondent ... was in any way an active agent in bringing about the death of Blanche Burns, but simply that he owed her a duty which he failed to perform, and that in consequence of such failure on his part she came to her death.'

> Upon this theory a conviction was asked and secured ....

> Seeking for a proper determination of the case at bar by the application of the legal principles involved, we must eliminate from the case all consideration of mere moral obligation, and discover whether respondent was under a legal duty towards Blanche Burns at the time of her death, knowing her to be in peril of her life, which required him to make all reasonable and proper effort to save her; the omission to perform which duty would make him responsible for her death ....

> It is urged by the prosecutor that the respondent 'stood towards this woman for the time being in the place of her natural guardian and protector, and as such owed her a clear legal duty which he completely failed to perform'. The cases cited and digested establish that no such legal duty is created based upon a mere moral obligation. The fact that this woman was in his house created no such legal duty as exists in law and is due from a husband towards his wife, as seems to be intimated by the prosecutor's brief. Such an inference would be very repugnant to our moral sense. Respondent had assumed either in fact or by implication no care or control over his companion. Had this been a case where two men under like circumstances had voluntarily gone on a debauch together and one had attempted suicide, no one would claim that this doctrine of legal duty could be invoked to hold the other criminally responsible for omitting to make effort to rescue his companion. How can the fact that in this case one of the parties was a woman, change the principle

of law applicable to it? Deriving and applying the law in this case from the principle of decided cases, we do not find that such legal duty as is contended for existed in fact or by implication on the part of respondent towards the deceased, the omission of which involved criminal liability."

## (ii) Duty imposed on public official

Holders of certain public offices may be under a duty to act to uphold the law by virtue of their office. **2.09** Hume mentions the case of *Thomas Mitchell*, December 15 and 26, 1698 (Hume, 1, 297). There the charge was that Mitchell, being a magistrate, was obliged to assist a messenger who had been taken prisoner by "a rabble" but that he failed on two occasions to do so "under frivolous shifts and pretences". The court held that he could be found art and part liable in the assault upon the messenger. *Cf. Bonar and Hogg v. McLeod*, 1983 S.C.C.R. 161.

## (iii) Duty to remove a danger one has created

### MacPhail v. Clark
### 1983 S.C.C.R. 395

The accused, a farmer, set about ploughing a stubble field next to a busy main road. Before **2.10** doing so, he set fire to a quantity of straw in the field. The ground at the time was very dry. The fire spread across the field and set alight vegetation on an embankment next to the road. As a result, thick smoke affected both carriageways, so that visibility on the road was severely reduced. The driver of a Volkswagen Beetle stopped because he could not see. A petrol tanker ran into his car which was pushed off the road and down an embankment, injuring the occupants of the car. The accused took no steps to control the fire which he had started.

SHERIFF MCINNES: " . . . It seems to me that the accused did nothing wrong in setting fire to a pile of straw by the gate into the field. It is what he failed to do thereafter which gives rise to this prosecution. He could have ensured that the fire which he had started had burned itself out and would not spread. He could have put it out but did not. I believe that he knew very well that the fire was spreading and did nothing to stop it. It was foreseeable that the closer the fire got to the public road the greater was the danger of smoke affecting the visibility of road users. It was also foreseeable that if the fire spread to the embankment there would be greater risk of smoke affecting visibility from combustion of the materials then to be found on the embankment. . . .

The accused has been charged with causing danger by his culpable negligence and recklessly endangering the safety and lives of the occupants of the Volkswagen car and the petrol tanker. It was not disputed that such conduct can be criminal. It was accepted that the standard is that set out in the cases of *Paton v. H.M. Advocate*, 1936 J.C. 19 and *Quinn v. Cunningham*, 1956 J.C. 22. In *Paton*, Lord Justice-Clerk Aitchison said: '[I]t is now necessary to show gross, or wicked, or criminal negligence, something amounting, or at any rate analogous, to a criminal indifference to consequences, before a jury can find culpable homicide proved' [at p. 22]. Although the Lord Justice-Clerk regarded that state of the law as one which might have to be reconsidered, his view of the law was confirmed in Quinn in which at p. 24 the Lord Justice General said this of the foregoing statement: 'This represents the standard of culpability which must be established in such cases in order to constitute a crime at common law, based not upon intent, but upon reckless disregard of consequences . . . .

The standard of culpability must be the same, whether its consequences are death or not . . . .' On p. 25 the Lord Justice-General says that for a complaint to be relevant it must libel 'recklessness so high as to invoke an indifference to the consequences for the public generally.'

The question is whether the accused's conduct reaches that standard. If it does not, I am bound to acquit. I have come to the conclusion that the accused's conduct does reach that standard. The dangers of straw burning when there is a wind are well known and would be particularly well known to a person such as the accused, who is a farmer in partnership with his father. To set fire to straw at the upwind side of a field creates an obvious risk of the fire and smoke spreading downwind. In this case there was, as the accused well knew, a dual carriageway just downwind of the field. To leave the fire to spread and to do nothing whatever about it for at least twenty minutes, when he must have seen what was happening, in my opinion demonstrates a reckless indifference to the consequences for the public generally and for the particular road users mentioned in the complaint. In these circumstances I find the accused guilty of the charge."

Accused convicted.

NOTE

**2.11**    **1.** *Cf. Miller* [1983] 2 A.C. 161.

**2.** It is important to note that there was nothing unlawful, let alone criminal, in the accused's initial act of setting fire to the straw. The accused's responsibility arose from his failure to remove the danger which his actions had created. *Cf. H.M. Advocate v. McPhee*, 1935 J.C. 46. There the accused was charged with murdering a woman by assaulting her and leaving her unconscious in a field, exposed "while in an injured and unconscious condition to the inclemency of the weather". The death resulted from a combination of the initial injuries, and the additional harm which flowed therefrom. Is this a case in which it is necessary to rely on the failure to remove the danger, or is it sufficient simply to state that the accused's initial act caused death?

## (b) Duty assumed by the accused

### (i) Duty assumed under contract

**2.12** Exceptionally, criminal responsibility may arise where the accused has assumed a duty under contract to perform certain obligations, and fails to carry out those obligations. In the case of *William Hardie,* the accused was appointed as an Inspector of Poor. His duties included receiving and acting upon applications received from poor persons for relief. He received an application from a woman who was destitute, but did not act upon it and she died as a result. He was found guilty of culpable homicide. Such cases are rare at common law in Scotland, although there are more examples to be found under English law. In the case of *Pittwood* (1902) 19 T.L.R. 37 the accused was employed as a railway crossing gate-keeper. He opened a gate to allow a cart to cross the railway line, and then went off to have his lunch, forgetting to close the gate. In his absence another cart attempted to cross the railway through the open gates and was struck by a train. The accused was convicted of manslaughter. In such cases it is probably the case that there must be a reckless failure on the part of the accused to discharge his contractual obligations. Note also that in such cases there may be questions as to the extent of the contractual obligation. (In *Pittwood*, for example, it was argued, unsuccessfully, that the accused did not owe a duty of care to third parties under the contract, but only to his employer.)

### (ii) Duty assumed towards the sick or helpless

**2.13** Even without a formal contractual undertaking, an accused may be held responsible for failing to discharge a duty of care which she or he has voluntarily assumed.

**R. v. Instan**
[1893] 1 Q.B. 450

**2.14** The accused was convicted of the manslaughter of her 73-year-old aunt. The facts are fully outlined in the case stated by Day J. for the Court for Crown Cases Reserved.

DAY J.: "At the time of the committal of the alleged offence, and for some time previous thereto, she had been living with and had been maintained by the deceased. Deceased was a woman of some 73 years of age, and until a few weeks before her death was healthy and able to take care of herself. She was possessed of a small life income, and had in the house in which she lived some little furniture, and a few other articles of trifling value. The two women lived together in a house taken by the deceased; no one lived with them or in any way attended to them.

The deceased shortly before her death suffered from gangrene in the leg, which rendered her during the last 10 days of her life quite unable to attend to herself or to move about or to do anything to procure assistance. No one but the prisoner had previous to the death any knowledge of the condition in which her aunt thus was. The prisoner continued to live in the house at the cost of the deceased, and took in the food supplied by the trades people; but does not appear to have given any to the deceased, and she certainly did not give or procure any medical or nursing attendance to or for her, or give notice to any neighbour of her condition or wants, although she had abundant opportunity and occasion to do so.

The body of the deceased was on August 2, while the prisoner was still living in the house, found much decomposed, partially dressed in her day clothes, and lying partly on the ground and partly prone upon the bed. The death probably occurred from four to seven days before August 3, the date of the post-mortem examination of the body. The cause of death was exhaustion caused by the gangrene, but substantially accelerated by neglect, want of food, of nursing, and of medical attendance during several days previous to the death. All these wants could and would have been supplied if any notice of the condition of the deceased had been given by the prisoner to any of the neighbours, of whom there were several living in adjoining houses, or to the relations of the deceased, who lived within a few miles. It was proved that the prisoner, while the deceased must have been just about dying had conversations with neighbours about the deceased, but did not avail herself of the opportunities thus afforded of disclosing the condition in which she then was."

LORD COLERIDGE C.J.: "We are all of the opinion that this conviction must be affirmed. It would not correct to say that every moral obligation involves a legal duty; but every legal duty is founded on a moral obligation. A legal common law duty is nothing else than the enforcing by law of that which is a moral obligation without legal enforcement. There can be no question in this case that it was the clear duty of the prisoner to impart to the deceased so much as was necessary to sustain life of the food which she from time to time took in, and which was paid for by the deceased's own money for the purpose of the maintenance of herself and the prisoner; it was only through the instrumentality of the prisoner that the deceased could get the food. There was, therefore, a common law duty imposed upon the prisoner which she did not discharge.

Nor can there be any question that the failure of the prisoner to discharge her legal duty at least accelerated the death of the deceased, if it did not actually cause it. There is no case directly in point; but it would be a slur upon and a discredit to the administration of justice in this country if there were any doubt as to the legal principle, or as to the present case being within it. The prisoner was under a moral obligation to the deceased from which arose a legal duty towards her; that legal duty the prisoner has wilfully and deliberately left unperformed, with the consequence that there has been an acceleration of the death of the deceased owing to the non-performance of that legal duty. It is unnecessary to say more than that upon the evidence this conviction was most properly arrived at."

Conviction affirmed.

NOTES

1. Gordon (3rd ed.) (para. 3.37) objects to Lord Coleridge's confusion of law and morality, and **2.15** suggests that a better *ratio* for *Instan* is that "where people related as were the accused and the deceased live in the circumstances in which they lived, the law imposes an obligation—perhaps because it implies an undertaking—on the healthy person to look after the invalid."

2. In such cases the existence of a family relationship is not necessary in order to establish the duty, although the existence of such a family tie may make it easier to infer that the accused has assumed a

duty towards the "victim". See the cases of *Stone and Dobinson* [1977] Q.B. 354; *Bonnyman* (1942) 28 Cr.App.R. 131.

3. The fact that A has assumed the responsibility of caring for B and has failed in that responsibility is not, of itself sufficient to make A criminally responsible for the harm which ensues to B. As Erle C.J. pointed out in *Charlotte Smith* (1865) 10 Cox C.C. 82 (at p. 94): "The law is undisputed that, if a person having the care and custody of another who is helpless, neglects to supply him with the necessaries of life and thereby causes or accelerates his death, it is a criminal offence. But the law is also clear, that if a person having the exercise of free will, chooses to stay in a service where bad food and lodging are provided, and death is thereby caused, the master is not criminally liable."

## (c) Discharging the duty

**2.16** This is a topic which has not received much consideration in the authorities. In *Russell* (*ante*, p. 30) McArthur J. suggested that the proper approach was to require only that accused take "all reasonable steps to prevent the commission of the crime". According to his Lordship, "A man is not bound to take steps which in the circumstances no reasonable man would take." Much will of course depend on the circumstances of the case—the nature of the harm to be averted, the risks to the accused, the likelihood of success are all factors which need to be taken into account. In *U.S. v. Knowles* 26 F. Cas. 800; 4 Sawy. 517 (1864) the captain of a ship was charged with the murder of a member of the crew who had accidentally fallen overboard. It was alleged that the accused "wilfully omitted" to stop the ship, or to take any steps to rescue the crewman. It was further alleged that the latter "would have been rescued" had the captain stopped the ship and lowered row boats. In charging the jury Field C. J. stated:

> "Now, in the case of a person falling overboard from a ship at sea, whether passenger or seaman, when he is not killed by the fall, there is no question as to the duty of the commander. He is bound, both by law and by contract, to do everything consistent with the safety of the ship and of the passengers and crew, necessary to rescue the person overboard ... nothing will excuse the commander for any omission to take these steps to save the person overboard, provided they can be taken with a due regard to the safety of the ship and others remaining on board. Subject to this condition, every person at sea, whether passenger or seaman, has a right to all reasonable efforts of the commander of the vessel for his rescue, in case he should by accident fall or be thrown overboard."

The jury acquitted the accused.

## C. States of Affairs

### R. v. Larsonneur
### (1933) 24 Cr.App.R. 74

**2.17** The appellant, a Frenchwoman, was granted leave to enter the United Kingdom on certain conditions. These conditions were subsequently varied, requiring her to leave the United Kingdom immediately. She went to the Irish Free State, from whence she was deported and brought under arrest to Holyhead by the Irish police, where she was handed over to English police officers. She was convicted of an offence contrary to the Aliens Order 1920, Arts 1(3)(g) and 18(1)(b) as amended, the terms of which are set out in the opinion of Hewart L.C.J. On appeal:

HEWART L.C.J.: "The fact is, as the evidence shows, that the appellant is an alien. She has a French passport, which bears this statement under the date March 14, 1933, 'Leave to land granted at Folkestone this day on condition that the holder does not enter any employment, paid or unpaid, while in the United Kingdom', but on March 22 that condition was varied and one finds these words: 'The condition attached to the grant of leave to land is hereby varied so as to require departure from the United Kingdom not later than March 22, 1933.' Then follows the signature of an Under-Secretary of State. In fact, the appellant went to the Irish

Free State and afterwards, in circumstances which are perfectly immaterial, so far as this appeal is concerned, came back to Holyhead. She was at Holyhead on April 21, 1933, a date after the day limited by the condition on her passport.

In these circumstances, it seems to be quite clear that Art. 1(4) of the Aliens Order 1920 (as amended by the Orders of March 12, 1923, and August 11, 1931), applies. The Article is in the following terms: 'An immigration officer, in accordance with general or special directions of the Secretary of State, may, by general order or notice or otherwise, attach such conditions as he may think fit to the grant of leave to land, and the Secretary of State may at any time vary such conditions in such manner as he thinks fit, and the alien shall comply with the conditions so attached or varied. An alien who fails to comply with any conditions so attached or varied, and an alien who is found in the United Kingdom at any time after the expiration of the period limited by any such condition, shall for the purposes of this Order be deemed to be an alien to whom leave to land has been refused.'

The appellant was, therefore on April 21, 1933, in the position in which she would have been if she had been prohibited from landing by the Secretary of State and, that being so, there is no reason to interfere with the finding of the jury. She was found here and was, therefore, deemed to be in the class of persons whose landing had been prohibited by the Secretary of State, by reason of the fact that she had violated the condition on her passport. The appeal, therefore, is dismissed and the recommendation for deportation remains."

Appeal dismissed.

NOTES

1. The decision in *Larsonneur* has been almost universally condemned for its refusal to consider how **2.18** or why Miss Larsonneur came to be in the United Kingdom (see, *e.g.* Gordon, (3rd ed.) para. 8.29 who describes the decision as "ludicrous"). For a reappraisal and attempted rehabilitation of the decision, see Lanham, "Larsonneur Revisited" [1976] Crim.L.R. 276.

2. In *Winzar v. Chief Constable of Kent, The Times*, March 28, 1983 (Divisional Court) the appellant was convicted of being found drunk in a highway, contrary to section 12 of the Licensing Act 1872. The appellant had been taken on a stretcher to a hospital. The doctor who examined him formed the impression that he was drunk but that he was fit to leave the hospital. Although he was asked to leave he did not do so immediately. He was eventually carried out of the hospital and when the police arrived they formed the view that he was drunk, and took him to the police station. The court held that he had been correctly convicted of the offence. Compare that decision, and that of *Larsonneur*, with the following case.

### O'Sullivan v. Fisher
[1954] S.A.S.R. 33

The respondent was charged with being unlawfully drunk in a public place contrary to s.74(1) **2.19** of the Police Act 1936–51. The respondent was in a room on private premises at about 10.30 p.m. when the police arrived. He had been drinking. After some conversation with the police the respondent and the officers left the building and went out into the street where he was very soon arrested. The complaint against him was dismissed by the magistrate. The prosecutor appealed.

REED J.: "Section 74(1) of the Police Act 1936–1951 (as amended in 1946) provides that 'any person who is drunk in any road, street, thoroughfare or public place shall be guilty of an offence'. It was contended for the appellant that (to use the commonly accepted expression) *mens rea* is no part of the offence. By that, as I understand the argument, is meant that it is not necessary for the prosecution to prove either that the defendant intended to get drunk, or intended to be in the public place, and further, that it is not obligatory for the prosecution to establish that the defendant knew where he was. I have no hesitation in holding that the prohibition contained in s.74(1) is absolute and is not conditional on the defendant having a guilty mind. If, therefore, a defendant to a charge under s.74(1) is proved to have been drunk in a road, street, thoroughfare or public place he will, in the usual case, be convicted. The question still remains, however, whether any defence, not founded on a denial of either of the two elements just mentioned, is nevertheless open on a charge under this section.

The Special Magistrate found that the respondent was in Morphett Street for the reason that 'the police told him to go there from a private house where they found him'. After saying that no justification for that order had been proved, but whether or not there was any justification, and whether or not there was any purported arrest of the respondent on the premises (as alleged by him), the Special Magistrate said that the respondent 'may well have felt under compulsion to comply'. The respondent's evidence was that one of the constables told him in the upstairs room that he was under arrest. That was denied by the two police officers who gave evidence for the prosecution, and although the respondent said there were three constables present, it does not appear to be at all probable that that part of his evidence was accurate. The decision of the Special Magistrate does not rest upon a finding on that disputed issue, as the question is excluded in so many words. What did influence him appears to be that he could not believe that 'by the amendment to s.74 (in 1946) on which the prosecutor relies, namely, the substitution of the words "who is" for the word "found", Parliament intended to give the police authority to order a drunken person into a public place and then arrest him and have him convicted for being there.' I may say that I share that view, as it is not to be supposed that by the alteration of s.74 effected in 1946 Parliament intended to confer upon members of the police force powers that they did not previously possess in relation to persons on private property. To say that, however, does not decide this case. Mr Chamberlain put the common occurrence of the closing of a hotel bar at 6 p.m., when those who are in it are required to leave. If a man who has been drinking in the bar is drunk, he may go through the door into a street, and his exit may be expedited by a policeman in the bar who has told him to go. In such a case, as it seems to me, it would clearly be no defence to a charge under s.74 of the Police Act for the defendant to answer that he had been ordered out of the bar by a police officer, or that he believed he had been so ordered out and for that reason only he had gone into the street. So also, if a licensee acts under the provisions of s.143 of the Licensing Act and turns out of his licensed premises a person who is drunk by obtaining the assistance of a member of the police force, or if that person is expelled by a member of the police force on the demand of the licensee (cf. subs. (3)), that person has been lawfully evicted, and surely cannot succeed, on a charge under s.74 of the Police Act, by answering that he was, or believed he was, in the street by the order of a police officer.

Then again a drunken person may be in a public place after leaving a private residence, having been ejected therefrom by the occupier, who has used such force only as was reasonable to get rid of an unwelcome visitor. Whatever the powers of a police constable may be, I see no reason why an occupier who desires to eject a drunken person from his property should not request a police officer to assist him in removing such a person, and give him authority to use reasonable force in doing so. In such a case I cannot see that the person so ejected would have a defence to a charge under s.74, on the ground that he was in the public place as the result of the action of the occupier or of the police officer.

In all the cases I have taken as examples, the drunken person is in the public place by reason of some act that is lawful. Whatever may be the limits of compulsion as an answer to a charge of an offence against the law (to which I will refer later) I am unable to agree that, as a general proposition, a drunken person who comes into a public place because of a lawful action on the part of some other person is entitled to succeed on a charge of being drunk in a public place on the ground that he was lawfully compelled to be there. It may be that if a man who is drunk is arrested in a house for some offence and is taken in custody into the street, where he is detained until a police vehicle arrives, he would have an answer to a charge under this section, if the zeal of some police officer led him to lay such a charge. Such a defence, if valid, would I think rest upon a general ground not of the same nature as that which has been discussed.

The question whether compulsion is a defence to this charge has been debated. Mr Chamberlain contended, for the appellant, that the charge was established upon proof that the defendant was drunk, and was in a public place, and it was irrelevant how he came to be there.

For the present purpose, however, it appears to be sufficient to say that actual physical compulsion is recognised as an answer to a charge of murder in certain circumstances, as where A by force takes the hand of B, in which is a weapon, and therewith kills C—this is murder in A, but B is not guilty: *cf.*1 Hale P.C. 434, *Russell on Crimes* (10th ed., 1950) Vol. 1, p. 60: *Archbold on Criminal Pleading* (32nd ed., 1949), p. 20. In *Halsbury's Laws of England* (2nd ed.), Vol. 9, p. 23, the rule is stated as being: 'A person compelled by physical force to do an act which, if voluntarily done, would be a crime, is free from criminal responsibility, but the person compelling him is criminally liable'. In the case of murder above supposed, A is guilty. If, on the other hand, B, who is drunk, is sitting on the verandah of his house, which abuts on the street and A by force, and without any lawful authority, takes him into the street, it does not appear to be just to hold that B is guilty of an offence against s.74 of the Police Act. Furthermore, A would not be guilty of that offence, although he might be charged with assault, or some other offence. Being called upon to express an opinion, I state my view as being that if the respondent in the present case proved that he was compelled by physical force, used by a person or persons having no lawful right or authority to remove him from the premises, to go out into the street, he has established an answer to the charge.

With all respect to any who may hold the contrary view, it seems to me that the answer of duress or compulsion to a charge of an offence rests upon the right of an accused person to show that the act is one which in law cannot be imputed to him, and that the answer may be made in certain cases even though the person exercising the compulsion is not guilty of the offence with which the accused is charged (*cf. Cambridge Law Journal*, Vol. 6, at p. 91).

For these reasons the appeal will be allowed, and the order of dismissal will be set aside. I think the proper course to take is to remit the matter for rehearing. There are passages in the evidence that suggest that the two police officers acted at the request and upon the authority of the occupier of the premises, and it is possible that the respondent left voluntarily without the use of any force."

Appeal allowed.

NOTES

1. See also *R. v. Van Achterdam*, 1911 E.D.L. 336. In the latter case the accused was found drunk in a **2.20** police officer's garden. The police officer put him out into the street and told him to go home. He was too drunk to do so, and so the police officer arrested him for being drunk in a public place. His conviction for being drunk in a public place was subsequently quashed on the ground that the accused was put in the public place by the act of the police officer. The case does not appear to draw a distinction between lawful and unlawful compulsion by the police officer.

2. Section 19(1) of the Criminal Law (Consolidation) (Scotland) Act 1995 provides, inter alia: "Where a public service vehicle is being operated for the principal purpose of conveying passengers to or from a designated sporting event, then— ... (c) any person who is drunk on the vehicle shall be guilty of an offence ...." Would an offence be committed by A if he was (a) carried on to such a vehicle by friends while unconscious through drink; (b) required to get on to the bus by a police officer who was trying to clear the crowd after a designated sporting event? Would it make any difference to the answers to these questions to apply the reasoning in (i) *Larsonneur*, (ii) *O'Sullivan v. Fisher*, (iii) *R. v. Van Achterdam*?

## 3. The Mental Element In Crime: *Mens Rea*

The analysis of crimes in terms of external and mental elements—the *actus reus* and the *mens rea*—was **2.21** noted above. This section deals with the forms of *mens rea* and a number of general issues relating to the mental element in crime. Issues which relate specifically to the mental element in statutory offences are considered in the next chapter.

## A. General approaches to the mental element

### (a) Normative and Descriptive Approaches

**Hume, i, 21–22**

**2.22 "Of the nature of crimes**

In determining the extent of that part of the Law of Scotland, which has relation to CRIMES, I shall take that term in its ordinary acceptation; and shall consider every act as a crime, for which our practice has appointed the offender to make some satisfaction to the public, beside repairing, where that is possible, the injury sustained by the individual. It is obvious, that in exacting any such atonement, the law always supposes that the delinquent has infringed, in some respect, those duties which he owes to the community: He has set a dangerous example of violence, dishonesty, falsehood, indecency, irreligion; or he has trespassed with respect to some of those other articles of wholesome discipline, or wise economy, which affect the public welfare, and are matters of general concernment.

It does not seem necessary for me to say more, in this place, concerning the nature of crimes, as distinguished from civil wrongs; and I therefore proceed to submit a few remarks on the character of that Dole, as it is called,—that corrupt and evil intention, which is essential (so the light of nature teaches, and so all authorities have said) to the guilt of any crime. Now, in delivering this precept, those authorities are not to be understood in this sense, as if it were always necessary for the prosecutor to bring evidence of an intention to do the very thing that has been done, and to do it out of enmity to the individual who has been injured. In this more favourable sense to the prisoner, the maxim cannot be received into the law, for it would screen many great offenders from the due punishment of their transgressions. And I think it is only true in this looser and more general, but a practical and a reasonable sense, in which an English author of the first judgment in those matters has explained it: that the act must be attended with such circumstances, as indicate a corrupt and malignant disposition, a heart contemptuous of order, and regardless of social duty."

**Scottish Law Commission:**
The Mental Element in Crime
(Scot. Law Com. No. 80)

**2.23 "The Scottish approach**

2.14 Some crimes in Scotland, whether common law or statutory, raise fairly clearly the question of mental element. We have already mentioned, for example, the element of knowledge in reset, and recklessness in murder; and, of course, some statutory crimes necessarily require consideration of a mental element, for example where words such as 'knowingly' or 'with intent' are used. Further, it is no doubt true in theory that every common law crime requires *mens rea* of a kind, even if it is only in the very limited sense that the accused did what he did in the knowledge that he was doing it. It seems to us, however, that the Scots common law approach to mental element has historically been, and at the present day remains, rather different from that in England and Wales. Until comparatively recent times the only concept to express mental element in Scotland was that of 'dole', described by Hume as 'that corrupt and evil intention, which is essential (so the light of nature teaches, and so all the authorities have said) to the guilt of any crime'. While this rather moralistic concept of general wickedness has to some extent disappeared from Scots law, no doubt largely because of the proliferation of statutory crimes using express words of *mens rea*, it still remains as the background against which the mental element necessary for most common law crimes is to be measured. Indeed the concept of wickedness is still regularly, and on authority, used when describing the crime of murder. This approach to mental element, coupled with the fact that so much of the criminal law of Scotland is still part of the common law, has had several consequences. It has made it unnecessary for courts to consider and to construe words of mental element in relation to a wide range of crimes, and this has in turn meant that Scotland has been spared the proliferation of judicial glosses on such words that has occurred in England. As a result Scottish courts and juries have usually been able to concentrate more objectively on the *actus reus* of a common law crime, and to draw more readily what appear to be appropriate inferences from these objective facts, than appears to have been the case in England. If a question involving mental element is raised in the course of a trial, that will usually be because an accused person has himself put it in issue by, for example, introducing the state of his belief in relation to a defence of self-defence. Even in such cases, however, the question of mental element rarely appears to give rise to problems.

2.15 By contrast, the impression which we form from the Law Commission Report [*The Mental Element in Crime* (Law Com. No. 89, 1978)] and from our examination of English cases is that it is a feature of the system south of the Border that much elaborate, and to the Scots lawyer conceptually difficult, consideration is given to the problem of mental element. Despite this difference of approach we suspect that the end result in conviction or acquittal is more often than not much the same. One recent example, which we shall examine in more detail later, is to be found in the cases of *Allan v. Patterson*, 1980 S.L.T. 77 and *R. v. Lawrence* [1982] A.C. 510. Both were concerned with the interpretation of the word "recklessly" in sections 1 and 2 of the Road Traffic Act 1972. In the Scottish case a rather more objective approach was favoured by the High Court, whereas in the English case a rather more subjective approach was taken. In the end the two approaches were not all that dissimilar and in the English case Lord Diplock said ([1982] A.C. 510 at 527):

'I do not think that . . . the practical result of approaching the question of what constitutes driving recklessly in the way that was adopted by the Lord Justice-General in *Allan v. Patterson* is likely to be any different from the result of instructing a jury in some such terms as I have suggested above.'

While in these cases the approach north and south of the Border was not in the end greatly dissimilar there are, so far as we can see, many other instances where the English courts, perhaps because of the statutory form of much of the criminal law involved, have had to consider the question of mental element to an extent, and in a manner, which finds no parallel in Scotland."

NOTES

Although the term "dole" is not regularly used today, Hume's conception of the mental element in **2.24** crime is still influential, and can be seen in the use of phrases such as "wicked recklessness" in murder (*Cawthorne v. H.M. Advocate*, 1968 J.C. 32, *post*, p. 391), "wicked intent" in murder (*Drury v. H.M. Advocate*, High Court, February 2, 2001, *unreported*, *post*, p. 407), "evil intent" in assault (*Gray v. Hawthorn*, 1961 J.C. 13), and "cruel excess" in self-defence (*Fraser v. Skinner*, 1975 S.L.T. (Notes) 84). See also the references to "murderous" violence in such cases as *Kabalu v. H.M. Advocate*, 1999 S.C.C.R. 348 (*post*, p. 153) and *Cosgrove v. H.M. Advocate*, 1991 S.L.T. 25.

The difference between the traditional conception of "dole" and the notion of *mens rea* as that term is used in Anglo-American legal theory and in modern Scottish law is more than simply a matter of terminology. There is here a fundamental difference in approach to the question of the mental element. In very general terms, the Humean concept of "dole" involves an approach in which terms such as "malice", "wicked recklessness" and "evil intent" may be used normatively, to infer moral culpability on the part of the accused. The modern approach to *mens rea*, on the other hand, abandons any judgmental element, and uses terms in a purely descriptive fashion. Thus issues such as "intent" or "recklessness" become matters of definition, with no reference to the issue of moral culpability. (*Cf.* G. P. Fletcher, *Rethinking Criminal Law* (Boston, 1978), pp. 396 *et seq*.)

Gordon's view is that the approach to the mental element revealed in Hume (which he terms "general *mens rea*": (3rd ed., para. 7–05) is open to "serious objections":

"Criminal responsibility is concerned with actions and not with character, and it is not concerned with motive, which is the clue whereby a man's character can be related to his actions. There is a difference between the man who commits bigamy out of a sense of religious duty and the man who commits it out of a desire to deceive and seduce, but both are equally guilty of the crime" (para. 7–05).

The difficulty with this argument is that it assumes much of what it sets out to prove. The actors are both "equally guilty" only because the law ignores the motivation behind the offence. Why should motive be irrelevant if, in having regard to motive, we can clearly distinguish the moral positions of two actors? In any event, it is not true that motive is so universally disregarded. If for example one takes the case of coercion (where an accused commits an offence because he or she has been subjected to threats of death or serious bodily harm), it is clear that the accused's motive (self-preservation) is directly linked to the question of guilt.

Whether one adopts a normative or descriptive approach to the mental element can have important practical consequences. As Fletcher (*op. cit.*, pp. 399–400) points out:

"First, ... the normative theory of culpability provides an important (though not essential) premise in the argument requiring the prosecution to disprove claims of duress, insanity and mistake by proof beyond a reasonable doubt. Secondly, a commitment to a descriptive or normative theory of *mens rea* shapes one's attitude toward negligence as a ground of liability. Descriptive theorists are likely to view negligence as an aberrant basis of liability; normative theorists are more inclined to view negligence as a proper ground for blaming an actor for making a mistake or causing an accident."

And as Gordon further points out (para. 7–05):

"The notion of general *mens rea* also makes possible legal doctrines which depend on the transferring of a criminal mind directed to one crime from that crime to another, so that a person who accidentally does X while criminally doing Y may be deemed to have done X criminally, but although there are traces of this in Scots law, it has never attained the importance, scope or rigidity of the common law felony-murder doctrine."

The major difficulty encountered in applying either theoretical approach to Scots law is the lack of consistency found in judicial pronouncement. It is clear, for example that the "normative" approach has been highly influential in relation to the law of murder. where the idea of "wicked recklessness" as a form of the *mens rea* for that crime is well-established and where the distinction between an intention to kill and a "wicked" intention to kill has recently emerged (see *Drury v. H.M. Advocate*, High Court, February 2, 2001, *unreported, post*, p. 407).

On the other hand, there is a tendency in some judgments to use phrases such as "evil intent", while at the same time redefining them in what might be described as a "descriptive" approach. Thus while the essence of the crime of assault is said to be "evil intent" (*Smart v. H.M. Advocate*, 1975 S.L.T. 65, *post*, p. 301), a phrase with clear judgmental overtones, that "evil intent" tends to be characterised as an intention to inflict bodily harm (*Smart, post*, p. 302).

Normative language is frequently criticised as being insufficiently precise for the requirements of the criminal law. According to this view, terms such as "wicked recklessness", "cruel excess" and "shameless indecency" lack the precision necessary for use in the definition of crimes. The lack of precision means that the accused is not given fair notice of what is or is not prohibited by the law, and, moreover, may lead to the inconsistent application of the criminal law (since the views of one judge or jury as to what is "wicked" or "cruel" or "shameless" might not be the same as those of another judge or jury). The weight of this criticism would, however, be difficult to judge without extensive research on how different judges and juries interpret such terms in the light of actual cases— research which simply does not exist. Moreover, there is no reason to suppose that purely descriptive terms provide any greater degree of information to the would-be criminal of what is or is not permitted by the criminal law.

The use of normative terms does, on the other hand, contribute to the declaratory and denunciatory role of the criminal law. Although modern criminal law does not confine crimes to conduct which would be regarded as morally wrong, there is no doubt that punishment under the criminal law is closely linked to moral condemnation, and in that sense there should be little objection to the use of language which carries with it the moral judgment of the community on what the accused has done.

## (b) Objective and Subjective Mens Rea

We have seen that, in accordance with the maxim *actus non facit reum nisi mens sit rea*, proof of a mental **2.25** element is, as a general rule, required in order to establish criminal liability. What this means is that the Crown must prove, in relation to the elements of conduct, (and, where relevant, the surrounding circumstances) which make up the *actus reus*, that the accused had the state of mind required for the offence. But in doing so, must the prosecutor prove the actual state of mind of the accused the time of the offence, or some inferred state of mind, or even some *presumed* state of mind. In *R. v. Hancock and Shankland* [1986] 1 All E.R. 641 the accused pushed a block of concrete off a bridge over a road, into the path of an oncoming vehicle. The block went through the windscreen of the vehicle, and killed the driver. The accused said that they did not intend to kill him and, indeed, did not intend to hurt him or anyone else. Their intention in pushing the block off the bridge was to intimidate a passenger whom they knew was in the back of the taxi. In such a case, is it necessary for the prosecutor to show that the accused did in fact intend to cause injury to the driver (or some other person), or can the prosecutor argue that such injury was the natural and probable consequences of such an act, and that the accused should therefore be presumed to have intended that consequence? Similarly, if the argument proceeds on the basis of recklessness, is it necessary for the prosecutor to prove that the accused were aware of the risk of injury, or would it be sufficient for the prosecutor to show that the risk was one which would have been obvious to any reasonable person in the circumstances?

Where proof of actual intent, or actual awareness of risks is required, responsibility is said to be based on a principle of "subjective" *mens rea*. Where presumed intent, or reliance on the obviousness of the risk, is sufficient for criminal liability, responsibility is said to be based on "objective" *mens rea*. The question which arises is whether Scots law adopts a subjective or an objective approach to *mens rea*.

In *Ross v. H.M. Advocate*, 1991 J.C. 210, Lord McCluskey commented at some length on the necessity of proving a mental element in order to establish criminal responsibility. Having noted that the *onus* of proving the mental element rested on the prosecutor, he continued (at p. 229):

> "How then is the Crown to discharge this burden? That is an everyday problem. The Crown discharges that burden by laying before the court evidence as to the behaviour of the accused person and as to the whole context in which he behaved. It might be possible, in a particular case, to add other evidence showing directly the accused's state of mind, being evidence of statements made by the accused person, whether before or after the event, which cast light directly upon his state of mind at the time when he acted. The behaviour itself at the material time might even include shouts or threats of words emanating from the accused person (*res gestae*) which make his state of mind, or his intention, crystal clear. These then are the normal ways in which *mens rea* is proved. It is either proved directly by leading evidence of what the accused person has said or it is proved indirectly as an inference from all the circumstances; quite commonly there is both direct and indirect evidence from which it may properly be said that his *mens rea* can be established. Mens rea is a subjective state of mind, as *Morgan* and *Meek* make clear, but objective proof is commonly a most important element in establishing the state of the accused's mind. What is abundantly clear is that there is no presumption that an accused person had *mens rea* at the material time.... It therefore appears to me to follow from the most basic principles applicable to our criminal law that it is for the Crown to establish by evidence that the subjective state of the accused's mind at the material time could properly be described as *mens rea*."

However, in the very same case, Lord Hope, in discussing the rule that voluntary intoxication cannot exclude criminal responsibility made the following observation (at p. 214):

> "I have already mentioned the exception on grounds of public policy which applies where the condition which has resulted in an absence of *mens rea* is self induced. In all such cases the accused must be assumed to have intended the natural consequences of his act."

The view that a person is taken to have intended the natural and probable consequences of his acts reflects a wholly objective approach to *mens rea*. This approach is not confined to the case where the accused attempts to rely on voluntary intoxication as an excuse. In *Brown and Another v. H.M. Advocate*, 1993 S.C.C.R. 382, Lord Marnoch adopted the same approach in charging the jury in a murder case.

There is, furthermore, a rule in the law of homicide that in certain circumstances in a murder case the judge is entitled to withdraw from the jury the possibility of returning a verdict of culpable homicide, where death has resulted from extreme violence, which again suggests a highly objective approach. (See *post*, Chapter 10.) It is also clear from the definition of recklessness (see *post*, pp. 46–50) that that concept is understood in an objective sense.

In general, then, it is, with respect, not correct to suggest, as Lord McCluskey does, that *mens rea* is a subjective matter in Scots law. On the contrary, it is for the most part a highly objective question. Those cases in which a subjective approach has prevailed (for example in relation to the mental element in rape—see *Jamieson v. H.M. Advocate*, 1994 S.L.T. 537, *post*, p. 357) are widely regarded as exceptional, and, indeed, anomalous.

## B. Particular forms of the mental element

### (a) Intention

**2.26** There has been very little discussion of the concept of intention in Scots law, in marked contrast to the extensive discussions of the concept in other jurisdictions. (Many of the relevant references are conveniently gathered together in Gordon (3rd ed.) para. 7.13, n. 37.) This is in part due to the fact that many common law crimes, and most older statutes, do not use the term "intention", but other terms (such as "maliciously", or "wickedly" or "wilfully"), and also to an unwillingness on the part of the Scottish courts to engage in what might be regarded as a somewhat empty debate about the meaning of terms. This is especially true where recklessness is available as an alternative form of *mens rea*, since there is little point in debating whether the accused "intended" a particular act or its consequences, when there is no doubt that his or her conduct could be characterised as "reckless".

There are, however, some offences which can only be committed intentionally, and in such cases it may be necessary to provide some guidance as to the meaning of the term. The following case provides one of the few examples of a Scottish court offering a definition of the term "intention".

**Sayers and Others v. H.M. Advocate**
1981 S.C.C.R. 312

**2.27** The appellants were charged, *inter alia*, with conspiring to further by criminal means the purpose of an association (the Ulster Volunteer Force) and to acquire unlawfully firearms, ammunition and explosive substances "intending by means thereof to endanger life or cause serious injury to property or to enable other persons by means thereof to endanger life or cause serious injury to property." In the course of his charge to the jury on this part of the indictment, Lord Ross offered the following explanation of the word "intending".

LORD ROSS: "Now, while dealing with this part of the indictment I should also just explain one or two of the expressions that have been used in this first part of the indictment. You will see that the first purpose is said to be to further by criminal means the purposes, and so on. Now, 'criminal' is the adjective of 'crime', and a crime is any act which is punishable by law.

Then you will see lower down it says '... and to acquire unlawfully firearms, ammunition and explosive substances'. Now the word 'unlawful' simply means contrary to law, without legal authority. In the next line you will see that the word appears 'intending', and this is a word which appears at several different portions of this indictment. You may feel that you don't really need any assistance in knowing what the word 'intending' means, but if assistance were needed I can perhaps do no better than quote to you what a distinguished judge has given as his interpretation of intention or intending when these words are used. What this judge said was as follows: 'An "intention" to my mind connotes a state of affairs which the party "intending" ... does more than merely contemplate, it connotes a state of affairs which, on the contrary he decides, so far as in him lies, to bring about, and which, in point of possibility, he has a reasonable prospect of being able to bring about, by his own act of volition' [*Cunliffe v. Goodman* [1950] 2 K.B. 237, Asquith L.J. at 253]. So it is a state of affairs which an individual decides so far as he can to bring about and which he has reason to think can be brought about by his own act."

NOTES

1. Although *Cunliffe v. Goodman* is a civil case, Asquith L.J.'s approach was quoted with approval by **2.28** Lord Hailsham in *Hyam v. DPP* [1974] 2 All E.R. 41 at pp. 51–52, It was adopted, or, more correctly, adapted, by the Court of Appeal in *Mohan* [1975] 2 All E.R. 193 as a basis for defining the intent required for attempted crime. In *Mohan,* James L.J. defined that intent as (at p. 200):

> "a decision to bring about, in so far as it lies within the accused's power, the commission of the offence which it is alleged the accused attempted to commit, *no matter whether the accused desired that consequence or not.*" (Emphasis added.)

The definition proposed by Lord Ross in *Sayers* may be described as "purposive," in that it relates to the aim or purpose of the accused, and should be contrasted with James L.J.'s gloss which makes it clear that a person can "intend" a consequence even though they do not "desire" it to happen. Indeed, intention, can embrace a much wider range of mental attitudes towards consequences, and even surrounding circumstances. Some examples will serve to illustrate the range of possibilities:

(1) A wants to kill B, but B has left the country. A knows that the only hope he has of achieving B's death is to manufacture a parcel bomb and send it to B. He knows that his chances of success are slight because (a) he has no experience of making such bombs, (b) B lives in the depths of the jungle where postal services are unreliable, and (c) he has no way of knowing if B will open the parcel if it reaches him. He makes the bomb and sends it to B.

Does A "intend" to kill B? The passage quoted by Lord Ross suggests not, because there is not, in this case, a reasonable prospect of A achieving what he wants to achieve. But if A's plan works why should we not say that he intended B's death? He has achieved what he desired. As Wilson points out (William Wilson, *Criminal Law: Doctrine and Theory*, p. 124), "Purposive action is the clearest possible case of intentional action". As Ashworth puts it, "The core of 'intention' is surely aim, objective, or purpose; whatever else 'intention' may mean, a person surely acts with the intention to kill if killing is the aim, objective, or purpose of the conduct causing death." (*Principles of Criminal Law*, 3rd ed., at p. 177).

There may, of course, be cases in which the means adopted by A to achieve his purpose are so highly improbable that we would begin to question whether he does "intend" those consequences—for example A's preferred method of assassination is to stick pins in a voodoo doll—but short of such fantastical methodologies, it is not unjust to hold that A intends those things which it is his purpose to achieve, even if his chances of success are remote.

(2) A puts petrol through B's letter box and sets fire to it. A does this in order to frighten B, but realises that it is (i) possible, (ii) probable, (iii) highly probable, (iv) virtually certain, that the occupants of the house will be injured. Does A intend to injure the occupants in any of these cases?

Two questions arise here: (a) Since in this case injury is not part of A's purpose can A nevertheless be regarded as intending that consequence, and, if so, (b) what degree of probability is needed before that conclusion can be reached? Although opinions differ, it can be argued that, with the possible exception of scenario 2(iv), A does not "intend" to cause injury to the occupants of the house. Foreseeing consequences as likely to follow from one's action, even to a high degree of probability, is not the same thing as intending them. However, such foresight may be treated as evidence from which intention may be inferred.

But outside the courts, would we not generally accept that in scenario 2(iv) A intends to cause injury. What could A say to us to dissuade us from holding that he intended injury in such a case? If we do not accept, in the abstract, that A intends injury in that case, then are we content to accept, for example, that the terrorist, who plants a bomb which injures a member of the bomb disposal team called to disarm his device does not "intend" to injure that person?

(3) A and B are born as "conjoined twins". They both have most of their vital organs, but there is only one functioning heart, which is in A's chest cavity. This heart supplies oxygenated blood to both of them. It is clear that A could survive independently of B, but that B could not survive independently of A. It is also clear that if they are left as they are, the demands of both children on the heart will cause it to fail. A decision is taken to separate the twins, in the knowledge that A will survive and B will die, but this is the only way in which A will survive. The operation is performed and B dies. Did the surgeon intend to kill

B? (*cf. Re A (children) (conjoined twins: surgical separation)* [2000] 3 F.C.R. 577.) Does it matter in such a case whether B's death is regarded as a necessary pre-condition to saving A's life, or as a necessary consequence of doing so?

In this case the surgeon's purpose is to save A's life. The only way in which this can be achieved is to adopt a course of action which will inevitably cause B's death. It is generally accepted that where an actor intends a particular purpose or end result, he intends those things which are done as a means to that end. This is true even if the actor would prefer if he or she could achieve those ends without the undesired consequence. (The doctor can avoid criminal responsibility by pleaded necessity, rather than by arguing that she did not intend to kill B.)

(4) A and B, two cowboys, are arguing about which of them is faster on the draw. They agree to test this, and A wins, by a fraction. B says, "I bet you don't have the nerve to shoot" and A, without thinking, pulls the trigger and shoots B, killing him. Did A intend B's death? (*Cf. Moloney* [1985] 1 All E.R. 1025.)

It might be argued, on the basis of Lord Ross's statement that A did not intend to kill B because he did not "decide" to bring about B's death. Again, this conclusion is one which would generally be rejected. In many instances we can fairly be said to act intentionally even though we make no decision to act, and our actions involve no reflection upon their consequences. "Instinctive" actions can be, and usually are, intentional, as where a driver breaks suddenly when a child runs out in front of him. We would have no difficulty in saying that the driver intended to stop.

Questions such as these have not troubled the Scottish courts. It remains to be seen, therefore, how the courts would define intention if called upon to do so. It is suggested that while Lord Ross's views in *Sayers* provide a convenient starting point, they leave many questions unanswered.

## (b) Recklessness

**2.29** Recklessness involves the idea of risk taking, in circumstances where to take the risk is unjustifiable. In English law it is regarded as a state of mind available as an alternative to intention in a range of offences. Much of the discussion in England has concentrated on the distinction between "subjective" and "objective" recklessness. The former requires proof that the accused was aware of the risks involved in what he was doing. The latter requires only that the risks were such as would have been obvious to a reasonable person. To the extent that the matter has been discussed at all in detail, the Scottish cases on recklessness indicate an objective approach. But those cases may reveal a more profound difference between the Scottish and English approach in that the Scottish cases tend to regard "reckless" and "recklessness" as terms which describe how the accused has behaved, rather than what was going on in his head at the time he committed the *actus reus*. This is apparent from the following case, and from the case law on reckless injury and endangerment set out in Chapter 8.

### Allan v. Patterson
1980 S.L.T. 77

**2.30** The respondent was charged with reckless driving, contrary to s.2 of the Road Traffic Act 1972, as amended by s.50 of the Criminal Law Act 1977. The sheriff acquitted the respondent, and the Crown appealed by way of stated case to the High Court. The circumstances of the offence, and the grounds for the sheriff's acquittal are outlined in the opinion of the court.

OPINION OF THE COURT: "In this appeal by the Crown this court is required for the first time to consider s.2 of the Road Traffic Act 1972 as that section has been amended by the Criminal Law Act 1977, s.50. Before the amendment the section read as follows: 'If a person drives a motor vehicle on a road recklessly, or at a speed or in a manner which is dangerous to the public, having regard to all the circumstances of the case, including the nature, condition and use of the road, and the amount of traffic which is actually at the time, or which might reasonably be expected to be, on the road, he shall be guilty of an offence.' It now reads: 'A person who drives a motor vehicle on a road recklessly shall be guilty of an offence.'

At the hearing before us the appellant and the respondent joined issue on the proper interpretation of this section and in particular as to the test to be applied by a judge or a jury in determining whether the offence created by s.2 in its amended form has been established by the prosecutor.

These questions come before us in this way, The respondent went to trial in the sheriff court at Jedburgh upon a summary complaint in which he was charged in these terms—that on September 11, 1978 on the Kelso to Ednam road and Edenside Road, Kelso, District of Roxburgh, you did drive a motor vehicle, namely a motor cycle, recklessly and at a place where a child on his way to or from school was seeking to cross the road, and having been required to stop said motor cycle by a school crossing patrol in uniform, and exhibiting a prescribed sign, did fail to stop said motor cycle: Contrary to the Road Traffic Act 1972, s.2.'

After trial the sheriff acquitted the respondent. According to the Crown the sheriff in so doing misdirected himself as to the meaning and implications for the prosecutor of s.2 as amended. The particular submission was that although the sheriff appears to have found in fact that the respondent drove his motor cycle with a high degree of negligence in all the circumstances of the case he acquitted the respondent only because on his construction of s.2 in its new form he concluded that no person can be convicted of driving 'recklessly' unless it is shown: (a) that he knew that there were material risks in driving in a particular manner and (b) that he deliberately decided to drive in that manner regardless of the possible consequences. In short, it was contended, the sheriff applied what has been called a subjective test. Upon the assumption that the sheriff so directed himself we shall now come to the competing submissions.

For the Crown the submission can be stated shortly. There is no doubt that the question whether a person has committed the offence created by s.3 of the Act, *i.e.* of driving a motor vehicle on a road without due care and attention or without reasonable consideration for other persons using the road, must be answered by the application of an objective test. A judge or a jury, accordingly, must simply ask themselves whether the particular act of driving established in evidence demonstrated a want on the part of the driver of that degree of care and attention or consideration for other persons to be expected of a competent and careful driver. In considering a charge brought under ss.1 and 2 of the Act in their unamended form (and such a charge normally included the word 'recklessly' as well as the succeeding words 'or at a speed or in a manner etc.') the simple task of a judge or a jury was to consider the act of driving which, by reason of speed or otherwise, was in their judgment dangerous to the public having regard to all the circumstances of the case including those specially mentioned in the sections. In its amended form there is nothing in the language of s.2 (and similar considerations apply to s.1 as amended) to indicate an intention on the part of Parliament that the test to be applied is no longer to be objective. The word 'reckless' in its ordinary meaning is well understood. The adverb 'recklessly' is an adverb of manner qualifying the verb 'drives.' In its context it plainly means a piece of driving which, judged objectively, is eloquent of a high degree of negligence much more than a mere want of due care and attention and supports the inference that material risks were deliberately courted or that these risks which ought to have been obvious to any observant and careful driver were not noticed by reason of gross inattention. Driving 'recklessly' accordingly, is driving which demonstrates a gross degree of carelessness in the face of dangers.

For the respondent counsel resolutely defended the proposition that no man can be said to drive 'recklessly' unless it is shown that he actually knew of certain material risks in driving in a particular way and nevertheless elected to drive in that way with complete indifference to the possible consequences.

We have no difficulty in reaching the conclusion that the Crown submission must receive effect. There is nothing in the language of s.2 as amended to suggest an intention on the part of Parliament to penalise thereunder only a course of driving embarked upon wilfully or deliberately in the face of known risks of a material kind. Inquiry into the state of knowledge of a particular driver accused of the offence created by the section as amended and into his intention at the time is not required at all. The statute directs attention to the quality of the driving in fact but not to the state of mind or the intention of the driver. If it were otherwise, the section, and indeed s.1, would virtually become inoperable in all but the rarest of instances. Neither is the skill or capacity of the particular driver in issue: the offence can be committed whether or not the event is followed or demonstrated by a casualty. All that is in issue and all that Parliament requires the court or the jury to consider and determine is the degree to which the driver in question falls below the standard to be expected of a careful and competent driver in all the circumstances of the particular case and whether the degree is such as properly to attach in the judgment of court or jury the epithet or label of 'reckless'.

Section 2, as its language plainly, we think, suggests, requires a judgment to be made quite objectively of a particular course of driving in proved circumstances, and what the court or a jury has to decide, using its commonsense, is whether that course of driving in these circumstances had the grave quality of recklessness. Judges and juries will readily understand, and juries might well be reminded, that before they can apply the adverb 'recklessly' to the driving in question they must find that it fell far below the standard of driving expected of the competent and careful driver and that it occurred either in the face of obvious and material dangers which were or should have been observed, appreciated and guarded against, or in circumstances which showed a complete disregard for any potential dangers which might result from the way in which the vehicle was being driven. It will be understood that in reaching a decision upon the critical issue a judge or jury will be entitled to have regard to any explanation offered by the accused driver designed to show that his driving in the particular circumstances did not possess the quality of recklessness at the material time.

We ought, we think, to mention that in the course of his submission the learned advocate-depute drew our attention to a passage in Wilkinson's *Road Traffic Offences* (9th ed.) p. 287, where the author suggests that in respect of the offence now defined by s.2, as amended, a court will require to consider a driver's state of mind. With that suggested construction we profoundly disagree. The author also declares that the following definition proposed by the Law Commission (of England) is perhaps as satisfactory as any other; 'A person is reckless if (a) knowing that there is a risk that an event may result from his conduct or that a circumstance may exist, he takes that risk, and (b) it is unnecessary for him to take it having regard to the degree and nature of the risk which he knows to be present.' The author goes on to say 'The test in (a) is subjective and the test of necessity of (b) is objective.' It will be appreciated from what we have said that the section is concerned with the quality of a proved course of driving and that there is nothing in its language to indicate that that quality is to be assessed otherwise than objectively. We cannot accordingly approve of the definition as an aid in deciding whether a s.2 offence has been committed. Apart from this it appears to us that the editor falls into the error of failing to appreciate that the proposed definition is apparently intended, as it says, to define a reckless person. What this statute is defining or seeking to define is a manner of driving—a very different matter. The Law Commission's definition is, in any event, one which, if it did not confuse a judge would bemuse most juries. Finally, we have only to add that although we were very properly referred to the English cases of *R. v. Clancy* [1979] R.T.R. 312 and *R. v. Davis (William)* [1979] R.T.R. 316, it is evident that in neither was the Court of Appeal called upon to decide whether the relevant test in respect of a s.2 offence is in whole, or even in part, subjective, and, indeed, there is much in the opinion delivered in the latter case by Geoffrey Lane L.J. (as he then was) to indicate that, as we think, the approach must be totally objective."

> Case remitted to the sheriff in order that he might inform the court whether, in the light of their opinion, he would have convicted; the High Court subsequently ordered him to convict.

NOTES

**2.31**    1. This case concerns the meaning of the word "reckless" as it appears in a modern statutory offence. It has been applied to other statutory offence, including the crime of vandalism (*Black v. Allan*, 1985

S.C.C.R. 11, *post*, p. 551) and maliciously causing an explosion contrary to section 2 of the Explosive Substances Act 1883 (*McIntosh v. H.M. Advocate*, 1994 S.L.T. 59). It was also accepted as providing the appropriate standard for recklessness in the common law offence of recklessly endangering others by discharging a firearm (*Gizzi and Another v. Tudhope*, 1982 S.C.C.R. 442. However, some more recent decisions have queried whether a test formulated for the construction of a statutory provision relating to reckless driving can appropriately be applied in the context of the common law offences of recklessly endangering the public by discharging a firearm (*Cameron v. Maguire*, 1999 S.C.C.R. 44—a case very similar to *Gizzi*) and reckless fire-raising (*Carr v. H.M. Advocate*, 1994 S.C.C.R. 521.)

In the latter case, the appellant was charged in the alternative with wilful fireraising or culpable and reckless fireraising. He had broken into a church hall. He lit a match in order to see, but that was not very effective. He then lit a roll of paper towels and when these began to burn his hands he dropped them and left the building. The burning towels set fire to some curtains and eventually the hall was burned to the ground. The accused was convicted of wilful fireraising. In upholding the appeal, the Lord Justice-General (Hope) commented on the appropriate directions on recklessness in such a case:

"We think that what [the sheriff] then said in order to define what was meant by recklessness in this context was not entirely satisfactory. The explanation which he gave was based on what was said by Lord Justice General Emslie in *Allan v. Patterson*, 1980 J.C. at p. 60; 1980 S.L.T. at pp. 79–80 about the adjective 'recklessly' in the context of a charge of reckless driving. That definition in both its branches is entirely in point in a case where the accused is charged with doing something which is otherwise lawful but with doing it in a manner which can be described as reckless. But in a case of fireraising it is not the manner of doing an act which would otherwise be lawful which is in issue but the question whether the accused had the *mens rea* necessary for the commission of a crime. It would have been more appropriate for the sheriff therefore to confine his definition to the question whether the accused's actions showed a complete disregard for any dangers which might result from what he was doing and in particular of the fire taking effect on the premises."

See also, in this respect, *Thomson v. H.M. Advocate*, 1995 S.L.T. 827. It is not clear whether such *dicta* should be taken as suggesting that there are two kinds of recklessness—a statutory form, which is based on *Allan v. Patterson*, and a common law form. Part of the problem in applying *Allan v. Patterson* to the common law offences is that the offence in *Allan v. Patterson* was a "conduct" offence whereas the offences discussed in *Maguire*, *Carr* and *Thomson* all required proof of a result. The definition of recklessness in *Allan v. Patterson* was shaped to meet the description of a driver driving recklessly, and it is not easily applied to offences which require proof of *mens rea* with regard to a particular result.

2. *Allan v. Patterson* certainly emphasises that what is at stake in recklessness is an objective assessment of the conduct in question, rather than the state of mind of the accused. This can be seen from the distinction drawn by the court between a "reckless person" and "reckless driving". Conduct which, judged objectively, creates substantial risks of injury to others, or damage to property can be adjudged reckless, even if the accused is not aware of those risks. The language used to describe the gravity of the risks tends to vary (see in this respect the language used in the case-law on reckless injury and reckless endangerment in Chapter 8 and the cases on culpable homicide in Chapter 10), but the overall picture is unmistakeable. Mere carelessness or negligence will not suffice for recklessness. The accused must be shown to have conducted himself in a way which manifests a complete disregard for the consequences of his conduct.

3. In *Allan v. Patterson*, the court was at pains to point out that before a finding of recklessness can be made, the Crown must prove that the manner of driving fell below "the standard to be expected of a careful and competent driver in all the circumstances of the particular case". This is an important element of recklessness. Put in less specific terms, it means that conduct can only be regarded as "reckless" if it is first established as being careless. In *Crowe v. H.M. Advocate*, 1990 S.L.T. 670, the appellant was convicted of causing death by reckless driving, by driving through a red stop light, entering a junction at excessive speed and colliding with another vehicle. The sheriff directed the jury that "if the accused here saw the lights were at red and went through them, that would undoubtedly be reckless driving." That was held to be a misdirection. The first question to be asked was whether the accused's driving fell below the standard to be expected of a careful and competent driver, "in all the

circumstances". While driving though a red traffic light at 40 miles an hour, at 5.30 p.m. on a busy Friday afternoon, might obviously be regarded as reckless, the same conclusion would not follow if the accused drove through the same red light at 10 miles an hour at 4 a.m. on a Sunday morning.

## (c) Knowledge and wilful blindness

**2.32** Some offences, both at common law and under statute, require proof of knowledge of facts and circumstances. It is, however, notoriously difficult to prove that A knew something, and as a result the courts have developed the idea of "wilful blindness" which performs the same function as knowledge. See, for wilful blindness in statutory offences, the cases of *Knox v. Boyd*, 1941 J.C. 82, *Thornley v. Hunter*, above, *Mackay Brothers and Company v. Gibb*, 1969 S.L.T. 216, and for wilful blindness in common law offences, *Latta v. Herron* (1967) S.C.C.R. Sup. 18, *post*, p. 521.

## D. Transferred *mens rea*

**2.33** The problem of transferred *mens rea* is well identified in the following passage from Hume.

### Hume, i, 22–23

"In the first place, a criminal charge may be good, though there is no evidence of a purpose to injure the very person who has been the sufferer on the occasion .... The same is true in a case even of homicide, that crime to which a special malice may seem more natural than to most others. If John make a thrust at James, meaning to kill, and George, throwing himself between, receive the thrust, and die, who doubts that John shall answer for it, as if his mortal purpose had taken place on James? Or if John lay poison in such circumstances, as shew it to be intended for a human creature, he shall certainly die for it, though it be accidentally taken by the person dearest to him upon earth, and whom, at the peril even of his own life, he would have redeemed from such a hazard. This was the opinion of the Court, and never doubted to be sound law, in the case of Carnegie of Finhaven, who, hastily thrusting at Lyon of Bridgeton, who had insulted him, happened to kill another person, the Earl of Strathmore, to whom he bore all manner of regard. Notice may be taken also of the case of Matthew Hay, who was convicted of murder, in the Circuit Court at Ayr, in May 1780. This man's malice was levelled at a young woman, who was with child to him. She, however, though she ate of the food in which the poison was mingled, survived the attempt, though sorely injured in her health; but her father and mother also ate of it, and died. Certainly the case was thus far more unfavourable to him, as he could not but see the hazard to the whole family; for he had thrown the poison into the vessel, where the common mess was cooking for their breakfast."

NOTES

**2.34** Two questions arise immediately arise: (1) Does the doctrine set out by Hume apply only to Homicide, or can it apply to other crimes, and (2) is it accepted in modern Scots law? Both are answered in the following case.

### Roberts v. Hamilton
### 1989 S.L.T. 399

**2.35** The appellant was charged with assaulting a man called Crawford with a pole. The blow which struck Mr Crawford was aimed not at him but at another man, Halliday, who was fighting with the appellant's son. The appellant was convicted of assaulting Mr Crawford and appealed.

OPINION OF THE COURT: "... Counsel submitted that these findings disclose actings of a criminal nature but not the crime of assault; he submitted that the appellant might have been guilty of recklessly injuring Mr Crawford but that she could not be guilty of the crime of assault. His contention was that the findings showed that there was no *mens rea* on her part directed against Mr Crawford, the victim of the incident. He submitted that the injury caused to Mr Crawford was really accidental and that the appellant accordingly fell to be acquitted.

The sheriff in his note explains that in finding the appellant guilty of the charge he relied upon a passage in Hume on *Crimes*, i, 22 [*supra*]. Counsel, however, maintained that the sheriff had drawn the wrong conclusion from the passage in Hume. At the end of the day, counsel's submission was that the doctrine of transferred intent does not apply in Scotland in relation to a crime such as assault which can only be committed if there is evidence of evil intent.

The advocate-depute on the other hand founded upon the passage in Hume, and submitted that the court should hold that the doctrine of transferred intent applied to assault. He stressed that having regard to the terms of charge 2 on the complaint no question of assault on Halliday arose. Likewise there was no question of whether the appellant was guilty of culpable or reckless conduct. The question was whether she was guilty of assaulting Crawford.

The starting point is the passage in Hume to which the sheriff referred in his note. In this passage it is stated: 'In the first place, a criminal charge may be good, though there is no evidence of a purpose to injure the very person who has been the sufferer on the occasion.' Counsel for the appellant pointed out that in the passage following that sentence, Baron Hume refers in the main to cases of homicide, and that cases of homicide are in a special position. It is true that Baron Hume does give a number of examples of cases of homicide, but the passage which we have just quoted appears in a chapter dealing with the nature of crimes in general. Moreover in the particular passage he is dealing with the character of dole which he explains is that corrupt or evil intention which is essential to the guilt of any crime. That being so we are quite satisfied that the sentence which we have quoted is not confined to cases of homicide, but is of general application. On p. 22 Baron Hume gives the following example: 'If John make a thrust at James, meaning to kill, and George, throwing himself between, receive the thrust, and die, who doubts that John shall answer for it, as if his mortal purpose had taken place on James?'

It is true that that is an example of homicide, but this may well be because Baron Hume goes on in the passage to quote the particular case of Carnegie of Finhaven which was a case of homicide. In our opinion, however, the example which he gives would be equally valid if the references to homicide were omitted and if the sentence read: 'If John makes a thrust at James, and George, throwing himself between, receive the thrust, who doubts that John shall answer for it?'

In Macdonald's *Criminal Law* (5th ed.) at p. 115 it is stated: 'Nor is it assault if some act of mischief, not directed against the person of any one, causes injury to another of whose presence the perpetrator of the mischief was not aware.' In our opinion, what is important in that statement is to observe that the act in question was not directed against the person of any one; the situation is not necessarily the same where, as here, the act in question was directed against one person although it took effect upon the person of another.

In Gordon's *Criminal Law* (2nd ed.), para. 9–12, the learned editor quotes from the passage in Hume at i, 22. He then proceeds to express certain criticisms of the passage. The matter is taken up again by Sheriff Gordon at para. 29–30, where he deals with *mens rea* in assault generally. He states: 'It is undecided whether if A throws a bottle at B and hits C instead, he is guilty of assaulting C or only of recklessly injuring him. This depends on whether the doctrine of transferred intent applies in Scotland in relation to a crime which can be committed only intentionally, and it is submitted that on principle it should not apply in such a case, and A should be guilty only of recklessly injuring C, a crime which is independent of his unfulfilled intention to assault B.'

Understandably counsel for the appellant founded strongly upon this passage. He submitted that there was no room for the doctrine of transferred intent except in cases of homicide where he said the doctrine could be justified on the grounds of public policy. Counsel also referred to *H.M. Advocate v. Phipps* (1905) 4 Adam 616. At the end of the day he invited us to answer the one question in the case in the negative.

The advocate-depute, on the other hand relied upon the passage in Hume to which we have referred. The advocate-depute also referred to *David Keay* (1837) 1 Swin. 543 and to Macdonald, p. 2 where it is stated: 'The principle is, that where the result which has happened was likely to occur, the perpetrator is answerable, and accordingly the circumstance of each case must determine the applicability of the rule.'

He submitted that whether the matter was approached from the point of view of transferred intent, or whether it was approached from the point of view that the result which happened was likely to occur, the sheriff had been entitled to find the appellant guilty in this case, and he invited us accordingly to answer the question in the case in the affirmative.

In our opinion the passage in Baron Hume at i, 22 which we have quoted is of general application and is not confined to cases of homicide. In particular his statement would apply to a case of assault. No doubt, as observed in Macdonald, if the act of the assailant is not directed against the person of anyone, he will not be guilty of assault because he will lack the necessary *mens rea*. If, however, his act is directed against the person of A, but he causes injury to another, B, in our opinion, he is guilty of assault. The difference between the two cases is that in the latter case the accused has the necessary dole or *mens rea*. In our opinion the statement by Sheriff Gordon at p. 825 to the effect that the doctrine of transferred intent does not apply in Scotland in relation to a crime which can only be committed intentionally is unsound. In our opinion the findings in fact in this case contain all the necessary elements of a charge of assault. The appellant carried out an attack upon the person of another; she picked up a pole and delivered a blow with it. Moreover she had the necessary evil intention; it was her intention to assault Mr Halliday. Her attack was carried out and took effect; the pole wielded by the appellant struck the complainer. In these circumstances, we are quite satisfied that the sheriff was justified in bringing in a finding of guilty of assault. ..."

Appeal refused.

NOTES

**2.36**     1. See also *Connor v. Jessop*, 1988 S.C.C.R. 624.

2. Suppose, in such a case, that A, acting in self defence, aims a blow at B, but accidentally strikes C. Does the defence "transfer" along with the criminal intent? Hume's view is that the defence also transfers:

> "On the other hand, where the *animus* is blameless or excuseable, the act is not a felony, though an innocent person happen to perish thereby. If a man strike in such circumstances as would have inferred culpable homicide only, or homicide in pure self-defence, if the blow had taken place, as intended, on the aggressor, it is still a case of self-defence only, or culpable homicide, though accidentally, or by excuseable mistake, the blow take place on a different person" (Hume, i, 22).

3. The idea of "transferring" the criminal intent inherent in act A to consequence B is facilitated by the "general *mens rea*" approach adopted by Hume (see *ante*, p. 40). But even Hume sets limits to the transmissibility of criminal intent. Having considered cases in which a criminal purpose takes an unintended, but not unforeseeable turn (as where the accused attacks an enemy intending to beat him severely but "mistakenly" kills him), Hume continues:

> "In these several instances, the event partakes, at least in some measure, of the nature of the original purpose, and is a natural fruit of the same disposition and temper of mind. But what shall be said, where a purpose to do a certain unlawful act is accidentally followed by an injury of a quite different kind and degree? In cases of this sort, according to certain English authorities, the guilt of the first purpose is to be considered; and the offender shall have judgment according to the character in law of that which he intended to do: So that if a man, shooting at a bird, happen

unfortunately to kill his neighbour, his sentence, shall be different, according to the kind of bird, and his purpose in shooting. If it be a tame fowl, but not his own, which he shot at for amusement, or his improvement as a marksman, it shall be manslaughter, because he meant to trespass on the property of another: But if he shot with an intention to steal and carry off the fowl, which is a felony, it shall be murder, by reason of that intention: And again, if the homicide happen in shooting at a wild pigeon, which is nullius in bonis, the person shall be entirely excused. But I have not found any thing in our records, which inclines me to believe that we should be disposed to assume this strained and artificial sort of principle, which conjoins things in their own nature different, and makes out the crime by coupling a purpose of lucre to an act which is only then criminal, when it is done out of malice and with a purpose to destroy: A disposition which the man has not shewn, and which cannot reasonably be inferred against him, as one who might probably be capable of such wickedness" (at p. 24).

Modern English law does not in fact follow the lines suggested by Hume: see *Latimer* (1886) 17 Q.B.D. 259, *Pembliton* (1874) L.R. 2 C.C.R. 119.

4. In *Blane v. H.M. Advocate*, 1991 S.C.C.R. 576, it was held that the doctrine of transferred intent does not apply in the crime of wilful fire-raising. This opinion was endorsed by a bench of five judges in *Byrne v. H.M. Advocate* 2000 S.C.C.R. 77 (*post*, p. 538). The reason why there is no room for the doctrine of transferred intent in wilful fire-raising appears to have been that wilful fire-raising can only be committed intentionally (see Lord Coulsfield in *Byrne*, *post*, p. 548).

But if this is so, why then does the doctrine apply in assault which likewise can only be committed intentionally?

5. What is the significance of the references to events which were "likely to happen" in this case and *Connor v. Jessop*, bearing in mind that the crime of assault requires proof of intention? Do these references suggest that if A foresees that injury is likely to happen as a result of what she is doing that she intends such injury?

# E. Error

## (a) Error of fact

Errors of fact (as opposed to errors of law) may be relevant to the issue of criminal responsibility in **2.37** different ways. In the first place, a mistake may have the effect of excluding all, or a part, of the mental element. Suppose, for example, that X takes Y's umbrella in the mistaken belief that it is his own. In such a case, X cannot be guilty of stealing the umbrella because his mistake excludes the necessary element of dishonesty. Viewed in this way, mistake is not a matter of "defence" to be established by the accused. It becomes part of the "definitional" aspect of the offence, in the sense that if the jury accept that the accused's mistake excludes an element of the offence which the prosecutor is required to prove (the mental element), then the prosecutor has failed to discharge the onus of proof placed upon him, and the accused is entitled to an acquittal. it also follows that if a mistake is relevant in that it excludes the mental element, regard must be had to the nature of the mistake. Suppose, for example, that the accused is charged with recklessly endangering the public by discharging a loaded gun. At the time of firing the gun, he believes that there is no one within range, and that no one is likely to be endangered. However, that belief is mistaken, and has been reached recklessly. In principle, the accused ought still to be guilty of the offence because his mistaken belief does not exclude the mental element.

Mistakes may also be relevant in other ways, as in the case of mistaken self-defence. Suppose for example that X stabs Y with a knife, in the mistaken belief that Y is about to carry out a lethal attack on him. In such circumstances, X is entitled to rely on a plea of self-defence (perhaps more correctly "mistaken self defence"). In this case the error does not exclude the *mens rea* but provides a basis for a plea of self-defence.

The general rule governing both categories of error is that the accused is entitled to be judged according to the facts as she or he believed them to be. So, for example, if A believes that the property which he has destroyed or damaged is his, he cannot be guilty of malicious mischief or vandalism. Those crimes require proof that the accused intentionally or recklessly destroyed property belonging to another, and a person who intends to destroy what he believes to be his own property does not have the required intention. Similarly, the accused who mistakenly believes that his adversary is attacking him with a knife would be entitled to act in self-defence to the degree that would be permitted if he had in fact been attacked by a person wielding a knife.

If the accused's erroneous belief does not produce a state of mind consistent with innocence of the crime, then it is irrelevant. Suppose, for example, that A shoots at B, thinking that he is C, his mortal enemy and kills him. Such an error would be regarded as irrelevant since the identity of the victim is irrelevant in a case of murder. But in some cases errors as to identity and quality are relevant. This would be true, for example, in the case of incest, where it is a defence for the accused to show that even though she had intercourse with her uncle (a person related to her within the prohibited degree required by that offence) she believed, on reasonable grounds, that the person in question was her cousin (a person not so related to her).

In *C. v. H.M. Advocate*, 1987 S.C.C.R. 104, the accused was charged with indecently assaulting an 11 year old girl. He claimed that he believed that she had consented to what had taken place. It was held that despite this belief he was still guilty of the offence. His belief was irrelevant because as a matter of law, an 11 year old girl cannot consent to indecent assault. In order for his error to have been reasonable he would have had to have believed (a) that the girl was 12 years of age or older and (b) that she consented.

Although mistakes going to "definitional" elements and mistakes going to defences are similar in the sense that they both allow the accused to be judged according to the facts as he believed them to be, there is a possible difference between the two types of error. It has long been held that an error of the latter kind—going to a positive defence—must be "reasonable" before it can provide the accused with a defence. (See, *inter alia*, *Crawford v. H.M. Advocate*, 1950 J.C. 67.) It has, however, been held, at least in the case of error as to consent in rape (*Jamieson v. H.M. Advocate*, 1994 S.L.T. 537) and indecent assault (*Marr v. H.M. Advocate*, 1996 J.C. 199) that such an error is relevant even if the accused does not have reasonable grounds for his erroneous belief. See *post*, Chap. 9.

## (b) Error of law

**2.38**  The maxim *ignorantia juris neminem excusat* is rigorously applied in the criminal law (see, for example, the case of *R. v. Bailey* (1800) Russ. & Ry. 1, in which ignorance of the criminal law was held to be no defence even where it was impossible for the accused to have known that what he did was against the law), but it is probably the case that a distinction ought to be drawn between ignorance of the criminal law and ignorance of the civil law.

## (i) Ignorance of the criminal law

### Hume, i, 26

**2.39**  [Having examined the question of motive, and having concluded that it was irrelevant to dole, Hume considers the effect of ignorance of the criminal law:]

"As little is it included in the notion of dole, that the offender have been in the knowledge of the punishment which the law annexes to his crime. Nay, though he thought that it was a lawful act, and liable to no punishment, (as some may imagine of the plundering of a wrecked vessel, or of rescuing their own goods when seized by the revenue officer,) he still has no defence in this sort of imperfect and corrupt belief: For he may, and is bound to know as much of the law as concerns the regulation of his own conduct; and he shall be judged on the presumption that he does so. And thus it is, that we reduce under the common principle of dole, certain cases of homicide and other offences, in which it may seem, at first sight, that a person is punished for mere error, not attended with any criminal intention. A judge, for instance, who pronounces an unlawful and utterly erroneous sentence of death, is not adjudged guilty of murder because he has erred, but because he has wilfully done wrong. The law, which cannot know the truth of his excuse, and which perceives the advantage that might be taken of such gross pretences, for the indulgence of malice, presumes his knowledge of that which he is not excuseable for being ignorant of, and judges him accordingly. As applicable to this matter, such seems to be the true meaning of that noted maxim of the Roman law, *culpa lata equiparatur dolo*."

## Dewar v. H.M. Advocate
### 1945 J.C. 5

The appellant, the manager of a crematorium, was convicted of the theft of two coffins and a **2.40** large number of coffin lids, which, along with the bodies contained therein, had been consigned to him for cremation. The lids had been disposed of "in various utilitarian ways". In his defence he stated that he believed that the coffins and their lids, once delivered to him, were completely within his jurisdiction for disposal, and also that he believed he was merely following a practice commonly adopted at other crematoria throughout Britain. On appeal:

LORD JUSTICE-GENERAL (NORMAND): The next objection was that there was no appropriation by the appellant of the coffins or of the lids. This is, in my opinion, an unstatable proposition—unstatable both in law and in fact. It is contrary to the appellant's own evidence that the coffins were completely under his jurisdiction for disposal, and that he was merely following a usual practice in removing the lids, storing them, and using them as firewood or employing them in some other 'economic way', as he called it, rather than destroying them. His evidence is a plain assertion to his unlimited right of property in a thing which he knew was sent to him under contract for the purpose of destruction, and of destruction only along with the bodies, and this applies both to the coffins and to the lids. Accordingly, in my opinion, there was misappropriation of property which he knew was sent to him merely for destruction by a prescribed method. That being so, there is no doubt that there was evidence upon which the jury were entitled to find the appellant guilty of theft, and I have very great doubt whether there was any relevance in the further contention that it was necessary to establish a guilty intent by other facts and circumstances. In my opinion, the presiding judge would have been perfectly entitled to instruct the jury that the evidence about the alleged practice in other crematoria and the evidence of the appellant's belief in the alleged practice was irrelevant and that they were bound to disregard it. That was not, however, the course taken by the learned judge, and he left to the jury the question whether the felonious intent was established by other evidence, or, more correctly, whether the appellant had by other evidence established that his intent had been innocent. There was evidence led on behalf of the appellant to show that he only did what others do elsewhere, or at least that he believed that he only followed the common practice in other crematoria, and further, that he had not practised any concealment. The presiding judge took a lenient view when he instructed the jury to consider whether the appellant might have entertained an honest and reasonable belief, based on colourable grounds, that he was entitled to treat the coffins, as 'scrap'. The presiding judge pointed out that the jury must not exculpate the appellant merely because he entertained an erroneous belief founded on some singular notions of his own but that they must discover some evidence that he had rational and colourable grounds for believing that he was entitled to remove, retain and dispose of the coffin lids. The direction could not have been more favourable to the appellant than it was. The onus is rightly placed on him. What had to be proved by him was stated and reiterated with the most careful moderation, and I think that there is no possible objection to the direction on the ground of unfairness."

Appeal dismissed.

NOTES

It is not entirely clear what sort of error Dewar made. It appears to have been a combination of errors **2.41** of fact (as to the practice at other crematoria) which induced an error of law (as to his entitlement to dispose of the property in the way that he did). On one view, this might be regarded as a claim of right—an "assertion of his unlimited right of property" in the goods. Viewed in this way a mistaken claim of right in theft ought to have the same effect as a well-founded claim of right, *viz.*, acquittal.

If, as appears from the decision of the Appeal Court, this is not to be treated as a claim of right case, then Dewar's claim "could be expressed ... as being that the accused believed that what he was doing was something he was entitled to do, and that therefore he acted without 'felonious intent'" (Gordon

(2nd ed.) para. 14–86). Gordon suggests that there is a difficulty with such a defence in that "it involves an error of law of a kind not normally accepted by the courts—a belief that the accused's conduct was not criminal—and can therefore be considered as being as irrelevant as the belief of an English uncle who sleeps with his niece in Scotland that his behaviour is not incestuous . . . But it is arguable that such a defence is relevant in theft in so far as it excludes the felonious intent which is part of the definition of the crime" (para. 14–86). It seems that the latter is the better view. Dewar's claim would seem to have been that because of his beliefs about what went on in other crematoria he was not dishonest, and in that sense this would be a mistake of fact negating an element of *mens rea* required for the offence. *Cf.* the following case, in which a mistake of civil law is held to have the same effect.

## (ii) Ignorance of the civil law

**2.42** It has been observed that "[a] misconception of legal rights, however gross, will never justify the substitution of the law of the jungle for rules of civilised behaviour". (Lord Justice-General Clyde in *Clarke v. Syme*, 1957 J.C. 32, *post* p. 536.)

In certain circumstances, however, ignorance of the civil law, or mistaken beliefs as to one civil law rights may be relevant to criminal responsibility. Suppose, for example, that A enters into a contract with B, a car dealer, for the purchase of a car. A believes that the agreement has the effect of transferring ownership of the car to him at that point. In fact, it is a hire-purchase agreement, under which ownership does not pass until the final payment under the contract is made. A then sells the car to C. In doing so, he has appropriated the property of another (since the car is not yet his to sell), but it is possible to argue that he is not guilty of theft, either because he has no intention to appropriate the property of another (he thinks it is his car) or, possibly, because of his mistaken understanding of the law, he is not acting dishonestly.

In the English case of *R. v. Smith (David)* [1974] 1 Q.B. 354 the accused was the tenant of a rented flat. He made various improvements to the flat, including the installation of roofing materials, wall panels and floor boards. When he was given notice to quit, he removed these materials, and as a result was convicted of criminal damage, contrary to section 1 of the Criminal Damage Act 1971. On appeal the conviction was quashed. In order to establish guilt under section 1 of the 1971 Act it must be proved that the accused intended to damage property belonging to another, or that he or she was reckless as to that result. Although as a matter of the civil law the material which he had installed in the flat became part of the freehold, and therefore the property of the landlord, the accused had not appreciated this. When he set about removing the material, he thought he was removing his own property. His failure to appreciate the civil law, therefore, meant that he did not have the *mens rea* for the offence.

## F. Motive

### Hume, i, 25

**2.43** "It is not material to the notion of guilt, that the offender have himself been fully conscious of the wickedness of what he did. Though he were persuaded that it was innocent, or even meritorious (such are the miserable effects of fanaticism in politics and in religion), yet still this cannot save him from the judgment of the law; which must be determined by the nature of the act, and its evil consequences to the public, and not by any allowance for those strange delusions, which are as dangerous as the vices of the most thorough malefactor. The judge cannot search into the heart of the prisoner, and even if he could, still be the cause what it may, which impels a man to do such things as are subversive of society, his will is not on that account the less inordinate, or his nature the less depraved: It is only the greater proof of his depravity, that he could do such things, without even feeling that they are wrong."

NOTES

1. The courts have frequently endorsed the view that "motive" is irrelevant to guilt. See, for example, **2.44**
*Palazzo v. Copeland*, 1976 J.C. 52, *post*, p. 214. But is it always correct to state that motive is irrelevant.
Suppose, for example, that A commits a crime because B has threatened to kill his wife and child and is
holding them at gun point. In such a case the accused would be able to plead the defence of coercion. He
can hardly say, if he commits the crime, that he did not have the *mens rea*. In a sense his defence is based
on a recognition that the accused's underlying motive for acting—protecting his family—provides him
with an excuse for what would otherwise be a crime.

2. In *Drury v. H.M. Advocate*, High Court, February 2, 2001, *unreported*, *post*, p. 407, the High Court
suggested that murder required proof of "wicked intention" to kill or "wicked recklessness" and held
that where the accused acted under provocation the element of "wickedness" was elided. Would it be
possible to apply this notion to other circumstances which might be said to affect the "wickedness" of an
accused intent? Suppose, for example, that A, with B's consent, takes B's life as an act of mercy and in
order to relief B's suffering. Does A have a "wicked" intention to kill, or do his motives affect the
evaluation of that intent?

## 4. COINCIDENCE OF *ACTUS REUS* AND *MENS REA*

The principle of *actus non facit reum nisi mens sit rea* is generally understood to require a coincidence of **2.45**
the two elements in point of time. In certain cases this may be quite problematic. A attacks B, intending
to kill B, and, thinking B is dead, disposes of the "corpse" in a river. In fact B is not dead when placed in
the river, but dies subsequently from drowning. Is A guilty of murder? Although at one stage A did
indeed have the *mens* rea for murder, the *actus reus* was not completed. By the time A carried out the
*actus reus* by killing B the *mens rea* was no longer present. There does not appear to be any Scottish
authority on the question. The following cases illustrate a number of possible approaches. For a general
discussion of this question, see Marston, "Contemporaneity of Act and Intention" (1970) 86 L.Q.R. 208
and A. R. White, "The Identity and Time of the Actus Reus" [1977] Crim.L.R. 148.

### Thabo Meli and Ors. v. The Queen
#### [1954] 1 W.L.R. 228

The appellants, acting on a preconceived plan, attacked a man and, believing him to be dead,
rolled his body over a cliff to make the death look like an accident. It was established that the
initial injuries were not sufficient to cause death, and that death was due in fact to exposure.
The appellants were convicted of murder, and appealed, arguing that the acts which caused
death were not accompanied with malice aforethought since they believed the victim to be
already dead. On appeal to the Privy Council from the High Court of Basutoland:

LORD REID: "The point of law which was raised in this case can be simply stated. It is said
that two acts were necessary and were separable: first, the attack in the hut; and, secondly, the
placing of the body outside afterwards. It is said that, while the first act was accompanied by
*mens rea*, it was not the cause of death; but that the second act, while it was the cause of death,
was not accompanied by *mens rea*; and on that ground it is said that the accused are not guilty
of any crime except perhaps culpable homicide.

It appears to their Lordships impossible to divide up what was really one transaction in this
way. There is no doubt that the accused set out to do all these acts in order to achieve their
plan and as parts of their plan; and it is much too refined a ground of judgment to say that,
because they were under a misapprehension at one stage and thought that their guilty
purpose had been achieved before in fact it was achieved, therefore they are to escape the
penalties of the law. Their Lordships do not think that this is a matter which is susceptible of
elaboration. There appears to be no case either in South Africa or England, or for that matter
elsewhere, which resembles the present. Their Lordships can find no difference relevant to
the present case between the law of South Africa and the law of England, and they are of
opinion that by both laws there could be no separation such as that for which the accused

contend, so as to reduce the crime from murder to a lesser crime, merely because the accused were under some misapprehension for a time during the completion of their criminal plot.

Their Lordships must, therefore, humbly advise Her Majesty that this appeal should be dismissed."

Appeal dismissed.

NOTES

**2.46**    Some earlier cases had adopted a different approach, holding that where the accused inflicted the initial injury with *mens rea*, but did not cause death, but subsequently caused death without *mens rea* it was not possible to convict of murder. A charge of attempted murder may have be possible, where the initial injury was caused with the appropriate *mens rea* for that crime. See *Khandu* (1890) I.L.R. 15 (India) and *Shorty* [1950] S.R. 280 (Rhodesia).

*Thabo Meli* was followed by the English Court of Appeal (Criminal Division) in *R. v. Moore and Dorn* [1975] Crim. L.R. 229. In both these cases, the final outcome resulted from a preconceived plan, and that for that reason it could be argued that they have no application where there is no such plan. That was the view adopted by the New Zealand courts in *Ramsay* [1967] N.Z.L.R. 1005, and at one time by the South African courts (*R. v. Chiswibo*, 1960 (2) S.A. 714) but see now the later case of *S. v. Masibela*, 1968 (2) S.A. 558. As the following case demonstrates, that limitation is not accepted by the English courts.

**R. v. Le Brun**
(1992) 94 Cr. App. Rep. 101

**2.47**  The appellant assaulted his wife by striking her on the chin. She fell to the ground. He attempted to pick her up and to drag her away from the scene of the assault, but she slipped out of his grasp and fell backwards. Her head hit the pavement, causing a fracture of the skull, which caused her death. The appellant was charged with murder, and convicted of manslaughter. On appeal against conviction:

LORD LANE C.J.: "The main thrust of [counsel for the appellant's] argument is to be found in ground 3 of the notice of appeal, which I will now read:

> 'The judge erred in law in directing the jury that they could convict the appellant of murder or manslaughter (depending on the intention with which he had previously assaulted the victim) if they were sure that, having committed the assault with no serious injury resulting, the appellant had accidentally dropped the victim causing her death whilst either: (a) attempting to move her to her home against her wishes, including any wishes she may have expressed prior to the previous assault, and/or (b) attempting to dispose of her body or otherwise cover up the previous assault.'

Problems of causation and remoteness of damage are never easy of solution. We have had helpful arguments from both counsel on this point, the point in the present case being, to put it in summary before coming to deal with it in more detail, that the intention of the appellant to harm his wife one way or another may have been separated by a period of time from the act which in fact caused the death, namely, the fact of her falling to the ground and fracturing her skull. That second incident may have taken place without any guilty mind on the part of the appellant.

The authors of Smith & Hogan, *Criminal Law*, 6th ed (1988) p. 320, say:

> 'An intervening act by the original actor will not break the chain of causation so as to excuse him, where the intervening act is part of the same transaction, but it is otherwise if the act which causes the actus reus is part of a completely different transaction. For example, D, having wounded P, visits him in hospital and accidentally infects him with smallpox of which he dies.'

The problem in the instant case can be expressed in a number of different ways, of which causation is one. Causation on the facts as the jury in this case must have found them—I say at the best from the point of view of the appellant—is in one sense clear. Death was caused by the victim's head hitting the ground as she was being dragged away by the appellant. The only remoteness was that between the initial unlawful blow and the later moment when the skull was fractured causing death.

The question can be perhaps framed in this way. There was here an initial unlawful blow to the chin delivered by the appellant. That, again on what must have been the jury's finding, was not delivered with the intention of doing really serious harm to the wife. The guilty intent accompanying that blow was sufficient to have rendered the appellant guilty of manslaughter, but not murder, had it caused death. But it did not cause death. What caused death was the later impact when the wife's head hit the pavement. At the moment of impact the appellant's intention was to remove her, probably unconscious, body to avoid detection. To that extent the impact may have been accidental. May the earlier guilty intent be joined with the later non-guilty blow which caused death to produce in the conglomerate a proper verdict of manslaughter?"

[His Lordship outlined the facts of, and the decision in, the case of *Thabo Meli* (*supra*) and continued:]

"That decision of course is not binding upon us. It is of very persuasive authority and it was adopted by another division of this court in 1975 in *R. v. Moore* [1975] Crim.L.R. 229.

However, it will be observed that the present case is different from the facts of those two cases in that death here was not the result of a preconceived plan which went wrong, as was the case in those two decisions which we have cited. Here the death, again assuming the jury's finding to be such as it must have been, was the result of an initial unlawful blow, not intended to cause serious harm, in its turn causing the appellant to take steps possibly to evade the consequences of his unlawful act. During the taking of those steps he commits the actus reus but without the *mens rea* necessary for murder or manslaughter. Therefore the *mens rea* is contained in the initial unlawful assault, but the actus reus is the eventual dropping of the head on to the ground.

Normally the *actus reus* and *mens rea* coincide in point of time. What is the situation when they do not? Is it permissible, as the prosecution contend here, to combine them to produce a conviction for manslaughter?

The answer is perhaps to be found in the next case to which we were referred, and that was *Reg v. Church* [1966] 1 Q.B. 59. In that case the defendant was charged with the murder of a woman whose body was found in a river. The cause of death was drowning. The defendant had it seemed attacked the woman and rendered her semi-conscious. He thought she was dead and in his panic he threw her into the river. He was acquitted of murder but convicted of manslaughter. Edmund Davies J, giving the judgment of this court, said, at p. 70:

> 'the conclusion of this court is that an unlawful act causing the death of another cannot, simply because it is an unlawful act, render a manslaughter verdict inevitable. For such a verdict inexorably to follow, the unlawful act must be such as all sober and reasonable people would inevitably recognise must subject the other person to, at least, the risk of some harm resulting therefrom, albeit not serious harm .... In the light of *Meli v. The Queen* [1954] 1 W.L.R. 228 it is conceded on behalf of the appellant that, on the murder charge, the trial judge was perfectly entitled to direct the jury, as he did: "Unless you find that something happened in the course of this evening between the infliction of the injuries and the decision to throw the body into the water, you may undoubtedly treat the whole course of conduct of the accused as one." But for some reason not clear to this court, appellant's counsel denies that such an approach is possible when one is considering a charge of manslaughter. We fail to see why. We adopt as sound Dr Glanville Williams's view in his book, *Criminal Law* (2nd ed., 1961), p. 174, that, "If a killing by the first act would have been manslaughter, a later destruction of the supposed

corpse should also be manslaughter." Had Mrs Nott [the victim] died of her initial injuries a manslaughter verdict might quite conceivably have been returned on the basis that the accused inflicted them under the influence of provocation or that the jury were not convinced that they were inflicted with murderous intent. All that was lacking in the direction given in this case was that, when the judge turned to consider manslaughter, he did not again tell the jury that they were entitled (if they thought fit) to regard the conduct of the appellant in relation to Mrs Nott as constituting throughout a series of acts which culminated in her death, and that, if that was how they regarded the accused's behaviour, it mattered not whether he believed her to be alive or dead when he threw her in the river.'

It seems to us that where the unlawful application of force and the eventual act causing death are parts of the same sequence of events, the same transaction, the fact that there is an appreciable interval of time between the two does not serve to exonerate the defendant from liability. That is certainly so where the appellant's subsequent actions which caused death, after the initial unlawful blow, are designed to conceal his commission of the original unlawful assault.

It would be possible to express the problem as one of causation. The original unlawful blow to the chin was a causa sine qua non of the later actus reus. It was the opening event in a series which was to culminate in death: the first link in the chain of causation, to use another metaphor. It cannot be said that the actions of the appellant in dragging the victim away with the intention of evading liability broke the chain which linked the initial blow with the death.

In short, in circumstances such as the present, which is the only concern of this court, the act which causes death, and the necessary mental state to constitute manslaughter, need not coincide in point of time...."

Appeal dismissed.

NOTES

**2.48**    There seem to be two principles combined in this opinion. On one view, the accused is guilty if the initial unlawful act and the act which causes death form part of the "same transaction". Alternatively, the person responsible for that initial act will be held responsible for that outcome, unless the subsequent event (in this case the dropping of the victim) can be regarded as breaking the chain of causation. What would the outcome be in a case such as *Le Brun* if it were to be shown that the death was caused by the assailant attempting to render assistance to the victim? Would an attempt to assist the victim (as opposed to an attempt to conceal what had happened) be regarded as part of the "same transaction"? Arguably not, since such an attempt is differently motivated and a quite different outcome is being pursued. That is how the trial judge directed the jury, and in that respect the trial judge's directions were accepted as correct by the Appeal Court.

What would be the position if the "causation" test is applied? Would dropping the victim in an attempt to assist her be regarded as a *novus actus*? In the sense that the actor is the same, and that dropping the victim would be a factual cause of death whatever the actor's intentions it is possible to argue that there is not a *novus actus*. If this is so, then the choice between the "same transaction" and the "causation" principles would seem to be of real significance. However, the Appeal Court, like the trial judge, appears to accept that if the victim were dropped while the appellant was trying to help her, then that would have been a *novus actus*.

### Fagan v. Commissioner of Metropolitan Police
[1963] 3 W.L.R. 1120

**2.49** The appellant was convicted of assaulting a police officer in the execution of his duty, and appealed by case stated to the Divisional Court. The circumstances of the offence are fully set out in the judgment of James J.

JAMES J.: "On August 31, 1967, the appellant was reversing a motor car in Fortunegate Road, London, N.W.1, when Police Constable Morris directed him to drive the car forwards to the kerbside and standing in front of the car pointed out a suitable place in which to park. At first the appellant stopped the car too far from the kerb for the officer's liking. Morris asked him to park closer and indicated a precise spot. The appellant drove forward towards him and stopped it with the offside wheel on Morris's left foot. 'Get off you are on my foot,' said the officer. 'Fuck you, you can wait,' said the appellant. The engine of the car stopped running. Morris repeated several times, 'Get off my foot.' The appellant said reluctantly 'Okay man, okay,' and then slowly turned on the ignition of the vehicle and reversed it off the officer's foot....

The justices at quarter session on those facts were left in doubt as to whether the mounting of the wheel on to the officer's foot was deliberate or accidental. They were satisfied, however, beyond all reasonable doubt that the appellant 'knowingly, provocatively and unnecessarily allowed the wheel to remain on the foot after the officer said "Get off, you are on my foot".' They found that on those facts an assault was proved.

Mr Abbas for the appellant relied upon the passage in Stone's Justices' Manual (1968), Vol. 1, p. 651, where assault is defined. He contends that on the finding of the justices the initial mounting of the wheel could not be an assault and that the act of the wheel mounting the foot came to an end without there being any *mens rea*. It is argued that thereafter there was no act on the part of the appellant which could constitute an actus reus but only the omission or failure to remove the wheel as soon as he was asked. That failure, it is said, could not in law be an assault, nor could it in law provide the necessary *mens rea* to convert the original act of mounting the foot into an assault.

Mr Rant for the respondent argues that the first mounting of the foot was an *actus reus* which act continued until the moment of time at which the wheel was removed. During that continuing act, it is said, the appellant formed the necessary intention to constitute the element of *mens rea* and once that element was added to the continuing act, an assault took place. In the alternative, Mr Rant argues that there can be situations in which there is a duty to act and that in such situations an omission to act in breach of duty would in law amount to an assault. It is unnecessary to formulate any concluded views on this alternative ...

To constitute the offence of assault some intentional act must have been performed: a mere omission to act cannot amount to an assault. Without going into the question whether words alone can constitute an assault, it is clear that the words spoken by the appellant could not alone amount to an assault: they can only shed a light on the appellant's action. For our part we think the crucial question is whether in this case the act of the appellant can be said to be complete and spent at the moment of time when the car wheel came to rest on the foot or whether his act is to be regarded as a continuing act operating until the wheel was removed. In our judgment a distinction is to be drawn between acts which are complete—though results may continue to flow—and those acts which are continuing. Once the act is complete it cannot thereafter be said to be a threat to inflict unlawful force upon the victim. If the act, as distinct from the results thereof, is a continuing act there is a continuing threat to inflict unlawful force. If the assault involves a battery and that battery continues there is a continuing act of assault.

For an assault to be committed both the elements of actus reus and *mens rea* must be present at the same time. The '*actus reus*' is the action causing the effect on the victim's mind (see the observations of Park B. in *Regina v. St. George* (1840) 9 C. & P. 483). The '*mens rea*' is the intention to cause that effect. It is not necessary that *mens rea* should be present at the inception of the *actus reus*; it can be superimposed upon an existing act. On the other hand the subsequent inception of *mens rea* cannot convert an act which has been completed without *mens rea* into an assault.

In our judgment the Willesden magistrates and quarter sessions were right in law. On the facts found the action of the appellant may have been initially unintentional, but the time came when knowing that the wheel was on the officer's foot the appellant (1) remained seated in the car so that his body through the medium of the car was in contact with the officer (2) switched off the ignition of the car, (3) maintained the wheel of the car on the foot and (4) used words indicating the intention of keeping the wheel in that position. For our part we cannot regard such conduct as mere omission or inactivity.

There was an act constituting a battery which at its inception was not criminal because there was no element of intention but which became criminal from the moment the intention was formed to produce the apprehension which was flowing from the continuing act."

Appeal dismissed.

NOTE

**2.50** The court in this case was rather constrained by the conclusion that it is not possible to commit assault by omission, which meant that it had to base its decision on some act attributable to the appellant. It is, however, possible to argue that in these circumstances the appellant, by driving onto the police officer's foot, even if accidentally, created a danger which, once he was aware of it, he was under a duty to remove. His failure to do so constituted a criminal omission. For a case in which this kind of analysis was applied, see *MacPhail v. Clark*, 1983 S.C.C.R. 395, *ante*, p. 33 and the decision of the House of Lords in *R. v. Miller* [19831 1 All E.R. 978.

## R. v. Cogan; R. v. Leak
[1976] Q.B. 217

**2.51** At the instigation of Leak, Cogan had intercourse with Leak's wife, without her consent. Cogan was charged with rape, and Leak with aiding and abetting that offence. They were both convicted, but Cogan's conviction was subsequently quashed on the ground that he had believed the victim to be consenting. Leak appealed against his conviction on the ground, *inter alia*, that since Cogan's conviction had been quashed he could, not stand convicted of aiding and abetting that offence.

LAWTON L.J.: "The only case which [counsel for Leak] submitted had a direct bearing upon the problem of Leak's guilt was *Walters v. Lunt* [1951] 2 All E.R. 645. In that case the respondents had been charged, under section 33(1) of the Larceny Act 1916, with receiving from a child aged seven years, certain articles knowing them to have been stolen. In 1951, a child under eight years was deemed in law to be incapable of committing a crime: it followed that at the time of receipt by the respondents the articles had not been stolen and that the charge had not been proved. That case is very different from this because here one fact is clear—the wife had been raped. Cogan had had sexual intercourse with her without her consent. The fact that Cogan was innocent of rape because he believed that she was consenting does not affect the position that she was raped.

Her ravishment had come about because Leak had wanted it to happen and had taken action to see that it did by persuading Cogan to use his body as the instrument for the necessary physical act. In the language of the law the act of sexual intercourse without the wife's consent was the *actus reus*: it had been procured by Leak who had the appropriate *mens rea*, namely, his intention that Cogan should have sexual intercourse with her without her consent. In our judgment it is irrelevant that the man whom Leak had procured to do the physical act himself did not intend to have sexual intercourse with the wife without her consent. Leak was using him as a means to procure a criminal purpose....

The reason a man cannot by his own physical act rape his wife during cohabitation is because the law presumes consent from the marriage ceremony: see *Hale, Pleas of the Crown* (1778), vol. 1, p. 629. There is no such presumption when a man procures a drunken friend to do the physical act for him. ... Had Leak been indicted as a principal offender, the case against him would have been clear beyond argument. Should he be allowed to go free because he was charged with 'being aider and abettor to the same offence'? If we are right in our opinion that the wife had been raped (and no one outside a court of law would say that she had not been), then the particulars of offence accurately stated what Leak had done, namely, he had procured Cogan to commit the offence. This would suffice to uphold the conviction. We would prefer, however to uphold it on a wider basis. In our judgment convictions should not be upset because of mere technicalities of pleading in an indictment. Leak knew what the case against him was and the facts in support of that case were proved. But for the fact that jury thought that Cogan in his intoxicated condition might have mistaken the wife's sobs and distress for expressions of her consent, no question of any kind would have arisen about the form of pleading. By his written statement Leak virtually admitted what he had done. As Judge Chapman said in *Reg v. Humphreys* [1965] All E.R. 689, 692: 'It would be anomalous if a person who admitted to a substantial part in the perpetration of a misdemeanor as aider and abettor could not be convicted on his own admission merely because the person alleged to have been aided and abetted was not or could not be convicted.' In the circumstances of this case it would be more than anomalous: it would be an affront to justice and to the common sense of ordinary folk. It was for these reasons that we dismissed the appeal against conviction."

Appeal dismissed.

NOTES

This case differs from the others discussed in this section in that there was no separation of *actus reus* **2.52** and *mens rea* in point of time, but rather in respect of the actors. What this case suggests is that if A commits the external elements of the offence, albeit without the necessary *mens rea*, and in doing so is encouraged by B who does have the necessary criminal intent, then between them,there is an *actus reus* accompanied by *mens rea* and there is thus a sufficient coincidence of *actus reus* and *mens rea*. (And what is more, the accused who provides one of the constituent elements of the offence is also to be held guilty of aiding and abetting it!) How far does this depart from the principle *actus non facit reum nisi mens sit rea*? After all, it was accepted that the accused who committed the *actus* did not have the *mens rea*, and in those circumstances it is not even correct to describe what Cogan did as an "*actus reus*".

The rule that a husband cannot in law be guilty of raping his wife was abrogated in England and Wales by the decision of the House of Lords in *R. v. R.* [1991] 4 All E.R. 481, which is now reflected in section 1 of the Sexual Offences Act 1956, as amended by section 142 of the Criminal Justice and Public Order Act 1994. A similar rule was removed from Scots law by the decision of the High Court in *S. v. H.M. Advocate*, 1989 S.L.T. 469. See *ante* p. 6.

# Chapter 3

## STRICT, VICARIOUS AND CORPORATE RESPONSIBILITY

There are good reasons for drawing together the different themes which are discussed in this chapter. There is a close relationship between the different forms of responsibility considered here. Strict responsibility involves the attribution of criminal responsibility without proof of *mens rea* in respect of all elements of the offence. This form of responsibility is in a sense inherent in many cases of vicarious responsibility, where one individual is held responsible for the criminal acts and omissions of another. It may be easier to find a company guilty of a strict responsibility offence, at least when compared with the difficulties that may arise when attributing responsibility to a company for an offence requiring proof of *mens rea*. Similarly, notions of vicarious responsibility have been influential in the development of theories of corporate criminal responsibility.

## 1. STRICT RESPONSIBILITY

**3.01** Offences of strict liability present an important exception to the general rule *actus non facit reum nisi mens sit rea*. Such offences are invariably created by legislation. There are no strict liability offences at common law.

Strict responsibility involves attributing responsibility for crime to a person who may not have intended to commit the prohibited acts, may not have been reckless or even negligent, and, indeed, may have been wholly unaware of facts proof of which might otherwise be regarded as essential to criminal responsibility. This is a serious step to take, since it raises the prospect of convicting individuals for often quite serious offences when they are not at fault. In *Mitchell v. Morrison*, 1938 S.L.T. 201, the Lord Justice-General (Normand) commented (at p. 204):

> "... [T]here is no novelty in holding that a statutory offence may be committed although there is a complete absence of *mens rea*. Nevertheless, the burden lies on the Crown of shewing that a statute imposes an absolute obligation, breach of which constitutes an offence and subjects to a penalty one who is entirely free from all moral culpability ... the Crown must always shew that the language of the statute is without distortion or strain habile to impose an absolute obligation."

### A. Strict responsibility and human rights

**3.02** As a preliminary to the discussion of the approach of Scots law to this issue, it is worth considering whether imposing strict responsibility is compatible with the European Convention on Human Rights. It might be argued, for example that imposing strict liability is incompatible with the presumption of innocence contained in article 6(2) of the Convention. Gordon (3rd ed.) states that "given the present state of the Convention jurisprudence, it is simply not possible to be certain whether strict or absolute liability is contrary to Article 5 or 6 of the Convention". The assumption is made (*ibid.*) that strict liability is not incompatible with Convention rights. Such statements as there are from the Court, suggest that this is indeed the case. In *Salabiaku v. France* (1991) 13 E.H.R.R. 379 the Court stated:

> "27. . . . in principle the Contracting States remain free to apply the criminal law to an act where it is not carried out in the normal exercise of one of the rights protected under the Convention . . . and, accordingly, to define the constituent elements of the resulting offence. In particular, and again in principle, the Contracting States may, under certain conditions, penalise a simple or objective fact as such, irrespective of whether it results from criminal intent or from negligence. Examples of such offences may be found in the laws of the Contracting States."

They did, however, state that such departures from the normal principles of criminal responsibility must be confined "within reasonable limits which take into account the importance of what is at stake and maintain the rights of the defence".

*Salabiaku* suggests that very strict conditions of responsibility will not be incompatible with the Convention. In that case, the applicant was convicted under article 392, paragraph 1 of the Customs Code, according to which "the person in possession of contraband goods shall be deemed liable for the offence". He had collected a package from an airport in France which he believed to contain foodstuffs sent to him on an Air Zaïre flight. In fact the package contained prohibited drugs. (His mistake appears to have been at least honest, since two days later a package containing food, sent to him via Air Zaïre did turn up. It had been delivered to Brussels by mistake.) The Court held that there had been no violation of article 6(2). This was not an "absolute offence", but one which created a presumption of responsibility. This presumption, according to the case law of the French courts, was not irrebuttable and there was, in the circumstances no breach of article 6(2).

However, it is clear that the conditions under which it could be rebutted were limited to *force majeure* (including "the absolute impossibility . . . of knowing the contents of [a] package") and (possibly) necessity and "unavoidable error", which suggests that mere ignorance of the contents of the package, albeit wholly innocent, would not be sufficient to avoid conviction. That is a form of strict responsibility. See also, in this connection *Pham Hoang v. France*, Series A, No. 243, another case involving French drugs legislation in which it appeared that the only way in which the accused could rebut not one but four presumptions raised against him was by demonstrating that he had "acted from necessity or as a result of unavoidable mistake". Again, the Court held that there was no breach of article 6(2).

The approach of the European Court of Human Rights to these issues should be contrasted with the views developed in the Canadian Supreme Court, particularly in relation to section 7 of the Canadian Charter of Rights and Freedoms. That section provides that "Everyone has the right to life, liberty and security of the person and the right not to be deprived thereof except in accordance with the principles of fundamental justice". This section has been applied so as to require proof of *mens rea* in all cases of serious crime. And even in less serious offences, if imprisonment is available as a penalty, there must at least be some minimum level of fault. See, for example, *Re British Columbia Motor Vehicle Act* [1985] 2 S.C.R. 486. For a summary of the Canadian position, see Gordon, (3rd ed.) paras 8.04 *et seq.* The English courts, by contrast, have made it quite clear that the fact an offence is punishable by imprisonment does not prevent it being treated as being one of strict liability: *Gammon Ltd v. A.-G. of Hong Kong* [1985] A.C. 1, *per* Lord Scarman at 17; *Harrow B.C. v. Shah* [2000] 1 W.L.R. 83, *per* Mitchell J. at 89.

## B. The presumption in favour of *mens rea*

It has been stressed in many cases both in Scotland and England that strict responsibility for a statutory **3.03** criminal offence is the exception rather than the rule, and that penal statutes should normally be construed as requiring *mens rea* as to the elements which give rise to guilt. As was said by Lord Justice-Clerk Cooper in *Duguid v. Fraser*, 1942 J.C. 1 at p. 5:

> "Our reports already contain many examples of cases in which it has been held that a *malum prohibitum* has been created by statutory enactment in such terms and under such circumstances as to impose an absolute obligation of such a kind as to entail this wider liability. In all such cases it

has, I think, been the practice to insist that the Crown should show that the language, scope and intendment of the statute require that an exception should be admitted to the normal and salutary rule of our law that *mens rea* is an indispensable ingredient of a criminal or quasi-criminal act; and I venture to think that it would be a misfortune if the stringency of this requirement were relaxed."

The House of Lords has also confirmed this view.

### Sweet v. Parsley
[1970] A.C. 132

**3.04** Cannabis was found on property let out by the appellant who did not know her tenants were using the premises for the purposes of smoking cannabis. She was convicted of being concerned in the management of premises used for smoking cannabis, under s.5 of the Dangerous Drugs Act 1965, and appealed to the House of Lords.

LORD REID: "Where it is contended that an absolute offence has been created, the words of Alderson B. in *Attorney-General v. Lockwood* (1842) 9 M. & W. 378, 398 have often been quoted: 'The rule of law, I take it upon the construction of all statutes, and therefore applicable to the construction of this, is, whether they be penal or remedial, to construe them according to the plain, literal, and grammatical meaning of the words in which they are expressed, unless that construction leads to a plain and clear contradiction of the apparent purpose of the Act, or to some palpable and evident absurdity.'

That is perfectly right as a general rule and where there is no legal presumption. But what about the multitude of criminal enactments where the words of the Act simply make it an offence to do certain things but where everyone agrees that there cannot be a conviction without proof of *mens rea* in some form? This passage, if applied to the present problem, would mean that there is no need to prove *mens rea* unless it would be 'a plain and clear contradiction of the apparent purpose of the Act' to convict without proof of *mens rea*. But that would be putting the presumption the wrong way round: for it is firmly established by a host of authorities that *mens rea* is an essential ingredient of every offence unless some reason can be found for holding that that is not necessary.

It is also firmly established that the fact that other sections of the Act expressly require *mens rea*, for example because they contain the word 'knowingly', is not in itself sufficient to justify a decision that a section which is silent as to *mens rea* creates an absolute offence. In the absence of a clear indication in the Act that an offence is intended to be an absolute offence, it is necessary to go outside the Act and examine all relevant circumstances in order to establish that this must have been the intention of Parliament. I say 'must have been' because it is a universal principle that if a penal provision is reasonably capable of two interpretations, that interpretation which is most favourable to the accused must be adopted.

What, then, are the circumstances which it is proper to take into account? In the well-known case of *Sherras v. De Rutzen* [1895] 1 Q.B. 918, Wright J. only mentioned the subject matter with which the Act deals. But he was there dealing with something which was one of a class of acts which 'are not criminal in any real sense, but are acts which in the public interest are prohibited under a penalty' (p. 922). It does not in the least follow that when one is dealing with a truly criminal act it is sufficient merely to have regard to the subject matter of the enactment. One must put oneself in the position of a legislator. It has long been the practice to recognise absolute offences in this class of quasi-criminal acts, and one can safely assume that, when Parliament is passing new legislation dealing with this class of offences, its silence as to *mens rea* means that the old practice is to apply. But when one comes to acts of a truly criminal character, it appears to me that there are at least two other factors which any reasonable legislator would have in mind. In the first place a stigma still attaches to any person convicted of a truly criminal offence, and the more serious or more disgraceful the offence the greater the stigma. So he would have to consider whether, in a case of this gravity, the public interest really requires that an innocent person should be prevented from proving his innocence in order that fewer guilty men may escape. And equally important is the fact that fortunately the Press in this country are vigilant to expose injustice and every manifestly unjust conviction made known to the public tends to injure the body politic by undermining public confidence in the justice of the law and of its administration. But I regret to observe that, in some recent cases where serious offences have been held to be absolute offences, the court has taken into account no more than the wording of the Act and the character and seriousness of the mischief which constitutes the offence.

The choice would be much more difficult if there were no other way open than either *mens rea* in the full sense or an absolute offence, for there are many kinds of case where putting on the prosecutor the full burden of proving *mens rea* creates great difficulties and may lead to many unjust acquittals. But there are at least two other possibilities. Parliament has not infrequently transferred the onus as regards *mens rea* to the accused, so that, once the necessary facts are proved, he must convince the jury that on balance of probabilities he is innocent of any criminal intention. I find it a little surprising that more use has not been made of this method: but one of the bad effects of the decision of this House in *Woolmington v. Director of Public Prosecutions* [1935] A.C. 462 may have been to discourage its use. The other method would be in effect to substitute in appropriate classes of cases gross negligence for *mens rea* in the full sense as the mental element necessary to constitute the crime. It would often be much easier to infer that Parliament must have meant that gross negligence should be the necessary mental element than to infer that Parliament intended to create an absolute offence. A variant of this would be to accept the view of Cave J. in *Reg. v. Tolson* (1889) 23 Q.B.D. 168, 181. This appears to have been done in Australia where authority appears to support what Dixon J. said in *Proudman v. Dayman* (1941) 67 C.L.R. 536, 540: 'As a general rule an honest and reasonable belief in a state of facts which, if they existed, would make the defendant's act innocent affords an excuse for doing what would otherwise be an offence.' It may be that none of these methods is wholly satisfactory but at least the public scandal of convicting on a serious charge persons who are in no way blameworthy would be avoided.

If this section means what the Divisional Court have held that it means, then hundreds of thousands of people who sublet part of their premises or take in lodgers or are concerned in the management of residential premises or institutions are daily incurring a risk of being convicted of a serious offence in circumstances where they are in no way to blame. For the greatest vigilance cannot prevent tenants, lodgers or inmates or guests whom they bring in from smoking cannabis cigarettes in their own rooms. It was suggested in argument that this appellant brought this conviction on herself because it is found as a fact that when the police searched the premises there were people there of the 'beatnik fraternity'. But surely it would be going a very long way to say that persons managing premises of any kind ought to safeguard themselves by refusing accommodation to all who are of slovenly or exotic appearance, or who bring in guests of that kind. And unfortunately drug taking is by no means confined to those of unusual appearance.

Speaking from a rather long experience of membership of both Houses, I assert with confidence that no Parliament within my recollection would have agreed to make an offence of this kind an absolute offence if the matter had been fully explained to it. So, if the court ought only to hold an offence to be an absolute offence where it appears that that must have been the intention of Parliament, offences of this kind are very far removed from those which it is proper to hold to be absolute offences."

LORD DIPLOCK: "The expression 'absolute offence' used in the first question is an imprecise phrase currently used to describe an act for which the doer is subject to criminal sanctions even though when he did it he had no *mens rea*, but *mens rea* itself also lacks precision and calls for closer analysis than is involved in its mere translation into English by Wright J. in *Sherras v. De Rutzen* [1895] 1 Q.B. 918, 921 as 'evil intention or a knowledge of the wrongfulness of the act'—a definition which suggests a single mental element common to all criminal offences and appears to omit thoughtlessness which, at any rate if it amounted to a reckless disregard of the nature or consequences of an act, was a sufficient mental element in some offences at common law.

A more helpful exposition of the nature of *mens rea* in both common law and statutory offences is to be found in the judgment of Stephen J. in *Reg. v. Tolson* (1889) 23 Q.B.D. 168, 187. He said: 'The full definition of every crime contains expressly or by implication a proposition as to a state of mind. Therefore, if the mental element of any conduct alleged to be a crime is proved to have been absent in any given case, the crime so defined is not committed; or, again, if a crime is fully defined, nothing amounts to that crime which does not satisfy that definition.'

Where the crime consists of doing an act which is prohibited by statute the proposition as to the state of mind of the doer which is contained in the full definition of the crime must be ascertained from the words and subject-matter of the statute. The proposition, as Stephen J. pointed out, may be stated explicitly by the use of such qualifying adverbs as 'maliciously', 'fraudulently', 'negligently' or 'knowingly'—expressions which in relation to different kinds of conduct may call for judicial exegesis. And even without such adverbs the words descriptive of the prohibited act may themselves connote the presence of a particular mental element. Thus, where the prohibited conduct consists in permitting a particular thing to be done the word 'permit' connotes at least knowledge or reasonable grounds for suspicion on the part of the permitter that the thing will be done and an unwillingness to use means available to him to prevent it and, to take a recent example, to have in one's 'possession' a prohibited substance connotes some degree of awareness of that which was within the possessor's physical control: *Reg. v. Warner* [1969] 2 A.C. 256.

But only too frequently the actual words used by Parliament to define the prohibited conduct are in themselves descriptive only of a physical act and bear no connotation as to any particular state of mind on the part of the person who does the act. Nevertheless, the mere fact that Parliament has made the conduct a criminal offence gives rise to some implication about the mental element of the conduct proscribed. It has, for instance, never been doubted since *McNaghten's* case (1843) 10 Cl. & F. 200, that one implication as to the mental element in any statutory offence is that the doer of the prohibited act should be sane within the McNaghten rules; yet this part of the full definition of the offence is invariably left unexpressed by Parliament. Stephen J. in *Reg. v. Tolson* (1893) 23 Q.B.D. 168 suggested other circumstances never expressly dealt with in the statute where a mental element to be implied from the mere fact that the doing of an act was made a criminal offence would be absent, such as where it was done in a state of somnambulism or under duress, to which one might add inevitable accident. But the importance of the actual decision of the nine judges who constituted the majority in *Reg. v. Tolson*, which concerned a charge of bigamy under section 57 of the Offences Against the Person Act, 1861, was that it laid down as a general principle of construction of any enactment, which creates a criminal offence, that, even where the words used to describe the prohibited conduct would not in any other context connote the necessity for any particular mental element, they are nevertheless to be read as subject to the implication that a necessary element in the offence is the absence of a belief, held honestly and upon reasonable grounds, in the existence of facts which, if true, would make the act innocent. As was said by the Privy Council in *Bank of New South Wales v. Piper* [1897] A.C. 383, 389, 390, the absence of *mens rea* really consists in such a belief by the accused.

This implication stems from the principle that it is contrary to a rational and civilised criminal code, such as Parliament must be presumed to have intended, to penalise one who has performed his duty as a citizen to ascertain what acts are prohibited by law (*ignorantia juris non excusat*) and has taken all proper care to inform himself of any fact which would make his conduct lawful.

Where penal provisions are of general application to the conduct of ordinary citizens in the course of their everyday life the presumption is that the standard of care required of them in informing themselves of facts which would make their conduct unlawful, is that of the familiar common law duty of care. But where the subject-matter of a statute is the regulation of a particular activity involving potential danger to public health, safety or morals in which citizens have a choice as to whether they participate or not, the court may feel driven to infer an intention of Parliament to impose by penal sanctions a higher duty of care on those who choose to participate and to place upon them an obligation to take whatever measures may be necessary to prevent the prohibited act, without regard to those considerations of cost or business practicability which play a part in the determination of what would be required of them in order to fulfil the ordinary common law duty of care. But such an inference is not lightly to be drawn, nor is there any room for it unless there is something that the person on whom the obligation is imposed can do directly or indirectly, by supervision or inspection, by improvement of his business methods or by exhorting those whom he may be expected to influence or control, which will promote the observance of the obligation (see *Lim Chin Aik v. The Queen* [1963] A.C. 160, 174).

The numerous decisions in the English courts since *Reg. v. Tolson* (1889) 23 Q.B.D. 168 in which this later inference has been drawn rightly or, as I think, often wrongly are not easy to reconcile with others where the court has failed to draw the inference, nor are they always limited to penal provisions designed to regulate the conduct of persons who choose to participate in a particular activity as distinct from those of general application to the conduct of ordinary citizens in the course of their everyday life. It may well be that had the significance of *Reg. v. Tolson* been appreciated here, as it was in the High Court of Australia, our courts, too, would have been less ready to infer an intention of Parliament to create offences for which honest and reasonable mistake was no excuse . . . .

It has been objected that the requirement laid down in *Reg. v. Tolson* (1889) 23 Q.B.D. 168 and the *Bank of New South Wales v. Piper* [1897] A.C. 383 that the mistaken belief should be based on reasonable grounds introduces an objective mental element into *mens rea*. This may be so, but there is nothing novel in this. The test of the mental element of provocation which distinguishes manslaughter from murder has always been at common law and now is by statute the objective one of the way in which a reasonable man would react to provocation. There is nothing unreasonable in requiring a citizen to take reasonable care to ascertain the facts relevant to his avoiding doing a prohibited act."

Appeal allowed; conviction quashed.

NOTES

1. Section 5 of the Dangerous Drugs Act 1965, under which Ms Sweet was charged, is no longer in **3.05** force. See now the Misuse of Drugs Act 1971, s.8.

2. *Sweet v. Parsley* is still to be regarded as an authoritative statement of principle, and was accepted as such in *Gammon Ltd v. A.-G. of Hong Kong* [1985] A.C. 1, where the Privy Council summarised the law as follows:

"(1) there is a presumption of law that *mens rea* is required before a person can be held guilty of a criminal offence; (2) the presumption is particularly strong where the offence is "truly criminal" in character; (3) the presumption applies to statutory offences, and can be displaced only if this is clearly or by necessary implication the effect of the statute; (4) the only situation in which the presumption can be displaced is where the statute is concerned with an issue of social concern, and public safety is such an issue; (5) even where a statute is concerned with such an issue, the presumption of *mens rea* stands unless it can also be shown that the creation of strict liability will be effective to promote the objects of the statute by encouraging greater vigilance to prevent the commission of the prohibited act."

For an application of these criteria, see *Harrow B.C. v. Shah* [2000] 1 W.L.R. 83, where it was held that the offence of selling a National Lottery ticket to a person under the age of sixteen was a strict liability offence.

3. In *B. v. DPP* [2000] 1 All E.R. 833, B, a fifteen-year-old boy, repeatedly asked a thirteen-year-old

girl to perform oral sex with him. He was charged with inciting a child under fourteen to commit an act of gross indecency with him, contrary to section 1(1) of the Indecency with Children Act 1960. His defence, that he honestly believed that the girl was over fourteen, was rejected by the magistrates and the Divisional Court, who both held that the offence was one of strict liability.

The House of Lords, however, ruled that there was nothing in the statute to justify displacing the presumption that *mens rea* is required, and his conviction was quashed.

**3.06**      This is a somewhat surprising decision in the context of the particular offence in question. Although their Lordships are at pains to point out that there is no general consistency of approach to the question of strict liability throughout the (English) Sexual Offences Act 1956, there has always been a widespread acceptance of the view that, subject to the statutory defences of reasonable error as to age, as set out in the legislation, sexual offences which have an age condition are offences of strict liability with regard to the age element. Why should the offence of having unlawful sexual intercourse with a girl aged between 12 and 13 be regarded as an offence of strict liability but the offence of inciting an act of gross indecency with the same girl be regarded as an offence requiring proof of knowledge of the girl's age?

The views expressed by their Lordships are influenced by the subjectivist approach to *mens rea* which is more readily accepted in English law, and it remains to be seen whether this judgment would be regarded as influential in Scotland in relation to statutory sexual offences. For a trenchant and persuasive critique of the decision in *B. v. DPP* see, J. Horder, "How Culpability Can, and Cannot, Be Denied in Under-age Sex Crimes", [2001] Crim.L.R. 15.

4. In *C.P.S. v. K.*, (2000) 144 S.L. L.B. 272 the Court of Appeal in England held that the offence of indecent assault on a female under the age of 16, contrary to section 14(1) of the Sexual Offences Act 1956 is one of strict liability as regards the age of the complainer, and that applying strict liability in this offence was not contrary to Article 6 of the European Convention on Human Rights.

## B. Terms implying *mens rea*

**3.07**      It is clear from the above discussion of strict responsibility that the mere absence of terms indicating that a mental element is required will not necessarily indicate that the offence is one of strict liability. At the same time, the presence of certain terms from which a mental element might be inferred does not necessarily mean that this is so. Some terms such as "intention", "knowledge", "recklessly" necessarily infer *mens rea*, but others are less certain. On a number of occasions the courts have had to determine whether or not words or phrases such as "cause" or "permit" or "possession" require proof of a mental element which, although not expressed, is implied by the nature of the term.

### (a) "Knowingly"

**Noble v. Heatly**
1967 S.L.T. 26

**3.08**      The licensee of a public house was convicted of knowingly permitting drunkenness on the premises, contrary to the terms of his licence and section 131 of the Licensing (Scotland) Act 1959. One of the statutory conditions of the licence was that the licence holder "shall not knowingly permit any ... drunkenness" on the premises. The police had found two people drunk in the pub and hour and twenty minutes after closing time. The licensee was not present at the time, and had no knowledge of the circumstances giving rise to the charge. He had delegated the running of the pub to an experienced supervisor, who had in turn appointed a manager who was in sole charge of the premises when the police arrived. He appealed to the High Court by stated case. The appeal was heard by five judges.

The Opinion of the Court: "This appeal was put out before a Court of five judges in order to consider the soundness of the decision in the case of *Greig v. Macleod* (1908) 5 Adam 445, particularly in the light of the recent decision in the House of Lords of *Vane v. Yiannopoullos* [1965] A.C. 486 ...."

It is clear in these circumstances that the appellant had himself no personal knowledge of the drunkenness that evening in this public house, and the question in the case is whether the magistrate was entitled to convict him of knowingly permitting the drunkenness which occurred there. The decision of the magistrate is sought to be justified by the decision of the Court in *Greig v. Macleod* 1908 S.C. (J.) 14. In that case the High Court upheld the conviction of the holder of a public house certificate charged with knowingly allowing an assistant in the premises to sell exciseable liquor to a girl under 14 years of age in breach of s.59 of the Licensing (Scotland) Act 1903. The sale took place outwith the certificate holder's presence and actual personal knowledge. He had given no sufficient instructions as to the supply of liquor to persons under 14. Lord Maclaren who gave the leading opinion with which the rest of the Court agreed stated his reason for upholding the conviction in the following words: "In the case of *Emary v. Nolloth* [1903] 2 K.B. 264 we have the authority of Lord Alverstone for this construction of the provisions of the section, that if a person in the position of the appellant delegates the conduct of his business to another, he is responsible for the acts of the person to whom he has given the institorial power as if he had made the sale himself. Now I think it is not an illegitimate extension of the rule thus laid down if I say that every licensee who delegates a part of his business is at least responsible to the extent that he must give instructions to his assistant as to compliance with Acts of Parliament which regulate the spirit trade."

Although the result at which the Court arrived in that case appears to be sound in the light of the facts found proved Lord Maclaren's grounds for reaching the decision are in our opinion unsound. In the first place, Lord Alverstone's observations were not necessary for the decision of the case of *Emary* (*supra*) which was not a case of delegation by the licence holder. They were therefore strictly obiter. In the second place, these dicta were pronounced in an English case, and related to rules of English law which have never been part of the law of Scotland, and which so far as appears from the decided cases reported in Scotland have never been applied in Scotland except in *Greig's* case. In the third place, Lord Maclaren in this latter case sought to extend the English rule in a way which would conflict with other passages in Lord Alverstone's opinion and for which there is no warrant in what Lord Alverstone had said.

In the result therefore knowingly must in our opinion mean what it says, and unless there is express statutory warrant for holding it to mean something else an offence is not committed where knowingly is of its essence unless there is personal knowledge on the part of the accused person. Considerable support for this conclusion is to be found in the speeches in the recent House of Lords decision in *Vane v. Yiannopoullos* (*supra*) regarding the meaning of "knowingly" in a similar provision in an English licensing Act. In the course of the argument before us reference was made to s.187 of the Licensing (Scotland) Act 1959. This section does not appear to have been founded upon in the Court below, and there are consequently no proper findings in regard to it in the present case. Counsel for the respondent very fairly conceded that he could not rely on the section to justify the conviction. Whatever meaning it may have—and parties were acutely divided on the matter in the argument before us—it would not be proper in these circumstances to determine the present issue by a consideration of whether it was applicable or what effect it had."

Appeal allowed.

NOTES

1. So "knowingly" means "knowingly", unless, of course, it does not. The Court does not actually **3.09** overrule *Greig v. MacLeod* (the correctness of which had already been doubted in *Thornley v. Hunter*, 1965 S.L.T. 206) since it appeared to think that on its facts it was correctly decided.

2. The requirement of knowledge in such statutory offences can be satisfied by proof of "wilful blindness". See, for example, *Knox v. Boyd*, 1941 J.C. 82; *Thornley v. Hunter, supra*; *Mackay Brothers and Company v. Gibb*, 1969 S.L.T. 216.

## (b) "Causing" and "Permitting"

### Smith of Maddiston Ltd v. MacNab
1975 S.L.T. 86

**3.10** OPINION OF THE COURT (nine judges): "The appellants are a limited company who carry on business as haulage contractors. They were convicted in the sheriff court at Greenock on a complaint that they caused or permitted to be used by their employee, John Lamont, a motor vehicle with an insecure load. On the same complaint, John Lamont pled guilty to using the vehicle whilst in this condition. The complaint bore that both offences were contrary to Regulation 90(2) of the Motor Vehicles (Construction and Use) Regulations 1973 . . . .

At the time of the offence the appellants had hired the vehicle with the driver Lamont for the purpose of transporting an 8-ton tiller from Greenock to Ardrossan. The appellants through their responsible officials knew that in order to secure the load safely and prevent it falling off, a chain and dwang should be used. They did not specifically instruct Lamont to secure the load by this means. He was an experienced driver and had done similar work before. Chains and dwangs were available in the appellants' central store depot. Lamont knew that he could, at any time, draw the equipment he required to secure a load from that depot. The appellants took it for granted that he would know to use a chain and dwang. Lamont did not do so but secured the load by a rope. In the course of the journey the load broke loose and fell off, struck a passing car and injured its occupants. Lamont admitted to the operations manager of the appellants that he had not used a chain and a dwang. He also said he was not satisfied with the way the load had been secured.

The sheriff convicted the appellants on the ground that the decision in *Hunter v. Clark*, 1956 J.C. 59, 1956 S.L.T. 188, compelled him to conclude that the obligation imposed by Regulation 90(2) of the 1973 Regulations as applied by s.40(5) of the Act of 1972 is absolute both upon the person who uses the vehicle and the person who causes or permits its use. In the sheriff court the Crown case was presented on the basis that the appellants were guilty if they caused the vehicle to be used although they were unaware that it was being used in breach of the regulation. In view of that, the Solicitor-General stated that he would not argue before this court that the conviction should, in any event, stand because the appellants had not given sufficient directions to Lamont as to how the load should be secured.

The case of *Hunter v. Clark* (*supra*) related to a breach of the Motor Vehicles (Construction and Use) Regulations 1955, made under the Road Traffic Act 1930. Regulation 104 created the offence by stating that if any person used or caused or permitted to be used on any road a motor vehicle in contravention of the regulations he should be liable to penalties. The regulations alleged to be contravened were Regulation 76 relating to the braking system and Regulation 61 relating to the painting of certain markings on vehicles. It was proved that the vehicle was used in contravention of these regulations. There was no proof that the owner knew of the defective brakes. He had given instructions to a painter to paint all his vehicles with the markings required by Regulation 61.

In dealing with the alleged contravention of Regulation 76 the Lord Justice-General stated that, in his view, the matter was analogous to the situation in the seven judge case of *Mitchell v. Morrison*, 1938 J.C. 64, 1938 S.L.T. 201. It was this observation which led to the present case being heard before a Bench of nine judges. In *Mitchell v. Morrison* (*supra*) the court were concerned with the provisions of the Road and Rail Traffic Act 1933 and the relevant regulations which required the holder of a licence for the carriage of goods to keep or cause to be kept certain records regarding drivers and others. It was held that these provisions imposed an absolute obligation. This obligation, however, is a direct personal one imposed by Parliament upon the holder of a licence and differs from the obligation considered in *Hunter v. Clark* where, as in the present case, the offence consisted in causing or permitting another to use a vehicle in contravention of regulations. *Mitchell v. Morrison* does not, therefore, require to be reviewed by this court. The Solicitor-General and counsel for the appellants both accepted this. The distinction between *Mitchell v. Morrison* and *Hunter v. Clark* was noted in the English case of *Ross Hillman Ltd v. Bond* [1974] Q.B. 435. The analogy sought to be drawn by the Lord Justice-General in *Hunter v. Clark* is therefore unsound.

In addition, the Lord Justice-General drew a distinction between causing and permitting as used in Regulation 104. His view was that in the case of causation responsibility remained with the person who caused the use even if he had no knowledge of the use in contravention; whereas permission to use in contravention necessarily involved knowledge of that contravention. We agree with the second part of this proposition but not the first. In our opinion a person cannot permit the use of a vehicle in contravention of a regulation unless he knows or should know of the contravention. In *Hunter v. Clark* the Crown conceded that this was correct and, in the present case, the sheriff, following the Lord Justice-General in *Hunter v. Clark*, accepted the accuracy of the proposition. Before this court the Solicitor-General did not renew the concession, but in our view the proposition is accurate and is supported by authority. We agree with the opinion of the majority of the court in *James & Son Ltd v. Smee* [1955] 1 Q.B. 78. That case was concerned with Regulation 101 of the Motor Vehicles (Construction and Use) Regulations 1951 which made it an offence for any person to use or cause or permit to be used on a road a motor vehicle in contravention of the regulations. The majority held that a charge of permitting the use in contravention imported a state of mind and required knowledge on the part of the person who permitted not only the use of the vehicle but its use in contravention. Knowledge in this connection includes the state of mind of a man who shuts his eyes to the obvious and allows another to do something in circumstances where a contravention is likely, not caring whether a contravention takes place or not. It may be inferred where the permittor has given no thought to his statutory obligations at all (*Houston v. Buchanan*, 1940 S.C. (H.L.) 17, 1940 S.L.T. 232, per Lord Wright, at p. 236).

Accepting that permission requires knowledge in the sense above described it is our opinion that the same consideration must apply to the interpretation of the word 'causes' in s.40(5) of the Road Traffic Act 1972. To 'cause' involves some express or positive mandate from the person 'causing' to the other person, or some authority from the former to the latter arising in the circumstances of the case (*Houston v. Buchanan* (*supra*), per Lord Wright, at p. 236; *Shave v. Rosner* [1954] 2 Q.B. 113). In *Lovelace v. D.P.P.* [1954] 1 W.L.R. 1468, Lord Goddard, C.J. applied this definition to a situation where the licensee and manager of a theatre was convicted of causing to be presented part of a play without the approval of the Lord Chamberlain. The departure from the approved script took place at the instance of one of the actors without the knowledge of the appellant. Indeed, it was contrary to his express instructions to adhere strictly to the script. In allowing the appeal Lord Goddard stated at p. 1471 that if a man is charged with causing or permitting something, it follows that that must result by reason of some act of his which is equivalent to causing, such as a command or direction to do the act. We respectfully agree with this proposition. It follows from it, in our opinion, that a person cannot be said to have caused another to do something in contravention of a regulation without knowledge, actual or constructive, that it will be done in such contravention. This view also appealed to the court in *Ross Hillman Ltd v. Bond* (*supra*).

For these reasons we do not agree with the distinction drawn by the Lord Justice-General in *Hunter v. Clark* between causing and permitting so far as the question of knowledge is concerned. Also, we do not agree with the conclusion of Lord Russell in the same case to the effect that if absence of knowledge were to be an offence the regulations would have said so. In our opinion the correct approach is to construe the regulation in the first instance. If that construction points to absolute liability on the part of the person who merely causes or permits the vehicle to be used on the road, the question of a statutory defence based on absence of knowledge may then be important. We prefer the approach and reasoning of Lord

Sorn in his dissenting judgment. His conclusion was that the words 'causes to be used ... in contravention' contained in Regulation 104 of the 1955 Regulations denote a person who causes not only use but use in contravention.

The Solicitor-General pointed out that in the present case the statutory provision under consideration, *viz.* s.40(5) of the Road Traffic Act 1972, is worded differently from Regulation 104 of the 1955 Regulations considered in *Hunter v. Clark*. Section 40(5) makes it an offence to use on a road a motor vehicle which does not comply with the regulations, or to cause or permit a vehicle to be so used. Regulation 104 provides that if any person uses or causes or permits to be used on any road a motor vehicle in contravention of the defined regulations he shall be liable to penalties. This distinction was not considered by the court in *Ross Hillman Ltd v. Bond.* The Crown argument was that the decision in *Hunter v. Clark*, whether correct or incorrect, was not directly relevant to the differently worded s.40(5) now being considered. It was said that as a matter of plain construction a breach of that section necessarily followed on proof of two facts—(a) that the vehicle was caused or permitted to be used on a road, and (b) that it did not comply with the regulations. This argument proceeded on the basis that knowledge of the second fact need not be established either in causing or in permitting. *Hunter v. Clark* and other Scottish decisions in which such knowledge was recognised as necessary to permitting were decided on a concession to that effect which was not made in the present case. It was also urged that the English decisions on the matter should not be followed. We do not consider that the difference in wording involves a different construction of the words 'causes or permits' in s.40(5) to that given to the same words in Regulation 104. Also, for the reasons already given, we are satisfied that a necessary ingredient of permission in this context is knowledge, actual or imputed, not only of the use of the vehicle on a road but of the use of that vehicle which does not comply with the relevant regulation. The Solicitor-General accepted that, if this were so, it is equally a necessary ingredient of causation in the same context and we so conclude.

We allow the appeal and answer the question in the stated case in the negative."

Conviction quashed.

NOTES

**3.11**   1. Offences of causing or permitting are often established even where persons in control simply do not care whether contraventions of statutes occur. See, for example, *Brown v. Burns Tractors Ltd*, 1986 S.C.C.R. 146 and *Carmichael v. Hannaway*, 1987 S.C.C.R. 236.

2. The case does, however, establish that, as a general rule both "causing" and "permitting" require proof of *mens rea*. For an exception, see *Lockhart v. National Coal Board, infra*.

3. See also *Macdonald v. Howdle,* 1995 S.L.T. 779. In this case, the appellant was convicted of causing or permitting another driver ('J.') to use her car without being insured to drive it, contrary to section 143(1) of the Road Traffic Act 1988. J. had assured her that he was insured to drive the car. He was not. The sheriff found that the appellant would not have allowed J. to drive the car if she had known that he was not insured. The sheriff convicted the appellant, taking the view that it was not necessary to show, under section 143, that she knew that J. was not insured. On appeal to the High Court it was held, following the English decision of *Newbury v. Davis* [1974] R.T.R. 367 (and the point being conceded by the Crown) that this was a case in which permission to drive the vehicle had been conditional on J. being insured. Since that condition was not fulfilled, the appellant had not permitted him to drive, and the conviction was quashed.

In delivering the opinion of the Court, the Lord Justice-General (Hope) observed that *Smith of Maddiston Ltd v. Macnab* was concerned with an alleged breach of the Construction and Use Regulations and that the wording of the relevant provision in the Act which creates the offence is different from that which is in issue in this case. As Sheriff Gordon points out, however, (*Commentary*, 1995 S.C.C.R. 220), the charge in *Smith of Maddiston Ltd* was not essentially different from the charge in this case.

It should, perhaps, be noted that in *DPP v. Fisher* [1991] Crim.L.R. 787 the Divisional Court was unwilling to follow *Newbury v. Davis*. In *Fisher*, F. agreed to lend his car to L. on the basis that L. could find someone insured to drive it. L. asked R. to drive, assuming that he was insured. He was not. The Court held that *Newbury* "must be regarded with extreme caution. Its *ratio* is capable of application only in exceptional circumstances .... It cannot be right in law that a person who lends his car to another can avoid liability merely by asking the other to be insured before using it."

### Lockhart v. National Coal Board
#### 1981 S.L.T. 161

The National Coal Board was charged on summary complaint with causing or knowingly **3.12** permitting, between October 21, 1979 and December 19, 1979, poisonous, noxious or polluting matter to enter various streams from ground on which they had carried out mining operations, contrary to s.22(1)(a) of the Rivers (Prevention of Pollution) (Scotland) Act 1951. They were acquitted after trial. The procurator fiscal appealed by stated case. The principal question before the High Court was whether the sheriff was entitled to find that the Board did not cause the pollution to enter the streams.

OPINION OF THE COURT: "The law applicable here was accepted by both parties to be the law laid down by the House of Lords in the English case of *Alphacell Ltd v. Woodward* [1972] A.C. 824 which related to the corresponding and identical section in the English Act, namely s.2(1)(a) of the Rivers (Prevention of Pollution) Act 1951. While what was said and decided in that case is not binding on this court, we, like counsel, fully accept the law as laid down therein. For present purposes we find it only necessary to refer to a few of the passages in the speeches of their Lordships. Lord Wilberforce said at p. 479: 'The subsection evidently contemplates two things—*causing*, which must involve some active operation or chain of operations involving as a result the pollution of the stream; *knowingly permitting*, which involves a failure to prevent the pollution, which failure, however, must be accompanied by knowledge. I see no reason either for reading back the word "knowingly" into the first limb, or for reading the first limb as, by deliberate contrast, hitting something which is unaccompanied by knowledge. The first limb involves causing and this is what has to be interpreted. In my opinion, "causing" here must be given a commonsense meaning and I deprecate the introduction of refinements, such as *causa causans*, effective cause or *novus actus*. There may be difficulties where acts of third persons or natural forces are concerned ... this is a clear case of causing the polluted water to enter the stream. The whole complex operation which might lead to this result was an operation deliberately conducted by the appellants'. His Lordship went on to say that the fact that there was no negligence involved did not entitle it to be said that this excluded causation in terms of the section, and that complication of the case by the infusion of the concept of *mens rea*, and its exceptions, was unnecessary and undesirable. Viscount Dilhorne said at p. 483: 'What, then, is meant by the word 'caused' in the subsection? If a man intending to secure a particular result, does an act which brings that about, he causes that result. If he deliberately and intentionally does certain acts of which the natural consequence is that certain results ensue, may he not also be said to have caused those results even though they may not have been intended by him? I think he can, just as he can be said to cause the result if he is negligent, without intending that result. I find support for my view in the observations of Bowen L.J. in *Kirkheaton District Local Board v. Ainley & Co.* He said [at p. 283]: 'It appears to me that any person causes the flow of sewage into a stream ... who intentionally does that which is calculated according to the ordinary course of things and the laws of nature to produce such flow.'"

We find it unnecessary to quote from the speeches of the other noble and learned Lords since they in effect lead to the same result in this matter of causation. The passages above cited seem to us to lead to this. In considering causation within the meaning of s.22(1) of the Scottish Act, (1) the prosecution must prove that the accused carried out some active operation or chain of operations the natural consequence of which is that polluted matter entered a stream; (2) knowledge and foreseeability are not matters which require to be proved; (3) a common sense meaning must be given to 'causing'; (4) neither negligence nor *mens rea* need be established; and (5) consideration has to be given to such things as natural forces, the act of a third party or an act of God, if the evidence justifies the bringing of such matters into consideration.

With these considerations in view we turn to examine the respective submissions of the parties and the evidence on which these submissions were made. This requires to be done on the basis of the decisions which we have already made, namely, (1) that the actings of the respondent to be looked at are those prior to the emergence of the polluted water into the streams on October 21, 1979 and (2) that the facts on which the issue is to be determined are those in the whole findings 1 to 20. The Lord Advocate submitted that the court was entitled to look at the respondent's mining operations from the time the mine was sunk in 1951 since this started a chain of operations which eventually resulted in and caused the overflow of polluted water into the streams. Counsel for the respondent argued that the court could only look at the activities of the respondent after November 1977 when the mine was closed on the exhaustion of workable coal resources. The Lord Advocate, in support of his contention, submitted that everything stemmed from the sinking of the mine in 1951. This in effect meant that the respondent dug a big hole in the ground. Water gathered in the workings and as a result of oxygen having been introduced into the mine pyrite became oxidised. While the mine was in working operation disposal of the water kept the oxidised pyrite latent. When the mine closed in 1977 all working by the respondent, including pumping, ceased, as a result of which the mine began to fill with water coming from the surface and this brought the oxidised pyrite product into a rich contaminated solution. In the absence of pumping the level of water containing the contaminated solution continued to rise until it broke the ground surface whereby the contaminated solution found its way into the streams. This was all part of a continuous chain of events deliberately carried out by the respondent which resulted in and caused the contamination of the streams as libelled. The respondent had set up a system under which pollution of the water was bound to occur and the polluted water was bound to overflow into the streams unless there were pumps of sufficient capacity to prevent this occurring. When there were no pumps the result was inevitable. On a commonsense approach this was a simple and straightforward case of 'causing'.

Counsel for the respondent maintained that since the polluted solution was kept under control so as not to constitute any danger when the pumps were operating, nothing which was done prior to the cessation of the working of the mine in 1977 (including the pumping) could be said to have caused the overflow of the polluted solution into the streams in October to December 1979. Accordingly all that the court was entitled to look at were the actings of the respondent after November 1977. Nothing which the respondent did or could do during that period could be said to have caused the overflow of the contaminated solution into the streams during the period libelled. Findings 8 and 20 showed that the respondent had no right of access to or over the surface of the ground referred to in the charge after the lease referred to in finding 1 had expired in 1978, that after the closure of the mine in 1977 the respondent had no right to go into the non coal-bearing strata at the mine, that the respondent had no right of access to the mine, and accordingly that the respondent had no right to instal and operate pumps underground. Thus since it was impossible for the respondent to operate pumps after the closure of the mine or do anything to control the level of the water, it cannot be said that subsequent to that point of time the respondent had by any positive act caused the overflow and consequential inflow of the contaminated water into the streams. That had been caused as a result of natural forces, to wit, the descent of surface water into the mine during the later period. Causation must be coupled with control, and the respondent had no control over what happened during that later period. The acquittal verdict was accordingly justified.

We agree with the submission made by the Lord Advocate. Looking back from the time when the polluted solution entered the streams one finds a continuous link of operations, actings and decisions by the respondent which were responsible for the contamination of the water and its eventual introduction into the streams. We need not repeat but simply adopt the Lord Advocate's history of the events. His submission seems to us to provide the common sense answer. The considerations stated by Lord Wilberforce and Viscount Dilhorne (*supra*) have been satisfied. The irrelevancies have been properly ignored. We find ourselves in further agreement with the Lord Advocate when he observed that the sheriff had gone wrong, as we think he did, by taking into consideration in relation to 'causation' factors which were relevant to 'permission' but not to 'causation'. Counsel for the respondent presented a meticulous and careful argument but we disagree with the premise underlying his principal submission. The respondent's decision to cease operations and stop pumping was a positive act. It resulted in a danger which had been created but kept latent becoming a real one which caused all the trouble. Reasonable foreseeability of the consequences does not come into account. It is the fact which matters. Nor is it an answer that the respondent was not in a legal position to do anything about pumping out the water after the mining operations had ceased and the lease had expired. That was something for which the respondent was responsible in entering upon such a lease. We do not consider that it is in the respondent's mouth to say: 'I have left myself in a position where I can do nothing about a danger which I have created, and so I cannot be held responsible for that danger'. The bringing into activity and hitherto latent danger was not just the forces of nature, namely the surface water continuing to come into the mine. It was the result of the respondent creating the latent danger and then leaving it to the mercy of the forces of nature which activated the danger.

Counsel for the respondent sought to distinguish the case of *Alphacell* (*supra*) in that the operations in that case were still continuing and the pumps were still in operation, albeit not properly, when the polluted material entered the river. This however, constitutes no ground for saying that what their Lordships said in their speeches had only applicability when these two things happened concurrently. While these dicta were expressed in the context of that case they are manifestly of general applicability. In support of his contention that causation had to be coupled with control, counsel for the respondent founded on the case of *Westhoughton Coal and Cannel Co. Ltd v. Wigan Coal Corporation Ltd*. That was a civil case and it is not clear, at least to us, what the basis of the claim for damages was. In any event it was decided on the particular facts of the case, and we do not consider that what was said and decided therein has any bearing on the present case where the facts were entirely different and the question at issue was an alleged contravention of a specific statutory duty, the considerations in respect of which were laid down by the House of Lords in the case of *Alphacell*.

Finally counsel for the respondent made what from one point of view was an argument on practicability and from another a plea ad misericordiam. He said that if the appeal succeeded on the ground of what happened here the respondent would be in continuous contravention of the section, since there was nothing which the respondent could do to prevent the continuation of what had already occurred. Furthermore, the respondent could be faced with the same problem every time a mine was closed. That may be so, but if what was done here constituted a breach of s.22(1) of the Act, as we hold that it does, then, standing the present law, it is no answer to say, so far as conviction is concerned, that it poses problems for the offender. It is for the respondent, not the court, to decide how such a position can be met.

Appeal allowed.
Case remitted to sheriff with direction to convict.

NOTES

1. The result may seem harsh for a body such as the N.C.B. who had no longer any legal right to enter **3.13** the mine and take the necessary precautions, but the court clearly felt that the danger originally created by them could not be ignored in assessing their guilt.

2. Suppose that the offence had been limited to "causing", without any reference to "knowingly permitting". What would the proper outcome of the case be then?

## (b) Possession

**3.14** Some offences which require proof of possession may be satisfied by the Crown proving that the accused knew that he had the prohibited article or substance. Others may require further proof that the accused was aware that of the characteristics of the object or substance which make it unlawful to possess it. So, for example, where a person was charged with possessing a firearm without the necessary firearms certificate, contrary to section 1(1) of the Firearms Act 1968, as amended, it was held that it was necessary for the Crown to show that the accused knew that the item which he possessed was a firearm: *Smith v. H.M. Advocate*, 1996 S.L.T. 1338. In some instances the statute will expressly state, for example, that the possession must be "knowing", in which case knowledge of the presence of the object, and of its prohibited quality, will be required. See, for example, *Black v. H.M. Advocate*, 1974 S.L.T. 247. Often, however, the statute will be silent on the question of knowledge, which then becomes a matter of construction.

### R. v. Warner
### [1969] 2 A.C. 256

**3.15** The appellant was charged with having drugs in his possession without being duly authorised contrary to s.1(1) of the Drugs (Prevention of Misuse) Act 1964. There was evidence that a police officer had stopped the appellant who was driving a van in the back of which were found three cases, one of which contained scent bottles and another a plastic bag containing 20,000 amphetamine sulphate tablets. The appellant had been to a café where he was accustomed to collect scent from B, was told by the proprietor that a parcel from B was under the counter, and had found two parcels there, namely the one containing scent and the other which was found to contain the drugs. He said that he had assumed that both contained scent. On the question of possession the judge directed the jury that if he had control of the box which turned out to be full of amphetamine sulphate, the offence was committed and it was only mitigation that he did not know the contents.

The accused was convicted and appealed, ultimately, to the House of Lords.

LORD REID (*dissenting*): "I understand that this is the first case in which this House has had to consider whether a statutory offence is an absolute offence in the sense that the belief, intention, or state of mind of the accused is immaterial and irrelevant. It appears from the authorities that the law on this matter is in some confusion, there being at least two schools of thought. So I think it necessary to begin by making some observations of a general character.

There is no doubt that for centuries *mens rea* has been an essential element in every common law crime or offence. Equally there is no doubt that Parliament, being sovereign, can create absolute offences if so minded. But we were referred to no instance where Parliament in giving statutory form to an old common law crime has or has been held to have excluded the necessity to prove *mens rea*. There are a number of statutes going back for over a century where Parliament in creating a new offence has transferred the onus of proof so that, once the facts necessary to constitute the crime have been proved, the accused will be held to be guilty unless he can prove that he had no *mens rea*. But we were not referred to any except quite recent cases in which it was held that it was no defence to a charge of a serious and truly criminal statutory offence to prove absence of *mens rea*.

On the other hand there is a long line of cases in which it has been held with regard to less serious offences that absence of *mens rea* was no defence. Typical examples are offences under public health, licensing and industrial legislation. If a person sets up as say a butcher, a publican, or a manufacturer and exposes unsound meat for sale, or sells drink to a drunk man, or certain parts of his factory are unsafe, it is no defence that he could not by the exercise of reasonable care have known or discovered that the meat was unsound, or that the man was drunk or that the premises were unsafe. He must take the risk and when it is found that the statutory prohibition or requirement has been infringed he must pay the penalty. This may well seem unjust but it is a comparatively minor injustice, and there is good reason for it as affording some protection to his customers or servants or to the public at large. Although this man might be able to show that he did his best, a more skilful or diligent man in his position might have done better, and when we are dealing with minor penalties which do not involve the disgrace of criminality it may be in the public interest to have a hard and fast rule. Strictly speaking there ought perhaps to be a defence that the defect was truly latent so that no one could have discovered it. But the law has not developed in that way, and one can see the difficulty if such a defence were allowed in a summary prosecution. These are only quasi-criminal offences and it does not really offend the ordinary man's sense of justice that moral guilt is not of the essence of the offence."

LORD PEARCE: "Lord Parker C.J. ([1967] 2 Q.B. 243, 248) was right (and this is conceded by both sides) in taking the view that a person did not have possession of something which had been 'slipped into his' bag without his knowledge. One may, therefore, exclude from the 'possession' intended by the Act the physical control of articles which have been 'planted' on him without his knowledge. But how much further is one to go? If one goes to the extreme length of requiring the prosecution to prove that 'possession' implies a full knowledge of the name and nature of the drug concerned, the efficacy of the Act is seriously impaired, since many drug pedlars may in truth be unaware of this. I think that the term 'possession' is satisfied by a knowledge only of the existence of the thing itself and not its qualities, and that ignorance or mistake as to its qualities is not an excuse. This would comply with the general understanding of the word 'possess'. Though I reasonably believe the tablets which I possess to be aspirin, yet if they turn out to be heroin I am in possession of heroin tablets. This would be so I think even if I believed them to be sweets. It would be otherwise if I believed them to be something of a wholly different nature. At this point a question of degree arises as to when a difference in qualities amounts to a difference in kind. That is a matter for a jury who probably decide it sensibly in favour of the genuinely innocent but against the guilty.

The situation with regard to containers presents further problems. If a man is in possession of the contents of a package, prima facie his possession of the package leads to the strong inference that he is in possession of its contents. But can this be rebutted by evidence that he was mistaken as to its contents? As in the case of goods that have been 'planted' in his pocket without his knowledge, so I do not think that he is in possession of contents which are quite different in kind from what he believed. Thus the prima facie assumption is discharged if he proves (or raises a real doubt in the matter) either (a) that he was a servant or bailee who had no right to open it and no reason to suspect that its contents were illicit or were drugs or (b) that although he was the owner he had no knowledge of (including a genuine mistake as to) its actual contents or of their illicit nature and that he received them innocently and also that he had had no reasonable opportunity since receiving the package of acquainting himself with its actual contents. For a man takes over a package or suitcase at risk as to its contents being unlawful if he does not immediately examine it (if he is entitled to do so). As soon as may be he should examine it and if he finds the contents suspicious reject possession by either throwing them away or by taking immediate sensible steps for their disposal . . . .

The direction to which the accused was entitled would, in my opinion, be approximately as follows. The Act forbids possession of these drugs. Whether he possessed them with an innocent or guilty mind or for a laudable or improper purpose is immaterial since he is not allowed to possess them. If he possessed them he is guilty. If a man has physical control or possession of a thing that is sufficient possession under the Act provided that he knows that he has the thing. But you do not (within the meaning of the Act) possess things of whose existence you are unaware. The prosecution have here proved that he possessed the parcel, but have they proved that he possessed its contents also? There is a very strong inference of fact in any normal case that a man who possesses a parcel also possesses its contents, an inference on which a jury would in a normal case be justified in finding possession. A man who accepts possession of a parcel normally accepts possession of the contents.

But that inference can be disproved or shaken by evidence that, although a man was in possession of a parcel, he was completely mistaken as to its contents and would not have accepted possession had he known what kind of thing the contents were. A mistake as to the qualities of the contents, however, does not negative possession. Many people possess things of whose exact qualities they are unaware. If the accused knew that the contents were drugs or were tablets, he was in possession of them, though he was mistaken as to their qualities. Again, if though unaware of the contents, he did not open them at the first opportunity to ascertain (as he was entitled to do in this case) what they were, the proper inference is that he was accepting possession of them. (It would be otherwise if he had no right to open the parcel.) Again, if he suspected that there was anything wrong about the contents when he received the parcel, the proper inference is that he was accepting possession of the contents by not immediately verifying them. (This would, in my opinion, apply also to a bailee.)"

Conviction affirmed,
although magistrates' direction defective.

NOTES

**3.16**   1. The legislation discussed in *Warner* was repealed and replaced by the provisions of the Misuse of Drugs Act 1971. Section 4(1) provides that it is unlawful for a person not authorised to do so to produce a controlled drug, or to offer or supply such a drug to another person. Section 5(1) of that Act provides that it is unlawful for a person not authorised to do so to have in his possession a controlled drug. Section 5(2) makes it an offence to possess a controlled drug in contravention of section 5(1). Section 5(3) makes it an offence to possess a controlled drug, whether lawfully or not, with intent to supply it to another in contravention of section 4(1).

Both the offence of possession under section 5(2) and the offence of possession with intent to supply under section 5(3) are subject to the provisions of section 28 of the 1971 Act. Section 28(2) provides that in proceedings for an offence under sections 5(2) or (3) "it shall be a defence for the accused to prove that he neither knew of nor suspected nor had reason to suspect the existence of some fact alleged by the prosecution which it is necessary for the prosecution to prove if he is to be convicted of the offence charged."

Section 28(3)(a) provides that where it is necessary for the prosecution to prove that the substance in question was a particular controlled drug, and that much is proved, it is not a defence for the accused to show that he neither knew nor suspected, nor had reason to suspect, that the substance was that controlled drug. But section 28(3)(b) provides that the accused is entitled to an acquittal if he proves that he neither believed nor suspected nor had reason to suspect that the substance was a controlled drug at all. Section 28(3)(b) also provides that it is a defence in such a case for the accused to prove that he believed that the substance he had in his possession was a controlled drug which, in the circumstances of the case, it would not have been unlawful for him to possess.

2. *Warner* states that proof of possession, at least under section 1(1) of the 1964 Act did not require proof of knowledge of the character of the substance which was proved to be a controlled drug. It was, however, necessary for the Crown to show that the accused was aware of the existence of the substance. In *McKenzie v. Skeen*, 1983 S.L.T. 121 the appellant was convicted under section 5(2) of the 1971 Act. She appealed, arguing that there was insufficient evidence to establish that she knew she was in possession of a drug. The Crown argued, on the basis of section 28(2) that it was not necessary, under the 1971 Act for the Crown to "establish that any possession of an article by an accused was with his knowledge". It was the Crown's contention that the effect of section 28(2) was to shift the onus of proof to the accused "to show, if he could, that he did not know that he had any particular article found on his person or repositories or otherwise under his control". The argument was rejected by the Court which held that under the 1971 Act if the Crown wished to prove possession it was still necessary for them to establish that the accused was aware that he or she had something in their possession, although it was not necessary for the Crown to prove that the accused knew that it was a controlled drug:

"There is no doubt that under the corresponding provisions of the Act of 1964 knowledge on the part of the alleged possessor was an essential element to be established in proof of a charge of unlawful possession of a substance specified in the Schedule to that Act. In this respect the word 'possession' was, not surprisingly the meaning commonly accepted in other statutory context, for example the Explosives Act 1883, and the English cases of *Lockyer v. Gibb* [1967] 2 Q.B. 243 and *R. v. Warner* [1969] 2 A.C. 256, which were concerned with s.1 of the Drugs (Prevention of Misuse)

Act 1964, show quite clearly that for the purposes of that section a person cannot be said to be in the possession of an article which he does not realise was there at all. What was required, therefore, was proof that the alleged possessor was aware of the existence of the thing which he is said to have possessed and since the section did not demand proof of knowledge of the quality of the thing possessed, if that thing turned out to be a controlled drug, proof of the offence was complete. Has the Misuse of Drugs Act 1971 made the fundamental change for which in this case the Crown contends? In my opinion the answer is emphatically in the negative."

3. Sections 5 and 28 have not always been easy to apply. In particular, the relationship between section 28(2) and 28(3), and the different functions that they are intended to perform, have not always been appreciated. These matters were, however, explored in considerable detail in the following case.

### Salmon v. H.M. Advocate; Moore v. H.M. Advocate
1999 S.L.T. 169

These two cases were not related, but were considered together by the High Court as they **3.17** raised similar issues. Salmon was charged with being concerned in the supply of cocaine, contrary to section 4(3)(b) of the Misuse of Drugs Act 1971. Moore was charged with possession of ecstasy with intent to supply it to another, contrary to section 5(3).

The relevant statutory provisions are as follows:

**Section**

**4.**—(1) Subject to any regulations under section 7 of this Act for the time being in force, it shall not be lawful for a person—

(a) to produce a controlled drug; or

(b) to supply or offer to supply a controlled drug to another ...

(3) Subject to section 28 of this Act, it is an offence for a person— ...

(b) to be concerned in the supplying of [a controlled drug] to another in contravention of subsection (1) above ...

**5.**—(3) Subject to section 28 of this Act, it is an offence for a person to have a controlled drug in his possession, whether lawfully or not, with intent to supply it to another in contravention of section 4(1) of this Act.

**28.**—(1) This section applies to offences under any of the following provisions of this Act, that is to say section 4(2) and (3), section 5(2) and (3), sections 6(2) and section 9.

(2) Subject to subsection (3) below, in any proceedings for an offence to which this section applies it shall be a defence for the accused to prove that he neither knew nor suspected nor had reason to suspect the existence of some fact alleged by the prosecution which it is necessary for the prosecution to prove if he is to be convicted of the offence charged.

(3) Where in the proceedings for an offence to which this section applies it is necessary, if the accused is to be convicted of the offence charged, for the prosecution to prove that some substance or product involved in the alleged offence was the controlled drug which the prosecution alleges it to have been, and it is proved that the substance or product in question was that controlled drug, the accused—

(a) shall not be acquitted of the offence charged by reason only of proving that he neither knew not suspected nor had reason to suspect that the substance or product in question was the particular controlled drug alleged; but

(b) shall be acquitted thereof—

(i) if he proves that he neither believed nor suspected nor had reason to suspect that the substance or product in question was a controlled drug; or

(ii) if he proves that he believed the substance or product in question to be a controlled drug, or a controlled drug of a description, such that, if it had in fact been that controlled drug or a drug of that description, he would not at the material time have been committing any offence to which this section applies.

(4) Nothing in this section shall prejudice any defence which it is open to a person charged with an offence to which this section applies to raise apart from this section.

Lord Justice General (Rodger): "...

## Section 28

[His Lordship set out the facts of the case, then the terms of section 4(1) and (3), section 5(3) and section 28, and continued:]

The first thing which strikes me, when I look at these provisions, is that Parliament intends s.4(3)(b) to be read along with, and subject to, s.28 and similarly intends s.5(3) to be read along with, and subject to, s.28. This emerges both from the opening words of s.4(3) and s.5(3) ("Subject to section 28") and from subs. (1) of s.28 which applies that section to offences under various provisions, including s.4(3) and s.5(3). Section 28 is therefore designed to put a qualification on the scope of those provisions.

The other point which strikes me is that ss.4(3) and 5(3) are to be read as being subject to s.28 as a whole. So far as s.28 was concerned, in the earlier stages of the hearing counsel tried to confine the argument to the effect of subs.(3). That subsection had been paraphrased by the trial judge in his charge to the jury in the Salmon case and, counsel argued, it should have been mentioned by the trial judge in the Moore case. In cleaving to subs.(3) and studiously averting their eyes from subs.(2) counsel were merely following the lead of distinguished judges in both Scotland (*McKenzie v. Skeen*, 1983 S.L.T. 121 and England (*R. v. Ashton-Rickhardt* [1978] 1 W.L.R. 37). The result of the courts' attitude is that s.28(2) has vanished into a legal black hole. To ignore a provision which Parliament has included in an Act is wrong in principle, but, worse still, by disregarding subs.(2), the courts are in danger of distorting the construction of s.28 as a whole. Indeed it is indispensable, even to a proper understanding of s.28(3), to bring s.28(2) back into the light and to examine its terms. As the opening words of subs.(2) show, Parliament intends subs.(3) to be read as qualifying subs.(2). That being so, one must understand subs.(2) if one is to understand subs.(3). Subsection (3) also provides invaluable clues to the construction of subs.(2). I begin by examining subs.(3).

### Section 28(3)

Section 28(3) introduces a defence. It therefore provides a basis on which an accused person is to be acquitted, even though he would otherwise fall to be convicted.

In approaching the construction of s.28(3) I start with the opening words of subs.(2), "Subject to subsection (3) below". Those words immediately indicate that, although the scope of subs.(2) is wider than the scope of subs.(3), subs.(3) is designed to apply a special legislative regime to a particular situation which would otherwise fall within subs.(2) and be regulated by it. So, by identifying what subs.(3) covers, you identify a particular example of the general kind of situation which subs.(2) is designed to cover.

The courts have tended to construe subs.(3) as if it applied in any case where an accused person is found in possession of a drug but says that he thought that the drug was something else. So, for instance, in *R. v. McNamara* (1988) 87 Cr.App.R. 246, Lord Lane C.J. considered that s.28(3) would be the basis upon which the appellant, if believed by the jury, could be acquitted in a case where he said that he thought that a cardboard box, which was on his motorcycle, contained pornographic or pirate videos rather than the 20 kilos of cannabis resin which it in fact contained. In my view, however, such a broad interpretation of subs.(3) is not justified by the very precise language used by Parliament.

The first part of subs.(3) shows that the subsection concerns the situation where it is necessary for the prosecution to prove that "some *substance or product* involved in the alleged offence was the controlled drug which the prosecution alleges it to have been, and it is proved that the *substance or product* in question was that controlled drug" (emphasis added). It is significant that Parliament uses the words "substance or product" rather than some more general word such as "article". In the clauses which I have quoted the words "substance or product" can refer only to a substance or product which is actually a controlled drug—so it must be, say, the *powder or tablets* in question. That meaning must be carried through to the remainder of the subsection. Therefore in subs.(3)(b)(i), for instance, Parliament is saying that an accused is to be acquitted if he proves that he neither believed nor suspected nor had reason to suspect that the powder or tablets in question were a controlled drug. It follows that the subsection is intended to deal with the limited situation where the Crown have proved that the accused person possessed or was concerned in supplying, say, tablets ("the substance or product"), which are proved to be ecstasy tablets, but he says that he was mistaken about the nature or quality of the tablets.

A person in that position may say one of three things about the tablets. First, he may say that he did not know that they were ecstasy tablets and had always thought that they were heroin. Even if the jury accept his evidence on this point, it does not constitute a defence, however, since he is not to be acquitted of possessing ecstasy tablets by proving that he did not know that the substance or product in question was the particular controlled drug alleged rather than another controlled drug (s.28(3)(a)). Secondly, the accused may prove that he thought that the tablets in the bottle were aspirin and that he neither suspected nor had reason to suspect that they were a controlled drug. In that situation he is to be acquitted (s.28(3)(b)(i)). Thirdly, there are situations where people are authorised to possess or supply particular drugs. For instance, although heroin is a class A drug, a doctor may "for the purpose of acting in his capacity as" a doctor have heroin in his possession (regs 8(2)(a) and 10(1)(a) of, and Sched. 2 to, the Misuse of Drugs Regulations 1985 (S.I. 1985/2066)). If a doctor were found to have ecstasy tablets in his possession, it would be a defence for him to prove that he believed that the tablets were heroin tablets which he had in his possession for the purpose of acting in his capacity as a doctor (s.28(3)(b)(ii)).

That being the scope of subs.(3), it is not apt to apply to the kind of case envisaged in *McNamara* where an accused says that he thought that the contents of a box on his motorcycle were pornographic or pirate videos rather than cannabis resin. In such a case the accused is not claiming that he did not know that the organic matter ("the substance or product in question") was a controlled drug. Rather, he is saying that he did not think that the cannabis resin was there at all: he thought that the box contained videos. It follows that, if the only possible basis for the motorcyclist's defence were s.28(3), he would have no defence.

As I noted, s.28(3) applies only where it is necessary "for the prosecution to prove that some substance or product involved in the alleged offence was the controlled drug which the prosecution alleges it to have been, and it is proved that the substance or product in question was that controlled drug". The subsection is therefore concerned with a situation where the Crown have to prove the existence of a particular fact, *viz* that the substance or product in question was a controlled drug. Similarly, as the wording of paras (a) and (b)(i) shows, the subsection applies where the accused proves that he neither knew nor suspected nor had reason to suspect the existence of the fact which it was necessary for the Crown to prove, *viz.* that the substance or product in question was a controlled drug. Therefore, as was envisaged above, subs.(3) turns out to be simply a particular example of the wider class of situations covered by subs.(2), *viz.* situations where the accused proves "that he neither knew of nor suspected nor had reason to suspect the existence of some fact alleged by the prosecution which it is necessary for the prosecution to prove if he is to be convicted of the offence charged".

### Section 28(2)

This brings me to s.28(2) itself. In view of what is said by Lord Justice General Emslie in *McKenzie* (1983 S.L.T. at p. 121), it is perhaps worth emphasising that subs.(2) of s.28 is concerned with the accused's state of knowledge as to some fact which the Crown must prove if it is to succeed in the prosecution rather than with the fact itself. So, for instance, in *McNamara* it was necessary for the Crown to prove that there was organic matter in the box on the back of the appellant's motorcycle and that it was cannabis resin. The function of subs.(2) is to give an accused person in the position of McNamara a defence—which subs.(3) does not afford him—if he proves that he neither knew nor suspected nor had reason to suspect that the organic matter was in the box. I note that subs.(3) was designed to provide a defence to someone who would otherwise fall to be convicted of an offence under, say, s.4(3) or s.5(2) or (3). In the same way, subs.(2) is designed to provide a defence to someone who would otherwise fall to be convicted of an offence under the same provisions. So, even if the

Crown established that the motorcyclist in *McNamara* was in possession of the box and of the cannabis resin inside the box, he would still have a complete defence to the charge if he proved that he thought that the box contained videos and that he neither knew nor suspected nor had reason to suspect that the organic matter, which was proved to be cannabis resin, was in the box. I therefore respectfully agree with the Court of Appeal in *McNamara* when they say that, if he proved that, a person in McNamara's position would have a defence, but the defence would arise, not—as the Court of Appeal thought—under s.28(3), but rather under s.28(2).

It is worth summarising the conclusions so far.

Subsections (2) and (3) of s.28 are both designed to come into play at a stage when the Crown have proved all that they need to prove in order to establish guilt either of a contravention of s.4(3)(b) or of a contravention of s.5(3). So the Crown will have proved that the accused was delivering a package containing cocaine, for example, and was thus concerned in the supplying of cocaine; or that he was in possession of a package containing ecstasy with intent to supply it. At that stage s.28(2) provides that the accused is nonetheless to be acquitted if he proves that he neither knew nor suspected nor had reason to suspect the existence of a fact which the Crown required to prove, for example, that there was powder—which proved to be cocaine—or that there were tablets—which proved to be ecstasy—in the package which he was delivering or in the package which he possessed.

The scope of that general defence in s.28(2) is qualified by s.28(3). Subsection (3) is concerned with one particular type of the general situation covered by subs.(2), *viz.* where the Crown establish that the accused was concerned in supplying the substance or product which turns out to have been a controlled drug, or that he possessed it, but the accused proves something about his absence of knowledge of the nature and quality of the substance or product which comprised the controlled drug. In that situation, even although the accused proves that he neither knew nor suspected nor had reason to suspect the existence of a fact which the Crown required to prove, *viz.* that the substance or product was a controlled drug, in one set of circumstances he is not to have the benefit of the kind of defence provided in s.28(2).

The set of circumstances is this. To succeed in a particular prosecution the Crown must prove the charge which they bring. In particular where they have alleged, say, that the accused possessed ecstasy with intent to supply it, they must prove that it was ecstasy, and not any other controlled drug, that the accused possessed. For obvious reasons, however, Parliament will not allow an accused person to escape conviction simply by proving that, though he knew that he had a controlled drug, he neither knew nor suspected nor had reason to suspect that the drug was ecstasy as opposed to some other controlled drug, say, cocaine. Section 28(3)(a) therefore qualifies the general defence in subs.(2) by providing that in such a situation the accused is not to be acquitted. Presumably, it was because of the need to cater for this case that subs.(3) was inserted. See *R. v. Shivpuri* per Lord Bridge of Harwich at [1987] A.C., pp. 16F–17C.

If, however, the accused proves that he neither believed nor suspected nor had reason to suspect that the pills which he had or which he was involved in supplying were a controlled drug, he is to be acquitted (s.28(3)(b)(i)). The same is to happen in the very special situation envisaged in s.28(3)(b)(ii) where, for instance, someone could legitimately possess a controlled drug or a particular controlled drug in certain circumstances. If he possessed a different drug, then it is a defence for him to prove that he believed that the substance or product was one which he had in his possession for the purpose of acting in his capacity as a doctor. The situations in para. (b)(i) and (ii) are dealt with on essentially the same basis as situations which fall under subs.(2).

It is perhaps worth stating explicitly that, even though subss(2) and (3) speak of the accused proving something, this does not imply that, to establish a defence, the accused must necessarily give evidence. Doubtless, that would often be the simplest mode of proof, but the necessary evidence might come, for example, from a "mixed" statement or from witnesses speaking to what the accused was told was in the container or to the accused's apparent astonishment when the contents of the container were revealed and found to be a controlled drug. It goes almost without saying that the facts necessary for any defence under s.28 can be proved on the basis of uncorroborated evidence.

### Section 28 and the burden of proof

As I mentioned, the courts in both England and Scotland have tended to ignore s.28(2). This appears to have happened as a result of somewhat incautious arguments which the Crown put forward in both jurisdictions in the years after s.28 came on the scene in the 1971 Act. The issue tended to arise in relation to charges involving possession of a controlled drug. It has long been accepted, rightly in my view, that in the context of drugs legislation, the term "possession" is not to be given any technical construction but is to be given its ordinary meaning. As Lord Diplock said in *D.P.P. v. Brooks* [1974] A.C. 862, an appeal to the Privy Council concerning the dangerous drugs legislation in Jamaica: "In the ordinary use of the word 'possession', one has in one's possession whatever is, to one's own knowledge, physically in one's custody or under one's physical control" ([1974] A.C., p. 866).

Similarly, in *McKenzie v. Skeen* Lord Cameron inferred that in the 1971 Act the concept of possession covered "an article subject to the control of the possessor", and he added (at p. 122): "the concept of control would imply knowledge that the article in question was subject to that control. Control is not a function of the unconscious". It follows that, before someone can be convicted of being in possession of a controlled drug, the Crown must prove that he had the necessary knowledge and control. This was the position under the Drugs (Prevention of Misuse) Act 1964. For the purposes of that Act the courts required, of course, to define what degree of knowledge and control the Crown needed to establish. This they did in a series of cases culminating in the decision of the House of Lords in *Warner v. Metropolitan Police Commissioner* [*ante*, p. 78].

Under the 1964 Act, on the other hand, there was never any doubt that the burden of proving the necessary knowledge and control rested on the Crown. With the advent of s.28 of the 1971 Act, however, the Crown began to argue that the effect of s.28(2) had been to shift the onus in regard to proving the necessary knowledge from the Crown to the defence. In other words, it was contended that all that the Crown required to do was to prove that, as a matter of fact, the drugs were in the custody or control of the accused and he would then be convicted, unless he proved that he had not known that the drugs were there. Not surprisingly, this kind of argument provoked a strong reaction from the courts, both in Scotland and in England. They rejected the argument for the Crown and affirmed that s.28(2) did not shift the onus of proving knowledge on to the defence (*McKenzie v. Skeen*, per the Lord Justice General (at p. 121) in Scotland and *Ashton-Rickhardt*, per Roskill L.J. ((1977) 65 Cr.App.R. at p. 67) in England). The courts were plainly right to reject the Crown's argument: as Roskill L.J. pointed out, the manifest purpose of s.28 was not to place a new onus on an accused person but "to afford a defence to an accused person where no defence had previously existed" (*Ashton-Rickhardt*, at p. 72). Unfortunately, having rejected the extreme argument advanced by the Crown as to the effect of s.28(2), the courts seem to have felt that there was no place left for that subsection in a system, such as they envisaged, where the burden of proving the necessary knowledge and control continued to rest on the Crown. Hence subs.(2) disappeared from view.

Once the proper but limited range of s.28(3) is appreciated, however, there is no inconsistency in holding both that the burden of proving the necessary knowledge and control rests on the Crown and that s.28(2) has a distinct role to play. There are cases, of course, where police officers searching a suspect or his house find pills comprising a controlled drug, not in any container, but perhaps in his hand or in his pocket or lying on his bedside table. In straightforward cases of that kind, in order to prove their case, the Crown must satisfy the jury that the accused knew that he had the pills and that he had control of them. Since the pills are not in any kind of container but can be seen directly, the Crown will be seeking to show that the accused knew that he had the pills themselves. In the nature of things, however, controlled drugs tend to be found in a container of some kind—in a bag or a parcel or a box or a tin, for example. In such cases the strict legal question comes to be whether the Crown require to prove not only that the accused knew that he had the container in question but also that he knew that there were controlled drugs inside the container. In broad terms the courts have decided that it is sufficient for the Crown to prove that the accused knew that he had the container and that there was something in it. In that situation, if he had the necessary control of the container and its contents, the accused is held to have been in possession of the contents even though he did not know that they were controlled drugs.

So far as England is concerned, this emerges most clearly from *McNamara*. The Lord Chief Justice began by drawing a number of propositions from the speeches in *Warner*, including ((1988) 87 Cr.App.R. at p. 251): "Fourthly, in the case of a container or a box, the defendant's possession of the box leads to the strong inference that he is in possession of the contents or whatsoever it is inside the box. But if the contents are quite different in kind from what he believed, he is not in possession of it."

Lord Lane goes on to point out that the 1971 Act was passed with a view to elucidating some of the problems which arise from the speeches in *Warner*. Referring to the situation in *McNamara* where the appellant had a box containing drugs on the back of his motorcycle, Lord Lane then says:

> "It seems to us, in order to make sense of section 28, and also to make as clear as can be possible the decision in *Warner v. M.P.C.* (*supra*), the draftsman of the Act intended that the prosecution should have the initial burden of proving that the defendant had, and knew that he had, in these circumstances the box in his control and also that the box contained something. That, in our judgment, establishes the necessary possession. They must also of course prove that the box in fact contained the drug alleged, in this case cannabis resin. If any of those matters are unproved, there is no case to go to the jury. The speeches in *Warner v. M.P.C.* (*supra*) then seem to have qualified that comparatively simple concept by saying that the defendant has the burden thereafter to show or suggest that he had no right or opportunity to open the box or reason to doubt the legitimacy of the contents and that he believed the contents were different in kind, and not merely quality, than what they actually were.
>
> "To implement those considerations as they stood, and explain them so the jury can understand them, would have been a daunting task for a judge. Accordingly, in our view, it is to those matters that the words of section 28, and particularly section 28(3)(b)(i) are directed."

Having quoted s.28(1) and (3), which embody part of the new approach, Lord Lane concludes (at p. 252): "Once the prosecution have proved that the defendant had control of the box, knew that he had control and knew that the box contained something which was in fact the drug alleged, the burden, in our judgment is cast upon him to bring himself within those provisions."

In my respectful opinion that passage states the law correctly, except that, for the reasons which I have explained, I consider that in *McNamara* the appellant required to bring himself within the scope of s.28(2) rather than of s.28(3)(b)(i).

A similar approach has been adopted in Scotland. In a passage in his opinion in *McKenzie v. Skeen* which is not reproduced in the *Scots Law Times* report, the Lord Justice General remarked: "In most cases possession of a container will support the inference of possession of its actual contents but it must always be a question to be decided in the particular circumstances of the particular case."

Lord Emslie's general approach is clear, even although he went on to say that on the particular—and very special—facts as stated in that case he was unable to draw the necessary inference that the appellant knew that there was a minute quantity of cannabis flakes in a jar containing cannabis seeds, the seeds not being a controlled drug.

In his opinion in the same case Lord Cameron expressed a similar view about the general approach. He cited *Warner* as authority for holding that "in proof of possession it was necessary for the prosecutor to establish that the 'possessor' had knowledge of the fact that he had the article which turned out to be a prohibited drug though it was not necessary to prove that he was aware that the article or substance was a drug far less the prohibited drug libelled".

I note *en passant* that, despite what is said in the *Scots Law Times* report, there is nothing in the papers which we have recovered from the Scottish Record Office to indicate whether Lord Johnston, the third member of the court, concurred with the Lord Justice General or with Lord Cameron. It is therefore not possible to identify the precise ratio of the decision. In practice, however, this passage from Lord Cameron's judgment has generally been followed by Scottish judges when charging juries. More recently, some uncertainty about the correct approach seems to have crept in after the decision of this court in *Sim v. HM Advocate* 1996 S.C.C.R. 77.

In *Sim* the appellant was charged with being in possession of temazepam capsules with intent to supply them. The capsules were in transparent self sealing plastic bags inside an opaque unsealed plastic grocery bag which was in the wardrobe in the appellant's bedroom. The trial judge directed the jury that: "The Crown must, however, prove that he knew that the bag, with contents, was in his physical control, and that he knew the general character of the contents of that bag." The appeal appears to have been based on another passage in the judge's charge which was said to be inconsistent with this passage. The contention was that there was a confusion between the statements which would be likely to have misled the jury. The court held that there was no confusion and that it was clear what the trial judge was saying. The Lord Justice General (Hope), giving the opinion of the court, added at 1996 S.C.C.R., p. 79: "He was basing his direction upon the opinions in *McKenzie v. Skeen*. What he was doing was to develop the matter, first by reference to an illustration and then by applying that illustration to the evidence which was before the jury in this case. He was making it clear how the principles in *McKenzie v. Skeen* fell to be applied to that evidence. The matter was summed up by him perfectly correctly, as a proper development of the previous passages, in the passage ... to which Mr McSherry quite rightly took no objection."
...

Plainly, the trial judge in *Sim* went further than Lord Cameron in *McKenzie* and, insofar as he directed the jury that the Crown must prove that the accused knew "the general character" of the contents of the bag, I consider that the direction was unduly favourable to the accused. For the reasons which I have given, I am satisfied that the Crown would have discharged their initial burden by proving that the accused knew that the bag was in the wardrobe, that it contained something which turned out to be temazepam capsules and that the bag and its contents were under his control. The judgment of the court in *Sim* proceeded on the basis that the approach in *McKenzie* was correct and the court regarded the passage in the trial judge's charge as having been intended to reflect that approach. Indeed it is clear that the focus of the appeal was not on the passage of the judge's charge which I have quoted, but on a supposed confusion arising out of another passage. In rejecting the criticism of the judge's charge, therefore, the court were not intending to lay down any rule which conflicted with what Lord Cameron had said in *McKenzie* and their opinion should not be read as doing so. The approach of Lord Cameron in this matter should be followed.

Even though that approach has been enshrined in our law for more than 20 years, it can still seem surprising that, technically, for instance, a taxi driver who agrees in all innocence to collect a suitcase, which obviously contains something, and carry it to some destination will, when carrying the suitcase, be in possession both of the case and of the controlled drugs which it contains. This makes it all the more important to stress that s.28(2) provides a complete defence for the taxi driver to any conceivable charge under s.5(3). The role of s.28(2) and (3) is therefore crucial in providing innocent people with a defence and it is therefore singularly unfortunate that the courts should have banished s.28(2), in particular, from their sight.

### Section 28 and possession

At the risk of some repetition, the way in which ss.5 and 28 of the 1971 Act are intended to operate may be more readily understood with the aid of simple examples. (In s.5(3) charges, of course, the Crown requires to prove not merely possession but an intent to supply—which they usually invite the jury to infer from surrounding circumstances or from the quantity or form of the drugs. For the sake of simplicity, however, I concentrate simply on the issue of possession.)

Suppose that police officers search a house where the accused lives with other people and in the course of the search the officers find a bag containing ecstasy tablets. The Crown prosecute the accused on a charge of being in possession of ecstasy. At his trial the accused may say a number of things.

First, he may say that he was completely unaware that the drugs were in the house and that, if they were, they must have belonged to one of the other occupants. It is for the Crown to establish that the accused knew that the bag was in the house, that he had control of it and that it contained ecstasy. If they fail to establish any of those elements, then the prosecution will fail, simply because the Crown will not have discharged the burden of proof which lies on them. So far as knowledge and control are concerned, in directing a jury, the judge will simply say that, if any of the evidence leaves them with a reasonable doubt as to whether the accused knew that the bag was in the house or as to whether he had it under his control, then the accused must be acquitted. No issue under s.28 arises.

Alternatively, if the Crown prove that there were ecstasy tablets in the bag, the accused may say that, although he knew that the bag was in the house and contained something, and although he had it in his control, nonetheless he did not know that it contained tablets. In that situation, since the accused is admitting knowledge and control of the bag and its contents, the Crown have discharged their burden of proof. The accused will therefore be convicted, unless he proves that he did not know nor suspect nor have reason to suspect that the tablets were in the bag. If he proves this, then, even though he was in possession of the tablets, he must be acquitted in terms of s.28(2). In a case like that the trial judge should direct the jury to consider whether they are satisfied, on a balance of probabilities, that the accused did not know nor suspect nor have reason to suspect that the tablets were in the bag. If they are so satisfied, they must acquit; if they are not so satisfied, they must convict.

Thirdly, if the Crown prove that there were ecstasy tablets in the bag, the accused may say that, although he knew that the bag was in the house and although he had it in his control and even although he knew that it contained tablets, nonetheless he did not know that the tablets comprised ecstasy. In that situation also, the accused is admitting that he was in possession of the ecstasy tablets and the Crown have discharged their burden of proof. The accused will therefore be convicted unless he brings himself within the scope of the defences in s.28(3). To do so, it will not be enough for him to prove that he thought that the tablets were a different controlled drug—heroin rather than ecstasy, for instance. As s.28(3)(a) shows, that is not a defence. But the accused will have a defence in terms of s.28(3)(b)(i) if he proves that, even though he knew that he had the tablets, he neither knew nor suspected nor had reason to suspect that they were a controlled drug. In that situation therefore the trial judge should direct the jury to consider whether they are satisfied, on the balance of probabilities, that the accused neither knew nor suspected nor had reason to suspect that the pills were a controlled drug. If they are so satisfied, they must acquit; if they are not so satisfied, they must convict. *Mutatis mutandis* the same applies in the special case covered by s.28(3)(b)(ii).

I do not suggest that these clear cut illustrations exhaust the possibilities. For example, a person accused of having ecstasy tablets in his possession with intent to supply might give evidence that an individual had been in the habit of leaving bags at his house and that he had always understood that they contained pornographic videos. He could go on to say that, on the occasion referred to in the charge, he had been staying at his girlfriend's flat and so had been unaware that the bag in question had been left in his house. The jury might reject the accused's evidence that he did not know of the presence of the bag on the particular occasion, but accept his evidence that he had believed that the bags left with him contained videos. They could therefore acquit him on the basis of the defence in s.28(2), *viz.* that he neither knew nor suspected nor had reason to suspect that the bag in question contained the pills which turned out to be ecstasy.

In such a case the judge would require to direct the jury that they should first consider whether, on the basis of all the evidence, including the evidence given by the accused, they are satisfied beyond reasonable doubt that, on the occasion in question, the accused knew that the bag was in his house, that he was aware that it contained something and that he had control of the bag and its contents. If they are not so satisfied, they should acquit the accused because the Crown would have failed to prove that the accused was in possession of the tablets. The judge should go on to direct the jury that, even if they are satisfied that the accused had possession of the bag and its contents, they should then go on to consider whether, on all the evidence, they are satisfied, on the balance of probabilities, that the accused neither knew, nor suspected nor had reason to suspect, that the ecstasy tablets were in the bag. If they are so satisfied, they must acquit the accused; if they are not so satisfied, they must convict him.

It is similarly possible to conceive of a defence being open under s.28(3)(b)(i) even although the accused's primary position is that he did not know that he had the tablets on the occasion in question.

For instance a person accused of possession of ecstasy tablets with intent to supply might give evidence that a friend had been in the habit of leaving bags at his house from time to time and that he (the accused) had known that they contained tablets, but had always understood that the tablets were some (uncontrolled) "lifestyle" drug which his friend was selling on the black market. In this case also he could go on to say that, on the occasion referred to in the charge, he had been staying at his girlfriend's flat and so had been unaware that the bag in question had been left in his house. Here too the jury might reject the accused's evidence that he did not know of the presence of the bag in his house on the particular occasion, but accept his evidence that he believed that the bags left with him contained tablets of some (uncontrolled) lifestyle drug. They could therefore acquit him on the basis of the defence in s.28(3)(b)(i), *viz.* that he neither knew nor suspected nor had reason to suspect that the tablets comprised a controlled drug.

In such a case the judge would require to direct the jury that they should first consider whether, on the basis of all the evidence, including the evidence given by the accused, they are satisfied beyond reasonable doubt that on the occasion in question the accused knew that the bag was in his house, that he was aware that it contained something and that he had control of the bag and its contents. If they are not so satisfied, they should acquit the accused because the Crown would have failed to prove that the accused was in possession of the tablets. The judge should go on to direct the jury that, even if they are satisfied that the accused had possession of the bag and its contents, they should then consider whether, on all the evidence, they are satisfied, on the balance of probabilities, that the accused neither knew, nor suspected nor had reason to suspect, that the tablets comprised a controlled drug. If they are so satisfied, they must acquit the accused; if they are not so satisfied, they must convict him.

### Section 28 and being concerned in supplying

I have so far discussed the application of s.28 to charges involving possession under s.5. But, as s.28(1) shows, s.28 also applies to charges of supply or of being concerned in supplying under s.4(3). Since s.28(1) does not indicate that s.28 is to operate differently in relation to different provisions, it must be intended to operate in the same way in all cases. This in turn means that, just as the initial onus remains on the Crown under s.5, so also the initial onus remains on the Crown under s.4(3). So, for instance, under s.4(3)(b) the Crown will require to prove both that the accused was concerned in supplying a product or substance and that the product or substance was the controlled drug libelled in the charge.

In the case of s.5, the use of the word "possession" entails the need for the Crown to establish the necessary degree of knowledge. In my view, equally, the use of the words "concerned in" in s.4(3)(b) shows that the accused person must have a degree of knowledge.

One cannot be "concerned in" supplying a controlled drug, if one is not aware of being involved in supplying .... But, just as with possession, so also in s.4(3) cases, the question arises as to the degree of knowledge which the Crown must establish. In my view, by a parallel train of reasoning to that which applies in s.5 cases, the Crown must establish that the accused knew that he was involved in supplying something, and must prove that the thing which he was concerned in supplying was the controlled drug libelled in the charge. Provided that the Crown establish those elements, they have done all that is required under s.4(3)(b). The accused will then be convicted unless he can establish one of the defences in s.28 ...."

NOTE

**3.18**    See also *Tudhope v. McKee,* 1988 S.L.T. 153. In *R. v. Lambert*; *R. v. Ali*; *R. v. Jordan* [2001] 2 W.L.R. 211 the Court of Appeal in England held that section 28(2) of the Misuse of Drugs Act 1971 was compatible with Article 6(2) of the European Convention on Human Rights (presumption of innocence) despite the fact that it places on the accused the onus of proving the defence set out in that section.

## 2. VICARIOUS RESPONSIBILITY

**3.19**    Apart from the doctrine of art and part (*post*, Chapter 5) the general rule is that an accused is only answerable for his own acts. In some circumstances, however, statute may impose liability on a superior (usually an employer) for the acts of persons under his direction and control.

Vicarious responsibility permits the attribution of responsibility for an offence to a person who did not intend to commit the offence, was not reckless, and who was not aware of the circumstances of the offence. What is more, a person who is held vicariously responsible has not, personally, done anything to commit the offence. Vicarious responsibility must therefore be based on the view that it is just in the circumstances to hold A responsible for the Acts of B.

Such justification may be found in the idea that although the superior has not directly committed the offence, he or she has failed to ensure that an employee does not commit the prohibited conduct. The superior enjoys and accepts the benefits derived from the conduct in question (for example, operating a public house, selling tobacco products or running a car dealership), and is therefore under an obligation to ensure that those activities are conducted according to the statutory regulatory framework. That responsibility cannot be avoided by delegating the day to day running of the business to a third party. And it is fair to expect that in the direction of the business, the superior ensures that there are proper procedures in place to ensure that those with day to day responsibility are (a) aware of the regulatory framework and (b) the importance of abiding by that framework.

### Bean v. Sinclair
### 1930 J.C. 31

**3.20**    LORD JUSTICE-GENERAL (CLYDE): "... If a trader is, in virtue of statutory restrictions, allowed to carry on his trade only under certain conditions, the trader is, in my opinion, answerable for any breach of those conditions committed in the course of trade. A breach is none the less committed in the course of his trade because the actual delinquent is a servant or other person acting within the authority committed to him by the trader. It is in this way that the maxim *qui facit per alium facit per se*, although it does not strictly apply in criminal cases, has been said to apply in the 'class of delicts in which, as in cases under the Licensing Acts, the offence is the acting in contravention of the trade conditions to which by Act of Parliament the master of the business is bound to conform' (*Hogg v. Davidson*, 1901, 3 F. (J.) 49, see *per* Lord M'Laren at p. 50; 3 Adam 335 at p. 338). If a trader is only allowed to carry on his trade on certain conditions and the conditions are breached in some particular, it follows that the trade is being carried on illegally in that particular; in other words, the trader is trading in a manner not permitted by law, and is therefore necessarily liable to the penalty for contravention, whether he commits the breach personally or not. This principle is familiar under the Licensing Acts (*Linton v. Stirling*, 1893, 20 R. (J.) 71; 1 Adam 61; *Hogg v. Davidson* (sup. cit.); *Hall v. Begg*, 1928 J.C. 29); but, as the opinions delivered in the cases referred to shew, it is by no means limited in its application to those Acts."

NOTES

1. The suggestion that vicarious responsibility has "no place" in the criminal law can be found in Lord **3.21** McLaren's opinion in *Linton v. Stirling* (1893) 1 Adam 61, at p. 70. It is true that the doctrine largely grew up in the context of licensing cases, but it is clear that it is no longer confined to such circumstances.

2. Vicarious responsibility may, of course, be expressly imposed by the language of the statute. (See, for example, section 67(2) of the Licensing (Scotland) Act 1976 which provides that if the employee or agent of a licensee commits certain offences proceedings may be taken against the licensee.) More often, however, the imposition of vicarious responsibility is a matter of construction of the statute in question.

### Duguid v. Fraser
1942 S.L.T. 51

A shopkeeper in Inverness was charged with selling an article, the price of which was fixed **3.22** under the Prices of Goods (Price Regulated Goods) Order, 1940, at a price which exceeded the permitted price, contrary to the Prices of Goods Act 1939, section 1. The accused did not sell the item personally. He was not present at the time of the sale and indeed took no part in the management of these particular premises. The goods were sold by an assistant, acting in the course of her employment. The sheriff acquitted the accused, holding that he was not legally responsible for the actings of his employee. The prosecutor appealed by stated case.

THE LORD JUSTICE-CLERK (COOPER): The charge against the respondent is that in his shop in Inverness he sold to a customer for 7s. [35p], a price-regulated article of which the permitted price was 4s. 9d. [24p], contrary to section 1 of the Prices of Goods Act, 1939 (2 & 3 Geo. VI, cap. 118). The sale and its surrounding circumstances are not in dispute. The sole specialty which gave rise to the argument in the Court below and before us depended upon the fact that the sale was made, not by the respondent in person, but in his absence by a subordinate, a servant, acting within the scope of her employment .... We are now asked to determine whether the Sheriff-Substitute was entitled so to find.

I pause to observe that the precise implications of the respondent's defence are not wholly clear to me. We are specifically told in the findings in fact that it was the respondent's shop; that he there carried on business in his own name as a draper, outfitter, and house furnisher; and that the shop assistant in question was his servant, which I take to mean that she was appointed and remunerated by him and answerable to his orders in the discharge of her duties.

We are further, I think, entitled to infer, though the findings are silent on the subject, that the stock displayed for sale was acquired with the respondent's money and that the proceeds of the sales went into his pocket. In these circumstances it is not easy to evaluate or interpret the respondent's uncorroborated statement, on which the Sheriff's judgment apparently proceeded, that "he took no actual part in the management of the business". This, however, is clear, that this is not a case, like many in the reports, in which the person in charge of a business, or owning a business, pleads that a statutory contravention occurred during his temporary absence, or against his orders and despite his best efforts to secure compliance with the law. The respondent's position, as it was cogently presented to us in argument, is that he personally had nothing to do with the sale in question, that he has chosen to delegate to subordinates the ordinary work of his shop and the conduct of the business transacted therein, and that he is not answerable for the admittedly illicit sale, for which his subordinate must accept sole responsibility. The Solicitor-General was content to meet the argument as so presented, and the case may therefore be described as one which raises anew the issue of vicarious responsibility for a statutory offence. I am not sure that I wholly agree with that method of describing the issue. I think the question in most cases can more accurately be formulated as a question whether, on a sound construction of a statute or order creating an offence, the obligation imposed by the statute is of such a character that an offence can be committed by, and a prosecution may be taken against, the person carrying on the business even although the act which is the subject of the prosecution may have been committed by some subordinate in his employment acting within the scope of his employment.

Our reports already contain many examples of cases in which it has been held that a *malum prohibitum* has been created by statutory enactment in such circumstances and under such terms as to impose an absolute obligation of such a kind as to entail this wider liability. In all such cases it has, I think, been the practice to insist that the Crown should shew that the language, scope, and intendment of the statute require that an exception should be admitted to the normal and salutary rule of our law that *mens rea* is an indispensable ingredient of a criminal or quasi-criminal act; and I venture to think that it would be a misfortune if the stringency of this requirement were relaxed. Upon the general principle I need say no more in view of the Full Bench decision in the recent case of *Mitchell v. Morrison* (1938 J.C. 64), except to observe that, in my view, the issue in every case is purely one of the interpretation of the statute or order under consideration, and further, that the commonest type of case in which so-called vicarious responsibility has been affirmed is where, as in the many decisions under the Licensing Acts, the Legislature intervenes in the public interest to lay down the conditions under which alone a trader may carry on his business.

In my view, the Crown have sufficiently discharged the *onus* of shewing that the Prices of Goods Act, 1939, falls within this category. The Act expressly bears to be a piece of war legislation which is to remain in force only until the end of the emergency which was the occasion of its enactment (section 23, subsection (2)). The price control at which it aims is manifestly part of the general financial and economic war policy of the country pursued in the national interest. In addition to penalties by way of fine and imprisonment, provision is made by section 7, subsection (2), on a third or any subsequent conviction, for the making of orders prohibiting the offender from carrying on, or being concerned in the carrying on of, the business in question or any similar business. By section 10, conviction of a contravention of the Act confers upon the buyer the option to avoid certain contracts made with the person carrying on the business or to recover the excess price. Section 12 contains various prohibitions against the holding up of stocks by the person carrying on the business in face of a tender of the permitted price. Finally, section 18 provides for the consequences of a conviction of a body corporate. In the light of these amongst other considerations, it appears to me that when this statute opens, as it does, with a general declaration that it shall be unlawful for any person to sell, agree to sell, or offer to sell any price-regulated goods in the course of any business at an excessive price, the intention was to impose an absolute obligation affecting the conduct of the trade or business. If this is so, it is idle for the respondent to seek to escape the responsibilities attaching to the business which he carries on in his shop through the medium of his servants by devolving responsibility for compliance with the Act upon paid employees, or by representing that a sale effected in contravention of the Act by one of those employees within the scope of her employment is not truly a sale by him. Incidentally, the general acceptance of such defences would, I fear, go far towards rendering the Act inoperative. Accordingly I am of opinion that, on the facts found proved, it was the duty of the Sheriff-Substitute to convict, and I move your Lordships that we answer the question put to us in the negative."

Appeal allowed.

NOTES

**3.23**   1. In cases of vicarious responsibility, it is possible to convict both the superior and the employee, although whether this is competent will depend upon the terms of the legislation in question. In *Stainton v. McNaughton,* 1993 S.L.T. 119, the holder of a restaurant licence and an employee working in the restaurant were convicted of supplying alcohol in the restaurant to persons who were not taking a meal on the premises, contrary to section 99(a) of the Licensing (Scotland) Act 1976. Section 99 provides, *inter alia*, that "The Holder of a restaurant licence or his employee or agent" may be found guilty of the offence. They appealed, arguing that they could not both competently be convicted. The appeal was refused. Given the term of section 67 of the 1976 Act, which provided for vicarious responsibility of the part of the licence holder under section 99(a), proceedings against both the licence holder and the employee were competent.

2. It is, of course, important in a case of vicarious responsibility for the prosecutor to show that the prohibited act was done in the course of the employee's employment, and as part of that employment. In *Simpson v. Gifford,* 1954 S.L.T. 39 the holder of a licence which included a hotel certificate was convicted on a charge of supplying alcohol to a customer for consumption off the premises, and not for his personal consumption, contrary to his certificate and section 60(1) of the Licensing (Scotland) Act 1903. The accused was not present at the time, and he had given clear instructions to his employees that the licensing laws were to be observed. The sale was carried out by one of his employees, who was a personal friend of the customer who bought them, and it was found as a fact that the sale would not have occurred if this had not been the case. Notwithstanding this finding, the High Court upheld the conviction.

3. Where the guilt of the superior is based on vicarious responsibilty for the acts of a subordinate, it is, of course, necessary to establish that the subordinate has committed the offence, before the superior can be convicted. In *Macnab v. Alexanders of Greenock Ltd and Another,* 1971 S.L.T. 121 a company and their sales manager were convicted of applying a false trade description to a second hand car. On appeal the Lord Justice-Clerk (Grant) noted: "Counsel were agreed that logically, in considering the appeal, one should look first at the case against the second respondent who was the first respondents' sales manager. That is clearly right because, if he was rightly acquitted, the case against his employers inevitably fails . . . ."

## 3. DEFENCES TO CHARGES INVOLVING STRICT AND VICARIOUS RESPONSIBILITY

Reliance on strict or vicarious liability is sometimes justified, or at least explained, on the ground that **3.24** requiring proof of *mens rea*, or active involvement of the superior, might in many cases thwart the social and legal policy pursued by the legislation. This is particularly so where the alleged offender is a company or other organisation where it might be difficult to identify individuals to whom the necessary mental element might be attributed, or where the superior takes no active part in the day to day activities of the business. At the same time, it is argued by some that the potential for injustice which is inherent in strict and vicarious responsibility can be mitigated by allowing the accused to avoid conviction by invoking certain defences. These include notions of "due diligence" or that the accused has taken "all reasonable steps" to avoid the proscribed outcome or event. In other words, the accused is permitted to argue that he has not been negligent.

### Tesco Supermarkets Ltd v. Nattrass
[1972] A.C. 153

Section 24 of the Trade Descriptions Act 1968 provides:                                    **3.25**
  "(1) In any proceedings for an offence under this Act it shall subject to subsection (2) of this section, be a defence for the person charged to prove—
   (a) that the commission of the offence was due to a mistake or to reliance on information supplied to him or to the act or default of another person, an accident or some other cause beyond his control; and
   (b) that he took all reasonable precautions and exercised all due diligence to avoid the commission of such an offence by himself or any person under his control.
  (2) If in any case the defence provided by the last foregoing subsection involves the allegation that the commission of the offence was due to the act or default of another person or to reliance on information supplied by another person, the person charged shall not, without leave of the court, be entitled to rely on that defence unless, within a period ending seven clear days before the hearing, he has served on the prosecutor a notice in writing giving

such information identifying or assisting in the identification of that other person as was then in his possession.

(3) In any proceedings for an offence under this Act of supplying or offering to supply goods to which a false trade description is applied it shall be a defence for the person charged to prove that he did not know, and could not with reasonable diligence have ascertained, that the goods did not conform to the description or that the description had been applied to the goods."

A supermarket company was charged under the Trade Descriptions Act 1968 and pleaded in defence that s.24(1) of the Act applied in that the offence was due to the act or default of their store manager and that they had taken all reasonable precautions and used due diligence to avoid breaking the law. The store manager did not hold a high executive position within the company which had however instituted a proper system for avoidance of offences under the Act. The store manager had been properly trained to operate the system and was supervised on a regular basis.

In the magistrates' court it was held that the defendants had complied with s.24(1)(b) of the Act in that the system was properly organised but that the manager had failed to carry out his part in the running thereof. The magistrates however convicted on the view that the store manager could not be "another person" within the wording of s.24(1)(a).

On appeal to the House of Lords:

LORD REID: "Over a century ago the courts invented the idea of an absolute offence. The accepted doctrines of the common law put them in a difficulty. There was a presumption that when Parliament makes the commission of certain acts an offence it intends that *mens rea* shall be a constituent of the offence whether or not there is any reference to the knowledge or state of mind of the accused. And it was and is held to be an invariable rule that where *mens rea* is a constituent of any offence the burden of proving *mens rea* is on the prosecution. Some day this House may have to re-examine that rule, but that is another matter. For the protection of purchasers or consumers Parliament in many cases made it an offence for a trader to do certain things. Normally those things were done on his behalf by his servants and cases arose where the doing of the forbidden thing was solely the fault of a servant, the master having done all he could to prevent it and being entirely ignorant of its having been done. The just course would have been to hold that, once the facts constituting the offence had been proved, *mens rea* would be presumed unless the accused proved that he was blameless. The courts could not, or thought they could not, take that course. But they could and did hold in many such cases on a construction of the statutory provision that Parliament must be deemed to have intended to depart from the general rule and to make the offence absolute in the sense that *mens rea* was not to be a constituent of the offence.

This has led to great difficulties. If the offence is not held to be absolute the requirement that the prosecutor must prove *mens rea* makes it impossible to enforce the enactment in very many cases. If the offence is held to be absolute that leads to the conviction of persons who are entirely blameless: an injustice which brings the law into disrepute. So Parliament has found it necessary to devise a method of avoiding this difficulty. But instead of passing a general enactment that it shall always be a defence for the accused to prove that he was no party to the offence and had done all he could to prevent it, Parliament has chosen to deal with the problem piecemeal, and has in an increasing number of cases enacted in various forms with regard to particular offences that it shall be a defence to prove various exculpatory circumstances.

In my judgment the main object of these provisions must have been to distinguish between those who are in some degree blameworthy and those who are not, and to enable the latter to escape from conviction if they can show that they were in no way to blame. I find it almost impossible to suppose that Parliament or any reasonable body of men would as a matter of policy think it right to make employers criminally liable for the acts of some of their servants but not for those of others and I find it incredible that a draftsman, aware of that intention, would fail to insert any words to express it. But in several cases the courts, for reasons which it is not easy to discover; have given a restricted meaning to such provisions. It has been held that such provisions afford a defence if the master proves that the servant at fault was the person who himself did the prohibited act, but that they afford no defence if the servant at fault was one who failed in his duty of supervision to see that his subordinates did not commit the prohibited act. Why Parliament should be thought to have intended this distinction or how as a matter of construction these provisions can reasonably be held to have that meaning is not apparent . . . .

LORD DIPLOCK: "What amounts to the taking of all reasonable precautions and the exercise of all due diligence by a principal in order to satisfy the requirements of paragraph *(b)* of section 24(1) of the Act depends upon all the circumstances of the business carried on by the principal. It is a question of fact for the magistrates in summary proceedings or for the jury in proceedings on indictment. However large the business, the principal cannot avoid a personal responsibility for laying down the system for avoiding the commission of offences by his servants. It is he alone who is party to their contracts of employment through which this can be done. But in a large business, such as that conducted by the appellants in the instant appeal, it may be quite impracticable for the principal personally to undertake the detailed supervision of the work of inferior servants. It may be reasonable for him to allocate these supervisory duties to some superior servant or hierarchy of supervisory grades of superior servants, under their respective contracts of employment with him. If the principal has taken all reasonable precautions in the selection and training of servants to perform supervisory duties and has laid down an effective system of supervision and used due diligence to see that it is observed, he is entitled to rely upon a default by a superior servant in his supervisory duties as a defence under section 24(1), as well as, or instead of, upon an act of default of an inferior servant who has no supervisory duties under his contract of employment . . . .

To establish a defence under section 24 a principal who is a corporation must show that it 'took all reasonable precautions and exercised all due diligence'. A corporation is an abstraction. It is incapable itself of doing any physical act or being in any state of mind. Yet in law it is a person capable of exercising legal rights and of being subject to legal liabilities which may involve ascribing to it not only physical acts which are in reality done by a natural person on its behalf but also the mental state in which that person did them. In civil law, apart from certain statutory duties, this presents no conceptual difficulties. Under the law of agency the physical acts and state of mind of the agent are in law ascribed to the principal, and if the agent is a natural person it matters not whether the principal is also a natural person or a mere legal abstraction. *Qui facit per alium facit per se: qui cogitat per alium cogitat per se.*

But there are some civil liabilities imposed by statute which, exceptionally, exclude the concept of vicarious liability of a principal for the physical acts and state of mind of his agent; and the concept has no general application in the field of criminal law. To constitute a criminal offence, a physical act done by any person must generally be done by him in some reprehensible state of mind. Save in cases of strict liability where a criminal statute, exceptionally, makes the doing of an act a crime irrespective of the state of mind in which it is done, criminal law regards a person as responsible for his own crimes only. It does not recognise the liability of a principal for the criminal acts of his agent: because it does not ascribe to him his agent's state of mind. *Qui peccat per alium peccat per se* is not a maxim of criminal law.

Due diligence is in law the converse of negligence and negligence connotes a reprehensible state of mind—a lack of care for the consequences of his physical acts on the part of the person doing them. To establish a defence under section 24(1)(b) of the Act, a principal need only show that he personally acted without negligence. Accordingly, where the principal who relies on this defence is a corporation a question to be answered is: What natural person or persons are to be treated as being the corporation itself, and not merely its agents, for the purpose of taking precautions and exercising diligence?

My Lords, a corporation incorporated under the Companies Act 1948 owes its corporate personality and its powers to its constitution, the memorandum and articles of association.

The obvious and the only place to look to discover by what natural persons its powers are exercisable, is in its constitution. The articles of association, if they follow Table A, provide that the business of the company shall be managed by the directors and that they may 'exercise all such powers of the company' as are not required by the Act to be exercised in general meeting. Table A also vests in the directors the right to entrust and confer upon a managing director any of the powers of the company which are exercisable by them. So it may also be necessary to ascertain whether the directors have taken any action under this provision or any other similar provision providing for the co-ordinate exercise of the powers of the company by executive directors or by committees of directors and other persons, such as are frequently included in the articles of association of companies in which the regulations contained in Table A are modified or excluded in whole or in part.

In my view, therefore, the question: what natural persons are to be treated in law as being the company for the purpose of acts done in the course of its business, including the taking of precautions and the exercise of due diligence to avoid the commission of a criminal offence, is to be found by identifying those natural persons who by the memorandum and articles of association or as a result of action taken by the directors, or by the company in general meeting pursuant to the articles, are entrusted with the exercise of the powers of the company . . . .

Any legal duty, whether arising at common law or imposed by statute, may generally be performed by the person upon whom it is imposed through the agency of some other person. But if it is not performed, the person upon whom the duty is imposed is liable for its non-performance. It is irrelevant that he instructed a servant or agent to perform it on his behalf, if that servant or agent failed to do so. All that is relevant is that the duty was not performed. When the duty is imposed upon a person by statute and non-performance is made a criminal offence without any requirement of *mens rea* this is what is meant by an offence of 'strict liability'.

The fallacy lies in the next step of the argument. Where Parliament in creating an offence of 'strict liability' has also provided that it shall be a defence if the person upon whom the duty is imposed proves that he exercised all due diligence to avoid a breach of the duty, the clear intention of Parliament is to mitigate the injustice, which may be involved in an offence of strict liability, of subjecting to punishment a careful and conscientious person who is in no way morally to blame. To exercise due diligence to prevent something being done is to take all reasonable steps to prevent it. It may be a reasonable step for an employer to instruct a superior servant to supervise the activities of inferior servants whose physical acts may in the absence of supervision result in that being done which it is sought to prevent. This is not to delegate the employer's duty to exercise all due diligence; it is to perform it. To treat the duty of an employer to exercise due diligence as unperformed unless due diligence was also exercised by all his servants to whom he had reasonably given all proper instructions and upon whom he could reasonably rely to carry them out, would be to render the defence of due diligence nugatory and so thwart the clear intention of Parliament in providing it. For, *pace R. C. Hammett Ltd v. London County Council*, 97 J.P. 105, there is no logical distinction to be drawn between diligence in supervising and diligence in acting, if the defaults of servants are to be treated in law as the defaults of their employer."

Conviction quashed.

NOTES

**3.26** 1. Here, the company were ultimately successful in establishing that the contravention was due to the act or default of another person and that they had used due diligence to prevent contraventions. On the question of corporate responsibility, see *post,* pp. 97 *et seq*.

2. The question of "due diligence" arises frequently in the context of offences directed towards the protection of consumers. It is an offence under section 1 of the Trade Descriptions Act 1968 to apply a

false trade description to goods, or to supply or offer to supply goods to which such a description has been applied, in the course of a trade or business. Section 24 of that Act provides that it is a defence in criminal proceedings under the Act for the person charged "to prove (a) that the commission of the offence was due to a mistake or to reliance on information supplied to him or to the act or default of another, and (b) that he took all reasonable precautions and exercised all due diligence to avoid the commission of such an offence by himself or any person under his control". The offences created by section 1 are offences of strict liability, subject to the defence set out in section 24: *Macnab v. Alexanders of Greenock Ltd and Another,* 1971 S.L.T. 121. A typical trade description offence is the application of false information to second-hand cars (for example by describing them as being "in good condition" when they are not (*cf. Aitchison v. Reith and Anderson (Dingwall and Tain Ltd)* 1974 S.L.T. 282) or by the use of false odometer readings (*e.g. Costello v. Lowe,* 1990 S.L.T. 760). For the application of the statutory defence, and in particular "due diligence" in such cases, see the above cases and *Ford v. Guild,* 1990 S.L.T. 502.

3. "Due diligence" may be established by the accused demonstrating that he or she has in place a system directed towards ensuring that the relevant regulations are observed. Such a system does not need to be foolproof. What is required is that the accused has exercised due diligence, not that the accused has established a system which would guarantee that the law is observed. See, for examples, *Barclay v. Clark*, 1957 S.L.T. 33, *Byrne v. Tudhope* 1983 S.C.C.R. 337 and *Ahmed v. MacDonald,* 1995 S.L.T 1094.

4. See also *Readers' Digest Association Ltd v. Pirie,* 1973 J.C. 42, where the appellants had been **3.27** convicted of a contravention of the Unsolicited Goods and Services Act 1971 by continuing to send to, and claim payment for, copies of a magazine from someone who had cancelled his subscription, "not having reasonable cause to believe that there was a right to payment". The conviction was quashed on appeal, with the Lord Justice-Clerk (Wheatley) observing (at 48) that:

> "It has been found that it was the policy and practice of the company not to send out unsolicited copies of the publication, not to demand from customers payment for goods not ordered by them or on their behalf, and not to ignore deliberately instructions from customers (which would include instructions to cancel a particular order). The company had set up a system of operations, whereby, if it was properly carried out, no improper demand for payment would be made. Here the improper demand for payment was made in respect of unsolicited goods not as a result of anything that was wrong with the company's policy, practice or system of operation, but because of a mistake or mistakes by relatively junior employees as a result of which the company's system of operation broke down, and its policy and practice were defeated. In these circumstances I do not consider that it can be said that the *company* did not have reasonable cause to believe that there was a right to payment. On the contrary I think that it has been shown that the *company* acted in good faith, but were let down by the mistakes of their junior staff. That seems to me to constitute reasonable cause within the meaning of the sub-section.
>
> The facts to which I have adverted clearly show that there was no *mens rea* on the part of the company, or anyone who could be said to be the 'mind' of the company in relation to the dispatch of the demand for payment. The observations of Lord Reid on the position of a company *vis-à-vis* its employees, and the limited circumstances in which the 'mind' of an employee can be said to be the 'mind' of the company (*Tesco Supermarkets Limited v. Nattrass* [1972] A.C. 153, at p. 170) are relevant to this point. I am therefore of the opinion that the Sheriff was wrong in holding that the appellants had no reasonable cause to believe that there was a right to payment. He based this finding on the proposition that the knowledge which was available to junior employees if they had carried out their duties properly can be imputed to the company. In this I think he erred. In the circumstances I find it unnecessary to consider the other aspects of the complaint, and in particular whether the company knew that the goods were unsolicited. I accordingly answer the third and fourth questions of law in the negative, finding it unnecessary to answer the other questions, and move your Lordships to quash the conviction."

## 3. CORPORATE RESPONSIBILITY

At one time, it was thought that corporations could not commit criminal offences. This view was **3.28** widespread. (See, for a comparative and historical account of the development of corporate criminal responsibility, Guy Stessens, "Corporate Criminal Liability: A Comparative Perspective" (1994) 43

I.C.L.Q. 493.) Various reasons have been suggested. A corporation has no mind, and therefore cannot have a "guilty" mind. A corporation cannot be subjected to the ordinary penalties of the criminal law. A corporation can only act within the terms of the rules governing its incorporation, and since no corporation could be created legally with the power to commit crimes, it must be *ultra vires* a corporation to commit an offence.

These arguments have, almost entirely, been rejected in most developed systems. So far as concerns the "guilty mind" of the corporation, the objection was only relevant to offences which required proof of *mens rea*, and with the advent of statutory crimes of strict responsibility its significance was much diminished. It is, in any event, now accepted in Scotland that a corporation can commit at least some offences requiring proof of *mens rea*. So far as concerns punishment, it is true that a corporation cannot be imprisoned or required to undergo other penalties which are directly linked to human attributes. (Could a company be required to undertake community service?) But the broad range of sentencing disposals available to the courts means that the only offence for which a corporation could not be punished is murder, and that is because the only sentence for murder is life imprisonment. The *vires* argument is also generally rejected. If, during the course of activities permitted by its articles of incorporation, a corporation does something which it would be criminal if done by any other person, then a corporation may be held criminally responsible.

In Scotland it has long been established that a corporation can be convicted of a statutory offence, both of strict responsibility and offences which require proof of *mens rea*. What was less clear was whether or not a company could be guilty of a common law offence requiring proof of *mens rea*. If one adopts the modern descriptive approach to *mens rea* there ought to be no difficulty in holding that a company can be guilty of both types of offence, there being no difference in philosophy between common law and statutory *mens rea*. As we have seen, however, there is at least a residual normative element in the *mens rea* of some common law offences, and the common law notion of "dole" has strong elements of moral culpability. Against that background it could be argued that it would not be appropriate to attribute to an artificial person the mental element required at common law. Some support for this view is to be obtained from the decision of the High Court in *Dean v. John Menzies (Holdings) Ltd*, 1981 J.C. 23, below to the effect that a limited company could not be convicted of the common law offence of shameless indecency. On the other hand, the case of *Purcell Meats (Scotland) Ltd v. McLeod*, 1986 S.C.C.R. 672, *post*, p. 109 makes it clear that there is no obstacle in principle to convicting a limited company of a common law offence requiring proof of *mens rea*.

### Dean v. John Menzies (Holdings) Ltd
### 1981 J.C. 23

**3.29** The respondent company were charged on summary complaint with conducting themselves in a "shamelessly indecent manner in respect that they did sell, expose for sale and have for sale 64 indecent and obscene magazines ... which magazines were likely to deprave and corrupt the morals of the lieges and to create in their minds inordinate and lustful desires". A plea to the competency of this complaint was upheld by the sheriff, and the procurator-fiscal appealed to the High Court. The question of competency for the High Court was whether a company could be guilty of the common law offence libelled in the complaint.

LORD MAXWELL: "It appears that, so far as is known, this is the first occasion on which a body corporate has been charged in Scotland with a crime at common law. The sheriff reached his decision on the broad principle that a body corporate, having no mind, cannot be guilty of a common law crime because of the requirement of *mens rea* or dole as an element of guilt in such a crime. In my opinion this is not a particularly appropriate case in which to attempt to decide that question as a generality. It is not necessary to do so. What is at issue is whether the particular crime charged here can competently be brought against a corporation. I should add, however, that I do not find the authorities on which the sheriff relied convincing support for the general proposition which he sustained. *Miles v. Finlay & Co.* (1830) 9 S. 18 is more fully reported in 6 Fac., December 11. The case concerned a complaint against a partnership. It was a complaint of contravention of statute. Lord Gillies merely said that he was clear 'that a company cannot be convened in such a complaint as the present' and gave as his reasons certain aspects of partnership law which are no longer the law. In any event there has been much development of the law since 1830. The passage in Green's *Encyclopaedia*,

Vol. 4 at p. 138, on which the sheriff also relied, is a bare statement that 'a company can neither prosecute nor be prosecuted for a crime'. It relies on Miles and I should have thought that the statement that a company cannot prosecute is plainly wrong. As to the problem raised by the requirements of *mens rea* as such, it may be that the sheriff attached a larger meaning to that expression than it necessarily has, at least as regards some crimes (Gordon, *Criminal Law*, ch. 7). The accused's counsel presented an argument to the effect that, as this was the first time a common law crime had been charged against a company, the court was, in effect, being asked to make new law and in this area legislation ought to be by Parliament. I have sympathy for the view that, in the realm of what is in substance censorship of certain types of magazines, literature, films, etc., on the grounds that they are socially unacceptable, it would perhaps be preferable that the matter be dealt with by statute rather than the existing common law, which was I think designed to meet rather different problems. I think that, in fairness, it might be better that conduct of the kind complained of should be controlled in appropriate cases by getting at the employer company rather than the employee, but I very much doubt whether, on this subject, any attempt to apply ancient common law principles to the activities of companies is likely to produce sensible results. However, I do not think that counsel's argument as stated is sound. The fact that the question raised in this case has never been raised before does not absolve the court from attempting to determine what the law now is. But I do think that the fact that the Crown here is seeking to do what it has never done before is of some significance in considering whether it is competent. In particular, while in theory a decision on competency does not necessitate a decision as to what would require to be proved to establish guilt, in my opinion it would be wrong to declare for the first time a particular kind of criminal responsibility without having a reasonably clear and precise idea of the circumstances in which that responsibility would arise. The crime charged in my opinion has certain characteristics which have a bearing on the present problem. It is a charge of 'shameless and indecent' conduct. This involves not merely, as in some crimes, the doing of a specific thing which the common law prohibits, but the doing of something which is defined by reference to a type of behaviour of which human beings alone are capable. I do not question the soundness of the decisions in *Watt v. Annan*, 1978 J.C. 84 and *Robertson v. Smith*, 1979 S.L.T. (Notes) 51 that such human behaviour can be displayed by the purveying or exhibiting of indecent books, magazines or films, but I suppose that in the past the crime usually concerned actual physical conduct of the human body. The crime further involves to an exceptional degree a subjective judgment upon which reasonably-held opinions can differ. It is true that in practice whether the crime has been committed will depend upon the subjective judgment of the judge or jury rather than of the accused, but a finding of guilt implies that the accused has used his judgment and discretion in an indecent and shameless fashion. The crime as charged also, in my opinion, necessarily involves knowledge of the contents of the particular magazines complained of. In the course of his argument the learned advocate-depute appeared to suggest that a general knowledge on the part of someone at an appropriate level in the accused's hierarchy of the contents of this 'type' of material would be sufficient. I agree that the necessary knowledge might be inferred and proved in various ways, but I do not think that on the wording of this particular charge, anything less than knowledge of the contents of the particular magazines in question would suffice. There might be cases where magazines, in edition after edition, have displayed pictures or writing of a quality that would justify conviction, where a person could properly be charged with shameful and indecent conduct for selling any edition. That is not what is charged here and, for all I know, the case if it proceeded might turn on whether one particular and uncharacteristic picture or sentence went too far.

We were referred to a number of authorities both Scottish and English. While the English cases and particularly the House of Lords case of *Tesco Supermarkets Ltd v. Nattrass* [1972] A.C. 153 (hereinafter referred to as *Tesco*) must be treated with very great respect, I think that caution must be used in applying dicta in those cases in relation to a matter with which they were not concerned, namely the common law of Scotland relating to crime and to a rather special type of crime.

It is accepted by the Crown that the common law does not recognise vicarious criminal responsibility (*Mackay Brothers v. Gibb*, 1969 J.C. 26 per Lord Justice-Clerk Grant) and that the complaint would not be competent unless the accused company, as such, could have committed the crime alleged. Whatever may be the position as regards other common law crimes, it is perfectly apparent that the company as a legal abstraction could not, as matter of fact, have the knowledge, exercise the judgment and conduct itself in the manner alleged in the complaint. Accordingly, the complaint can only become competent by the employment of a fiction (*Tesco, per* Lord Reid). Fiction has frequently been employed both in England and Scotland to attribute to a corporation human characteristics which it cannot have, but the fiction which has been employed is not always the same fiction. It seems to me that the approach of the courts has been this. Where the plain requirements of justice, the express provisions of statute, or the presumed intentions of Parliament require human characteristics to be attributed to corporations, the courts provide the necessary fictions tailored to what is necessary to give effect to those requirements, provisions, or intentions. In *Tesco*, Lord Diplock, after examining the statutory consumer protection provisions with which the case was concerned in a practical light, reached a construction of the provisions and stated that: 'So construed these sections provide for a rational and just system of enforcement of the penal provisions of the Act.' Later he stated that to establish a defence under s.24 a principal who is a corporation must show that it 'took all reasonable precautions and exercised all due diligence". A corporation is an abstraction. It is incapable of doing any physical act or being in any state of mind, yet in law it is a person capable of exercising legal rights and of being subject to legal liabilities which may involve ascribing to it not only physical acts which are in reality done by a natural person on its behalf but also the mental state in which the person did them.' He then rejected, as inapplicable in the context of the Act in question the fiction of an agent's state of mind being attributable to his principal and, along with the other Lords of Appeal, adopted as appropriate the fiction of what I might call for short 'the controlling mind'. This, I think, though it is not entirely clear, is the fiction which the Crown argues is applicable in the present case. It was not, of course, a new fiction in 1972. It had in particular been developed by Lord Denning in *H. L. Bolton Engineering Co. Ltd v. J. T. Graham & Sons Ltd* [1956] 1 Q.B. 159 in a well-known passage likening a company to a human body. However, what Lord Diplock says in the passage I have quoted is that the exercise by a corporation of legal rights and the subjection of it to legal liabilities 'may involve' the need to use a fiction. This seems to me a different thing from saying that for all purposes in law the 'controlling mind' fiction or any other particular fiction has to be applied.

The circumstances in which the problem has arisen vary greatly. It has long been established that a company can be negligent so as to incur civil liability. We were, rightly, not afforded a detailed examination of the development of this fiction, but I suppose it was largely designed to overcome the rigidities of the law of common employment which had become intolerable with changing attitudes towards labour. This fiction, though in theory it ascribes a state of mind to a company, does not usually present much difficulty, since in practice, to give it effect, it is normally only necessary to show that something has not been done. If a safe system of working has not been set-up it is both unnecessary and pointless to inquire who it was who failed to set it up.

The authorities to which we referred included two in which it was held possible to ascribe to a corporation the peculiarly human failing of 'malice'. In *Gordon v. British and Foreign Metaline Co.* (1886) 14 R. 75 a company was sued for damages for judicial slander alleged to have been made in a sheriff court process. The defenders pled 'privilege', to which the pursuers answered 'malice'. The defenders argued unsuccessfully that they could not be guilty of malice having no mind. The result was hardly surprising. The defenders could not well claim privilege, but deny to the pursuers any possibility of establishing a qualification on the privilege. This case takes one no further in establishing the nature of the fiction required. *Triplex Safety Glass Co. Ltd v. Lancegaye Safety Glass (1934) Ltd* [1939] 2 All E.R. 613 established, as a necessary preliminary to certain English procedure, that a company could be guilty of a criminal slander which apparently involves malice. I doubt if this is of any assistance in the Scottish courts, but I get the impression from the judgments that the fiction there employed was not the same as the 'controlling mind' fiction referred to in *Tesco*.

I turn to some of the cases involving a fictional imputation of knowledge. In *Clydebank Co-operative Society Ltd v. Binnie*, 1937 S.L.T. 114, a company was charged with 'permitting' an employee to use a vehicle as an express carriage without an appropriate licence as required by the Road Traffic Act then in force. There are two elements in permitting. One is knowledge and the other is, as with the civil law negligence cases, a sin of omission in respect of failure to prevent. Knowledge was the aspect at issue in the case. Lord President Normand held that the required knowledge was brought home to the company by the knowledge of the then transport manager who was in charge of their vehicle hiring establishment. Lord Fleming appears to have gone further and held that knowledge, not only of the transport manager but even so lowly an individual as the vehicle driver, was to be imputed to the company. I do not question the soundness of the decision in its statutory context, but the fiction used for the purposes of imputing knowledge seems to have little relationship to the controlling mind fiction discussed in *Tesco*.

*Mackay Brothers & Co. v. Gibb*, 1969 J.C. 26, concerned a charge against a partnership of permitting a vehicle to be used with its tyres in a certain condition contrary to motor vehicle regulations. For present purposes the question was whether the accused firm 'knew' of the condition of the tyres. It was held that knowledge was brought home to them through the 'wilful blindness' of their garage controller. The Lord Justice-Clerk appears to have considered that knowledge of any employee would have sufficed. Lord Wheatley, making it clear that he was proceeding on the presumed intention of Parliament, took the view, as I read his judgment, that the knowledge of any employee on a matter within the responsibilities delegated to him would be knowledge of the company. A similar approach was taken by Lord Milligan. Again I do not question the decision in its statutory context, but it is far from the 'controlling mind' fiction as discussed in *Tesco*.

*Smith of Maddiston Ltd v. Macnab*, 1975 S.L.T. 85, is of little help, since it was concerned with the question of whether a statutory offence of causing or permitting a motor vehicle to be used in a certain way required knowledge of someone that the vehicle was not only being used, but was being used in a prohibited manner. In the earlier motor vehicle cases referred to, an affirmative answer to this question had been assumed, at least as regards 'permitting'. In *Smith of Maddiston Ltd* the court did not require to consider what was the appropriate fiction for the purposes of imputing knowledge to the company.

*Readers Digest Association Ltd v. Pirie*, 1973 S.L.T. 170, I think in substance involved the question of imputing a kind of knowledge, but it was concerned with a statutory qualification or defence on what would otherwise have inferred statutory guilt. The statute makes it an offence for a trader to demand payment for what are known to be unsolicited goods. The court found it unnecessary to consider whether knowledge that the goods were unsolicited could be attributed to the company. The statute, however, qualifies the offence by providing that a person is only guilty if he is a person 'not having reasonable cause to believe that there is a right to payment'. Certain of the junior employees did not have reasonable cause to believe that there was a right to payment, but policy and procedure had been laid down by someone in some managerial or higher position designed specifically to prevent demands for payment for unsolicited goods. It was a temporary breakdown in that policy and procedure, caused by a combination of a computer failure and some inattentiveness on the part of junior employees, which gave rise to the complaint. The court held that the company was not a person 'not having reasonable cause to believe'. Their Lordships were to some extent guided by *Tesco* but, while they considered, as I understand it, that the intention of Parliament required a distinction to be made between those persons whose belief and cause to believe could or could not be imputed to the company. The circumstances of the case did not require any attempt to draw the dividing line and it does not follow that the court, if it had had to make the attempt, would necessarily, for the purpose of the Act in question, have adopted the 'controlling mind' fiction as defined in *Tesco*. Lord Milligan was evidently concerned to rationalise the distinction between the *Readers Digest* case and other cases where knowledge of an employee at more or less any level has been held imputable. He did so by observing a difference between 'knowing' and 'having cause to believe'. With respect, I find this a rather thin distinction and suggest the problem is more satisfactorily resolved by conceding that the appropriate fiction depends on the presumed intention of Parliament as ascertained by an examination of the statutory scheme in question.

One other Scottish case to which we were referred is *MacNab v. Alexanders of Greenock*, 1971 S.L.T. 121. A company and its sales manager were charged with the statutory offence of applying a false trade description by selling a motor car with a mileometer which gave an untrue reading. The statute provides a defence that the person charged took all or reasonable precautions and exercised all due diligence to avoid the commission of the offence. The statute in terms applies to companies and the court held that the statutory offence was established on the simple ground that, on the facts, no precautions were taken and no diligence was exercised by anyone. As regards the appropriate fiction the case is accordingly similar to common law cases of negligence where it is unnecessary to impute to the company the actions of any particular individual or class of individuals.

Turning now to the English cases in which the 'controlling mind' fiction has been developed, while the principle has been repeatedly stated by the highest authorities in relation to the cases under consideration, it appears to me that its practical application in relation to common law crimes in Scotland of the kind with which we are concerned would give rise to great difficulty. While the dicta are highly authoritative there appear to me to be differences in emphasis and degree. It was suggested in the course of the argument that once the possibility of the company being competently charged is accepted the rest is all matter of fact. I am not wholly satisfied that this is wholly correct. Fiction by definition is not fact. Lord Reid in *Tesco* emphasised that it was a question of law, and, as I have already stated, I find it difficult to hold that the present complaint is competent because of a fiction, without knowing with reasonable precision what the fiction is.

*Lennard's Carrying Co. Ltd v. Asiatic Petroleum Co. Ltd*, [1915] A.C. 705, was a civil claim for damages under the Merchant Shipping Act. It was not disputed that the company could be liable and the question was whether the company had proved that the loss and damage arose without the company's 'actual fault or privity'. The defence failed. It was held that there was fault or privity of a person who was managing director of a company who managed the ship in question and who was also a director of the defendant company. The Lord Chancellor, Viscount Haldane, said that the actions of persons who were 'the directing mind and will, the very ego and centre of the corporation' were to be treated as actions of the company. Lord Dunedin said that it could not be that the only way one could find fault and privity in the company would be by a decision of the whole board of directors. This case was decided against a statutory background which gave no option but to find some circumstances in which actual fault and privity could be attributed to the company.

*Rudd v. Elder Dempster & Co.* [1933] 1 K.B. 566 was a civil case under the Workman's Compensation Act. The question was whether there was 'personal negligence' or 'wilful act' on the part of the company. Again the statute demanded a fiction. The fiction demanded could not be one which attributed to the company the act of any employee. Lawrence L.J. held that there could be attributed to the company the acts of the managing director or general manager 'or other person having authority from the Board of Directors to conduct the company's business'. This last expression seems to me to go further than some of the judicial definitions of the controlling mind in, for example, *Tesco*. Greer L.J. on the other hand adopted, perhaps somewhat uncertainly, 'the directors (or possibly general manager)'.

*Wheeler v. New Merton Board Mills* [1933] 2 K.B. 669 involved a statutory civil claim. The question was whether the presence of a dangerous machine was due to the wilful act of the employers. It was held that, as an obviously dangerous machine was in fact present, the company was guilty. It was not necessary to enter into any attempt to define the fiction, and the case therefore resembles the cases on civil negligence.

*D.P.P. v. Kent and Sussex Contractors Ltd* [1944] K.B. 146 was a charge under the wartime emergency legislation concerned with producing false petrol rationing documents with 'intent to deceive'. In this case it appears to have been held that the knowledge and intention of the accused servants could be imputed. This was no doubt appropriate against the particular statutory background, but bears no relationship to the controlling mind fiction.

*H. L. Bolton Engineering Co. Ltd v. T. J. Graham & Sons Ltd* [1957] Q.B. 159 concerned civil proceedings under the Landlord and Tenant Act 1954 and the question was whether the landlords, as a company, had shown an 'intention' to occupy certain premises for their own purposes. Denning L.J., after likening a company to a human body, said: 'Some of the people in the company are mere servants or agents who are nothing more than the hands to do the work and cannot be said to represent the mind and will. Others are directors and managers who represent the directing mind and will of the company and control what they do.' My anxiety as regards this fiction, so stated, as a test of criminal responsibility in respect of a crime of the kind with which this case is concerned is that the reference to that manager introduces an element of uncertainty in that, particularly in large companies, there can be persons with managerial functions of a kind at many grades and levels, and the concept gives no clear indication as to where in fact the line is to be drawn.

The matter was considered in great detail in *Tesco*. The statutory provision makes it an offence to offer to supply goods with an indication that they are being offered at a price less than that at which they are in fact being offered. There is then a provision that it shall be a defence for the person charged to prove: (a) that the commission of the offence was due to, *inter alia*, the act or default of 'another person', and (b) that 'he' (*i.e.* the person charged) took all reasonable precautions and exercised all due diligence to avoid the commission of the offence. Despite the rubric, I have the impression that the issue before the House of Lords was not whether the local store manager, who was in default, was 'another person' within the meaning of (a) above, but whether the accused company took all reasonable precautions. In any event it was a question, not of proof of guilt, but establishment of a defence and it seems that the particular statutory scheme necessitated the finding of a dividing line below which a person's acts could not be said to be the acts of the company. Lord Reid said that 'normally the board of directors, the managing director and perhaps other superior officers carry out the functions of the management and speak and act as the company. Their subordinates do not.' This puts the dividing line somewhere slightly lower than the level of directors but higher than the level of any person with management functions. Lord Morris of Borth-y-Gest found it sufficient to determine that in any event the store manager was below the dividing line. Viscount Dilhorne proposed, at least as one test, that the person whose acts by fiction are the acts of the company is: 'a person who is in actual control of the operations of the company or part of them and is not responsible to another person in the company for the manner in which he discharges his duty in the sense of being under his orders.' This, taken literally, would suggest drawing the line no lower than the directors. Lord Pearson, as I understand it, considered that if a company had one shop and appointed a manager, that manager might be the controlling mind, but that the same would not apply where a company had a number of shops and appointed a manager for each. Lord Diplock took a somewhat different line. He said that 'the obvious and only place to look to discover by what natural persons its [a company's] powers are exercisable is in its constitution'. He referred to a provision in 'Table A' which, where 'Table A' applies, provides that a company is to be managed by directors and they may exercise all powers of the company other than those allocated exclusively at a general meeting. He concludes: 'What natural persons are to be treated in law as being the company for the purposes of acts done in the course of its business including the taking of precautions and the exercise of due diligence to avoid the commission of a criminal offence is to be found by identifying those natural persons who by the memorandum and articles of association or as a result of action taken by the directors or by the company in general meeting pursuant to the articles are entrusted with the exercise of the powers of the company.' I do not find this, so to speak, constitutional approach to the problem reflected in other dicta and it puts the dividing line possibly at a higher level than at least some of the other dicta in the cases appear to suggest.

The uncertainty which appears to me to surround any attempt to extract from the authorities any one clear and precise fiction is increased by various possible propositions suggested by the learned advocate-depute at various stages of his address. This is not intended to be, and I hope will not be taken as being, a criticism. The advocate-depute was concerned to give the court every assistance in a difficult and important matter, and this he certainly did. According to my notes, and I apologise if I have misnoted and therefore misquoted him, he suggested at different stages of his address *inter alia* (1) 'If there is alleged against a company a common law crime of the present kind it must be proved that there is a policy decision of a company's directorate to sell the material.' He went on to explain that, as question of fact, certain matters might be inferred. (2) 'If it is a question for the company's decision as to what the company sells, the conduct and knowledge of those who are vested with the responsibility of selling the material and who acquire knowledge is the conduct and knowledge of the company.' (3) 'It must be proved that it was company policy to sell such things. I am not suggesting that if selection is left to managers as matter of policy that would involve guilt.' Of these propositions, no. (2) might in practical terms provide the most sensible basis for criminal responsibility. It seems to me that no. (2) is quite different from, and inconsistent with, nos (1) and (3).

In the light of the authorities cited to us, I am not satisfied that the common law of Scotland recognises any clear single fiction which would, for purposes of criminal responsibility, in all matters attribute to a company the kind of human characteristics and conduct alleged in this complaint. It appears to me unrealistic to suggest that the accused company will be guilty if, but only if, some individuals or individual, whose status is not precisely defined but who must be vaguely at or near director level had knowledge of the contents of the magazines in question and acted in a shameless and indecent manner in deciding to sell them. That, however, seems to be the result of applying the controlling mind fiction. If some other fiction is to be applied I do not know what it is. I accordingly consider that the complaint here is incompetent. It may be that the criminal law of England would reach a different result (*Rex v. I.C.R. Haulage Ltd* [1944] K.B. 531). If so, it would not be the first time . . . ."

LORD STOTT: "It is, I think, self-evident that there are certain crimes and offences which cannot be committed by a corporate body. Murder is such a crime, not only, as the advocate-depute conceded, because a company cannot be imprisoned, but because it is incapable of having that wicked intent or recklessness of mind necessary to constitute the crime of murder. Other examples which come to mind are reset and perjury. In my opinion the offence of conducting oneself in a shamelessly indecent manner falls into the same category.

There is, I think, no doubt that a company is held in law to be capable of some degree of delictual or criminal intent. A corporate body can be guilty of negligence in failing to provide a safe working place for its employees (*McMullan v. Lochgelly Iron & Coal Co.*, 1933 S.C.(H.L.) 64). It can have an intent to deceive (*D.P.P. v. Kent and Sussex Contractors* [1944] K.B. 146). It can act in such a way as to infer malice in law (*Gordon v. British and Foreign Metaline Co.* (1886) 14 R. 75). It can permit the use of a vehicle on a road (*Mackay Bros. v. Gibb*). It can sell products by retail (*Patterson v. Camnethan Oatmeal*, 1948 J.C. 16). It can buy wild rabbits (*Behling v. McLeod*, 1949 J.C. 25). It can supply utility furniture to a customer (*Muir v. Grant*, 1947 J.C. 42). On these and similar analogies it was argued by the advocate-depute that an allegation of selling and exposing for sale the obscene magazines may properly be made against a company. He conceded that it was not sufficient for the purpose of this charge for the Crown to prove that the company exposed obscene magazines for sale. Such conduct might be indecent, but as was made clear in *Watt v. Annan* it is not the indecency of conduct which makes it criminal but the quality of 'shamelessness.' If that is the test (and I do not read the later case of *Robertson v. Smith* as qualifying or detracting from it), it would follow in my opinion (and I understood the advocate depute to assent to this) that not only must a publication be indecent but it must be known to be indecent. It should be noted that the complaint does not relate to a type of magazine; it relates simply and solely to specified issues, and the relevant knowledge must therefore be knowledge of the allegedly indecent material comprised in these four issues. Furthermore, since there is no vicarious liability for crime, liability could arise only through the knowledge not of a mere employee or shop assistant but of a person or persons who may be regarded as the 'directing mind and will of the company' (*Tesco Supermarkets v. Nattrass*; *Reader's Digest Association v. Pirie*).

What the Crown therefore are seeking to prove (although unfortunately this does not appear *ex facie* of the complaint but from a gloss on the expression 'shamelessly indecent') is that either the respondents' board of directors or (possibly a less spectacular flight of fancy) some senior officer to whom had been delegated full responsibility for dealing with such matters has perused the four magazines libelled, along with the other publications currently on sale in the respondents' branches, has observed in the contents of the four magazines something that he ought to have realised was obscene, and nevertheless had been so lost to any sense of shame as to authorise or at all events permit their sale in the respondents' shop at Dumbarton. The inference of shamelessness being thus brought home to a person or persons who may be looked upon as the controlling mind of the company must then be imputed to the company itself. Whatever may be thought about the earlier stages of this argument, and about the application (if any) to common law crime of the somewhat nebulous doctrine of 'controlling mind,' this final conclusion is to my mind a non sequitur and one which does not accord with realities. Many as are the attributes which have been imputed to a company, a sense of shame has never been regarded as one of them; and nothing that has been said by the advocate-depute has persuaded me that it must or could be so regarded.

It was submitted that as matter of public policy it would be unfortunate if a small shopkeeper or shop assistant were to be liable to prosecution on this charge whereas more culpable offenders could shelter behind the cloak of incorporation. I am not satisfied, however, that that would be a necessary consequence of our holding this complaint to be incompetent. To obtain a conviction, the Crown would have to bring home to the company the requisite degree of knowledge and intent. In order to do so, it would seem that the Crown would require to identify the controlling person or persons by whom the knowledge was acquired and the intent conceived; and if they are in a position to do that they should be in a position to proceed against these persons as individuals. In any event I cannot think that it would be sound public policy to introduce an additional element of fiction into an area of law in which (as is perhaps indicated by the archaic and faintly ludicrous wording of the complaint) common sense is not noticeably at a premium."

LORD CAMERON (*dissenting*): "... The criminal law has long recognised that a corporate body may be guilty of breaches of statute and incur a penalty, and therefore be susceptible to prosecution as a person recognised in the eyes of the law. Further, the law has also recognised that an incorporation may be guilty of statutory offences the commission of which is the result of intended or deliberate action or inaction. It was not Parliament which specifically provided that corporate bodies such as limited companies should be subject to prosecution. The various statutes assumed that no distinction in capacity to offend should exist between natural and other persons recognised by law as legal entities with capacity to discharge certain functions and perform certain actions. The responsibility of both for breaches of statute is the same, and the individual and the company alike can be cited and charged in their own names. No doubt in s.333 of the Criminal Procedure (Scotland) Act 1975 provision is made for certain responsible individuals to be cited in the case of a firm or limited company: this provision is permissive and not mandatory, while the books are full of cases where firms and limited companies have been cited and charged in their own proper names without further addition or without reference to the hand or actions of a particular individual whose physical act or omission occasioned the breach. Thus the accountability of limited companies in the matter of statutory offences is beyond argument, and does not in any sense arise out of precise legislative provision to that effect. Section 333, which re-enacts earlier legislation, makes no distinction between statutory and common law offences and in particular contains nothing to indicate that its provisions only relate to breaches of statute or regulations. If Parliament had intended that a company in its individual capacity should not be liable to prosecution in respect of common law offences it could have said so, and at the same time prescribed where and on what natural persons within the structure or employment of the company responsibility and consequent criminal liability should fall. But Parliament has not so provided, and the authorities cited by the advocate-depute illustrate the extent to which companies in Scotland can be and are rendered liable to criminal prosecution, even where commission of the offence libelled involves a conscious exercise of will or demonstration of intent. It would seem therefore to follow that there should be no obstacle in principle to the same liability to prosecution where the offence is *malum in se* and not *malum prohibitum*. This distinction lay at the root of Mr Kerrigan's argument that the question of common law liability was a matter for Parliament and not for the courts. The fallacy of this argument, however, would seem to lie in the fact this is not a case of creating or declaring a new crime or offence which never existed before, nor of extending the boundaries of criminal responsibility to a group of legal persons on whose shoulders criminal responsibility had not been rested before. If, therefore, a limited company has the capacity to form an intention, to decide on a course of action, to act in accordance with that deliberate intent within the scope and limits of its articles, it is difficult to see on what general principle it should not be susceptible to prosecution where that action offends against the common law. It must no doubt be conceded that this principle could not be applied to a crime where the law prescribes only one and that a custodial penalty; but the fact that *lex non cogit ad impossibilia* in a particular instance does not imply that as a consequence it follows that *lex non cogit ad possibilia* in other instances where penalties for breaches of the common law can be effectively imposed. It has long been settled in our civil law that a company can be guilty of malice: malice implies a harmful intention deliberately directed against another person or persons. The parallel between malice in the field of defamation and the essence of this *mens rea* which is essential to criminal liability at common law appears to me close. What then is criminal intent? While it is of course true that the 'wicked intent' (which is *mens rea*) is a matter of proof in which the burden of proof lies upon the Crown, 'the wicked intent is an inference to be drawn from the circumstances of the deed, as well as from any explanations by the man. Although a man considers his deed meritorious, the law may hold him to have acted wickedly and feloniously. Whenever a person does what is criminal, the presumption is that he does so wilfully' (*Macdonald* (5th ed.), p. 1). Further it was put by Hume in writing on the nature of dole thus: 'It is not material to the notion of guilt, that the offender have himself been fully conscious of the wickedness of what he did' (*Hume on Crimes*, i.25). No distinction is drawn by Hume between the concept of 'dole' and that of *mens rea*: dole being defined as 'that corrupt and evil intention, which is essential ... to the guilt of any crime' (*op. cit.*, i.22). These are general principles applicable to all common law crimes and offences and therefore it follows that the presumption of law is precisely the same in all cases—whatever the degree of moral obliquity involved in the commission of the offence. Therefore the bald submission that a company cannot in Scotland in any circumstances be guilty of a common law offence does not commend itself to me as sound in principle. It is without an authority and if it be argued that a company cannot possess the capacity to exhibit *mens rea* it can be sufficiently answered that *mens rea* is no more than that 'wicked intent' which is the presumed element in all acts which are criminal at common law. It is trite law also that a company is legally capable of many deliberate actions within the limits of its powers as set out in its articles of association, these powers being exercised by those who are the 'directing mind' or 'will' of the company. In the case of *Lennard's Carrying Co. v. Asiatic Petroleum Co.* Lord Chancellor Haldane, with whom his colleagues, including Lord Dunedin, concurred, in analysing the elements which taken together demonstrate the basis on which a company can be held responsible as an entity for deliberate acts or omissions where these acts or omissions are those at least in the field of civil liability, said: 'A corporation is an abstraction. It has no mind of its own any more than it has a body of its own; its active and directing will must consequently be sought in the person of somebody who for some purposes may be called an agent, but who is really the directing mind and will of the corporation, the very ego and centre of the personality of the corporation. That person may be under the direction of the shareholders in general meeting; that person may be the board of directors itself, or it may be, and in some companies it is so, that that person has an authority co-ordinate with the board of directors given to him under the articles of association, and is appointed by the general meeting of the company, and can only be removed by the general meeting of the company.' This may well indicate that difficulties of proof will arise when a charge of criminal conduct at common law is brought against a limited company, but nothing to suggest that such a charge may not be competently brought and that without the necessity in all cases of specifying in the complaint or indictment which particular officer or employee of the company was in fact responsible for the act or omission charged. The argument put forward by Mr Kerrigan, who cast aside any support which he might get from *Miles v. Findlay* and the passage in *Green's Encyclopaedia* founded on by the sheriff, that there is no reported authority in Scotland supporting the Crown's contention on competency, does not seem to me to carry the matter very far: stood on its head the argument on the absence of direct authority is equally potent—that the absence of authority indicates that the matter is beyond argument. But the authorities demonstrate that a company can be guilty of *mala prohibita* even where the offence involves knowledge, intentional action or permission. Further, in the field of civil liability a company can be held liable in reparation for defamation where malice has to be established, while in England there is authority for the proposition that a company may be guilty of criminal libel. If a company can by law—by legal fiction if you will—be endowed with a mind and will exerciseable by natural persons acting within the confines of the company's legal competence, and be held responsible for actings in pursuance of the exercise of that mind and will, then if those actings are contrary to the common criminal law, I find it difficult to see upon what basis of principle it can be said that the company is free of criminal liability however this may be enforced. The wicked intent in all common law crimes is the intent to perform the criminal act. The motive or moral depravity of the actor are alike irrelevant to the quality of that act in the eye of the law. Therefore if the act is intentional the criminal intent is presumed whatever the motive which inspired the actor.

The rules of law as to a company's capacity to exercise a conscious mind and will enunciated in the case of *Lennard's Carrying Co.* have been further illustrated in the recent and important case of *Tesco Ltd v. Natrass*. No doubt the decision is concerned with a statutory charge and with the defences open to a company charged with a contravention of that statute, but in my view its importance lies in the extent to which the House of Lords held that a company could be susceptible to criminal proceedings whether under statute or at common law. In that case Lord Reid at p. 171, after citing the passage I have quoted from the speech of Lord Haldane, went on to refer to a passage from the judgment of Lord Denning in *H. L. Bolton Engineering Co. v. T. J. Graham & Sons Ltd* where he said: 'A company may in many ways be likened to a human body. It has a brain and nerve centre which controls what it does. It has also hands which hold the tools and act in accordance with directions from the centre. Some of the people in the company are mere servants and agents who are nothing more than hands to do the work and cannot be said to represent the mind or will. Others are directors and managers who represent the directing mind and will of the company and control what it does. The state of mind of these managers is the state of mind of the company and is treated by the law as such.' Having quoted that passage, Lord Reid went on to say: 'In that case the directors of the company only met once a year, they left the management of the business to others and it was the intention of those managers which was imputed to the company. I think that was right.' I draw particular attention to the word 'intention'. Later in his speech Lord

Reid referred to the case of *D.P.P. v. Kent and Surrey Contractors* cited by the advocate-depute and also *Rex. v. I. C. R. Haulage Ltd* where it was held that a company can be guilty of common law conspiracy. Lord Reid added in relation to this latter case: 'I think that the true view is that the judge must direct the jury that if they find certain facts proved then as a matter of law they must find the crucial act of the officer, servant or agent including his state of mind, intention, knowledge or belief, is the act of the company. I have already dealt with the considerations to be applied in deciding when such a person can and when he cannot be identified with the company. I do not see how the nature of the charge can make any difference.'

No doubt the decision in the case of *Tesco* is one concerned with English criminal law, but the statute under which the prosecution was brought is a United Kingdom statute effective in Scotland, and the judgment and opinions in the case if technically not binding in this country are necessarily to be treated with the highest respect. One thing may be taken as clear, that in England a charge of common law crime may be competently laid against a company, and while I agree that there is no reason why the criminal jurisprudence of the two countries should necessarily fall into line, at the same time I see no reason in principle why a different rule of law should operate in Scotland, the same statute governing the structure, powers and functioning of limited companies in both countries. In both countries the rules and principles governing the civil liabilities of companies are the same, in both countries the rules and principles governing criminal liability in respect of statutory offences are the same, and it is therefore not easy to see upon what principle of Scots criminal law that a company created by statute should not be amenable to the common law in matters criminal—the only authority for the contrary view which appealed to the sheriff was thrown overboard by Mr Kerrigan and in my opinion rightly—particularly as in both countries the capacity of a company to form an intent, to carry it into effect, to exercise a will and to make a conscious choice of courses of action or inaction is undoubted and is precisely the same. In my opinion the competency of the present charge is not open to successful challenge on the broad general principle that a company cannot in Scots law be guilty of a common law offence.

This however is not an end of the matter. It must necessarily be conceded that certain criminal conduct cannot be ascribed to a company. Thus, where the only penalty prescribed or permitted by law is custodial or personally physical, it may be presumed that no charge will lie, but no such objection could be levelled here and that is a question that does not arise in the present case. The narrower question is whether this charge can be brought against a limited company, and it is to this particular aspect of the matter that Mr Kerrigan's subsidiary argument was directed. Whatever might be the general liability of a limited company this charge, it was submitted, was not one which could be competently brought. Mr Kerrigan's argument in brief was that as this charge involved as a critical element an accusation of 'shamelessness' it went far beyond any acceptable limits. His argument could be put in very simple form. He said that 'shame' or a 'sense of shame' was something which could not be attributed to a fictional person. Therefore a fictional person could not possess the capacity to act 'shamelessly'. But the charge was one of 'shameless' conduct. The accused was a fictional person, therefore the charge lacked its essential content because no fictional person could have a sense of shame. The simplicity of the argument thus presented is attractive. But the 'shameless' quality of the conduct here libelled is essentially an objective and not a subjective quality. It is of the essence of this offence that the conduct be directed towards some person or persons with an intention or in the knowledge that it should corrupt or be calculated or be liable to corrupt or deprave in the manner libelled, those towards whom the conduct is directed. It is this which determines the shameless quality of the act, with which the moral obliquity of the actor—if any—has nothing to do. In the present ease the qualification of the conduct is that the exposure for sale or sale to persons, members of the public, was done with the knowledge or intention of the company—knowledge of the calculated consequences or those liable to follow or intention that such consequences should follow. Now the respondents here are primarily a commercial company concerned in the sale of *inter alia* magazines. It may be presumed that the selection of stock is not a matter of accident but at least dictated to some extent by commercial considerations and in the hope and expectation that the articles exposed will be attractive and saleable and that the selection is at the will and intention of the seller. The transactions under consideration therefore represent conduct which is directed and deliberately directed to members of the public to influence them to purchase articles for sale. In these circumstances I do not see why that conduct directed as it admittedly would be, towards members of the public as potential purchasers, should not be capable of bearing the qualitative description which the Crown seeks to put upon it. In effect, the test of criminality is objective and not subjective and it is here that Mr Kerrigan's subsidiary or 'subjective' argument appears to me unsound, because it is ill founded. The question is not whether a company is an entity which is endowed with a conscience to be appeased or a capacity for moral sensation or an absence of a sense of shame or even a capacity to overcome a sense of shame by the prospect of financial profit. It may well be that the offence libelled is one which falls within the category of offences against public morals, but in order to commit it the offender does not require to be possessed of capacity to feel a sense of personal shame or even to lack it. What however is of the essence of the offence is that the action itself of an indecent character should be directed towards a person or persons with certain intentions or knowledge of the consequences or likely consequences to that person or those persons—the intention or knowledge that it should corrupt or be calculated or liable to corrupt or deprave those towards whom the conduct is directed. If these matters can be established by relevant and sufficient evidence then the qualification and therefore the criminal character of the actions themselves is also proved.

In my opinion therefore Mr Kerrigan's two main attacks on the competency of this charge as directed against the respondents fail. By libelling this offence against the respondents it cannot be said the prosecutor is seeking to create a new offence. The offence is one known to the common law, as Mr Kerrigan conceded. Further I do not think that he succeeded in demonstrating that a company cannot possess a capacity in law to intend its actions and therefore be incapable of forming the wilful intent essential to the commission of a common law offence, and as I have already indicated, I think his argument on 'shamelessness' of conduct was misconceived. I do not intend to imply however that a limited company is in law to be regarded as capable of the commission of any and every common law offence, other than those for which the only penalty is custodial, or of offences—such as rape—which are obviously and necessarily physical acts of a natural person. In my opinion, and as at present advised, so to hold would go much further than is necessary for a decision as to the competency of libelling this offence against a limited company. Having considered the arguments presented in this case I am of opinion that a company may competently be charged with an offence at common law, where that offence consists of action purposely taken by the company within its statutory powers and in pursuance of its objects as defined and set out in its articles, and where such action if taken by a natural person would constitute a common law offence. Thereupon I consider that a charge of this nature—*i.e.* shamelessly indecent conduct in the particulars libelled may be competently and relevantly libelled against a company."

Appeal dismissed.

### Purcell Meats (Scotland) Ltd v. McLeod
1986 S.C.C.R. 672

Lord Justice-Clerk (Ross): "The appellants were charged on a summary complaint with a **3.30** charge which was originally in the following terms:

'[T]hat between September 27 and October 9, 1985, both dates inclusive, at the premises at Blakely Road, Saltcoats, occupied by you, you did attempt to obliterate the premium certification stamp on nine carcasses of beef and apply on said carcasses a facsimile of an I.B.A.P. exemption stamp and did thereafter present said carcasses for inspection to officers of the Meat and Livestock Commission and did attempt to induce said officers to certify said carcasses as exempt from repayment of the beef premium clawback amounting to £411 and did thus attempt to defraud the Intervention Board of Agricultural Produce of said sum.'

In the course of the hearing before the sheriff the procurator fiscal obtained leave to amend that complaint by inserting the words 'by the hands of persons unknown' between the words 'did' and 'attempt' in the [third] line of the complaint and also to make a further amendment by the insertion of the words 'to the Intervention Board for Agricultural Produce' after the word 'certify' in the [fourth] last line of the complaint.

The appellants had taken objection before the sheriff to the competency and relevancy of the complaint. Having heard the parties the sheriff repelled the pleas to competency and relevancy and it is against his decision that the appellants have now appealed to this court. In the note of appeal three grounds are stated, but Mr Boag-Thomson for the appellants made it plain that he was departing from the third ground of appeal. Accordingly, it has only been necessary for us to consider two grounds of appeal. The two grounds of appeal are in the following terms:

'(a) The complaint is incompetent in that a limited company cannot be charged with an offence at common law being incapable of forming the *mens rea* for the offence set out in the complaint;

(b) the complaint is totally lacking in specification; that there is no specification of the person or persons through whom or by whom the limited company operated and accordingly the action should be dismissed.'

In support of the appeal Mr Boag-Thomson addressed himself to these two grounds of appeal and he emphasised that the principal submission which he made was related to the need for *mens rea*. He drew attention to a number of authorities and in particular the case of *Dean v. John Menzies (Holdings) Limited*. He also referred to a number of English authorities which had been reviewed by the court in that case. At the end of the day he summarised his submissions as follows. He contended first that for the offence libelled in the complaint *mens rea* was necessary. Secondly he contended that one could not impute to the company knowledge on the part of persons when you did not know who these persons were. Thirdly he submitted that a limited company was not in itself capable of knowledge, and fourthly that the Crown could only succeed on what had been referred to in the case of *Dean* as the fiction principle, but that the Crown could not do so if it did not know who the persons were who had acted on behalf of the company. In reply to these submissions the advocate-depute accepted that since this was a charge of attempted fraud *mens rea* was necessary. Accordingly, he did not demur to the first submission put forward by Mr Boag-Thomson. So far as imputing knowledge is concerned the advocate-depute indicated that in the present case the Crown were not in a position to identify the particular employees who had done the relevant acts on behalf of the company. It was for that reason that the amended complaint libelled that the company had, by the hands of persons unknown, made the attempts in the charge. The advocate-depute accepted that at the end of the day it would all depend upon whether it could be shown that the acts libelled had been done by an employee of such status and at such a level that the sheriff could reasonably conclude that the acts had been done by the company. In this connection he drew attention to a passage from the speech of Lord Reid in *Tesco Supermarkets Ltd v. Nattrass* [1972] A.C. at p. 170. In that passage of his speech Lord Reid said this:

'I must start by considering the nature of the personality which by fiction the law attributes to a corporation. A living person has a mind which can have knowledge or intention or be negligent and he has hands to carry out his intentions. A corporation has none of these; it must act through living persons, though not always one or the same person. Then the person who acts is not speaking or acting for the company. He is acting as the company and his mind which directs his Acts is the mind of the company. There is no question of the company being vicariously liable. He is not acting as a servant, representative, agent or delegate. He is an embodiment of the company or, one could say, he hears and speaks through the persona of the company, within his appropriate sphere, and his mind is the mind of the company. If it is a guilty mind then that guilt is the guilt of the company. It must be a question of law whether, once the facts have been ascertained, a person in doing particular things is to be regarded as the company or merely as the company's servant or agent. In that case any liability of the company can only be a statutory or vicarious liability.'

Having regard to what Lord Reid said in that passage we are of opinion that in the present case it will only be once the facts have emerged that it will be possible to conclude whether the persons by whose hands the particular acts were performed were of such a status and at such a level in the company's employment that it would be open to the sheriff to draw the conclusion that the acts fell to be regarded as acts of the company rather than acts of the individual. It may not be easy for the Crown to establish its ease, but in our opinion from the point of view of the competency and specification of this charge, it is sufficient now that the charge libels that the acts in question were done by the hands of persons unknown. If the acts were done by persons who were not employed by the company or by employees who had no authority to do the acts, the Crown may fail. The charge, as amended, however, in our view is a competent charge and having regard to the fact that the Crown are unable to identify which particular employees did the acts libelled, sufficient specification has been given to the appellants of the persons by whom the company had acted at the material time. It follows that in our view the sheriff was well founded in repelling the pleas to competency and relevancy and accordingly the appeal at the instance of the appellants is refused."

Appeal dismissed.

NOTES

1. The net result of these two cases is that while a company can commit certain common law offences, **3.31** it cannot generally be said that a company can be guilty at common law of an offence requiring proof of *mens rea*.

2. Corporate responsibility is really of two sorts. In the first place—and this was typical in the development of corporate criminal responsibility—a company can be held vicariously responsible for the offences of its employees. But the cases set out here concern what might be termed "primary" responsibility—that is, where the company is alleged to be directly responsible for the commission of the offences. In neither *Dean* nor *Purcell Meats* was it suggested that the company's responsibility was dependent upon conviction of an employee.

3. It remains to be seen which other offences can and cannot be committed by a company. There are some offences which, it is suggested, cannot be committed by a company because it is not capable of forming the required *mens rea*. Shameless indecency is one of these, and in *Dean v. John Menzies (Holdings) Ltd* Lord Stott suggests that this would be true also of murder and, it would seem, reset and perjury, although if a company can be guilty of fraud it is difficult to see why it cannot be guilty of reset, and if a company can, through its officers, make a false statement, it can arguably do so while they are under oath and giving evidence in the capacity of "controlling minds" of the company.

Both Lords Stott and Cameron point to a general class of offences which cannot be committed by a company, *viz.* those for which there is only one penalty, imprisonment, a penalty which cannot be enforced against a company. Lord Cameron also mentions a category of cases in which the offence necessarily involves the "physical acts of a natural person", such as rape.

In *McKendrick v. Sinclair*, 1972 S.L.T. 110 it appears to have been accepted, or at least assumed, that a company could be guilty of culpable homicide (the difference between this crime and murder lying in the degree of recklessness involved). In *R. v. H.M. Coroner for East Kent* (1987) 88 Cr.App.Rep. 10 it was accepted that a corporation could be indicted for manslaughter under English law. In *R. v. P&O Ferries (Dover) Ltd* (1990) 93 Cr.App.Rep. 72 a company was prosecuted, along with seven of its employees, on charges of manslaughter arising from the sinking of the *Herald of Free Enterprise* in Zeebrugge harbour on March 6, 1987, with the loss of nearly 200 lives. The accused were acquitted when the judge withdrew the case from the jury for lack of evidence.

Companies are prosecuted under the Health and Safety at Work, etc., Act 1974 for offences which have resulted in death. See, for example, *Procurator Fiscal v. Aberdeen City Council*, High Court, July 2, 1999, *unreported*.

4. The court in *Purcell Meats* appears to assume that the "controlling mind" test is applicable in Scots law, but this must be read in the light of, (a) the scant discussion of authority in that case, and (b) Lord Maxwell's doubts on that issue in *Dean v. John Menzies (Holdings) Ltd.*

5. Is the "controlling mind" test an appropriate or satisfactory approach to determining criminal responsibility in the case of a corporation? Following the sinking of the Herald of Free Enterprise the Secretary of State for Trade and Industry ordered a formal investigation under section 55 of the Merchant Shipping Act 1970, which was conducted by Sheen J. The immediate cause of the sinking of the ship was that it was allowed to set sail with her bow doors open and her nose down. Water entered the vehicle decks, leading to a rapid capsize of the boat. In paragraph 14.1 of his Report Sheen J. stated:

> "At first sight the faults which led to this disaster were the aforesaid errors of omission on the part of the Master, the Chief Officer and the assistant bosun, and also the failure of Captain Kirby to issue and enforce clear orders. But a full investigation into the circumstances of the disaster leads inexorably to the conclusion that the underlying or cardinal faults lay higher up in the company ... All concerned in management, from the members of the Board of Directors down to the junior superintendents, were guilty of fault in that all must be regarded as sharing responsibility for the failure of management. From top to bottom the body corporate was infected with the disease of sloppiness ..."

Where a company is so badly run, does the "controlling mind" theory have much relevance? In a sense, the responsibility is less narrowly focused, and more dispersed throughout the company. One might almost argue, indeed, that there was no controlling mind at all. That, indeed, was the problem with the company.

# Chapter 4

# CAUSATION

As far as criminal responsibility is concerned, the question of causation has most frequently been **4.01** discussed in the context of causing death in homicide. The problems of causation are not, of course, confined to this area, and may be encountered in relation to other offences against the person, such as causing real injury (*Khaliq v. H.M. Advocate*, 1984 S.L.T. 137, *post*, p. 459). Issues relating to causation may also crop up in the context of fraud (*Mather v. H.M. Advocate* (1914) 7 Adam 525, *post*, p. 605) and offences of damaging property.

## 1. FACTUAL AND LEGAL CAUSATION

All issues of causation involve a consideration of two questions. In the first place it must be established **4.02** whether the accused's conduct, as a matter of fact, contributed to the completion of the *actus reus*? In a case of fraud, did the accused's misrepresentations contribute to the victim doing something that she or he would not otherwise have done? In a case of murder, did the accused's conduct contribute to the death of the victim?

But factual causes can be many and various. The accused's conduct may not have been the only factor contributing to the proscribed outcome. There may have been other actors, and other events, some of which are connected with the accused's conduct, and others which are quite independent. The victim himself may have contributed to the network of causes. That being so, it is necessary to ask a further question, namely, was the accused's conduct a legally relevant contribution to the completion of the *actus reus*.

In determining criminal responsibility, it is for the court to determine whether or not a factual cause is to be regarded as a legally relevant cause. Whether a legally relevant cause did in fact contribute to the result is a matter for the jury (or the judge in summary proceedings), on the basis of all the evidence presented. Witnesses, even expert witnesses, should not be invited to express views on matters of causation in a way which would usurp the function of the jury in this respect: *Hendry v. H.M. Advocate*, 1988 S.L.T. 25. *Cf. H.M. Advocate v. McGinlay*, 1983 S.L.T. 562 and *Paxton v. H.M. Advocate*, 2000 S.L.T. 771.

## 2. CAUSAL CRITERIA

In determining whether a cause is legally relevant the law can adopt different criteria. It may, for **4.03** example, ask whether the causal factor contributed directly to the outcome (or, putting it the other way round, did the outcome flow directly from the causal factor(s) in issue). It may, on the other hand, ask whether the outcome is proximately, or remotely, linked to the causal factor(s) in issue. And remoteness can be invoked to place a limit on the causal effect of directly contributing causes. The more remote a cause, the easier it is to argue that it is not legally relevant, even if it can be shown that it has a direct link to the outcome under consideration. There is a tendency in criminal cases in which issues of causation arise to favour directness as the test of causation. It is extremely rare to find cases in which a causal factor, directly linked to the outcome, is excluded as being too remote, at least when the causal factor is a wrongful act or omission on the part of the accused.

The issue of intention is also relevant to causation, in the sense that it is easier to ascribe a causal link between the accused's conduct and an outcome where that outcome is intended. Suppose, for example, that A intends to murder her husband. She puts poison in his evening meal, which makes him ill. He is taken to hospital where he contracts an infection from another patient and dies. Suppose, on the other hand, that B, driving recklessly, knocks C down in the street. C is taken to the hospital where he too contracts an infection from another patient and dies. In practice the courts are more likely to treat A as the cause of her husband's death than they are to treat B as the cause of C's death.

The blameworthiness of the accused will often result in his or her conduct being treated as a cause sufficient to attribute responsibility, even if there are contributing causes that are as important or even more important. So, for example, the deliberate refusal of the victim to seek or accept medical treatment, even when it is known that this is both necessary and sufficient for the victim's recovery, will not be regarded as the cause of death where the need for treatment arises from an assault on the victim. (See, for example, the case of *R. v. Blaue* [1975] 3 All E.R. 446, *post*, p. 115.) Similarly, where the death of the victim results directly from the act of a third person, the accused may still be held responsible, where that act is provoked by the unlawful conduct of the accused. (See, for example, the case of *Pagett* (1983) 76 Cr.App.Rep. 279, *post*, p. 134 and also *Lord Advocate's Reference (No. 1 of 1994)* 1995 S.L.T. 248.

## 3. SUBSISTING CONDITIONS

### A. Medical conditions

**4.04** Suppose, in a case of assault or murder, that the victim suffers from an existing medical condition which makes him or her more susceptible to injury or death. Can the accused argue that the victim's medical condition is the true cause of injury or death?

### H.M. Advocate v. Robertson and Donoghue
### High Court, August 1945, *unreported*

**4.05** The accused were charged with, *inter alia*, assault, robbery and murder. The case against the first accused was that he had assaulted an elderly shopkeeper in his shop, struggled with him and inflicted certain slight injuries on him. As a result of this attack the old man died of heart failure. The first accused was also charged with assaulting the deceased's wife, and stealing a sum of money from the shop. The case against a second accused was that he was art and part guilty in these offences. The medical evidence disclosed that the deceased had a very weak heart. In his charge to the jury the presiding judge made the following remarks on the question of causation:

LORD JUSTICE-CLERK (COOPER): "... The first point you have to address your mind to is not, I think, the question whether murder or culpable homicide was committed, but whether the old man died as a direct result of the violence used against him—for this reason, ladies and gentlemen: whether the criminal taking of life is charged as murder or culpable homicide, in either event it is indispensable that the victim should have died as a result of the injury inflicted—obviously so. The death must result from real violence used against the victim. To take obvious examples, if in any case death was due to, say, natural causes, or to some subsequent accident or maltreatment or neglect, which broke the chain of causation between the so-called crime and the death, then the death cannot be laid to the door of the assailant. Such a death would be, to borrow [counsel's] phrase, an act of God or a mischance. On the other hand, you have to keep very steadily in view that somewhat different considerations apply in a case like this if it be the case that the assailant was engaged at the time in committing a crime of violence. What I mean is this: we know that Mr Demarco (the deceased) was an old man of 82, we know as a result of the post-mortem examination what probably nobody knew, not even Mr Demarco, before that examination was made ... that his heart was in a very serious condition, and that he was, to use Dr Wright's words, a frail, old man. Now it cannot be sufficiently emphasised, ladies and gentlemen, that if an intruder or aggressor, acting from some criminal intent and in pursuance of some criminal purpose, makes a violent attack upon any man or woman he must take his victim as he finds him. It is every whit as criminal to kill a feeble and infirm old man, or a new born infant as it is to kill an adult in the prime of life. However precarious the victim's hold on life may be, no person dare extinguish the spark by violent means but at his peril. It would never do for it to go forth from this Court that house-breakers or robbers, or others of that character, should be entitled to lay violent hands on very old or very sick or very young people, and, if their victim died as a result, to turn round and say that they would never have died if they had not been very weak or very old or very young. That is not the law, and I think you will agree with me that it is not common sense. And so this point, ladies and gentlemen, very much turns on the view you as a jury take both of the background and general circumstances under which the assault was committed and of the evidence we have heard with regard to Mr Demarco and his condition . . . .

On that medical evidence it is for you to consider . . . whether, so to put it, the violence which I assume you hold proved to have been inflicted by Robertson on Mr Demarco was or was not the direct cause of his death, or whether, to put it from the opposite standpoint, Mr Demarco's death was a pure mischance and an act of God . . . . The question is for you on the medical and other evidence, but . . . if you are satisfied that the applied violence, the violence applied by Robertson, was the effective cause of Mr Demarco's death, then you would pass to the next stage, which is to consider whether . . . Robertson is answerable for the crime of murder or only for the lesser crime of culpable homicide. It was said by one of the witnesses . . . that Demarco might have died any moment in his sleep. I suppose the same is true of any of us, although in a lesser degree I hope, but the point I wish to make is that it is none the less homicide to accelerate or precipitate the death of an ailing person than it is to cut down a healthy man who might have lived for fifty years."

Verdict: Robertson guilty of culpable homicide; case against Donoghue found not proven.

NOTES

Similar statements of the law are to be found in *H.M. Advocate v. Rutherford*, 1947 J.C. 1, *post*, **4.06** p. 388, *Bird v. H.M. Advocate*; 1952 J.C. 23, *post*, p. 435. The rule that an assailant cannot rely on the weakness or illness of his victim as an exculpatory circumstance applies even where the weakness is self-induced, or due to some fault on the part of the victim. In *James Williamson* (1866) 5 Irv. 326, *post*, it was argued by the accused that the victim's health had been impaired by excessive drinking, so that a blow which might not otherwise have been very serious proved fatal to her. The Lord Justice-Clerk (Inglis) rejected the argument, stating, "because a person is weaker than his neighbours, either from natural constitution or bad habit, can never make the slightest difference in the question of guilt or innocence in a case of this kind".

## B. Other personal circumstances or conditions

### R. v. Blaue
[1975] 3 All E.R. 446

The appellant was charged, *inter alia*, with the murder of a young woman, by stabbing her. At **4.07** his trial the evidence disclosed that the victim was a Jehovah's Witness, who, on being taken to hospital, refused the blood transfusion which she was advised was essential if she was to survive. She did not receive a transfusion and died four hours later. It was accepted that she would have survived if she had accepted the transfusion when it was suggested. The appellant was found to be suffering from diminished responsibility, and was convicted of manslaughter. On appeal against conviction:

LAWTON L.J.: "The physical cause of death in this case was the bleeding into the pleural cavity arising from the penetration of the lung. This had not been brought about by any decision made by the deceased girl but by the stab wound.

Counsel for the appellant tried to overcome this line of reasoning by submitting that the jury should have been directed that if they thought the girl's decision not to have a blood transfusion was an unreasonable one, then the chain of causation would have been broken. At once the question arises—reasonable by whose standards? Those of Jehovah's Witnesses? Humanists? Roman Catholics? Protestants of Anglo-Saxon descent? The man on the Clapham omnibus? But he might well be an admirer of Eleazor who suffered death rather than eat the flesh of swine or of Sir Thomas Moore who, unlike nearly all his contemporaries, was unwilling to accept Henry VIII as Head of the Church of England. Those brought up in the Hebraic and Christian traditions would probably be reluctant to accept that these martyrs caused their own deaths.

As was pointed out to counsel for the appellant in the course of argument, two cases, each raising the same issue of reasonableness because of religious beliefs, could produce different verdicts depending on where the cases were tried. A jury drawn from Preston, sometimes said to be the most Catholic town in England, might have different views about martyrdom to one drawn from the inner suburbs of London. Counsel for the appellant accepted that this might be so; it was, he said, inherent in trial by jury. It is not inherent in the common law as expounded by Sir Matthew Hale and Maule J. It has long been the policy of the law that those who use violence on other people must take their victims as they find them. This in our judgment means the whole man, not just the physical man. It does not lie in the mouth of the assailant to say that his victim's religious beliefs which inhibited him from accepting certain kinds of treatment were unreasonable. The question for decision is what caused her death. The answer is the stab wound. The fact that the victim refused to stop this end coming about did not break the causal connection between the act and death.

If a victim's personal representatives claim compensation for his death the concept of foreseeability can operate in favour of the wrongdoer in the assessment of such compensation, the wrongdoer is entitled to expect his victim to mitigate his damage by accepting treatment of a normal kind: see *Steele v. R. George & Co. Ltd* [1942] A.C. 497. As counsel for the Crown pointed out, the criminal law is concerned with the maintenance of law and order and the protection of the public generally. A policy of the common law applicable to the settlement of tortious liability between subjects may not be, and in our judgment is not, appropriate for the criminal law.

The issue of the cause of death in a trial for either murder or manslaughter is one of fact for the jury to decide. But if, as in this case, there is no conflict of evidence and all the jury has to do is to apply the law to the admitted facts, the judge is entitled to tell the jury what the result of that application will be. In this case the judge would have been entitled to have told the jury that the appellant's stab wound was an operative cause of death. The appeal fails."

Appeal dismissed.

NOTES

**4.08**     1. Is it only religious conviction that is to be accorded this respect? Suppose that the victim was a racial bigot and refused to accept treatment because the only available medical staff were black, or because they could not guarantee that he would not receive blood donated by a member of a racial group of which he disapproved? Would this be materially different from *Blaue*?

2. What was the victim's contribution here? Was it her pre-existing "condition" (*i.e.* her religious convictions) or her decision to refuse treatment, based on those convictions? Is it correct to apply the rule that the accused takes his victim as he finds her in this case? Is this not different from cases such as *Robertson and Donoghue*? In that case (and other cases involving a subsisting medical condition) the rule operates irrespective of an action or decision on the part of the victim. But that could not have been the case in *Blaue*. The doctrine is only applicable because of the decision to refuse medical treatment. Or

can it be argued that in the case of deeply-held religious convictions there is no real "choice" for the believer?

## C. Other subsisting conditions

Although the relevance of subsisting conditions is generally discussed in the context of offences **4.09** involving personal injury, there is no reason, in principle, why it should not be applied, for example, in the case of damage to property. Suppose, for example, that A decides to break into B's house. He uses a crowbar to force the back door. Unknown to him there is a gas leak in the house. As he forces the door he causes a spark which ignites the gas, causing an explosion. The means used to enter the house would not, normally, destroy it. But on this occasion they do. Must A accept responsibility for the effect of his actions on the pre-existing conditions in the house?

In *State v. Jansing*, 186 Ariz. 63, 918 P. 2d 1081 (1996) the accused, considerably under the influence of alcohol, drove her pickup truck through a stop sign at forty miles an hour and struck another pickup which burst into flames upon impact. The driver of the other truck was killed, and the defendant's son, who was travelling with her, sustained burns and other injuries. She was charged, *inter alia*, with the manslaughter of the other driver and aggravated assault on her son. At her trial she sought to lead evidence of a possible design defect in the fuel tank of the vehicle she struck, but the judge ruled this inadmissible as irrelevant. On appeal it was argued that the trial judge had erred. She asserted that "evidence of the alleged defective placement of the sidesaddle gas tank was relevant to the manslaughter charge because it could have led the jury to conclude that her actions were not the proximate cause of the victim's death". The Arizona Court of Appeals rejected her appeal. Even if there had been an unforeseeable design defect in the placing of the fuel tank, it was not unforeseeable that a truck would catch fire when struck by another vehicle travelling at forty miles an hour.

## 4. SUPERVENING CAUSES: *NOVUS ACTUS INTERVENIENS*

Probably the most commonly encountered question in the context of causation is the effect of **4.10** supervening acts and events.

## A. The victim's contribution

### (a) Consumption of harmful substances supplied to the victim

#### Khaliq v. H.M. Advocate
1984 S.L.T. 137

The appellants were charged, *inter alia*, that they did, on various occasions between February **4.11** 1, 1981 and April 6, 1983, at a shop occupied by them, "culpably, wilfully and recklessly supply to [18 named children, variously aged from 8 years to 15 years] ... and to other children under the age of 16 years whose identities are to the prosecutor unknown, quantities of solvents, and in particular Evo-stik glue, in or together with containers, such as tins, tubes, crisp packets and plastic bags, for the purpose of inhalation of the vapours of said solvents from within said containers, well knowing that said children intended to use said solvents and said containers for said purpose and that the inhalation by said children of the vapours of solvents was or could be injurious to the health of said children and to the danger of their lives and in consequence of your said actions you did cause or procure the inhalation by said children of vapours from said quantities of solvents to the danger of their health and lives". Objections to the relevancy and specification of these charges were repelled by Lord Avonside at a preliminary diet. On appeal:

Lord Justice-General (Emslie): "... Objection was taken to the relevancy and specification of these charges. In relation to charge (1) the major proposition was that the facts libelled do not disclose a crime known to the law of Scotland, and it was contended that in any event the charge was bad for want of specification and fair notice in a number of important respects ....

After debate the trial judge, Lord Avonside, repelled the objections presented on behalf of the appellants, and sustained the relevancy of both charges, holding that the facts libelled in charge (1) did disclose a crime already known to our law, and that the whole other criticisms levelled against both charges were without substance. I have only to add, at this stage, that although in the course of the debate some attention was given to the question whether it was any longer within the power of the High Court to declare that certain conduct constitutes a new crime, *i.e.* one hitherto unknown to our law, the trial judge decided that he, at least, sitting alone, had no such power.

Against the decision of the trial judge the appellants have appealed to this court and on the appellants' behalf counsel has contended that the trial judge erred in concluding that charge (1) libelled a crime known to our law and that [charge (1) was] not defective for any lack of essential specification or fair notice.

Before examining the important question posed by the contention for the appellants that charge (1) does not disclose any crime known to the law of Scotland, it is, I think, desirable to understand what are the essential features of the charge.

(i) There is libelled expressly the culpable wilful and reckless supply to 18 named children and other unnamed children, all under 16 years of age, of solvents for the purpose of their abuse by these children.

(ii) It is averred in particular that the solvents were supplied in or together with containers for the purpose of that abuse, namely, for inhalation from within the containers of the vapours of the solvents.

(iii) The charge then proceeds to libel the state of knowledge of the appellants at the time of supply and the averments are that they well knew that the children intended to use the solvents and the containers for the purpose of abuse, and that the particular abuse was or could be injurious to the health of the children and to the danger of their lives.

(iv) The concluding words of the charge are these: "and in consequence of your said actions you did cause or procure the inhalation by said children of vapours from said quantities of solvents to the danger of their health and lives." In other words, what the Crown offers to prove is that the children did abuse the solvents by inhaling them and that what the appellants did caused or procured that inhalation to the danger of the health and lives of the inhalers.

In introducing the appellants' primary objection to the relevancy of charge (1), counsel for the first appellant reminded us quite correctly that Parliament has not yet subjected solvents to statutory control, fenced by criminal penalties. There are, further, no statutory provisions restricting the supply of solvents to children. Such provisions have, of course, been made in relation to, for example, alcohol and tobacco. He reminded us, too, that it has not yet been held that the deliberate abuse of solvents is a criminal offence. The only step taken by Parliament, so far, was taken in the Solvent Abuse (Scotland) Act 1983 which did not come into force until long after the end of the period with which the indictment is concerned. All that was done was to add an additional sub-paragraph to s.32(2) of the Social Work (Scotland) Act 1968 in terms of which a child may be found to be in need of compulsory measures of care if 'he has misused a volatile substance by deliberately inhaling, other than for medicinal purposes, that substance's vapour'. In this state of the law it accordingly follows that what the children are alleged to have done, *i.e.* inhale the vapours of the solvents, was not a criminal offence, and that the supply of solvents to them was not a criminal offence either.

Against this background the submission, which I shall attempt to summarise fairly, was that there is no warrant in precedent or authority for the view that the supply of a potentially harmful substance, even in circumstances such as those libelled in charge (1), including the knowledge that it would be used or abused by the recipient to the danger of his health, constitutes a crime recognised by the common law of Scotland. Had our common law treated such a supply as criminal one would have expected that some attempt might have been made to prosecute suppliers of drugs, well known to be dangerous to health, before such drugs were brought under statutory control. This is a supply case and not an administration case. The supply allegedly made endangered no one. The risk of injury could arise only if the person supplied performed a voluntary act after the substance had passed out of the control of the supplier. The abuse of the substance by the persons supplied is to be seen as remote for that reason, so far as the supplier's responsibility is concerned, and that abuse, if it occurs, is not itself a crime. It will be observed too, said counsel for the first appellant, that none of the named children in the charge is said to have been under the age of criminal responsibility and it is not averred that any of them was ignorant of the dangers of inhalation which are said to have been known to the appellants. It cannot be presumed that they were so young as to be inevitably ignorant of the dangers of what they intended to do and did. While the administration of a noxious substance to another may well be a crime in certain circumstances, including the age and understanding of the alleged victim, or where the administration is against the will of that person, mere supply of a noxious substance to a person with which, if he chooses, he may injure himself without committing an offence, has never been held to be criminal by the common law of Scotland. The relevancy of charge (1) cannot be supported by recourse to the law which renders criminal reckless acts to the danger of the lieges in general. Under reference to Macdonald, Criminal Law (5th ed.), pp. 141 and 142, this chapter of the criminal law has no application to circumstances in which the alleged danger only arises as the result of the voluntary acts of such persons. The relevancy of the charge cannot be supported either, as the Crown seeks to support it, by recourse to the law relating to offences against the person discussed in *Hume*, Vol. i (3rd ed.), p. 327. That passage, properly understood, is concerned only with acts which inflict real injury to the person, of the nature of assaults, whatever their kind may be. The Crown case appears to be that what the appellants did caused real injury to the children mentioned in the charge but that proposition cannot survive critical examination. This is not a case in which the appellants are said to have administered the noxious vapours to the children. Their only act was the act of supply which, at best for the Crown, merely provided for the children the occasion for the possible abuse of the solvents. It did not cause injury to anyone and from the moment that each transaction was complete, the solvents and the use to which they might be put passed out of the control of the appellants and into the sole control of the child supplied. The essential link between the supply and the inhalation is inevitably broken by the voluntary act of the child supplied and it would not, accordingly, be open to the judges of fact to find that the supply caused the alleged injury. They could only do so if the sequence of events between the alleged cause and the alleged injury is unbroken, and the sequence in the narrative in charge (1) is plainly broken by the dependence of the libel upon the voluntary acts of the persons supplied who must be assumed to be responsible for what they did. The trial judge's opinion, in which he *inter alia* cites the passage in *Hume* upon which the Crown relies, is plainly unsound for the view upon which he sustained the relevancy of charge (1) was that mere supply of a substance to another in full knowledge that that person will use it to the danger of his health and life is criminal. Not even the Crown submission went so far. Whatever the knowledge of the supplier and the intention of the customer, supply is not criminal where the intended use is not itself a crime.

As so often happens after full and well conducted debate the critical questions become readily identifiable. The first and perhaps the only critical question to be answered in this case is whether the Crown's primary submission in support of the relevancy of charge (1) is well founded. The Crown's position is that what is libelled here is not a new crime but merely a modern example of conduct which our law has for long regarded as criminal. Such conduct is described by Hume in the passage to which reference has already been made and consists in actions of any kind which cause or are a cause of real injury to the person. The Crown case is, in short, that the actions of the appellants, in the particular circumstances libelled, were a cause of real injury to the children referred to resulting from their inhalation of the intoxicating and dangerous fumes emitted by the solvents supplied to them for that specific purpose. The particular question for us to answer, accordingly, is whether in the particular circumstances libelled in charge (1) it would be open to the judges of fact to conclude that the supply by the appellants of solvents and containers for the intended purpose of abuse by the children, caused or procured the inhalation of their vapours which occurred, and was, accordingly, a cause of injury which they suffered thereby.

'It would be a mistake', as the Lord Justice-General (Clyde) observed in the case of *McLaughlan v. Boyd*, 1933 S.L.T. at p. 631, 'to imagine that the criminal common law of Scotland countenances any precise and exact categorisation of the forms of conduct which amount to crime. It has been pointed out many times in this Court that such is not the nature or quality of the criminal law of Scotland. I need only refer to the well-known passage of Baron Hume's institutional work, in which the broad definition of crime—a doleful or wilful offence against society in the matter of "violence, dishonesty, falsehood, indecency, irreligion"—is laid down'.

Section 44 of the Criminal Procedure (Scotland) Act 1975, repeating the language of the earlier statute of 1887, provides that it shall not be necessary in any indictment to specify by any nomen juris the crime which is charged but it shall be sufficient that the indictment sets forth facts relevant and sufficient to constitute an indictable crime. No nomen juris is specified in charge (1) and it is accordingly to the facts set forth that one must look to see whether they are relevant and sufficient to constitute an indictable crime. It is of course not an objection to the relevancy of a charge alleged to be one of criminal conduct merely to say that it is without precise precedent in previous decisions. The categories of criminal conduct are never to this extent closed. 'An old crime may certainly be committed in a new way; and a case, though never occurring before on its facts, may fall within the spirit of a previous decision, or within an established general principle'. So said Lord Cockburn in his dissenting judgment in the case of *Bernard Greenhuff* (1838) 2 Swin. 236 at p. 274. In the case now before us it is to an established general principle that the Lord Advocate resorts in defence of the relevancy and sufficiency of the facts libelled to constitute an indictable crime, and that general principle is to be found in *Hume*, Vol. i (3rd ed.) p. 327 and, in particular, in the passage quoted by the trial judge in his opinion which I do not find it necessary to repeat. The general principle to be discovered from that passage is that within the category of conduct identified as criminal are acts, whatever their nature may be, which cause real injury to the person. Does this case, though never before occurring on its facts, fall within that general principle as the Lord Advocate contends? In my opinion it does, although the nature of the injury and the act alleged to be a cause of that injury may be new. Let me now try to explain why I am of this opinion.

There is ample authority for the view that the wilful and reckless administration of a dangerous substance to another causing injury or death is a crime at common law in Scotland. Examples are to be found in cases such as *H.M. Advocate v. Brown and Lawson* (1842) 1 Broun 415, *H.M. Advocate v. Jean Crawford* (1847) 1 Arkley 394. In these cases the victims were young children but it does not appear to me that the relevancy of the charges there made depended essentially on the age, state of knowledge, or attitude of the victim. In the passage in Alison, *Criminal Law*, Vol. 1, p. 629, dealing with this topic it is not suggested that the criminal character of the administration is affected by the absence of any pretence as to the nature of the substance administered, or by the knowledge of the victim of the properties of the substance administered. The case of *H.M. Advocate v. Milne and Barry* (1868) 1 Couper 28 throws further light upon the problem. In that case a charge libelling the wicked and felonious administration of jalap a powerful purgative, dangerous when taken in quantity—to an adult to his injury was held to be irrelevant because it was not said to have been administered with criminal intent. The point was that the jalap could have been administered for a good medical reason. Lord Cowan was of opinion that had the charge libelled that the jalap had been administered 'wilfully and culpably' it might have amounted to a criminal charge, and it is to be noted that the charge did not libel any pretence nor that the jalap was administered without the knowledge and consent of the victim. Upon the matter of the consent of a victim to conduct causing injury to him, or his death, the law is perfectly clear. Consent on the part of the victim even instigation by the victim—is of no importance at all. Clear authority is to be found for that proposition in the cases of *H.M. Advocate v. Rutherford*, 1947 J.C. 1 (murder); *Smart v. H.M. Advocate*, 1975 J.C. 30 (assault); and *Finlayson v. H.M. Advocate*, 1979 J.C. 33 (culpable homicide by injection of a controlled drug causing death). In light of what I have said so far I have no doubt whatever that had charge (1) libelled that the appellants had, culpably, wilfully and recklessly, held the containers supplied to the noses of the children to enable them to inhale the vapours of the solvents to their injury, the relevancy of such a charge, bearing in mind the state of knowledge attributed to the appellants, would be beyond question. I go further and say that the relevancy of such a charge would not have been impaired had the alleged consenting victims of the alleged conduct of the accused been of full age. It is nothing to the point either that the victims might, without committing any criminal offences, have inflicted the same injury upon themselves, for the question is simply whether the accused has, by wilful and reckless conduct on his part, caused real injury to a third party.

As counsel for the first appellant has repeatedly reminded us however, this is not an administration case. What is libelled is culpable, wilful and reckless supply, and the injuries with which the charge is concerned were self-inflicted by the voluntary acts of the persons supplied, after the solvents and the containers had passed out of the immediate control of the appellants. I am not persuaded that these considerations are fatal to the relevancy of charge (1) in this case. Whether the supply was a cause of the injury is a matter of fact and in the particular circumstances averred it would, in my opinion, be open to the judges of fact to hold that the supply not merely of solvents, but of what the press vividly describe as 'glue-sniffing kits', was a cause of injury to the person supplied who proceeded to employ them for the known, intended, and expected purpose, namely inhalation of the injurious vapours of the solvents from the containers. That the persons supplied were children is not, as I have already indicated, essential to the relevancy of the charge but the age of such persons in a charge of this kind will be a circumstance which may be taken into account in deciding whether the supply complained of ought, upon the evidence, to be held to have been a cause of the injury suffered. Turning to the more important obstacles to relevancy founded upon on the appellants' behalf, it is my opinion that the facts and circumstances libelled in charge (1) are such as to permit the judges of fact to conclude that there was no material distinction between what the appellants are said to have done, and direct administration of the noxious fumes. The supply of 'glue-sniffing kits' was sought or invited for the particular purpose of abuse of the solvents. The purpose and the intention of the supply libelled was that the solvents should be abused, employing the means of abuse provided. The solvents were, it is averred, abused, and this could be regarded as the expected, intended and probable consequence of the supply. There are undoubtedly circumstances in which the distinction between supply and administration of a noxious substance will not be material and I do not regard the distinction as material for the purpose of relevancy in the particular circumstances of this case. As the Lord Justice-Clerk (Aitchison) pointed out in the case of *H.M. Advocate v. Semple*, 1937 S.L.T. at p. 50: 'Of course supply by itself does not amount to a crime but here it is coupled with use, and the distinction between supply and administration does not appear to me to be material in a case where the supply is closely related to the use by words of instigation or by some act of instigation on the part of the panel'. In this case, upon the facts libelled, it would in my opinion be open to the judges of fact to conclude that the supply libelled was closely related to the use, even in the absence of words of instigation on the part of the suppliers. The purpose of the supply was no proper purpose and, it may appear, was obviously intended to be carried out. It was abuse of the solvents and, in the circumstances averred, no words or acts of instigation are necessary to demonstrate the close relationship of the supply and the abuse which occurred. I am fully satisfied, further, that it is not fatal to the relevancy of charge (1) that a voluntary act on the part of the recipients of the 'glue-sniffing kits' was required to produce the injurious consequences which they are alleged to have suffered. The causal link is not, of necessity, broken by that circumstance. In a supply case the extent to which the supplier may have a *locus poenitentiae*, and the extent to which extraneous and intervening circumstances dictate or influence the actions of the recipient of the supply, are of course, not unimportant considerations. The doctrine of the *novus actus interveniens*, familiar in the field of delict or the law of contract, if it is to be relevant and exculpatory, must involved that the intervening actus is truly *novus* and *ultroneous* (see, for example, the speech of Lord Wright in *The Oropesa* [1943] p. 32 quoted in *Finlayson v. H.M. Advocate*). Where, as in the case of charge (1), there is no intervention of third party action, or of an unexpected event entirely external to the transaction between the parties directly concerned, there appears to be no ground upon which it can be successfully maintained, upon the basis of *novus actus interveniens*, that the inhalation of the noxious fumes of the solvents by the voluntary and deliberate acts of the recipients of the supply, is fatal to the relevancy of such a charge as is exemplified by charge (1) in this indictment. According to the facts and circumstances libelled in this charge, which is of a course of conduct over a long period, the actions of the recipients which it was known that they intended to carry out, were entirely to be expected, and were, indeed, the known specific purpose of the supply. The true question is whether the charge relevantly libels a causal connection between the alleged supply and the abuse and its consequences, that is to say, whether it would be permissible for the judges of fact to conclude that the supply provided not merely the occasion for the abuse of the solvents by the recipients, but was a cause of that abuse. To that question, for the reasons which I have endeavoured to explain, I give an affirmative answer .... ."

Appeal dismissed.

NOTES

**4.12**     1. The Lord Justice-General describes this as a new example of the principle recognised by Hume (*viz.* that it is a crime to cause real injury). But, as has already been pointed out (Chapter 1, *ante*) the development of the criminal law in this manner cannot be justified simply on the ground that this is a new way of committing an old crime. Some new ways of committing old crimes are so novel as to exceed the permissible limits of judicial development of the criminal law and to fall foul of Article 7 of the European Convention on Human Rights.

2. The appellants subsequently pleaded guilty and were sentenced to three years' imprisonment. These sentences were reduced on appeal to two years' imprisonment. The court took into account the fact that the appellants genuinely believed that their conduct was not criminal, and appeared to have been aware of the decision in *Skeen v. Malik*, Sheriff Court of Glasgow and Strathkelvin, August 1977, *unreported*. In that case the accused was charged with selling to various children and young persons between the ages of 12 and 16 years quantities of "Evo-stik" glue "well knowing that they were purchasing said cans and tubes intending to inhale the vapours of said glue to the danger of their health and lives, and this you did wilfully, culpably and recklessly, and they did inhale said vapour to the danger of their health and lives." A plea taken to the relevancy of the complaint was upheld by the sheriff. See the second edition of this work, p. 453.

3. *Khaliq* was followed in *Ulhaq v. H.M. Advocate*, 1991 S.L.T. 614. That case marks a development of the decision in *Khaliq* in that the "victims" in that case were adults to whom quantities of gas lighter fluid were supplied. In *Ulhaq* it was argued that a distinction could be drawn between a case of supply to children and a case of supply to adults. That argument was rejected, it being pointed out that in *Khaliq v. H.M. Advocate* Lord Emslie said that the fact that the persons supplied were children was not essential to the relevancy of the charge. The age of the persons was merely a circumstance which might be taken

into account in deciding whether the supply complained of ought, upon the evidence, to be held to have been a cause of the injury suffered. *Khaliq* was also the foundation of the following decision.

### Lord Advocate's Reference (No. 1 of 1994)
1995 S.L.T. 248

An accused supplied a quantity of amphetamine to a number of young women, all of whom **4.13** used the drug. One of them died as a consequence of ingesting the drug. As a consequence, the accused was charged, *inter alia*, with culpable homicide. The trial judge held that there was no case to answer on this charge on the ground that the accused's act of supplying the drugs could not be regarded as the cause of death. Following the accused's acquittal on this charge, the Lord Advocate referred the following question to the High Court for its opinion:

"On the basis of the evidence (a) that X supplied amphetamine to the deceased for the purpose of abuse; (b) that this purpose was achieved inasmuch as the deceased ingested the drug; and (c) that this ingestion caused her death, was the judge entitled to acquit X of culpable homicide in terms of s.140A of the Criminal Procedure (Scotland) Act 1975 on the basis that it was not open to the jury to conclude that X caused the deceased's death?"

In his report to the High Court the trial judge (Lord Coulsfield) explained his ruling on the basis that the evidence led clearly showed that the decision to take amphetamine was one taken jointly by all the persons concerned and that the deceased participated in that decision entirely voluntarily without any persuasion or suggestion. He rejected any argument that the supply of amphetamine by the accused to the deceased was either a cause of her ingesting the drug or a cause of her death. He distinguished *Khaliq* (*supra*) on the ground that in that case there was an element of instigation and encouragement; and he distinguished *Ulhaq* (*supra*) on the ground that it was not intended there to lay down any general approach to questions of causation.

The following opinion of the court was delivered by the Lord Justice Clerk (Ross):

OPINION OF THE COURT: " ... Before this court, the advocate depute accepted that the Crown required to prove that the supply of the controlled drug caused the ingestion of it by the deceased. He also recognised that it was not averred in the charge that X knew that the controlled drug was lethal or potentially lethal in the quantity supplied, but he maintained that it was unnecessary to prove that X should have foreseen what occurred.

The advocate depute also maintained that since the issue had been determined in the context of a submission under s.140A of the Criminal Procedure (Scotland) Act 1975, the critical question was whether there was sufficient evidence to support the part of the libel alleging culpable homicide. The advocate depute drew attention to what the trial judge stated in his report. He pointed out that in his report the trial judge expresses the view that the chain of causation was broken because (i) the deceased actually sought the supply of the drug, and when it was obtained divided it and selected the dose which she would take; and (ii) because X did not instigate, suggest or encourage the ingestion of the drug.

The advocate depute maintained that these two factors referred to by the trial judge did not have the effect of stopping the chain of causation from starting nor did they interrupt the chain of causation. He submitted that the trial judge was in error in not recognising that the present case was governed by the principles laid down in *Khaliq v. H.M. Advocate* and *Ulhaq v. H.M. Advocate*. In these two cases the charges libelled culpable and reckless conduct, but the advocate depute maintained that the principles laid down in these cases were equally applicable to the present case. In the present case, it was libelled that the supply of the controlled drug was illegal, and the advocate depute submitted that supply in these circumstances amounted to culpable and reckless conduct which caused a real risk of injury, and that injury and death had in fact resulted. In that situation he maintained that there was sufficient evidence to entitle the jury to convict of culpable homicide.

In essence the advocate depute's submission was that the case of *Khaliq v. H.M. Advocate* was to all intents and purposes on all fours with the present case. He also contended that his submissions derived further support from *Ulhaq v. H.M. Advocate.*

Senior counsel, however, who appeared for X along with junior counsel, maintained that the trial judge had reached the correct decision in this case. He contended that the illegal act which amounts to culpable homicide must be proved to have had direct physical effect upon the victim, causing his death. In the present case he submitted that for X merely to have supplied the drug to the deceased was not sufficient to justify a charge of culpable homicide. For the Crown to succeed there must be proof that the death of the deceased was the direct result of the supply. Senior counsel accepted that in the present case there had been supply of the controlled drug to the deceased, and he also conceded that on the authority of *Khaliq v. H.M. Advocate*, supply might equal administration. However he maintained that, as regards ingestion of the controlled drug, it all depended upon the quantity which the deceased chose to take. He also submitted that *Khaliq v. H.M. Advocate* and *Ulhaq v. H.M. Advocate* were different to the present case in that in each of these cases there were averments of recklessness. However, he pointed out that in the present case there was no averment of recklessness. Senior counsel also founded upon *R. v. Dalby*, and submitted that this court should follow what was stated by the Court of Appeal in England in that case. Senior counsel also referred to Gordon's *Criminal Law* (2nd ed.), para. 26–26 and *H.M. Advocate v. Sutherland* 1994 S.L.T. 634. In *H.M. Advocate v. Sutherland* reference had been made to *Finlayson v. H.M. Advocate* 1978 S.L.T. (Notes) 60.

In all the circumstances senior counsel submitted that the trial judge had been entitled to hold that evidence that X had supplied the controlled drug was not sufficient to support a charge of culpable homicide, and that he was accordingly well founded in acquitting X of charge 11 insofar as it libelled culpable homicide.

We have come to the conclusion that the argument of the advocate depute is to be preferred. In our opinion the trial judge was in error when he concluded that the present case was not covered by *Khaliq v. H.M. Advocate* and *Ulhaq v. H.M. Advocate*. He appears to have distinguished these two cases upon the view that in *Khaliq v. H.M. Advocate* there was an element of instigation and encouragement of the abuse of the substance supplied, and because there was no discussion in these cases of causation in general.

In our opinion there are close similarities between the present case and *Khaliq v. H.M. Advocate*, and the observations of the court in *Khaliq v. H.M. Advocate* are highly pertinent in the present case. In both cases the accused had knowledge of the purpose for which the substance in question was to be used; in both cases there was no question of the supplier instigating the abuse of the substance; and in both cases the amount of the substance which was abused was at the discretion of the person abusing it.

Of course *Khaliq v. H.M. Advocate* was not a case of culpable homicide but was a case of culpable and reckless conduct. There are, however, similarities between charges of culpable and reckless conduct on the one hand and cases of culpable homicide based on culpable and reckless conduct. It is clear that the trial judge was indeed in error when he held that *Khaliq v. H.M. Advocate* could be distinguished from the present case because there had been an element of instigation on the part of the accused and because in the present case the deceased had actually sought the supply of the drug.

[The Lord Justice-Clerk quoted a passage from *Khaliq*, 1984 J.C. 23 at 32–33 and continued:]

In these circumstances we are satisfied that the reasons which the trial judge gave for distinguishing the case of *Khaliq v. H.M. Advocate* are unsound. That case was decided upon principles which in our opinion are equally applicable to the present case, and the observations of the Lord Justice General in *Khaliq v. H.M. Advocate* appear to us to support the Lord Advocate's contention in this case that there was sufficient evidence to support the libel of culpable homicide.

The same is true of *Ulhaq v. H.M. Advocate*. There again there was no evidence of instigation on the part of the accused. In that case at p. 615J the Lord Justice General said:

'The essence of the charge therefore was that the appellant knew that the purpose of the acquisition of the solvents was their abuse and that the supply of them to their recipients was a cause of that abuse. That is sufficient for the conduct to be criminal, because once that is established then there is no material distinction between the supply of the solvents and the direct administration of their fumes to the purchasers which, it was accepted, would plainly be criminal."

Of course we recognise that, as senior counsel submitted, there is in charge 11 no express averment of culpable and reckless conduct. However in charge 11 it is libelled that the supply was unlawful, and that the supply was of a controlled and potentially lethal drug. It is also libelled that the drug was supplied in a lethal quantity. It is clear from what is said in the reference and in the trial judge's report that X supplied a quantity of the controlled drug to a number of people including the deceased, and that the purpose of that supply was so that the deceased and others could take doses of the drug. In our opinion such conduct on the part of X is the equivalent of culpable and reckless conduct. No doubt the extent of any injurious consequences would depend upon the quantity of the drug which the deceased ingested, but since the purpose of the supply was obviously for the drug to be ingested by those to whom it was given by X, it does not appear to us that this affects the matter. As the Lord Justice General pointed out in *Khaliq v. H.M. Advocate*, the causal link is not broken merely because a voluntary act on the part of the recipient of the drugs was required in order to produce the injurious consequences.

So far as *R. v. Dalby* is concerned, the Court of Appeal held that where a charge of manslaughter was based on an unlawful and dangerous act which inadvertently caused death, the act had to be directed at the victim and be likely to cause him immediate injury in order to constitute the *actus reus* of manslaughter.

Senior counsel founded upon this case, but we are not persuaded that the decision in that case has any relevance to the present case. We cannot affirm that the law in England relating to manslaughter is the same as the law in Scotland relating to culpable homicide. In any event, having regard to the nature of this charge, we would see no difficulty in holding that the act of X was directed at the deceased, if indeed that was a requirement of the law relating to culpable homicide. Insofar as the Court of Appeal appear to have held that it was necessary to show that the unlawful act was not only directed at the victim but was likely to cause immediate injury, we are not persuaded that that is a rule of our law so far as culpable homicide is concerned. Under Scots law the test is not one of foreseeability. In Gordon's *Criminal Law* (2nd ed), para 26–02, Sheriff Gordon states: 'For the purposes of the crime of involuntary culpable homicide A will be held to have caused B's death where B's death results directly from an act or omission by A, and whether or not it was a foreseeable result of that act or omission. There are some kinds of culpable homicide which require negligence on A's part and for that reason are confined to circumstances where B's death was foreseeable, but that is a question of *mens rea*; so far as the *actus reus* of the crime is concerned the criterion is that of directness and not that of foreseeability.'

We agree that that is a correct statement of the law, and we have no difficulty in concluding that *R. v. Dalby* gives no assistance in determining the present case.

For the foregoing reasons we are satisfied that the trial judge was wrong to acquit X on charge 11 insofar as it contained an allegation of culpable homicide. We shall accordingly answer the question in the Lord Advocate's petition in the negative."

NOTES

1. Suppose that A supplies drugs to B and B supplies those drugs to C. C ingests the drugs and dies. **4.14** Who caused C's death? Suppose that A supplies heroin to B. B usually smokes his heroin, and A knows this. But on this occasion B injects the heroin and, because he is less experienced at this method of consumption, dies of an overdose. Did A cause B's death? Suppose that B told A that he was going to smoke the heroin, but injected it, would that affect matters?

2. A sells B forty cigarettes a day for fifteen years, at the end of which period B dies of lung cancer. Is A guilty of culpable homicide?

3. A supplies LSD to B. B ingests the drug. The drug induces horrific hallucinations, and reacting to these B kills C in the belief that C is a monstrous creature which is attacking him. Has A caused C's death? If not, then why does B's act in taking the drug break the causal link in this case, but not in the case where B ingests the drug and dies? Presumably because C's death results from an intervening cause in the shape of B's actions while under the influence of the drug. But is that an "act", when he has no awareness of what he is doing? See the discussion of intoxication and automatism in Chapter 7.

4. It has been suggested (Hart and Honoré, *Causation in the Law*, pp. 326 and 361) that in the acts of the victim may break the chain of causation if they are "free, deliberate and informed". Surely this is a reasonable criterion on which to distinguish *Khaliq* from *Ulhaq* and *The Lord Advocate's Reference (No. 1 of 1994)*? The decision of a child or young person to abuse solvents would not satisfy that test. The decision of an adult to do the same would (unless by the relevant point they were no longer capable of exercising rational judgment in the matter). The decision of a 19-year-old to consume amphetamine, especially in the current level of social awareness of the effects of drugs and the risks associated with their use, ought also to be regarded as capable of satisfying that test.

5. *Cf.* the English case of *R. v. Kennedy* [1999] Crim. L.R. 65 in which the case of *Dalby* is distinguished. In that case the accused supplied heroin to the deceased, but went further and prepared the heroin for injection and handed the needle to the deceased, waited while he injected himself and then retrieved the needle. The deceased died as a result of injecting the drug. It was held that this was more than merely supply and involved an element of encouragement to the deceased sufficient to found a charge of manslaughter.

## *(b) Disregard of medical advice by the victim*

### Jos. and Mary Norris
### (1886) 1 White 292

**4.15** Two accused were charged with the culpable homicide of a man by striking him with their fists and stones, and knocking him to the ground and kicking him about the back and head. It appeared that none of the wounds inflicted by the accused were serious, and that he received prompt medical treatment. However, the victim died eight days later, of lockjaw (tetanus). Evidence was led on behalf of the accused that the victim had not followed medical advice by consuming alcohol, and also that he had removed his own bandages. On two occasions he walked home late at night, having consumed a quantity of beer. In his charge to the jury the presiding judge gave the following direction:

Lord Craighill: "If you are of opinion that the prisoners inflicted the wounds on the deceased, the medical testimony is clear that wounds of so apparently trivial a character have been known to cause tetanus, and had produced tetanus in this case. There is also no doubt at all that the deceased died of tetanus.

If therefore you believe that tetanus was the natural result of the injuries the deceased received on that occasion, and would have ensued whether the deceased had behaved in the manner spoken to by the witnesses Keith and Taylor or not, then it is my duty to tell you that the legal result is that the prisoners are liable for the consequences of their assault on the assumption that it was unjustifiable. On the other hand, if you believe that the tetanus was not a natural result, but was brought on by the deceased's own indiscretion, then the prisoners would be entitled to a verdict in their favour."

Verdict: not proven.

Notes

**4.16** 1. In this case the victim appears to have deliberately ignored medical advice. What would be the result if he had not received any such advice but had acted as he did?

2. What is a "natural result" of an injury in the context of modern medical treatment? If A stabs B, infection is a "natural result" if B is not effectively treated with antibiotics. If B refuses such treatment,

and his condition deteriorates, is that a "natural" result? Would it matter *why* B refused such treatment? *Cf. R. v. Blaue, ante,* p. 115.

## (c) Measures of self-protection by the victim: escape

If A attacks B, and B, in seeking to escape, harms himself, the question whether A caused the harm **4.17** depends, it would seem, on the foreseeability of B's actions in seeking to escape. The only reported Scottish case which touches on this point is *Patrick Slaven and Others,* (1885) 5 Couper 694. In that case the accused attacked a woman intending to rape her. She ran away and the accused pursued her. She fell over a cliff and died. There is no difficulty in such a case in holding that the accused caused the victim's death. But what would the position be if she had *jumped* over the cliff? In the English case of *R. v. Roberts* (1971) 56 Cr. App. Rep. 95 the accused assaulted a young woman in a car and she jumped out of the car, while it was moving, in order to escape from him. He was convicted of assault occasioning actual bodily harm. It was held that if her action in doing so was so unexpected that no reasonable person could be expected to foresee it, then it would be regarded as her own voluntary act, and would break the chain of causation. See also *Beech* (1912) 7 Cr. App. Rep. 197 where the victim was injured after jumping out of a window to escape from a man whom she had reason to fear and *R. v. Mackie* (1973) 57 Cr. App. Rep. 453.

See also the discussion of this question by the High Court of Australia in *Royall v. The Queen* (1991) 172 CLR 378.

## (d) Self-endangerment by the victim: rescue cases

What happens if the victim's injuries result from self-endangerment by attempting to effect a rescue? **4.18** Suppose that A sets fire to a building. B is inside, and C enters the building in an attempt to rescue B. If C is injured or killed has A caused that result? There are no reported Scottish criminal cases on this point. Such civil authority as there is suggests that the test here is one of foreseeability. If C's attempts at rescue were foreseeable, then they do not constitute a *novus actus: Steel v. Glasgow Iron and Steel Co.,* 1944 S.C. 237.

In the well-known American case of *State v. Glover* 330 Mo. 709 (1932) the accused was held to have caused the death of a firefighter who was called to put out a fire at the accused's home. The accused had set fire to the house in order to make a fraudulent insurance claim on the property. See also *Commonwealth v. Rhoades,* 379 Mass. 810, 401 N.E.2d 342 (1980).

Is the question of the "reasonableness" of the victim's actions (as opposed to its reasonable foreseeability) relevant here? Suppose that in a case such as the above, the firefighter was given instructions not to enter the building, but disobeyed them? Or suppose that a person attempting to effect a rescue took wholly unreasonable risks, should the fire-raiser be held responsible in that case? Might it not be foreseeable that a person—such as a distraught parent trying to rescue a trapped child—might take wholly unreasonable risks?

## (e) Deliberate self-harm by the victim

### People v. Lewis
124 Cal. 551; 57 Pac. 470 (1899) (Supreme Court of California)

Following an altercation the accused shot his brother-in-law in the stomach, inflicting a **4.19** wound which, according to medical evidence, would have resulted in death within one hour. The victim was put to bed, and a few minutes later cut his own throat, inflicting a wound which, according to medical evidence, must necessarily have resulted in death within five minutes. The deceased died a few minutes later. The accused was convicted of manslaughter, and appealed.

TEMPLE J.: "Now, it is contended that this is a case where one languishing from a mortal wound is killed by an intervening cause, and therefore deceased was not killed by Lewis. To constitute manslaughter, the defendant must have killed someone, and if, though mortally wounded by the defendant, Farrell actually died from an independent intervening cause, Lewis, at the most, could only be guilty of a felonious attempt. He was as effectually prevented from killing as he would have been if some obstacle had turned aside the bullet from its course, and left Farrell unwounded. And they contend that the intervening act was the cause of death, if it shortened the life of Farrell for any period whatever.

The Attorney-General does not controvert the general proposition here contended for, but argues that the wound inflicted by the defendant was the direct cause of the throat-cutting, and therefore defendant is criminally responsible for the death. He illustrates his position by supposing a case of one dangerously wounded, and whose wounds had been bandaged by a surgeon. He says, suppose, through the fever and pain consequent upon the wound, the patient becomes frenzied, and tears away the bandage, and thus accelerates his own death, would not the defendant be responsible for a homicide? Undoubtedly he would be, for in the case supposed the deceased died from the wound, aggravated, it is true, by the restlessness of the deceased, but still the wound inflicted by the defendant produced death. Whether such is the case here is the question.

The Attorney-General seems to admit a fact which I do not concede, that the gunshot wound was not, when Farrell died, then itself directly contributing to the death. I think the jury were warranted in finding that it was. But, if the deceased did die from the effect of the knife wound alone, no doubt the defendant would be responsible, if it was made to appear, and the jury could have found from the evidence, that the knife wound was caused by the wound inflicted by the defendant, in the natural course of events. If the relation was causal, and the wounded condition of the deceased was not merely the occasion upon which another cause intervened, not produced by the first wound, or related to it in other than in a casual way, then defendant is guilty of a homicide. But, if the wounded condition only afforded an opportunity for another unconnected person to kill, defendant would not be guilty of a homicide, even though he had inflicted a mortal wound. In such case, I think, it would be true that the defendant was thus prevented from killing.

The case, considered under this view, is further complicated from the fact that it is impossible to determine whether deceased was induced to cut his throat through pain produced by the wound. May it not have been from remorse, or from a desire to shield his brother-in-law? In either case the causal relation between the knife wound and the gunshot wound would seem to be the same. In either case, if defendant had not shot the deceased, the knife wound would not have been inflicted.

Suppose one assaults and wounds another, intending to take life, but the wound, though painful, is not even dangerous, and the wounded man knows that it is not mortal, and yet takes his own life to escape pain, would it not be suicide only? Yet the wound inflicted by the assailant would have the same relation to death which the original wound in this case has to the knife wound. The wound induced the suicide, but the wound was not, in the natural course of things, the cause of the suicide.

Though no case altogether like this has been found, yet, as was to have been expected, the general subject has often been considered. In I Hale, P.C. 428, the law is stated. So far as material here, his views may be thus summarised: (1) If one gives another a dangerous wound, which might, by very skillful treatment, be cured, and is not, it is a case of homicide. (2) If one inflicts a dangerous wound, and the man dies from treatment, 'if it can clearly appear that the medicine, and not the wound, was the cause of the death, it seems it is not homicide; but then it must appear clearly and certainly to be so'. (3) If one receives a wound, not in itself mortal, and fever or gangrene sets in because of improper treatment or unruly conduct of the patient, and death ensues, it is homicide, 'for that wound, though it was not the immediate cause of his death, yet it was the mediate cause thereof, and the fever or gangrene was the immediate cause of his death, yet the wound was the cause of the gangrene or fever, and so, consequently, is *causa causati*'. (4) One who hastens the death of a person languishing with a mortal disease is guilty of a homicide, for the death is not merely by a visitation of Providence, but the hurt hastens it, and the wrongdoer cannot thus apportion the responsibility, etc. It would make no difference, I presume, if the person killed was languishing from a mortal wound, rather than from an ordinary disease . . . . In *Bush v. Commonwealth*, 78 Ky. 268, the deceased received a wound not necessarily mortal, and, in consequence, was taken to a hospital where she took scarlet fever from a nurse and died of the fever. The court said: 'When the disease is a consequence of the wound, although the proximate cause of the death, the person inflicting the wound is guilty, because the death can be traced as a result naturally flowing from the wound and coming in the natural order of things; but when there is a supervening cause, not naturally intervening by reason of the wound, the death is by visitation of Providence, and not from the act of the party inflicting the wound . . . . If the death was not connected with the wound in the regular chain of causes and consequences, there ought not to be any responsibility.'

[That] case, in my opinion, so far as it goes, correctly states the law.

The facts of this case do not bring it strictly within any of the propositions found in I Hale, P.C. 428. The second and third propositions both predicate a wound not necessarily mortal. What the law would have been in the second case, had the wound been mortal, and the applications had hastened the death, is not stated. It seems to me, however, the case of a person already languishing from a mortal wound is precisely that of one suffering from a mortal disease. Certainly, the willful and unlawful killing of such a person would be a felony, and it cannot be true that the first offender and the last can each be guilty of murdering the same man, if they had no connection with each other, and both wounds were not actively operating to produce death when it occurred.

But why is it that one who inflicts a wound not mortal is guilty of a homicide, if through misconduct of the patient or unskillful treatment gangrene or fever sets in, producing a fatal termination, when if it can be clearly made to appear that the medicine, and not the wound, was the cause of the death, he is not guilty of a homicide? In each case, if the wound had not been, the treatment would not have been, and the man would not then have died. In each case the wound occasioned the treatment which caused or contributed to the death. The reason, I think, is found in the words advisedly used in the last sentence. In the one case the treatment caused the death, and in the other it merely contributed to it. In one case the treatment aggravated the wound, but the wound thus aggravated produced death. In the other the wound, though the occasion of the treatment, did not contribute to the death, which occurred without any present contribution to the natural effect of the medicine from the wound. Take, for instance, the giving of a dose of morphine, by mistake, sufficient to end life at once. In such case it is obvious that the treatment produced death as it would have been had the physician cut off his patient's head. But see *People v. Cook*, 39 Mich. 236. In this case it appears that defendant had inflicted a dangerous wound, but it was contended by the defence that death was caused by an overdose of morphine. Defendant asked an instruction as follows: 'If the jury believe that the injury inflicted by the prisoner would have been fatal, but if death was actually produced by morphine poisoning, they must acquit.' The instruction was refused, but the jury were told that if the wound was not in itself mortal, and death was caused solely by the morphine, they must acquit. The action of the trial court was sustained on the ground that a mortal wound had been given, which necessitated medical treatment, that the physicians were competent, and acted in good faith; and that it was not made clearly to appear that the morphine solely produced death, and that the wound did not at all contribute to the death at that time. Under the authorities, this was equivalent to a finding that the wound did not contribute to the death.

This case differs from that in this: that here the intervening cause, which it is alleged hastened death, was not medical treatment, designed to be helpful and which the deceased was compelled to procure because of the wound, but was an act intended to produce death, and did not result from the first wound in the natural course of events. But we have reached the conclusion by a course of argument unnecessarily prolix, except from a desire to fully consider the earnest and able argument of the defendant, that the test is—or, at least, one test—whether, when the death occurred, the wound inflicted by the defendant did contribute to the event. If it did although other independent causes also contributed, the causal relation between the unlawful acts of the defendant and the death has been made out. Here, when the throat was cut, Farrell was not merely languishing from a mortal wound; he was actually dying; and after the throat was cut he continued to languish from both wounds. Drop by drop the life current went out from both wounds, and at the very instant of death the gunshot wound was contributing to the event. If the throat-cutting had been by a third person, unconnected with the defendant, he might be guilty; for, although a man cannot be killed twice, two persons, acting independently, may contribute to his death, and each be guilty of a homicide. A person dying is still in life, and may be killed; but, if he is dying from a wound given by another, both may properly be said to have contributed to his death."

Appeal dismissed: conviction affirmed.

NOTES

**4.20**    1. There appear to be two reasons why the accused caused the death of his brother-in-law. Either the original wound was still an operating cause at the time of death, or, the original injury caused the deceased to cut his own throat. Either way, the accused's action was sufficiently causally related to the death to attribute responsibility to him. *Cf. U.S. v. Hamilton*, 812 F.Supp. 548 (1960).

2. Suppose that the first wound had not been fatal. How should the court have dealt with the causation problem then? How would the Scottish courts approach the situation faced by the Supreme Court? If, as appears to be the case from *Finlayson v. H.M. Advocate*, 1978 S.L.T. (Notes) 60, *post*, p. 384, and the case of *Khaliq v. H.M. Advocate*, 1984 S.L.T. 137, *ante*, p. 117, the question seems to be whether the victim's act is wholly unforeseeable, then the case is a marginal one.

3. In *Ex Parte Die Minister Van Justisie: In re S. v. Grotjohn*, 1970 (2) SA 355 an accused had a quarrel with his wife. She threatened suicide, and he handed her a gun, saying "Shoot yourself if you want to, because you're a nuisance". She shot herself. The accused was acquitted on a charge of homicide. The case was referred to the Appellate Division by the Minister of Justice. Steyn C.J., delivering an opinion with which the other members of the court agreed, stated:

> "I would prefer not to approve a general doctrine that the last 'voluntary and independent act' of the person committing suicide must always bring about the acquittal of the appellant, without some reservation in regard to the independence of the act. There is no doubt that the act of another which is the immediate cause of the result necessarily interrupts or excludes the causality of the perpetrator's act. To have this effect it would have to be a completely independent act, in the sense that it should be one which is totally unconnected and has no relationship to the act of the perpetrator; and this would not be the case where this act or behaviour is indeed the primary cause of the act, although the act in itself is innocent . . . ."

For a discussion of this type of problem, see D. J. Lanham, "Murder by Instigating Suicide" [1980] Crim. L.R. 215.

4. For a case involving elements of self-harm and self-neglect, see *R. v. Dear* [1996] Crim. L.R. 595.

**Commonwealth v. Atencio and Marshall**
189 N.E. 2d. 223 (1963) (Supreme Judicial Court of Massachusetts)

**4.21** The defendants were convicted, *inter alia*, of the manslaughter of a third man, Britch, with whom they had been playing "Russian roulette". The circumstances of the death are outlined in the judgment of Wilkins C.J., on appeal.

WILKINS C.J.: "Facts which the jury could have found are these. On Sunday, October 22, 1961, the deceased, his brother Ronald and the defendants spent the day drinking wine in the deceased's room in a rooming house in Boston. At some time in the afternoon with reference to nothing specific so far as the record discloses, Marshall said, 'I will settle this', went out, and in a few minutes returned clicking a gun, from which he removed one bullet. Early in the evening Ronald left, and the conversation turned to 'Russian roulette'.

The evidence as to what happened consisted of testimony of police officers, who took statements of the defendants, and testimony of one defendant, Atencio. The evidence did not supply all the facts. For example, the source and ownership of the revolver were not made clear. The jury could have found that it was produced by the deceased and that he suggested the 'game', or they might have found neither to be the fact. There was evidence that Marshall earlier had seen the revolver in the possession of the deceased, and that the latter handed it to Marshall, who put it in the bathroom under the sink. Later when the deceased accused him of stealing it, he brought it back from the bathroom, and gave it to the deceased. Any uncertainty is not of prime importance. The 'game' was played. The deceased and Atencio were seated on a bed, and Marshall was seated on a couch. First, Marshall examined the gun, saw that it contained one cartridge, and, after spinning it on his arm, pointed it at his head, and pulled the trigger. Nothing happened. He handed the gun to Atencio, who repeated the process, again without result. Atencio passed the gun to the deceased, who spun it, put to his head, and pulled the trigger. The cartridge exploded, and he fell over dead ...

There is no controversy as to definition. Involuntary manslaughter may be predicated upon wanton or reckless conduct. *Commonwealth v. Bouvier*, 316 Mass. 489, 494, and cases cited. 'The essence of wanton or reckless conduct is intentional conduct, by way either of commission or of omission where there is a duty to act, which conduct involves a high degree of likelihood that substantial harm will result to another.' *Commonwealth v. Welansky*, 316 Mass. 383, 399. Restatement: Torts, at 500.

We are of opinion that the defendants could properly have been found guilty of manslaughter. This is not a civil action against the defendants by the personal representative of Stewart Britch. In such a case his voluntary act, we assume, would be a bar. Here the Commonwealth had an interest that the deceased should not be killed by the wanton or reckless conduct of himself and others. *State v. Plaspohl*, 239 Ind. 324, 327. Such conduct could be found in the concerted action and cooperation of the defendants in helping to bring about the deceased's foolish act. The jury did not have to believe testimony that the defendants at the last moment tried to dissuade the deceased from doing that which they had just done themselves.

The defendants argue as if it should have been ruled, as matter of law, that there were three 'games' of solitaire and not one 'game' of 'Russian roulette'. That the defendants participated could be found to be a cause and not a mere condition of Stewart Britch's death. It is not correct to say that his act could not be found to have been caused by anything which Marshall and Atencio did, nor that he would have died when the gun went off in his hand no matter whether they had done the same. The testimony does not require a ruling that when the deceased took the gun from Atencio it was an independent or intervening act not standing in any relation to the defendants' acts which would render what he did imputable to them. It is an oversimplification to contend that each participated in something that only one could do at a time. There could be found to be a mutual encouragement in a joint enterprise. In the abstract, there may have been no duty on the defendants to prevent the deceased from playing. But there was a duty on their part not to cooperate or join with him in the 'game'. Nor, if the facts presented such a case, would we have to agree that if the deceased, and not the defendants, had played first that they could not have been found guilty of manslaughter. The defendants were much more than merely present at a crime. It would not be necessary that the defendants force the deceased to play or suggest that he play.

We are referred in both briefs to cases of manslaughter arising out of automobiles racing upon the public highway. When the victim is a third person, there is no difficulty in holding the drivers, including the one whose car did not strike the victim (*Brown v. Thayer*, 212 Mass. 392; 99 N.E. 237), or in whose car a victim was not a passenger. *Nelson v. Nason*, 343 Mass. 220, 221; 177 N.E.2d 887.

In two cases the driver of a non-colliding car has been prosecuted for the death of his competitor, and in both cases an appellate court has ruled that he was not guilty of manslaughter. In *Commonwealth v. Root*, 403 Pa. 571; 170 A.2d 310, 82 A.L.R.2d 452, the competitor drove on the wrong side of the road head-on into an oncoming truck and was killed. The court held (p. 580; 170 A.2d p. 314) that 'the tort liability concept of proximate cause has no proper place in prosecutions for criminal homicide and more direct causal connection is required for conviction . . . . In the instant case, the defendant's reckless conduct was not a sufficiently direct cause of the competing driver's death to make him criminally liable therefor.' In *Thacker v. State*, 103 Ga. App. 36, 117 S.E.2d 913, the defendant was indicted for the involuntary manslaughter of his competitor in a drag race who was killed when he lost control of his car and left the highway. The court said (p. 39, 117; S.E.2d p. 915) that the indictment 'fails to allege any act or acts on the part of the defendant which caused or contributed to the loss of control of the vehicle driven by the deceased, other than the fact that they were engaged in a race at the time.'

Whatever may be thought of those two decisions, there is a very real distinction between drag racing and 'Russian roulette'. In the former much is left to the skill, or lack of it of the competitor. In 'Russian roulette' it is a matter of luck as to the location of the one bullet, and except for a misfire (of which there was evidence in the case at bar) the outcome is a certainty if the chamber under the hammer happens to be the one containing the bullet.

Each defendant excepted to the denial of a request to the effect that if he urged the deceased not to pull the trigger, the jury would be warranted in finding that the defendant did not show a reckless disregard of the deceased's safety, and would be warranted in finding him not guilty. We do not agree with the defendants' contention that the request was not given in substance. Very near the close of the charge the judge instructed the jury, 'If any one of these defendants abandoned or quit the roulette before it was completed, before the shot was fired, then, of course, he would not be responsible or guilty of the shooting.'

Appeal dismissed: conviction affirmed.

NOTES

**4.22** This case differs from the other cases in which the victim has taken his own life in the sense that the deceased presumably did not intend to do so, and no doubt fervently hoped that the gun would not go off. Nor was it the intention of any of the other parties that the deceased should die. So in what sense did the accused "kill" the deceased?

If one adopts the position of the court in *Khaliq v. H.M. Advocate, ante*, p. 117 (and, of course, the *Lord Advocate's Reference (No. 1 of 1994)*, *ante*, p. 123 this could be treated as a case in which the accused supplied to the deceased the means by which the deceased took his own life, and, indeed a case of instigation by the accused. The deceased's action in putting the gun to his head and pulling the trigger could hardly be regarded as truly extraneous. If, therefore, such a case were to arise in Scotland, it is difficult to see how the court could avoid reaching the conclusion that the accused caused the death.

## B. Third party interventions

### (a) Medical treatment

**4.23** The situation where the victim refuses medical treatment, or ignores treatment advice was noted above (p. 126). The cases which follow are just a few of the many which have arisen where the result (usually death) is produced by a combination of the accused's conduct and medical treatment.

It is possible to distinguish a number of issues here. (1) What is the causal significance of bad medical treatment? (2) Can the accused escape responsibility by demonstrating that better, or more appropriate, medical treatment could have prevented death? (3) What is the causal significance of "collateral" injury arising from medical treatment, such as an illness or infection, not related to the original injury, contracted while receiving treatment? In general, the courts are reluctant to shift the responsibility for death or further harm from the original blameworthy act to those who are doing their best, albeit in some instances their negligent best, to help the victim.

### James Williamson
### (1866) 5 Irv. 326

The panel was charged with the murder, or alternatively culpable homicide, of a woman by **4.24** stabbing her. On his behalf it was argued, *inter alia*, that the wound only proved fatal because of the bad medical treatment she received. In his charge to the jury the presiding judge made the following remarks:

LORD JUSTICE-CLERK (INGLIS): "Then, in the second place, it is said that this woman, after she received the wound was not well treated, and that if she had been better treated she would have recovered. Now, it is necessary to explain to you how the law stands about this. If a person receives a wound from the hand of another which is not fatal in itself—it may be a simple and easily cured wound—and then afterwards by unskilful and injudicious treatment this wound assumes a more serious aspect, and finally terminates in death, it is possible to say, and to say with perfect truth, that the wound inflicted by the hand of the prisoner is not the cause of death, because it would not by itself have produced death but for the bad treatment which followed on it. But it will never do, on the other hand, if a wound calculated to prove mortal in itself is afterwards followed by death, to say that every criticism that can be made on the treatment of the patient after the wound is received is to furnish a ground for aquitting the person who inflicted the wound of either murder or culpable homicide."

Verdict: guilty of culpable homicide.

NOTES

1. In *James Wilson*, (1838) 2 Swin. 16 (*post*, p. 137) Lord Cockburn states as a general rule that if an **4.25** accused administers a blow to another, he must "stand the peril of the consequences of his act". What *Williamson* holds is that this rule does not apply where a non-serious injury is aggravated by "unskilful and injudicious treatment" to the point at which it becomes fatal. If, however, the original injury is "calculated to prove mortal in itself", then negligent treatment of such an injury will not serve to exonerate the person who inflicted the original injury. There are no reported modern cases which deal with this question.

2. The English courts adopt a strict approach to such questions. Although in *R. v. Jordan* (1956) 40 Cr. App. R. 152 it was held that "palpably wrong" medical treatment could break the causal link between an unlawful injury and death, in *R. v. Smith* [1959] 2 All E.R. 193 that case was described as "a very particular case depending on its own facts". In *Smith* the court stated that if at the time of death the original injury was still an "operating cause and a substantial cause" it would be treated as the cause of death. Only where a subsequent cause "is so overwhelming as to make the original wound merely part of the history" can it be said to be the cause of death. In *R. v. Cheshire* [1991] 3 All E.R. 670 it was alleged that negligence on the part of medical staff treating the victim for gunshot wounds was the true cause of death. In dismissing the accused's appeal against conviction, the Court of Appeal accepted that even negligent treatment will not break the causal link between the original injury and death. "[W]hen the victim of a criminal attack is treated for wounds or injuries by doctors or other medical staff attempting to repair the harm done, it will only be in the most extraordinary and unusual case that such treatment can be said to be so independent of the acts of the accused that it could be regarded in law as the cause of the victim's death to the exclusion of the accused's acts." See also *R. v. Malcherek*; *R. v. Steel* [1981] 2 All E.R. 422.

## (b) Other "therapeutic" interventions

The discussion of the consequences of failed therapeutic intervention are all confined to cases of medical **4.26** intervention. But clearly the same kind of problem could arise in other contexts. Suppose, for example, that A sets out to break into B's house. In order to do so he attempts to disable the burglar alarm. His efforts cause an electrical short circuit which causes a small electrical fire in the alarm which is on an external wall. B's neighbour, C, sees the fire and attempts to put it out using a water-based fire extinguisher. This is quite inappropriate and causes an explosion which sets the whole house on fire. The house is burned to the ground. Who is responsible for destroying the house? Would it matter if it could be shown that the original fire would have burned itself out without affecting the rest of the building?

## (c) Non-medical intervention by a third party

**4.27** In what circumstances will a third party intervention, other than medical intervention, affect the causal link between the accused's conduct and the final outcome?

### R. v. Pagett
(1983) 76 Cr. App. Rep. 279

**4.28** The appellant formed a relationship with a young woman called Gail Kinchen. Ms Kinchen was six months pregnant by him and after various domestic upsets left him to go back to her parents' house. The appellant armed himself with a shotgun and went looking for her. When he found her he assaulted her and took her against her will to his flat. When the police arrived he threatened to kill Ms Kinchen. Armed police were called, but the appellant refused to give himself up or release Ms Kinchen. Eventually he emerged from the flat, using Ms Kinchen as a shield. He fired his gun at the police who, although they could not see clearly what was happening, fired back. Ms Kinchen was shot three times by the police and died from her wounds. The appellant was unharmed. The appellant was convicted of, *inter alia*, manslaughter, in respect of the death of Ms Kinchen and appealed.

ROBERT GOFF L.J. (delivering the unanimous opinion of the Court): " ... The present appeal against conviction is concerned only with the conviction of the manslaughter of Gail Kinchen .... The question of law relates to the direction given by the learned judge to the jury in respect of the count of murder, and the alternative count of manslaughter, of Gail Kinchen. He directed the jury as follows. First he gave them the full definition of murder in the following terms: 'A person who unlawfully and deliberately causes the death of another person intending to kill or to do serious bodily harm to that person is guilty of murder, and so in the present case the prosecution have to prove beyond all reasonable doubt two things: first that by his unlawful and deliberate acts the defendant caused Gail's death or was a cause of her death. Secondly, in doing those acts he intended to kill or to do serious bodily harm to her.'

Next he considered with the jury the two acts of the appellant which the prosecution contended were unlawful and deliberate and which caused her death, *viz.* (1) the firing of the gun at the police officers (which he explained could constitute an assault), and (2) the physical force applied to Gail so that her body could be used as a shield (which again he explained could constitute an assault). Then the learned judge turned to the question of causation. On this, he directed the jury as follows:

> "Now, members of the jury, if you were satisfied that he did those two unlawful and deliberate acts, the question now becomes whether by those acts he caused or was a cause of Gail's death. It sometimes happens that difficult questions arise when a jury has to decide whether something is a cause of the death of the victim. This is just such a case. In those circumstances it is for me to decide as a question of law whether by his unlawful and deliberate acts the defendant caused or was a cause of Gail's death, but the answer to that question of law depends upon findings of fact which you alone can decide, and accordingly I have to direct you that if you find the facts I am about to mention proved beyond all reasonable doubt, then the defendant would have caused or been a cause of Gail's death .... I turn now to the question whether the defendant caused or was a cause of Gail's death. I am going to mention the facts. If you are sure that the following facts have been proved beyond all reasonable doubt, then the defendant would have caused or would have been a cause of Gail's death. First of all, that he fired the shot-gun deliberately at the police officers before any shot was fired by them. In other words, you must be sure that he fired first. Secondly that his act in firing at the police officers caused them to fire back with the result that bullets from their weapons shot Gail and caused her

death. Next, that in firing back for that reason the police acted reasonably either by way of self-defence or in the performance of their duty as police officers, or both. I will explain that in a little more detail in a moment. Lastly, that from the beginning to the end of the firing Gail was being used against her will and by force by the defendant as a shield to protect him from any shots fired by the police. If you are not sure about any of those matters, acquit him, and you will acquit him of course because the chain which links his deliberate and unlawful acts with Gail's death will have been broken."


The criticism of the summing-up, advanced in this Court by Lord Gifford (to whose argument we are much indebted), was directed primarily to the direction to the jury on causation, which was of course equally applicable to the count of murder and the alternative count of manslaughter. The three specific points raised on behalf of the appellant were as follows (we quote from the grounds of appeal):

(1) The learned judge erred in law in directing that the jury must as a matter of law find that the appellant caused the death of the deceased, if they were satisfied as to the four matters of fact which he set out. The learned judge ought rather to have left it to the jury to determine as an issue of fact whether the defendant's act in firing at the police officers was a substantial, or operative, or imputable, cause of the death of the deceased.

(2) In the alternative, if the learned judge was correct in himself determining as a matter of law what facts would amount to causation of the death by the appellant, he ought to have held that the appellant had not in the circumstances of this case caused the death of the deceased. The learned judge, in directing himself upon the law, ought to have held that where the act which immediately resulted in fatal injury was the act of another party, albeit in legitimate self-defence, then the ensuing death was too remote or indirect to be imputed to the original aggressor.

(3) If the learned judge's direction as to causation was correct, then he erred in law in directing the jury that they could bring in an alternative verdict of manslaughter. The requirement that the jury had to be satisfied that the deceased was being used by the appellant as a shield required the jury to apply a test which was the same or very similar to the test of *mens rea* in murder. ...

We turn to the first ground of appeal, which is that the learned judge erred in directing the jury that it was for him to decide as a matter of law whether by his unlawful and deliberate acts the appellant caused or was a cause of Gail Kinchen's death ....

In cases of homicide, it is rarely necessary to give the jury any direction on causation as such. Of course, a necessary ingredient of the crimes of murder and manslaughter is that the accused has by his act caused the victim's death. But how the victim came by his death is usually not in dispute .... Occasionally, however, a specific issue of causation may arise. One such case is where, although an act of the accused constitutes a *causa sine qua non* of (or necessary condition for) the death of the victim, nevertheless the intervention of a third person may be regarded as the sole cause of the victim's death, thereby relieving the accused of criminal responsibility. Such intervention, if it has such an effect, has often been described by lawyers as a *novus actus interveniens*. We are aware that this time-honoured Latin term has been the subject of criticism. We are also aware that attempts have been made to translate it into English; though no simple translation has proved satisfactory, really because the Latin term has become a term of art which conveys to lawyers the crucial feature that there has not merely been an intervening act of another person, but that that act was so independent of the act of the accused that it should be regarded in law as the cause of the victim's death, to the exclusion of the act of the accused. At the risk of scholarly criticism, we shall for the purposes of this judgment continue to use the Latin term.

Now the whole subject of causation in the law has been the subject of a well-known and most distinguished treatise by Professors Hart and Honore, *Causation in the Law*. Passages from this book were cited to the learned judge, and were plainly relied upon by him; we, too, wish to express our indebtedness to it. It would be quite wrong for us to consider in this judgment the wider issues discussed in that work. But, for present purposes, the passage which is of most immediate relevance is to be found in Chapter XII, in which the learned authors consider the circumstances in which the intervention of a third person, not acting in concert with the accused, may have the effect of relieving the accused of criminal responsibility. The criterion which they suggest should be applied in such circumstances is whether the intervention is voluntary, *i.e.* whether it is 'free, deliberate and informed'. We resist the temptation of expressing the judicial opinion whether we find ourselves in complete agreement with that definition; though we certainly consider it to be broadly correct and supported by authority. Among the examples which the authors give of non-voluntary conduct, which is not effective to relieve the accused of responsibility, are two which are germane to the present case, *viz.* a reasonable act performed for the purpose of self-preservation, and an act done in performance of a legal duty.

There can, we consider, be no doubt that a reasonable act performed for the purpose of self-preservation, being of course itself an act caused by the accused's own act, does not operate as a *novus actus interveniens* .... If authority is needed for this almost self-evident proposition, it is to be found in such cases as *Pitts* (1842) C. & M. 284, and *Curley* (1909) 2 Cr.App.R. 96. In both these cases, the act performed for the purpose of self-preservation consisted of an act by the victim in attempting to escape from the violence of the accused, which in fact resulted in the victim's death. In each case it was held as a matter of law that, if the victim acted in a reasonable attempt to escape the violence of the accused, the death of the victim was caused by the act of the accused. Now one form of self-preservation is self-defence; for present purposes, we can see no distinction in principle between an attempt to escape the consequences of the accused's act, and a response which takes the form of self-defence. Furthermore, in our judgment, if a reasonable act of self-defence against the act of the accused causes the death of a third party, we can see no reason in principle why the act of self-defence, being an involuntary act caused by the act of the accused, should relieve the accused from criminal responsibility for the death of the third party. Of course, it does not necessarily follow that the accused will be guilty of the murder, or even of the manslaughter, of the third party; though in the majority of cases he is likely to be guilty at least of manslaughter. Whether he is guilty of murder or manslaughter will depend upon the question whether all the ingredients of the relevant offence have been proved; in particular, on a charge of murder, it will be necessary that the accused had the necessary intent ....

No English authority was cited to us, nor we think to the learned judge, in support of the proposition that an act done in the execution of a legal duty, again of course being an act itself caused by the act of the accused, does not operate as a *novus actus interveniens* .... Even so, we agree with the learned judge that the proposition is sound in law, because as a matter of principle such an act cannot be regarded as a voluntary act independent of the wrongful act of the accused. A parallel may be drawn with the so-called 'rescue' cases in the law of negligence, where a wrongdoer may be held liable in negligence to a third party who suffers injury in going to the rescue of a person who has been put in danger by the defendant's negligent act. Where, for example, a police officer in the execution of his duty acts to prevent a crime, or to apprehend a person suspected of a crime, the case is surely *a fortiori*. Of course, it is inherent in the requirement that the police officer, or other person, must be acting in the execution of his duty that his act should be reasonable in all the circumstances: see section 3 of the Criminal Law Act 1967. Furthermore, once again we are only considering the issue of causation. If intervention by a third party in the execution of a legal duty, caused by the act of the accused, results in the death of the victim, the question whether the accused is guilty of the murder or manslaughter of the victim must depend on whether the necessary ingredients of the relevant offence have been proved against the accused, including in particular, in the case of murder, whether the accused had the necessary intent."

Appeal dismissed.

NOTES

Was the action taken by the police in this case compatible with article 2 of the European Convention on **4.29** Human Rights? Was the force used "no more than absolutely necessary"? See, in this context, *Andronicou and Constantinou v. Cyprus*, (1998) 25 EHRR 491 which concerned a death resulting from attempts by the police to rescue a hostage. The Court held that in the circumstances there was no violation of article 2. In such a situation, the authorities were required, in the planning and control of the rescue, to take appropriate care to ensure that any risk to the lives of the couple [the hostage-taker and the hostage] had been minimised and to demonstrate that they were not negligent in their choice of action.

## C. Supervening events

To what extent may occurrences, other than human actions, which occur after the accused's wrongful **4.30** conduct, be regarded as affecting the causal link between that conduct and the final result? The question has typically arisen where the victim of an attack has succumbed to an infection or some other illness.

### James Wilson
(1838) 2 Swin. 16

The panel was charged, along with another man, with culpable homicide or, alternatively, **4.31** assault to the danger of life. The charge of culpable homicide alleged that they struck the deceased with their fists and feet and cut him with a bayonet, "or at least [the deceased] in consequence of the injuries so suffered ... contracted or was infected with erysipelas of the head ... and of which disease he died ..." and was thus killed by the accused. It appeared that there was a mild case of erysipelas in the hospital to which the deceased was taken for treatment. The medical witnesses took the view that the deceased did not contract the disease through infection from the other patient, although it was possible that he might have done so. In his charge to the jury the presiding judge made the following remarks:

LORD COCKBURN: "[I]t is argued by the public prosecutor, that but for the wounds inflicted by the panel, the sufferer never would have died, and they are, therefore, not only the remote, but, properly speaking, the real and only cause of his death. For the panel, on the other hand, it is argued, that the wounds cannot be blamed for the effects of a disease, which is not the natural consequence of them, and but for which they would have proved comparatively harmless. Now, this latter doctrine is not to be taken without some limitation. Suppose a man to die of apoplexy, but that apoplexy to have been produced by a blow. It will not, surely, do for the prisoner, in that case, to say, I gave you a blow, but I did not give you apoplexy. He must stand the peril of the consequences of his act. Death seldom follows directly from a blow, or even a wound. Some supervening disease is generally the immediate cause ... You must apply this principle to the present case. If the wound caused the disease, the panel must be found guilty of culpable homicide. If it had no effect in producing it—the verdict cannot go that length. Now, the medical witnesses tell us that the disease was not contracted by infection, and their report describes the wounds as the primary cause of death. Before you can acquit the panel of the more serious charge standing against him, you must be satisfied that the disease was an entirely new disease—not produced by the wounds, but by infection, or some other external cause."

Verdict: guilty of assault as libelled.

## Heinrich Heidmeisser
### (1879) 17 S.L.R. 266

**4.32** The panel was charged with the murder of a man by stabbing him. The view of the medical witnesses was that the wounds were not necessarily fatal, but that they were dangerous. It was argued on behalf of the panel that the cause of death was not the wounds but improper medical treatment. It was established that his nurses had been replaced by an old man described as "quite inefficient", and that his condition might have been seriously affected by exposure to a chill, the hospital being a draughty building. One of the medical witnesses was of the view that the deceased was "out of danger" when the improper treatment began.

LORD JUSTICE-CLERK (MONCREIFF): "The first point to consider is, what was the cause of this man's death. The defence as to this seemed to be that the deceased with proper treatment in the hospital would have recovered, but that his death had resulted from improper treatment after the danger from the wound had been removed. This defence is what is technically known as *mal regimen*—that is to say, where an injury has become mortal or fatal by reason of improper treatment. With regard to such a defence there are distinctions to be observed, which I think have been properly and clearly laid down in the cases referred to—*A. Dingwall*, September 1867, 5 Irv. 466, *J. Williamson*, November 1866, 5 Irv. 326 and which will commend themselves to your common sense. If a man inflicts an injury on another which is not in itself mortal, or which if left to its own operation could not be said to be likely to lead to death, and if that injury becomes fatal by reason of improper treatment, then it does not necessarily follow that the man who inflicted the wound was the cause of death. I do not lay it down more strongly than that, because every case depends on its own circumstances. On the other hand, if a man inflicts an injury which if left to itself will result in death, or of which death is the probable result—which is calculated to lead to death, though it may be capable of cure by the best attention of the best medical skill—then though the man might have recovered if he had had these, it will not relieve the person who inflicted the wound from the guilt of homicide that that best medical skill or care had not been got. That is the general rule, and it will, I think, commend itself to your own common sense, as well as being a sound legal proposition. If a man fights a duel and wounds his antagonist, and by reason of the mode of carrying him off the field haemorrhage set in, though the wound might not in itself have caused death, and haemorrhage is the direct cause, the man who inflicts the wound is responsible.

To apply this doctrine to the present case, you will see that it is a hard one for the prisoner. This man had not recovered from the injury in any popular or reasonable sense, but he was fairly within the grasp of proper medical care. He had been brought through the danger, and nothing more was required but ordinary skill and care, but he had not recovered, and if a chill was sufficient to carry him off, as in point of fact it seems to have done, the man who put his fellow-man in a position where a chill would carry him off is responsible."

Verdict: guilty of culpable homicide.

NOTES

**4.33**     1. Gordon's view (3rd ed., para. 4.46) is that Lord Moncrieff's view in *Heidmeisser* is wrong, and that the better approach is to be found in Lord Moncrieff's statements in *James Wilson*. But Lord Moncrieff's charge seems to imply that there may be cases of non-mortal injury followed by improper treatment where the original wound might be treated as the cause of death. Is that consistent with the view of Lord Inglis in *James Williamson*?

2. In *Bush v. Commonwealth*, 78 Ky. 268 (1880) the accused shot and wounded his victim. The latter was infected with scarlet fever by a member of the medical staff treating him, and died. It was held that death had been caused by the disease, and not by the accused's wound, which was not in itself mortal. This suggests a distinction between subsequent illness (or other event) which is a response to the original act, and events which are merely coincidental. In *State v. Hall*, 129 Ariz. 589, 633 P.2d 398 (1981) the Court explained this distinction in the following way:

"An intervening act is a *coincidence* when the defendant's act merely put the victim at a certain place at a certain time, and because the victim was so located it was possible for him to be acted upon by the intervening cause . . . . By contrast, an intervening act may be said to be a *response* to the prior actions of the defendant when it involves a reaction to the conditions created by the defendant . . . . But, while a response usually involves human agency, that is not necessarily the case . . . ." (quoting LaFave, *Criminal Law* para. 35, pp. 257–258.)

Would the deaths in *Wilson* or *Heidmeisser* be regarded as coincidental in this sense?

# Chapter 5

# ART AND PART LIABILITY

**5.01** The origins of the term "art and part" are obscure (see Hume, ii, 225) but its significance is clear. The phrase denotes participation in the commission of a crime. According to Hume (*ibid*):

> "[Art and Part] includes, in the first place, all those relative and less immediate degrees of guilt, the *ope et concilio* of the Roman law, wherein one is involved, who is concerned in occasioning, preparing, or facilitating the criminal deed... This, however, is but a small portion of what in our practice falls under the compass of such a charge: It relates equally to all interference and assistance *in ipso actu*, at the very time of perpetration; whereby the person concerned is not an accessory, but a principal offender."

"Art and part" guilt thus includes many forms and degrees of participation in the offence, ranging from full participation in the commission of the offence, to less immediate (but not necessarily less important) involvement by, for example, supplying the means whereby the offence is to be committed.

The breadth of the concept of art and part has been commented upon by the Scottish Law Commission (*Art and Part Guilt of Statutory Offences*, Scot. Law. Com. No. 93, Cmnd. 9551 (1985), para. 6):

> "While the law recognises anything within these extremes as constituting art and part guilt, it may be thought that such a wide concept does not draw an appropriate distinction between, on the one hand, minor involvement by way of prior assistance without any active participation in the crime itself, and on the other hand, full participation as a principal at the time when the crime is committed."

It should be remembered, however, that the point in time at which an accused is involved in the offence may not necessarily be as significant as the degree of participation. A person who manufactures and supplies a bomb which is used by another to kill someone bears a heavy degree of responsibility for the death, even though he or she may be a thousand miles away when the bomb goes off.

Older Scottish indictments expressly stated that the accused was "guilty actor or art and part." The Criminal Procedure (Scotland) Act 1887 dispensed with this requirement. Section 46 of the Criminal Procedure (Scotland) Act 1975 expressly stated that in an indictment or complaint "it shall not be necessary to state that a person is 'guilty, actor or art and part' but such charge shall be implied." A similar provision dealing with summary complaints was found in section 312(d) of the 1975 Act. Those provisions were not repeated in the consolidating Criminal Procedure (Scotland) Act 1995, apparently on the view that they were no longer necessary in modern practice. See *H.M. Advocate v. Meikleham*, 1998 S.C.C.R. 621, *per* Lord Eassie. Although the legislation (Criminal Procedure (Consequential Provisions) (Scotland) Act 1995, s.6 and Scheds 5 and 6) is by no means clear, it is probably the case that a charge of art and part guilt is implied in all modern indictment and complaints.

Notwithstanding the rule that art and part liability is implied in any complaint or indictment, there may be cases where it is necessary to charge the accused as an accessory, where, for example, he or she cannot be guilty as a principal offender (for example, where a woman assists a man to commit rape, or where a person, not within the prohibited degrees of relationship, assists in the commission of incest).

# 1. THE BASIC PRINCIPLE

### H.M. Advocate v. Lappen
### 1956 S.L.T. 109

Lappen and five others were charged, *inter alia*, with assault and robbery. In the course of his **5.02** charge to the jury the presiding judge gave the following directions on the question of art and part guilt:

LORD PATRICK: "The Crown's case is that all the accused except Thomson together with this man George Grey of whom we have heard so much, were parties to a common plan to rob the van and to assault the guard. If that was proved, that they were parties to such a common plan, each of those five with whom I am now dealing would be responsible for the acts of all the others in carrying out the robbery and the assault; the acts of each of them in that case would in law be the acts of every one of them, and it would not matter at all that all of them did not actually take part in the attack and seizure of the property, or were not proved to have taken part in the attack and the seizure of the property. To illustrate this doctrine of the law, ... if a number of men form a common plan whereby some are to commit the actual seizure of the property, and some according to the plan are to keep watch, and some according to the plan are to help to carry away the loot, and some according to the plan are to help to dispose of the loot, then, although the actual robbery may only have been committed by one or two of them, every one is guilty of the robbery, because they joined together in a common plan to commit the robbery. But such responsibility for the acts of others under the criminal law only arises if it had been proved affirmatively beyond reasonable doubt that there was such a common plan and that the accused were parties to that common plan. If it has not been proved that there was such a common plan, or if it has not been proved that the accused were parties to this previously conceived common plan, then in law each is only responsible for what he himself did, and bears no responsibility whatever for what any of the other accused or any other person actually did.

It becomes, ladies and gentlemen, a somewhat difficult business when a jury is considering such a case as this, where a common plan to commit a crime is alleged, ... to keep what each has done quite clearly and separately before the jury's eyes, so that there is always a danger, unless one is careful, that ... before they have arrived at the conclusion that there was a common plan to which the accused were parties, they might ... tend to ascribe to some of the accused acts which had been done by others, and that would be wrong. The way to approach the problems you have to decide is this: you should first of all consider each of the accused quite separately and one after the other. Make up your minds what each of these accused is himself proved to have done, then take all these facts which you find each of the accused severally and separately is proved to have done, and against the general background of circumstances which are proved in the case, and which have no particular reference to one or the other, say whether you are convinced beyond reasonable doubt that there was a common plan to commit this robbery, and whether it is proved that the accused, or some of them, and if so, which of them were parties to that common plan ....

Suppose you do not, as I have said to you before, hold that a common plan has been proved, then no question can possibly arise of holding any man responsible except for what he himself is proved to have done, but if you do hold that there was here a common plan between some, more than one, and possibly a good number more than one, persons to commit this robbery then the next question which you will have to determine is which, if any of the accused is proved to have been a party to that common plan. Any one of the accused, again I am speaking of the first five—any one of them whom you hold to have been a party to a common plan to commit this robbery would then be responsible for the commission of the robbery, and would be guilty of the fifth charge, no matter what part he played in the actual execution of the robbery, and no matter though it had not been proved that he played a part in the actual execution of the robbery. The critical things are, has it has been proved that there was such a common plan, and secondly, is it proved that the accused, and if so, which of them, were parties to that common plan?"

Verdict: three accused convicted.

NOTES

**5.03**    1. A person will generally only be held criminally responsible for his or her own acts and omissions, but where the accused acts as part of a group he or she can be held responsible for the acts of the group as a whole. But if there is no common purpose, it appears that two people cannot be guilty, independently, of the same crime: *Greig v. Muir*, 1955 J.C. 20, *per* the Lord Justice-Clerk Thomson (at p. 23).

2. The existence of a common purpose does not depend upon a prior agreement between the parties, nor does it require express agreement between the parties. A common purpose may arise spontaneously, for example, where A observes B in the commission of a criminal act and assists in its commission. See below, pp. 151–153.

3. The existence of a criminal purpose is very useful (from the perspective of the prosecution) in attributing responsibility where it is not clear which of a number of accused persons actually committed the offence. The common purpose allows responsibility to be attached to all of the accused, but it is always crucial that a common purpose is established. See the following cases.

**H.M. Advocate v. Welsh and McLachlan**
(1897) 5 S.L.T. 137

**5.04**    The two accused were charged, *inter alia*, with the murder of an old woman by striking her on the head with an iron bar or other weapon, having broken into her house and stolen certain articles therein. In the course of his charge to the jury, the presiding judge, Lord Young, stated that there could be no doubt on the evidence that the house ... was broken into. Neither did there appear to be any question that the men, whoever they were, who broke into the house, struck [the victim], so that she died within a fortnight. The question was—whether or not it was proved that both or either of the prisoners were the persons who broke into the house, and whether both or either of them struck the old woman? If the jury held it proved that the prisoners were the men who broke into the house, and that one of them struck the blow which proved fatal, then the further question arose as to whether both the prisoners could be held legally responsible for the violent act of one of them. If one of the prisoners in this case struck the woman, that would not necessarily lead to the conviction of both on the charge of murder. If two men, both with pistols, stop a man on the highway and demand his money or his life, and one shoots the man, then both would be responsible. If two housebreakers went with pistols or knives, or anything which satisfied the jury that they were prepared, by violence, to overcome any resistance which was offered, regardless of human life, then, though only one inflicted the fatal injury, both would be responsible. That did not appear to his lordship to be applicable in the present case, in which a helpless, feeble old woman who could not offer any resistance was struck by one of the men, and there was no evidence by which of them. In such a case the other could not be held responsible. If the jury were convinced that both prisoners went into the house with the intent to inflict such violence as was inflicted upon the woman, then both the prisoners would be responsible if only one had done what both were prepared to do. There was no evidence to indicate a case of that kind here, and the jury would take it that, in law, they could not convict either prisoner of the murder without being satisfied that he was the man who had inflicted the blow. It was sad enough if they should come to the conclusion that one or other did the deed, but they could not tell which. Still, if that were so, it would be their duty not to convict either. The evidence was as weak and slender as his lordship had seen on so serious a charge.

Verdict: not proven on the charge of murder.

## Docherty v. H.M. Advocate
### 1945 S.L.T. 247

The appellant was convicted of murder. The circumstances of the offence and the grounds of **5.05** appeal are fully set out in the opinion of Lord Moncrieff:

LORD MONCRIEFF: "In this case the appellant was charged on an indictment, the charge against him being that he, while acting in concert with a person whose name and address were to the prosecutor unknown, on a day in December last and in a one roomed house occupied by him at an address in Greenock, did assault a man named Davies, offering him various acts of violence, and in particular attacking him with a hatchet, did rob him of a cigarette case and other property, and did murder him. He was tried before the High Court in Glasgow, and on March 1 of this year was convicted of murder by the verdict of a jury and was sentenced to death. It is against that conviction that this appeal is taken.

In the note of application for leave to appeal, three reasons of appeal are set forth. The third of these reasons is that the verdict was contrary to the evidence. Senior counsel, however, eventually found himself unable to withhold an admission that, subject to affirming concert which the jury were entitled to affirm, there was material in the evidence upon which the jury could competently return that verdict; but he insisted—and this was the proposition upon which he particularly relied—that unless concert was so affirmed, there was no evidence which could support the verdict.

The special feature of this case is the need for affirming concert in the circumstances in which the act is said to have occurred. That need arose as follows. When the blow with the hatchet which caused death was struck, assuming that it in fact was struck in the house and in the presence of the appellant, there were present in that single room not only Davies, who lost his life, and the appellant, but also and along with them the unknown associate referred to in the indictment. For all that appears in the evidence the fatal blow may as well have been struck by the associate as struck by the appellant. To establish guilt on the part of the appellant it was thus conceded that it was essential to prove concert; and this in order that, if he was not guilty in respect of his own act, he might yet remain guilty under the doctrine of law which ascribes to associates in crime in certain cases responsibility for the criminal acts of their associate. As might thus be expected, the reasons of appeal which are still maintained are two reasons which are both associated with the concert which is alleged as a principal element in the indictment; and both of these reasons are founded upon objections to the charge to the jury by the presiding judge.

The first reason of appeal, which is that the presiding judge failed to give adequate directions, was, I think, expanded so as to become a complaint of what amounted to misdirection. That this was the purport of the objection is made clear by the case which was relied on in support of this objection, namely, the case of *Tobin* (1934 J.C. 60). In that case a charge to a jury was given by a learned sheriff in a case in which concert was alleged; and it was held that his failure as presiding judge to direct the jury to consider the evidence against each of the accused separately, and to explain that it was competent to convict certain of the accused without convicting the others, had amounted to a misdirection. It was argued that a similar misdirection was to be found in the charge of the presiding judge to the jury in this case. I have great difficulty in understanding what is supposed to be the foundation of that objection. The learned judge at the outset of his charge proceeds to deal with legal questions, and in particular with the legal consequences of an individual act by one of two parties who are acting in concert; and he points out that proof of a previous plan or arrangement to commit the act is not required, and that concert may be demonstrated by the fact that people have joined together in doing what is done. Then he says in terms, 'Although a number of persons are charged as acting in concert, it does not follow that all may be found guilty. Some may be guilty and some may not be guilty, and, just because of that, where concert is charged the first thing a jury has to determine is whether each—and they must consider each separately—whether each is in the concert or in the plot or took part in the crime which was committed.' I cannot think of words which could more clearly direct a jury to have in view the plea in defence which the learned judge had failed to bring to the notice of the jury in the case of *Tobin* (*supra*); and accordingly, so far as this reason of appeal is dependent upon a contention that the error made in the case of *Tobin* was again made in this case, it is one which very clearly, in my opinion, should not be sustained."... [His Lordship then dealt with a further aspect of this part of the appeal, which is set out *post*, pp. 156–158, and continued:]

Turning now to the second of the reasons of appeal, I find that, as it appears in the note of application for leave to appeal, this reason is not too lucidly phrased. If, however, all the words in the second line, as the reason appears in type, should be deleted after the first two words in that line, it becomes clear what is the purport of this objection. The reason then would run: 'That the presiding judge failed to direct the jury as to their duty in the event of their finding concert not proved.'... I have examined the charge of the presiding judge carefully, and I do not find that the direction desiderated is anywhere explicitly given ....

Having asked the jury to consider whether the facts do or do not demonstrate that the appellant participated in the crime, the learned judge goes on: 'On the other hand, if you think that the accused had nothing to do with it'—and then one notes the word *'or'*—'or if you think that the Crown have failed beyond reasonable doubt to prove their case and to bring home guilt to Docherty, then your verdict would be a verdict of not guilty or not proven.' It was claimed that in that direction it was at least suggested that such an alternative verdict should be brought in, not in a single case, but in two separate cases. The second case is 'If you think that the Crown have failed beyond reasonable doubt to prove their case and bring home guilt to Docherty'; the first case is 'If you think that the accused had nothing to do with it'. It was argued that the first case was applicable to the event of the jury having negatived concert, while the second dealt with the case they would still require to consider if, having disposed in his favour of the plea of concert, they should regard the appellant as a single person charged under the indictment, and therefore as answerable only for his own acts. While for my own part I would be inclined to understand the direction as indicating only the contrasted circumstances in which a verdict of not guilty or a verdict of not proven would be appropriate, I think that that is a view of the charge which might perhaps be taken by others chosen from among qualified legal practitioners who should have had an opportunity of reading and considering what the learned judge had said; but I fail to find in that sentence, or to find elsewhere in the charge, an explicit direction as to what the jury should do with the evidence in the event of their negativing concert, and fail in any event to find an explicit direction such as has been desiderated upon the very exacting standard which has been fixed in previous cases, as requiring from a presiding judge a direction so clear as to be unmistakable even by persons who are without experience of legal process, doctrine or phrasing ....

It was maintained for the appellant, and in my opinion was rightly maintained, that the jury ought to have been directed that, if they failed to find proof of concert, they were bound on the evidence to return a verdict of acquittal. I find that there is an absence from the charge of any explicit direction to that effect; and it thus only remains to consider whether the direction desiderated is on a matter of critical importance. If concert was not proved, I do not think it was maintained against the appellant that there was any evidence to shew whether the blow had been struck by himself or by his associate; and in such a case there is abundant authority in law which affirms that evidence in that position is not relevant to support a charge against either party. In the case of *Robertson* (2 Adam, 92) a husband and wife were tried for the murder of their infant son, and the Lord Justice-Clerk (Lord Kingsburgh) directed the jury that if there was no evidence of concurrence between them and no satisfactory evidence to prove which of the panels inflicted violence, then the jury must find the charge not proven against either of them. In his charge that learned judge says this: 'The prosecution is not entitled to content itself with bringing proof that there is a likelihood that the crime was committed by one of the accused. The rule of our law is that if a crime has been committed by one or other of two persons, and must have been the act of one of them, but the prosecutor is unable to prove which did it, then neither can be found to have been proved guilty.' And then the learned judge proceeds to consider a case which he does not name but which is apparently the case of *Peterson* (2 Coup. 557), in which the point is referred to as the subject of a ruling by the presiding judge in a single paragraph on page 560 which summarises the position as follows: 'The case having been closed, the jury, under the direction of Lord Deas, returned a verdict of not proven. His Lordship pointed out that in the dark the knife might have been used by one of the prisoners—it was impossible to say which of them—without the knowledge of the other. The prisoners were accordingly assoilzied and dismissed from the Bar.' Again, as recently as the case of *Alexander v. Adair* (1938 J.C. 28), it was, in the view of the late Lord Justice-Clerk, almost too clear for argument that where two possible delinquents or one or other of them had been concerned in a motor accident, and there was no proof whether one or other or both of them had been the cause of the accident, then in law there was no evidence relevant to support the conviction against either of them. That this is a matter upon which juries may fall into disastrous error unless guided is apparent from the circumstance that, in the case to which I have last referred, the very mistake which requires to be guarded against has been made by a learned and experienced sheriff who, while sitting as a jury, has misdirected himself to that effect.

Accordingly, it seems to me to be beyond question that the matter is one of critical importance; and that any defect in the charge in respect of failure to contain an explicit direction for the guidance of the jury upon the question is a defect which may have affected the very substance of their verdict. Seeing that there was in this case no evidence to shew, if there had not been concert, whether the appellant or his associate struck the blow, the only possible verdict in defect of concert was a verdict of acquittal .... "

Appeal allowed; conviction quashed.

NOTES

As Lord Carmont observed in the above case (at p. 251), "The effect of proof of acting in concert is of **5.06** far-reaching importance, and particularly so when the crime has been committed in such circumstances as point to a single hand having dealt the fatal blow. Such proof will turn one who would otherwise be found to be a mere onlooker or bystander into *socius criminis* ...." The case also emphasises the importance of the judge making clear the consequences in such a case of a failure on the part of the prosecutor to prove concert.

Other aspects of this case are considered *post*, pp. 156–158.

## 2. ACQUITTAL OF CO-ACCUSED

Art and part guilt is based on the idea of concert, that the accused acted along with others. Does it follow **5.07** from this that an accused cannot be found guilty art and part if the other alleged offenders are acquitted, or never discovered? Or can one be found guilty art and part without the conviction of others?

As Hume indicates, the idea of art and part guilt is capable of embracing two rather different notions. The first of these is where one or more of the parties can properly be regarded as principal offenders, and others as accomplices. The second is where all parties involved in the offence are properly to be regarded as joint principals. So far as concerns the degree of responsibility of those who are convicted, this is a distinction without any difference. However, this distinction may be relevant where not all parties to the offence are convicted. If, in the former case, the "principal" offender is acquitted, it may not be logical to convict the accomplice. If, however, the parties are all properly regarded as principal offenders in their own right, then the acquittal of one should have no bearing on the guilt or innocence of the others. The following cases illustrate this distinction.

## Young v. H.M. Advocate
1932 J.C. 63

**5.08** The appellant was charged along with a number of other persons with, *inter alia*, making a fraudulent allotment of shares in a limited company. The appellant's co-accused were all associated with the company either as directors or, in one case, as secretary, but he had no such connection with the company. He was convicted on this charge, while the other accused were all acquitted. On appeal against conviction:

LORD JUSTICE-GENERAL (CLYDE): Charge (2).—This is a charge of fraud upon the new company, and of fraudulent misappropriation of its funds to an extent exceeding in all £500,000. The fraud upon the new company is said to have consisted in the directors going to allotment at all in the circumstances known to them, and particularly in allotting shares to certain of the applicants; and the fraudulent misappropriation is said to have consisted in the making of certain payments by the said directors out of the new company's funds, for their own purposes, and without value or consideration. The appellant Todd was the new company's secretary, and he is charged along with the directors. The appellant Young was not a director of, or otherwise officially connected with, the new company; but he is charged with being 'art and part,' both in the fraud and in the fraudulent misappropriation, and—as regards the latter—the charge was laid against the directors and secretary, and all of them, 'acting in concert' with the appellant Young. The verdict was one of not guilty in favour of all the accused except the appellant Young, who was found guilty of the charge 'but not guilty of acting in concert with the others'.

The result thus arrived at is a remarkable one; and counsel for the appellant Young not only subjected it to attack, but (not unnaturally) used it to reinforce the argument (already dealt with in connection with charge (1)) that there was an unjust discrimination in the verdict against the appellant Young. Dealing, however, with charge (2), the result was to convict the appellant Young of being art and part in acts (namely, the allotment of the company's shares, and the sanction of payments out of its funds) to which—whether inspired by fraudulent intent or not—he (not being a director) could not possibly be a party, and, moreover, of being art and part in a fraud which the principal persons charged with it are found by the jury not to have committed. That the charge of concert between the directors and secretary and the appellant Young was disposed of by the verdict in his favour may have been due to the general direction given by the trial Court to the jury that there was no evidence of any common fraudulent design among the accused; but, inasmuch as (particularly as regards the fraudulent misappropriation of the company's funds) the only possible link between the exclusive domain of the directors and the actings of the appellant Young was the alleged concert, it is difficult to understand how a verdict could be arrived at against him on this charge at all. The Crown sought to justify the conviction on the ground that a person accused as art and part might be convicted notwithstanding the failure of the prosecutor to bring home the commission of the crime to the principals charged, provided the fact that the crime was committed (even by persons unknown) is proved. It was suggested that the jury may have been convinced that fraud and fraudulent misappropriation had been committed, although not by the directors and secretary who were indicted. This is an afterthought. If the crime was committed at all, it must have been by some person or persons who were in the position of directors; and it is incredible that individual directors, who were either not charged in the indictment, or whose names were withdrawn from it by the Crown, could be sanely regarded as the guilty parties. Whatever be the explanation of what happened in connection with this charge, it is clear that the conviction of the appellant Young under it is neither reasonable nor intelligible, and it must be quashed accordingly."

Appeal allowed, quoad conviction on charge (2).

## Capuano v. H.M. Advocate
### 1984 S.C.C.R. 415

The appellant was charged along with two other men with assaulting two persons by throwing **5.09** bricks and stones or other missiles at their motor car. One of the occupants of the car was struck on the head by a stone and injured. There was evidence that all three had participated in the attack on the car, and some evidence that the appellant had thrown, or attempted to throw, something at the car. The appellant's co-accused were acquitted. On appeal to the High Court:

LORD JUSTICE-GENERAL (EMSLIE): This appeal is brought to challenge the appellant's conviction on [the charge outlined above] only. The grounds stated in the note of appeal were these:

'1. Insufficient evidence in law to entitle the jury to convict the appellant.

2. The verdict of the jury was perverse, unreasonable and contrary to the law, as well as unsupported by the evidence. The jury acquitted both co-accused in a situation where the Crown presented its case against the appellant on the basis of art and part participation.'

At the hearing of the appeal the submission was short and clear. There was not sufficient evidence to entitle the jury to find the appellant guilty as *actor* in the events libelled in charge (12) and indeed the Crown sought his conviction upon the basis that there was sufficient evidence to establish that he was guilty art and part of acts committed by Douglas in particular, while he was part of a group which included the appellant and Todd. The jury, however, acquitted both Douglas and Todd, the only two persons with whom it was contended the appellant was guilty art and part, and in the result the conviction of the appellant cannot stand.

In our judgment this submission is unsound and must be rejected. There are undoubtedly cases in which if the only persons who could have committed an offence, as actors, have been acquitted an accused cannot be found guilty, art and part with them (see, for example, *Young v. H.M. Advocate*, 1932 J.C. 63). This, however, is not such a case. There was ample evidence that a group of three or more youths acting together of common criminal purpose ran to intercept the car driven by Mr Cardle, that bricks and stones were thrown at the car by members of the group, and that one of the group threw a brick or stone which smashed the windscreen and struck Miss Mitchell. There was also evidence that other missiles were thrown at this car by other members of this group, and there was ample evidence that the appellant was a member of the group, and some evidence that he threw a stone at this car by other members of this group, and there was ample evidence that the appellant was a member of the group, and some evidence that he threw a stone towards the car. The Crown set out to satisfy the jury that Douglas and Todd were also members of the group and that Douglas, in particular, was the person who threw the brick or stone which caused the injury to Miss Mitchell. The jury, as their verdicts show, were not so satisfied beyond reasonable doubt, but that does not mean that in the circumstances of this case they were not entitled to convict the appellant as a participant in the proved crime of assault committed by a group, and a member or members of a group, to which he belonged. By section 45 of the Criminal Procedure (Scotland) Act 1975 the words 'all and each or one or more' are implied in a charge such as [this], and the failure of the Crown to satisfy the jury that Douglas and Todd were sufficiently identified as members of the group which undoubtedly committed a group crime did not deprive the jury of their right to convict the only identified member of the group, namely, the appellant. The situation which arose in this case is not an unfamiliar one. A typical example which is encountered in practice is where the Crown charges four named persons as the perpetrators of a masked robbery which on the evidence was carried out by four persons, three of whom entered the target premises leaving one outside as the driver of the escape vehicle. In such a case the problem is identification of the participants and if the jury hold that the driver has been sufficiently identified as one of the four-man team, but are not satisfied that the other named accused have been identified as the remaining members of that team, it cannot seriously or reasonably be maintained, and so far as we are aware there has never been an attempt to maintain, that they would not be entitled to convict the only member of the four-man team whose identification as one of the perpetrators of the crime is not in doubt.

For these reasons the appeal will be refused."

Appeal dismissed.

NOTES

**5.10** 1. The difference between *Young's* case and *Capuano* appears to be this: In *Young* the appellant could not be charged as a principal offender, since he was not a director of, or otherwise connected with, the company. The only basis, therefore, on which he could be found guilty was as an accessory to the offences allegedly committed by his co-accused. Since they had all been acquitted there was, in effect, no offence to which he could be an accessory. In *Capuano*, the appellant's liability was not, in this sense, dependent on that of his co-accused. This was a case of art and part of the second category suggested by Hume, *viz.* where all accused are really principal offenders. Thus the acquittal of two of the accused did not affect the position of the third (principal) offender.

2. Apart from special circumstances of the kind illustrated by *Young v. H.M. Advocate* there is no rule which would prevent an accused being convicted of an offence along with a person who has already been acquitted of the crime in question. In the case of *McAuley v. H.M. Advocate*, 1946 J.C. 8 Lord Cooper stated that it was not proper for the Crown to indict an accused for having committed an offence with a person who had previously been tried for that offence and acquitted. However, that case was overruled in *Howitt v. H.M. Advocate; Duffy v. H.M. Advocate*, 2000 S.L.T. 449. (*Duffy v. H.M. Advocate* is discussed, *post*, in Chapter 6.)

3. Since the jury are required to consider the evidence against each accused separately, there is no objection to the conclusion that while it is proved that A acted in concert with B, it is not proved that B acted in concert with A: *Low and Reilly v. H.M. Advocate*, 1994 S.L.T. 277.

## 3. ESTABLISHING THE COMMON PURPOSE

### (a) Assistance prior to the commission of the offence

#### H.M. Advocate v. Johnstone and Stewart
1926 J.C. 89

**5.11** The two accused were charged with procuring an abortion while acting in concert. The accused were in fact unknown to each other. The first accused took no part in the actual operation, which was performed by the second accused, but had merely passed on her name (which she had received from a third party) to persons interested in obtaining an abortion. She received no reward for such referral. In his charge to the jury the presiding judge gave the following directions on the issue of art and part guilt:

LORD MONCRIEFF: "If you are satisfied that Mrs Johnstone and Mrs Stewart were entire strangers, and are further satisfied that no money passed, then I think it would be straining the law to hold that the mere communication of a name by a party who was not in actual communication with the party named was actual participation in the illegal act .... Accordingly, on the question raised, you have to consider, Is there any evidence, of association between these two women? If you find there is not such evidence, you must next consider, Is there proper legal proof which can be relied on that money had passed for the giving of the name? And if you find in the negative on that question also—that there was nothing except, upon solicitation, communication of the name to the parties—then I have to direct you that it will be your duty in that case to find a verdict in favour of the prisoner Johnstone."

Verdict: Johnstone, not guilty, Stewart, guilty.

NOTES

1. The *nexus* required for art and part guilt was not present in this case, but how much more was **5.12** required to make the accused part of a joint criminal activity? There is the clear suggestion that if money had changed hands the situation would have been different, and if the first accused had actively procured clients for the second accused no doubt the court could have held that they were both parties to the unlawful abortions carried out by the latter.

2. In this case the first accused knew that the second accused carried out unlawful abortions. The obstacle to conviction was that there was no common purpose. What is the position where one party assists another in a criminal purpose, but at the time of the assistance is unsure what that purpose might be? In *R. v. Bainbridge* [1959] 1 Q.B. 129 the appellant bought oxygen cutting equipment on behalf of some thieves who used it to break into and rob a bank. He was convicted of being an accessory before the fact. He admitted that he suspected the equipment was to be used for something unlawful, perhaps the breaking up of stolen metal, but it was his contention that he did not contemplate its use for the purpose of breaking into and stealing from the bank.

On appeal it was held that while it must be proved that the accomplice knew the "type" of offence intended, it was not necessary to show that he knew precisely the crime intended, in the sense of knowing (for example) which particular branch of which bank was to be robbed and on what date.

In *DPP for Northern Ireland v. Maxwell* [1978] 3 All E.R. 1140 the appellant, a member of the U.V.F., was charged with doing an act with intent to cause an explosion by a pipe bomb, contrary to section 3(a) of the Explosive Substances Act 1883 and possession of a bomb contrary to section 3(b) of the same Act. The appellant had guided other members of a U.V.F. group to a public house where a bomb was planted. He claimed that although he suspected that there was going to be an attack, he did not know what form it would take, nor did he know that the persons whom he guided to the public house had a bomb in their possession. In dismissing his appeal against conviction, the House of Lords held that in such a case, "the guilt of an accessory springs . . . from the fact that he contemplates the commission of one (or more) of a number of crimes by the principal and he intentionally lends his assistance in order that such a crime will be committed" ([1978] 3 All E.R. 1140, *per* Lord Scarman at pp. 1150–1151). This formulation avoids the difficult problems associated with the question of what is an offence of the "type" intended. It also extends the law somewhat beyond Bainbridge, since it was accepted that it could not be proved that the appellant knew that a bomb attack on the public house was contemplated and thus it could not be said that he knew the type of offence intended. This type of problem is touched upon, but not resolved, by Hume (i, 157–158) and Gordon suggests that "Scots law may require more exact knowledge" than was required in *Bainbridge* (Gordon, p. 143, note 80). This would seem to follow from *Johnstone and Stewart*, but would the alternative approach of the House of Lords in *Maxwell* be any more acceptable in Scots law?

## (b) Participation in the commission of the offence

### H.M. Advocate v. Kerr
#### (1871) 2 Couper 334

Three accused were charged with assault with intent to ravish. One of them, Donald, was **5.13** charged with being "present, in company with" the principal offender, "aiding and abetting him whilst he was attempting to ravish" the victim, "by looking on and failing to interfere in her behalf, or to call for assistance." The accused had taken no direct part in the attack, but had stood at the other side of a hedge, watching the attack. He did not speak either to the girl or to his companions during the attack.

The accused Donald objected to the relevancy of the charge against him.

LORD ARDMILLAN: "I noticed the peculiarity in respect of which this objection has been taken when I first read this indictment, and think it has been properly brought under consideration of the Court. I will not attempt to decide the general question which has been adverted to, whether a man is a *particeps criminis* who sees a crime committed and passes by or looks on without doing anything. The answer to that question can not be given in general terms, for it may depend upon a variety of circumstances. Here I think it proper that the charge should go to the Jury in order that all the circumstances may be disclosed in evidence. It may be, that Donald actually encouraged the other prisoners by his language, or by his presence—being in such a position as to indicate readiness to give assistance, not to the girl but to her assailants, if necessary, and thus intimidating the girl. This is quite possible, and is not excluded by the terms of the indictment. It may yet be proved. If nothing of that kind appears in the course of the evidence for the prosecution, that will be for the benefit of the accused, who can raise, with reference to the ascertained facts, the objection which he has now stated on the relevancy."

The indictment having been held relevant, the case went to the jury. In his charge to the jury, Lord Ardmillan gave the following directions with regard to the accused Donald:

LORD ARDMILLAN: "If Donald had been in the field standing close beside the other panels, and during the commission of their offence on the girl, the English authorities quoted would not have deterred me from regarding the present case against Donald as a case to go to the Jury, leaving it to them to decide on the question of participation, for if there was participation the case is a serious one. But it seems to be proved that he was not in the field, but only looking through the hedge; and although this was an improper thing to do, it would, I think, not be safe for you to convict the prisoner Donald on this charge."

Verdict: the jury found the charge against Donald not proven.

NOTES

**5.14**     1. In discussing art and part guilt in homicide Hume discusses the case of a premeditated group assault in which one person strikes the victim:

> "Properly speaking, he is their instrument with which they strike, and they by their presence are consenting, aiding and abetting to him in all he does, having all come hither on purpose to have it done, and being ready to lend their aid, if need shall be. Their presence on the occasion is substantially an assistance. It adds to the terror and the danger of the person attacked, who, in case of an assault by one only, not supported by the attendance of others, might happen successfully to defend himself; as on the other side the invader is heartened in the enterprise, by his knowledge of the force which is at hand to sustain him" (Hume, i, 264).

Hume's comments must, of course, be read in the context of a premeditated assault, where the purpose of the group is to attack and kill the victim. But it is possible to apply similar reasoning in a case where there is no such premeditation, provided that it is the intention of the onlookers to encourage the perpetrator of the offence and that they do in fact encourage the perpetrator. *Cf. R. v. Clarkson and Carroll* [1971] 3 All E.R. 344.

2. There will be circumstances in which mere presence at, or failure to prevent, the commission of an offence by a third party will result in art and part liability. Thus where the onlooker is under a duty to prevent the offence, failure to do so may result in liability. Hume mentions the case of *Thomas Mitchell*, December 15 and 26, 1698 (Hume, 1, 297). There the charge was that Mitchell, being a magistrate, was obliged to assist a messenger who had been taken prisoner by "a rabble" but that he failed on two occasions to do so "under frivolous shifts and pretences". The court held that he could be found art and part liable in the assault upon the messenger. *Cf. Bonar and Hogg v. McLeod*, 1983 S.C.C.R. 161.

**Webster v. Wishart**
1955 S.L.T. 243

**5.15** The appellants stole seven cwts of coal from a distillery and made their escape in a lorry belonging to the second appellant. The lorry was involved in a collision with a car and a motor cycle. Both the appellants were charged with reckless driving, contrary to s.11(1) of the Road

Traffic Act 1930. There was no evidence as to who was driving at the time of the offence. The sheriff convicted them both, and they appealed by stated case to the High Court.

LORD JUSTICE-CLERK (THOMSON): "Counsel for appellants' next point was that ... there was not enough evidence to convict [on the second charge] because one did not really know anything about the situation, who was driving, or who was the passenger, or how these offences came to be committed. The Solicitor-General put before us the broad proposition that where people are engaged in a criminal enterprise and make their escape from the scene of the crime by car all the occupants of the car become liable for such breaches of the Road Traffic Act as the driver commits, and that that doctrine applied even in a case of this kind where it is not known who the actual driver was. The Solicitor-General's proposition is that all the parties who were acting in concert took the risk of the driver's conduct. It seems to me that that is too wide a proposition. I have no doubt at all that there may be cases where a passenger in a car which is being used for criminal purposes may become liable for what the driver does, but before convicting such a passenger one would require to know something about the facts. One would have to apply this doctrine with some knowledge of the particular facts. It does not seem to me that it is a doctrine which one can apply indiscriminately and I am not prepared to apply it here where we do not know which was driving or the circumstances surrounding the commission of the offence."

Appeal allowed.

NOTES

1. Presumably the concert involved in the theft did not extend to the escape from the scene of the crime. But would this be so if, for example, the theft had been an armed robbery necessitating a speedy escape? **5.16**

2. A and B spend the evening drinking together and consume a substantial quantity of alcohol. At the end of the evening A tells B that he is going to drive home. B asks if he can get a lift, and A agrees. B knows how much alcohol A has consumed. A is stopped by the police and his breath alcohol reading is well above the permitted limit. A is subsequently charged with an offence under section 5(1)(a) of the Road Traffic Act 1988. Is B guilty art and part? *Cf. Winnick v. Dick*, 1981 S.L.T. (Sh.Ct.) 101. In that case a group of friends went drinking together. At the end of the evening one of them drove the others home, but on the way lost control of the car, injuring his passengers. He was subsequently convicted of offences arising from his drunk driving.

One of the passengers sued the driver who argued, *inter alia*, that public policy ought to preclude the recovery of damages "where the parties were engaged in a criminal enterprise". In rejecting this argument the sheriff principal observed (at p. 103):

"This was plainly an afterthought, which had not been argued before the sheriff. There being no objection, I allowed counsel for the appellant to add by amendment a new plea-in-law to support this case. I am not, however, prepared to sustain it. In my opinion it is a misuse of language to say that the respondent, because he was being driven by one with excess alcohol in his blood, was engaged in a criminal enterprise. The appellant was convicted of contraventions of ss.3 and 6 (1) of the Road Traffic Act 1972, but the respondent was not charged with acting art and part. There is no finding that he was acting art and part, and I am not prepared to proceed upon the assumption that he was. Even where a car has been used to escape from the scene of a crime (which is far from the facts of this case), a passenger will not lightly be held responsible for road traffic offences committed by the driver (*Webster v. Wishart*, 1955 S.L.T. 243)."

## (c) Joining in an offence already under way

Is it possible to argue that an accused who joins in the commission of an offence thereby adopts what any other offender has done before he becomes a party to the offence? **5.17**

## McLaughlan v. H.M. Advocate
### 1991 S.L.T. 660

**5.18** The appellant was charged along with her husband with assaulting another woman to her severe injury and to the danger of her life. The complainer gave evidence that she was jumped on from behind by the appellant's husband who punched her, knocking her unconscious to the ground. When she regained consciousness she saw the accused's husband holding her arm while the accused was on her left side. Both accused punched and kicked her. A blow to the complainer's head resulted in a fracture to the base of her skull which increased the risk of permanent damage and risk to her life.

In his charge to the jury the sheriff stated, *inter alia*, that "if someone comes on a scene in which ... a group of parties are assaulting another by punching and kicking that person, and elects to join in their support, he becomes responsible for all that has taken place". The accused was convicted of the charge and appealed on the ground of misdirection. The opinion of the Court was delivered by the Lord Justice-Clerk (Ross).

OPINION OF THE COURT: "We entirely agree with counsel that that statement [quoted above] did constitute a misdirection. It might have been a proper direction if the sheriff's closing words had been "He becomes responsible for all that has taken place thereafter." But that is not what the sheriff said. On the contrary the sheriff appears to have been advancing a proposition that if someone joins in where an assault has already been started by someone else, he in some way adopts or homologates what has gone before. If that is what the sheriff meant, and it does indeed appear to be what he was conveying to the jury, such a direction is not in accordance with our law. The learned Solicitor-General, under reference to Hume on Crimes, i, 281, conceded that what the sheriff had said constituted a fundamental misdirection .... The sheriff unfortunately makes the matter worse in his report because when facing up to [this] ground of appeal he remains completely unrepentant. Indeed he seeks to justify what he says in his report by referring to Gordon, Criminal Law (2nd ed.), at p. 146, where there is set out a portion of the charge delivered by Lord Keith in the case of *Gallacher and others* [*H.M. Advocate v. Gallacher and Ors.*, High Court, Glasgow, October 1950, *unreported*, Gordon (3rd Edn) paras 5.34 *et seq.*]. We have read the portion of the charge quoted by the sheriff but we are quite unable to see that it justified the words which the sheriff used in this case.

The effect of this misdirection must next be considered. There is no doubt from what the sheriff tells us in his report that there was ample evidence to entitle the jury to conclude that the second appellant was guilty of assaulting the complainer .... There is no doubt that as a result of this assault the [complainer] suffered serious injuries and the sheriff in his report refers to the evidence given by the neurosurgeon. There is no doubt also from what he says that the life threatening injury was a result of a blow to the head. The difficulty is that because of the misdirection which the sheriff gave, the jury were not required to direct their attention to the question of whether the injury which was life threatening had been caused before or after the ... appellant had joined in the assault. Putting the matter in another way it can be said that having regard to the directions which were given in this case, the Crown are not in a position now to maintain that it was established beyond reasonable doubt that the life threatening injury to the complainer occurred after the appellant had joined in the assault.

For these reasons we are satisfied that the conviction of the ... appellant for assault to severe injury and danger of life cannot stand. We shall accordingly set aside her conviction on charge 2 as libelled, and for that conviction we shall substitute a verdict of guilty of assault to injury."

Appeal allowed; conviction quashed and conviction
for assault to injury substituted therefor.

NOTES

1. This decision is, with respect, the correct one. In the absence of any evidence to suggest that the **5.19** appellant had agreed with her husband to carry out an attack with this degree of violence it must follow that she was not responsible with him for the injuries inflicted before she joined the fray. It is worth comparing this case with the observations of the Court in *Kabalu v. H.M. Advocate*, 1999 S.C.C.R. 348.

In that case the appellant was convicted of murder, along with three co-accused. Following an altercation at a club the deceased was pursued by a group of youths and subjected to a concerted attack by several of them in which they repeatedly kicked and punched him about the head and body and stamped on his head. The medical evidence showed that it was unlikely that any single blow caused death, but the cumulative effect of the blows was to cause substantial diffuse injury to the brain from which death resulted.

The appellant joined in the attack near its end and although there was evidence that he kicked or stamped on the deceased's head, he did not participate in the earlier stages of the attack in which murderous violence was used. There was no direct evidence that the appellant had taken part in the formulation within the club of any plan to attack the deceased, but there was evidence from which the jury could have concluded that the appellant must have known that the youths setting off from the club in pursuit of the deceased were intending to settle what they regarded as a score with him and to assault him. There was a possibility that the accused could have seen the extreme violence as he approached the scene of the attack. It was accepted that the appellant could only be guilty of murder on the basis that he was a party to the earlier stages of the assault on the deceased.

On appeal it was accepted that the jury were entitled to find that the appellant formed part of a concerted plan to attack the deceased, and that he assaulted the deceased by kicking him. However, it was argued that it was not shown that he had witnessed the earlier stages of the attack and therefore the blows which he struck could not be linked to that attack from which death resulted.

The Court held that there was not sufficient evidence to entitle the jury to hold that the appellant had witnessed the extreme violence to which the deceased was subjected and which caused his death before the appellant kicked him. The Court stated (at p. 357E–F):

> "It therefore cannot be affirmed that by kicking the deceased as he did he joined in, and took part in, the earlier concerted attack which was delivered with the extreme violence that caused the deceased's death. It follows that there was in our opinion not sufficient evidence to entitle the jury to convict the appellant of murder."

Does this statement suggest that, contrary to *McLaughlan*, it is possible for an accused to "adopt" what has gone before, and to be held responsible for acting prior to his becoming a party to the common purpose? That it does indeed suggest this is to some extent borne out by those earlier passages in the court's opinion where it considered whether there was sufficient evidence to hold that the appellant had witnessed the attack on the deceased. Those passages plainly suggest that if such evidence had been available, the court might well have held that the accused was a party to the common murderous purpose.

If this is so, then, it is suggested, the approach of the court should be resisted to the extent that it countenances the "adoption" of prior actions by a person not party to them. Even if Kabalu was a party to the original scheme to exact some retribution on the deceased, there was nothing to indicate, at that stage, that Kabalu was a party to a common purpose to inflict murderous violence on the deceased.

What offence did Kabalu commit? Presumably, if he intended to kill, or the violence he used could be regarded as wickedly reckless, then he could be guilty of attempted murder.

## (d) Assistance after the offence

Hume included in his description of art and part guilt the idea of "approving of, or ratifying" the offence **5.20** after its commission. However, subsequent passages in Hume make it clear that he did not consider simple accession after the fact to be a form of art and part guilt. Things done after the commission of an offence could not amount to accession if they were "unconnected with any earlier knowledge of, or concern in the deed" (Hume, i, 282).

It is accepted that there is no guilt by accession after the event in modern Scots law (*Martin v. Hamilton*, 1989 S.L.T. 860) although such participation may suggest complicity at an earlier stage in the commission of the offence (see Hume, i, 281–282). In *Collins v. H.M. Advocate*, 1991 S.C.C.R. 898 a number of accused were charged with murdering a man by shooting him. It was not clear whether two of the accused had shot the deceased before he died, or after death. In his charge to the jury Lord Allanbridge stated, *inter alia* (at p. 903E–F):

> "If you reach a stage where you consider that either or both of Mr Currie or Mr Collins shot a dead body then the legal position is as follows: as the advocate-depute correctly said, shooting a dead man is not a crime, or at least it is not a crime libelled in this indictment. However, it is one of many factors or facts which you may consider occurred after the victim's death. There could be shooting at a dead body. There could be burial of the body. There could be disposal of clothes after the shooting .... However, these are all matters of fact you can take into account in assessing the vital question as to whether or not at the time of death either Mr Currie or Mr Collins was acting art and part or in concert with the actor or actors, with the killer or killers.
>
> Thus, while in Scots law we have no room for the doctrine of what is called in other systems of law accession after the fact, a jury in Scotland can consider anything an accused does after the victim dies to see if such evidence assists them as a jury to determine whether or not that accused was acting in previous concert with the killer or killers at the time of death."

Of course, a person who assists another who has committed an offence may be independently guilty of another offence. A person who helps the murderer to hide the body will not be art and part guilty of the murder merely for doing so. But she or he will be guilty of an attempt to defeat the ends of justice. (See *post*, Chap. 17.) A person who hides stolen goods for the thief will be guilty of reset. (See, *post*, Chap. 14.)

## 4. WITHDRAWAL FROM THE COMMON PURPOSE

### MacNeil v. H.M. Advocate
1986 S.C.C.R. 288

**5.21** The appellant and seven other accused were charged with, *inter alia*, importing, or being concerned in the importation of, a quantity of cannabis, contrary to s.50(3) of the Customs and Excise Management Act 1979 and s.3 of the Misuse of Drugs Act 1971. He had been engaged as engineer on a vessel which sailed from Oban to West Africa. Off the coast of Nigeria, the ship took on a cargo of cannabis, which the appellant subsequently helped to store in one of the ship's fuel tanks. On its way back to Scotland the ship put in at the Spanish port of Law Coruña where the appellant left the ship and, along with another of the accused, travelled back to England where he tried to obtain his wages for the voyage.

His defence to the charges of importing or being concerned in the importation of, the cannabis was that he was unaware that the cargo was cannabis until after it had been loaded, and that as soon as he became aware of this he dissociated himself from the enterprise and urged his fellow seamen to dump it overboard.

The trial judge directed the jury to ask themselves what the appellant's state of mind was at various times, and whether he took part in concealing the cargo or was innocent on the view that he would have nothing to do with its carriage to the United Kingdom. The appellant was convicted and appealed on the ground that the trial judge should have directed the jury that a person who withdraws from a criminal enterprise and seeks to dissuade others at a time when, if his advice is taken, the contemplated crime will not be committed, has the defence of dissociation, and that if the appellant had dissociated himself from the enterprise when he left the vessel he should be acquitted, regardless of the degree of his earlier involvement. The Crown argued that the perpetration of the crime had begun before the appellant left the vessel, and that he could not escape liability for the completed crime by withdrawing when he did.

LORD JUSTICE-GENERAL: "... There is, said counsel, oddly enough, very little authority on the matter but under reference to a short passage in Macdonald, *The Criminal Law of*

*Scotland* (5th edn), p. 5 (dealing with the position of an instigator of a contemplated crime), a similar passage in Gordon, *Criminal Law* (2nd edn), para. 5–24, an English decision, *Antonio Becerra*; *John David Cooper*, and the dictates of common sense and public policy (which must provide an inducement to persons to avoid committing a planned crime and to try to dissuade others from doing so), [he argued that] the law can be taken to be that a person who is an instigator of a contemplated crime or a participator in preparation for it, may successfully dissociate himself from criminal responsibility in the crime, if it is committed by others, if he clearly intimates to them that he is withdrawing, and seeks to discourage them from proceeding with the plan, at a stage when, if his advice were followed, the crime would not be committed. In such circumstances he cannot be guilty of the crime if it is nevertheless committed regardless of the importance of the part he may have played in the preparations for its commission. ...

For the Crown the learned advocate-depute correctly, in our opinion, submitted that there was no such thing as the defence of dissociation. The true question is to be seen in the context of possible concert. This explains the dearth of authority to which counsel for Socratous referred. If a crime is merely in contemplation and preparations for it are being made, a participator who then quits the enterprise cannot be held to act in concert with those who may go on to commit the crime because there will be no evidence that he played any part in its commission. If, on the other hand, the perpetration of a planned crime or offence has begun, a participant cannot escape liability for the completed crime by withdrawing before it has been completed unless, perhaps, he also takes steps to prevent its completion. In this case the perpetration of the offence libelled in charge (1) (import into the United Kingdom) had begun long before the *St Just* reached La Coruña—perhaps even when the vessel sailed from Oban to collect its sinister cargo, but in any event once the cargo had been taken on board in order to import it into the United Kingdom. In these circumstances the appellant was not entitled to any such direction as he sought because Socratous's departure from the enterprise came too late. All that was required were proper directions on concert which were duly given with particular reference to the evidence relating to the part played by Socratous. In any event these directions, which were in fact given, were unduly favourable to the appellant in that they appeared to give to the jury the opportunity to acquit Socratous if they held that he would have nothing to do with the carriage of the cargo to the United Kingdom.

We entirely agree that evidence of 'dissociation' by a participant in the preparation of a crime or offence in contemplation will be highly relevant in any decision as to whether he can be held to be in concert with those who proceed to commit it and that there is no warrant in our law for speaking of a defence of 'dissociation' ... "

Appeal dismissed.

NOTES

The court rejects any notion of a "defence" of dissociation, but does suggest that once the point of **5.22** perpetration had been reached an accused might escape liability for the completed offence if he dissociates himself from its commission and also takes steps to prevent its completion. It is not clear if the court means by this that the accused should have taken effective steps to prevent the completion of the offence, or whether they mean simply that reasonable steps would be demanded.

# 5. RESPONSIBILITY FOR THE CONSEQUENCES

Once it is established that the accused have taken part in the commission of an offence, it is necessary to **5.23** determine the responsibility of each accused for what has happened. The essential question here is what was contemplated by the parties to that common purpose. The issues are best illustrated by some examples:

1. A, B and C set out to murder D. They are all carrying weapons. They all attack D and D dies as a result. All three are responsible for D's death, since it was their common purpose to kill D. The same

result would be achieved even if it could be shown, for example, that death actually result from a blow struck by A. And, similarly, if it transpired that B took no part in the attack, but kept a look out and prevented anyone from coming to D's assistance, A would still be responsible for D's death, along with B and C.

This is the paradigm case. There is a clear common purpose, everyone contributes, and nothing happens which was not agreed to. Much more difficult problems arise where one or more of the parties does something which was not the subject of agreement between them but which might reasonably have been within their contemplation. Consider the following example.

2. A, B and C set out to commit robberies in a city centre park. They agree that if necessary they will use sufficient force to rob their victims, but no weapons will be carried. One of their intended victims, D, refuses to hand over his wallet when told to do so, and begins to struggle with A and B. C picks up a stone and hits D over the head, killing him. Are A and B responsible for the death, or is that the sole responsibility of C?

This is less clear, since the agreement to use sufficient force to overcome the victim might be construed as an agreement to use the degree of force employed by C. But death was certainly not an intended consequence of the common purpose and it can be argued that there was an understanding that weapons would not be used.

3. A and B set out to confront C. Neither are carrying weapons, but on the way to meet C, A picks up an iron bar which he finds lying in the street. B is clearly aware of this. When they encounter C, A hits C on the head with the bar, killing him. Is A alone responsible, or are they both responsible for the death? Suppose (a) that A had said he would use the bar in this way, (b) A said that he would not, and B broke off the attack as soon as the weapon was used, and (c) A said that he would not use the weapon in this way but did, and B persisted in the attack after he became aware of the fact that A was using the bar to assault C.

A is clearly responsible for the use of the weapon. B's responsibility may depend upon whether he foresaw that B might use the iron bar in such a way as to inflict fatal injuries on C. It may also depend on whether B was prepared to "go along" with such use, once it emerged, even though there was no prior understanding to that effect between them.

The cases which follow illustrate the current practice of the courts in such cases. The decisions which have emerged over the last 20 years or so suggest an increasingly sophisticated view of art and part responsibility than formerly, and this is particularly true in the case of homicide resulting from a group attack. While at one time it may have been correct for a court to state that "if any of the accused was part of a crowd engaged in a common purpose of assaulting the deceased, each is responsible for his death, although only one of them may have delivered the fatal blow" (*H.M. Advocate v. Gallacher and Ors*, Glasgow High Court, October 1950; unreported: see Gordon, 3rd ed. para. 5–55), that would today be regarded as an over-simplification.

## Docherty v. H.M. Advocate
### 1945 S.L.T. 247

**5.24** The appellant was convicted of murder while acting with a person unknown. The Court considered two grounds of appeal. The first related to the trial judge's directions on the doctrine of concert, the second to an alleged failure on the part of the judge to direct the jury on what to do if they did find concert established. The facts of the case, the first aspect of the first ground of appeal, and the second ground of appeal, are set out above at pp. 143–145. This excerpt deals with a second aspect of the first ground of appeal, relating to the judge's charge on responsibility for the consequences of action taken in concert.

LORD MONCRIEFF: "But then there is maintained under this reason a further objection to the charge; because it was urged by learned counsel that a particular illustration which the learned judge immediately proceeds to give is one which does not correctly formulate the law, and which therefore gives a misdirection on a point of law which may properly have been thought of critical importance by the jury. The illustration is in the following terms: 'If without premeditation two or three men set on to someone in the street with the intention, just perhaps entered into at the time of causing him injury, and one stabs him fatally, then all are equally guilty although there was not really an intention, until the man came along, to attack him at all.' Now, if one were considering the academic question of whether that illustration correctly formulates a doctrine of law, I think it might be recognised that perhaps the proposition is too widely and too unguardedly framed. I think the proposition should have been stated less universally. It is true that if people acting in concert have reason to expect that a lethal weapon will be used—and their expectation may be demonstrated by various circumstances, as, for example, if they themselves are carrying arms or if they know that arms and lethal weapons are being carried by their associates—they may then under the law with regard to concert each one of them become guilty of murder if the weapon is used with fatal results by one of them. In view of their assumed expectation that it might be used, and of their having joined together in an act of violence apt to be completed by its use, they will be assumed in law to have authorised the use of the fatal weapon, and so to have incurred personal responsibility for using it. If, on the other hand, they had no reason so to expect that any one among them would resort to any such act of violence, the mere fact that they were associated in minor violence will not be conclusive against them; and the lethal act, as being unexpected, will not be ascribed to a joint purpose so as to make others than the principal actor responsible for the act.

This distinction has the support of many authorities. In his Commentaries on the Law of Crimes, at page 270 of the first volume, Baron Hume, after dealing with the question of joint liability for the act of one member of a group of persons using violence, says: 'In all that has been said this limitation is plainly implied, that to affect all concerned, the homicide must be done in pursuance of the common enterprise. For if the killer strike on some accidental and peculiar quarrel of his own, nowise connected with or subservient to the original design; or, though it be in some sort connected with that design, if a resolution of the whole party to accomplish their object by such extreme means cannot reasonably be inferred in the whole circumstances of the case certainly all the reasons fail for which, by the construction of law, the act of one of them may be carried over into the persons of his associates.' In like manner Lord Anderson, in his work on the Criminal Law of Scotland, at page 48, lays down the laws as follows: 'But persons acting together are not always guilty of the acts of one of them. If a sudden brawl arise, *rixa per plures*, sticks and fists being used, and one draws a knife and stabs another, the friends of the man who used the knife are not guilty of murder if the injured man dies.' In this passage Lord Anderson thus gives a concise illustration of the doctrine that secondary responsibility for a criminal act arises only in cases of reasonable expectation. The case of *Welsh* ((1897) 5 S.L.T. 137) affords an excellent illustration of the limitation of the application of the doctrine to cases in which the special act of violence might reasonably be anticipated. In that case two men broke into a house, the old lady of the house was wakened, and one of the men, seizing a crowbar, assaulted her so violently that she died from her injuries. It was suggested that the act of the man who used the crowbar should be regarded, under the doctrine of concert in violence, as being the act also of the man who did not use the crowbar; but Lord Young negatived that view, and told the jury that so unexpected an act as such a violent attack upon one who was so incapable of resistance, need not be within the reasonable expectation of anyone other than the man who himself did the act. Upon consideration of these authorities, if one were dealing with the exact formulation of a proposition in law, it might thus be open to comment whether the illustration put before the jury by the presiding judge was not too broadly and too generally stated; and had this been a case in which the act of violence which caused death had been perpetrated with a weapon which had been concealed by the man who used it and had been suddenly and unexpectedly produced, then I think that the illustration might well have been regarded as misleading. But in this case the weapon which was used was a hatchet which was the property of the appellant and which must have been present visibly in the room; and it seems to me that in these circumstances either of the assailants must have ascribed against him a common expectation that in the stress of the event the other might snatch up anything which was handy and which was adapted to achieve the joint purpose. I am thus enabled to take the view that, while the illustration might have been a misleading one in certain circumstances, it in this case rather acted as a useful guide to the jury, and did not operate as a misdirection. In any event, I regard the giving of the illustration as one which in the circumstances could in no sense have caused a miscarriage of justice; and so, if there should be thought to be any ground for this attack upon the charge, it is one which I think may be disregarded under the provisions of section 2 (1) of the Act of 1926 (16 & 17 Geo. V. cap. 15)."

Appeal allowed, conviction quashed.

NOTES

**5.25**   1. The appellant's conviction was quashed on the ground that the trial judge had failed to direct the jury adequately on the proper course to adopt if they did not find that concert had been proved (see above, pp. 143–145). There was no direct evidence to show who struck the blow and it was therefore essential to the Crown's case against the appellant to establish at least that the appellant was art and part responsible for the death. It was the court's view that the jury should have been directed that if they failed to find concert they were obliged, on the evidence, to return a verdict of acquittal.

2. Compare this case with *Humphries v. H.M. Advocate*, 1994 S.C.C.R. 205. In that case Humphries and another person, Cassidy, were charged with murdering M while acting in concert by stabbing him. Death resulted from a single stab wound. Both accused had knives, but the wound could not have been inflicted by the appellant's knife. There was some evidence that Cassidy had inflicted the fatal wound, but there was also evidence that he had not. The trial judge essentially told the jury that if they found concert the accused stood or fell together. They could convict both accused of murder, or culpable homicide, or acquit both. But they could not acquit one and convict the other. On appeal it was held that this was a misdirection leading to a miscarriage of justice. There was "ample" evidence to distinguish the two accused, and the jury should have been given the option of drawing a distinction between them.

**O'Connell v. H.M. Advocate**
1987 S.C.C.R. 459

**5.26**   LORD JUSTICE-CLERK: "The appellant is Gary O'Connell who along with three co-accused was found guilty of culpable homicide under charge (2) on an indictment under certain deletions which were made on the direction of the presiding judge. He has appealed against his conviction. In opening the appeal Mr Daiches has explained what the background to the matter was. The victim, one George Conlan, and a companion, William McAllister, were apparently in Conlan's house on the evening in question. They were under the influence of drink. At some stage someone unknown threw a brick through the window into the house. This enraged Conlan and his companion McAllister and they went out in search of the perpetrators of the offence of throwing the brick and they armed themselves. McAllister apparently had some form of axe and Conlan had a hammer. Thereafter, at some stage, they pursued the appellant and his three co-accused and then the chase was reversed and the four accused chased McAllister and Conlan. That was the background, it was said, to the assault which is described in charge (2). There was evidence of a medical nature to the effect that Conlan had died as a result of blows on the head from a hammer and Mr Daiches accepted that the evidence was to that effect. This was referred to by the trial judge in his charge to the jury. Mr Daiches, however, maintained that there was insufficient evidence to justify the jury concluding that blows with the hammer had been administered during the assault by the four accused. He pointed out that the source of the hammer was the victim himself, because the hammer which caused the fatal injuries was proved to be the hammer which he had taken from his house when he left to pursue those who he had thought had thrown the brick. Mr Daiches maintained that since that was the source of the hammer, this was not a situation where any of the accused would have had the hammer in his possession for any length of time to the knowledge of his companions. Mr Daiches maintained that the jury would have had to address their minds to the question of whether the use of a hammer in the assault was contemplated. There was evidence that boys in the group had armed themselves with sticks of wood but he maintained that there was insufficient evidence to justify the conclusion that the use of a hammer was contemplated. He stressed that a hammer was a different kind of weapon from a stick of wood.

In our opinion there was evidence from which the jury could infer that the blows with the hammer were delivered during the assault by the appellant and his three co-accused. In his charge the trial judge referred to the evidence of a taxi driver, Mr McNeilly, who was driving his fare near to the locus. When he was some distance away he saw four boys carrying on with sticks, all standing thumping them down, hammering something. As he passed, he said, the boys were moving away and he saw what he described as a boy lying crouched up on his side on the pavement. He said the boys carried the sticks away. There was also evidence from a Mrs McGoldrick, who gave evidence that she had been lying in bed and had been wakened by noises outside. It was accepted that her house was near the locus. She spoke to hearing noises and to hearing somebody say, 'Hit him on the head with a hammer'. In the light of that evidence, together with the evidence of what the appellant himself had said to the police, we are satisfied that there was sufficient evidence to justify the jury in holding that the blows by the hammer had been delivered during the time when the victim was being assaulted by these boys. The appellant, after being cautioned, said, 'I didn't kill him, they all had sticks but I only punched him and kicked him. I didn't kill him'. The evidence is also sufficient to justify the jury in concluding that the four accused took part in a concerted attack upon the deceased with weapons in the form of sticks. As I have just indicated, the appellant himself spoke to the fact that his companions all had sticks and accordingly he must have known that they were armed even if it be correct, as he maintained in his statement, that he merely punched and kicked the victim.

The critical question which arises is as to whether there was concert as regards the use of the hammer. The matter was dealt with by the trial judge at some length. He told the jury that if they took the view that the victim was hit on the head with a hammer during the assault by the four boys, none of them could be found guilty unless they were acting in concert because there was no evidence as to which of the boys actually used the hammer. The trial judge put the issue to the jury in the following terms:

'Let me remind you that the law is if these four boys formed a common plan to assault Conlan with weapons which were capable of causing death or serious injury, or were aware that such weapons were likely to be used in such an assault, then in the course of that assault if someone gets hold of another weapon which is broadly of a similar nature and equally capable of causing death or serious injury, and uses it, all the people involved in that assault would be guilty of what the man who had obtained the other weapon did.'

Subsequently in his charge the trial judge returned to this theme and he said this to the jury:

'[W]here the weapons are of a broadly similar nature and all capable of causing death or serious injury, it is open to you—and I emphasise this—it is open to you to decide whether each or all of the persons involved in the common plan of assaulting with sticks and bricks should have anticipated the use of a weapon of a nature which was broadly similar. That would apply at whatever stage in the assault that weapon was obtained. But let me emphasise, ladies and gentlemen, that whether the use of a hammer was part of a common plan is a matter entirely for you.'

Finally ... the trial judge summarised this critical issue as follows:

'So if all the boys knew or ought to have anticipated that a weapon such as that might be used in an assault on Conlan, it would be open to you to hold that a similar weapon, if you think it is a similar weapon, such as a hammer might be used even if that wasn't anticipated at the time that they were running down the road with their sticks and possibly a brick.'

In our opinion these directions which the trial judge gave to the jury were sound directions. The matter was left to the jury to determine whether on the evidence they were satisfied that the hammer which had caused the fatal blows was similar to the sticks of wood. Mr Daiches argued strongly that a hammer is a different kind of weapon from a stick of wood, but in our opinion it must depend upon the circumstances. The trial judge gave various examples to the jury. If, for example, the sticks with which the group had armed themselves had been light bamboo cane it might well be that one could not regard a hammer as a similar weapon. The sticks of wood here, however, were more substantial than that. The trial judge reminded the jury that Label No. 54 was a length of wood which might be described as a rectangular piece of wood about three or four feet long. If sticks of that kind were involved then, in our opinion, the jury would be well entitled to regard such sticks as lethal weapons capable of causing death or serious injury. The hammer likewise could be categorised as a weapon capable of causing death or serious injury. Whether or not the hammer should be regarded as a similar weapon to the sticks of wood was a question of fact for the jury. The matter was left to the jury to determine. It was entirely a matter for them. The jury were given proper and adequate instructions upon the issue and, in our opinion, there was evidence before the jury sufficient to entitle them to reach the conclusion that the hammer was similar to the other lethal weapons in the form of the sticks. Accordingly, the attack which is made upon this conviction has failed and the appeal against conviction is refused."

Appeal dismissed.

NOTES

**5.27**    1. The appellants appear to have been willing collectively to use dangerous weapons against the victim, with the result that the court was able to leave the question of the similarity of the weapons to the jury. The case would, of course, have been different had the scope of their concerted action not included the use of weapons, or at least not weapons of a lethal nature. Suppose that the accused had collectively assaulted the victim with sticks and hammers and one of them had then stabbed the victim. Would they have been liable collectively? What would the case have been if he had used a gun to shoot the victim?

2. Can the decision in this case be reconciled with the example given by Macdonald, and quoted in *Docherty* (*ante*) to the effect that "If a sudden brawl arise, . . . sticks and fists being used, and one draws a knife and stabs another, the friends of the man who used the knife are not guilty of murder if the injured man dies". That example was accepted by Lord Moncrieff as correctly stating the law. Can it be distinguished from what happened here by reference to the fact that the accused in *O'Connell* prepared themselves by arming themselves for a fight?

3. What would be the position of an accused who initially engages in an attack, without using weapons, but who, on seeing a weapon produced, breaks off his engagement in the attack? In *Mathieson and Another v. H.M. Advocate*, 1996 S.C.C.R. 388 the appellants, Mathieson and Murray, and three other youths, were charged with murder. They had all formed a group which attacked the deceased, knocking him off his bicycle, punching and kicking him. While the assault was under way, one of the other accused, Swan, produced a knife and stabbed the deceased several times. One of the stab wounds proved fatal. Swan was convicted of murder and the appellants of culpable homicide. In his charge the trial judge told the jury that before they could hold the appellants responsible for the death of the victim, they had to be satisfied that there was concert in the use of the knife. That could be established if they had known at the outset that Swan had a knife and that he was likely to use it, but there was insufficient evidence to support that conclusion. He went on to say, however, that if the appellants persisted in the attack after the point at which they knew that a knife had been produced and that it was being used to inflict injury on the deceased they could be convicted of murder or culpable homicide.

The appeal to the High Court on this aspect of the case was concerned with the question whether there was sufficient evidence to support the conclusion that the appellants knew, or must have known, that Swan was using the knife to stab the deceased while they were still engaged in the assault. In holding that there was the High Court accepted as correct the trial judge's charge.

See also *Walker and Raiker v. H.M. Advocate*, 1985 S.C.C.R. 150. In that case the Lord Justice-Clerk (Wheatley) suggested that what was relevant in such a case was whether the accused knows, or should have known, that a weapon was being used by the other party and still persisted in the attack: 1985 S.C.C.R. 150 at p. 156.

### Codona v. H.M. Advocate
### 1996 S.L.T. 1100

The appellant was a party to an assault which resulted in the death of the victim. However, she **5.28** did so only to a minor extent (by kicking the victim on the feet), and only at the beginning of the assault. The other participants went on to use extreme violence, which caused the death. Although she had been present earlier the same evening when the other assailants had assaulted and robbed two men, neither of these earlier assaults had involved the kind of murderous violence displayed in the final assault. The appellant was convicted of murder. The evidence against her relied in part on a statement she made to the police in which she admitted kicking the victim, but on appeal it was held that that statement had been unfairly obtained and should not have been left to the jury. In allowing the appeal the Lord Justice-General (Hope) stated:

"Her appeal against this conviction on the ground that there was a miscarriage of justice has been brought on three grounds. The first is that the trial judge erred in allowing the evidence of an admission which she made to police officers during an interview to be admitted in evidence. ... In the course of the interview which she gave ... the appellant was asked several times whether she had kicked the deceased. She continued to deny this until a later stage in the interview when, in answer to the question, 'Did you kick the man?' she replied, 'Aye, once on the back ae the feet.' In response to further questions she said that she had done this once only at the start of the incident. The Crown case that she was guilty of murder was based on her admission in the course of this part of the interview, together with other information which she gave to the police which indicated that she was present throughout the attack. Corroboration was said to be provided by evidence of spots of blood on her T-shirt, indicating that she was in close proximity to the victim when he was being assaulted.

We should say at once that in our opinion the evidence which was relied upon by the Crown was insufficient to entitle the jury to convict the appellant of murder. Assuming for the moment that her admission was admissible against her in evidence, what it amounted to was an admission that she kicked the deceased once on the back of his feet at the start of the attack. It was put to her, in a passage which we shall quote more fully in a later part of this opinion, that she did this when they were all kicking into him, to which she replied 'Once'. While these admissions were plainly enough, if corroborated, to entitle the jury to convict her of assaulting the deceased and, as she knew what had happened to the other two victims, of acting in concert with the others in an assault in which he was likely to sustain injury, there was no indication in these answers that, when she kicked the victim once at the start, she was participating in an attack which she had reason to think was murderous in character. There was nothing in the nature of the assaults which had been perpetrated on the other two victims to indicate that the deceases was likely to be subject to an attack of such savagery and wicked recklessness as ensued after he was first kicked.

The only other evidence against the appellant, apart from evidence that she was present at the time, came from the spots of blood on her T-shirt. These were small spots mainly on the lower front of it, which were consistent with her being close to the victim when blood was coming from him aerially in the form of a spray. The position of this blood on her T-shirt suggests that this occurred at a stage when the victim was punched on the face and was still on his feet before reaching the ground. There was no evidence that she had blood on the lower part of her body or on her shoes. The evidence of the bloodstains was clearly enough to corroborate her admission that she participated in an assault on the deceased. But in our opinion it did not provide the further circumstantial evidence which was needed in this case, in view of the limited character of her admission, to convict her of murder."

Appeal allowed.

NOTES

**5.29**    1. In *Mathieson* there was no prior understanding that a knife would be used, and the appellants' responsibility for the death of the victim depended upon their having persisted in the attack after they knew that a knife was being used. In this case the victim of the first assault was struck on the head with a bottle, and threatened with a knife. The victim of the second assault was struck with a knife which he had produced in an attempt to defend himself. The third victim was stabbed with the knife taken from the second victim. Everything which preceded the final fatal attack had been witnessed by the appellant. The victim in the final attack was killed by blows with fists and feet to the head and body. What would the situation have been if that victim had died as a result of the use of a bottle and a knife? Would that have affected the responsibility of the appellant?

2. Even if, in such cases, the accused are held responsible for the homicide, it does not follow than they are all equally responsible. It is possible in such cases to distinguish between the accused and found some guilty of murder and others guilty only of culpable homicide.

**Melvin v. H.M. Advocate**
1984 S.L.T. 365

**5.30**    The appellant and another man, McFarlane, were charged with robbery and murder. Both accused attacked an elderly man. There was no evidence of a prior agreement to attack the victim or rob him. There was evidence that the appellant played the major role in the offence. McFarlane was convicted of culpable homicide. The appellant was convicted of murder and robbery. McFarlane did not appeal against his conviction. On appeal, Melvin argued, *inter alia*: "[8] The verdicts returned by the jury against the appellant and the co-accused William McFarlane were inconsistent since the Crown case was based on concert and presented to the jury upon the basis that the fatal blow was struck by the appellant accordingly, *esto* the co-accused McFarlane was held responsible art and part for causing the death of the deceased, the crime of which he was guilty fell to be determined by the nature and quality of the actings of the appellant, and a verdict of guilty of culpable homicide against the co-accused McFarlane excluded a verdict of guilty of murder against the appellant."

LORD CAMERON: "The argument of counsel for the appellant in support of this eighth and final ground of appeal was succinctly presented. The second accused had been charged with assault and murder in concert with the appellant. The appellant had been convicted of murder as libelled, while McFarlane had been convicted art and part with him of culpable homicide. If that verdict was justified, then the verdict returned against the appellant could not stand. The verdict was fatally self-contradictory. Where two parties were convicted of a homicidal assault, acting in concert, it was impossible to convict one of murder and the other of culpable homicide arising out of precisely the same joint criminal enterprise. There was here a fatal and insoluble logical inconsistency. The presiding judge had properly drawn the attention of the jury to the circumstances in which, on a certain view of the evidence as directed against the second accused, it could be open to them to return a verdict of assault and robbery or even of simple assault against him. But if that view of the evidence was rejected by the jury, as plainly it was, then there was no basis on which a verdict of guilty in respect of the assault could be returned against both accused acting in concert, which discriminated as to their measure of guilt. The verdict returned could only be interpreted as one which found the second accused guilty art and part in this particular assault with the appellant. The modus was identical in the case of both, and no deletions were made on the libel in the verdict returned. If the verdict of culpable homicide was one which the jury were entitled to return upon the evidence before them in the case of McFarlane, it was clearly inconsistent and insupportable having regard to the evidence to return a verdict of murder against the appellant. The conviction of murder should therefore be quashed and one of culpable homicide substituted in its place.

For the Crown the learned advocate-depute submitted that there was no substance in this ground of appeal. The evidence of the participation of the appellant in the assault on May was adequate to enable and entitle the jury to conclude that his guilt was of murder. The test to be applied by the jury in considering the quality of the crime had been properly put to the jury by the presiding judge and his direction had not been challenged. The appellant's argument, that if the jury's verdict on the second accused was justified that against the appellant could not be supported, was unsound. It did not assist the appellant merely to point to an alleged inconsistency in the verdict on the second accused, because there was no necessary logical inconsistency between the two verdicts. It was open to the jury to consider the precise degree of participation by each accused in determining whether their conduct in their judgment displayed that degree of utter recklessness (assuming no proved intention to kill) necessary to entitle a jury to return a verdict other than that of culpable homicide. They had done that in this case, and on the unchallenged evidence as to the individual actings of the appellant and McFarlane they were entitled to do so. . . .

In my opinion the argument submitted by Mr Daiches in support of this last and independent ground of appeal fails. In the first place, it is not necessarily to be assumed that the verdict returned in the case of McFarlane is sound, but let that be assumed. The charge against both accused was murder and they were charged acting in concert. Under such a charge, if a jury were satisfied that it was proved that the actions of both accused contributed to the death of the victim, a verdict of homicide against both would be competent. In determining the quality of the crime, *i.e.* as between culpable homicide and murder, a jury would be entitled, in a case where intent to kill was not suggested or established or indeed any antecedent concerted intention to carry out an assault and robbery on the deceased or any other person, to consider and assess the degree of recklessness displayed by each participant and return, if their judgment so required, a discriminating verdict in accordance with their assessment. This is precisely what the jury has done in this case, having been given full and careful directions by the presiding judge. Therefore the fact that on this indictment the jury have discriminated as to the measure of guilt of the two accused does not by itself amount to a 'logical inconsistency' which inevitably so taints the verdict that it cannot stand. In the present appeal it was not denied by Mr Daiches that the evidence before the jury did demonstrate that the participation of the two accused in this crime was far from equal, that there was no previous concert or intention to assault and rob the deceased, that the initial assault on the deceased was by the appellant alone without support or encouragement from McFarlane, and that it was only at a later stage in the episode that McFarlane was proved to have taken part by inflicting a few kicks to the deceased as he was lying in the close. In these circumstances I am of opinion that a verdict as in this case, discriminating as to the quality of the crime where two or more are indicted of murder on the same indictment, is not of itself indicative of such inconsistency as to make that verdict self contradictory and so to be fatal to a conviction of murder of one and of culpable homicide of the other even where, as here, the two persons convicted have been indicted acting in concert. . . .

LORD AVONSIDE: "I wholly agree with your Lordship's reasoning and conclusion in the appeal directed to the merits of the case. The real question of interest and importance was in the submission made by Mr Daiches in support of his last ground of appeal, which does not relate to the merits as such.

His submission can be put very shortly and I hope to do no injustice to him in setting it out in this manner: A and B are charged jointly with murdering C; A is found guilty of murder, B of the lesser and different crime of culpable homicide: it is apparent from the verdicts that both played a part in bringing about the death of C; therefore A can have played no greater a role than B and his offence can only be that of culpable homicide.

In my opinion so to argue displays immediately a logical non sequitur. If one pushes formal logic further it could lead to the result that if B had been convicted of assault only, then A should only have been so found guilty. The fundamental fallacy of the argument lies in the assumption that there could be no distinction between the actings of A and B as these actings were demonstrated in the evidence in the case. In this case there was a very clear distinction and I need not elaborate what has been said by your Lordship.

I am anxious to stress that, in my opinion, the facts of this case were very special. The decision in this appeal must not be thought to encourage or licence in future cases inquiry into minute or unimportant differences between the actings of those who are charged jointly with acts of violence. It is only relevant, at the most, to situations in which there might be demonstrated striking differences of relevant conduct. It does not, in any way, alter the existing rules of law."

Appeal dismissed.

NOTES

**5.31**    1. The parties are distinguished in this case according to the degree of recklessness displayed in their attacks on the victim. What would be the situation in the following case: A and B go to visit C to extort money from him. B has a gun of which A is aware. A thinks that B will only use it to threaten C, but B uses it to shoot C, which he has all along intended to do. Is A art and part guilty of the killing of C? If so, is he guilty of murder or culpable homicide? *Cf. Betts and Ridley* (1930) 22 Cr. App. Rep. 148; *Larkin* [1943] 1 All E.R. 217.

2. In *Malone v. H.M. Advocate*, 1988 S.C.C.R. 498 the Lord Justice-General commented (at p. 508):

> "Where two are charged with murder in concert there is no doubt no logical inconsistency between a verdict of guilty of murder against one and a verdict of guilty of culpable homicide against the other where there is no evidence of any antecedent intention to carry out the crime of assault and robbery. If the evidence permits it a jury are entitled to assess the relative degree of recklessness attributable to each accused (see *Melvin v. H.M. Advocate*). But if a distinction is to be made in a case involving a joint assault causing death it could normally reasonably be justified only if, on the evidence, ... there were striking differences in the relevant conduct of each of the assailants."

**Brown and Another v. H.M. Advocate**
1993 S.C.C.R. 382

**5.32**  The appellants, Brown and a man called Holmes, were convicted of murdering Brown's husband. Brown was separated from her husband and living with Holmes. There was evidence that they had gone to the deceased's house seeking some sort of confrontation with him, although this was disputed by the appellant Brown. There was evidence that both appellants had attacked the deceased. Holmes admitted that he had struck him on the head with an iron bar which he had picked up on the way to the deceased's house. Death was caused by a single stab wound to the heart which, it was accepted, must have been sustained during the course of this attack. There was no evidence as to who struck the fatal blow, and both appellants denied any knowledge of how the fatal injury was inflicted. Both accused implied that it must have been the other who was responsible. There was evidence that Brown had previously threatened her husband.

The trial judge told the jury that because of the nature of the injury this was not a case in which a verdict of culpable homicide could be returned. He also told them that before they could return a verdict of murder against either accused on the basis of concert, they would have to be satisfied that there had been a concerted attack by the two appellants and that, considering the case against each separately, it was proved that the use of murderous weapons was within the foreseeable scope of the joint attack so as to make death or serious injury within the contemplation of each accused.

Both accused were convicted of murder and appealed to the High Court. Both argued that the judge had erred in law in withdrawing the verdict of culpable homicide from the jury. The opinion of the Court was delivered by the Lord Justice-General (Hope).

OPINION OF THE COURT: ... It is clear that it was the nature of the stab wound which persuaded the trial judge that it was not appropriate to leave it to the jury to consider whether this was a case of culpable homicide. He has drawn our attention to the details which are set out in the post-mortem report. It is recorded here that the wound, which was inflicted on the left side of the chest, had completely divided the fourth rib on the left side. Its direction was slightly upwards and medially into the heart, and the total depth from the skin surface to the point of its termination in the left atrium was approximately 11.6 centimetres. It was not unreasonable for the trial judge to describe this wound as the result of someone plunging the knife into the very heart of the deceased. It could not be suggested that this was an accident, and there was no question of provocation or of diminished responsibility. There might, in these circumstances, have been something to be said for the view that the jury were bound to convict of murder had it not been for the fact that more than one person was involved in the attack.

The alternative verdict of culpable homicide is one which should be withdrawn from the jury only with great caution, because the onus is on the Crown to prove its case and all questions as to the weight or quality of the evidence are for the jury and not for the trial judge. The correct approach to the questions raised by the direction as to what constitutes murder should normally be to leave it to the jury to decide whether the necessary degree of wicked recklessness has been established by the Crown. Nevertheless there may be cases where the number or nature of the blows struck or the weapons used are of such a character that there is no room for a verdict of culpable homicide, in the absence of any other basis for that verdict in the evidence . . . .

[His Lordship referred to the cases of *Parr v. H.M. Advocate* 1991 S.L.T. 208, and *Broadley v. H.M. Advocate* 1991 S.L.T. 218, *post*, p. 396, and continued.]

The best that can be said is that the question is ultimately one of fact, and that the trial judge should not take this course unless he is satisfied that there is no basis at all for the verdict in the evidence.

The problem in the present case, however, is that there was only one stab wound and there were two assailants. The force and depth of the stab wound might be said to indicate nothing less than the necessary degree of wicked recklessness in the mind of the person who inflicted it. This no doubt was what the trial judge was thinking about when he said that whoever did that act was guilty of the crime of murder. But what about the other party to the attack? What evidence was there that he or she was acting with the same degree of wicked recklessness, and that in his or her case also murder was, on the evidence, the only possible verdict? The jury had to be satisfied that he or she was aware that a knife was likely to be used in the attack to take the verdict beyond one of assault. But what was there to show, once this point was reached, that he or she anticipated that the knife would be used to inflict a wound of this character? The answers to these questions are to be found later in the charge when the trial judge was dealing with the question of concert. He reminded the jury of the various pieces of evidence which had been relied on by the Crown to implicate each accused. But it is significant that when he was dealing with this matter he told the jury that the question was whether this was a joint attack in which murderous weapons were to be used so as to make death or serious injury within his or her contemplation because these weapons could inflict death or serious injury. He did not tell them that they had to be satisfied that they both had in contemplation, as part of their joint purpose, an act of the necessary degree of wicked recklessness such as that the deceased would be stabbed by plunging a knife into his heart. This was unnecessary on the approach he had taken, since he had removed from them the verdict of culpable homicide. On the other hand, if all that was in contemplation was to use weapons to inflict serious injury, there was room for the view that this was a case of culpable homicide, since the murderous act went beyond the joint purpose and there was no evidence to show which of the two assailants used the knife. The evidence other than that relating to the force and depth of the stab wound was not such as to exclude the possibility that one of the accused had acted with a greater degree of wicked recklessness than was in the reasonable contemplation of the other at the time of the assault. It appears that this point was overlooked by the trial judge when he said that whoever did the stabbing was guilty of the crime of murder. In any event there was here a question of fact which should have been left to the jury to decide.

For these reasons we are in no doubt that the direction which deprived the jury of this opportunity was a misdirection, and that it has resulted in a miscarriage of justice. For these reasons we must allow these appeals, and we shall do so by setting aside the verdict of guilty to murder in each case and substituting therefor an amended verdict of guilty of culpable homicide."

Appeals allowed; verdicts of culpable homicide<br>substituted.

NOTES

**5.33**    1. One of the very curious features of the decision by the appeal court is that it does not discuss any of the authorities on art and part guilt, although the issue was central to the trial judge's directions, and to resolving the difficult question of attributing responsibility to the parties.

Since the parties were clearly engaged in a joint assault which resulted in death, there was no difficulty in holding that they were at least guilty of culpable homicide. The difficulty in convicting either party of murder arose from a combination of factors: (a) There was no evidence as to who struck the fatal blow; (b) there was no evidence of a common purpose to use lethal force before the attack; (c) there was no evidence of a common purpose to use lethal force during the attack.

It might have been possible to convict both of murder if it could have been shown that one of them produced the knife and the other persisted in the attack after the knife was produced (*cf. Mathieson, ante*). But even in that case, since there was only one blow struck with the knife, it would have been difficult to demonstrate that the person not wielding the knife had an opportunity to withdraw from the attack before the fatal blow was struck.

Could it be argued that there was a common purpose to use dangerous weapons, based on the evidence that Holmes had picked up, and used, a substantial iron bar to assault the deceased? The evidence showed that the bar was used to strike the deceased on the head prior to his death. In answer to that it presumably could be argued that (a) there was no evidence that the weapon was used with murderous intent, or that Brown "endorsed" such use of the bar by Holmes even if that was Holmes' intention in using it, and (b) even if there was a common purpose to use the bar, it was not a weapon of the same kind which produced the fatal wound—although that argument would have to be considered in the light of the court's decision in *O'Connell*, above.

2. See Gordon's comments on this case at 1993 S.C.C.R at pp. 392–393. See also the observations of Lord Coulsfield on the correctness of this decision in relation to the law of murder in *Coleman v. H.M. Advocate*, 1999 S.L.T. 1261.

## 6. EXCLUSION OF ART AND PART GUILT

### A. Victims and art and part guilt

**5.34**    Can an accused be guilty art and part of an offence of which he or she is the victim? In *Sutherland v. H.M. Advocate*, 1994 S.L.T. 634 the appellant was charged with setting fire to his own property with intent to defraud insurers, and with the culpable homicide of an accomplice who had helped to set fire to the property and who was killed in the fire. The accused was convicted and appealed, contending, *inter alia*, that the accused could not be guilty where the deceased was acting in concert with the accused in pursuance of the criminal purpose to set fire to the house. The Court held that it was not a defence to the charge for the accused to say that the deceased was participating with him in the common criminal purpose which caused his death since the fact that he was a willing participant was irrelevant. That is hardly surprising, since consent cannot be a defence to a charge of criminal homicide. (See *post*, Chapter 10.) Suppose that A and B enjoy participation in sadomasochistic practices. A encourages B to beat him, for their mutual gratification. B is guilty of assault, because A's consent is disregarded (unless, of course, this is treated as an indecent assault, in which case consent would be relevant: *Smart v. H.M. Advocate*, 1975 S.L.T. 65, *post*, p. 301). Is A guilty art and part in the assault?

In certain circumstances it appears that Parliament may have created offences where the possibility of a willing victim being guilty art and part is excluded. These are offences which have been created to protect members of a particular "class". In such a case, a member of the "class" may not be guilty art and part of an offence committed against him or herself.

### R. v. Tyrrell
### [1894] 1 Q.B. 710

The defendant was convicted of aiding and abetting a man to have unlawful carnal knowledge **5.35** of her, contrary to s.5 of the Criminal Law Amendment Act 1885. The case was reserved for the Court for Crown Cases Reserved, the question for the opinion of the court being, "Whether it is an offence for a girl between the ages of thirteen and sixteen to aid and abet a male person in the commission of the misdemeanor of having unlawful carnal connection with her, or to solicit and incite a male person to commit that misdemeanor."

LORD COLERIDGE C.J.: "The Criminal Law Amendment Act, 1885, was passed for the purpose of protecting women and girls against themselves. At the time it was passed there was a discussion as to what point should be fixed as the age of consent. That discussion ended in a compromise, and the age of consent was fixed at sixteen. With the object of protecting women and girls against themselves the Act of Parliament has made illicit connection with a girl under that age unlawful, if a man wishes to have such illicit connection he must wait until the girl is sixteen, otherwise he breaks the law; but it is impossible to say that the Act, which is absolutely silent about aiding or abetting, or soliciting or inciting, can have intended that the girls for whose protection it was passed should be punishable under it for the offences committed upon themselves. I am of opinion that this conviction ought to be quashed."

MATHEW J.: "I am of the same opinion. I do not see how it would be possible to obtain convictions under the statute if the contention for the Crown were adopted, because nearly every section which deals with offences in respect of women and girls would create an offence in the woman or girl. Such a result cannot have been intended by the legislature. There is no trace in the statute of any intention to treat the woman or girl as criminal."

Conviction quashed.

NOTES

1. *Cf.* Gordon's view (para. 5–05) that: "So far as sexual offences are concerned the law probably is **5.36** that where an offence is created in order to protect a particular class of persons a member of that class cannot be convicted of being art and part in its commission against herself." It is difficult to see why this should be so if the "victim" genuinely encourages the offence. The practical problem alluded to by Mathew J. may be overcome by the discretion not to prosecute where the "victim" is required as a witness.

2. The rule in *Tyrrell* only applies where the member of the protected class is the "victim" of the offence. Where A, a fifteen-year-old girl, provides her fifteen year old friend, B, with a room in which to have sexual intercourse with her (B's) boyfriend and provides them with contraceptives, she may be guilty, art and part, with the boyfriend.

## B. Offences excluding art and part liability

There are some offences in which it is either not possible, or inappropriate, to apply the doctrine of art **5.37** and part guilt. Thus it has been stated that the crime of concealment of pregnancy (see *post*, Chapter 10) cannot be committed art and part. See Hume, 1, 299, Alison, 1, 158 and the case of *Alison Punton* (1841) 2 Swinton 572. But see also the discussion of this point by Gordon (2nd ed.) at para. 27–04. In *H.M. Advocate v. Hamill*, 1998 S.L.T. 164 Lord Marnoch held, in respect of the statutory offence of being concerned in the supply of a controlled drug (Misuse of Drugs Act 1971, s.4(3)(b)),

"[t]he breadth of the statutory charge is such that there is, ... no place for an application of the common law doctrine of concert. If, for example, there was a statutory charge of "being concerned in the robbing of a bank" it would, as I see it, be quite unnecessary to invoke the doctrine of concert in order to implicate or convict the "getaway" driver."

## 7. Art and part in statutory offences

## Criminal Procedure (Scotland) Act 1995, s.293

**5.38** "**293.**—(1) A person may be convicted of, and punished for, a contravention of any enactment, notwithstanding that he was guilty of such contravention as art and part only.

(2) Without prejudice to subsection (1) above or to any express provision in any enactment having the like effect to this subsection, any person who aids, abets, counsels, procures or incites any other person to commit an offence against the provisions of any enactment shall be guilty of an offence and shall be liable on conviction, unless the enactment otherwise requires, to the same punishment as might be imposed on conviction of the first mentioned offence."

NOTES

**5.39**    1. There is no reason in principle why the rules of art and part guilt should not apply to statutory offences in the way that they apply to common law offences. Hume states (ii, 239) that "The charge of art and part is suitable alike to accusations of every sort; to an indictment on a British statute, which creates some new offence, as to one laid at common law, or on any of our old Scottish acts". There were, however, some cases during the nineteenth century which cast doubt upon this issue: *Isabella Murray and Helen Carmichael or Bremner* (1841) 2 Swin. 559, *Colquhoun v. Liddell* (1876) 3 Couper 342, *Stoddart v. Stevenson* (1880) 4 Couper 334. For this reason section 31 of the Criminal Justice (Scotland) Act 1949 provided that a person might be convicted of a statutory offence, notwithstanding that he was only guilty art and part. That provision is now reproduced in section 293(1) of the 1995 Act.

2. The background to section 293(2) is to be found in the Scottish Law Commission's Report on *Art and Part Guilt of Statutory Offences* (Scot. Law Com. No. 93, Cmnd. 9551 (1985)). Certain statutory offences specifically provide for a separate offence of aiding, abetting, counselling or procuring the offences which they create. The Law Commission recommended that there should be a general statutory offence of this kind, which is now contained in section 293(2). So, for example, in a case of vandalism, contrary to section 52 of the Criminal Law (Consolidation) (Scotland) Act 1995, a person who has encouraged the commission of the offence may be charged as art and part guilty of the statutory offence, or guilty of the statutory offence (under section 293(2)) of aiding and abetting the commission of the offence of vandalism, contrary to section 52 of the 1995 Act. Whether this really provides much of an improvement on the law, or any additional "ammunition" for the prosecutor is unclear.

3. One area in which some uncertainty remains is in relation to offences which can only be committed by persons acting in a "special capacity". There is a line of authority dating from *Robertsons v. Caird* (1885) 5 Couper 664 that where a statute created an offence which could only be committed by a person in a special capacity, a person not acting in that capacity could not be guilty art and part of the offence. See, for examples of the operation of this rule, *Phyn v. Kenyon* (1905) 4 Adam 528 and *Graham v. Strathern*, 1927 J.C. 29. The attempt made by section 31 of the Criminal Justice (Scotland) Act 1949 to apply the principles of art and part guilt to statutory offences did not remove this obstacle to conviction. See, for example, *McIntyre v. Gallacher*, 1962 J.C. 20.

More recent authorities, however, suggest either that *Robertsons v. Caird* is to be limited in application, or even that it is wrongly decided. In *Vaughan v. H.M. Advocate*, 1979 S.L.T. 49 a man was convicted of being art and part guilty of incest even though he was not within the prohibited degrees of relationship for that crime. That case suggested that only exceptionally would a statute be so framed as to limit art and part guilt to those who shared the "special capacity". See also *Templeton v. H.M. Advocate*, 1987 S.C.C.R. 693 in which it was stated that the decision in *Robertsons v. Caird* "turned upon the particular provisions of the Debtors (Scotland) Act 1880" and that it was not an authority on the general issue of art and part guilt of statutory offences (see the Lord Justice-Clerk (Ross) at p. 697).

In *Reid v. H.M. Advocate*, 1999 S.L.T. 1275 the appellant, a woman, was charged with two male co-accused with knowingly living on the earnings of prostitution, contrary to section 11(1)(a) of the Criminal Law (Consolidation) (Scotland) Act 1995. That section makes it an offence for "Every male person" to live on the earnings of prostitution, and an objection was taken to the charge on the ground that the offence under section 11(1)(a) could not competently be libelled against her as she was a woman. In support of that contention it was pointed out that section 11(5) of the Criminal Law (Consolidation) (Scotland) Act 1995 made special provision for women who controlled or influenced prostitutes for gain. The sheriff, relying on section 293(1) held the charge competent, and his decision was upheld on appeal. In delivering the opinion of the Court, the Lord Justice-Clerk (Cullen) observed that:

> "Section 293(1) is expressed in general terms and is not stated to be subject to a contrary intention appearing in the terms of any statutory offence."

Notwithstanding the fairly general terms in which the Court expressed itself in *Reid*, Gordon argues (3rd ed. at para. 5.11) that "it must be conceded that Parliament *can* restrict art and part guilt to members of a particular class, or to a particular person, but it is contended that to achieve this result clear and express provisions should be necessary."

# Chapter 6

# INCHOATE OFFENCES

**6.01** A person who conceives of a criminal purpose, but who keeps it to himself, and takes no steps to bring it to fruition, is not guilty of any crime. But once he takes steps to commit the crime he may be guilty of an offence even if the proposed crime is not committed. Depending upon the circumstances he may be guilty of attempting to commit the crime, or, if he seeks to involve others in its commission, he may be guilty of incitement, or conspiracy. Attempting to commit a crime, inciting others to commit a crime or conspiring with others to commit a crime are all "inchoate offences".

It is important to notice that what is "inchoate" or "incomplete" about an inchoate offence is the substantive offence which is the accused's criminal purpose. Suppose for example, that A sets out to murder B. He finds B and stabs him, but B does not die. What is incomplete here is the murder of B. The "inchoate" offence of attempting to kill B is itself complete, at the latest, when A stabs B. (It may be that an attempt is complete at an earlier stage, depending upon the rules which determine what an accused must do in order to "attempt" a crime.)

This chapter considers, in turn, incitement, conspiracy and attempt. It also considers the problem of impossibility in relation to each of these offences. Is it an offence to incite, conspire or attempt to commit an offence which, in the circumstances, it is impossible to carry out?

## 1. INCITEMENT

### Baxter v. H.M. Advocate
1997 S.C.C.R. 437

**6.02** The appellant was charged with inciting a man, I, to murder another man, G. The incitement was alleged to have taken place during a conversation between the appellant and I (which was secretly recorded by I), in which possible methods of killing G were discussed, as well as the fee for carrying this out. The desirability of making the death look like an accident, and of having the killing carried out while the appellant was working offshore, were also discussed, since the appellant thought that if the death looked like murder he would probably be investigated and he appeared to have a motive for killing G. However, there was no agreement on these matters, no direct instruction to kill was given and matters were left on the basis that the appellant would give I a call. The appellant's defence was that there was never any real intention to have G killed, and that the conversation was part of a 'stunt'. G gave evidence of having previously been threatened by the appellant.

In his charge to the jury the trial judge stated (*inter alia*):

"[I]ncitement in the common sense of the word is effectively encouragement and instruction to commit an act. It is not sufficient simply that it be talked about, it's not sufficient that it be expressed as a desire on the part of the person who is allegedly making the incitement, it's not sufficient that in relation to this type of case the incitement should be based simply upon a wish that, in this case, [G] be got rid of; what you have to spell out of the tape contents beyond reasonable doubt is a serious, earnest and pointed attempt by the accused to encourage and instruct a crime and unless you can spell that out of the conduct, if it falls anything short of that, then you must acquit because not crime has been committed.

It matters not that nothing was done, but the fact nothing was done in the sense of the furtherance of the instruction, it bears very much upon how serious and how realistic you think the instruction was, and that again is entirely a matter for you to assess upon the evidence and it is a high test, so unless you are satisfied effectively beyond reasonable doubt that when these two gentlemen parted ... [I] knew that he had received an instruction to kill which was seriously intended, unless you are so satisfied, what he did doesn't matter ... then there is no crime and you will acquit and, of course ... you must be equally satisfied that [the appellant] was serious in the intention that he is alleged to have expressed."

The appellant was convicted, and appealed on the ground that the evidence was not sufficient to entitle the jury to convict.

LORD JUSTICE-GENERAL (RODGER): "Incitement to commit a crime is rarely encountered in our courts except in cases where the incitement has taken effect and the crime has been committed. Somewhat surprisingly we were told that neither side had found any authority on what could be regarded as incitement. There is in fact quite a body of authority on what constitutes incitement in the context of art and part guilt of a completed crime, as a glance at paragraphs 5–22 and 5–23 of Gordon's *Criminal Law* shows. While not everything which is said in the context of art and part guilt can be applied to the situation where the incitement has not been followed by the commission of a crime, the general approach must be the same. For present purposes it is sufficient to note that a person may be guilty of incitement without actually instructing another to commit the crime in question. Hume, who defines the crime narrowly, requires:

"a direct and a special counsel; a persuasion to kill by employment of the topics calculated to work on the particular man, and relative, less or more, to some near occasion of doing the deed, so as to excite *him* to an immediate course of action" (Commentaries, vol. i, p. 279).

Alison speaks of 'counsel or instigation' but adds:

"What will infer advice, instigation, or order, in such cases, must depend on the terms used, the consideration or promise given, and the other circumstances of the case, joined to the relative situation of the parties. Less counsel will implicate a party, who has any authority or control over the person to whom it is addressed, than if addressed to an indifferent person (Principles, p. 57).

Even allowing for any possible difference in emphasis, the protean nature of the concept is captured in Holmes J.A.'s description of an inciter as

"one who reaches and seeks to influence the mind of another to the commission of a crime. The machinations of criminal ingenuity being legion, the approach to the other's mind may take various forms, such as suggestion, proposal, request, exhortation, gesture, argument, persuasion, inducement, goading or the arousal of cupidity. The means employed are of secondary importance; the decisive question in each case is whether the accused reached and sought to influence the mind of the other person towards the commission of a crime" (*S. v. Nkosiyana and Another* 1966 (4) S.A. 655 (A.D.) at pp. 658H–659A, quoted in part in Smith and Hogan, *Criminal Law* (8th edn), p. 273).

The trial judge was clearly correct to stress the importance of the jury being satisfied that the appellant seriously intended [I] to kill [G], but in our view it was not necessary for the jury to find that he specifically instructed him to do so. A person can incite another to commit a crime without actually instructing him to do so. Depending on the circumstances it may be enough if, for example, he encourages or requests him to do so and the offer of a reward for the commission of the crime will obviously be a factor which the jury can take into account when deciding whether the accused person seriously intended the other party to commit the crime."

[Having reviewed the evidence, including the tape-recording, his Lordship continued:]

"The only question for us is whether on all the evidence the jury were entitled to infer that the appellant had incited [I] to kill [G]. In our view they were. The conversation between the appellant and [I] could be viewed by them in the context of the evidence about the appellant's motive and about the threat which he had made to [G]. Especially against that background the jury were entitled to infer that in the conversation the appellant was requesting and encouraging [I] to kill [G]. We should observe, of course, that it was not suggested to the jury at the trial that they should acquit the appellant on the basis that he had not finalised his instructions to [I]—the defence was that this was a stunt and that he had never intended to have [G] killed at all. Be that as it may, the fact that the details of the method and of the payment had not been finalised were simply factors which the jury would have been entitled to consider when deciding whether he seriously intended that [I] should kill [G] and that in this conversation he was inviting him to do so."

                                                                        Appeal refused.

NOTES

**6.03**    1. This is one of the few modern authorities on incitement in Scots law, and the only case in which, outside the context of art and part guilt, the concept of incitement has been discussed. In *H.M. Advocate v. Tannahill and Neilson,* 1943 J.C. 150 Lord Wark stated, in his charge to the jury, that "instigation to a crime may in itself be criminal even although the crime is never committed and never attempted to be committed", but there was no discussion of what constitutes "instigation" for these purposes.

2. It is clear that the inciter must intend that the crime in question be carried out, and the inciter must also intend that it be carried out by the person incited as a result of the incitement. Idle musings by A which are taken up by B ought not to constitute incitement by A, since A has not sought to reach B's mind. Presumably also wishes expressed in anger or exasperation, but which are not seriously intended, would not amount to incitement for the same reason. Was Henry II's alleged outburst against Thomas à Becket ("Who will rid me of this turbulent priest?") incitement to murder?

3. The state of mind of both the inciter (A) and the person incited (B) need to be considered. Clearly, as the case of *Baxter* demonstrates, there can be incitement even though B has no intention of committing the offence provided A believes that B is open to persuasion. A must also be aware of (or, where recklessness is a sufficient *mens rea* for the crime incited, reckless with regard to) all of the circumstances which would make the act incited an offence if carried out by B. So, for example, if A is charged with inciting B to rape a woman, A must know that the woman would not consent, or at least have no honest belief that she would. What would be the position if A incites B to have sexual intercourse with a woman who would in fact consent, although A thinks that she would not?

4. Some difficult questions arise with regard to A's state of mind about B's state of mind. If, for example, A incites B to have sexual intercourse with a non-consenting woman, knowing that B thinks she is consenting, is that incitement to commit rape? If A knows that B would not have the *mens rea* for the offence, then arguably there can be no incitement since an essential element of the offence incited is missing. But see, *R. v. Cogan and Leak* [1976] Q.B. 217 (*ante*, p. 62).

# 2. CONSPIRACY

The idea of conspiracy is not a difficult one to grasp. A criminal conspiracy is simply an agreement **6.04** between two or more persons to engage in conduct which, if carried out by one of them, would be a crime. What makes the Scots law of conspiracy, or at least Scottish conspiracy cases, is the form of indictment commonly used in conspiracy cases. The typical Scottish conspiracy indictment charges the conspirators with conspiring to do X, and in pursuance of that conspiracy doing A, and B and C, etc. This can lead to lengthy and complicated indictments.

Conspiracy charges have frequently been the subject of judicial criticism. In *Macdonald v. H.M. Advocate,* 1988 S.L.T. (Notes) 85, 1987 S.C.C.R. 581 the police arrested and charged the accused with conspiracy to commit robbery. The police then proceeded to question him about various other robberies not mentioned in the charge. He was eventually indicted on charges of robbery and not conspiracy. At the trial objection was taken to the evidence of statements made by the accused after he had been charged, in relation to the robberies for which he was standing trial. The objection was repelled by the trial judge. In upholding the trial judge's decision, Lord Ross commented:

> "In my opinion, the trial judge was fully justified in repelling the objection which was taken on behalf of the appellant to the admissibility of the evidence, and the first ground of appeal is ill founded. No problem would have arisen if the police had not charged the appellant with conspiracy. It is difficult to see why they did charge him with conspiracy although this is not the first occasion when it has appeared that a conspiracy charge has been made unnecessarily. In my experience, complications often arise through the use of conspiracy charges, and difficulties could often be avoided if the Crown and the police refrained from charging conspiracy when the circumstances do not make such a charge necessary. The question of what charges should be made against an accused is, however, a matter for the Crown (and the police) and not for the court."

## A. The general definition of conspiracy

### Sayers and Others v. H.M. Advocate
#### 1981 S.C.C.R. 312

The accused were charged with conspiring to further by criminal means the purpose of the **6.05** Ulster Volunteer Force and to acquire unlawfully firearms, ammunition and explosive substances intending by means thereof to endanger life or cause serious injury to property or to enable other persons by means thereof to endanger life or cause serious injury to property. The indictment then proceeded to libel various acts done in pursuance of the conspiracy. In charging the jury Lord Ross gave the following directions on the meaning of conspiracy.

LORD ROSS: "... The accused are all charged with conspiracy. The question which arises on which I now have to give you directions is what is conspiracy. Ladies and gentlemen, a criminal conspiracy arises if two or more persons agree to render one another assistance in doing an act whether as an end in itself or as a means to an end which would be criminal if done by an individual. Now, judges in the past have often explained conspiracy to juries in the following terms, and I am going to quote this to you because it is perhaps as convenient a way as I can find of explaining to you what conspiring means. Conspiracy when regarded as a crime is the crime of two or more persons to effect any criminal purpose whether as their ultimate aim or only as a means to it, and the crime is complete if there is such agreement even though nothing is done in pursuance of it. The crime consists in the agreement though in most cases overt acts done in pursuance of the combination are available as proof of the fact that they have agreed.

Now, I will just say to you one or two more things about this: firstly, you will appreciate from what I have said that you can have a criminal conspiracy even if nothing is done to further it. Of course, actings often do follow on a plot and in this case, as I pointed out to you, the Crown has libelled that in pursuance of the alleged conspiracy certain of the accused committed a whole series of criminal acts. But remember, you can have a criminal conspiracy even though nothing is done to further it, and that is the first point I have to make. The next point is this:

from the very nature of conspiracy there will seldom be direct evidence available to you of the making of the agreement. As one judge put it, essentially conspiracy means agreeing in stealth and secrecy so one would not perhaps expect to hear eye-witnesses who heard the plot being hatched, and in most cases one must look at the overt acts done and determine from them whether in fact there was a conspiracy. In other words, it will often have to be a matter of inference and the question for the jury will be whether the conspiracy can be inferred from the known facts, and as a jury you will have to consider the evidence and ask yourselves whether on the facts proved it is established beyond reasonable doubt that there was a conspiracy. That is to say, whether it has been established beyond reasonable doubt that two or more of the accused took part, formed a conspiracy as libelled.

Now, when you look at the actings of the accused in order to determine that question, this will include looking at the actings which are said to have been done in pursuance of the alleged conspiracy. In other words, here the charge is firstly that they conspired and, secondly, that in pursuance of the conspiracy they did certain things which are themselves offences against the law. But in determining the first question as to whether or not it is conspiracy it is legitimate to consider all the evidence of the actings of the alleged conspirators including the actings that are said to have been done in pursuance of the conspiracy. Of course, if conspiracy is established you will then have to consider some of that evidence again in order to determine whether the acts libelled as being done by certain of the accused in pursuance of the alleged conspiracy were done. Of course, the evidence of actings said to have been done in pursuance of the conspiracy is not the only evidence upon which you may rely on this issue. You can consider the whole evidence including the general evidence regarding the actings of the accused even though it is not directed specifically to any of the sub-heads said to have been done in pursuance of the conspiracy.

Now, of course, although it is open to you to consider evidence of acts said to have been done in pursuance of the alleged conspiracy you have to look at them from the point of view of seeing whether they enable to conclude that there was an antecedent agreement: that is to say, whether they enable you to determine that before any acts were done that two or more of the accused had conspired together . . . .

Now, the other thing I have to say to as regards this part of the case is this: I have already explained that it is legitimate for you to consider all the evidence of the actings of the alleged conspirators including the actings which are said to have been done in pursuance of the conspiracy. But when you come to consider the case of the various accused you must consider the case against each of the accused separately. Therefore as regards any particular accused you can only have regard to the actings under the latter sub-heads or charges which involve that particular accused. To put it another way: if the evidence relating to a particular sub-head did not implicate or involve a particular accused at all, then you could not have regard to that evidence when you are considering whether that particular accused has been proved to have been involved in the alleged conspiracy: you might think that is really very obvious. On the other hand, if the evidence in relation to a particular sub-head did involve or implicate that particular accused then you could have regard to that evidence when you are considering whether that particular accused has been proved beyond reasonable doubt to have been involved in the alleged conspiracy.

Now, still dealing with the subject of conspiracy the next thing which I have to say to you is this, and it really follows from the definition which I gave you of conspiracy which I gave you a short time ago: it is not essential in the formation of the conspiracy that it should be conceived and planned by all the alleged conspirators together at the same time because one may conceive a plot initially and others may join later, so all the conspirators need not join a conspiracy at the same time or at the same place. All need not meet together at any one time or at any one place. For example, if A and B conspire together and hatch a plot between them, and then A goes off and brings in C and B goes off and brings in D to the plot, all four may then be in one conspiracy, but they may never have all met together at all.

It follows too, as I mentioned, that they alleged conspirators don't require to have been at all the places libelled in the indictment as places where the accused conspired. Just as all conspirators don't have to join at the same time, so all of them don't have to be present at all the places where the alleged conspiracy is said to have taken place . . . .

Now, there is another aspect of conspiracy which I just want to touch on, . . . . In law a man is normally responsible only for his own actions, he is not responsible for the actions of another person, but there may be exceptions to that rule; and sometimes if two or more persons are engaged together in the commission of some criminal purpose or sometimes as conspirators the law may hold each responsible for and guilty of the acts of each other in carrying out the common criminal purpose or in furthering the conspiracy.

However, in the present case the Crown is not asking you to hold one man responsible for the actions of another. As you will see in the charges or sub-heads in this indictment the Crown is not suggesting that each of the alleged conspirators is liable for all the acts alleged to have been done in furtherance of the conspiracy, because in each sub-head certain only of the accused are named. Accordingly in this case there is no question of one accused being held responsible for the actions of another. The Crown in this case is only seeking to hold each accused responsible for his own actions. So you must examine the evidence with that in mind, considering the case against each of the accused separately.

Now, still dealing with conspiracy, ladies and gentlemen, may I mention another point? Even where two or more persons are shown to be engaged upon a conspiracy together it is essential to determine the scope of the conspiracy to which each of them is a party, and the scope need not be the same for every conspirator. For example, on the present indictment if a number of persons are proved to be in the conspiracy they need not necessarily be involved in the whole conspiracy as libelled. Thus one might be involved in all the purposes libelled in the first half of page 1 [of the indictment], that is to say, to further by criminal means the purposes of an association of persons known as the Ulster Volunteer Force, and so on, and to acquire unlawfully firearms, ammunition and explosive substances, with the intention stated; whereas another might be involved, let us say, only in the acquisition of arms but might not be involved in the earlier purpose stated of furthering the purposes of the U.V.F. So you must determine the scope of the conspiracy to which each conspirator acceded, if there was a conspiracy. So you will appreciate the first question really must be—was there a conspiracy; and the second question would be—if there was a conspiracy, what was its scope . . . ."

NOTES

1. Lord Ross's charge is one of the few reported examples of a modern charge in a conspiracy case. **6.06** The general definition of conspiracy has not been considered in detail by the Appeal Court, although in *Maxwell and others v. H.M. Advocate,* 1980 J.C. 40 that court did offer the following general definition of conspiracy:

> "That crime is constituted by an agreement of two or more persons to further or achieve a criminal purpose. A criminal purpose is one which if attempted or achieved by action on the part of an individual would itself constitute a crime by the law of Scotland. It is the criminality of the purpose and not the result which may or may not follow from the execution of the purpose which makes the crime a criminal conspiracy."

Lord Ross's charge broadly follows that of Lord Grant to the jury in the unreported case of *H.M. Advocate v. Wilson, Latta and Rooney,* High Court, February 1968, *unreported,* which is reproduced at pp. 203–206 of the second edition of this book. That charge, in turn, relies in part on statements of the law by Viscount Simon in *Crofter Handwoven Harris Tweed v. Veitch,* 1942 S.C. (H.L.) 1.

3. An accused's participation in a conspiracy can be established without any express agreement on his part. Participation in the conspiracy can be inferred from the accused's conduct. (*Coleman and Others v. H.M. Advocate,* 1999 S.C.C.R. 87). Merely being in the company of others as they enter into a conspiracy, however, will not be sufficient to infer participation in the conspiracy.

In *West v. H.M. Advocate,* 1985 S.C.C.R. 249, the appellant was charged with conspiring with another man to assault and rob people working in certain named premises. The indictment alleged that in furtherance of this conspiracy the men loitered in the vicinity of these premises "for a period exceeding thirty minutes" and that thereafter they entered the premises while in possession of a blade from a pair of scissors, and an open razor, "all with intent to assault said employees with said weapons and rob them of money". The evidence supported the allegations in the indictment. There was evidence that the appellant approached the glass doors to the premises and peered in through the glass. There was also evidence that when the appellant and the other man became aware that they were being observed by the police they walked quickly away from the premises. The jury convicted both men of conspiracy to rob. On appeal it was held that there was sufficient evidence to justify the jury's verdict. Would it have been possible, in these circumstances, to convict the men of attempted robbery?

4. Conspiracy requires an agreement to do something which would be criminal if carried out by a person acting alone. There are early cases which suggest that it may be a criminal conspiracy to agree to commit certain acts which it would not be criminal for a single person to do (confined to cases of workers combining to obtain better wages by going on strike—see Burnett, pp. 237–238 and Hume, i, 494). But the modern view is that it is not a crime to agree to achieve a purpose by means which are not criminal, albeit that such means might be civilly unlawful. (*Cf.* in this respect the English common law crime of conspiracy to defraud which does not require proof of an agreement to commit an act which would be criminal if carried out by a person acting alone: *Scott v. Metropolitan Police Commission* [1974] 3 All E.R. 1032. It may also be the case that the offences of conspiracy to corrupt public morals and conspiracy to outrage public decency may be committed even though the conduct in question would not be a crime if carried out be a single person—although the position here is less clear, since it may be an offence at common law for one person to engage in conduct that corrupts public morals—*Shaw v. DPP* [1962] A.C. 220; *Knuller v. DPP* [1973] A.C. 435, and it probably is a crime at common law for one person to outrage public decency—*Gibson* [1991] 1 All E.R. 439.)

## B. The requirement of more than one party

**6.07** A conspiracy requires an agreement between two or more people. Most of the time this presents few problems. Difficulties may arise, however, where the co-conspirator lacks legal capacity (for example, because he or she is insane or below the age of criminal responsibility) or where the co-conspirator has a defence (for example, because he or she has been coerced into the agreement). Such questions have not been fully discussed by the Scottish courts in the context of conspiracy.

It appears to be accepted that where A uses B to commit an offence A is guilty of the offence even though B lacks criminal capacity, or benefits from a defence personal to B (such as coercion). But it does not necessarily follow that A could be guilty of *conspiring* with B in such cases. Since the question in conspiracy is whether there has been an agreement to commit a criminal act, this would seem to pre-suppose, at least, that the parties to such an agreement are legally capable of committing the criminal act agreed upon. It may, therefore, be that where A agrees with B to commit a crime, there is no conspiracy. The case should, however, be otherwise where B has the capacity but benefits from a defence such as coercion, and in *H.M. Advocate v. Sayers and others* (*supra*) it appears to have been accepted that a person coerced into a conspiracy was nevertheless a party to the conspiracy.

The question also arises as to whether or not it is a defence for A, charged with conspiring with B to commit a crime, that B has been acquitted of that crime, or that B's guilt has not been established. Consider, in this regard, the following case.

### Howitt v. H.M. Advocate; Duffy v. H.M. Advocate
2000 J.C. 284

**6.08** The appellant Duffy was charged with conspiring with another man, Miller, to set fire to a house and murder its occupants and with setting fire to the house, thereby endangering the lives of the occupants. Prior to the appellant's trial Miller had appeared on an indictment libelling the same charges, and the Crown had accepted a plea of guilty to conspiracy to set fire to the house, under deletion of the conspiracy to murder the occupants. At the appellant's trial the Crown led Miller in evidence against the appellant. Miller stated that he had purchased petrol but that he had given it to the appellant to go and burn down the house. Miller denied any intention of going with the appellant to set fire to the house, or that he had been in the company of the appellant after he had bought the petrol. At no time did the Crown allege that the appellant had conspired with anyone else in relation to the matters with which he was charged. The appellant was convicted and appealed. It was argued that since the Crown had accepted Miller's plea of guilty to a charge of conspiring with the appellant to set fire to the house (but no conspiracy to murder) it was now wrong in law, incompetent and oppressive for the Crown to seek the conviction of the appellant in respect of a conspiracy with Miller to murder the occupants of the house. The appeal was heard by a Bench of five judges.

OPINION OF THE COURT (LORD McCLUSKEY): "... In [this] appeal, the principal argument rested upon a statement in the opinion delivered by Lord Justice-Clerk Cooper and concurred in by the other judges in *McAuley* [*McAuley v. H.M. Advocate*, 1946 J.C. 8, 1946 S.L.T. 50]. In that case the appellant was indicted in the sheriff court on a charge which set forth

> 'that having, while acting in concert with James Preston ... and Archibald Ralston ... formed a fraudulent scheme to secure interference with the running of certain greyhounds ... by administering or causing to be administered to them prior to a race in which such greyhounds were listed to race ... drugs which would adversely affect their running ... [did] ... induce Alexander Brownlie ... and Robert Fraser Hughes ... to administer to three of said greyhounds ... a quantity of chlorotone or other drug ... with intent that said three ... greyhounds should be adversely affected in their running ...'.

McAuley was convicted as libelled. However, Preston and Ralston had previously been tried summarily upon a charge of forming and carrying out, in concert with McAuley, the same scheme; and in those proceedings Preston had been acquitted. (The report of the case in 1946 J.C. does not disclose whether Ralston was found guilty in respect of his own actings or on the basis of concert.) In McAuley's appeal against conviction the court did not find it necessary to pronounce upon the main point argued in the appeal, namely that all three men should have been tried together. The court, however, allowed the appeal upon the ground that Preston, one of the alleged *socii*, had been acquitted in the summary proceedings. The Lord Justice-Clerk said [at p. 11]:

> '(Once) that happened it seems to me to be quite unjustifiable for this Court to applaud or countenance the subsequent service of an indictment upon McAuley for having engaged in a fraudulent scheme with a person who after, I must presume, a fair and proper trial was found not guilty of having fraudulently conspired with McAuley in that very scheme.'

In the present appeals, counsel argued that the Lord Justice-Clerk had there stated a rule that was applicable in all such cases, including those now before the court. In each of the present cases the Crown had sought and obtained a conviction that rested upon evidence that the appellant had been guilty on the basis of concert with a *socius* who had been acquitted in earlier proceedings—wholly acquitted in the case of McKay and partly so in the case of Miller. Thus what the Crown had done in each case was to lead evidence as to the involvement and guilt of the *socius* contradictory of the verdict in, or result of, the earlier proceedings. This was something that the Crown could not properly do, in the light of McAuley. The verdict of the jury in the case in which McKay was acquitted was described in the submission of counsel for Howitt as 'a verdict at large'. As to the proceedings against Robert Miller, it was submitted by counsel for Duffy that the Crown, by accepting a restricted plea from Miller, had expressly accepted that he was not guilty of conspiring with Duffy 'to murder the occupants' of the house; it was wholly inconsistent with that acceptance by the Crown of Miller's restricted plea to invite the jury in Duffy's trial to hold that Duffy, had conspired with Miller 'to murder the occupants'. This, it was submitted, was an even stronger case than McAuley because conspiracy 'is constituted by the agreement of two or more persons to further or achieve a criminal purpose', per Lord Cameron in *Maxwell v. H.M. Advocate* 1980 J.C. 40 at p. 43. Accordingly, as the Crown had effectively accepted in the earlier proceedings that Miller had not agreed with Duffy to murder the occupants, they could not in Duffy's trial invite the jury to hold that Duffy, had agreed with Miller to murder the occupants. While it was accepted, as was clear from the opinions in *H.M. Advocate v. O'Neill* 1992 J.C. 22 and the decision in *Elder v. H.M. Advocate* 1995 S.L.T. 579, that the Crown might be justified in certain circumstances in changing their position between two related trials, they could not do so in a way that entirely contradicted either the verdict of the jury in the earlier related proceedings or the terms of a conviction obtained in such proceedings in consequence of the Crown's accepting a restricted plea of guilty. The Crown, it was submitted, could not ignore or seek to contradict the result of the earlier proceedings. For the Crown to proceed in such a way was obnoxious and oppressive and transgressed the overriding principle of fairness; it amounted to 'abhorrent' tactics. Counsel for Duffy submitted that it was clear that, if both he and Miller had appeared on the same indictment, a verdict by the jury in their trial that they were both guilty of conspiracy, on the express basis that Duffy was guilty of the whole conspiracy but that Miller was guilty, only of a lesser conspiracy, would have had to be rejected as self-contradictory. In both appeals counsel submitted that the earlier verdicts were 'binding' and had to be respected by the Crown ....

On the main issue it was submitted that *McAuley* was wrongly decided. In any event, it should not be universally applied. It was noteworthy that the Lord Justice-Clerk in *McAuley* had referred to no authority in support of the proposition upon which the appeal was decided. There was no authority for it. On the contrary, there was now clear authority for convicting one person of an assault committed by a group, including that person, acting in concert, even although the only other identified members of the group had been charged along with that person and acquitted in the same trial: *Capuano v. H.M. Advocate* 1985 S.C.C.R. 414. It was accepted that that case was not exactly in point, as the jury's verdict there could be supported on the basis that the convicted accused was acting in concert with others not named and not identified in the indictment. However, the observations of the Lord Justice-General in giving, at p. 418, a 'typical example', provided strong support for the Crown's position. The example given was of a case in which the Crown indicted four persons as robbers acting in concert, three of them entering the target premises and the fourth, the getaway driver, waiting to drive them from the scene. If the evidence adduced identified only the driver then, as the Lord Justice-General said [at p. 418]:

'(It) cannot seriously or reasonably be maintained, and so far as we are aware there has never been an attempt to maintain, that they would not be entitled to convict the only member of the four-man team whose identification as one of the perpetrators of the crime is not in doubt.'

Reference was also made to *H.M. Advocate v. Fairweather* (1836) 1 Swin. 354 and to *Pollock v. H.M. Advocate*, Criminal Appeal Court, February 1967, *unreported*, referred to in footnote 59 at paragraph 5–18 of Gordon's Criminal Law (2nd ed.). At one point the Lord Advocate advanced the suggestion that it might be open to the Crown to avoid the difficulty presented by *McAuley* by the device of not naming the previously acquitted person as a *socius* in the second indictment. However, he did not persist with this suggestion when it was pointed out that fairness would usually require the Crown to name in the indictment any person with whom the accused was alleged to have acted in concert, if that person's identity was known to the Crown when framing the indictment.

In our opinion, the Crown were entitled to proceed as they did in both of the cases now under consideration. The proposition that underlies the submissions for the appellants appears to us to be that when, in a criminal trial, the jury, applying the ordinary rules as to onus and standard of proof, determines a particular matter on the basis of the evidence presented to it that determination thereby becomes a 'fact' in its own right with validity and evidential value in other proceedings; or the verdict itself is of evidential value in criminal proceedings subsequently brought against persons not indicted in the trial in which the verdict was obtained. That, we consider, is a mistaken view. The result of a trial obviously has a continuing validity for certain purposes even after the jury has been discharged. Clearly a person acquitted by the verdict of the jury cannot be tried again on the same matter. Likewise a conviction following the jury's verdict has consequences that survive the conclusion of all proceedings relating to the trial itself. Thus, for example, a conviction can be libelled as a previous conviction in later criminal proceedings. A conviction may have direct significance in civil proceedings, for example, under the Rehabilitation of Offenders Act 1974, or in connection with defamation proceedings (*cf. Gatley on Libel and Slander* (9th ed.) chapter 7), or for the purposes of section 10 of the Law Reform (Miscellaneous Provisions) (Scotland) Act 1968.

A jury does not, however, make or issue findings in fact that have validity outwith the context of the trial itself. The jury's function is reflected in the oath taken by the jurors to return a true verdict according to the evidence; the verdict is on the charge or charges before the jury, and the evidence is that led during the course of the trial. The jurors, of course, have to resolve disputes on matters of fact as they consider what verdict the jury is to return; but, when their deliberations are complete, juries simply deliver verdicts; they have no competence to make pronouncements or findings of general application about the particular issues of fact on which they have heard evidence and which they may have had to decide before reaching their verdicts. Thus if A faces trial alone, but on an indictment in which he is charged expressly on the basis that he acted in concert with B, then, if he is convicted as libelled, the jury in that trial must have been satisfied on the evidence adduced in that trial that concert has been proved. If, however, B is thereafter brought to trial on a separate indictment containing the same charges *mutatis mutandis*, neither the prosecutor nor the defence can found upon the circumstances that the earlier jury must have held that concert was proved. The fact that the jury in A's trial was satisfied on the evidence before it as to proof of concert is not an evidential fact in B's trial; evidence that the jury in A's trial had decided that issue of fact would not be admissible in B's trial. In short, the character of an accused's involvement in the commission of an alleged crime charged in an indictment on which he goes to trial is a matter to be determined on the basis of the evidence competently adduced in that trial. Although an admission of guilt by a person in one trial might be proved in later proceedings, a finding in one trial as to the character of the involvement of an accused person has no relevance to the determination of the guilt in other proceedings of any person not then on trial on the same indictment.

Indeed, it goes further than that, and for the same reason. For even if A and B go to trial on the same indictment the jury has to consider the case against each accused separately. If they are charged with acting in concert with each other, and with no one else, there may be clear evidence against A consisting of one piece of direct evidence from a single witness that A and B agreed to carry out the joint criminal enterprise, corroborated by A's extra judicial admission of that fact. On such evidence, the jury would be entitled to find A guilty in respect of the whole criminal enterprise, by reason of concert with B. However, A's extra-judicial admission would not be competent evidence against B; so, if B had made no self-incriminating admission and the only evidence available to prove that B had entered into such an agreement with A was that of the same single witness, the case against B would fail for lack of evidence. But that would not be a good reason for the jury (assuming that it accepted all the incriminating evidence competently adduced in respect of A) to depart from the finding— applicable to A only—that A had acted in concert with B. In such a case concert has to be proved individually against each accused on the basis of the evidence that is admissible against him. The failure of the evidence to show that one was involved in the criminal enterprise does not necessarily mean that the other was not. This is what the Lord Justice-General made clear in *Capuano*. Even if the evidence against B was such that he had to be acquitted under section 97(2) of the Criminal Procedure (Scotland) Act 1995, the case against A could still proceed upon the basis that A had acted in concert with B.

Underlying this analysis is the recognition that a 'fact' in a criminal trial is something that is established to the satisfaction of the jury by competent and sufficient evidence adduced, and in relation to a person indicted in that trial. A 'fact' of that character has no existence outside the context of the trial; and the facts established at a trial against one accused may well differ from the facts established against a co-accused in the same proceedings; they commonly do. So there is no necessary contradiction between a jury's finding that there is convincing evidence, applicable to A only, to show that A acted in concert with B and a contemporaneous jury finding that the evidence applicable to B has failed to demonstrate that he acted in concert with A. The same phenomenon is familiar in civil proceedings. Thus, in an action of divorce or separation, if adultery was the ground of action, it formerly had to be proved beyond reasonable doubt and by corroborated evidence. Accordingly the court could find the defender guilty of adultery with the co-defender, but assoilzie the co-defender because there was no evidence sufficient in law to prove that he had committed adultery with the defender: *Creasey v. Creasey*. The Lord President there referred to a passage in Lord Fraser's *Husband and Wife* (vol. ii, pp. 1173–1174):

> 'The confessions of the wife, defender, may warrant the Court in finding that adultery is proved against her, while, not being evidence against the co-defender, he escapes; and thus divorce may be granted against the wife for adultery committed by her with him, while he himself is assoilzied from the action.'

The situation, considered in the example discussed earlier, of a criminal case where the only alleged *socii* are on trial together is distinguishable from that seen in the 'Silks' case—*Young v. H.M. Advocate* 1932 J.C. 63—in which the trial judge directed the jury that there was no evidence of any common fraudulent design involving Young and his co-accused; it followed, as the appeal court made clear, that Young could not be held criminally responsible for those acts (the allotment of shares and the sanctioning of certain payments from company funds) which Young, not being a director of the company concerned, could not personally have carried out.

It was suggested that the Crown was somehow 'barred' by what had happened in the proceedings against the first *socius* from proceeding against the second *socius* in terms that appeared to be at odds with the results of those proceedings; but we were referred to no authority—other than *McAuley*—in support of that submission. This submission appears to reflect a widespread but mistaken view that a person acquitted by the jury's verdict in a criminal trial is thereby declared to be 'innocent' of the charges he has faced at the trial, so that he thereby acquires an unimpeachable certificate of innocence. He does not. An acquittal on a charge in a criminal trial means only that the charge has not been established beyond reasonable doubt; it is not a positive proof that the acquitted person did not commit the crime charged. Proof of guilt is the issue in a criminal trial; innocence is not. The accused, though acquitted, may still be sued in the civil courts: for example, a person acquitted in a criminal trial on a charge of murder can be sued by the victim's relatives for reparation for the wrong done to them by his murdering of the victim.

It was also suggested that it was 'oppressive' for the Crown to proceed against the [appellant], ... on indictments framed as [this was]. In our opinion, however, for the reasons already given, it cannot be said to be oppressive for the Crown to indict the accused with a view to laying before the jury all competent evidence relevant to the accused's participation in the criminal activities libelled.

In our opinion, the ground upon which *McAuley* was decided was unsound and the decision should accordingly be overruled. The submissions for the [appellant] ... based upon the opinion of the Lord Justice-Clerk fall to be rejected.

The other subsidiary arguments presented were entirely dependent upon the submission that McAuley was correctly decided and that therefore the Crown had been guilty of fundamental error or unacceptable conduct in proceeding as they did in the cases of the appellants. They accordingly fall to be rejected along with the main submission."

Appeal refused.

NOTES

1. Although *Duffy* concerned a case of conspiracy, the point raised in this appeal applies to other cases **6.09** where the accused is alleged to have acted in concert with an accused who has been acquitted. This is clear from the case of *Howitt v. H.M. Advocate* which was heard and determined accordingly along with the appeal in *Duffy*.

2. *Duffy*'s case is distinguishable from *McAuley* in that in that case there was at least one other accused who was convicted of conspiring with McAuley, whereas in *Duffy* there was no other alleged conspirator. If the Crown were prepared to accept, when Miller was brought to trial, that Miller did not conspire with Duffy to commit murder, on what basis can they consistently argue, at Duffy's trial, that they had conspired to commit murder? It is, with respect, not really to the point for the court to argue that juries may reach different verdicts in respect of co-accused, or co-conspirators. The point about this case was that the question whether Miller was guilty of conspiracy to murder was not put to a jury: the Crown accepted a plea of guilty, an acceptance which explicitly ruled out one of the parties to the alleged conspiracy. Since there was no other conspirator, the Crown's actions in respect of Miller placed them in the position of saying that D conspired with M to commit murder, but M did not conspire with D to commit murder. So with whom did D conspire? This, it is submitted, is quite different from the situation where the Crown attempt to prove that A and B conspired together, but are only able to prove the guilt of one of them.

3. The approach of the court in this case raises interesting and difficult questions in relation to the presumption of innocence as set out in Article 6(2) of the European Convention on Human Rights. In *Duffy* Miller was called as a witness by the Crown, who suggested that he had conspired with Duffy to commit murder. Is this compatible with Miller's rights under Article 6(2)? It has been held that where the state drops criminal proceedings against a person, without matters reaching the stage of a formal acquittal, it is not incompatible with Article 6(2) for the state, including the courts, to voice continuing suspicions about the accused's guilt. See *Englert v. Germany,* Series A, No. 123, (1991) 13 E.H.R.R. 392, paras 34–41 and *Nölkenbockhoff v. Germany*, Series A No. 123, (1991) 13 E.H.R.R. 360, paras 37–421. However, it has also been stated by the Court that "the general aim of the presumption of innocence . . . is to protect the accused against any judicial decision or other statements by State officials amounting to an assessment of the applicant's guilt without him having previously been proved guilty according to law." (*Ashan Rushiti v. Austria*, judgment of March 23, 2000. See also, *Allenet de Ribemont v. France*, (1996) 22 E.H.R.R. 582, para. 35, and cases there cited).

While clearly this does not mean that the state is not entitled to accuse someone of a crime, it would seem to be inconsistent with this general principle for the Crown to seek to allege that A is guilty of an offence for which they have declined to place him on trial. Even if this is not the case, it would certainly seem to be incompatible with article 6(2) for the Crown to attempt, in a case such as *Duffy*, to demonstrate that the accused has committed an offence along with an accused who has previously been *acquitted* of that offence. In *Ashan Rushiti v. Austria* the Court re-affirmed the rule stated in the case of *Sekanina v. Austria* (1994) 17 E.H.R.R. 221 that, following a final acquittal, even the voicing of suspicions by State officials regarding an accused's innocence is incompatible with the presumption of innocence.

## C. Conspiracy and the "sub-heads"

As indicated above, conspiracy indictments generally allege the agreed purpose of the conspiracy, and **6.10** matters done in pursuance thereof. This can lead to indictments which are complex and difficult to explain to juries. (See, for example, Lord Ross's charge in *Sayers, supra*.) These difficulties are exacerbated by indictments in which not all conspirators are necessarily charged with having done the same acts in pursuance of the conspiracy. Even more difficulties arise from the fact that some of the acts done in pursuance of the conspiracy may be separate crimes, while others may not. So, for example, an indictment alleging a conspiracy to rob may state that the parties A, B and C conspired to carry out a robbery at specified premises. It may go on to say that in pursuance of the conspiracy A stole a car, B equipped himself with a sawn-off shotgun and C purchased three balaclava helmets and a sports hold-all.

The range of verdicts which, it appears, can properly be returned on such indictments is substantial. It is clear, first of all, that the jury could find in respect of each conspirator that they were party to the conspiracy, and that they carried out any sub-headings alleged against them. It appears that this is an acceptable form of verdict even though the sub-head in question was in itself a separate crime. See *H.M. Advocate v. Milnes and others*, High Court, Glasgow, January 1971, *unreported* (but see the second edition of this book at pp. 207–209). This feature of the law has been subjected to frequent criticism, and in *H.M. Advocate v. Al Megrahi and another*, 2000 S.C.C.R. 177 it was argued that it was not competent to libel a charge of conspiracy to murder and murder cumulatively. That argument was, however, rejected by Lord Sutherland (2000 S.C.C.R. 177, at 189, D–F):

> "The next point that was taken by defence counsel was an attack on the general relevancy of charge (1) on the basis that it charged both conspiracy and murder cumulatively and that that is not competent.
>     Reference was made to the cases of *Cordiner v. H.M. Advocate* 1993 S.L.T. 2; *Young v. H.M. Advocate* 1932 J.C. 63; and *H.M. Advocate v. Wilson, Latta and Rooney* Glasgow High Court, February 1968, *unreported*, and in these cases the court had stressed that separate offences should be libelled in separate charges. Reference was also made to Gordon's Criminal Law (2nd edn) at paragraphs 6–55 to 6–59, where he points to the great possibility of confusion when conspiracy charges are combined with substantive charges.
>     The use of conspiracy charges with other substantive charges, being said to have been carried out in pursuance thereof, is now a fairly regular practice; whether it is a desirable practice is another matter, but it is a regular practice, and this is shown by the indictments in a number of terrorist-type cases. It is now recognised that the approach to these is to deal separately with the conspiracy and the various substantive charges by returning verdicts separately on each of these charges. As I have said, the practice may be somewhat regrettable and may cause confusion, certainly to juries, but I am satisfied that it cannot be said to be incompetent."

It was accepted in *H.M. Advocate v. Wilson, Latta and Rooney*, High Court, February 1968, *unreported* (but see the second edition of this book at pp. 203–206) that the jury might acquit an accused on the charge of conspiracy, but convict him or her of any of the sub-heads which were themselves crimes (and which were allegedly carried out in pursuance of the conspiracy).

## D. Conspiracies with a foreign element

**6.11** In general, Scots law adopts a territorial approach to jurisdiction over crime. Unless an offence is committed at least in part in Scotland, the Scottish courts, generally, do not have jurisdiction over the offence. By its nature, conspiracy is susceptible of crossing national boundaries. What is the position where a conspiracy is entered into outside Scotland, to commit criminal acts in Scotland? What if the acts do not take place in Scotland? What is the situation where the conspirators agree to commit acts which would be criminal in Scotland, and which take place in Scotland, although the conspirators did not intend this. And what is the situation where the conspiracy is entered into in Scotland, to commit criminal acts outside Scotland?

### H.M. Advocate v. Al Megrahi and Another
### 2000 S.C.C.R. 177

**6.12** The accused were charged with conspiring to further the purposes of the Libyan Intelligence Service by criminal means and, in particular, by the destruction of a civil passenger aircraft and the murder of its occupants. The formation of this conspiracy, and all of the acts alleged to have been done in pursuance of this conspiracy, were carried out outside Scotland. The indictment did, however, allege that the actions carried out by the accused in pursuance of the conspiracy culminated in a bomb being placed on board an aircraft while it was outside the United Kingdom, which subsequently exploded on board that aircraft near to Lockerbie, as a result of which the passengers and crew were killed, and that the accused did murder them.
    The accused took a plea to the competency of the charge on the ground, *inter alia*, that in the absence of any averment of actings by the accused in Scotland, the Scottish courts had no

jurisdiction to try the charge of conspiracy. The opinion of the High Court at Camp Zeist in the Netherlands, repelling the plea to competency, was delivered by Lord Sutherland:

LORD SUTHERLAND: "At this stage of the preliminary diet a number of objections have been taken to the competency and relevancy of parts of the indictment. I deal first with the submission that charge (1) on the indictment is not a charge which is subject to the jurisdiction of a Scottish court.

The definition of 'conspiracy' is best contained in the speech of Viscount Simon LC in *Crofter Hand Woven Harris Tweed Company v. Veitch* 1942 S.C. (H.L.) 1 [at p. 5]. That definition is that:

> 'Conspiracy, when regarded as a crime, is the agreement of two or more persons to effect any unlawful purpose, whether as their ultimate aim, or only as a means to it, and the crime is complete if there is such agreement, even though nothing is done in pursuance of it.'

I accept, of course, that the crime is complete once agreement has been reached and can be charged as such once agreement has been reached.

Defence counsel submitted that because the conspiracy is complete as soon as agreement is reached, and because in lines [1] to [14] of [charge (1)] of the indictment the only locations which are specified are outwith Scotland, then it must follow that no part of the conspiracy took place in Scotland and, therefore, the Scottish court has no jurisdiction.

In my view, however, just because the crime has been completed when agreement has been reached and can be charged at that stage, it does not follow at all that the crime is necessarily spent.

[His Lordship referred to the cases of *R. v. Doot* [1973] A.C. 807 and *Somchai Liangsiriprasert v. Government of the United States* [1991] 1 A.C. 225, where it was held that the English courts had jurisdiction over conspiracies to commit offences in England even though the conspiracy was entered into outside England, and continued:]

I accept that the situations posited in the cases of *Doot* and *Liangsiriprasert* rely to some extent on the specific target being the country seeking jurisdiction, and it might be argued that a country not a specific target cannot have jurisdiction. If the conspiracy never reached fruition and if there was no overt act to carry on the conspiracy in the country concerned, I appreciate that that would be a formidable objection.

Where, however, a crime of the utmost gravity has been in fact committed in a particular country and it can be shown that that crime is the culmination of a long-drawn-out and complex conspiracy, it appears to me quite illogical to say that that country has no interest in putting the conspirators on trial for their part in what has happened, even though their activities were all carried out abroad. Defence counsel recognise that this is undoubtedly so in relation to the charge of murder in Scotland. I see no logical reason why the same principle should not apply to the charge of conspiring to commit the final criminal act, which is alleged to be the culmination and the whole purpose of the conspiracy. That view, in my opinion, is consistent with what has been said in the cases of *Doot* and *Liangsiriprasert* which, although they deal with the English law of conspiracy, appear to me to be entirely consistent with the law in Scotland.

Counsel submitted, however, that there were certain authorities which should prevent me from coming to this conclusion.

In the case of *H.M. Advocate v. Witherington* (1881) 8 R. (J.) 41 a distinction was made between result crimes and conduct crimes and the implication was that conduct crimes committed abroad would not be justiciable in Scotland because the whole crime was committed abroad. The example given in that case was forgery, and uttering; and I would accept that a person could not be tried in Scotland for the crime of forgery and uttering committed in England. That, however, does not address the question of what would be the position if the forged document was used to commit a fraud in Scotland and the accused was charged with conspiring to defraud and, in pursuance of that conspiracy, forging the document in England. That, in my view, would be justiciable in Scotland and a perfectly permissible extension of the rule. That would also be following the case of *Dumoulin v. H.M. Advocate* 1974 S.L.T. (Notes) 42, where it was said that foreign offences could only be charged if there was a nexus between them and the crime committed in Scotland. That, in my view, would be so even if conspiracy should not be regarded as a continuing crime.

I was also referred to the case of *Maxwell v. H.M. Advocate* 1980 J.C. 40. In that case Lord Cameron said [at p. 43]:

> 'That crime is constituted by the agreement of two or more persons to further or achieve a criminal purpose. A criminal purpose is one which if attempted or achieved by action on the part of an individual would itself constitute a crime by the law of Scotland. It is the criminality of the purpose and not the result which may or may not follow from the execution of the purpose which makes the crime a criminal conspiracy.'

It was suggested that in that passage Lord Cameron was indicating that what one has to look to is the original agreement to commit the crime rather than look to the result to see if the crime has been committed. It should, however, be noted that his Lordship's observations were in the context of a case where the argument was that as the purpose of the conspiracy was one which was impossible of achievement, no offence could have been committed. Accordingly, all that Lord Cameron was pointing out was that a successful conclusion to the conspiracy is not a necessary part of the commission of the offence and that the offence has been committed when the agreement has been entered into. I do not read what Lord Cameron has said as meaning that the result of the conspiracy is something which can simply be ignored.

In the case of *Clements v. H.M. Advocate* 1991 S.C.C.R. 266 the Lord Justice-General, Lord Hope, said, in connection with an offence under section 4(3)(b) of the Misuse of Drugs Act [at p. 274C–D and p. 275C–D]:

> 'On the other hand the nature of the offence which is created by section 4(3)(b) suggests strongly that all those who participated in the chain should be subject to the jurisdiction of the courts of the place in the United Kingdom where the chain comes to an end. For the criminal enterprise with which they were concerned was the whole network or chain of supply, right up to the end of the chain. It is at the end of the chain that the harmful effects will be felt, and the single purpose, with which all those involved were in their own way concerned, was to bring this about . . . .
>
> 'The underlying mischief at which these provisions are directed is the supply or offer to supply of a controlled drug to another, and to look to the place of the mischief as the place where jurisdiction can be established against all those involved would be consistent with the idea that the courts of the place where the harmful acts occur may exercise jurisdiction over those whose acts elsewhere have these consequences.'

Counsel referred to Lord Coulsfield's observations on result and conduct crimes. What his Lordship said was [at p. 277A–C]:

> 'The general rule undoubtedly is that "In the absence of legislation to the contrary, the jurisdiction of the Scottish criminal courts is limited to crimes committed in Scotland" (Gordon, Criminal Law (2nd edn), paragraph 3–39). In the ordinary case, a crime may be held to have been committed in Scotland either if there has been conduct in Scotland which amounts to a crime there or there has been conduct abroad which has had as its result an *actus reus* in Scotland. In considering questions of jurisdiction, therefore, crimes may be classified as "conduct crimes" and "result crimes" although, as has been pointed out, it must not be forgotten that conduct on the part of the accused is an essential

element in both types of crime ... I do not, however, think that it could be said that all offences under section 4(3)(b) of the 1971 Act must be either conduct crimes on the one hand or result crimes on the other. Section 4(3)(b) has a very wide scope and covers many different types of conduct .... According to circumstances, section 4(3)(b) may apply where what is charged is conduct in Scotland or conduct which leads to a result in Scotland, or both. To decide whether the court has jurisdiction to try a particular accused on a charge under section 4(3)(b), therefore, it is necessary, in my view, to consider the precise conduct which is the subject of the charge in the particular case.'

In my opinion this passage does not go so far as to say that on no view could a conduct crime committed abroad ever be justiciable in Scotland. As Lord Coulsfield pointed out [at p. 277C–D]:

'(It) is necessary ... to consider the precise conduct which is the subject of the charge in the particular case.'

I do not therefore consider that anything said by the Scottish authorities to which I have referred detracts from the general principles relating to jurisdiction in conspiracy which are set out in the speeches in the cases of *Doot* and *Liangsiriprasert*, and I am satisfied that on the basis of what is set out in charge (1) of this indictment the Scottish courts do have jurisdiction in this matter."

Plea to competency repelled.

NOTE

As Lord Sutherland notes, this case is somewhat different from cases such as *Doot* and **6.13** *Liangsiriprasert* in that in those cases the "target" of the conspirators was the country seeking to assert jurisdiction. It was not averred in *H.M. Advocate v. Al Megrahi and Another* that the conspirators intended to commit any offence in Scotland. Nevertheless, there is little objection in terms of international law to a state asserting jurisdiction over extraterritorial offences which take effect on their territory. Lord Sutherland's opinion appears to accept that a conspiracy to commit criminal acts in Scotland would be triable in Scotland even though no acts in furtherance of the conspiracy have taken place in Scotland. The much more difficult question arises where the state is not able to show that the offence took effect on its territory or at least (as in *Liangsiriprasert*) that it was intended to do so.

There can be little doubt that many states would have been in a position to exercise jurisdiction in respect of the murder of the passengers and crew of the aircraft, given the terms of articles 1 and 5 of the *Convention for the Suppression of Unlawful Acts against the Safety of Civil Aviation* (1971) (the "Montreal Convention"). However, a great many states would not have been able to assert jurisdiction in respect of a conspiracy to murder, since many states do not have a general offence of conspiracy to commit another offence.

## 3. ATTEMPTS

Section 294 of the Criminal Procedure (Scotland) Act 1995 provides: "(1) Attempt to commit any **6.14** indictable crime is itself an indictable crime. (2) Attempt to commit any offence punishable on complaint shall itself be an offence punishable on complaint." Section 294 does not, however, offer any definition of what constitutes an attempt. That is left to the common law.

### A. The *actus reus* of attempted crime

The question here is: What does a person have to do before it can be said that he or she has attempted to **6.15** commit an offence? Clearly some external act is required, and that act must be linked in some way to the commission of the full offence (subject to what is said below about the problem of impossibility). But in what way must it be linked? Scots law adopts what has generally been described as a "stage" approach. According to this view, an individual commits an attempt once he or she has reached a certain "stage" or point on a linear progression from conceiving the idea to committing the full offence. The test currently favoured is whether the accused has moved beyond the stage of preparation to the stage of perpetration.

## (a) Moving from preparation to perpetration

### H.M. Advocate v. Camerons
#### 1911 S.C. (J.) 110

**6.16** Two persons, husband and wife, formed a scheme to defraud insurance underwriters by insuring a necklace, staging a fake robbery, and claiming the insurance money by pretending to the underwriters that the necklace had been stolen. They were charged with attempting to defraud the underwriters of the sum of £6500. At the trial, however, the Crown failed to prove that a claim had actually been made. In charging the jury the Lord Justice-General gave the following directions on attempt:

LORD JUSTICE-GENERAL (DUNEDIN): "You must take it that it is a blunder; but it is a bad blunder, because you are bound to take it from me that it is not proved that any claim was made against the underwriters by Mrs Cameron. It is not only that no formal claim has been made but no claim has been made. As I tell you, I foresaw this some time ago—as it happened really, I think, on the first day of the trial—and it gave me very great anxiety, because it certainly was a question whether it did not ruin the case altogether. I not only considered the matter very carefully myself, but I did what I have a perfect right to do, I consulted with several of my brethren on the matter, and therefore what I am now to lay down to you is very carefully considered law, and at any rate, as you know, you are bound to take the law from me. I am bound to say that although I have nothing to complain of—I have already said what I thought of counsel's speeches—I cannot say that the law here was correctly stated by either of the learned counsel who addressed you. Mr Morison said that there was no crime at all unless a claim had been put forward, and Mr Clyde said that four things had to be proved before you could make a conviction, and the fourth was the making of the claim. Now, I cannot lay down either of those propositions as correct law. The thing that is charged here is an attempt, it is not success. The underwriters have not been defrauded, because they have not paid a penny. Fraud and an attempt to commit a fraud are both crimes according to the law of Scotland. Now, I am going to read to you first the words of a writer who wrote more than a hundred years ago, and who is still one of the greatest authorities on the criminal law in Scotland, *viz.*, Baron Hume. What he said is this: 'I have now said enough concerning the nature of that inordinate and vicious will which is essential to the guilt of every crime. But the vicious will is not sufficient, unless it is coupled to a wrongful act. And here the question arises, How far must the culprit have proceeded in the prosecution of his wicked purpose to make him answerable in the tribunals of this world? This may on many occasions be a difficult inquiry.' Then he goes on thus, after giving some illustrations of where a person trying to do one thing did something less, I mean trying to murder and only wounding: 'Even when no harm ensues on the attempt, still the law rightly takes cognisance of it . . . if there has been an inchoate act of *execution* of the meditated deed.' After going through many cases, and in particular the case of *Maciver and Macallum* for boring holes in a ship's bottom and drawing the plugs to sink the vessel and cheat the insurers, he goes on: 'Between these extremes there lie a great variety of ambiguous cases with respect to which it is very difficult to say where preparation ends and perpetration begins.' Now, that is really the root of the whole matter; it is to discover where preparation ends and where perpetration begins. In other words, it is a question of degree, and when it is a question of degree it is a jury question, a question for you.

Applying these observations to the matter in hand, mere conception of a fraudulent scheme is not enough; that fraudulent scheme, in order to be criminal, must be carried into some effect by overt act; but if it has begun to be carried into effect by overt act it need not come to final fruition. The mere conceiving of the scheme—if you think a scheme was conceived—is not enough; but if that scheme is so far carried out as that a false insurance is taken, and that a false robbery is gone through, very little more will do. At the same time you must remember that the actual claim has not been made. I give an illustration to show you how particular this is. Supposing that after getting that letter from Price & Gibbs saying that they wanted a formal claim, Dundas & Wilson had gone down to the parties and said, 'We want a formal claim ' and they said, 'No, we have changed our minds, and we give it up; we are not to claim at all'—do you think there would have been much chance of convicting them? Well, of course, they are not in that happy position, but, through the omission of the Crown to prove any claim, they are in the same position, as you must just take it, as if they had been arrested after they had made the communications to which I am now going to refer. Now, the communications which are libelled other than those which you must read out as not proved—you must read out the Dundas & Wilson letters—are, first of all, an intimation to Mr Munt by telegram on the night of the occurrence, 'Regret to report pearl necklace snatched off wife's neck in street 6.15 p.m. tonight local police informed immediately. Will you set your own detectives to work?' And then that is followed by a confirming letter: 'In confirmation of my wire of tonight I greatly regret to report that my wife's pearls were snatched from her today in the circumstances explained in the enclosed statements.' Then the two statements are enclosed in that letter. They do not say anything about asking for money, but they given an account of the robbery in the street. I do not read them again, because they have been read before. Then there is a letter of February 14, which is after Mr Leach had been down. 'Mr dear Mr Munt,—We are disappointed at the result of your man's visit. He only stayed one day and seemed even sceptical because the thing seemed so wonderful. My solicitors here, Dundas & Wilson, who keep the policy up to the mark and take charge of my papers, would very much like a copy of the policy just for form. May I have one please?' And he gets the copy of the policy. The last letter is the one in which he says that Mr Munt is quite right in his story, and then he says, 'We will not be able to show our hand more or less, and, if necessary, declare war.' Well, now, you are entitled to take all those communications into consideration, and you are entitled to consider what is the true meaning of them. You do not as a rule write to an insurance broker to say that there has been a theft except with a view to following it up by making a claim. Mr Munt is not the actual representative of the underwriters, as counsel were quite right in saying, but still there you are, and that is how the matter rests. Assuming that you find that there is a conspiracy at all, you have to consider whether what was done had got beyond the stage of preparation into the stage of perpetration."

Verdict: both accused were found guilty.

## NOTES

1. The Court states that the question is "to discover where preparation ends and perpetration begins". **6.17** Despite its apparent simplicity, this approach is problematic. Quite apart from the problem of determining when that point is reached (as to which, see Gordon (3rd ed.), para. 6–19 *et seq* and the cases which follow), it is not always clear that determining that point will lead to the conclusion that A has attempted an offence.

Suppose, for example, that A is observed trying the door handles on various cars parked in a car park. Eventually he gets into one and at that point he is challenged. Can it be said that he has attempted to steal the car? What if he says that he was looking for something to steal from the car? And what if his answer when challenged is that he was simply looking for a place to sleep? (See *Guthrie v. Friel*, 1993 S.L.T. 899)

2. English law applies a very similar test of attempt. Section 1(1) of the Criminal Attempts Act 1981 provides that the stage of attempt is reached if the accused "does an act which is more than merely preparatory to the commission of the offence".

3. For further examples of cases applying the "preparation to perpetration" test see *Guthrie v. Friel*, *supra*; *Barrett v. Allan*, 1987 S.C.C.R. 479; *Burns v. Allan*, 1987 S.C.C.R. 449. This is not, however, the

only test that has from time to time been applied by the Scottish Courts. Different approaches have been adopted, sometimes as the sole test and sometimes in conjunction with, the preparation to perpetration test. The following cases are illustrative of the different approaches adopted.

## (b) The last act required of the accused for completion of the crime

**6.18** In some cases the court has held that the accused has committed an attempt once he or she has carried out the last act that is required by the accused in order to complete the commission of the offence. The fact that something happens thereafter to prevent the offence is neither here nor there. The advantage of this test is that, in some cases, that point may be more easily identified than the point at which one moves from preparation to perpetration. The disadvantage is that it may not allow a sufficiently early intervention in the development of a criminal scheme.

### Samuel Tumbleson
### (1863) 4 Irv. 426

**6.19** The accused was charged with attempting to murder his wife by giving a quantity of poisoned oatmeal to an innocent third party to give to his wife. Objections were taken to the relevancy of the indictment, on the ground, *inter alia*, that there was no averment that the poisoned food had reached, or been taken by the intended victim, or, at least, that it had been placed, by some overt act, beyond the control of the accused.

LORD NEAVES: "With regard to the second objection, it is true that the mere resolution to commit a crime is not indictable. It requires, of course, to be expressed in some overt act, more or less proximate, before the law can take cognizance of it; but when, as in the present case, machinery is put in motion, which, by its own nature, is calculated to terminate in murder—when this agency is let out of the party's hands to work its natural results—that is a stage of the operation by which he shows that he has completely developed in his own mind a murderous purpose, and has done all that in him lay to accomplish it."

LORD DEAS: "As regards the major proposition, which in substance charges an attempt to administer poison with the intent of committing murder, or with the intent of committing great bodily injury, I have no doubt at all, any more than your Lordship, that the attempt to administer poison with either of these views is a crime according to the law of Scotland. It has always, I think, been so held, and it is common sense that it should be so. So much for the major proposition. But the more important question relates to the minor proposition, namely, whether, assuming that such an attempt as I have mentioned is a crime in law, the facts set forth in the minor amount to that offence? Now, the facts stated just come to this—that the panel mixed in a quantity of oatmeal this strychnia or other deadly poison, and that he gave it to the woman (Mrs Tumbleson) named in the indictment, directing and instructing her to give it (that is to say, the meal containing the poison) to his wife, 'in order that it might be partaken of by her as an article of food'. Now I can have no doubt that if the wife had partaken of the oatmeal and died, the panel would have been guilty of murder. I recollect a case from Dundee conducted by myself as Advocate-Depute, in which the circumstances were very analogous. There the man (Leith I think was his name) was indicted in the High Court for the murder of his wife by means of poison. The mode of administration libelled was the mixing the poison with a quantity of oatmeal, and leaving the oatmeal in a place where he expected his wife would find it and use it, which she did, and consequently died. The panel was convicted and executed. Here, as there, the panel, if what be said is true, had done his part. He had mixed the poison with the meal, and given it to a third party, to be handed to his wife, intending and expecting that she would partake of it as food. If the woman to whom the panel gave the meal had done what he intended her to do, and his wife had used the meal, his alleged purpose would have been accomplished, and it was not owing to him, so far as we can see, that these results did not follow. Now, it would be a sad state of the law, if, after a man has done all which it lies with him to do to poison his wife or anybody else, and put the result beyond his own power, but through some providential cause over which he had no control, the result intended does not follow, it should be held that the law cannot take cognizance of what has been done with a view to punishment, but must allow him to repeat the attempt with impunity as often as he pleases, until he ultimately succeeds. I cannot hold this to be the law of this country."

Objection to relevancy repelled.

NOTE

This case and that of *H.M. Advocate v. Mackenzies, infra*, suggest that the completion of the attempt is **6.20** reached quite late. Lord Macdonald in *Mackenzies* talks of the situation where the forger has so put the forged document out of his possession "that there is no longer any *locus poenitentiae*", and in *Tumbleson* Lord Deas refers to the situation where the accused has "done all which it lies with him to do . . . and put the result beyond his own power". What this suggests is that the stage of attempt is not reached until matters are beyond redemption by the act of the accused. If this is correct then, as Gordon points out (para. 6–34), it may be objected that such an approach: "allows too many prospective criminals to escape punishment, and allows even those it does punish to advance very far in their criminal purpose before it can intervene to punish them for attempting to commit a crime."

What, according to the views expressed in these cases, would be the result in the following situation? A puts poison in a cup of coffee which he gives to B. Just as B is about to drink it A repents and knocks the cup out of B's hand. Is A guilty of attempting to poison B? In the following case (*Baxter*) the court uses the expression "there was plenty of room for going back on what was done". Does this help to clarify matters in any way? Suppose that there was plenty of room for going back on what was done, but not in the sense of effectively stopping what has been put in motion?

## (c) *The opportunity for effective repentance*

The following cases suggest that there is no attempt, even where the accused is well advanced in the **6.21** commission of the offence, while there is still an opportunity for the accused to repent and stop the commission of the full offence. This test must be regarded as unsatisfactory since it leads to the conclusion that the would-be murderer who, having stabbed his victim, repents and rushes his still breathing victim to the hospital in time to save her life is not guilty of attempted murder.

**H.M. Advocate v. Baxter**
(1908) 16 S.L.T. 475

In order to procure an abortion for a pregnant woman, the accused obtained a quantity of **6.22** drugs, which he sent to a third party with instructions on how they were to be administered in order to bring about an abortion. He was charged with attempting to procure an abortion. An objection was taken to the relevancy of the indictment.

LORD JUSTICE-CLERK (MACDONALD): "This is a very peculiar case, but I have no difficulty in holding that the indictment is irrelevant. It appears on the face of it to be a charge of an attempt to commit a crime. The attempt consisted solely in supplying a person with a drug which, if used in a certain way, would be likely to cause a pregnant woman to abort. It is not said the drug ever reached the person to whom it was sent; indeed, we are told at the bar that it never did reach him, and I should have gathered that from the indictment without being told it. The indictment is based on this, that one person sent to another person something which, if used in the way directed, would be likely to cause abortion. No one can doubt that is a reprehensible act, and if Parliament were to make such a thing illegal by statute, probably no one would be found to express disapproval of the enactment. But the sole question we are now dealing with is whether at common law this constitutes an attempt to commit a crime. There are many crimes for which preparation is necessary; but mere preparation is not enough to constitute attempt. Suppose a man is employed by housebreakers to make instruments for the purpose of housebreaking. It is not a crime at common law to make a jemmy or a brace or any other housebreaking tool, or to sell it to a man who is going to commit housebreaking. But it is said by the Advocate-Depute that if the man knows that the tools are to be used for the purpose of breaking into a house, and hands them to the housebreaker for that purpose, then he renders himself liable to a charge of attempt. That can be tested in this way. If it were so, the attempt to commit housebreaking could only be at the place the housebreaker told the man that the tools were to be used, and nowhere else. Now, no burglar could be charged with housebreaking because the police found him going along the street to the house he intended to break into, and were able to prove that it was his intention to break into the house. Supposing he had gone to the house and peeped through the keyhole, and then, because he had seen a watchman, went away again. Could it be said he had made an attempt at housebreaking? I do not think it could. And if the burglar went to another house and broke into it with the tools, the man who made the tools could certainly not be charged with attempt to break into that house, because they were not made for that purpose. There must be some direct act applied at the place where it could be said the manufacturer of the tools intended them to be used, before he could be charged with attempt as art and part. The moment the instrument has been used on the house for which it was intended, then that moment you have something on which a jury can say whether the two men were engaged in attempting to break into it. Up to the time when something is done there is no attempt, because there is nothing except the burglar with his tools being in the particular locality.

Unless it is said that an attempt is made at the time of serving out the drug or other article for use to commit the crime to some man who may thereafter commit it, I do not see how what is not a crime can become one by anything which subsequently happens, except where conspiracy can be charged and proved to do the particular deed. And I am unable to see how it can be said that there was an attempt to commit crime. There was plenty of room for going back on what was done. The sender of the drugs might immediately afterwards have sent a letter to the man to whom they were sent forbidding him to use them for the purpose for which he sent them, and saying that, if he did not get an undertaking at once that they would not be so used, he would himself inform the police of the matter. It is quite plain that, if he had done that, it could not be said that an attempt to commit the crime had been made. If that is so, it is equally plain that it cannot be said an attempt was made if nothing took place. The fact that he did not or did express repentance could not make what was done a crime or not a crime.

Cases have been referred to where a person, being himself a principal in the act, did something which if followed out was such as could be dealt with as a completed crime. It is sufficient to say that these cases seem to me to have no bearing on the present question. A man who has done something by way of overt act with the purpose of committing a crime, but does not complete it, is punishable for attempt to commit the crime. Examples were cited of putting poison in a teapot or sending explosives addressed to a person in such a way that they would go off when the packet was opened. But these were acts done by a person who is in course of committing the full crime, and the person attempting had by overt act directly taken steps, not merely to prepare for the perpetration of a crime, but to put his machinations into practical action. It could not be said that he made an attempt to commit the crime of murder by buying the poison or the explosives unless he followed that up by making use of what he had bought, so as to be in the act of perpetrating the crime, which, failing to effect it, reduced the case to an attempt only.

The Advocate-Depute was in a difficulty about the different cases of an accessory and a principal But this is not a case of an accessory, but entirely one of a principal, and being so, I cannot say that it can be said on the facts stated in the indictment that he made an attempt to commit the crime of abortion when he supplied a person with materials for that purpose and nothing further took place. It might be well if such an act was made criminal by the legislature although no actual attempt was made. But it certainly does not constitute an attempt at common law."

Objection to relevancy sustained.

NOTES

1. Lord Macdonald poses the following question: Suppose that a burglar goes to a house, intended to **6.23** break in and peeps through the keyhole. Because he sees a watchman he goes away. Can he be guilty of attempted housebreaking? His Lordship thought not. Compare this with *Burns v. Allan*, 1987 S.C.C.R. 449. Burns was charged, along with a co-accused, with attempted housebreaking. The accused had gone to the premises they intended to break into, and had disconnected a burglar alarm. This set off an alarm at a police station, and the police arrived at the locus within one minute, to find Burns at the far end of the lane adjacent to the premises in question. Referring to Macdonald, *Criminal Law of Scotland* (5th ed.), p. 50, it was held that for there to be an offence of housebreaking there must be a "violation of the security of the building", and that disconnecting the fire alarm was plainly an attempt to overcome the security of the building. *Cf.* also *H.M. Advocate v. Innes* (1915) 1 S.L.T. 105.

2. Were the accused in *Camerons* above any nearer to the completion of their criminal scheme than the accused was in this case?

### H.M. Advocate v. Mackenzies
#### 1913 S.C.(J.) 107

A husband and wife were charged on an indictment which, *inter alia*, charged the husband **6.24** with making copies of certain secret recipes which he had taken from his employers, in breach of his contractual obligations to his employers, "with intent to dispose of said copies for valuable consideration to trade rivals". An objection was taken to the relevancy of this charge.

LORD JUSTICE-CLERK (MACDONALD): I am quite unable to hold that this is a relevant charge of crime, either completed crime or attempted crime. It is a charge covering a preparation for crime only—assuming that the completed act or actual attempt would infer crime—but it is not a charge of anything done that can be called an overt act. The law does not strike at preparation to commit a crime unless by special statutory enactment such preparation is placed in the category of crime. The analogy which comes nearest to the present case is that of forgery. No successful prosecution can take place so as to secure punishment for the preparation of a forgery. The overt act of uttering is essential to a conviction. The forger is not amenable to the law because he had made a forgery or has a forgery in his possession, whatever may be his intent to make use of it to effect a felonious end. Thus in the indictments, although forgery and uttering were charged, there could be no conviction of the forgery unless the uttering was proved. It must have gone beyond his power to abstain from using by his having used it, by actually presenting it, or posting it, or so putting it out of his own possession that there is no longer any *locus poenitentiae*. Till this is done, however much the making or the possession of the fabricated document may indicate moral delinquency, his act does not bring him within the grasp of the law. He had not proceeded to put his nefarious intention into operation. He is like a man who has prepared false keys in order to enter the premises of another for a felonious purpose, but has never used them. This well-established and most just rule of law, which does not allow of punishment for unfulfilled intents and preparations which have not culminated in an irrevocable act of commission or attempt, is only, as I have said, set aside in certain cases by statutory enactments for special reasons. Thus the manufacture of spurious banknotes is constituted a criminal offence without there being any proof of uttering. The statute strikes at the manufacture of false banknotes as being a thing highly dangerous to the general community, and calling for special State intervention. That a statute should be necessary to check such wholesale manufacture illustrates the rule that the preparation of a fraudulent document, or a document intended to be fraudulently used, is not in itself a punishable crime, and that it requires an overt act of use to constitute an indictable offence. In this indictment the statement that he made the copies with an intent to dispose of them to trade rivals, is not an averment of any act done, but only of a state of mind, which might be gone back upon, and nothing done to carry out the intent. I have therefore no hesitation in holding the second charge against the male prisoner to be irrelevant."

Objection to the relevancy of the second charge sustained.

NOTES

**6.25**    1. In what sense had the Camerons proceeded further in their scheme than Mackenzie (given that the Camerons had not made a claim)?

2. See also *Morton v. Henderson*, 1956 J.C. 55, where Lord Justice-General Clyde suggested that, although the test is indeed whether the accused has crossed the line between preparation and perpetration, that line will not be crossed until there has been some "overt act, the consequences of which cannot be recalled by the accused" (at 58, quoting *H.M. Advocate v. Tannahill and Neilson*, 1943 J.C. 150, *per* Lord Wark at 153). If this is correct, is there any difference between the various theories on the *actus reus* of an attempted crime?

## B. The mental element in attempted crime

**6.26**    The word "attempt" suggests purpose. One would not normally say that a person has attempted to do something that he or she did not intend to do. If while running to catch a train I slip and almost fall under a bus, it would be stretching language to suggest that I had attempted to commit suicide.

English law requires that the conduct required for an attempt must be done with intent to commit the full offence (see Criminal Attempts Act 1981, s.1). This is so even if the completed crime can be committed with a state of mind less than intention. In *Whybrow* (1951) 35 Cr.App.R. 141 the Court of Criminal Appeal held that an accused could not be guilty of attempted murder unless it was proved that he or she intended to kill. In *Mohan* [1975] 2 All E.R. 193 it was held that, on a charge of attempting to cause grievous bodily harm by "wanton driving", in order to secure a conviction the prosecution had to prove an intention to cause grievous bodily harm. Foresight of such harm, or recklessness as to that consequence were not sufficient.

The situation in Scots law is quite different. In *Cawthorne v. H.M. Advocate*, 1968 J.C. 32, *post*, p. 391, it was held that wicked recklessness was sufficient *mens rea* for a charge of attempted murder. Essentially the reasoning in that case was that there was no difference between murder and attempted murder, other than the fact that in the latter case the victim did not die. This approach was facilitated by the court's approach to the question of the mental element in the crime of murder in general, and its acceptance that intention to kill and wicked recklessness were alternative forms of the "wicked intent" required for murder; see, in particular, Lord Guthrie, *post*, pp. 392–394. The result of *Cawthorne* is that Scots criminal law recognises the possibility of the reckless attempt.

See, on some of the problems which flow from the acceptance of reckless attempts, Scottish Law Commission, Consultative Memorandum No. 61, *Attempted Homicide* (September 1984).

## 4. IMPOSSIBILITY

**6.27**    Impossibility is one of the classical problems of the criminal law, and has led to lengthy academic and judicial debate in many jurisdictions. It is generally discussed in the context of criminal attempts, but it is clearly a problem that can arise in the context of other inchoate offences. (In the case of *Maxwell and Others v. H.M. Advocate,* 1980 J.C. 40, the issue was discussed in the context of conspiracy.) Impossibility can arise in a variety of ways. The attempt may be "factually" impossible: the property which the thief intends to take may not exist; the intended murder victim may already be dead, and so on. Such impossibility may be "absolute" (as in the two examples given) or "relative", where the impossibility arises because of the inadequacy of the means adopted—the safebreaker who uses inadequate means to open the safe. These are all examples of so-called "factual" impossibility—where the accused has set out to commit an offence but has failed, as a matter of fact, to do what he set out to do. These are sometime contrasted with so-called "legal impossibility". This is said to arise where the accused has set out to commit what he believes to be an offence, has done everything that she or he intended to do, but what is done turns out not to be an offence (or at least the intended offence). The classic example is the person who buys property which she believes to be stolen but which is not in fact stolen. Is this a case of attempted rest?

Prior to the case of *Docherty v. Brown*, 1996 S.L.T. 325 (*infra*) there was a clear conflict in the Scottish authorities. In *H.M. Advocate v. Anderson,* 1928 J.C. 1 Lord Anderson held that there could not be a relevant charge of attempting to procure an abortion when it was not alleged that the woman was pregnant. That view was supported by the opinion of Lord Justice-Clerk Aitchison in *H.M. Advocate v. Semple,* 1937 S.L.T. 48, where his Lordship stated that "it is an essential element of the crime of attempting to procure abortion that there be something there to abort; in other words, the woman must be pregnant" (at p. 51). However, it was held in *Lamont v. Strathern,* 1933 S.L.T. 118 that a person could be guilty of attempting to steal from another person's pocket even though it was not proved that there was anything in the pocket. In that case Lord Sands attempted to distinguish attempted theft from attempted abortion (at p. 120):

> "A charge of attempt at criminal abortion is a charge of an attempt to make a pregnant woman abort. A charge of attempt to steal is a charge of attempting to steal anything of value that might be found. The completed acts may be on the same footing. One cannot cause abortion if the womb be empty, or steal a valuable if the pocket be empty. But the attempts may be on a different footing. As regards abortion, I understand that the view taken was that attempt to commit abortion must be an attempt to cause a pregnant woman to abort. A pregnant woman is a condition of the offence. On the other hand, in the case of attempted theft from a pocket, that is an attempt to steal whatever may be found there. A pocket which may contain something of value is the only condition."

Interestingly, the comparison between attempted abortion and attempted theft was discussed in the New Jersey case of *State v. Moretti*, 52 N.J. 182 A. 2d 499, 37 A.L.R. 3d 364. In that case, the accused were convicted of conspiracy to carry out an unlawful abortion on a woman who was not in fact pregnant, although this fact was not known to them. It was argued at the trial, and again on appeal to the Supreme Court of New Jersey, that they could not be guilty of conspiracy to commit an abortion in circumstances where the full offence could not have been committed. In refusing the appeal the court stated (37 A.L.R. 3d 364, at 370):

> "In our view, this case is indistinguishable in principle from cases such as *State v. Meisch*, 86 N.J. Super. 279 .... In *Meisch*, defendant was convicted of attempted larceny. It was held that it was no defense that the drawer into which the defendant thrust his hand contained no property which could be the subject of larceny. Likewise, it should be no defence in an attempted abortion case that the woman, because not pregnant, could not be the subject of an abortion."

The court also referred to the Illinois decision in *People v. Huff*, 339 Ill. 323, 171 N.E. 261, in which it was held that it was possible to commit an attempted abortion by performing an operation on a woman with the intent to procure a miscarriage, even though the woman was not pregnant.

An opportunity to address the conflict in the Scottish cases arose in the case of *Maxwell and Others v. H.M. Advocate*, 1980 J.C. 40, but although the conflict was noted, the circumstances of the case were not such as required its resolution. The question of impossibility in attempted crime was authoritatively determined in following case.

### Docherty v. Brown
### 1996 S.L.T. 325

The appellant took possession of a quantity of tablets which he believed contained a class A **6.28** controlled drug, with intent to supply them to others. The tablets did not in fact contain the drug. He was charged with attempting to have a class A drug in his possession with intent to supply them to others in contravention of s.4(1) of the Misuse of Drugs Act 1971, contrary to sections 5(3) and 19 of the 1971 Act. He objected to the relevancy of the complaint on the ground that it did not disclose a crime. That objection was repelled by the sheriff. On appeal to the High Court the case was remitted to a Bench of Five Judges so that the conflict between the earlier cases of *H.M. Advocate v. Anderson*, 1927 J.C. 651, *Lamont v. Strathern*, 1933 S.L.T. 118 and *H.M. Advocate v. Semple*, 1937 S.L.T. 48 could be resolved. The leading opinion was delivered by Lord Ross.

THE LORD JUSTICE CLERK (ROSS): [Having reviewed the arguments of counsel for the accused and the Crown] " ... It appears to me that the issue raised in this appeal falls to be decided as a matter of principle. In his *Criminal Law* (2nd ed.), Sheriff Gordon at para 6–49 states:

> 'One of the most controversial problems in the law of attempt is the question of responsibility for attempts to commit crimes which are impossible of achievement.'

In a footnote he observes that the amount of literature on this topic is out of proportion to its practical importance, and I respectfully agree with him. So far as the law of Scotland is concerned, the starting point is Hume on *Crimes*, i, 26–30. At p. 26, Baron Hume having dealt with dole or *mens rea*, goes on to consider "Attempt, when punishable". He states:

> 'I have now said enough concerning the nature of that inordinate and vicious will, which is essential to the guilt of every crime. But the vicious will is not sufficient, unless it is coupled to a wrongful act. And here the question arises, how far must the culprit have proceeded in the prosecution of his wicked purpose, to make him answerable in the tribunals of this world?'

Baron Hume then goes on to consider various instances where enough has been done to constitute an attempt.

At p. 27 Baron Hume states:

> 'But further, even when no harm ensues on the attempt, still the law rightly takes cognisance of it, *si deventum sit ad actum maleficio proximum*; if there has been an inchoate act of *execution* of the meditated deed; if the man have done that act, or a part of that act, by which he meant and expected to perpetrate his crime, and which, if not providentially interrupted or defeated, would have done so; and more especially still (but this is *not* indispensable), where he has done something which must have its own course, and puts repentance out of his power. Under this rule falls the case of one who mingles a draught of poison, and offers the cup to the intended victim; or who kindles combustibles, and tosses them upon or among the stacks in his neighbour's barn-yard; or who, to defraud the underwriters on his ship, bores holes in the ship's bottom, and draws the plugs when at sea, and abandons the ship; or who instigates others, though ineffectually, to raise fire; or seriously endeavours to suborn false witnesses, or to bribe a public officer, or to seduce a servant to poison or to rob his master, or to un-fasten the bolts and locks of his master's shop, that the thief may enter in the night and steal. In such cases, not only is the wickedness of the man's heart disclosed (that is *not* sufficient): But the business takes a definite and more active shape, and this in pursuance of a new, a *final*, and a more *resolute* act of the delinquent's will, which is quite distinct from all his previous contrivances and meditations, how long and laborious soever. On all such occasions, the law therefore justly and wisely interferes, because the ultimate and meditated act is in part done; and it is not good for the public, nor for the delinquents themselves, that they should be encouraged with the belief that they may go such lengths, unpunished.'

That passage supports the advocate depute's proposition that an attempt occurs when a person has *mens rea*, and takes some positive act towards executing it. Although Baron Hume does not expressly deal with the question of an attempt to commit a crime which is impossible of achievement, that situation is, in my opinion, covered by his reference to a man having done the act by which he meant to perpetrate the crime but which has been 'providentially interrupted or defeated'. Support for the view that a relevant charge of attempt to commit a crime can be committed although it is in fact impossible to commit the completed crime, can be found in Bell's *Supplemental Notes*, p. 3. After dealing with a case of attempted murder where the indictment had been accepted as relevant, Baron Hume adds:

> 'It was observed, that if a tube filled with gunpowder, which had become unexplosive, were used, or a gun out of which the ball had fallen, there would be no real danger, but a grave attempt to kill, and so a relevant charge would lie. The ineffectual attempt to explode a gun having a bad lock, was viewed in a similar light.'

These appear to me to be all examples of situations where the completed crime was impossible of achievement. If the gunpowder had lost its explosive quality or if the ball had fallen out of the gun, or the gun had a defective lock, then killing would not have been achieved. Nonetheless Baron Hume observes that the court's view was that a relevant charge would lie.

In Alison, *Criminal Law*, i, 165, it is stated:

> 'In attempts at murder, the crime is to be held as completed if the pannel has done all that in him lay to effect it, although, owing to accident or any other cause, the desired effect has been prevented from taking place. If a person fired a pistol at his neighbour's head, but it miss fire, or the ball does not hit the object at which it was directed; or he strike with a dagger, but it light on a button and produce no injury, still the offender has done all that he could to effect his purpose, and he should be judged guilty of attempt to murder. Accordingly, in the case of Hume and Justice, July 30 1744, the libel was laid as for an attempt to murder, in consequence of discharging a pistol which missed its aim.'

In my opinion in the passage quoted above the words 'or any other cause' would cover the situation of an attempt to commit a crime which it was impossible to commit.

In this century the first case where the aspect of impossibility was considered appears to be *H.M. Advocate v. Anderson*. The charge in that case libelled that the panel

> 'did insert pieces of slippery elm bark or other substances into the private parts of Agnes M'Kain, wife of and residing with the said Falconer M'Kain, in the belief that she was then pregnant, and for the purpose of causing her to abort, and did attempt to cause her to abort'.

An objection to the relevancy of that charge was taken in respect that the indictment did not set forth that the complainer was in fact pregnant at the time of the alleged crime. Lord Anderson held that since it was not alleged that the complainer was in point of fact pregnant, he was bound to assume that she was not pregnant. He expressed the view that an allegation of pregnancy was an essential part of a charge of procuring or attempting to procure abortion, and that it was not enough that the accused believed there was pregnancy if in point of fact there was none. At one point of his opinion he stated: 'To attempt to do what is physically impossible can never, in my opinion, be a crime.' *H.M. Advocate v. Anderson* was cited in *Lamont v. Strathern*. In that case the accused had been charged with theft, and had been found guilty of, while acting in concert, attempting to steal money from the complainer's person. Lord Sands explained in his opinion that the sole question was whether the sheriff was warranted in convicting the accused of an attempt to steal money in the absence of satisfactory evidence that the complainer's pocket contained money. He stated at 1933 JC, p. 36; 1933 SLT, p. 119:

> 'I am not, I confess, impressed by the metaphysical argument that, whereas one cannot take what is not there, therefore one cannot attempt to take what is not there. I

apprehend that, if men were charged with illegally attempting to take salmon with a net from a certain pool, contrary to any Act which declared any such attempt to be illegal, it would be a futile defence that, as they caught nothing, the pool proving to be empty, they did not attempt to take the salmon. Nor, I think, would it be reasonable to deny to Mother Hubbard the credit of an attempt to fetch a bone for her dog.'

Subsequently he pointed out that the would-be thief may have no knowledge of what, if anything, is in the complainer's pocket, and he stated: "He attempts to steal whatever he may happen to find there." Later in his opinion at pp. 37–38 (p. 120) Lord Sands proceeded to distinguish *H.M. Advocate v. Anderson*:

'A charge of attempt at criminal abortion is a charge of an attempt to make a pregnant woman abort. A charge of attempt to steal is a charge of attempting to steal anything of value that might be found. The completed acts may be on the same footing. One cannot cause abortion if the womb be empty, or steal a valuable if the pocket be empty. But the attempts may be on a different footing. As regards abortion, I understand that the view taken was that attempt to commit abortion must be an attempt to cause a pregnant woman to abort. A pregnant woman is a condition of the offence. On the other hand, in the case of attempted theft from a pocket, that is an attempt to steal whatever may be found there. A pocket which may contain something of value is the only condition.'

Lord Blackburn stated at p. 38 (p. 121):

'In short, I am of opinion that, although the crime of theft cannot be completed unless the thief obtains possession of something belonging to another, nevertheless an attempt to commit a theft may be proved independently of any transfer of property or indeed of there being any property to transfer. It would, I think, be enough to justify a conviction of attempt to steal that the thief had reason to think there might be something to take possession of.'

The report makes it plain that the Lord Justice General concurred, and that must mean that he concurred with both Lord Sands and Lord Blackburn.

In *H.M. Advocate v. Semple*, *Lamont v. Strathern* was referred to in the argument, but the only reference to it appears in the opinion of Lord Fleming. As already observed there were charges where it was libelled that the appellant had supplied to a woman in the belief that she was then pregnant a number of powders and pessaries with intent to cause her to abort, and had instigated and caused her to take and use the same which she did, and that he had done this with intent to cause her to abort. The Lord Justice Clerk observed that attempt to procure abortion was not libelled in these charges. He added:

'I think it was rightly not libelled, because it is an essential element of the crime of attempting to procure abortion that there be something to abort; in other words, the woman must be pregnant.'

The Lord Justice Clerk went on to consider the case of *H.M. Advocate v. Anderson* where the charge was laid as a charge of attempting to procure abortion. He stated:

'I have not the slightest doubt that Lord Anderson was right in holding, on the terms of the libel with which he had to deal, that it did not set out the crime of attempt to procure abortion. Now, in this case the Crown has not libelled pregnancy, only a belief in the mind of the panel that the woman was pregnant, and it is said that what was done was done in that belief and with the intent to cause an abortion. In my judgment, that does not disclose a crime as the law of Scotland at present stands.'

Lord Fleming, when dealing with these charges, referred to the dictum of Lord Sands in *Lamont v. Strathern*. He agreed that the two charges in *H.M. Advocate v. Semple* to which I have referred were not relevant apparently because it was not alleged that the woman was in fact pregnant, or that the powders and pessaries were noxious or calculated to endanger health or life, or that the woman suffered any harm from taking them. Lord Moncrieff expressed similar views.

There is no doubt that these cases raise sharply the question of whether it is necessary for the relevancy of a charge of attempting to commit a crime, that the completed crime was capable of being committed. In my opinion, it is essential to bear in mind that an attempt to commit a crime is a different offence from committing the complete crime. There can be no question of an accused committing an offence which it is impossible to commit. When the crime is impossible of achievement, the most that an accused can be guilty of is an attempt to commit that crime. It is the fact that it is impossible to commit the complete crime which has resulted in the accused being charged with an attempt to commit that crime. But the fact that it is impossible to commit the complete crime does not, in my opinion, preclude the Crown from charging an accused with an attempt to commit the crime. I see nothing illogical in an accused being charged with attempting to commit a crime which is impossible of achievement. In my opinion *Lamont v. Strathern* was correctly decided, and a man may be convicted of attempt to steal by putting his hand towards another man's pocket with the object of stealing money therefrom, even though there was nothing in the pocket to steal. The fact that there was nothing in the pocket to steal means that the accused cannot be convicted of theft, but provided that he has had the necessary *mens rea*, and has taken sufficient positive steps towards the perpetration of the crime, he can be convicted of attempted theft, and it does not matter that the pocket was empty.

In *H.M. Advocate v. Anderson* Lord Anderson stated: 'To attempt to do what is physically impossible can never, in my opinion, be a crime.' In my opinion that is an unsound statement of the law. The fact that something is physically impossible will prevent an accused from being convicted of the complete crime, but it does not prevent him being relevantly charged with attempt to commit that crime provided that he has the necessary *mens rea*, and does some positive step towards executing his purpose.

Although *Lamont v. Strathern*, was, in my opinion, correctly decided, I am not persuaded that the approach favoured by Lord Sands towards the end of his opinion is well founded. He described a pocket which may contain something of value as a condition of the offence which he was considering. In my opinion that is not the proper approach. It is unnecessary to consider whether, as Lord Anderson thought, an allegation of pregnancy was an essential part of the charge which he was considering, or, as Lord Sands thought, whether a pocket which might contain something of value was a condition of the charge which he had under review, and indeed such an approach is misleading. When considering whether a relevant charge of attempting to commit a crime has been laid, it is not necessary to consider whether or not it was impossible for the complete crime to be committed. All that the court requires to do is to consider whether the accused has the necessary *mens rea*, and has taken matters further by doing some positive act towards execution of his purpose. That is not to say that what the accused believes is irrelevant. As Sheriff Gordon points out in para 6–49 [2nd Edition], where the accused knows of the impossibility of doing what he is attempting to do there can be no attempt. In a charge such as the present charge, the charge would be irrelevant unless it were libelled that the accused believed that the tablets of which he had taken possession contained controlled drugs. If he did not believe that, the charge of attempting to commit the crime could not in the circumstances succeed.

With the greatest respect to the distinguished judges in the House of Lords who decided *R. v. Smith* [1975] A.C. 476 and the other cases already referred to, it appears to me that they have failed to give proper weight to what requires to be proved for an attempt, and have treated an attempt as requiring the same *actus reus* as the completed crime. In *R. v. Smith* at p. 499 Lord Reid said:

'But this theory attaches a very different meaning to the word 'attempt'. The accused has done, as he did here, everything which he intended to do. There is no question of drawing a line so that remote acts of preparation are not attempts but acts proximate to the crime are attempts. The crime is impossible in the circumstances, so no acts could be proximate to it. The theory confuses attempt with intent. If the facts had been as he believed they were the man would have committed a crime. He intended to commit it. But he took no step towards the commission of a crime because there was no crime to commit.'

In my opinion if it is impossible to commit the complete crime, it does not follow that an accused can carry out no acts which are perpetration or are acts proximate to the crime which is being attempted.

In the course of their speeches in *R. v. Smith* and the other House of Lords decisions [*Anderton v. Ryan* [1985] A.C. 560 and in *R v. Shivpuri* [1987] A.C. 1], a number of hypothetical examples were considered. These included a pickpocket who puts his hand into another man's pocket only to find it empty; a man who attempts to assassinate a corpse, or a bolster in a bed, believing it to be the living body of his enemy; or a man who fires into an empty room believing that it contained an intended victim; and a man who takes away an umbrella from a stand with intent to steal it believing it not to be his own, although it turns out to be his own. As I understand it, the view was expressed that none of these were examples of attempts which were criminal because it was impossible in the circumstances to commit the complete offence. For my part, I am satisfied that all these instances would constitute relevant charges of attempt to commit the complete offence because the accused had the necessary *mens rea*, and had taken positive steps to carry out his purpose. The only reason that his purpose was not carried fully into effect was that it was impossible to commit the complete crime. I am not persuaded that the fact that it was impossible to commit the complete crime would prevent a relevant charge of attempt to commit that crime being laid.

It would be supererogatory to attempt to examine all the literature on the subject of attempts to do the impossible, but it is worth recording that the opinion which I have formed appears to find support in the articles written by Mr Brian Gill (as he then was) ["Impossibility in Criminal Attempts", 1965 J.R. 136] and Professor Glanville Williams, ["The Lords and Impossible Attempts or *Quis Custodiet Ipsos Custodes?*" (1986) C.L.J. 33] ... and in Gordon, *Criminal Law*, para 6–54 [2nd Edition].

Despite the confusion which emerges from the trilogy of House of Lords cases to which I have referred, it is interesting to see that in earlier times the English approach appears to have been very similar to that described by Baron Hume for Scotland. In *R. v. Scofield* (1784) Cald. Mag. Cas. 397, Lord Mansfield said:

'So long as an act rests in bare intention it is not punished by our laws, but immediately when an act is done, the law judges, not only of the act done, but of the intent with which it is done, and if it is coupled with an unlawful and malicious intent, though the act itself would otherwise have been innocent, the intent being criminal, the act becomes criminal and punishable.'

It is also interesting to see how, in relation to drugs, similar questions have been dealt with in New Zealand and Australia. In *R. v. Willoughby* [1980] 1 N.Z.L.R. 66 which was a case of conspiracy, it could not be proved that the packet in question contained controlled drugs. Speight J. in the Supreme Court, Auckland observed:

'Ordinarily where there is evidence that a person has attempted to commit an offence but it has proved factually impossible, a verdict of attempt can be sustained, for example, the pickpocket case and the cases of supplying the means of procuring an abortion which in fact, unknown to the offender, prove innocuous' (at p. 68).

Even though there was no evidence that the material handed over was heroin, Speight J. said:

> 'If, therefore, in the terms of s.72 an accused person has an intention to commit that offence, that is intends to have heroin in his possession, and does an act such as purchasing or attempting to purchase to that end, or, as here, pays over money, then in my view he comes within the plain wording of s.72 read in the context of the Misuse of Drugs Act.'

In *Britten v. Alpogut* [1987] V.R. 929, the defendant believed that he was importing and intended to import into Australia a prohibited import, namely cannabis, but the substance which he believed to be cannabis and which he imported was another substance which was not a prohibited import. The Full Court of the Supreme Court of Victoria held that *R. v. Smith* did not state the common law in Victoria applicable to criminal attempts, and that there was a case to answer. Murphy J. at p. 935 said:

> 'In my opinion, it can be said that before *Haughton v. Smith* the law of attempt punished a manifest criminal intention to commit a crime which was not accomplished.'
>
> For some inexplicable reason the law of attempt became involved with the question whether or not the crime attempted could have been in fact accomplished by the accused.
>
> 'It was thought by some that the accused could not be convicted of an attempt to commit a particular crime, when on the facts of the case it would not have been possible for the accused to commit the crime in question.
>
> 'Immediately, there was a confusion demonstrated between a relevant step in the commission of a possible crime and a relevant step in the commission of an intended crime, but one not capable of being accomplished.
>
> 'Courts began to ignore the importance of the intention of the accused and tended to concentrate on the question whether what was done was a step towards a crime, which if uninterrupted, would have been committed.'

Subsequently at p. 934, Murphy J. added:

> 'For if the evil intent of the actor can make a sufficient proximate though objectively innocent act criminal, so as to amount to an attempt, it would seem irrelevant to have to go on to see whether the attempt could or would have succeeded. At common law, if the intent was to commit a recognised and not an imagined crime, and the act done was not merely preparatory but sufficiently proximate, then at that stage an attempt to commit the recognised crime has been committed, and it seems to me it is not necessary to go further.'

At p. 938, Murphy J. stated:

> 'It would also be to recognise that at common law a criminal attempt is committed if it is proven that an accused had at all material times the guilty intent to commit a recognised crime and it is proven that at the same time he did an act or acts (which in appropriate circumstances would include omissions) which are seen to be sufficiently proximate to the commission of the said crime and are not seen to be merely preparatory to it. The 'objective innocence' or otherwise of those acts is irrelevant.
>
> Impossibility is also irrelevant, unless it be that the so-called crime intended is not a crime known to the law, in which case a criminal attempt to commit it cannot be made.'

In my opinion the logic expressed in these two cases is undoubted. Speight J. and Murphy J. appear to me to be expounding principles which are in line with the approach of the court in Scotland in *Lamont v. Strathern*. I accordingly agree with the advocate depute that for a relevant charge of an attempt to commit a crime, it must be averred that the accused has the necessary *mens rea*, and that he has done some positive act towards executing his purpose, that is to say that he has done something which amounts to perpetration rather than mere preparation. If what is libelled is an attempt to commit a crime which is impossible of achievement, impossibility is irrelevant except that there can be no attempt to commit the crime if the accused is aware that what he is trying to do is impossible. Except to that extent, impossibility has no relevance.

In the present case, it is libelled that the accused not merely had possession of tablets which he believed to contain a controlled drug with intent to supply that controlled drug to another or others, but that he had taken possession of these tablets. I am accordingly satisfied that the terms of charge 1 disclose that the appellant had the necessary *mens rea*, and that he took a positive step towards carrying out his purpose, namely, he took possession of the tablets in question. That being so, the necessary ingredients are present to support the charge that he attempted to have the controlled drug in his possession with intent to supply it to another in contravention of s.5(3) of the Act of 1971. In my opinion the objections taken to the relevancy of this charge are not soundly based, and the sheriff was correct to repel the objections to the relevancy.

The objections put forward were based upon *H.M. Advocate v. Anderson* and *H.M. Advocate v. Semple.* So far as *H.M. Advocate v. Anderson* is concerned I am of opinion that the charge in that case was a relevant charge of attempting to cause the complainer to abort, and that the decision of Lord Anderson should be disapproved. In my opinion this court should expressly disapprove of the statement in his opinion to the effect that to attempt to do what is physically impossible can never be a crime.

I would also disapprove of various dicta in *H.M. Advocate v. Semple.* I would disapprove of the statement of Lord Justice Clerk Aitchison at 1937 J.C., p. 45; 1937 S.L.T., pp. 50–51 to the effect that it is an essential element of the crime of attempting to procure abortion that there be something to abort, in other words, that the woman must be pregnant. I would also disapprove of the final paragraph of Lord Fleming's opinion which proceeds upon the basis that the charge was irrelevant because it had not been alleged that the woman was in fact pregnant.

Although I am satisfied that the case of *Lamont v. Strathern* was correctly decided, and that the appellant was correctly convicted of attempted theft, I have already indicated that the approach of Lord Sands in the latter part of his opinion is unsound. In particular it is incorrect to hold that a pregnant woman is a condition of a charge of attempt to commit abortion.

In my opinion these three cases will in future all require to be read in the light of the decision of the court in the present case. I would accordingly refuse the appeal and affirm the decision of the sheriff."

LORD SUTHERLAND: [His Lordship agreed with the opinion of the Lord Justice-Clerk. In discussing the cases of *Lamont v. Strathern* and *Anderson* his Lordship made the following observation on Lord Sands' attempt to distinguish between an attempt to steal from an empty pocket and an attempt to abort the pregnancy of a non-pregnant woman:] "... The attempt to distinguish between an empty womb and an empty pocket does not appear to me to be convincing. An attempt to abort what may be in the womb is surely as valid an attempt as an attempt to steal what may be in a pocket. If it is not a condition of attempted theft that the pocket should have some contents then equally it should not be a condition of attempted abortion that the womb should have some contents. What matters is that in both cases the perpetrator takes active steps to achieve his goal with the evil intent of committing a criminal offence. Having done so he has committed the indictable offence of attempt to commit a crime. Reading between the lines of Lord Sands' judgment it appears that he was not wholly convinced of the correctness of the decision in *Anderson*. It is perhaps unfortunate that he did not say so in terms which would have forced the court in *Semple* to consider the matter in detail. In my opinion, however, *Anderson* was wrongly decided. The actual decision in *Semple* was sound insofar as the Crown refrained from libelling an attempt to procure abortion, but I consider that the dicta supporting *Anderson* are unsound . . .".

LORD CAMERON OF LOCHBROOM: [Lord Cameron delivered an opinion which agreed with that of the Lord Justice-Clerk on the general question of impossibility. He did, however, reserve his opinion on the following point:] "Like Sheriff Gordon in his *Criminal Law* (2nd ed.) at p. 196, I find the distinction which at times has been attempted to be made between 'factual' and 'legal' impossibility, unjustifiable in principle for the reasons which he there sets out. But I would reserve my opinion on whether in a case where a crime can only be committed if a person is within a certain class of person, such as licensees, that is to say that the accused has to have a specified personal capacity which is required to be libelled as a part of the charge, it is relevant to libel an attempt to commit such a crime by one who merely believes himself to be within that class. Since these are more likely to be offences created by statute, the question may turn upon the provisions of the particular statute. It is sufficient to say that there is no such restriction to a specified class in the offence created by the provisions of the Misuse of Drugs Act with which this appeal is concerned . . .".

Appeal refused.

NOTES

1. The Lord Justice-General (Lord Hope) and Lord Johnston delivered concurring opinions. In his **6.29** opinion the Lord Justice-General made the following observation on the problem of "absurd" attempts:

> "I appreciate that difficult questions can arise where, for some absurd reason, the completed crime could not have been committed. Examples were mentioned in the argument of cases where a person stabs a person who is already dead or where on the true facts the notion that a crime could have been committed was fanciful. I do not think that these difficulties affect the principle. There will no doubt be cases where no good purpose would be served in prosecuting a person who acted in this way, because his actings were so wholly misconceived as to cause no risk of harm to anybody."

2. The conclusion is, with respect, correct. However, it is not easy to reconcile its predominantly subjective foundation, which places great emphasis on the intentions and beliefs of the accused, with the essentially objective approach of Scots law to questions of criminal responsibility.

3. Impossibility of the types discussed in *Docherty v. Brown* does not extend to criminalising conduct which is not prohibited merely because the accused believes it to be so. If A mistakenly believes that he is B's brother and has intercourse with her he can be convicted of attempted incest when it turns out that she is not his sister. However, if A believes that it is incest to have sexual intercourse with his cousin (which it is not) he is not guilty of attempted incest if he has intercourse with her.

4. For a detailed discussion of the decision in *Docherty v. Brown*, see Sheldon, "Impossible Attempts and Other Oxymorons" (1997) 1 E.L.R. 250.

5. Although the decision in *Docherty v. Brown* is confined to impossibility in the context of attempts, it is clear that impossibility is not a defence to a charge of conspiracy (*Maxwell and Others v. H.M. Advocate* 1980 J.C. 40). There seems to be no good reason in principle why impossibility should be a defence to incitement, but there is as yet no case law on this point.

# Chapter 7

## DEFENCES

---

## 1. THE NATURE OF DEFENCES

### A. Introduction: How defences work

**7.01** This chapter deals with defences to crime which are capable of application to more than one offence or category of offences. Defences which are applicable only to particular offences are dealt with in the context of those offences. Thus the plea of diminished responsibility is discussed in the context of homicide, since in modern practice it is only relevant as a defence to a charge of murder. Similarly, the plea of provocation is discussed in the context of assault and murder.

Although there is a significant body of law relating to the various defences, Scots law has not yet developed a coherent theory of defences. Thus the courts have only recently begun to analyse the function of defences in the attribution of criminal responsibility, and the approach of the High Court remains inconsistent in this respect. In *Drury v. H.M. Advocate*, High Court, February 2, 2001, *unreported, post*, p. 407, for example, the High Court held that the plea of provocation in murder negated the *mens rea* of the offence—in other words, the presence of an excusing factor was treated as part of the definition of the offence. In *Lord Advocate's Reference No. 1 of 2000*, High Court, March 30, 2001, *unreported, post*, p. 217, however, the defence of necessity was regarded as a matter extrinsic to the definitional elements of the offence of malicious mischief.

It is also worth noting that the idea of a "defence" to a criminal charge may take various forms, and that the term is used rather loosely. In one sense, a "defence" is any argument which the accused may adduce to raise a reasonable doubt about his or her guilt. It may take the form of a denial that the accused was, in factual terms, responsible for the commission of the *actus reus* alleged. Thus an accused may argue, as a defence, quite simply that she did not commit the alleged offence.

Taking matters one step further, an accused may seek to support the denial of guilt by reference to circumstances which positively support the accused's innocence in fact. The classic examples of this kind of defence are alibi and impeachment. In the former, the accused claims not only that he or she did not commit the offence, but positively asserts that he or she was elsewhere at the time of the offence. In the latter, the accused not only asserts that he or she is not guilty, but suggests that a third party is responsible for the commission of the offence.

In both of the foregoing examples, the nature of the defence is that the accused did not commit the *actus reus* of the alleged offence. However, circumstances will arise in which the accused, while not denying the commission of the *actus reus*, argues that criminal responsibility for that *actus reus* should not be attributed to him or her. This chapter is concerned with the arguments of the latter kind.

### B. Special defences

**7.02** The discussion of defences in Scots law has been complicated, and at times confused, by a special category of defence known as "special defences". In *Adam v. Macneill*, 1972 J.C. 1, Lord Walker said (at p. 5): "Generally speaking, a special defence is one which puts in issue a fact (1) which is not referred to in the libel, and (2) which, if established, necessarily results in acquittal of the accused." But the term "special defence" should properly be regarded more narrowly than this statement suggests. Correctly understood, the term "special defence" refers to a narrow category of defences of which the accused must give advance notice to the Crown. (See section 78 of the 1995 Act.) In other words, "special defence" is really a procedural category, rather than a substantive classification. Strictly understood, the special defences are alibi, incrimination, self defence, and insanity at the time of the offence. (See, generally, Renton and Brown, 6th ed., paras 14–26 *et seq.*). In addition, however, section 78(2) of the 1995 Act provides that the defences of automatism (*i.e.* non-insane automatism) and coercion are to be treated as if they were "special defences".

Properly understood, then, the classification of these defences as "special" defences should be distinguished from their legal effect. It should also be distinguished from the question of whether any other defence is capable of excluding criminal responsibility. Unfortunately, this has not always been the case, and in *H.M. Advocate v. Cunningham*, 1963 J.C. 80 the failure to maintain this distinction led the court to exclude a plea of automatism because it was not within the category of recognised special defences. The court pointed out that in order to qualify as a "special defence", it is a plea which, if established, leads to a verdict of not guilty. The court then went on to state that the categories of special defence were well-known, that the accused plea (non-insane automatism) was an attempt to extend the category of special defence beyond the established limits, and that the court would not permit this.

It is, of course, true that in order to qualify as a "special defence" an allegation must be something which, if established, would result in an acquittal. But it does not follow that, in order to result in an acquittal, an allegation must be a "special defence". If this were so, then the simple argument that the accused did not have the *mens rea* for the offence would require to be added to the category of special defence.

This, and several other aspects of *Cunningham* were overruled by the decision of the High Court in *Ross v. H.M. Advocate*, 1991 S.L.T. 564 (*post*, p. 245), and it should now be accepted that an accused may rely, by way of defence, on any plea which would have the effect of excluding guilt, or raising a reasonable doubt as to guilt, whether or not it is a "special defence".

## C. Justification and Excuse

There has been no extended discussion in Scots law of the distinction between justification and excuse. **7.03** Fletcher, explains the distinction in the following terms:

> "Claims of justification concede that the definition of the offense is satisfied, but challenge whether the act is wrongful; claims of excuse concede that the act is wrongful, but seek to avoid the attribution of the act to the actor. A justification speaks to the rightness of the act; an excuse to whether the actor is accountable for a concededly wrongful act" (*Rethinking Criminal Law*, p. 759).

Greenawalt offers a similar explanation:

> "Most reasons why otherwise criminal acts, such as A's intentional shooting of B, may be noncriminal fall roughly into the categories of justification and excuse. If A's claim is that what he did was fully warranted—he shot B to stop B from killing other people—A offers a justification; if A acknowledges that he acted wrongfully but claims he was not to blame—he was too disturbed mentally to be responsible for his behavior—he offers an excuse." (K. Greenawalt, "The Perplexing Borders of Justification and Excuse" (1984) 84 Columbia L.R. 1897, at p. 1897.)

The distinction between justification and excuse is conceptually useful, but does it have any "practical" relevance or is it merely of theoretical interest? After all, the accused is probably not very interested in whether his or her defence is a justification or an excuse. All that is of interest is whether it "works". But there are important practical consequences to the distinction between justification and excuse.

In the first place, excuses are "personal" to the accused, but justifications may be invoked by persons other than the actor. Greenawalt explains the distinction in the following way:

"Some of the typical features of justification and excuse may be generalized in the following way. Justified action is warranted action; similar actions could properly be performed by others: such actions should not be interfered with by those capable of stopping them; and such actions may be assisted by those in a position to render aid. If action is excused, the actor is relieved of blame but others may not properly perform similar actions; interference with such actions is appropriate; and assistance of such actions is wrongful." (K. Greenawalt, *loc. cit.*, at p. 1900.)

This difference between justified and excused actions can be illustrated as follows:

(1) A presents a gun at B and demands her purse. This is observed by C. In such a situation it would generally be accepted that B is justified in resisting A's demands, and, indeed, using reasonable force to do so. Since B's action in resisting A's threats is justified, C would also be justified in using force to protect B. Furthermore, since B is acting in a justified manner, it would be wrong for C to interfere with B's use of force, or for C to assist A.

(2) A and B return to B's house where they discover B's wife committing adultery with C. B is provoked by what he has discovered and attacks C. A joins in the attack and C is killed. In such circumstances, B would be entitled to plead provocation as a defence to a charge of murder. (See *post*, Chapter 10.) But provocation is only an excuse, not a justification. The killing is wrong, but by way of concession to "human frailty" provocation reduces the gravity of the offence from murder to culpable homicide. But as an excuse, provocation is personal to B. It cannot be relied upon by A, and A's assistance of B in the attack may render him liable to a conviction for murder. Indeed, A would be *justified* in using force against B to bring to an end his assault on C.

That last point illustrates further the usefulness of the distinction between justification and excuse. In allows us to resolve problems which may arise where there are competing or conflicting defences. Suppose, for example, that A instructs B to beat up C, and backs up his instruction by telling B that he will be killed if he does not comply. In such circumstances, if B carries out the instruction and assaults C, he would be entitled to plead, as an excuse, that he was coerced into committing the assault. But C is not expected to suffer passively the assault simply because B's conduct is excused. In such circumstances, C would be entitled to use force to resist the assault, and it would not be unlawful for him to do so. The reason why it would not be unlawful for C to use force to resist the attack, even though B would not be guilty of a crime in carrying out the attack, is because C would be justified in using force to resist the attack, while B's assault would only be excused. In that sense, a justification "trumps" an excuse. (See also, in this context, the discussion of the case of *R. v. Dudley and Stephens* (1884) 14 Q.B.D. 273, *post*, p. 268.)

The above examples suggest that the distinction between justification and excuse is neat and clear. Unfortunately life is not as simple as that.

In the first place, there is no universal consensus as to how to allocate all defences. It is accepted, generally, that private defence and the prevention of crime would be regarded as justifications. But some defences are less easily allocated, not least because they manifest elements of justified conduct and excused conduct, depending upon the circumstances in which they arise. Necessity is such a defence.

In some circumstances we would regard a person's conduct as being entirely warranted by the necessity of the situation: A uses B's mobile phone without permission to summon an ambulance to the scene of a serious accident. Consider, on the other hand, the circumstances of the Canadian case of *R. v. Perka and Others* (1985) 13 D.L.R. (4th) 1. In that case, the accused were engaged in smuggling a large quantity of drugs from Colombia to Alaska by boat. While off the coast of Canada their boat got into difficulties and a decision was taken to head for the Canadian coast, where the ship ran aground and began to take in water. The captain, fearing that the ship would be lost, ordered the crew to offload the cannabis. The accused were arrested and charged with unlawfully importing cannabis into Canada and pleaded necessity. It is unlikely that in such a case the accused's conduct would be regarded as justified. We would not applaud the accused's actions in offloading the cannabis—but we might accept that in the circumstances they were excusable.

For further discussion of these problems see, in addition to the materials set out below, Leo Katz, *Bad Acts and Guilty Minds: Conundrums of the Criminal Law*, Chicago U.P., 1987, Chapter 1, William Wilson, *Criminal Law: Doctrine and Theory*, Longman, 1998, pp. 206–219, and J. C. Smith, *Justification and Excuse in the Criminal Law*, Stevens, 1989.

# 2. Justification

## A. The use of force in private defence and the defence of public interests

The criminal law seeks to restrict the use of force and violence to very limited circumstances. One of **7.04**
these is the use of force by an individual to protect himself or herself from violence. In some systems
there is a more general rule that an individual may use reasonable force in the prevention of crime.

### (a) Private defence

"Private defence" arises where the accused has used force or violence in order to protect personal
safety, and (possibly) property interests. Although the commonest example of this is "self-defence" the
term "private defence" is used here. This is because private defence extends to the case where the
accused has acted to protect a third party. It is also apt to cover the limited circumstances in which force
may be used to defend property.

### (i) General principles of private defence

#### H.M. Advocate v. Doherty
1954 J.C. 1

Doherty was charged with the culpable homicide of a man called Cairns, by stabbing him in **7.05**
the eye with a bayonet. A special defence of self-defence was lodged by the panel, to the effect
that he killed Cairns while defending himself from an attack by the latter with a hammer. In
his charge to the jury the presiding judge made the following comments on the plea of
self-defence:

LORD KEITH: "Now we come to the point that has really been put before you, and that is
that Doherty acted in self-defence. Self-defence has been very fairly and fully put before you
both by the Advocate-depute and by Mr MacDonald for the accused, but it is my duty to state
what the law of the matter is with regard to self-defence, and, although there may be some
repetition in this, it will, at any rate, refresh your minds, and it is a duty that I cannot avoid.

If the defence of self-defence is held to be established, that results in the complete
exculpation of the accused, that is to say, the accused is held to be not guilty of culpable
homicide. That is the result of holding self-defence established, but you have got to consider
very carefully the limits of this doctrine of self-defence. It is my duty in the first place to
consider whether there is evidence at all on which you might hold that self-defence could be
established. I have had considerable difficulty in this case in deciding whether this was a
matter that I should leave to you, but, in the whole circumstances of the case, I think there is
evidence on which you will have to consider this question of self-defence and to decide
whether you think the defence has been established, subject to such directions as I am now
about to give you upon the law of the matter.

Let me remind you first of all of the limits of self-defence in a case of this kind. First of all,
there must be imminent danger to the life or limb of the accused, to the person putting
forward this defence; there must be imminent danger to his life and limb; and, secondly, the
retaliation that he uses in the face of this danger must be necessary for his own safety. Those
are two fundamental things you will keep in mind, that there is imminent danger to life and
limb and that the retaliation used is necessary for the safety of the man threatened. You do
not need an exact proportion of injury and retaliation; it is not a matter that you weigh in too
fine scales, as had been said. Some allowance must be made for the excitement or the state of
fear or the heat of blood at the moment of the man who is attacked, but there are limits or tests

that are perfectly well recognised and which will help you to understand this doctrine by way of illustration. For instance, if a man was struck a blow by another man with the fist, that could not justify retaliation by the use of a knife, because there is no real proportion at all between a blow with a fist and retaliation by a knife, and, therefore, you have got to consider this question of proportion between the attack made and the retaliation offered. Again, if the person assaulted has means of escape or retreat, he is bound to use them. If he has these means, then it is not necessary in self-defence to stand up against the other man in retaliation use a lethal weapon against him. He could defend himself by escape, which is really just another way of ridding yourself of the danger. He could escape or retreat, and then no necessity arises to retaliate by the use of a lethal weapon or in any other way, and, accordingly, that is another of the things in this case that you have got to consider, and to consider very carefully.

Just let me apply the law, as I have endeavoured to indicate it, to the circumstances of this case. Consider the application of those rules here. First of all, it is undoubtedly favourable to the accused that he was attacked or threatened by a hammer, because I do not think you will have any doubt at all that a hammer was a very dangerous thing to be threatened or attacked with, and, therefore, that is a feature favourable to the accused. If the accused had been cornered and had had a bayonet in his hand, it might well have justified a thrust with the bayonet in his self-protection to defend his own life, or to defend himself from very serious injury from the hammer, that is, if the accused were cornered and there was no other method open to him of saving his life or limb. But in this case the circumstances are not all that favourable. First of all, you know he was handed this bayonet by McNulty and told to defend himself, and that suggests something—it is for you to consider, it is not for me, but I am only putting this forward as a matter you have got to keep in view—that is suggests something of the nature of a duel, and that is not permissible; you cannot start up a duel with another man and then say, 'But I killed him or injured him in self-defence.' He had friends round about him whom you may think—and it is for you to consider—whom you may think might have helped him or dissuaded Cairns or disarmed Cairns, and again you may think he had a means of retreat. He had an open door to this stair behind him, the stairs down to the yard, and certainly there does not seem to have been any attempt to make an escape by the door, or to get behind his companions Moffat and McNulty, or anything of that sort. Those are circumstances in this case to which you will have to apply your minds, and you will have to decide whether in the light of all those circumstances this was a proper case of self-defence, in which the accused really had no other alternative in his own safety but to thrust at Cairns with the bayonet in the way which has been spoken to in evidence, if you think it is established in evidence that some such thrust was made. It is quite true that you may think that the accused was not altogether to blame, that he was provoked and that he used this bayonet in the heat of the moment. That is perfectly true, and I recognise that, but it is not provocation that has been put forward here; it is self-defence. Provocation is a very different matter, and it really is the provocation that has made this a case of culpable homicide and not of murder; the provocation in that sense has been taken into account, and, of course, provocation would be taken into account in the matter of sentence if you thought that self-defence did not apply here and that the accused is guilty of culpable homicide. In that case, of course, the whole circumstances in which this assault was made by the accused, in which those injuries were caused, the whole question of provocation, heat of blood, and that sort of thing, are proper matters for others to take into account, but you are not really here to consider the question of whether the accused was provoked. I recognise that it may well be said that he was provoked, but the question is, Do you think that he was acting in self-defence?"

Verdict: Guilty.

NOTES

**7.06**    1. Lord Keith's directions continue to provide a general statement of the law, and the language used by Lord Keith is frequently relied upon by judges in charging juries. However, as Lord Cameron observed in *Fenning v. H.M. Advocate* 1985 S.L.T. 540, it is important to distinguish between the central principle of the law, and what is said in order to illustrate that principle:

> "The degree of force which is in law permissible to repel an unprovoked attack, escape from which is not reasonably possible and the use of which will warrant an acquittal on the ground of self defence, must be adjusted to the violence and quality of the attack which has to be repelled. That is the essence of the matter. No doubt in giving direction to a jury on this matter and by way of illustration, phrases such as 'not to weigh in too fine scales', 'making allowances for the excitement or state of fear or heat of blood at the moment of attack' may be used by the judge—but, while such phrases have their uses, they are not statements of the law to be applied, but illustrative of it.... No doubt judges frequently find it helpful to make use of the language used by Lord Keith in the case of *H.M. Advocate v. Doherty* (1954 S.L.T. at p. 170) and the use of such illustrations may be of assistance to the jury, but such picturesque or illuminative phrases do not become mechanical but mandatory shibboleths to be uttered in every case of murder where the defence of self defence is presented, under penalty, in the case of omission, of a quashing of the verdict of the ground of misdirection" (at pp. 544–545).

2. The nature of the "retreat rule" has been the subject of some discussion. In *McBrearty v. H.M. Advocate* 1999 S.L.T. 1333 the trial judge, in directing the jury on self-defence, stated:

> "Secondly, an accused can only use violence as a last resort. He must have no means of escape or retreat, that is going, ladies and gentlemen. If there are other way of avoiding attack he should take them. If, for example, he could have run away, he should have done so, and you may think that in this case, ladies and gentlemen, that is a significant factor."

On appeal it was argued that this was a misdirection. The jury should have been told that the appellant should have had no "reasonable" means of escape or retreat.

The appeal court held that in the circumstances of the case there was no material misdirection but the decision suggests that it would, generally, be wrong for a judge to state the "retreat" rule in absolute terms. In *McBrearty* the Lord Justice-General noted that "it would have been more precise if the trial judge had explained to the jury that the means of escape required to be 'reasonable'" (at p. 1336). In *Fenning v. H.M. Advocate* Lord Cameron referred to an attack "escape from which is not reasonably possible" (see the passage quoted above). The question is always whether, in the circumstances, the degree of force used was excessive. The availability of a means of escape is, it is suggested, simply a matter to be taken into account in determining whether or not the use of force was excessive to the degree that would exclude the plea of self-defence.

The English courts have abandoned the "retreat rule" and, following the views of the High Court of Australia in *Howe* (1958) 100 C.L.R. 448, now hold that a failure to retreat is only an element in the considerations on which the reasonableness of an accused's conduct is to be judged, as a factor to be taken into account in deciding whether it was necessary to use force, and whether the force used was reasonable: *Julien* [1969] 1 W.L.R. 843, *McInnes* [1971] 1 W.L.R. 1600, *Bird* [1985] 2 All E.R. 513.

3. Private defence is not limited to "self" defence. In *H.M. Advocate v. Carson*, 1964 S.L.T. 21 Carson and another man were charged with assaulting a third man "to his severe injury". In the course of his charge to the jury Lord Wheatley stated: "If a man sees another man being unlawfully attacked he is entitled to try to stop that unlawful attack, and if within reason he uses methods that otherwise would constitute an assault he will be excused because his intention is not to commit a criminal assault on the victim but to prevent the victim from carrying out an assault, an illegitimate assault, on another person." See also *Whyte v. H.M. Advocate* 1997 S.L.T. 24 and *Boyle v. H.M. Advocate* 1993 S.L.T. 577.

4. The fact that an accused person started a fight, or went willingly into a fight, does not mean that they cannot for that reason plead self-defence. In *Burns v. H.M. Advocate* 1995 S.L.T. 1090 the court stated (at p. 1093):

> "It is not accurate to say that a person who kills someone in a quarrel which he himself started, by provoking it or entering into it willingly, cannot plead self defence if his victim then retaliates. The question whether the plea of self defence is available depends, in a case of that kind, on whether the retaliation is such that the accused is entitled then to defend himself. That depends upon whether the violence offered by the victim was so out of proportion to the accused's own actings as to give rise to the reasonable apprehension that he was in an immediate danger from which he had no

other means of escape, and whether the violence which he then used was no more than was necessary to preserve his own life or protect himself from serious injury."

See also the case of *Boyle v. H.M. Advocate* 1993 S.L.T. 577.

## (ii) The permissible degree of force

**7.07** The defence of self-defence ceases to be available to the accused when she or he uses excessive force. The test which is commonly applied to determine whether the use of force has been excessive is that of "cruel excess". In *Fenning v. H.M. Advocate* (above) the trial judge told the jury, *inter alia*, that "there must be no cruel excess of violence on the accused's part. If he goes further than is necessary for his defence and uses cruel excess that cannot in law constitute self-defence". In considering the accused's appeal against conviction in that case, Lord Cameron stated:

> "It is, ... clearly the duty of the judge to explain to the jury that the benefit of the defence is lost where the force used to repel the attack is excessive, and in my opinion where, as here, the language is precise and positive and the degree of excess characterised which will elide the defence is specifically stated to be 'cruel', then it is not mandatory for the judge to illustrate by examples the meaning of these words" (at p. 545).

The test of "cruel excess" has been approved in relation to self-defence in cases of assault: *Fraser v. Skinner* 1975 S.L.T. (Notes) 84. It should be noted that whether or not the force used is "cruelly excessive" depends upon the circumstances. It may well be that in some cases even moderate force could be regarded as a cruel excess.

Article 2(1) of the European Convention on Human Rights prohibits the intentional deprivation of life (subject to an exception for the death penalty where this is permitted by law). Article 2(1) provides:

"Deprivation of life shall not be regarded as inflicted in contravention of this article when it results from the use of force which is no more than absolutely necessary:

(a) in the defence of any person from unlawful violence;

(b) in order to effect a lawful arrest or to prevent the escape of a person lawfully detained;

(c) in action lawfully taken for the purpose of quelling a riot or insurrection."

Two questions arise here. Firstly, is the Convention standard for the use of lethal force the same as, stricter, or more lenient, than the test of "cruel excess"? It would certainly be possible to argue that the Scots law test is less strict than the Convention test. In *Ogur v. Turkey*, European Court of Human Rights, judgment of May 20, 1999, the Court stated (at para. 78):

> "... the use of the term 'absolutely necessary' in article 2(2) indicates that a stricter and more compelling test of necessity must be employed than that normally applicable when determining whether State action is 'necessary in a democratic society' under paragraph 2 of article 8 to 12 of the Convention. In particular, the force must be strictly proportionate to the achievement of the aims set out in sub-paragraphs 2(a), (b) and (c) of Article 2."

It is possible to envisage a case in which the use of force has been more than absolutely necessary, but which does not amount to cruelly excessive force. Certainly the Court has taken the view that article 2(2) appears to impose a stricter standard than a rule which permits the taking of life where this is "reasonably justifiable". See *McCann and Others v. United Kingdom* (1996) 21 E.H.R.R. 97, at para. 154.

The second question that arises is whether article 2 applies to private citizens, or only to public authorities (such as the police or the military and those assisting them in the execution of their duty). This, of course, is linked to the general question of whether the Convention rights have "horizontal effect" and is one of the few areas of the criminal law in which this question arises. If Article 2 does not apply to the taking of life by private citizens exercising the right of private defence, then it may be that the standard for the acceptable use of violence applicable in such cases will differ from that applicable in cases involving the use of lethal force by public authorities. There is the further related question: What standard is to be applied by a police officer who acts in self defence, as opposed to the defence of another? The "cruel excess" test, or the "no more than is absolutely necessary" test?

## (iii) What interests may be protected?

### McCluskey v. H.M. Advocate
1959 J.C. 39

The panel was charged with the murder of a man called Ormiston. He stated a special defence **7.08** of self-defence to the effect that he killed the deceased while resisting an attempt by the latter to commit sodomy upon him. The trial judge directed the jury that on a charge of murder self-defence was only available if the accused killed in order to save his life. The jury returned a verdict of guilty of culpable homicide, and the panel appealed on the ground, *inter alia*, of misdirection.

LORD JUSTICE-GENERAL (CLYDE): "The first question for this Court arises in regard to the ambit in the law of Scotland of a plea of self-defence. It is contended for the accused that the learned Judge at the trial misdirected the jury in directing them as a matter of law that homicide in this case could only be justified by self defence if the homicidal act was done by McCluskey to save his own life. ...

In the present case it is argued that although McCluskey had no grounds for thinking that his life was in any way in danger, a forcible attempt was made by Ormiston to commit sodomy with him, and this was such as to justify McCluskey in defending himself to the extent of taking Ormiston's life. The basis for this extension of the doctrine of self-defence, is, as I follow it, that an attack on the appellant's virtue is as much a justification for taking another man's life as an attack upon his life would have been. No authority was quoted for this extension of the plea of self-defence and I can see no logical nor indeed any other justification for it. Murder is still one of the most serious crimes in this country, for no man has a right at his own hand deliberately to take the life of another. Indeed it is because of this principle of the sanctity of human life that the plea of self-defence arises. Just because life is so precious to all of us, so our law recognises that an accused man may be found not guilty, even of the serious crime of murder, if his own life has been endangered by an assailant, or if he has reasonable grounds for apprehending such danger, and if the steps which he takes to protect his life are not excessive, although they have led to fatal consequences. But I can see no justification at all for extending this defence to a case where there is no apprehension of danger to the accused's life, and indeed, very little evidence of any real physical injury done to the accused himself, but merely a threat, pushed no doubt quite far, but none the less still only a threat, of an attack on the appellant's virtue. Dishonour, it is suggested, may be worse than death. But there are many ways of avoiding dishonour without having to resort to the taking of a human life, and, so far as I am concerned, I do not see how the taking of a human life can ever be justified by the mere fact that there have been threats of dishonour or indignities or even of some bodily harm, which falls short of creating reasonable apprehension of danger to life. Indeed this seems to be recognised in the authorities quoted to us. In Alison's *Criminal Law*, Vol. i, p. 132, the learned author says: 'A private individual will be justified in killing in defence of his life against imminent danger, of the lives of others connected with him from similar peril, or a woman or her friends in resisting an attempt at rape.' It seems to me impossible to assimilate the present case to a woman threatened with rape. For rape involves complete absence of consent on the part of the woman. This is not the situation in sodomy. Hume on *Crime*, Vol. i, p. 223, says: 'The general notion of homicide in self-defence is, that it is committed from necessity, in the just apprehension, on the part of the manslayer, that he cannot otherwise save his own life, and without alloy of any other excusable motive.' The decisions of the Court do not advance the matter since the point has not really arisen in any of them ....

In my view, therefore, where an attack by an accused person on another man has taken place and where the object of the attack has been to ward off an assault upon him it is essential that the attack should be made to save the accused's life before the plea of self-defence can succeed. For myself I would be slow indeed to suggest that people in this country are justified in taking human life merely because their honour is assailed by someone else. It would be a retrograde step if we were to widen the scope of self defence so as to enable an accused person to escape altogether in such circumstances. In my view, therefore, the direction given by the learned Judge to which exception is taken was a sound direction, and this ground of appeal is without substance."

Appeal refused.

Notes

**7.09**  1. It appears to be accepted by Lord Clyde that a woman may use such force in protecting herself from rape. But why should this be recognised as an exception to the general rule proposed by Lord Clyde? So far as concerns Lord Clyde's reasoning in this case, it is difficult to accept the distinction which he draws between rape and sodomy. The fact that the latter offence may be committed with the consent of both parties, while the former necessarily implies absence of consent on the woman's part ought to be irrelevant in a case involving forcible sodomy.

The real question is whether or not a person is entitled to use this degree of force in order to resist forcible sexual penetration. Viewed in that light, it is submitted that there is no difference between rape and forcible sodomy. That said, *McCluskey* was followed in *Elliott v. H.M. Advocate*, 1987 S.C.C.R. 278 and if the above argument is correct this must call into question the view that a woman may kill to protect herself from rape.

2. Would it ever be lawful to kill in defence of property? In principle this ought to be excluded on the view that it could never be a reasonable use of force to take human life merely in defence of property, and this view seems to be supported by what Lord Clyde says above. The householder who kills a burglar merely to stop the latter taking property should, it is submitted, be regarded as committing murder. If, however, the householder kills the burglar because she or he believes that their life is in danger, or that the life of some other person in the house is endangered, should be entitled to plead self-defence, provided the defence is otherwise made out in the circumstances. The terms of Article 2 of the European Convention on Human Rights make it clear that a public authority (such as the police or the military) or any person assisting a public authority cannot use lethal force merely in order to protect property, and there seems to be no good reason for applying a different rule in respect of private defence of property. On the other hand, the use of lethal force is permissible where this is absolutely necessary to defend a person from "unlawful violence", so that the rule that a person may kill to prevent rape (provided taking life was "absolutely necessary") would not fall foul of article 2.

3. Self-defence may be available as a defence to a charge of breach of the peace. In *Derrett v. Lockhart*, 1991 S.C.C.R. 109 two accused were convicted of breach of the peace by fighting. Derrett appealed on the ground that he was acting in self-defence at the time. The sheriff held that since the circumstances of the alleged breach, as narrated in the complaint, libelled an assault, the appellant was entitled to plead self-defence as a defence to the charge of breach of the peace. The High Court agreed. But is this limited to the situation in which the Crown have, as a matter of specification in the complaint, alleged that the breach took the form of an assault? Surely the accused would be entitled to argue, in such a case, that the reason why he committed the breach was because he was acting in self-defence, whether or not an assault is specified in the complaint?

## (iv) Mistaken self-defence

### Owens v. H.M. Advocate
### 1946 J.C. 119

**7.10**  Owens was charged with the murder of a man called Falconer by stabbing him. The panel lodged a special defence of self-defence and gave evidence to the effect that he thought Falconer was attacking him with a knife and stabbed him. The jury found him guilty of murder. On appeal, on the ground, *inter alia*, of misdirection in relation to his mistaken belief about the attack made by the deceased:

Lord Justice-General (Normand): "I will now turn to the passage in the charge where the presiding Judge directs the jury on the essentials of a special defence. The learned Judge said: 'If he was completely wrong in thinking'—that is if the appellant was completely wrong in thinking—'there was an object of a dangerous sort in Falconer's hand when he sprang out of bed and there was no such object, then any attack by Falconer following him into the lobby would not have justified the use of a lethal weapon. As I will tell you in a moment with authority the defence must be against an attack which reasonably is understood to be one likely to cause danger to life before it justifies the use of a lethal weapon.'

The first of these two sentences is, in our opinion, a misdirection on the essential elements of self-defence. In our opinion self-defence is made out when it is established to the satisfaction of the jury that the panel believed that he was in imminent danger and that he held that belief on reasonable grounds. Grounds for such belief may exist though they are founded on a genuine mistake of fact. In the present case, if the jury had come to the conclusion that the appellant genuinely believed that he was gravely threatened by a man armed with a knife but that Falconer actually had no knife in his hand, it would, in our opinion, have been their duty to acquit, and the jury ought to have been so directed. Here in the first of the two sentences they are plainly instructed to the opposite sense, and the effect of that direction is not taken off by the obscure sentence which follows and which holds out the unfulfilled expectation of a more complete treatment of the law on the question in a later passage of the charge. The result is that the jury were misdirected on the essential nature of the defence which they were considering, and if they had been properly directed they might have acquitted the appellant. The verdict therefore cannot stand."

Appeal allowed: conviction quashed.

NOTE

1., Two issues require consideration here: (a) the requirement that a mistaken belief should in this **7.11** context be "reasonable", and (b) the restriction of self-defence to cases of actual or perceived "imminent" danger.

On the first of these, the Lord Justice-General in *Crawford v. H.M. Advocate*, 1950 J.C. 67 commented (at p. 71):

> "As regards the argument urged upon us that the appellant rightly or wrongly thought that he was in danger of his life and the reliance placed upon the case of *Owens*, 1946 J.C. 119 [below], I should like to say that, when self-defence is supported by a mistaken belief rested on reasonable grounds, that mistaken belief must have an objective background and must not be purely subjective or of the nature of a hallucination. I am of opinion that the appeal fails; and on the question of sentence I see no reason to disturb the discretion exercised by the presiding Judge."

In other words, it appears that a belief in self-defence may be fairly subjective and still be "reasonable" for these purposes. On the other hand, it appears that a merely "honest" belief may not be sufficient. In *Jones v. H.M. Advocate*, 1990 S.C.C.R. 160 both Lord Ross and Lord Wylie approved the following passage from Lord Strachan's charge to the jury in *McCluskey v. H.M. Advocate*, 1959 J.C. 39, at 39–40:

> "Before you could find that the accused was justified in killing [the deceased] you would have to be satisfied that he struck the fatal blow for his own protection and to ward off danger to himself, either danger which was actually threatened or danger which might reasonably be anticipated by him. It would not be necessary to find that there was actual danger to the accused; you could uphold the special defence, ... if you were satisfied that the accused believed that he was in danger and if you were satisfied that he had reasonable grounds for so thinking."

In *Jamieson v. H.M. Advocate*, 1994 J.C. 88 it was held that an accused was entitled to an acquittal on a charge of rape if he honestly believed that the woman consented to sexual intercourse, notwithstanding the absence of reasonable grounds for that belief. However, the court expressly refrained from applying this subjective approach to mistakes to the case of mistaken self-defence. See *post*, p. 357.

It should be noted that in England the courts have held that the principles established in *Morgan* [1976] A.C. 182, upon which the decisions in *Meek* and hence *Jamieson* are based, apply to cases of mistaken self-defence: *Williams*, (1984) 78 Cr.App.R. 276, *Beckford v. R.* [19871 3 All E.R. 425.

So far as concerns the question of the "imminence" of the danger, compare the views expressed in *Owens* (and *Doherty* 1954 J.C. 169) with those of the Privy Council in *Beckford v. R.*, *ante*, in which it is suggested that a man who is about to be attacked does not have to wait for his assailant to launch the attack, but may in appropriate circumstances make a "pre-emptive strike" in self-defence.

## (v) Withdrawing the defence from the jury

### Crawford v. H.M. Advocate
### 1950 J.C. 67

**7.12**  THE LORD JUSTICE-GENERAL (COOPER): "The withdrawal of a special defence is always a strong step, but there are circumstances in which it is the duty of the presiding Judge to take that step . . . . I am prepared to affirm that it is the duty of the presiding Judge to consider the whole evidence bearing upon self-defence and to make up his own mind whether any of it is relevant to infer self-defence as known to the law of Scotland. If he considers that there is no evidence from which the requisite conclusion could reasonably be drawn, it is the duty of the presiding Judge to direct the jury that it is not open to them to consider the special defence. If, on the other hand, there is some evidence although it may be slight, or even evidence about which two reasonable views might be held, then he must leave the special defence to the jury subject to such directions as he may think proper."

NOTE

**7.13**     See also *Whyte v. H.M. Advocate*, 1997 S.L.T. 24 in which the Lord Justice-General (Hope) stated, on the basis of what Lord Cooper said in *Crawford*, that "a special defence of self-defence should be left with the jury to consider if there is some evidence, however slight, on which a jury might properly come to the view that that defence was made out" (at p. 25).

## (vi) Self-defence and provocation

**7.14**  There has in the past been confusion between the effect of the pleas of self-defence and provocation, especially where there has been excessive violence. In such cases it is possible for a verdict of culpable homicide to be returned, and it is sometimes, quite erroneously, thought that this is because "excessive self-defence" results in a verdict of culpable homicide. As was noted by Lord Lloyd of Berwick in the case of *R. v. Clegg* [1995] 1 All E.R. 334 (at 342): "It is sometimes said that the law of Scotland allows a verdict of excessive force in cases of excessive force in self-defence. Thus in the House of Lords Select Committee Report on Murder and Life Imprisonment (H.L. Paper (1988–89) No. 78-I), para 89 the committee recommended that there should be a qualified defence of excessive force in self-defence, and noted that this would bring the law of England and Wales into line with the law of Scotland." His Lordship went on to note, however, the observations of Lord Cooper in the following case:

### Crawford v. H.M. Advocate
### 1950 J.C. 67

**7.15**  The appellant was charged with the murder of his father by stabbing him. He tabled a special defence of self-defence, and also led evidence of provocation. The special defence was withdrawn from the jury by the judge, but he left open to them the issue of provocation. The jury returned a verdict of guilty of culpable homicide. On appeal against conviction:
     THE LORD JUSTICE-GENERAL (COOPER): [Having outlined the circumstances in which a trial judge would be justified in withdrawing the special defence from the jury:] "It is next to be observed that in this case self-defence is pleaded in answer, not to a simple assault, but to an

act of homicide, admittedly committed by the appellant, and it is so pleaded with the intent of exculpating the appellant upon the view that in the proved circumstances the homicide was justified. Exculpation is always the sole function of the special defence of self-defence. Provocation and self-defence are often coupled in a special defence, and often I fear confused: but provocation is not a special defence and is always available to an accused person without a special plea. The facts relied upon to support a plea of self-defence usually contain a strong element of provocation, and the lesser plea may succeed where the greater fails; but when in such a case murder is reduced to culpable homicide, or a person accused of assault is found guilty subject to provocation, it is not the special defence which is sustained but the plea of provocation. I, of course, respectfully agree with Lord Justice-Clerk Aitchison in *Hillan*, 1937 J.C. 53 that self-defence and provocation 'in many cases overlap', and with Lord Jamieson in *Kizileviczius*, 1938 J.C. 60, that 'in many respects the considerations which apply to them are the same'; but I desire to emphasise that the pleas are not identical but entirely separate and distinct, and that the special defence of self-defence must either result in complete exculpation or be rejected outright ... ."

Appeal dismissed.

NOTES

The distinction between self-defence and provocation in homicide was re-emphasised in *Fenning v.* **7.16** *H.M. Advocate*, 1985 S.L.T. 540 where Lord Cameron pointed out that the plea of provocation could only arise for consideration if the jury rejected the plea of self-defence. In the case of assault, it appears that, at least historically, provocation may have been accepted as a complete defence and this much was stated by Lord Justice-Clerk Aitchison in *H.M. Advocate v. Hillan*, 1939 J.C. 53. Although his Lordship's views in this respect were severely criticised by Lord Cooper in *Crawford*, they were somewhat rehabilitated by Lord Rodger in *Drury v. H.M. Advocate*, High Court, February 2, 2001, *unreported, post*, p. 407. His Lordship noted that Lord Justice-Clerk Aitchison was probably correct to state that at one time provocation could operate as a complete defence to assault, while accepting that in modern practice it could operate only as a mitigating factor. See *post*, p. 410.

## (vii) Accident and self-defence

It is not uncommon for an accused person to put forward a defence along these lines: "I was attacked by **7.17** the deceased. There was as struggle. During the struggle I had a knife in my hand, and during the struggle the knife went into the deceased. I did not mean to stab him. I was just trying to get him off me." In some cases 'it was an accident' and 'I was acting in self-defence' may be regarded as mutually contradictory defences, and in *Surman v. H.M. Advocate*, 1988 S.L.T. 371. Lord Morrison directed the jury that self-defence could not be relied upon by an accused who claimed that the fatal injuries were accidental. This was because "self-defence is a deliberate act intended by the victim of an attack for his own protection" and could not be relied upon by an accused who stated that he had not deliberately inflicted the fatal injuries for the purpose of self defence. On appeal it was held that this was a misdirection. Whether or not self-defence and accident are mutually exclusive defences is a matter which depends upon the circumstances of each case. Compare, in this respect, *MacKenzie v. H.M. Advocate*, 1983 S.L.T. 220 where the court held that, on the facts, accident and self-defence were mutually exclusive, and *H.M. Advocate v. Woods*, 1972 S.L.T. (Notes) 77 in which it was held that they were not.

## B. Other cases of use of force

There is no general statutory provision governing the use of force in the furtherance of justice in **7.18** Scotland. (In England, section 3 of the Criminal Law Act 1967 provides that a person may use "such force as is reasonable in the circumstances in the prevention of crime, or in effecting or assisting in the lawful arrest of offenders or suspected offenders or of persons unlawfully at large".)

## (i) Prevention of crime

**Palazzo v. Copeland**
1976 J.C. 52

**7.19** The appellant fired a shotgun in the air in the early hours of the morning to disperse a crowd of youths who were creating a disturbance in the street outside. He was convicted of breach of the peace, and appealed by stated case to the High Court.

OPINION OF THE COURT: "The appellant was convicted after trial on summary complaint upon a charge of breach of the peace. The particulars of the charge were that at a late hour at night, indeed in the early hours of the morning on November 29, he discharged a shotgun into the air to the alarm of the lieges. The Sheriff, as we have indicated, convicted and the question in the case is whether on the facts stated he was entitled so to do. Mr Booker Milburn has argued that it is perfectly plain from the case that the gun was fired in the air to try to stop a breach of the peace which was being committed by a number of unsavoury and drunken youths in the vicinity. The findings show that the appellant had been caused trouble before by youths who had damaged his property and that in course of the breach of the peace some of the drunken youths were shouting abusive expressions in the direction of his premises. The proposition was that an act which is committed to stop a breach of the peace ought not to be regarded itself as a breach of the peace. While the proposition is attractive, however, we regret to say that we cannot give effect to it in law. Undoubtedly a gun was fired in the air in an urban situation in the early hours of the morning. Undoubtedly certain lieges, however undesirable they might have been, were put in a state of fear and alarm. But more importantly, the act of firing a gun in the air in an urban situation at that time in the morning was calculated to be likely to put lieges in general in a state of fear and alarm. In these circumstances the fact that the appellant's motive was the sound one of trying to stop a breach of the peace is irrelevant. The fact that the only persons put in a state of fear and alarm were those committing the breach of the peace is equally irrelevant. A man may not take the law into his own hands. Furthermore a man may not commit an offence in an attempt to stop another. In the event, as the case shows, what the appellant did, did not end the fracas outside his premises, and it might be thought to have aggravated an already unsatisfactory situation. In the whole matter, while we have considerable sympathy for the appellant, we have no alternative but to answer the question in the case in the affirmative."

Appeal dismissed.

NOTES

**7.20**     1. *Palazzo* states that it is not a defence to a charge of breach of the peace that one was merely trying to prevent a breach of the peace. If the accused's conduct is such as is calculated, in an objective sense, to give rise to alarm or annoyance, the fact that it was done for some good purpose is not a defence. But is this a convincing decision? Suppose that A sees B stealing C's purse from her shopping back in the street. He attempts to stop B, who struggles with him. A struggles with B, and shouts at him to stop struggling. Many passers-by, who, of course, do not know what is happening, are alarmed. Is A guilty of a breach of the peace? Surely it is much too sweeping a statement of the law to suggest that "a man may not take the law into his own hands"? The general proposition that "a person may not commit an offence in an attempt to stop another" was endorsed by the High Court in *Lord Advocate's Reference (No. 1 of 2000)*, High Court, March 30, 2001, *unreported, post*, p. 217 (at para. 37). That case makes it clear, however, that this proposition is subject to the general principles of the defence of necessity, and that where the conditions for that defence are made out, then a person may "commit an offence in order to prevent another".

2. See also the case of *Ralston v. H.M. Advocate*, 1989 S.L.T. 474 in which it was held that the accused's motive in committing a breach of the peace, namely to protest about prison conditions, was not a defence to the charge.

## (ii) Arresting offenders: the police

So far as concerns arrest, and the lawful exercise of powers ancillary to arrest (such as search) the **7.21** common law recognises that a reasonable degree of force may be necessary and therefore permissible. If, however, unnecessary force is used, then this may amount to an assault. The degree of force which will render unlawful an arrest or search has not been clearly spelt out in any authority, and since much will depend on the circumstances of a case it is probably not possible to go further than saying that only "reasonable" force is permissible.

In *Bonar and Hogg v. McLeod*, 1983 S.C.C.R. 161 the High Court held that a police officer who grasped an arrested person by the throat, twisted his arm up his back and "quick marched" him down a corridor had used excessive force in view of the fact that the prisoner was neither resisting arrest nor struggling with the officer at the time. *Marchbank v. Annan*, 1987 S.C.C.R. 718 the appellant, a police officer, was convicted of assaulting a 16-year-old youth, D. D had been pursued by the police, at high speed, while driving a car. D was forced off the road, and the appellant smashed his window with his baton, hit D on the head, dragged him out and kicked him on the ground. It was held that the appellant, albeit that he was angry as a result of D's conduct, had gone far beyond the limit of permissible force when arresting a suspect.

It is worth noting that the degree of force which would be unlawful in such cases is less than that which would defeat a plea of self-defence, where only "cruel excess" will have that consequence (see *Fraser v. Skinner*, 1975 S.L.T. (Notes) 84).

A certain latitude is, however, allowed to the police where they act in good faith, but in error, when using force to effect what they believe to be a lawful arrest. In *McLean v. Jessop*, 1989 S.C.C.R. 13, the appellant, a police officer, was convicted of assaulting C by repeatedly striking him with his police baton. The appellant had been called to a suspected housebreaking and had seen two persons running out of a garden at the rear of the premises. One of them was C. The appellant caught hold of C who struggled and tried to explain he was a neighbour who had called the police. The appellant had then struck C with his baton. On appeal the conviction was quashed. The High Court held that the appellant had reasonable grounds to suspect that an offence had been committed, and, on seeing C running from the garden, to suspect that C was implicated. Since C had struggled with the appellant, the latter had not acted unlawfully in using his baton to effect an arrest.

But compare that decision with *Cardle v. Murray*, 1993 S.L.T. 525. Two police officers saw the respondent was breakdancing in a busy shopping precinct. He accidentally bumped into an elderly woman, nearly knocking her down. One of the police officers approached him to speak to him about his conduct. but the respondent danced away from the police officer. The police officer put his hand on the respondent's arm and said "Excuse me". The respondent swore at the police officer, and carried on dancing away from him. The police officer kept hold of the respondent's arm and tried to calm him down. The respondent shouted and tried to draw away from the police officer, at which point he was arrested for breach of the peace. He continued to shout, struggle and swear as he was taken away, and when he arrived at the police station. He was charged with breach of the peace and resisting the police in the execution of their duty. A submission of no case to answer in respect of all charges was upheld by the sheriff who acquitted the respondent. The prosecutor appealed to the High Court, but the appeal was refused. Since the respondent was not committing an offence, and the police had no reasonable grounds to apprehend the commission of an offence, he had been unlawfully detained by the police and was therefore entitled to use force in order to resist their unlawful action in taking hold of him.

Appeal refused.

## (iii) "Citizen's arrest"

A citizen is entitled to use force to effect an arrest, but the circumstances in which this is lawful are **7.22** narrowly stated.

### Bryans v. Guild
1989 S.L.T. 426

OPINION OF THE COURT (LORD HOPE): "The appellant ... appeared in the District Court at **7.23** Kirkcaldy on a ... charge of assault. The matter arose out of an incident which had taken place outside the appellant's house in Buckhaven .... What had happened was that his house had been subjected to an assault by various articles which had been thrown at it by a group of youths numbering some 12 persons who had been shouting and creating a disturbance outside the premises. It so happened that the victim of the alleged assault by the appellant was in a separate group of three who happened to be walking on the opposite side of the road at or about the time the assault on the house was taking place. When the assault on the house was over the appellant ran from his home after the group of youths who had been responsible for throwing the articles at his house. They ran past the man B.T. and those with him who, although not part of the group, were on the road at the time. What happened next was that the appellant grabbed B.T., who on the findings appears to have been innocent of the disturbance outside the appellant's house, grabbed him by the arm, twisted his arm up his back and caused certain bruising. Later when he was cautioned and charged the explanation which the appellant gave was this: "I took him by the arm and brought him in as a group were causing bother outside." The result of the trial was that the justice convicted the appellant of the charge of assault subject to a deletion which we need not trouble with, and admonished the appellant.

The appeal has been brought against conviction. It has been brought upon the basis that this was what was known as "a citizen's arrest" and that in the circumstances of the case the appellant was justified in the action which he took. In other words if the question was asked "was this a deliberate attack with criminal intent?", the answer would be no, because the appellant had reasonable grounds for believing B.T. had committed an offence against him.

In his reply the learned advocate-depute has reminded us of the limits of the rule which permits in certain special circumstances what is known as "a citizen's arrest". The matter has been the subject of comment recently by this court in the case of *Codona v. Cardle* 1989 S.L.T. 791. In the course of his opinion (at p. 792) the Lord Justice-Clerk referred with approval to a statement in Renton & Brown, *Criminal Procedure* (5th ed.), para. 5–19, in the following terms: "A private citizen is entitled to arrest without warrant for a serious crime he has witnessed, or perhaps where, being the victim of the crime, he has information equivalent to personal observation, as where the fleeing criminal is pointed out to him by an eye witness."

The particular circumstances of the case of *Codona v. Cardle* need not detain us, but it was emphasised by the Lord Justice-Clerk that the appellant had failed to bring himself within the categories described in the passage which he quoted because he had not actually witnessed the incident and it could not be affirmed that he had any information equivalent to personal observation. So far as the present case is concerned the alternative about information equivalent to personal observation does not arise. The particular circumstance here was one where the appellant saw certain youths committing this assault on his house and ran out and indeed thought that the man he was apprehending was one of those responsible. The fact remains however, that on the findings which are before us, the appellant could not be said to have witnessed an offence committed by B.T. because B.T. was not himself a party to the offence that was being committed. We do not find it possible to say that this is a case where the appellant has brought himself within either of the two categories which have been recognised as setting the limits to the circumstances in which a private citizen may resort to an arrest. We accept the proposition which the learned advocate-depute has made that the limits of the rule should not be departed from lightly. In the circumstances we have no alternative but to answer the question which asks whether the conviction was justified in the affirmative ...."

Appeal refused.

NOTES

**7.24** 1. In *Codona v. Cardle,* the accused purported to effect a "citizen's arrest" on a youth whom he suspected was responsible for breaking a window in an amusement arcade which the accused operated along with his father. He did not see the youth break the window, but said that he had witnesses who were prepared to state that he had done it. The purported arrest was attempted at some distance from the arcade and some time after the window was broken.

2. These cases make it clear that a citizen's arrest is subject to a "reasonable force" condition (as any arrest by a police officer would be). They also make it clear that merely suspecting that a person is responsible, will generally not be sufficient to justify a citizen's arrest. In *Codona v. Cardle* the Court observed that "at best the appellant had a suspicion that the complainer was the perpetrator of the offence" (the breaking of the window) and that that was not sufficient to entitle the accused to pursue the complainer in the way that he did.

## C. Human Rights

The Convention, by protecting certain rights and freedoms, provides accused persons with a defence to **7.25** a criminal charge based on those rights. While states "remain free to apply the criminal law to an act where it is not carried out in the normal exercise of one of the rights protected under the Convention" (*Salabiaku v. France*, (1991) 13 E.H.R.R. 379 at para. 27) the state cannot enforce the criminal law where to do so would interfere with the exercise of a Convention right, except to the extent that the Convention permits such interference. By enforcing the criminal law in such circumstances the Crown would be acting *ultra vires* in terms of section 57(2) of the Scotland Act 1998 (unless it was able to invoke section 57(3) of that Act). It would also be acting unlawfully in terms of section 6(1) of the Human Rights Act 1998. The relevance of the Convention rights to the general principles of criminal responsibility and specific offences is noted at the appropriate points throughout this work.

## D. Compliance with European Union Law

Where a provision of domestic criminal law conflicts with a directly effective rule of the law of the **7.26** European Union, the latter, in line with the principle of supremacy of European Union law, must prevail. It would therefore be a defence for a person charged under such a provision to demonstrate that the provision of Scots law conflicted with European Union law. See, for examples, *Conegate v. Customs and Excise Commissioners* [1987] Q.B. 254; *Criminal Proceedings against Brandsma* [1996] 3 C.M.L.R. 904; *Criminal Proceedings against Forsakringsaktiebolaget Skandia* [1999] 2 C.M.L.R. 933; *Criminal Proceedings against Webb (Alfred John)* [1982] 1 C.M.L.R. 719. *Cf. R. v. Dearlove, R. v. Druker* (1988) 88 Cr. App. R. 279.

## E. Compliance with International Law

A question which has emerged recently is the extent to which it is a defence to a criminal charge to argue **7.27** that one is acting in order to uphold a superior norm derived from international law.

### Lord Advocate's Reference (No. 1 of 2000)
#### High Court, March 30, 2001, *unreported*

Three accused were acquitted on charges of theft and malicious damage arising from direct **7.28** action taken by them against Trident nuclear weapons deployed at a Royal Naval base in Scotland. The actions were taken in good faith, based on the belief that the deployment of Trident missiles by the United Kingdom Government is a breach of customary international law, and as such, criminal, in Scots law. In particular it was argued that securing compliance with certain international legal obligations (derived from the Nuremberg Principles enunciated by the United Nations following the Trial of the Major German War Criminals) provided a justification for committing offences against domestic law.

Following their acquittal, the Lord Advocate referred a number of questions to the High Court for their opinion under section 123 of the Criminal Procedure (Scotland) Act 1995, including the following:

"2. Does any rule of customary international law justify a private individual in Scotland in damaging or destroying property in pursuit of his or her objection to the United Kingdom's possession of nuclear weapons, its action in placing such weapons at locations within Scotland or its policies in relation to such weapons?

3. Does the belief of an accused person that his or her actions are justified in law constitute a defence to a charge of malicious mischief or theft?

4. Is it a general defence to a criminal charge that the offence was committed in order to prevent or bring to an end the commission of an offence by another person?"

OPINION OF THE COURT: "[Having rejected the argument that the United Kingdom's possession and deployment of Trident was contrary to customary international law, and the argument that the accused had acted in circumstances of necessity:]

*Intervention to prevent crime*

[87] As we have indicated at paragraph 32 above, the respondents rely upon customary international law not merely as showing that what the Government were doing was illegal, but as providing a justification (not otherwise to be found in Scots law, and quite apart from any justification by necessity) for what they did. We come now to that question.

[88] The respondents claim to have "acted in the knowledge that the only effective remedy open to us to prevent a nuclear holocaust was to join with other 'global citizens' in an effort to enforce the law ourselves as the Government, judiciary, police and other institutions of the State were not willing to do it themselves, despite high level delegations asking them to do so." Leaving aside the question of whether what they did could seriously be seen as helping to prevent a nuclear holocaust, and stripping this claim of some of its vaguer and more tendentious implications, the underlying proposition appears to be that if the law is being broken, and is not being enforced by public institutions empowered to enforce it, individuals have the legal right to enforce it, or to take steps contributing to its enforcement, notwithstanding that what they do would otherwise itself be criminal. As we have indicated, the law in relation to necessity confers no such general right. What is contended is that customary international law confers such a right. Indeed it is that contention which appears, even more than alleged necessity, to underlie the respondents' claim to be justified in what they did. Its basis is much less clear.

[89] The argument advanced in support of this proposition, in particular on behalf of the second respondent, was at one stage founded upon the Nuremberg Principles. But these clearly have nothing to do with this matter, and the argument based on them was not insisted in. Counsel for the second respondent, and Ms Zelter, submitted however that the proposition had a basis in principles revealed at the Nuremberg trials themselves. It was not explained how or why any rule or principle applied in the conduct of those trials, but not incorporated in the Nuremberg Principles, should be regarded as established customary international law. The cases relied upon, both by Ms Zelter and by counsel for the second respondent, were cases where an accused person pled justification by extreme necessity, arising from the plight of Germany at certain stages in the war, or by superior orders at times of grave emergency. Those defences were rejected, and the argument here appeared to be on the lines that as some kind of corollary or implication, deriving from the fact that neither orders nor necessity excused an individual's participation in actions alleged to be criminal at international law, the individual in question should be seen as having had a right to take action (itself otherwise criminal) designed to prevent the military or civilian authorities from committing the crimes in which the accused had in fact implicated himself.

[90] That does not appeara to use to have been an issue at the Nuremberg trials in question. And while interesting questions of law might no doubt arise, in relation, say, to a German citizen during the war who in breach of German law chose to kill his officer rather than obey him in committing a crime against humanity, the cases to which we were referred do not appear to us to have determined any such issue.

[91] Particular emphasis was laid upon the case of a Swiss national, Paul Grueninger, who had been dismissed from office and convicted in a local court on the ground of disregard of Swiss federal directives and laws in allowing refugees from Nazi persecution to enter Switzerland. We were told by Ms Zelter that his trial was re-opened in 1995 and that he was acquitted posthumously. The facts of the case appeared clearly from Ms Zelter's narrative, but the grounds of judgment did not. On the material available his actions appear to have had the character of rescue. There is nothing to support the notion that the case demonstrates some right, as a matter of customary international law, to prevent crime by committing what would otherwise be a criminal act. We see no real analogy between any of these cases and the situation in which the respondents find themselves. What we have referred to as a "notion" is in our opinion no more than that. It has no foundation in law. Unless the respondents' actions are justified by the law of necessity, they cannot be seen as justified ..."

NOTES

1. Similar arguments were presented by the accused in *John v. Donnelly*, 2000 S.L.T. 11. There, the **7.29** accused was charged with vandalism contrary to section 52(1) of the Criminal Law (Consolidation) (Scotland) Act 1995. It is not an offence under section 52(1) if the accused has a "reasonable excuse" for destroying or damaging the property in question. The accused cut part of the perimeter fence surrounding the Royal Navy base at Coulport. She pleaded by way of defence that she believed she had a reasonable excuse for doing so. As the Court explained:

> "In her view nuclear weapons were illegal. She found support for that view in that nuclear weapons were unable to distinguish between combatants and non-combatants and would pollute the atmosphere, and posed a massive ecological threat. She also said that it was not lawful, in her view, to target nuclear weapons at innocent non-combatants and that this was a contravention of humanitarian law. She had tried alternative methods of protesting, such as subscribing petitions, but without result. She took the view that her actions were justified in terms of international law, the Nuremberg Principles, the Geneva Conventions and humanitarian law" (*per* Lord Coulsfield at pp. 12–13).

In the event, the court did not find it necessary to address the question whether compliance with international law was a defence to the charge. It had not been demonstrated that the possession of nuclear weapons would in itself be unlawful. In these circumstances, the accused's defence amounted to a sincere belief in the illegality of nuclear weapons coupled with "anxiety at their potentially appalling effects", but this, the court held, could not amount to a "reasonable excuse" in terms of section 52(1).

A similar argument was also raised, unsuccessfully, in *Hipperson v. DPP*, Queen's Bench Division, July 3, 1996 (*unreported*) C.L.Y. 96/1445. In that case the appellant, with others, broke into the Nuclear Weapons Establishment at Aldermaston. They were convicted, *inter alia*, of criminal damage, contrary to section 1 of the Criminal Damage Act 1971. On appeal it was argued that the accused had a "lawful excuse" for their actions, which were carried out in the honestly held belief that they were attempting to prevent the crime of genocide or conspiracy to commit genocide by preventing the design, production or refurbishment of Trident nuclear weapons.

This defence was likewise rejected. The accused had acted under a mistaken belief as to what constituted "genocide" as defined by the Genocide Act 1969 (which adopts the definition of Genocide in the United Nations Convention on Genocide (1948). The work carried out at Aldermaston was not capable of amounting to the crime of genocide or conspiracy to commit genocide.

2. Discussion of this topic has tended to focus on the legality of nuclear weapons. However, the issue is more far-reaching, and includes the question whether it is a defence under domestic law for a person to commit an offence in order to avoid or bring to an end the commission of a crime against international law such as genocide or grave violations of the Geneva Conventions.

There is authority for the view that the *use* of nuclear weapons would generally be contrary to international law. As the High Court pointed out in its opinion (paras 79 *et seq.*) the International Court of Justice stated in its *Advisory Opinion on the Legality of the Threat or Use of Nuclear Weapons*, July 8,

1986, that while the threat or use of nuclear weapons was not specifically authorised by treaty or customary international law, there was equally no conventional or customary "comprehensive and universal prohibition of the threat or use of nuclear weapons as such". The Court held (by eight votes to seven) that the threat or use of nuclear weapons would generally be contrary to the rules of international law applicable in armed conflict, and in particular the principles and rules of humanitarian law. However, it left open the question whether the threat or use of nuclear weapons would be unlawful "in an extreme circumstance of self-defence, in which the very survival of the State would be at stake".

The argument that it is permissible to break domestic criminal law in order to uphold international law is, at least in part, based on the view that there is a general obligation in international law to prevent and punish crimes against international law. The extent of this obligation is, however, disputed. (See, for example, Diane F. Orentlicher, "Settling Accounts: The Duty to Prosecute Human Rights Violations of a Prior Regime", 100 Yale L.J. 2537 (1991) and compare with the decision of the South African Constitutional Court in *Azanian Peoples Organisation (AZAPO) and Others v. President of the Republic of South Africa and Others* 1996 (8) BCLR 1015. In any event, the obligation to prevent and punish is one which, in principle, is placed upon states, rather than individuals, and there is no clear authority for the view that an individual is under any obligation to prevent the commission of such crimes. See, in this connection, the opinion of Martin J. in *Limbo v. Little*, 65 N.T.R. 19.

## 3. EXCUSES

### A. Lack of capacity

**7.30** *(a) Non-age*

#### Criminal Procedure (Scotland) Act 1995
**7.31**     **41.** It shall be conclusively presumed that no child under the age of eight years can be guilty of any offence.

NOTES

**7.32**     1. Section 41 ought not to be construed as meaning that once the age of criminal responsibility is reached, the age of a child ceases to be relevant to criminal responsibility. Where, for example, *mens rea* is a necessary element of an offence, the youthfulness of a child even over the age of eight ought to be relevant in determining whether the child formed the requisite intent. All that section 41 does is to establish a rule that below the age of eight a child is not criminally responsible for his or her conduct. This does not mean to say that a child over that age is necessarily as responsible as an older person. The question must always be whether, in the circumstances, the child *as a matter of fact* has sufficient understanding and knowledge to justify attributing to him or her criminal responsibility for what he or she has done. *Cf. H.M. Advocate v. S.*, High Court, July 9, 1999 (unreported, but discussed by C. Connelly and C. McDiarmid, "Children, Mental Impairment and the Plea in Bar of Trial" (2000) 5 S.L.P.Q. 157.

2. The rule contained in section 41 is a rule of substantive law, rather than procedure, despite its appearance in the 1995 Act. See, in this respect, *Merrin v. S.*, 1987 S.L.T. 193 in which it was held that since it was a rule of law that a child under the age of eight is incapable of committing an offence, a child under that age could not be referred to a children's hearing on the ground that he had committed an offence.

3. A child who is alleged to have committed an offence may be dealt with by means of a children's hearing under Part 3 of the Children (Scotland) Act 1995 (which is not a criminal proceeding) or by prosecution. The latter course may only be adopted on the instructions of the Lord Advocate or at his instance, and no court other than the High Court or the sheriff court has jurisdiction in such cases: Criminal Procedure (Scotland) Act 1995, s.42. Criminal prosecutions involving children are governed by the Criminal Procedure (Scotland) Act 1995.

4. For the above purposes, a "child" is defined, principally, as a person under the age of 16 years: Criminal Procedure (Scotland) Act 1995, s.307(1) and Children (Scotland) Act 1995, s.93(2)(b). Presumably, a person who is over the age of 16, but whose mental age is below 16 does not fall within the

definition. *(Cf. State v. Schabert,* 24 N.W. 2d 846 (1947): on a murder charge, a defendant whose chronological age was 28 years, but whose mental age was only eight years, sought to avail herself of a rebuttable statutory presumption that children over seven and under 12 years of age were incapable of committing crime. The court held that "age" referred to chronological age.) A case such as this might, however, raise questions of diminished responsibility (see *post,* Chap. 10).

5. At eight, the age of criminal responsibility in Scotland is one of the lowest in Europe. It appears that only Cyprus, Switzerland and Liechtenstein have a lower age of criminal responsibility (at seven). The age of criminal responsibility is 13 in France, 14 in Germany, Austria, and Italy, 15 in the Scandinavian countries, 16 in Portugal, Poland and Andorra and 18 in Spain, Belgium and Luxembourg. See *T. v. United Kingdom,* (2000) 30 E.H.R.R. 121, at para. 48. Ireland introduced legislation in 1999 to raise the age of criminal responsibility from seven to 12.

6. The applicants in *T. v. United Kingdom* and *V. v. United Kingdom* were convicted in the Crown Court in England of murdering a two-year-old child. At the time of the offence, both were aged ten, which is the age of criminal responsibility under English law. They were 11 at the time of the trial. Both argued, *inter alia,* that the attribution of criminal responsibility at an age as low as 10, coupled with their public trial in an adult court, amounted to a violation of Article 3 of the European Convention on Human Rights. The majority of the Court, noting that there was not, as yet, a prevailing consensus amongst European States with respect to the age of criminal responsibility, rejected this argument.

"70. The Court has considered first whether the attribution to the applicant of criminal responsibility in respect of acts committed when he was ten years old could, in itself, give rise to a violation of Article 3. In doing so, it has regard to the principle, well established in its case-law that, since the Convention is a living instrument, it is legitimate when deciding whether a certain measure is acceptable under one of its provisions to take account of the standards prevailing amongst the Member States of the Council of Europe (see *Soering v. United Kingdom,* judgment of July 7, 1989, Series A no. 161, p. 40, § 102; and also the *Dudgeon v. United Kingdom* judgment of October 22, 1981, Series A no. 45, and the *X, Y and Z. v. United Kingdom* judgment of April 22, 1997, *Reports* 1997-II).

71. In this connection, the Court observes that, at the present time there is not yet a commonly accepted minimum age for the imposition of criminal responsibility in Europe. While most of the Contracting States have adopted an age-limit which is higher than that in force in England and Wales, other States, such as Cyprus, Ireland, Liechtenstein and Switzerland, attribute criminal responsibility from a younger age. Moreover, no clear tendency can be ascertained from examination of the relevant international texts and instruments (see paragraphs 43–44 above). Rule 4 of the Beijing Rules which, although not legally binding, might provide some indication of the existence of an international consensus, does not specify the age at which criminal responsibility should be fixed but merely invites States not to fix it too low, and Article 40(3)(a) of the UN Convention requires States Parties to establish a minimum age below which children shall be presumed not to have the capacity to infringe the criminal law, but contains no provision as to what that age should be.

72. The Court does not consider that there is at this stage any clear common standard amongst the Member States of the Council of Europe as to the minimum age of criminal responsibility. Even if England and Wales is among the few European jurisdictions to retain a low age of criminal responsibility, the age of ten cannot be said to be so young as to differ disproportionately from the age-limit followed by other European States. The Court concludes that the attribution of criminal responsibility to the applicant does not in itself give rise to a breach of Article 3 of the Convention."

*(T. v. United Kingdom,* paras 70–72). See also *V. v. United Kingdom,* paras 72–74.

The Court went on to hold that "the particular features of the trial process as applied to [the applicants] caused, to a significant degree, suffering going beyond that which would inevitably have been engendered by any attempt by the authorities to deal with the applicant[s] following the commission by [them] of the offence in question" (at paras 77 (*T. v. United Kingdom*) and 78 (*V. v. United Kingdom*).

Five members of the Court, however, dissented on the question of the age of responsibilty:

"As far as the age of criminal responsibility is concerned, we do not accept the conclusion of the Court that no clear tendency can be ascertained from the development amongst European States and from international instruments. Only four Contracting States out of forty-one are prepared to find criminal responsibility at an age as low as, or lower than, that applicable in England and Wales. We have no doubt that there is a general standard amongst the Member States of the Council of Europe under which there is a system of relative criminal responsibility beginning at the age of thirteen or fourteen—with special court procedures for juveniles—and providing for full criminal responsibility at the age of eighteen or above. Where children aged from ten to about thirteen or fourteen have committed crimes, educational measures are imposed to try to integrate the young offender into society. Even if Rule 4 of the Beijing Rules does not specify a minimum age of criminal responsibility, the very warning that the age should not be fixed too low indicates that criminal responsibility and maturity are related concepts. It is clearly the view of the vast majority of the Contracting States that this kind of maturity is not present in children below the age of thirteen or fourteen. In the present case, we are struck by the paradox that, whereas the applicants were deemed to have sufficient discrimination to engage their criminal responsibility, a play area was made available for them to use during adjournments."

(Joint partly dissenting opinions of Judges Pastor Ridruejo, Ress, Makarczyk, Tulkens and Butkevych.)

7. Rule 4.1 of the "Beijing Rules" to which reference is made above states "In those legal systems recognising the concept of the age of criminal responsibility for juveniles, the beginning of that age shall not be fixed at too low an age level, bearing in mind the facts of emotional, mental and intellectual maturity" (United Nations Standard Minimum Rules for the Administration of Juvenile Justice, Adopted by General Assembly Resolution 40/33, 1985, see Gane and Mackarel, *Human Rights and the Administration of Justice*, Kluwer, 1997, at pp. 469–477).

8. The United Nations Committee on the Rights of the Child, in its Report on the United Kingdom (CRC/C/15/add.34) dated February 15, 1995, stated, *inter alia*:

> "35. The Committee recommends that law reform be pursued to ensure that the system of the administration of juvenile justice is child-oriented .... 
> 
> 36. More specifically, the Committee recommends that serious consideration be given to raising the age of criminal responsibility throughout the areas of the United Kingdom ...."

In 2000, the Scottish Executive referred the question of the age of criminal responsibility in Scotland to the Scottish Law Commission.

## (b) Insanity

**7.33** Insanity may arise either as a defence to a criminal charge, or as a plea in bar of trial. In the first case the issue is whether or not the accused's mental condition at the time of the offence was such as to justify a verdict of acquittal on the ground of insanity. In the second the issue is whether the panel is presently fit to stand trial, irrespective of his mental condition at the time of the offence. Strictly speaking, therefore, the plea of insanity in bar of trial is not a defence to a charge, but a plea which prevents the accused being tried on that charge. Following a successful plea in bar of trial the accused is not, of course, acquitted. He or she may, however, be detained under a hospital order and indeed may subsequently be put on trial should his or her condition improve sufficiently. (See, for example, *H.M. Advocate v. Bickerstaff*, 1926 J.C. 65.) The cases discussed below are concerned only with the defence of insanity at the time of the alleged offence.

### Hume, i, 37–44

*"Nature of the Plea of Insanity*

**7.34**    II. We may next attend to the case of those unfortunate persons, who have to plead the miserable defence of idiocy or insanity. Which condition, if it is not an assumed or imperfect, but a genuine and thorough insanity, and is proved by the testimony of intelligent witnesses, makes the act like that of an infant, and equally bestows the privilege of an entire exemption from any manner of pain; *'Cum alterum innocentia concilii tuetur, alterum fati infelicitas* *excusat.*' I say, where the insanity is absolute, and is duly proved: For if reason and humanity enforce the plea in these circumstances, it is no less necessary to observe such a caution and reserve in applying the law, as shall hinder it from being understood, that there is any privilege in a case of mere weakness of intellect, or a strange and moody humour, or a crazy and capricious or irritable temper. In none of these situations does or can the law excuse the offender: Because such constitutions are not exclusive of a competent understanding of the true state of the circumstances in which the deed is done, nor of the subsistence of some steady and evil passion, grounded in those circumstances, and directed to a certain object. To serve the purpose of a defence in law, the disorder must therefore amount to an absolute alienation of reason, '*ut continua mentis alienatione, omni intellectu careat*'—such a disease as deprives the patient of the knowledge of the true aspect and position of things about him—hinders him from distinguishing friend or foe—and gives him up to the impulse of his own distempered fancy.

Whether the man must have utterly lost the knowledge of good and evil, right and wrong, is a more delicate inquiry, and fit perhaps to be resolved differently, according to the sense in which the question is put. If it is put in this sense—in a case, for instance, of murder, Did the panel know that murder is a crime? Would he have answered, on the question, that it is wrong to kill a fellow creature? this is hardly to be reputed a just criterion of such a state of soundness, as ought to make him answerable to the law for his actions. Because a person may happen to answer in this way, who yet is so absolutely insane as to have lost all power of observation of facts, all discernment of the good or bad intentions of those who are about him, or even the knowledge of their persons. But if the question is put in another and a more special sense, as relative to the act done by the panel, and his knowledge of the situation in which he did it, Did he, as at that moment, understand the evil of what he did? Was he impressed with the consciousness of guilt, and fear of punishment?—it is then a pertinent and a material question, but one which cannot be rightly answered, without taking into consideration the whole circumstances of the situation. Every judgment in the matter of right and wrong supposes a case, or state of facts, to which it applies. And though the panel have that vestigate of reason, which may enable him to answer in the general, that murder is a crime; yet if he cannot distinguish a friend from an enemy, or a benefit from an injury, but conceives every thing about him to be the reverse of what it really is, and mistakes the illusions of his fancy in that respect for realities, '*absurda et tristia sibi dicens atque fingens*;' these remains of intellect are of no sort of service towards the government of his actions, or enabling him to form a judgment of what is right or wrong on any particular occasion. If he does not know the person of his friend, or is possessed with the vain conceit that his friend is there to destroy him, and has already done him the most cruel wrongs, and that all about him are engaged in a conspiracy to abuse him, as well might he be utterly ignorant of the quality of murder. Proceeding, as it does, on a false case, or a conjuration of his own fancy, his judgment of right and wrong is, as to the question of responsibility, truly the same as none at all. It is therefore only in this special sense, as relative to the particular thing done, and the condition of the man's belief and consciousness on that occasion, that an inquiry concerning his intelligence of moral good or evil seems to be material to the issue of his trial . . . .

But although the distemper must thus be absolute in degree, it is not indispensable that it be also continual in respect of time. The quality of the deed depends entirely on the man's state of mind at the time he does it; so that whether his malady is constant and unremitting, or only returns at intervals, still his defence shall be equally available, if he was then utterly furious, and void of reason. And here I may cite the case of Sir Archibald Kinloch; who, having had his senses injured by the acute delirium of a West India fever, was afterwards liable to occasional fits of derangement of mind, though at considerable intervals, and at length, in a state of utter furiosity, had the misfortune to kill his brother. This violent fit of distemper had lasted only for a few days; and soon after the fact, he settled into his ordinary condition. The jury were, nevertheless, unanimous in acquitting him."

Note

**7.35** The interesting question is how far the courts have progressed since Hume's time in their approach to the question of insanity. "Not very far" seems to be the answer from the following case.

### Brennan v. H.M. Advocate
1977 S.L.T. 151

**7.36** The appellant was charged with the murder of his father by stabbing him. On the day on which the killing took place the appellant had consumed between twenty and twenty-five pints of beer, a glass of sherry and, about half-an-hour before the killing, a microdot of LSD. A special defence of insanity was lodged on his behalf, and it was also contended that the effect of his self-induced intoxication might be to reduce the quality of the crime from murder to culpable homicide. At the trial, Lord Wylie withdrew the special defence from the jury, and directed them that the evidence of the accused's state of intoxication did not entitle them to return a verdict of culpable homicide. The accused appealed against conviction.

Opinion of the Court (Full Bench): "What was said was that the appellant, at the time he stabbed his father, was so much under the influence of the drink and the drug he had taken as to be insane. This case accordingly is one in which the state of the appellant's mind was, according to the evidence, attributable merely to the transitory effects of alcohol and LSD deliberately consumed by the appellant with knowledge, from his previous experience of both, that they were bound to intoxicate him. It will be seen therefore that the first submission for the appellant raises the single and important question whether a temporary impairment of mental faculties, resulting merely from self-induced intoxication, may in our law amount to insanity for the purposes of a special defence such as the appellant tabled in this case ....

In the development of the first submission the particular proposition was that if a person suffers total alienation of reason as the result of self-induced intoxication he will be regarded by our law as insane and thus free from any criminal responsibility. On the assumption that this proposition was sound it was then argued that there was evidence on which a jury would have been entitled to hold on a balance of probability that the special defence had been made out.

We ask ourselves first of all the fundamental question: 'What is insanity, according to the law of Scotland, for the purpose of a special defence of insanity at the time?' The question has nothing to do with any popular view of the meaning of the word insanity nor indeed is it a question to be resolved upon medical opinion for the time being. It is, on the contrary, a question which has been resolved by the law itself as a matter of legal policy in order to set, in the public interest, acceptable limits upon the circumstances in which any person may be able to relieve himself of criminal responsibility.

In discovering what is insanity within the meaning of our criminal law we cannot do better than begin by noticing that Hume treated the nature of the plea, in vol. 1, p. 37, of the third edition of his work on *Crimes*, thus: 'Which condition, if it is not an assumed or imperfect, but a genuine and thorough insanity, and is proved by the testimony of intelligent witnesses, makes the act like that of an infant, and equally bestows the privilege of an entire exemption from any manner of pain.... I say, where the insanity is absolute, and is duly proved: For if reason and humanity enforce the plea in these circumstances, it is no less necessary to observe such a caution and reserve in applying the law, as shall hinder it from being understood, that there is any privilege in a case of mere weakness of intellect, or a strange and moody humour, or a crazy and capricious or irritable temper. In none of these situations does or can the law excuse the offender: ... To serve the purpose of a defence in law, the disorder must therefore amount to an absolute alienation of reason ... such a disease as deprives the patient of the knowledge of the true aspect and position of things about him—hinders him from distinguishing friend or foe—and gives him up to the impulse of his own distempered fancy.' It is a clear from the discussion which follows that Hume is speaking of absolute alienation of reason in relation to the act charged. It is abundantly clear, too, whatever may be comprehended within the word 'disease' as Hume used it that it does not include deliberate and self-induced intoxication, for in the passage immediately following his treatment of insanity, Hume (p. 45) contrasts insanity with 'that sort of temporary madness, which is produced by excess in intoxicating liquors', and says of the latter: 'certain it is, that the law of Scotland views this wilful distemper with a quite different eye from the other, which is the visitation of Providence; and if it does not consider the man's intemperance as an aggravation, at least sees very good reasons why it should not be allowed as an excuse, to save him from the ordinary pains of his transgression. Not to mention that one cannot well lay claim to favour, on the ground of that which shows a disregard of order and decency . . . .'

We have no doubt that the law as stated by Hume is and has always been the law of Scotland, and neither our own researches nor those of the learned Solicitor-General and senior counsel for the appellant, have revealed that the accuracy of Hume's statement has ever been called in question. On the contrary it has constantly been accepted and applied, and with the increasing misuse of drugs in these times, it would be wholly irresponsible to alter or modify it in any way . . . .

In 1890, in the case of *H.M. Advocate* v. *McDonald*, (1890) 2 White 517 the Lord Justice-Clerk (Macdonald) in charging the jury re-affirmed the clear distinction between total alienation of reason caused by unsoundness of mind, which will constitute insanity in law, and the mere effects of drink which will not, and he did so in these terms:

'A defence of insanity can only be supported by proof that the prisoner was actually of unsound mind at the time. It is said that he had taken so large a quantity of ardent spirits that he was insane. Now, a man who is merely drunk is not held by the law to be insane merely because he is drunk. On the contrary, if a man when sober has no signs of insanity about him, gets himself into a state of intoxication, the presumption is that any abnormal acts he may commit when in that state, are to be attributable to the effects of the drink he has taken, and not to mental disease of which there has been no indication previously.

It is the present presence of a poison in him which causes his brain to suffer, and his mind to wander and go away from its course of sober action, just as the body of a man is controlled by a hurricane of wind: he cannot control himself. But observe, the temporary cause of the disease is not anything in the brain itself, but a quantity of drink which he has taken which affects the brain. . . .'

From this charge emerges clearly the necessity for unsoundness of mind, or disease, in the concept of what he calls "real" insanity, *i.e.* insanity in the legal sense, and we need hardly add that if there is present the essential prerequisite of such unsoundness of mind it is both unnecessary and irrelevant to inquire what caused it. Further, running throughout all more recent cases, and in all statements of the law on diminished responsibility, that necessity has invariably been reiterated. To illustrate what we have just said we simply draw attention to one example, the case of *H.M. Advocate* v. *Kidd*. In that case Lord Strachan in his charge to the jury on the special defence of insanity posed the question: "What degree of mental illness is sufficient in law to excuse a person from responsibility for his actions?" and told the jury to ask themselves whether the accused was "of unsound mind" and stressed that "there must have been an alienation of the reason in relation to the act committed. There must have been some mental defect . . . by which his reason was overpowered." . . . .

In short, insanity in our law requires proof of total alienation of reason in relation to the act charged as the result of mental illness, mental disease or defect or unsoundness of mind and does not comprehend the malfunctioning of the mind of transitory effect, as the result of deliberate and self-induced intoxication. As we understand it the law of England in spite of its different definition of insanity—the so-called McNaghten Rules which form no part of our law (see *Breen* v. *Breen*)—has reached precisely the same conclusion . . . ."

Appeal refused.

NOTES

**7.37**    1. To the extent that voluntary intoxication cannot found a plea of insanity at the time of the offence, the charge to the jury in *H.M. Advocate v. Aitken*, 1975 S.L.T. (Notes) 86 was disapproved by the court in *Brennan*. See also, *McGowan v. H.M. Advocate*, 1976 S.L.T. (Notes 8).

2. See below under "intoxication" for the court's views on the appellant's alternative plea. *Brennan* should also be considered in relation to automatism or "temporary dissociation". See H.M. *Advocate v. Ritchie (infra)* and *H.M. Advocate v. Cunningham.*

3. For some time the accepted approach to insanity was to be found in Lord Strachan's charge to the jury in the case of *H.M. Advocate v. Kidd*, 1960 J.C. 61. In that case his Lordship stated, *inter alia* (at p. 70):

> "The question really is this, whether at the time of the offences charged the accused was of unsound mind. I do not think you should resolve this matter by inquiring into all the technical terms and ideas that the medical witnesses have put before you. Treat it broadly, and treat the question as being whether the accused was of sound or unsound mind. The question is primarily one of fact to be decided by you, but I have to give you these directions. First, in order to excuse a person from responsibility for his acts on the ground of insanity, there must have been an alienation of the reason in relation to the act committed. There must have been some mental defect, to use a broad neutral word, a mental defect, by which his reason was overpowered and he was thereby rendered incapable of exerting his reason to control his conduct and reactions. If his reason was alienated in relation to the act committed, he was not responsible for that act, even although otherwise he may have been apparently quite rational. What is required is some alienation of the reason in relation to the act committed. Secondly, beyond that, the question in this case whether the accused's mind was sound or unsound is to be decided by you in the light of the evidence, in the exercise of your common sense and knowledge of mankind, and it is to be judged on the ordinary rules on which men act in daily life. Thirdly, the question is to be decided in the light of the whole circumstances disclosed in the evidence. You must have regard to the evidence which has been given by the medical witnesses, but the medical evidence by itself is not conclusive. The question is to be decided by you and not by the mental specialists. In coming to your decision you are entitled, and indeed bound, to regard the whole evidence. You are entitled in particular to consider the nature of the act committed and the conduct of the accused at and about the relevant times, and his previous history. Those are the directions which I give you on this matter.
>
> At one time, following English law, it was held in Scotland that if an accused did not know the nature and quality of the act committed, or if he did know it but did not know he was doing wrong, it was held that he was insane. That was the test, but that test has not been followed in Scotland in the most recent cases. Knowledge of the nature and quality of the act, and knowledge that he is doing wrong, may no doubt be an element, indeed are an element in deciding whether a man is sane or insane, but they do not, in my view, afford a complete or perfect test of insanity. A man may know very well what he is doing, and may know that it is wrong, and he may none the less be insane. It may be that some lunatics do an act just because they know it is wrong. I direct you therefore that you should dispose of this question in accordance with the directions which I have given, which briefly are, that there must be an alienation of reason in regard to the act committed, otherwise the question is one for you to decide whether the accused was at the time of sound or unsound mind."

4. Lord Strachan's rejection of a test of insanity based on the M'Naghten Rules of English law (*M'Naghten's Case* (1843) 10 Cl. & F. 200) was confirmed by the approach of the Second Division in the civil case of *Breen v. Breen,* 1961 S.C. 158 and by the High Court in *Brennan*. But in *Brennan*, Lord Emslie seems to lay more stress on alienation of reason, and less on unsoundness of mind. Is this not a move towards the *M'Naghten* approach, despite the court's explicit rejection of the Rules? *Cf.* the remarks of the Butler Committee on Mentally Abnormal Offenders (Cmnd. 6244, 1975), para. 18.6: "the main defect of the M'Naghten test is that it was based on the now obsolete belief in the pre-eminent role of reason in controlling social behaviour."

5. Is there a difference between "alienation of reason" (which is the test applied in *Kidd*) and "total alienation of reason" which is the test applied in *Brennan*, and if so, what is the correct formulation? As to this, see *Cardle v. Mulrainey,* 1992 S.L.T. 1152, *post*, p. 251.

6. The onus of establishing the defence of insanity rests on the accused: *Kidd*, above, *Lambie v. H.M. Advocate,* 1973 S.L.T. 219. In both solemn and summary proceedings, the prosecutor has a duty to bring before the court such evidence as may be available of the mental condition of the accused, where it appears to the prosecutor that that person may be suffering from mental disorder: Criminal Procedure (Scotland) Act 1995, s.52(1). The situation may therefore arise in a trial where the Crown pursue a verdict of acquittal on the ground of insanity. This may, indeed, be opposed by the defence for whom a verdict of guilty might be preferable. In *H.M. Advocate v. Harrison,* High Court, Dundee, October 1967, *unreported* (but see the second edition of this work, pp. 300–301) it was held that where the Crown seek to establish that the accused is insane they need only prove this on a balance of probability (which is the same standard as when the accused seeks to establish the defence). Should there be a higher standard on the Crown, given that the defence is seeking to avoid the verdict of insanity?

7. A person may, of course, be insane and entitled to acquittal on other grounds. Suppose, for example, that a person charged with murder pleads self-defence. There is also evidence to the effect that he was insane at the time. Section 54(6) of the 1995 Act provides that if, in such a case, the accused is acquitted, the court must (a) in proceedings on indictment, direct the jury to find, or, in summary proceedings state, whether the accused was insane at the time, and if so, to declare whether he was acquitted on the ground of insanity.

8. Where a person has been acquitted on the ground of insanity in a case other than murder, the court may (a) make an order for that person to be detained in a hospital (specified by the court), with or without special restrictions, (b) make an order placing the person under the guardianship of a local authority or of a person approved by a local authority, (c) make an order for supervision and treatment, or (d) make no order at all. Where the offence with which the person was charged was murder, the court has no discretion, but must make an order for the accused's detention in a hospital, with restrictions. See Criminal Procedure (Scotland) Act 1995, s.57.

9. If the Crown were to be successful in obtaining a verdict of not guilty by reason of insanity in a case such as *Harrison*, by what means could the accused obtain a review of this finding? He cannot, after all, appeal against his acquittal. *Cf.* the English Criminal Appeal Act 1968, s.12, of which gives a right of appeal in such cases. See also the Second Report of the Thomson Committee on Criminal Procedure in Scotland (Cmnd. 6218/1975), paras 52–18—52–23. (It should be noted that although an accused cannot appeal against an acquittal on the ground of insanity he may appeal against any order made by the court pursuant to such a finding: 1995 Act, s.62(1)(c)).

## (c) Diminished responsibility

**7.38** The plea of diminished responsibility—a form of mental abnormality verging upon but falling short of the complete alienation of reason required for insanity—was at one time accepted as a defence to a wide range of offences. (See the discussion in Gordon, Chapter 11, especially at para. 11–05.) However, it was held in *H.M. Advocate v. Cunningham*, 1963 J.C. 80, that the defence was applicable only in charges of murder, and that continues to be the practice today. The defence of diminished responsibility is, therefore, considered in the context of murder and culpable homicide, in Chap. 10.

## (d) Automatism

**7.39** This term is used to indicate a condition in which the accused, although apparently acting, cannot properly be described as doing so because his or her conduct is not conscious and therefore not within their control.

There are differing views as to how automatism affects criminal responsibility. Some writers take the view that since the accused is not conscious at the time of the conduct upon which the criminal charge is based, there is no *actus reus*. But as Ashworth (*Principles of Criminal Law*, 3rd ed., p. 101) notes "[a]utomatism is often regarded as a defence to crime rather than as an essential component of criminal conduct" and observes that it has much in common with various excuses such as mental disorder and intoxication. (*Cf.* Wilson, *Criminal Law: Doctrine and Theory* (Longman, 1998), who discusses involuntary behaviour (including automatism) under the general heading of "excuses".) To treat automatism as an excuse, however, is to assume that the basic requirements of *actus reus* and *mens rea* are present, notwithstanding the accused's lack of consciousness. Automatism may, however, raise more "fundamental" questions:

> "Automatism is not merely a denial of fault. It is more a denial of authorship, a claim that the ordinary link between mind and behaviour was absent; the person could not be said to be acting as a moral agent at the time—what occurred was set of involuntary movements of the body rather than 'acts' of [the accused]." (Ashworth, *ibid*.)

It is not difficult to accept that a person has not acted in any morally significant fashion if, for example, they have a heart attack while driving, so that they fail to stop at a pedestrian crossing. It could also be accepted without much difficulty that a person who lashes out with their arms and legs in the course of an epileptic episode is not "acting" in a sense that the criminal law should punish.

But some people may have greater difficulty in accepting that an accused has not "acted" where the accused claims to have been unconscious and yet has managed to perform some complex action with apparent skill. In *R. v. Parks* [1992] S.C.R. 871, for example, the respondent attacked his parents-in-law, killing one and severely injuring the other, while they were asleep in their beds. He claimed that at the time he was asleep, although prior to the attack he had driven some 23 kilometres from his home to the home of his parents-in-law. Such cases are clearly different from those in which injury or damage is caused by a wholly uncontrollable muscle spasm or reflex action. Sleepwalkers such as Parks are examples, rather, of cases in which the accused's consciousness has been so substantially impaired that the accused should not be held responsible for events which he has caused while in that condition.

Treating the matter as one of impaired consciousness makes it easier to treat automatism as a matter of excuse: the accused carried out the prohibited acts, brought about the events which the criminal law proscribes, but did so in circumstances where she or he may be excused because of their mental condition at the time.

That appears to be the current approach of the Scottish courts at least since the case of *Ross v. H.M. Advocate*, 1991 S.L.T. 564, *post*, p. 245. Although treating automatism as a matter affecting *mens rea*, they have applied to it a test of mental impairment derived from the defence of insanity—which is generally regarded as an excusing condition.

Recognising automatism as a defence does raise important issues of public policy. Where the accused's condition is due to some external factor, over which he had no control, then there are few risks in simply acquitting her. But where automatism results from some inherent condition which is prone to recur, the courts have displayed considerable unease about the consequences of simply acquitting the accused. This is understandable. The accused may have caused significant harm to other persons while 'acting' involuntarily, and may do so again if not subjected to measures of control. But if the accused is to be acquitted, then how can such measures be imposed or enforced. Early cases such as *Simon Fraser* demonstrate the difficulties faced by the courts. In modern practice this issue is more easily addressed by treating cases of automatism due to "inherent" conditions as cases of insanity. This approach is reinforced by the application to all cases of automatism of a standard of mental dissociation derived from the plea of insanity.

It is now possible, indeed, necessary, to distinguish between cases of automatism depending upon their origins, not from the point of view of the effect on criminal responsibility—automatism should result in an acquittal whatever its origin—but from the point of view of disposal. Automatism arising from "internal" factors will generally be treated as raising questions of insanity, and the appropriate verdict is therefore not guilty by reason of insanity. Automatism arising from external factors and which is not "self-induced" (as to which see *Ross v. H.M. Advocate*, 1991 S.L.T. 564, *post*, p. 245) will result in a simple acquittal.

At one time, however, it was not possible to make this distinction, because of the decision in *H.M. Advocate v. Cunningham*, 1963 J.C. 80. In that case the accused was charged with taking and driving away a van without the owner's consent or other lawful authority, contrary to section 217 of the Road Traffic Act, 1960, driving the van recklessly, causing it to mount a footpath and collide with several persons (one of whom was so severely injured that he died immediately thereafter), contrary to section 1 of the Act, and driving while unfit through drink or drugs, contrary to section 6(1) of the Act.

The accused pleaded not guilty and lodged what was described as a "special defence" to the effect that throughout the period during which the crimes were allegedly committed he was not responsible for his actings "on account of the incidence of temporary dissociation due to an epileptic fugue or other pathological condition".

The Court was not prepared to accept this defence. The Lord Justice-General (Clyde) stated:

"In my opinion, this present defence is not a competent special defence at all. To constitute a valid special defence the proof of the factors in it should lead to a verdict of 'not guilty'. Proof of all the factors in the present special defence would not, in my opinion, justify a verdict of not guilty. On the contrary, these factors only bear upon mitigation of sentence and not upon guilt ....

It follows that if this present so-called special defence is to be made into a true special defence, as understood in the law of Scotland, it would require to include an averment of insanity at the time the offence was committed .... Any mental or pathological condition short of insanity—any question of diminished responsibility owing to any cause, which does not involve insanity—is relevant only to the question of mitigating circumstances and sentence."

In rejecting the accused's defence, the Court disapproved the charge given to the jury by Lord Murray in the case of *H.M. Advocate v. Ritchie* 1926, J.C. 45, *infra*. That was a case of automatism arising from the effect exhaust fumes on a driver, which caused him to lapse into unconsciousness. It was, therefore, a case of automatism arising from *external* factors, and quite easily distinguished from the circumstances of *Cunningham*. The effect of *Cunningham* was, therefore, to treat all cases of automatism in the same manner, and to exclude the defence of automatism if the circumstances could not be brought within the defence of insanity.

This decision, driven largely by considerations of public policy and public safety, was capable of generating considerable injustice. While it was applied uncritically in some cases (see, for example, *H.M. Advocate v. Murray*, 1969 S.L.T. (Notes) 85) it was clearly not approved of by some judges, and some sheriffs in particular made efforts to avoid it. See, for example, *Carmichael v. Boyle*, 1985 S.C.C.R. 58 and *Farrell v. Stirling*, 1975 S.L.T. (Sh.Ct) 71.

Notwithstanding the criticisms made of *Cunningham* it remained the law until it was over-ruled in *Ross v. H.M. Advocate*. There a bench of five judges held that *Cunningham* was wrongly decided "in so far as it held that any mental or pathological condition short of insanity is relevant only to the question of mitigating circumstances and sentence". The Court went on to state that a verdict of acquittal would be an appropriate verdict if the jury are not satisfied beyond reasonable doubt as to the accused's ability to form the intention to commit the crime with which he is charged and that in appropriate circumstances a defence of automatism could be admitted.

## (i) Automatism arising from external factors

### H.M. Advocate v. Ritchie
### 1926 J.C. 45

The panel was charged with the culpable homicide of a pedestrian by reckless driving. A **7.40** special defence was tendered to the effect that "by the incidence of temporary mental dissociation due to toxic exhaustive factors he was unaware of the presence of the deceased on the highway and of his injuries and death, and was incapable of appreciating his immediately previous and subsequent actions". In the course of his charge to the jury, the presiding judge gave the following directions:

LORD MURRAY: [After a summary of the facts] "Now, however, you have to consider the more difficult aspect of the case—the special defence, which is a somewhat novel one, based upon the alleged abnormal and irresponsible condition of the accused at the time of the accident. Such irresponsibility may create criminal immunity and form the ground of a good defence; but there is a strong presumption in favour of normality and responsibility. The presumption may be overcome, but the onus of proof lies, as indeed was conceded by counsel for the defence, upon the person who pleads that he is abnormal and irresponsible.

Turning now to the question of a man's responsibility or irresponsibility for his actions, irresponsibility need not be confined to what to us is the most familiar example, *viz.*, the case of a person who is, in popular language, 'out of mind'. It may be useful for me to remind you of the general basis on which the defence of irresponsibility rests. Putting it in language which is both legal and intelligible, it amounts to this, that, owing to some disordered condition of the mind which affects its working, the afflicted person does not know the nature of his act, or, if he does know what he is doing he does not know that what he is doing is wrong. The most familiar case is where reason has been upset and the person is, in common parlance, out of his mind, a condition which may be permanent or passing. This condition may be induced by various causes. It may be congenital; it may be induced by illness, fever, palsy, accident, injury, or shock; all these may induce a condition in which, in popular language, a man is 'not fully responsible for his action'. This condition may be brought about by a man's own action, *e.g.* over-indulgence in drink; but in the present case I am glad to say we are relieved from considering that question, as both sides are in agreement that the question of drink does not enter into the case. It being then the law that there may be irresponsibility—temporary or permanent—where the reason is so affected as to make the person who has committed the act unaware of the nature of his act, I must remind you shortly of conditions which fall short of inferring irresponsibility. As was pointed out by counsel for the Crown, there are certain things which will not excuse. If a person, being normal, runs over someone because he did not see him, the fact that he did not see the person he ran over affords no excuse, for the law holds that he ought to have seen him. If a person is abnormal, in the sense merely that he is below the ordinary or average standard, that affords no excuse. The degree of care which the law imposes is always proportionate to the risk of the operation. In the event of an accident it would be no defence for a man to say, 'I happened to be tired and rather exhausted and therefore less attentive'. It would be no defence for a woman to say, 'I had overestimated the strength of my nerves; a situation arose in which my nerves were unequal to the strain, and that was the cause of the accident'. The law says to such persons that they were bound to take account of such possibilities. But where the defence is that a person, who would ordinarily be quite justified in driving a car, becomes—owing to a cause which he was not bound to foresee, and which was outwith his control—either gradually or suddenly not the master of his own action, a question as to his responsibility or irresponsibility for the consequences of his action arises, and may form the ground of a good special defence. The question, accordingly, which you have to determine is whether, at the time of the accident, the accused was or was not master of his own action. So put the question becomes a pure question of fact.

Now it is not disputed that there may be such a thing as a condition of irresponsibility induced by what has been referred to as mental dissociation. The admission, however of the possibility of such a condition does not relieve the case of difficulty. As regards the period immediately following the accident, it is common ground between the factors examined on behalf of the Crown and the accused respectively that the actions of the accused during this period are typical of a state of mental dissociation. The period to which you must turn your attention is the crucial period which elapsed from the time the accused left the young lady at her door until the moment of the accident. What happened thereafter, it is common ground, may be regarded as typical of mental dissociation. You must draw your conclusions as best you can from the facts, as the question you have to decide does not admit of definite proof. Upon the facts proved you must decide whether after leaving the young lady and until the accident, the accused, being then in a normal condition, was just driving carelessly and inattentively, and whether it was not the shock of the accident which induced a state of dissociation; or whether, on the contrary, the state of dissociation, which admittedly existed after the accident, was not a continuation of a state which had existed prior to the accident, and which had supervened and was in operation from some time after the accused left the young lady at her house. On leaving her house did something supervene in the mind and condition of the accused for which he was not responsible and which he could not foresee, and did this something exist at the time of the accident; or is the true view that it was not until after the accident that the abnormality supervened? That appears to me to be the problem with which you are confronted. Admittedly, the facts in the case are open to more than one interpretation. For instance, take the question of excessive speed. It is within your knowledge that persons, who as a rule are careful, are sometimes careless, and it is a perfectly rational view of the facts in this case that we have here an instance of a careful man betrayed from mere fatigue into a situation in which he was not paying proper attention. On the other hand, as the defence contends, the apparent carelessness may not have been carelessness at all, but the result of some abnormal influence at work in the accused from some time after he left the young lady and became the sole occupant of the car. It is between these two views you have got to choose, and I shall now touch on the facts which I think you should keep in mind as bearing on the situation. [His Lordship reviewed the facts, drawing the jury's attention, *inter alia*, to the marked inconsistency between the reckless and apparently callous conduct of the accused at the time of, and immediately after, the accident and the character and record of the accused up to that date.]

Upon the question of the form of verdict which you are to return, it would be competent for you, under my direction, to return a special verdict; but I prefer the course suggested by counsel for the defence, that you should return a general verdict. If there were no question of abnormality in the case, I have little doubt your verdict would be one of guilty, but the question of abnormality is present and must be dealt with. If you think that, at the time of the accident, the accused was master of his own actions, it is your duty to return a verdict of guilty. If, on the other hand, you think that the condition of mental dissociation, which admittedly was present after the accident, was also actively present prior to the accident, then your view would preclude the existence of culpability on his part. If you affirm irresponsibility there can be no culpability, and the proper verdict for you to return is one of 'not guilty'. I do not think that there is any difficulty on the law of the case, but only on its application to the facts. The question you have to solve is really one of fact, and it is for you to arrive at a just inference from the facts laid before you."

Verdict: Not guilty.

NOTES

1. As noted above, Lord Murray's charge was expressly disapproved by the High Court in *H.M.* **7.41** *Advocate v. Cunningham*, but that decision in its turn was disapproved in part, and Lord Murray's direction "rehabilitated", by the High Court in *Ross v. H.M. Advocate*.

2. It is important, of course, in cases such as *Ritchie* that the accused is not guilty of any prior fault of a kind which could attract criminal responsibility. If, for example, the accused had failed to maintain his car in a proper roadworthy condition, and drove it on the road in a manner which showed a reckless disregard for the safety of other people, then the result would be quite different. If, in such circumstances, the driver of a vehicle were to be overcome by the fumes from the exhaust, then it would be possible to hold her responsible for the injury or damage which results from the loss of control over the vehicle. See, in this respect, *Watmore v. Jenkins* [1962] 2 Q.B. 572.

3. Compare *H.M. Advocate v. Ritchie* with the American case of *People v. Newton*, 87 Cal. Rptr 394 (1970). The defendant was charged, *inter alia*, with the murder of a police officer. His defence included the claim that the police officer had shot him first, and that the firing of the defendant's gun was involuntary. Evidence was led to the effect that the defendant had been shot in the abdomen shortly before he fired any shots, and that such a wound could have provoked unconsciousness or the involuntary discharge of the accused's gun. This defence was not put to the jury by the trial judge. On appeal this was held to be a prejudicial error, since the judge's failure deprived the defendant of his constitutional right to have the jury determine all material issues presented by the defence.

## (ii) Automatism arising from internal factors

The origins or cause of involuntariness have no bearing on whether or not the accused should be held **7.42** responsible except where those origins demonstrate prior fault on the part of the accused. But they are regarded as highly significant when one comes to address the question of disposing of the accused. If, for example, the accused's involuntary conduct arises from a condition which the law would describe as insanity, then the demands of public safety are such that the accused will not be entitled to a simple acquittal, but to an acquittal on the ground of insanity. Particular difficulties have been encountered where the accused's mental condition suggests that there may be a risk of the circumstances giving rise to the offence recurring, but where it is not established that his mental condition amounts to insanity.

### 3. Simon Fraser
(1878) 4 Couper 70

**7.43** The panel was charged with the murder of his eighteen-month-old son by fracturing his skull. A special plea was entered that at the time the crime was committed the panel was asleep. The panel stated that he had had a nightmare during which he believed he was being attacked by an animal. He had a history of somnambulism, accompanied on occasions by violent behaviour. Medical witnesses, however, disagreed on the question of his sanity. In addressing the Jury:

THE LORD JUSTICE-CLERK: "I suppose, gentlemen, you have not the slightest doubt that the prisoner at the time was totally unconscious of the act that he was doing. There is not the slightest doubt that he was labouring under one of those delusions which occurred in a state of somnambulism—he was under the impression that some animal had got into the bed. I see no reason to doubt, and I do not suppose you, gentlemen, have any doubt, that the account as given is correct. It is a matter of some consequence to the prisoner whether he is found responsible or not, because you are aware that his future must to a great extent depend upon the verdict you shall return. The question whether a state of somnambulism such as this is to be considered a state of insanity or not is a matter with which I think you should not trouble yourselves. It is a question on which medical authority is not agreed. But what I would suggest is, that you should return a verdict such as this—that the Jury find the panel killed his child, but that he was in a state in which he was unconscious of the act which he was committing by reason of the condition of somnambulism, and that he was not responsible."

NOTES

**7.44**     1. The jury having returned a verdict in accordance with the above direction, the Solicitor-General proposed that the case should be adjourned for two days so that there might be an opportunity for "consultation as to what arrangements should be made with reference to the accused". The Lord Justice-Clerk agreed to this proposal and the case was adjourned. The accused subsequently gave an undertaking that in future he would sleep alone, an undertaking supported by his father, and he was accordingly dismissed from the bar. When the case was called again the following minute of procedure was recorded:

> "In respect the Counsel for the Crown does not move for sentence, and in respect the panel has come under certain obligations satisfactory to Crown Counsel, the Court deserted the diet *simpliciter* against the panel, and dismissed him from the Bar."

The case is not very satisfactory. While there seems to have been an acceptance that the accused was not responsible for what took place, there seems equally to have been a reluctance to accept the consequences of this—namely that the accused was not guilty of an offence. And if the accused was not guilty of an offence, on what basis could the Crown have moved for sentence? (In *Ross v. H.M. Advocate* (*post*, p. 245) the Lord Justice-General (Hope) expressed the view that Fraser was not acquitted— a view supported by the reference to the court deserting the diet in the above-mentioned minute.)

2. A similar approach appears to have been adopted in the unreported case of *H.M. Advocate v. Hayes*, High Court, November 1949. In this case the accused was charged on an indictment which libelled culpable homicide, or alternatively reckless driving, contrary to section 11 of the Road Traffic Act 1930. The facts alleged were that he was the driver of a bus which, due to his neglectful driving, collided with two stationary vehicles and overturned, killing some of the passengers, and injuring several others. A special defence was tabled to the effect that the accused pleaded not guilty "and further pleads ... that at the time the crime charged is said to have been committed by the incidence of temporary dissociation due to masked epilepsy or other pathological condition, he was unaware of the presence of the stationary motor lorries with which the motor bus driven by him collided".

The presiding judge (Lord Carmont) directed the jury that in returning their verdict they should answer the following questions:

(1)  Has the Crown proved against the accused the charge of culpable homicide, or the alternative charge of reckless driving and if so, which?

If the answer to question 1 is that either charge has been proved, the jury must go on to answer the following question:

(2) Do you find the special defence proved or do you not so find?

The jury found the charge of culpable homicide proved against the accused, and also found the special defence proved. After some debate as to the effect of the jury's findings the verdict was allowed to stand. In respect of the difficulty occasioned by the findings of the jury, as to their correct interpretation and the consequent disposal of the case, Lord Carmont, in accordance with a memorandum previously issued by the Lord Justice-General, certified the case to the High Court (Full Bench). In delivering its opinion the court stated:

> "If we had been left in any doubt as to the true effect of the verdict returned by this jury under the special circumstances which have been described by Lord Carmont, it would have been necessary to re-affirm the salutary rule that, once a verdict has been recorded and assented to, it is no longer open to challenge or discussion except through the medium of an appeal under the Act of 1926. That, however, is a matter which has ceased to be significant in this case, because it is sufficiently plain from the record and from the shorthand note that the view of the jury was that, if the panel had been a normal man, they would have found him guilty of culpable homicide, but that they were satisfied on the medical evidence that the special defence was established and therefore that he was not a normal man. It is on the footing that that was the jury's conclusion that we approach the question as to the advice we should give to Lord Carmont as to his duty in this case.
>
> We are faced, as always happens in these cases, with a twofold responsibility, our duty to the panel on the one side, and our duty to do what in us lies for the protection of the public interest on the other side; and the proposal I am about to announce is the one that seems appropriate in this case but is by no means to be regarded as a necessary precedent in any other case. Our advice is that, if the panel will give an undertaking of the type indicated by his learned counsel, namely, that he will now surrender his public service licence and his driving licence and undertake that he will engage no more in driving cars or public service vehicles of any kind, he should be discharged from the bar; and we also consider that an intimation of the decision should be sent to the Licensing Authority and to the Road Traffic Commissioners. With that conclusion and advice we shall adjourn to enable Lord Carmont to carry through the concluding stages of the trial."

3. The obvious problem with the approach adopted in both *Simon Fraser* and *Hayes* would be securing compliance with the undertakings demanded of the accused. In practical terms it is impossible to see how the undertaking in *Fraser's* case could ever be enforced. Those suggested in *Hayes* are a little less problematic. It is implicit in the course of action suggested in both cases that, if the accused refused to give the undertakings suggested by the court, a different outcome would follow. In practical terms that could only mean a finding of guilt, which simply raises the question of the effect of automatism on criminal liability. If the accused were unconscious at the time of the alleged offence, can they properly be held responsible for those actions?

4. The question which does arise is how Fraser and Hayes would be dealt with today. There is little doubt that Hayes would be regarded as suffering from insane automatism. (See *H.M. Advocate v. Mitchell*, 1951 S.L.T. 200 (in which it was held that a person suffering from "psychic epilepsy" which resulted in a loss of consciousness on the part of the accused, during which he killed a woman) and, indeed, *Cunningham*.)

The position is perhaps less clear with regard to Fraser. In *R. v. Parks, supra*, five expert witnesses called by the defence testified to the effect that the respondent was sleepwalking and that sleepwalking is not a neurological, psychiatric or other illness. The trial judge put only the defence of automatism to the jury, which acquitted the respondent of first degree murder and then of second degree murder. The judge then acquitted the respondent of the charge of attempted murder. The Court of Appeal unanimously upheld the acquittal. Other Commonwealth courts have reached similar conclusions. See *Ryan v. The Queen* (1967), 40 A.L.J.R. 488 (Australia), *R. v. Cottle* [1958] N.Z.L.R. 999 (New Zealand) and *R. v. Naidoo*, 1971 (3) S.A. 605 (N) (South Africa).

In at least one English case, however, the Courts have held that a person who commits an offence while sleepwalking is not entitled to a simple acquittal. Sleepwalking in that case is regarded as manifesting a "disease of the mind", with the result that if the accused is to be acquitted, this must be done on the basis of a plea of insanity, rather than non-insane automatism. See *R.* v. *Burgess* [1991] 2 All E.R. 769 (and the *obiter* statements in *R.* v. *Sullivan* [1983] 2 All E.R. 673 which suggest a similar conclusion).

### Finegan v. Heywood
2000 S.C.C.R. 460

**7.45** The appellant was convicted of driving a motor vehicle after consuming so much alcohol that the proportion of it in his breath exceeded the prescribed limit; secondly, taking and driving away a motor vehicle without the owner's consent, and driving without insurance. He appealed against his conviction. The circumstances of the offence and his grounds of appeal are set out in the opinion of the Court, delivered by the Lord Justice-General (Rodger).

OPINION OF THE COURT: "[2] The facts on which we have to proceed in this unusual case are those found by the Sheriff and stated in the case. The appellant has been prone to sleepwalking (parasomnia) since he was a teenager. For some months before May 1997 he had been suffering from stress, much of it related to worries about the impending birth of a child. In due course his wife had a son and, on May 23, 1997, the appellant and two friends, one of them a Mr Gregor White, went out to celebrate. Before going out, Mr White, who had arranged to stay overnight at the appellant's home, left a Mercedes Benz car, belonging to his employers, outside the appellant's house. The appellant and his friends visited various licensed premises in and around Dundee where the appellant consumed not less than six pints of beer. During the course of the evening the appellant became separated from his friends who returned to the appellant's home, went to bed and went to sleep. Mr White slept in a bed in the appellant's bedroom and the keys to the Mercedes Benz were on a dressing table in that room. The appellant returned home at about 1 a.m. and, having sat down to watch television in the living-room, fell asleep. While in a parasomniac state, the appellant went to his bedroom, took the car keys from the dressing table and drove the Mercedes Benz some 1.5 miles to Strathmore Street, where police officers found it sitting in the roadway with its front at an angle of 45 degrees to the kerb. The engine was running and the appellant was asleep in the driver's seat. The police officers had difficulty in waking him and, when they managed to do so, he tried to put the automatic gearbox into the drive position. The car moved a very short distance, whereupon the officers ordered the appellant to stop the car. He did so, opened the door and came out of the car. He spoke incoherently to the officers who could make no sense of what he was saying other than that he was constantly repeating a postcode. They believed that he was very drunk. The appellant co-operated with the officers' request to provide a breath sample, which proved positive. He was arrested and taken to police headquarters. On arriving there he spoke intelligibly to the police officers and told them who owned the car and where the person with authority to use it was to be found. The officers found the keys to the car among the items of the appellant's property. The appellant provided two specimens of breath for testing by the Camic device. The lower reading showed that the proportion of alcohol in his breath was 79 microgrammes in 100 millilitres of breath.

[3] On the basis of expert evidence led on behalf of the appellant, the Sheriff found that stress can promote instances of parasomnia. He also found that consumption of alcohol is often associated with parasomniac episodes, because alcohol can induce deep sleep in which such episodes take place. They are therefore more likely to occur after the consumption of alcohol. The disinhibiting effect of alcohol also increases the likelihood of persons who are prone to parasomnia being put into such a state. The appellant was aware that at least three of his recent experiences of parasomnia had been preceded by the consumption of amounts of alcohol similar to the quantity which he took on the evening in question. The Sheriff's overall conclusion was that 'The alcohol consumed by the appellant on May 23 had induced the parasomniac state in which he was when he took the car key and [which] persisted throughout that time until the car came to a halt at the kerbside.'

[4] The sleepwalker is a familiar figure in romance and literature, including the literature of the law. He features somewhat less often in actual decisions of the courts, although one of the most famous examples is, of course, the nineteenth-century Scottish case of *Simon Fraser* (1878) 4 Coup. 70. But, as Lord Justice-General Hope pointed out in *Ross v. H.M. Advocate* 1991 J.C. 210 at p. 217, that case cannot be regarded as anything other than very special in view of the manner in which the court interpreted the jury's verdict. In advancing his submissions on behalf of the appellant in the present case, therefore, Mr Shead did not suggest that the court could derive much guidance from the approach of Lord Justice Clerk in *Simon Fraser*.

[5] Mr Shead's argument can be summarised in this way. It is a basic principle of criminal law that only those who act voluntarily should be punished. A person who is in a state of somnambulism is unconscious and so his actions are not voluntary. In the present case, therefore, at the relevant time, the appellant was not "driving" the car since his conscious mind was not controlling his actions. There was no evidence before the Sheriff which would justify the view that somnambulism was a disease of the mind. The appellant should therefore be acquitted on the ground of non-insane automatism. In formulating his submissions Mr Shead relied extensively on the wide-ranging survey of the authorities in *R. v. Parkes* [1992] 2 S.C.R. 871. In that case the Canadian Supreme Court was concerned, above all, to decide whether the appellant's sleepwalking should be regarded as giving rise to a defence of insane, rather than of non-insane, automatism. That is not an issue which we find it necessary to explore in this case.

[6] In *Bratty v. Attorney-General for Northern Ireland* [1963] A.C. 386 at p. 409 Lord Denning observed obiter:

"No act is punishable if it is done involuntarily: and an involuntary act in this context—some people nowadays prefer to speak of it as 'automatism'—means an act which is done by the muscles without any control by the mind, such as a spasm, a reflex action or a convulsion; or an act done by a person who is not conscious of what he is doing, such as an act done whilst suffering from concussion or whilst sleep-walking."

He went on to say that the point had been well put by Stephen J. in *R. v. Tolson* (1889) 23 Q.B.D. 168 at p. 187:

"To take an extreme illustration, can anyone doubt that a man who, though he might be perfectly sane, committed what would otherwise be a crime in a state of somnambulism, would be entitled to be acquitted? And why is this? Simply because he would not know what he was doing."

In that passage his Lordship was giving judicial expression to the earlier extrajudicial observation of Sir James Fitzjames Stephen in his *History of the Criminal Law of England* Volume 2 (1883), p. 100:

"For legal purposes it is enough to say that no involuntary action, whatever effects it may produce, amounts to a crime by the law of England. I do not know indeed that it has ever been suggested that a person who in his sleep set fire to a house or caused the death of another would be guilty of arson or murder."

Mr Shead readily acknowledged that the words of Stephen J. in Tolson encapsulated his submission in this case.

[7] We accept that, on the facts found by the Sheriff, when the appellant took the car and drove it while drunk, his normal conscious mind was not controlling his actions. In that sense his actions were "involuntary". We also accept that, if these were the only relevant facts, for

the reasons given by Stephen J. and Lord Denning, the appellant could not properly be held criminally responsible for his actions while he was in this transitory state of parasomnia.

[8] Mr Shead argued indeed that these were the only relevant facts since sleepwalking constituted a unique category in our law: once it was established that an accused had been in a state of parasomnia at the relevant time, there was no need to enquire further into the antecedents of his condition because the only proper conclusion was that he should be acquitted. We see no reason in principle, however, why in the case of parasomnia the court should necessarily disregard the surrounding circumstances and, in particular, any circumstances which explain why the accused was in the state of parasomnia on the occasion in question. If those circumstances could be legally relevant, they should be considered—and we see no *a priori* reason why such circumstances could not indeed be of relevance.

[9] In the present case the Sheriff found that the alcohol consumed by the appellant induced the parasomniac state in which he took the keys and drove the car. In addition, the Sheriff found that the appellant had been aware that at least three of his recent experiences of the condition had been preceded by his consuming approximately the same amount of alcohol as he consumed on the occasion in question.

[10] In our law these factors have to be considered in the light of the approach to intoxicants adopted by the Full Bench in *Brennan v. H.M. Advocate* 1977 J.C. 38. In that case, which concerned the law of insanity and diminished responsibility, the court said of insanity (1977 J.C. at pp. 42–43) that its meaning is

> "a question which has been resolved by the law itself as a matter of legal policy in order to set, in the public interest, acceptable limits upon the circumstances in which any person may be able to relieve himself of criminal responsibility".

Approaching the matter in that way and having reviewed the relevant authorities, the court held (1977 J.C. at p. 46):

> "In the law of Scotland a person who voluntarily and deliberately consumes known intoxicants, including drink or drugs, of whatever quantity, for their intoxicating effects, whether these effects are fully foreseen or not, cannot rely on the resulting intoxication as the foundation of a special defence of insanity at the time nor, indeed, can he plead diminished responsibility."

Although their Lordships were not, of course, thinking of the situation where the voluntary consumption of alcohol for its intoxicating effect induced a transitory state of parasomnia, we consider that the same approach should be applied in such a case. If insanity in our law "does not comprehend the malfunctioning of the mind of transitory effect, as the result of deliberate and self-induced intoxication" and if the defence of diminished responsibility cannot be "established upon mere proof of the transitory effects upon the mind of self-induced intoxication" (1977 J.C. at pp. 45–46), then, equally, the defence of automatism cannot in our view be established upon proof that the appellant was in a transitory state of parasomnia which was the result of, and indeed induced by, deliberate and self-induced intoxication. In that regard the decision on automatism in *Ross v. H.M. Advocate* is distinguishable since it dealt only with those cases where there was no disease of the mind "and where the factor which had caused the impairment was not self-induced" (1991 J.C. at p. 213 per the Lord Justice General).

[11] Applying our conclusion on the law to the facts of the present case, we hold that, since the appellant's consumption of alcohol induced the parasomniac state in which he took the keys and drove the car, the Sheriff was correct to reject the appellant's defence and to convict him of the three charges. The appeal against conviction must therefore be refused."

Appeal against conviction refused; appeal against
sentence allowed.

NOTES

1. The Court held that the circumstances under which the drink-driving offence was committed **7.46** amounted to "special reasons" for not disqualifying him and allowed the appeal against sentence by quashing the period of disqualification and imposing six penalty points instead.

2. The court appears to treat the accused's defence as one of automatism, but if automatism is, as *Ross* suggests, a matter affecting *mens rea*, then what is the relevance of the accused's defence to the offences of strict liability with which the accused was charged?

3. This is a case of prior fault leading to automatism. What would be the position if the accused was aware of his propensity to sleep walk, and to commit acts of violence in his sleep, but took no steps to prevent this happening. Would there be prior fault in that case? That, in fact, was the position in *Simon Fraser's* case. Indeed, so concerned was Fraser's wife that she regularly hid knives and other implements, prior to going to bed at night, which could cause harm.

## (e) Intoxication

As an exculpatory plea, intoxication presents substantial difficulties for the criminal justice system. In **7.47** the first place, there is an understandable reluctance to allow a person to plead intoxication as a defence since, as a general rule, intoxication results from the ingestion of substances which, to the knowledge of the user, may result in diminished capacity to conform ones behaviour to the requirements of the criminal law. Why should a person who voluntarily consumes a known intoxicant be entitled to rely on the consequent intoxication as a defence to a criminal charge? Secondly, there is a perceived link between intoxication, or at least alcoholic intoxication, and certain forms of criminal behaviour, most importantly offences of violence and offences of damage to property.

Both of these arguments suggest a strong policy in favour of holding responsible a person who knowingly consumes an intoxicant and, under the influence of that intoxicant, commits the *actus reus* of an offence. There is, however, a problem, which stems from the fundamental axiom of the criminal law, *actus non facit reum nisi mens sit rea*. If an individual commits an offence while so intoxicated that he or she does not have the *mens rea* required for the offence in question, the logic of the criminal law suggests that he or she should not be convicted, at least of an offence requiring proof of *mens rea*.

The policy issues can be addressed in part by distinguishing between voluntary and involuntary intoxication since in the latter case there is at least no question of prior fault.

## (i) Voluntary intoxication

### Brennan v. H.M. Advocate
### 1977 S.L.T. 151

(For the facts of this case, see above under "Insanity".)                                      **7.48**

THE COURT: "The second and alternative submission for the appellant was that in any event the trial judge should have left to the jury the possibility of returning a verdict of guilt of culpable homicide because, it was said, there was evidence on which the jury would have been entitled to conclude that the appellant was intoxicated to such a degree that he was deprived of all capacity to form the 'specific intent' which is of the essence of the crime of murder.

The argument for the appellant in support of this submission was necessarily founded upon the cases of *H.M. Advocate v. Campbell*, 1921 J.C. 1 and *Kennedy v. H.M. Advocate*, 1944 J.C. 171 in which it was said that, according to the law of Scotland, if a man accused of murder was shown to have been incapable, by reason of self-induced intoxication, of forming the intention to kill or do serious injury to the deceased, he will be guilty only of culpable homicide. According to these cases the laws of Scotland and England are the same on this matter, and attention was drawn to the case of *D.P.P. v. Beard* [1920] A.C. 479, the judgment in which has recently been explored and explained in the case of *D.P.P. v. Majewski* [1977] A.C. 443 to which reference has already been made. Before us the correctness of the statements of the law to be found in *Campbell* and *Kennedy* was challenged by the Crown and fully debated, but before we come to examine these cases it is, we think, important to remind ourselves of the law as it clearly appeared to be when Campbell went to trial on September 27, 1920, and to notice certain differences between the laws of Scotland and England.

As we have already shown, impairment of the mental faculties of an accused person caused merely by self-induced intoxication however gross the impairment may be, is not insanity in our law. Further, proof of the mere effects of such intoxication, whatever their degree, cannot in our law support a defence of diminished responsibility—a defence available only where the charge is murder and which, if it is established, can result only in the return of a verdict of guilt of the lesser crime of culpable homicide. In both branches, insanity and diminished responsibility, the attitude of the law of Scotland has accordingly been entirely consistent, and has remained true to the sound general rule enunciated by Hume and Alison that self-induced intoxication is no defence to any criminal charge, at least for an offence in itself perilous or hurtful. In these circumstances it would be surprising if our law were to admit proof of self-induced intoxication as a defence to a charge of murder in circumstances in which it could not be held that the criminal responsibility of the accused was in law diminished.

The law of England was as we understand it was until the late 19th century at one with the law of Scotland in refusing to countenance self-induced intoxication as any kind of defence to a criminal charge, and embarked upon the same search for a modification and mitigation of the law in those cases where the only penalty for the crime of murder was capital. In Scotland the search led to the recognition of the concept of diminished responsibility as early as 1867 in the case of *H.M. Advocate v. Dingwall*—a concept which was only introduced into the law of England by statute in the latter half of this century. In England, it appears, the law took a different route and the formula adopted was that of permitting, where the charge was murder, a verdict of guilty of manslaughter to be returned where it was shown that the effects of self-induced intoxication had deprived the accused of all capacity to form the 'specific intent' which had to be proved to establish the crime of murder (*D.P.P. v. Beard*). This relaxation was, it seems, applied to all crimes involving proof of 'specific intent' as distinct from 'basic intent' but to no others, and the rule in *Beard* which was conceived in the days of capital punishment has rightly been recognised as illogical. We have only to add that in crimes of 'basic intent' we understand the law of England to be at one with the law of Scotland in refusing to admit self-induced intoxication as any kind of defence.

The next matters to be noticed before we proceed to an examination of the cases of *Campbell* and *Kennedy* are these. Our law has never recognised a distinction between 'specific' and 'basic' intent in crime. Further, the definition of the crime of murder in Scotland is not the same as the definition of that crime in the law of England. In England the crime involves 'malice aforethought' a technical expression which requires proof of either the specific intention to kill or to do serious injury. In the law of Scotland, however, the crime of murder is constituted by any wilful act causing the destruction of life whether intended to kill or displaying such wicked recklessness as to imply a disposition depraved enough to be regardless of the consequences. Our definition of murder includes the taking of human life by a person who has an intent to kill or to do serious injury or whose act is shown to have been wickedly reckless as to the consequences.

The case of *Cawthorne v. H.M. Advocate*, 1968 S.L.T. 330, where the charge was of attempted murder by a man who fired rifle shots at random into a room where he knew that there were several persons, is a good example of acting's so wickedly reckless that if they resulted in the taking of life the crime would be murder. The charge of the trial judge in that case was affirmed by the court on appeal and the following passage appears in the opinion of the Lord Justice-General (Clyde) at p. 331: 'The crimes of murder and attempted murder are common law crimes in Scotland and I do not find it helpful to seek to draw analogies from alien systems of law where the rules may for various reasons be different. The issue must be determined by the rules applicable to Scots law. In our law murder is constituted by any wilful act causing the destruction of life (Macdonald, *Criminal Law* (5th ed.), p. 89). The *mens rea* which is essential to the establishment of such a common law crime may be established by satisfactory evidence of a deliberate intention to kill or by a satisfactory evidence of such wicked recklessness as to imply a disposition depraved enough to be regardless of consequences. (See Macdonald in the same passage.) The reason for this alternative being allowed in our law is that in many cases it may not be possible to prove what was in the accused's mind at the time, but the degree of recklessness in his actings, as proved by what he did, may be sufficient to establish proof of the wilful act on his part which caused the loss of life.'

Finally we must dispel any suspicion that what was said in *Campbell* and *Kennedy* was merely an echo of a passage in the charge of the Lord Justice-Clerk in *McDonald*, in which he directed the jury that 'if the means adopted were not of themselves likely to lead to bad results and if there were no malice aforethought then the fact that the man was in a drunken state may be considered in determining the question between murder and culpable homicide'. The initial hypothesis presented to the jury is of crucial importance: (1) absence of malicious or criminal intent to kill; and (2) use of modes of assault not of themselves likely to lead to bad results. The case of *McDonald* therefore lays down and professes to lay down no general principle of law, and the direction is one related precisely to a particular combination of facts. It might indeed have been argued that without any evidence of drunkenness that combination of facts would have made a verdict of culpable homicide a proper one.

We come now to the case of *Campbell*. In that case the Lord Justice-Clerk was dealing with a charge of murder by violent blows of the fist. There was no evidence to support a contention that the accused was in any way suffering from mental disease or disorder causing total or partial alienation of reason related to the crime charged. The only alleged mitigating circumstance was the accused's intoxication at the time of the event. It was pleaded for the accused that his drunkenness was of such a degree as to warrant the jury in returning a verdict of culpable homicide. The report bears that 'Counsel for the Crown contended that the drunkenness of the accused did not reduce the crime from that of murder to culpable homicide. Reference was made to *H.M. Advocate v. McDonald* and *Director of Public Prosecutions v. Beard*.' It also appears that counsel for the accused founded on the passage in the charge in *McDonald* which we have already examined. There is in the report no trace of any argument that *Beard* did not represent the law of Scotland and in directing the jury without having had the advantage of a full debate or further examination of the relevant Scots authorities on the place of self-induced intoxication in our law, the Lord Justice-Clerk said this: 'If a man strikes and wounds another and a fist may be just as dangerous, if it is sufficiently used, as a weapon—if he strikes him in such a way and kills him there and then on the spot, with the intent to kill, that is murder. But it is also the law that if a man proceeds to strike another fellow-being, it may be without the intent to kill, but with the intent to cause serious injury, then, although he did not mean to kill, or had no intention of killing, if he is struck with the intent to bring about serious injury, and the result is that his victim died, then that too is murder. The question which you have to consider is whether from the blows which this man undoubtedly inflicted upon this woman, his wife, who was six months gone in pregnancy at the time—whether he had the intention to cause her serious injury. If you think he was so drunk that he could not form any intention about it, you may reduce it to culpable homicide; the question for you is, was he so drunk as to be incapable of forming any intention on the subject, or was there any other intention on the part of this man but to cause serious injury to the woman.'

Later he referred to the case of *Beard* and said this: 'Quite recently there was a very important case . . . decided in England, by the House of Lords, where this question came up as to what was the effect of drunkenness when a man had killed a fellow human being, and the case was considered of such importance that it was dealt with by eight judges in the House of Lords. Two of them were Scotsmen, one being a Scottish lawyer, Lord Dunedin, and the other Lord Haldane, and one judgment was delivered expressing the views of the whole Court. On this matter there is no difference between the law of England and the law of Scotland. It would be most unfortunate indeed if, as to the effect of drunkenness, where injuries are due to the violence of a drunk person, there was such a difference; but there is no difference at all. The result of that case may be summed up thus—that insanity, of course, is a complete answer, to this effect, that the man or person who has committed a crime cannot be found guilty if he was insane at the time even though the insanity is caused by drink, and he will be dealt with as an insane person; but so far as drunkenness was concerned, their lordships said this, that evidence of drunkenness which renders the accused incapable of forming the specific intent required to constitute the crime—that is in this case the intention to kill or to do serious injuries—should be taken into consideration with the other facts proved in order to determine whether or not he had that intention.'

From our examination of the charge as a whole and in particular the passages we have quoted it is plain that the Lord Justice-Clerk omitted to notice that *Beard* was a special case not involving a need to prove specific intent as that is understood by the law of England for by that law, differing from the law of Scotland, it was only necessary to show that the act of causing death was done in furtherance of rape. He omitted to notice also that the definition of murder in Scotland is not the same as that of the law of England and that the concept of 'specific intent' is only intelligible if the crime may only be constituted by proof of actual intention to kill or do serious injury. Further he gave no reasons why what was said in *Beard* coincided with the law of Scotland, unless perhaps it was because two of the eight judges were Scotsmen! Finally he did not appreciate that there was no trace in the law of Scotland before 1920 of self-induced intoxication being a recognised defence to a charge of murder, and that evidence of the effects of such intoxication, by itself, was not even admitted by our law to be a foundation for a plea of diminished responsibility. The charge accordingly contained for the first time a proposition of law contrary to the whole tract of previous authority on the subject, and inconsistent with the broad general principle upon which self induced intoxication had always been treated in the law of Scotland. If according to our law the *mens rea* in murder may be deduced from the wicked recklessness of the actings of the accused, it is extremely difficult to understand how actings may lose the quality of such recklessness because the actor was in an intoxicated state brought about by his own deliberate and conscious purpose .... .

The case of *Campbell* was however approved in the later case of *Kennedy*, but here again it was apparently agreed by both prosecution and defence for the purposes of the argument that the law with regard to the effects of drunkenness upon criminal responsibility was accurately set out in *Campbell*. *Kennedy* involved a charge of murder by stabbing, and the defence was that the verdict should be one of culpable homicide in respect of the accused's drunkenness which, it was maintained, had deprived him of the capacity to form the specific intent to kill or inflict serious injury. The presiding judge refused to allow that plea to be considered by the jury on the ground that, in his opinion, there was no relevant evidence to support it. The appeal was concerned only with the question whether the judge was entitled to take the course he did. It is clear therefore that the appeal was conducted before the Full Bench of five judges of eminence and long experience upon agreement and concession as to the applicability of the law as it was stated in *Campbell's* case and as to the applicability in Scotland of the ratio of *Beard*. This is expressly recorded in the Lord Justice-General's opinion. In particular there was no reference at all to, or examination of, the differences and distinctions between the elements which constitute the crime of murder in the criminal law of Scotland, and those which, according to *Beard*, constitute that crime in England. More important still, there was no discussion or examination of the applicability to the law of Scotland of the distinction drawn in *Beard's* case between crimes of 'specific intent' of which murder is apparently one, and all other crimes described as crimes of 'basic intent'. We have already pointed out how inappropriate that distinction is in any proper consideration of the crime of murder in the law of Scotland. In the result, notwithstanding the great weight which is normally to be accorded to any statement of the law by Lord Justice-General Normand and his distinguished colleagues, we are unable to find in *Kennedy's* case any more sound foundation for the law stated in *Campbell*. We have no doubt that the law was therein incorrectly stated, and that what was said in *Beard's* case as to the effect of self-induced intoxication in relation to a charge of murder, does not and never did represent the law of Scotland. There is nothing unethical or unfair or contrary to the general principle of our law that self-induced intoxication is not by itself a defence to any criminal charge, including in particular the charge of murder. Self induced intoxication is itself a continuing element and therefore an integral part being the evidence of the actings of the accused who uses force against his victim. Together they add up or may add up to that criminal recklessness which it is the purpose of the criminal law to restrain in the interests of all the citizens of this country.

For the reasons we have given, the learned trial judge gave directions to the jury which were entirely in accordance with our law and which were in the circumstances properly given. We shall accordingly refuse the appeal."

Appeal refused.

NOTES

1. The meaning of *Brennan*.                                                                    **7.49**

Now that it has been accepted (in *Ross, post*) that a condition of complete alienation of reason through intoxication is inconsistent with evil intent, it is clear that the decision in *Brennan* is essentially one of public policy (as accepted by Lord Hope in *Ross, post* pp. 246 and 247). What distinguishes the appellant in *Brennan* from the appellant in *Ross* was not his mental condition at the time he attacked his father, but how he came to be in that condition. In *Ross* the appellant was not at fault in becoming intoxicated, since he was unaware of the true nature of the intoxicant which he was consuming. In *Brennan* there was no suggestion that the appellant was unaware of what he was consuming, or that he did not understand the likely effects of the alcohol and other drugs which he consumed.

The recognition of the policy foundation of *Brennan* makes it easier to understand as a decision, since the reasons given in the opinion of the court for upholding the conviction are not, with respect, wholly clear or convincing. It is possible to read the decision in *Brennan* in two ways:

## (a) Intoxication as a form of recklessness:

The first is to emphasise those passages in which the court, clearly influenced by the much-criticised **7.50** English decision of *Majewski*, treats the voluntary consumption of alcohol to the point at which a person is no longer in control of their actions as a form of recklessness, at least where it is accompanied by violence:

> "Self-induced intoxication is itself a continuing element and therefore an integral part being the evidence of the actings of the accused who uses force against his victim. Together they add up or may add up to that criminal recklessness which it is the purpose of the criminal law to restrain . . . ."

Does this passage suggest that acute voluntary intoxication is only to be regarded as reckless where it is associated with violence, or is it to be read as meaning that intoxication supplies the mental element which, along with violence, would be sufficient to constitute an offence?

If intoxication is being equated with recklessness, then, arguably, *Brennan* is relevant only to those cases in which recklessness is a sufficient *mens rea*, and it would not (paradoxically) be applicable to such crimes as assault which cannot be committed recklessly. Does this mean, then, that a person who, while acutely intoxicated, stabs someone with a knife, can only be guilty of reckless injury? In practice, of course, this is not the case, and another interpretation of *Brennan* must be sought.

This conclusion is supported by reference to another hypothetical situation. Suppose that A, while running along the street, accidentally bumps into an elderly woman who suddenly steps out of a close into his path. She is knocked over, so that she strikes her head on the kerb and dies as a result of a fractured skull. In those circumstances the death is not criminal: A's conduct does not display the degree of recklessness that is sufficient even for culpable homicide. Suppose now that A had been acutely intoxicated at the time. Does the reasoning in *Brennan* suggest that A should now be guilty at least of culpable homicide and possibly of murder because his intoxication supplies the kind of recklessness required for these crimes? Again, it is submitted that it ought not to be the law that what would otherwise be regarded as an accident can be converted into a serious crime against the person because the actor in question was drunk at the time.

## (b) The irrelevance of voluntary intoxication

**7.51** These examples suggest that the better interpretation of *Brennan* is not that acute intoxication can supply the degree of recklessness required for certain offences, but that voluntary intoxication (of whatever degree) is simply to be disregarded in determining the responsibility of the accused. There is some support for this in other passages in the Court's opinion:

> "If according to our law the *mens rea* in murder may be deduced from the wicked recklessness of the actings of the accused, it is extremely difficult to understand how actings may lose the quality of such recklessness because the actor was in an intoxicated state brought about by his own deliberate and conscious purpose."

If this approach is adopted then the difficulties set out above are avoided.

2. The major objection in principle to *Brennan* is, of course, that it cannot be reconciled with the maxim *actus non facit reum nisi mens sit rea*. However one interprets *Brennan* one is left with the conclusion that an acutely intoxicated offender can be found guilty of a crime for which he has not formed the necessary *mens rea*. Lord Hope, in *Ross* attempts to overcome this objection by relying on the suggestion that where the absence of *mens rea* results from a self-induced condition, "the accused must be assumed to have intended the natural consequences of his act" (*post*, p. 247). This argument proceeds on an assumption about the link between the consumption of intoxicants and what a person does when intoxicated which is not necessarily born out in fact (as to which, see *infra*, note 5). It is also a fiction, and it is undesirable that persons should be convicted of serious offences, and deprived of their liberty, on the basis of a fiction. Suppose that X consumes a large amount of alcohol, and in his acutely intoxicated condition falls down a flight of stairs and breaks his neck. Would we really accept that he had committed suicide? That is the conclusion which follows from the presumption relied upon by Lord Hope.

3. Is the rule in *Brennan* compatible with the rule contained in Article 6(2) of the European Convention on Human Rights? Article 6(2) provides that everyone charged with a criminal offence "shall be presumed innocent until provided guilty according to law". The phrase "according to law" means, in addition to the rules of evidence and procedure, that the prosecutor must prove the elements of the offence. If the Crown are able to convict the accused without proving the *mens rea*, has Article 6(2) been complied with? It might be argued that the Crown are entitled to rely on a presumption of criminal intent (as *per* Lord Hope in *Ross*), and the use of presumptions is not incompatible with Article 6(2). (See, *inter alia, Salabiaku v. France* (1991) 13 E.H.R.R. 379.) However, Article 6(2) requires States to confine such presumptions within reasonable limits which take into account the importance of what is at stake and maintain the rights of the defence (*Salabiaku v. France*, para. 28). Suppose, then, that an accused is convicted of murder, while acutely intoxicated. Is the use of a presumption of criminal intent in such a serious crime reasonable?

4. The defence of voluntary intoxication has been problematic for most jurisdictions:

(a) England

English law, as exemplified by the decisions of the House of Lords in *Beard* and *Majewski*, draws a distinction between crimes of "specific intent" and crimes of "basic intent". According to this distinction, in crimes which require proof of "specific intent", voluntary intoxication to a degree which excludes that intent is a defence. But in crimes which require proof of "basic" intent only, intoxication is no defence. As a matter of policy this might be defensible, in the sense that intoxication might be accepted as a defence to certain offences but not others. However, it is clear that the distinction drawn by the House of Lords in *Majewski* has no logical basis. Neither the courts, nor commentators on the efforts of the courts, have been able to put forward a rationally justifiable distinction between crimes of specific intent and crimes of basic intent. And if it is not possible to explain the distinction which is fundamental to the analysis proposed, then it is difficult to defend the outcome of that analysis.

(b) Australia

In *R. v. O'Connor* (1980) 146 C.L.R. 64, the High Court of Australia declined to follow the distinction between crimes of "basic intent" and crimes of "specific intent" and held that voluntary intoxication could be a defence to a charge of unlawful wounding contrary to s.423 of the Crimes Act 1958 (Victoria). According to the Court, evidence of self-induced intoxication, whether induced by alcohol or other drugs, was relevant and admissible in determining whether the accused had the mental element required for the offence with which he was charged.

In delivering his judgment, Barwick, C.J. observed (at para. 15) that intoxication was not a "defence" to a criminal charge, in the sense of furnishing an excuse for the accused's conduct. At most, intoxication is "merely part of the totality of the evidence which may raise a reasonable doubt as to the existence of essential elements of criminal responsibility". If such doubt was not removed by the Crown, intoxication could result in an acquittal, not because the accused was intoxicated, "but because the charge will not have been proved beyond reasonable doubt".

(c) New Zealand

In *R. v. Kamipeli* [1975] 2 N.Z.L.R. 610, the Court of Appeal of New Zealand came to the same conclusion as the High Court of Australia in *O'Connor*.

(d) South Africa

Prior to the decision in *S. v. Chretien*, 1981 (1) S.A. 1097 (A) the law in South Africa followed the English "specific intent" rule, but this was rejected by the Appellate Division in the case of *Chretien*. In that case, the court held that the idea of specific intent did not form part of the law of South Africa. A more 'principled' approach was to be preferred. In the words of Rumpff C.J. (1981 (1) S.A. 1097 at p. 1105):

> "In my opinion, it is preferable to accept that, should it appear from the evidence that an accused was really so intoxicated that he in fact had no appreciation of what he was doing, public policy does not require that pure legal principle should be deviated from and an accused be punished simply because he had voluntarily reached a state in which he could not act, juridically speaking, or lacked criminal capacity."

(Translation by J. Burchell and J. Milton, *Cases and Materials on Criminal Law*, (2nd ed.), 1997, p. 289.)

(e) Canada

*Majewski* was followed by a majority of the Canadian Supreme Court in *Leary v. The Queen* (1977) 74 D.L.R. (3d) 103. In *R. v. Daviault* [1994] 3 S.C.R. 63, however, the same court held that the rule that the *mens rea* of a general intent offence cannot be negated by drunkenness was contrary to the Canadian Charter of Rights and Freedoms.

In the views of the majority, the strict application of the rule established in *Leary* was contrary to both sections 7 and 11(d) of the *Canadian Charter of Rights and Freedoms*. (Section 7 of the Charter provides that everyone has the right to life, liberty and security of the person and the right not to be deprived thereof "except in accordance with the principles of fundamental justice". Section 11(d) of the Charter provides that everyone charged with an offence has the right to be presumed innocent until proven guilty according to law in a fair and public hearing by an independent and impartial tribunal.)

The effect of the rule which excluded intoxication as a defence effectively relieved the prosecutor of the burden of proving an essential element of the offence by substituting an intention to get drunk for the intention which must normally be proved in order to establish the offence. It was recognised in *R. v. Vaillancourt*, [1987] 2 S.C.R. 636 that in some cases substituting proof of one element for proof of an essential element will not infringe the presumption of innocence, but only if "the existence of the substituted fact leads inexorably to the conclusion that the essential element exists, with no other reasonable possibilities". In the view of the majority of the Court:

> "The substituted *mens rea* set out in *Leary* does not meet this test. The consumption of alcohol simply cannot lead inexorably to the conclusion that the accused possessed the requisite mental element to commit a sexual assault, or any other crime. Rather, the substituted *mens rea* rule has the effect of eliminating the minimal mental element required for sexual assault. Furthermore, *mens rea* for a crime is so well recognised that to eliminate that mental element, an integral part of the crime, would be to deprive an accused of fundamental justice. See *R. v. Vaillancourt* [1987] 2 S.C.R. 636."

The majority found a further objection to the exclusion of intoxication as a defence:

> "In [*R. v. Vaillancourt*] it was found that s.11(d) would be infringed in those situations where an accused could be convicted despite the existence of reasonable doubt pertaining to one of the essential elements of the offence; see *Vaillancourt, supra*, at pp. 654–656. That would be the result if the *Leary* rule was to be strictly applied. For example, an accused in an extreme state of intoxication akin to automatism or mental illness would have to be found guilty although there was

reasonable doubt as to the voluntary nature of the act committed by the accused. This would clearly infringe both ss.7 and 11(d) of the *Charter*."

(f) United States

In the United States, the approach appears to vary from state to state. In *Roberts v. People*, 19 Mich. 401, the defendant was convicted of assault with intent to commit murder. On appeal, the court considered the question of the effect of intoxication upon the formation of the intent required for this crime:

> "In determining the question whether the assault was committed with the intent charged, it was ... material to inquire whether the defendant's mental faculties were so overcome by the effect of intoxication, as to render him incapable of entertaining the intent."

Similarly, in *People v. Waler*, 38 Mich. 156, a case of theft, the court expressed the view that intoxication was relevant to the question of guilt:

> "While it is true that drunkenness cannot excuse a crime, it is equally true that when a certain intent is a necessary element in a crime, the crime cannot have been committed when the intent did not exist. In larceny the crime does not consist in the wrongful taking of property, for that might be a mere trespass; but it consists in the wrongful taking with felonious intent, [in the absence of which] the crime cannot have been committed."

In other states, however, a different approach is adopted. In *McDaniel v. State*, 356 So 2d 1151 (Mississipi, 1978) it was held that proof of intoxication was permissible only to show that the accused was in a state of automatism at the time of the offence (and not simply to negate the required *mens rea*). In *State v. Vaughn*, 268 S.C. 119, 232 SE 2d 328 (1977, South Carolina) it was held that proof of intoxication was only relevant if it was led to establish permanent insanity.

5. The objections to permitting a defence of voluntary intoxication are based on (a) assumptions regarding the link between intoxication and offending, and more particularly on a link between alcohol intoxication and offences of violence, and (b) an assumption that juries would too willingly acquit when faced with this defence.

So far as concerns the first of these, there is a considerable body of evidence (from within the United Kingdom and elsewhere) that while "[e]xperience may suggest that alcohol makes it easier for violence to occur by diminishing the sense of what is acceptable behaviour ... [alcohol] is not in itself a cause of violence". (*R. v. Daviault*, [1994] 3 S.C.R. 63, *per* Cory J. See, in this respect, the *Interim Report of the Commission of Inquiry into the Non-Medical Use of Drugs* (1970), c. 3.; "*The Le Dain Interim Report*", referred to by S. H. Berner, in *Intoxication and Criminal Responsibility* (Law Reform Commission of Canada, 1975); The Law Commission, *Intoxication and Criminal Liability*, Consultation Paper No. 127 (1993), at pp. 4 and 67; C. N. Mitchell, "The Intoxicated Offender—Refuting the Legal and Medical Myths" (1988), 11 Int. J. L. & Psychiatry 77, at p. 89.

So far as concerns the second objection, experience (and research) in Australia and New Zealand apparently suggest that in practice juries are slow to give effect to voluntary intoxication defences. See the Law Commission, *Intoxication and Criminal Liability, ante,* at pp. 60–63.) See also the opinion of Barwick C.J. in *O'Connor*, at para. 45.

## (c) Alternative approaches

**7.52** In *O'Connor*, Barwick C.J. considered alternatives to the approach adopted in *Majewski*, and in particular some statutory alternative:

> 67. "There would be good sense, it seems to me, in a statutory provision which gave to a jury who were driven to the conclusion that an accused, due to the result of self-induced intoxication, was not culpable of the crime with which he is charged to be able to bring in an alternative verdict that he, by his own conduct, had brought himself to a state where he was not responsible for his acts. There should be a substantial penalty provided for his conviction of this alternative charge, a penalty of

confinement which would include both an element of punishment and provide an opportunity for treatment for the tendency to take alcohol or drugs. It would, it seems to me, be quite just to make the accused responsible for his act of having taken alcohol or other drug to the point I have described."

In South Africa, following the decision in *S. v. Chretien*, 1981 (1) S.A. 1097 (A), the legislature, concerned about the implications of that decision, passed the Criminal Law Amendment Act 1 of 1988. Section 1(1) of that Act provides that "Any person who consumes or uses any substance which impairs his faculties to appreciate the wrongfulness of his acts or to act in accordance with that appreciation, while knowing that such substance has that effect, and who while such faculties are thus impaired commits any act prohibited by law under any penalty, but is not criminally liable because his faculties were impaired as aforesaid, shall be guilty of an offence and shall be liable on conviction to the penalty ... which may be imposed in respect of the commission of that act". The offence under section 1(1) may be charged as an offence in its own right, or may be treated as an alternative verdict where an accused has successfully relied upon a defence of intoxication: section 1(2).

See also A. Ashworth, "Intoxication and General Defences", [1980] Crim. L.R. 556, The Law Commission, Consultation Paper No. 127, "Intoxication and Criminal Liability" (1993), Criminal Law Revision Committee, 14th Report, "Offences Against the Person", Cmnd. 7844, the Report of the Committee on Mentally Abnormal Offenders, 1975, Cmnd. 6244 and R. D. McKay, *Mental Condition Defences in the Criminal Law*, 1995.

## *(ii) Involuntary Intoxication*

### Ross v. H.M. Advocate
1991 S.L.T. 564

THE LORD JUSTICE-GENERAL (HOPE): "The appellant went to trial in the High Court at **7.53** Glasgow on a charge of malicious damage, nine charges of assault involving the use of a knife in all but two of which he was also charged with attempted murder, one charge of breach of the peace and a charge of assaulting police officers in the execution of their duty contrary to the Police (Scotland) Act 1967, s.41(1)(a). Most of the facts were agreed by joint minute except those relating to the charge of police assault, and the jury found the appellant not guilty on that charge. They found him guilty on all the other charges under deletion of the references to attempted murder, and subject to the rider that at the time of these offences he was acting under the influence of drugs administered to him without his knowledge. He has appealed against his conviction on the ground that the trial judge misdirected the jury that they could not acquit him of the charges of which he was convicted.

There was evidence that on the day in question the appellant had been drinking lager from a can. Unknown to him five or six tablets of temazepam and a quantity of LSD had been squeezed into the can and he ingested these drugs along with the lager which he was drinking. Within about half an hour he started to scream continuously and to lunge about in all directions with a knife. Various people who were complete strangers to him were struck by him with the knife, and in most cases the injuries which they received were severe. The police arrived, but when they approached the appellant he continued to scream and he resisted arrest until he was handcuffed. He struggled continuously for about two hours until he was eventually taken to hospital where a drug was administered which brought him under control. Temazepam is a hypnotic drug which in most cases has a tranquillising effect, although in rare instances it may cause a person to overreact in a disinhibited way. LSD on the other hand is an hallucinogen, whose effect initially is that of arousal. It tends to generate feelings of fear or anxiety, together with visual distortions. This may give rise to behavioural reactions in the form of paranoia and aggression, especially in the case of persons who are not aware that they have taken the drug. To a large extent the reaction depends on the individual, and it is not capable of being predicted.

The argument for the defence in this case was that the effect of the ingestion of these drugs was to deprive the appellant of his self control to such an extent that he was incapable of *mens rea*, and that it should be left to the jury to consider whether or not they should acquit him on this ground. The Crown contended that, standing the agreed facts, there was no room for an acquittal because the only defence which could have been put forward to support such a verdict was a plea of insanity at the time. This argument was based on the decisions in *H.M. Advocate v. Cunningham*, 1963 S.L.T. 345 and *Carmichael v. Boyle*, 1985 S.L.T. 399; see also *Clark v. H.M. Advocate*, 1968 J.C. 53. Since no plea of insanity had been offered and no evidence to that effect had been led, it followed that verdicts of guilty had to be returned. The trial judge took the view that he could not distinguish *Cunningham* and *Carmichael* from the present case, so he directed the jury that the evidence about the appellant's mental state at the time could not result in his acquittal.

The basis for that direction was the following passage in the opinion of Lord Justice-General Clyde in *Cunningham* at 1963 J.C., p. 84: "Any mental or pathological condition short of insanity—any question of diminished responsibility owing to any cause, which does not involve insanity—is relevant only to the question of mitigating circumstances and sentence." That was a case where the appellant had claimed that he was not responsible for his actings on account of the incidence of temporary dissociation due to an epileptic fugue or other pathological condition. In *Carmichael v. Boyle*, where the respondent was a diabetic of low intelligence, the sheriff held that he had committed the acts charged when in a state of hypoglycaemia and acquitted him on the ground that he lacked *mens rea*. His decision was reversed on appeal, and the court took the opportunity to point out that *Cunningham* was completely general in its terms and that its authority had to be accepted and followed until its authority was superseded by an Act of Parliament or by a larger court. We are now in a position, as a court of five judges, to re-examine the decision in *Cunningham* especially in its application to the facts of the present case.

It should be noted that counsel for the appellant did not seek to challenge the soundness of that decision on its own facts. He recognised that reasons of public policy might exist for insisting that, where the mental condition which is said to affect *mens rea* is a pathological condition which might recur, it must be the subject of a special defence of insanity at the time. A similar view has been taken in England, where in *R v. Sullivan* [1984] A.C. 156 it was held that in cases of a disorder amounting to a disease of the mind, whether permanent or transient, such as epilepsy, the proper verdict of acquittal is one of not guilty by reason of insanity .... There may be cases, such as those where the condition is due to epilepsy or hypoglycaemia, where any period of detention of the accused in a state or other hospital might seem to be unjustified. But that is not an issue which arises in this case. We are concerned here only with a mental condition of a temporary nature which was the result of an external factor and not of some disorder of the mind itself which was liable to recur. Nor does any issue arise in this case, having regard to the jury's verdict, about the effect on the accused's mental condition of an external factor which is self-induced. Counsel for the appellant accepted that there were clear reasons of public policy for holding, as in *Brennan v. H.M. Advocate* [1977 J.C. 38], that a person who voluntarily and deliberately consumes known intoxicants cannot rely on his own action either as a foundation for a special defence of insanity at the time, let alone as a basis for the argument that he did not have the *mens rea* necessary for a finding that he was guilty of the crime charged. The jury's rider was that the drugs were administered to the appellant without his knowledge. We are concerned here therefore only with those cases where there is no disease of the mind and where the external factor which has caused the impairment is not self-induced.

In principle it would seem that in all cases where a person lacks the evil intention which is essential to guilt of a crime he must be acquitted. Hume, i, 21 describes dole or *mens rea* as "that corrupt and evil intention, which is essential (so the light of nature teaches, and so all authorities have said) to the guilt of any crime". So if a person cannot form any intention at all because, for example, he is asleep or unconscious at the time, it would seem impossible to hold that he had *mens rea* and was guilty in the criminal sense of anything he did when he was in that state. The same result would seem to follow if, for example, he was able to form intention to the extent that he was controlling what he did in the physical sense, but had no conception whatever at the time that what he was doing was wrong. His intention, such as it was, would lack the necessary evil ingredient to convict him of a crime. Insanity provides the clearest example of this situation, but I do not see why there should be no room for the view that the lack of evil intention in cases other than insanity, to which special considerations apply, should not also result in an acquittal. Indeed, since it is for the Crown to prove *mens rea* as well as the actus reus of the offence, it would seem logical to say that in all cases where there is an absence of *mens rea* an acquittal must result.

I have already mentioned the exception on grounds of public policy which applies where the condition which has resulted in an absence of *mens rea* is self-induced. In all such cases the accused must be assumed to have intended the natural consequences of his act. As Lord Justice-General Emslie said in *Brennan* at 1977 S.L.T., p. 155, a person who voluntarily and deliberately consumes known intoxicants cannot rely on the resulting intoxication as the foundation of a special defence of insanity at the time, nor can he plead diminished responsibility. Standing the decisions in *Cunningham* and *Carmichael*, these were the only defences which might be thought to be available in such cases, and no doubt it was for that reason that it was felt unnecessary to go further in disposing of the argument that a person who suffers total alienation of reason as a result of self induced intoxication is free from any criminal responsibility. In my opinion the reasons why, in the phrase used by Hume, i, 46, "our custom utterly disowns any such defence", exclude also any defence based upon the argument that self induced intoxication has resulted in the absence of *mens rea*.

But we are concerned in this case with a situation to which that exception does not extend, and where there is no continuing disorder of the mind or body which might lead to the recurrence of the disturbance of the appellant's mental faculties. Counsel for the appellant's argument was that in all such cases where there is a loss of self control which is not self induced and is not due to any continuing physical or mental disorder, it should be left to the jury to consider whether *mens rea* has been established by the Crown, without the lodging of a special defence directed to this issue. Much of what he said to us was not in dispute, because the learned Solicitor-General accepted that there was a basis in the evidence which was led in this case for the jury to find that the appellant was totally without responsibility for his actions due to the effects of the drugs which he had unknowingly consumed. I understood him to accept that there was evidence that the appellant had no control over his actions with the result that they were involuntary. So I think that we can treat this case as one where the accused committed the acts with which he was charged while he was not conscious of what he was doing, and that he was in the state which has been described in some of the cases as that of non-insane automatism.

The Solicitor-General went on to accept that the court could, consistently with principle, recognise that an accused person could be acquitted on the ground that he was totally irresponsible for his actings on a ground other than that of insanity at the time. He emphasised the need for a total alienation of reason resulting in a complete loss of control over his actions before an acquittal could be justified on the ground that there was an absence of *mens rea*. If this was the extent of the irresponsibility resulting from their effects, then the fact that this was due to the consumption of drink or drugs or to other external factors such as toxic exhaust fumes was of no consequence, so long as this was not self-induced. He invited us to approach the points raised by counsel for the appellant's argument on the view that the total alienation of reason which was required was the same in its effect on *mens rea* as insanity. He submitted that, as in the case of the special defence of insanity at the time, there was an onus on the accused to establish that the presumption that a person was responsible for his actions had been overcome. But if that onus was satisfied a verdict of acquittal would be consistent with principle and not open to objection on grounds of public policy.

The first point to be considered is whether it is consistent with principle for a person to be acquitted where he claims to have entirely lost his self-control for reasons which are not due to a disease of the mind and in circumstances which are not self-induced. Dicta which favour this approach are to be found in three cases, all at first instance, where the point was made by the trial judge in the course of his charge. In *H.M. Advocate v. Ritchie*, the driver of a motor car who was charged with causing death by reckless driving lodged a special defence that he was not guilty because of temporary mental dissociation due to toxic exhaust factors. He claimed that he was unaware of the presence of the deceased on the highway and of his injuries and death and that he was incapable of appreciating what he was doing. Lord Murray said of this special defence that it was "a somewhat novel one, based upon the alleged abnormal and irresponsible condition of the accused at the time of the accident. Such irresponsibility may create criminal immunity and form the ground of a good defence; but there is a strong presumption in favour of normality and responsibility. That presumption may be overcome, but the onus of proof lies, as indeed was conceded by counsel for the defence, upon the person who pleads that he is abnormal and irresponsible" (1926 S.L.T., at p. 309).

Having reminded the jury of the basis for the defence of irresponsibility, which was that owing to some disordered condition of the mind which affected its working, the affected person did not know the nature of his act or, if he did know what he was doing, he did not know that what he was doing was wrong, he referred first to conditions which fell short of inferring irresponsibility. He then said this at p. 309: "But where the defence is that a person, who would ordinarily be quite justified in driving a car, becomes—owing to a cause which he was not bound to foresee, and which was outwith his control—either gradually or suddenly not the master of his own action, a question as to his responsibility or irresponsibility for the consequences of his action arises, and may form the ground of a good special defence. The question, accordingly, which you have to determine is whether, at the time of the accident, the accused was or was not master of his own action. So put, the question becomes a pure question of fact."

This direction has not been referred to with approval in any subsequent Scottish case to which we were referred, and it was expressly disapproved in *Cunningham* at 1963 S.L.T., p. 347 for reasons to which I shall return. But it was referred to by Lord Denning in *Bratty v. Att. Gen. for Northern Ireland* [1963] A.C. 386 at p. 410 in support of the proposition that a person may have a defence if he can show that what he did was an involuntary action in the sense that he was unconscious at the time and did not know what he was doing. It was the basis also for a submission in *Watmore v. Jenkins* [1962] 2 Q.B. 572 that automatism is a defence to a charge of dangerous driving, provided the person takes reasonable steps to prevent himself from acting involuntarily in a manner dangerous to the public and provided it was caused by some factor which he could not reasonably foresee and not by a self induced incapacity. That submission was referred to with approval in *R. v. Quick* [1973] Q.B. 910, which was concerned with a malfunctioning of the mind caused by the taking of insulin. The defendant Quick, who was a nurse in a mental hospital, had assaulted a patient there while in a condition which, according to his medical evidence, was consistent with hypoglycaemia. The judge at the trial ruled that the evidence could only support a defence of insanity and not a defence that he was suffering from automatism. But it was held on appeal that the question whether he was suffering from automatism should have been left to the jury to decide. And Lord Murray's direction was referred to in *R. v. Cottle* [1958] N.Z.L.R. 999 by Gresson P. at p. 1017, in the course of an extensive analysis of cases from various Commonwealth countries in support of the defence of automatism. It was held in that case, where the defence was based on evidence about epileptic fits, that if there is sufficient evidence on which a finding of automatism could be based the jury should be told that they must consider whether they are satisfied that the Crown has discharged its onus of proof of the guilt of the accused. It is worth noting at this point that in *R. v. Sullivan* at p. 172, Lord Diplock mentioned the possibility of non-insane automatism, for which the proper verdict would be a verdict of not guilty, in cases where temporary impairment, not being self-induced by consuming drink or drugs, results from some external factor such as a blow on the head causing concussion, or the administering of an anaesthetic for therapeutic purposes. He did not think it appropriate in that case to explore possible cases of non-insane automatism and the two examples which he gave are distinct from the circumstances in *Ritchie* and from those in the present case. Nevertheless it is significant that Lord Murray's direction is consistent with the approach taken in these various cases in other countries which favour this defence in cases other than that of insanity.

In *McGregor v. H.M. Advocate* (1973) S.C.C.R. Supp. 54, Lord Fraser was dealing with charges of assault to the danger of life and of reckless driving. The defence was that the accused had formed no intention of doing the acts with which he was charged because he was unable to form this intention due perhaps to drugs. He admitted to having consumed some drink voluntarily before the incidents took place, but the question was raised whether drugs had also been administered to him without his knowledge. This was not the subject of a special defence, and Lord Fraser did not suggest that it should have been or that there was any onus of proof on the accused. He directed the jury at p. 57 to consider the question whether the case came within the category of cases where the person was unable to form an intention to do anything at the time. The typical case which he described was that of a robot or of automatism as where the person is unconscious due to an anaesthetic or is asleep. This approach received no encouragement when the case was taken to appeal, the accused having been found guilty but with a finding that drugs administered to him without his knowledge was a factor on all charges. His charge was said to have gone further than the propositions desiderated and, on the face of it, to be even more favourable to the accused than that which it was said he should have given. The court made it clear at p. 59 that it was not to be taken as having endorsed the correctness of the charge.

There was some discussion in the hearing before us as to the soundness of some of what Lord Fraser said in that case. *H.M. Advocate v. Simon Fraser* (1878) 4 Coup. 70 was referred to by counsel for the appellant as providing support for his approach, this being one of the very rare examples of a crime having been committed while the accused was asleep. It was suggested to the jury by Lord Justice-Clerk Moncreiff at p. 75 that they should find that the panel killed his child "but that he was in a state in which he was unconscious of the act which he was committing by reason of the condition of somnambulism and that he was not responsible". The verdict which was recorded in that case was in accordance with this direction. We have been shown a copy of it, and it is in these terms: "The jury unanimously find that the panel killed his child when he was unconscious of the nature of the act which he committed, by reason of a condition of somnambulism, and that the panel was not responsible at the time. The court (delayed pronouncing sentence in the meantime) continued the diet against the panel till Wednesday first the seventeenth current at 3 o'clock; and ordained him in the meantime to be detained in the prison of Edinburgh."

Evidently this was not seen as a verdict of acquittal, otherwise there would have been no question of the panel's being detained after it was pronounced. I do not think that this case can be regarded as anything other than a very special one, and it does not provide authority for the argument that a verdict of acquittal is appropriate where *mens rea* is absent because of automatism. Nevertheless, I find Lord Fraser's remarks to the jury in *McGregor* of some assistance in the present case, especially where he talks about the person being "unable" to form the intention to do the acts with which he is charged. This is in accordance with the Solicitor-General's argument that what one should be looking for is a total alienation of reason with the result that the accused had no idea of what he was doing at the time.

The third case in this chapter is *H.M. Advocate v. Raiker* 1989 S.C.C.R. 149, where the trial judge, Lord McCluskey, directed the jury at p. 154, in regard to a defence which had been advanced by the accused Skellet, that where a person acts under a real, genuine and justifiable fear that if he does not act in accordance with the orders of another that other person will use life threatening violence against him, he cannot be said to have the evil intention which the law regards as the necessary ingredient in the carrying out of a crime. Having thus dealt with the defence of coercion, he went on to say this: "Ladies and Gentlemen, the same rule, the same idea, applies not just to a person acting under genuine serious fear of physical violence, it applies even if he was acting, for example, under hypnosis or wholly and completely under the influence of some drug which was administered by force or by stealth without his consent, if it was a drug which like hypnosis put his will as it were under the control of another."

That direction was not, I think, consistent with either *Cunningham* or *Carmichael*, according to which that defence, since it falls short of a defence of insanity at the time, would have to be rejected and regarded as relevant only to mitigation of sentence. But it is, nevertheless, in accordance with the principle which was noted in both *Ritchie* and *McGregor* that a necessary element in every crime is the existence of *mens rea* and with its corollary that where evil intention is entirely absent there can be no *mens rea* and a verdict of acquittal must result.

The question then is whether *Cunningham* was correctly decided on this point, and especially whether the court was right to disapprove of Lord Murray's charge in *Ritchie*. I should stress again that we were not invited to reconsider the soundness of *Cunningham* as a decision on its own facts. We are not concerned in this case with a pathological condition such as epilepsy or with the questions of public policy which may affect how such cases should be approached. The discussion in Lord Justice-General Clyde's opinion at 1963 S.L.T., pp. 346–347, is directed principally to the question whether the categories of special defences should be extended to include what he saw as a new one which, although short of insanity, would lead to an acquittal. There is no discussion of the principle that *mens rea* is a necessary ingredient of any crime. The whole approach seems to be one directed to grounds of public policy. It is said that to allow such a novel type of defence could lead to serious consequences so far as the safety of the public is concerned, and Lord Murray's approach is criticised on the ground that "To affirm or even extend that decision would lead to laxity and confusion in our criminal law which could do nothing but harm". In my opinion these strictures are not justified in cases where the defence is based, as it was in *Ritchie*, on an inability to form *mens rea* due to some external factor which was outwith the accused's control and which he was not bound to foresee. I do not see why laxity or confusion should result if we were to recognise that, where the point is sufficiently put in issue, an accused should be acquitted if the jury are not satisfied that the Crown has proved *mens rea*. That would be entirely consistent with the principle that the onus rests throughout on the Crown. The requirements that the external factor must not be self-induced, that it must be one which the accused was not bound to foresee, and that it must have resulted in a total alienation of reason amounting to a complete absence of self-control, provide adequate safeguards against abuse . . . ."

[His Lordship then considered the Crown's argument that an accused who sought rely on a defence of involuntary intoxication should be required to establish it on a balance of probabilities. His Lordship considered, *inter alia*, the cases of *Ritchie* (*supra*, p. 229, and *Lambie*, 1973 S.L.T. 219. He also considered the views of various Commonwealth courts on this question, including *Bratty v. Attorney-General for Northern Ireland* [1963] A.C. 386, *The Queen v. O'Connor* (1980) 146 C.L.R. 64, *R. v. Cottle* [1958] N.Z.L.R. 999, *S. v. Trickett* 1973 (3) S.A. 526 (T) and *S. v. Hartyani* 1980 (3) S.A. 613 (T). His Lordship concluded that no onus could be placed upon the accused to prove on a balance of probabilities a defence of involuntary intoxication. His Lordship then continued:]

For these reasons I consider that we should now overrule *Cunningham* to the extent indicated by this opinion, and with it the decisions in *Clark* and in *Carmichael* in so far as they proceeded on an acceptance of the decision in *Cunningham* to this extent. The trial judge was right to regard himself as obliged by *Cunningham* to direct the jury that the evidence about the appellant's mental state at the time could not result in his acquittal. But the jury should have been invited to consider this evidence and, since it is not disputed that there was evidence which would have entitled them to acquit the appellant on this ground, I think that we must now quash his conviction on all charges on the ground that a miscarriage of justice has occurred."

NOTES

1. The other members of the Court agreed with Lord Hope that the appellant's conviction should be **7.54** quashed, and that involuntary intoxication of the degree referred to by Lord Hope could exclude criminal responsibility. There was some difference of opinion as to whether involuntary intoxication should be treated as a "special defence" in the procedural sense, that is, as a defence which required to be notified to the Crown in advance of the trial. That matter is now dealt with by section 78(2) which provides that the rules regarding notification of "special defences" apply to automatism (and coercion) "as if" they were special defences.

2. In this case the High Court holds that complete alienation of reason resulting from involuntary ingestion of drugs can provide a defence, because such alienation of reason precludes the formation of *mens rea*. If that is the correct basis of the defence of automatism, then logically it has no place to play in relation to offences of strict liability. Is this satisfactory? If, because of automatism, the accused is not able to control his vehicle, does it matter whether the offence is one of strict liability or one which requires proof of *mens rea*? This is the question addressed in *Kilbride v. Lake* (noted *ante*, pp. 27–28) and, it is submitted, correctly decided in favour of the view that involuntariness is an obstacle to conviction for any offence, and not just those which require proof of *mens rea* (*cf. Finegan v. Heywood, ante*, p. 234).

### Cardle v. Mulrainey
### 1992 S.L.T. 1152

The respondent was charged with unlawfully taking and driving away a motor vehicle, driving **7.55** without insurance, opening a lockfast vehicle with intent to steal from it, attempting to steal a number of motor vehicles, and theft from a vehicle. The offences were all committed within a short time of each other. In his defence, he pleaded that he committed the offences while under the influence of alcohol to which, without his knowledge, a quantity of amphetamine had been added. Evidence was led as to the effects of amphetamine and the sheriff found that ingestion of amphetamine can lead to the failure on the part of the person taking it to appreciate the consequences of his action. There was no evidence, other than that provided by the accused, to suggest that he was acting under the influence of amphetamine. The sheriff found that the accused was aware of his actions while interfering with the various vehicles to which the charges related, that he was aware that these actions were wrong, but that he was unable to refrain from these actions by reason of his ingestion of the amphetamine. The sheriff did not find, however, that there had been a total alienation of reason. The sheriff acquitted the accused. The prosecutor appealed.

LORD JUSTICE-GENERAL (HOPE): " . . . The Lord Advocate submitted that the sheriff ought not to have acquitted the respondent because, on the findings, there was no evidence that he was suffering from the kind of total alienation of reason which was essential if this defence was to succeed. . . . The sheriff's conclusion that the respondent's ability to reason was to some extent affected, in that he was unable to take account of the fact that he knew what he was doing was wrong and to stop himself, fell short of the total alienation of reason which was required. The most that could be said in the respondent's favour was that, as in the case of provocation, his inability to control himself from doing what he knew to be wrong might mitigate the offence.

In her reply counsel drew attention to the difficulty which the sheriff had had in determining whether the inability of the respondent to stop himself fell within the ambit of the third requirement in *Ross* that there must be a total alienation of reason. The particular difficulty which he experienced here had not arisen in Ross because, on the evidence in that case, the appellant had not been conscious of what he was doing at all. It was possible in that case to regard his actions as involuntary and to say that he had a total alienation of reason because he had no idea of what he was doing at the time. But the phrase 'total alienation of reason' was an incomplete description of the various situations in which there could properly be said to be an absence of *mens rea*. All that was needed in order to make out the defence was evidence sufficient for there to be a reasonable doubt about the existence of evil intent. This was the point Lord Murray had been making in *H.M. Advocate v. Ritchie*, 1926 S.L.T. at p. 309

in his discussion of the defence of irresponsibility. The condition which he described at p. 309 was that the accused was 'not fully responsible for his actions'. In *H.M. Advocate v. Kidd*, 1960 S.L.T. at p. 86 Lord Strachan directed the jury, in regard to the defence of insanity, that there must have been some mental defect, that what was required was 'some alienation of reason in relation to the act committed'. Her suggestion was that the phrase 'a total alienation of reason' was too strongly expressed. Applying these submissions to the facts of the present case her argument was that the sheriff was right to conclude that a reasonable doubt had been raised about the respondent's responsibility for his actions. No doubt he knew that what he was doing was wrong, but he was unable to apply that knowledge in order to stop himself from performing the criminal acts and this meant that he was not truly responsible for what he did.

The question is whether, since the facts of this case are clearly very different from those in *Ross*, the respondent has nevertheless brought himself within the limits of the defence. On this point there can be only one answer and, while we acknowledge the anxious consideration which the sheriff gave to the case, we must disagree with him and answer in the negative. Where, as in the present case, the accused knew what he was doing and was aware of the nature and quality of his acts and that what he was doing was wrong, he cannot be said to be suffering from the total alienation of reason in regard to the crime with which he is charged which the defence requires. The sheriff found in finding 16 that the respondent's ability to reason the consequences of his actions to himself was affected by his ingestion of the drug. The finding narrates that he was unable to take account in his actions of the fact that they were criminal in character and to refrain from them. But this inability to exert self-control, which the sheriff has described as an inability to complete the reasoning process, must be distinguished from the essential requirement that there should be total alienation of the accused's mental faculties of reasoning and of understanding what he is doing. As in the case of provocation, which provides another example of a stimulus resulting in a loss of self-control at the time of the act, this may mitigate the offence but it cannot be held to justify an acquittal on the ground that there is an absence of *mens rea*.

As for counsel's suggestion that the requirement that there must be a total alienation of reason has been too strongly stated, we need say only this in light of the relatively brief argument to which we listened on this point. The phrase has, as she pointed out, been in use for a very long time. An early example of its use is to be found in Hume on *Crimes*, vol. i at pp. 37 and 42. In these passages Hume made it clear that in his view the insanity required to be absolute to make out the defence. 'To serve the purpose of defence in law, the disorder must therefore amount to an absolute alienation of reason.' He went on to say in the latter passage that, however unaccountable the condition might be, the defence was available only 'if the utter alienation of reason for the time is proved'. An insistence in such absolute terms upon an utter or total alienation of reason may appear to be absent from some of the more recent discussions of the defence of insanity, and in particular from the passage in Lord Strachan's charge to the jury in *H.M. Advocate v. Kidd*, 1960 S.L.T. at p. 86 on which the sheriff relied. As Lord Strachan put it:

'(In) order to excuse a person from responsibility for his acts on the ground of insanity, there must have been an alienation of the reason in relation to the act committed. There must have been some mental defect, to use a broad neutral word, a mental defect, by which his reason was overpowered, and he was thereby rendered incapable of exerting his reason to control his conduct and reactions. If his reason was alienated in related to the act committed, he was not responsible for that act, even although otherwise he may have been apparently quite rational. What is required is some alienation of the reason in relation to the act committed.'

But in the Full Bench case of *Brennan v. H.M. Advocate*, 1977 S.L.T. at p. 154 Lord Justice-General Emslie, after a review of the authorities, including *Kidd*, in which the requirements for the defence of insanity were discussed, said this:

'In short, insanity in our law requires proof of total alienation of reason in relation to the act charged as the result of mental illness, mental disease or defect or unsoundness of mind ... The only distinction between insanity and the state of diminished responsibility recognised by our law is that for the latter state to be established something less than total alienation of reason will suffice.'

It is clear therefore that not every weakness or aberration of the mind will amount to insanity. So it is in the case of the defence with which the decision in *Ross* was concerned. Not every weakness or aberration induced by the external factor will provide the defence. Hence the insistence in *Ross* on a total alienation of reason in relation to the crime charged. This is necessary in order to distinguish the condition from other conditions which may be regarded at best as merely mitigating the offence. What will amount to a total alienation of reason or, as was said in *Ross*, 1991 S.L.T. at p. 572A, a total loss of control of the accused's actions in regard to the crime with which he is charged, must be a question of fact in each case. But so far as the present case is concerned the sheriff has made express findings in regard to several of the crimes with which the respondent was charged that he intended to do what he did. There are findings that he intended to start the motor vehicles, steal them and drive them away. In the light of these findings the sheriff's conclusion that the respondent's ability to reason the consequences of his actions to himself was affected by his ingestion of the drug and that he was unable to refrain from them was relevant at best only to mitigation. He should have held that the respondent's reason in relation to the crimes charged was not totally alienated and that he did not have a proper basis for the defence.

For these reasons we consider that on the facts stated the sheriff was not entitled to acquit the respondent. Accordingly, we must allow this appeal and we shall answer the question in the negative and remit the case to the sheriff to proceed as accords.

Appeal allowed.

Notes

1. Although this case concerns the effect of "involunary" intoxication (as to which, see *Ross v. H.M.* **7.56** *Advocate, ante,* p. 245) it is relevant also to the defence of insanity. This is because the defence of involuntary intoxication requires "alienation of reason" in the same way that insanity does, albeit arising from a different source.

2. Does this case mark a shift towards the M'Naghten Rules of English law, despite their rejection in *Kidd, Breen v. Breen* and *Brennan*? The court's reference to the fact that "the accused knew what he was doing and was aware of the nature and quality of his acts and that what he was doing was wrong" is very close indeed to the M'Naghten Rules. This is further borne out to the extent that the Court holds that a person whose mental condition is such that he or she cannot control their actions or conform their behaviour to the requirement of the law is still responsible. One of the characteristics of the M'Naghten approach was to exclude "volitional" insanity, and to concentrate on the accused's ability to understand the nature and quality of his or actions. See, in this respect, *Kopsch* (1925) 19 Cr. App. R. 50; *Sodeman* [1936] 2 All E.R. 1138.

3. It is accepted that where a person is irresponsible owing to the effect of drugs knowingly consumed by him, he is nonetheless to be treated as being "involuntarily" intoxicated, if he has taken those drugs under medical supervision, and has acted in accordance with his medical adviser's directions. (See *Carrington v. H.M. Advocate*, 1994 J.C. 229.) But if a person, without medical supervision, consumes drugs in a reckless fashion, even if this is done for the purpose of relieving pain (rather than becoming intoxicated) this will be regarded as voluntary intoxication. See *Ebsworth v. H.M. Advocate*, 1992 S.L.T. 1161.

4. The Court in *Ross* was clearly concerned to ensure that their decision did not produce a flood of spurious intoxication defences. In order further to ensure that the defence of involuntary intoxication is not abused, the High Court has imposed exacting evidential requirements in respect of this type of defence. See the following case:

## Sorley v. H.M. Advocate
### 1992 S.L.T. 867

**7.57** The appellant was charged with assault and breaches of the peace. There was evidence that he appeared to be hopelessly drunk at the time. The appellant gave evidence that he had been given a small amount to drink by an acquaintance, Stace, before the time of the offences, but that he had then suffered a blackout and had no recollection of what happened between taking the drink and waking up in the police station the next morning. Stace gave evidence that, without the appellant's knowledge, he had put LSD and sleeping tablets into the drink which he had given to the appellant. Stace also gave evidence that in his experience the effect of LSD was to produce hallucinations. S had not observed the appellant after he had taken the drink. Relying upon *H.M. Advocate v. Cunningham*, 1963 J.C. 80, the sheriff withdrew the appellant's defence from the jury and the appellant was convicted. He appealed to the High Court on the ground that on the authority of *Ross v. H.M. Advocate, ante*, the defence should have been left to the jury. In refusing the appellant's appeal, the Court stated:

OPINION OF THE COURT: "... The test which was laid down in *Ross* falls into three parts ... On the evidence which was given by the appellant and by Stace in this case there is no difficulty about the first two. The learned Solicitor-General accepted that they gave evidence of an external factor, namely the consumption of the LSD tablets by the appellant, which was not self-induced and whose presence in the can of lager the appellant was not bound to foresee. It was to the third point that the argument was directed. Mr Drummond said that there was evidence that the presence of the LSD resulted in a total loss of control by the appellant over his actions in regard to the crimes charged. The learned Solicitor-General submitted that there was no evidence at all to support this proposition, and accordingly it would have been the duty of the sheriff to direct the jury that it was not open to them to consider this defence...

This case should be seen as an illustration of the warning which was given in *Ross* about the strict limits which must be applied to this defence. Two of the three requirements may be relatively easy to satisfy. All that is needed is some evidence which would entitle the jury to consider whether there was present some external factor which was not self-induced and which the accused was not bound to foresee. But the whole point of the defence is that the accused was suffering from a total loss of control over his actions in regard to the crime with which he is charged. Unless there is evidence directed to this essential point, the defence is not available. It is a point of such importance that it cannot be left to speculation, and a few casual remarks or hints by lay witnesses will not do. There must be clear evidence to support it, and this means that the evidence must be specific on all details which are material. The evidence must relate to the state of mind of the accused. It must relate to the time at which the crime charged was committed. And it must provide a causative link between the external factor and the total loss of control. It is unlikely that these requirements will be satisfied unless there is some expert evidence, since the essence of the defence is a state of mind which requires to be precisely diagnosed, and the cause of it must be explained. A genuine case will have the basis for it carefully laid, by eliciting from the eyewitnesses who observed the accused's condition at the critical time all the elements which are necessary for an informed diagnosis to be made.

Having examined the evidence which was led in this case, which may be contrasted with that in Ross as described by the Lord Justice-General in the second paragraph of his opinion, we are satisfied that the sheriff's direction did not result in any miscarriage of justice, and for this reason the appeal is refused."

Appeal refused.

NOTES

**7.58** See also *Macleod v. Napier,* 1993 S.C.C.R. 303, and *Carrington v. H.M. Advocate*, 1995 S.L.T. 341.

# B. Consent

Consent may provide a defence in a number of offences, such as theft, rape and indecent assault. In each **7.59** of these cases, the core activity of the offence must be carried out without consent. In theft, the appropriation of the property must be done without consent. In rape, sexual intercourse must take place without the victim's consent, and there can be no indecent assault if the victim consents to what takes place. In all of these cases, the absence of consent is an element of the *actus reus* of the offence, so that consent functions as a defence by excluding an element of the *actus reus*. As a matter of law, consent cannot be pleaded as a defence to a charge of homicide, nor is it a defence to non-sexual assault. The scope of consent is discussed in the context of each of these offences.

# C. Threats and compulsion

The defences discussed in this section have certain characteristics in common. They are all defences **7.60** which rely, to a greater or lesser extent, on the argument that the accused has committed an offence when his or her will was overcome as a result of some threat, express or implied, arising from a human agency (as in coercion and superior orders) or a natural event or occurrence (as in necessity). This similarity in the defences has led to a certain assimilation of coercion and necessity. (See *Moss v. Howdle*, 1997 S.L.T. 782, *post*, p. 261.) Whether this is correct is another matter.

## (a) Coercion

### Hume, I, 51

*"Of the Plea of Subjection* **7.61**
[Having discussed various special cases in which the defence of coercion had been recognised, Hume concludes with the following general statement of principle:] "But generally, and with relation to the ordinary condition of a well-regulated society, where every man is under the shield of the law, and has the means of resorting to that protection, this is at least somewhat a difficult plea, and can hardly be serviceable in the case of a trial for any atrocious crime, unless it have the support of these qualifications: an immediate danger of death or great bodily harm; an inability to resist the violence; a backward and an inferior part in the perpetration; and a disclosure of the fact, as well as restitution of the spoil, on the first safe and convenient occasion. For if the pannel take a very active part in the enterprise, or conceal the fact, and detain his share of the profit, when restored to a state of freedom, either of these replies will serve in a great measure to elide his defence."

### Thomson v. H.M. Advocate
1983 S.C.C.R. 368

The appellant was convicted of armed robbery. At his trial, he admitted driving the van **7.62** containing the robbers to the locus of the offence. He also admitted that he had driven them and the stolen property away after the offence. He claimed that on the outward journey, he did not know that there was going to be a robbery, and that it was only when they reached the locus of the crime that he realised what was going to happen. He stated in evidence that he tried to get away but a gun was produced, and that the gun went off when he tried to get out of the van, and that he was hit on the hand. He stated that he was terrified of the other men. The trial judge left the defence of coercion to the jury. The jury convicted the appellant of armed robbery. On appeal to the High Court:
LORD JUSTICE-CLERK (WHEATLEY): "This appeal raises the question of the extent to which a defence of 'coercion' plays a part in the criminal law of Scotland. ...

In directing the jury on this defence the trial judge, Lord Hunter, read to them the passage from Hume on *Crimes*, Vol. i, p. 53 which deals with this matter, interposing some observations of his own. [The court set out the relevant passages from Lord Hunter's charge and continued:]

The basic ground of appeal advanced by the appellant's counsel was: misdirection by the trial judge of the defence of coercion in directing the jury that the danger must be immediate and the threat has to be of present and not future violence. As a corollary of that, it was submitted, where present violence is combined with threats of future violence it is for the jury to decide whether these present and future threats combine to produce the legal threat of violence.

It has to be noted that what the trial judge was dealing with was what constituted a complete defence of coercion in what was undoubtedly in Hume's words an atrocious crime. It was in that situation that he directed the jury that the danger must be immediate. In the result he allowed the defence of coercion to go to the jury, restricted to immediate danger to life in a threatened situation, because there was some evidence from the appellant to that effect.

As the judge had directed the jury in the words of Hume, counsel for the appellant was in a difficulty. He did not wish to argue the bold proposition that Hume was wrong, although if all else failed he was prepared to do so. His main line was that the trial judge had construed too strictly what Hume had said, and that the passage in Hume was not as rigid as the judge had made out. He submitted that Hume was speculating and was at the best laying down guidelines rather than enunciating legal principles. In the last resort he was prepared to argue that Hume was wrong through lack of clarity.

Our views on the passage from Hume under consideration are these. The passage has to be looked at in its context. The immediately preceding passage deals with the case of James Graham who claimed that he had been forced by Rob Roy and his gang to take part in an armed robbery, and this was in an age of lawlessness when recourse to the forces of law and order for protection was often not available. By contrast Hume set out to define the law of coercion in the context of the type of society in which we live today. He accordingly starts by saying: 'But generally, and with relation to the ordinary condition of a well regulated society, where every man is under the shield of the law, and has the means of resorting to that protection, this (*i.e.*, coercion) is at least a somewhat difficult plea.' This, in our view, explains the thinking underlying Hume's subsequent words, and is the key to the use of the word 'immediate'. What he was saying was that it is only where, following threats, there is an immediate danger of violence in whatever form it takes that the defence of coercion can be entertained, and even then only if there is an inability to resist or avoid that immediate danger. If there is time and opportunity to seek and obtain the shield of the law in a well regulated society, then recourse should be made to it, and if it is not then the defence of coercion is not open. It is the danger which has to be 'immediate' not just the threat. It will be a question of circumstances in each case whether the conditions permitting the invocation of that defence have been satisfied. 'Immediate danger' may have to be construed in the circumstances in which it is threatened, but clearly if there is the opportunity to run away or to seek the protection of the forces of law and order before the crime is committed, then the accused cannot claim to have been coerced. Hume recognised that the rule could not be made absolute because of the imponderable situations which might arise in the country's history. Hence the qualifications, prefaced with 'generally, and with relation to the ordinary condition of a well regulated society'. We have already dealt with the first two of these, namely immediate danger and inability to resist violence. With regard to the third, a backward and inferior part in the perpetration, we consider that the part which is taken in the perpetration, which can take place in a whole variety of ways and degrees, is simply one factor in the amalgam of factors which may point to the accused's voluntary or coerced conduct. If a man opens a safe, which is the major feature of the crime, but only does so because he has a revolver pointed at his head and he is told that his head will be blown off if he does not open it, it is difficult to see why the defence is not open to him because he played a major and not a backward or inferior part in the perpetration of the crime. So far as the fourth is concerned, disclosure of the fact as well as the restitution of the spoil on the first safe and convenient occasion, that is not something which could positively affirm or disprove that the accused was acting under coercion. Rather it is a test of whether such actings are or are not consistent with his proposed defence of coercion. This seems clearly what was meant when regard is had to the passage which follows: 'For if the panel take a very active part in the enterprise, or conceal the fact, and detain his share of the profit when restored to a state of freedom, either of these replies will serve in a great measure to <u>elide his defence</u>' (the underlining is ours).

In so expressing himself Hume was setting down in characteristic manner what he conceived to be the criminal law of Scotland on this subject. He was plainly not seeking to lay down any absolute rule, but he was adumbrating the very strict conditions under which a defence of this nature could be sustained. He obviously appreciated the great danger to the proper administration of justice if a facile defence of this nature was not subjected to strict control. The four 'qualifications' to which he refers are tests of the validity of such a defence. The first two are conditions to be satisfied before the defence gets off the ground. It is only if it does get off the ground that the other two tests came into play as measures of the accused's credibility and reliability on the issue of the defence. So far as the passage quoted is concerned, it only remains for us to say that Hume was not rejecting the defence of coercion as incompetent, he was only seeking to set out the very strict confines within which it could be sustained. This is underlined by his use of such phrases as 'a somewhat difficult plea' and 'can hardly be serviceable ... unless ...'. The advocate-depute seemed to have a point when he argued that 'hardly' there had to be read as meaning 'surely not'.

As counsel for the appellant was not prepared to accept these limitations on the defence of coercion, and was prepared to argue that Hume was unclear or indeed wrong in what he said, we feel it incumbent on us in the light of what we have already said to repudiate these assertions. This may seem a needless exercise to many who have fled to Hume as the fount of knowledge on the criminal law of Scotland when judicial pronouncements have appeared to be conflicting or unclear. A defence of coercion is recognised in the law of Scotland. Doubts have been expressed on whether it extends to murder cases, but that does not arise here and we express no opinion on that point. Hume restricts it to 'atrocious crimes', and whether a particular crime falls into that category will depend not only on the nature of the crime but on its attendant circumstances. A fine balance may have to be struck between the nature of the danger threatened and the seriousness of the crime, calling for a value judgment. The facile manner in which it could be invoked, and the consequential effects on the proper and fair administration of justice if its use was unfettered demonstrate clearly the need for the restrictive conditions and considerations which Hume saw fit to impose. As previously noted, all this has to be considered against the background of the ordinary condition of a well-regulated society where recourse is available to the forces of law and order for protection. If that situation does not for any reason exist, then different considerations may have to apply, but we are dealing here with the ordinary position. In the light of the examination of the passage in Hume which we have made we are satisfied that it represents the law of Scotland at the present time when it states that the defence of coercion is normally only open when it is based on present danger from present threats, and is properly tested by the answers to the four qualifications posed. In saying this we are conscious that even in the ordinary condition of a well-regulated society there may be circumstances where a person is exposed to a threat of violence to himself or a third party or even the security of the state from which he cannot be protected by the forces of law and order and which he is not in a position to resist. If such a situation arose it would have to be determined on its facts and no profit can be gained from an exercise in hypothetical cases.

It is only but right to point out that our attention was drawn to four Scottish cases and two English ones where the law of coercion or duress played a part. The first of the Scottish cases was *H.M. Advocate v. Peters, Garvie and Tevendale* (November 1968, unreported). There a special defence of coercion was received under reservation, but it was not allowed to go to the jury through lack of evidence to support it, and nothing can be gained from that case in relation to the current issue. The second was the case of *H.M. Advocate v. Peter Docherty & Ors.* (June 3, 1976, unreported). The trial judge (Lord Keith) in his charge to the jury said that a defence of coercion was open to an accused 'when his will has been overcome by a threat to him, that he had reason to believe—and believed—it would be carried out'. At a later stage he repeated this general direction but added 'or threats to his mother'. It was said by counsel for the appellant here that this was at least a case of a mixture of present and future threats. Even if this be so, and the judge's charge does not disclose whether it is, the direction in law was given without reference to what Hume had said, and we cannot find in the generality of the direction anything to alter our view on the law. The third of these cases was *H.M. Advocate v. John McCallum* (May 19, 1977, unreported). In that case the trial judge, Lord Allanbridge, cited to the jury the passage in Hume, *supra* and laid emphasis on the fact that it was the immediate and not the future threats which they had to look at. To buttress this he quoted a passage from Anderson's Criminal Law (2nd edition), p. 16—'The threats must have had reference to present, not to future injury'. In answer to a question from a juror whether all four of Hume's tests [*sic*] should be satisfied the judge replied that the jury had to consider the whole evidence and apply the four tests. The fourth case was *Sayers & Ors. v. H. M. Advocate*, 1981 S.C.C.R 312. The defence of coercion was advanced in that case and was dealt with by the trial judge. Although the case was appealed to the appeal court it was not on this point. The trial judge, Lord Ross, having given the general directions on coercion to the jury referred them to a number of occasions when threats were uttered. It would appear that these related either to the first of Hume's qualifications or to the fourth. The point of immediate danger from an immediate threat was not canvassed, and once again nothing emerges from the case to support the arguments on one side or the other.

From this review of the Scottish cases cited to us, the case of *McCallum* supports the view taken by Lord Hunter in the present case while the others do not really advance the argument one way or the other, as the point at issue here was not raised and expressly dealt with. Only in the passage in Anderson is there a correlation between immediate threat and immediate danger to be found.

Reference was made by counsel for the appellant to two English cases which dealt with the English term duress. These were *R. v. Hudson* [1971] 2 Q.B. 202 and *D.P.P. v. Lynch* [1975] A.C. 653. These cases were naturally cited not as binding authorities on us but as cases of persuasive influence. Many of the English cases dealing with the law of duress were canvassed and discussed in *Lynch* and we confine ourselves to a consideration of the broad matters of identity and difference between them and the Hume view. Both agree that it is a competent defence in limited circumstances. There is mutual agreement of the dangers of facile resort to such a type of defence and for the need to have strict limits monitoring its application. There is unanimity of view that coercion or duress must have dominated the mind at the time of the act and that it was by reason of that domination that the act was committed. It has been said that the duress must be real and effective at the time when the decision to commit the act was made. Where the difference creeps in is in the relationship between the threats and the danger. The English cases seem to keep the emphasis on the threat whereas Hume places it on the immediate danger arising out of the threat. Thus in the case of *R. v. Kray (Ronald)* (1969) 53 Cr. App. R. 569 at p. 578 Widgery, L.J. propones the test as 'that by reason of threats he was so terrified that he ceased to be an independent actor'. As we see the existing Scottish law, the basic question is whether there was immediate danger of the threat being implemented in the event of non-compliance at the point of time when the decision had to be made. Other considerations may arise where there is an inability to have recourse to the protection of the law or to any other form of reasonably practical means to prevent the threat being implemented in the present or in the future. These considerations do not seem to have been taken into account in the case of *Hudson, supra*, where the fact of the threats having been spoken to in evidence, coupled with the allegation that a man of violence, who was one of a group of men who had made the threats, was in the public gallery of the court, was sufficient to satisfy the Court of Appeal that the issue of duress should have been left to the jury. We freely accept that if there is evidence in the case which supports a defence in law it ought to go to the jury, but evidence must have that attachment. If it does not, then that evidence should not go to the jury. If the law of Scotland is the law set out by Hume, then with all due respect we cannot see how Hume's first two qualifications would be held to be satisfied if corresponding facts to those in *Hudson* appears in a Scots trial, unless of course there was evidence to the effect that the process of law and order could not afford a reasonable protection against the threats being carried into effect at some future date. Here again the emphasis on threats as distinct from danger from the threats comes into play. In *Hudson* the Court of Appeal held that the jury should have been left to decide whether the threats had overborne the will of the defendants at the time when they gave the false evidence—and when, we may add—they were presumably under no fear of the threats then being implemented immediately.

Having regard to all these circumstances we have reached the conclusion that we should proceed on the basis of the traditional law of Scotland expounded by Hume as we have interpreted it *supra*. This is in essence the view of the law taken and applied by the trial judge, who confined the issue of coercion to immediate danger from threats. In our view, he gave the proper direction in the circumstances of the case in a careful and meticulous manner, and we reject the contention that he misdirected the jury in his presentation of the law to them. The appeal is accordingly refused."

Appeal dismissed.

NOTES

## (i) The nature of the threat

In his charge to the jury, Lord Hunter stated that the threat must be one of death or great bodily harm. **7.63** His Lordship added the further qualification that the threats must be such "as would overcome the resolution of an ordinarily constituted person of the same age and sex as the accused". It is not clear what purpose this further qualification serves. Lord Hunter states: '[the accused] doesn't need to be a hero: on the other hand, the law does not make allowance for excessive cowardice or timidity." But if the only kind of threat which can amount to coercion is one of death or great bodily harm, in what circumstances will the court hold that such a threat cannot provide a defence because the ordinarily constituted person of the same age and sex as the accused would not have been overcome by it? See, further, *Cochrane v. H.M. Advocate*, High Court, June 13, 2001, *unreported*.

## (ii) The immediacy of the harm

The decision makes it clear that threats of future harm will not constitute coercion. It is submitted, **7.64** nevertheless, that the approach of the court in *Hudson and Taylor* is logically defensible and fairer to the accused. If, as the court suggests, what matters is the overcoming of the accused's will by threats, it is difficult to see why the defence should be limited to threats of immediate harm. If A is told to commit a robbery under threat of his wife and children being shot within 24 hours if he does not, then the issue is simply one of whether or not there is a reasonable prospect of that consequence being avoided without the commission of the crime by the accused. It is of course right that the defence of coercion should not be available where the accused could protect himself in other ways. But that is not a reason for ruling out *a priori*, threats of future harm. It is not correct to suggest that the availability and practicability of alternative methods of preventing the threat being implemented were not taken into account in *Hudson and Taylor*. As Lord Widgery pointed out, it is always open to the Crown to "prove that the accused failed to avail himself of some opportunity which was reasonably open to him to render the threat ineffective, and that upon this being established the threat in question can no longer be relied upon by the defence" (p. 207).

See also in this connection *R. v. Carker (No. 2)* [1967] 2 C.C.C. 190, which adopts the same approach as Scots law. In *Hébert v. R.* [1989] 1 S.C.R. 233 the appellant committed perjury. He claimed that he had given false evidence in the face of death threats made against him. The Canadian Supreme Court held that a death threat which a person could easily escape and could render unenforceable when giving evidence could not provide the basis for a defence of compulsion provided for in section 17 of the Canadian Criminal Code. But see also *R. v. Ruzic* 128 C.C.C. 3d 97 (1999) in which the Ontario court of appeal held that, as a matter of common law (as opposed to the defence of compulsion under section 17 of the Code), that the plea of duress was available to an accused who, charged with illegally importing drugs into Canada, claimed that she had done so because of threats to kill her family living in Serbia. The persons making the threats were at all times in Serbia, and did not accompany her to Canada.

## (iii) The foundation of the plea

**7.65** Lord Hunter expresses this in terms of the will of the accused being overborne by the threats, and in this respect he followed what was said by Lord Keith in *H.M. Advocate v. Docherty and Others*, Glasgow High Court, June 1976, unreported (but see the first edition of this book, pp. 234 *et seq.*). See also *Sayers v. H.M. Advocate*, 1981 S.C.C.R. 312 at pp. 318–319. There are, however, *dicta* to the effect that duress functions so as to exclude the *mens rea* for an offence. See, for example, Lord McCluskey's charge to the jury in *H.M. Advocate v. Raiker and Others*, 1989 S.C.C.R. 149, at p. 154 B–C. There his Lordship suggests that a person who acts under duress "he cannot be said to have the evil intention which the law says is a necessary ingredient in the carrying out of a crime".

## (iv) The scope of the plea

**7.66** According to the court, Hume "restricts [the plea] to 'atrocious crimes'". This, with respect, is not what Hume says. Hume makes it clear that the plea will be a difficult one to sustain in the case of atrocious crime. As the court points out, there may be some doubt as to its applicability in a case of murder. The House of Lords has held that on a true reading of the English authorities the defence of duress is not available to anyone who participates in murder, thus overruling the earlier decision of the House in *Lynch v. D.P.P. for Northern Ireland* [1975] 1 All E.R. 913: *R. v. Howe, ante.*

In *Collins v. H.M. Advocate*, 1993 S.L.T. 101, 1991 S.C.C.R. 898 Lord Allanbridge, in his charge to the jury, stated, *inter alia* that the defence of coercion was not available, as a matter of law, in a case of murder:

> "I direct you [that] as a matter of law coercion is not a defence in Scotland to the crime of murder and the reason is quite simple. It is because of the supreme importance that the law affords to the protection of human life. It is repugnant that the law should recognise in any individual in any circumstances however extreme the right to choose that one innocent person should be killed rather than any other person including himself. So, ladies and gentlemen, it is as simple and it is as clear as that, that in the law of Scotland as I understand it coercion is not open as a defence to murder."

The direction was, *obiter*, since neither of the accused in the instant case actually relied upon the defence, and Lord Allanbridge's statement of the law cannot, therefore be accepted as an authoritative statement of the modern law. The court in *Thomson v. H.M. Advocate*, 1983 J.C. 69 reserved its opinion on this question. It may be of some significance that Hume, while in large measure adopting the views of Hale, clearly did not go so far as to accept Hale's exclusion of the defence in the case of murder.

In the case of *Erdemović v. Prosecutor*, I.T.–96–22, October 7, 1997, the Appeal Chamber of the International Tribunal for the former Yugoslavia considered the question of whether or not coercion could be relied upon as a defence to a charge of committing crimes against humanity where the crime took the form of murdering civilian detainees. After an extensive consideration of the legal systems of more than twenty countries the tribunal determined, by a majority, that the defence of coercion would not be available in such circumstances.

## (v) Voluntary exposure to the risk of coercion

**7.67** One of the concerns which is frequently raised in the context of the defence of coercion is the risk that it presents of criminals effectively conferring defences upon their associates by coercing them into committing offences. This, however, is not a very significant risk since, as has happened in several jurisdictions, the defence can be excluded where a member of a group engaged in criminal activities performs such an act under duress emanating from the group. This was the position adopted by the court in *R. v. Fitzpatrick* [1977] N.I. 20 in excluding the defence of duress where a member of the I.R.A. committed a robbery under duress which took the form of threats by that organisation against his family.

In *R. v. Calderwood and Moore* [1983] N.I. 361 it was held that the principle established in *Fitzpatrick* applied not only to a person who voluntarily joined an illegal association, but also to a person who voluntarily associated himself with such a group or organisation and thereby exposed himself to the risk of being subjected to threats. See also *R. v. Sharp* [1987] 3 W.L.R. 1. In *R. v. Shepherd* (*The Independent*, May 29, 1987), the Court of Appeal held that if an accused voluntarily joined a group dedicated to the use of violence, and was subsequently subjected to threats from members of that group, he could not plead duress. If, however, an accused joined a criminal enterprise which did not at the outset alert the accused to the possibility of violence being used, but which subsequently manifested violence, the accused was not necessarily deprived of the possibility of pleading duress.

See also, in this context, *Lynch v. DPP; People v. Merhige* (1920) 212 Mich. 601, 180 N.W. 418; *Ross v. State* (1907) 169 Ind. 388; 82 N.E. 781; Law Commission Working Paper No. 55, para. 26.

## (b) Necessity

### Hume, I, 54–55

"Last of all, let me take notice of another sort of constraint, that which arises from the **7.68** pressure of extreme want: I mean where the person has done some thing which serves to the support of nature for the time. As might be expected, lawyers have differed about the justice of punishing in such a case: some affirming that the notion of dole is excluded in these circumstances of personal distress, or at least that they afford a good plea for a mitigation of the ordinary pains; while others deny that such considerations are at all available in law. [Hume considers the difficulties associated with framing a defence of necessity, particularly where it is pleaded as a defence to the taking of another's property, and the problems of determining when a case of necessity is truly made out. He then continues:]

But there are truly far higher considerations against admitting such a rule—a rule which would subvert all security of property, by confounding the common notions of honesty among our people, and throwing into every man's own hand the estimation of his own wants and distresses, and of the impossibility of relieving them in any more lawful course. It is grounded, therefore, in sound reason, and substantial justice, and is, as I understand, the settled law of Scotland, that the judge shall apply the ordinary pains of law in this, as in every other case, where a person knowingly, and for his own advantage, has taken the property of his neighbour; leaving it to the necessitous offender to supplicate his relief from his Majesty, who is the source of mercy, and will not refuse to listen, in any case where it is fit for him to interpose. Thus the rigid and salutary precept of the law is maintained entire; and humanity is at the same time consulted, without the risk of any of those manifold evils and disorders, which would follow on a more enlarged scheme of indulgence."

NOTES

1. Compare Hume's views to the views of Lord Denning in *London Borough of Southwark v. Williams* **7.69** *and Another* [1971] Ch. 734.

2. Is it consistent for Hume to accept the possibility of a defence of coercion, but to reject out of hand the plea of necessity? What (apart from the source of the "threat") is the difference between the two pleas? See the comments of Lord Hailsham in *R. v. Howe* [1987] 1 All E.R. 771 at p. 777 and *Moss v. Howdle*, 1997 S.L.T. 782, *infra*.

### Moss v. Howdle
### 1997 S.L.T. 782

LORD JUSTICE-GENERAL. "On October 31, 1995 the appellant, Mr Roland Maurice Moss, was **7.70** driving his car south on the A74(M) Glasgow to Carlisle road. He had as a passenger a Mr

William Pearson, not a close friend, but someone who shared his interest in market trading. Before they reached the slip road to Kirkpatrick Fleming, Mr Pearson suddenly and without prior warning began to shout out in pain, but did not explain the cause of his pain. Mr Moss believed that Mr Pearson had been taken seriously ill. At that time he could have pulled to the side of the road to discover the nature of Mr Pearson's distress and, if necessary, to summon assistance. Mr Moss thought of using his mobile telephone to summon assistance but remembered that the batteries were flat. What he in fact did was to drive at a speed in excess of the 70 m.p.h. limit with a view to reaching a service area as soon as possible. For nearly three-quarters of a mile his speed was recorded as averaging 101.70 m.p.h. He was followed by police officers in a police car, who saw his car move from the outside lane across the other lanes and into the slip road leading to the services at Gretna, which were the closest to the point where the incident had begun. By the time Mr Moss parked his car there Mr Pearson had recovered enough to tell him that he had suffered an attack of cramp. Mr Pearson got out of the car and walked to the services building in order to use the toilet facilities there. Meanwhile the police officers spoke to Mr Moss and cautioned and charged him with a contravention of the Motorway Traffic (Speed Limit) Regulations 1974. He made no reply and in particular did not mention Mr Pearson.

In due course the appellant went to trial on a charge alleging a contravention of regulation 3 of the Motorway Traffic (Speed Limit) Regulations 1974 and of sections 17 and 134 of the Road Traffic Regulation Act 1984. He was convicted and fined £100, but, in view of the circumstances, the sheriff decided not to disqualify him from driving. He has appealed against his conviction by way of stated case.

In the sheriff court the solicitor appearing for Mr Moss argued that in Scots law necessity could be a defence to a charge of this kind. The sheriff accepted that necessity could constitute a defence but, having examined the appellant's actings, he went on to hold that a medical emergency could not constitute necessity for these purposes in Scots law. He therefore held that, on the facts of the case, the defence had not been made out. In the appeal to this court Miss Scott renewed the submission that a defence of necessity could apply in such cases and argued further that a medical emergency could amount to necessity. Here, she submitted, Mr Moss had been compelled to drive in excess of the speed limit because he believed—not unreasonably, as the sheriff had found—that Mr Pearson had been taken seriously ill and he wished to take him to the nearest service area as quickly as possible. So the defence had been established . . . .

A convenient starting-point is the crisp observation of Lord Justice-Clerk Wheatley in *Thomson v. H.M. Advocate* at 1983 J.C., p. 78 that 'A defence of coercion is recognised in the law of Scotland'. The equivalent defence in English law is generally referred to as duress. Some indication of the scope of the defence in Scots law is to be found in Hume's Commentaries, where the author goes through a range of cases in which arguments had been put forward that an accused person should be acquitted because he acted under compulsion of various kinds. One thing which emerges is that Scots law as known to Hume, was cautious in admitting such kinds of defence. None the less he does recognise that in certain situations a defence of this type may be made out. He starts with situations of great commotion, or extensive danger, in time of war or rebellion where the forces of law have been overpowered and individuals may be forced to do things for their self-preservation. He then applies a similar approach to situations of less extensive commotion where mobs may roam around, take possession of someone and compel him to take part in their criminal adventure. Sailors who are captured by pirates and compelled to take part in their criminal adventures are treated in the same way (Commentaries, vol. i, p. 52). He adds, however, that

'There may even be situations, though not so common now as formerly, of a more special and private sort of violence, which shall be judged by the same rule.'

The contrast therefore seems to be between cases where there is some fairly widespread breakdown of order and cases where, even though there is no general disorder, the accused has committed a crime as a result of being subjected to violence. Hume admits that a defence may be open in such cases, but says [at p. 53] that in the ordinary condition of a well-regulated society,

'this is at least somewhat a difficult plea, and can hardly be serviceable in the case of a trial for any atrocious crime, unless it have the support of these qualifications: an immediate danger of death or great bodily harm; an inability to resist the violence; a backward and an inferior part in the perpetration; and a disclosure of the fact, as well as restitution of the spoil, on the first safe and convenient occasion. For if the pannel take a very active part in the enterprise, or conceal the fact, and detain his share of the profit, when restored to a state of freedom, either of these replies will serve in a great measure to elide his defence'.

What Hume says in the last sentence has to be read in the light of the comments of their Lordships in *Thomson,* but, leaving that aside, we deduce from the passage that, although the plea of coercion may be 'somewhat ... difficult', even in the case of an atrocious crime an accused may be acquitted on the ground that he was compelled to commit it—provided that certain conditions are fulfilled. Rather surprisingly, in *Thomson* the court interpreted Hume's words as showing that he would have allowed the defence to apply *only* in the case of 'atrocious crimes' (at p. 78). If that were so and his view represented the law today, then plainly the defence would not be available in a motoring offence such as the present. We are satisfied, however, that the comment in *Thomson* was both obiter and unsound. It puts a false gloss on Hume's words. Their plain implication is, rather, that the defence of coercion is more generally available but, in the case of atrocious crimes, it will not in practice be sustained unless the particular qualifications which he mentions are made out. It would be an odd legal system indeed which, as a matter of principle, allowed coercion to elide guilt of the crime of armed robbery, but not guilt of the offence of exceeding the speed limit.

Among the qualifications which Hume mentions is that the accused acted under 'an immediate danger of death or great bodily harm'. That requirement is apt to delimit the scope of the defence and to keep it within narrow bounds. Miss Scott did not suggest that any lesser threat would do and we have found nothing in the authorities to which we were referred which would suggest otherwise. On the contrary, in *McNab v. Guild* 1989 S.C.C.R. 138 at p. 141 the court held that if a defence of necessity could be advanced to a charge of reckless driving, it could be made out only where 'at the material time the appellant was in immediate danger of life or serious injury'. A similar qualification is found in other systems. See, for example, *R. v. Conway* [1989] Q.B. 290 at p. 297E–F, per Woolf L.J. We therefore proceed on the basis that the minimum requirement of any defence of this kind is that the accused acted in the face of an immediate danger of death or great bodily harm.

Counsel argued, however, that the immediate danger of death or great bodily harm did not require to arise out of a threatened assault by a third party. An accused should equally be acquitted if he acted to avoid danger of death or great bodily harm which arose out of a threatened natural disaster or from illness. Similarly, she said, the threat did not need to be to the accused himself. If an accused could be acquitted when acting to avoid danger of death or great bodily harm to himself, he should likewise be acquitted when he acted to avoid such danger or harm to a companion. So, she argued, in this case Mr Moss should be acquitted since he exceeded the speed limit because he not unreasonably believed that Mr Pearson was suffering from a serious illness and he wanted to get him to the nearest service area as soon as possible.

Plainly counsel's argument takes the scope of the defence further than is envisaged in the passage of Hume which we have quoted. But that passage does not purport to give a full description of the defence as it is to be applied in all circumstances. As the Lord Justice-Clerk noted in *Thomson* [at p. 380], Hume plainly was not seeking to lay down any absolute rule'. So the entire law of Scotland on the topic is not set out in these few lines of Hume, though they provide an invaluable pointer to the general basis on which it rests. What Hume envisages is a situation where a third party threatens the accused with death or serious injury if he does not commit a particular offence or participate in a criminal adventure—and the accused commits the offence or participates in the adventure. In such cases the threat is directed at compelling the accused to commit a particular offence or to participate in a criminal adventure. But in other cases, where that is not the purpose of the threat, the accused may claim to have committed an offence in order to escape from an immediate threat of death or serious injury. The term 'duress of circumstances' has been used to describe the defence of this kind of case in English law. *Tudhope v. Grubb* 1983 S.C.C.R. 350 (Sh.Ct.) is such a case in Scots law. The accused was charged with attempting to drive with an excess of alcohol in his blood, contrary to section 6(1) of the Road Traffic Act 1972. He had been assaulted by three men, knocked to the ground and kicked and punched on the body. He was injured as a result. He escaped from them, but eventually found himself in his car which was attacked by the men kicking it and trying to smash its windows. The accused tried to drive off to escape them. This resulted in the charge under section 6(1). The sheriff held that the accused had attempted to drive in an effort to save himself further injury and that he had made a full disclosure of the facts to the police at the first opportunity. The sheriff found the defence, described as a defence of necessity, established and acquitted the accused. (It would indeed have been enough if the Crown had failed to rebut the defence.) The Crown appealed but abandoned their appeal. The advocate-depute did not suggest that the general approach in *Grubb* had been incorrect. A similar defence was put forward to charges of reckless driving in *MacLeod v. MacDougall* 1988 S.C.C.R. 5 and *McNab v. Guild* 1989 S.C.C.R. 138, in both of which the accused contended that they had been escaping from assailants. They were convicted and this court refused their appeals on the facts, without deciding whether the defence was available to such a charge. The general approach in *Grubb* is, however, in line with authorities in other systems such as *R. v. Willer (Mark Edward)* [1987] R.T.R. 22 (reckless driving to escape a gang) and *R. v. Conway* [1989] Q.B. 290 (reckless driving to escape police officers whom the accused believed to be potential assailants). Moreover, such an approach appears to be consistent with the requirement of our law of self-defence that a person who is attacked should take any reasonable opportunity to escape from his attackers.

If the defence is available where the accused committed the crime in order to escape a threat of death or great bodily harm from a third party, we see no reason why it should be excluded simply because the immediate threat of death or great bodily harm which the accused is trying to evade arises from, say, a natural disaster or from illness, rather than from the actings of a third party. On this matter we respectfully adopt the reasoning of Lord Hailsham L.C. in *R. v. Howe* [1987] A.C. 417 at p. 429C–D. He was dealing with an argument that cases on duress could be distinguished from cases on necessity, such as the famous case of *R. v. Dudley and Stephens* (1884) 14 Q.B.D. 273 where two shipwrecked sailors were convicted of murdering a cabin boy whom they had killed and eaten to preserve their own lives. The Lord Chancellor rejected that argument and said:

'There is, of course, an obvious distinction between duress and necessity as potential defences; duress arises from the wrongful threats or violence of another human being and necessity arises from any other objective dangers threatening the accused. This, however, is, in my view, a distinction without a relevant difference, since on this view duress is only that species of the genus of necessity which is caused by wrongful threats. I cannot see that there is any way in which a person of ordinary fortitude can be excused from the one type of pressure on his will rather than the other.'

The passage was applied by Woolf L.J. in *R. v. Conway* at pp. 297–298. Since the hearing in the present appeal we have noticed that Lord Hailsham's reasoning was also adopted by Lamer C.J. in the Supreme Court of Canada in *Hibbert v. R.* [1955] 2 S.C.R. 973 at pp. 1012–1013, where he said:

'The defences of self-defence, necessity and duress all arise under circumstances where a person is subjected to an external danger, and commits an act that would otherwise be criminal as a way of avoiding the harm the danger presents. In the case of self-defence and duress, it is the intentional threats of another person that are the source of the danger, while in the case of necessity the danger is due to other causes, such as forces of nature, human conduct and other than intentional threats of bodily harm, etc. Although this distinction may have important practical consequences, it is hard to see how it could act as the source of significant juristic differences between the three defences.'

Approaching the matter in this way, we consider that, where an accused commits a crime in an endeavour to escape an immediate danger of death or great bodily harm, it makes no difference to the possible availability of any defence that the danger arises from some contingency such as a natural disaster or illness rather than from the deliberate threats of another. Indeed the advocate-depute readily accepted that in principle the defence could be based on medical emergency. So, an accused may drive dangerously in order to avoid an immediate threat of death from an incipient heart attack, or to avoid an immediate threat of death by drowning in a flood or to avoid an immediate threat of death by drowning due to the deliberate actings of a third party. For the purposes of deciding whether they afford a defence to a charge of dangerous driving, the law should regard all of these threats in the same way.

In the present case, of course, the appellant does not argue that he himself was under any threat. Rather, his argument at its highest is that he should be acquitted because he not unreasonably believed that Mr Pearson was seriously ill and he drove as he did in order to bring him as quickly as possible to a place where he might receive assistance. In other words, the appellant exceeded the speed limit in order to try to save Mr Pearson from the effects of what he believed to be a serious illness. Again this involves a certain development from the core case since the accused is not escaping a danger to himself but is helping his passenger to escape what the accused not unreasonably believes to be an immediate danger. But once more the approach is consistent with the ethos of our system. The law recognises that 'Danger invites rescue' in Scotland just as surely as in New York: *Wagner v. International Railroad Co.* (1921) 232 N.Y. 176 at p. 180, per Cardozo J.; *Steel v. Glasgow Iron and Steel Co.* 1944 S.C. 237 at p. 248, per Lord Justice-Clerk Cooper. So Scots law has never been so mean-spirited as to confine the defence of self-defence to situations where the accused acts to save himself. It has always recognised that the defence may be available in situations where the accused acts in an altruistic fashion to save a companion: Hume, Commentaries, vol. i, p. 218. In the same way, if a defence of duress would be open to someone who committed a crime to try to escape immediate danger to his own life or health, it should be open to someone who does the same to try to ensure that his companion escapes such danger. An illustration given by Simon Brown J., as he then was, in *Martin* [1989] 1 All E.R. 652 at p. 654B–D is particularly instructive for present purposes.

'[W]e can see no distinction in principle between various threats of death; it matters not whether the risk of death is by murder or by suicide or, indeed, by accident. One can illustrate the latter by considering a disqualified driver being driven by his wife, she suffering a heart attack in remote countryside and he needing instantly to get her to hospital.'

It may be useful at this stage to dispose of the more general issues raised in the present case, before turning to consider how any defence should be regarded on the particular facts. In the stated case the first question which the sheriff puts to this court is: 'Was I correct in law to proceed upon the basis that a defence of necessity could be available for a road traffic offence of this nature?' Miss Scott submitted that this question should be answered in the affirmative and the advocate-depute accepted that. In the light of the general considerations which we have discussed, the answer should indeed be in the affirmative, provided that a 'defence of necessity' is interpreted as referring to a defence based on an immediate danger of death or great bodily harm. The third question in the case was: 'Did I err in concluding that medical emergency is relevant to sentence only?' Again counsel for the appellant and the advocate-depute were agreed that the question should be answered in the affirmative and, for the reasons which we have given, we are satisfied that this is correct.

There is much discussion in the cases and in the books about the juridical basis of a defence of coercion or duress. Happily there is no reason even to try to add to it in this case. It is sufficient to concentrate on one point which the advocate-depute stressed. He emphasised that, for the defence to operate, the coercion or duress must have dominated the mind at the time of the act and that it was by reason of that domination that the act was committed': *Thomson* at p. 382. As the court recognised in *Thomson,* the law of England is to the same effect. So, in the context of a driving case Woolf L.J. held that the defence could arise only 'where the defendant was constrained by circumstances to drive as he did to avoid death or serious bodily harm to himself or some other person': *R. v. Conway* at p. 297E–F. Where the defence applies, an accused

> 'has control over his actions to the extent of being physically capable of abstaining from the act. Realistically, however, this act is not a "voluntary" one. His "choice" to break the law is no true choice at all; it is remorselessly compelled by normal human instincts' (*Perka v. R.* at p. 249, per Dickson J. giving the majority opinion of the Supreme Court of Canada).'

It follows that the defence cannot apply where the circumstances did not in fact constrain the accused to act in breach of the law. Again the point is focused by Dickson J. in another passage from the judgment in *Perka* [1984] 2 S.C.R. 232 at pp. 251–252:

> 'Given that the accused had to act, could he nevertheless realistically have acted to avoid the peril or prevent the harm, without breaking the law? *Was there a legal way out?* I think this is what Bracton means when he lists "necessity" as a defence, providing the wrongful act was not "avoidable". The question to be asked is whether the agent had any real choice: could he have done otherwise? If there is a reasonable legal alternative to disobeying the law, then the decision to disobey becomes a voluntary one, impelled by some consideration beyond the dictates of "necessity" and human instincts' (emphasis as in the original).

Counsel did not dispute that the availability of the defence had to be tested this way, nor that, if Mr Moss had had an alternative course of action which was lawful, the defence could not apply. What the sheriff says in his note is this:

> 'I accepted that the suddenness of Mr Pearson's attack of cramp afforded the appellant little opportunity to reach a considered decision on what action he should take, given that he was already driving, but I could not conclude that the appellant's will had been overcome by the perceived danger to Mr Pearson's well-being, so that he (the appellant) had no option but to drive in the manner libelled. It seemed to me that the appellant's conduct was quite deliberate. It also seemed to me that the appellant had available to him the option (and, in my opinion, the prudent option) of driving his vehicle to the side of the road in order to ascertain the nature of Mr Pearson's distress.'

The starting-point for the sheriff's reasoning is the fact that Mr Moss proceeded on the basis of a not unreasonable belief that his passenger was seriously ill, when in fact he was suffering from nothing worse than a severe bout of cramp. There is no finding that the appellant asked him what was wrong. The sheriff takes the view that the prudent thing for the appellant to have done would have been to drive to the side of the road, find out what was wrong with Mr Pearson and then decide what he should do in the light of that. The sheriff appears to have concluded that the appellant had a real choice. Certainly the fact that he thought about using his mobile telephone shows that the appellant was able to consider alternative courses of action. The sheriff concludes his note by saying that the appellant 'had available to him at least one option short of driving at excessive speed, but he did not avail himself of that option'. He must therefore be proceeding on the very understandable basis that 'if Mr Moss had pulled over and found out what was actually the matter with Mr Pearson, he would not have felt the need to drive above the speed limit and would not have done so. Since the sheriff has found that the appellant could have prudently followed an alternative course of action which would not have involved committing the offence in question or any offence at all, we too must proceed on the basis that he had a real choice and was not constrained to commit the offence. That being so, the defence of coercion or duress is not available to him.

For these reasons we are satisfied that the sheriff was correct to reject the defence of necessity and was entitled to find the appellant guilty. We shall therefore answer questions 2 and 4 in the stated case in the affirmative and dismiss the appeal.

Appeal dismissed.

NOTES

1. This case firmly establishes the defence of necessity in Scots law. One of the most interesting aspects **7.71** of the case, however, is the extent to which it draws upon the defence of coercion, including Hume's views, and ignores entirely Hume's unqualified rejection of the defence of necessity.

2. The defence of necessity was further considered in *Lord Advocate's Reference (No. 1 of 2000)*, High Court, March 30, 2000, *unreported*. In that case the court identified a number of principles governing the plea of necessity (in addition to those set out in *Moss v. Howdle*). The court emphasised the need for the immediacy of danger: "Immediacy of danger is an essential element in the defence of necessity." (para. 37). There must be reasonable grounds for the view that the action taken is necessary. The actor must have "good cause to fear that death or serious injury *would* result unless he acted; that cause for fear must have resulted from a reasonable belief as to the circumstances; the actor must have been impelled to act as he did by those circumstances; and the defence will only be available if a sober person of reasonable firmness, sharing the characteristics of the actor, would have responded as he did" (para. 42). The court also took the view that the actor must, at the material time, "have reason to think that the acts carried out had some prospect of removing the perceived danger" (para. 46).

The reliance on coercion as a foundation of the defence in *Moss v. Howdle* leads the Court to conclude that necessity is limited to cases in which the accused acts in order to avoid death or serious harm to the person. Is this a justifiable limitation of the defence? Suppose, for example, that a fire breaks out in A's kitchen. Major damage can be avoided if the fire is extinguished quickly, but there is no fire service near to his house. He knows that his next door neighbour has a fire extinguisher. He runs to his neighbour's house to borrow it, but his neighbour is out. He breaks into his neighbour's house, and uses the extinguisher to put out the fire. Should A be entitled to rely on the defence of necessity?

3. The references to the case of *Perka v. The Queen* suggest that the Court was inclined to accept that the foundation of the plea of necessity is that of "moral involuntariness" in the sense that the accused acted as he did because he or she was deprived of any realistic choice in the face of an overwhelming threat. That being so, it seems to follow that in order to take advantage of the defence of necessity the accused must have been motivated by the circumstances from which the necessity arose. If the accused would have committed the criminal offence in any event, the fact that it could be excused by circumstances of necessity is irrelevant.

4. In *Dawson v. McKay*, 1999 S.L.T. 1328, a firefighter was charged with driving a fire-engine while his breath alcohol was above the prescribed limit. The accused had been off-duty, and had been drinking in the company of another fire-fighter, who was summoned to the scene of a serious road accident. The accused went along with him, and drove a fire appliance to the scene of the accident. At the scene of the accident it became necessary to move the fire appliance which had been driven to the scene by the accused in order to allow an ambulance to take a seriously injured patient to hospital. The accused was asked by the paramedics to move the vehicle, which he did. In doing so he collided with a police car. His defence of necessity was rejected by the sheriff. On appeal the High Court upheld the conviction. In delivering the opinion of the Court, Lord Sutherland considered the cases of *Moss v. Howdle* and *Perka v. The Queen,* and stated:

"It is in our view clear ... that the defence of necessity only arises when there is a conscious dilemma faced by a person who has to decide between saving life or avoiding serious bodily harm on the one hand and breaking the law on the other hand. If, in the circumstances of the case, he elects to break the law rather than risk life, the defence of necessity may well be open to him. Applying that principle to the present case it can be seen that there was no question of the appellant making any choice at all. It never occurred to him that he should not be driving, and the reason why he drove at the locus was simply because he was the driver of that pump. The question is not why did he drive, but is why did he drive with excess alcohol and carelessly? No doubt he drove because he was asked to do so, and he did so in a situation where there was some urgency. That, however, does not answer the question as to why he drove with excess alcohol in his blood. The reason he did that was because it never crossed his mind that he was unfit to drive, and he would have driven anyway. In these circumstances it cannot be said that his mind was dominated at the time of the act by the extreme urgency of the situation which overrode the normal requirements that a driver should not drive with excess alcohol in his blood. We are therefore satisfied that in the circumstances of this case the defence of necessity was not available to the appellant."

5. Does it matter, in case of necessity, that the conditions of necessity arise from the commission of an offence by the accused? In *Perka v. The Queen*, the appellants were drug smugglers. While engaged in delivering a boatload of cannabis from Colombia to a point off the coast of Alaska they ran into difficulties. The ship's engines malfunctioned, as did their navigation equipment. In worsening weather it was decided to make for the Canadian coast and take shelter there. While sheltering in a bay off Vancouver Island, the ship ran aground and began to list severely. The captain of the ship, fearing that the vessel would be lost, ordered the crew to off load the cannabis (332 tons in all). The ship and the appellants were subsequently arrested by the Canadian police. The appellants were charged with importing cannabis into Canada, and possession of cannabis for the purpose of trafficking, contrary to the Narcotic Control Act 1961. At their trial the appellants successfully relied on a defence of necessity. The Crown appealed against that acquittal, which was reversed on appeal. On appeal the Supreme Court of Canada held that involvement in criminal or immoral activity did not disqualify the accused from relying upon the defence of necessity.

6. There is a general reluctance to accept coercion as a defence to a charge of homicide. What is the situation with regard to necessity? Consider the following well-known case.

### R. v. Dudley and Stephens
#### (1884) 14 Q.B.D. 273

**7.72** The defendants, along with a third man called Brooks and a seventeen-year-old boy called Parker were cast adrift in an open boat after their yacht went down in a storm 1,600 miles from the Cape of Good Hope. On the twentieth day after the shipwreck, when they had been for eight days without food and for six without water, the defendants killed the boy. The latter did not consent to their act, but did not offer any resistance, being already too ill to do so. The defendants and Brooks fed on the flesh and blood of the boy until they were picked up four days later. At the trial the jury returned a special verdict which stated, *inter alia*:

> "If the men had not fed upon the body of the boy, they would probably not have survived to be so picked up and rescued, but would within the four days have died of famine; the boy, being in a much weaker condition was likely to have died before them; at the time of the act in question there was no sail in sight nor any reasonable prospect of relief; under the circumstances there appeared to the prisoners every probability that, unless they then fed, or very soon fed, upon the boy or one of themselves, they would die of starvation; there was no appreciable chance of saving life except by killing someone for the others to eat; assuming any necessity to kill anybody, there was no greater necessity for killing the boy than any of the three men."

LORD COLERIDGE C.J.: From these facts, stated with the cold precision of a special verdict, it appears that the prisoners were subjected to terrible temptation, to suffering which might break down the bodily power of the strongest man, and try the conscience of the best . . . . But nevertheless this is clear, that the prisoners put to death a weak and unoffending boy upon the chance of preserving their own lives by feeding upon his flesh and blood after he was killed, and with the certainty of depriving *him* of any possible chance of survival. The verdict finds in terms that 'if the men had not fed upon the body of the boy they would *probably* not have survived,' and that 'the boy being in a much weaker condition was *likely* to have died before them'. They might possibly have been picked up next day by a passing ship; they might possibly not have been picked up at all; in either case it is obvious that the killing of the boy would have been an unnecessary and profitless act. It is found by the verdict that the boy was incapable of resistance, and, in fact, made none; and it is not even suggested that his death was due to any violence on his part attempted against, or even so much as feared by, those who killed him ... [His Lordship dealt with certain objections taken on behalf of the defendants which are not relevant to the present question, and the state of the authorities on the question, and then continued:] ... Now except for the purpose of testing how far the conservation of a man's own life is in all cases and under all circumstances, an absolute, unqualified, and paramount duty, we exclude from our consideration all the incidents of war. We are dealing with a case of private homicide, not one imposed upon men in the service of their Sovereign and in the defence of their country. Now it is admitted that the deliberate killing of this unoffending and unresisting boy was clearly murder, unless the killing can be justified by some well-recognised excuse admitted by the law. It is further admitted that there was in this case no such excuse, unless the killing was justified by what has been called 'necessity'. But the temptation to the act which existed here was not what the law has ever called necessity. Nor is this to be regretted. Though law and morality are not the same, and many things may be immoral which are not necessarily illegal, yet the absolute divorce of law from morality would be of fatal consequence, and such divorce would follow if the temptation to murder in this case were to be held by law an absolute defence of it. It is not so. To preserve one's life is generally speaking a duty, but it may be the plainest and highest duty to sacrifice it. War is full of instances in which it is a man's duty not to live, but to die. The duty, in case of shipwreck, of a captain and his crew, of the crew to the passengers, of soldiers to women and children, as in the noble case of the *Birkenhead*; these duties impose on men the moral necessity, not of preservation, but of the sacrifice of their lives for others, from which no country, least of all, it is to be hoped, in England, will men ever shrink, as indeed, they have not shrunk. It is not correct, therefore, to say that there is any absolute or unqualified necessity to preserve one's life .... It is not needful to point out the awful danger of admitting the principle which has been contended for. Who is to be the judge of this sort of necessity? By what measure is the comparative value of lives to be measured? Is it to be strength, or intellect, or what? It is plain that the principle leaves to him who is to profit by it to determine the necessity which will justify him in deliberately taking another's life to save his own. In this case the weakest, the youngest, the most unresisting, was chosen. Was it more necessary to kill him than one of the grown men? The answer must be 'No'—

'So spake the Fiend, and with necessity,
The tyrant's plea, excused his devilish deeds.'

It is not suggested that in this particular case the deeds were 'devilish', but it is quite plain that such a principle once admitted might be made the legal cloak for unbridled passion and atrocious crime. There is no safe path for judges to tread but to ascertain the law to the best of their ability and to declare it according to their judgments; and if in any case the law appears to be too severe on individuals, to leave it to the Sovereign to exercise that prerogative of mercy which the Constitution has intrusted to the hands fittest to dispense it.

It must not be supposed that in refusing to admit temptation to be an excuse for crime it is forgotten how terrible the temptation was; how awful the suffering; how hard in such trials to keep the judgment straight and the conduct pure. We are often compelled to set up standards we cannot reach ourselves, and to lay down rules which we could not ourselves satisfy. But a man has no right to declare temptation to be an excuse, though he might himself have yielded to it, nor allow compassion for the criminal to change or weaken in any manner the legal definition of the crime. It is therefore our duty to declare that the prisoners' act in this case was wilful murder, that the facts as stated in the verdict are no legal justification of the homicide; and to say that in our unanimous opinion the prisoners are upon this special verdict guilty of murder."

Verdict: Guilty.

NOTES

**7.73**    1. For some time the difficulty with this case lay in determining the ground on which the court convicted the accused. Did Lord Coleridge hold that as a matter of law necessity was not available as a defence to murder, or that it was not a defence to any charge, or only that on the facts of this case the defendants had no defence?

In *R. v. Howe* [1987] 1 All E.R. 771 Lord Hailsham made the following remarks while discussing the defence of duress:

> "[*R. v. Dudley and Stephens*] is generally ... regarded as an authority on the availability of the supposed defence of necessity rather than duress ... There is, of course, an obvious distinction between duress and necessity as potential defences: duress arises from the wrongful threats or violence of another human being and necessity arises from any other objective dangers threatening the accused. This, however, is, in my view, a distinction without a relevant difference, since on this view duress is only that species of the genus of necessity which is caused by wrongful threats. I cannot see that there is any way in which a person of ordinary fortitude can be excused from the one type of pressure on his will rather than the other" (at p. 777).

If his Lordship's analysis is correct, then this suggests that the reason for excluding the defence of necessity in *Dudley and Stephens* was that while necessity may be a defence, it is not a defence to a charge of murder. This view tends to be confirmed by the court's concerns about the possibility of might becoming right if the defendants were to be acquitted.

*R. v. Abdul-Hussain* [1999] Crim. L.R. 570 confirms that necessity in English law is not available on a charge of murder or attempted murder. In *Re A (children) (conjoined twins: surgical separation)* [2001] 2 W.L.R. 480 two children were born conjoined in such a way that they both relied upon certain vital organs. One of the twins, Jodie, enjoyed good health, and if separated from her twin, Mary, had a good prospect of a relatively normal life. Mary, on the other hand, had very poor prospects of survival, no prospect of independent survival and would have had a very poor quality of life. It was clear that not separating them would result in the death of both, but it was also clear that separating them would inevitably result in the death of Mary. Would it be lawful to perform an operation in order to separate them in such circumstances, given that, in these circumstances, it could be argued that the doctors performing the operation could be said to be intentionally killing Mary? Does the doctrine of necessity apply here, or is it excluded by the view that it is not available in a case of murder?

2. Would the accused in a case such as *Dudley and Stevens* be entitled to an acquittal under Scots law? In *Lord Advocate's Reference (No. 1 of 2000)*, High Court, March 30, 2000, *unreported*, the court expressed the view that the accused must, at the time of committing the offence "have reason to think that the acts carried out had some prospect of removing the perceived danger". Would that condition be satisfied here? Would a "sober person of reasonable firmness, sharing the characteristics of the accused" have reacted in the way that Dudley and Stephens did? Would it matter, in answering this question, that the accused were experienced sailors, and aware of a general acceptance amongst sailors at the time that resort to cannibalism in such circumstances was a necessary evil? See, in this connection A. W. B. Simpson, *Cannibalism and the Common Law*, which discusses *Dudley and Stephens* in its historical context.

**7.74**    3. Even if it were to be accepted that it was necessary in a case such as *Dudley and Stephens* for someone's life to be sacrificed, how is the choice of victim to be made? In *U.S. v. Holmes*, 26, Fed. Cas. 360 (1842) a ship, the *William Brown* struck an iceberg and sank while *en route* to Philadelphia from Liverpool. Nine of the crew (including Holmes and the mate) and 32 passengers crowded into the ship's longboat. About 24 hours after the wreck, Holmes, along with other members of the crew, acting on the orders of the mate, began to throw out some of the male passengers in order to lighten the boat which was in serious danger of being swamped by the rising sea. In all, fourteen male passengers (and possibly two female passengers) were thrown out. None of the crew members suffered this fate. All those who were in the boat were picked up by another ship the following morning. Holmes was charged with the manslaughter of one of the men he put overboard. The judge's charge to the jury made it clear that the crew owed a duty of care towards the passengers, and that they ought to have sacrificed themselves, rather than the passengers. But suppose that there had only been passengers, or only crew in the boat? On what basis could such choices decently be made? The judge in *Holmes* suggested that there might be a resort to the drawing of lots which he justified as in some sense being an appeal to divine intervention in the selection of those to be cast overboard.

But would this method completely validate the proceedings? How should a person who refuses to draw a lot be dealt with? Suppose that it became necessary to eject some passengers and the wife of a victim attacked those who were trying to eject her husband. Would that attack be a criminal assault?

## (c) Superior orders

### Hume, i, 54–55

"It only remains to take notice of the case of soldiers, who are trained to a still stricter **7.75** discipline, and are bound to obedience of orders by far higher penalties. It is obvious nevertheless, that any plea which may be grounded upon these favourable considerations, must at least be received under certain provisions, without which it would be both dangerous and unjust. The order must be such as falls within the officer's commission, and known line of duty and though given in his own province, it must be at least an excusable order, or such as may be the subject of different opinions; not a manifest injury and aggression on his part. If an officer order out a party to rescue him from a messenger, who has him in custody for debt, any homicide or other injury which ensues on so irregular an enterprise, would at the hazard even of all the private men concerned in the execution of it. Or put the case, that being on guard with his party, an officer orders them to fire on an inoffensive meeting of the people—a command which he is punishable for giving, and which they may lawfully disobey: Certainly they, as well as he, are answerable for the consequences. The case of William Ferguson and others, soldiers in the Earl of Errol's regiment of militia, was an unfavourable one in both those respects: For the pannels and their party had been sent out to poind for deficiencies in the quota of militia-men, upon the warrant of their officer only, who had no sort of right to give such a warrant; and they had been guilty of great excess and precipitancy in putting it to execution. But cases of such outrageous wrong have not often occurred with us. And in those, which sometimes happen, of a more ambiguous character, a humane regard to the situation of the soldier, who has acted under the impression of duty, and the constraint of military habits, has generally had the effect of limiting the prosecution to the officer alone, as true author of the wrong. This was the course in the case of Captain Wallace; and in the still more noted case of Captain Porteous; though in both the order to fire had been obeyed by all, or many of the party, under the officer's command. But I do not wish to enter more at large into an article of such delicate discussion."

### H.M. Advocate v. Hawton and Parker
#### (1861) 4 Irv. 58

The accused were, respectively, a boatswain in the Royal Navy, and a marine. They were sent **7.76** out at night with a party of seamen to intercept persons who were illegally trawl fishing in Lochfyne. On the orders of the boatswain the marine fired on the trawlers to make them stop fishing and come to the shore. Blank shot was used at first, then live rounds were fired, with the intention of going wide of the trawlers. One shot, however, hit and killed one of the fishermen. The accused were charged with murder or alternatively culpable homicide. The Crown passed from the charge of murder, but sought a conviction on the latter charge.

LORD JUSTICE-GENERAL (McNEILL): "There was no doubt, on this occasion, the prisoners went out in the performance of their duty, and that they were armed in the usual manner; and also, that the fishermen were at the time engaged in an unlawful occupation; and it was also beyond question that a person in one of these boats had been killed by a shot fired by Parker. The question was, were either of the prisoners responsible?

The prisoners were enlisted in the naval service of the country, and were bound to follow the rules of that service. It was not necessary to discuss how far the employment of persons in the naval service in such a duty as suppressing trawling, imported into that employment the rules of the naval service. But subordinate officers or privates were not persons who were entitled to consider whether the rules to which they had been accustomed were imported into this duty, unless that were explained to them by their superior officers. One of the prisoners on this case had a certain command, the other was in the position of a subordinate; and it was the duty of the subordinate to obey his superior officer, unless the order given by his superior was so flagrantly and violently wrong that no citizen could be expected to obey it. But that principle extended also to the other prisoner, the officer then in command, because he was there also as a subordinate to fulfil the duty entrusted to him according to the rules of the service. And, therefore, if, when the prisoners fired the shots with the view of making the fishermen yield to legal authority, they were acting in accordance with the usage of the naval service, they were not guilty of any violation of the law.

But then in doing that it was incumbent on them to take due care of the lives of the fishermen; their object in firing was not to produce death or injury, but merely to give notice to these persons that they were required to submit to the law; and they were bound to take care that the shots fired for that purpose were not so carelessly fired as to produce injury or death .... [If the jury] were of opinion that the prisoners had acted in accordance with the rules of the naval service, and had not acted carelessly or recklessly, the prisoners were entitled to an acquittal. If, on the other hand, they were of opinion that they had deviated from the rules of the service, or that, in acting according to the rules of the service, they had failed to use due caution, they were then bound to give a verdict against the prisoners."

Verdict: Not guilty.

### H.M. Advocate v. Sheppard
### 1941 J.C. 67

**7.77** The accused, a private in the Pioneer Corps, was part of an escort under the charge of a lance-corporal, whose duty it was to return a deserter from the Corps to their regiment. The accused was left alone with the deserter for a few minutes, during which time the deserter tried to escape and the accused shot and killed him. It appeared from the evidence that no clear orders had been given as regards shooting at escaping prisoners, but it was established that the lance-corporal had told the accused to stand no nonsense and to shoot if necessary. The accused explained that he had not intended to kill, but merely to frighten, the prisoner who had already made two abortive attempts to escape (both of which had been thwarted by the accused). The accused was charged with assault and murder (the latter being reduced by the Crown to culpable homicide during the trial).

In his charge to the jury the presiding judge made the following remarks.

LORD ROBERTSON: "Now, first of all, about culpable homicide. Here, the killing of Fitzgerald is not in dispute, but the question for you on the charge of culpable homicide that is made against the accused is: Was the accused culpable, and was he culpable in the degree required to make the crime ... of culpable homicide? Now that degree of culpability is higher than mere negligence such as would suffice to substantiate, for instance, a civil claim of damages by let me say, the widow of a person who had been killed by negligence on the part of the person accused. The degree is higher than that. To make the crime of culpable homicide, the degree of culpability must be what is described by Lord Justice Clerk Alness in the case to which the learned Dean of Faculty referred me (*H.M. Advocate v. Cranston*, 1931 J.C. 28) as 'gross and palpable carelessness'; or, to take an expression from another judge, Lord Justice-Clerk Aitchison ... the position is this, that 'a person is not criminally liable for a mere act of negligence. He may be civilly liable, but he would not be criminally liable. Before you can convict of the second charge'—that is, culpable homicide—'you must be able to say that the accused acted with such gross and wicked recklessness that his conduct ought properly to be regarded as criminal conduct'.

Now that is the position which you have to consider generally before you come to the facts of the case on the charge made against the accused of culpable homicide; and I would just like to add a little as to what Lord Justice-Clerk Aitchison said in the case to which I have referred, *H.M. Advocate v. Macpherson* (Edinburgh High Court, September 1940, *unreported*). It was the case of a soldier not on duty, but on leave. He had come up from the south, somewhere in England, to Edinburgh, and in the course of the black-out, and while an air-raid alert was in progress, he took it upon himself, having a rifle and ammunition, to shoot at a motor-car which was proceeding along the road, as he thought at an excessive rate of speed, and, as he thought, with its lights not sufficiently dimmed. It so happened that the motor-car was a police car, and contained the Assistant Chief Constable of Edinburgh, and the Assistant Chief Constable was shot and killed, and the accused man was accused of culpable homicide. In that case what Lord Aitchison said to the jury, amongst other things, was this: 'If the shot was deliberately directed at the car, as it was, in which these people were travelling, that was criminal recklessness in the sense of the indictment unless there are proved facts in the case that will justify you in saying that the act of the accused can be excused upon some reasonable ground, but I must emphasise the words "upon some reasonable ground". It won't do for a soldier on leave to discharge a loaded rifle in the public street and take human life and then seek to evade the responsibility for his act by saying that he thought he was doing his duty. You must as, yourselves whether there were any reasonable grounds, such as might influence a man in his sober senses, for the accused acting as he did.' ... His Lordship went on: 'Now I am bound to tell you that there are no facts proved in this case that would justify a plea of justifiable homicide.' You will remember, however, the soldier there was on leave with no duty to perform at the moment. He added: 'We are not in the region of justifiable homicide at all. The question is not—Was the accused justified in taking Thomson's life?'—Thomson was the Assistant Chief Constable—'That is not the question. The question is—Is it proved that he acted with criminal recklessness? And that just comes down to the other question—Had he, looking at it broadly, some kind of just excuse for what he did?' And then I ask you to note that his Lordship added this: 'Even in a case where the soldier was on leave and had no specific duty to perform, if you are to say that the accused acted under a mistaken sense of duty and that he had some reasonable cause for what he did, you would be entitled to acquit him.' ... Now the accused was on duty, unlike the accused in the case of Macpherson when the Assistant Chief Constable of Edinburgh was shot. The accused was on duty, and his immediate duty was to keep in custody, and to deliver up, the man whom he was escorting. In such a case it is obviously not impossible by any means for a jury to take the view that, if the circumstances were such as to require the accused, for the due execution of his duty, to shoot in order to keep this man in custody, then the homicide was justifiable, and so to acquit the accused entirely of the crime charged against him. The question is—and it is a question for you, the jury—whether on the facts the conclusion that there was no crime in the matter, but only the execution, painful as it might be, of a duty imposed upon the accused—whether that conclusion is a proper one. In considering it, it will be right for you to keep in view the situation in which the accused was placed. He was a soldier on duty in charge of a deserter and under obligation to deliver up the body of the deserter to headquarters. It would be altogether wrong to judge his actings, so placed, too meticulously—to weigh them in fine scales. If that were to be done, it seems to me that the actings of soldiers on duty might well be paralysed by fear of consequences, with great prejudice to national interests ....

[His Lordship referred to Hume's treatment of superior orders (Hume, *Commentaries*, i, p. 205) and continued:] and on the facts now the question for you will be whether, making the allowance to which the accused as a soldier on duty is properly entitled, you must nevertheless convict him of the crime of culpable homicide: or whether you can acquit him entirely of crime. Now that comes down to this, I think. Was this shooting, in a proper sense, in the line of the accused's duty as reasonably understood by him, or was it an act which, while falling short of murder, is yet proved to have been of such gross and wicked recklessness that the conduct of the accused must properly be regarded as criminal conduct? These are the two alternatives. In the former case, that is, if the shooting was in the line of the accused's duty, then the homicide was justified and the proper verdict would be one of not guilty—applying to the whole of the indictment. In the latter case, that is there is to your satisfaction proof of gross and wicked recklessness, then the proper verdict, as it seems to me, would be one of guilty as libelled on the whole indictment, as now restricted to an indictment of assault and culpable homicide."

Verdict: Not guilty.

NOTES

**7.78**     1. What would have been the position if the Crown had proved that there was a general order not to shoot at escaping prisoners? Would the more immediate order of the lance-corporal have provided a defence? See Gordon (3rd ed.), para. 13–33.

2. Lord Robertson suggests that acting in the line of duty and criminal recklessness are "alternatives". How does this compare with the views of the Lord Justice-General in *Hawton and Parker*?

3. The defence of superior orders is generally limited by reference to the "manifest illegality" test. According to this test, an order which is "manifestly unlawful" should not be obeyed, and will not provide a defence to a criminal charge. In *United States v. Calley,* 22 U.S.C.M.A. 534; 48 C.M.R. 19 (1973) Lieutenant William Calley was convicted of the premeditated murder of 22 women, children, infants and old men, and of assault with intent to murder a child of about 2 years of age. All the killings and the assault took place on March 16, 1968 in the area of the village of May Lai in the Republic of South Vietnam. The Army Court of Military Review affirmed the findings of guilt. Calley petitioned the United States Court of Military Appeals arguing, *inter alia* that the trial judge had not adequately directed the court-martial on the defence of superior orders. In rejecting the appeal and confirming Calley's conviction, the Court approved the following direction given by the trial judge:

"... A determination that an order is illegal does not, of itself, assign criminal responsibility to the person following the order for acts done in compliance with it. Soldiers are taught to follow orders, and special attention is given to obedience of orders on the battlefield. Military effectiveness depends upon obedience to orders. On the other hand, the obedience of a soldier is not the obedience of an automaton. A soldier is a reasoning agent, obliged to respond, not as a machine, but as a person. The law takes these factors into account in assessing criminal responsibility for acts done in compliance with illegal orders.

The acts of a subordinate done in compliance with an unlawful order given him by his superior are excused and impose no criminal liability upon him unless the superior's order is one which a man of ordinary sense and understanding would, under the circumstances, know to be unlawful, or if the order in question is actually known to the accused to be unlawful."

See also *S. v. Banda and Others* 1990 (3) S.A. 466 for a detailed historical and comparative review of the defence of superior orders. The "manifestly unlawful" test was also applied in that case.

4. English law, in common with law of several other Commonwealth jurisdictions, does not recognise the defence of superior orders. The matter was discussed by the House of Lords in the case of *R. v. Clegg* [1995] 1 A.C. 482, [1995] 1 All E.R. 334, [1995] 1 Cr.App.Rep. 50.

5. At one time the defence of superior orders was ruled out *a priori* in the case of war crimes, crimes against humanity. This was the approach adopted in the Charters of the Nuremberg and Tokyo Tribunals established to try the major German and Japanese war criminals at the end of the Second World War. More recently, however, a less absolute position has been adopted both in relation to international tribunals and in the domestic criminal law of certain states. Thus, Article 33 of the Statute of the International Criminal Court provides:

"1. The fact that a crime within the jurisdiction of the Court has been committed by a person pursuant to an order of a Government or of a superior, whether military or civilian, shall not relieve that person of criminal responsibility unless:

    (a) The person was under a legal obligation to obey orders of the Government or the superior in question;

    (b) The person did not know that the order was unlawful; and

    (c) The order was not manifestly unlawful.

2. For the purposes of this article, orders to commit genocide or crimes against humanity are manifestly unlawful."

See also *R. v. Finta* [1994] 1 S.C.R. 701 in which the Canadian Supreme Court held that defence of superior orders was available in prosecutions for war crimes and crimes against humanity under the Canadian criminal code. The defence was available, subject to the manifest illegality test. The Court also held that the defence was available even in the case of a manifestly unlawful order where the accused had no moral choice as to whether to follow the order. (That is, "where there was such an air of compulsion and threat to the accused that he or she had no alternative but to obey the order".)

# D. Provocation

Provocation is not a general defence, but operates as an excuse in the crime of murder, where it has the **7.79** effect of reducing the crime from murder to culpable homicide. It may also have the effect of reducing a charge of attempted murder to assault or assault to severe injury, under provocation: *Brady v. H.M. Advocate,* 1986 S.C.C.R. 191, *Salmond v. H.M. Advocate,* 1992 S.L.T. 156. It is accepted as having a mitigatory effect in assault. The plea of provocation is discussed in the context of homicide (Chapter 10) and non-fatal offences against the person (Chapter 8).

# E. Entrapment

The defence of entrapment arises where the accused pleads that the offence in question was committed **7.80** at the instigation of a police officer (or other individual acting for the law enforcement agencies) and that without such instigation he would not otherwise have committed the offence. Entrapment may take various forms, but typically it consists in the police approaching a suspect and asking him or her to engage in conduct which would constitute an offence. Occasionally, however, it may take the form of the police offering criminal services and arresting those who approach them to take advantage of those services.

As a defence this plea has its origins in the United States. See, *Sorrells v. U.S.* 287 U.S. 435, 77 L. ed. 413 (1932) *Sherman v. U.S.,* 356 U.S. 369, 2 L. Ed 848 (1958), *Masciale v. U.S.,* 356 U.S. 386, 2 L. Ed. 859 (1958), *Grohman v. State,* (1970) 41 A.L.R. 3d. 406, *U.S. v. Russell* 411 U.S. 423 and *Mathews v. U.S.,* 56 U.S.L.W. 4183 (1988).

It has been held that there is no defence of entrapment as such in Scotland: *H.M. Advocate v. Harper,* 1989 S.C.C.R. 472, and it is accepted that the police may engage in what would generally be regarded as an offence in order to gather evidence of offending by others. The limits of such practices are presently determined by reference to the "fairness" test of the admissibility of the evidence so gathered. See, for example, *Weir v. Jessop* 1992 S.L.T. 533, *Marsh v. Johnston* 1959 S.L.T. 28, *Cook v. Skinner* 1977 S.L.T. (Notes) 11, *MacDonald v. Skinner Ming v. H.M. Advocate* 1987 S.C.C.R. 110

It has also been held that there is no defence of entrapment in English law: *R. v. Mealey and Sheridan,* [1974] Crim. L.R. 710, *R. v. McEvilly,* [1974] Crim. L.R. 239. The fact of entrapment may, however, be taken into account as a mitigating factor in sentencing. See, for examples, *R. v. Mealey and Sheridan,* above, *R. v. Springer* [1999] 1 Cr.App.R.(S.) 217, *R. v. Tonnessen* [1998] 2 Cr.App.R. (S.) 328 and *R v. Beaumont,* (1987) 9 Cr.App.R.(S.) 342. In *R. v. Latif (Khalid)* [1996] 1 All E.R. 353 it was accepted that the court would have the power to stay criminal proceedings where it appeared to the court that the accused had been entrapped. The court is not, however, obliged to do so, and in that case did not.

The fact that the police have engaged in entrapment may give rise to an issue under article 6(1) of the European Convention on Human Rights:

**Case of Teixeira de Castro v. Portugal**
European Court of Human Rights
(1999) 28 E.H.R.R. 101

**7.81** The applicant complained of entrapment. Two police officers, working under cover, approached a small-time drug dealer, V.S., and offered to buy hashish from him. V.S. offered to put them in contact with a supplier, but despite being pressed by the police officers was unable to do so. On a later occasion they approached V.S. and told him that they were interested in buying heroin. V.S. agreed to put them in touch with the applicant, which he did with the assistance of another man. All four went to meet the applicant. The police told him that they wanted to buy 20 grams of heroin for 200,000 escudos. The applicant agreed to obtain the heroin. He went to yet another person's house, obtained 20 grams of heroin and then went back to his own house, where the police officers were waiting. When he produced some of the heroin the police revealed their identity to him and he was arrested. He was subsequently convicted of dealing in heroin and sentenced to six years' imprisonment.

OPINION OF THE COURT:

"28. Mr Teixeira de Castro applied to the Commission on October 24, 1994. He relied on Article 6(1) of the Convention, complaining that he had not had a fair hearing as police officers had incited him to commit the offence of which he was subsequently convicted. In his view those circumstances also amounted to breaches of Articles 3 and 8. He considered that he had in addition been subjected to discriminatory treatment because he had been given a heavy sentence whereas the other people implicated in the case were either not prosecuted or had received a light sentence.

29. On June 24, 1996 the Commission declared the application admissible in so far as it concerned the fairness of the proceedings and inadmissible as to the remainder. In its report of February 25, 1997, it expressed the opinion that there had been a violation of Article 6(1) ..., but not of Article 3 ... and that it was unnecessary also to examine whether there had been a violation of Article 8 ....

30. In their memorial the Government asked the Court to "hold that there had been no violation of Article 6(1) of the Convention in the instant case".

AS TO THE LAW

Alleged violation of Article 6(1) of the convention.

31. Mr Teixeira de Castro complained that he had not had a fair trial in that he had been incited by plain-clothes police officers to commit an offence of which he was later convicted. He relied on Article 6(1) of the Convention, of which the part relevant in the present case reads as follows:

> "In the determination of ... any criminal charge against him, everyone is entitled to a fair ... hearing ... time by [a] ... tribunal ... ."

He maintained that he had no previous convictions and would never have committed the offence had it not been for the intervention of those "*agents provocateurs*". In addition, the police officers had acted on their own initiative without any supervision by the courts and without there having been any preliminary investigation.

32. The Government submitted that a large number of States, including most members of the Council of Europe, accepted the use of special investigative measures, in particular in the fight against drug trafficking. Society had to find techniques for containing that type of criminal activity, which destroyed the foundations of democratic societies. Article 52 of Legislative Decree no. 430/83, which was applicable to the facts of the present case—and indeed the United Nations Convention against Illicit Traffic in Narcotic Drugs and Psychotropic Substances of 1988 and the Council of Europe Convention of 1990 on

Laundering, Search, Seizure and Confiscation of the Proceeds from Crime—thus allowed the use of undercover agents, whose role had however nothing in common with the activity of *"agents provocateurs"*. Furthermore, Article 126(1) and (2)(a) of the Code of Criminal Procedure laid down high standards that had to be met if the means used for obtaining evidence were to be considered legitimate and lawful.

The two police officers involved in the present case could not be described as *"agents provocateurs"*. A distinction had to be drawn between cases where the undercover agent's action created a criminal intent that had previously been absent and those in which the offender had already been predisposed to commit the offence. In the instant case, the officers had merely exposed a latent pre-existing criminal intent by providing Mr Teixeira de Castro with the opportunity of carrying it through. F.O. (one of the co-accused) had not pressed the applicant, who had immediately shown interest in obtaining the drugs and carrying out the transaction. In addition, when arrested, the applicant had been in possession of more drugs than had been requested by the "buyers".

Lastly, during the proceedings Mr Teixeira de Castro had had an opportunity to question both the two police officers and the other witnesses and to confront them. The Supreme Court had based its assessment not only on the police officers' intervention but also on other evidence. There was nothing to suggest that the fairness of the trial had been undermined.

33. The Commission considered that the offence had been committed and the applicant sentenced to what was a fairly heavy penalty essentially, if not exclusively, as a result of the police officers' actions. The officers had thus incited criminal activity which might not otherwise have taken place. That situation had irremediably affected the fairness of the proceedings.

34. The Court reiterates that the admissibility of evidence is primarily a matter for regulation by national law and as a general rule it is for the national courts to assess the evidence before them. The Court's task under the Convention is not to give a ruling as to whether statements of witnesses were properly admitted as evidence, but rather to ascertain whether the proceedings as a whole, including the way in which evidence was taken, were fair (see, *inter alia*, the *Van Mechelen and Others v. The Netherlands* judgment of April 23, 1997, *Reports of Judgments and Decisions* 1997-III, p. 711, para. 50).

35. More particularly, the Convention does not preclude reliance, at the investigation stage of criminal proceedings and where the nature of the offence so warrants, on sources such as anonymous informants. However, the subsequent use of their statements by the court of trial to found a conviction is a different matter (see, *mutatis mutandis*, the *Kostovski v. The Netherlands* judgment of November 20, 1989, Series A no. 166, p. 21, para. 44).

36. The use of undercover agents must be restricted and safeguards put in place even in cases concerning the fight against drug trafficking. While the rise in organised crime undoubtedly requires that appropriate measures be taken, the right to a fair administration of justice nevertheless holds such a prominent place (see the *Delcourt v. Belgium* judgment of January 17, 1970, Series A no. 11, p. 15, para. 25) that it cannot be sacrificed for the sake of expedience. The general requirements of fairness embodied in Article 6 apply to proceedings concerning all types of criminal offence, from the most straightforward to the most complex. The public interest cannot justify the use of evidence obtained as a result of police incitement.

37. The Court notes, firstly, that the present dispute is distinguishable from the case of *Lüdi v. Switzerland* (see the judgment of June 15, 1992, Series A no. 238), in which the police officer concerned had been sworn in, the investigating judge had not been unaware of his mission and the Swiss authorities, informed by the German police, had opened a preliminary investigation. The police officers' role had been confined to acting as an undercover agent.

38. In the instant case it is necessary to determine whether or not the two police officers' activity went beyond that of undercover agents. The Court notes that the Government have not contended that the officers' intervention took place as part of an anti-drug-trafficking operation ordered and supervised by a judge. It does not appear either that the competent authorities had good reason to suspect that Mr Teixeira de Castro was a drug trafficker; on the

contrary, he had no criminal record and no preliminary investigation concerning him had been opened. Indeed, he was not known to the police officers, who only came into contact with him through the intermediary of V.S. and F.O. ...

Furthermore, the drugs were not at the applicant's home; he obtained them from a third party who had in turn obtained them from another person (see paragraph 11 above). Nor does the Supreme Court's judgment of May 5, 1994 indicate that, at the time of his arrest, the applicant had more drugs in his possession than the quantity the police officers had requested thereby going beyond what he had been incited to do by the police. There is no evidence to support the Government's argument that the applicant was predisposed to commit offences. The necessary inference from these circumstances is that the two police officers did not confine themselves to investigating Mr Teixeira de Castro's criminal activity in an essentially passive manner, but exercised an influence such as to incite the commission of the offence.

Lastly, the Court notes that in their decisions the domestic courts said that the applicant had been convicted mainly on the basis of the statements of the two police officers.

39. In the light of all these considerations, the Court concludes that the two police officers' actions went beyond those of undercover agents because they instigated the offence and there is nothing to suggest that without their intervention it would have been committed. That intervention and its use in the impugned criminal proceedings meant that, right from the outset, the applicant was definitively deprived of a fair trial. Consequently, there has been a violation of Article 6(1)."

Notes

**7.82**   1. The applicant did not pursue his complaints under article 3, and in light of its conclusion on article 6, the Court did not consider it necessary to express a view on the alleged violation of article 8.

2. In the case of *Lüdi v. Switzerland*, European Court of Human Rights, Series A, No. 238 the applicant complained of a violation of articles 6(1), 6(3)(d) and 8 of the Convention. The applicant, a Swiss national, was known to the German police as a drug trafficker. The German police notified the Swiss police that the applicant was seeking funds to finance the purchase of a substantial quantity of cocaine in Switzerland. An investigation was launched by the Swiss authorities, during which the applicant's telephone was tapped, and he was approached by a Swiss police officer, acting under cover, who introduced himself to the applicant as a potential drug purchaser. The applicant and the agent met on five occasions, on each occasion at the instance of the agent. The applicant was eventually arrested. According to the agent's reports the applicant had promised to him, as intermediary, 2 kg of cocaine worth 200,000 Swiss francs, and had borrowed 22,000 Swiss francs from a third person for the purchase of cocaine or other narcotics. The applicant was convicted of drug trafficking. He complained to the Commission that the interception of his telephone conversations combined with his manipulation by an undercover agent had infringed the right to respect for his private life under Article 8.

The Commission held that there had been a violation of article 8. The Court disagreed. In the opinion of the Court there was no doubt that the telephone interception was an interference with Mr Lüdi's private life and correspondence, but it was not in breach of the Convention because there was a legal basis for it, it was aimed at the prevention of crime and the Court had "no doubt whatever as to its necessity in a democratic society" (para. 39).

The Court also thought that the use of an undercover agent in the present case was not an interference with the applicant's private life:

> 40.... [The agent's] actions took place within the context of a deal relating to 5 kg of cocaine. The cantonal authorities, who had been warned by the German police, selected a sworn officer to infiltrate what they thought was a large network of traffickers intending to dispose of that quantity of drugs in Switzerland. The aim of the operation was to arrest the dealers when the drugs were handed over. [The agent] thereupon contacted the applicant, who said that he was prepared to sell him 2 kg of cocaine, worth 200,000 Swiss francs ... Mr Lüdi must therefore have been aware from then on that he was engaged in a criminal act punishable under [Swiss law] and that consequently he was running the risk of encountering an undercover police officer whose task would in fact be to expose him.
>
> 41. In short, there was no violation of Article 8.

3. In *R. v. Shannon (John James), The Times*, October 11, 2000 the English Court of Appeal held that there was no general objection to evidence provided by an *agent provocateur* independent of the issue of fairness. The Court referred to *Texeira de Castro*, and held that it was clear from that case that national courts were given considerable discretion in the admissibility of such evidence, subject to the duty of the court to ensure that the accused had a fair trial. They also noted that *Texeira* concerned the actings of police officers, whereas the accused in the instant case has been induced to supply drugs to a newspaper journalist posing as an Arab sheikh.

# Chapter 8

# NON-FATAL OFFENCES AGAINST THE PERSON

**8.01** This chapter considers a range of common law and statutory offences directed at protection of individuals from conduct which causes harm, whether in the sense of physical injury or in the sense of apprehension of injury. It also deals with offences of endangerment, and some "preventive" offences, the purpose of which is to reduce the potential for serious harm by punishing the possession of knives and other weapons.

Modern practice has tended to draw distinctions between offences against the person, depending upon the criminal intent with which the harm has been caused, or the nature of the harm. There is thus a distinction between a person who carries out a deliberate attack on another (assault) and one who recklessly causes injury. Similarly, there is a distinction drawn between a person who places a person in fear by pointing a gun at them (again, assault) and one who brings about the same result by uttering written or verbal threats to kill or seriously injure them. It is worth, recalling, however, that in *Khaliq v. H.M. Advocate*, 1984 S.L.T. 137, the High Court held that it is, generally, a crime to cause "real" (that is, personal) injury to another, by whatever means. (See, *ante*, p. 117.)

## 1. ASSAULT

**8.02** Assault may be very simply defined as an attack upon the person of another (Gordon (2nd ed.) para. 29–01; Macdonald, 115). For these purposes, an "attack" ranges from the violent infliction of personal injury to very trivial "attacks", and indeed need not involve any personal injury at all—as where a blow is aimed but does not connect, or a gun pointed without being fired.

### A. The *actus reus* of assault

**David Keay**
(1837) 1 Swin. 543

**8.03** The panel was charged with assaulting a boy who was riding a pony in that he did "wickedly, culpably, and reckless of the consequences, whip the said pony, and did give it with his driving whip repeated lashes on its back or other parts, whereby the animal becoming alarmed, run away with the [rider], and threw him off its back, or fell with or above him, ... and from [the rider] having fallen off, or fallen with or under the said pony, or from the said pony, in rising from the ground after it fell, having planted one or more of its feet on the body of the [rider], his right leg was severely wounded, to the serious injury of his person, and the great effusion of his blood". An objection was taken to the relevancy, on the ground, *inter alia*, that "In the case of assault, the party strikes at the individual assaulted. Direct personal injury is intended, whereas here the immediate object was to quicken the pace of the pony, and the ultimate result was imputable to accident."

LORD MONCREIFF: "It is assumed by the counsel for the pannel that no injury was intended to the boy. But I cannot see what purpose the pannel could have, except either to do him a direct injury, or to put him in alarm. I cannot go quite so far as to say, that every case must be one of assault, which, if death had followed, would be culpable homicide. If a person throws a stone out of a window into the street, and thereby kills a passer by, he would be guilty of culpable homicide. Yet this act, done without intention to hurt anyone, could not be charged as assault. Although I have some difficulty, I think the charge of assault is relevant in this case."

LORD COCKBURN: "I have no doubt at all upon the subject. It may appear on proof that the pannel had no actual intention of injuring the boy. But there may be a constructive intention. If he had seized the boy in his arms and carried him away, that would most clearly have constituted an assault, and the fact of his having made the pony the instrument of carrying him off makes no difference. The maxim *qui facit per alium facit per se* makes the act of the pony the act of the pannel."

Objection to relevancy repelled.

NOTES

This case is a good illustration of how even indirect injury may constitute an "attack" for the purposes **8.04** of assault. The reference to vicarious responsibility is, of course, quite inappropriate. The only 'acts' upon which criminal responsibility can be founded are the acts of human beings. Applying the doctrine in the circumstances of this case is equivalent to saying that an accused who hits another person with a stick is responsible for the 'act' of the stick. The fact that the instrument with which the attack is carried out is not an inanimate object but a living creature is irrelevant. See, in this respect *Kay v. Allen* (1978) S.C.C.R. Supp 188 and *Quinn v. Lees* 1994 S.C.C.R. 159 (both cases involving assault by setting a dog on the victim).

**Atkinson v. H.M. Advocate**
1987 S.C.C.R. 534

Atkinson and another man were charged that they did, on a certain date, "with faces masked, **8.05** break into the shop premises at the Mayfield Service Station, ... jump over the counter and there assault Charles Gilmour, cashier there, *present a knife or other similar instrument at him, seize hold of him, demand that he open the till, repeatedly push his head down onto a counter and hold said knife or other similar instrument against his neck* and did rob him of £798.73 or thereby of money". The jury returned a verdict of guilty, under deletion of the italicised passage. On appeal to the High Court:

LORD JUSTICE-CLERK (ROSS): "The appellant is Gary Atkinson who was found guilty on charge (1) on an indictment under certain deletions.... Charge (1) was a charge of assault and robbery. He has appealed against conviction and sentence and his appeal against conviction is to the effect that all that he should have been convicted of in respect of charge (1) was robbery and not of assault and robbery. The basis for making this submission is that the jury deleted part of the first charge....

The important question is whether what remains in that charge is sufficient to support a conviction of [assault and] robbery. In our opinion what remains is sufficient for that purpose. We say that because the part of the indictment on which he was convicted libels that he and a co-accused, with faces masked, broke into specified shop premises and jumped over the counter and there assaulted the complainer. In our opinion, for the appellant to act in that way was sufficient to support the proposition that he carried out an assault upon the complainer. An assault may be constituted by threatening gestures sufficient to produce alarm. For someone with his face masked to come into a shop and jump over a counter towards the cashier in the shop, in our opinion, could constitute an assault according to the law of Scotland, and the jury were entitled to hold that an assault did in the circumstances take place. Accordingly, the sole ground put forward for attacking the conviction is unsound and the appeal against conviction is refused."

Appeal dismissed.

NOTES

**8.06**    1. The court stated that an assault may be constituted by threatening gestures "sufficient to produce alarm". Presumably this does not mean that they need cause actual alarm on the part of the person to whom they are directed but simply that they be of a nature likely, in an objective sense, to cause alarm. If A brandishes a bayonet at B the latter has been assaulted even though he is not in fact alarmed.

A more difficult question arises, however, if the victim is not aware of the accused's threatening gestures. It is well-established that a person may be assaulted without knowing it (for example because he or she is asleep or unconscious: *H.M. Advocate v. Logan,* 1936 J.C. 100; *Sweeney v. X.,* 1982 S.C.C.R. 509 (*post,* Chap. 9)) but these are cases in which there has been a "physical" as opposed to a "psychic" assault. If there is no physical attack on the victim, and the victim is unaware of the threatening behaviour, can it be said that the victim has been assaulted? If the answer to that question is "no" then, presumably, it would not be an assault to point a gun at a blind person, or, indeed to point a gun at the victim's back, without at the same time announcing the presence of the threatening gesture in such a way as to bring it home to the victim.

2. Would it be possible to commit an assault by omission? In *Fagan v. Metropolitan Police Commissioner,* [1969] 1 Q.B. 439 (*ante,* p. 61) the appellant accidentally parked his car on a policeman's foot, and, when made aware of what had happened, deliberately refrained from moving the vehicle. His conviction for assault was upheld because the court was able to discern a "continuing act" in the appellant's conduct, but it remains the case that the assault consisted in a wilful failure to get off the officer's foot which comes close to assault by omission. Scots law requires an "attack" for assault and while that term receives a fairly wide interpretation it is not immediately clear how one can "attack" by omission. If the circumstances of *Fagan's* case were to be repeated in Scotland it seems that there would be more appropriate charges than assault. "Causing real injury" would be one possibility since clearly injury may be caused by an omission as well as by positive conduct. (On causing real injury, see, *post,* p. 325.)

3. Is it possible to commit an assault without being physically proximate to the victim? In *R. v. Ireland* [1997] 4 All E.R. 225 the defendant made repeated silent telephone calls, generally at night, to three women, causing psychiatric injury to all three of them. The House of Lords upheld a conviction for assault occasioning actual bodily harm, contrary to section 47 of the Offences Against the Person Act 1861. (For these purposes, English law regards an assault as any act which causes the victim to apprehend violence then and there or at least in the immediate future.) In *Constanza* [1997] Crim. L.R. 576 in which it was held that assault occasioning actual bodily harm could be constituted by sending threatening letters.

So far as concerns Scots law, there would seem to be no reason to give such a strained interpretation to the law. Written and verbal threats of death or serious bodily harm, or even serious damage to a person's property, are in themselves criminal (see *Kenny v. H.M. Advocate,* 1951 J.C. 104 and *James Miller* (1862) 4 Irvine 238, *post,* pp. 336–339). Less serious threats are not criminal, unless they are done for a criminal purpose (such as perverting the course of justice—see *Kenny, ante*). But, since it is apparently an offence at common law to cause 'real injury' to another by any means, causing 'psychic' harm by means of threats is presumably criminal (provided always that 'psychic' injury is 'real') which would allow the possibility of a charge of causing real injury were a case such as *Ireland* to arise in Scotland.

## The *mens rea* of assault

### H.M. Advocate v. Phipps
(1905) 4 Adam 616

**8.07**    Two men discharged sporting guns at a group of men they believed to be poaching salmon from their father's fishings. One of the men was hit in the eye and seriously injured. At the time of the shooting the suspected poachers were on the opposite bank of the river from the accused, at a distance of about 40 to 50 yards. The shooting took place at night. The accused were charged with assault, or, alternatively, reckless discharge of firearms to the injury of the person. In charging the jury the presiding judge gave the following directions on assault and reckless discharge of firearms:

LORD ARDWALL: "Three views are presented to you in this case. The first is that this is a case of assault, or a verdict to that effect is asked by the Advocate-Depute on behalf of the Crown. On that I agree with Mr Shaw, that evil intent is of the essence of the charge. The second possible view is that the accused were guilty of recklessness of a criminal character, and the third is the view presented for your acceptance by the defence, that the facts of the case disclose mere misadventure, for which the accused are not responsible in a criminal sense.

On the first of these views of this case I agree, as I have said, with Mr Shaw, and the authority quoted by him, that in order to entitle you to affirm a verdict of guilty to the charge of assault you must find evil intent proved. Unless you find it proved as a matter of fact that there was evil intent in the minds of the panels, an intention to do bodily injury to these men, you will not return a verdict of guilty of assault by discharging loaded firearms, which is the first charge in this indictment.

On the other hand I cannot agree with the proposition stated to you by Mr Shaw, that there can be no crime of reckless discharge of firearms merely because the result was unexpected. On the contrary there have been several cases where a verdict of reckless discharge of firearms was found justified in our law where the result was quite outwith the expectation of the accused. Thus a poacher on a dark night seeing something moving fired at it, thinking it was a hare. It turned out to be a man whom he had thus hit. The poacher was convicted of reckless discharge of firearms. Again, on an occasion when crime was the last thing present in the accused's mind, at a wedding festivity, the accused had fired off a gun loaded blank by the way of a salute, and injured a member of the public passing by, who was struck by the cotton wad. Conviction followed. Another case which comes nearer the kind of facts we are dealing with in this case was this. An Aberdeenshire farmer, being disturbed by the too frequent nocturnal visits of a man to his kitchen premises, attempted to surprise him, and when he took refuge in flight, fired his gun at him without any intention to wound him, and hit him in the legs. The farmer was charged with and convicted of reckless discharge of firearms. That shows the sort of case you have to hold has been made out under the charge of reckless discharge of firearms, and that is a possible view which you may quite competently see yourselves bound to take of the facts which have been proved before you.

There is yet another possible view which you may take, and which Mr Shaw has asked you to take. You may come to the conclusion that there was neither evil intent present nor such an amount of recklessness as would justify a verdict of reckless discharge of firearms, but that the facts amount to mere misadventure or an unfortunate chain of misadventures; the unauthorised presence of these men netting this pool; the unfortunate failure of the men to answer when challenged, and the regrettable mischance by which one of the pellets lodged in the eye of one of the men. Was this a mere chain of accidents which the accused could not foresee, and which they were not bound to foresee?

These, then, are the three views on which it is your duty to make up your minds in returning your verdict in this case, and I shall attempt shortly to go over the facts which have been proved, and indicate, as far as I can, their bearing on these questions.

First, then, with reference to the charge of assault. What evidence have you of evil intent? The attitude of the accused has from the first been quite consistent. They said that night at the Castle, they said to the police, and lastly they said in their declaration before the Sheriff, that they had no intention of injuring any one. Now is there any evidence contrary to that? It is suggested that the distance from which they fired was far too short, and that they should not have fired at all. Now as to that you have the evidence both of the gun-maker and of Lord Lovat, and can judge for yourselves, that in the night-time and in uncertain light, as one sees in duck-shooting in early morning, distances are very deceptive and illusive. Even taking it that the distance was only fifty yards, this was an ordinary sporting-gun, and in ordinary circumstances could do not much more than tickle a man hit at that distance, unless some of the shot lodged in such a delicate organ as the eye. Again it is said that the accused knew this river so well that they should have been able to calculate to a nicety the distance across at this point. On the other hand you have it said that they were agitated by the natural excitement of a possible resistance, and the haste of their approach through the brushwood, as they ran down to scare these persons, whom they took for poachers. Turning again to the state of the light. The night is said to have been dark but clear, and what is more important, on the bank behind the men was a clump of wood standing out against the horizon and therefore dimming the light coming thence and making it impossible to say how far the men might seem to one on the opposite bank. For there is no perspective in darkness. It is for you to say whether you find anything proved either in the distance or in the state of the light, which entitles you to say that these gentlemen knew, or ought to have known, that the persons they saw in the shadow on the opposite bank were within shooting distance, and that they fired intending to injure them. I can only say that such a conclusion does not commend itself to my mind.

That is all that seems necessary to say in regard to the question of assault. You are quite entitled to take into consideration the evidence as to the relations which subsisted between the panels and the men whom they are said to have assaulted—to consider whether these men, and especially the fishing ghillie, John Fraser, Cruives—were not the last persons in the world whom the accused would intentionally seek to injure; and whether it is not a more natural explanation to find, that taking them for poachers, they sought to scare them away by firing off shots, and so do what is always considered of importance in such cases, drive the poachers away and secure their nets or some other tangible evidence of their offence. It is said that for this purpose it was unnecessary to fire off four or more shots, as is evidenced by the three empty cartridges found on the ground. That seems to me just the course two men would follow when they were attempting to scare away a larger number of poachers—fire off as many shots as possible and so make a demonstration of force which might impress the poachers with the idea that they had a larger number than two to deal with. It was the safest thing to do, as it might induce the poachers to believe that they were outnumbered and therefore render resistance less likely. Poachers often carry guns, and therefore the fact that the accused fired off so many cartridges seems to me to strengthen the supposition that they fired to scare and not to injure the men at the boat."

NOTES

The requirement of "evil intent" in assault is further discussed in *Smart v. H.M. Advocate*, 1975 S.L.T. 65 *post*, p. 301 and in the following case. *Cf.* the English rule that assault may be committed intentionally or recklessly: *Venna* [1976] Q.B. 421, *R. v. Ireland*, *ante*, and the comments of Lord Moncreiff in *Keay* (*ante*). Causing reckless injury and recklessly endangering the public are further discussed *post*, pp. 309–324.

## Lord Advocate's Reference (No. 2 of 1992)
### 1992 S.L.T. 460

**8.08**     An accused person was tried on indictment for a contravention of sections 17(2) and (5) of the Firearms Act 1968 and attempted robbery by assaulting two shopkeepers, presenting an imitation handgun at them, placing them in a state of fear and alarm for their safety, demanding money and demanding that they lie on the ground. The accused admitted entering the shop, presenting an imitation firearm at the complainers, stating that this was a hold-up, demanding money from the complainers, and telling them to lie on the floor. Both complainers stated that they were alarmed by the accused's conduct. The accused accepted this, but stated that his actions were a joke and that he had no evil intent to assault or rob. The complainers gave evidence that they did not consider this to be a joke. The trial judge directed the jury that if they believed the accused when he said that his actions were a joke and that he had no evil intent they would acquit him.

The accused was acquitted and the Lord Advocate presented a petition to the High Court to obtain the court's opinion on whether the evidence of the accused to the effect that his admitted actions were carried out as a joke constituted a defence to the charge of assault. The opinion of the Court was delivered by the Lord Justice-Clerk.

THE LORD JUSTICE CLERK (ROSS): " ... The advocate depute supported the submission which is contained in the petition to this court. He maintained that the trial judge had confused intent with motive, and that motive was irrelevant to criminal responsibility. He contended that if a person carries out an *actus reus* with *mens rea*, he is guilty of the crime, and that his motive is irrelevant to the question of guilt. The advocate depute drew attention to *H.M. Advocate v. Elizabeth Edmiston* (1866) 5 Irv. 219 where it was held that the writing and sending of threatening letters was a crime, whatever may have been the motive. He contended that the same principle should be applied here. In charging the jury in that case the Lord Justice Clerk said: "The writing or sending of letters expressed in these terms is in itself in the eye of the law a crime, no matter what the motive. Supposing it to be perfectly true that all that was designed was frolic, the writing and sending of such letters as these would still be a crime, and the counsel for the prisoner seriously misunderstood the true and proper meaning of those words which expressed the quality of the act charged against the panel, that she did wickedly and feloniously write and send these letters. Every crime is wicked and felonious, and the moment you arrive at the conclusion that the act charged against the prisoner is a crime, that of itself is sufficient proof of wicked and felonious intent. The words mean no more than that the act is criminal. If the act is shown to be criminal, from the nature of the act itself there is no necessity for any proof of malice as regards any of the ordinary crimes."

The advocate depute submitted that the same principles should be applied to the present case, and that the trial judge ought to have directed the jury that it was no defence to say that it had all been a joke. He also referred to *Ralston v. H.M. Advocate* 1989 S.L.T. 474. In that case the appellant maintained that the sheriff had erred in giving directions to the jury to the effect that even if they thought that the appellant's motives were blameless, nonetheless they must convict him. In the course of my opinion I stated at 1989 S.L.T., p. 476: "Whether or not any particular acts amount to a breach of the peace is a question of fact depending upon the particular circumstances of the case. Since it is a question of fact, it was for the jury to determine that matter. Whatever the appellant's motives may have been, it was for the jury to decide on the evidence whether his actings amounted to a breach of the peace."

The advocate depute maintained that in the present case the actions of X had been deliberate, and that accordingly they constituted the crime of assault. The advocate depute recognised that in some areas of human activity difficult situations might arise. He submitted that to bring another person down by means of a rugby tackle would not constitute assault in the course of a game of rugby, but that it would be criminal if the person tackled was a stranger in a public street. He also maintained that between friends no crime would be committed if one friend perpetrated a joke upon another. The situation he submitted was different where strangers were involved. At the end of the day his submission was that the crime of assault was committed once it was plain that the appellant was acting deliberately. He contended that there was a risk that the direction given by the trial judge could become a "Robbers' Charter".

Counsel for X on the other hand contended that the directions given by the trial judge were sound and proper. He submitted that it was necessary for the jury to consider all the circumstances before they could determine whether there had been evil intent or dole. He maintained that the accused's assertion that it was a joke was one factor which had to be taken into account in the overall evaluation of the existence of dole; if the jury accepted that that factor negatived evil intent, they were entitled to acquit. He submitted that the assertion that it was a joke was not relevant to the issue of motive; it was a factor which required to be considered when the jury determined whether or not there had been evil intent. All that was decided in *H.M. Advocate v. Elizabeth Edmiston* was that the prosecutor was not required to establish a motive for the crime (Macdonald's *Criminal Law* (5th ed.), p. 1). He also referred to *Atkinson v. H.M. Advocate*, 1987 S.L.T. 534 and *Young v. McGlennan*, 1991 S.C.C.R. 739. Senior counsel further submitted that it was not the correct approach to hold that the accused's assertion that it was a joke came too late, that is, after the assault had been committed. He maintained that there was no justification for any cut off point in evaluating the overall circumstances of the incident. It was necessary to look at the whole circumstances when determining whether or not the necessary evil intent was present.

In my opinion the accused's assertion that it was a joke means no more than that it was his motive or ulterior intention in acting as he did. It has often been said that evil intention is of the essence of assault (Macdonald's *Criminal Law*, p. 115). But what that means is that assault cannot be committed accidentally or recklessly or negligently (Gordon's *Criminal Law* (2nd ed.), para 29–30). In the present case, it is plain that when the accused entered the shop, presented the handgun at Mrs Daly and uttered the words which he did, he was acting deliberately. That being so, in my opinion, he had the necessary intent for his actions to amount to assault, and his motive for acting as he did was irrelevant. I agree with the advocate depute that the principle laid down by the Lord Justice-Clerk in *H.M. Advocate v. Elizabeth Edmiston* would apply to the present case, and that even if the accused was believed when he stated it was a joke, his acting as he did would still constitute the crime of assault.

The advocate depute raised the question of there being possible difficult situations. I agree with him that it would be a crime to rugby tackle a stranger on the public street, although a rugby tackle in the course of a game of rugby would not amount to an assault. The reason for that is that for conduct in a sporting game to be criminal, it would require to be shown to be outwith the normal scope of the sport (*Butcher v. Jessop*, 1989 S.L.T. 598). As regards a joke between friends, if a friend, for example, deliberately tripped up his companion as a joke, the crime of assault would still have been committed although if it took place in the context of joking between friends, any prosecution would be unlikely.

I am not persuaded that the approach of counsel for X is a sound one. It is clear that even where conduct has taken place against the background of good natured joking, an assault may be committed if an accused has acted deliberately when he has carried out an attack upon another (*Young v. McGlennan*). It is well established that an assault may be constituted by threatening gestures sufficient to produce alarm (*Atkinson v. H.M. Advocate*). The actings of the accused in the present case included threatening gestures and produced fear and alarm in the two complainers.

When he gave his evidence at the trial, X stated that after he had told the complainer Mrs Daly that it was a hold up, that she should get the money and get down on the floor, he started laughing and stated "I'm only kidding" as he left the shop. Neither of the complainers spoke to this; they did not say that he started laughing or that he said "I'm only kidding". On the other hand, the jury may have accepted X's evidence in this regard, but even if they did, I am satisfied that by the time he claims to have started laughing, the crime of assault had been committed; his laughing and statement to the effect that it was a joke came too late to alter the quality of his conduct ...."

Lord Cowie: "... The point is a short one and it depends upon what is meant by the words "evil intent" insofar as they form an essential element in the crime of assault. In my opinion the meaning of the words in the context of this offence is not to be obtained from a wide review of the circumstances surrounding the incident but is to be derived directly from the quality of the act in the first place, and in the second place, whether that act was committed deliberately as opposed to carelessly, recklessly or negligently. It is the quality of the act itself, assuming that there was no justification for it, which must be considered in deciding whether it was evil. That was the position in the case of Edmiston where the Lord Justice Clerk indicated that it was the quality of the act which justified the description of the writing and sending of the threatening letters as "wicked and felonious". Having established that the act is an evil one all that is then required to constitute the crime of assault is that that act was done deliberately and not carelessly, recklessly or negligently.

Accordingly, in my opinion, the approach of counsel for the panel was too wide and in relation to the facts is not appropriate in deciding whether evil intent had been established in the present case.

The evil intent was established when the panel deliberately and without justification pointed the hand gun at the person in the shop premises and said: "Get the money out of the till and lay on the floor." At that point the crime of assault was established and the subsequent actions suggesting that it was all a joke were wholly irrelevant as a defence to that crime. For these reasons I have no hesitation in saying that in the present case, the trial judge misdirected the jury ...."

LORD SUTHERLAND: "... The words "evil intent" have an eminently respectable pedigree, being used by Hume when he describes dole or *mens rea* as "that corrupt and evil intention which is essential to the guilt of any crime". It is however perfectly possible to have an intention to perform particular acts without necessarily intending evil consequences from those acts. The use of the word "intention" may therefore be confusing in itself. If intention means motive then plainly it is irrelevant. If on the other hand intention means nothing more than wilful, intentional or deliberate as opposed to accidental, careless or even reckless, then plainly it is relevant in that a criminal act cannot be performed other than deliberately. This latter view appears to commend itself to Macdonald, *Criminal Law*, p. 115 and Gordon, *Criminal Law*, para 29–30. If, therefore, a person deliberately performs an act which would in itself be criminal then both the *actus reus* and the *mens rea* co-exist and a crime has been committed. The pointing of a gun at a shop assistant accompanied by words such as those used by the panel would undoubtedly constitute the *actus reus* of the crime of assault, and if these things are done deliberately and intentionally as they were done here the *mens rea* is also, in my opinion, established. The panel undoubtedly knew what he was doing and knew that what he did would be likely to cause alarm and distress. That is sufficient to constitute the crime of assault and his motive for doing it was quite irrelevant. I am therefore satisfied that at least as far as the crime of assault is concerned the trial judge misdirected the jury in leaving open to them consideration of the alleged defence that it was all a joke ...."

The Court answered the question referred by the Lord Advocate in the negative.

## NOTES

1. See also *Quinn v. Lees*, 1994 S.C.C.R. 159 in which the appellant was convicted of assaulting three **8.09** boys by setting a dog on them. The dog knocked over one of the boys and bit him on the leg. The appellant claimed that he had set the dog on them 'as a joke'. Relying upon the case of *Lord Advocate's Reference (No. 2 of 1992)* the court held that the accused was guilty of assault since he had acted deliberately in setting the dog on the boys. Similarly, in *Gilmour v. McGlennan*, 1993 S.C.C.R. 837, the appellant was convicted of assault where he had presented a toy gun at the complainer and said "Gie me your money or I'll shoot you". The gun was not obviously a toy, and the sheriff found as a fact that the complainer thought that the gun was real and that the appellant was going to shoot him. As the complainer ran away, the appellant shouted after him "Jim, I'm only kidding". The appellant's defence was that the events had been intended as a joke, and that the complainer had over-reacted. The sheriff convicted. On appeal the conviction was upheld. The Court, again applying *Lord Advocate's Reference (No. 2 of 1992)*, confirmed that an assault may be committed even against the background of 'good-natured joking', and that since the accused had deliberately engaged in conduct which included threatening gestures, and which produced fear and alarm on the part of the complainer, the fact that it may have been intended as a joke was irrelevant.

2. The instant case is not entirely satisfactory. It is not clear precisely what the nature of the accused's defence was in this case. If it was that he intended to frighten the complainers, but only as part of an ill-considered "joke", then clearly he ought to have been convicted, since he would have had the intention to place the complainers in a state of fear and alarm, and that would satisfy the *mens rea* requirement for assault. But matters ought surely to be different if the accused's defence was that he had never intended to frighten the complainers and that he had not expected them to be frightened. He might, for example, have thought that they would recognise him and realise that he was not being serious. In such a situation he could fairly be described as acting recklessly with regard to the effect of his actions on the complainers, but that ought not to be a sufficient *mens rea* for assault in the light of *H.M. Advocate v. Phipps*.

3. Suppose that at a pantomime performance 'the villain' makes threatening gestures at the audience, points a gun at them and discharges it causing a loud bang and a great deal of smoke. Most of the

audience recognise this for what it is, a theatrical performance, but a number of young children attending the performance are genuinely frightened by it. Is the villain guilty of assault? The villain's actions are deliberate in the sense that that word is apparently used in *Lord Advocate's Reference (No. 2 of 1992)*. He has deliberately carried out the actions which have placed the children in fear. If it is an assault to do this even in the context of "good-natured joking" it is presumably an assault to do this in the context of a theatrical performance.

## 2. AGGRAVATED ASSAULTS

**8.10** Assault may be aggravated in a variety of ways, most commonly by the degree of injury actually or potentially inflicted on the victim, by the use of a weapon such as a knife or by the character of the victim. Cases in the first two categories often shade into each other, for example, where the accused is charged with assaulting his victim with a weapon to his "severe injury" or "permanent disfigurement". Assault "to the danger of life" is also encountered, and this may be established even in the absence of actual injury: *Jane Smith or Thom* (1876) 3 Couper 32 (*cf. Kerr v. H.M. Advocate*, 1986 S.C.C.R. 91). So far as concerns assault aggravated by the character of the victim, the commonest case in practice is in relation to police assault. This is usually prosecuted as a contravention of section 41(1) of the Police (Scotland) Act 1967 which provides that "any person who (a) assaults, resists, obstructs, molests or hinders a constable in the execution of his duty ... shall be guilty of an offence". The terms of this subsection have been examined in a series of cases. In the context of this offence "obstruction" involves some physical element akin to assault, while "hindering" may be satisfied by minimal physical interference: *Skeen v. Shaw*, 1979 S.L.T. (Notes) 58. On the interpretation of the phrase "in the execution of his duty", see *Monk v. Strathern*, 1921 J.C. 4; *Twycross v. Farrell*, 1973 S.L.T. (Notes) 85, and the following two cases.

### Cardle v. Murray
1993 S.L.T. 525

**8.11** The accused was breakdancing in a busy shopping precinct. He accidentally bumped into an elderly lady, nearly knocking her down. A police officer walked towards the accused in order to warn him about his conduct. The accused continued to break dance and backed away from the officer as he approached. At that point the officer took hold of the accused's arm and said "Excuse me". The accused swore at the officer and continued to dance away so that the officer could not speak to him. The officer kept hold of the accused's arm and tried to calm him down but the accused shouted and tried to draw away, whereupon he was arrested for committing a breach of the peace. The accused continued to resist the police as he was handcuffed and walked to the police car, in the police car and at the police station.

The accused was charged with breach of the peace and resisting a police officer in the execution of his duty, contrary to section 41(1)(a) of the Police (Scotland) Act 1967. A submission that the accused had no case to answer was upheld by the sheriff, who acquitted the accused on the ground that when the accused was first restrained by the police officer this was unlawful and the accused was accordingly entitled to use reasonable force to resist. The Crown appealed. The opinion of the court was delivered by the Lord Justice-General (Hope):

OPINION OF THE COURT: "... There was ample evidence that the respondent behaved in a disorderly manner and shouted and swore both in Main Street and in the police station, and that he resisted the police officers by struggling with them when he was being arrested. But the question is whether, before any of the alleged offences had been committed, he was unlawfully detained by the police officer who first went over to speak to him. There is no dispute that if this was the position the respondent was entitled to resist him as he did. As Lord Cameron pointed out in *Swankie v. Milne*, 1973 S.L.T. (Notes) at p. 29, an arrest is something which in law differs from a detention by the police at their invitation or suggestion: "In the latter case a person detained or invited to accompany police officers is, at that stage, under no legal compulsion to accept the detention or invitation. It may well be that in a particular case refusal to comply could lead to formal arrest, but until that stage is reached there is theoretical freedom to exercise a right to refuse to accept detention at the hands of police officers who are not armed with a warrant. I think it is important always to keep clear the distinction between arrest, which is a legal act taken by officers of the law duly authorised to do so and while acting in the course of their duty, carrying with it certain important legal consequences, and the mere detention of a person by a police officer".

These comments must of course now be read subject to the point that, under s.2(1) of the Criminal Justice (Scotland) Act 1980, a constable who has reasonable grounds for suspecting that a person has committed or is committing an offence punishable by imprisonment may detain that person for the purposes which that subsection describes. But the principle remains that a person has the right to refuse to accept detention at the hands of a police officer unless the officer is armed with a warrant or is exercising a statutory right to detain him upon suspicion that he has committed or is committing an offence.

In *Twycross v. Farrell*, 1973 S.L.T. (Notes) 85, the appellant was asked by a police constable what he was doing and asked for his name and address. When he made no answer, swore at the constable and started to run away the constable seized hold of him, whereupon the appellant struggled and shouted and was only with difficulty detained until further police constables arrived. His conviction of resisting, obstructing, molesting and hindering the constable in the execution of his duty and of attempting to resist arrest was quashed on appeal. The report of the case does not set out the terms of the opinion which was delivered, but it is stated in it that in allowing the appeal and quashing the conviction the court indicated that, since there were no findings in the case to support the existence of a reasonable belief by the constable that the appellant had committed an offence, the constable had no right to attempt to stop the appellant from moving smartly away from the spot and that the appellant, having been so stopped, was entitled to struggle as he did.

The sheriff took the view, on a consideration of these and other authorities, that at the initial stage of the incident the respondent was restrained or detained or arrested unlawfully by the police officer. In his view it did not matter what label was given to the restraint because no form of restraint was justified. It followed that the police officers, when restraining the respondent, were not in the execution of their lawful duty, and their actions continued to be unlawful until he was released. And the respondent was entitled to use reasonable force to resist his detention. Any action by him within these limits which was directly referable to his unlawful detention was not an offence.

The advocate depute submitted that the police constable had seen circumstances which would have justified the making of a complaint, since the respondent was behaving irresponsibly by break dancing among the shoppers in the street. She accepted that no formal complaint had yet been made, and that the police constable was not attempting to arrest the respondent or to detain him in terms of the statute. Nevertheless the sheriff ought to have held in all the circumstances, looked at objectively, that the constable's actions in laying his hand on the respondent to restrain him were lawful. He was justified in taking the action which he did, so that he could talk to the respondent about his conduct. He was simply trying to settle him down so that he could speak to him, which was reasonable since the respondent was continuing to break dance all the time and to move away. In support of her argument she referred to *McFarlane v. Valentine*, High Court of Justiciary, November 20, 1990, *unreported*, 1991 G.W.D. 7–379, in which the appellant appealed unsuccessfully against his conviction for breach of the peace. He was convicted of shouting and swearing in a public place when he was spoken to by police officers who asked for his name, and he continued to do so when he was warned by them that he might be taken to the police station. But there was no suggestion in that case that the police officers laid their hands on him or attempted to restrain him by any other means before he had committed the breach of the peace. She referred also to *Ingram v. Cuthbertson*, High Court of Justiciary, July 2, 1991, *unreported*, 1992 G.W.D. 26–1488, where, on being asked to move on by the police, the respondent shouted and swore at them and was then arrested for committing a breach of the peace. He was acquitted by the sheriff of that charge and of resisting arrest, but on the latter point the sheriff's decision was reversed on appeal. That case also is of no assistance here, because there was no attempt by the police to restrain the appellant until after he had begun to shout and swear at them in a manner which, in their opinion, amounted to a breach of the peace.

In the present case, as counsel for the respondent emphasised in the course of his argument, the police constable's action in laying his hand on the respondent was not preceded by any complaint by anybody or by any conduct which, in the view of the police officer, gave reasonable grounds for his suspecting that the respondent was committing or had committed an offence. There is no doubt either that his purpose in laying his hand on the respondent was to restrain or to detain him, even although this was, initially at least, for the purpose only of speaking to him to warn him about his conduct. We agree with the sheriff that the respondent was entitled to protest at this action and to back away from the police constable, who had no right to stop him from continuing to move away. The police constable's action in holding on to him at this point was clearly unlawful, and the respondent cannot be said to have been committing an offence when he continued to protest and struggle as he did. It follows that his actions thereafter, as he was being taken under arrest to the police car and from the car into the police station, must be seen also as lawful conduct on his part in his attempts to resist the unlawful actions by the police.

We have some sympathy with the police constable, who was sufficiently concerned at what he saw to think it right to go over to the respondent to warn him about his conduct in break dancing in this busy street. There was no doubt a risk that as he moved among the shoppers in this way he would knock into other people, as he had just done when he knocked accidentally into the elderly lady as he was being watched by the police. A caution about the risk to others and the need to take care would not have been unreasonable. There was however no justification at that stage for the police constable to take hold of the respondent which, in the circumstances, could not have been seen as anything other than an attempt to restrain or detain him unlawfully against his will. It is on this short point that the case depends, and we consider that the sheriff was right to conclude that the respondent had no case to answer on any of the charges in the complaint, which were the result of his attempts to resist the actions of the police constable.

Accordingly we shall answer all five questions in the case in the affirmative and refuse the appeal."

Appeal refused.

NOTE

**8.12**    Clearly, since the accused was not acting in a disorderly manner prior to being approached by the police, they were not entitled to lay hands on him. Even if he had bumped into another shopper it is not clear that the police would have been entitled to intervene, unless it could be said that his conduct amounted to a breach of the peace (and is that likely in this context?) or some other offence which would have justified the police arresting him, or detaining him under section 14 of the Criminal Procedure (Scotland) Act 1995. *Cf. Lochrie v. Jessop*, 1992 S.L.T. 557; *Logan* v. *Jessop*, 1987 S.C.C.R. 604 and *McLeod v. Lowe*, 1993 S.L.T. 471.

Given the above, what steps could the police officer have taken to ensure that the accused did not injure other users of the shopping precinct, while remaining within the scope of his duty, given that the accused was clearly unwilling to listen to what the police officer had to say but had not, at that point, committed an offence justifying his arrest or detention?

**Stirton v. MacPhail**
1983 S.L.T. 34

**8.13**    LORD JUSTICE-CLERK: "The appellant was charged with a contravention of s.41 of the Police (Scotland) Act 1967, which provides inter alia that: 'Any person who (a) assaults, resists, obstructs, molests or hinders a constable in the execution of his duty ... shall be guilty of an offence.' The charge alleged 'that on December 20, 1980, at the house at 104b Glengarry Road, Perth, you did obstruct and hinder Ian Cantwell, Detective Constable, and Neil McPherson, Police Constable, then engaged in the execution of their duty, namely apprehending James Lindsay Stirton, in that you did lock the outside door of said house, remove and conceal the key from the lock of said door and refuse to open said door when requested to do so by said officers thereby preventing them from leaving said house with said James Lindsay Stirton; contrary to Section 41 of the Police (Scotland) Act 1967'.

The sheriff found the appellant guilty and fined her £25. She has appealed against that conviction by way of stated case and the only question posed for the opinion of this court by the sheriff is: 'On the facts admitted or proved, was I entitled to convict the appellant?' It appears from the additional report from the sheriff called for by this court that a further question should have been included in the case, namely: 'On the facts admitted or proved, was I entitled to make finding-in-fact 9?' ... [Finding 9 was in the following terms: 'The police officers were acting properly in the course of the execution of their duty and had made the appellant sufficiently aware of this at the material time.']

Counsel for the appellant submitted that it was essential to a conviction under this subsection that the prosecution should have proved first, that the police constables involved were in fact engaged in the execution of their duty as distinct from them having a reasonable belief that they were so acting, and secondly, that the appellant knew or might reasonably be inferred to have known that the police constables were acting in the execution of their duty. Whether these vital prerequisites were satisfied depended on the facts of the particular case, and in his submission they were not satisfied in this case.

In furtherance of the first of these contentions it was argued that in this context it was necessary for the prosecution to prove by requisite evidence that there was a valid warrant (or valid warrants) in existence, that the police officer was carrying that valid warrant with him, and that it was produced particularly if there was a request for its production. If this was not done it could not be said that the police officer was acting in the execution of his duty within the meaning of s.41. It was argued that these matters had not been established here and that accordingly no conviction should have been recorded. Reference was made to Hume on *Crimes* (3rd ed.), vol. 2, p. 78, Alison's *Criminal Law*, vol. 2, p. 124, and Macdonald's *Criminal Law* (5th ed.), p. 199. It was particularly necessary for the police officer to have the warrants with him, because these were fine warrants, and if the person in respect of whom the warrants were issued then paid the fines on the spot the warrants fell. The sheriff had proceeded on the basis that since the police officers here had acted in the honest belief that there were warrants in existence and that they were acting under the authority of such warrants they were acting in the execution of their duty.

Counsel for the appellant was well founded in submitting that it was not proved that there were in existence four extract conviction warrants against the appellant's husband in respect of unpaid fines. It is clear from finding 3 that none of the police officers concerned had first-hand knowledge of their existence, and it appears from the sheriff's note that the information about them was second or third hand so far as these officers were concerned. It is equally clear from that finding that none of these officers ever had possession of these warrants. Thus the factual basis on which counsel based his argument is established by the findings. But of what relevance have these facts to the question whether the police officers were acting in the execution of their duty in the circumstances of this case?

In finding 3 it is recorded that D.C. Cantwell had been informed of these four warrants in the course of his duties and he in turn informed the other officers involved. The procedure was elaborated on by the sheriff in his note when he was discussing what the evidence revealed on that matter. It was to the effect that so far as the police force at Perth is concerned the system is that when the court grants a warrant for the non-payment of fines (an extract conviction warrant) the actual warrant itself is sent to one police officer whose duties include the duty of extracted warrants officer. He in turn informs the appropriate duty officer of the existence of such warrants for his area, and the duty officer then instructs members of the force under his control to execute the warrants. The practice seems to differ as to whether the police officers so instructed take the warrant with them when they go to arrest the subject of the warrant. D.C. Cantwell who had received the instruction said that the normal procedure was not to see or have the actual warrant but to rely on the information passed to him by his instructing officer. P.C. McPherson on the other hand thought it was not necessary for the actual warrant to be taken on execution, but he normally took it with him. It was against that background that D.C. Cantwell and P.C. McPherson with their two colleagues went to the house to arrest the appellant's husband. Their purpose was to arrest him because of the four extract conviction warrants against him in respect of unpaid fines. They did not have the warrants but they had the second-hand information from Cantwell about them. After some difficulty in gaining admittance to the house the police officers were admitted by the appellant who was informed by Cantwell about the four warrants which were out for her husband and that he was to be arrested. The appellant at first denied that her husband was in the house, although in fact he was, and asked two or three times if they had the warrants. The wording in finding 6 that she asked to see the warrants is wrong, according to the sheriff. His note appended to the stated case sets out the true position, as he explains in his report to us. The appellant did not ask to see the warrants; she asked if they had the warrants. Cantwell again explained the purpose of the visit and he and McPherson walked past her into the house. Her husband was found in a bedroom and eventually had to be manhandled to the front door. It was there that the incidents related in the charge took place.

Despite the well-presented argument by appellant's counsel I consider that it was vitiated by the fact that it proceeded on a wrong basis. The issue in this case is not whether the warrants in question were valid quoad the appellant's husband, but is whether the police officers were acting in the execution of their duty when the appellant obstructed and hindered them as she did. They had been instructed by their superior officer to go and arrest the appellant's husband in respect of four warrants of which they were apprised but did not see. It was their duty to carry out these instructions. They were in the course of carrying out their orders when they were obstructed and hindered by the appellant. That was a clear contravention of s.41(1)(a). The fact that it was not proved that such warrants were in existence, that they did not have these warrants in their possession at the time, and that their knowledge of them rested only on hearsay might be relevant when considering a complaint by the appellant's husband that he had been illegally arrested, but are not criteria in considering whether in the circumstances here present the police officers were acting in the execution of their duty when carrying out their orders. If it were otherwise a police officer who was ordered to make an arrest on a warrant with which he was supplied but which was eventually found not to be valid, could not be said to be in the execution of his duty when assaulted by a person other than the person he was attempting to arrest under the warrant. I do not consider that s.41(1)(a) should be so construed. That being so, I do not find it necessary to consider the authorities referred to by counsel in support of his submission, since in my view they have no relevance to the real issue in the case.

That leaves for consideration the second of counsel's submissions, namely that the Crown failed to prove that the appellant knew or might reasonably be inferred to have known that the police officers were acting in the execution of their duty. This was founded on the following points. Cantwell was a detective not in uniform and McPherson had a coat over his uniform. The other two officers were at the rear of the house. The time when the police arrived at the house was 3.50 a.m., and when she asked several times if they had warrant cards none was produced, nor was any form of identification. As against that, she was informed several times that the men were police officers. The purpose of their visit was disclosed, as was the fact that they had four extract conviction warrants for her husband. Despite this, the appellant initially lied when she said that her husband was not in the house. There is no finding that she attempted to prevent the officers from entering the house, and she only offered resistance when her husband required to be manhandled towards the door. Then, significantly, after refusing to produce the key of the door which she had secreted she eventually produced it. She did not give evidence, and so did not proffer any evidence from which it could even be inferred that she had no reason to believe that the men were police officers. All she said in answer to the caution and charge was: 'How did I molest or obstruct you, you never had a warrant?' In these circumstances I am of the opinion that the sheriff was entitled to hold, as he did, that the appellant was aware, or ought to have been aware, that the police were acting in the execution of their duty.

In all these circumstances I move your Lordships to answer in the affirmative both the question of law contained in the stated case and the question in law regarding finding 9 which the sheriff on reflection thought ought to have been incorporated, and to refuse the appeal."

Appeal refused.

NOTES

1. Since it was never proved that the warrants referred to actually existed, and there being no common **8.14** law or statutory power of arrest without warrant in the circumstances of the case, the case must be regarded as one in which the officers were carrying out an unlawful arrest. It might well be argued that it is no part of a police officer's duty to carry out an unlawful arrest, but that view must be open to doubt in the light of the Lord Justice-Clerk's view that they were acting within the scope of their duty because they were carrying out orders given to them by a superior officer. His lordship pointed to the situation of an officer who is in possession of a warrant which is subsequently found to be invalid as supporting his argument.

Nevertheless, it is submitted that there are difficulties with the approach adopted by the court in this case. Certainly the fact that a police officer is acting on the instructions of his or her superior ought not in itself to be determinative of the issue. The case should be read as applying only to those instructions which a superior may lawfully give, or at the very least those instructions which the superior honestly and reasonably believes may be given. Thus an officer may instruct his subordinates to execute a warrant which he has in his possession, but could not, for example, instruct them to "execute" a warrant which he knew did not exist.

The problem is made more complex if one takes into account the state of knowledge of the subordinates. Suppose, for example, that a constable is instructed by a superior officer to do something which the constable knows to be unlawful. Surely he cannot be allowed to shelter behind the instructions of his superiors, even if the latter honestly and reasonably believe that the instruction is one which may lawfully be given?

Conversely, suppose that the police officer is not in fact acting in the execution of his duty, but believes that she is. In England it has been held that it is not enough for a police officer to hold such a belief. The test is an objective one: *Kerr v. D.P.P.* [1995] Crim. L.R. 394.

2. Compare *Stirton* with *R. v. Purdy* [1974] 3 All E.R. 465. A police officer was sent to arrest the appellant for non-payment of fines, a warrant having been issued by a justice of the peace. At the time of the arrest the police officer did not have the warrant on his person having left it in his car, which was some 60 yards away. The appellant, along with some other men, assaulted the police officer. The appellant was convicted, *inter alia*, of assaulting a police officer in the execution of his duty. On appeal it was argued that since the officer did not have the warrant in his possession at the time of the attempted arrest, that arrest was unlawful and the appellant was entitled to resist. The court held that the arrest was lawful, since the warrant, although not on the person of the officer, was sufficiently available to be in his possession. The court went on to add that if the arrest had not been lawful, the appellant could not have been guilty of assaulting a police officer in the execution of his duty, although he could have been guilty of other offences of violence, such as assault occasioning actual bodily harm, or affray.

3. For comments on the mental element in this offence, see the notes to *Annan v. Tait*, 1982 S.L.T. (Sh.Ct) 108, *post*, p. 295.

4. Entry by the police officers into a person's home without their consent will generally constitute an interference with the right to respect for that person's home under Article 8 of the European Convention on Human Rights. As such, it will be an unlawful act in terms of section 6 of the Human Rights Act, unless it can be justified in terms of Article 8(2) of the Convention. While entry into a home in order to investigate or prevent a serious crime, or to prevent a breach of the peace (see, for example *Robert Moffat v. P.F. Edinburgh*, High Court, May 13, 1999, *unreported*) would probably be justified, (see, for example, *McLeod v. United Kingdom*, R.J.D., 1998-VIII, [1999] E.H.R.L.R. 125), it is not at all

clear that entry without permission into a home to effect detention in respect of a minor offence is justified (*Cf. McLeod v. United Kingdom, supra*). It might be regarded as being a disproportionate interference with the right to respect for the home. But, of course, different considerations apply where the police are acting in pursuance of a search warrant or a warrant to arrest.

5. More generally, since it cannot be any part of a police officer's duty to engage in an unlawful act, the exercise of police powers in a way which is incompatible with *any* of the Convention rights ought to result in the conclusion that the police officer is not acting in the execution of his or her duty. This should provide an additional incentive to police officers to ensure that they act in compliance with those rights. Consider, in this context, the case of *Gellatly v. Heywood*, 1997 S.C.C.R. 300. The accused was charged with obstructing a police officer in the execution of his duty. He had been arrested in the late afternoon, subjected to a strip search and placed in a cell. In the early hours of the following morning he was seen to be in possession of a tin box containing two cigarettes. He was also in an agitated condition. A decision was taken to conduct a further strip search, ostensibly for his own protection since it was feared that he might have other, harmful, substances in his possession. He was told that he was to be searched, but was not given any reason why (although in his condition it might have been difficult to explain the reasons). The appellant resisted the search and that resulted in the charge of obstruction. The sheriff convicted and the conviction was upheld by the High Court. Such a search would arguably be an interference with the accused's right to privacy under article 8(1) of the Convention, particularly given the intrusive nature of the search. If so, it would be an unlawful act, unless justified in terms of article 8(2) of the Convention. Could it be said in this case that it was "necessary" to engage in a search of this kind, without explanation? And for what purpose? The reason preferred by the police officers in this case is not one set out in article 8(2), unless it is covered by the reference to protection of health.

6. Where the legal basis for detention of a suspect has ceased to exist, an attempt to interfere with the liberty of the suspect will be unlawful, and the suspect will be entitled to resist. Such resistance will not, then, amount to assaulting, obstructing or resisting the police in the execution of their duty. See *Stocks v. Hamilton*, 1991 S.C.C.R. 190.

## Mens rea *in aggravated assault*

**8.15** It may be necessary here to distinguish those cases in which the aggravation is one of causing severe injury or endangering life from those in which the aggravation relates to the character of the victim. In the first category of cases it appears that it is not necessary to show that the accused intended, or was even reckless as to, any such consequence (*cf.* the cases of *Jane Smith or Thom* (1876) 3 Couper 332 and *Kerr v. H.M. Advocate*, 1986 S.C.C.R. 91, *ante*, p. 288).

So far as concerns the second category of cases, involving the identity or character of the victim, two issues arise: (1) is knowledge as to identity an element of the offence, and (2) if so, is this something which the prosecutor must establish, or is it for the accused to prove ignorance? These are issues on which no decisive answer has been given by the High Court, but recent cases suggest that it is for the Crown to prove knowledge on the part of the accused, and it is submitted that this accords with principle. However, as the matter is not settled, a range of authorities is included here.

### Alexr. and James Alexander
#### (1842) 1 Broun 28

**8.16** The accused were engaged in removing goods illegally from a ship lying in the Firth of Clyde when a revenue officer intervened. They attacked him, and eventually threw him in the river and struck him with an oar. They were charged with assault "especially when committed on an Officer of the Revenue in the execution of his duty". An objection was taken on the relevancy of the charge on the ground that it did not aver that they knew the victim to be an officer of the revenue in the execution of his duty.

LORD MONCREIFF: "I do not think that our decision in this case will settle any general question, although it will serve to regulate the drawing of indictments. I hold the major proposition to be correctly laid. I agree also that it is not necessary to set forth, in so many words, that the pannels knew who the individual assaulted was. There may certainly be equivalents. Scarcely one, however, of the many indictments which have been quoted, does not furnish a clearer inference than the present. All that is stated in this libel may have taken place, and yet the pannels have been ignorant of the main fact charged in the aggravation. It is not set forth that the removal of the casks from the ship was by smuggling. A person might have been stationed on board of the vessel, and have attempted to prevent the removal of casks or bags, although he was not a customhouse officer. It is not charged against the pannels, that they did wilfully obstruct or deforce the said officer in the execution of his duty, but merely, that they wickedly and feloniously attacked and assaulted him. Where, then, is it to be collected from this indictment, that the pannels knew this party, and what he was doing? No such necessary inference follows. It seems to me, that the libel should have contained such averments, as to make it perfectly plain, that the pannels were made aware, at the time, of the situation and character of the person whom they assaulted. I admit the point to be attended with doubt, but, on the grounds already stated, my opinion is, that this particular indictment, so far as the aggravation is concerned, is bad."

The Lord Justice-General (Boyle): "The objection which has been started, in the criticism upon this indictment, is a most important one. I am satisfied that there have been numerous cases, where the same fundamental deficiency, supposing it to be so, has occurred, but in which the indictments have been sustained, and punishments inflicted. In judging of the relevancy of the present libel, we must read the whole minor. The assertion made by the prosecutor, that the pannels had removed from the ship, which the customhouse officer was appointed to guard, several casks or bags, with the intention of conveying them ashore, coupled with the positive averment, that this was done illegally, just amounts to a charge of smuggling. In these circumstances, I agree with the Solicitor-General, that the *onus* of proof is shifted, and that, instead of the prosecutor being required to prove the knowledge of the pannels, it is for them to establish, that they did *not* know the person, whom they assaulted, to be an officer engaged in protecting her Majesty's revenue. It is absurd to suppose, that this person was to walk up and down the vessel, crying aloud every quarter of an hour that he was a customhouse officer. There is enough set forth to satisfy me, that the pannels must well have known his true character, and the object of his interference with their illegal proceedings. I am therefore of opinion, that the aggravation is relevantly charged."

> The court being equally divided, the presiding judge,
> as is usual in such circumstances gave no vote, and
> the objection to the relevancy was therefore sustained.

Note

*Cf. Helen Yuill* (1842) 1 Broun 480 where Lord Mackenzie's view was that "the minor proposition of **8.17** indictments, charging the obstructing or assaulting officers of the law in the execution of their duty, must either contain an express statement that they were known to the pannels as such, or set forth such circumstances as necessarily imply this knowledge". In that case it was held that an averment that the accused assembled "for the purpose of obstructing and assaulting" the officers satisfied this requirement. See also, *George McLellan* (1842) 1 Broun 478. In *O'Brien v. McPhee* (1880) 4 Couper 375 the view was expressed (*obiter*) that once the Crown had established that the accused had assaulted the constables, and that the latter were acting in the execution of their duty, it was for the accused to show "by positive evidence—or that the probability from the whole facts and circumstances disclosed was—that although the persons to whom they offered and used violence were in truth police constables in the execution of their duty, they had no suspicion of that". However, to require such exculpatory proof conflicts with the general principles of onus of proof (Chapter 1, *ante*; *cf.* Gordon, para. 29–21, n. 72) and should be regarded as incorrect.

## Annan v. Tait
### 1982 S.L.T.(Sh.Ct) 108

Sheriff Poole: "The relevant facts in this case are that on October 16, 1980, acting detective **8.18** constable Martin of the Lothian and Borders Police and woman detective constable Smith of the same force, who were in plain clothes, in an unmarked police vehicle, witnessed a fight amongst a group of young people in West Main Street, Armadale, West Lothian. They radioed for assistance. In fact the fight seemed to have stopped of its own volition. But thereafter a further fight developed between Mr Bonnar, one of the co-accused, and a third party. Very properly, acting in the course of their duty, the two police officers went over to the fight and detective constable Martin pulled Mr Bonnar and the other youth apart. Mr Bonnar's friends, including Mr Tait, believing this to be a further attack on Mr Bonnar, started to pull at Mr Bonnar and at detective constable Martin. Detective constable Martin shouted that he was a police officer. Detective constable Smith pulled out her warrant card and showed it to Miss Bonnar, one of the co-accused, who in any event does not seem to have taken an active part in the struggle which by now was crossing the road. Mr Bonnar broke free at that point, but later tripped and fell and detective constable Martin was able to secure him.

Detective constable Martin himself very fairly said, on oath in the witness box, that Mr Tait did not stop struggling with him 'until eventually he did stop when it got through to him that I was a police officer'. This was confirmed by Mr Tait and the defence witnesses. Mr Stephen explained that it was he who had informed Mr Tait that detective constable Martin had said he was a police officer, and to stop and that Mr Tait had done so. In other words, at the relevant time Mr Tait was ignorant of the fact that constable Martin was a police officer.

There is little doubt that the Crown had established that constable Martin was a police officer, that Mr Bonnar was in his lawful custody and that Mr Tait had tried to rescue Mr Bonnar.

It was contended for the Crown that that was sufficient to secure a conviction and that it mattered not that Mr Tait was unaware of the fact that detective constable Martin was a police officer at the time of his actions. There was nothing in the statute which showed that a lack of knowledge was exculpatory, although of course it might be mitigatory. The contrary position was contended for by the defence.

The fundamental principle of our Scottish criminal law lies within the concept of *actus non facit reum nisi mens sit rea*, although in dealing with statutory cases it may well be necessary to refer to the terms of the statute itself to inquire whether Parliament intended to abrogate that fundamental principle in that particular statute.

As Lord Reid said in the House of Lords case of *Sweet v. Parsley* [1969] 2 W.L.R. 470 at p. 473: 'Our first duty is to consider the words of the Act: if they show a clear intention to create an absolute offence that is an end of the matter. But such cases are very rare. Sometimes the words of the section which creates a particular offence make it clear that *mens rea* is required in one form or another. Such cases are quite frequent. But in a very large number of cases there is no clear indication either way. In such cases there has for centuries been a presumption that Parliament did not intend to make criminals of persons who were in no way blameworthy in what they did. That means that whenever a section is silent as to *mens rea* there is a presumption that, in order to give effect to the will of Parliament, we must read in words appropriate to require *mens rea*.'

Further, Lord Reid in *R. v. Warner* [1968] 2 W.L.R. 1303 at p. 1307 said: 'There is no doubt that for centuries *mens rea* has been an essential element in every common law crime or offence. Equally there is no doubt that Parliament, being sovereign, can create absolute offences if so minded. But we were referred to no instance where Parliament in giving statutory form to an old common law crime has or has been held to have excluded the necessity to prove *mens rea*. There are a number of statutes going back for over a century where Parliament in creating a new offence has transferred the onus of proof so that, once the facts necessary to constitute the crime have been proved, the accused will be held to be guilty unless he can prove that he had no *mens rea*. But we were not referred to any except quite recent cases in which it was held that it was no defence to a charge of a serious and truly criminal statutory offence to prove absence of *mens rea*. On the other hand there is a long line of cases in which it has been held with regard to less serious offences that absence of *mens rea* was no defence. Typical examples are offences under public health, licensing and industrial legislation .... These are only quasi criminal offences and it does not really offend the ordinary man's sense of justice that moral guilt is not of the essence of the offence.'

The charge libelled against Mr Tait is under s.41(1)(b) of the Police (Scotland) Act 1967. That section provides: 'Any person ... who rescues or attempts to rescue, or assists or attempts to assist the escape of, any person in custody, shall be guilty of an offence'. 'Custody' is defined in s.41(2)(a) as 'lawful custody'. It enacts in statutory form an old common law crime of rescuing or attempting to rescue prisoners from officers of the law' (Anderson's *Criminal Law of Scotland*, p. 85; Gordon's *Criminal Law* (2nd ed.), p. 1084).

It is quite clearly a serious and truly criminal offence.

The question which then fell to be considered was whether, if Mr Tait held an honest and reasonable belief in his ignorance of constable Martin's capacity, was he entitled to be acquitted? In my view, in the confused circumstances at that time, and given the fact that both police officers were in plain clothes, Mr Tait held an honest belief on reasonable grounds. There was nothing in the words of s.41(1)(b) to suggest that Parliament had intended to exclude any element of *mens rea*, such as the exclusion of a defence of an honest mistake in fact: see Diplock L.J. in *Sweet v. Parsley, supra*, at p. 486.

In my view therefore, the Crown has not established the guilt of Mr Tait and he is entitled to be acquitted."

Verdict of not guilty.

NOTE

It is unfortunate that the learned sheriff did not deal with any of the authorities more closely in point. **8.19** Nevertheless, as a statement of principle the case is very welcome. It does not, of course, deal with a charge under section 41(1)(a), but it is submitted that it adopts the approach which ought to be applied to charges under that subsection. This is to some extent supported by the statements of the court in *Stirton v. MacPhail*, 1983 S.L.T. 34, *ante* p. 290, where the Lord Justice-Clerk appears to accept the proposition that for a conviction under section 41(1)(a), it is necessary for the Crown to prove that the appellant "knew or might reasonably be inferred to have known" that the officers were acting in the execution of their duty.

# 3. JUSTIFICATION AND EXCUSE IN ASSAULT

The principles applicable to general defences, and their application in particular crimes are discussed in Chapter 7, and reference is made to that chapter for a discussion of private defence and other lawful authority as defences to a criminal charge. This section deals with one defence which is peculiar to assault—the lawful chastisement of children—and two defences which, while they are encountered in respect of certain other offences, give rise to particular issues in the context of assault—consent and provocation.

## A. Lawful chastisement

### (a) The limits of lawful chastisement

At common law certain adults are entitled to inflict corporal punishment on children for the purposes of **8.20** correction. The consequence of this is that conduct which would otherwise be an assault is not criminal. The same defence would be available to a person charged with assaulting or ill-treating a child contrary to section 12 of the Children and Young Persons (Scotland) Act 1937 (see *post*, p. 328). This rule, however, needs to be kept within established limits.

(a) In the first place, it is restricted to punishment administered by parents on their children, or by school teachers on pupils. Parents may expressly (or perhaps by implication also) confer on others the authority to administer such punishment. In *Stewart v. Thain*, 1981 S.L.T. (Notes) 2 the parents of a 15-year-old boy called in his headmaster to deal with the boy who seemed to be beyond the control of his parents. The headmaster administered several strokes to the boy's bare buttocks, and was subsequently charged with indecently assaulting him. It was held that there was no offence since the punishment had been administered by a person *in loco parentis* and for the purpose only of chastising the boy.

(b) Secondly, the punishment must be kept within reasonable bounds and must not be excessive. In determining whether or not the punishment is reasonable, the court will have regard to the age of the child and the nature and severity of the punishment. In *Gray v. Hawthorn*, 1964 J.C. 69, the appellant, the headmaster of a school, administered nine blows with a leather strap to the hands of an eleven-year-old boy within a period of one hour. In holding that the appellant had been correctly convicted of assault, Lord Guthrie stated: "When a headmaster or teacher is charged with assault on a pupil, such matters as the nature and violence of the punishment, the repetition or continuity of the punishment, the age, the health and the sex of the child, the blameworthiness and the degree of blameworthiness of the child's conduct, and so on, are all relevant circumstances ...." See also *Brown v. Hilson*, 1924 J.C. 1, *McShane v. Paton* 1922 S.L.T. 251, *Byrd v. Wither*, 1991 S.L.T. 206 and *Peebles v. MacPhail*, 1990 S.L.T. 245.

(c) The punishment must also be administered for the correction of the child. Even moderate punishment administered for an improper purpose, such as the sexual gratification of the adult, would thus be unlawful. (*Cf. Stewart v. Thain, ante.*)

(d) So far as concerns school teachers, although school teachers do not commit a criminal offence if they administer reasonable punishment to pupils in their charge, corporal punishment is no longer in use in state schools. The matter is now effectively determined by section 48A of the Education (Scotland) Act 1980, as inserted by section 48 of the Education (No. 2) Act 1986. Section 48A provides, *inter alia*:

> "(1) Where, in any proceedings, it is shown that corporal punishment has been given to a pupil by or on the authority of a member of the staff, giving the punishment cannot be justified on the ground that it was done in pursuance of a right exercisable by the member of the staff by virtue of his position as such.
> (2) Subject to subsection (3) below, references in this section to giving corporal punishment are references to doing anything for the purposes of punishing the pupil concerned (whether or not there are also other reasons for doing it) which, apart from any justification, would constitute physical assault upon the person.
> (3) A person is not to be taken for the purposes of this section as giving corporal punishment by virtue of anything done for reasons which include averting an immediate danger of personal injury to, or an immediate danger to the property of, any person (including the pupil concerned).
> (4) A person does not commit an offence by reason of any conduct relating to a pupil which would, apart from this section, be justified on the ground that it was done in pursuance of a right exercisable by a member of the staff by virtue of his position as such."

What this means in effect is that while in other proceedings a teacher cannot rely on his "right" to administer corporal punishment, the administration of such punishment within the limits of lawful chastisement, will not amount to an offence.

For the purposes of this section, the term "pupil" includes a person for whom education is provided at a public school, at a grant-aided school or at an independent school maintained or assisted by a Minister of the Crown which is a school prescribed under regulations made under section 48A. Where a corporal punishment is still administered in schools (essentially schools wholly within the private sector), section 294 of the Education Act 1993 provides that the punishment should not be "inhumane or degrading".

## (b) The legal foundation of the defence

**8.21** There is a divergence of opinion as to why a parent or teacher who administers moderate corporal punishment to a child is not guilty of an assault. The discussion of this issue in a number of cases appears to suggest that where a child is beaten for the purpose of chastising him then the person administering the punishment is not guilty of assault because he or she does not have the 'evil intent' necessary for assault. (See, for example, *Gray v. Hawthorn, supra*; *B. v. Harris*, 1989 S.L.T. 208; *Byrd v. Wither,* 1990 S.L.T. 206; *Peebles v. MacPhail,* 1990 S.L.T. 245.)

If one were to accept the 'normative' nature of the term 'evil intent' then this would be a defensible position. A person who strikes a child for the purpose merely of inflicting pain arguably has a different kind of intent from one who does so for the purpose of correcting the child's behaviour. However, both inflict the blow deliberately, and in the knowledge that it will cause the child pain. (That, after all, is how corporal punishment is meant to work—the child reacts to the pain by resolving, like all children, never to be naughty again.) In that sense, and clearly in the sense intended by the court in *Lord Advocate's Reference (No. 2 of 1992), ante*, p. 284, and cases which have followed that decision, a person who deliberately inflicts a blow on another demonstrates the evil intent necessary for assault and the reason why it is done does not affect the presence of that state of mind. (But *cf.* also the views of the High Court in *Drury v. H.M. Advocate*, High Court, February 2, 2001, *unreported*, *post*, p. 407.)

It is suggested that the proper approach is this: the fact that a parent or teacher strikes a child for the purpose of chastising the child is nothing to do with whether or not the parent has the *mens rea* for assault, but rather offers a justification for what would otherwise be an offence. In other words, parents who smack their children do have 'evil intent' (in the sense of deliberately inflicting the injury), but they do so for a purpose which the law recognises as acceptable and for that reason they are not guilty of an offence. See *Kennedy v. A.*, 1993 S.L.T. 1134.

## (c) Corporal punishment and human rights

**8.22** Judicial corporal punishment or "birching"—not a lawful punishment in Scotland but until relatively recently in use on the Isle of Man—was condemned by the European Court of Human Rights as being necessarily incompatible with Article 3 of the Convention—see *Tyrer v. United Kingdom*, (1978) 2 E.H.R.R. 1. The use of corporal punishment in schools and within the family has been the subject of a number of challenges on human rights grounds.

In *Campbell and Cosans v. United Kingdom*, (1982) 4 E.H.R.R. 293 it was held that the use of corporal punishment in state schools in Scotland, without the consent of the child's parent, violated the parent's rights under Article 2 of the First Protocol which provides that "[I]n the exercise of any functions which it assumes in relation to education and to teaching, the State shall respect the right of parents to ensure such education and teaching in conformity with their own religious and philosophical convictions". In the same case it was argued that the use of such punishment violated the child's right under article 3 not to be subjected to inhumane or degrading treatment or punishment. That part of the case was declared inadmissible and the issue was therefore not developed before the Court. The decision in this case did, however, lead to the passing of section 48A of the Education (Scotland) Act 1980, referred to above.

In *Costello-Roberts v. United Kingdom*, (1995) 19 E.H.R.R. 112 the Court considered an application based on article 3, but held that the punishment administered (by a teacher in a private school) had not reached the level of severity prohibited by Article 3. In the following case, however, the Court held that the punishment administered to a nine-year-old boy was sufficiently severe, and that the United Kingdom was in violation of the Convention for failing to protect the child from punishment of this kind.

### A. v. United Kingdom
### (1999) 27 E.H.R.R. 611

**8.23** The applicant, who was nine years old at the time, was beaten by his step-father, using a garden cane. A medical examination of the applicant revealed bruises on the backs of his legs and thighs and on his bottom. The paediatrician who examined the boy stated that these injuries were consistent with the use of a garden cane, "applied with considerable force, on more than one occasion". The step-father was charged with assault occasioning actual bodily harm. At his trial he admitted that he had caned the applicant on a number of occasions, but he argued that this had been necessary and reasonable since the applicant "was a difficult boy who did not respond to parental or school discipline". In his summing up the judge told the jury that it was a defence to the charge of assault that the accused was correcting the applicant's behaviour provided that the correction was reasonable. The jury returned a verdict of not guilty.

A applied to the European Commission on Human Rights claiming that the United Kingdom had failed to protect him from ill-treatment by his step-father, in violation of Articles 3 and/or 8 of the Convention; that he had been denied a remedy for these complaints in violation of Article 13; and that the domestic law on assault discriminated against children, in violation of Article 14 in conjunction with Articles 3 and 8.

The Commission expressed the opinion that there had been a violation of Article 3; that it was not necessary to consider the complaint under Article 8, that there had been no violation of Article 13 and that it was not necessary to consider the complaint under Article 14 in conjunction with Articles 3 and 8.

OPINION OF THE COURT:

"19. The applicant asked the Court to find a violation of Article 3 of the Convention, which provides:

"No one shall be subjected to torture or to inhuman or degrading treatment or punishment."

Both the Commission and the Government accepted that there had been a violation of Article 3. Despite this, the Court considers it necessary itself to examine the issues in this case (see, for example, the *Findlay v. United Kingdom* judgment of February 25, 1997, Reports of Judgments and Decisions 1997-I, p. 263). As is its usual practice, this examination will be limited to the specific facts of the case before it.

20. The Court recalls that ill-treatment must attain a minimum level of severity if it is to fall within the scope of Article 3. The assessment of this minimum is relative: it depends on all the circumstances of the case, such as the nature and context of the treatment, its duration, its physical and mental effects and, in some instances, the sex, age and state of health of the victim (see the *Costello-Roberts v. United Kingdom* judgment of March 25, 1993, Series A no. 247-C, p. 59 para. 30).

21. The Court recalls that the applicant, who was then nine years old, was found by the consultant paediatrician who examined him to have been beaten with a garden cane which had been applied with considerable force on more than one occasion . . . .

The Court considers that treatment of this kind reaches the level of severity prohibited by Article 3.

22. It remains to be determined whether the State should be held responsible, under Article 3, for the beating of the applicant by his step-father.

The Court considers that the obligation on the High Contracting Parties under Article 1 of the Convention to secure to everyone within their jurisdiction the rights and freedoms defined in the Convention, taken together with Article 3, requires States to take measures designed to ensure that individuals within their jurisdiction are not subjected to torture or inhuman or degrading treatment or punishment, including such ill-treatment administered by private individuals (see, *mutatis mutandis*, the *H.L.R. v. France* judgment of April 29, 1997, Reports 1997-III, p. 758, §40).

Children and other vulnerable individuals, in particular, are entitled to State protection, in the form of effective deterrence, against such serious breaches of personal integrity (see, *mutatis mutandis*, the *X and Y v. The Netherlands* judgment of March 26, 1985, Series A no. 91, pp. 11–13, §§21–27, the *Stubbings and Others v. The United Kingdom* judgment of October 22, 1996, Reports 1996-IV, p. 1505, §§62–64 and also the United Nations Convention on the Rights of the Child, Articles 19 and 37).

23. The Court recalls that under English law it is a defence to a charge of assault on a child that the treatment in question amounted to "reasonable chastisement" (see paragraph 14 above). The burden of proof is on the prosecution to establish beyond reasonable doubt that the assault went beyond the limits of lawful punishment. In the present case, despite the fact that the applicant had been subjected to treatment of sufficient severity to fall within the scope of Article 3, the jury acquitted his step-father, who had administered the treatment (see paragraphs 10–11 above).

24. In the Court's view, the law did not provide adequate protection to the applicant against treatment or punishment contrary to Article 3. Indeed, the Government have accepted that this law currently fails to provide adequate protection to children and should be amended.

In the circumstances of the present case, the failure to provide adequate protection constitutes a violation of Article 3 of the Convention."

Notes

1. The Court decided that in view of its finding in respect of Article 3, that it was not necessary to **8.24** examine "whether the inadequacy of the legal protection provided to A. against the ill-treatment that he suffered also breached his right to respect for private life under Article 8" (para. 28). Since the applicant accepted the Commission's finding of no violation of Article 13 of the Convention and did not pursue his claim under Article 14 of the Convention taken in conjunction with Articles 3 and/or 8 the Court did not think it necessary to consider these complaints (paras 29–30). The Court awarded the applicant £10,000 compensation in respect of non-pecuniary damage.

2. The decision in this case can be read as holding that the defence of reasonable chastisement is inconsistent with the rights of the child, in the sense that it prevents the state from effectively protecting the child from severe punishment. It is probably more correct, however, to read it as stating that if parental chastisement is permitted, then the state must ensure that punishment which is inhuman and degrading cannot be regarded legally as reasonable chastisement.

3. The Scottish Executive has proposed that the law should make it clear, by express provision, that physical punishment which constitutes 'inhuman and degrading treatment' can never be justified as 'reasonable chastisement'. They have also proposed that the law should explicitly set out that, in considering whether or not the physical punishment of a child constitutes reasonable chastisement, a Court should always have regard to (a) the nature and context of the treatment, (b) its duration and frequency, (c) its physical and mental effects, and, in some instances (d) the sex, age and state of health of the victim. (Scottish Executive Justice Department, *The Physical Punishment of Children in Scotland—A Consultation*, February 2000, p. 17.) Whether such legislative provisions would effect any significant change in the interpretation of lawful chastisement must, however, be open to question in view of the existing principles of the law.

4. More radical suggestions for limiting the punishment of children were proposed by the Scottish Law Commission (*Report on Family Law*, Scot. Law. Com. No. 135 (1992)). There the Commission proposed that the defence of reasonable chastisement should not be available where the child was struck with an object, struck in such a way as to cause, or risk causing, injury, or struck in such a way as to cause, or risk causing, pain or discomfort lasting more than a very short time. The Scottish Executive has sought views on whether there are forms of punishment which should never be considered as 'reasonable', including blows to the head, shaking children, using implements such as canes, belts and slippers and the physical punishment of very young children.

# B. Consent

### Smart v. H.M. Advocate
1975 S.L.T. 65

The appellant and another man agreed to have a "square-go" during the course of which the **8.25** appellant inflicted a number of injuries on the other party. He was charged with assault, and in his defence he claimed (a) that since the other party had consented to the fight he could not be convicted of assault, and (b) that his actings were in self-defence. The jury were directed that consent could not provide a defence to the charge, and the appellant was convicted. He presented an application for leave to appeal against conviction.

Opinion of the Court: "The applicant was found guilty by a majority verdict of the Jury of a charge of assault. The charge libelled was that he assaulted Isaac Wilkie, kicked him on the private parts, punched and kicked him about the head and body, pulled out his hair and bit him on the left arm to his injury.

The argument in support of the application proceeded on the basis that the applicant had invited Wilkie to have a 'square go' and that Wilkie consented to this. There was evidence, said to be disputed by the applicant, that Wilkie had been invited on several occasions to have a 'square go' before he finally consented. It is not necessary, in our view, to have regard to this allegation to determine the issues canvassed before us.

Two lines of defence were submitted at the trial. The first was that since Wilkie had consented to fight with the applicant the latter could not be guilty of assault in respect of his actions in that combat by consent. The second was that since the applicant had tabled a special defence of self-defence, that special defence should have gone to the jury. Normally it could only be determined on the evidence whether such a direction was justified, but as this case was presented it appeared that the self-defence founded on was simply that the applicant was participating in an agreed-upon fight and that anything he did was done either to get the better of his opponent or to defend himself against the attack of his opponent. In the course of his charge to the jury the presiding sheriff refused to give effect to these submissions. These arguments were repeated by counsel for the applicant at the hearing of the application. For support of his first contention, based on the parties' consent to fight, counsel said that there was a complete dearth of authority, and he relied principally on a passage in Gordon's *Criminal Law*, at p. 774, where the learned author says: 'If A and B decide to fight each other they cannot be guilty of assaulting each other, so long as neither exceeds the degree of violence consented to or permitted by law.' The author then goes on to say: 'Where the assault does not involve another crime the position appears to be that consent is a good defence provided that not more than a certain degree of injury is caused (*R. v. Donovan* [1934] 2 K.B. 498). What that degree is undecided and unknown. Consent is not a defence to the charge of murder (*H.M. Advocate v. Rutherford*, 1947 J.C. 1, 1947 S.L.T. 3), and the ratio of *H.M. Advocate v. Rutherford*, that the attitude of the victim is irrelevant, was applied in the unreported case of *Ian Gordon Purvis* (1964) to exclude a defence of consent in a charge of an assault with a knife to the danger of the victim's life. But it is submitted that consent is a defence to minor assaults whether inflicted for sexual, sporting or other purposes.' We have quoted these passages at length because they represent in effect the argument presented by the applicant's counsel. Leaving aside the question of what constitutes a minor assault, the apparent contradiction in the two passages quoted, and whether the *ejusdem generis* rule applies to his illustrations, we are of the opinion that the conclusion which Professor Gordon reaches and the submission which he makes are wrong.

An assault is an attack on the person of another. Evil intention is of the essence of assault—Macdonald's *Criminal Law* (5th ed.) p. 115. This was reiterated by Lord Justice-Clerk Cooper (as he then was) in *H.M. Advocate v. Rutherford* (*supra*) at p. 6. That is what the presiding sheriff said in the present case. Lord Cooper said that consent was not a defence in a case of murder or culpable homicide. In this he was following the view of Baron Hume in his treatise, *Crimes*, Vol. i, at p. 230. This view was followed in *Purvis* (*supra*) in regard to an assault with a knife to the danger of life. Is there any justification for applying this line of authority to serious assaults but not to minor assaults? In our opinion there is not. Apart from the obvious difficulty of knowing where to draw the line there is nothing in principle to justify the distinction. If there is an attack on the other person and it is done with evil intent, that is, intent to injure and do bodily harm, then, in our view, the fact that the person attacked was willing to undergo the risk of that attack does not prevent it from being the crime of assault. If A touches B in a sexual manner and B consents to him doing so (and there is nothing else involved which would constitute a crime under statute or at common law) there is no assault because there is no evil intention to attack the person of B. So, too, if persons engage in sporting activities governed by rules, then, although some form of violence may be involved within the rules, there is no assault because the intention is to engage in the sporting activity and not evilly to do harm to the opponent. But where the whole purpose of the exercise is to inflict physical damage on the opponent in pursuance of a quarrel, then the evil intent is present, and consent is elided. This view consists with the English view as expressed by Swift, J., in giving the judgment of the court in *R. v. Donovan* (*supra*), at p. 506 *et seq*. This was recognised in the case of duelling when the intention of the participants was to kill the opponent, and we see no reason why it should be different when the duellists have the evil intent of inflicting physical injury on the opponent.

In the circumstances of this case as explained to us we are of the opinion that the sheriff was fully justified in directing the jury that there was no relevant evidence to support the plea of self defence. It is, accordingly, unnecessary for us to consider the broader question of whether self-defence could ever be a defence in the case of a combat which started by consent.

The applicant's counsel sought to invoke a further argument from the civil law and submitted that the *maxim volenti non fit injuria* should apply to a case like this and result in an acquittal. In our view, the reasons for rejecting consent as a defence equally dispose of this submission. It follows that the criticisms of the directions in law given by the presiding sheriff in the circumstances of this case are not well-founded and that the application must be refused.

Before parting with the case we wish to make one final observation. It is said that the consent was to have a 'square go'. There is no definition, classical or otherwise, of the phrase, and it seems unlikely that any normal person would consent to a fight which could legitimately involve what is contained in the charge, but for the purposes of the argument we accepted that Wilkie did so. We are only too aware of the prevalence of what is alleged to be a 'square go' in one form or another, often leading to serious results. Accordingly, apart from the private interests involved in this case, it is in the public interest that it should be decided and made known that consent to a 'square go' is not a defence to a charge of assault based on that agreed combat."

Application refused.

## NOTES

1. The difficulties associated with this decision are legion. For a general consideration of the problems **8.26** which it provokes, see Gordon, "Consent in Assault" (1976) 21 J.L.S. 168. See also the discussion of consent in relation to sexual offences, Chap. 9, *post*.

2. Suppose that A and B agree that in order to settle their differences they will have a boxing match, rather than a fight in the car park of the pub. They agree that the fight will be properly conducted according to recognised rules and with an independent referee. A breaks B's nose and knocks him out. Can it be said that "there is no assault because the intention is to engage in the sporting activity and not evilly to do harm to the opponent", or is this a case in which "the whole purpose of the exercise is to inflict physical damage on the opponent in pursuance of a quarrel" in which evil intent is present and consent is elided?

At what point in a sporting activity does "evil intent" take over from an intention to engage in the sporting activity? A certain degree of violence is a part of many games such as rugby, football and even cricket. Suppose, for example, that the bowler in a cricket match bowls with the intention of intimidating his opponent, but bowls within the rules of the game. Is he guilty of assaulting the opponent if one of his balls hits the opponent (or even if it does not, as, for example, where the opponent is put in fear for his safety)? The answer to that question may, of course, be that there is no "evil intent" since there is no intention to injure.

3. In England it appears that one may consent to an assault, provided that actual bodily harm is neither intended nor caused: *Attorney-General's Reference (No. 6 of 1980)* [1981] 2 All E.R. 1057. Consent to greater degrees of harm is only effective in certain socially approved situations, and where the injuries are inflicted "for no good reason" the consent of the victim is irrelevant. The great difficulty with this approach, however, is to determine what are and what are not "good reasons" for inflicting injury on another person. It is clear that therapeutic medical operations are lawful and, as was pointed out by Lord Templeman in *R. v. Brown* [1993] 2 All E.R.75, at p. 79b "[O]ther activities carried on with consent by or on behalf of the injured person have been accepted as lawful notwithstanding that they involve actual bodily harm or may cause serious bodily harm. Ritual circumcision, tattooing, ear-piercing and violent sports including boxing are lawful activities."

4. But clearly similar (or even less serious) injuries are unlawful if the context in which they are inflicted is not socially (that is to say, judicially?) approved. In *R. v. Brown*, (*supra*) the applicants engaged in consensual sado-masochistic practices with each other, and with other men, from which they derived sexual gratification. Although their activities involved maltreatment of the genitalia with a variety of implements, beatings and brandings, which on occasion led to the flow of blood and scarring, they did not lead to any instances of infection, permanent injury or the need for medical attention. The applicants' activities became known to the police and they were charged with assault occasioning actual bodily harm and unlawful wounding, contrary to sections 47 and 20 of the Offences Against the Person Act 1861. At their trial the applicants pleaded guilty to the assault charges when the judge ruled that they could not rely on the consent of the "victims" as an answer to the prosecution case. The applicants were sentenced to periods of imprisonment. These were reduced on appeal, but the convictions were

upheld by the Court of Appeal and, ultimately, by the House of Lords which held that assault occasioning actual bodily harm and wounding were criminal notwithstanding the consent of the "victim".

6. That decision may be contrasted with the case of *Wilson (Alan)*, [1996] 2 Cr.App.R. 241 in which it was held that the appellant should not have been convicted of assault occasioning actual bodily harm when he branded his initials on his wife's buttocks with her consent. The instant case differed from the circumstances revealed in *Brown*, which concerned sado-masochism, and torture. There was also a risk of serious injury. Here, all that the appellant had done, in the view of the court, was to assist his wife in acquiring a desired physical adornment, and it was not easy to distinguish this logically from a tattoo. (See also *Emmett*, Court of Appeal, Criminal Division, June 18, 1999, *unreported*).

5. A number of the unsuccessful appellants in *Brown* claimed that their prosecution and conviction interfered with their privacy rights under Article 8(1) of the European Convention on Human Rights.

### Laskey, Jaggard and Brown v. United Kingdom
### (1997) 24 E.H.R.R. 39

(For the background to this case, see *supra.*)

**8.27**    The applicants complained to the European Commission on Human Rights that their convictions resulted from an unforeseeable application of a provision of the criminal law in violation of Article 7 of the European Convention on Human Rights which, in any event, amounted to an unlawful and unjustifiable interference with their right to respect for their private life, contrary to Article 8 of the Convention. The Commission held the application admissible only under Article 8, and expressed the view that there had been no violation of that provision.

OPINION OF THE COURT:

**8.28**    "35. The applicants contended that their prosecution and convictions for assault and wounding in the course of consensual sado-masochistic activities between adults was in breach of Article 8 of the Convention, which provides:

> "1. Everyone has the right to respect for his private and family life, his home and his correspondence.
> 2. There shall be no interference by a public authority with the exercise of this right except such as is in accordance with the law and is necessary in a democratic society in the interests of national security, public safety or the economic well-being of the country, for the prevention of disorder or crime, for the protection of health or morals, or for the protection of the rights and freedoms of others."

It was common ground among those appearing before the Court that the criminal proceedings against the applicants which resulted in their conviction constituted an "interference by a public authority" with the applicants' right to respect for their private life. It was similarly undisputed that the interference had been "in accordance with the law". Furthermore, the Commission and the applicants accepted the Government's assertion that the interference pursued the legitimate aim of the "protection of health or morals", within the meaning of the second paragraph of Article 8.

36. The Court observes that not every sexual activity carried out behind closed doors necessarily falls within the scope of Article 8. In the present case, the applicants were involved in consensual sado-masochistic activities for purposes of sexual gratification. There can be no doubt that sexual orientation and activity concern an intimate aspect of private life (see, *mutatis mutandis*, the *Dudgeon v. United Kingdom* judgment of October 22, 1981, Series A no. 45, p. 21, §52). However, a considerable number of people were involved in the activities in question which included, *inter alia*, the recruitment of new "members", the provision of several specially-equipped "chambers", and the shooting of many video-tapes which were

distributed among the "members" .... It may thus be open to question whether the sexual activities of the applicants fell entirely within the notion of "private life" in the particular circumstances of the case.

However, since this point has not been disputed by those appearing before it, the Court sees no reason to examine it of its own motion in the present case. Assuming, therefore, that the prosecution and conviction of the applicants amounted to an interference with their private life, the question arises whether such an interference was "necessary in a democratic society" within the meaning of the second paragraph of Article 8.

"Necessary in a democratic society"

37. The applicants maintained that the interference at issue could not be regarded as "necessary in a democratic society". This submission was contested by the Government and by a majority of the Commission.

38. In support of their submission, the applicants alleged that all those involved in the sado-masochistic encounters were willing adult participants; that participation in the acts complained of was carefully restricted and controlled and was limited to persons with like-minded sado-masochistic proclivities; that the acts were not witnessed by the public at large and that there was no danger or likelihood that they would ever be so witnessed; that no serious or permanent injury had been sustained, no infection had been caused to the wounds, and that no medical treatment had been required. Furthermore, no complaint was ever made to the police—who learnt about the applicants' activities by chance ....

The potential for severe injury or for moral corruption was regarded by the applicants as a matter of speculation. To the extent that issues of public morality had arisen—with reference to Mr Laskey's conviction for keeping a disorderly house and for the possession of an indecent photograph of a child (see paragraph 11 above)—these had been dealt with under the relevant sexual offences provisions and appropriately punished. In any event, such issues fell outside the scope of the case as presented before the Court.

39. The applicants submitted that their case should be viewed as one involving matters of sexual expression, rather than violence. With due regard to this consideration, the line beyond which consent is no defence to physical injury should only be drawn at the level of intentional or reckless causing of serious disabling injury.

40. For the Government, the State was entitled to punish acts of violence, such as those for which the applicants were convicted, that could not be considered of a trifling or transient nature, irrespective of the consent of the victim. In fact, in the present case, some of these acts could well be compared to "genital torture" and a Contracting State could not be said to have an obligation to tolerate acts of torture because they are committed in the context of a consenting sexual relationship. The State was moreover entitled to prohibit activities because of their potential danger.

The Government further contended that the criminal law should seek to deter certain forms of behaviour on public health grounds but also for broader moral reasons. In this respect, acts of torture—such as those at issue in the present case— may be banned also on the ground that they undermine the respect which human beings should confer upon each other. In any event, the whole issue of the role of consent in the criminal law is of great complexity and the Contracting States should enjoy a wide margin of appreciation to consider all the public policy options.

41. The Commission noted that the injuries that were or could be caused by the applicants' activities were of a significant nature and degree, and that the conduct in question was, on any view, of an extreme character. The State authorities therefore acted within their margin of appreciation in order to protect its citizens from real risk of serious physical harm or injury.

42. According to the Court's established case-law, the notion of necessity implies that the interference corresponds to a pressing social need and, in particular, that it is proportionate to the legitimate aim pursued; in determining whether an interference is "necessary in a democratic society", the Court will take into account that a margin of appreciation is left to the national authorities (see, inter alia, the *Olsson v. Sweden (No. 1)* judgment of March 24,

1988, Series A no. 130, pp. 31–32, §67), whose decision remains subject to review by the Court for conformity with the requirements of the Convention.

The scope of this margin of appreciation is not identical in each case but will vary according to the context. Relevant factors include the nature of the Convention right in issue, its importance for the individual and the nature of the activities concerned (see the *Buckley v. United Kingdom* judgment of September 25, 1996, [23 E.H.R.R. 101] §74).

43. The Court considers that one of the roles which the State is unquestionably entitled to undertake is to seek to regulate, through the operation of the criminal law, activities which involve the infliction of physical harm. This is so whether the activities in question occur in the course of sexual conduct or otherwise.

44. The determination of the level of harm that should be tolerated by the law in situations where the victim consents is in the first instance a matter for the State concerned since what is at stake is related, on the one hand, to public health considerations and to the general deterrent effect of the criminal law, and, on the other, to the personal autonomy of the individual.

45. The applicants have contended that, in the circumstances of the case, the behaviour in question formed part of private morality which is not the State's business to regulate. In their submission the matters for which they were prosecuted and convicted concerned only private sexual behaviour.

The Court is not persuaded by this submission. It is evident from the facts established by the national courts that the applicants' sado-masochistic activities involved a significant degree of injury or wounding which could not be characterised as trifling or transient. This, in itself, suffices to distinguish the present case from those applications which have previously been examined by the Court concerning consensual homosexual behaviour in private between adults where no such feature was present (see the *Dudgeon v. United Kingdom* judgment cited above, the *Norris v. Ireland* judgment of October 26, 1988, Series A no. 142, and the *Modinos v. Cyprus* judgment of April 22, 1993, Series A no. 259).

46. Nor does the Court accept the applicants' submission that no prosecution should have been brought against them since their injuries were not severe and since no medical treatment had been required.

In deciding whether or not to prosecute, the State authorities were entitled to have regard not only to the actual seriousness of the harm caused—which as noted above was considered to be significant—but also, as stated by Lord Jauncey of Tullichettle ... to the potential for harm inherent in the acts in question. In this respect it is recalled that the activities were considered by Lord Templeman to be "unpredictably dangerous" ....

47. The applicants have further submitted that they were singled out partly because of the authorities' bias against homosexuals. They referred to the recent judgment in the *Wilson* case ... where, in their view, similar behaviour in the context of a heterosexual couple was not considered to deserve criminal punishment.

The Court finds no evidence in support of the applicants' allegations in either the conduct of the proceedings against them or the judgment of the House of Lords. In this respect it recalls the remark of the trial judge when passing sentence that "the unlawful conduct now before the court would be dealt with equally in the prosecution of heterosexuals or bisexuals if carried out by them" ....

Moreover, it is clear from the judgment of the House of Lords that the opinions of the majority were based on the extreme nature of the practices involved and not the sexual proclivities of the applicants ....

In any event, like the Court of Appeal, the Court does not consider that the facts in the *Wilson* case were at all comparable in seriousness to those in the present case ....

48. Accordingly, the Court considers that the reasons given by the national authorities for the measures taken in respect of the applicants were relevant and sufficient for the purposes of Article 8 §2.

49. It remains to be ascertained whether these measures were proportionate to the legitimate aim or aims pursued.

The Court notes that the charges of assault were numerous and referred to illegal activities which had taken place over more than ten years. However, only a few charges were selected for inclusion in the prosecution case. It further notes that, in recognition of the fact that the applicants did not appreciate their actions to be criminal, reduced sentences were imposed on appeal (see paragraphs 15–17 above). In these circumstances, bearing in mind the degree of organisation involved in the offences, the measures taken against the applicants cannot be regarded as disproportionate.

50. In sum, the Court finds that the national authorities were entitled to consider that the prosecution and conviction of the applicants were necessary in a democratic society for the protection of health within the meaning of Article 8 §2 of the Convention.

51. In view of this conclusion the Court, like the Commission, does not find it necessary to determine whether the interference with the applicants' right to respect for private life could also be justified on the ground of the protection of morals. This finding, however, should not be understood as calling into question the prerogative of the State on moral grounds to seek to deter acts of the kind in question.

FOR THESE REASONS, THE COURT UNANIMOUSLY:

Holds that there has been no violation of Article 8 of the Convention.

CONCURRING OPINION OF JUDGE PETTITI:

I concurred with all my colleagues in finding that there had been no violation of Article 8 of the Convention. However, my reasoning differs from theirs in some respects.

Firstly, the Court implicitly accepted that Article 8 was applicable since it assumed there had been an interference, and the application referred to State interference under Article 8— "the institution of criminal proceedings infringed that Article".

In my view, that Article was not even applicable in the instant case. The concept of private life cannot be stretched indefinitely.

Not every aspect of private life automatically qualifies for protection under the Convention. The fact that the behaviour concerned takes place on private premises does not suffice to ensure complete immunity and impunity. Not everything that happens behind closed doors is necessarily acceptable. It is already the case in criminal law that the "rape" of a spouse where there is doubt whether consent was given may lead to prosecution. Other types of behaviour may give rise to civil proceedings (internal telephone-tapping for example). Sexual acts and abuse, even when not criminal, give rise to liability. ...

The dangers of unrestrained permissiveness, which can lead to debauchery, paedophilia or the torture of others, were highlighted at the Stockholm World Conference (cf. paragraph 11 of the judgment). The protection of private life means the protection of a person's intimacy and dignity, not the protection of his baseness or the promotion of criminal immoralism.

NOTES

1. There is an important difference between the approach of the majority and that of Judge Pettiti. **8.29** While the majority considered that there had been an interference with the applicants' private lives (albeit rather doubtfully, see para. 36), but that the state's interference was justified, judge Petiti's view was that the applicants' activities were not embraced by paragraph 1 of Article 8. Is what took part in *Wilson* protected by article 8?

2. That it was not the applicants' sexual orientation, but the nature of the activities in which they indulged that was objectionable is substantially confirmed by the decision of the Court in *A.D.T. v. United Kingdom*, (2000) 9 B.H.R.C. 112, *post*, Chap. 9.

# C. Provocation

The principles governing provocation in assault are in some ways similar to those governing provocation **8.30** in homicide (see Chapter 10, *post* and *H.M. Advocate v. Callander*, 1958 S.L.T. 24, *infra*). There are, however, some important differences. The first is that verbal insults may constitute provocation in cases of assault, where this is not the case in homicide: *Thomson v. H.M. Advocate*, 1985 S.C.C.R. 448, *post*, p. 419 (but see also *Berry v. H.M. Advocate* (1976) S.C.C.R. Supp. 156, discussed *post*, p. 422 and *Stobbs v. H.M. Advocate*, 1983 S.C.C.R. 190, discussed *post*, p. 422). On verbal provocation in assault, see Hume, i, 333, Alison, 1, 176 177 and Gordon, para. 29–46.

The second difference may relate to the effect of the plea in provocation. In *Hillan v. H.M. Advocate*, 1937 J.C. 53, it was suggested that provocation could provide a complete defence. This case was subjected to severe criticism in *Crawford v. H.M. Advocate*, 1950 J.C. 67, but was not expressly over-ruled. The distinction between the exculpatory plea of self-defence and the plea of provocation was authoritatively restated in *Fenning v. H.M. Advocate*, 1985 S.L.T. 514, but only in the context of the law relating to homicide. Technically, the question remains open, but it is accepted today that the effect of provocation in assault is merely to mitigate the penalty imposed in the event of provocation. (See, in this regard, *Drury v. H.M. Advocate*, High Court of Justiciary, February 2, 2001, *unreported*, *post*, p. 407.)

## H.M. Advocate v. Callander
### 1958 S.L.T. 24

**8.31** The accused was charged with assaulting his wife and another woman to their severe injury. Evidence was led to the effect that the assault was committed under provocation when the accused discovered his wife and the other woman engaging in lesbian practices. In the course of his charge to the jury, the presiding judge gave the following directions on provocation:

LORD GUTHRIE: [After dealing with other matters] "The next question which we have to consider together is this: Are the circumstances disclosed in evidence today such as would reasonably entitle you on a certain view of the facts to hold that they amounted to provocation? You heard the story told by the accused of the unhappy circumstances of his married life after 1955, after his wife had formed her association with Mrs O'Neill and had indulged with Mrs O'Neill in those unnatural practices between females to which the name of Lesbianism has been given. Ladies and gentlemen, if a husband discovers his wife in the act of adultery or if a husband learns of his wife's adultery and immediately or shortly thereafter inflicts blows upon his wife, her conduct would amount to provocation. Lesbianism is not adultery, but I do not think that anyone would hold that it is a less serious infringement of the duty of a wife than adultery is, and consequently if you are satisfied that the husband's actions were influenced by the discovery of his wife under circumstances which indicated that she was pursuing her course of Lesbianism with Mrs O'Neill, that would entitle you to form the opinion that he assaulted her and Mrs O'Neill under provocation. I want to add to that, however, that the mere fact the Lesbianism was the unfortunate background to this married life would not of itself amount to provocation because, if a husband has known of his wife's adultery or of her unnatural conduct and does not act under the immediate impulse of his discovery, then, if he assaults her later that is not an act under provocation, but one of revenge, and if you thought that the accused here was not acting under the influence of the discovery of his wife in a compromising situation with Mrs O'Neill, but was merely acting under the influence of what he had known for a long time, then that would not amount to provocation."

NOTES

**8.32** *Cf. H M. Advocate v. Hill*, 1941 J.C. 59 and *McDermott v. H.M. Advocate*, 1974 S.L.T. 206. *Cf.* English law which maintains that it is only in murder that provocation may operate to reduce the quality of an offence. Thus it cannot operate to reduce a charge of malicious wounding (*Cunningham* [1959] 1 Q.B. 288) or even attempted murder (*Bruzas* [1972] Crim.L.R. 367).

## 4. RECKLESS INJURY AND RECKLESS ENDANGERMENT

As has been pointed out (*ante*, pp. 282–288) assault cannot be committed recklessly or negligently. **8.33** Recklessly injuring another, or recklessly endangering the safety of others are not, however, beyond the reach of the criminal law. At one time, it was thought that reckless conduct was only criminal where it was libelled to be "to the danger of the lieges": *Quinn v. Cunningham*, 1956 J.C. 22. But that view was departed from in the following Full Bench case.

## A. The *actus reus* of reckless injury

### H.M. Advocate v. Harris
#### 1993 S.L.T. 963

The accused, a bouncer at a discotheque, was charged with assaulting a young woman to her **8.34** severe injury and permanent disfigurement by seizing hold of her, pushing her on the body and causing her to fall down a flight of stairs and onto the roadway as a result of which she was struck by a motor vehicle. The indictment also libelled an alternative charge to the effect that the accused culpably, wilfully and recklessly seized hold of his victim and did all of the acts libelled in the assault charge to her severe injury and permanent disfigurement. The accused objected to the relevancy of the alternative charge on the ground that it did not disclose a crime known to the law of Scotland. At a preliminary diet the sheriff sustained the objection and dismissed the alternative charge. The Crown appealed, contending that reckless conduct resulting in actual injury constituted a crime and that it was not essential that the conduct be to the danger of the lieges. The accused argued that the alternative charge was merely a duplication of the assault charge. The Lord Justice-Clerk (Lord Ross), along with Lords Murray, Morison and Prosser, rejected this view. Lord McCluskey dissented.

THE LORD JUSTICE-CLERK (ROSS): "... In opening the appeal, the Lord Advocate explained that the respondent was what is commonly called a bouncer or steward at a discotheque, and as such was expected to exercise control over persons frequenting such an establishment; in particular it had to be recognised that on occasions in the course of his duties a bouncer might find it necessary to seize and take hold of those frequenting the premises with a view to removing them therefrom. The sheriff had upheld the plea to relevancy upon the view that *Quinn v. Cunningham* laid down that reckless conduct was not a crime at common law unless it was libelled to be "to the danger of the lieges". That was not libelled in the alternative charge in this indictment, and accordingly on the authority of *Quinn v. Cunningham*, the sheriff had sustained the plea to relevancy. The Lord Advocate submitted that it was not necessary in all cases to libel danger to the lieges; reckless conduct would be criminal if it was libelled either as being to the danger of the lieges or as having resulted in actual injury. He referred to a number of cases where charges had been held to be relevant on the basis that the reckless conduct in question had caused actual injury.

In *Ezekiel McHaffie*, a case of careless navigation of a ship was allowed to go to a jury where the accused was charged with "recklessly managing or directing a vessel or steampacket, so as to cause it to run down, sink and destroy another boat or vessel, thereby seriously wounding and injuring the person of a man sailing in such boat or vessel". In *H.M. Advocate v. Latto* (1857) 2 Irv. 732, a railway signalman pled guilty to a charge of culpable violation of duty in consequence of which an accident happened and several persons were injured. In *H.M. Advocate v. Robert Young* (1839) 2 Swin. 376, a plea to relevancy was taken of a charge which libelled "culpable and reckless neglect of duty by a workman in the management or use of machinery or mechanical apparatus whereby lives were lost or bodily injuries suffered or the safety of the lieges put in danger". The plea was taken upon the ground that it was not relevant to libel merely that the safety of the lieges was put in danger, because in order to constitute a crime, there must be a result produced or intended. The court recommended that the words "or the safety of the lieges put in danger" should be struck out of the indictment, and that was done. This case is accordingly clear authority for the view that culpable and reckless conduct which causes actual injury is criminal. In *Smith and McNeil* (1842) 1 Broun 240 a charge of wickedly, recklessly and culpably discharging loaded firearms into an inhabited house to the imminent danger of the lives of the persons within the house was held to be a relevant charge. The Lord Justice-Clerk observed that to make a relevant charge of reckless conduct it was not necessary to show that there had been actual injury to a person. The Lord Advocate contended that these cases showed that reckless conduct resulting in actual injury would constitute a crime by the law of Scotland. The Lord Advocate also referred to Macdonald, *Criminal Law of Scotland* (5th ed.), pp 141–142. The view appears to be accepted that reckless conduct to the danger of the lieges is criminal, and that such offences are "more heinous when injury results to the lieges". The learned editors add: "In other cases, in order to make a relevant charge of danger to the lieges, it may be necessary to specify that injury resulted to some of them."

I agree with the Lord Advocate that these authorities support the proposition that reckless conduct which results in injury constitutes a crime under the law of Scotland. There was no dispute before this court regarding that, and indeed senior counsel for the respondent expressly accepted that reckless conduct causing injury was a crime under our law. That being so, I see no need to embark on any detailed analysis of the theories which may be thought to justify the law being what I have held it to be, particularly when no detailed arguments were presented to us on that matter.

In *Quinn v. Cunningham,* the accused was charged on a summary complaint with riding a pedal cycle in a reckless manner and causing it to collide with a pedestrian and injure both parties. The court held that as the conduct was not libelled as being "to the danger of the lieges" the complaint was irrelevant. In the course of delivering his opinion the Lord Justice General described the charge as consisting of two separate parts, "firstly riding a pedal cycle in a reckless manner, and secondly causing it to collide with someone whereby slight injury resulted". For myself I would have thought that the proper way to read the charge was that it libelled riding a pedal cycle recklessly so that it collided with a pedestrian and injured him. However that may be, the Lord Justice General went on to say (at 1956 S.L.T., p. 57): "As the law stands therefore this complaint can only be relevant if it libels that degree of recklessness which constitutes the crime at common law, that is to say a recklessness so high as to involve an indifference to the consequences for the public generally."

After citing a passage from the Lord Justice General in *McAllister v. Abercrombie* (1907) 15 S.L.T. 70, Lord Justice General Clyde said: "Judged by this standard the present complaint fails to satisfy what is required, for the words 'to the danger of the lieges' as a qualification of the recklessness, are not libelled in this complaint. It charges the appellant therefore with a degree of recklessness which does not constitute a crime."

It is thus clear that Lord Justice General Clyde was holding that in order to make a relevant charge of reckless conduct, it was necessary to libel that the conduct had been "to the danger of the lieges". He went on to say: "Mere recklessness by a pedal cyclist followed by an injury to a foot passenger does not constitute a crime in Scotland, any more than mere recklessness by driving followed by death would constitute culpable homicide". He added: "In the present case the injury to the foot passenger is in no way connected up with the recklessness, and is not libelled as an element of that recklessness."

Lord Sorn had some doubt as to whether the charge did not disclose riding a bicycle recklessly to the danger of the lieges, although the words "to the danger of the lieges" did not appear.

In my opinion, since there is ample authority for the view that reckless conduct causing injury is a crime by the law of Scotland, the case of *Quinn v. Cunningham* is an unsatisfactory decision. Insofar as it supports the proposition that it is not enough for the Crown to libel reckless conduct causing actual injury, I am of opinion that it was wrongly decided. Insofar as *Quinn v. Cunningham* supports the proposition that it is necessary in all cases to aver reckless conduct "to the danger of the lieges" I am also of opinion that it was wrongly decided. In my judgment there are two ways in which reckless conduct may become criminal. Reckless conduct to the danger of the lieges will constitute a crime in Scotland, and so too will reckless conduct which has caused actual injury. Being satisfied that it was wrongly decided in these respects, I would move your Lordships to overrule *Quinn v. Cunningham*.

The relevancy of the charge was challenged upon another ground. Senior counsel for the respondent maintained that the respondent was being charged with the same crime in both the principal charge and the alternative. He appreciated that in the principal charge the respondent is said to have assaulted the complainer and seized hold of her and pushed her on the body and caused her to fall, whereas in the second charge he is libelled to have culpably, wilfully and recklessly seized hold of the complainer, pushed her on the body and caused her to fall. He submitted that both charges libelled assault and that it did not matter that the word "assault" did not appear in the alternative charge because it was not necessary in any indictment to specify by any nomen juris the crime which was charged provided that the indictment set forth facts relevant and sufficient to constitute an indictable crime (section 44 of the Act of 1975). The alternative charge was a charge of assault. There was no need for the Crown to have included the words "wilfully" or "culpably and recklessly" as these words would be implied in a charge of this nature (section 48 of the Act of 1975). In both the principal charge and the alternative charge precisely the same conduct on the part of the respondent was averred. Senior counsel further explained that the defence to both charges would be that the respondent had been carrying out his ordinary duties as a bouncer, and lacked the *mens rea* necessary for assault.

The Lord Advocate accepted that the words "culpably" and "wilfully" added nothing to the alternative charge and were superfluous. He also accepted that if the respondent had merely been acting carelessly, that would not be sufficient to render his conduct criminal. He did submit however that the Crown were entitled to libel these alternative charges. If the Crown did not succeed in establishing that the appellant had the necessary *mens rea* for assault, they might still be able to show that he had been guilty of reckless conduct which had caused injury.

I have come to the conclusion that the argument of the Lord Advocate is to be preferred. I appreciate that both the principal charge and the alternative charge libel precisely the same conduct on the part of the respondent, but in my opinion a different *mens rea* is required for each charge. As Sheriff Gordon points out in his Criminal Law (2nd ed.), para. 29–30: "Assault is a crime of intent and cannot be committed recklessly or negligently."

"Evil intention being of the essence of assault, it differs from culpable homicide in so far as injuries happening from carelessness, however culpable, are not assaults" (Macdonald, *Criminal Law of Scotland* (5th ed.), p. 115).

The law draws a distinction between intent and recklessness (*H.M. Advocate v. Phipps*, (1905) 4 Adam 616, *ante*, p. 282). Accordingly, I am satisfied that the charges truly are alternatives. It will be for the jury to determine whether the accused acted in the manner described in the indictment, and if that is established, then although the accused was acting as a bouncer, the jury may conclude that when he seized hold of the complainer and pulled her, he had the intent necessary for assault; alternatively they may conclude that he lacked the intent necessary for assault but had displayed recklessness which caused her to fall and sustain injury. Of course, if the Crown fail to establish that the accused acted in the manner libelled or that he had the *mens rea* required for either of the alternative charges, they will acquit the accused. I would not anticipate that a sheriff would have any difficulty in giving a jury comprehensible directions in relation to this indictment. In my opinion a jury which has received proper directions should be well able to understand the difference between the alternative charges.

The sheriff sustained the preliminary plea and dismissed the alternative charge on the basis of *Quinn v. Cunningham* which was of course binding upon him. As I have already indicated, in my opinion the alternative charge in this indictment is a relevant charge. I would accordingly move your Lordships to sustain this appeal, to reverse the decision of the sheriff dated September 23, 1992 and to remit to the sheriff to proceed as accords."

LORD MCCLUSKEY (*dissenting*): "... From that discussion of the first charge, I now turn to the so-called alternative charge. What it does is to set forth precisely the same averments of fact without, however, any specification of a nomen juris. What it also does, however, is to use a number of familiar adverbs, namely "culpably, wilfully and recklessly". As to these adverbs, it may be marked that when this case was first indicted the alternative charge did not contain the word "wilfully". Further, the Lord Advocate submitted to this court that the words "culpably" and "wilfully" added nothing at all to the charge and it would, he submitted, be a relevant charge if they were simply omitted. He also acknowledged that all these words, whether expressly included or not, were implied into the charge by virtue of s.48 which provides, *inter alia*: "It shall not be necessary in any indictment to allege that any act of commission or omission therein charged was done or omitted to be done 'wilfully' or ... 'culpably and recklessly' ... or to use any similar words or expressions qualifying any act charged, but such qualifying allegation shall be implied in every case."

The express inclusion in the alternative charge of these adverbs seems to me to risk obfuscating and confusing the issue because, in the context of the averments of fact, the word "wilfully" is quite contradictory of the word "recklessly"; and the role of the word "culpably" is wholly obscure because it contradicts "wilfully" and is, in effect, no more than a milder version of "recklessly". However, the Lord Advocate submitted that what was really being averred was that the specified acts were recklessly done and that to do such acts recklessly whether to the danger of the lieges or to the actual injury of one of them (as here) was to commit an indictable crime. He gave us examples of indictable crimes of this character. Senior counsel for the respondent conceded that certain kinds of reckless conduct causing injury or danger to the lieges would constitute an indictable crime. This concession was, in my opinion, properly given, and like your Lordships I am content to accept it and need not here reiterate the examination of the case law on this matter by your Lordship in the chair and Lord Prosser. In certain circumstances, reckless conduct which causes injury or endangers the lieges may well constitute an indictable crime. For that reason alone, I have no difficulty in agreeing with your Lordships that the reasoning of the Lord Justice General in *Quinn v. Cunningham* is not supportable in the light of the full citation of authority which we were privileged to have.

But, and this I consider to be an essential point, what is averred in the alternative charge in the present case is a series of facts that do not constitute the crime of assault: otherwise the alternative charge would be a mere duplication of the first charge and the indictment would then be incompetent. So if it is not assault which is charged in the alternative, what is it? It is said to be—and it would have to be—something less than assault. The Lord Advocate acknowledged that it was not averred as a crime of negligence; he submitted, as I understood him, that the libel showed that it was a crime of intention. That being so, it appears to be it might have been appropriate to use the word "wilfully" and omit the words "culpably" and "recklessly". However, we have to take the charge as we find it, with the Lord Advocate's acknowledgment that what was libelled was that the accused acted intentionally: the accused, in other words, intended to seize hold of Jane Breen; he intended to push her on the body. I do not see how it could be said that what is libelled does not involve intention. You cannot unintentionally "seize hold" of a person and unintentionally "push" her. That must be conduct which results from, and perhaps evidences, an intention. But if the accused intended to seize hold of Jane Breen and intended to push her on the body and did both these things, in that order, then that must be an assault, if the intent is found to have been evil. If it is not an assault, I do not know what it is. In the course of the debate the word "manhandle" was used in order to avoid begging the question at issue; but the charge does not talk about manhandling that was culpably excessive. It talks about wilful seizing and pushing. There is an obvious logical fallacy in using the term "manhandling" as a synonym for what is actually averred well in the words actually used in the indictment. A man who wilfully, intentionally seizes hold of a woman and pushes her on the body, thereby causing her to fall down a flight of stairs, is guilty of common law assault, provided he has the necessary evil intent, which is an essential ingredient in such a crime. (I have used the word "thereby" because the Lord Advocate in his submission said that that word fell to be implied before the word "cause".) Although evil intent is a necessary ingredient in the crime of assault, "evil intent" is not averred when the Crown charges an accused with assault. No doubt that is because the evil intent is treated, for the purposes of proof, not as a primary fact of which notice has to be given but as a secondary fact which falls to be proved by inference from the primary facts (principally the actings of the accused on the occasion in question).

I would have equal difficulty in understanding how one can "recklessly" seize hold of a person and push her on the body thereby causing her to fall down a flight of stairs. That just does not seem to me to make sense. If I were the trial judge and I had to direct the jury as to what the alternative crime was, to tell them how they were to differentiate it from assault, and what state of mind it was necessary to prove on the second charge I should not know how to begin. There was no reported case found in the careful researches of the Lord Advocate and senior counsel for the respondent in which a person who intended to seize another and manhandle that other by seizing, pushing and causing that other to fall, and who did these things, had ever been charged with any crime other than that of assault. I do not believe there is such a crime. It is of course not the function of this court nowadays to invent new crimes, nor indeed were we being avowedly invited to do so. This court can acknowledge, and characterise as criminal, conduct which is really a new way of committing an old crime. But it cannot be said that wilfully and recklessly seizing hold of a woman and pushing her on the body causing her to fall down a flight of stairs is a new way of committing an old crime. It is just an old, and all too common, way of committing an all too common crime, the crime of assault. It is always essential to give consideration before charging a jury as to the directions which are appropriate in relation to *mens rea*. On this indictment it would be necessary to explain to the jury what constituted *mens rea* in relation to the first charge bearing the nomen juris "assault". It would then be necessary to explain to the jury that, in relation to the second or alternative charge, they would reach that charge if, but only if, they had held that they could not infer the *mens rea* of assault. What then is the *mens rea* (not being that appropriate to the crime of assault) which turns the wilful seizing and pushing of the victim, thereby causing her to fall, into an innominate crime? Lord Prosser's discussion of the concepts of recklessness and danger, intent, gross negligence and the existence and foreseeability of possible harm to others—all of which the trial judge would have to consider explaining to the jury—serves to illustrate how unnecessarily sophisticated and remote from reality we are in danger of rendering the law when, in a matter of this kind, it should be simple and easy for juries to grasp.

I can well understand how in the past the court, applying the principles which Lord Clyde referred to in *McLaughlan v. Boyd*, discovered various innominate crimes, the common characteristic of which was that the conduct was reckless and unconscionable because it exposed the lieges to unacceptable dangers. Thus, as noted by Sheriff Gordon in his *Criminal Law* (2nd ed), at para. 29–55, the court had recognised as indictable crimes such activities as the reckless discharge of firearms, the negligent driving of horses and railway engines, the negligent navigation of vessels, the negligent use of explosives and negligence in erecting buildings. But it appears to me that this series of extensions of the criminal calendar was necessary only when there was no known crime which fitted the facts. Where one has got an averment of wilful seizing of a person and pushing her on the body thereby causing her to fall down a flight of stairs there is absolutely no need to invent any innominate crime. The familiar crime of assault fits the bill perfectly. I should simply be repeating myself if I sought to take the matter any further. In my opinion, the alternative charge in the indictment is irrelevant on the ground that it does not disclose a crime known to the law of Scotland. In my opinion, there is no crime known to the law of Scotland consisting of wilfully seizing another human being, pushing her on the body and causing her to fall down a flight of stairs, except the crime of assault. As ex hypothesi the alternative charge does not contain a charge of assault it cannot be relevant.

I appreciate that it is possible for a libel to contain averments of fact, proof of all of which would entitle the jury to convict of one crime or alternatively of another: the obvious example is a murder charge containing a narrative of violent assault. On such a libel the jury can return a verdict of murder or a verdict of culpable homicide, the difference between the two being warranted by the difference between the *mens rea* required for the respective crimes, or because some circumstance such as provocation warrants a reduction from murder to culpable homicide. But that is, I believe, a special case. Indeed in that type of case there is never an alternative charge of culpable homicide set forth in the indictment (and based upon the same species facti). The trial judge nonetheless will direct the jury that, if the necessary *mens rea* for murder is not established, the alternative verdict of culpable homicide is open to them. I have never known it to be suggested, however, that on an assault charge, particularly one libelling wilful seizing and pushing, the judge should direct the jury that it is open to them to return a verdict not of assault but of wilful, culpable and reckless conduct to the danger of the lieges or to the actual injury of any of them. I can also readily envisage circumstances— quite distinct from those of common assault—in which culpable and reckless conduct involving physical manhandling of others could be charged as a crime. For example, if a person, whether acting out of high spirits or to escape the police or just for bravado, ran the wrong way down an upward moving escalator crowded with people, thus barging into people, he might be guilty of wilful, culpable and reckless conduct. But I doubt very much if that is how such conduct would be charged. It would obviously be charged as a breach of the peace. Similarly, in circumstances not amounting to assault, where a person is accused of manhandling the lieges in such a way as to put them in danger he could certainly be charged with a breach of the peace. Accordingly what the court is being asked to do is to sanction the inclusion in the indictment of a charge which is innominate, has no real precedent, and, if it is a crime, is properly to be described either as an assault or a breach of the peace. I see no reason to lend my support to such a novel and unnecessary step.

We were informed that the accused was employed as a "bouncer" or steward in the premises at which the incident described in the indictment took place. In my view, the character of the accused's employment has no bearing whatsoever upon any matter of law that we have to decide at this stage. There is not one law for bouncers and another law for the rest. The common law in relation to conduct that might be characterised as constituting the crime of assault or of breach of the peace is the same for all persons, even although it is obvious that some, such as policemen, may well find themselves roughly manhandling persons whom they have to restrain in the course of their duty, without themselves being guilty of assault: the legal justification for not regarding as criminal their use of force in such circumstances would be the absence of the *mens rea* of assault. It may be that others, such as club stewards, might similarly receive the benefit of the doubt from the tribunal of fact if the evidence showed that their genuine and only aim was to preserve the peace and maintain good order at the place where they were employed. The evaluation of *mens rea* is a jury function to be exercised with common sense. None of this, however, has anything to do with the correct analysis of what this indictment properly means."

Appeal allowed; decision of Sheriff reversed.

NOTES

**8.35**    1. It is difficult to disagree with Lord McCluskey's views in this case concerning the overlap between the first and second charges in the indictment. The difficulty seems to arise because the indictment does not really make clear the distinction between acts and their consequences. It seems clear from the terms of the indictment that the accused either deliberately seized the victim and pushed her down the stairs, intending to do so, or that he deliberately seized her and pushed her, but that he was reckless with regard to whether she falls down the stairs or not. In either case, of course, he seems at most to have been reckless with regard to the injuries which resulted.

2. It is very welcome to see the court's encouragement to the Crown to abandon the contradictory labelling of conduct as being both wilful and reckless.

### Kimmins v. Normand
### 1993 S.L.T. 1260, 1993 S.C.C.R. 476

The appellant was charged that, having been informed by a police officer (W) that he was **8.36** about to be searched, and having been asked if he was in possession of any needles, syringes or any sharp instruments, he, knowing that there was an unguarded hypodermic needle and syringe in his jacket pocket, did culpably and recklessly and with an utter disregard for the safety of the lieges, and in particular the police officer, deny being in possession of any such instruments and that he permitted the police officer to place his hand in his jacket pocket with the result that the hypodermic needle entered the police officer's hand to his injury, exposing him to the risk of infection.

A plea to the relevancy of the charge on the ground that it did not libel a crime known to the law was repelled by the sheriff. On appeal, the opinion of the Court was delivered by the Lord Justice-General (Hope).

OPINION OF THE COURT: "... It can be seen from this carefully framed charge that it contains within it the following elements. First, that the complainer was advised that he was to be searched in terms of the statutory provision; second, that he was asked whether he was in possession of any needles, syringes or any sharp instruments; third, that he knew very well that he had an unguarded needle and syringe in the pocket of his jacket; and, fourth, that he denied having any such article in his possession. These being the four elements, it is then said that he permitted the constable to place his hand in the pocket whereby the constable sustained injury and was exposed to the risk of infection.

[Counsel for the appellant] submitted that the sheriff erred in two respects in the view which he took of this charge. The first was that there was no crime committed as known to the law of Scotland, in that no act was performed by the appellant in the sense that he did not do anything. In our opinion that argument is not capable of being supported, because the complainer, having been asked the question, in the light of the advice he was given as to why it was being put to him, denied being in possession of any such instruments. By making that denial he was undoubtedly doing something and we consider that it can properly be said that there was the commission by him of something which, if the circumstances were appropriate, could amount to criminal conduct.

The other point which [counsel for the appellant] raised was whether there was a causal connection between the denial and the end result. On this matter we consider the facts are perfectly clear in the light of the narrative given in the charge. The denial must be seen against the background of the advice that the appellant was to be searched. He had no choice but to submit to the search in terms of the statute [Misuse of Drugs Act, 1971]. It must have been clear to him that the reason why the question was being put to him was that the police officer was about to put his hand into the pocket of his jacket with a view to conducting the search. It is a reasonable inference from the denial in these circumstances that it would lead directly to the police officer doing what he in fact did, that is, putting his unprotected hand into the appellant's pocket with the result that it was injured by the needle in the pocket. The chain of events follows naturally from one end of the charge to the other and we are satisfied that on these averments in the libel there was a causal connection between the denial and the end result.

For these reasons the view taken by the sheriff was, in our opinion, the correct one and we shall give effect to this decision by refusing this appeal."

Appeal dismissed.

NOTES

**8.37** 1. *Cf. Normand v. Morrison*, 1993 S.C.C.R. 207, in which it was held that an accused, knowing that she and her property were about to be searched and having been questioned as to whether there were any sharp objects on her person or in her property, had culpably and recklessly denied to two police officers that she had an unprotected needle in her handbag.

2. In *Donaldson v. Normand*, 1997 S.C.C.R. 351, the appellant, in circumstances similar to *Kimmins* and *Morrison,* denied that he was in possession of any sharp instruments when he was about to be searched. He claimed that, due to the effects of the voluntary consumption of Temazepam and heroin, he had forgotten that he was in possession of an unguarded hypodermic, which he had hidden in his sock prior to taking the drugs. The Court held, relying upon *Brennan v. H.M. Advocate*, 1977 J.C. 38, *ante*, p. 237, that where the accused's lapse of memory was due to the self-induced effects of the drugs, it was no defence for him to say that he had forgotten the presence of the needle. But what would the case have been if this had been a simple lapse of memory as a result of which the accused had forgotten that he had anything dangerous in his pocket? That would presumably have raised a question of error of fact, and the accused's criminal responsibility would have had to be judged according to the facts as he believed them to be.

3. Suppose in *Kimmins* and *Morrison* the accused had refused to answer the police officer's question. They would not then have 'done' anything. Could they then have been charged with endangering the person conducting the search by their failure to respond? In order to reach that result it would have to be established that the accused was under a duty to reply. There are two problems involved in holding that there would be such a duty.

The first is that it is difficult to see what the basis of any legal duty might be. The case does not fall within any of the recognised duty relationships, although it might just be argued that by carrying with him an unguarded hypodermic in circumstances where he might be searched, the accused had created a dangerous situation which, when asked by the police officer if there was any such danger, he was under a duty to avert by warning the police officer.

The second difficulty is that in such circumstances the person being searched has no duty to reply to questions put to him or her by a police officer, especially if the reply is likely to be incriminating. That point was taken by the accused before the sheriff, but since the sheriff, like the High Court, held that there had been a positive act on the part of the accused, the point was not answered. If the sanction for not answering is that the accused exposes himself to the risk of prosecution for reckless injury or endangerment, is this consistent with the presumption of innocence and the privilege against self-incrimination under Article 6(1) of the European Convention on Human Rights? See, in this context, *Saunders v. United Kingdom*, 23 E.H.R.R. 313; *Murray v. United Kingdom*, 22 E.H.R.R. 29; *Funke v. France*, 16 E.H.R.R. 297 and *Brown v. Stott*, 2001, S.L.T. 59.

## B. The *actus reus* of reckless endangerment

**8.38** It is a crime recklessly to endanger the lieges, that is, the public, or a section of the public. Like reckless injury, it may take many forms. One commonly encountered charge is that of recklessly discharging firearms, but as the following cases illustrate, the offence may be committed in any way which presents a sufficiently high risk to the public.

### David Smith and William McNeil
#### (1842) 1 Broun 240

**8.39** The accused were charged with wickedly, recklessly and culpably discharging loaded firearms into a house, to the imminent danger of the lives of the persons in the house. An objection was taken to the relevancy of this charge on the grounds, inter alia, that the indictment did not aver knowledge of the presence of persons in the house or that any injuries were caused.

THE LORD JUSTICE-CLERK (HOPE): "I am of opinion that the act libelled is a crime, and correctly charged as such. Furious driving upon a public road, even when no passengers are to be seen upon it is an offence, although it may not be worthwhile to try the case in the Court of

Justiciary, unless some person has been injured. The same remark may be made as to Reckless Steering, which has occasioned a collision between two ships, unattended by injury either to persons or lives. If by the argument which was stated in the case of *Young* (1839) 2 Swin. 380, it is meant that in order to constitute an indictable offence, there must be injury to the person, this is clearly erroneous. But if, on the other hand, the doctrine merely is, that there must be a completed act on the part of the pannel, then, in the present case, a sufficient result has been set forth in the alleged act of firing into an inhabited house. The averment that the house, into which the gun was discharged, was 'inhabited', is explicit enough, and renders an additional averment, that the pannel knew that persons were in the house at the moment, unnecessary. The prosecutor cannot be expected to prove that, before committing the criminal act, the pannel first rung the bell, and inquired if any one was at home. By firing into an inhabited house, the pannel took his chance of that."

Objection to relevancy repelled.

THE LORD JUSTICE-CLERK, in charging the jury, directed them: "That in order to constitute the particular crime charged, it was not necessary to prove against the pannel by separate evidence any intention to injure either persons or property. The act of discharging loaded firearms into an inhabited house, if proved was of itself sufficient to infer recklessness. It was unnecessary, also, under the present libel, to prove real danger to individuals within the house. The mere firing of the gun into the house constituted the crime, the pannel having taken his chance of the consequences. It would, therefore, be no defence, that the inmates of the house had accidentally left the room when the shot was fired into it, far less that there happened to be a screen which possibly might shield them from danger. If a person standing upon one side of a wall, and hearing the noise of a crowd collected upon the other, threw over some heavy substance, the act was equally criminal, though the crowd chanced at the moment to have moved back from the wall. In the present case, the act done was one by which lives were endangered, and would in all probability have been lost, had it not been for circumstances which the pannel could not have foreseen."

Verdict: The jury found the accused McNeil guilty.

NOTE

Whether it would today be correct to state that discharging a loaded firearm into an uninhabited **8.40** house is of itself sufficient to constitute reckless endangerment is questionable, and in the circumstances of this case such statements are clearly *obiter*.

## Normand v. Robinson
### 1994 S.L.T. 558

Two accused were charged on summary complaint with culpably and recklessly promoting **8.41** and organising a rave in a derelict warehouse to the danger of the lieges. The complaint stated that the premises were unsafe in the following respects: (a) there was no mains electricity and lighting was provided by candles; (b) there was no means of giving an alarm of fire and no adequate route of escape; (c) there was no operative fire-fighting equipment or emergency lighting; (d) there was no running water; (e) there were holes in some areas of floor and in other areas of floor there was flooding and debris. The complaint concluded that the accused "did thus recklessly endanger the safety and lives of those attending said 'rave' or similar event".

The sheriff held that the complaint did not disclose an offence known to the law of Scotland. The procurator fiscal brought a bill of advocation praying the High Court to recall the sheriff's order. On appeal the opinion of the Court was delivered by Lord Murray.

OPINION OF THE COURT: "... In his report the sheriff summarises the contentions of the parties and lists the authorities to which he was referred. He states that it was submitted for the respondents that the matters libelled in the charge did not disclose manifest wilfulness and general danger to the lieges of a standard required to make the crime one of culpable and reckless conduct. In the present case it was said for the respondents that the danger was too remote for the libel to be relevant. While the circumstances libelled might infer a breach of duty, to constitute a crime more would require to be libelled. Further, it was said, in the case of *Khaliq v. H.M. Advocate* an immediacy of causation was libelled which was absent in the present case. The Crown were attempting to extend the concept of culpable and reckless conduct which was a matter for Parliament and not for the courts. In any event the Civic Government (Scotland) Act 1982 by s.41 provided for licensing of public entertainment which a rave would appear to be.

The sheriff then narrates that the procurator fiscal depute initially attempted to amend the complaint to disclose that there were 60 persons inside the premises when the police arrived. The sheriff states that he refused this motion on the ground that the submissions already made were on the basis of the libel as it stood. He then narrates that it was submitted for the complainer under reference to the case of *Khaliq* that the question of recklessness was one for evidence and that the libel in relation to parts (a) to (e) of the charge sufficiently disclosed dangers from which culpable recklessness could be inferred. A rave, it was suggested, was an event which might involve acts such as misuse of drugs and the dangers in those circumstances were very real.

In his report the sheriff explains his decision as follows:

> "In reaching my decision on the matters complained of, I took into account that the Crown attitude appeared to be unclear as to whether the purpose of the charge was indicative of public policy to stop 'raves' or whether it was to prevent the use of places for raves which might constitute a danger. From what had been said in the submissions my understanding of a rave was that it might involve riotous or criminal conduct and accordingly, if this were happening in a derelict warehouse, it might constitute danger. However, the specification given was of apparent failures to meet fire and building regulations and I questioned whether this was not a matter for the application of the Civic Government (Scotland) Act rather than common law. I also took into account the situation where participants might be there willingly and queried whether the failure to provide what might be considered satisfactory premises could amount to culpable and reckless conduct since there were no standards indicative of what requirements should be met in a situation where a rave took place.
>
> "In the circumstances, I therefore held that the libel did not specify a sufficient causal link between the act of promoting and organising the rave and the causation of danger to the lieges. I also indicated that even if the complaint had been amended to disclose that 60 persons were attending the rave my view of the relevancy would not have been altered and I consider that if persons promoting and organising raves were to be prosecuted in such circumstances for culpable and reckless conduct, this should be a matter either for the High Court or for parliamentary legislation."

The advocate depute for the Crown submitted that the charge relevantly averred culpable and reckless conduct in the organisation of an event involving a gathering of persons to which the public were invited, in premises of the character and with the defects narrated, with the actual attendance of people to their danger. Read as a whole the libel was sufficient to infer "gross, or wicked, or criminal negligence, something amounting, or at any rate analogous, to a criminal indifference to consequences", in terms of *Paton v. H.M. Advocate*, 1936 J.C. at p. 22; 1936 S.L.T. at p. 299; *W. v. H.M. Advocate*, 1982 S.C.C.R. at p. 155; 1982 S.L.T. at p. 420; *Allan v. Patterson*; and *Gizzi v. Tudhope*, 1983 S.L.T. 214. It was sufficient for relevancy that the charge could infer recklessness of the necessary criminal standard but it was a matter of evidence, not relevancy, whether that standard was met. The sheriff had misdirected himself on this aspect of relevancy and he had wrongly directed his attention to whether a rave might constitute a danger and whether there were alternative statutory ways of dealing with such danger. In the face of what was said in *Khaliq*, at 1983 S.C.C.R., p. 493; 1984 S.L.T., p. 144, the sheriff was wrong to hold as he did that the libel did not specify a sufficient causal link between the act of promoting and organising the rave and the danger to the lieges. He was wrong to refuse the prosecution motion to amend the charge to give further specification of the danger arising from the attendance of some 60 persons. In any event the Crown now moved to amend the charge by deleting the words "those attending" in the second last line and substituting therefor "the 60 persons who did attend". The bill should be passed, the decision of the sheriff recalled and the case remitted back to the sheriff in terms of the complainer's plea in law.

Counsel who appeared for both respondents opposed the Crown's motion to amend on the basis that it came too late and that the sheriff in the exercise of his discretion had refused a similar amendment. He submitted that the sheriff had not erred in dismissing the complaint as irrelevant. The law set a high standard for culpable and reckless conduct, requiring more than mere recklessness to be libelled. To be relevant the recklessness libelled had to be in connection with a danger which was obvious and very real or known to the persons accused of culpable recklessness. The narrative here fell short of that standard, nor was it averred that the respondents were aware of the danger or that they had any responsibility for the premises. The significance of (a) to (d) in the charge depended on there being a fire. There had to be manifest danger: *W. v. H.M. Advocate* and *Normand v. Morrison*. Lord Justice General Clyde, in *Quinn v. Cunningham*, referring to *Paton v. H.M. Advocate* said, 1956 J.C. at the foot of p. 24 to the top of p. 25; 1956 S.L.T. at p. 56, after quoting the foregoing passage at p. 22 (p. 299) of *Paton*: "This represents the standard of culpability which must be established in such cases in order to constitute a crime at common law, based not upon intent, but upon reckless disregard of consequences."

Even with all the elements specified in the charge in the present case the libel fell short of that standard. It had not been shown that the sheriff erred in law in dismissing the complaint as irrelevant.

With some hesitation we have come to the conclusion that the sheriff did err in law in dismissing this complaint as irrelevant. The fact that the Crown might have brought charges under the Civic Government (Scotland) Act 1982 was no reason for concluding that it might not also proceed under common law. The libel narrates that the premises in question were a derelict warehouse awaiting demolition which had been secured by padlock and had been broken into within three days of the date on which the rave was to be held. The rave is said to involve a gathering of persons, which would be apt to cover a crowd of people as well as a small group, and the first four defects specified in the premises have a clear bearing on the safety of such persons in event of a fire. In addition it is averred that there were holes in some areas of floor, and flooding and debris in other areas. The substance of the charge, in our opinion, was that it was culpably reckless to organise such a gathering in derelict premises with the potentially dangerous defects specified so as to endanger those actually attending, With charges of culpable and reckless conduct it must always be a matter of fact and degree whether the standard of wicked or criminal culpability has been established, but at the stage of relevancy the issue is whether sufficient has been averred to enable such an inference to be drawn. In the present case we consider that the risk of fire in derelict and unoccupied premises which are no longer secured may be a manifest and obvious one, particularly with the use of candles and with debris lying about, and that, if it were established that the premises had the specific defects narrated in the charge, it would be open to a court to hold that there was an obvious danger in organising a gathering of any significant size in such premises. We agree with the advocate depute that instead of directing his attention to the foregoing matters the sheriff misdirected himself in the respects which he identified. Whether the defects and dangers narrated, if proved, are of a sufficient degree to warrant the inference that there was "criminal indifference to the consequences" is a matter of fact to be decided at the trial, but in our view there is sufficient specification in the complaint to allow evidence to be led which might justify such an inference, bearing in mind that a high standard of evidence is required.

Accordingly we shall pass the bill, recall the decision of the sheriff and remit the case back to him. In light of our decision the Crown's proposed amendment of the charge is not strictly necessary. However, although the motion to amend was opposed by counsel for the respondents, we consider it to be in the interests of justice that this further specification of the charge should be given. In remitting the case we therefore direct the sheriff to allow the amendment proposed by the Crown, to call upon the respondents to plead to the charge as amended and thereafter to proceed as accords."

> Bill passed, decision of the sheriff recalled and case remitted to the sheriff to proceed as accords.

### C. The *mens rea* of reckless injury and reckless endangerment: what kind of recklessness is required?

**8.42** The question here is what is the appropriate standard or degree of recklessness to be applied? Reckless injury and reckless endangerment are generally discussed in the context of objective recklessness, and the courts have insisted on a high degree or recklessness (although the language used has not always been consistent). It appears, also, that the appropriate formulation of the test may depend upon the context in which the reckless conduct occurs. If it occurs in a situation with which the trier of fact is likely to be familiar, for example in the context of reckless driving of a motor vehicle, then the test laid down in *Allan v. Patterson* (*ante*, Chapter 2) may be appropriate. But if it occurs in situations with which the trier of fact is less likely to be familiar, then it appears that the formulation adopted in *Quinn v. Cunningham* is to be used. The following cases illustrate this point, and the standard of recklessness currently applied by the courts.

**R.H.W. v. H.M. Advocate**
1982 S.C.C.R. 152

**8.43** LORD HUNTER: "The charge against the appellant was that he did on May 23, 1981, in the house occupied by Mary Fraser or McFarlane on the fifteenth floor of the block of flats known as Butterburn Court, Dundee, with wicked disregard for the consequences, culpably and recklessly drop or throw a bottle from said house which bottle struck and severely injured Barry James Gall, 14B James Street, Carnoustie. It was conceded by counsel for the appellant that this was a relevant charge although it did not contain the words 'to the danger of the lieges'. There are indications in the opinions of the Lord Justice-General and Lord McLaren in *McAllister v. Abercrombie* (1907) 5 Adam 366 at pp. 370 and 371, that if the equivalent of these words can be found in the substance of the complaint there may be a relevant charge of a crime at common law. In the present case the words chosen were 'with wicked disregard for the consequences'. It was accepted by counsel for the appellant that this phrase, in the context of the present complaint, was adequate to fill the gap left by omission of the words 'to the danger of the lieges'.

The jury after a trial unanimously found the appellant guilty as libelled. He has appealed against that conviction on the sole ground of misdirection by the sheriff who presided at the trial. The ground of appeal is that the trial judge erred in law in that he misdirected the jury on the nature and quality of behaviour necessary to constitute the charge libelled in the indictment.

The crime charged is of a relatively unusual character and it is not altogether easy to rationalise the authorities in this branch of the criminal law. It emerges, however, from the decisions to which we were referred that the degree of culpability and recklessness which is required to constitute the necessary mental element is high, and that it is of the essence that there should be criminal recklessness in the sense of a total indifference to and disregard for the safety of the public. This idea was at one time imported into charges of this nature by attaching to the words 'culpably and recklessly' the concept of danger to the lieges. The phrase which we would select from the authorities cited to us as best expressing the degree of culpability and recklessness which is required to establish a charge of the nature libelled in the present case is taken from the opinion of the Lord Justice-General (Clyde) in *Quinn v. Cunningham*, 1956 J.C. 22 at p. 24. His Lordship there defined the degree of culpability and recklessness required to constitute a crime at common law, in cases where an intention to commit a wrong was not present, as 'an utter disregard of what the consequences of the act in question may be so far as the public are concerned'. This definition is in our view well suited to application in the case of a common law crime of the type with which the appellant was charged.

The attack on the sheriff's charge to the jury was, as we have said, that he failed to give clear directions as to the degree of culpability and recklessness which the law requires in such a case. Counsel for the appellant pointed to more than one passage in the charge, which taken out of their context could perhaps lend some force to this argument, but reading the charge as a whole, including in addition to the passages against which the main criticism were directed both the introductory passages and the final observations before the jury retired, we are of opinion that the sheriff brought to the attention of the jury with sufficient clarity the high degree of culpability and recklessness which is required to constitute a crime of this nature. The sheriff pointed out to the jury that it was not disputed that the accused had deliberately thrown the bottle out of the window fifteen storeys up. He also drew the attention of the jury to evidence that the accused had been warned by an older boy against the risk which was eventually taken with near fatal consequences to a member of the public. In describing the prosecution case the sheriff pointed out to the jury that it was to the effect that the accused had quite deliberately and with a total disregard for the consequences thrown the bottle out of the fifteenth-storey flat. Against that background the sheriff gave the jury the particular directions which have been subjected to criticism. This part of the charge was brought to a point in a passage in which the jury were directed that they must be satisfied that in throwing the bottle out of the window the accused had a total indifference to the consequences which in the circumstances was criminally irresponsible, 'that he displayed a recklessness which was so depraved as to be regardless of the consequences'. We consider that this passage certainly did not understate the degree of culpability required by the law in such a case. Moreover, in the following sentence the sheriff drew express attention to the requirement that the culpably reckless conduct should have caused danger to other persons and should at least show a reckless disregard of the consequences. This was emphasised in the final part of the charge. It may be that the charge of the sheriff on these matters could be criticised as having been somewhat repetitious and over-elaborate and that he would on this aspect of the case have been better advised to confine himself to the simple phraseology of the passage which we have quoted from the opinion of the Lord Justice-General in *Quinn v. Cunningham*. However, we are not persuaded that the directions given by the sheriff to the jury were such as to leave them in any doubt as to the high degree of culpability and recklessness which must be proved by the Crown in such a case.

In the circumstances, despite the able argument which was presented on behalf of the appellant, the court is of opinion that the appeal must be refused."

Appeal dismissed.

NOTES

1. *Cf. MacPhail v. Clark*, 1983 S.C.C.R. 395, *ante*, p. 210; *Gizzi v. Tudhope*, 1983 S.L.T. 214 and *Skeen* **8.44** *v. Malik*, Sheriff Court of Glasgow and Strathkelvin, August 1977, *unreported* (but see the second edition of this work at p. 453).

2. In *Gizzi v. Tudhope*, the court stated, in a case of recklessly endangering the lieges, that they found the standard of recklessness referred to in *Allan v. Patterson*, 1980 J.C. 57, *ante*, p. 46, "preferable" to that adopted in this case. That observation must now be read in the light of cases subsequent to *Gizzi*, particularly *Cameron v. Maguire*, 1999 S.C.C.R. 44, *post*, p. 322.

3. What would have been the appropriate charge if the injured person had died as a result of his injuries? The *mens rea* of murder has been described as including a state of mind displaying such

"wicked recklessness as to imply a disposition depraved enough to be regardless of consequences". The same words were used by the sheriff in the instant case, but it is inconceivable that the accused would be guilty of murder in the case suggested. The modern law seems to be that reckless killing will not constitute murder unless the accused intended to cause some personal injury (although not necessarily to the victim). See the discussion of the mental element in murder, *post*, Chap. 10.

### Cameron v. Maguire
### 1999 S.C.C.R. 44

**8.45** The appellant was charged with recklessly discharging a firearm in the direction of open woodland to the danger of the lieges who might reasonably be expected to be walking there. He was convicted and appealed by stated case. The facts of the case are fully set out in the opinion of Lord Marnoch, delivering the opinion of the Court.

LORD MARNOCH: "[I]t was not disputed that the sheriff was entitled to make the following findings in fact:

> "1. The Appellant resided at Eastside Cottage, Killiechronan, Isle of Mull. The area in which he resided is a remote rural area. His cottage formed part of a building in which there were two other dwellinghouses, both occupied. One dwellinghouse, about 15 feet from the Appellant's dwellinghouse, was occupied by Mr Iain Slade and his wife and the other, between these houses by Mrs Ishbel Lamb.
>
> 2. Within 300 yards of the Appellant's house was a dense wooded area to which access might be gained by a pathway leading from the Appellant's house into the wooded area. There was a hotel within 200 yards lying on the main road.
>
> 3. It was possible for persons to walk within the wooded area and to have used the path to emerge from it at or adjacent to the Appellant's house.
>
> 4. The Appellant's house lay about 50 yards from the main public road. Access to the Appellant's house from the said road also gave access to the houses occupied by Mr and Mrs Slade and by Mrs Ishbel Lamb.
>
> 5. The Appellant was the owner of Crown Label 1, a high calibre rifle capable of killing a person of [*sic*] a range of up to 3 miles.
>
> 6. On May 31, 1996 in the early hours of the evening the Appellant had fired the said rifle in the yard of his house at Eastside Cottage. He had fired the weapon on up to 10 occasions within the space of 20 minutes both into a high banking of earth and at a target situated in front of the said banking. Said target was situated approximately 1 foot from an open pathway leading into the woodland area which was not obstructed by the said banking.
>
> 7. At the time the Appellant was firing his weapon Mr and Mrs Iain Slade were in their dwellinghouse approximately 15 feet from the Appellant's house.
>
> 8. There was a danger of ricochet of bullets from the banking in the direction of the public road adjacent to the Appellant's house. A person could have walked round the corner of the Appellant's house into the area where the Appellant was firing his weapon. Persons could have been using woodland area within 300 yards of the Appellant's house unseen by the Appellant. Mr and Mrs Slade used the said woodland area for walking from time to time.
>
> 9. Upon being charged with the reckless discharge of the said rifle the Appellant had replied,
>
> 'I can't deny I was shooting and at the time I thought it was safe. On looking at it again now, I wouldn't do it again, no.'

10. The Appellant held a firearms certificate for *inter alia* the said rifle. The Appellant had

been shooting for about 30 years. Prior to firing the Appellant had checked the immediate area of his dwellinghouse and had found no persons in the area.

When the Appellant had first shot the said rifle he had not been aware of its accuracy and had been carrying out a 'zeroing' test on the rifle. The Appellant was aware of the risk of ricochet. The Appellant test [*sic*] the accuracy of the weapon simply by firing it into the banking.

11. Any persons using the woodland area in the direction of the path and out of sight of the Appellant would have been at risk of death or serious injury from any stray bullet fired by the Appellant from his weapon.

12. Any person entering the yard area of the Appellant's house unexpectedly whilst the Appellant was firing his weapon at the banking or in the direction of the target would have been at the risk of injury or death from a bullet ricochet."

The questions stated for the opinion of this Court were:

"(1) Was I entitled to repel the submission of no case to answer?
(2) On the facts found was I entitled to convict the Appellant as libelled?"

Since, however, all the findings, with the exception of the penultimate sentence of Finding in Fact 10, appear to have been made on evidence led by the Crown, it seems to us that in this case these two questions raise precisely the same issue.

Before the sheriff, and before us, reference was made to the case of *Gizzi and Another v. Tudhope* 1982 S.C.C.R. 442 where the appellants were similarly convicted of the reckless discharge of a firearm and where the facts were not wholly dissimilar from the circumstances of the present case. As to the proper test to be applied, reference was made in *Gizzi* to what had been said by Lord Justice-General (Clyde) in *Quinn v. Cunningham* 1956 J.C. 22 at p. 24 regarding what was required to render recklessness a crime at common law, namely "an utter disregard of what the consequences of the act in question may be so far as the public are concerned". The court in *Gizzi* did not disapprove that test but, somewhat curiously to our minds, expressed a preference for the form of wording used in relation to a charge of reckless driving under section 2 of the Road Traffic Act 1972 in *Allan v. Patterson* 1980 J.C. 57 at p. 60. What was said in that case was as follows:

"Section 2, as its language plainly, we think, suggests, requires a judgment to be made quite objectively of a particular course of driving in proved circumstances and what the Court or a jury has to decide, using its common sense, is whether that course of driving in these circumstances had the grave quality of recklessness. Judges and juries will readily understand, and juries might well be reminded, that before they can apply the adverb 'recklessly' to the driving in question they must find that it fell far below the standard of driving expected of the competent and careful driver and [our underlining] that it occurred either in the face of obvious and material dangers which were or should have been observed, appreciated and guarded against, or in circumstances which showed a complete disregard for any potential dangers which might result from the way in which the vehicle was being driven".

The difficulty, as it seems to us—and we say this with great respect to Lord Justice-General (Emslie) who delivered the Opinion of the Court in both *Gizzi* and *Allan v. Patterson*—is that while the standard of driving to be expected of a competent and careful driver may well be within the knowledge of judge or juror, the matter of the discharge of a firearm may not be so familiar to either. It follows that expert evidence would be required in every such case and, indeed, evidence, in the form of testimony by a police officer with many years of experience of firearms, was led in the present case. However, in so far as we are dealing here with a crime at common law and in so far as the discharge of a firearm "in the face of obvious and material dangers" must, as it seems to us, always fall within the common law test formulated by Lord Justice-General Clyde, we, for our part, are content to adopt and apply as applicable to cases such as the present the test laid down in *Quinn v. Cunningham, supra*, namely that there should be "an utter disregard of what the consequences of the act in question may be so far as the public are concerned" or, as re-formulated on the following page of the report (p. 25), that there should be "a recklessness so high as to involve an indifference to the consequences for the public generally".

Applying that test, or those tests, to the facts found proved in the present case we are in no doubt that the answer which should be returned to the two questions asked of us is in the affirmative. In saying that we would emphasise, first, that this was a high calibre rifle with a range of three miles; second, that there was clearly a risk that a bullet would miss the target by one foot to the right and that, if it did, it would, as the sheriff says in his note, "have led to a stray bullet travelling in the direction of the track and into the woodland area"; third, that the rifle was new to the appellant and he did not know its accuracy—he had indeed been zeroing it; fourth, that there was in any event a risk of ricochet in the vicinity of other habitations and a public road; and, fifth, that it may not be wholly without significance that in answer to the Charge the appellant himself said:

"I can't deny I was shooting and at the time I thought it was safe. On looking at it again now, I wouldn't do it again, no."

We would add, for the avoidance of doubt, that our conclusions would be the same even if we were to disregard the presence in the vicinity of either or both of the public road and other habitations.

Appeal refused.

NOTES

**8.46**    1. See also, *Robson v. Spiers*, 1999 S.L.T. 1141. In that case, the appellant was convicted of culpably and recklessly chasing nine bullocks, causing them to escape from a field onto a railway line adjacent to the field, proceed along the railway line and thereafter onto a main road, thereby endangering persons using the railway line and the road. The appellant was admonished. He appealed against conviction, arguing, *inter alia*, that there was insufficient evidence to entitle the magistrate to find the necessary standard of recklessness to render the appellant's conduct criminal, the assessment of recklessness involving an assessment of the foreseeability of potential harm to the lieges. Under reference to *Quinn v. Cunningham*, 1956 J.C. 22, *H.M. Advocate v. Harris* and *Cameron v. Maguire*, the High Court held that the magistrate was entitled to hold that the utter recklessness required was proved.

2. It is clear that the test for recklessness is an objective one. It is not necessary for the prosecutor to show that the accused was aware of the facts and circumstances which would make his or her conduct reckless to the degree required. In *O'Neill v. Stott*, 1999 G.W.D. 23–1090, the appellant was convicted of recklessly discharging a rifle. The appellant had been shooting rabbits. Two shots he fired passed very close to the complainers, two railway workers, to their danger. At the time the shots were fired the appellant was about two hundred yards from the complainers. They were out of sight of the appellant. In support of the contention that the appellant had not been reckless, it was stated that there was no evidence to show that the appellant appreciated the range of his rifle. In answer to this point the court observed:

"The next question is whether the appellant knew what the range of the rifle was. In our view what the appellant might have thought himself is neither here nor there because any person who is engaged in using a rifle which is obviously a dangerous weapon ought to ascertain, before using it, what its potential range was in order that he could satisfy himself that when he fired it it was safe to do so. Quite plainly this rifle did have a range of at least 200 yards because of the evidence of the witnesses who heard the bullets whistling past them."

## 5. CAUSING REAL INJURY

### Hume, 1, 327

"Let us now attend to those offences against the person, which remain on the footing of the **8.47** common law, and are punishable only with some inferior pain, at the discretion of the Court. These are various in kind and degree; and the law is provided with sundry corresponding terms for them, more or less comprehensive, and commonly employed in libels, such as assault, invasion, beating and bruising, blooding and wounding, stabbing, mutilation, demembration and some others. But although the injury do not come under any of those terms of style, nor be such as can be announced in a single phrase, this circumstance in nowise affects the competency of a prosecution. Let the libel, in the major proposition, give an intelligible account of it in terms at large; and, if it amount to a real injury, it shall be sustained to infer punishment, less or more, *pro modo admissi*; no matter how new or how strange the wrong."

NOTES

1. This passage was relied upon by the High Court in *Khaliq v. H.M. Advocate*, 1984 S.L.T. 137, in **8.48** reaching the conclusion that it was a crime at common law to supply "glue-sniffing kits" to a number of children and young persons aged under 16, knowing that the recipients intended to use these kits to inhale the vapours from the glue to the danger of their health and lives, and thereby causing or procuring the recipients to inhale the vapours to the danger of their health and lives. That decision was followed in *Ulhaq v. H.M. Advocate*, 1991 S.L.T. 614. That case also involved supply of substances which the accused knew the recipients were going to inhale to the danger of their health and lives. It did, however, mark a development of the decision in *Khaliq* in that the recipients in *Ulhaq* were adults. *Khaliq* also forms the basis of the decision in *Lord Advocate's Reference (No. 1 of 1994)*, 1996 J.C. 76, in which it was held that where a person died as a result of using drugs which had been unlawfully supplied to them, the supplier was guilty of culpable homicide. (See, *ante*, Chap. 4.) See also *Jamieson v. H.M. Advocate,* 1987 S.C.C.R. 484.

2. Essentially these cases is based on the propositions that (a) it is an offence to cause real injury to a third party, by whatever means, and (b) injury may be "caused" by supplying to the victim the means to injure himself in circumstances where it is foreseeable that the means will be used in that way."

3. The decision in *Khaliq*, and hence the passage from Hume above appears, therefore, to have been limited to "supply" cases, although clearly "causing" injury to another person is not, as Hume makes clear, limited to supply. Indeed, the one type of case which is not referred to in this passage is supply, and causing injury to someone by supplying them with the means to injure themselves is not the most obvious or compelling example of causing injury.

## 6. ABDUCTION

### Elliot v. Tudhope
### 1987 S.C.C.R. 85

The appellant, a police officer, was charged on complaint that he did "assault Francis Stewart **8.49** ... seize hold of his clothing, wrongfully arrest him for an alleged breach of the peace, unlawfully detain him there and in a police car in the course of a journey to Chester Street Police Office Glasgow, and occasion his unlawful detention at said police office by other officers."

It appeared that the appellant was being given a lift to a police station for a refreshment break, when the officers on duty in the vehicle stopped a car being driven by Stewart and made certain inquiries of him. The appellant intervened in the inquiry to ask Stewart some questions. The latter gave a false answer on at least two occasions, and the appellant became angry and aggressive towards him. After a further altercation between the appellant and Stewart, the appellant marched Stewart to the police vehicle and placed him in it beside one of the other officers. The appellant did not inform Stewart why he was being detained, but at the police station he preferred a charge of breach of the peace against him. The appellant was aware that there was no justification for this charge. Stewart was detained in the police station for about 75 minutes.

Pleas to the competency and relevancy of the charge of assault and abduction were repelled by the sheriff who subsequently convicted the accused on the charge of abduction, under deletion of the words "other officers" and the substitution of "the duty bar officer". An appeal to the High Court on the ground that the sheriff erred in rejecting the pleas to the competency and relevancy of the charge of assault and abduction was lodged but not pursued. In his note the sheriff stated:

"The first ground of appeal alleges that I erred in law in rejecting the pleas to the competency and relevancy of the second charge and in holding that the said charge was competent and relevant ....

[The appellant's solicitor] submitted in support of his plea to the competency and relevancy of charge (2), first, on the basis that that charge libelled assault and wrongful arrest and unlawful detention. His submission was that wrongful arrest and unlawful detention were not crimes at common law. [The appellant's solicitor] referred to Walker on Civil Remedies at p. 1008. The only remedy for wrongful arrest and unlawful detention lay in the civil law and not the criminal law. The remedy was a civil action of damages. [He] referred to *Dahl v. Chief Constable, Central Scotland Police.*

It may, however, be possible in appropriate circumstances for a prosecutor to proceed with a criminal case under statute alleging a breach of s.44(2) of the Police (Scotland) Act 1967. This had not been done in this case. Accordingly, as wrongful arrest and unlawful detention taken either separately or together did not amount to a crime or crimes at common law, all the words occurring after the word 'clothing' did not form a competent charge known to the criminal law of Scotland.

[The appellant's solicitor] submitted, secondly, that on the basis that this charge was one of assault, all the words occurring after the word 'clothing' were irrelevant. The words complained of could not relevantly form part of a charge libelling assault. The reasoning was the same. Wrongful arrest and unlawful detention were not crimes at common law. [He] referred to *McLeod v. Shaw* which, he said, did not assist in the circumstances, and to Sheriff Gordon's commentary thereon at 1981 S.C.C.R. p. 59.

As I understood him, [his] point was that the law of delict and the criminal law were entirely separate, and since the words complained of were not an actual consequence of an assault (such as "to injury") or an aggravation of assault, they had no place in the charge.

Furthermore, [he] submitted that if the respondent had introduced the words complained of as part of the narrative then the words were superfluous as they were *ex post facto* and added nothing and could add nothing to the charge of assault which had been libelled.

Accordingly, under reference to *McCallum v. Hamilton*, the words complained of were irrelevant and should be deleted from the charge.

[The appellant's solicitor] submitted, thirdly, that if the words complained of were intended to libel a charge of abduction then the charge lacked specification. There were two questions to be answered. The first was: 'Was the accused acting in the course of his duty?' and the second: 'Did the accused do it wrongfully?' The charge did not allege that the appellant was a police officer and had unlawfully arrested the complainer in the course of his duty, the truth being that he well knew that the complainer had not committed a breach of the peace. The charge did not libel an unlawful arrest. [He] referred to the unreported case of Jas. McLean, Glasgow High Court. The charge there was a charge of abducting a little girl and also a charge of raping her. Sheriff Gordon records that Lord Kincraig directed the jury on the abduction charge that: "It is a crime to carry off or confine any person forcibly against their will without lawful authority." Here there was no allegation of carrying off the complainer forcibly against his will without lawful authority. The fact that the appellant may have made a mistake in arresting the complainer did not amount to a crime, nor did it amount to the crime of abduction. If the words complained of were intended to libel a charge of abduction then a test of relevancy had not been satisfied. While it may be abduction for a police officer to detain a person forcibly against his will without lawful authority in a house up a back alley, it was not a relevant charge of abduction to allege that the complainer had wrongfully been arrested for an alleged breach of the peace and unlawfully detained there and in a police car and at a police office. The arrest was not alleged to be unlawful; for all these reasons the words complained of were irrelevant and should be deleted from the charge.

Furthermore, as I understood [the appellant's solicitor], if the charge was intended to libel a species of the crime of attempting to pervert the course of justice then, again, the libel containing the words complained of did not pass the test of relevancy.

In the reply, the respondent's depute referred to s.312(b) of the Criminal Procedure (Scotland) Act 1975. She submitted, and [the appellant's solicitor] accepted, that in terms of that subsection 'it shall not be necessary to specify by any *nomen juris* the offence which is charged, but it shall be sufficient that the complaint sets forth facts relevant and sufficient to constitute an offence punishable on complaint'.

The respondent's depute submitted that the essence of the crime of abduction was to carry off a person against his will without lawful authority. The respondent's depute referred to Macdonald, Criminal Law (4th ed.), p. 428. [The appellant's solicitor] accepted that that was the essence of the crime of abduction.

The respondent submitted that it was not necessary to libel the words 'against his will' in the circumstances of this case. The charge was not one of a continuing assault. An assault had been libelled, but an assault can be part of all sorts of crime—for example, robbery. The respondent's depute submitted that the words 'wrongfully arrest him for an alleged breach of the peace' were narrative but that the crucial words followed beginning with 'unlawfully detain him' to the end of the charge. This, the respondent's depute submitted, relevantly libelled a species of abduction and was the gravamen of the charge. The assault was merely part of the modus of achieving the relevant crime of unlawful detention.

In reply, [the appellant's solicitor] reiterated the points which he had made earlier.

I gave careful consideration to these submissions and repelled the plea to the relevancy and competency taken in respect of charge (2). It humbly seemed to me that the respondent's submissions were to be preferred to those of the appellant. It was accepted that the essence of abduction was to carry off a person against his or her will without lawful authority. It humbly seemed to me that abduction for any purpose is criminal. I refer to Macdonald and to the 5th ed. at p. 124. I reached the view that unlawful detention was a recognised crime at common law—see Macdonald. So far as the complaint of lack of specification is concerned, I reached the view that while the complaint could, perhaps, have been better drafted, there was sufficient specification. It could not be said that the appellant had no fair notice of the charge against him. I took account of the terms of s.312(e) of the 1975 Act. Although the charge did not libel that the appellant was a police officer, it humbly seemed to me that this was implicit in the charge. For a police officer to unlawfully detain someone, it was implicit that his arrest was both wrongful and illegal and, in my view, the appellant had sufficient and fair notice that charge (2) libelled assault and unlawful detention of the complainer at the places specified in the charge.

It is but right to record that at the close of the respondent's case at the trial, [the appellant's solicitor] made a submission in terms of section 345A of the 1975 Act and reviewed, in considerable detail, the authorities on wrongful arrest. He did so in considerably more detail than he did at the debate, but I have confined myself to reporting the arguments which were advanced at the debate. I would only observe that in making his no-case-to-answer submission, [the appellant's solicitor] referred to *Shields v. Shearer* and to the speech of Lord Shaw of Dunfermline. This authority is not mentioned in Professor Walker's treatment of the subject of wrongful apprehension at p. 1008 of his *Civil Remedies* and, having read that case, I must respectfully question whether Professor Walker has accurately stated the law of wrongful apprehension."

Pleas to competency and relevancy dismissed.

Notes

**8.50**    1. Older authorities such as Hume appeared to suggest that abduction was only criminal if carried out against a woman for the purpose of forcing her to enter into marriage (Hume, I, 310), or possibly for the purpose of rape. This case makes it clear that the forcible abduction of any person, and for any purpose, is criminal.

2. Abduction of a pupil child may be charged as theft at common law; see Chapter 9, *post*. In appropriate circumstances there may also be an offence under Pt II of the Child Abduction Act 1984.

## 7. Ill-treatment of persons under sixteen

### Children and Young Persons (Scotland) Act 1937

**8.51** **12.**—(1) If any person who has attained the age of sixteen years and who has parental responsibilities in relation to a child or to a young person under that age or has charge or care of a child or such a young person, wilfully assaults, ill-treats, neglects, or exposes him, or causes or procures him to be assaulted, ill-treated, neglected, abandoned, or exposed, in a manner likely to cause him unnecessary suffering or injury to health (including injury to or loss of sight, or hearing, or limb, or organ of the body, and any mental derangement), that person shall be guilty of an offence ....

(2) For the purposes of this section—
  (a) a parent or other person legally liable to maintain a child or young person or the legal guardian of a child or young person shall be deemed to have neglected him in a manner likely to cause injury to his health if he has failed to provide adequate food, clothing, medical aid or lodging for him, or, if, having been unable otherwise to provide such food, clothing, medical aid or lodging, he has failed to take steps to procure it to be provided under the enactments applicable in that behalf.

### A. What constitutes 'neglect'?

#### H. v. Lees; D. v. Orr
1994 S.L.T. 908

**8.52** LORD JUSTICE-GENERAL (HOPE): "The appellants in each of these two cases were found guilty of a contravention of section 12(1) of the Children and Young Persons (Scotland) Act 1937, in respect that, being persons having the custody, charge and care of a child under the age of sixteen years, they wilfully neglected the child in a manner likely to cause unnecessary suffering or injury to the child's health. They have appealed against their convictions on the ground that the charges were not made out on the evidence. When the appeals came before us on the first occasion, the advocate-depute informed us that the Crown did not wish to support the convictions. But we were sufficiently concerned about the circumstances of these cases, and in particular that of [PH] which appeared to us to raise issues of some general interest and importance, to express doubt about the soundness of the decision that the convictions were not to be supported. We decided to continue the appeals to a later date so that the Crown could give further consideration to the matter and in order that the proper disposal of these appeals could be decided upon after the presentation of full argument on both sides of the case. We have now had the benefit of the detailed argument, as a result of which we are persuaded that it would be appropriate for us to quash these convictions, as we were invited to do by the Lord Advocate. Although the decisions in these cases thus proceed on a concession by the Crown, it is nevertheless right that we should explain the basis for them in view of the care with which the sheriff in each case has explained his reasons for deciding that it was his duty to convict.

The circumstances of the two cases are different, the only common link between them being that they were both said to involve contraventions of the same provision in the same Act. Section 12(1) of the 1937 Act provides [his Lordship quoted the terms of section 12(1), above, and continued]:

The references to the assault, ill-treatment, abandoning and exposure are thereafter left to speak for themselves. No further definition is given in the section of what is meant by these words. The word 'neglect' must, however, be read together with the provisions of section 12(2)(a), which provides that, for the purposes of that section [his Lordship quoted the terms of section 12(2)(a) above, and continued],

Where this deeming provision applies, the only remaining question is whether what was done or omitted to be done was wilful. But the present cases are not concerned with a failure to provide adequate food, clothing, medical aid or lodging for the child. In these cases it was accordingly necessary for the Crown to prove that the appellants neglected the children, that they did so in a manner likely to cause unnecessary suffering or injury to the child's health and, further, that this was done wilfully, in order to establish that they were guilty of the offence.

In [PH's] case the child was her son [MH] who was a baby aged nine months. The child's father was a student who lived a short distance away in another house. The father regularly cared for the child and when he did so he usually stayed overnight with the appellant. But they retained their separate accommodation and they were not residing together on a full-time basis at the time of the alleged offence. The appellant had left the child in the care of its father and gone to the funeral of a relative, from which she returned at about midnight substantially under the influence of drink. Shortly after her return, the father returned to his own house, leaving the appellant in sole charge of the child. A short time later, just after midnight, the appellant arrived at the father's house still considerably under the influence of drink, having left the child alone in her house. There was an argument because she wanted him to return to her house and he was unwilling to do so. She returned to her own house without him and was there on her own with the child when, shortly before 1 a.m., police officers arrived there, following a report by the father. He had become concerned at the appellant's condition and behaviour and had contacted the police. The police were unable to obtain a response from the appellant when they knocked at the door and shouted through the letter box. After two or three minutes they used the key which the father had given them to enter the house and went into the living-room. They found the appellant sitting on a couch there, very intoxicated, and when they spoke to her she had difficulty in comprehending what they were saying. There were no other persons in the house apart from the child, who was sound asleep and, when checked by the police officers, was found to be quite safe and healthy and well wrapped up in a cot upstairs.

The police were, however, unhappy about the appellant being alone with the child because of her intoxicated condition. After an incident in the house which led to her being charged with a breach of the peace, the appellant's step-father was contacted and brought to the house and she was taken to the police station. The charge against her alleged that she

'did wilfully neglect said [MH] in a manner likely to cause him unnecessary suffering or injury to health and did leave him alone and unattended and without proper supervision in the said house; and further, while in said house, you were drunk and incapable of looking after him'.

At the conclusion of the Crown case the charge was amended on the unopposed motion of the prosecutor by the deletion of the words 'and did leave him alone and unattended and without proper supervision in the house; and further' and the appellant was found guilty of the charge, as amended.

In [BD's] case, the child was his daughter [CAD], who was aged thirteen years and six months at the time of the alleged offence and was in her third year at secondary school. She was living in family with her father and a brother aged eleven, the appellant having been divorced from the child's mother .... After the child had returned from school and the family had had their evening meal, the appellant said that he was going to Elgin to visit and that the child and her brother should go with him. There then followed an argument because the child refused to go with the appellant to Elgin. He then left with the son at about 6 p.m., leaving the child alone in the house. He said that he would be home about midnight. He made no arrangements for anyone to stay with her that evening or for anyone to look in on her and the house had no telephone. But the child knew where the appellant was going and the appellant had told her previously, although not on the evening in question, to go and see a neighbour who lived nearby if she was in trouble. The neighbour happened to look in that evening and found the child in the sitting-room watching television, having done her homework. The sitting-room was warm, with an open coal fire which the child was capable of replenishing and stoking as required. There was no other form of heating in the rest of the house and the weather was very cold outside and it was dark, it being February.

At about 9.40 p.m. the police called at the house, having been informed that a young girl was alone there. They knocked on the door and were admitted to the house. They had previously knocked on both the front and back doors of the house and shouted 'Police' through the keyhole. When she admitted the police to the house the child was upset and crying and she was taken by the police to Inverness where she spent the night in a children's home. The charge in this case alleged that the appellant

'did wilfully neglect said child in a manner likely to cause her unnecessary suffering or injury to health, in respect that you left her unattended by any responsible person'.

The appellant was found guilty of the charge as libelled.

It can be seen from this narrative that in both of these cases reports were made to the police and that, when the police arrived, they were sufficiently concerned about the circumstances to feel it appropriate to take action to safeguard the interests of the child. The Lord Advocate submitted, however, that in neither case, on the facts which were found by the sheriff to have been established by the evidence, had an offence under section 12(1) of the 1937 Act been committed and he invited us, as did the appellants' counsel, to quash the convictions.

In order to constitute an offence under this subsection, where neglect is alleged, it must be shown that the child was neglected, that he was neglected in a manner likely to cause him unnecessary suffering or injury to health, and that this was done wilfully. No question has been raised in either of these cases as to whether what was done, if it was neglect of the child, was done wilfully. It is not suggested that the appellants were unable to appreciate what they were doing at the time. In *R. v. Senior* at pp. 290–291 Lord Russell of Killowen C.J. said:

' "Wilfully" means that the act is done deliberately and intentionally, not by accident or inadvertence, but so that the mind of the person who does the act goes with it.'

Mr Di Rollo for [PH] accepted that he could not suggest that her state of intoxication was other than voluntary and he did not seek to make anything of the question whether she expected to be left alone with the child. Mr Smart for [BD] accepted that it was a deliberate decision on his part to leave the child alone in the house when he and his son went to Elgin. The question is whether what happened in either case could be described as neglect of the child and, if so, whether this was in a manner likely to cause the child unnecessary suffering or injury to health. Neglect on its own, even if wilful, is not enough to constitute the offence, so it was necessary also to show that it was of such a character, or of such a duration, as to be likely to have that effect. It was not suggested in either case that there was actual suffering or injury to health on the part of the child.

The Lord Advocate submitted that the verbs used in section 12(1) to describe the offence are all powerful words and that, in order to understand what was meant by neglect in this context, the maxim *res noscitur a sociis* should be applied. He pointed out that the heading of Part II of the 1937 Act in which section 12 appears is in these terms:

'Prevention of cruelty and exposure to moral and physical danger.'

He drew our attention also to section 22 of the Act, under which it is an offence for a person to allow a child under seven to be in a room containing an open fire grate which is not sufficiently protected against the risk of injury and the child is killed or suffers serious injury. A person convicted under that section is liable only to a small fine as compared with the substantial fines and periods of imprisonment to which a person is liable if convicted under section 12(1). He said that something more than trivial was required to amount to neglect in this context and that a child had to be seen to be neglected in order to constitute the offence. He submitted that merely to leave a child alone and unattended for a time, whether in the child's own house or outside it, could not be said to amount to neglect of the child.

Each of the words used in section 12(1) suggests that the conduct must be more than transient or trivial. But the element of cruelty which is indicated by the head note is to be found in the manner, or the likely effect, of the conduct, which must of course be wilful. Each verb taken separately has a reasonably clear and distinct meaning. We do not think that it is helpful to attempt to attach any particular weight or gravity to any of them by reference to others in the group. As Lord Diplock pointed out in *R. v. Sheppard* at p. 403[D], four of the verbs in this subsection refer to positive acts, while the word 'neglect' refers to failure to act, and it is preferable where the word 'neglect' is in issue to confine attention to the ordinary meaning of that word.

In *Clark v. H.M. Advocate* at p. 56 Lord Justice-Clerk Grant quoted with approval the definition of 'neglect' which had been given to the jury by the sheriff-substitute. This was itself a quotation from the definition of the word by Lord Russell of Killowen in *R. v. Senior* at p. 291 in these terms:

'Neglect is the want of reasonable care—that is, the omission of such steps as a reasonable parent would take, such as are usually taken in the ordinary experience of mankind.'

That definition was criticised by Lord Diplock in *R. v. Sheppard* at p. 406[C–D] on the ground that it invited confusion between, on the one hand, neglect and on the other hand negligence. Nevertheless, he was content to accept it, if all it meant was that a reasonable parent who was mindful of the physical welfare of the child and possessed a knowledge of all the relevant facts would have taken steps that the accused omitted to take, to avoid the risk of unnecessary suffering by the child or injury to his health. There was a difference of view in that case as to whether the offence required proof that the parents were aware of the probable consequences of their neglect. The majority view, which included that of Lord Diplock, was that this was a necessary part of the offence, having regard to the use of the word 'wilfully' in the subsection. That issue aside, however, there was no difference of view about the ordinary meaning of the word 'neglect'. Lord Diplock said at p. 40[F] that to neglect a child is to omit to act, to fail to provide adequately for its needs. Lord Keith of Kinkel said at p. 417[D] that:

'neglect of a child means, according to the ordinary use of language, a failure to bestow proper care and attention upon the child'.

Lord Fraser of Tullybelton at p. 416 and Lord Scarman at p. 423 were content with the meaning given to the word by Lord Russell. In *Kennedy v. S.* the test which commended itself to the court in *Clark v. H.M. Advocate* was applied. The Lord Justice-Clerk said at p. 682[J] that the sheriff erred in confining 'neglect' to what can be seen. As he put it,

'Children may give the appearance of being clean and well fed and yet may have been the victims of neglect within the meaning of the statutes.'

In our opinion, in light of these authorities, the approach to this word which was taken by the Lord Advocate tended to set rather too high a standard for what may amount to neglect for the purposes of the statute. But there is no doubt, as Lord Keith pointed out in *R. v. Sheppard* at p. 417[E], that parents may take widely varying views about what constitutes proper care and attention for their children. So it is not possible to set any absolute standard as to what may amount to neglect. This must depend upon the circumstances. In a case to which the deeming provision in section 12(2)(a) applies, the standard to be applied is that of adequacy. Thus, if a parent or other person legally liable to maintain the child fails to provide the child with adequate food, to take just one example of the types of provision mentioned in this subsection, he will be deemed to have neglected the child in a manner likely to cause injury to the child's health. In cases such as the present which fall outside the deeming provision, the appropriate standard is what a reasonable parent, in all the circumstances, would regard as necessary to provide proper care and attention to the child. Failure to achieve that standard may reasonably be described as neglect, whether this was due to a deliberate decision or a positive act on the one hand or to an omission to do what was required on the other. But the offence will only be constituted if it is also shown by the evidence that this was done in a manner likely to cause the child unnecessary suffering or injury to health.

The sheriff was satisfied in [PH's] case that her degree of intoxication was such, when combined with the fact that she was alone in the house and would not have anyone else there when asked to agree to this by the police officers, as to amount to neglect of the child. He was also satisfied that, although there was no evidence that any actual harm had occurred to the child, the degree of intoxication of the appellant had created a situation which was likely to cause unnecessary suffering or injury to the child. Mr Di Rollo submitted that the mere fact that the child's mother was intoxicated did not constitute neglect of the child and that there was no evidence to show that it was likely that the child would be caused unnecessary suffering or injury to his health because of this. He pointed out that it was an offence under section 50(2) of the Civic Government (Scotland) Act 1982 for a person to be drunk in a public place while in charge of a child under the age of ten years. But there was no provision to the effect that a person who was drunk in private while in charge of a child committed an offence. In the absence of any finding that the child was in need of anything, or was likely to suffer unnecessarily or to be injured in his health in some way before the appellant became sober, there was no basis for a conviction.

The Lord Advocate associated himself with these submissions, pointing out that there were no special circumstances established by the evidence to show that the child was likely to suffer in these respects. As to the meaning of the word 'likely' in this context, he submitted that in *R. v. Sheppard* at p. 405[C] Lord Diplock had gone too far when he said that it should be understood as excluding only what would fairly be described as 'highly unlikely'. He pointed out that it would be a contradiction in terms to say something which, although not highly unlikely, was nevertheless unlikely to occur was likely to do so. We were referred to the Australian case of *Boughey v. The Queen* at p. 21, where Mason, Wilson and Deane J.J. said that the ordinary meaning of the word was to convey the notion of a substantial, a real but not remote, chance regardless of whether it was less or more than 50 per cent. In the New Zealand case of *R. v. Piri* Cooke P. noted at p. 78 that The Concise Oxford Dictionary includes in its definition of 'likely' the phrase 'such as may well happen'. At p. 84 McMullin J. referred to 'a real or substantial risk' which need not be more probable than not, but should be more than a bare possibility. The Lord Advocate submitted that there was no evidence in this case to indicate that there was a substantial risk that the child would be caused unnecessary suffering or injury to his health as a result of the appellant's incapacity.

It is the absence of any findings that, in any specific and substantial respect, the child was likely to be caused unnecessary suffering or injury to his health that persuades us that, in this case, it was not proved that there was a contravention of section 12(1) of the 1937 Act. We accept that for a person to be drunk when in charge of a young child does not, in itself, constitute an offence under this subsection. Drunkenness may well, however, be regarded as irresponsible conduct and if it is of such a degree that the person is, for all practical purposes, incapable of looking after the child, this may indeed be thought to be such as to amount to neglect. This is because a reasonable parent could not be expected to leave a young child alone with a person while he or she was in that state. A person who is so intoxicated, whether through drink or drugs, as to be incapable of looking after the child might as well not be there at all. He or she may indeed be said to have abandoned the child and may also be liable to create risks for the child which would not arise if he or she were sober.

Nevertheless, it cannot be assumed that such neglect will be likely to cause the child unnecessary suffering or injury to health, as this cannot be left to speculation. There must be some evidence to support the inference that this was likely to occur. The child in the present case was found to be quite safe and healthy and well wrapped up in a cot upstairs at about 1 a.m., while the mother was sitting intoxicated in the living-room. There are no findings as to when the child was likely to require attention, whether for feeding or changing or for some other reason, while the mother remained intoxicated, nor are there findings of any other respect in which the child might be at risk of suffering or of injury. Moreover, the allegation in the charge that the appellant left the child alone and unattended and without proper supervision in the house was deleted by the prosecutor, so the only remaining point in the charge at the stage of conviction was that the appellant was so drunk as to be incapable of looking after him, with the result that unnecessary suffering or injury to health was likely to occur. In these circumstances, although with some hesitation, we are prepared to accept the decision of the Lord Advocate, taken in the public interest, that the conviction in this case cannot be supported. We shall allow this appeal of consent and quash the conviction.

The position in [BD's] case is, as Mr Smart pointed out, completely different. The sheriff was willing to accept that the child was a mature and sensible thirteen-and-a-half-year-old. She was left on her own in the house for the evening, having refused to go with her father and brother to Elgin, as had been his intention. There was no telephone in the house, it was cold and dark outside had she been in need of seeking help for any reason from the neighbour, and her father had told her that he would not be home until about midnight. We doubt whether a person who left a child of that age alone in her own house for about six hours on a single occasion in these circumstances could be said to have neglected her. There was nothing to suggest that she was not in good health or was otherwise not well cared for. But in any event, there was no evidence that in any specific and substantial respect what was done in this case was likely to lead to unnecessary suffering or injury to the child's health. The sheriff said that the specific risks were insubstantial but not entirely absent, by which we understand him to mean that it was possible that an accident might happen or that the child might fall ill while her father was away. But the risk of being unable to deal with accident or illness, should it occur, is not the test. The question is whether the neglect itself was likely to lead to injury to health or to unnecessary suffering and there are no findings that in this case this was likely to result merely from the father's absence that evening. Although the child was upset and crying when she admitted the police to the house, there are no findings that this was due to the fact that her father was away. When the neighbour looked in earlier that evening, she found the child watching television, having done her homework. We consider that there was insufficient evidence for a conviction in this case, and since the Lord Advocate did not seek to support it, we shall allow the appeal in this case also and quash the conviction.

We should not like it to be thought, however, from the decision which has been taken in these two cases that we are offering encouragement to persons having the custody, care or charge of children to leave them alone and unattended, or to become drunk or render themselves for any other reason incapable to such an extent as to be unable to look after them. Nor are we to be taken as being in any way critical of those who contacted the police, or of the police themselves, who acted responsibly and out of a proper concern for the child in each case. If any harm had happened to the children while they were unattended, so that there was evidence of actual suffering or actual injury to health, it might have been a relatively simple matter for the Crown to establish that an offence under section 12(1) of the Act had been committed. As the Lord Advocate has indicated, it ought not to be assumed that an offence is being committed simply because a child is left alone. But the purpose of the subsection is to prevent harm being caused to the child due to neglect. Thus, to leave a child, especially of a very young age, unattended for a substantial period in circumstances where no reasonable parent would do this, may properly be regarded as amounting to neglect of the child. Those who may be tempted to do this should be aware that they are at risk of being held to have committed an offence, if there is evidence that to do so will cause the child, in some specific respect, unnecessary suffering or that it will cause injury to the child's health."

Appeals allowed, convictions quashed.

NOTES

**8.53**    1. In *McF. v. Normand*, 1995 S.C.C.R. 380, the appellant left his eighteen-month-old son in the family car for about an hour while he and his wife and another child went to do some Christmas shopping. The car was parked in Bath Street, Glasgow and was securely locked. The child was strapped in a car seat, and partly covered by a blanket. The child was observed by passers-by, by a traffic warden and eventually the police were called. The police remained at the car until the appellant returned. At no time did the child appear to be upset or distressed. The appellant was convicted of wilfully neglecting and abandoning his child in a manner likely to cause him unnecessary suffering or injury to health. In convicting the appellant, the sheriff found, *inter alia*, that in leaving the child in this way, the appellant exposed the child to various risks "including the sudden illness of the child while alone, a break-in to the car or its theft with the child inside, another vehicle colliding with the car of the child being taken by an evilly disposed or perverted person".

The High Court held that these considerations were "speculative" and that they should not have been taken into account by the sheriff when considering whether this was a case of neglect of the child likely to cause it unnecessary suffering. The appellant's conviction was quashed. (See also *W. v. Clark*, 1999 S.C.C.R. 775.)

## B. What is 'wilful' neglect?

**Clark v. H.M. Advocate**
1968 J.C. 53

**8.54**  The appellants neglected to provide food and medical aid for their child, as a result of which the child was caused suffering and injury to health, and eventually died. They were convicted under s.12 of the Children and Young Persons (Scotland) Act 1937 of "wilfully neglecting the child in a manner likely to cause her unnecessary suffering and injury to health".

LORD JUSTICE-CLERK (GRANT): "The applicants were convicted by a jury in the sheriff court in Edinburgh on a charge under section 12(1) of the Children and Young Persons (Scotland) Act, 1937, to the effect that they did 'wilfully neglect' their infant child 'in a manner likely to cause her unnecessary suffering and injury to health'. The neglect libelled was failure to provide adequate food and medical aid, and in the outcome the child died. In the course of the defence case the defending solicitor sought to adduce as a witness Dr Parry, a psychiatrist, who had seen the applicants for the first time on the previous Saturday and had no personal knowledge of the facts of the case. After argument the sheriff substitute, on the ground that Dr Parry's proposed evidence was not relevant to the question of guilt or innocence, refused to allow him to be called as a witness at that stage, but without prejudice to the right of the defence to call him to give evidence in mitigation in the event of the accused being found guilty.

Even assuming that the proposed evidence was irrelevant to the question of guilt or innocence, it would, I think, have been preferable to allow Dr Parry to give evidence, so far as relevant to mitigation before the jury retired, in order that, if they thought fit and as they were entitled to do, they might add a recommendation to leniency when returning their verdict. Indeed, it would appear from the transcript that the basic objection of the procurator-fiscal was not to the witness being adduced at that stage, but to the relevance of the proposed line of evidence to the question of guilt or innocence. However, it appears that in passing sentence the sheriff-substitute took into account Dr Parry's report, no complaint is made in regard to sentence, and this procedural matter is not in issue in the present applications.

From the transcript, the grounds upon which the defending solicitor sought to uphold the relevance of the proposed evidence to the merits of the case are not wholly clear. Insanity was not pleaded, there was no question of diminished responsibility in the legal sense, and it appears that the object of the evidence was to establish some lesser state of mental irresponsibility which would negative wilfulness and justify an acquittal. The sheriff-substitute in rejecting the defence submission followed the dicta of the Lord Justice-General (Clyde) in *H.M. Advocate v. Cunningham*, 1963 J.C. 80 at p. 84, to the effect that 'any mental or pathological condition short of insanity—any question of diminished responsibility owing to any cause, which does not involve insanity—is relevant only to the question of mitigating circumstances and sentence ... diminished responsibility is a plea applicable to murder. It is not open in the case of a lesser crime ....'

Before us, Mr Gow did not challenge the dicta above quoted but contended that, so far as the present case is concerned, '*Cunningham* is a red herring'. His argument centred on the word 'wilful' and was to the effect that, just as the Crown have to establish wilful neglect here, equally the defence were entitled to plead psychiatric evidence of a mental state on the part of the applicants, short of insanity, which would justify the jury in holding that the acts and omissions constituting the neglect complained of, if established, had not been shown to be wilful. He equiparated such evidence with evidence tending to establish accident, but conceded that, if his argument be right, it was an argument which would be open, not merely in the case of statutory offences which are not absolute but involve wilfulness, but also in the field of common law crimes and offences in which *mens rea* is of the essence. In that event, the new hazards and difficulties involved in accepting the argument would be immense.

It is not disputed that the applicants neglected their child, that they failed to provide adequate food and medical aid for her and, as I understand it, that unnecessary suffering and injury to her health were caused as a result and that she died. Nor is it suggested that the medical evidence sought to be led was designed to counter any of these facts. What is said is that evidence would have been to the effect that the applicants were so feckless and incompetent that they did not appreciate what the result of their failure would be and that accordingly their neglect was not wilful. On that basis, it was said the jury would have been entitled to acquit. Although the passage was not cited to us, I think that the argument for the applicants can be found, put in a nutshell, in Gordon's Criminal Law at p. 208. The passage in a paragraph dealing with 'Wilful Neglect' reads thus:

> 'Neglect may be negligent or intentional: the man who neglects his children by deliberately keeping them short of food and clothing has neglected them wilfully; the man who keeps them short of food and clothing because he is too feckless to look after them properly has neglected them negligently.'

That, in my opinion, is not the test to apply in a case of an offence under section 12(1) of the 1937 Act. The argument for the applicants seems to me to proceed on a confusion between the two ingredients of such an offence: (a) that there should be neglect (or ill-treatment, abandonment, assault, etc.) which is wilful—though it is difficult to conceive of conduct which is not wilful constituting assault; and (b) that this should be in a manner likely to cause the child unnecessary suffering or injury to health. As the sheriff-substitute pointed out, 'neglect is the want of reasonable care, that is the omission of such steps as a reasonable parent would take, such as are usually taken in the ordinary experience of mankind. That is what neglect is, but before you can bring a criminal charge, you have got to prove that it was wilful in the sense of being deliberate or intentional, but ... without necessarily having any intent to harm the child.' In other words, while proof of wilfulness is essential to establish head (a), the test under head (b) is an objective one. That test is whether the neglect was 'in a manner likely to cause ...' and not whether it was 'in a manner intended to cause ...'. It is not suggested here that the applicants did not appreciate the nature of their acts or omissions or that these were not deliberate and intentional. The argument is, and the evidence proposed to be led was, to the effect that the consequences were not intended or foreseen. Mr Gow in support of his argument founded mainly on the case of *Reg. v. Senior*, [1899] 1 Q.B. 283, which was an appeal which was concerned with the effect and meaning of certain statutory provisions which were, for all relevant purposes, in the same terms as section 12(1) of the 1937 Act. That decision, however, seems to me to be against the applicants' contentions here. Mr Senior, who was an affectionate parent, had taken all reasonable steps for the care of his dangerously ill child except the vital step of calling in medical aid. This he had deliberately omitted to do, not because he wished or intended any harm to the child (who in fact died), but because of religious convictions which he held as a member of a sect known as the 'Peculiar People'. Nevertheless his conviction was upheld. In the words of Lord Russell of Killowen C.J. (at pp. 290–291), ' "Wilfully" means that the act is done deliberately and intentionally, not by accident or inadvertence, but so that the mind of the person who does the act goes with it'. The test of 'wilful neglect' was thus satisfied (head (a) referred to above) and it was no defence that, acting on strongly held religious principles, he had no intention of causing unnecessary suffering or harm. The absence of such intention where, as is said to be the case here the actings or omissions are due, not to religious principles (however mistaken), but to fecklessness and incompetence is, in my opinion, equally no defence. This present case is, in my opinion, an attempt, wholly lacking in any merit, to prise ajar a door which was firmly shut in Cunningham. I agreed and still agree with what was said in Cunningham and I would refuse both applications for leave to appeal."

Application for leave to appeal dismissed.

NOTES

**8.55**   *Cf. Sheppard and Another* [1980] 3 All E.R. 899. In that case the appellants were a young couple, described as being of low intelligence. Their 16-month-old son died of hypothermia and malnutrition. The appellants were charged under s.1(1) of the Children and Young Persons Act 1933 with wilfully neglecting the child in a manner likely to cause him unnecessary suffering or injury to health. It appeared that they had neglected to obtain medical assistance for the child, but they claimed that they did not realise that the child was ill enough to need a doctor, and that although they knew the child was unable to keep its food down, they "had genuinely thought that this was due to some passing minor upset to which babies are prone, from which they recover naturally without medical aid and which medical treatment can do nothing to alleviate or to hasten recovery" (*per* Lord Diplock at p. 901). The appellants were convicted before the Crown Court. Their appeal to the Court of Appeal was dismissed, that court considering itself bound by a line of authority to the effect that the question in such cases was: "Would a reasonable parent with knowledge of the facts that were known to the accused, appreciate that failure to have the child examined was likely to cause him unnecessary suffering or injury to health?" (*emphasis added*). On appeal to the House of Lords, it was held that the test in such cases was not the objective test of the "reasonable parent". What was required was proof that the child needed medical aid at the time when the parent failed to provide it and, either that the parent was aware at that time that the child's health might be at risk if it was not provided with medical aid or that the parent's failure to appreciate this was due to his not caring whether his child's health was at risk or not (*per* Lord Diplock at pp. 906–907). For a discussion of this case see C. Gane, " 'Wilful Neglect' in the Children and Young Persons Act 1933", (1981) 3 Liverpool Law Review 79.

## 8. ISSUING THREATS

**8.56**   "Threatening gestures sufficient to produce alarm" may constitute an assault (*Atkinson v. H.M. Advocate*, 1987 S.C.C.R. 534 (*ante*, p. 281)). The following cases deal with written and oral threats of violence.

**James Miller**
(1862) 4 Irvine 238

The accused was charged on an indictment which libelled the "wickedly and feloniously **8.57** writing and sending threatening letters". An objection was taken to the relevancy of this charge in respect that it did not set forth any crime known to the law of Scotland.

THE LORD JUSTICE-CLERK (INGLIS): "The Court having formed an opinion in this case, they have requested me to state the grounds of it. The major proposition charges the accused with the 'wickedly and feloniously writing and sending, or causing to be written or sent, to any of the lieges, any threatening letter'. Now it is necessary to consider whether this major proposition, as regards its relevancy, obtains support from the use of the words 'wickedly and feloniously', and it must be observed that, properly speaking, these words have no place in the major proposition. The proper place for these words in an indictment is in the minor proposition, and when they occur in the minor, they express a quality of the act which is there specifically charged; they express that which is essential to the constitution of the crime—a certain condition of mind on the part of the accused at the time of committing the act libelled. I do not say that it is impossible, that these words should have any force or effect in a major proposition; but whatever force or effect they may have, it cannot alter their settled meaning, which is what I have now endeavoured to explain.

Abstracting these words, the crime charged is, 'writing and sending a threatening letter.' Now, that the use of threats is, in certain well-known cases, a crime in the eye of the law of Scotland, will not admit of dispute. A threat to burn a man's house is undoubtedly criminal, and so is a threat to put him to death, or to do him any grievous bodily harm, or to do any serious injury to his property, his fortune, or his reputation. These are all criminal threats; and, any one who uses such threats may be punished for the use of them, although he had no intention of carrying them into effect, and no purpose to serve in using them, except it may be the gratification of his own malice or his own caprice. The very using of the threat is in these cases itself a crime. But then, while there is a certain class of threats that are undoubtedly criminal in the eye of the law, there is another and a much larger class of threats that are not so; and even threats that are immoral and unjust may not be of such a kind as to amount to a crime. It is therefore absolutely indispensable, when the criminal law deals with the use of threats as a ground of punishment, that care should also be taken to distinguish between these two classes of threats. It seems to follow from this, as a necessary consequence, that the major proposition of a libel which charged the using and uttering of threats would not be relevant, assuming that that means the using and uttering of threats verbally, because there may be the using and uttering of threats in a great variety of cases which would not amount to a crime; and the major proposition which I have supposed, therefore, would be a bad major proposition. On the other hand, it seems clear enough that the using and uttering of a threat verbally of such a kind as I have already adverted to—a threat to burn a man's house, or to take his life, or to do him some grievous harm—would be a relevant point of dittay, and a major proposition setting forth that would set forth a crime known in the law of Scotland.

But here we have the element of writing, and it is that which gives to this case its peculiar importance. The threats here are contained in letters, and the question comes to be, whether the crime of writing and sending threatening letters, or the writing and sending of a threatening letter, is a relevant statement of a crime in a major proposition. Here, again, it seems abundantly clear, that the writing and sending of a threatening letter, in the popular sense of these words, is not in every case criminal, any more than the use of verbal threats is always criminal. For it is only certain threats that are criminal; and it is only if threats of that kind are conveyed in writing, that such writing becomes criminal. It may be also that the threats so conveyed are used for an unlawful purpose, such as extorting money, and thus they may acquire in another way a criminal character. But if in the natural and popular sense these words, 'writing and sending a threatening letter', do not in themselves amount to a statement of what is criminal, the only question remaining is, whether writing and sending threatening letters, or rather, properly speaking, the term 'threatening letters', has a technical and fixed meaning in law, and signifies the writing and sending of letters containing threats of that particular kind of which the use is criminal? Now, we have considered the various authorities and the cases that have been cited to us, and upon the whole we have come to the conclusion that there has been no such fixed understanding or practice as to give any definite technical meaning to the term 'threatening letters', and, consequently, that the major proposition of this indictment, which we read, for the reasons I have already stated, as simply libelling the writing and sending of a threatening letter, is not a relevant major proposition. The objection to the libel is therefore sustained."

*Objection to relevancy sustained.*

Note

**8.58**    In *Hill v. McGrogan*, 1945 S.L.T. (Sh. Ct) 18 (*post*, p. 499) the accused was charged with sending a letter to a woman in which he demanded her resignation from her job as a school cleaner, failing which he would write to the Ministry of Education to have her charged with theft of Government property, all for the purpose of forcing her to leave her job. The sheriff held that this was not a criminal threat since what was threatened was not criminal in itself (since it did not threaten violence), nor was it used for an improper purpose (since it did not seek financial gain for the accused). Whether this decision can today be regarded as sound is questionable, especially in light of the decision of the High Court in *Rae v. Donnelly*, 1982 S.C.C.R. 148, *post*, p. 498.

### Kenny v. H.M. Advocate
1951 J.C. 104

**8.59**    The appellants were charged on indictment with, *inter alia*, threatening a man with violence "all with intent to intimidate him and to deter him from giving evidence" against the appellants in a criminal trial. On this charge, the jury returned a verdict of guilty of threatening violence, but without the intent libelled. An application for leave to appeal against conviction on the third charge was presented to the High Court.

Lord Keith: "Various points have been taken by the applicants in this appeal, and I can dispose at once of certain of the objections which do not seem to bulk very largely in the case. The facts are that a fracas took place on a common stair in Glasgow, in which the applicants were involved and in the course of which serious injury by cutting with a sharp instrument, a knife or a razor, was occasioned to one of the witnesses, a man Welsh. Welsh was taken to hospital, and some time after his return from hospital—in fact two and a half months after the incident—the two accused called at his house, looked into the house through the top of a window, made certain remarks to him of a threatening character, came round to the door of the house, which Welsh had by this time closed, and made further remarks to him, including one which was that if Welsh came out the accused would mark his face. The charge that was made against the accused on this latter incident (the third in the indictment) was that 'you did climb on to the window ledge of and peer into said house, did shout, knock at the door and threaten said William Welsh with violence, all with intent to intimidate him and to deter him from giving evidence against you in your trial ....'

On a suggestion of the Sheriff who was the presiding Judge at the trial, the jury brought in a verdict from which the latter part of the charge was excised, the verdict being that on charge 3 they found the accused guilty of threatening violence without the intent libelled. Such a verdict is, however, open to serious objection. Had the indictment charged the accused with merely threatening violence, the charge would, I think, have been irrelevant and could not have proceeded to trial. In these circumstances, looking to the verdict that the jury has returned, I think the proper course here would be to find that the verdict did not amount to a verdict of a crime of which the accused can be found guilty. Accordingly, so far as the third charge is concerned, I think the accused are entitled to succeed in their appeal."

Lord Russell: "I am of the same opinion. I desire to add only a few words with regard to the conviction on the third charge. It is not every verbal threat that is a criminal offence. It appears to me that the verbal threat libelled in the third charge of this indictment was clearly serious and criminal by reason of the purpose or intent with which the threat was alleged to have been made, that purpose being to intimidate the victim so as to deter him from giving evidence against the accused in their trial due to take place a few days later. I am satisfied that, as framed, that charge did disclose a relevant criminal charge. If that charge had been established by the evidence, it would have been, as it is, a serious offence. As it happened, however, in the evidence adduced relating to the circumstances in which the verbal threat was made, there was no proof of any reference having been made by the accused to the forthcoming trial or of any language used by way of deterring the recipient of the threats from appearing as a witness at the trial. In that situation, since the jury were of opinion that the intent to intimidate and deter was not proved, the result of their verdict was to convict the accused merely of uttering a verbal threat to do violence, without any further specification relevant to infer grievous bodily harm or sinister intent. The failure of the Crown to prove the substance of the sinister purpose contained in the threat so waters down the charge that I have, with some hesitation, come to the conclusion that what was left of the charge did not, on the evidence by which it was supported, amount to a criminal offence. I therefore agree that the conviction on the third charge should be quashed."

Conviction quashed.

NOTES

1. Not every threat will amount to a crime at common law. Threats of death, serious bodily harm, or **8.60** serious damage to property may be criminal. But since not every threat will amount to an offence, merely to charge a person with "writing and sending a threatening letter" is not a relevant charge. Where the threat in question is one which is, as it were, criminal *per se*, the reason for uttering the threat is irrelevant. But as *Kenny v. H.M. Advocate* makes clear, there will be circumstances in which a threat, not otherwise criminal, becomes criminal when it is made for a purpose such as to intimidate a witness and deter him or her from giving evidence.

2. One issue not considered by the Scottish authorities is the effect of words when combined with gestures. We have seen (*ante*, pp. 281–282) that threatening gestures which cause alarm may amount to an assault. What is the position of an *ex facie* "innocent" or "neutral" gesture accompanied by oral threats? Suppose that A walks towards B, and at the same time starts to remove his (A's) jacket. Presumably no assault? But what if A, at the same time says, "Right, let's fight it out here and now". Is there an assault?

What is the effect of the converse situation, *i.e.* an apparently threatening gesture accompanied by words which indicate no present intention to injure? Suppose A picks up a stick and brandishes it at B, while stating, "If it wasn't for the fact that there was a policeman across the street I'd knock your teeth out." Is that an assault? Is it a criminal threat? *Cf. Tuberville v. Savage* (1669) 1 Mod. Rep. 3.

# 9. Stalking and harassment

Stalking and harassment as types of threatening or intimidating behaviour have come to the fore over **8.61** the last ten years. The Protection from Harassment Act 1997 prohibits harassment and, for England and Wales, creates a new statutory offence of harassment. At the time the Act was passed it was thought unnecessary to create such a statutory offence for Scotland since most types of harassment could already be dealt with by the common law, largely by an appropriately worded charge of breach of the peace. Section 9 of the Act does, however, create a new offence of "breach of non-harassment order".

**Protection from Harassment Act 1997**
*Scotland*

**Harassment**

8.—(1) Every individual has a right to be free from harassment and, accordingly, a person **8.62** must not pursue a course of conduct which amounts to harassment of another and—

(a) is intended to amount to harassment of that person; or

(b) occurs in circumstances where it would appear to a reasonable person that it would amount to harassment of that person.

(2) An actual or apprehended breach of subsection (1) may be the subject of a claim in civil proceedings by the person who is or may be the victim of the course of conduct in question; and any such claim shall be known as an action of harassment.

(3) For the purposes of this section—

"conduct" includes speech;

"harassment" of a person includes causing the person alarm or distress; and

a course of conduct must involve conduct on at least two occasions.

(4) It shall be a defence to any action of harassment to show that the course of conduct complained of—

(a) was authorised by, under or by virtue of any enactment or rule of law;

(b) was pursued for the purpose of preventing or detecting crime; or

(c) was, in the particular circumstances, reasonable.

(5) In an action of harassment the court may, without prejudice to any other remedies which it may grant—

(a) award damages;

(b) grant—

    (i) interdict or interim interdict;

    (ii) if it is satisfied that it is appropriate for it to do so in order to protect the person from further harassment, an order, to be known as a "non-harassment order", requiring the defender to refrain from such conduct in relation to the pursuer as may be specified in the order for such period (which includes an indeterminate period) as may be so specified,

but a person may not be subjected to the same prohibitions in an interdict or interim interdict and a non-harassment order at the same time.

(6) The damages which may be awarded in an action of harassment include damages for any anxiety caused by the harassment and any financial loss resulting from it.

(7) Without prejudice to any right to seek review of any interlocutor, a person against whom a non-harassment order has been made, or the person for whose protection the order was made, may apply to the court by which the order was made for revocation of or a variation of the order and, on any such application, the court may revoke the order or vary it in such manner as it considers appropriate.

(8) In section 10(1) of the Damages (Scotland) Act 1976 (interpretation), in the definition of "personal injuries", after "to reputation" there is inserted ", or injury resulting from harassment actionable under section 8 of the Protection from Harassment Act 1997".

### Breach of non-harassment order

**8.63**    9.—(1) Any person who is found to be in breach of a non-harassment order made under section 8 is guilty of an offence and liable—

(a) on conviction on indictment, to imprisonment for a term not exceeding five years or to a fine, or to both such imprisonment and such fine; and

(b) on summary conviction, to imprisonment for a period not exceeding six months or to a fine not exceeding the statutory maximum, or to both such imprisonment and such fine.

(2) A breach of a non-harassment order shall not be punishable other than in accordance with subsection (1) ....

NOTES

1. Section 11 of the 1997 Act inserts a new section 234A into the Criminal Procedure (Scotland) Act **8.64** 1995. Under section 234A, where a person is convicted of an offence involving harassment of a person ("the victim"), the prosecutor may apply to the court to make a non-harassment order against the offender requiring him to refrain from such conduct in relation to the victim as may be specified in the order for such period (which includes an indeterminate period) as may be so specified, in addition to any other disposal which may be made in relation to the offence. Before making such an order the court must be satisfied, on a balance of probabilities, that it is appropriate to do so in order to protect the victim from further harassment. A person who is found to be in breach of such an order is guilty of an offence under section 234(a)(4) and liable to the same penalties as are set out in section 9 of the 1997 Act.

2. For an example of how a charge of breach of the peace may be framed in a case of harassment, see *Elliott v. Higson*, High Court, on appeal, May 12, 1999, *unreported*.

3. The absence of an express offence of harassment in Scotland has been criticised as providing inadequate protection for victims. The Scottish Executive launched a consultation exercise on the law in March 2000. See Scottish Executive, Justice Department, *Stalking and Harassment—A Consultation Document*.

# 10. PREVENTIVE OFFENCES: KNIVES AND OTHER WEAPONS

## Criminal Law (Consolidation) (Scotland) Act 1995

### Prohibition of the carrying of offensive weapons

**47.**—(1) Any person who without lawful authority or reasonable excuse, the proof whereof **8.65** shall lie on him, has with him in any public place any offensive weapon shall be guilty of an offence ...

(4) In this section "public place" includes any road within the meaning of the Roads (Scotland) Act 1984 and any other premises or place to which at the material time the public have or are permitted to have access, whether on payment or otherwise; and "offensive weapon" means any article made or adapted for use for causing injury to the person, or intended by the person having it with him for such use by him or by some other person.

### Offence of having in public place article with blade or point

**49.**—(1) Subject to subsections (4) and (5) below, any person who has an article to which **8.66** this section applies with him in a public place shall be guilty of an offence ...

(2) Subject to subsection (3) below, this section applies to any article which has a blade or which is sharply pointed.

(3) This section does not apply to a folding pocketknife if the cutting edge of its blade does not exceed three inches (7.62 centimetres).

(4) It shall be a defence for a person charged with an offence under subsection (1) above to prove that he had a good reason or lawful authority for having the article with him in the public place.

(5) Without prejudice to the generality of subsection (4) above, it shall be a defence for a person charged with an offence under subsection (1) above to prove that he had the article with him—
    (a) for use at work;
    (b) for religious reasons; or
    (c) as part of any national costume ....

(7) In this section "public place" includes any place to which at the material time the public have or are permitted access, whether on payment or otherwise.

**Offence of having article with blade or point (or offensive weapon) on school premises**

**8.67**    **49A.**—(1) Any person who has an article to which section 49 of this Act applies with him on school premises shall be guilty of an offence.

(2) Any person who has an offensive weapon within the meaning of section 47 of this Act with him on school premises shall be guilty of an offence.

(3) It shall be a defence for a person charged with an offence under subsection (1) or (2) above to prove that he had good reason or lawful authority for having the article or weapon with him on the premises in question.

(4) Without prejudice to the generality of subsection (3) above, it shall be a defence for a person charged with an offence under subsection (1) or (2) above to prove that he had the article or weapon in question with him—

> (a) for use at work,
> (b) for educational purposes,
> (c) for religious reasons, or
> (d) as part of any national costume ...

(6) In this section ... of this Act, "school premises" means land used for the purposes of a school excluding any land occupied solely as a dwelling by a person employed at the school; and "school" has the meaning given by section 135(1) of the Education (Scotland) Act 1980.

NOTES

**8.68**    1. Section 47(4) divides "offensive weapons" into three categories: articles (a) made for use for causing injury to the person, (b) those adapted for use for causing injury to the person and (c) those intended by the person having it with him for such use by him or by some other person.

*Category (a)*: Articles which fall into this category are frequently described as offensive weapons *per se*. Whether or not an article has been made for the purpose of causing injury will in many cases be a relatively straightforward question, especially if there is no other lawful use to which the article might be put. Thus guns whose construction indicates that they have been made for causing injury to the person, such as military rifles, machine guns and most pistols, will be regarded as offensive *per se*. But shotguns (see *Hodgson* [1954] Crim.L.R. 379) and other guns intended for hunting game, airguns, and possibly competition pistols have other lawful uses and ought not, therefore, to be regarded as offensive weapons *per se*. Other weapons which the courts have held to be offensive *per se* include coshes (see *Smith v. Vannet*, 1998 S.C.C.R. 410), swordsticks (see *Davis v. Alexander* (1970) 54 Cr.App.R. 398; *Butler* [1988] Crim.L.R. 695); flick-knives (see *Tudhope v. O'Neill*, 1982 S.C.C.R. 45), nunchaca sticks (see *Hemming v. Annan*, 1982 S.C.C.R. 432 and also *Copus v. D.P.P.* [1989] Crim.L.R. 577 and *Malnik* [1989] Crim.L.R. 451), 'shuriken' or 'Chinese throwing stars' (*McGlennan v. Clark*, 1993 S.C.C.R. 334). In *Coull v. Guild*, 1985 S.C.C.R. 421, Lord Ross appeared to accept that knuckledusters are offensive weapons *per se* (at p. 423).

In some instances whether the article is to be regarded as offensive *per se* is a matter of circumstance and degree. Not all knives will be regarded as offensive *per se*. In *Coull v. Guild*, 1985 S.C.C.R. 421 the weapon was a sheath knife. It was held that in the absence of evidence that sheath knives in general, or the particular knife in question, were made for causing personal injury, the sheriff had erred in holding that the knife was an offensive weapon *per se*. In contrast, in *Houston v. Snape*, 1993 S.C.C.R. 995, the High Court held that the sheriff had erred in not treating a knife as offensive *per se*. In that case the knife was a sheath knife with a seven inch blade, sharp on one side only, and pointed. The High Court took the view that this was more of a "dagger" than a sheath knife.

Other articles, similarly, may or may not be regarded as offensive weapons *per se* depending upon their characteristics. In *McKee v. MacDonald*, 1995 S.C.C.R. 513 the article was a light wooden baton, about eighteen inches long and in the shape of a police truncheon. The words "View sun from Spain" were painted on it, and it had a coloured cord threaded through the handle. It was very light for an object of its material and size. The sheriff convicted the appellant on the basis that this was an offensive weapon *per se*. In doing so, he founded upon the case of *Houghton v. Chief Constable of Greater Manchester* (1987) 84 Cr.App.R. 319, and a *dictum* in that case by May L.J. to the effect that a truncheon cannot be said to have any innocent quality since, if it is to be used at all, it can only be used for causing personal injury. The High Court disagreed. As Lord Sutherland observed in delivering the opinion of the Court: "If we look at the weapon concerned it does not appear to us to be designed for the purposes of offence and to have only that quality. It appears to us to be in the form of a souvenir, comparatively light for its nature and does not contain the qualities which would equiparate it with a police truncheon." That case should be contrasted with *Latham v. Vannet*, 1999 S.C.C.R. 119, which also concerned a wooden baton, but one which was much more substantial and which appeared to have "the infliction of injury as its primary purpose" (*per* Lord Sutherland, delivering the opinion of the Court). Having regard to "the size of the article, its weight and the solidity of the wood from which it was made" the High Court held that the sheriff had been entitled to treat this as an offensive weapon *per se*.

Where an article is made for a dual purpose—both as a weapon and for some other purpose such as a tool—it cannot be said that it is an offensive weapon *per se*. In *Woods v. Heywood*, 1988 S.C.C.R. 434 the weapon was a machete. The Shorter Oxford English Dictionary defines a machete as a "broad and heavy knife or cutlass used, esp. in Central America and the West Indies, both as a tool and a weapon". The sheriff treated the weapon as offensive *per se*. The High Court held that the sheriff had erred in doing so: "Where there are, as in the present case, twofold purposes, namely one which is for causing personal injury and the other for an innocent purpose, it cannot properly be affirmed that the weapon in question was one which was made for use for causing injury. It might have been made for the innocuous purpose, *i.e.*, as a tool" (*per* Lord Ross, delivering the opinion of the Court).

*Category (b)*: This category includes such things as a bottle or glass broken for the purpose of causing injury, a sharpened comb, a belt to which metal studs have been added. The fact that an article has undergone modification, or has been altered from its original form, is not sufficient to bring the article within this category. It is not clear if the intentions of the person adapting the article (who may or may not be the person charged with having the article with him) are relevant here. *McLaughlin v. Tudhope*, 1987 S.C.C.R. 456 suggests that it must at least be proved that any modification was effected in the course of adapting the article for use for causing injury.

*Category (c)*: This category may include any article which the accused has with him in a public place, with the intention that it be used to cause personal injury. Whether such intent is present is a question of fact and circumstance (*Lopez v. MacNab*, 1978 J.C. 1; *Owens v. Crowe*, 1994 S.C.C.R. 310). The nature of the article itself is important. In *Lynn v. McFadyen*, 1999 G.W.D. 24–1142, the appellant was found in possession of a baseball bat in circumstances which did not suggest that he was about to use it for sporting purposes. Lord Prosser observed: "Much will turn on the particular nature of the implement. A baseball bat has a limited number of likely uses. It is not suggested that baseball was one of these in the circumstances; and it seems to us that it will require only quite limited facts to justify the inference, with such an implement carried not for its primary design purpose."

The manner in which the weapon is carried may be significant: *Miller v. Douglas*, 1988 S.C.C.R. 565, where the weapon was a knife with a seven inch blade, carried in the pocket of the accused, where it might come readily to hand; *Kane v. H.M. Advocate*, 1988 S.C.C.R. 585, where the weapon was a Stanley knife, carried in the pocket with its blade exposed rather than retracted into the handle; *Brown v. Kennedy*, 1999 S.C.C.R. 574, where the weapon, a small kitchen knife, was found concealed in the accused's hat in the early hours of the morning; *Lynn v. McFadyen, supra*, where the baseball bat was carried in a bin bag among clothing. (It is worth observing from the above cases that the fact that the weapon is concealed and the fact that it is carried openly may both contribute to the inference that it is intended to be used to cause personal harm.)

Where it is being carried may also be relevant: *Owens v. Crowe*, above, where the weapon was a 'lock-knife' carried in a discotheque. Here the sheriff held that had the knife been carried during the day and the accused had been making his way along a street, he would not have been prepared to draw the inference of an intention to use the knife to cause personal injury. See also *Wallace v. Ruxton*, 1998 S.C.C.R. 701.

The possibility of the weapon being used may also be relevant. In *Orme v. Ruxton*, 1999 S.C.C.R. 344, the appellant was seen brandishing a large piece of wood, possibly a table leg, above his head, in the street at about 11.30 p.m. There were other young persons in the vicinity, but no suggestion of violence or antagonism. The accused threw the piece of wood away when he saw the police coming. The High Court held that there was not sufficient evidence here for the sheriff to draw the inference of an intention to use the piece of wood to cause personal injury. On the other hand, the fact that the accused has had the opportunity to use the weapon in the face of aggression, and refrained from doing so does not necessarily exclude the inference that he carried it with the intention of using it: *Miller v. Douglas, supra*.

It is extremely important to determine into which category the alleged weapon falls. If it falls into categories (a) or (b) all that the prosecutor need show is that the accused had the weapon with him or her in a public place. It is then for the accused to establish, on a balance of probabilities, that he or she has lawful authority or a reasonable excuse for having the weapon with him or her. If, however, the weapon does not fall into either of those categories, then it is for the prosecutor to prove the intention to use the article to cause personal injury.

2. Although, as noted above, a knife will not always be regarded as an offensive weapon *per se*, a person who has a knife in a public place with the intention that it be used to cause personal harm will fall foul of section 47(1) for that reason. They may alternatively be guilty of an offence under section 49 or, depending upon the circumstances, section 49A.

3. '*Has with him*': A person may be found to have a weapon with him or her even though they are not actually carrying it or in possession of it at the time. In *Smith v. Vannet*, 1998 S.C.C.R. 411, the accused had a cosh and a knife in his car. The car was parked in a lane and he was about six feet from the car when he was stopped and searched by the police, with the keys to the car in his pocket. The High Court held that the sheriff had been entitled to hold that the accused had the weapons with him. See also *Pawlicki and Swindell*, [1992] 3 All E.R. 902. *Cf. McVey v. Friel*, 1996 S.C.C.R. 768 and *Murdoch v. Carmichael*, 1993 S.C.C.R. 444.

4. '*Public place*': The fact that the accused is found with a weapon in a place which is not a public place, does not prevent the inference being drawn that in order to get there he or she must have passed through a public place with the weapon: *Wallace v. Ruxton*, 1998 S.C.C.R. 701; *McKernon v. McGlennan*, 1999 S.C.C.R. 255. On what is a "public place"; see *Normand v. Donnelly*, 1994, S.L.T. 62 (treatment cubicle in a hospital casualty department not a "public place").

5. '*Lawful authority*': It is likely that very few persons charged under sections 47, 49 or 49A will be able to claim that they have 'lawful authority' to have the weapon (or article with a point or blade) in a public place. In England it has been suggested that 'lawful authority' refers to those people 'who from time to time carry an offensive weapon as a matter of duty—the soldier with his rifle and the police officer with his truncheon' (*Bryan v. Mott* (1975) 62 Cr.App.Rep. 71, *per* Lord Widgery C.J. at p. 73).

6. '*Reasonable excuse*': This is a much wider concept than 'lawful authority', but is one which should be interpreted with regard to the purpose of the legislation which is to deter the carrying of weapons. It is not, therefore, a 'lawful excuse' that the accused feared that he might be attacked, and carried the weapon 'just in case': *Grieve v. Macleod*, 1967 J.C. 32; *Miller v. Douglas, supra*; *Kincaid v. Tudhope*, 1983 S.C.C.R. 389; *Hemming v. Annan, supra*; *Glendinning v. Gould*, 1987 S.C.C.R. 304.

It may, however, be a lawful excuse that the accused had picked up the weapon with the intention of using it to fend off an imminent attack. See *Evans v. Hughes* [1972] 1 W.L.R. 1452; *Miller v. Douglas, supra*.

7. '*Good reason*' or other reasons for having an article with a blade or point:

In *Crowe v. Waugh*, 1999 S.L.T. 1181, the respondent was arrested for breach of the peace. On the way to the police station he told the police that he had a knife in his jacket pocket. The jacket was one which he normally wore when he went fishing, and the knife was one which he used when fishing. The sheriff held that the respondent had a 'good reason' for having the knife with him. The procurator-fiscal appealed to the High Court. In delivering the opinion of the court, upholding the prosecutor's appeal, Lord Prosser made the following observations:

> "[T]he question in terms of section 49(4) is whether the accused has proved that 'he had a good reason' for having the article with him in a public place. The question of whether an accused 'had' a good reason can in our view be distinguished from the question of whether there was a good reason, and is perhaps suggestive of those reasons which are not external and objective, but are a matter of intention or purpose. We would not, however, see that as sufficient to rule out the possibility that a good reason might be found not in an accused's intentions, but in the whole facts and circumstances which brought the situation about. But there is a more important question: according to what criteria is one to consider and decide whether a particular reason is to be held as 'good'? We would respectfully accept what is said by the court in *Lister v. Lees,* 1994 S.C.C.R. 548 at page 552, that 'it is important to bear in mind the purpose of the legislation'. The opinion of the Court continues as follows:
>
> > 'The legislation contains a general prohibition against carrying in a public place an article with a blade or point, and the purpose of the legislation must be to protect the public from persons who may use such articles to cause injury or threaten others. In these circumstances before a reason put forward can be regarded as 'good reason' it must be a reason which would justify an exception to the general prohibition contained in the statute .... We are satisfied that in determining whether

any reason put forward amounts to 'good reason' the court should not be making any moral judgment".

And at page 553, it is said that the court must determine whether the reason advanced appears to constitute "a justifiable exception to the general prohibition", and that since each case depends upon its facts and circumstances, the court does not find it possible to give any greater guidance as to what is meant by "good reason" in the statute.

The problem for an accused person such as Mr Waugh seems to us to lie not merely in the general purpose of the legislation: a provision designed to protect the public from persons who might use such articles to cause injury or to threaten others could at least arguably achieve its full purpose while treating proof that one did not know one had the object, and had no such intention, as a defence. But in section 49, Parliament appears to us to have adopted a means of achieving its purpose which casts the net very wide. By ignoring knowledge and intent in subsection (1), Parliament is not merely telling those who contemplate taking a knife or the like into a public place that they must refrain from doing so. It is telling everyone, including the careless and the casual and the thoughtless and the forgetful that they will be guilty of an offence under section 49(1), unless they can establish a defence under subsection (4) or (5). Such a provision is in our view not merely a "prohibition", to be obeyed, but is effectively designed to bring it home to the public in general that some care will have to be taken in the way they run their day to day lives, if they are to avoid committing the offence through casualness, carelessness and the like. In that context, it does not appear to us that "good reason" could be constituted in terms of subsection (4), in situations such as the present where there is no knowledge and intent, and where the reason for the presence of the knife is to be found in the background and circumstances, except in what we think would be rather unusual circumstances. An example of such unusual circumstances could be where the accused had at no time had any knowledge of the article, and his having it with him resulted from the acts of others or some very immediate circumstance. Given the terms of the general section (1), it is necessary to look at the background and circumstances with some care. If one owns a garment which one is likely, or even liable on occasion, to wear in a public place, then the pockets of that garment are not a suitable place to keep something like a knife ...

In *Johnston v. Gilchrist*, 1999 G.W.D. 22–1032, the appellant was found with a knife tucked into his waistband. When questioned about this he stated that he was carrying it for his friend. He subsequently claimed that he had taken the knife from his friend who had been brandishing it in an aggressive manner and that he was acting, as it were, as peacemaker. The appellant was indeed seen and heard trying to calm the situation. He explained that he had intended to dispose of the knife, but had not had time to do so before the police searched him. The High Court held that the Sheriff had been entitled to convict, since the appellant's line of defence was not accepted, but the case appears to suggest that had it been accepted that he had taken the knife in an attempt to prevent its unlawful use, that would have been a "good reason" for having the knife.

# Chapter 9

# SEXUAL OFFENCES

**9.01** This is an area fraught with difficulties, although these are frequently matters of policy rather than substantive law. One of the major sources of difficulty lies in the fact that in relation to sexual matters the criminal law is invoked for a range of quite different purposes. Thus it is expected to protect the individual from sexual aggression or exploitation, or to enforce "morality," or to curb behaviour which is offensive or annoying.

## 1. RAPE

**9.02** Rape is widely regarded as the most serious sexual offence. The victim may suffer serious harm, both physical and psychological, and the crime may carry with it the risk of infection or pregnancy. The "essential guilt" of the crime, however, is well summarised by para. 263 of the California Penal Code as consisting in "the outrage to the person and feelings of the victim".

The generally accepted statement of the law is that a man is guilty of rape if he has sexual intercourse with a woman by overcoming her will (see Hume, i, 301; Gordon, paras 33–02 to 33–08; *William Fraser* (1847) Ark. 280, *infra*, p. 353; *Charles Sweenie* (1858) 3 Irv. 109, *post*, p. 348; *H.M. Advocate v. Logan*, 1935 J.C. 100, *post*, p. 352).

## A. The *actus reus* of rape

### (a) Sexual intercourse

**9.03** For these purposes the requirement of sexual intercourse is satisfied by any degree of penetration of the woman's body, and this need not be accompanied by emission of semen (*Alexr Macrae*, January 7, 1841, Bell's Notes 83; *Muldoon v. H.M. Advocate*, 1967 S.L.T. 237, *per* Lord Walker at p. 240.)

Penetration must be intended to effect "genital" intercourse, that is to say penetration of the vagina by the penis, so that forcible anal or oral intercourse, or forcible penetration of the victim's body with the hand or an object such as a stick or bottle is not rape, but indecent assault.

An expansion of the concept of rape has been considered, and rejected, on several occasions in England. See, for earlier discussions, the Criminal Law Revision Committee's *Working Paper on Sexual Offences* (October 1980) and their final *Report on Sexual Offences*, Cmnd. 9213 (1984) at para. 2–47.

The definition of rape was again reviewed in considerable detail by the independent Review of Sex Offences established by the Home Office:

## Setting the Boundaries: Reforming the Law on Sex Offences
Report of the Review of Sex Offences
Home Office, July 2000

*Rape*                                                                          **9.04**

2.8.1 The first issue we thought about was the criminal behaviour that should be included in the crime of rape. We considered the various sexual violations that are perpetrated on men and women by other men and women, and the impact of differing kinds of sexual assaults on the victim in order to assess the relative seriousness of the different kinds of behaviour. We also wondered how the public might understand the law. We looked at what solutions other countries had adopted and sought information on how effective they had been. (The latter was particularly difficult as the letter of the law is only one of many variables in the way the criminal justice process operates.)

2.8.2 We decided that the essence of rape was the sexual penetration of a person by another person without consent. However, penetration comes in many forms. Men put their penis into the vagina, anus and mouth. Other parts of the body (notably fingers and tongues) are inserted into the genitalia and the anus. Objects are inserted into the vagina and anus of victims. Both men and women may perform such penetration. These are all extremely serious violations of victims which can leave them physically and psychologically damaged for many years. We did consider whether there was evidence that a woman could force a man to penetrate her against his will but, although we found a little anecdotal evidence, we did not discover sufficient to convince us that this was the equivalent of rape. (However we do recognise the existence of such coercive behaviour and think it should be subject to the criminal law. We make separate recommendations about offences of compelling sexual penetration . . . .)

2.8.3 Having decided that all coerced sexual penetration was very serious, the question was how the law should best deal with it. There seemed to be two potential approaches—that of defining any sexual penetration as rape, and that of treating penile penetration separately from other forms of penetration.

2.8.4 We were uneasy about extending the definition of rape to include all forms of sexual penetration. We felt rape was clearly understood by the public as an offence that was committed by men on women and on men. We felt that the offence of penile penetration was of a particularly personal kind, it carried risks of pregnancy and disease transmission and should properly be treated separately from other penetrative assaults. We therefore set aside our presumption of gender-neutrality as regards the perpetrator for offences for the crime of rape and propose that it be limited to penile penetration. We also recognised the concerns of transsexuals that the law could except them from the protection of the criminal justice system. If modern surgical techniques could provide sexual organs, the law should be clear enough to show that penetration of or by such organs would be contained within the scope of the offence. The law must give protection from all sexual violence. Whether or not sexual organs are surgically created, the law should apply. Accordingly we thought to put it beyond doubt that the law should apply to surgically constructed organs—whether vaginal or penile.

2.8.5 The present crime of rape is limited to the penile penetration of the anus and vagina. Forced oral sex is treated as an indecent assault. We thought that inappropriate. Forced oral sex is as horrible, as demeaning and as traumatising as other forms of forced penile penetration, and we saw no reason why rape should not be defined as penile penetration of the anus, vagina or mouth without consent.

NOTES

An extremely important change in English law has already been effected by section 142 of the **9.05** Criminal Justice and Public Order Act 1994, which re-defined the crime of rape so as to include non-consensual anal intercourse by a man with a woman or another man. Section 1(1) of the Sexual Offences Act 1956 (as amended by the 1994 Act) now provides that it is an offence for a man to rape a woman or another man. Section 1(2)(a) provides that a man commits rape if he has intercourse, whether vaginal or anal, with a person who at the time of the intercourse does not consent to it.

Several American states have extended the definition of rape and sexual assault to include non consensual oral-genital contact and vaginal or anal penetration with an object. See, for example, Arkansas Criminal Code, paras 5–14—103 and 5–14—101, Delaware Criminal Code, para. 761 (a) and (g), Kansas Statutes, 21–305 (1), Michigan Penal Code, para. 750.520a (1), Nebraska Statutes, Chapter 28–318 (6). Similar developments have taken place in some European jurisdictions. See, for example the Spanish *Código Penal*, article 179, the French *Nouveau Code Pénal*, art. 222–223 (and see, in this respect, Cass. Crim. 22 février 1984, *Bull. Crim.* No. 171, Dalloz 1984, IR 228 (oral penetration); Cass. Crim. 24 juin 1987, *Bull. Crim.* No. 265 (anal penetration); Cass. Crim. 5 septembre 1990, *Bull. Crim.* No. 313, Dalloz 1991, 13, J.C.P. 1991, II 21629 ('object' rape)). *Cf.* the Italian *Codice Penale*, artice 609*bis*.

## (b) 'By a man with a woman'

**9.06** It follows from the definition of rape that in Scots law this crime can only be committed by a man upon a woman. It is not rape for a man to force another man to submit to anal intercourse, nor is it rape for a woman to force a man to have sexual intercourse with her. (*Cf.* in this respect the views of the New York Court of Appeals which held, in *People v. Liberta*, 64 NY 2d 152, 474 NE 2d 567 (1984), that a woman could be guilty of raping a man and the circumstances of *Vaughan v. H.M. Advocate*, 1979 S.L.T. 49.) In France the crime of rape, which required *pénétration sexuelle* (article 332 of the old penal code now replaced by *aggression sexuelle* in the *Nouveau Code Pénal*) has been held to apply to acts by both men and women against men or women: Cass. Crim. 4 janvier 1985, *Bull. Crim.* No. 10, *Gaz. Pal.* 1986, 1. 19 (rape committed by a woman); Cass. Crim., 24 juin 1987 and 3 juillet 1991, *Droit Pénal* 1991, 314 (rape committed on a man).

## (c) Without consent

**9.07** Consent, or more correctly the absence of consent, is central to the crime of rape. This is undoubtedly the most problematic and contentious issue surrounding both the definition of the crime. The following problems arise: Firstly, is it sufficient for a conviction for the Crown to show that the victim did not consent to intercourse, or is it necessary for the prosecutor to go further and show that sexual penetration took place against the will of the victim? Secondly, since consent is in many instances a difficult question of fact for the jury to determine, are there any legal rules to determine when apparent consent is not effective? The third problem relates to the *mens rea* for rape. Since consent on the part of the woman excludes rape, a belief in consent will exclude the *mens rea* for rape. But need that belief be based on reasonable grounds, or is it sufficient that that belief was in fact held by the accused? This matter is discussed *post* pp. 356–359.

## (i) 'Without consent' or 'against her will'?

### Charles Sweenie
(1858) 3 Irv. 109

**9.08** An accused person was charged with raping a sleeping woman and also with "wicked and feloniously having carnal knowledge" of a sleeping woman. He objected to the relevancy of the indictment.

Lord Deas: "I have no doubt at all that the act charged in this indictment, is a crime cognizable by this Court. To suppose the contrary, would be to suppose that any female—it may be a virgin, pure in thought and in act—may, while asleep, without her knowledge or consent, be deprived of her virtue, rather than have yielded which, she would have yielded her life, and may even, by being made a mother, be brought to open shame, and yet that the perpetrator of this grievous wrong shall be liable to no punishment. This is a proposition too repugnant, not only to our moral nature, but to the plainest principles of our criminal jurisprudence, to be for a moment entertained. Let it be—as was held by the only Judge who dissented from the judgment in the gambling case of Greenhuff and others (2 Swin. 236), and who was so scrupulously jealous of what has been called the native vigour of our criminal law—that we are not to introduce new crimes—that an offence, to be indictable, must either come within the range of some known term, or fall within the spirit of some previous decision, or within some established general principle; still, I can see no difficulty in holding, that the wickedly and feloniously invading, by stealth (as is said in this indictment), the bed of a woman while asleep, and having carnal knowledge of her person without her consciousness or consent, is an offence of an aggravated kind, which might easily enough be brought (if that were necessary), within the range of more than one known term and which certainly falls as well within the spirit of previous decisions, as within the established general principle, that everyone who inflicts upon another, without that other's consent, a grievous and irreparable personal injury, must be answerable for having done so at the bar of criminal justice.

The more difficult question, however, remains, whether the offence be the crime of rape?

The prosecutor defines rape to be carnal knowledge of a woman without her consent. This, he says, is all that it is necessary to libel as a general rule, and that the cases where anything more has been stated, or requires to be stated, are exceptional. It is obvious, if this be so, that nearly all the cases that have occurred have been exceptional, and that we have scarcely had an example of the general rule. Accordingly, it is said, that all the cases of adults who have a will, are exceptional, and that it is because such cases are exceptional, that force has been and must be libelled as having been used to overcome the person, or the will. I cannot concur in this views. It appears to me that, according to all practice and authority, the libelling of force or concussion, applied either to the person or the will, is necessary, as a general rule, to the relevancy of the charge of rape; and that the cases where this is dispensed with, are exceptional. The prosecutor holds the case of infants to be rather an instance of the general rule than an exception. But, on his own shewing, it would not be a good instance, for it goes beyond his definition of the crime—the libel in such cases, never bearing, 'without her consent', but being, in modern practice at least, altogether silent on the subject of consent, of which an infant is presumed to be incapable. Of the alleged general rule, as applied to the case of an adult (I mean the mere libelling that carnal knowledge was had of the woman without her consent), we have really no instance; not even in the case mentioned by Hume, of the bedfast cripple of sixteen, whose alleged inability to make resistance, can only have been inability to make successful resistance, for what was charged against the panel was, 'the shameful deflowering, *forcing*, and abusing' of the girl.

I do not say that force must, in every instance, be libelled. The case of girls of tender years is an instance to the contrary; resting, however, not so much on the fact, that they have neither appetite nor will in the matter (for in some cases, and to some extent, they may have both), as on a presumption of law, introduced and established to prevent the evils to society and the demoralization which might otherwise follow, and which presumption, accordingly, is not allowed to be reargued. It may be that idiots fall within the same principle. (I say nothing of insane persons who are not idiots, whose cases may depend on their own circumstances and on degree). But I regard instances of children and of idiots as exceptional; and it does not follow, that, because an exception is made of cases in which by law, or both by law and nature, the parties are totally disqualified from consenting, an exception shall equally be made of the case of a woman who might have consented if awake, although she neither did nor could consent, being asleep.

Beyond the case of parties whom the law holds incapable of consent, we have no recorded instance of the element of force being altogether omitted in the libel. I mean force different from that which is necessarily implied in the act of sexual intercourse—for there is a plain fallacy in confounding what is essential to the act, even when consented to, with the force necessary to obtain opportunity to perform the act."

Charge of rape held irrelevant, but indictment
nonetheless held to disclose a crime.

NOTES

**9.09** 1. Other jurisdictions which at one time shared the view rape required that penetration took place against the will of the victim have abandoned that position. See, for example, *Larter* [1995] Crim.L.R. 75, where the Court of Appeal held that the appellants had rightly been convicted of rape notwithstanding that the victim had remained asleep throughout the offence. All that is required in English law is absence of consent. See the cases of *Lang* (1975) 62 Cr.App.R. 50 and *Olugboja* (1981) 73 Cr.App.R. 344. However, the rule established in *Sweenie* was confirmed by the High Court in *Sweeney and Thomson v. X.*, 1982 S.C.C.R. 509. In that case, the accused had sexual intercourse with the victim while she was unconscious. The Crown alleged that she had been rendered unconscious by her assailants, but the evidence did not support this. There was, however, sufficient evidence to establish that the victim was unconscious at the time of intercourse, possibly through the consumption of alcohol earlier in the evening. In his charge to the jury the trial judge, stated, *inter alia*, that it is not rape to have intercourse with a woman who is sleeping or unconscious, and the jury returned a verdict of guilty of indecent assault. The trial judge's statement of the law was confirmed by the appeal court.

2. In *Sweeney,* Lord Justice-General Emslie describes the offence of having sexual intercourse with an unconscious woman as a type of indecent assault. In *H.M. Advocate v. Grainger and Rae*, 1932 J.C. 40, (*post*, p. 359) Lord Anderson described it as "the crime of inflicting clandestine injury on a woman", and that description appears to be acquiring a *nomen juris* in its own right. See *post*, pp. 359–360.

3. If the accused has rendered the victim unconscious for the purpose of overcoming her resistance the situation is quite different, and in that case, sexual intercourse will constitute rape. See *H.M. Advocate v. Logan*, 1936 J.C. 100, *post*, p. 352. (Although it is interesting to note that in *H.M. Advocate v. Fraser* (1847) Ark. 280, *post*, p. 353, Lord Cockburn suggested that it would be rape for a man to have intercourse with a woman who was in a "faint" "though [this] may not have been produced by the ravisher".)

4. *Sweenie* and *Sweeney* demonstrate the resistance of the Scottish courts to defining rape simply as sexual intercourse without the consent of the woman. See also the case of *H.M. Advocate v. Watt*, High Court at Aberdeen, *unreported*, March 22–23, 2001, where it appears to have been held that it is insufficient for the Crown to show that the complainer did *not* consent even if she was *not* asleep or insensible as in *Sweenie* and *Sweeney*. Something more (such as force, the threat of force, or drugging, which are discussed below) must be shown to demonstrate that the victim's will was overcome. The case generated considerable comment and the Lord Advocate indicated that he would refer issues arising from the judge's ruling to the High Court under section 123 of the 1995 Act.

5. Would defining the law in terms of "without consent" be an improvement? Doing so would extend the protection which the law of rape affords. This point should not be overlooked, since although non-consensual intercourse with a woman may constitute the offence of indecent assault, there is a strong "symbolic" argument that conduct of the kind encountered in *Sweenie* and *Sweeney*, being as invasive of the rights and person of the woman as sexual intercourse achieved by overcoming her will, ought to be treated as rape. However, defining the crime in terms of absence of consent is not free from difficulty. What is meant by 'consent'? What if the victim does not consent but does not manifest this? The matter was considered by the *Review of Sex Offences* (see *ante*, p. 347), who reached the conclusion that there should be a statutory definition of consent, and that legislation should also set out a non-exhaustive set of circumstances where consent was not present. The definition of consent suggested by the Review is simply that consent should be defined as "free agreement" (see section 2.10). The list of circumstances where consent would be deemed not to be present would include:

- Where a person submits or is unable to resist because of force, or fear of force;
- Where a person submits or is unable to resist because of threats or fear of serious harm or serious detriment of any type to themselves or another person.
- Where a person was asleep, unconscious, or too affected by alcohol or drugs to give free agreement;
- Where a person did not understand the nature of the act, whether because they lacked the capacity to understand, or were deceived as to the purpose of the act;
- Where the person was mistaken or deceived as to the identity of the person or the nature of the act;
- Where the person submits or was unable to resist because they are abducted or unlawfully detained;

- Where agreement is expressed by a third party not the victim.

The list is illustrative only, and the *Review* suggests that it is supported by standard directions on the question of consent, which the courts would be expected to use, no doubt adapted to the circumstances of individual cases. Such an approach is presently used in the Australian state of Victoria (see *Review*, *para.* 2.11.1).

Many of the above situations are, of course, recognised in Scots law. Would this approach satisfy the criticisms of such cases as *Sweenie*, while at the same time avoiding the problems which are encountered in defining rape simply in terms of absence of consent?

6. For an alternative approach to this problem in rape, see Tadros, "No Consent: A Historical Critique of the Actus Reus of Rape", (1999) 3 Edinburgh Law Review, 317.

## *(ii) Force and threats*

On the question of what force (if any) is required for rape, Lord Ardmillan in *Sweenie* at p. 137 said "any **9.10** mode of overpowering the will, without actual personal violence, such as the use of threats, or drugs, is force in the estimation of the law—and ... any degree of force is sufficient in law to constitute the crime of rape, if it is sufficient in fact to overcome the opposing will of the woman".

References such as these to force in the definition of rape may have the effect of suggesting that there is no rape unless the victim resists and her resistance is physically overcome. This is not the modern view or practice. A man may be guilty of rape even though the woman puts up no resistance at all. In *Barbour v. H.M. Advocate*, 1982 S.C.C.R. 195, the appellant was charged with repeatedly raping and committing other serious sexual assaults on a woman whom he had threatened with violence. The complainer accepted that she had not offered any resistance. In his charge to the jury Lord Stewart stated:

> "... First of all, what is rape. Now, the crime of rape consists in the carnal knowledge of a woman against her will, her resistance having been overcome. There must be penetration of the body of the woman, that is the vagina, by the private member of the assailant.
>
> The important matter is not the amount of resistance put up but whether the woman remained an unwilling party throughout. The significance of resistance is only as evidence of unwillingness ....
>
> Now, let me just say a little more than I have on the question of unwillingness and resistance to these sexual advances. Now, as to all these things that she says were done to her Miss (X) says that she was an unwilling party.
>
> Now, you may think, ladies and gentlemen, you heard her give evidence for most of a day, that she was an intelligent woman, and you remember that when she was asked in cross-examination whether these things had not been done to her with her consent I recollect her hesitating and saying something like 'It depends what you mean by consent'. What she was indicating was that she did not resist, she said she did not resist but she allowed these things to happen to her, but she emphasised, and it is for you whether you believe her or not, that she did not voluntarily agree and was not a willing participant."

Threats of serious harm will be regarded as sufficient legally to overcome the victim's will. It is probably the case that they need not be directed at the victim herself. To coerce a woman into submitting to sexual intercourse by threatening to harm her child, for example, ought to be rape. But what if the victim submits under lesser threats? Suppose, for example, that the victim's employer demands that she have sexual intercourse with him and threatens her with the loss of her job if she does not? Or suppose that the accused has an affair with a married woman. She tells him she wants to end it but he says that he will tell her family if she does not continue to have sexual relations with him? Are such threats legally sufficient to overcome the victim's will?

Procuring a woman to have sexual intercourse by threats or intimidation is an offence under section 7(2) of the Criminal Law (Consolidation) (Scotland) Act 1995. The a maximum penalty under this section is two years' imprisonment (as opposed to life imprisonment for rape) so arguably the offence is targeted at much less serious threats than would be required for rape. But would a maximum penalty of two years always be sufficient for such cases? In *S. v. Volschenk*, 1968 (2) PH. H. 283 the accused, a police officer, took a black woman from her home. He drove her to a remote spot where he offered her the choice of having sexual relations with him or being prosecuted on a criminal charge. The woman allowed intercourse to take place. It was held that the accused was guilty of rape. The court's view was that a threat of prosecution and possible imprisonment was more serious than, for example, a threat to dismiss a woman from her employment, and sufficient to negate consent on her part. (See J. Burchell and J. Hilton, *Cases and Materials on Criminal Law* (2nd ed.), p. 559.)

## (iii) Drugging

### H.M. Advocate v. Logan
### 1936 J.C. 100

**9.11** A man was charged with raping a woman "while she was in a state of insensibility from the effects of intoxicating liquor supplied to her by you for the purpose of rendering her incapable of resistance". In the course of charging the jury:

LORD JUSTICE-CLERK (AITCHISON): "The Crown case is that the woman was doped with drink. If you thought that the Crown had proved that the woman was plied with drink, and drink of a deadly kind, the nature of which was concealed from her, in order to overcome her resistance, you could find a verdict of guilty of rape; but if the position was that the woman was not given the drink for the purpose of overcoming her or making her incapable of resistance, but had taken it of her own free will, and it had not been given to her for a criminal purpose, and she became insensible, and advantage was then taken of her in her insensible condition, then, in the eye of the law, the crime would not be rape but indecent assault only. Now, you think that a very odd distinction, but it is there on the authorities. A similar question arose many years ago, as far back as 1858, in what is known as the case of *Sweenie* (1858) 3 Irv. 109. That was a case where a man took advantage of a woman while she was asleep. There was no drugging of her to put her to sleep, and the Court held that it was a crime by the law of Scotland. The crime, so far as it is possible to define it, comes within the category of indecent assault. There may have been a reason for the decision in *Sweenie's* case, because in 1858 rape was one of the pleas of the Crown (as it still is), but also it was a capital offence, and the judges were very unwilling to extend the definition of rape so as to bring any new class of crime within the category of a capital offence. That may explain the decision, and, in any event, it is binding on me; and, applying it here in this case, it comes to this, that if you are satisfied on the evidence that Logan was a party to doping this woman for the purpose of overcoming her resistance, so that advantage might be taken of her, and advantage was taken of her, then he would be guilty of rape and there would be no answer to it. On the other hand, if the woman through indulgence—even if she was being invited or coaxed to drink—voluntarily took drink and just got insensible through it, and it was not doped or given her for the purpose of making her insensible, and advantage was taken of her in her insensible condition, then the crime is not rape, but indecent assault."

The accused was convicted of indecent assault.

NOTES

**9.12** The reference to "pleas of the Crown" is of no significance today, except as a reminder that rape is in the exclusive jurisdiction of the High Court.

Where the victim has consumed alcohol (or other intoxicants) not supplied to her by the accused for the purpose of overcoming her will, the fact that she is intoxicated may be factually relevant to the question of whether or not her will was overcome. An accused intent upon having sexual relations may find that his victim is more easily overcome. But if, because of intoxication, the victim is more easily persuaded to consent to sexual intercourse, such sexual intercourse will not be rape: *W. v. H.M. Advocate*, 1995 S.L.T. 685. See also Lord Ross's charge to the jury in *Sweeney and Thomson v. H.M. Advocate*, 1982 S.C.C.R. 509.

## (iv) Fraud

### William Fraser
(1847) Ark. 280

A man was charged with raping a woman by having intercourse with her while inducing her to **9.13** believe he was her husband, and alternatively with "fraudulently and deceitfully obtaining access to and having carnal knowledge of a married woman" by pretending to be her husband, or otherwise conducting himself, and behaving towards her so as to deceive her into the belief that he was her husband. The accused objected to the relevancy of the indictment.

LORD COCKBURN: "Now, I can gather nothing from our books, except that the crime of rape consists in having intercourse *without the woman's consent*. It is sometimes said that it must not only be without her consent, but *forcibly*. But this is plainly said loosely; merely because where consent is withheld, force is generally resorted to. It is not meant that there must be positive physical force, as a substantive element; but only that constructive force which is implied in the absence of consent. It is in the absence of consent that the essence of the crime consists. Force is only the *evidence*, and the *consequence*, of the want of consent, but is not necessary for the constitution of the crime. Hence, the crime is unquestionably committed wherever consent is *impossible, though there may be no force*; as in the case of intercourse with children, or lunatics or with women in intoxication, or in faints, though these may not have been produced by the ravisher. An insane woman, instead of requiring force, may actively concur; but because she cannot consent, the connection is rape.

In applying this principle to the case before us, there is a statement in the indictment which, in one view, settles, or at least supersedes, the question at issue. It is averred, and of course offered to be proved, that the intercourse was '*against, or without her will*'. If this is to be assumed, no question of relevancy is raised. But this interpretation of the libel would not decide, but might only postpone, the decision of the point. If the prosecutor was to maintain that the constructive want of consent implied in the fraud was sufficient, or if the Jury were to ask instructions on this matter, the question would arise on the trial. Moreover, I presume that the prosecutor does not mean to say that there was any *positive* dissent, or any *positive* absence of consent, but only intends to set forth that want of consent which is implied in the alleged deception practised on the woman. If this be the proper view of the libel, then the question may be held to be regularly raised now.

And my opinion upon it is, that obtaining access to the person of a female by this deception, does not amount to the crime of rape. I reach this result solely because the want of the woman's consent is not implied, either legally or practically, in the circumstance of her yielding from misrepresentation.

There is nothing better known to the law, or more familiar to its practice, than the difference between consent *withheld*, and consent given, but *given through fraud*. It would be idle to state examples of a distinction so certain and so common.

Now, the prosecutor's argument proceeds entirely on confounding these two things. Its substance is, that there was no consent, and indeed that the prisoner's fraud reduced his victim to a state of non-free agency, exactly as if he had taken advantage of her having been in childhood, or in lunacy, or as if he had drugged her himself. The plain fallacy of this, however, is, that it assumes consent given; an assumption not warranted by legal principle, and repugnant to the actual truth.

There is certainly nothing impossible or absurd in the idea of a person being induced to consent by a trick. And this very indictment states a fact which necessarily implies that this was the case here. It sets forth, that 'you (the prisoner) *did deceive her into the belief that you were her husband*'. If this was her belief, it includes her consent. No doubt it was a consent procured by deceit; but still it was procured. The victim was not in the condition of a female intoxicated, deranged, or under age, where there is no consent *de facto*. It is said that there was no consent to intercourse *with the prisoner*. But there was; only the consent was given on the erroneous conviction that he was her husband. She was misled as to his name and identity, but her consent to intercourse with the very individual beside her, is involved in the fact of her believing that she was his wife."

> Charge of rape held irrelevant, but alternative charge relevant.

NOTES

**9.14**    1. This is quite a shocking decision. What it holds is that so long as the woman understands that what is happening is sexual intercourse it does not matter that she is mistaken as to the identity of the other person. Now, unless it is suggested that women do not in general discriminate on this matter, that the identity of a woman's sexual partner is a matter of indifference to her, it seems quite wrong to hold that a fundamental deception as to a matter likely to affect the woman's decision whether or not to consent to intercourse is irrelevant. Suppose, for example, that the accused is a person to whom the woman has made it absolutely clear that she would not have sexual relations with him. What about other factors affecting the woman's choice? Suppose, for example, that the man is suffering from a sexually-transmittable disease which he conceals from her. Is the woman to be taken as consenting to intercourse even in this case? (*Cf. R. v. Clarence* (1888) 16 Cox C.C. 511 and see also *H.M. Advocate v. Kelly*, High Court at Glasgow, *unreported*, February 13–23, 2001, where a man who concealed from his girlfriend the fact that he was HIV-positive was convicted of culpably and recklessly infecting her with the virus by having sexual intercourse with her).)

2. The particular crime charged in *Fraser* is now a statutory form of rape. Section 7(3) of the Criminal Law (Consolidation) (Scotland) Act 1995 (which derives from the Criminal Law Amendment Act 1885) provides as follows: "A man who induces a married woman to permit him to have sexual intercourse with him by impersonating her husband shall be deemed to be guilty of rape." *H.M. Advocate v. Montgomery*, 1926 J.C. 2, *cf.* where this offence was held to cover impersonation of a former husband.

While overturning the objectionable features of decisions such as *Fraser* with regard to married women and their husbands, section 7(3) in a sense reinforces the attitude which lies behind that decision. Why should it only be rape to induce a married woman to have sexual intercourse by impersonating her husband, but not rape in other cases of deception as to identity?

3. This question has arisen in other jurisdictions, with quite different results. At one time it was held in England that it was not rape to have sexual intercourse by impersonating the woman's husband: *Barrow* (1868) 11 Cox C.C. 191. The effect of that decision was reversed by section 4 of the Criminal Law (Amendment) Act 1885, and in *Elbekkay* [1995] Crim. L.R. 163 the Court of Appeal held that it was rape for a man to have intercourse with a woman by impersonating the complainant's boyfriend (with whom she had been living for 18 months). Section 4 of the 1885 Act was passed in part to resolve a conflict between the decision of the English court in *Barrow* and the Irish decision in *Dee* (1884) 15 Cox C.C. 579 in which it was held that it was rape to have intercourse with a woman by impersonating her husband. The same conclusion was reached by the South African courts in *R. v. C.* 1952 (4) S.A. 117.

4. The deception in *Fraser* related to the identity of the man. What is the situation where the deception relates to the nature of the act? In *Flattery* (1877) 2 Q.B.D. 410 the victim was persuaded to allow sexual intercourse in the belief that it was a medical procedure. In *Williams* [1923] 1 K.B. 340 the accused, a choir master, pretended to the victim that the procedure was one which would improve her singing voice. In both cases the court held that the accused was guilty of rape. Compare those decisions with the South African case of *R. v. Williams* 1931 (1) P.H. H. 38 (E.) in which the complainer agreed to have sexual intercourse with the accused after he spuriously pretended to her that this would remedy a gynaecological disorder. The court held that this was not rape. The complainer, as a married woman was not deceived as to the act, but only as to the consequences. See also *Linekar* [1995] 3 All E.R. 69 (L's fraudulent claim that he would pay the complainant, a prostitute, for intercourse did not vitiate her consent to the act).

5. In *Gray v. The Criminal Injuries Compensation Board* 1998 S.C.L.R. 191 the reclaimer, G, became friendly with a man, W. W asked to have sexual intercourse with her, but she refused. He also asked her to marry him, and although at first she refused she eventually agreed. The parties had intercourse on one occasion before they went through the marriage ceremony, and on about six occasions thereafter. A few months after the marriage W disappeared. G found out that at the time of the marriage ceremony W was already married. Discovering that her marriage was bigamous severely affected G's health, and she claimed compensation from the Criminal Injuries Compensation Board. She argued that the consent

she had given to sexual intercourse with W was ineffective, having been induced by fraud. She had therefore been the victim of rape, and thus of an offence of violence, for which compensation was payable under the Criminal Injuries Compensation Scheme. Her claim was rejected, and that decision was upheld by the Court of Session.

The Court appears to have accepted that the effect of the fraud perpetrated on G was covered by the decision in *Fraser*. Her consent was not vitiated by the deception practised by W. Is this strictly correct? G was never deceived as to the identity of the person with whom she had intercourse. She knew all along that it was the person known to her as W. In that sense the case is clearly and easily distinguished from *Fraser*. The true question in G's case was whether a deception as to the "quality" of the intercourse (marital or non-marital) or, more broadly, a deception as to some precondition to intercourse vitiated consent. The question so put does not seem to have been discussed in any of the Scottish authorities. Given the approach adopted in *Fraser* the court might well have reached the same conclusion. If G's case had been based on the argument that her religious or moral scruples were such that she would not have consented if she had realised that her "marriage" was void, that might have been a stronger argument, but one which, on the facts, it would have been impossible to sustain.

To have upheld the argument that W was guilty of rape would have made most male bigamists into rapists, since only the most punctilious bigamous is honest about his marital status. That consideration appears at least to have influenced the High Court of Australia in *Papadimitropoulos v. R.*, 98 C.L.R. 249 (1958). In that case the accused induced the complainer to agree to sexual intercourse by pretending to her that certain proceedings which had taken place between them at a registry office was a ceremony of marriage (which it was not). The High Court held that the accused's conviction for rape should be quashed: "... rape is carnal knowledge of a woman without her consent: carnal knowledge is the physical fact of penetration; it is the consent to that which is in question; such a consent demands a perception as to what is about to take place, as to the identity of the man and the character of what he is doing. But once the consent is comprehending and actual the inducing causes cannot destroy its reality and leave the man guilty of rape."

## (v) Rape in marriage

According to Hume (i, 305–306) a husband could not be guilty of raping his wife because, on marriage, **9.15** she gave an irrevocable consent to sexual relations with her husband. That view (which was probably borrowed by Hume from Hale's *Pleas of the Crown*, i, 628–629) was accepted as a correct statement of the law by later writers (Burnett, 102, Macdonald, 119 and Alison, i, 218) until it was unchallenged by Sheriff Gordon who argued that the rule as stated by Hume was out of keeping with contemporary attitudes towards the relationship between husband and wife (Gordon, para 33–12).

In *H.M. Advocate v. D.*, 1982 S.C.C.R. 182 and *H.M. Advocate v. Paxton*, 1985 S.L.T. 96, it was held that a husband could be guilty of raping his wife, at least where the parties were no longer cohabiting. The matter was finally settled by the Appeal Court in the case of *S. v. H.M. Advocate*, 1989 S.L.T. 469 in which it was held that a husband could be found guilty of raping his wife, even where the parties were living together as husband and wife. In that case, the Court held that, whatever may have been the correctness of Hume's statement of the law at the end of the 18th century, the proposition that a husband was entitled to have sexual intercourse with his wife, even if she did not consent in fact, was out of keeping with contemporary attitudes. In the words of the Court:

> "A live system of law will always have regard to changing circumstances to test the justification for any exception to the application of a general rule. Nowadays it cannot seriously be maintained that by marriage a wife submits herself irrevocably to sexual intercourse in all circumstances. It cannot be affirmed nowadays, whatever the position may have been in earlier centuries, that it is an incident of modern marriage that a wife consents to intercourse in all circumstances, including sexual intercourse obtained only by force. There is no doubt that a wife does not consent to assault upon her person and there is no plausible justification for saying today that she nevertheless is to be taken to consent to intercourse by assault" (1989 S.L.T. 469 at p. 473).

The English courts took a similar view of the law in *R. v. R.* [1992] 1 A.C. 599. In that case the House of

Lords held that the marital rape exemption enjoyed by husbands (as stated in Hale) no longer formed part of the English law of rape for broadly similar reasons.

That decision, and the decision in a related English case, were challenged before the European Court of Human Rights. (No such challenge was mounted to the decision in *S. v. H.M. Advocate*.) In *C.R. v. United Kingdom*, Series A, No. 335-C and *S.W. v. United Kingdom*, Series A, No. 335-B, (1996) 21 E.H.R.R. 363 the applicants claimed that the courts had retrospectively extended the criminal law by removing the husband's privilege, in violation of Article 7 of the European Convention on Human Rights. (See *supra*, Chap. 1) The Court rejected this argument. The Court noted that the absolute privilege previously enjoyed by husbands in this respect had been subjected to various qualifications and exceptions by the English courts over the last fifty years. (See, in this respect, *R. v. Clarke* (1949) 33 Cr.App.R. 216; *R. v. Miller* [1954] 2 Q.B. 282 and *R. v. Steele* (1976) 65 Cr.App.R. 22.) The decision in *R. v. R.* was, in the view of the Court, a predictable culmination of this process, and did not, therefore, violate article 7 since the applicants in both *C.R. v. United Kingdom* and *S.W. v. United Kingdom* could reasonably have foreseen the possibility that their conduct would be regarded as criminal.

Although that conclusion might be viewed with some scepticism, the removal of the husband's immunity was, as a matter of legal policy, entirely correct. A rule which permits a man to have sexual relations with his wife without the latter's consent, based upon a legal fiction, is patently absurd and discriminatory. Moreover, the marital rape exemption was probably contrary to the European Convention on Human Rights in that it violated the woman's right to privacy within the meaning of Article 8 of the Convention. Article 8(1) states that: "Everyone has the right to respect for his private and family life . . . ." It is well-established in the case law of the European Court of Human Rights that a person's "sex life" is an intimate part of his or her "private life" within the meaning of Article 8(1): see, *e.g. X and Y v. Netherlands*, Series A, vol. 91 (1985) at para. 22. The Court has also accepted that Article 8(1) may impose on a state the positive obligation to protect individuals from interference with their private life, including interference by other individuals: *Marckx v. Belgium* (1979) 3 E.H.R.R. 330; *Airey v. Ireland* (1979) 2 E.H.R.R. 305, and *X and Y v. Netherlands, supra*). That being so, it is arguable that to fail to apply normal criminal sanctions to a man who has intercourse with a woman by overcoming her will, on the ground that the woman is his wife, is a failure to ensure respect for that woman's private life, and there is some suggestion of this in the Court's decision in *C.R. v. United Kingdom, supra*, at para. 42.

## (vi) Capacity

**9.16** A person cannot consent to sexual relations without the legal capacity to do so. A person's capacity may be affected by such matters as age or mental condition. So, for example, a girl under the age of 12 cannot give effective consent to sexual intercourse, with the result that in all conditions, sexual intercourse with a girl who has not reached that age is rape—even if in fact she consents. See Hume, i, 303 and, in the context of indecent assault, *H.M. Advocate v. C.*, 1988 S.C.C.R. 104. In *William v. Fraser, ante*, p. 353, Lord Cockburn stated that "the crime [of rape] is unquestionably committed wherever consent is *impossible, though there may be no force*; as in the case of intercourse with children, or lunatics or with women in intoxication, . . . . An insane woman, instead of requiring force, may actively concur; but because she cannot consent, the connection is rape."

## B. The *mens rea* of rape

**9.17** The mental element in rape has not been the subject of much judicial consideration in Scotland. To have sexual intercourse with a woman who does not consent, knowing that she does not consent, is clearly rape. General principles of *mens rea* in Scottish common law crimes would suggest that it is also rape if the man is reckless as to consent. This appears to be confirmed, at least in part, by the decision of the High Court in *Jamieson v. H.M. Advocate* 1994 S.L.T. 537, *post*, p. 357. If the accused has sexual intercourse with a woman who does not consent, without a positive belief in consent, he will be guilty of rape. Thus a man who does not consider whether or not the woman is consenting, or is indifferent to whether or not she consents, has the *mens rea* for rape. But if he *believes* that she is consenting then he is not guilty. The critical question here, however, is whether that belief must be based on reasonable grounds. That point is addressed in the following case:

## Jamieson v. H.M. Advocate
### 1994 S.L.T. 537

The appellant was convicted of rape. His defence at the trial was that the complainer had **9.18** consented to sexual intercourse, and, alternatively, that even if she had not consented, he believed when he had intercourse with her that she was consenting. The trial judge directed the jury that "reasonable belief, and that is to say a belief based on reasonable grounds, on the part of the male to the effect that the woman was a consenting party is a defence even though the belief was, in fact, mistaken". The accused was convicted and appealed on the ground of misdirection. On behalf of the Crown the Solicitor-General conceded that there had been a misdirection.

THE OPINION OF THE COURT: "... The crime of rape consists in the carnal knowledge of a woman forcibly and against her will. Thus the *mens rea* of this crime includes the intention to have intercourse with the woman without her consent. The absence of a belief that she was consenting is an essential element in it. If a man has intercourse with a woman in the belief that she is consenting to this he cannot be guilty of rape. Now, the question whether the man believed that the woman consented is a question of fact. It is a question which the jury must decide, if it is raised, on the evidence. The grounds for his belief will be important, and if he has reasonable grounds for it the jury may find it easier to accept that he did honestly believe that the woman consented. But it will be open to the jury to accept his evidence on this point even if he cannot give grounds for it which they consider to be reasonable, and if they accept his evidence they must acquit him. This is because the question is whether he genuinely or honestly believed that the woman was consenting to intercourse. It will not do if he acted without thinking or was indifferent as to whether or not he had her consent. The man must have genuinely formed the belief that she was consenting to his having intercourse with her. But this need not be a belief which the jury regards as reasonable, so long as they are satisfied that his belief was genuinely held by him at the time.

These observations are consistent with the comment in *Meek v. H.M. Advocate*, 1983 S.L.T. 280 at p. 281, that the court had no difficulty in accepting that an essential element in the crime of rape was the absence of an honest belief that the woman was consenting. It was noted in that case that the absence of reasonable grounds for such an alleged belief would however have a considerable bearing upon whether any jury would accept that such an honest belief was held. The same points were made by Lord Fraser of Tullybelton in *D.P.P. v. Morgan* [1976] A.C. 182 at p. 237E–F where he said: "It seems to me that ... the *mens rea* of rape is an intention to have intercourse with a non-consenting woman or to have non-consensual intercourse. If that is so, then the logical difficulty of requiring a belief in the woman's consent to be based on reasonable grounds arises sharply. If the effect of the evidence as a whole is that the defendant believed, or may have believed, that the woman was consenting, then the Crown has not discharged the onus of proving commission of the offence as fully defined and, as it seems to me, no question can arise as to whether the belief was reasonable or not. Of course, the reasonableness or otherwise of the belief will be important as evidence tending to show whether it was truly held by the defendant, but that is all."

A direction that the man must have reasonable grounds for thinking that the woman consented is therefore a misdirection as to the law on this matter. But the jury should be directed to consider whether there were reasonable grounds for the belief in reaching their decision as to whether in fact it was genuinely or honestly held by him at the time.

As the trial judge points out in his report, there is ample authority that a person who claims that he acted in self-defence because he believes that he was in imminent danger must have reasonable grounds for his belief: *Owens v. H.M. Advocate*, 1946 J.C. 119; *Crawford v. H.M. Advocate*, 1950 J.C. 67; *Jones v. H.M. Advocate*, 1990 J.C. 160. He suggests that *Meek* is inconsistent with this line of authority. As the Solicitor-General conceded that there was a misdirection in this case and that a direction on the lines indicated by *Meek* was appropriate here, we were not addressed to any extent on this point. We wish to say however that we are not to be taken, from what we have said in this opinion, as casting any doubt on the soundness of the *dicta* in those cases. Nor are we to be taken as suggesting that in any other case, where a substantive defence is based on a belief which is mistaken, there need not be reasonable grounds for that belief. The reason why, in rape cases, the man's belief need not be shown to be based on reasonable grounds for his belief to be relevant as a ground of acquittal is because of the particular nature of the *mens rea* which is required to commit the crime. Difficult questions of fact may arise as to whether, if he can give no reasonable grounds for his belief, the accused genuinely believed at the time that the woman was consenting or was reckless or indifferent as to the matter of consent. These questions are however for the jury to resolve, on proper directions by the trial judge, in the light of the evidence.

In view of the position which the Solicitor General has adopted in the light of the evidence in this case, we shall allow the appellant's appeal against his conviction on charge 1 by setting aside the verdict of the trial court and quashing the conviction. The Solicitor General did not ask us to grant authority to the Crown to bring a new prosecution on this charge."

Appeal against conviction for rape allowed.

NOTES

**9.19**   1. This is a problematic decision both in terms of its doctrinal foundation, and the legal policy which it appears to pursue. *Jamieson* states that where an accused holds a mistaken belief in a fact (in this case the consent of the victim) he is entitled to the benefit of that mistaken belief, even though there are no reasonable grounds for that belief. In the context of rape, therefore, the accused is entitled to an acquittal if he believes that the victim is consenting, even if that belief is based on nothing other than, for example, a wholly unreasonable belief in his own attractiveness to women ("no woman would ever refuse me") or other objectionable beliefs about the sexual autonomy of women ("even though they say 'no' they really mean 'yes' "). It is true that the jury may take the view that a person who offers such a weak justification for a belief in consent may not genuinely have believed that the woman consented. But if the jury accept that the accused did indeed believe that the victim was consenting, then he is entitled to an acquittal.

This approach to mistake of fact is unsupported by any Scottish authority. Such authority as there is on mistakes of fact has consistently required reasonable grounds for any mistaken belief put forward in exculpation. The Court avoids this problem by insisting that their decision should not be read as having any bearing on those cases involving mistaken self-defence. These cases can, of course, be distinguished on the ground that they do not concern mistakes affecting *mens rea* but mistakes affecting an affirmative defence.

2. It is unfortunate that the Court's attention was not drawn to any authority on mistakes of the former kind. Such authority can be found, it is submitted, in *Dewar v. H.M. Advocate*, 1945 J.C. 5, *ante*, p. 55. In that case the accused, the manager of a crematorium. appropriated to his own use property (coffins and coffin lids) which had been consigned to him for cremation. As part of his defence he argued that he was only doing what was common practice in other crematoria, or at least that he believed such to be the common practice elsewhere. It was held that this belief was no defence unless it was "reasonable [and] based on colourable grounds".

Evidence relating to Dewar's belief in the practice pursued in other crematoria appears to have been put forward in order to sustain the argument that he had no theftuous intent. If that is correct, then *Dewar* would appear to run contrary to the approach adopted in *Jamieson*. Or, suppose a more straightforward case: Suppose that A appropriates B's property in the wholly unreasonable belief that B has consented to the taking. Does it follow from *Jamieson* that A is not guilty of theft, or from *Dewar* that A is guilty? For discussion of this issue, see S. McCall, "Acquaintance Rape: Time for Reform?" 2000 S.L.T. (News) 123 and J. Chalmers, "Acquaintance Rape: A Reply" 2000 S.L.T. (News) 163.

3. *Jamieson* may not be easy to reconcile with the approach Scots law takes to intoxication and criminal responsibility (as to which, see *ante*, Chapter 7). Suppose, for example, that A has sexual intercourse with B without her consent. He gives evidence to the effect that he honestly believed that B was consenting, and that the reason why he failed to appreciate that she was not was because he was extremely drunk at the time, or otherwise under the influence of drugs. The absence of an honest belief in consent is an essential element in the crime of rape. A honestly (but drunkenly) believes that A is consenting. Presumably, therefore, A is not guilty of rape, unless, of course, a drunken belief is not an

"honest" one. In this context it is interesting to note that while the Canadian Supreme Court held in *Pappajohn v. The Queen* [1980] 2 S.C.R. 120 that the accused's belief in consent need not be reasonable for it to afford a defence, section 273.2 of the Canadian Criminal Code now provides that a belief in consent is not a defence in sexual assault cases where, *inter alia*, the accused's belief arose from self-induced intoxication.

# 2. CLANDESTINE INJURY TO WOMEN

### H.M. Advocate v. Grainger and Rae
### 1932 J.C. 40

Two men were charged on indictment with assaulting a woman, having carnal knowledge of **9.20** her person while she was in a state of insensibility or unconsciousness from the effects of intoxicating liquor, and ravishing her. They objected to the relevancy of the indictment on the ground that these averments were not relevant to infer the crime of rape.

LORD ANDERSON: "Rape (save in the exceptional cases of pupils and idiots) is the carnal knowledge of a woman forcibly and against her will—Macdonald's *Criminal Law* (4th ed.) p. 175; Hume on *Crimes*, vol. i., pp. 301–302; Alison's *Criminal Law*, vol. i., p. 209. Accordingly, it was urged by the accused, the crime cannot be committed unless a woman is in a condition, physically and mentally, to exercise her will power and offer resistance. In the present case the libel sets forth that the woman was in a condition when she was incapacitated, by reason of intoxication, from offering any resistance to her assailants or from exercising her will power in the way of giving or refusing consent. The offence charged, accordingly, it was said, does not amount to rape. This contention seems to me to be well-founded. It is not alleged that the accused supplied the woman with the liquor with which she became intoxicated. Had this allegation been made, the charge of rape might have been sustained, as it has been decided that it is rape to have connection with a woman whose resistance has been overcome by drugging her—Macdonald's *Criminal Law* (4th ed.) p. 176; Hume on *Crimes*, vol. i., p. 303; Alison's *Criminal Law*, vol. i., p. 212; *Fraser* (1847) Ark. 280; *Sweenie* (1858) 3 Irv. 109. It might be suggested that the present case falls to be assimilated to that of an idiot female; but this does not seem to me to be a true analogy. The idiot has, in law and in fact, no will; in the present case the woman assaulted had a will, the activity of which was but temporarily suspended by her intoxication. The true analogy seems to me to be the case of the woman who is taken advantage of while asleep. Such an offence is not rape—Macdonald's *Criminal Law*, p. 175, *Sweenie*. Just as a sleeping woman is temporarily in a state of unconsciousness wherein she is incapable of exercising her will-power, so here it seems to me that the woman was in the same temporary condition of unconsciousness by reason of intoxication.

The objection to relevancy must therefore be sustained.

As I have indicated, what is said to have been done by the accused, although not rape, is a criminal offence—the crime of inflicting clandestine injury on a woman—Macdonald's *Criminal Law* (4th ed.) p. 178. But the crime must be indicted as such, and not as rape."

Objection to relevancy sustained.

NOTES

There is some doubt as to whether this is a crime in its own right, or merely a particular form of **9.21** indecent assault. In *H.M. Advocate v. Logan, ante*, p. 352, the Lord Justice-Clerk (Aitchison) stated that this offence "so far as it is possible to define it, comes within the category of indecent assault" (1936 J.C. 100, at p. 102). In *Sweeney and Thomson v. X*, 1982 S.C.C.R. 509 it was accepted that the appropriate verdict where an accused had sexual intercourse with an unconscious woman was "indecent assault". It appears, however, that Parliament has accepted that the *nomen iuris* "clandestine injury" is appropriate and that it is distinct from "indecent assault". See, for example, the Criminal Procedure (Scotland) Act 1995, s.274 and Schedule 1, paragraph 2(1)(a) of the Sex Offenders Act 1997. If "clandestine injury" is an offence distinct from indecent assault, then this creates difficulties in relation to section 14 of the Criminal Law (Consolidation) (Scotland) Act 1995 which provides for alternative verdicts which may be returned on an indictment for rape where the Crown have failed to prove that crime. Although the alternatives listed include indecent assault, there is no reference in section 14 to "clandestine injury". In *Sweeney and Thomson v. X.*, 1982 S.C.C.R. 509, the accused were originally charged with rape but convicted of indecent assault. Would it be any objection today to such an alternative verdict that (a) Parliament has recognised "clandestine injury" as a distinct crime and (b) that offence is not referred to in section 14 of the 1995 Act?

## 3. INDECENT ASSAULT

**9.22** "Indecent assault" is generally described simply as an assault accompanied by circumstances of indecency. (See, for example, *Barbour v. H.M. Advocate*, 1982 S.C.C.R. 195, *per* Lord Stewart at 198, *Sweeney and Thomson v. X*, 1982 S.C.C.R. 509, *per* Lord Ross at 511.) Just when an assault is "indecent" is a matter of fact and circumstance, but what must be proved is an assault of a sexual character—see *Young v. McGlennan*, 1991 S.C.C.R. 738.

There are, however, some important qualifications to the general statement that indecent assault is an assault in circumstances of indecency. In the first place, although consent does not, in general, negative an assault, consent can negate what would otherwise be an indecent assault. In *Smart v. H.M. Advocate*, 1975 J.C. 30, the court stated that "If A touches B in a sexual manner and B consents to him doing so (and there is nothing else involved which would constitute a crime under statute or common law) there is no assault because there is no evil intention to attack the person of B". (1975 J.C. 30, at p. 33.) This is, with respect, not a very convincing explanation of the supposed difference between assault and indecent assault. If a man puts his arm round a woman's shoulder and touches her breasts, that is an indecent assault, unless the woman consents. He may hope she consents, he may not care, he may expect her to consent. But in each case there has been a deliberate touching of her in a sexual manner and that is sufficient for indecent assault if she does not in fact consent. What makes the difference is not his intent, but the presence or absence of consent on the part of the woman.

Once it is accepted that consent may negative indecent assault, it becomes necessary to determine in what circumstances such consent would be operative. The cases discussed *ante* in the context of rape will presumably apply, *mutatis mutandis*, to indecent assault. So, for example, consent to touching in an indecent manner would be negatived by fraud as to the nature of the act. If, for example, a doctor were to carry out an examination of a patient which involved touching the patient's sexual organs, this would not be an assault if carried out with consent. But if the touching were not a necessary part of the medical procedure, and were carried out for the doctor's own sexual gratification, that should be treated as an indecent assault (*cf. Hussain v. Houston*, 1995 S.L.T. 1060).

**9.23** What would be the decision of the Scottish courts in a case such as *R. v. Brown* [1993] 2 All E.R. 75, *ante*, Chap. 8? Presumably the courts would say that the degree of harm was relevant in such cases, and that for that reason consent should be disregarded. But suppose that the injuries inflicted were minor, but that otherwise the circumstances were similar. Would that be a case of indecent assault?

Secondly, while "ordinary" assault merely requires a deliberate attack upon the victim, indecent assault may require proof that the accused was aware of the circumstances of indecency, and may require proof of an "indecent intent" as well. In *Morrow v. Vannet*, 1999 G.W.D. 8-378, it was held that the sheriff was entitled to find that "fondling" three young girls over their clothing on the shoulder and thigh amounted to indecent assault. It is doubtful that it is always an indecent asssault to rub a child's thigh—what if the accused in that case had shown that he was trying to comfort a girl who had fallen over and hurt herself? Presumably this would not be indecent assault and, if not, that suggests that at least in cases of this kind (where the act is not overtly sexually indecent) the accused's purpose may be relevant in deciding whether or not the conduct is indecent. This interpretation is supported by the court's use of the word "fondling" (defined by the Oxford English Dictionary as "an affectionate handling")—which carries with it an implication of a certain motive—unlike "touching", which does not (*c.f.* the English cases of *George* [1956] Crim. L.R. 52 and *Court* [1988] 2 All E.R. 221 and the South African case of *R. v. Abrahams* 1918 C.P.D. 590).

For a full discussion of indecent assault, see Gane, *Sexual Offences* (1992), Chap. 3.

# 4. OFFENCES INVOLVING CHILDREN AND YOUNG PERSONS

Sexual offences such as rape or indecent assault can, of course, be committed against persons of any age. **9.24** The criminal law has, however, identified children and young persons as a group requiring special protection, and a number of offences exist, both at common law and under statute, for the protection of children and young persons.

## A. Sexual intercourse with girls under 16

At common law, intercourse with a girl under the age of 12 is rape. It is irrelevant that she may have **9.25** consented, since the law assumes that she is incapable of giving a valid consent: Hume, i, 303; Alison, i, 213; Gordon, para. 33–14. *Cf. C. v. H.M. Advocate*, 1987 S.C.C.R. 104. A girl who has reached the age of 12 is considered to be incapable of giving such consent, so that consensual intercourse with a girl of or above that age is not rape. Since the 19th century, however, it has been a statutory offence to have unlawful sexual intercourse with a girl under 16, even where she is a fully consenting party. The two most important offences in this category are now contained in section 5 of the Criminal Law (Consolidation) (Scotland) Act 1995.

### 1. Criminal Law (Consolidation) (Scotland) Act 1995
**"Intercourse with girl under 16**
**5.**—(1) Any person who has unlawful sexual intercourse with any girl under the age of 13 **9.26** years shall be liable on conviction on indictment to imprisonment for life.

(2) Any person who attempts to have unlawful sexual intercourse with any girl under the age of 13 years shall be liable on conviction on indictment to imprisonment for a term not exceeding ten years or on summary conviction to imprisonment for a term not exceeding three months.

(3) Without prejudice to sections 1 to 4 of this Act, any person who has, or attempts to have, unlawful sexual intercourse with any girl of or over the age of 13 years and under the age of 16 years shall be liable on conviction on indictment to imprisonment for a term not exceeding ten years or on summary conviction to imprisonment for a term not exceeding three months ....

NOTES

1. In this context sexual intercourse is "unlawful" if it is extra-marital: *Henry Watson* (1885) 5 Couper **9.27** 696. *Cf. Abinet v. Fleck* (1894) 2 S.L.T. 30; *Chapman* [1959] 1 Q.B. 100.

2. It is a defence to a charge under section 5(3) that the accused has reasonable cause to believe that the girl was his wife, or that he had reasonable cause to believe that the girl was of or above the age of 16 (s. 5(5)). He may not plead the latter of these defences, however, unless he is under the age of 24 and has not previously been charged with a "like offence", which is defined in s. 5(6). These provisions imply that it can *never* be a defence to a charge under s. 5(1) or s. 5(2) that the accused believed that the girl was over the relevant age, no matter how reasonable that belief might have been.

On reasonable beliefs for the purposes of section 4(2)(b), see *H.M. Advocate v. Hoggan* (1893) 1 Adam 1, *H.M. Advocate v. Macdonald* (1900) 3 Adam 180 and *Clark v. Gallagher*, 1999 G.W.D. 25–1185.

## B. Lewd, indecent and libidinous practices and behaviour

It has long been accepted that it is an offence at common law to engage in "lewd, indecent and libidinous **9.28** practices and behaviour" towards children (girls and boys) below the age of puberty. Section 6 of the Criminal Law (Consolidation) (Scotland) Act 1995 extends the common law rule to girls aged 12 to 16:

## 1. Criminal Law (Consolidation) (Scotland) Act 1995

**9.29** **6.**—Any person who uses towards a girl of or over the age of 12 years and under the age of 16 years any lewd, indecent or libidinous practice or behaviour which, if used towards a girl under the age of 12 years, would have constituted an offence at common law, shall, whether the girl consented to such practice or behaviour or not, be liable on conviction on indictment to imprisonment for a term not exceeding two years or on summary conviction to imprisonment for a term not exceeding three months.

NOTES

**9.30**     1. So far as concerns a girl under the age of 12, the common law disregards the question of consent, since a child under that age cannot consent. Section 6 makes it clear that for the purposes of the statutory offence, consent is likewise irrelevant.

2. The implication of section 6 is that, without it lewd practices with a girl over the age of 12 would not be criminal at common law, provided, of course, that she consented. Certainly at one time it was generally accepted that common law offence of using lewd, indecent or libidinous practices or behaviour towards girls could only be committed in respect of a girl under the age of puberty. In the case of boys, the offence could possibly be committed in respect of boys below, or somewhat above the age of puberty—see *David Brown*, (1844) 2 Broun 261; *Andrew Lyall*, (1853) 1 Irvine 218. It is also worth noting that in *Boyle v. Ritchie*, 1999 S.C.C.R. 278, Lord Prosser noted that section 4 of the Criminal Law Amendment Act 1922 (from which section 6 is derived) extended to girls between 12 and 16 the protective measures which had previously been available for those under the age 12.

In *Batty v. H.M. Advocate*, 1995 S.C.C.R. 525, however, the Court reserved its opinion on the question whether "the common law crime of lewd, libidinous and indecent practices and behaviour must be confined to cases where the complainer is under the age of puberty". The Court did, however, observe, *obiter*, that "the balance of authority is now in favour of the view that the age of the complainer is not of the essence of the crime of lewd, libidinous and indecent practices and behaviour". The case concerned alleged indecencies with girls all aged between 12 and 16 engaged in by a house-parent at their school. The case was treated as an example of shameless indecency (see *post*, p. 365) on the basis of the "breach of trust" involved (*cf. H.M. Advocate v. Roose*, 1999 S.C.C.R. 259, where it was held that a substantial age difference between the accused and the complainer is not in itself sufficient to imply a breach of trust). See also the Sexual Offences (Amendment) Act 2000, s.3, which creates a statutory offence of abuse of a position of trust. This is committed where a person over the age of 18 has sexual intercourse or engages in other sexual activity "with or directed towards" a person under that age, if they are in a position of trust in relation to that person. "Position of trust" has a statutory definition (s.4). It remains to be seen whether Scottish prosecutors will make use of this statutory provision, or if they will continue to rely on charges of shameless indecency in such cases.

**9.31**     3. While it is an offence at common law for any person to engage in lewd practices towards a boy under the age of puberty, the situation is rather less clear with regard to boys who have reached that age. In the case of homosexual acts, there is authority that lewd practices between males are criminal at common law irrespective of the ages of the parties (*McLaughlan v. Boyd*, 1934 J.C. 19, *post*, p. 365, which, in this respect, is something of an extension of the earlier cases of *Brown* and *Lyall*, *supra*). Section 13(5) of the Criminal Law (Consolidation) (Scotland) Act 1995 also creates a statutory offence of committing a homosexual act with a person under the age of 16. However, where both parties are over the age of 16, consent to the act, and the act takes place in private, s.13(1) of the 1995 Act 9 *post*, p. 370) would apply and the act would be lawful regardless of the common law rule.

4. So far as concerns heterosexual acts, unless the conduct amounts to shameless indecency (as, for example, where the adult is the boy's mother, or teacher) it may not be an offence at all for a woman to engage in indecent practices with a boy who has reached the age of puberty and who consents. The accuracy of this statement may, however, depend upon the correctness of the *dicta* in *Batty* (above) concerning the age of the child, and whether or not those *dicta* apply to boys as well as girls.

5. As to what may amount to "lewd, indecent and libidinous" practices or behaviour, see *Boyle v. Ritchie*, 1999 S.C.C.R. 278, where the accused was convicted of a breach of section 6 of the 1995 Act by having kissed a 15-year-old girl on the lips (after the sheriff had deleted various allegations of further indecent activity from the complaint). On appeal, it was argued that "a kiss is just a kiss" and incapable of amounting to a breach of s.6. The court refused the appeal, holding that:

"We are not persuaded that any act such as a kiss is ruled out from being lewd and libidinous. It will depend entirely on the circumstances. The circumstances here appear to us generally to have been lewd and libidinous in a wider sense.

At the time the appellant, who was 18, was in bed with both his girlfriend and the complainer on this charge. He appears to have been naked, or perhaps at an earlier stage at least, wearing boxer shorts only. It appears clear that there had some sexual activity with his girlfriend. There is no doubt that his intentions when he kissed the appellant went beyond a mere kiss. There had been some discussion with his girlfriend in which he said that he wanted to "have a threesome" or various other ways of putting the matter; and when he eventually kissed the complainer it was on the mouth and lasted something like a minute. It appears to us that one is entitled to take into account the whole surrounding circumstances, the background, the expressed intention and also the understanding of the complainer which was, as the Solicitor General pointed out, that she had heard that the appellant had had these further intentions and knew of them when he kissed her on the lips and she did not respond. It does not appear to us that any general principle is involved here. There was ample evidence on which the Sheriff was entitled to see this particular kissing episode as falling within the statutory words and the appeal is refused."

## C. Incest and related offences

The crime of incest is today justified largely on the need to protect children from sexual abuse within the **9.32** family. A number of offences created by Parliament when the law on incest was reformed by the Incest and Related Offences (Scotland) Act 1986 are specifically directed towards the protection of children and young persons from sexual abuse within the family. These offences are discussed below.

## 5. INCEST AND RELATED OFFENCES

Until 1986 the law of incest was based, if not entirely then for all practical purposes, on the Incest Act of **9.33** 1567. The Incest and Related Offences (Scotland) Act 1986 replaced the old law with a new statutory offence of incest, and at the same time created two new offences closely related to incest—intercourse with a step-child and intercourse by a person in a position of trust with a child under 16. The Act's provisions, which were closely based on recommendations contained in the Scottish Law Commission's *Report on the Law of Incest in Scotland* (Scot. Law Com. No. 69, Cmnd 8422 (1981)) are now contained in the Criminal Law (Consolidation) (Scotland) Act 1995.

### (a) Incest (section 1 of the 1995 Act)

A person who has sexual intercourse with a close relative of the opposite sex commits the crime of **9.34** incest. The applicable degrees of relationship are specified in a table at the end of s.1(1). It is notable that they do not include "cousin" (although they do include aunts, uncles, nieces and nephews), they do not include relationships by affinity (*e.g.* step-parent and step-child—but *cf.* s.2), and although they include both adoptive (and former adoptive) parents and children, they do not include adoptive siblings. It is irrelevant whether a relationship is of the full blood or the half blood, and it is also irrelevant that the relationship is traced through or to any person whose parents are not or have not been married to one another.

It is a defence for the accused to prove (on the balance of probabilities) that he or she did not know and had no reason to suspect that the person with whom they had sexual intercourse was a close relative (s.1(1)(a)); that they did not consent to sexual intercourse or did not consent to sexual intercourse with that person (s.1(1)(b)); or that they were validly married to that person (s.1(1)(c)).

### (b) Intercourse with a step-child (section 2 of the 1995 Act)

Section 2 of the 1995 Act provides that "[any] step-parent or former step-parent who has sexual **9.35** intercourse with his or her step-child or former step-child shall be guilty of an offence if that step-child is either under the age of 21 or has at any time before attaining the age of 18 lived in the same household and been treated as a child of his or her family".

It is a defence for the accused to prove (on the balance of probabilities) that he or she did not know and had no reason to suspect that they were related in this way (s.2(a)); that they believed on reasonable grounds that the person with whom they had intercourse was 21 or over (s.2(b)); that they did not consent to have sexual intercourse or to have sexual intercourse with that person (s.2(c)); or that they were validly married to that person (s.2(d)).

The Scottish Law Commission had originally proposed that this offence should only apply where the step-child or former step-child was under the age of 16, but it was necessary to amend the Bill as it passed through Parliament in order to take account of the provisions of the Marriage (Prohibited Degrees of Relationship) Act 1986. That Act permits marriage between former step-parents or grandparents and former step-children or grandchildren, provided that both parties have reached the age of 21 at the time of the marriage and the younger party has not at any time before attaining the age of 18 lived in the same household as the other party and been treated by that party as a child of his family. If the Law Commission's original proposals had been enacted against this background, there would have been cases where the parties could lawfully engage in sexual intercourse, but could not marry (as in the case of a man and his 17-year-old step-daughter).

### (c) Intercourse with a child under 16 by a person in a position of trust (s.3 of the 1995 Act)

**9.36**    Section 3 of the 1995 Act provides that a person of 16 or over who has sexual intercourse with a child under 16, and is a member of the same household as that child, and is in a position of trust and authority in relation to that child, shall be guilty of an offence.

It is a defence for the accused to prove (on the balance of probabilities) that he or she believed on reasonable grounds that the person with whom they had intercourse was 16 or over (s.3(2)(a)); that they did not consent to have sexual intercourse or to have sexual intercourse with that person (s.3(2)(b)); or that they were validly married to that person (s.3(2)(c)).

This provision recognises the need to protect children and young persons from sexual abuse within the family where such children do not fall within the scope of the offence of incest or the special provisions relating to step-children. Clear examples are foster-children or children of one party to an unmarried relationship who are at risk from the other party.

The range of relationships which might be included in this section is unclear, and the scope of the term "household" is unsettled. For a discussion of these problems, see Gane, *Sexual Offences*, Chapter 5. See also *McGregor v. Haswell*, 1983 S.L.T. 626, and *Simmons v. Pizzey* [1977] 2 All. E.R. 432.

This offence can only be committed when the younger person is under 16. *Cf. H.M. Advocate v. R.K.*, 1994 S.C.C.R. 499, however, where Lord MacLean held that an accused who had sexual intercourse with his foster daughter after she had reached the age of 16 could be convicted of shameless indecency.

**9.37**    It should be noted that all of these offences require proof of "sexual intercourse", which, although it is not defined in the Criminal Law (Consolidation) (Scotland) Act 1995, is probably limited to the meaning given to that term in other offences such as rape or unlawful sexual intercourse contrary to section 5 of that Act. What this means, then, is that all of these offences are "heterosexual", and that forms of sexual acts other than sexual intercourse are not covered by these provisions. What this means is that it is incest for a man to have sexual intercourse with his daughter or niece, even if they are both adults and both consent. It is not, however, incest, for a man to have sexual relations with his son or nephew in similar circumstances. Such sexual relations would presumably be regarded as shameless indecency, at least in the case of father and son, but as such the parties would be entitled to invoke the provisions of section 13 of the Criminal Law (Consolidation) (Scotland) Act 1995, according to which homosexual acts (including shameless indecency) are not criminal if and both parties have reached the age of 18.

Some of these issues might be addressed by the creation of a more general offence of "familial sexual abuse", which has recently been proposed for England and Wales. See Home Office, *Setting the Boundaries: Reforming the Law on Sex Offences* (2000), Chap. 5.

# 6. SHAMELESSLY INDECENT CONDUCT

Shameless indecency is one of the most remarkable judicial creations in the criminal law. It is derived **9.38** from an *ex cathedra* statement by Macdonald in the first edition of his *Criminal Law* (1866) that "all shamelessly indecent conduct is criminal", which was not true then and is not true today. Although this *dictum* was given the seal of judicial approval in the case of *McLaughlan v. Boyd* 1934 J.C. 19, *infra*, it did not really come into its own until the decision of the High Court in *Watt v. Annan*, 1978 J.C. 84 (*post*, Chapter 16).

Shameless indecency can be committed in a wide variety of circumstances. It ranges from acts of a sexual nature between two (or presumably more) parties, to indecent exposure, to selling or exposing for sale obscene literature. It also includes the purely private exhibition of obscene matter to persons who have consented to the exhibition (as in *Watt v. Annan*). The cases which follow are examples of sexual conduct between individuals which have been held to be shamelessly indecent. Cases involving public indecency, and the publication of obscene or indecent material are considered in Chapter 16 below.

## McLaughlan v. Boyd
### 1934 J.C. 19

A publican was charged in the police court, *inter alia*, with using lewd, indecent and libidinous **9.39** practices towards a number of persons who came to his bar in the course of their work. In each case the evidence was that he had seised the other person's hand and placed it on his own private parts. There was no evidence of the age of these persons. He was convicted by the magistrate. On appeal by stated case, the charges were challenged on the ground that the words "lewd, indecent and libidinous practices" could not be used to describe an assault on a person of the age of puberty.

LORD JUSTICE-GENERAL (CLYDE): "To deal only with the charges in the indictment on which conviction followed, it appears that the accused over a considerable period of time has given himself up to conduct with other men of a grossly and shamelessly indecent kind. The incidents were repeated and followed each other at short intervals. Some of the charges on which conviction was pronounced were libelled as assaults by the appellant placing his hand upon the private parts of certain persons named; in other cases the charge was libelled as the use of lewd, indecent, and libidinous practices by the accused 'seizing [the hand of his victim] and placing it on [the appellant's own] private parts.'

The main question which has been debated is as to whether there is in Scotland, at common law, any such offence as indecency or lewdness when committed upon a person who is not proved to be below the age of puberty. In support of the argument that indecent or lewd conduct in such circumstances is not a crime by the common law of Scotland, reference was made to the statutory provision introduced by section 11 of the Criminal Law Amendment Act of 1885, which affirms that gross indecency between two male adults, or indecency committed by one male adult on another male adult, is a crime. But it is, in my opinion impossible to maintain on the authorities that, by the common law of Scotland, indecent conduct committed by one person upon another only constitutes a crime when the victim of that conduct is below puberty. Whether the victim is male or female, it has, no doubt, always been a serious aggravation that the victim was near the age of puberty or below it. There are obvious reasons for this but the cases quoted to us negative the idea that indecency or lewdness ceases to be a crime as soon as the victim is proved to be above the age of puberty. If a hard-and-fast line at that age is not warranted by the authorities, it is impossible in principle to fix any standard of age; although (according to circumstances) the age of the victim may be an important consideration.

It would be a mistake to imagine that the criminal common law of Scotland countenances any precise and exact categorisation of the forms of conduct which amount to crime. It has been pointed out many times in this Court that such is not the nature or quality of the criminal law of Scotland. I need only refer to the well known passage in the opening of Baron Hume's institutional work (Hume on *Crimes* (3rd ed.) ch. i), in which the broad definition of crime—a doleful or wilful offence against society in the matter of 'violence, dishonesty, falsehood, indecency, irreligion' is laid down. In my opinion, the statement in Macdonald's *Criminal Law* (4th ed., p. 221), that 'all shamelessly indecent conduct is criminal', is sound, and correctly expresses the law of Scotland. No doubt there may be in particular cases circumstances of aggravation, but I am not prepared to rule out of the category of crime any shamelessly indecent conduct, and I am not prepared to infer from the circumstances that section 11 of the Act of 1885 affirmed the proposition that shamelessly indecent conduct by one male adult in relation to another was criminal, that such conduct was not, or could not have been, the competent subject of prosecution in Scotland before.

That being so, the only question that remains in this stated case is whether the magistrate, by convicting of assault in the modus libelled in some of the charges, and of lewd practices in the modus libelled in the others, has gone wrong. I do not think so. It is not material that the charges are stated as charges of assault attended with indecency, or as charges of lewd practices. It is, in short plain to my mind that it is impossible to attribute to the conviction as it stands any injustice to the accused at all.

Lastly, complaint was made that the magistrate, in narrating the facts proved under the various charges, has not stated in so many words that the indecent assaults or lewd practices were committed against the consent and without the will of the victims. But it is impossible to read the findings in fact in relation to the charges made as consistent with the notion that there was any consent on the part of the persons who were abused in this way. I suggest that both the first and second questions ought to be answered in the affirmative."

Appeal dismissed.

NOTES

**9.40**    1. Macdonald provided no authority for his assertion that "all shamelessly indecent conduct is criminal". It is probably the case that *certain* forms of behaviour were criminal, if they took place in circumstances which could properly be described as "shamelessly indecent", but that there was no general offence of conducting one's self in a shamelessly indecent manner.

Some support for this can be found in Schedule 19 to the Summary Jurisdiction (Scotland) Act 1908 which sets out the form of charge to be used in summary proceedings. Amongst these is an example of indecent exposure in the following terms: "You did publicly expose your person in a shameless and indecent manner in the presence of the lieges." It is worth observing that the form of the charge is not that the accused conducted himself in a shamelessly indecent manner by publicly exposing his person, but rather than he exposed his person publicly in a shamelessly indecent manner. The case of *Poli v. Thomson*, 1910 S.L.T. 197 which discusses Schedule 19 appears to support the view that the offence was one of indecent exposure, rather than shameless indecency.

2. Was there any need to resort to shameless indecency in this case? The complaint seems to narrate a relevant charge of indecent assault either by touching the victim's private parts, or by grabbing the victim's hand and placing it on the accused's private parts. Either was there is an assault in circumstances of indecency.

**R. v. H.M. Advocate**
1988 S.C.C.R. 254

**9.41** The accused was charged with conducting himself in a shamelessly indecent manner which his sixteen-year-old daughter. The acts in question involved simulated sexual intercourse, but did not involve sexual penetration. An objection to the relevancy of the indictment was repelled by the sheriff. The case went to trial, and in the course of his charge to the jury the sheriff (I. D. MacPhail) stated that they were not called upon to consider whether or not the acts in question were, in their view, shamelessly indecent, but simply whether they found that the accused had deliberately engaged in the acts libelled in the indictment. The accused was convicted, and appealed.

OPINION OF THE COURT: " . . . [T]he first ground of appeal is that the sheriff erred in repelling the plea to the relevancy of [the charge of shameless indecency] .... The ground of appeal goes on to say that whereas shamelessly indecent conduct is a crime known to the law of Scotland, the specification in relation to charge 2 is such that it does not and cannot amount to shamelessly indecent conduct even if that conduct were proved. The charge is therefore irrelevant and should have been withdrawn from the jury's consideration.

Counsel for the appellant supported that ground of appeal in his submission to us and referred to a number of authorities and decided cases beginning with *Macdonald on Criminal Law* (5th ed.) at p. 150, and ending in effect with the case of *Watt v. Annan* [1978 J.C. 84 (*post*, p. 57). But we do not need to trouble ourselves with a consideration of these cases because counsel very properly and correctly accepted that the sheriff had extracted from the authorities five unassailable propositions with which he entirely agreed. These propositions are set out in the sheriff's report to us, and he has this to say: "(1) It is a principle of the law of Scotland that all shamelessly indecent conduct is criminal. (2) The scope of the offence is quite deliberately imprecise. (3) The offence may be committed in private. (4) The person against whom the conduct is directed may participate in or consent to or offer no objection to the conduct. (5) It is not the indecency of the conduct which makes it criminal, but the quality of shamelessness."

In this case, the sheriff's decision on relevancy was that the quality of shamelessness appeared to arise not from the physical conduct itself considered simply as sexual behaviour between any male and female, but from the nature of the relationship of father and lawful daughter which existed between the now appellant and the other party. It followed, said the sheriff, from that relationship that the appellant's behaviour as averred in each of charges 1 and 2 had been incestuous in quality, and he considered, as he tells us in his report, that a father who so conducted himself towards his lawful daughter would inescapably merit description as being lost to any sense of shame or as using his judgment and discretion as to his conduct in an indecent and shameless fashion. The reasons for the sheriff's decision on relevancy clearly appear and we observe that he seems to be saying what has been said by jurists since the time of Hume, namely, that a sexual relationship between a parent and child is in the law of Scotland regarded as behaviour which is repugnant to society. Counsel for the appellant argued that the sheriff was entirely wrong in disposing of the matter in that way and, as we understood his argument, it was that the conduct itself was not indecent and therefore the relationship could not aggravate conduct which was otherwise lawful. On the averments in this case the practices are not indecent or illegal without the relationship of father and daughter and therefore, with the relationship, they cannot be shamelessly indecent either. We have no hesitation in rejecting the submission under head 1 of the grounds of appeal, and endorsing fully the decision of the sheriff which was given for the reasons set out in his report.

The next ground of appeal is concerned with the manner in which the sheriff directed the jury on the performance of their task in returning a verdict on charge 2. From the report we take the directions which were in fact given. They are an exact quotation from the transcript of the trial judge's charge from pp. 9D to 10E. By way of introduction let it be said that in addressing the jury both the procurator fiscal and the solicitor for the now appellant, addressed the jury on the basis that if the jury found that the conduct libelled in charge 2 had been proved, it was still for the jury to decide whether that conduct was shameless.

The directions given by the sheriff did not follow that pattern at all. What he had to say was this: "Now, ladies and gentlemen, I have to give you some directions as to what this charge means" (and he is talking about charge 2). "And I will ask you to attend to this with particular care because I have the misfortune to take a slightly different simpler line on this matter than the two gentlemen who have addressed you and it is my directions which you must follow. If these turn out to be wrong it can be put right elsewhere but as far as you are concerned, it is the directions which I am giving to you now which matter and which you must follow. Ladies and gentlemen, it is really quite straightforward. By the law of Scotland all shamelessly indecent conduct is criminal and it has already been decided in this court at an earlier stage of this case that what is libelled in charge 2 is a species or kind of shamelessly indecent conduct, in other words, it has already been decided earlier that if a father deliberately conducts himself towards his daughter in the manner described in charge 2, he behaves in what the law regards as an indecent and shameless fashion. The shamelessness arises from the nature of the relationship with father and daughter. I should also say that it does not matter whether the conduct is in public or in private, and the attitude of the daughter is immaterial whether she resists it or not, it does not matter a scrap. If you find that the acts libelled were deliberately committed by the accused then it follows that he was conducting himself in a shamelessly indecent manner and you are not called upon to make any value judgment as to whether it was shamelessly indecent, you are entitled to find the accused guilty."

Counsel's submission for the appellant was that that was a misdirection. The sheriff erred in taking away from the jury an alleged right to make a value judgment on the proved conduct. Counsel's submission was that it was for the jury to decide not only whether the conduct was proved to have been deliberately engaged in by the appellant, but whether, in their judgment, that conduct deserved to be categorised as shamelessly indecent. In our opinion that submission does not persuade us that the sheriff misdirected the jury at all. It has already been said in this opinion that sexual practices indulged in by a father to a daughter deliberately are regarded in Scots law at least as repugnant to society. They have been so regarded for centuries and so far as we know there is no law to the contrary which has been cited to us or of which we are aware. In our judgment the direction was a perfectly proper one. The question for the jury was simply whether this father deliberately committed the acts of a sexual kind towards and with the daughter because if he did deliberately engage in the practices described in the libel, then as matter of law he was behaving in a manner which the law has always regarded as shamelessly indecent. In the result we refuse the appeal against conviction on both grounds.

Appeal refused.

NOTES

**9.42**    1. While one can have little sympathy for the accused, there is little doubt that this decision marked a substantial development in the law. An extension of the crime of shameless indecency was the only route by which criminal sanctions could be brought to bear on this accused. Since there was no intercourse it was not possible to rely on charges of incest. (See now section 1 of the Criminal Law (Consolidation) (Scotland) Act 1995, *ante*, p. 363.) Since the indictment did not allege that the acts took place without the daughter's consent it was not possible to charge the father with indecent assault, and since she was 16 at the time of the alleged offence it would not have been possible to bring charges of lewd practices under what is now section 6 of the Criminal Law (Consolidation) (Scotland) Act 1995.

There does not appear to have been any precedent for the prosecution in *R. v. H.M. Advocate*, and given the understanding of the prevailing law at the time, it is possible to argue that the decision in that case violated article 7(1) of the European Convention on Human Rights, as construed by the Court in *C.R. v. United Kingdom; S.W. v. United Kingdom* and *Kokkinakis v. Greece* (above, Chap. 1).

2. *R. v. H.M. Advocate* establishes that the question of whether or not conduct is "shamelessly indecent" is a question of law, to be determined by the Court. It is not the jury's function to determine whether or not the conduct is of that character. In some ways this is curious, since whether or not conduct is of a kind which the community regards as repugnant would seem to be precisely the kind of question that juries are there to answer. However, since the crime consists in conduct which is shamelessly indecent, what is or is not "shamelessly indecent" behaviour is part of the definition of the offence which is therefore a matter of law and not fact.

3. In *H.M. Advocate v. R.K.*, 1994 S.C.C.R. 499, the accused was charged with conducting himself in a shamelessly indecent manner by having sexual intercourse with a young woman who had been his foster

daughter since the age of eight. The intercourse was alleged to have taken place on various occasions when the foster daughter was aged 16- to 18-and-a-half. An objection to the relevancy of the indictment was repelled by Lord MacLean who noted that the parties remained in a "family relationship" and held that this case was analogous to that of *R. v. H.M. Advocate*. Is this correct given that (were he to divorce his wife or become a widower), the accused could lawfully have married his foster daughter?"

4. In *H.M. Advocate v. Roose*, 1999 S.C.C.R. 259, the accused (who was 38) was charged with **9.43** shameless indecency by having sexual intercourse with a 13-year-old girl. Although this would normally be charged as a violation of s.5(3) of the Criminal Law (Consolidation) (Scotland) Act 1995, prosecutions under that section must be taken within one year of the offence (s.5(4)). The Crown attempted to circumvent the time-bar by prosecuting R for shameless indecency instead of the statutory offence. Lord Marnoch held that the indictment was irrelevant, observing that ...

"... it is, in my opinion, clear that formerly, at least, intercourse with a child over the age of puberty was permitted by the common law of Scotland and it may, indeed, be instructive that until 1929 a child of 12 could actually enter into marriage. As to the state of the common law generally prior to 1885 I refer to *H.M. Advocate v. Watson* (1885) 5 Coup. 696, particularly at p. 702. However, the Advocate Depute, in seeking to uphold the libel, submitted, firstly, that, whatever may have been the common law in 1885, the crime of shameless indecency was flexible enough to embrace a change in the public perception of what constituted wholly unacceptable behaviour and, secondly, that the differential in ages between the accused and the complainer (some 20 years) [*sic*] might itself be sufficient to infer a relationship of trust such as had been founded on in *Batty v. H.M. Advocate*, 1995 S.C.C.R. 525. In support of his first proposition the Advocate Depute referred me to the obiter remarks of Lord Cameron in *Watt v. Annan* 1978 J.C. 84, at pp. 88–89, which include Lord Cameron's approval of the statement in McDonald's *Criminal Law* that "all shamelessly indecent conduct is criminal".

While, however, I see the force of the advocate-depute's submissions it seems to me a very far reaching proposition that it should, in effect, be left to a jury to declare criminal for the first time conduct formerly regarded as non-criminal. This is particularly so bearing in mind that we are in an area which Parliament has expressly legislated for as recently as 1995 in the Criminal Law Consolidation (Scotland) Act of that year. As for the advocate-depute's second submission I am simply not satisfied that an age differential *per se* is a sufficient basis for inferring a relationship of trust such as to bring the case within the ratio of *H.M. Advocate v. Batty, cit. sup.* While "shameless indecency" can doubtless cover a variety of conduct and will often be dependent on the facts and circumstances of a particular case, it must in the end be a question of law as to what is or is not capable of constituting the crime and the citizen is entitled to clear notice in the indictment of the facts and circumstances which are said to render his particular conduct criminal. If a difference of age *per se* is said to be material I have great difficulty in seeing where the line is to be drawn."

This decision must be read in the light of other recent cases where the High Court has proved reluctant to expand the scope of the crime of shameless indecency. See, in this respect, *Paterson v. Lees*, 1999 J.C. 159 and *Geddes v. Dickson*, 2000 S.C.C.R. 1007. Shameless indecency is discussed further in Chap. 16.

NOTES

1. Lord Marnoch was clearly unwilling to sanction an extension of the crime of shameless indecency. **9.44** In view of the terms of Article 7 of the European Convention on Human Rights it is, with respect, submitted that he was entirely correct to adopt the approach which he did. It is worth comparing Lord Marnoch's careful observation of the principles of legality with the decisions in *R. v. H.M. Advocate*, *ante*, p. 366 and *H.M. Advocate v. K.*

2. The case of *Batty* was hardly relevant. That was a case in which there was clearly a relationship of trust and authority between the accused and the girls whom he abused. There was nothing in the indictment in this case to reveal any such relationship, and it must surely be correct to state that such cannot be inferred merely from a substantial difference in the ages of the accused and the young person. (Although Lord Marnoch refers to an age difference of 20 years, the accused was in fact born in May 1960.)

3. What the Crown were attempting to achieve here was to circumvent the time-limit on the statutory offence of having unlawful sexual intercourse with a girl aged between 13 and 16 (section 5 of the Criminal Law (Consolidation) (Scotland) Act 1995). Should it be permissible at all for the Crown to do so?

## 7. HOMOSEXUAL OFFENCES

### A. Sexual acts between men

#### 1. Criminal Law (Consolidation) (Scotland) Act 1995

**9.45** 13.—(1) Subject to the provisions of this section, a homosexual act in private shall not be an offence provided that the parties consent thereto and have attained the age of eighteen years.

(2) An act which would otherwise be treated for the purposes of this Act as being done in private shall not be so treated if done—

(a) when more than two persons take part or are present or

(b) in a lavatory to which the public have, or are permitted to have, access whether on payment or otherwise.

(3) A male person who is suffering from mental deficiency which is of such a nature or degree that he is incapable of living an independent life or of guarding himself against serious exploitation cannot in law give any consent which, by virtue of subsection (1) above, would prevent a homosexual act from being an offence; but a person shall not be convicted on account of the incapacity of such a male person to consent, of an offence consisting of such an act if he proves that he did not know and had no reason to suspect that male person to be suffering from such mental deficiency.

(4) In this section a "homosexual act" means sodomy or an act of gross indecency or shameless indecency by one male person with another male person.

(5) Subject to subsection (3) above, it shall be an offence to commit or to be party to the commission of, or to procure or attempt to procure the commission of a homosexual act—

(a) otherwise than in private;

(b) without the consent of both parties to the act; or

(c) with a person under the age of eighteen years.

(6) It shall be an offence to procure or attempt to procure the commission of a homosexual act between two other male persons.

(8) It shall be a defence to a charge of committing a homosexual act under subsection 5(c) above that the person so charged being under the age of 24 years who had to previously been charged with a like offence, had reasonable cause to believe that the other person was of or over the age of 18 years.

NOTES

**9.46**     1. Prior to 1980 all sexual acts between men were criminal, irrespective of the ages of the parties, the fact that the parties consented and that the acts took place in private. The criminal law was based on a combination of the common law offences of sodomy and shameless indecency, and statutory offences of gross indecency. Following upon the *Report of the Committee on Homosexual Offences and Prostitution* (chaired by Lord Wolfenden) (Cmnd. 247, 1957) most consensual homosexual acts between adult men in private were de-criminalised in England and Wales by the Sexual Offences Act 1967. That legislation was not, however, applied to other parts of the United Kingdom, although in practice sexual acts between men were not prosecuted in Scotland where such acts would not be unlawful in England and Wales. The law in Scotland was eventually changed by section 80 of the Criminal Justice (Scotland) Act 1980 which de-criminalised "homosexual acts" between men provided that they took place in private, were consensual and both parties were over 21. That age was reduced to 18 by the Criminal Justice and

Public Order Act 1994. Section 80 was replaced by section 13 of the Criminal Law (Consolidation) (Scotland) Act 1995, and the age of consent was again reduced, this time to 16, by the Sexual Offences (Amendment) Act 2000, s.1(3). This statute is intended to equalise the age of consent for heterosexual and homosexual acts in light of the decision of the European Commission of Human Rights in *Sutherland v. United Kingdom* (App. No. 25186/94, 1995). Complete equalisation has yet to be achieved in Scots law, however, as while it is an offence for a male to have sexual intercourse with a girl under the age of 16 (s.5 of the 1995 Act), it is probably not an offence for a female to have sexual intercourse with a boy under the age of 16. If the boy is under (or perhaps slightly over) the age of puberty (14), then the female would be committing the offence of lewd practices (see *supra*, p. 362).

It remains the case that all sexual acts between men are unlawful unless the provisions of section 13 of the 1995 Act apply. The relevant offences are still found in a combination of common law and statute:

## (a) Sodomy

Sodomy consists in anal intercourse between two male persons (Alison, i, 566; Macdonald, p. 149). **9.47** Other forms of sexual act, such as oral intercourse do not constitute sodomy: Alison, i, 566, relying upon the English case of *R. v. Jacobs* (1817) Russ. & Ry. 331.

## (b) Lewd practices

It is an offence at common law for a man to engage in lewd practices with or towards a boy under or **9.48** "about" the age of puberty (*i.e.* 14 at common law): *David Brown*, (1844) 2 Broun 261; *Andrew Lyall*, (1853) 1 Irvine 218.

## (c) Shameless indecency

It is an offence at common law for a man to engage in "lewd, indecent or libidinous practices" with or **9.49** towards another man: *McLaughlan v. Boyd*, 1934 J.C. 19, *ante*, p. 365.

## (d) Offences involving "homosexual acts" under section 13 of the Criminal Law (Consolidation) (Scotland) Act 1995

Section 13 of the 1995 Act creates a number of offences involving "homosexual acts" (as defined by **9.50** section 13(4) to include sodomy and shameless indecency, as well as "gross indecency"). There is thus a substantial overlap between these statutory offences and the common law offences. It would, for example, be an offence both at common law and under section 13(5) for a man to commit sodomy with another man (subject to the de-criminalising provisions of section 13(1)). There are, however, important differences between the statutory offences and the common law offences in terms of procedure and penalties. Thus prosecutions for the statutory offences must be commenced within 12 months of the date of the offence (1995 Act, s.13(9)), whereas there is no such statutory time-limit on the prosecution of the common law offences. The penalties for the statutory offences are also different. Thus the maximum penalty for sodomy as a homosexual act within the meaning of section 13(5) is two years' imprisonment (1995 Act, s.13(5)), whereas the maximum penalty at common law is life imprisonment.

2. Consensual homosexual acts are, in terms of section 13(1) and (2)(a) only rendered lawful if they take place in "private". Section 13(2)(a) provides that an act shall not be treated as having taken place in private if "more than two persons take part or are present". The equivalent restriction in English law (found in section 1(2) of the Sexual Offences Act 1967) was successfully challenged before the European Court of Human Rights in *A.D.T. v. United Kingdom* (2000). Clause 10 of the Convention Rights (Compliance) (Scotland) Bill, which is before the Scottish Parliament at the time of writing, is expected to amend the 1995 Act to conform with this decision. If this Bill passes into law as it currently

stands, the rule that consensual homosexual acts must take place in private in order to be lawful will remain, but the restriction that an act can never be considered to take place in private if more than two persons were present will be removed.

## B. Sexual acts between women

**9.51** 1. Sexual relations between women have never been regarded as criminal. Certainly sexual relations between adult women, as such, would appear to be beyond the reach of the criminal law, although in appropriate circumstances sexual acts between adult women might be regarded as shamelessly indecent (if, for example, these were to occur in circumstances involving public indecency). It must be remembered, however, that the various decisions of the European Court of Human Rights holding that criminal prohibitions on sexual relations between adult men are incompatible with Article 8 of the Convention (see the cases referred to, *supra*, in *A.D.T. v. United Kingdom*) would apply to the case of sexual relations between adult women.

2. There would seem to be no reason in principle why sexual relations between an adult woman and a female child could not be the subject of criminal proceedings. It is an offence at common law for any person to engage in acts of sexual indecency with a girl under puberty (since the girl cannot consent) and section 6 of the Criminal Law (Consolidation) (Scotland) Act 1995 makes it an offence for "any person" to use lewd, indecent or libidinous practices towards a girl aged between 12 and 16 where such conduct would have been criminal at common law.

## 8. OFFENCES RELATING TO PROSTITUTION

**9.52** Offences relating to prostitution are not easily categorised. For some the purpose of such offences is to control prostitution which is regarded as an evil in itself. For others, the law should concern itself only with the public manifestation of prostitution, the public solicitation of sexual acts. Others again take the view that the law concerns in this area should embrace the protection of sex workers themselves from violence and exploitation.

## A. Soliciting for the purpose of prostitution

### Civic Government (Scotland) Act 1982

**9.53** **46.**—(1) A prostitute (whether male or female) who for the purposes of prostitution—
   (a) loiters in a public place;
   (b) solicits in a public place or in any other place so as to be seen from a public place; or
   (c) importunes any person who is in a public place,
shall be guilty of an offence ...

(2) In subsection (1) above, "public place" has the same meaning as in section 133 of this Act but includes—
   (a) any place to which at the material time the public are permitted to have access, whether on payment or otherwise; and
   (b) any public conveyance other than a taxi or hire car within the meaning of section 23 of this Act.

NOTES

**9.54**    1. A prostitute is a person who offers their body for the sexual gratification of others in return for payment: *De Munck* [1918] 1 K.C. 635; *Smith v. Sellers*, 1978 S.L.T. (Notes) 44. This definition was devised originally in relation to female prostitutes, but there is no reason why it should not be applied in the case of a male prostitute.

2. Section 133 of the Civic Government (Scotland) Act 1982 defines a "public place" as any place, whether a thoroughfare or not, to which the public have unrestricted access, including doorways and entrances abutting on any "public place" and common closes, passages, stairways, etc.

## B. Living on the earnings of prostitution

### Criminal Law (Consolidation) (Scotland) Act 1995

**11.**—(1) Every male person who—                                                           **9.55**

(a) knowingly lives wholly or in part on the earnings of prostitution; or

(b) in any public place persistently solicits or importunes for immoral purposes,

shall be liable on conviction on indictment to imprisonment for a term not exceeding two years or on summary conviction to imprisonment for a term not exceeding six months.

(2) ...

(3) Where a male person is proved to live with or to be habitually in the company of a prostitute, or is proved to have exercised control, direction or influence over the movements of a prostitute in such a manner as to show that he is aiding, abetting or compelling her prostitution with any other person, or generally, he shall, unless he can satisfy the court to the contrary, be deemed to be knowingly living on the earnings of prostitution.

(4) Every female who is proved to have, for the purposes of gain, exercised control, direction or influence over the movements of a prostitute in such a manner as to show that she is aiding, abetting or compelling her prostitution with any other person, or generally, shall be liable to the penalties set out in subsection (1) above.

(5) Any person who—

(a) keeps or manages or acts or assists in the management of a brothel; or

(b) being the tenant, lessee, occupier or person in charge of any premises, knowingly permits such premises or any part thereof to be used as a brothel or for the purposes of habitual prostitution; or

(c) being the lessor or landlord of any premises, or the agent of such lessor or landlord, lets the same or any part thereof with the knowledge that such premises or some part thereof are or is to be used as a brothel, or is wilfully a party to the continued use of such premises or any part thereof as a brothel,

shall be guilty of an offence.

**13.**— (9) A person who knowingly lives wholly or in part on the earnings of another from male prostitution or who solicits or importunes any male person for the purpose of procuring the commission of a homosexual act within the meaning of subsection [13(4)] above shall be [guilty of an offence]

(10) Premises shall be treated for the purposes of sections 11(1) and 12 of this Act as a brothel if people resort to it [*sic*] for the purposes of homosexual acts within the meaning of subsection (4) above in circumstances in which resort thereto for heterosexual practices would have led to its being treated as a brothel for the purposes of those sections.

NOTES

1. Although the offence under s.11 can only be committed by a "male person", this does not prevent a **9.56** woman from being guilty of the offence art and part: *Reid v. H.M. Advocate*, 1999 J.C. 54 (*ante*, p. 168). Presumably, however, the prostitute herself cannot be guilty art and part.

2. On who is "male" for the purposes of the offence of living on the earnings of a male prostitute, see *R. v. Tan* [1983] 2 All E.R. 12.

### Soni v. H.M. Advocate
#### 1970 S.L.T. 275

A landlord owned or controlled about 22 furnished houses in Glasgow of which he let eight to **9.57** women whom he knew to be prostitutes. He was charged with and convicted of knowingly living in part on the earnings of prostitution, contrary to s.1(1)(a) of the Immoral Traffic (Scotland) Act 1902. He appealed to the High Court on three grounds: (1) that the sheriff misdirected the jury in that he directed them that they would be entitled to convict if the evidence showed that the accused was participating and assisting in the activities of the prostitutes notwithstanding that the charges made for the houses were reasonable and normal and not exorbitant; and (2) in any event there was no evidence upon which the jury could have found that he was participating and assisting in the activities of the prostitutes and (3) that there was no evidence of exorbitant charges.

LORD JUSTICE-CLERK (GRANT): "The applicant was charged on indictment and convicted of a contravention of s.1(1)(a) of the Immoral Traffic (Scotland) Act 1902 as amended by the Criminal Law Amendment Act 1912, s.7. The conviction, in terms of the jury's verdict, was that during the period libelled he had knowingly lived in part on the earnings of prostitution. He was sentenced to nine months' imprisonment. Against both conviction and sentence he now seeks to appeal .... The first ground of appeal is in the following terms: 'The presiding judge misdirected the jury in that, having correctly directed them on s.1(3) of the Immoral Traffic (Scotland) Act 1902, that there was no sufficient evidence that the applicant had been proved *inter alia* "to have exercised control direction or influence over the movements of a prostitute in such a manner as to show that he was aiding and abetting or compelling her prostitution with any other person or generally" he then directed them in law that the applicant would be guilty of the offence libelled if the evidence showed that he was participating and assisting in the activities of the prostitutes notwithstanding that the charges made for the houses were reasonable and normal and not exorbitant.' It is right to say here that what the sheriff substitute did in fact say was not that 'the applicant would be guilty' but that the jury 'would be entitled to convict'.

Before turning to examine and determine the arguments submitted on this ground of appeal it is desirable to give a digest of the facts. The applicant owned or controlled about 22 furnished houses in Glasgow. Eight of these he rented to women he knew to be prostitutes. At the trial the Crown maintained that the rents charged for these latter houses were exorbitant or 'prostitute rents' and that in the circumstances the applicant by receiving the rents was living at least in part on the immoral earnings of the prostitutes who rented the houses.

Counsel for the applicant argued strongly that where a house was rented for occupation to a prostitute, and was not provided solely and specifically by the landlord to enable the prostitute to carry on her trade, then the only way by which the landlord could be convicted of a contravention of s.1(1)(a)(*supra*) was to establish that the rent charged was exorbitant, or what has been described in other cases as a 'prostitute rent'. In support of this submission he founded on a passage from the speech of Viscount Simonds in *Shaw v. Director of Public Prosecutions*, [1962] A.C. 220 at p. 266; (1961) 45 Cr.App.R. 113 at p. 146. If this were well-founded, then the learned sheriff-substitute had obviously misdirected the jury in law when he told them the applicant could be guilty of the offence libelled even if the evidence showed that the charges made for the houses were reasonable and normal and were not exorbitant.

In our view the limitation which counsel for the applicant sought to place on the conditions under which a conviction can be obtained in circumstances such as prevailed here is too restrictive. Each case must be considered on its own facts. The authorities indicate that where a landlord lets a room specifically and exclusively for the purpose of enabling a prostitute to carry on her trade an offence under the section may be held to be committed: see *R. v. Thomas* [1957] 1 W.L.R. 747, (1957) 41 Cr.App.R. 117 and the observations thereon by Viscount Simonds in Shaw (*supra*). The same situation arises where knowing that the woman is a prostitute and likely to carry on her trade in the premises, the landlord charges a rent in excess of normal, extorting it from the prostitute upon no other ground than that she is a prostitute—Lord Reid in Shaw, at p. 271. And, of course, a person may be convicted if he is brought within the provisions of s.1(3) of the Act as amended. These, however, are not the exclusive ways in which the section may be attracted. Circumstances may vary infinitely and in any given case the question is whether in the words of the subsection it is proved that the person accused has been living in whole or in part on the earnings of prostitution.

We were informed that this is the first case of its kind which has come before the courts in Scotland for an authoritative determination. There have, however been a number of cases in England under kindred statutes, and, in consequence of these, and in particular of the case of Shaw, it was accepted (and properly so) by both sides of the Bar that there could not be a contravention of the subsection simply if the premises were let for occupation, even if the landlord knew that the tenant was a prostitute and must be assumed to have known that she would ply her trade there. Something more than that is required. Counsel for the applicant maintained that the only thing that could be 'something more' was exorbitant rent. Why should there be such a limitation? There seems to be no reason in principle. The passage from Viscount Simonds in Shaw, at p. 226, on which the whole argument was hinged, must be read in its context. His Lordship was there dealing with a case such as that of *R. v. Silver* [1956] 1 W.L.R. 281, 40 Cr.App.R. 32, where the facts were that in the various charges libelled the landlord had let a flat at a high rate to a prostitute, knowing that she was a prostitute and that she intended to use the flat for the purposes of prostitution. Viscount Simonds, who found *Silver* (*supra*) a difficult case and expressed no final opinion on it, said that it was a tenable view that in such a case the landlord could be convicted of an offence upon the ground that the rent is exorbitant. He did not say that in another set of circumstances no other determining factor could apply. Elsewhere in his speech the noble Lord, after pointing out that a prostitute is entitled to be provided with goods and services in the same way as other people, without an offence being committed, goes on to make a distinction. He says at p. 263: 'I would say, however, that, though a person who is paid for goods or services out of the earnings of prostitution does not necessarily commit an offence under the Act, yet a person does not necessarily escape from its provisions by receiving payment for the goods or services that he supplies to a prostitute. The argument that such a person lives on his own earnings, not hers, is inconclusive. To give effect to it would be to exclude from the operation of the Act the very persons, the tout, the bully or protector, whom it was designed to catch.' The latter category is not confined to those who might be caught by virtue of s.1(3). At p. 264 he adopts with approval terms used in previous cases such as 'coadjutor' (*i.e.* an assistant) and 'trading in prostitution'. All this points to a wider range of possibilities than counsel for the applicant asserted. When the case of *Shaw* was in the Court of Criminal Appeal, Ashworth, J., who read the judgment of the court stated (at p. 229): 'It was further submitted that there was no evidence that the appellants charged inflated prices for the prostitute's advertisements, and that therefore *Thomas's* (*supra*) case was distinguishable. This submission is not well founded, and involves a misunderstanding of the relevance of the inflated rent in that case. The purpose of tendering evidence as to the rent was to show that the room was not let for normal accommodation, but for the prostitute's professional purposes, and although, in the absence of such evidence or other evidence implicating the accused, it might be difficult to prove the charge in the case of a room being let to a prostitute, such evidence was not, in our view, an essential element in the prosecution's case.'

In the House of Lords, Lord Reid said at p. 271: 'But I am far from saying that a landlord can never be guilty of living on the immoral earnings of his tenant. To my mind, the most obvious case is where he takes advantage of her difficulty in getting accommodation to extract from her in the guise of rent sums beyond any normal commercial rent. In reality he is not then merely acting as a landlord; he is making her engage in a joint adventure with him which will bring to him a part of her immoral earnings over and above rent. And there may well be other ways in which he can make himself a participator in her earnings not merely a recipient of rent. The line may be a difficult one to draw, but juries often have to decide broad questions of that kind.'

While proof of payment of an exorbitant rent may be a factor, and possibly a telling factor, in the issue, it is not an essential one. In its absence, proof that the accused was living on the immoral earnings of prostitution might be difficult, but that is not to say it is impossible. We therefore reject this argument by counsel for the applicant ....

So far as the second ground of appeal is concerned, it was agreed that there was ample evidence to support the point that the applicant knew that the women concerned were prostitutes. Counsel for the applicant submitted, however, that there was not sufficient evidence to warrant a reasonable jury finding that the applicant was participating and assisting in the activities of the prostitutes in such a manner as would bring him within the terms of s.1(1)(a) of the statute. It is not necessary to go into all the evidence in detail. There is, however, ample evidence that the sole reason why some of the prostitutes came to Glasgow was to carry on their trade there, that the applicant was aware of this and that he gave them priority as tenants. There is also clear evidence that the dominant purpose of the lets was not to provide a place to live in but to provide a place where the prostitutes could carry on their trade. At least two of them speak to obtaining a change of house, not because their accommodation was unsuitable for living in, but because the new accommodation was more suitable for prostitution. The prostitutes had no means of support other than prostitution and it was, to say the least of it, in the applicant's interest that their earnings should cover their rent as well as their other outgoings—and that their earning power should be reasonably substantial and should be affected, on a conviction for soliciting, by a fine and not by imprisonment ....

In our opinion the evidence that he was participating and assisting in such ways as we have just described and that, for example, he was giving them premises more suited for their activities, discussing the installation of a telephone to facilitate bookings and counselling them against conduct which might get them involved with the police and a possible cutting off of their income, can properly be regarded as showing a personal involvement with their immoral activities designed to secure and advance his own financial interests. This is a view which the jury were entitled to take. The matters which we have mentioned clearly distinguish the position of the applicant from the ordinary case of a person providing services at a normal rate in the normal way. We are accordingly of opinion that the second ground of appeal also fails.

In support of the third ground of appeal counsel for the applicant argued that it was impossible for the jury to come to any decision that the rents were exorbitant in the admitted absence of any evidence of comparative rents for comparative properties. He made a similar submission at the trial, and the presiding judge left it to the jury to decide whether they should accept that, but indicated that there was other evidence, albeit not very much, which would entitle them to find the point proved in the absence of such comparative evidence.

We are of the opinion that while comparative evidence might have been the best way of establishing that the rents were exorbitant, it is not necessarily the only way. We are also of the opinion that although the evidence on the point is not strong there was sufficient to entitle the jury to hold that the exorbitancy had been established. The evidence about the applicant's proposal to 'cook' the returns to the Inland Revenue, wherein the rents would be shown as being about only half of the rents actually being charged could be regarded as a legitimate touchstone of what normal rents ought to have been ....

In the whole circumstances therefore we are of the opinion that the application for leave to appeal against conviction should be refused and that the conviction should stand."

Appeal refused.

NOTES

**9.58**   Section 1(1)(a) of the Immoral Traffic (Scotland) Act 1902 is now section 11(1)(a) of the Sexual Offences (Scotland) Act 1976.

# 9. SEXUAL OFFENCES OUTSIDE THE UNITED KINGDOM

Concern over what has become known as "sex tourism" has prompted Parliament to take steps to **9.59**
control the activities of those travelling from the United Kingdom to various countries to engage in
sexual relations with children and young persons, and those who, in the United Kingdom, arrange or
facilitate such activities. Section 6 of the Sexual Offences (Conspiracy and Incitement) Act 1996
inserted into the Criminal Law (Consolidation) (Scotland) Act 1995 a new section 16A, concerning
conspiracy or incitement to commit certain sexual acts outside the United Kingdom. That provision was,
in turn, amended by the Criminal Justice (Terrorism and Conspiracy) Act 1998, s.9(1) and Schedule 1,
which removed from section 16A the references to conspiracy to commit sexual offences outside the
United Kingdom. Section 7 of the 1998 Act inserts a new section 11A into the Criminal Procedure
(Scotland) Act 1995 which deals generally with conspiracy to commit offences outside the United
Kingdom and which therefore renders redundant the special provisions concerning conspiracy to
commit sexual offences outside the United Kingdom, formerly contained in section 16A of the Criminal
Law (Consolidation) (Scotland) Act 1995. The particular provisions in section 16A relating to
incitement remain in force.

Part II of the Sex Offenders Act 1997 takes the more radical step of extending the extra-territorial
jurisdiction of the United Kingdom courts to try certain sexual offences committed entirely outside the
United Kingdom (*i.e.*, irrespective of any element of incitement or conspiracy within the United
Kingdom). Extra-territorial competence is conferred by section 16B of the Criminal Law (Consolidation) (Scotland) Act 1995, as inserted by section 8 of the Sex Offenders Act 1997.

# Chapter 10

## HOMICIDE AND RELATED MATTERS

**10.01**  Homicide is the killing of a living human being (other than oneself). As such it may be criminal or non-criminal. Criminal homicide includes the common law crimes of murder and culpable homicide, as well as the statutory offences of causing death by dangerous driving (Road Traffic Act 1988, section 1) and causing death by careless or inconsiderate driving while under the influence of drink or drugs (Road Traffic Act 1988, section 3A).

Criminal homicide may also form a constituent element of genocide under the Genocide Act 1969 (giving effect to the Genocide Convention of 1948), an offence under the Geneva Conventions Act 1957 and, in certain limited circumstances, murder carried out in violation of the laws and customs of war is a crime under the War Crimes Act 1991.

Non-criminal homicide includes cases of justifiable or excused killing and "casual" homicide, that is, where a person kills unintentionally, when lawfully employed and without culpable carelessness. This chapter is principally concerned with murder and culpable homicide, although other forms of homicide are touched on.

## 1. THE *ACTUS REUS* OF HOMICIDE

**10.02**  The *actus reus* of all forms of homicide is the destruction of a living human being. This gives rise to a number of questions. At what point does a human being begin to exist for these purposes? What protection does the criminal law afford before this point is reached? At what point does a person cease to exist for the purposes of the law of homicide? How does the law fix the causal connection between the death of the victim and the accused's act or omission? The last question is discussed in Chapter 4. The remaining questions are considered below.

### A. The beginning of life

**10.03**  The general question "when does life begin?" is a difficult one to answer. According to some, the point of conception provides at least an identifiable starting point. The American Convention on Human Rights, for example, states (article 4(1)) that the right to life is protected by law "in general, from the moment of conception". While it may be difficult in any given case to determine precisely when conception occurs, the fact that it has occurred can be demonstrated reliably from an early stage. The view that life starts at conception is not without its critics. John Harris argues in *The Value of Life* (London, 1985) that even before conception both the egg and the sperm are alive, and that it might be more correct to consider life as "a continuous process that proceeds uninterrupted from generation to generation" (*op. cit.* at p. 10)). The criminal law takes a less metaphysical approach and settles upon birth as the starting point for the law of homicide. However, even this approach is not without its problems.

## Jean McCallum
(1858) 3 Irv. 187

The panel was charged with the murder of her newly-born child by strangling it with a piece of **10.04** tape. The evidence showed that the child had breathed, but was not conclusive on whether it had been fully born alive.

LORD JUSTICE-CLERK (INGLIS): There is no kind of homicide that can be committed except upon a living human being, and, in order to establish here a charge of murder, which is the highest kind of homicide, you must be satisfied on the question, Whether there was a living child, murdered after its birth. The indictment sets forth, in logical sequence, the facts that the prosecutor undertakes to prove, and which are indispensable to his case. After stating time and place, it proceeds: 'You, the said Jean McAllum or McCallum, having been delivered of a living female child, did immediately or soon after the birth of said child . . . . '

You see, therefore, that the prosecutor must prove that the prisoner was delivered of a living female child, and that the assault leading to the murder of the child was committed after its birth . . . .

The prosecutor must thus prove, as indispensable to his case, that the subject so attacked—the child round whose neck this ligature was tied—was born a living child.

As to what is a living child, there is no difficulty about the law. A child that is not fully born has no separate existence from the mother, and is not, in the eye of the law, a living human being. It is in a state of transition from a foetus *in utero* to a living human being, and it does not become a living human being until it is fully born and has a separate existence of its own.

You may destroy a foetus *in utero*. It has a principle of vitality. And you may destroy it on the eve of birth; or you may destroy it in the course of being born. And all these are very serious offences, and are punishable by law. But they are not murder. And murder is the only charge in this indictment. Now this is extremely important, because unless you are satisfied that that child was alive after birth—that it was completely born a living child—you cannot find a verdict against the prisoner . . . . Everything depends upon what opinion you have as to whether the child was born alive. The case rests entirely on that."

Verdict: Not proven.

## H.M. Advocate v. Scott
(1892) 3 White 240

The accused was charged with the culpable homicide of her newly-born child by strangling it **10.05** immediately after birth, or alternatively by refraining from calling for assistance at the birth. Evidence was led by the Crown to the effect that the child had been born alive, had breathed, and had died as a result of manual strangulation. A medical witness for the defence was of the opinion that the injuries could have been caused by the accused delivering herself of the child, or alternatively that they might have been inflicted before the child was wholly separated from the person of its mother. Counsel for the accused argued that unless the injuries were proved to have been inflicted after complete delivery, there could be no conviction of culpable homicide. In his charge to the jury, the presiding judge gave the following directions.

LORD YOUNG: "If, then, you think that no blame attaches to the prisoner for the death of her child, you will, as I have said, acquit her. If you think that blame does attach to her, then culpable homicide is the name for that blame, resulting as it did in the death of a child which had both cried and breathed. It does not matter in the least, so far as the criminality of the accused is concerned if the injuries were inflicted when the child was partly in its mother's body, and no suggestion of that kind was made at the time by the girl herself."

Verdict: Not guilty.

NOTES

**10.06**     1. Is it possible to reconcile these two cases? Gordon accepts that they conflict and, in common with Macdonald, prefers Lord Young's approach: "There is a gap between abortion which consists in inducing a miscarriage, and the murder of a living child … and this gap can be shortened although not completely closed by adopting Lord Young's view which avoids the necessity of distinguishing between destroying a viable child the moment before it completely leaves the mother's body and destroying it a moment later, a distinction that appears to be without a difference" (para. 23–02). How far can this argument be taken? If fatal injuries are inflicted on a child during delivery, does it make any difference if these are inflicted before any part of its body is expelled from the body of the mother? Should it make a difference? If it does not, then the distinction between homicide and the destruction of at least a viable foetus becomes rather more difficult to justify.

2. In some systems it is accepted that the killing of a child *in utero* is homicide. In *Keeler v. People*, 470 P. 2d 617, the Supreme Court of California held that it was not murder where the accused attacked a pregnant woman and inflicted such serious injuries on her unborn child that it was delivered stillborn. Following that decision the California legislature amended section 187 of the Penal Code so as to include the "unlawful killing of a fetus" within the definition of murder.

The Michigan Penal Code, Chapter 750, section 322 provides that "The wilful killing of an unborn quick child by any injury to the mother of such child, which would be murder if it resulted in the death of such mother, shall be deemed manslaughter."

2. In English law, if a child is born alive, but dies as a result of injuries inflicted on it before birth, this is treated as homicide: Hawkins, *Pleas of the Crown*, Chap. 31, s.16, Hale, *Pleas of the Crown*, 1, 433; *R. v. West* (1848) 2 C. & K. 784; *Attorney-General's Reference (No. 3 of 1994)* [1997] 3 All E.R. 936. The same rule has been adopted in other common law jurisdictions. See, for examples, *State v. Anderson*, 343 A. 2d 505 (1975) (Approved on appeal: 413 A.2d 611, (1980)); *Clarke v. State*, 23 So. 671 (1898); *Morgan v. State*, 256 S.W. 433 (1923); *Cotton v. State*, 321 Ariz. Adv. Rep. 19 (2000); *Keeler v. People*, 470 P. 2d 617 (1970); *Williams v. State*, 561 A.2d 216 (1989); *State v. Hammett*, 192 Ga. App. 224; 384 S.E.2d 220, (1989); *Jones Movant v. Commonwealth*, 830 S.W.2d 877 (1992). Section 223 (2) of the Canadian Criminal Code provides that "A person commits homicide when he causes injury to a child before or during its birth as a result of which the child dies after becoming a human being."

English law also provides, in the Infant Life (Preservation) Act 1929, that it is an offence to kill an unborn child where that child is capable of being born alive. A similar provision is found in section 182 of the New Zealand Crimes Act 1961 which provides 182 that it is an offence to cause the death of "any child that has not become a human being in such a manner that he would have been guilty of murder if the child had become a human being". In *R. v. Henderson* [1990] 3 N.Z.L.R. 174 it was held that this provision did not require proof that the child was "capable of being born alive". See also *Wilcox v. Police* [1994] 1 N.Z.L.R. 243.

4. What is the position in Scots law where a child, born alive, dies as a result of ante-natal injuries? Hume doubts if such a case could be proved (Hume, i, 187). Gordon suggests (para. 23–02) that it might be an innominate offence. The matter is now (probably) resolved by the following case.

**McCluskey v. H.M. Advocate**
1989 S.L.T. 175

**10.07**     The appellant was charged with causing the death of 'another person' by reckless driving contrary to s.1 of the Road Traffic Act 1972 which provided that "A person who causes the death of another person by driving a motor vehicle on a road recklessly shall be guilty of an offence". The appellant was driving a car which collided with another vehicle in which a pregnant woman was a passenger. The woman and the child she was carrying (who had reached 35 weeks' gestation) were both injured in the collision. As a result of these injuries the child was delivered alive by emergency caesarian section but died thereafter. At a preliminary diet the appellant objected that the charge was irrelevant on the ground that the 1972 Act was concerned solely with causing the death of a person who was in independent life at the time of the act of reckless driving. The sheriff repelled the objection. On appeal:

OPINION OF THE COURT: "Before us counsel for the appellant renewed the submissions which the sheriff rejected. This, he said was the first time the Crown had charged anyone with a contravention of s.1 where the person who died was an unborn child at the time of the driving which was alleged to be reckless. In rejecting the appellant's submission the sheriff adopted an over-simplified approach to the construction of s.1. A sound construction of that section requires one to have regard to the principles of the common law of Scotland governing the crime of culpable homicide—causing the death of a person by an unlawful act. So approaching the construction of s.1, the words "the death of another person" relate only to a person in life at the time of the driving which is alleged to have caused his death. If Parliament had intended s.1 to make provision for the situation in which the person who died was still unborn when he or she sustained the injuries alleged to have caused death after birth it would have expressly provided for this situation. This could readily have been done (see, *e.g.* s.2 of the Congenital Disabilities (Civil Liability) Act 1976).

As the *actus reus* of homicide is indistinguishable from the *actus reus* of an offence under s.1, Parliament cannot be presumed to have intended in s.1 to penalise a reckless driver who injures a child *in utero* even if he dies as a result after being born alive. A charge of culpable homicide would not lie upon a libel of inflicting injury upon a foetus which dies *in utero* and it would offend against logic and common sense if a relevant charge could be laid merely because the child injured in the womb is born alive and dies later. It would be anomalous, it was said, if the particular criminal responsibility of a citizen (at common law or under statute) were to depend upon the mere chance, perhaps as the result of successful medical intervention, that the injured foetus survives long enough to be born alive. If the sheriff's construction of s.1 is correct it would be difficult to draw the line in any sensible way. Would s.1 apply to a case of injury to a child, just viable, in the womb of a mother who was not even aware of her pregnancy? The correct construction of s.1 must be that it is concerned only with causing the death of a person in life at the time of the act of reckless driving. There has been no case of a charge of culpable homicide, in Scotland at least, where the circumstances were similar to those in this indictment, *i.e.* the death of a child born alive as the result of injuries sustained before birth.

In our opinion for the reasons given by the learned advocate-depute the submission on behalf of the appellant must be rejected. Charge 1 is a charge of contravention of a statutory provision. We are concerned only with the relevancy of that charge. Its relevancy falls to be tested in the same way as that of any other statutory charge .... To be relevant a charge of contravention of s.1 requires to libel three matters: (1) the death of "another person", (2) reckless driving by the accused, and (3) a causal connection between the reckless driving and the death. All three requirements are met in the libel of charge 1 in this indictment and it is nothing to the point that the appellant's driving caused the injuries, which are said to have caused the child's death, shortly before his live birth. The Crown properly accepted that the offence created by s.1 is a statutory form of homicide and, further, that it would be anomalous to say that a relevant charge of contravention could lie if at common law on similar facts it were not culpable homicide to cause the death of a person born alive by injuries inflicted before birth. There is no authority in the law of Scotland to the effect that a relevant charge of culpable homicide would not lie in such circumstances. In Hume on *Crimes* (3rd ed.), Vol. 1, p. 187, the following passage appears: "One case is indeed stated in some of the English law-books, about which there may be room for argument; the case of a child which is born alive, but dies immediately on the birth, in consequence of deleterious medicines, previously administered to the mother. But it is difficult to imagine (and no more need be said on such a case), that in these circumstances a decisive proof can ever be obtained of the true cause of the death of the child." The sheriff considered that in that passage Baron Hume implied that a charge of that nature would be relevant. He was, we think, wrong about that. The implication is merely that such a charge might be relevant but the important matter is that Baron Hume did not say that a relevant charge would not lie, in our law, in these circumstances.

Since the Road Traffic Act is a United Kingdom statute it is legitimate to consider the common law position in England. As we understand the position a charge of manslaughter would in such circumstances be relevant. Our understanding proceeds upon the full consideration of English authority in the case of *Kwok Chak Ming (No. 1) v. The Queen*, at first instance, and on appeal at p. 349. Support for the view taken of the law of England in that case is to be found in Glanville Williams, *Text Book of Criminal Law* (2nd ed., 1983), p. 289, and in Russell on *Crime* (12th ed.), p. 401. In this state of the common law in Scotland and in England it is impossible to find, in the enactment of s.1 in a United Kingdom statute, that the words "the death of another person" must relate only to the death of a person who was a person in life at the time of the act of reckless driving."

Appeal refused.

NOTES

**10.08**     1. Although this case concerned the statutory offence of causing death by reckless driving, there would seem to be no logical reason for not applying the same approach in the case of common law homicides.

2. The approach adopted by the Court in *McCluskey* has been followed in relation to delictual liability for death resulting from ante-natal injuries: *McWilliams v. Lord Advocate*, 1992 S.L.T. 1045, 1992 SCLR 954.

3. *McCluskey* concerns only the *actus reus* of homicide, although it necessarily accepts that a person can be guilty of "recklessly" killing a person of whose existence he or she is unaware. Where the case is one of killing at common law, would the crime be murder or culpable homicide? Some rather complex issues arise here. It is possible to distinguish the following situations:

(a) The accused injures the child, intending to do so; (b) The accused injures the child, intending to kill the mother, while unaware of the existence of the child; (c) The accused injures the child, intending to kill the mother, while accepting a risk that the child might be killed or at least seriously harmed; (d) The accused injures the child, being reckless as to the death of the mother and the child.

Suppose, in each of the above, the child is born alive but subsequently dies as a result of the injuries it has received. Should the characterisation of the child's killing depend upon (a) the accused's *mens rea* with regard to the injuries inflicted on the mother, or (b) the accused's *mens rea* with regard to the injuries inflicted on the child? Can the doctrine of transferred intent assist here?

In *Attorney-General's Reference (No. 3 of 1994)* [1997] 3 All E.R. 936 a baby girl, S, was born prematurely as a result of injuries inflicted upon her mother, M, when M was 22 to 24 weeks pregnant. The injuries (stab wounds) were inflicted by B, the child's father, who knew that M was pregnant. M made a good recovery from her injuries, but two weeks after the attack went into labour and gave birth to S. The likely period of gestation was 26 weeks, and the medical evidence was that S only had a 50 per cent chance of survival. S survived in intensive care, but died after 121 days. She died because her lungs could not perform satisfactorily, due to her premature birth. One of the stab wounds inflicted on M penetrated her uterus and injured S, but it was accepted that this injury did not contribute to S's death.

The House of Lords held that the *mens rea* of murder was not established. The intention to do serious harm to the mother could not be 'transferred' in such a way as to establish the *mens rea* for a charge of murdering the child. It was however possible to hold that 'unlawful act' manslaughter could be committed in these circumstances, since, in the views of Lord Hope with whom the rest of the Court agreed, "it is sufficient that at the time of the stabbing the defendant had the *mens rea* which was needed to convict him of an assault on the child's mother." The attack on M was an unlawful act, and it was also an act which was dangerous in the sense that it was an act which was likely to harm another person.

4. Suppose that the accused does an act which is intended to kill the child, while it is unborn. The child is then born alive and survives. Is that attempted murder? If murder requires a living human being, does the attempt also require that? In the Canadian case of *R. v. Drummond* (Ontario Court (Provincial Division)), 1996 Ont. C.J.P. LEXIS 4 (December 23, 1996) this was held not be attempted murder.

## B. The end of life

**10.09**     At what point can it be said that a person is dead? This is a difficult question since medical understanding and definition of death have changed with the development of new techniques of life support. As Lord Lane C.J. pointed out in the case of *Malcherek* [1981] 2 All E.R. 422 (at pp. 426–427):

"Modern techniques have undoubtedly resulted in the blurring of many of the conventional and traditional concepts of death. A person's heart can now be removed altogether without death supervening; machines can keep the blood circulating through the vessels of the body until a new heart can be implanted in the patient, and even though a person is no longer able to breathe spontaneously a ventilating machine can, so to speak, do his breathing for him .... There is, it seems, a body of opinion in the medical profession that there is only one true test of death and that is the irreversible death of the brain stem, which controls the basic functions of the body such as breath. When that occurs it is said that the body has died, even though by mechanical means the lungs are being caused to operate and some circulation of blood is taking place."

The Criminal Law Revision Committee, in their fourteenth Report on *Offences Against the Person*, Cmnd. 7844 (1980) considered the possibility of a statutory definition of death in English law. While recognising that there was a general level of agreement among the medical profession that brain death was an appropriate test of death, and also on what constitutes brain death, the Committee declined to recommend the introduction of a statutory definition of death based on brain death:

"We are ... extremely hesitant about embodying in a statute (which is not always susceptible of speedy amendment) an expression of medical opinion and knowledge derived from a field of science which is continually progressing and inevitably altering its opinions in the light of new information. If a statutory definition of death were to be enacted there would, in our opinion, be a risk that further knowledge would cause it to lose the assent of the majority of the medical profession. In that event, far from assisting the medical profession, for example in cases of organ transplants, the definition might be a hindrance to them. Moreover, while there might be agreement that the statutory definition was defective, there might be differences of view about the proper content of any new definition. An additional reason for not recommending a definition of death is that such a definition would have wide repercussions outside offences against the person and the criminal law. A legal definition of death would also have to be applicable in the civil law. It would be undesirable to have a statutory definition confined only to offences against the person."

In some jurisdictions, however, a statutory definition of death has been attempted. Section 7180(a) of the California Health and Safety Code provides that "An individual who has sustained either (1) irreversible cessation of circulatory and respiratory functions, or (2) irreversible cessation of all functions of the entire brain, including the brain stem, is dead".

The High Court of Justiciary has not addressed itself to the question of an appropriate test of death. Some indication of the current approach of the courts may, however be discerned from *Law Hospital N.H.S. Trust v. Lord Advocate*, 1996 S.L.T. 848 the relatives of a woman who was in a "persistent vegetative state" sought a declarator that it would not be unlawful to withdraw feeding and hydration from her, with the result that she would die. The Lord President, Lord Hope, described her condition in the following terms (at p. 851):

"It is not in doubt that the patient has been in a persistent vegetative state for at least the past three years and that there is no prospect of any improvement in her condition. This is the result of irreversible damage to the cerebral cortex. The function of consciousness has been lost completely and for ever. The patient is wholly unaware of her surroundings. She cannot see, hear, feel pain or pleasure, communicate by word or movement or make voluntary movements of any kind. The brain stem structures are preserved and so long as this continues she remains clinically alive. The vegetative reflexes which control such functions as breathing, cardiac action and digestion are maintained. Involuntary movements of the eyes and the ability to make sounds give the impression of apparent wakefulness. This is followed by periods of apparent sleep with the eyes closed. But she is now permanently insensate, and she remains alive only because feeding and hydration are provided to her artificially and because of the nursing care which she continues to receive in the hospital."

Although the court was not concerned in this case with determining when death would ensue, it was central to the case that the patient was, in this condition, still "alive". There may also be some significance in the Lord President's observation that so long as the brain stem structures were preserved, the patient was "clinically alive".

It is not clear, however, whether the "brain death" criterion is accepted as the test in criminal cases.

**Finlayson v. H.M. Advocate**
1978 S.L.T. (Notes) 60

**10.10** The appellant was convicted of culpable homicide by injecting into another man (with his consent) a mixture of morphine and diazepam. There was evidence after that after the deceased had been injected with the drugs he had been taken to a hospital where he was placed on a life-support machine. A decision had subsequently been taken to switch the machine off and the patient died. The appellant argued that the trial judge should have directed the jury to find him not guilty, since the chain of causation between his unlawful act and death was broken by the actions of the doctors.

LORD JUSTICE-GENERAL (EMSLIE): "Before we come to the alleged misdirection it is proper to give a brief summary of the essential background against which the argument was presented. The result of injecting the drug into the person of Wilson was that it caused such serious brain damage that brain death occurred and that the heart would have inevitably failed for lack of oxygen unless means were available and taken to prolong heart function and to delay physical death by artificial mechanisms. In the event, when Wilson was taken to hospital he was placed on a life support machine in, we imagine, the intensive care unit of the hospital concerned. After a relatively short period on the life support machine and after serious consultation among responsible and highly qualified consultants, and after discussions with the parents of Wilson himself, a decision was taken to discontinue the artificial life support on the grounds that the brain damage was seen to be complete and irreversible and that all that a life support machine could do in the circumstances was to prolong the physical life of a person who was by then in a totally vegetative state. The decision having been taken the artificial life support was discontinued. Nature took control and the patient in due course died. For the applicant the submission of counsel was this. Even if the reckless injection of the drug would have led to the death of the deceased had matters been left to nature, matters were not left to nature. In short once the deceased had been placed on the life support machine it was the fact that his physical life could have been maintained indefinitely. In these circumstances what caused the death of the deceased was not the act of the applicant, but the deliberate discontinuance of the life support treatment which had been applied. This then, it was said, was an extraneous and extrinsic act which broke any chain of causation between the act of the applicant which caused the brain injury and the patient's death. That being so the trial judge should have directed the jury to bring in a verdict of not guilty of culpable homicide. This it was said, and by this we mean the act of discontinuing the life support treatment, was a deliberate act which could not be foreseen. In presenting this submission counsel for the appellant relied upon the case of *R. v. Smith* [1959] 2 Q.B. 35 and he cited it in particular for the quotation by Parker L.J. with approval of a test enunciated by Lord Wright in the well-known case of The Oropesa. The test is in these terms. 'To break the chain of causation it must be shown that there is something which I will call ultroneous something unwarrantable, a new cause which disturbs the sequence of events, something which can be described as either unreasonable or extraneous or extrinsic.'

In our judgment the argument for the applicant is unsound. On the face of it, it appears that the effects of the applicant's act were a substantial and operating and continuing cause of the death which occurred. It must be remembered that the decision which was taken to place the patient on a life support machine was taken, no doubt, with a view to keeping the patient physically alive until it could be ascertained with certainty whether there were any prospects of recovery of brain function. The argument further conceded that the decision to discontinue life support was in all the circumstances a perfectly reasonable one. It follows accordingly that the act of disconnecting the machine can hardly be described as an extraneous or extrinsic act within the meaning of these words as they were used by Lord Wright in their context. Far less can it be said that the act of disconnecting the machine was either unforeseeable or unforeseen and it certainly cannot be said that the act of disconnecting the machine was an unwarrantable act. If we read the definition or test of Lord Wright properly the key to the test is to be found in the word unwarrantable. Once the initial reckless act causing injury had been committed the natural consequence which the perpetrator must accept is that the victim's future depended on a number of circumstances, including whether any particular treatment was available and if it was available whether it was medically reasonable and justifiable to attempt it and to continue it. Having said all that, we are perfectly satisfied that upon the evidence led in this case it was not in any event a matter for the judge to determine *ab ante* whether, as matter of fact, it could be said that the chain of causation had been broken. That was a matter inexplicably bound up with the other facts in the case which were for determination by the jury and what the judge did was to leave the very question of the chain of causation to the jury with, as we see it, proper directions. We have little doubt that the jury reached the correct conclusion, but, in any event, no misdirection has been demonstrated and we have not the slightest hesitation in saying that it would have been a gross misdirection if the judge had, in the circumstances we have narrated, directed the jury that they must on his instruction return a verdict of not guilty of culpable homicide."

Appeal dismissed.

NOTES

1. The difficulty with this case is the loose way in which the court uses terms such as "alive", **10.11** "physically alive", "died" and "death". The court seems to assume that "death" did not occur until after the life support system was removed and the appellant's argument is dealt with on principles of causation. On this view the disconnection of the machine is simply treated as a foreseeable consequence of the initial injury and not something ultroneous or unforeseeable. But would it not have been simpler for the court to accept that the deceased was already dead when he was coupled up to the life support system? It was accepted by the court that brain death had occurred before that point. Naturally doctors and others having an interest in the life of the victim will want to establish carefully the true condition of a person in the situation of the deceased in such a case, and it would not be surprising to see life support measures being taken, perhaps over an extended period. But if in the end brain death is confirmed, then it is submitted that the point of death is the point at which brain death ensued rather than the removal of the life support system consequent on the establishment of brain death.

2. For a full discussion of the problems involved in such cases, see: Skegg, "The Termination of Life Support Measures and the Law of Murder" (1978) 41 M.L.R. 423; Watson *et al.*, "Brain Stem Death" (1978) 23 J.L.S, 433; and Kennedy. "Switching Off Life-Support Machines: The Legal Implications" [1977] Crim.L.R. 443.

3. The fact that the victim may remain alive, albeit unconscious, or in a severely impaired state for some time after the initial assault means that when the victim eventually dies, the assailant may face criminal charges in respect of that death, even though he or she has already been prosecuted on charges of assault in respect of the injuries which caused death: *Tees v. H.M. Advocate*, 1994 S.L.T. 701; *McNab v. H.M. Advocate*, 1999 S.C.C.R. 930. Nor does it matter whether the accused is convicted or acquitted on the earlier indictment. See also *Isabella Cobb or Fairweather* (1836) 1 Swin 354; *John McNeill* (1826) Shaw 162; *H.M. Advocate v. O'Connor* (1882) 5 Couper 206; *H.M. Advocate v. Stevens* (1850) J. Shaw 287 and *H.M. Advocate v. Stewart* (1866) 5 Irv. 310. A substantial delay between the original assault and prosecution for killing the victim may give rise to claims of oppression at common law or a violation of the right to a trial within a reasonable time under Article 6–1 of the European Convention on Human Rights. See *Tees* and *McNab*, above.

## C. The protection of the unborn child

We have seen that the law of homicide concerns itself with the protection of living human beings, and **10.12** that for these purposes life begins at birth. The unborn child is not, therefore, protected by the law of homicide. But this does not mean to say that the destruction of an unborn child is beyond the scope of the criminal law. The unborn child is protected by (a) the law relating to abortion and (b) the law relating to concealment of pregnancy.

## (a) Abortion

**10.13** Procuring an abortion is a crime at common law: Hume, i,186–187; Gordon, para. 28–02; *H.M. Advocate v. Anderson*, 1928 J.C. 1; *H.M. Advocate v. Semple and Others*, 1937 J.C. 41. It consists in procuring the miscarriage of a foetus at any time between conception and birth. A woman who co-operates in the procuring by another of her own miscarriage may be guilty art and part, and there appears to be no reason in principle why a woman who procures her own miscarriage should not be guilty of the offence.

It was probably not a crime at common law to procure an abortion where this was necessary in order to preserve the life or (perhaps) health of the mother; Gordon, para. 28–01; Macdonald, 114; *cf. R. v. Bourne* [1939] I K.B. 687. The legality of abortion is now governed by the terms of the Abortion Act 1967, as amended by the Human Fertilisation and Embryology Act 1990.

### Abortion Act 1967
**"Medical termination of pregnancy**

**10.14** **1.**—(1) Subject to the provisions of this section, a person shall not be guilty of an offence under the law relating to abortion when a pregnancy is terminated by a registered medical practitioner if two registered medical practitioners are of the opinion, formed in good faith—

> (a) that the pregnancy has not exceeded its twenty-fourth week and that the continuance of the pregnancy would involve risk, greater than if the pregnancy were terminated, of injury to the physical or mental health of the pregnant woman or any existing children of her family; or
>
> (b) that the termination is necessary to prevent grave permanent injury to the physical or mental health of the pregnant woman; or
>
> (c) that the continuance of the pregnancy would involve risk to the life of the pregnant woman, greater than if the pregnancy were terminated; or
>
> (d) that there is a substantial risk that if the child were born it would suffer from such physical or mental abnormalities as to be seriously handicapped.

(2) In determining whether the continuance of a pregnancy would involve such risk of injury to health as is mentioned in paragraph (a) or (b) of subsection (1) of this section, account may be taken of the pregnant woman's actual or reasonably foreseeable environment.

(3) Except as provided by subsection (4) of this section, any treatment for the termination of pregnancy must be carried out in a [National Health Service hospital] or in a place approved for the purposes of this section by ... the Secretary of State.

(4) Subsection (3) of this section, and so much of subsection (1) as relates to the opinion of two registered medical practitioners, shall not apply to the termination of a pregnancy by a registered medical practitioner in a case where he is of the opinion, formed in good faith, that the termination is immediately necessary to save the life or to prevent grave permanent injury to the physical or mental health of the pregnant woman.

NOTES

**10.15** 1. The question has arisen in a number of cases as to whether or not a third party, such as the father of the unborn child, may take any legal steps to prevent the termination of a pregnancy under the terms of the Abortion Act. The Act certainly makes no mention of the rights or interests of the unborn child, or of any person who would have legal standing to act on behalf of the child. It was held in England that provided the statutory requirements are observed, it appears that the father of an unborn child has no standing to prevent the termination of the pregnancy: *Paton v. Trustees of the British Pregnancy Advisory Board* [1978] 2 All E.R. 987, as confirmed by *C. v. S.* [1988] QB 135. A similar conclusion was reached by the Supreme Court of Canada *Tremblay v. Daigle* [1989] 2 S.C.R. 530 and by the Court of Session in the case of *Kelly v. Kelly*, 1997 S.L.T. 896.

2. The "rights of the foetus" figure prominently in discussions of abortion. Article 2–1 of the European Convention on Human Rights provides:

> "Everyone's right to life shall be protected by law. No one shall be deprived of his life intentionally

save in the execution of a sentence of a court following his conviction of a crime for which this penalty is provided by law."

Two questions arise: (a) does the unborn child have a right to life which is protected by law, and (b) if so, are there any circumstances in which the unborn child may lawfully be deprived of that right?

The question as to when life begins has not yet come before the Court, and the Commission, although faced with the question on more than one occasion in the context of abortion, has, perhaps understandably, avoided dogmatic or categorical statements.

In *Paton v. United Kingdom*, Application 8416/78, 19 DR 244 (1980) the Commission held that Article 2 does not recognise an absolute right to life on the part of an unborn child. The Commission left open the question of whether an unborn child had *any* rights under Article 2, or whether the unborn child had some rights, subject to limitations—such as the countervailing rights of the mother.

In *H. v. Norway*, Application 17004/90 (1992), unreported, the Commission recalled the point made in *Paton v. United Kingdom* that the "general usage of the term 'everyone' in the Convention" and the particular context in which that term is used in article 2 "tend to support the view that it does not include the unborn" ("The Law", para. 1). In particular, the limitations on the right to life recognised by article 2 itself "by their nature, concern persons already born and cannot be applied to the foetus" (*ibid.*).

Having said that, the Commission, also noted that "the first sentence of Article 2 imposes a broader obligation on the State than that contained in the second sentence" an obligation which includes an obligation "to take appropriate steps to safeguard life". While stating that in the instant case it did not have to decide whether the foetus enjoyed "a certain protection" under the first sentence of Article 2, it also held that it would not "exclude that in certain circumstances this may be the case notwithstanding that there is in Contracting states a considerable divergence of views on whether or to what extent Article 2 protects the unborn life."

In the case under consideration the abortion was carried out only after the mother had been interviewed by two medical practitioners, who had approved the termination of her pregnancy, having regard to her situation, including her ability to provide care for the child in a satisfactory way, as provided for by Norwegian law. In the circumstances, the Commission thought that the respondent state had not gone beyond the limits of the discretion which it enjoyed in such sensitive matters.

The legal protection of the right to life may, therefore, in some circumstances, protect the unborn child. A legal system which afforded no protection whatsoever to the unborn child might therefore be incompatible with the positive obligation imposed by that article. The issue would arise, for example, where a legal system confers on the pregnant woman a right to termination without having to demonstrate medical or social reasons. But even in such a case it is arguable that the interests of the unborn child would have to be set against, and balanced with, the rights of the mother. This balance may be relatively easily struck where the unborn child's right to life is set against the same right of the mother, or where it is set against the health of the mother, where, it is submitted, the latter should prevail. The balance may be more difficult where the right to life is set against less compelling arguments, such as the right to respect for private life. In *Brüggeman and Scheuten v. Federal Republic of Germany*, Application No. 6959/75, 10 DR 100 (1978) the Commission took the view that the privacy rights of the pregnant women could not be invoked so as to establish unfettered access to abortion.

## (b) Concealment of pregnancy

**Concealment of Birth (Scotland) Act 1809**

"And if after the passing of this Act, any woman in Scotland shall conceal her being with child **10.16** during the whole period of her pregnancy and shall not call for and make use of help or assistance in the birth, and if the child be found dead or be amissing, the mother, being lawfully convicted thereof, shall be imprisoned for a period not exceeding two years."

NOTE

This Act replaced an earlier, and much more severe provision, the Act 1690, c. 50, which provided that in such circumstances "the mother shall be holden and repute the murderer of her own childe". In the case of *Ann Gall* (1856) 2 Irv. 366 the jury returned a special verdict in which they found that the accused had, while she was pregnant, informed the man she believed to be the child's father of her condition, and left to the court the question of whether this provided a defence to a charge under the 1809 Act. By a majority the court held that it did and that the jury's verdict was substantially one of not guilty. See also *Jean Kiellor* (1852) Shaw 577.

## D. The death of another: Suicide, assisted suicide and related questions

**10.17** "Self-murder" may at one time have been regarded as a crime: Mackenzie, I, tit. XIII. For the successful suicide's heirs and successors this meant escheat of property which then was in the gift of the Crown. For the unsuccessful suicide, there was the possibility of prosecution for the attempt: Mackenzie, I, tit. XIII, iii. Whatever may have been the historical position, however, suicide is no longer regarded as crime in Scotland nor is the attempt—although the latter may in exceptional circumstances be prosecuted as breach of the peace. See Christie, *Breach of the Peace* (1990), para. 3.33.

Does it follow from the conclusion that a person who takes their own life is not guilty of homicide, that third-party involvement in suicide is likewise not a crime? Suppose, for example, that A owes a duty of care to B, and that, in the presence of A, B attempts to take his own life. Is A guilty of homicide if she does not intervene? (See, for example, the case of *R. v. Russell* [1933] V.L.R. 59, *ante*, Chapter 2.) What would the situation be where the victim takes their own life at the instigation of a third party? Would the third party be guilty of homicide, or would the victim's own act be regarded as the legal cause of death? If A's will is completely overborne by B, so that A takes his own life, there may be an argument for saying that B has caused A's death. It was suggested, for example, in *John Robertson* (1854) 1 Irv. 469 that it might be homicide for A to frighten B into committing suicide.

A more practical question does arise in the context of assisted suicide. Suppose that A is suffering from a terminal illness which causes her great pain and distress. She wishes to end her own life, but is not able to do so. Would it be criminal for B to assist? It would certainly be criminal—indeed it would be murder—for B to assist by intentionally taking A's life, since A's consent would be irrelevant. See the following case.

### H.M. Advocate v. Rutherford
#### 1947 J.C. 1

**10.18** The accused was charged with the murder of a young woman by strangling her with his tie. He gave evidence that the young woman had asked him to strangle her to death, and had put the tie round her own neck. He admitted pulling the tie, but alleged that he did so only to humour her or frighten her. He did, however, admit that he must have used considerable force, and also that he was aware of the dangers involved in what he did. In his charge to the jury the presiding judge gave the following directions:

LORD JUSTICE-CLERK (COOPER): The first thing I would say to you is this—rejecting one of the propositions that Mr Milligan asked me to pronounce—the first direction is this, that, even if you accepted the defence on its face value, there is no material before you in this case which would entitle you to treat the accused as guiltless and to acquit him, and I will tell you why. Mr Milligan said that this is a case to be accounted for as a mere accident, a pure misadventure, what is called in our law casual homicide. Now, casual homicide is a well-recognised category in the criminal law of Scotland, as in other countries; and I am going to read you a short passage from an authoritative work which explains what it is, and when I read it you will see why I decline this direction. The passage is this, 'It is casual homicide where a person kills unintentionally, when lawfully employed, and neither meaning harm to anyone, nor having failed in the due degree of care and circumspection for preventing mischief to his neighbour'. Note well the conditions. The writer proceeds, 'Under this class are comprehended all those cases, unfortunately too numerous, in which death ensues, not from any fault in any quarter, but from some misfortune or accident, and where, consequently, the person who is the innocent cause of another's death is more the subject of pity than punishment'. And then he proceeds to give examples. 'Thus, if a person's gun burst in his hand and kill his neighbour; or if the trigger be caught in going through a hedge, and the contents of the piece lodge in his breast; or a horse run away with its rider, in spite of all his efforts, and, though he had no good reason to have believed he would not manage it, and kill a passenger on the road,' and so on—cases, ladies and gentlemen, of pure misadventure. Now, the responsibility is mine, and if I am wrong I shall be set right elsewhere, but I have to direct you in law that on no view of the evidence in this case would you be entitled to accept Mr Milligan's submission that this is a case of misadventure or pure accident or casual homicide as known to the law, and therefore no question of acquitting the accused altogether on that ground can arise.

So much for that. The next point which I have to direct you upon is this—it is a point the Solicitor-General raised, and the direction he asked was that anyone who wilfully kills another person at the latter's request or command is guilty of murder. That, in my opinion, is sound law, and I do so direct you; but I would rather put it more specifically with reference to this case in this form, that, if life is taken under circumstances which would otherwise infer guilt of murder, the crime does not cease to be murder merely because the victim consented to be murdered, or even urged the assailant to strike the fatal blow. To put the matter in popular terms; if there was nothing in this case except the woman's request, and you held that proved, that would not suffice to take the edge off the guilt which otherwise attaches to the assailant. The attitude of the victim is irrelevant. What matters is the intent of the assailant. I think you will see ladies and gentlemen, that it must be so. It would be a most perilous doctrine to introduce into the law of Scotland, or of any civilised country, that any person was entitled to kill any other person at that other person's request."

Verdict: Guilty of culpable homicide.

NOTES

1. This was a straightforward case of killing. But what would have been the case if Rutherford had **10.19** been a party to a suicide pact with the deceased? In his evidence to the Royal Commission on Capital Punishment, his Lord Cooper stated: "The suicide pact would never be charged as murder in Scotland" (para. 5430). Presumably this is because the circumstances are not such as would "otherwise infer guilt of murder". Nevertheless, problems remain. His Lordship did not rule out the possibility of a charge of culpable homicide (*cf.* the position in English law under section 4(1) of the Homicide Act 1957 which provides that the survivor of a suicide pact is guilty of manslaughter if he or she kills the suicide or is a party to the killing by someone else).

2. *Rutherford* was discussed in *Sutherland v. H.M. Advocate*, 1994 S.L.T. 634.

3. *Rutherford* deals with the case where the accused has directly killed the victim with her consent. But what is the position where the accused has not killed the victim, but has assisted, for example, by providing the would-be suicide with the means of taking his or her life? This situation is not dealt with in *Rutherford* and since suicide is not a crime in Scots law, and there is no separate offence of aiding suicide, arguably this level of involvement is not criminal. The problem with this view is the approach currently adopted by the High Court to questions of causation and in particular the cases of *Khaliq v. H.M. Advocate* and *Lord Advocate's Reference (No. 1 of 1994) ante,* Chapter 4. In *Khaliq* the court held that A could be guilty of causing "real injury" to B by supplying to him an injurious substance which B uses to his injury. In *Lord Advocate's Reference (No. 1 of 1994)* the court held that A could be held guilty of causing B's death where B's death resulted from the use of controlled drugs unlawfully supplied to her by A.

Suppose, then, that A knowing that his wife, B, wishes to take her own life to relieve herself of the severe pain and distress of the last stages of a fatal illness. A acquires a large quantity of pain killers and supplies them to his wife who uses them to take her own life. A is, on the basis of the authorities referred to above, guilty of at least culpable homicide. Might this be regarded, indeed, as murder? In the *Lord Advocate's Reference,* there was no intention on anyone's part that the victim should die, or even cause herself serious harm. But in the example under discussion, the "victim" consumes the drugs with that intention and they are supplied for that purpose. If it is accepted that A has caused his wife's death, then he has done so with intention to bring about that death, and that would appear to satisfy the definition of murder.

4. If a person cannot consent to his or her own death, it should presumably follow that consent of third parties is equally irrelevant. But is that the view of the courts? In *Law Hospitals NHS Trust v. Lord Advocate*, 1996 S.L.T. 848, the Court of Session was faced with the question of the legality of removing food and hydration from a patient who was in a persistent vegetative state (PSV). The patient had been in this condition for a prolonged period and there appeared to be no realistic prospect of her recovering consciousness. The patient's family applied to the Court of Session for authority to discontinue the food and hydration. The Court held that this would not be unlawful where to do so would be in the best interests of the patient. The feeding and hydration were subsequently discontinued and the patient died. The Inner House was at pains to point out that they could make no declaration which would have any consequences in relation to the criminal law, that being a matter for the High Court and the Lord Advocate. The Lord Advocate subsequently issued a public statement in the following terms [see 1996 S.L.T. at p. 867]:

> "In the light of the views expressed by the Inner House of the Court of Session in the case of *Law Hospital NHS Trust v. Lord Advocate*, the Lord Advocate has considered what approach the prosecuting authorities in Scotland should take when life sustaining treatment or other medical treatment is withdrawn or discontinued for patients who are incapable of consenting to such withdrawal or discontinuation.
>
> "The Lord Advocate has decided that he will not authorise the prosecution of a qualified medical practitioner (or any person acting upon the instructions of such a practitioner) who, acting in good faith and with the authority of the Court of Session, withdraws or otherwise causes to be discontinued life sustaining treatment or other medical treatment from a patient in a persistent, or permanent, vegetative state, with the result that the patient dies."

The approach of the Court and the statement of the Lord Advocate make it clear that to remove treatment necessary for life remains a criminal offence. See also the Adults with Incapacity (Scotland) Act 2000.

## 2. MURDER

### A. The distinguishing feature of murder

**10.20** Murder is simply one form of unlawful homicide. For many years, the accepted definition of murder was that contained in Macdonald's *Criminal Law* (5th ed., at p. 89):

> "Murder is constituted by any wilful act causing the destruction of life, whether intended to kill, or displaying such wicked recklessness as to imply a disposition depraved enough to be regardless of consequences."

This definition must now be read in the light of *Drury v. H.M. Advocate*, High Court, February 2, 2001, *unreported*, (*post*, p. 407) in which it was held that a mere intention to kill is not sufficient for murder. Any such intention—like recklessness—must be "wicked".

There are, therefore, two alternative forms of *mens rea* for murder—a wicked intention to kill and wicked recklessness. The qualification of the term "recklessness" makes it clear that a higher degree of recklessness is required for murder than for culpable homicide. The qualification of the term "intention" is more problematic, and is discussed *post*, p. 391.

This definition distinguishes murder from lesser forms of criminal homicide by reference solely to the mental element which must be proved in order to establish murder. But is that the only appropriate way to distinguish murder? In some jurisdictions the mental element is not the only criterion by which murder is distinguished from other forms of criminal homicide.

In some systems murder is defined by reference to the circumstances in which it is committed, rather than the intention of the accused. An example of this is the "felony murder" doctrine, which, until it was abolished by the Homicide Act 1957, was part of English law, and which is found in several American jurisdictions today. According to this doctrine, a killing is murder if it is committed in the course of committing another serious crime, or at least a crime involving personal injury. Thus the Illinois Criminal Code provides that a person is guilty of first-degree murder if, in performing the acts which cause the death, "he is attempting or committing a forcible felony other than second degree murder": 720 Illinois Compiled Statutes, 5/9–1(a)(3). In some states the felony murder rule has even been extended beyond killing in the course of a violent felony. In Indiana, for example, a person is guilty of murder if he or she kills another human being while dealing in cocaine or other narcotic drug or controlled substance: Indiana Code, 35-42-1-1 (3).

## B. Intentional killing

**10.21** An intention to kill is probably the most obvious form of *mens rea* of murder. It is important to appreciate that murder does not require premeditation (Hume, i, 254–255; Macdonald, p. 89) so that a person who (without any justification or excuse), intentionally kills another, is guilty of murder whether the killing was carried out as part of a pre-conceived plan, or in a sudden explosion of violence.

In *Drury v. H.M. Advocate*, High Court, February 2, 2001, *unreported*, (*post*, p. 407), it was suggested that reference to an "intention to kill" is not sufficient for murder, and that a distinction can be drawn between those who have an intention to kill and those who have a "wicked" intention to kill. A mere intention to kill is not sufficient for murder. A "wicked" intention is required. This is a surprising suggestion, there being no indication in any prior decision of the court that a "wicked" intention to kill was required to establish murder. Macdonald's definition of murder has been repeated to juries for most of the last 100 years, and by the appeal court in numerous cases, without any suggestion that it was in some way incomplete. It was expressly adopted by the appeal court in *Cawthorne v. H.M. Advocate*, 1968, J.C. 32, *infra*, and was referred to apparently with approval by a bench of seven judges in *Brennan v. H.M. Advocate*, 1977 S.L.T. 151. The adoption of "wicked intent" is also difficult to reconcile with the views of the court in *Scott v. H.M. Advocate*, 1995 S.C.C.R. 760. In that case, the court referred to Macdonald's definition as the "classic definition of murder"; it described the definition of murder as "well known"; and the court observed that it did not "consider that it would normally be appropriate for a judge to give a jury directions regarding the level of wickedness required for either branch of the classic definition of murder" (1995 S.C.C.R. at p. 765B–C).

The introduction of the notion of "wickedness" is problematic in a number of ways. How, for example, are we to distinguish between an "ordinary" intention to kill and a "wicked" intention to do so? Does the introduction of this term, for example, permit an inquiry into the motivation of the accused when he or she killed the victim. It is clear that this is so where provocation is in issue. This much is accepted by the Lord Justice-General in *Drury* who observes (at para. 11 of his opinion) that "in a case ... where provocation is in play, it is of some importance to consider the state of mind by which a murderer is actuated in committing the intentional or reckless act (*post*, p. 408).

Does *Drury* require an inquiry into the motives of other killers? Is a distinction to be drawn, for example, between a person who kills out of motives of greed or revenge and one who kills out of compassion and concern for the suffering of the victim?

It may well turn out that the introduction of this new concept will have little practical effect except where the accused argues that some excusing or justifying factor negates the "wickedness" required for murder. Support for this interpretation of *Drury* may be found in the opinion of the Lord Justice-General where he suggests that "wicked intention" "is just a shorthand way of referring to what Hume (Vol. 1, p. 254) describes as the murderer's 'wicked and mischievous purpose' in contradistinction to 'those motives of necessity, duty, or allowable infirmity, which may serve to justify or excuse' the deliberate taking of life." (*Drury*, para. 11.) If this is so, then clearly an inquire into motive will not be appropriate, but equally clearly much will depend upon what is embraced by "motives of necessity, duty, or allowable infirmity".

## C. Wicked recklessness

### (a) Wicked recklessness and intention to kill

**Cawthorne v. H.M. Advocate**
1968 J.C. 32

**10.22** The accused was charged with attempting to murder four people by firing shots from a rifle at random into a room in which they had barricaded themselves. His intention was apparently to frighten them, rather than kill any of them. At his trial, the presiding judge gave the following directions on the *mens rea* of murder:

LORD AVONSIDE: "In our law the crime of murder is committed when the person who brings about the death of another acted deliberately with intent to kill, or acted with intent to do bodily harm, or, and this is the third leg, acted with utter and wicked recklessness as to the consequences of his act upon his victim. Intent to kill, intent to do bodily harm, acting with utter and wicked recklessness as to the consequences of his act. In murder the Crown need never establish motive or premeditation or plot. Murder is a question of fact within the law, the occurrence of death within the law. It is impossible, ladies and gentlemen, to look into the mind of a man, and when, therefore, you are seeking to evaluate the effect of the evidence in regard to the nature and purposes of an act, you can only do so by drawing an inference from what that man did in the background of all the facts of the case which you accept as proved. In short, you look at all the proved circumstances and events disclosed by the evidence and draw what inference is disclosed as to the nature of the act. Mr Cowie, as I understand it, suggested that in Scots law the crime of attempt to murder was limited to cases in which the Crown had proved intent to kill. That is the first and most obvious branch of the definition of a murderous act. Again I do not agree, and you will take my direction in this matter. Attempt to murder is a charge brought against a man who is alleged to have made an attack on another or other people in circumstances in which, had his victim or victims died as a result of the attack, his offence would have been murder. Thus in my view, and you must accept my view in this court, the law holds it to be murder if a man dies as a result of another acting with utter and wicked recklessness, and that because the very nature of the attack, the utter and wickedly reckless attack, displays a criminal intention. If such an act does not result in death, none the less the criminal intention has been displayed and is of a quality and nature which results in its properly being described as an attempt to murder. And thus, in this case if you hold it proved that any of the three possible elements of murder have been established, you are entitled to convict the accused man of attempt to murder one or other, some of those named."

The jury returned a verdict of guilty, and the panel was sentenced to nine years' imprisonment. On appeal against conviction:

LORD JUSTICE-GENERAL (CLYDE): "The ground upon which the present appeal against conviction is taken is that under our law, so it is contended, a jury cannot find the appellant guilty of attempted murder unless they are satisfied beyond reasonable doubt that the appellant discharged the firearm at any of the persons named with the deliberate intention to kill. A direction to this effect was asked from the trial judge, who refused to give it, and the question is whether he was correct in so refusing. In my opinion he was.

The crimes of murder and attempted murder are common law crimes in Scotland and I do not find it helpful to seek to draw analogies from alien systems of law where the rules may for various reasons be different. This issue must be determined by the rules applicable to Scots law. In our law murder is constituted by any wilful act causing the destruction of life (Macdonald on the Criminal Law of Scotland, (5th ed.) p. 89). The *mens rea* which is essential to the establishment of such a common law crime may be established by satisfactory evidence of a deliberate intention to kill or by satisfactory evidence of such wicked recklessness as to imply a disposition depraved enough to be regardless of consequences. (See Macdonald in the same passage.) The reason for this alternative being allowed in our law is that in many cases it may not be possible to prove what was in the accused's mind at the time, but the degree of recklessness in his actings, as proved by what he did, may be sufficient to establish proof of the wilful act on his part which caused the loss of life."

LORD GUTHRIE: "The main ground of this application for leave to appeal against conviction is set forth in the first reason. The other reasons which were not abandoned at the hearing were subsidiary, and really dependent on the success of the first.

The first part of the first reason is that the trial judge misdirected the jury in respect that he equiparated the *mens rea* necessary for murder. As it is stated, I have difficulty in understanding that submission. *Mens rea*, or dole, in our criminal law is the wicked and felonious intention which impels the criminal to commit a crime. It is a state of mind which results in a criminal act, and I fail to see how there can be a distinction between the wickedness resulting in murder, and the wickedness resulting in an attempt to murder. Hume in his book on Crimes, vol. i, p. 21, describes dole as 'that corrupt and evil intention, which is essential (so the light of nature teaches, and so all authorities have said) to the guilt of any crime'.

During the argument, however, it appeared that the complaint of the applicant was against that part of the charge of the trial judge in which he dealt with the intention which is necessary to constitute an attempt to murder. The trial judge stated that 'in our law the crime of murder is committed when the person who brings about the death of another acted deliberately with intent to kill, or acted with intent to do bodily harm, or, and this is the third leg, acted with utter and wicked recklessness as to the consequences of his act upon his victim.' It was not disputed that this is a correct statement of the law in relation to murder if the word 'grievous' is inserted before 'bodily harm'. But it was submitted for the applicant that in a case of attempted murder a jury is not entitled to infer intent to murder from 'utter and wicked recklessness as to the consequences of his act upon his victim'. Therefore, it was argued, the Crown can only succeed in an indictment of attempted murder if it proves deliberate intent to kill or to inflict grievous bodily harm. This contention is expressed in the second part of the first reason. Counsel for the applicant accordingly maintained that the trial judge erred when he directed the jury in these terms: '. . . the law holds it to be murder if a man dies as a result of another acting with utter and wicked recklessness, and that because the very nature of the attack, the utter and wickedly reckless attack, displays a criminal intention. If such an act does not result in death, none the less the criminal intention has been displayed and is of a quality and nature which results in its properly being described as an attempt to murder.'

In my opinion this direction is soundly based in principle and is supported by authority. An attempt to murder is an occurrence, a fact, which can be proved by any competent evidence sufficient to establish it beyond the reasonable doubt of a jury. The intention involved in the attempt cannot, as the trial judge pointed out, be proved by an examination of the mind of the accused. The existence of the intention is a matter of the inference to be drawn from the accused's words, or acts, or both. The inference is easy when the accused has threatened his victim, or has stated his intention to third parties. Again, even in the absence of such statements, the intention may be deduced from the conduct of the accused. Admittedly this deduction will properly be drawn if he has been seen to aim a deadly blow at his victim. Thus it becomes a matter for the jury to decide whether the actions of the accused satisfy them that he intended to murder the victim. A reckless act may well be such as to lead to that inference. For example, as was suggested by your Lordship in the debate, a jury would be entitled to hold intention to murder proved if a criminal recklessly sprayed a courtroom with machine-gun bullets, even if all their Lordships fortunately escaped injury, and it was not proved that the criminal aimed at any one or more of them. As it is put in Macdonald on Crimes, (5th ed.) p. 108, the act manifests the intention. I refer also to Alison on Criminal Law, vol. i, p. 163, where he said: 'In judging of the intention of an accused who has committed an aggravated assault, the same rules are to be followed as in judging of the intent in actual murder, *viz.* that a ruthless intent, and an obvious indifference as to the sufferer, whether he live or die, is to be held as equivalent to an actual attempt to inflict death.' I think that that is a correct statement of the law of Scotland, and that it fully supports the charge as given by the trial judge.

The view of the trial judge is, in my opinion, in accordance with the fundamental rule of our criminal law that dole may be presumed from the perpetration of the wicked act. The evaluation of the act and the inference to be drawn from it are essentially matters for the jury. I agree with your Lordship that the applicant's attack on the charge of the trial judge fails, and that the application for leave to appeal against conviction should be refused."

LORD CAMERON: "I agree that this application fails. In my opinion those portions of the presiding judge's charge which were submitted to attack by Mr Cowie correctly stated what our law requires to establish the crime of attempt to murder. There are necessarily three elements in murder as defined in our law, (first) proof of death resulting from certain acts, (second) that these acts should be the wilful acts of the accused, and (third) proof of the necessary criminal intent. This intent can be established in the law of Scotland either by proof of deliberate intention to cause death, or by inference from the nature and quality of the acts themselves, as displaying, in the classic words of Macdonald, 'such wicked recklessness as to imply a disposition depraved enough to be regardless of consequences'. Such reckless conduct, intentionally perpetrated, is in law the equivalent of a deliberate intent to kill and adequate legal proof of the requisite *mens rea* to constitute that form of homicide which is in law murder.

Where death does not follow from such an act or acts, Mr Cowie conceded that, where a deliberate intention to kill is established, that was enough to constitute the crime of attempt to murder. This would necessarily be so whether injury was sustained by the party against whom the attempt was made or not. It was contended, however, that the mere commission of acts directed towards another or others which did not result in death or injury, but were wilful acts of such reckless character that, if death had resulted, the necessary criminal intent sufficient to constitute the crime of murder would be established, did not fall within the category of criminal conduct defined as attempt to murder. This contention, however, appears to me to seek to base a distinction in quality of the crime committed upon a difference in fact which is fortuitous and, in my opinion, irrelevant. It was not suggested by Mr Cowie that such actings would not constitute a crime, but it was maintained that they would do no more than constitute the crime of assault, possibly to the danger of life. I am not able to accept that contention. It seems to me that on principle the quality of the *mens rea* in a case of attempt to commit the crime of murder is not affected by the consequences of the acts constituting the criminal conduct if the *mens rea* necessary to constitute the completed act can be established either by proof of deliberate intent to kill or by the nature of the acts themselves. It would seem both to be logical and to consist with common sense that if the intent to commit the crime of murder can be established in two ways, both should be equally available in proof of the requisite intent of an attempt to commit that crime. After all, the subsumption of a charge of attempting to commit a crime must be that the criminal acts constituting the crime were perpetrated with the intent to commit the complete crime, an intent which was frustrated by circumstances outside or beyond the perpetrator's deliberate control. Therefore it would seem that the quality of the intent is the same in both cases and consequently in principle the proof of intent in both should be the same. This view of the matter would appear to get support from our most recent text writers of authority. Both in Macdonald (5th ed.) p. 108, and in Anderson (2nd ed.) p. 155, it is made plain that the necessary intent can be inferred from the acts of the accused. As Lord Anderson put it in dealing with the crime of attempt to murder, 'the intent to murder is held to be proved when the injury done shows utter recklessness as to the life of the victim . . .'. This appears to me necessarily to be so, and to be applicable even where by the accident of events no injury has followed upon the acts, because the quality of the criminal intent remains the same, whatever the consequences. The statements of the law contained in Macdonald and Anderson to which I have referred stand without contradiction or doubt cast upon their accuracy in any decided case, nor is there anything in Hume which is inconsistent with them (see, for example, Hume on *Crimes*, Vol. i, pp. 179, 256) and they are entirely in accord with the passage from Alison which your Lordship in the chair has quoted. I therefore think that this attack on the accuracy of the direction given by the presiding judge fails."

Application for leave to appeal refused.

NOTES

**10.23**   1. As Gordon has pointed out ("*Cawthorne* and the *Mens Rea* of Murder", 1969 S.L.T. (News) 41) the court vacillates between treating wicked recklessness as an alternative form of *mens rea* for murder, or as conduct from which intention to kill may be inferred. Indeed, there are suggestions of a second or third form of *mens rea*, the intention to do grievous bodily harm. It seems that the balance of views in the court tended towards the idea that "wicked recklessness" was something from which the required "criminal intent" might be inferred. But that is not particularly helpful, since the "criminal intent" seems to be capable of more than one meaning, *viz.* a generalised criminal intent, which includes intention to kill but is not restricted to such an intent, and a more particular form of *mens rea*, the intention to kill.

2. Despite these confusions, it is today accepted that "wicked recklessness" is a distinct and independent form of the *mens rea* for murder, and not simply something from which an intention to kill is to be inferred. See, in this connection, the evidence given to the House of Lords Select Committee on Murder by Lord Emslie and Lord Ross, *Report of the House of Lords Select Committee on Murder*, H.L. Paper 78-III, pp. 486–476, the evidence given by the Faculty of Advocates, *ibid.*, pp. 364–376 and the Scottish Law Commission, *ibid.*, pp. 385–397. In *Scott v. H.M. Advocate*, 1995 S.C.C.R. 760 the Lord Justice-Clerk (Ross) expressed the opinion that wickedly reckless conduct was "in law" the equivalent of a deliberate intent to kill, rather than the equivalent in fact of a deliberate intent to kill (1995 S.C.C.R. 760 at 765A).

## (b) Recklessness and 'wicked' recklessness

Gordon suggests (para. 23–17) that the reason why the person who kills with wicked recklessness is **10.24** treated as a murderer is because wickedly reckless killing is the moral equivalent of intentional killing: "Wicked recklessness is recklessness so gross that it indicates a state of mind which is as wicked and depraved as the state of mind of a deliberate killer". In *Scott v. H.M. Advocate, supra*, the High Court disagreed with this statement, preferring the following formulation: "Wicked recklessness is recklessness so gross that it indicates a state of mind *which falls to be treated* as wicked and depraved as the state of mind of a deliberate killer" (at p. 764–765, *emphasis added*). Whichever formulation is preferred, it is clear that a "merely reckless" killer is not a murderer. Reckless killing may be culpable homicide, but it is not the legal or moral equivalent of intentional killing. But what distinguishes 'wicked' recklessness from 'mere' recklessness?

### H.M. Advocate v. Robertson and Donoghue
### High Court, August 1945, unreported

(For the facts of this case see *ante*, p. 114.) **10.25**

In charging the jury:

LORD JUSTICE-CLERK (COOPER): "Now, every charge of murder, ladies and gentlemen, impliedly includes the lesser charge of culpable homicide. The choice is generally open to a jury—and in this case it certainly is open to a jury—and the matter to which I am now going to direct your attention is the question of the choice in this case between a verdict of murder and a verdict of culpable homicide. The critical factor in determining whether a given act of homicide is murder or culpable homicide only is the view which you take as to the intent with which the assailant acted. Of course, intent is something in a man's mind and can only be proved by inference from his conduct and from the whole surrounding circumstances of the case as these may be established in evidence, but will you please note very particularly that to justify a verdict of murder in this or any other case it is indispensable that the accused should have acted either with the intent to kill or, what is much more common, with wicked and reckless indifference to the consequences to his victim. May I repeat these words—wicked and reckless indifference to the consequences to his victim—and in judging whether that reckless indifference is present you would take into account the nature of the violence used, the condition of the victim when it was used, and the circumstances under which the assault was committed. I have already referred to the medical report, and it is a material point, of course, upon this issue of murder or culpable homicide that the injuries were slight—undoubtedly very slight. The doctors told us what we could have inferred for ourselves without their aid, that an ordinary adult would never have died as the result of those injuries alone. That fact that small injuries were inflicted is obviously in favour of the view that the recklessness—the wicked recklessness—was not present.

The next thing is—what were the weapons employed? Well, so far as the evidence goes, if you accept it, the weapons employed, apart from Robertson's fists or fingers, were bottles—empty bottles—and that is a factor which you may regard as rather indicative of recklessness, because an empty bottle of the size, weight and type exhibited in court before us during these last two days is not the thing which any responsible person breaks over the head of another human being—or tries to.

There is next the condition of the victim. What I mean is this, ladies and gentlemen, if this fracas had occurred between Robertson and a fit young man like Weatherston, the soldier [a witness for the Crown], for one thing there would have been no fatal consequences, and, even if there had been, it would not have been easy I think—it might not have been easy—for a jury to infer reckless indifference to consequences from the infliction of such injuries on a fit young man. But the point which you will have to consider carefully is this, that much less violence if applied to a feeble, old man, to a person whom the assailant must have known was a feeble, old man—if you think he must have known—it may suffice to justify an inference of wicked indifference to consequences. Much less violence in such a case would suffice than would suffice if the victim was a normal healthy adult ... and you will, accordingly, have to devote some thought to the question—what inference is to be drawn from the fact that this struggle took place and this violence was used, if it was used ... against this man of 82 whose photograph you have seen ... and whose description you have heard from his doctor .... On the other hand, it is right to add ... that Professor Sydney Smith did indicate that for his age he was a very muscular man. At p. 160 he said, 'He had good muscular development for 81 years. He was a fine, strong-looking fellow'. So that has certainly to be taken into account against the view of his family doctor ... that he was a frail old man."

The jury found Robertson guilty of culpable homicide.<br>The case against Donoghue was found not proven.

NOTE

**10.26**     Lord Cooper treats the various factors to which he refers—the use of weapons, the age and condition of the victim, the relative strength of the killer—as matters from which the jury might *infer* wicked recklessness. But such factors have not always been treated as matters of inference. The courts are prepared to hold that in some instances factors such as the use of weapons or the nature of the attack necessarily result in a finding of murder.

**Broadley v. H.M. Advocate**
1991 S.L.T. 218

**10.27** The appellant was convicted of murdering his wife by repeatedly stabbing her with a knife on the head, throat and body. There was no evidence of provocation or diminished responsibility. In his charge to the jury the trial judge stated:

> "I direct you that if you hold it proved beyond reasonable doubt on corroborated evidence that the accused assaulted, as I have defined it, his wife with a knife such as that in label 3 and inflicted injuries as described by Professor Busuttil and Dr Purdue in their report and evidence, then you would be bound to convict of murder, however reluctant you may be to do so, because as a matter of law no verdict of culpable homicide would be open to you in those circumstances."

The accused was convicted of murder and appealed to the High Court. The opinion of the Court was delivered by the Lord Justice-Clerk (Ross):

OPINION OF THE COURT: "Counsel maintained that where the jury required to consider whether there had been wicked recklessness, that went to the quality of the act, and was therefore a matter for the jury and not the judge to determine. Counsel maintained that the test for wicked recklessness was a subjective one and he founded upon the following factors:

(1) The appellant's marriage to the victim had been a long and tragic one, and indeed it had been described by him as 14 years of hell. (2) The appellant was a weak man. (3) The appellant's wife had left him. (4) Their child had been abandoned by the wife. (5) The appellant had sought medical assistance. (6) He had taken a knife with him to show to his wife and his father in law, and to tell them to leave him alone; he then intended to hand it to the police. (7) He had become involved in an argument with his father-in-law, and his wife had then become involved in the matter.

Counsel's submission was that it was for the jury to evaluate the evidence; they must look at the whole background, and ask whether the appellant had displayed wicked recklessness. He also maintained that the severity of the injuries was not the only thing that mattered. It was a practical question for the jury to assess the quality of the appellant's act. He accordingly submitted that the trial judge had erred in directing the jury that it was not open to them to return a verdict of guilty of culpable homicide. He stressed that there was no question of the appellant being acquitted of the charge, and in the circumstances he invited the court to allow the appeal, to set aside the verdict of the jury on charge 6 and to substitute an amended verdict of guilty of culpable homicide ....

On the authorities we are satisfied that in certain circumstances a trial judge has a duty to withdraw culpable homicide from the jury ....

[His Lordship then referred to the Lord Justice-Clerk's charge to the jury in *H.M. Advocate v. McGuinness* (above), the judge's charge to the jury and the opinion of the Lord Justice-General in *Miller and Denovan v. H.M. Advocate*, 1991 S.L.T. 211, *post*, p. 404), *Thomson v. H.M. Advocate*, 1986 S.L.T. 281 (*post*, p. 419), *H.M. Advocate v. Hartley*, 1989 S.L.T. 135, and *Parr v. H.M. Advocate*, 1991 S.L.T. 208 and continued:]

We recognise that in a number of these cases the violence which had been used had been in order to perpetrate the crime of robbery. In Gordon's *Criminal Law* at para. 23–26, the view is expressed that *Miller and Denovan* should be restricted to robbery, and that there is no sufficient warrant in earlier statements of the law for treating the wicked recklessness in simple assault cases so objectively as to make it a question of law for the judge in each case. However, the learned author adds: "The *ratio* of the lethal weapons cases must be that the evidence so overwhelmingly pointed to wicked recklessness that the jury could not but convict of murder." The learned author goes on to observe that this ratio may be thought to be unsatisfactory.

In *Parr v. H.M. Advocate* the Lord Justice-General observed that the matter cannot be reduced to categories. The Lord Justice-General added: "There is no doubt that there are limits to what a judge may properly do, since questions as to the weight or quality of the evidence are not for him. But if there is no basis at all for the point in the evidence then there is no ground in law for the jury to consider it, and it is the duty of the trial judge to intervene by giving a direction to that effect."

Counsel sought to rely upon the seven factors listed above; he maintained that having regard to these factors the jury would have been entitled to return a verdict of culpable homicide.

We do not agree with counsel that the matter falls to be tested subjectively. It is plain from *Miller and Denovan* that the test for distinguishing between murder and culpable homicide is an objective one, and we do not agree that what was said in that case should be restricted to robbery. Moreover when one considers the factors relied upon by counsel, it appears to us that most of them are in no way inconsistent with wicked recklessness. The fact of the matter is that the attack in this case was an attack of great determination involving the use of a lethal weapon with which repeated blows were delivered upon the body of the victim. Any question of accident could be eliminated, and it was accepted that there was no question of provocation or diminished responsibility. We were not referred to any other aspect of the evidence which might be said to modify the quality of recklessness involved. In the circumstances of this case we are accordingly satisfied that the jury were correctly directed that if they were satisfied that the appellant had carried out this assault, then they were bound to convict of murder and there was no room for a verdict of culpable homicide. We would, however, stress that every case depends upon its own facts, and we recognise that in many cases where an accused has used a lethal weapon which has caused fatal injuries, it will be for the jury to determine whether the proper verdict is one of murder or culpable homicide. The present case, however, is one where the trial judge was correct in withdrawing culpable homicide from the jury.

As this was the only ground of appeal put forward on behalf of the appellant his appeal against conviction falls to be refused.

Appeal refused.

NOTES

**10.28**    1. Although it is competent for the court to withdraw the verdict of culpable homicide from the jury, and there may be cases in which the court has a duty to do so (*Parr* and *Broadley, ante*), "the question [murder or culpable homicide] is ultimately one of fact, and that the trial judge should not take this course unless he is satisfied that there is no basis at all for the verdict in the evidence": *Brown and Another v. H.M. Advocate*, 1993 S.C.C.R. 382, *per* Lord Hope at p. 391D.

2. In his evidence to the House of Lords Select Committee on Murder and Life Imprisonment, Lord Emslie gave as an example of circumstances from which wicked recklessness could be inferred, an accused (A) punching a victim (B) whom he knew to be a haemophiliac, knowing that he would be bound to bleed, thus creating a risk that the victim might die. (HL Paper, 78-III, p. 469.) What would the situation be if , for example, A did not know that B was a haemophiliac? Is A wickedly reckless? If "wicked recklessness" is determined objectively, does it matter that A was unaware of B's condition? (*Cf.* the charge to the jury in *H.M. Advocate v. Robertson and Donoghue, ante*, p. 395.)

**Halliday v. HM Advocate**
1999 S.L.T. 485

**10.29** Two brothers were convicted of murder and appealed against their conviction. They admitted killing the deceased, and the only issue at the trial was whether this was a case of murder or culpable homicide. The circumstances of the killing and the appellants' argument are set out in the opinion of the Court which was delivered by the Lord Justice-General.

OPINION OF THE COURT: "... At their trial the appellants admitted killing the deceased. The issue for the jury was whether the conviction should be for murder or culpable homicide. The killing occurred after an incident involving a young woman. The deceased left the house where the incident had taken place and the appellants then left and met up with the deceased. A scuffle followed and the deceased landed up on the ground. Andrew Halliday immediately started kicking the deceased a number of times on the head with full force. At this stage Paul Halliday got up and punched and kicked him on the upper part of the body with considerable force. The deceased was motionless after this. The appellants went back in the general direction of the house and, at about this time, were seen to shake hands and say that they were great brothers. They then returned to the deceased and started kicking him again in the face a number of times with considerable force. They also jumped or stamped on his head. Two girls who were present shouted to them to stop and they did so, after delivering some more blows. Paul Halliday then put the deceased in the recovery position and the appellants returned to the house where various attempts were made to wash their clothes.

In the meantime someone who had seen what happened telephoned for an ambulance. The ambulance attended, as did the police, but, because it was dark and raining heavily, the ambulance officers and the police were unable to find the deceased. Some time later the appellants and two girls went out again to see the deceased. He was motionless in the place where they had left him. They felt for a pulse but there was none. Paul Halliday panicked and told his brother to go and telephone for an ambulance. He did so, using a false name. The ambulance came with police officers and the deceased was soon found. He was pronounced dead. Paul Halliday had left the scene and eventually went back to his sister's house where he told his mother that he thought that his brother had just killed someone.

In his charge to the jury the trial judge gave a standard direction on the distinction between murder and culpable homicide. Counsel did not criticise that direction, which ended by referring to a person being guilty of murder if he used life-threatening violence in such a way 'as to display a complete, utter and wicked disregard for the consequences to his victim'. When the jury sought further directions, the foreman agreed that the question concerning them was 'Whether that total disregard'—in the definition of murder— 'has to be at the time of the assault or thereafter'. The trial judge gave this direction:

'So, ladies and gentlemen, what you are considering here is the nature of the fatal assault itself and whether that meets the legal requirements for murder, the degree of recklessness, the total disregard that I spoke about earlier. So you are considering the assault itself, but as I said to you in my charge in considering that matter, whether the legal requirements for murder are met and there was this total disregard or the wicked disregard for the consequences that I spoke of, in considering that matter you must take account of all the evidence that you heard about the surrounding circumstances, whether before the event, during the event or after the event insofar as they throw light on the event itself and the nature of that event. Now does that answer your difficulties?

'So you are considering the assault itself but you consider it in the light of all the circumstances and it may be that for example if you highlight what happened thereafter it may be that what happened thereafter throws light on the nature of the assault in which case of course it throws light on the nature of the assault and it would be for you to consider in that light, but it may be that it doesn't throw any light on the nature of the assault and then obviously you will discount it. Does that help?'

The transcript is characterised by some of the apparent lack of coherence which is typically to be found when unscripted remarks are written down, even though they will have been quite well understood by the persons to whom they were addressed. Counsel made nothing of the form of the direction, nor indeed did he seek to argue as a general proposition that events following an assault could never be relevant to a determination of the character of that assault. What he submitted was that in this particular case there were no events following the assault which could properly be taken into account by the jury and in particular that they should have been directed that they could not take into account certain events which the Solicitor-General of the day had emphasised when addressing the jury.

The Solicitor-General was said to have emphasised three matters: the fact that the appellants shook hands and said that they were great brothers; the washing of the clothes which the appellants had been wearing at the time of the attack; and the failure to telephone for an ambulance until a considerable time after the attack. Counsel explained that he was treating the attack as one event, even though the appellants broke off, shook hands and then returned to assault the deceased once more. He accepted that the fact that they had resumed the attack in a determined manner was a factor which the jury would be entitled to take into account when reaching a view on the nature of the attack. But, for the rest, he submitted that the matters highlighted by the Solicitor General were irrelevant.

So far as the appellants' action in shaking hands and saying that they were great brothers is concerned, that took place between the two stages of the attack. In our view evidence of the appellants shaking hands and saying what they did was evidence which the jury would have been entitled to consider as casting light on the attitude of the appellants in attacking the deceased and in particular in considering whether they displayed complete, utter and wicked disregard of the consequences of their attack on the deceased. The evidence that, once the attack was over, the appellants failed to call an ambulance and proceeded instead to see to the washing of their clothes, is again evidence which the jury could properly regard as casting light on the attitude of the appellants at the time of the attack and as tending to show that they had been wickedly indifferent to the consequences of the attack on the deceased. For these reasons we are satisfied that the trial judge was correct not to direct the jury that they should leave the matters referred to by the Solicitor-General out of account. We have already noted that the direction which the trial judge gave the jury as to the manner in which they could use evidence of subsequent events was not criticised.

In the circumstances there is no merit in the ground of appeal advanced by counsel. We shall therefore refuse the appeals.

Appeals refused.

Notes

**10.30**    1. This decision proceeds on the basis of a concession by the appellants' counsel that it is permissible to have regard to what happens after the attack as evidence of the nature of the attack. Whether that concession is correct is open to question. If what matters in murder is the subjective state of mind of the accused at the time she or he carried out the acts which caused death this might be correct. But that is not what matters in the Scots law of murder, or at least not in a case such as this one where the Crown appear to have proceeded on the basis of wicked recklessness, rather than intention to kill. The test of wicked recklessness is an objective one, and what happens after the fatal assault is surely irrelevant to the question whether, objectively speaking, the fatal injuries were inflicted in a wickedly reckless manner.

2. *Halliday* was followed in *Reid (Gordon John) v. H.M. Advocate*, 1999 G.W.D. 19–871. There the appellant was convicted of murder on an indictment which charged him with killing the victim by knocking him down with a motor car. The victim was the owner of the car, and he was killed when he attempted to prevent the appellant stealing it by standing in its path. The appellant made no attempt to avoid the deceased but rather accelerated as he drove towards him. He did not stop after he struck the deceased, but drove the car to visit a friend and then went to Butlins Holiday Camp in Ayr, where they met two women and went to a dance. Although the possibility of an accident was left to the jury, it was accepted by counsel for the appellant that the real question was whether this was murder or culpable homicide.

The Crown had argued at the trial that the evidence of what the accused did after running down the deceased suggested "that the accused had behaved in a callous way which demonstrated that not merely had he not been involved in a mere accident, but that his attitude at the time of the driving was such as to display a wicked recklessness in regard to the life of the victim". The appellant's explanation had been that he had panicked. The High Court held that reliance upon what happened after the event was unobjectionable.

The court also referred to the case of *McDowall v. H.M. Advocate*, 1998 S.C.C.R. 343, which was concerned with a contravention of section 2 of the Road Traffic Act. There, it was held that the fact that immediately after the accident the appellant, the driver, showed utter disregard for the victim and drove with his bonnet up, was a factor which the jury were entitled to take into account along with his driving in the period before the accident when assessing his state of mind at the time of the accident.

See also *Reid (Donald) v. H.M. Advocate*, High Court, June 16, 1999, *unreported*.

3. Presumably, if it is permissible to look at what has happened after the event in order to support the conclusion that the accused was wickedly reckless, it is permissible to do so in order to overcome the inference of wicked recklessness which is to be drawn from the manner of the attack? Would evidence or remorse and immediate attempts to summon help have made any difference in *Halliday*? Surely not, given the persistent and brutal nature of the attack.

## (c) Wicked recklessness and indifference to the consequences

**10.31**    The classic formulation of the law requires "a disposition depraved enough to be regardless of consequences". What is the position of the depraved killer who is not "regardless of consequences"? Suppose, for example, that A tortures B to get information from him. A takes great care to keep B alive so that he can get the information he needs, but B has a heart attack and dies. A did not intend to kill, and he was not, in a very obvious sense, "regardless of consequences". But surely this is murder. The terrorist bomber who kills, having given a warning of the bomb might equally argue that he is not "regardless" of the consequences.

People who are wickedly reckless should be found guilty of murder if they kill, not because they are regardless of the consequences but because, either they are willing to run the risk of causing death, or because, objectively speaking, their conduct creates an obvious and serious risk of death.

## D. Intention to do bodily harm

The relevance of an intention to bodily harm as part of the *mens rea* for murder is uncertain. Two **10.32** questions arise: (i) Is an intention to do (serious) bodily harm in itself a sufficient *mens rea* for murder and (ii) Where the Crown do not allege intention to kill, and rely on wicked recklessness, must there also be an intention to do at least some bodily harm?

### (a) *Intention to do serious bodily harm as a third form of* mens rea

So far as concerns the first of these questions, *dicta* can certainly be found to support the view that an **10.33** intention to do serious, or grievous, bodily harm is a sufficient *mens rea* for murder.

In *H.M. Advocate v. William Marshall* (1896) 4 S.L.T. 313 the accused was charged with murdering a man by stabbing him. In the course of his address to the jury Lord Young stated, *inter alia*:

> "All unlawful killing or destroying the life of a human being is culpable homicide; but the term murder is technically applied to that culpable homicide which is done maliciously ... if the death inflicted—the destruction of life—is the consequence of a cruel act done wilfully and intended either to destroy life or to do grievous bodily harm—to inflict serious injury on the body—that is murder. A cruel act, done wilfully, which does destroy life, and which was either so intended, or, short of that, to inflict serious bodily injury—that is murder .... Where a lethal weapon, a deadly instrument is used (such as a knife), and the illegal act is a stab with that deadly weapon, the intention either to take life or to do grievous bodily injury is implied. If anybody stabs another wilfully, sending a knife, plain and sharp, into his heart, and he dies upon the spot, or within a short time, it is very hard to resist the conclusion of the general legal proposition that intent at least to do very grievous bodily harm is plain on the fact."

In *H.M. Advocate v. George Paterson* (1897) 5 S.L.T. 13 the accused was charged with murdering a woman by beating her with a red hot poker and inserting that instrument into her rectum and vagina. The same judge directed the jury that "if death was the consequence of a cruel act done wilfully, and intended either to destroy life or to do grievous bodily harm, that was murder. A cruel act, done wilfully, which destroyed life, and which was intended to inflict serious bodily injury, was murder."

The trial judge in *Carraher v. H.M Advocate* 1946 S.L.T 225 appears to have directed the jury in terms of an intention to kill or do grievous bodily harm (at p. 226), and in *H.M. Advocate v. Kidd,* 1960 J.C. 61 Lord Strachan described murder to the jury in the following terms: "Murder is the taking of human life by a person who either (a) has a malicious and wilful intent to kill or do grievous bodily harm, or (b) is wickedly reckless as to the consequences of his act upon his victim."

In *H.M. Advocate v. Hartley,* 1989 S.L.T. 135, Lord Sutherland directed the jury that 'murder is constituted by any wilful, that is to say intentional act causing the destruction of life either with the intent to kill or cause serious bodily harm, or when acting with such wicked recklessness as to show a disposition depraved enough to be regardless of the consequences' and at a later point in his charge stated:

> "Now, as you will see, ladies and gentlemen, murder can be constituted in two separate ways, either with intention to kill or cause serious bodily harm. So that if you declare your intention of killing somebody and go out and shoot him, then that is very plainly murder. If you declare your intention to maim somebody seriously and go out and do so and unfortunately go too far and he dies, that is murder, because you had the intent to cause serious bodily harm. That is the first branch of murder."

Although all of these statements of the law are to be found in charges to juries by a single judge, and are not therefore authoritative, similar statements have from time to time emanated from the appeal court. In *Cawthorne v. H.M. Advocate, ante,* the trial judge directed the jury that "murder is committed when the person who brings about the death of another acted deliberately with intent to kill, or acted with intent to do bodily harm, or, and this is the third leg, acted with utter and wicked recklessness as to the consequences of his act upon his victim". In the appeal court Lord Guthrie stated that this would be a correct statement of the law provided that the word "grievous" was inserted before "bodily harm". In *Brennan v. H.M. Advocate*, 1977 S.L.T. 151, the Lord Justice-General (Emslie) stated that the Scottish definition of murder "includes the taking of human life by a person who has an intent to kill or to do serious injury, or whose act is shown to have been wickedly reckless as to the consequences".

Despite these statements, the generally accepted view of the law is that an intention to serious bodily harm, or grievous bodily harm, is not a separate *mens rea* for murder. The only statements in support of this as a form of *mens rea* to come from the appeal court are to be found in the passages from *Cawthorne* and *Brennan* quoted above, but these cases must, it is suggested, be treated with considerable caution.

So far as concerns *Brennan*, when Lord Emslie was questioned on his statement of the law by the House of Lords Select Committee on Murder and Life Imprisonment he indicated clearly that he did not consider his statement of the law in *Brennan* accurately to reflect the law. The joint memorandum submitted by Lord Emslie and Lord Ross, and their oral evidence to the Committee, make it clear that in their view an intention to serious harm is not in itself sufficient. (See *Report of the Select Committee on Murder and Life Imprisonment*, Volume III, Oral Evidence Part 2, p. 469 H.L. Paper 78-III (1989).) Taken in the context of his opinion as a whole, it would be difficult to regard the brief passage from *Brennan* quoted above as supporting the view that the essentially English formulation—"grievous bodily harm"—is a sufficient intent for murder.

Although the appeal court in *Cawthorne* held that the trial judge had not misdirected the jury on the mental element in attempted murder, direct support for grievous bodily harm as a separate form of *mens rea* in *Cawthorne* is only found in the opinion of Lord Guthrie. The other members of the court do not express an opinion on the question, and the discussion of the law in that case is directed more to the question of whether wicked recklessness is a sufficient *mens rea* for attempted murder, rather than the issue of intention to serious bodily harm as a form of *mens rea* for murder.

Most commentators on the law also take the view that an intention to cause grievous bodily harm is not by itself a sufficient *mens rea* for murder. See Jones and Christie, *Criminal Law*, 2nd ed. (1996), pp. 210–211; Gordon, para. 23–20 and *Memorandum* to the House of Lords Select Committee on Murder and Life Imprisonment, *Report*, above, Volume III, p. 553–554; written memoranda and oral evidence to the same committee by the Faculty of Advocates, Sheriff Nicholson, the Scottish Law Commission and the Scottish Home and Health Department and the Crown Office, *Report*, Volume III, pp. 364 *et seq.*, 377 *et seq.*, 385 *et seq.* and 398 *et seq.* respectively. See, however, the views of Lord Goff, "The Mental Element in the Crime of Murder", (1988) 104 L.Q.R. 30 and Jones, "The Scottish Law of Murder" (1989) 15 L.Q.R. 516. Lord Goff accepts, on the basis of *Cawthorne* that an intention to serious bodily harm is sufficient. Jones appears to reach the same conclusion on the basis of Lord Sutherland's direction to the jury in *Hartley*. Lord Goff's comments must, with respect, be seen as emanating from a judge with no particular training in Scots law. Jones's claim that Lord Sutherland's comments about intention to do serious harm in *Hartley* are "certainly the orthodox view among the judiciary" (15 L.Q.R. 516 at 517) finds little support from the case law.

If it were to be accepted that an intention to do serious bodily harm is sufficient for murder, it would mean that the scope of the crime would be much wider than it is commonly conceived to be in modern practice. Suppose, for example, that A deliberately cuts off B's index finger. There would be no doubt about an intention to do serious harm in such a case. Suppose, further, that the wound inflicted on B becomes infected, septicaemia sets in and B eventually dies of blood poisoning. If intention to do serious bodily harm were to be sufficient for murder, that would be a case of murder, and that, it is suggested, would not be accepted as such in Scots law today.

## (b) Intention to do bodily harm in wicked recklessness cases

**10.34** The issue here is whether or not the *mens rea* for murder is made out where the accused acts with a high degree of recklessness, but where there is no evidence of any intention to do harm. Suppose, for example, that A consumes a large amount of alcohol, gets into his car and drives off at high speed in a built-up area. He drives at high speed through a red light at a busy junction and collides with another car, killing the occupants. Is A guilty of murder? It can certainly be argued that A has shown a "disposition depraved enough to be regardless of the consequences". Or suppose that A, a terrorist, puts a bomb in a building. He gives the authorities an hour's warning and the building is cleared. However, the bomb goes off killing B, a rough sleeper who has crept into the building to get out of the rain. Is A guilty of murder?

Gordon suggests, in his written *Memorandum* to the House of Lords Select Committee (above), that "[i]t is ... implicit in the law as it has developed that for reckless killing to be murder, death must be caused by assault or at least by the intentional infliction of some physical harm". (*Report*, Volume III, p. 554.) See also Gordon, paras 23–14 *et seq*. McCall Smith and Sheldon, on the other hand, suggest that at least in the terrorist-type case the accused should be found guilty of murder even in the absence of an intention to cause harm to anyone. (McCall Smith and Sheldon, *Scots Criminal Law* (2nd ed.) pp. 178–180.) Jones and Christie appear to confine wicked recklessness killing to cases where the accused intended to do serious harm and was wickedly reckless with regard to the consequences. (Jones and Christie, *Criminal Law* (2nd ed.), pp. 209 *et seq*.)

The point has not been considered in any modern Scottish authority. Hume's position on the question is uncertain. On the one hand, most of the examples he gives of cases involving wickedly reckless conduct are cases in which the accused has attacked the victim in circumstances which show "if not a determination to kill him, at least an absolute indifference whether he live or die". (Hume, i, 257.) On the other hand, however, he quotes with approval (at p. 23) the case of *James Niven*, December 21, 1795 as an example of murder. In that case the accused loaded a small cannon with powder and a piece of iron and fired it up a street, knowing that there were persons in the street, killing one of the latter. This is not, however, a case in which the accused deliberately attacked the victim in a way which showed an indifference to life. It is a culpably dangerous thing to do, but it is different in quality from the other examples he gives. It is much nearer to the example of the reckless drunken driver given above.

## E. Constructive murder? Killing in the course of other crimes

The term "constructive murder" is used here to describe killings which are treated as murder, not **10.35** because of state of mind of the accused the accused but because of the context in which the killing occurs. The clearest example of this type of case is to be found in the "felony-murder" doctrine mentioned above (p. 390).

In principle, Scots law does not expressly recognise constructive murder in that broad form. There are, however, suggestions that a limited form of constructive murder does exist in the law of Scotland.

### H.M. Advocate v. Fraser and Rollins
1920 J.C. 60

The accused were charged with the murder of a man they had assaulted and robbed. The **10.36** injuries inflicted on the victim made it clear that a considerable degree of violence had been used. In his charge to the jury the presiding judge made the following comments on the law of murder.

LORD SANDS: "If a person attempts a crime of serious violence, although his object may not be murder, and if the result of that violence is death, then the jury are bound to convict of murder. A striking illustration of this is the case of criminal abortion. There the man has no intention or desire to injure or kill the woman, it is the last thing he wants to do, but if he uses instruments to bring about a criminal abortion and in result kills the woman, that, by our law, is murder. Or, again, take the crime of rape. A man ravishes a woman but has no desire to kill her, yet, if he uses such violence as causes her death, then that is murder. And so it is with regard to the crime you are here concerned with, robbery, and it would be no answer—it was rather suggested in cross examination—it would be no answer that the violence was connected with the man's seeking to defend himself. If a man is assaulted with violence and those who are assaulting him seek to rob him, he is entitled to defend himself, and, if they use such violence to overcome his efforts to defend himself that they kill him, then that is murder. That aspect of the matter, however, was not pressed so much by the learned counsel; they rather dwelt upon the question of intention. Did the prisoners intend to kill the man? Now, as I have already told you, under the law of Scotland when you have a violent crime like rape or robbery, then in order to convict of murder it is not necessary to show there was intention to kill. No doubt, intention may be taken into account in certain cases where the violence is very slight and the death is as it were a sort of mischance; then, even although the violence is criminal, if there was no intent to kill it would not be murder. I might take the illustration of a thief who tries to snatch somebody's watch. He tries to pull it away and in doing so upsets the man's balance and the man falls on the kerb and has the misfortune to strike his head against the stone and is killed. That would not be murder because there is a certain mischance in the matter. There is no probability or likelihood that you will kill a man by trying to snatch his watch. Then again, if you take the case of somebody who threw a snowball at a man and as a result the man had a shock and it killed him, again, I say, that is a mischance and not what is contemplated and expected. But if a man uses reckless violence that may cause death, and uses that violence in perpetrating a crime, it is murder. You do not require the deliberate intention to kill, but you must have reckless use of force without any consideration of what the results of that use of force may be. It is in that view that you must regard this matter.

You have heard the evidence in regard to the injuries this man suffered, and you must consider whether there was or there was not such reckless violence as shows that these men were determined to rob this man and did not really care what happened to him. There is one aspect of the case which I am afraid you must take into account. I cannot tell you—I should not be stating the law correctly if I were to tell you—that, if a man attacks another man in a park or in the street, and holds his throat so as to prevent him from calling out, or throws him down or pins him to the ground so as to rob him, and the man through that violence suffers death—I am not able to tell you that that would not be murder. It might, however, be in some cases a question of circumstance if the violence were not very great, but this case is on a more unfavourable footing. It is quite clear that this man was not merely held by the throat, he was not merely held down for the purpose of robbing him, but it is perfectly clear, I think, that the evidence shows that the object of the violence was to stun him at all events, if not to kill him, to render him unconscious and I think that is borne out by the nature of what was done afterwards— taking away the boots and coat. He was struck in the face and on the head, there can be no doubt with the object either of stunning or paralysing him. It was not the case of a struggle to prevent the man calling out or protecting his own; the intention appears clearly to have been to reduce him to such a state that he was incapable either of calling out or resisting the removal of his clothes or anything else, or pursuing and giving the alarm—to make him, as I say, unconscious; and it is for you to judge whether that violence was or was not of that reckless character, regardless of consequences, which involves the crime of murder."

Verdict: Guilty of murder.

### Miller and Denovan v. H.M. Advocate
High Court, December 1960. Noted, 1991 S.L.T. 211

**10.37**  LORD JUSTICE-GENERAL (CLYDE): "These are two appeals against the verdict of a jury in the High Court in Glasgow. The jury unanimously found each of the appellants guilty of murder. They were both charged with assaulting John Cremin, striking him on the head with a piece of wood, knocking him down, robbing him of certain articles including a sum of £67 of money and of murdering him.

So far as the first named appellant Miller is concerned, as the jury must have found that he struck the fatal blow the verdict was one of capital murder within the meaning of the Homicide Act 1957, s.5(1)(a)—that is to say a murder done in the course of furtherance of theft.

But in regard to the second appellant Denovan there was no evidence that he struck the actual blow and the jury were therefore directed, and rightly directed, that he could only be guilty of non-capital murder owing to the provisions of s.5(2) of the Act. The jury found him guilty of non-capital murder.

As the presiding judge said in the course of his charge 'This case arises on a background of vice, depravity and violence,' and to appreciate the grounds of appeal it is necessary briefly to set out the circumstances as disclosed in the evidence.

In the indictment the two accused were charged with a series of assaults and robberies on men whom they accosted late in the evening in the Recreation Ground where this murder is alleged to have taken place. Before the evidence was all led the two appellants pled guilty to all the charges against them respectively in the indictment with the sole exception of the murder charge relating to Cremin.

On the night of Cremin's murder the two appellants had gone to the Recreation Ground late in the evening with the avowed intention of robbing someone. They waited in the vicinity of the public lavatory, Denovan going in to act as the decoy. Cremin visited the lavatory and as he and Denovan were on their way from it Miller suddenly came up and without any warning is alleged to have hit Cremin on the head with a large block of wood some 3 feet 3 inches long which with one blow knocked Cremin senseless to the ground. The two appellants then proceeded to go through his pockets, taking out anything of value. When they had secured all they could find they ran off and left him dead or dying. His body was found a short time afterwards.

My Lords, this cowardly and utterly unprovoked assault was unexplained and unexplainable except as being 'a deliberate attempt to overcome any risk of resistance by Cremin' and so to enable the two appellants in safety to rob his unconscious body of whatever possessions they could find upon it. There was no suggestion of any quarrel or dispute with Cremin or of any resistance on his part which could justify the attack. He was struck down without warning. Both appellants displayed a callous disregard of whatever injuries they may have done him. They centred their whole attention upon snatching all they could from his pockets, rolling his body over on the grass in order to get easier access to them. Once their purpose was achieved they fled into the night and left him to his fate.

But apart from this aspect of the matter there was medical evidence in the case as well. The medical evidence established that the cause of death was a single blow on his head which fractured his skull and caused a haemorrhage of or into the brain. The blow, according to the medical evidence, was 'a severe one' and 'a violent one' causing, as one of the doctors said, a large fracture and haemorrhage all over the brain. An attempt was made in cross-examination of this doctor to suggest that the fracture might have been caused by Cremin falling forward, to which the doctor replied 'Unless he is struck by a motor car and precipitated on to the ground you would not produce such an injury as this'.

In these circumstances the presiding judge directed the jury that 'If you come to the conclusion that that blow was delivered as a result of Miller hitting Cremin over the head with this large piece of wood in order to overcome his resistance in order that robbery might take place then I direct you in law that there is no room for culpable homicide in this case. If it was homicide at all, in that situation it was murder.' This direction by the presiding judge is attacked in this appeal upon the ground that the judge should have directed the jury that it was open to them on the evidence to return a verdict of culpable homicide.

In our opinion the presiding judge was amply justified in giving the direction which he did give in this case, and there is no basis on the evidence for a finding of culpable homicide. Murder is constituted by any wilful act causing the destruction of life whether intended to kill or displaying such wicked recklessness as to imply a disposition depraved enough to be regardless of consequences. That definition is a well-known one in Scotland. Obviously, therefore it is not essential for the establishment of murder to prove intent to kill. It may still be murder though that intent be absent. For it can still be murder if the jury are satisfied that there was a wilful act displaying utter recklessness of the consequences of the blow delivered. In the present case in our view there was ample evidence to justify a conclusion of that sort.

But it is argued on behalf of Miller that the presiding judge should have left it to the jury to find on the facts whether or not this crime was something less than murder, namely, culpable homicide. In our opinion the evidence of the present case required the presiding judge to direct them that there was no room for a verdict of culpable homicide. If it was homicide at all it was murder. My Lords, there are cases, of course, where the evidence of the circumstances in which the crime occurred is so conflicting that it would be appropriate to leave such a matter to the jury after the distinction between murder and culpable homicide had been pointed out. If, for instance, the issue between these two possible verdicts depended on the weight to be given to conflicting evidence as to the amount of violence used, or upon a question whether death might have been in that particular case a mischance, there may be room for leaving both murder and culpable homicide to the jury for their decision. But it is no part of the function of a judge at a trial to avoid his responsibility by leaving the issue in all cases to the jury to work out for themselves, and that in effect was the contention put before us on behalf of Miller this morning.

The judge has a duty to consider the evidence and has a duty to make up his mind whether any of it is relevant to infer that culpable homicide has been committed. If he arrives at the conclusion that there is no evidence in the case from which such a verdict could reasonably be reached, it is his plain duty to direct the jury that it is not open to them to consider culpable homicide. On the other hand if he finds that there is evidence which might reasonably entitle the jury to return a verdict of culpable homicide then, subject to suitable directions, it is his duty to leave the issue on the weight to be given to the evidence to the jury. (Compare in this connection the decision of the full bench in *Kennedy v. Lord Advocate*, 1944 J.C. 171, per Lord Justice-General at p. 177.)

In the present case the judge's direction in regard to culpable homicide is challenged on behalf of Miller in particular upon the ground that the judge did not put to the jury certain theories as to how the injuries leading to Cremin's death might have been caused. These theories had no basis in the evidence but were founded upon assumed states of fact for which there was no proof of any kind by anybody. The directions of a judge in a trial must be related to the circumstances of the case as disclosed in the evidence. In the present case there was no scintilla of evidence in support of any of these theories and the presiding judge in his charge very properly completely ignored them. In the present case accordingly in our view this attack upon the presiding judge in regard to his directions relating to culpable homicide completely fails."

Appeals dismissed.

NOTES

**10.38**    1. What is it that these cases decide? Is it that killing in the course of robbery (and certain other crimes) is murder, or are these merely examples of cases in which the degree of violence is such that it would be appropriate for the judge to withdraw from the jury any possibility of a verdict of culpable homicide? In cases such as *Parr, Broadley* and *Brown* (above, pp. 396–398) the decision in *Miller and Denovan* appears to be treated as a particular example of the latter, and certainly there are passages in Lord Clyde's opinion which would support that approach.

2. There are similar passages in *Fraser and Rollins* and there are, equally, passages in which Lord Sands appears to say, simply, that murder can be committed even in the absence of an intention to kill, provided there is the requisite degree of recklessness. However, it is difficult to ignore the opening passages of his Lordship's opinion in which he suggests that it is murder if death results from a crime of violence such as rape or robbery, and, especially, the suggestion that it is murder if death results from an unlawful abortion. These are classic examples of a constructive murder rule. If Lord Sands really does say that it is necessarily murder if death results from rape or abortion or robbery, then, with respect, this is incorrect. In principle, it should only be murder if the accused intended to kill or acted with wicked recklessness.

3. The difficulty with both of these cases is that while the court seems to suggest a form of "constructive" liability for murder there is ample evidence in both cases to support a conviction for murder on ordinary principles of *mens rea*. In both cases the attacks were carried out with a callous disregard for the victim, as indeed Lord Clyde points out in *Miller and Denovan*.

## 3. CULPABLE HOMICIDE

**10.39**    Culpable homicide comprises those homicides which are criminal at common law, but which are not murder. It has traditionally been accepted that there are two categories of culpable homicide: those which are "mitigated murder"—murder under provocation or when suffering from diminished responsibility—and those criminal homicides which are not committed with an intention to kill or with wicked recklessness, namely, killing by unlawful act and reckless killing). The first category—the "mitigated murder" cases—has generally been known as "voluntary culpable homicide" and the second category "involuntary culpable homicide".

The category of "mitigated murder" must now be revised in the light of the decision in *Drury v. H.M. Advocate*, 2001 S.C.C.R. 2000. In that case, the High Court treated provocation as a matter which could exclude the *mens rea* of murder, and, indeed, some members of the court likewise treated diminished responsibility. (See, for example, Lord Nimmo Smith.) If this is the correct analysis, then the effect of provocation (and diminished responsibility) is not to mitigate what would otherwise be murder, but to exclude the possibility of murder *ab initio*. What this means is that "voluntary" culpable homicide now embraces those cases of criminal homicide which are committed intentionally or with a high degree of recklessness, but which, because of provocation or diminished responsibility lack the quality of "wickedness" required for a murder conviction.

## A. Voluntary culpable homicide or "mitigated murder"

### (a) Killing under provocation

#### Drury v. H.M. Advocate
High Court, February 2, 2001, *unreported*

The appellant killed his ex-partner by hitting her on the head with a claw-hammer. The **10.40** parties had lived together for sixteen months, and although they were living apart at the time of the killing it was accepted that there was still a relationship entitling the accused to expect sexual fidelity on the part of the deceased. On the evening of the killing the accused went to the deceased's house and encountered a man leaving the premises. He suspected that this man and the deceased had been having sexual relations. He confronted her and, on being asked what was going on, she replied "What do you think?" He then killed her. At this trial he argued, first that he had not intended to kill and had not displayed the degree of wicked recklessness for murder. He also argued that he was acting under provocation. The jury convicted him of murder. On appeal it was argued that the trial judge had misdirected the jury, in relation to the defence of provocation, by telling them that while sexual infidelity could provide a basis for a plea of provocation, there must be a "reasonable relationship" between the provocation offered and the violence used by the accused.

LORD JUSTICE-GENERAL (ROGER): "... [8] Although the issue in the appeal is apparently narrow, it cannot be resolved without looking into wider aspects of the doctrine of provocation and, more generally, into the law of murder and culpable homicide. In doing this, I shall examine the account of the law given by Hume and Alison. As Mr. Prais [counsel for the appellant] was at pains to point out, both of these authors wrote rather a long time ago. I, for one, would not think it right to accord to their writings any superstitious reverence which left no room for evaluating their exposition of the law in the light of later experience, later developments or more modem analysis. Nevertheless, if approached with these factors in mind, Hume's account, in particular, is useful because it helps to fit provocation into the overall scheme of our law on murder and culpable homicide. One cannot help feeling that some at lest of the difficulties of the subject have arisen because provocation has sometimes tended to be treated as an isolated topic rather than in its proper place within that wider context.

[9] Since the issue between the Crown and defence at the trial was the issue between murder and culpable homicide the trial judge had to give the jury directions on the definition of both of these crimes. What he said was this:

'An assault is any deliberate attack on the person of someone else, whether it results in injury or not, and evil intent is of the essence of the crime of assault. Now, murder according to our law is constituted by any wilful act causing the destruction of life, either intending to kill or displaying such wicked recklessness as to imply a disposition depraved enough to be regardless of the consequences. So murder is any wilful act causing the destruction of life, either intending to kill or displaying such wicked recklessness as to imply a disposition depraved enough to be regardless of the consequences; that is, the assailant didn't care whether the victim lived or died. So evil intent is of the essence of the crime of murder, either acting with a deliberate intention to kill or at least with reckless indifference to the consequences to the victim of the violence.

Now, in this connection one cannot of course, see into someone's mind. You can only draw an inference from what he's done against the background in which he acted. So the necessary intention to kill or wicked recklessness would have to be capable of being inferred from the actings of the assailant, and you have to decide whether that is an inference which can properly be drawn in the circumstances of this particular case. Now, you heard counsel refer to the alternative verdict of guilty of culpable homicide. Now, culpable homicide is the term applied to a case where a person is assaulted and dies as a result of the assault but where the killing is not so grave as to constitute murder but which is, nevertheless, culpable and not justified; a case where there was no intention to kill and where the circumstances fall short of displaying the required degree of wicked recklessness to constitute murder but, as I say, where the killing is still culpable and results from a criminal act such as assault. So, as I say, culpable homicide applies where a person is assaulted and dies but the assailant did not intend to kill and did not display the required degree of wicked recklessness to constitute murder.'

[10] It may be useful to bring out what these directions say and do not say. First, the trial judge gives a direction on assault, including the need for evil intent. I agree with Lord Mackay of Drumadoon that such a direction will not always be necessary and may indeed be confusing in a case of this kind. Next, so far as murder is concerned, the judge directs the jury that it is constituted by any wilful act, causing the destruction of life, by which the perpetrator either intends to kill or displays wicked recklessness. This direction is modelled on a passage in Macdonald's Criminal Law (fifth edition), p. 89 which itself reflects, in part, the rubric to the first section of Alison's account of murder (Vol. 1, p. 1). In may cases—as, for instance, where the only real issue in dispute is the identity of the killer—a jury will need no further guidance. Nevertheless, as it stands, the definition in the direction is at best incomplete and, to that extent, inaccurate. Most obviously, someone who is subject to a murderous attack may defend himself by intentionally killing his assailant. He therefore falls within the terms of the first part of the judge's direction. But, of course, a person who intentionally kills in a self-defence is not guilty of murder or indeed of any other crime.

[11] The definition of murder in the direction is somewhat elliptical because it does not describe the relevant intention. In truth, just as the recklessness has to be wicked so also must the intention be wicked. Therefore, perhaps the most obvious way of completing the definition is by saying that murder is constituted by any wilful act causing the destruction of life, by which the perpetrator either wickedly intends to kill or displays wicked recklessness as to whether the victim lives or dies. Saying that the perpetrator "wickedly" intends to kill is just a shorthand way of referring to what Hume (Vol. 1, p. 254) describes as the murderer's 'wicked and mischievous purpose' in contradistinction to 'those motives of necessity, duty, or allowable infirmity, which may serve to justify or excuse' the deliberate taking of life. See also Vol. 1, p. 256. Alison (Vol. 1, pp. 1–2) adopts Hume's approach. For reasons which I explain below, in a case like the present where provocation is in play, it is of some importance to consider the state of mind by which a murderer is actuated in committing the intentional or reckless act.

[12] When he comes to define culpable homicide, the trial judge again gives a definition which is incomplete and, to that extent, misleading. He says that culpable homicide occurs in a case 'where there is no intention to kill and where the circumstances fall short of displaying the required degree of wicked recklessness to constitute murder. . . .' It applies where a person

is assaulted and dies 'but the assailant did not intend to kill and did not display the required degree of wicked recklessness to constitute murder.' In these directions the trial judge describes one particular kind of culpable homicide. This was indeed the kind of culpable homicide for which defence counsel was contending when he submitted to the jury—plainly, without success—that, even in the absence of provocation, they should conclude that the appellant had not intended to kill the deceased and that, moreover, he had not displayed the wicked recklessness required for murder. For dealing with that first aspect of the case the direction was entirely appropriate.

[13] But what the trial judge describes is merely one type of situation that is covered by culpable homicide. As its name suggests, according to the current usage in our law (Burnett, *Criminal Law*, pp. 26–27) the crime of culpable homicide covers the killing of human beings in all circumstances, short of murder, where the criminal law attaches a relevant measure of blame to the person who kills. For instance, it covers cases where a person who is suffering from diminished responsibility intends to kill someone and does so. Even though the killing is intentional, the appropriate verdict is one of culpable homicide. Similarly, where the deceased has provoked the accused and the accused, under the influence of that provocation, kills him, the accused will be guilty of culpable homicide even though he intended to kill the deceased. Hume (Vol. 1, p. 239) describes these as cases where the accused

> 'has a mortal purpose, and yet is not in the first degree of guilt as a murderer. Because he is not actuated by wickedness of heart, or hatred of the deceased, but by the sudden impulse of resentment, excited by high and real injuries, and accompanied with terror and agitation of spirits.'

Similarly, Alison (Vol. 1, p. 92) gives as the first way of committing culpable homicide:

> 'By the intentional infliction of death, in circumstances which law deems blameable, though not so much as to amount to murder.'

Under that heading he goes on to discuss cases where the killing takes place as a result of provocation (Vol. 1, pp. 92–94). 11

[14] Perhaps the clearest modern example of this kind of case is *H.M. Advocate v. Hill* 1941 J C. 59. The events took place in January 1941 and at the time the accused was a corporal in the military police stationed in England. When he returned home to Springburn, his wife was in the house and another man, who was serving in the Navy at Greenock, came into the house. In the ensuing discussion it emerged that the wife and the other man had had sexual relations in the matrimonial home on at least one occasion. The accused went to another room, got the service revolver which he was bound to carry, shot the man and then shot his wife, before giving himself up to the police. Although the accused said that he had been "driven to it", it is plain that he intended to kill both of his victims. None the less, in accordance with the trial judge's direction that it was open to them to do so, the jury convicted the accused of culpable homicide.

[15] Since culpable homicide covers cases of intentional killing carried out under provocation, it must also cover cases where the assault displays a degree of recklessness which, but for the provocation, would lead to the inference that the accused had acted wickedly. That being so, in this case the trial judge's charge to the jury on the matter of culpable homicide was not simply incomplete: it actually failed to give them any direction on the very kind of culpable homicide which was in issue under the second leg of the defence case, viz. that the appellant had killed while under the influence of provocation. If the jury had duly absorbed and faithfully tried to apply the trial judge's directions on culpable homicide, they might have been left in some doubt as to whether they could convict the appellant of culpable homicide if, for instance, they concluded that, in response to discovering her infidelity, the accused had intentionally killed the deceased. What the trial judge should have

done was to give the jury further directions dealing with culpable homicide on the basis of provocation. The fact that this very experienced trial judge omitted to do so is in itself a testimony to the somewhat confusing state of some aspects of our law on provocation.

[16] So far as homicide is concerned, in Scots law provocation has always operated as an excuse and never as a justification. In other words, an assailant who kills in response to provocation has never been entitled to be acquitted; he has merely been entitled to be convicted of culpable homicide rather than of murder. But the doctrine of provocation applies also in cases of assault. Where A assaults B in response to an assault by B, it has been suggested that, in the law of today, the assault by B cannot justify A's assault, but may merely serve as an excuse which can be taken into account in mitigation of sentence. See Gordon, *Criminal Law* (second edition), pp. 830–831. In the time of Hume, however, provocation in the form of an assault could indeed justify retaliation of a suitable level, to deter as well as to punish the initial assailant. Therefore, the person who retaliated by an assault of the appropriate level and merely injured his assailant was entitled to be acquitted. If he went too far, the initial assault would still operate as a factor in mitigation. See Hume Vol. 1, pp. 334–335. Despite some subsequent criticism of his judgment (*Crawford v. H M Advocate* 1950 J.C. 67 at p. 70 per Lord Justice General Cooper), this is undoubtedly the doctrine which Lord Justice Clerk Aitchison had in mind when he held, in *Hillan v. H M Advocate* 1937 J C. 53 at pp. 57–58, that provocation in the form of an assault could sometimes operate as a complete defence. The same approach is reflected in the original text of what is now to be found in Macdonald's *Criminal Law*, p. 116 where he states that 'Provocation by blows will justify retaliation *in self-defence* if not excessive.' If account is taken of the context, it requires no great application of thought to the textual criticism of the sentence to detect that the words which I have put in italics are not part of the original text. And, of course, they were not to be found, for instance, in the version cited by the Lord Justice Clerk in *Hillan* (1937 J.C. at pp. 57–58). They are in fact an interpolation by the editor of the (later) fifth edition. Moreover, with unfeigned respect to Sir Gerald Gordon (*Criminal Law*, p. 825), I detect in the relevant passage of Hume no 'terminological error' on his part. On the contrary, it appears clear to me—not least from his references to punishment—that Hume was not confusing retaliation in response to provocation with self-defence. Rather, he was expounding a doctrine as to the operation and effect of the law of provocation which was regarded as valid in his day—and apparently as late as 1937—but which has now fallen into disfavour. The reason for any change is, presumably, that it is nowadays thought that, with an organised police force throughout the land, an individual can never be justified in resorting to violence to deter and punish his assailant. Be that as it may, for present purposes it is useful to notice that, whether operating as a complete defence or as an excuse in mitigation, *ex hypothesi* in cases of assault provocation applied where the accused was intentionally attacking his assailant. That remains the position when it operates in mitigation today.

[17] In his charge, the trial judge directed the jury that, if they found that the appellant killed the deceased as a result of provocation, they should convict him of culpable homicide. But he did not really explain why this should be so, given the definitions of murder and culpable homicide which he had already given them. He merely said that:

'if the accused would otherwise be guilty of murder but you take the view that he was acting under provocation, then that would reduce the crime from murder to culpable homicide and you would find him guilty of culpable homicide.'

By saying that, if provocation were established, this would reduce the crime from murder to culpable homidice, the judge could be thought to give the impression that provocation acts as some kind of laissez-passer by virtue of which an accused, who displays the hallmarks of a murderer and would otherwise find himself convicted of murder, is entitled to escape from that predicament to the somewhat less serious predicament of a conviction of culpable homicide. While the terminology of 'reducing murder to culpable homicide' is frequently encountered, it is essentially misleading, as Lord Cameron of Lochbroom observed in the course of the hearing of the appeal. In particular, it suggests that the jury would first conclude that, absent provocation, the accused would have been guilty of murder, and only at that stage would they consider provocation. In reality, however, evidence relating to provocation is simply one of the factors which the jury should take into account in performing their general task of determining the accused's state of mind at the time when he killed his victim.

[18] In this case, the question for the jury was whether the Crown had proved beyond a reasonable doubt that the appellant had acted with the necessary *mens rea* for murder. If so, the jury would convict him of murder. If not, they would convict him of culpable homicide. In reaching their conclusion the jury had, of course, to draw inferences from all the relevant evidence, including the appellant's evidence relating to provocation. In effect, that evidence was simply one of the factors—the principal factor, perhaps—upon which the defence invited the jury to infer that the appellant had not had either the wicked intention to kill the deceased or the necessary wickedly reckless indifference as to whether she lived or died, to justify a conviction of murder. Rather, taking all the relevant factors into account, they should conclude that his action, though culpable, was not wicked or, at lest, that they had a reasonable doubt as to whether it was wicked: they should therefore convict him of culpable homicide.

[19] This analysis, which fits provocation into the overall scheme of our law on murder and culpable homicide, is consistent with Hume's account of the relevant aspect of culpable homicide. In the introductory passage (Vol. 1, p. 239) which I have already quoted in paragraph 13, Hume observes that, where the accused kills in response to provocation, he is 'not actuated by wickedness of heart, or hatred of the deceased, but by the impulse of resentment, excited by high and real injuries, and accompanied with terror and agitation of spirits.' He goes on to expound his thinking in a passage (Vol. 1, pp. 239–240) which is of considerable importance for the issues in this appeal:

> 'It is true, it could not well be maintained, that such a homicide shall be judged as a pure involuntary act, like that of a brute or a madman, the object of neither praise nor blame. For although, like other animals, we are subject to the feeling of resentment on injuries, which is necessary to our preservation; yet it is not in our species, as in theirs, a blind and an ungovernable impulse; but has been placed by the Author of our nature, under the control of a superior principle, which may serve to restrain it within those just and salutary bounds, where it answers its proper ends; and by means of which, if duly and habitually exerted, not only the conduct of the individual may be regulated, but even the feeling itself may in a great measure be chastened and subdued: So that the very things which he does in self-defence, shall be done calmly and with temperance, and less out of anger or revenge, than from considerations of justice and necessity. To gain this state of self-command is a part of every man's duty, according to the degree attainable in his way of education and course of life; and so far to fall short of it, as mortally to avenge any insult or injury not attended with danger to one's life, and not impossible to be repelled and chastised by gentler means,—this is certainly a criminal excess, such as ought to be the source of much distress to the survivor, and cannot be passed over by the magistrate without serious reprehension. A conclusion which will be the more confirmed, when he reflects on the great frequency of such scenes of provocation, and how strong the propensity to feel too keenly on occasion of all wrongs of this description. To put men therefore on their guard in this respect, and form them, as far as may be, to a previous habit and disposition on the subject, which may serve as a corrective of sudden passion, the law of most civilized countries has condemned all homicide that is done on provocation, though grievous and difficult to bear, as a high crime, and the fit subject of exemplary discipline.
>
> But while we thus entertain a well-grounded jealoudy of every man's partiality in his own case, and have a due regard to the peace and order of society, which are so deeply

concerned in the repressing of such excesses; yet, on the other side, we cannot as men be insensible to the wide difference between that homicide which has no incentive but wickedness of heart, and that which is in retaliation only of grievous and alarming injuries suffered upon the spot, and has thus the double excuse of bodily smart, and perturbation of spirits.

'Tis true, it may be argued, that in one point of view, there is more need of severity in the case of sudden than of wilful and malicious homicide; on account of the greater frequency of the inferior offence. But no more on this than on other occasions, can we, in judging of human conduct, put the feelings of human nature out of question on views of policy; or forget what the degree of perfection is, to which our constitution permits us to aspire. It is, indeed, a right and a necessary course, to keep the allowance for the frailties of our condition within as narrow bounds as may be; because by means of this wholesome discipline, men may improve and be corrected. But to have some consideration of those frailties, so as to punish them only in their degree as such, and not in the same rank with the foulest and most odious crimes,—this also is alike a just and a salutary rule; if the punishment is to have its due effect as an example, and the people are to be conciliated to the course of criminal justice; And here let me add, that in one point of view, those who argue for the reception of such a plea, are not, as at first it might seem, pleading purely on the side of mercy. For if the manslayer has in every case to make atonement with his life, without regard to the provocation, however high, which he has suffered; then may it be expected that juries will find a general verdict of *not guilty*, whensoever they cannot reconcile their conscience to such severity; and thus (as actually happened in Finhaven's case,) the offender shall be dismissed without even that punishment, which his intemperance deserves. Now, by acknowledging the inferior sort of homicide, the law saves indeed the manslayer's life, but still exposes him to some correction, proportioned to his fault, and maintains this great wrong in its due place in the public opinion as a crime.

All considerations issue, therefore, in one conclusion: The invader, who offered the injury, knowing as he did the resentment which it must excite, was therein guilty of a wrong; and he justly deserved to receive, upon the spot, a severe chastisement of his person. And although, on the other part, the due measure has been far exceeded, yet it were (I had almost said) no less excessive, to condemn this person to die for it; since he has not sinned out of cruelty or wickedness of heart, and is neither that object of aversion with his neighbours, nor the like irreclaimable felon, as the wilful murderer, on whom mercy would be thrown away. Punished he ought to be, that he may stand corrected, and others be taught the lesson of forbearance by the example; but it would not be right that he should seal his repentance with his blood, which in civilized times, neither the frequency of such incidents nor the public opinion will require.'

[20] I shall return to examine Hume's reasoning in more detail but, for present purposes, I simply draw attention to the wide difference which he sees 'between that homicide which has no incentive but wickedness of heart' (murder) and 'that which is in retaliation only of grievous and alarming injuries suffered upon the spot, and has thus the double excuse of bodily smart, and perturbation of spirits' (culpable homicide). Hume employs the same analysis when he says that it would be excessive to prescribe the death penalty for a person who kills under provocation 'since he has not sinned out of cruelty or wickedness of heart'. In other words, Hume sees the pain and the perturbation of spirits experienced by the person who has been assaulted as prompting his action in killing his assailant. Because of these factors, even if he intentionally kills his assailant, his state of mind is not of the same wicked character as that of a murderer. He has, of course, acted wrongly and deserves to be punished, but in a manner which reflects both his lack of wickedness and the actual degree of his wrongdoing in the circumstances. In my view, for the reasons which I have already given, in its essentials Hume's analysis remains valid for our law today: the person who kills under

provocation is to be convicted of culpable homicide rather than of murder because, even if he intentionally kills his victim, he does not have that wicked intention which is required for murder.

[21] But, of course, there is no rule that, simply because a man has been assaulted and then kills his assailant he *ipso facto* lacks the *mens rea* necessary for murder. As Bowen L.J. remarked so memorably in *Edgington v. Fitzmaurice* (1885) 29 Ch. D. 459 at p. 483, 'the state of a man's mind is as much a fact as the state of his digestion.' So, the state of the mind of the accused at the moment when he kills his assailant is a fact. This has always been recognised in the context of provocation. See, for example, Burnett's *Criminal Law*, pp. 17–18. So, for instance, if the accused simply takes the opportunity of the assault to kill his assailant, against whom he has previously harboured a grudge, the appropriate verdict will be one of murder, since he will in fact have had the necessary wicked intention for murder. Equally, if after the assault the accused waits until he has calmed down and then kills his assailant, that will equally be murder since, by deliberately and coldly killing his victim, he will in fact have displayed the wickedness required for murder. Indeed, where the position is sufficiently clear, a trial judge will have a duty to withdraw the issue of provocation from the jury on the view that on the evidence the accused's state of mind at the time of the killing *could not* have been materially affected by any antecedent provocative act. In the present case the trial judge left the issue for the jury to determine. Taking all the relevant evidence into account, the jury had to determine what the appellant's state of mind was at the time when he killed the deceased. More particularly, they had to decide whether the Crown had proved that at the relevant time he had a wicked intention or acted with wicked recklessness. If, because of his evidence of discovering the deceased with the other man, or for any other reason based on the evidence in the case, they had not been satisfied beyond reasonable doubt that the appellant had acted wickedly, then they would have convicted him of culpable homicide. The determination of the appellant's state of mind was as much a determination of a matter of fact as, for instance, the determination of the existence and nature of any relationship between the appellant and the deceased in September 1998.

[22] When the appeal first came before the court, senior counsel who then appeared in effect argued that, in any case where provocation is successfully advanced, the accused has lost all control of his actions. For that reason, he said, it was wrong in principle and indeed really nonsensical, to inquire further into the accused's state of mind. In advancing this argument counsel referred, of course, to the oft-quoted passage from Macdonald's *Criminal Law*, p. 94. 'The defence of provocation is of this sort—"Being agitated and excited, and alarmed by violence, I lost control over myself, and took life when my presence of mind had left me, and without thought of what I was doing."'

[23] In particular, since the accused had *ex hypothesi* completely lost control over himself, his actions were those of someone who had no control. Since he had no control of his actings, he could not keep them within any particular bounds. It was therefore wrong to say that provocation was of no avail if the accused's act of retaliation was disproportionate to the provocation offered to him. The trial judge had misdirected the jury in this respect.

In my view that particular argument against the introduction of a concept of proportionality falls to be rejected as being inconsistent with the approach which our law takes to provocation. It really amounts to saying that a person who has been provoked has no control whatever—is in effect in a state of frenzy or temporary insanity. But if that were indeed how our law understood the situation, then provocation should lead to acquittal on the ground of temporary insanity. Needless to say, provocation has never been understood to have this effect. On the contrary, in the passage which I have quoted from Hume in paragraph 19, he proceeds on the basis that, unlike the animals, men have the capacity to restrain their acting within due bounds. It could therefore not well be maintained, he says, that homicide under the influence of provocation was to be judged as a pure involuntary act (Vol. 1, p. 239). So, if a man overreacts to an assault, this is a criminal excess which requires punishment for a great wrong and high crime. One purpose of punishing such acts is to deter others by encouraging them to correct and control their sudden passions. While the law recognises that human nature is frail and men may in fact fail to master their passions, in principle they should—and their failure to do so is blameworthy. Hume's doctrine is inconsistent with any suggestion that men acting under provocation are in effect in a state of frenzy where their reason cannot operate.

[24] Essentially the same argument was addressed to the Privy Council in *Phillips v. The Queen* [1969] 2 A.C. 130, an appeal from Jamaica. Giving their Lordships' advice and under reference to Section 3c of the Offences against the Person (Amendment) Law (Jamaica), No. 43 of 1958, Lord Diplock said this (at pp. 137G–138B):

> 'Before their Lordships, counsel for the appellant contended, not as a matter of construction but as one of logic, that once a reasonable man had lost his self-control his actions ceased to be those of a reasonable man and that accordingly he was no longer fully responsible in law for them whatever he did. This argument is based on the premise that loss of self-control is not a matter of degree but is absolute; there is no intermediate stage between icy detachment and going berserk. This premise, unless the argument is purely semantic, must be based upon human experience and is, in their Lordships' view, false. The average man reacts to provocation according to its degree with angry words, with a blow of the hand, possibly if the provocation is gross and there is a dangerous weapon to hand, with that weapon.'

For the reasons discussed by their Lordships in *R. v. Smith (Morgan)* [2000] 3 W.L.R. 654, in this context it may be preferable to think in terms of the ordinary man or woman rather than of the reasonable man. In particular, it requires a considerable effort of the imagination to envisage a reasonable man actually killing someone in circumstances where the law provides that he ought not to do so. See, for instance, the remarks of Lord Hoffmann ([2000] 3 W.L.R. at p. 677 H). In Scots law, unlike English law, there is no statutory wording to hinder us from framing any test in terms of the ordinary man or woman, if we think it appropriate. But, subject to that minor qualification of Lord Diplock's reasoning. Mr. Prais accepted that he had been correct to reject the argument that there is no intermediate stage between icy detachment and going berserk. I agree with Mr. Prais. Moreover, the views of their Lordships in the Privy Council, based on their view of human experience, are similar to those of Hume and reflect the approach which our law has always adopted to these matters. The passage in Macdonald's *Criminal Law*, p. 94 falls to be interpreted accordingly.

[25] In matters of homicide Scots law admits the plea of provocation only within certain bounds which are considerably narrower than those within which it operates in English law. In Scots law it applies only where the accused has been assaulted and there has been substantial provocation. In English law, by contrast, even a slight blow or mere jostling may be sufficient to admit the plea. In Scots law, no mere verbal provocation can palliate killing. The same applied in England until the law was changed by Section 3 of the Homicide Act 1957. The difference in scope of the doctrine of provocation in the two systems does not arise, it should be stressed, because Hume and the Scottish judges are unaware that people may react violently to minor physical provocations or to insults. Rather, as a matter of policy, the law has taken the view that in such cases the person assaulted or the person insulted should be expected to control himself, at least to the extent of not killing his tormentor. To this policy Scots law admits only one exception: the law recognises that when an accused discovers that his or her partner, who owes a duty of sexual fidelity, has been unfaithful, the accused may be swept with sudden and overwhelming indignation—which may lead to a violent reaction resulting in death. In such cases the law provides that, where the jury are satisfied that this is in fact what happened, they should return a verdict of culpable homicide on the ground that, because of the effect of the provocation. The accused did not act with the wicked state of mind required for murder. ..."

[26] In Hume's time the plea of provocation applied only where the accused had actually

discovered his wife and the other party in the act of committing adultery. But in *Hill*, the plea was admitted when his wife and her paramour had told the accused of their adultery. More recently, of course, the scope of the plea has been extended to relationships where fidelity can be expected, even though the parties are not married. Nevertheless, this type of case remains an exception to the general rule that provocation arises only where the deceased assaulted the accused in a substantial fashion. Hume quite expressly treated it as an exception, one which was indeed already well established and which might have been recognised as early as 1510. See Vol. 1, p. 245 n. 3. Describing the case of James Christie who was tried in the High Court in 1731, he says (Vol. 1, pp. 245–246):

> 'This man had stabbed with a sword; but excused the deed on this ground, that he had found the deceased in the act of adultery with his wife, and sacrificed him to his resentment on the spot. This defence, the Court justly found relevant to restrict the libel to an arbitrary pain, yet, as reasonable as this judgment is, what other view can be taken of such a case, than as a case of homicide on high provocation? And though the provocation is high, yet is it in some respects not so favourable as that of some other injuries; because the homicide is here done on the principle of rage and revenge, unaccompanied with that fear of further violence, or that trepidation and alarm, which in the ordinary case of an assault on the body of the killer, concur with his resentment, and materially strengthen his defence.'

Similarly, a few pages further on, when he is contrasting the English and Scottish law, Hume says (Vol. 1, p. 248):

> 'In short, it is to be understood, that it is no excuse in our law, that the pannel is in rage and heat of blood, though excited by some rude or contemptuous freedom taken with his person: This passion must be occasioned by some adequate and serious cause, some severe and continued assault, such as is attended with trepidation and a dread of further harm, as well as with present smart and pain of body, so that the sufferer is excusable for the loss of his presence of mind, and exceeds of the just measure of retaliation. Excepting the peculiar case of a husband killing the adulterer caught in the fact, there seems to be no instance of culpable homicide in our record, which is not less or more of this description; not a case of passion only, but of passion excited by bodily suffering and mingled with terror, and perturbation of spirits.'

The law, he says, should aim to curb and repress a jealous, choleric or quarrelsome humour, so far as this can be done without injustice in any particular case, and Scots law best achieves this

> 'when it has consideration of human infirmity in those difficult and agitating situations, which require a more than ordinary strength of mind, and command of temper to withstand them; not in those, where the pride more than the person of the man has been offended' (Vol. 1, p. 149).

[27] These passages suggest that Hume recognised that provocation stemming from the discovery of adultery differed from other cases of provocation because the provocation arose only from rage and a desire for revenge, whereas in other cases these sentiments were reinforced by a fear of further violence and by the trepidation and alarm to which the assault had given rise. Even though these other aspects were not present, in this one case the law was prepared to make allowance simply for the rage and desire for revenge which swept over the killer. In *Smith (Morgan)* ([2000] 3 W.L.R. at p. 674 F–G) Lord Hoffmann suggests that, in certain circumstances at least, 'male possessiveness and jealousy should not today be an acceptable reason for loss of self-control leading to homicide.' But whatever the policy

arguments may be one way or the other, they must be for consideration by the legislature and they are not a matter for us to address in this case. Rather, what we have to decide is whether, in the (exceptional) case of provocation stemming from the discovery of sexual infidelity, and the trial judge was correct to direct the jury that they had to consider whether the degree of violence used by the accused was, or was not, grossly disproportionate to the provocation and that, if it was, the plea of provocation could not succeed.

[28] In my view the trial judge was wrong to give that direction. It invites the jury to measure, albeit not with too fine a scale, the degree of violence used by the appellant against the provocation offered by the supposed sexual activity of the deceased and the other man. The Advocate Depute argued that a jury could readily do this by taking account of all the circumstances, including the nature of any subsisting relationship between the appellant and the deceased. But, when pressed, 'he was—inevitably—unable to explain how the jury could do this since the sexual activity and the appellant's attack on the deceased are actually incommensurable. This is recognised, for instance, by *Russell on Crime* (twelfth edition by J.W.C. Turner) vol. 1, p. 549 and by Gordon, *Criminal Law*, p. 775 n. 69. Not surprisingly either, the diligence of counsel on both sides of the bar was unable to discover any case in which this court had laid down that the degree of violence was to be measured against the circumstances of the sexual activity giving rise to it so as to determine whether the violence was proportionate to the sexual activity. Lord Patrick gave the jury no such direction in *Hill*. Similarly, in *H.M. Advocate v. Callander*, 1958 S.L.T. 24, Lord Guthrie simply directed the jury that they would be entitled to form the opinion that the husband assaulted his wife and the other lady, if they were satisfied 'that the husband's actions were influenced by the discovery of his wife under circumstances which indicated that she was pursuing her course of Lesbianism with Mrs O'Neill.' He made no mention of the proportionality of the husband's response. I therefore reject the Advocate Depute's argument as both misconceived and unworkable.

[29] So tenaciously did the Advocate Depute cling to his test of proportionality that it seemed as if he believed that, without it, any killing, whatever its nature, would fall to be treated as culpable homicide, provided only that it occurred in the immediate aftermath of the provocation. Certainly, he offered no other yardstick by which the matter might be judged. Mr Prais, on the other hand, while arguing that the test of proportionality should be rejected, insisted that abandoning this test would not have such a drastic effect. Rather, the accused's act in killing the deceased would fall to be treated as culpable homicide only if the ordinary man (or woman, as the case might be) would have been liable to act in the same way in the same circumstances. Since in the present case it is not said that the appellant had any special characteristics which would have affected the way in which he acted, I do not need to consider how such a test is to be applied in the case of an accused who comes, for instance, from a particular minority ethnic background or who suffers from a particular physical handicap or defect in personality which might have affected his reaction. In other systems, where matters are regulated by statute, these questions have been hotly debated and they have recently divided the Privy Council, the New Zealand Court of Appeal and the House of Lords. I therefore prefer to express no view on the point, unless and until it arises for decision. In the meantime I simply refer to the discussions in *Luc Thiet Thuan v. The Queen* [1997] A.C. 131, *R. v. Rongonui* [2000] 2 N.Z.L.R. 385 and *R. v. Smith (Morgan)*.

[30] I am satisfied that the approach outlined by Mr. Prais is not only workable but is also consistent with our law as a whole.

[31] Hume's account of the operation of provocation depends on seeing it as an allowance which the law makes for ordinary human frailty. It would be better if every man could exercise the self-command to be expected of him 'according to the degree attainable in his way of education and course of life', but experience shows that in certain circumstances human beings are liable to give way and to over-react. The situations are such that they 'require a more than ordinary strength of mind and command of temper to withstand them' (emphasis added). In Hume's scheme, of course, people kill in circumstances where they would have

been justified in taking some lesser step to punish the assailant by inflicting blows upon him. Their fault lies in going further than the law permits. On the approach which the law is said to adopt today, we see no room for this measure of self-help in punishing assaults or adultery. In the case of an assault we would expect the ordinary man to defend himself, if necessary, and to summon the police, but to go no further, while a man or woman who finds that his or her partner has been unfaithful should, at most, take whatever—steps the civil law may provide to deal with the situation.

[32] But even though the *mores* of society may have altered in this way and, with them, the expectations of how the reasonable man or woman should deal with such situations, the fact remains that ordinary men and women will continue to fall short of the ideal. In particular, in some cases, when provoked, they may resort to violence and kill their assailant or their unfaithful partner. The law does not condone this. But, for essentially the same reasons of policy as Hume put forward almost two hundred years ago, the law acknowledges that, even with the best will in the world, ordinary men and women will not always be able to adhere to the ideal path which it prescribes. So, when an accused over-reacts in the way that ordinary men and women may tend to over-react, the law recognises that the accused is weak rather than wicked. It is because he reacts in a way in which other ordinary individuals would also be liable to react that Hume realises that juries would not be prepared to convict him of murder. It is also for this reason that he is not 'that object of aversion with his neighbours ... as the wilful murderer.' He is therefore to be treated not as a murderer but as a killer whose fault and crime are less serious, though still grave. But that approach, which is based on 'the feelings of human nature' and the recognition of the frailties of ordinary men and women, must equally mean that, if the killer reacts in a more extreme manner than the ordinary man or woman, he is not entitled to that strictly limited allowance which the law makes for the human frailty of ordinary men and women. Where, therefore, the accused has reacted to provocation in a way in which no ordinary man or woman would have been liable to react, a jury can rightly conclude that he acted with that wickedness which justifies a conviction for murder.

[33] This was also the effect of the final direction on provocation which Lord Justice General Cooper gave to the jury in *H.M. Advocate v. Smith*, Glasgow High Court, 27 February 1952, unreported. Smith was convicted of murder and appealed unsuccessfully, the appeal being reported on another point (1952 J.C. 66). The Appeal Court did not comment on this aspect of the Lord Justice General's direction on provocation. Since the passage in the charge has some bearing on another issue which I mention in paragraph 35 below, I quote it in full. Lord Cooper suggested to the jury that they might find some element of provocation in certain parts of the evidence and continued:

'Now, on that, I have to tell you this, that factor —although neither counsel has alluded to it, but I feel it my duty to do it—that factor, if it arises, arises in answer to a charge of stabbing a man to death, and I have got to tell you that in law it takes a tremendous amount of provocation to palliate stabbing a man to death. Words, however abusive or insulting, are of no avail. A blow with the fist is no justification for the use of a lethal weapon. Provocation, in short, must bear a reasonable relation to the resentment which it excites, and you would have to consider from that point of view whether there was anything in the evidence sufficient to raise in your minds even a reasonable doubt as to whether there was in this case provocation of such a kind as I have endeavoured to indicate. Remember the provocation that you would have to discover is not the provocation which might produce consequences in a pugnacious and an excitable man under the influence of a good many drinks; it has got to be such provocation as would induce an ordinary, reasonable man to act as this man did, and, unless you can find in the evidence as a whole sufficient to raise a reasonable doubt in your minds as to whether such provocation exists, you would not be justified in taking it into consideration as a means of reducing the offence from murder to culpable homicide.'

I have already indicated that, in my view, the invocation of the concept of the reasonable man is not helpful in this context, but in substance Lord Cooper was telling the jury that, to be legally relevant, the provocation would have had to be such as to induce an ordinary man to act in the way in which the accused acted. To put the same point in another way, the jury could conclude that, in stabbing the deceased, the accused had acted with the wickedness of a murderer if they considered that an ordinary man would not have reacted to the provocation in the same way.

[34] If there is evidence of a relationship entitling the accused to expect sexual fidelity on the part of the deceased, the jury should be directed to consider two matters. First, they should consider whether, at the time when he killed the deceased, the accused had in fact lost his self-control as a result of the preceding provocation. If they conclude that he had not lost his self-control, then the plea of provocation must fail and the jury will have to consider, on the basis of all the rest of the evidence, whether the appropriate verdict is one of murder or culpable homicide. If, on the other hand, the jury come to the conclusion that he had indeed lost his self-control due to the provocation, then they should ask themselves whether an ordinary man, having been thus provoked, would have been liable to react as he did. The nature and degree of the violence perpetrated by the accused will, of course, be relevant to the jury's consideration of that issue. If they conclude that the accused's reaction was more extreme than was to be expected of the ordinary man, then again the plea of provocation will fail and the jury will have to consider, on the basis of all the rest of the evidence, whether the appropriate verdict is one of murder or culpable homicide. If, however, they conclude that the accused reacted in the way in which an ordinary man would have been liable to react in the same circumstances, or the evidence on provocation leaves them in reasonable doubt as to whether he acted wickedly, the jury will return a verdict of culpable homicide.

[35] For the sake of completeness, I should add that in the course of the hearing we were referred to a number of cases of provocation by assault where this court has indicated that, for a plea of provocation to succeed, the accused's reaction in killing the deceased must not have been grossly disproportionate to the provocation. In the passage in his charge in *Smith* quoted above, Lord Cooper told the jury that 'Provocation, in short, must bear a reasonable relation to the resentment which it excites.' In *Lennon v. H.M. Advocate* 1991 S.C.C.R. 611 at p. 614F Lord Justice General Hope said that 'cruel excess, or a gross disproportion between the provocation offered and the retaliation by the accused, will bar the plea because in that situation it can be of no effect.' A somewhat similar approach was followed in a number of subsequent authorities which were reviewed by Lord Justice Clerk Ross, giving the opinion of the court, in *Robertson v. H.M. Advocate* 1994 J.C. 245. He concluded (at p. 249G–H) that the trial judge had been correct to direct the jury that 'there had to be a reasonable or reasonably proportionate—that is, not grossly disproportionate—relationship between the acts consti-tuting the provocation and the appellant's reaction to them.' This line of cases was obviously in the trial judge's mind when he gave the directions in the present case. This bench of Five Judges was indeed convened so that we could, if need be, review those earlier cases. For the reasons which I have given, I am satisfied that the trial judge was in fact wrong to direct the jury to apply that test in the present case where the provocation did not take the form of an assault. But, precisely because the present case is distinguishable in this way, we did not in the event hear any substantial argument as to the validity of the requirement, as a matter of law, that in the case of provocation by assault the retaliation should not be grossly disproportion-ate to the assault constituting the provocation. I accordingly express no view on the point, except to notice that, even if England and New Zealand, where there is no requirement that, as a matter of law, the response should be proportionate to the provocation, the nature and degree of the accused's response are none the less aspects of the evidence to which the jury can have regard when deciding whether the accused reacted in the way in which an ordinary man would have been liable to react. I refer to *Phillips v. The Queen* [1969] 2 A.C. per Lord

Diplock at p. 138C–D; *R. v. Campbell* [1997] 1 N.Z.L.R. 16 *per* Eichelbaum C.J. at p. 26, lines 10–15; *R. v. Rongonui* [2000] 2 N.Z.L.R. *per* Elias C.J., at pp. 426 lines 24 and 427 line 9, paragraphs 136–138.

[36] For the foregoing reasons I am satisfied that the trial judge was wrong to direct the jury in this case that the plea of provocation could succeed only if the degree of violence used by the accused was not grossly disproportionate to the provocation to which he had been subject. The misdirection was material and I have reached the conclusion that there has been a miscarriage of justice, even though the jury must have been satisfied that the appellant acted with the wickedness of a murderer. The judge's directions may have led them to leave the evidence of provocation out of account in reaching that conclusion in circumstances where that evidence would have been relevant. I would therefore invite your Lordships to allow the appeal, set aside the verdict of the trial court, quash the conviction and grant the Crown authority to bring a new prosecution in accordance with Section 119 of the Criminal Procedure (Scotland) Act 1995."

Appeal allowed. Authority for new prosecution
granted.

### Thomson v. H.M. Advocate
1986 S.L.T. 281

LORD JUSTICE-CLERK (ROSS): "The appellant went to trial on an indictment libelling that he **10.41** murdered a former business associate. The charge was that the appellant had assaulted the deceased by repeatedly stabbing him on the legs, arms and body with a knife or similar instrument, and that he had murdered him.

It was not disputed that the appellant had stabbed the deceased, but in the course of his submissions to the jury, counsel for the appellant submitted that there was evidence, if accepted, which would entitle the jury to find the appellant guilty of culpable homicide instead of murder because of provocation. The trial judge took the view that the circumstances of the case as disclosed in the evidence would not entitle the jury to reduce the offence from murder to culpable homicide on the grounds of provocation, and he directed the jury that it was not open to them to reduce what would otherwise be a verdict of guilty of murder to one of culpable homicide because of provocation. The jury then convicted the appellant of murder. He has now appealed against conviction on the ground of alleged misdirection by the trial judge. The grounds of appeal are in the following terms: 'The learned judge withdrew from the consideration of the jury the question of provocation which would have entitled them, if they so found in fact, to bring in a verdict of guilty of culpable homicide; in so doing the learned judge misdirected the jury in law.'

In support of the appeal, counsel for the appellant drew attention to the evidence given by the appellant which, as he submitted, was the most favourable account of the circumstances, which the jury were entitled to accept. So far as the facts were concerned, there was evidence, if the jury accepted it, to the effect that the deceased had acted dishonestly towards the appellant. The appellant was a plumber, and had entered into a business arrangement with the deceased whereby they joined forces to run a business called 'Culture Kitchens'. As counsel put it, the appellant had been defrauded by a man he trusted, he had been threatened with unjustifiable legal action, and in order to get peace he had signed away his business to the deceased on the basis that he himself would retain certain materials and equipment so as to resume business again on his own account. Subsequently he received a telephone call from a third party suggesting that all was not well as regards this agreement; the next morning he went to the premises of Culture Kitchens to obtain recovery of his materials, and the deceased told him he was reneging on the arrangement and that the appellant was to get nothing. He thus felt that he was facing financial ruin due to the conduct of the deceased he remonstrated with the deceased who laughed at him; the appellant then got up to leave and the deceased physically restrained him. This physical restraint, which constituted in law an assault, was what counsel described as the proverbial last straw which broke the camel's back. The appellant, when he got up to leave, had picked up some books which he had brought from home; he then dropped them. Among the books was a knife which he had brought with him from home. He stated in evidence that he had taken the knife for his own protection 'in case it was needed and if it was needed to threaten anybody or any person who might stop me from getting in to get my materials'. At that stage he stabbed the deceased, and the evidence was that the deceased suffered eleven stab wounds.

The question raised in this appeal is whether the judge was well-founded in directing the jury that it was not open to them to reduce what would otherwise be a verdict of guilty of murder to one of culpable homicide because of provocation. ...

Even allowing for the fact that the law on provocation has been developing, there is no doubt that a number of the cases reported on this issue are difficult to reconcile with the statements of Hume, Alison and Macdonald. These cases include, *inter alia, H.M. Advocate v. McGuinness*, 1937 J.C. 37, *Crawford v. H.M. Advocate*, 1950 J.C. 67; *Berry v. H.M. Advocate* (1976) S.C.C.R. Supp. 156; *H.M. Advocate v. Greig, unreported* [*post*, p. 423], and *Stobbs v. H.M. Advocate*, 1983, S.C.C.R. 190. However, it is not necessary in this appeal to reach any concluded opinion upon the soundness of the views expressed by the trial judges in these cases in relation to the facts which obtained in each particular case. Nor is it necessary or desirable to attempt to define comprehensively all the circumstances in which a plea of provocation may prevail to the effect of reducing murder to culpable homicide. All that requires to be considered is whether the facts of the present case were sufficient to entitle the jury to consider provocation.

On that issue I am in no doubt. Whether looked at individually or together, I am clearly of opinion that the evidence of the business dealings and of the minor assault were not sufficient to entitle the jury to consider provocation. The history of the business dealings was not sufficiently immediate to support provocation; the appellant had been aware of the situation for some days; there had been a heated meeting on the Monday, but he had gone home and spent the night there; a further meeting which preceded the assault took place on Tuesday. His evidence was that he arrived for the meeting on Tuesday 'pretty relaxed'; 'I thought everything was "okay"; 'everything seemed normal'. That evidence suggests that the prior business dealings were no longer affecting the appellant's self-control. In any event, if knowledge of these business dealings was still affecting him, since he was acting under the influence of what he had known for several days, that would not amount to provocation (*H.M. Advocate v. Callander*, 1958 S.L.T. 24). Indeed, far from supporting a plea of provocation, the evidence of the breakdown in the business relations, and the appellant's belief that he was being cheated, would provide a clear motive for murder. In all the reported cases, where provocation has been allowed to be considered by the jury, there has been some element of immediate retaliation to provocative acts. In the present case, that element is absent.

So far as the minor assault is concerned, the highest that can be said is that the deceased pulled the appellant as he was about to leave. A minor assault of that kind, whether or not one also takes into account the history of the business dealings, is clearly insufficient to found a plea of provocation which would palliate the taking of the deceased's life by stabbing. Where the victim has used force, there must be some relation between that force and the violence of the retaliation. In *H.M. Advocate v. Smith* (unreported on this point but referred to in Gordon, *supra*, p. 772), the Lord Justice-General told the jury: 'It takes a tremendous amount of provocation to palliate stabbing a man to death. Words, however abusive or insulting are of no avail. A blow with the fist is no justification for the use of a lethal weapon. Provocation, in short, must bear a reasonable retaliation to the resentment which it excites.' It is significant that no stage in his evidence did the appellant suggest that he was provoked into doing what he did. He said that he snapped, but that is all. He also indicated that there was no question of an argument preceding the fatal assault. In his evidence he stated, 'We never argued and when I went to leave the place John just pulled me back in again. I don't remember if we were talking or shouting or anything like that, while it was going on.'

In my opinion, even taking the evidence at its highest for the appellant, it falls far short of satisfying the test of provocation contained in the passage from Macdonald quoted above.

Accordingly, although in some cases it may well not be easy to draw the line between what will be sufficient for provocation and what will not be sufficient, I am clearly of opinion that the evidence relied on in the present case falls short of what is required to support a plea of provocation. In my opinion, the trial judge was well-founded in the directions which he gave to the jury, and I accordingly propose to your Lordships that this appeal should be refused."

Appeal refused.

NOTES

1. *The basis and legal effect of provocation*: A person who kills under provocation cannot be convicted **10.42** of murder but only of culpable homicide. (The argument that a person who killed while acting under provocation might be found guilty only of assault was authoritatively rejected in *McDermott v. H.M. Advocate*, 1974 S.L.T. 206.)

Why should a person who kills under provocation be acquitted of murder? There are two possible explanations. The first is that, as a concession to "human infirmity" (see Hume, i, 249) a person who acts under provocation is allowed a partial excuse for what would otherwise be murder. According to this view, provocation excuses notwithstanding the fact that the accused has intended to kill. That, indeed, is clear from a number of the early authorities from which the modern doctrine is derived in which it was clear that the accused had acted with a "mortal purpose". (See, for example, *Richard Firmin and Allan Macfarlane*, 1788, Hume, i 246, and other cases there discussed.) Modern practice for long regarded provocation as reducing murder to culpable homicide, and language to that effect can be found in many reported cases. (See, for examples, *McDermott v. H.M. Advocate, supra*; *Thomson v. H.M. Advocate, ante*; *Stobbs v. H.M. Advocate*, 1983 S.C.C.R. 190, *per* Lord Cowie at p. 199; *Graham v. H.M. Advocate*, 1987 S.C.C.R. 20, *per* Lord Cullen at p. 22.)

The alternative explanation is that provocation operates by removing the "murderous intent" required for conviction for that crime. This is suggested as the basis of the doctrine by Macdonald's who states (at p. 94): "The defence of provocation is of this sort—'Being agitated and excited, and alarmed by violence, I lost control over myself, and took life, when my presence of mind had left me, and without thought of what I was doing.'" (*cf.* Lord Mayfield's charge to the jury in *Fenning v. H.M. Advocate*, 1985 S.C.C.R. 219 at p. 220.)

*Drury* confirms that provocation operates by excluding the *mens rea* for murder, although not in quite the same way as suggested by Macdonald. The latter suggests that the provoked person is not guilty of murder because he or she did not intend to kill (although this does not explain why a provoked person could not be said to act with wicked recklessness). *Drury* accepts that the provoked accused is entitled to a verdict of culpable homicide notwithstanding an intention to kill (or wicked recklessness) because murder requires a wicked intent (or wicked recklessness) and provocation excludes the element of wickedness.

2. *The provocation offered*: Both *Thompson* and *Drury* confirm that, with the exception of sexual infidelity, only physical violence can provide a foundation for the plea of provocation. This is in line with the older authorities. See, in particular, Hume, i, 248 *et seq*. The limitation of provocative conduct to acts of violence is intended to ensure that provocation is not too readily admitted as an excuse for the taking of human life. It cannot be avoided, however, that there are bound to be circumstances in which abuse and taunts are at least as provocative as a physical assault, and, for some, more provocative.

In *Cosgrove v. H.M. Advocate*, 1991 S.L.T. 25 the appellant was convicted of murdering another man. The appellant gave evidence that he had fought with the victim, and that immediately before the fight the deceased, had admitted to him that he had sexually interfered with a girl, and that in doing so he had shown no remorse, but had "smirked". In directing the jury the judge told them that "words of abuse or insults, or such things as smirking are not enough" to constitute provocation. This direction was given substantially in the context of telling the jury that there must be a reasonable relationship between the provocation and the retaliation. In dismissing the appeal, the appeal court held that the judge had been correct to state the law as he did, which was substantially in terms of Macdonald's statement of the law.

But suppose, for example, that in such a case the deceased were to admit to the accused that he had sexually abused the accused's child. Faced with this sudden revelation the accused loses self-control and kills the deceased. No matter how painful or provocative such a statement might be, the accused would not be entitled to rely upon it as providing a foundation for the plea of provocation.

Despite the clarity of the rule, it appears that on occasions the courts have allowed juries to consider provocation based on words alone. In *Berry v. H.M. Advocate*, 1976 S.C.C.R. Supp. 156 the appellant was convicted of the murder of a woman. He gave evidence that the deceased had taunted him when he had tried unsuccessfully to have intercourse with her, and that he had retaliated by striking her on the head with a brick. Lord Keith left the plea of provocation to the jury, asking them to consider whether these taunts were, in their opinion sufficient provocation for what the accused had done. The appeal court expressed "grave doubts" as to whether it had been correct to leave provocation to the jury on this basis. On the other hand, in *Stobbs v. H.M. Advocate*, 1983 S.C.C.R. 190 no objection was raised to the suggestion that a threat by a young girl addressed to a man to tell the latter's wife that the parties had had sexual intercourse might amount to provocation.

In light of the opinions in *Thomson* and *Drury v. H.M. Advocate* it must be accepted that these cases are incorrect to the extent that they depart from the rule that provocation by words alone is irrelevant in relation to murder.

Section 3 of the Homicide Act 1957, which does not apply to Scotland, provides that in English law provocation may be constituted by things said, or things done, or both together. It appears that this provision was not applied to Scotland because of erroneous advice given to the Royal Commission on Capital Punishment and to Parliament by the then Lord Advocate. See Gordon, paras 25–26 *et seq*.

3. *The effect of provocation on the accused*: The provocation offered must have had the effect of causing the accused to lose self-control. See in this connection the case of *Low v. H.M. Advocate*, 1994 S.L.T. 277. In that case the appellant was convicted of murder. He appealed on the ground that the trial judge had misdirected the jury by withdrawing the plea of provocation from their consideration. The evidence showed that the deceased had died of multiple stab wounds, some of which had been inflicted after death. At the trial the appellant claimed that the deceased had come at him with a knife, and then made sexual overtures to him. He claimed that a struggle had ensued, during the course of which the deceased might have been stabbed. The trial judge withdrew the defence of provocation on the ground that there was no reasonable relationship between the provocation offered and the retaliation of the accused. In dismissing the appeal, the appeal court, while agreeing that the violence used by the accused was "out of all proportion to the violence which the deceased was alleged to have used", stated: "In our judgment when regard is had to the evidence given by the first appellant there is nothing to suggest that there was any loss of control on his part. On the contrary, what his evidence appears to have been was that the stabbing of the deceased was accidental. The evidence of the appellant does not fit the description of provocation given by Macdonald, and for that reason we are satisfied that the trial judge was entirely correct in directing the jury as he did." (1994 S.L.T. 277, *per* the Lord Justice-Clerk (Ross) at pp. 285–286.)

4. *The effect of the provocation on the "ordinary person"*: *Drury* makes it clear that it is not enough that the accused was provoked so as to lose his or her self-control. The jury must also ask themselves whether an ordinary person, having been provoked in the way that the accused was provoked, would have been liable to react as he or she did. If the jury conclude that the accused's reaction was more extreme than was to be expected of the ordinary man, then the plea of provocation fails. (However, the jury will still have to consider whether, on the basis of all the rest of the evidence, the appropriate verdict is one of murder or culpable homicide.)

An important question which is raised in *Drury*, but left open for future consideration, is whether the "ordinary person" is a wholly objective creation, or whether that person should be imbued with the "characteristics" of the accused (and if so, what "characteristics" would be relevant). The problem is perhaps less pressing in Scots law since provocation is confined to acts of violence, although it has caused considerable difficulty in English law where provocation may consist in words as well as acts, and provocative acts are not confined to violence. (See the Homicide Act 1957, s.3.) In such circumstances, it becomes important to consider the relevance of an individual's characteristics both as regards the provocative effect of the victims conduct (see *Camplin*, [1978] A.C. 705) and the accused's capacity to control his or her behaviour in the face of provocation (see *R. v. Smith (Morgan)* [2000] 3 W.L.R. 654).

5. *The immediacy of the retaliation*: The retaliation must be immediate. This restriction can be explained in two ways. The first is that after a lapse of time the accused is no longer acting in the heat of passion, so that the pre-condition for the defence—loss of self-control by the accused—is no longer present. Alternatively, it is a rule designed to avoid revenge killings—see Hume, i, 254, Alison, i, 8. Both explanations, however, assume a certain model of human behaviour in which provocative behaviour is met with instant, violent, retaliation. This model gives no recognition to the fact that human responses to

provocation are not in this sense uniform. For some, the reaction may be instantaneous, for others there may be a smouldering resentment which eventually boils over into a violent response. Nor does this model give any recognition to those who make an unsuccessful effort to restrain themselves. The rule, as presently constructed appears to favour the accused whose immediate response to provocation is violence.

The rule appears to be applied with some flexibility in the context of sexual infidelity cases. See, in this respect, the case of *Rutherford v. H.M. Advocate*, 1998 S.L.T. 740, *infra*.

6. *The relationship between the provocation and the retaliation*: It takes a great deal of provocation, so it is said, to palliate the taking of a human life. This rule (like the reference to the reaction of the ordinary person) introduces an element of objectivity into the defence of provocation. An accused person might be genuinely provoked to lose his or her self-control by a minor assault, but if the response is to take human life, then the plea of provocation will not be available. It must be asked whether, in the light of the introduction of the "ordinary man" test what additional function this rule now serves. Is it not now open to the jury simply to conclude that although the accused was provoked, no reasonable person, offered slight provocation, would react by killing?

How this issue of the relationship between the provocation and the retaliation is expressed has varied from time to time. There is an equivalent rule in relation to self-defence which says that the plea of self-defence is excluded if the accused has acted with "cruel excess" (see *ante*, Chap. 7). The same language has from time to time been used in the context of provocation, but the preferred formulation now is that the retaliation is not "grossly disproportionate". In *Low v. H.M. Advocate*, 1994 S.L.T. 277 the appeal court explained why this formulation was to be preferred:

> "We confess to being unhappy with the use of the expression 'cruel excess' in relation to provocation. These words are, of course, often used with regard to self-defence. For many years there was confusion between self-defence and provocation, but the importance of distinguishing between them has for some time now been recognised (*Crawford v. H.M. Advocate*; *Fenning v. H.M. Advocate*). The phrase 'cruel excess' does not appear to us to be entirely appropriate for the plea of provocation. Provocation involves loss of control, and where there has been loss of control, there may well be retaliation which is at least to some extent excessive. For that reason we prefer the alternative words used by the Lord Justice-General in *Lennon v. H.M. Advocate* [1991] S.C.C.R. 611]: 'a gross disproportion'. It is well established that where a plea of provocation is taken, there must be some equivalence between the retaliation and the provocation so that the violence used by the accused is not grossly disproportionate to the evidence constituting the provocation. Accordingly, we feel that the words 'cruel excess' should be confined to cases of self-defence."

The court did, however, go on to say that "whatever language is used to describe the limitation to the plea of provocation, it must always be a question of circumstances, and a question of degree." See also *McCormack v. H.M. Advocate*, 1993 S.L.T. 1158 and *Robertson v. H.M. Advocate*, 1994 S.L.T. 1004.

The requirement of immediate retaliation when coupled with the rule that the retaliation must not be grossly disproportionate to the provocation creates particular problems in relation to the question of "cumulative provocation". This is a phrase used to describe the gradual accumulation of provocative behaviour, the individual elements of which may not be sufficient to constitute provocation, but the overall effect of which is to cause the accused eventually to lose his or her self-control, often in the face of a relatively trivial final provocative act by the deceased.

This has proved to be a problem particularly for women who have suffered prolonged, violent behaviour at the hands of their spouses and partners (although it is clearly not a problem confined to this type of case—see *Thomson* and *Parr v. H.M. Advocate*, 1991 S.L.T. 208). Such cases are difficult to accommodate within the existing law and the problems to which they give rise have not been fully considered by the appeal court. They were touched upon in the case of *H.M. Advocate v. Greig*, High Court, May 1979, unreported. In that case the accused was charged with the murder of her husband by stabbing him. The deceased was a heavy drinker, and there was a history of violence against the accused at his hands when he had been drinking. The panel had on occasions left the matrimonial home, and had only returned to the home about a week before the killing. On the evening in question the deceased had been drinking, but he had not offered any violence toward the accused, although he was "nagging" at her, and she gave evidence to the effect that she was afraid that he would become violent. When the fatal blow was struck the deceased was sitting in a chair, probably dozing. A special defence of self-defence was tabled. Lord Dunpark withdrew the defence of self-defence but allowed the jury to consider provocation. In doing so he observed:

> "The essence of provocation is that the conduct of the deceased which immediately preceded—and I emphasise 'immediately preceded' the killing was so violent or threatening as to drprive the accused momentarily of his self-control—so that in this case she lashed out without stopping to think what she was doing. If this is what happened, it would be quite wrong to find the accused either intended to kill or was so wickedly—and I emphasise the word 'wickedly—reckless that she should be found guilty of murder—because provocation, in that sense, provoked the act and deprives it of the element of that murderous intent which is of the essence of murder ...
>
> Now, there is evidence before you that the deceases was a drunkard, if you like, not an alcoholic but a drunkard in the general sense, that he was a bully, that he assaulted his wife from time to time and that he made her life a misery. But, hundreds, indeed thousands of wives in this country, unfortunately, suffer this fate. The remedy of divorce or judicial separation or factual separation is available to end this torment. But, if, one day the worm turns, if I may use that phrase, not under the immediate threat of violence but by taking a solemn decision to end her purgatory by killing her husband, and by doing that very thing, is she not to be found guilty of murder?
>
> If you are satisfied beyond reasonable doubt that this is what this woman did then you would find her guilty of murder. If, on the other hand you can find some evidence, which I frankly cannot, that the accused was provoked in the sense in which I have defined it, you could return a verdict of guilty of culpable homicide; but only if you can find evidence which either satisfies you that she was so provoked or leaves you with a reasonable doubt as to whether she was so provoked, because, I repeat what I have said before, that you can only convict of murder if you are satisfied beyond reasonable doubt that the accused killed her husband with that intent which is of the essence of murder.

The jury returned a verdict of culpable homicide, and the accused was sentenced to six years' imprisonment. Given the views expressed in *Thomson*, it seems unlikely that a judge would be prepared today to leave such a case to the jury as one of provocation.

In practice, such cases are frequently dealt with by the Crown accepting a plea of guilty to culpable homicide. See, for example, the case of *Walker v. H.M. Advocate*, 1996 S.C.C.R. 818 and the cases discussed by Connelly, "Women who Kill Violent Men", 1996 J.R. 215. The approach of the Crown (and the courts) in these cases shows considerable sympathy for the position of women who kill in circumstances which do not "fit" the legal definition of provocation. But this approach means that the wisdom of the rule, which is avoided by recourse to plea-negotiation, is not properly considered. In several such cases the courts have held that the appropriate disposal is a non-custodial one. Does that not suggest that the definition of provocation itself requires some revision?

Scots law is not alone in finding these cases difficult to accommodate to traditional conceptions of provocation. See, *inter alia, Thornton*, [1992] 1 All E.R. 306; *Ahluwalia* [1992] 4 All E.R. 889 and *Ibrams and Gregory* (1981) 74 Cr.App.R. 154.

*Drury* states authoritatively that this restriction on the plea of provocation does not apply in the case of provocation by sexual infidelity. The explanation for this appears to be that there can be no reasonable relationship of proportionality between the revelation or discovery of sexual infidelity and the use of fatal violence. The court's conclusion is that since there can be no such relationship, it cannot form any part of the conditions for a successful plea of provocation in such cases. There is, however, an alternative conclusion. Since provocation requires a reasonable relationship between the provocation offered and the manner in which the accused responds, and since there can be no such relationship between sexual infidelity and the use of lethal violence, sexual infidelity should not be accepted as a form of provocation excusing murder.

7. *Sexual infidelity and provocation*: One clear exception to the rule that only violence will suffice for provocation in murder is to be found in the rule that in certain circumstances sexual infidelity may constitute provocation. This appears to be an ancient rule (Hume refers to the cases of *Robert Shanke* in 1510 and the case of *James Christie* in 1731: Hume, i, 245), and one which has been adapted and developed in modern practice.

The rule appears to have originally been based on the sudden resentment arising from finding a spouse in the act of adultery. However, in *H.M. Advocate v. Gilmour*, 1938 J.C. 1 the trial judge (Lord

Justice-Clerk Aitchison) directed the jury that they were entitled to return a verdict of culpable homicide, rather than murder, if they were satisfied "that the accused found his wife in the act of adultery, or in circumstances that reasonably conveyed to his mind that his wife had just committed adultery or was just about to commit adultery when discovered".

The rule was further relaxed in *H.M. Advocate v. Hill* 1941 J.C. 59. Here the accused, a soldier who was stationed in England, received a letter from his wife which led him to suspect that she had been unfaithful. He obtained leave and went home to Glasgow to confront his wife. When he got home he found her alone in the house, but they were soon after joined by another man, H. According to the accused, his wife and H confessed to him that they had committed adultery, and he shot them both with the service revolver which he was carrying as a part of his military equipment. The accused was charged with their murder. In his charge to the jury Lord Patrick gave the following directions on the question of provocation:

> "Now, the law ... has for several centuries recognised that, if a man catches his wife and her paramour in the act of adultery and in the heat of passionate indignation then and there kills them, his crime is a very serious one, but it is not murder, it is culpable homicide. The same is the law where the man does not actually catch his wife and the paramour in the act of adultery, but where he discovers that they have committed adultery; the discovery is exactly the same thing as if he caught them in the act. If, then, a wife and her paramour were to confess to the husband—who did not previously know that they had committed adultery—that they had committed adultery, and if he then and there killed them in the heat of passionate indignation, the crime would not be murder, it would be the serious crime of culpable homicide."

Hardly surprisingly, the jury returned a verdict of guilty of culpable homicide. What had originated as an exception based on finding a spouse in the act of adultery has been expanded to include not only circumstances which reasonably suggest that a partner has just committed adultery, or is about to do so, but confession of past adultery.

In *McDermott v. H.M. Advocate*, 1974 S.L.T. 206 the doctrine was extended to cover relationships where the parties were not married, but where there was an mutual expectation of sexual fidelity, and were further extended, in *H.M. Advocate v. McKean*, 1996 S.C.C.R. 402 to a same-sex couple.

In *McCormack v. H.M. Advocate* 1993 S.L.T. 1158 the appeal court held that where the provocation consists in an alleged confession of infidelity, there must be a "clear and unequivocal admission" of infidelity, which is accepted as such by the accused. In that case the appellant claimed that his wife had stated, repeatedly, that he was not the father of their baby daughter. The court was not prepared to accept that this could constitute provocation. These were merely "insulting remarks, uttered in the course of a violent quarrel, which at first the appellant did not take seriously and then only raised doubts in his mind. It appears that it was because he did not wish to continue to hear these allegations, and not because he actually believed them, that he then tried to silence his wife and ultimately caused her death."

The fact that information of this kind is communicated in a humiliating way, and, indeed, is intended to humiliate, will not, however, prevent them from constituting provocation if they convey information of a kind which reveals sexual infidelity: *Rutherford v. H.M. Advocate*, 1998 S.L.T. 740.

In *Rutherford v. H.M. Advocate* (above) the appellant killed the woman with whom he had been living for more than twelve years. The parties had separated, and while the appellant hoped that they might resume cohabitation the deceased appeared to have decided not to return. Two days before the killing the parties met, and the deceased told the appellant that she had had "an affair" with another man, that they had had sexual intercourse on two occasions, but that she was tiring of the relationship and was going to bring it to an end. The appellant was upset and angry at hearing this revelation. Two days later the parties met again, and the deceased told the appellant that relationship with the other man had been going on for much longer and that she had been "screwing that guy for months right under [the appellant's] nose". The appellant lost control and killed the deceased. The trial judge withdrew the plea of provocation from the jury, on the ground that at the time of the killing he was already aware of the deceased's infidelity, so that her statement immediately prior to the killing about her relationship with another man did not have the necessary element of discovery which was essential to a plea of provocation in such circumstances.

The appeal court disagreed with the trial judge. On the earlier occasion the deceased had indicated that she had only had intercourse with the other man on two occasions and that the affair was at an end. Immediately prior to her death, however, she had given a significantly different account of the relationship with the other man, that it had been much more than a passing affair and, indeed, that it was still going on. The appeal court considered that, "this fresh account of the nature and extent of the deceased's infidelity was one which could in itself have caused a reaction of sudden and overwhelming indignation which was separate from any reaction to the original account" and for that reason it could be accepted as provocation.

Whether sexual jealousy should be regarded as a sufficient reason to partially excuse the deliberate taking of human life is an interesting and difficult question, not least because, although sexual infidelity may be relied upon by both men and women, it is, in practice, a rule which tends to excuse male violence. (*cf.* Lord Nimmo Smith in *Drury*.) In *R. v. Smith (Morgan)* Lord Hoffmann questioned whether "male possessiveness and jealousy" should be regarded as "an acceptable reason for loss of self-control leading to homicide." ([2000] 3 W.L.R. 654 at 674F–G.)

Suppose that A confesses to B that (i) that he has murdered B's wife, and produce a photograph of her dead body to back this up and (ii) that he committed adultery with her just before he killed her. If B, enraged and distressed by the first confession, waits until he hears the second confession before killing A he could raise the plea of provocation. But if he reacts immediately and kills A after hearing the first confession he cannot. What arguments can be marshalled to justify this?

8. *Provocation and attempted murder*: What is the correct verdict if the accused commits attempted murder under provocation? If the only difference between murder and attempted murder is that the victim did not die (a conclusion which appears to follow from *Cawthorne v. H.M. Advocate, ante*, p. 391), then it might be expected that in a case of attempted murder, provocation might have an effect analogous to the effect it has on a charge of murder. If an accused who kills under provocation is guilty of culpable homicide, then, it should follow logically that if the victim does not die the appropriate verdict is 'attempted culpable homicide'. The courts, however, have not accepted the logic of the situation, and have held instead that the appropriate verdict is assault, or assault to severe injury, under provocation: *Brady v. H.M. Advocate*, 1986 S.C.C.R. 191; *Salmond v. H.M. Advocate*, 1992 S.L.T. 156. No authority was stated for this view in *Brady*. The only authority referred to in *Salmond* was *Brady* and the argument proposed by the Lord Justice-Clerk (Ross) in *Brady* is, with respect, hardly convincing. His Lordship states (1986) S.C.C.R. 191 at p. 200):

"Now it is well settled that the same mens rea is required for attempted murder as for murder. If the charge is murder and the accused is successful in a plea of provocation the offence is reduced to culpable homicide. There is no question of such an accused being found guilty of murder under provocation upon the view that the killing under provocation is not deliberate or the result of wicked recklessness. If that is so I am of opinion that when the charge is one of attempted murder, if the plea of provocation succeeds there could be no question of a verdict of being returned of guilty of attempted murder under provocation."

This, with respect, is undoubtedly the case. What is surprising, however, is the conclusion which his Lordship draws from these propositions (*ibid.*):

"Accordingly, although the jury were directed that they could bring in a verdict of guilty under provocation, I am of opinion that such a verdict was not competent in relation to charge (2) [the charge of attempted murder]. If the jury were satisfied that there was provocation as regards charge (2) their verdict should have been one of assault to severe injury under provocation."

Surely the more obvious conclusion to be derived from the initial stages of Lord Ross's argument would be that, by direct analogy with the law of murder, that the appropriate verdict was 'attempted culpable homicide'. What objections would there be to such a verdict? (For a possible explanation, see the Commentary to *Brady* at 1996 S.C.C.R. p. 201.)

What impact the decision in *Drury* has in this respect remains to be seen. If provocation can remove the "wickedness" required for a conviction for murder, why does it not remove the "evil intent" in assault? And if it does, then would a verdict of assault be competent?

## (b) Diminished responsibility

**10.43** It is suggested in *Drury ante*, p. 407, that diminished responsibility, like provocation, excludes the "wickedness" required for murder. The plea of diminished responsibility is based on the proposition that the accused was suffering from a mental abnormality at the time of the killing sufficiently serious to justify reducing the quality of the crime, but not serious enough to completely excuse the offender.

It first emerged in its modern form in *Alexander Dingwall* (1867) 5 Irv. 466.

### H.M. Advocate v. Alexander Dingwall
(1867) 5 Irvine 466

The accused, who was an alcoholic, killed his wife in the early hours of New Years Day **10.44** following a quarrel with the deceased, whom he suspected of having hidden his money and his whisky bottle. The accused and his wife were generally on good terms. He had consumed some whisky before the attack on his wife, but was not drunk. There was evidence of mental abnormality, but probably not enough for the jury to conclude that he was insane at the time of the offence. The circumstances of the case, however clearly generated some sympathy for the accused, and Lord Deas left open to the jury the possibility of convicting the accused of culpable homicide. In the words of the report:

"4th, There remained the question whether the offence was anything short of murder? And here his Lordship said that it was very difficult for the law to recognise it as anything else. On the other hand, however, he could not say that it was beyond the province of the jury to find a verdict of culpable homicide if they thought that was the nature of the offence. The chief circumstances for their consideration with this view were, 1st, The unpremeditated and sudden nature of the attack; 2nd, The Prisoner's habitual kindness to his wife, of which there could be no doubt, when drink did not interfere; 3rd, There was only one stab or blow, while not perhaps like what an insane man would have done, was favourable for the prisoner in other respects; 4th, The prisoner appeared not only to have been peculiar in his mental condition, but to have had his mind weakened by successive attacks of disease. It seemed highly probable that he had had a stroke of the sun in India, and that his subsequent fits were of an epileptic nature. There could be no doubt that he had had repeated attacks of *delirium tremens*, and if weakness of mind could be an element in any case in the question between murder and culpable homicide, it seemed difficult to exclude that element here. His Lordship had anxiously considered that question, and had come to the conclusion that the element was not inadmissible.

Culpable homicide in our law and practice, included what, in some countries, was called murder with extenuating circumstances. Sometimes the crime of culpable homicide approached the very verge of murder, and sometimes it was a very minor offence. The state of mind of a prisoner might, his Lordship thought, be an extenuating circumstance, although not such as to warrant an acquittal on the ground of insanity, and he could not therefore exclude it from the consideration of the jury here, along with the whole other circumstances, in making up their minds whether, if responsible to the law at all, the prisoner was to be held guilty of murder or of culpable homicide."

The jury returned a verdict of guilty of culpable homicide.

NOTES

1. Before *Dingwall*, it had been accepted that mental weakness falling short of insanity could be **10.45** regarded as a factor in mitigating punishment. In cases of murder this was achieved by relying on the accused's mental weakness to make a recommendation for mercy. (See the cases referred to in Bell's Notes to Hume (page 5), the cases of *Bonthorn*, (1763), Hume, 1, 38 and *Ainslie*, (1842) 1 Broun 25, and the discussion in Gordon, paras 11–10 — 11–12.) The significance of *Dingwall* is that it allowed the jury to change the category of the offence by returning a verdict of culpable homicide, rather than a verdict of murder, coupled with a recommendation to mercy.

2. As a plea in mitigation, as a opposed to a defence which changes the nature of the offence, mental weakness is not logically confined to murder. In *H.M. Advocate v. Cunningham*, 1963 J.C. 80 (*ante*, Chap. 7), the court held that as a defence which changes the nature of the crime, diminished responsibility is confined to murder. (See also *Brennan v. H.M. Advocate*, 1977 S.L.T. 151 (*infra*.) In

*H.M. Advocate v. Blake*, 1986 S.L.T. 661, Lord Brand directed the jury that in a case of attempted murder diminished responsibility could reduce the crime to assault, or serious assault.

3. In *Lindsay v. H.M. Advocate*, 1997 S.L.T. 67, the appeal court expressed the opinion that diminished responsibility is not a "defence" but a plea in mitigation. This opinion appears to have been based on the views expressed in Gordon, paras 11–01—11–03. In the sense that diminished responsibility mitigates what would otherwise be murder, this is true. And if there were no fixed penalty for murder it could operate in the way that any other mitigatory consideration might. But for so long as there is a fixed penalty for murder it continues to be necessary to distinguish between murder and culpable homicide, and diminished responsibility can only do that by operating as a defence to a charge of murder by reducing the offence to a lower category of crime. As noted above, it was suggested in *Drury* that diminished responsibility does that by excluding the "wickedness" required for murder. Is this consistent with *Lindsay*?

4. Although diminished responsibility as a defence to murder was generally accepted by the Scottish courts by the end of the nineteenth century, its acceptance was not universal. In *H.M. Advocate v. Higgins* (1913) 2 S.L.T. 258, however, Lord Johnston refused to recognise what he described as "mental degeneracy" as a mitigating circumstance. Although a lone voice in going so far as to reject the plea, he was not alone in seeking to confine the plea within narrow limits. This can be seen in the generally accepted definition of diminished responsibility which derives from the charge to the jury in the following case.

5. An accused who seeks to rely on diminished responsibility must establish the plea on a balance of probabilities: *Lindsay v. H.M. Advocate*, 1997 S.L.T. 67.

## H.M. Advocate v. Savage
### 1923 S.L.T. 659

**10.46** The accused was charged with murder. After the evidence had been led, it was argued on his behalf that even if he had killed the deceased, his mental condition was such that the proper verdict should be one of culpable homicide rather than murder.

THE LORD JUSTICE-CLERK (ALNESS) " ... In many murder cases you have a simple and indeed a single issue, namely, did A kill B. This, ladies and gentlemen of the jury, is not a case which can be solved along such simple lines as these. There is not one question to answer in this case but three. The first question you have to answer is—Is it proved to your satisfaction that the accused killed Jemima Grierson? That is the first question. If you are satisfied upon the evidence that he did, you will then proceed to consider the second question, which is—Has the prisoner proved to your satisfaction that he was insane at the time? But a third question remains behind these two, and it is this— Even if the prisoner has not proved that he was insane at the time, has he proved that his mental condition was such as to reduce his crime from the crime of murder—which has only one penalty, well known to you, attached to it—to the crime of culpable homicide, which varies in degree? These are the three questions which you will have to consider most carefully. [After dealing with the first and second questions, his Lordship proceeded:]

If, on the other hand, you are unable to hold it proved that he was then insane, you will pass on to the third and last question which you have to consider, and that is whether the crime of which the prisoner is guilty—if he be guilty of a crime—is reduced from that of murder to that of culpable homicide in respect of the state of his mind. You will have to say whether the state of the mind of the prisoner at the time, while not amounting to insanity, was such as to render appropriate, and indeed proper and necessary, a verdict of culpable homicide rather than of murder.

Now, that there may be such a state of mind of a person, short of actual insanity, as may reduce the quality of his act from murder to culpable homicide is, so far as I can judge from the cases cited to me, an established doctrine in the law of Scotland. It is a comparatively recent doctrine, and, as has at least twice been said from the bench to a jury, it must be applied with care. Formerly there were only two classes of prisoners—those who were completely responsible and those who were completely irresponsible. Our law has now come to recognise in murder cases a third class, the class which I have described, namely those who, while they may not merit the description of being insane, are nevertheless in such a condition as to reduce the quality of their act from murder to culpable homicide ....

It is very difficult to put it in a phrase, but it has been put in this way: that there must be aberration or weakness of mind; that there must be some form of mental unsoundness; that there must be a state of mind which is bordering on, though not amounting to, insanity; that there must be a mind so affected that responsibility is diminished from full responsibility to partial responsibility—in other words, the prisoner in question must be only partially accountable for his actions. And I think one can see running through the cases that there is implied ... that there must be some form of mental disease."

The jury returned a verdict of guilty of murder.

### Connelly v. H.M. Advocate
1991 S.L.T. 397

The accused was convicted of murder. His defence had included suggestions of self-defence **10.47** and provocation, which were apparently rejected by the jury. A defence of diminished responsibility was also advanced. Two expert witnesses testified that the accused was not suffering from any mental illness. A third (Dr Antebi) expressed the opinion that while the accused was not suffering from a mental illness, he was suffering from diminished responsibility because of an immature and inadequate personality. The trial judge withdrew the plea of diminished responsibility from the jury, who convicted the accused. On appeal against conviction:

THE LORD JUSTICE-GENERAL (HOPE): " ... The trial judge decided that he was not obliged to allow the question of diminished responsibility to go to the jury simply because the witness had applied this term to the state of mind of the appellant.

Counsel submitted on the appellant's behalf that the trial judge was wrong to take this view and that the question of diminished responsibility should have been left to the jury. He agreed that a presiding judge would be entitled to take this course if it was clear that on no construction of the evidence was there any basis in law for the jury to hold that diminished responsibility had been established. But he contended that Dr Antebi had said enough in his report and in his evidence to leave this matter open and that it should have been left to the jury to consider it. He said that dicta in the cases on this subject tended to overstate the need for some sort of mental disease or illness to be established and that it should now be affirmed that this was not necessary for there to be diminished responsibility. He asked us to re-examine the dicta of Lord Justice-Clerk Alness in *H.M. Advocate v. Savage*, at 1923 S.L.T., pp. 660–661, Lord Justice-Clerk Cooper in *H.M. Advocate v. Braithwaite*, at 1945 S.L.T., pp. 209–210, and Lord Brand in *H.M. Advocate v. Blake*, at 1986 S.L.T., p. 662. We were also referred to the opinion of Lord Justice-General Normand in *Carraher v. H.M. Advocate*. In *H.M. Advocate v. Savage* at 1923 S.L.T., p. 660 Lord Justice-Clerk Alness expressed the matter in this way: "It is very difficult to put it in a phrase, but it has been put in this way: that there must be aberration or weakness of mind; that there must be some form of mental unsoundness; that there must be a state of mind which is bordering on though not amounting to insanity; that there must be a mind so affected that responsibility is diminished from full responsibility to partial responsibility—in other words, the prisoner in question must be only partially accountable for his actions. And I think one can see running through the cases that there is implied ... that there must be some form of mental disease."

It is pointed out that the Lord Justice-Clerk had listed four criteria in order to indicate to the jury what had to be proved in order to establish that the crime which would otherwise be murder is only culpable homicide. Counsel submitted that these should be read as alternatives and not cumulatively. The last referred to "a mind so affected that the responsibility is diminished from full responsibility to partial responsibility". Dr Antebi had given an opinion to that effect, and even although he had been unable to say that the other three criteria were satisfied or to justify his opinion on psychiatric grounds that was enough to entitle the jury to return a verdict of culpable homicide in the present case.

In my opinion it is clear that Dr Antebi's evidence fell far short of what has always been required by our law in order to establish diminished responsibility. His opinion that the appellant's responsibility was diminished would have been appropriate for consideration by the jury if he had been able to justify that opinion on psychiatric grounds. He would then have been expressing an opinion as a psychiatrist on a matter within his expertise and his views would have been available for consideration upon that basis. But by his own admission he was not able to do so, precisely because he found no form of mental illness in this case. As he put it, he did not feel that the appellant's judgment or mind was so disturbed as to be able to say to himself or to the court that he was suffering from a mental illness at the time of the offence. This being so, his opinion that the appellant was nevertheless of diminished responsibility was, I think, worthless and strictly speaking it was not competent evidence of anything at all. Once he had dissociated himself from any psychiatric basis for expressing this opinion he had no proper basis whatever for expressing an opinion as a psychiatrist on the very issue which, in so far as it was a question of fact, was ultimately for the jury to decide. This is not to say that he was disabled from giving evidence about such views as he may have formed about the personality of the appellant and his immaturity or vulnerability to stress. But the conclusion, as to whether or not this could amount to diminished responsibility within the accepted meaning of that term, was one of law for the trial judge and not for him. As Lord Justice-General Normand remarked in *Carraher v. H.M. Advocate*, at 1946 S.L.T., p. 226, in not dissimilar circumstances: "The court has a duty to see that trial by judge and jury according to law is not subordinated to medical theories".

The fact that Dr Antebi's view as to what amounts to diminished responsibility seems to be at odds with the commonly accepted psychiatric definition of this expression is a good indication that this is a dispute about medical theory and not about the facts relating to the appellant's condition or state of mind. As it happens all three psychiatrists who gave evidence in this case were agreed that there was no question of any mental disorder in relation to the appellant. For these reasons I reject the suggestion which has been made in this case that the mere fact that Dr Antebi said that in his opinion the appellant's responsibility was diminished was sufficient to oblige the trial judge to leave this issue for the jury to decide.

I also reject counsel's suggestion, which was an essential part of his argument, that the concept of diminished responsibility is so out of touch with modern medical science that it should be redefined. He made much of the fact that social conditions have changed since 1923 when the case of *Savage* was before the court and that the teaching and practice of psychiatric medicine has advanced considerably since those days. For my part, however, I do not think that changes of this sort provide grounds for a difference of approach. On the whole I should have thought that a greater knowledge and understanding of the human mind has made it somewhat easier for the concept in its present form to be applied, but I would not wish to form a concluded view on this point without a much closer examination of the subject than we have been able to undertake in this case. It is sufficient to say that in my opinion it would be quite wrong, as I think counsel was suggesting, to isolate one part of Lord Justice-Clerk Alness's description in *Savage* as expressing the concept and to discard the others, or to treat his description as listing four criteria which can be regarded as alternatives so that if one only—and particularly the last—is met that is enough. This could be to place far too much emphasis on one phrase which is, as it happens, the least helpful of all those in the description because it is so obviously tautologous. The passage must be read as a whole with all its elements, and it must be read together with the remark at the end that running through all the cases one can see that there must be some form of mental disease. In my opinion it is the presence or absence of that particular characteristic, which has itself been variously described, which marks the borderline between what is acceptable and what is not. In *H.M. Advocate v. Braithwaite*, at 1945 S.L.T., p. 210, Lord Justice-Clerk Cooper said: "You will see, ladies and gentlemen, the stress that has been laid in all these formulations upon weakness of intellect, aberration of mind, mental unsoundness, partial insanity, great peculiarity of mind, and the like."

It was with that in mind that he went on to say that it will not suffice in law merely to show that an accused person has a very short temper or is unusually excitable and lacking in self-control. In my opinion the concept has been defined in terms which are sufficiently elastic or flexible to avoid the dangers of rigidity while at the same time preserving the doctrine from abuse. The question for the expert medical witness will be whether there is something in the mental condition of the accused which can properly be described as a mental disorder or a mental illness or disease. It is hard to see how the criteria for diminished responsibility could ever be met in the absence of evidence to this effect. But one thing is certain and that is that evidence of the kind given by Dr Antebi in this case will not suffice. The criminal conduct of the accused may be explained by immaturity on his part or by his vulnerability or lack of self-control when faced with stress, but these cannot in law diminish his responsibility for what he has done.

For these reasons I consider that the trial judge took the only course which was properly open to him in the circumstances in withdrawing the question of diminished responsibility from the jury. I would refuse this appeal.

Appeal refused.

NOTES

1. The description of diminished responsibility given in *Savage* is thus approved by the Appeal Court. **10.48** There must be evidence of mental illness or disease. Evidence of a condition bordering on mental disease or mental unsoundness is insufficient, even if it suggests that at the time of the offence the accused was in a very disturbed frame of mind and that his normal judgment was impaired: *Martindale v. H.M. Advocate*, 1994 S.L.T 1093.

2. To restrict diminished responsibility to cases where there is a "mental illness" has profound consequences for accused who are not mentally ill in the sense of suffering from a psychotic illness, but who are psychopathic or who display some other personality disorder. The exclusion of psychopathy from diminished responsibility was established in the following case.

### Carraher v. H.M. Advocate
1946 J.C. 108

The appellant was charged with the murder of a man by stabbing him. Evidence was led at the **10.49** trial to the effect that the appellant suffered from a psychopathic personality, and that on the day in question he had taken a considerable amount of drink. He was convicted of murder and appealed. The circumstances of the appeal are outlined by the Lord Justice-General who gave the opinion of the High Court (Full Bench).

LORD JUSTICE-GENERAL (NORMAND): "I come next to the question of diminished responsibility. The ground of appeal here is that the presiding Judge erred in his directions to the jury on the issue of diminished responsibility. The facts are that there was evidence that the appellant had that evening taken a considerable amount of drink, and that there was also evidence of opinion by medical men that he was suffering from a psychopathic personality which they said was associated with diminished responsibility. The presiding Judge's direction on diminished responsibility is as follows:— 'The accused, as I say, is perfectly sane, but our law does recognise, and it is a comparatively recent introduction into our law, that, if a man suffers from infirmity or aberration of mind or impairment of intellect to such an extent as not to be fully accountable for his actions, the result is to reduce the quality of the evidence in a case like this, which, if you think so, would be otherwise murder, to reduce it to culpable homicide.'

That is an adequate formulation of the law as it has been recognised in previous decisions. The learned Judge then goes on to describe by reference to previous decisions the essential elements in diminished responsibility. He quotes from an opinion of the Lord Justice-Clerk in *Braithwaite's* case (*H.M. Advocate v. Braithwaite*, 1945 J.C. 55). The Lord Justice-Clerk there cites with approval the following passage from the charge of Lord Justice Clerk Alness in *Savage's* case (*H.M. Advocate v. Savage*, 1923 J.C. 49): 'It is very difficult to put it in a phrase, but it has been put this way: that there must be aberration or weakness of mind; that there must be some form of mental unsoundness, that there must be a state of mind which is bordering on, although not amounting to, insanity; that there must be a mind so affected that responsibility is diminished from full responsibility to partial responsibility—in other words, the prisoner in question must be only partially accountable for his actions. And I think one can see running through the cases that there is implied that there must be some form of mental disease.' The presiding Judge in a later passage directed the jury to treat as tests of the responsibility possessed by the appellant these elements which he had taken from previous decisions. Another element was a condition of partial insanity, and yet another the existence of a condition of great mental peculiarity of mind.

He dealt with the medical evidence in this case, and he says that the evidence of one of the witnesses was to the effect that he was inclined to place the accused in the category of a psychopathic personality; that a psychopathic personality is a clinical condition in which are included persons who from childhood or early youth show all the gross abnormality in their social behaviour and emotional reaction, and who do not as a rule show enough insanity to be certifiable as insane; that, broadly speaking, it is a condition in which there is an inability on the part of the person affected to adapt himself to the ordinary social conditions, that it is usually less than certifiable insanity, and that it is associated with emotional instability. The charge also reminds the jury of this passage in the evidence of the same witness:— 'If you asked me does the accused know the difference between right and wrong intellectually, does he know if he commits a wrong act he is liable to punishment, I say yes, and then he is responsible, but if responsibility means that he has a proper appreciation of his social responsibility, that he is capable of resisting temptation, capable of exercising control over his actions, then, in my opinion, he is not as responsible as a normal person.'

The presiding Judge, after a direction dealing with the question of drink, comes back again to the question of diminished responsibility, and he says:— 'On the remaining elements which the doctors described as amounting to diminished responsibility they referred to various peculiarities which they said they found in the accused, or at least suspected, that he did not seem to appreciate the consequences of the charge hanging over him, that he had difficulty in resisting temptation, that he could not withstand frustration, and the description, you may remember, was such that it led me to ask whether there were not a great many people in this country who do not act just as good citizens, and whether he would include these in the category of psychopathic personality, and he said "Yes".' The learned Judge felt, as he says, difficulty about remitting this evidence for consideration to the jury as a ground for reducing the charge from one of murder to one of culpable homicide. I also have great doubt whether it was evidence of anything approaching to mental disease, aberration or great peculiarity of mind, and whether the Judge might not have been warranted in withdrawing the issue from the jury. The Court has a duty to see that trial by judge and jury according to law is not subordinated to medical theories; and in this instance much of the evidence given by the medical witnesses is, to my mind, descriptive rather of a typical criminal than of a person of the quality of one whom the law has hitherto regarded as being possessed of diminished responsibility."

Appeal refused.

Notes

**10.50**     Although a strict reading of *Carraher* suggests that the Courts might at one time have been prepared to include some instances of psychopathy within diminished responsibility (and see, in this respect, *H.M.*

*Advocate v. Cordon* (1967) 31 J.C.L. 270), the emphasis on mental illness in recent cases makes it clear that personality disorders, unless accompanied by mental illness, will not amount to diminished responsibility. See, in this respect, *Williamson v. H.M. Advocate*, 1994 S.L.T. 1000.

NOTES

See also Lord Hamilton's charge to the jury in *Lindsay v. H.M. Advocate*, 1997 S.L.T. 67.

### H.M. Advocate v. Macleod
1956 S.L.T. 24

The panel was charged with the murder of his wife. It was contended on his behalf, *inter alia*, **10.51** that at the time of the killing he was under the influence of drink and suffering from diminished responsibility. In the course of his charge to the jury the presiding judge gave the following directions:

LORD HILL WATSON: "My direction is in these terms, if a man is not shown by the evidence to be within the category of one with a diminished responsibility when sober he cannot place himself within the category of diminished responsibility by taking drink. That is a direction in law, and I give you that. My view is this on the law, because it was definitely done in that case about psychopathic personality (*Carraher v. H.M. Advocate*, (*ante*)) that you had to leave drink out of account, that if you found upon the evidence that this man suffered from a diminished responsibility without any question of drink at all then that would be a good defence, but if on the evidence you came to the conclusion that this diminished responsibility resulting in what he calls these blackouts only arises when the man takes drink then it is not diminished responsibility as known to the law of Scotland, and it would be your duty not to give effect to the plea.... You see, there is a recognised category of diminished responsibility that is a ground in the law of Scotland for reducing a charge of murder to one of culpable homicide, but if an accused person can only seek to take advantage of that doctrine by proving that he took drink, even if only a little drink, and so lost the restraint which he otherwise would have had, then that in the law of Scotland does not amount to a good defence of diminished responsibility."

NOTE

Certain of the statements in *Carraher v. H.M. Advocate* on the issue of intoxication must be read with **10.52** caution in the light of *Brennan v. H.M. Advocate* (*post*). As regards the relationship between intoxication and diminished responsibility, however, Brennan confirms *Macleod*. *Cf. R. v. Fenton* (1975) 61 Cr.App.R. 261; *R. v. Cittens* [1984] Q.B. 698 and *R. v. Atkinson* [1985] Crim.L.R. 314.

For evidential and procedural problems involved in setting up diminished responsibility, see *Gemmill v. H.M. Advocate*, 1979 S.L.T. 217.

## B. "Involuntary" Culpable Homicide

This is something of a misnomer. "Involuntary" in this context does not mean that the accused was not in **10.53** control of his or her actions. The term is used to describe two broad categories of killing—killing by unlawful act and reckless killing. The law in this area is not easy to state concisely since the term "involuntary culpable homicide" covers such a wide range of unlawful homicides. Some of these come close to murder, as, for example, where the killing shows a high degree of recklessness, but not sufficient to amount to "wicked" recklessness. At the other end of the scale, some examples are only slightly removed from accidental killings, where results from an unlawful act, but is a wholly unforeseeable result of that act.

## *(a) Reckless killing*

**10.54**  This category of culpable homicide comprises those cases in which the accused has caused the death of another through some reckless conduct which is not otherwise criminal at common law. For that reason it is frequently term "lawful act" culpable homicide. But this terminology is confusing (since by definition we are concerned with an allegedly criminal homicide) and the term reckless culpable homicide seems preferable.

**Paton v. H.M. Advocate**
1935 J.C. 19

**10.55**  Paton was charged, *inter alia*, with the culpable homicide of a pedestrian by driving his car in a "reckless and culpable manner" and at an excessive speed, so that he mounted a grass verge, collided with two pedestrians, injuring one and killing the other. The jury found the appellant guilty, and he was sentenced to six month's imprisonment. On appeal:

LORD JUSTICE-CLERK (AITCHISON): There is evidence in the case that the appellant was driving his car at a fairly high speed, and there is also evidence in the case that there was, perhaps, a want of care. The difficulty that the case presents is whether there was evidence that the appellant was guilty of criminal negligence in the sense in which we use that expression. At one time the rule of law was that any blame was sufficient, where death resulted, to justify a verdict of guilty of culpable homicide. Unfortunately, this law has to some extent been modified by decisions of the Court, and it is now necessary to show gross, or wicked, or criminal negligence, something amounting, or at any rate analogous, to a criminal indifference to consequences, before a jury can find culpable homicide proved. It may be that the law on this matter has got to be reconsidered."

Appeal allowed: conviction of culpable homicide
quashed; conviction of a contravention of section 11 of
the Road Traffic Act 1930 substituted.

NOTES

**10.56**  1. The terminology used in these cases is confusing. *Paton* refers to criminal negligence, while in other cases the term "recklessness" is used.

If the term negligence is used, then it is essential that it is not confused with the civil standard of negligence—that is, failing to achieve the standard of care expected of a reasonable person. If, on the other hand, the term "recklessness" is used, it is important that the distinction between recklessness and "wicked" recklessness—the standard for murder—is maintained.

It is possible to express the appropriate standard of care without reference to either term. In *Sutherland v. H.M. Advocate*, 1994 S.L.T. 634 the accused was charged with the culpable homicide of another man. The accused and the deceased had both been engaged in burning down the accused's house, this being done with a view to defrauding insurers. The deceased was killed when the house exploded. The prosecution proceeded on the basis that this was a case of reckless culpable homicide because of the manner in which the accused went about destroying the property. In his charge to the jury the trial stated that the question was whether the fireraising "was done in the face of obvious risks which were or should have been appreciated and guarded against, or in circumstances which showed a complete disregard for any potential dangers which might result".

3. Although many of the "lawful act" homicide cases arise from road traffic cases, the doctrine is not confined to such cases. See, for example, *H.M. Advocate v. Sheppard*, 1941 J.C. 67 (*ante*, p. 272); *Angus MacPherson and John Stewart*, (1861) 4 Irvine 85 (reckless navigation of a boat). A case such as *Paton* would today probably be charged as causing death by dangerous driving, under section 1 of the Road Traffic Act 1988.

In the English case of *Adomako*, [1994] 3 All E.R. 79 an anaesthetist failed to notice that a tube supplying oxygen to his patient, who was undergoing an eye operation, had become disconnected. The patient was deprived of oxygen for about six minutes, as a result of which he suffered a cardiac arrest and died. The anaesthetist was charged with manslaughter. An expert witness at the trial described the standard of care provided by the accused as "abysmal". Another stated that a competent anaesthetist ought to have recognised the signs of such a disconnection within 15 seconds, and stated that the accused's conduct amounted to a "gross dereliction of care". The House of Lords held that the accused was properly convicted of manslaughter.

## (b) Death resulting from an unlawful act: assault resulting in death

Perhaps the commonest example of unlawful act culpable homicide is death resulting from an assault. It is settled law that, in the absence of some justification or excuse, death resulting from an assault is always culpable homicide: *H.M. Advocate v. Delaney*, 1945 J.C. 138; *McDermott v. H.M. Advocate*, 1973 J.C. 8. The assault need not be one which was likely to cause death, or even serious injury. The consequences can be harsh, especially when combined with the rule that the accused "takes his victim as he finds him", as in the following case. **10.57**

### Bird v. H.M. Advocate
1952 J.C. 23

The appellant, a petty officer in the navy, who had been drinking, was under the impression **10.58** that a woman had taken money belonging to him. He pursued her along a road, and caused her such alarm and apprehension that she tried to stop and enter a passing car, whereupon she collapsed and died of shock. It appeared that she had a weak heart. In his charge to the jury the presiding judge gave the following directions, which were subsequently upheld on appeal:

LORD JAMIESON: "The crime with which the accused is charged is culpable homicide, and I think I can best help you by saying a word or two as to what that crime means. As its name implies, it is simply bringing about the death of another by a criminal act of culpa nor fault. It differs from the crime of murder in this, that in murder there must either be an intent to kill or a reckless disregard as to the consequences of one's act. In culpable homicide these factors may be absent. It takes many forms, but you here are only concerned with death resulting from violence or assault, and I shall have to explain to you later what exactly I mean by assault. Violence may take many forms. It may be a savage attack causing physical injury resulting in death or it may be a very slight assault. If, having a grievance against a man, another gives him a push, although a slight push, and that knocks him over and he hits his head against a kerb and dies, it may be culpable homicide, and it is no defence to the charge to say that a serious injury was not intended or that death was not in contemplation, and that in that sense the death was accidental. I am going to read to you what was said by one of our Judges, who was at one time Lord Justice Clerk, in charging a jury. He said [*H.M. Advocate v. Delaney*, 1945 J.C. 138 at p. 139]: 'That being so and life having been taken, it is clear that there must be a conviction, unless you are satisfied on the evidence that the taking of life was merely an innocent accident. It may be that those who offer violence, especially violence which is subject to be followed by death, have not had in view the taking of life. They, however, are not accidental in their use of violence. They are responsible for the violence they use, so far as the violence is concerned; and, if consequences follow which they do not anticipate or apprehend, they are also responsible for these consequences. One cannot say "I chose to exercise violence against a person against whom I thought I had a grievance, and it was merely accidental that a probable consequence of that violence followed."'

Now the degree of violence that has been used, as I have told you, may be very slight, but if there was any violence or if there was any assault and death results from it, directly results from it, then the accused person is guilty of culpable homicide. The question of the degree of violence is not really a question for the jury. It is a question for the Judge, if the accused is found guilty, in considering what punishment is to be meted out. Nor is it any defence that the victim was an old person, an infirm person, or a person that suffered from a bad heart, and that if he had been young and healthy the consequences would not have happened. If a person commits an assault, he must take his victim as he finds him. It is not necessary that the death should result from physical injuries. If the result of the treatment that the deceased person has received has been to cause shock and that person dies of shock, then the crime has been committed. If a person is assaulted, although to a slight degree, but is put in fear of serious bodily injury and dies as a result, then the crime has been committed and the person who has committed the assault is guilty of it.

Now I have been talking about assault. Assault, in law, is in some ways a technical term. One talking in ordinary parlance about an assault is rather inclined to think of some serious violence being used, but that, in law, is not necessary. The learned Advocate-depute referred to a well-known book on Criminal Law [Macdonald, at p. 115], in which it is said that every attack upon the person of another is an assault, whether it injure or not; and then it gives an example, that even spitting upon another is assault. Later on it says, 'Gestures threatening violence so great as to put another in bodily fear, whether accompanied by words of menace or not, constitute assault. That threatening language was used may be an element in estimating how far the fear of the person attacked was reasonable; but mere words cannot constitute an assault.' So, when I speak about an assault, do not run away with the idea it means something of a very violent nature. The same applies when I speak to you about violence. The matter was very well illustrated in a case to which the learned Advocate-depute referred me, where an attempt was made to rob a woman. Some force was used but there was no serious physical injury, but she had a weak heart and she died, I think it was a few days later. She died some time later from shock, and in charging the jury a very eminent Judge said this [*H.M. Advocate v. Brown* (1879) 4 Coup. 225 at p. 227], 'Anyone attacking a person with a view to robbery, and causing his or her death, was guilty of culpable homicide at the least. It was no defence at all that the victim was suffering from heart disease. Therefore, if they were of opinion that this woman died from the shock occasioned by the prisoner's criminal attempt to rob her, he was guilty, not merely of assault with intent to rob, but of culpable homicide.'

Death, however, must result directly from the assault or from the violence used. It must be a direct result, although there may be factors operating such as a diseased heart, and when I speak of it being direct it need not necessarily be the direct result of physical violence, that is to say, the physical injuries received. If a person has been assaulted and there is violence used or if the victim is put in reasonable fear of his or her safety, reasonable fear of further violence, and is suffering from a bad heart which operates as one cause, and as a result dies from shock or emotional shock, as the doctors call it here, that would be enough. So, when you come to consider the facts, you should, I think, direct your attention to this: Did the accused strike the deceased woman? Do you hold that proved? If you do not hold that she was actually struck, did he molest her? Did he lay hands on her and, by his actings, did he put her in a reasonable dread of being attacked to such an extent as caused her to suffer from shock? And, if you find either of these, the other question you have to direct your attention to is this, Was her death a direct result of that?"

Verdict: Guilty.

NOTES

**10.59**     1. *Cf.* the cases of *H.M. Advocate v. Robertson and Donoghue* (*unreported, ante*, Chap. 3) and *McDermott v. H.M. Advocate*, 1974 S.L.T. 206 (*supra*), and comments thereon. In *D.P.P. v. Newbury and Jones* [1976] 2 All E.R. 365 the House of Lords held that English law did not require actual foresight of the consequences of the unlawful act in such cases. All that was required was an unlawful and dangerous act, *i.e.* an act which was likely to endanger another.

2. The harshness of the rule that death resulting from an assault is always at least culpable homicide may be mitigated by the approach of the courts to sentencing. In *Burns v. H.M. Advocate*, 1998 S.C.C.R. 281 the appellant pleaded guilty to culpable homicide and was sentenced to two years' imprisonment. The deceased died as a result of a single blow, delivered with little force, to the deceased's neck. The blow, which was not aimed, severed the deceased's cerebral artery. The deceased had consumed a substantial amount of alcohol, and medical experts testified that consumption of alcohol can make the

cerebral artery more susceptible to injury. Death was not a foreseeable result of a blow of this kind. On appeal the sentence was reduced to 240 hours' community service.

## (c) Death resulting from an unlawful act: other cases

Not every unlawful act which results in death will amount to culpable homicide. The act must be **10.60** criminal. A merely delictual act will not suffice. It must also be one which, by its nature, presents a foreseeable risk of personal injury (as, for example, in the case of fire-raising resulting in death) or one which, although not in the ordinary course of events presenting any risk of personal injury, is carried out with such recklessness as to make personal injury reasonably foreseeable.

### Mathieson v. H.M. Advocate
1981 S.C.C.R. 196

OPINION OF THE COURT: "This is an appeal by Peter Andrew Mathieson against conviction. **10.61** Mathieson, who is now sixteen, was convicted in the High Court of the crime of culpable homicide and as the charge shows what happened was that the appellant set fire to combustible liquid at the rear entrance of certain premises known as the Talbot Centre in Glasgow. The charge further goes on to allege that this was done culpably and recklessly and the story unfolds with an account of the fire which followed which engulfed the building resulting in the death of a number of the occupants. As matter of admission the deaths resulted from the fire started by the accused. About that there is no question, and, accordingly, it followed that if the appellant's act was in law an unlawful act then the appellant was guilty of the crime libelled against him, namely, culpable homicide. The conviction of the appellant is however attacked upon the ground that it proceeded upon a misdirection by the trial judge consisting in a fundamental omission. As Mr Stirling put it to us, the judge gave a careful and correct instruction to the jury as to the ingredients of the crime of culpable homicide. The jury were accordingly left in no doubt that if the deaths which occurred as the result of the fire as the result of the appellant's act were the results of an unlawful act by the appellant then the crime charged had been established. What then was the unlawful act upon which the Crown relied? According to the charge it was culpable and reckless fire-raising. In this case there should, accordingly, have been defined for the jury by the trial judge the constituent and necessary elements of that particular crime and it should have been pointed out to the jury that that was the question they had to consider. The issue for us is whether the judge's omission to charge in these terms amounted to a misdirection. There is no doubt that he did not address himself precisely to the question focused by Mr Stirling. What he did instead was to examine the evidence. Having done so we find that in his charge at page 16 and further on page 17 that he first of all said to the jury, 'if you accept [certain evidence which he had just summarised] then you could [say] that this was a deliberate act by the accused'. He was well entitled to say this upon the evidence including a statement made by the appellant himself to this effect 'In the cellar I seen all the paint and that and I decided to light it. It went up right away.' So that was the first thing the trial judge did. The judge then went on to say all he had to say about the kind of deliberate act that act might have been and he examined carefully certain passages in evidence indicating the state of mind and the state of knowledge of the appellant. In particular he dealt with evidence which had been given by the appellant's two companions. In the first place there was a statement at the scene of the setting fire to the paint, 'Well, let's see what happens. Let's see what happens if we light it.' The trial judge then went on to say, 'If you accept that evidence you would be in a position to hold that the act of the appellant was an unlawful one'. In amplification of that proposition the trial judge reminded the jury that if someone lights a fire on the ground floor of that kind of property anything might happen and that that had been the evidence, if the jury accepted it, of certain fire officers. But more importantly he went on to remind the jury of what the young boy ... one of the appellant's companions, had said. And what he had said, according to the trial judge, was that both he and ... the appellant's brother had said before the appellant had set fire to the paint, 'Don't light this. Anything might happen. It may cause a fire.' In the context of this case we have to ask ourselves whether the trial judge sufficiently directed the jury that what they had to look for was evidence which entitled them to conclude that an unlawful act on the part of the appellant had been committed when he set fire to the paint in all the circumstances which the judge had described. In our judgment looking at the circumstances of this case the judge's approach cannot be faulted for he left it to the jury to decide upon relevant and sufficient evidence which he drew to their attention whether any unlawful act had been committed and what the jury were, in short, invited to do was to decide whether to accept the evidence. In all the circumstances the judge's omission to give the direction desiderated was not in any sense fatal to a conviction which was returned by the jury after a charge which was sufficient in the context of the case for the assistance of that jury."

Appeal dismissed.

NOTE

**10.62**    *Cf.* the case of *Sutherland v. H.M. Advocate*, 1994 S.L.T. 634.

# Chapter 11

# THEFT, EMBEZZLEMENT AND RELATED OFFENCES

This chapter discusses offences involving the appropriation of property and offences which are **11.01** preparatory thereto. Appropriation may consist in "taking" the property, in the sense of taking possession of it, or of using the property in a way which is not permitted by the owner or even simply retaining possession of property once one is aware that one is not legally entitled to do so.

The law in this area has undergone significant changes since the beginning of the nineteenth century, and it is still in the process of developing. Thus the crime of theft has changed from one in which the essence of the offence consisted in taking possession of the property of another and carrying it away to a much more broadly conceived offence, based on the idea of "appropriation" of property, which does not require the taking of possession, let alone the carrying away, of the property.

Equally important developments have taken place with regard to the *mens rea* of theft which, for most of the last 100 years has required proof of an intention permanently to deprive. In the absence of such an intention there was no theft, so that "borrowing" of property, even without the consent of the owner, could not be theft, no matter how great the inconvenience or loss caused by this temporary deprivation. The judicial response to this limitation was to recognise, in the case of *Strathern v. Seaforth*, 1926 J.C. 100 (*post*, p. 483) the existence of (or, more properly, to create) a separate common law offence of "clandestinely taking and using" the property of another. (This judicial development was later paralleled in the legislative creation of the offence of taking and driving away a vehicle without the owner's consent—an offence now contained in section 178(1) of the Road Traffic Act 1988.) More recently, however, the courts have re-defined the offence of theft so as to substantially modify, and some might say remove, the requirement of an intention permanently to deprive in the crime of theft.

Developments such as these call into question the need for a distinction between the crimes of theft and embezzlement. The offence of embezzlement, which consists in the dishonest appropriation to one's own use of property entrusted to one for a particular purpose developed in part as a response to the rule that theft required a taking of possession of property—a requirement difficult to fulfil in the case of persons who misappropriated property which had already been entrusted to their possession. Once theft was extended to embrace those who appropriate property which has already come into their possession, it is difficult to justify the retention of a separate offence of embezzlement. And the modification of an intention permanently to deprive renders questionable the need certainly for the common law offence of "clandestine taking and using" of property.

One further, separate, development has implications for the boundaries of the crime of theft, and that is the extension of the crime of malicious mischief to include cases where the accused has interfered with property belonging to another in such a way as to cause economic loss to the owner. This development clearly extends the overlap between the crime of theft and that of malicious mischief. This point is further discussed in the notes to the case of *Black v. Carmichael; Carmichael v. Black, post*, p. 449.

# 1. Theft

## A. The *Actus Reus* of Theft

### *(a) From "taking" to "appropriation"*

#### Hume, 1, 57

**11.02** "In considering that class of offences which affect individuals in their property, I naturally begin with the crime of theft, that sort of invasion of property, which being attended with a profit to the offender, as well as a damage to the owner, is more frequently committed than any other. And first, of the nature of the crime. All the necessary characters seem to be set forth in that short description of it, given in the civil law, *contrectatio fraudulosa rei alienae, lucri faciendi gratia;* the felonious taking and carrying away of the property of another, for lucre.

I. The fundamental circumstance here . . . is this of the *taking* . . . . In which it is implied, that the thing has not been previously in the possession of the thief, but in that of the owner, or some person for him, out of which the thief, without the consent of the owner, removes it. Now, with this article, simple as it first appears to be, there opens a wide field of discussion; as upon due understanding of this matter, depends, in some measure, the distinction between theft, and those other criminal, but as the law deems them, lower offences, of fraud, swindling, and breach of trust, which are nearly allied to theft, and very liable to be confounded with it. And here, without pretending to furnish an invariable criterion, or to resolve all those nice debates, which have exercised the ingenuity of the ablest lawyers, I shall content myself with stating, on the one and the other part, certain descriptions of cases, which are clearly referable to different denominations of crime: In this course, the circle of controversy may, I hope, at least be narrowed, if not some notion be attained of the true principle, which may serve to the decision of still more difficult situations.

1. In the first place, All those cases seem to fall under the notion of fraud or swindling only, and not of theft, in which the offender gets possession of the thing on a finished bargain for the *property*, upon *credit*, though the transaction have been accomplished by means of cozenage and falsehood. As in the case of one, who falsely pretends to be a partner of a certain thriving house, and thus buys and gets delivery of goods, to be paid for at a future day. Or take the case of Thomas Hall, tried in July 1789, who came to Edinburgh, falsely pretending to be a trader, and in prosecution of this plan hired and opened a shop, and having thus obtained goods from sundry dealers upon credit, suddenly eloped, and ran away with the goods, leaving his shelves furnished with a show of false bales and empty boxes, to deceive such as might inquire. In cases of this description, the offender's wrong lies only in the false and fraudulent inducement, which he has held out to the owner for prevailing with him to sell. But how unfair soever the way in which he obtained it, he has actually had the consent of the owner to convey that thing to him in property, to be his, and in all respects at his disposal, till the day of payment come . . . .

2. Put the case even that the owner does deliver the thing, but on some lower title than that of property; as in the case of a watch being given in loan, or a horse let to hire, or a pack of goods sent by a carrier, to be delivered at a certain place: Still the after-conversion of this thing to the possessor's own use, by selling the watch or horse, or opening the pack and taking the contents, though it is a wrong, and even a criminal act, does not however amount to the crime of theft. The reason is obvious, That there had been no felonious *taking* out of the owner's possession. The man, in all these instances, had at first obtained the thing honestly, by a fair contract, in the ordinary course of business, and meaning, as at that time, to restore or deliver it in terms of his agreement. At the instant, therefore, of the delivery made him in pursuance of that contract, the owner's possession ceased. The receiver was thenceforward in the lawful possession; and when he converts the thing to his own use, in pursuance of a

purpose which is only taken up afterwards, and is probably suggested by his command of the thing, he only breaks his contract, and abuses his power as possessor . . . .

4. The same principle which protects the trespasser in the case of delivery for some temporary use, still more strongly applies in his favour, in proportion as he had the thing upon a higher interest of his own, and under a contract which vests him with a fuller management and command of it. A creditor who has his debtor's property lying in pledge with him, is not guilty of theft if he irregularly use or sell it; for such is his interest in the thing, that the owner would be guilty of a crime, and, as some allege, guilty of theft even in certain circumstances, if he should secretly withdraw the thing from his possession. The same is true of the case of him who takes a furnished house for a term, and afterwards disposes of some of the articles of furniture. Take the case, in like manner, of a footman, whose clothes are furnished by his master: The clothes are not indeed the footman's property for he must surrender them when he leaves the service: But still he has a much higher interest in them than in his master's pate, or other things committed to his keeping, and such an interest, as shall at least hinder any prosecution of him as a thief, if he run off with them upon him, or sell them while in the service. . . .

In general, it seems to be true of all who are in a responsible state as officers, and are entrusted not with the *custody* only, but the *possession* of money, such as cashiers and tellers of banks, collectors of taxes or parochial rates, treasurers of bodies corporate, judicial factors and the like, that they are not punishable *as thieves*, but as delinquents of a lower order, for any dishonesty or malversation in their charge. . . .

In the case even of a shopkeeper's clerk, bookkeeper, or other such person, who does the business of the shop, pays occasional demands, and receives payment of, and discharges, in his employer's name, accounts due to the shop, there is room to doubt whether he is guilt of theft at common law, when he secretes and applies to his own use part of the money which thus comes into his hands. The money, in such a case, has never been properly in the master's possession; and besides, this free permission to touch and meddle with the money implies a special reliance on the individual, as one who is worthy of trust and able to account; . . . .

5. In all the cases which have yet been put, the offender is supposed to have got the thing by the act and will of the owner. But it seems also to be an available defence, that the thing came to him, though against the owner's will, in some lawful and warrantable manner, and without *tort* or transgression on his party in laying hold of it. A landholder finds a stray animal in his field, or a treasure in his grounds, or has wrecked goods thrown in upon his shore; or a passenger finds a pocket-book upon the highway, which has the owner's name marked in it; or a hackney-coachman finds a parcel in his coach left there by a passenger, who he had some time ago set down. It seems not to be a theft in any of these cases, if tempted by the opportunity, the man finally hide this thing, and keep it to himself: Because there is no felonious intention, nor even a *trespass* in the first occupying of the thing, which is lying vacant, and inaccessible to the owner, and may lawfully be taken possession of for the sake of custody, or till offer of a reward . . . .

II. There must not only be a taking, but a carrying away. For it seems to be in the nature of this offence . . . that the thing must have been brought into a situation, in which it was less under the owner's power and command than before. In general, the law intends that the thing must be removed from the place and state of keeping in which it had been; and that without some such alteration, nothing done by the pannel, how decisive soever of is felonious purpose, amounts to theft, but to an attempt or misdemeanour only, which may be greater or less, according to the circumstances of the fact."

NOTE

In virtually every case discussed by Hume, modern practice would hold the person appropriating the **11.03** property to be guilty of theft. The only exception to this is in that category of cases where the owner has entrusted the property to the "thief" to manage on behalf of the owner. In this type of case modern practice still relies upon charges of "breach of trust" or, as it is more commonly known in modern practice, embezzlement. The following cases illustrate the departure of the common law from the principles set out by Hume and the development of the modern crime of theft.

### John Smith
(1838) 2 Swinton 28

**11.04** The accused was charged with theft of a pocket book, £112 in cash and a bill of exchange in that he did "find the said money and other articles, and did then and there, or at some other time and place to the prosecutor unknown, appropriate the same to his own uses and purposes, he well knowing the same to be the property of the said John Buchanan and did wickedly and feloniously steal and theftuously away take the said articles".

He objected to the relevancy of the indictment.

LORD MEADOWBANK: "The Counsel for the pannel has almost admitted himself out of Court; for he admits, that if the pannel had seen the articles drop from the person of the owner, the immediate appropriation of them would have amounted to the crime charged. Now, just take the point a little farther. Suppose, that on the outside of the pocket book he had seen the name of the owner written in legible characters. It must be held that, after this, to pick it up and appropriate it, would be same thing as to do so after seeing it drop from the owner's person. Now, what is the difference in the circumstance that he goes one step farther? He does not see the name of the owner on the outside, but, having opened the book, he finds it written in the inside; and, having thus taken the only means in his power to discover who the owner is he immediately forms the intention of appropriating it. Suppose the case of a carrier, one of whose parcels had lost the address—he opens it in order to discover to whom it belongs, and after having done so, forms the design of appropriating it. Can it be doubted, after the decisions which we have given, that he would be held guilty of theft? The principle on which the cases of horse stealing, referred to in the Information, have been decided, is not—as is maintained for the pannel—that the *malus animus* existed at the time of the hiring. It is of no consequence of what character the original possession of the property is. The moment the intention of appropriating the property of another is formed, then the theft is committed. Such appearing to me to be the principle of our recent decisions, it is a source of satisfaction to find, that, although some very vague notions on the subject have at one time been held by those great men who, in England, have adopted the same views as Baron Hume, the more modern practice in that country is the same as our own."

LORD MONCREIFF: "I apprehend it to be quite clear, that the general principle originally laid down by Baron Hume on this subject has been, I do not say altered, but greatly qualified, by recent decisions. A servant who breaks through a trust and appropriates his master's property has, in innumerable cases, been found guilty of theft. So, also, the case of appropriation by a clerk who has the custody of goods, even with the power to sell them, has been held to be theft. Then the case of a person hiring a horse and appropriating it to his own use, is one very much in point. It is argued, in the Information for the pannel, that to constitute the crime of theft, the felonious intention must have existed from the beginning. I am not prepared to go that length. I think a person may have hired a horse for an honest purpose, and subsequently resolved to steal him; and I am not prepared to say that that would not be a case of theft, although the taking must be libelled in some different way, that if it had taken place at the period of the first hiring. So, also, in the case of theft by a carrier of goods entrusted to his care, the time and place of the offence is not when and where he received the goods, but when and where he formed the felonious intention of appropriating them. Suppose a flock of sheep are found straying on the public road, with the owner's mark on them, surely we should not hesitate to find, that the appropriation of them by another person was theft. The case of a man seeing a person drop a pocket-book, and picking it up and keeping it, is admitted to be a case of theft. But put another case—that he does not see it drop, but sees a person resting by the side of the road, and when he comes to the spot finds a pocket book there; and suppose that he either knows the person by sight or finds his name written in the book—can it be doubted that the moment he resolves to appropriate it to himself, that moment he commits theft? It is by accident that he has got possession of the goods of another, but so soon as he discovers who the owner is, it is his duty to restore them. It is a very nice question, whether, if the appropriation did not take place till long after the finding, the case would be the same. Whatever may be my opinion as to the alternative charge, I think the libelling of time and place would not, in that case, be sufficient, too great a latitude being taken in both respects. But the case before us may be decided on the assumption, that at, or immediately after the period of finding, the knowledge of the owner was acquired, and the design of appropriating formed. In that view, I can have no doubt that the Indictment is relevant."

LORD COCKBURN: "The definition which our law gives of theft, is, that it is *contrectatio fraudulosa rei alienae, lucri faciendi causa*—fraudulent taking of the property of another for the sake of lucre. Now, what is meant by this word *taking*? I know no authority, and no principle, for confining it to the act of first possessing. *Lifting* is not *taking*, at least not necessarily; a person may be the recipient of a commodity involuntarily or unconsciously—as by having it put into his pocket secretly, or delivered to him by mistake. He is the *possessor* after this, but not the *taker*. I don't conceive that there can be any taking, in the sense of this definition, without an intention to take. It means appropriation. Accordingly, there are innumerable cases, such as that of servants stealing things committed to their charge, in which the original possessing was quite innocent, but in which *beyond all doubt*, theft is committed merely by the subsequent application of the property to their own use. There is no bringing these cases within the rule, either in its words or in its meaning, without referring it to the appropriation, *no matter when it may occur*, as to the only act of taking. If this be correct, then the original innocence of possessing an article, is not merely no exclusion of the idea of theft afterwards committed by a new act of criminal application, but it has no tendency to exclude it. The guiltlessness of the first occupancy seems to me to be totally irrelevant in reference to the question of subsequent theft. There are two objections stated to this, as applied to the present case. 1st. That there must be an *animus furandi in the first taking*. I agree to this, provided the word *taking* be left to its correct legal sense, of appropriation. But when extended so as to include the original *reception*, it is *quite certain* that the objection is groundless. For there are various cases of clear, and indisputable theft—such as that of a carrier abstracting a bale committed to him for conveyance—where property is held to be stolen, because, though got innocently, it is withdrawn by the receiver from its proper destination, and converted to his own use. If the purity of the first acquisition be a defence against a charge of subsequent theft, it would not be easy to say how many have been illegally convicted of stealing. 2nd. The other objection is, that there can be no theft, where the owner, though he retains the property, happens for a time to have *lost the possession*. It would require very strong and positive authority to support a doctrine so full of danger. The import of this principle is, that *lost property can never be stolen*. And if this be law, then it is not theft to pick up a watch the instant that it is dropped and to run; nor to carry off the goods of a known owner which have been thrown ashore from a wrecked vessel whose whole crew has perished, nor for a police officer sent to discover the stolen goods of a known proprietor, and finding them in custody of the thief, concealing this fact and keeping them to himself. This principle would protect the case, where there was a theftuous intention from the first; for if possession by the owner be necessary, the absence of this element cannot be supplied by the motive of the taker. So, if lost goods were advertised, and a person were to search for them with the view of appropriating, and were to find, and to keep them, even this would not be theft. Nor would it be theft for a person observing a man bathing to sink and be drowned, to run off with his clothes lying on the shore, for the old owner, by death, had lost possession of them. I know no authority for such a principle. Rather than adopt it, the law supposes every man who voluntarily takes, or who even accidentally obtains possession of the property of another; to be a sort of trustee or custodier for him. In the cases of servants, clerks, porters, &c. this principle may be thought not to apply, because these persons obtain possession under a direct employment by the owner. But there are cases where this circumstance does not occur. Take the case of property *never received*. An unknown stranger holds a packet addressed to the real proprietor. He gives it to a porter to be delivered to that person, who does not know of its existence. The porter keeps it. I think that this would be theft and that it would be well charged as such, if the crime were set forth as committed not against the unknown stranger, but against the real owner; because, though not employed by him, the porter having got the parcel, held it as his custodier. I conceive a trust of an analogous description to be imposed by the law upon everyone who happens to take possession, or to find himself in possession, of the property of another; but especially where this is the result of his own act. It may not be his duty to lift the property of another; or, if he should happen to do so, he may lay it down again; but from the moment that he begins to keep possession, knowing whose it is, he holds it for that person; and hence would be entitled to resist its being taken from him."

Charge of theft held relevant.

NOTE

**11.05** The significance of the decision in *John Smith* lies in the fact that it dispensed with the requirement of an initial "felonious taking", thus paving the way for the *actus reus* of theft to be regarded in terms of appropriation. For some time, however, the courts were unwilling to follow the decision in *John Smith* to its logical conclusion.

In *Angus McKinnon* (1863) 4 Irvine 398, the accused was charged with theft by appropriating to his own use a pocket-book and bank-notes belonging to B, which he had found, knowing that they belonged to B, "or at all events that the same were not the property of you" the accused. The court held that this indictment was irrelevant. Lord Justice-Clerk Inglis distinguished this case from *John Smith* by pointing out that in that case it was alleged that the accused knew who the owner of the found property was at the time "or almost at the time" when he first took the property, and that the case advanced the law no further than that. The indictment in *Angus McKinnon* did not require the Crown to show that the accused knew whose property it was at the time of the initial finding, but merely that it did not belong to him, and this, Lord Inglis thought, led to the conclusion that an accused could be found guilty of theft if he found property and, not knowing whose it was, and not being able to discover this, subsequently decided to keep it. While this might be regarded as dishonest, it was not, in his Lordship's view, theft.

A similar reluctance was displayed by the Court in *Campbell v. MacLennan* (1888) 1 White 604. In that case the accused was also charged with stealing property which he had found, the complaint alleging that the accused, "having on the November 14, 1887 within the Inn at Dunvegan, found in money one pound, . . . did deny having found the same and did appropriate, and thus steal the same". The Court again held the complaint to be irrelevant. There was, however, some confusion as to just why this did not amount to theft. Lord McLaren, for example, did not think that the mere finding of a banknote, coupled with a denial of having found it was sufficient to constitute "felonious appropriation", especially since there was no indication that the person to whom the accused was alleged to have denied having found it was entitled to ask the question. Lord Young, on the other hand, appears to have thought that to find property and to deny having done so might not necessarily be sufficient to infer the necessary "*animus furandi*", that is, the intention to steal. He gave the following example: "A man of large property may find money in the street, and may give it in the way of alms to the next beggar; that is undoubtedly appropriation. Yet who would call it theft, even if the finder had denied having found it?" It is difficult, however, to see why this would not be theft, unless the argument is that the finder was not acting dishonestly—an analysis which is not entirely free from difficulty since at the time *Campbell v. MacLennan* was decided dishonesty does not appear to have formed part of the definition of the crime of theft. The argument may, of course, have been influenced by the old notion, still extant in Hume's time, that theft required that the appropriation be "*lucri faciendi causa*", that is, for the material advantage of the thief.

Lord Rutherford Clark dissented, holding that "if a person finds a £1 note and appropriates to his own use, . . . that is plainly theft and nothing else".

In modern practice there is no doubt that the charges in all of the above cases would be accepted as relevant charges of theft. A person who finds property, and, knowing that it is not his or her own, keeps the property, or otherwise deals with it as their own to dispose of, is guilty of theft.

To hold that a person who finds and keeps property, knowing that he or she is not entitled to do so, is guilty of theft, involved a departure from the principle that theft required an initial "felonious taking". It was probably easier to take this step in the case of stealing by finding than in the case where the thief is already in lawful possession of the property. After all, those who find property and keep it for themselves really have no claim whatsoever to be entitled to do so. The case was at least arguably different where the alleged thief converted to his own use property which had already been entrusted to them by the owner. However, the step taken in *John Smith* was fairly rapidly applied to the latter type of case as well, as the following case illustrates.

## George Brown
### (1839) 2 Swin. 394

The accused was charged that, having been employed as a watchmaker, and nine people **11.06** having delivered to him watches for repair between August and December 1838, he did on January 7, 1839 steal the watches. He objected to the relevancy of the charge.

LORD JUSTICE-CLERK (BOYLE) (dissenting): "I am, in this case, of the opinion that the proper charge against the pannel would have been one of breach of trust. In all these cases, to which I have referred, in which the charge of theft was found relevant, there was a limited mandate, for a temporary purpose, and for a short time. But when I look to the *species facti* in this Indictment, namely that the watches which the pannel is said to have appropriated, were delivered to him, either to be cleaned or to be repaired, I cannot help supposing that it was in the contemplation of all parties, that the operation would require a lengthened possession."

LORD MACKENZIE: "I think that we have already in numerous cases, departed from the authority of Mr Hume in this matter. One of the most remarkable instances of this was the case in which we found that the appropriation, by a pannel, of an article found on the highway, the owner of which is well known to him, is theft. We have also decided that a carrier, who appropriates goods given to him to be conveyed to a certain destination, is guilty of theft. The opinion of Mr Hume in regard to this offence is, that in the case of a regular carrier, it is not theft. So also in the case of a horse hired without any felonious purpose, and afterwards carried off by the hirer, we have decided that a theft is committed. But that decision is contrary to the opinion of Baron Hume, who makes the distinction between theft and breach of trust depend on the character of the first acquiring. Then looking to the charge contained in the present Indictment, I am not able to think that it is less than theft. I cannot see any difference—except a difference which adds to the difficulty of the theft—between the case of a watchmaker and that of a carrier. I presume that if a party gave goods into the charge of a carrier, which, instead of being delivered to another person were to be delivered to himself, the Court would not hold that this made any difference as to the crime committed by the carrier, supposing that he abstracted them. And why shall we say that delivery of a thing, without transferring either the property or the possession, does not bar theft, when the operation to be performed is removal over a certain space, and that it does bar theft, when the operation is the cleaning or repairing of the article. It may be true that there is no absolute limitation in the time which the operation, in the case before us, might require. But in a case such as that before us, the time is not unlimited. It is known that the operation can be performed within a certain time; and it is in the expectation of that time proving sufficient, that the article is given out of the owner's custody. There is this farther circumstance to be taken into account, that in the case of the carrier, the article remains more under the eye of the owner, than it does in that of the watchmaker. On the whole, I am of opinion that we have gone so far, that it is not possible for us to stop. I think we must hold here, as we have done in those other cases to which I have referred, that there was no such transference of the possession as to make the appropriation a less crime than theft. It may be that in practice we have sustained cases as breach of trust, which might properly have been tried as theft. Now, in regard to the argument thus raised, the only answer that occurs to me, is, that theft and breach of trust have not been considered opposed to one another, and that the Court has held them to be similar crimes, to the extent at least of admitting confession of the one, when the *species facti* libelled might perhaps have amounted, in strictness, to the other. I am the more inclined to think that this may have been the opinion of the Court, because I find an opinion to that effect in my own notes. And I am not yet convinced that the conclusion is illogical, which holds that the same act may sometimes fall under two different kinds of offences. If a butler steal wine from his master's cellar, and an indictment is raised against him, under the *nomen juris* of breach of trust, it cannot surely be held that that is equivalent to a decision that the crime was not theft. I agree with the Lord Justice-Clerk, that we are bound to look at indictments, even although no objection is taken, before pronouncing an interlocutor of relevancy. But it is a different thing to say, that if the Prosecutor is satisfied to try the pannel for the lesser crime, the Court ought to interfere with the objection that the *species facti* might have been tried under a harsher name."

LORD MONCREIFF: "I do not think that, consistently with our late decisions, we can come to any other determination than that this is a case of theft. If the principle were, that this crime could not be committed, when the article came into the power of the pannel with the consent of the owner, that principle would exclude from the category of theft the cases of the carrier, the porter, the hirer of the horse. But I apprehend that the decisions which we have given in these cases, proceeded on the fact, that the owner's consent to the transference of the possession is only a qualified and conditional consent, for a special and particular purpose. In the case before us, the pannel gets the watch solely for the purpose of cleaning or repairing it, with the clear expectation and intention of the owner, that it is to be restored to him so soon as that operation is completed. Now, I do not think we can hold this appropriation of the watch, in these circumstances, to be anything but the crime of theft. Although the article came at first lawfully into his possession, the principle of law is, that the felonious taking is at the moment he forms the resolution of appropriating it to his own use."

Charge of theft held relevant.

NOTE

**11.07**    See also the cases of *Elizabeth Anderson* (1858) 3 Irvine 65 and *John Martin* (1873) 2 Couper 501. In these cases the accused committed theft by appropriating clothes which had been given to them for their temporary use by the authorities responsible for the relief of the poor. Such decisions clearly contradict Hume's opinion that a footman could not be guilty of stealing the livery provided by his employer. In *O'Brien v. Strathern*, 1922 S.L.T. 440, the appellant, who ran a second hand clothes shop, was charged, *inter alia*, with resetting a kilt which, it was alleged, had been obtained by theft. The kilt had been sold by a soldier in the Argyll and Sutherland Highlanders to the appellant, who subsequently displayed it for sale in her shop. The kilt formed part of the soldier's uniform, and he was not authorised to sell it. At first instance the sheriff found the appellant guilty, holding that "when an article, lent for a specific use only, is appropriated and sold for his own benefit by the person to whom it has been so lent, the crime of theft is committed". On appeal, the High Court was unanimous in its opinion that the soldier, by selling his kilt to the appellant, was guilty of theft.

### Carmichael v. Black; Black v. Carmichael
1992 S.L.T. 897

**11.08**  The appellant, Black, was charged on summary complaint with extortion and, alternatively, theft of two cars. So far as concerns the theft charges, the complaint alleged that the accused attached wheel clamps to two cars and "did thus steal the same". The cars were parked in a private car park, without permission. A joint minute was lodged recording certain agreed facts, in the following terms:

"(1) The car park at Townhead Street, Hamilton, is an off street private car park used to service shops in Townhead Street, Roger Way and Quarry Street, Hamilton. There is no barrier to prevent the vehicular access to said car park. (2) On July 6, 1991 two notices were displayed within said car park bearing the following intimation: 'Private Property—unauthorised and unlawfully parked vehicles will be immobilised and a levy of £45 charged for release. South Coast Security (0506–873077). Agents to the Owner.' (3) That, on July 6, 1991, devices (commonly known as 'wheel clamps') were attached to motor vehicles registered numbers C77 JGA and D54 SGG then parked in said car park without authority and notices of levy in the terms stated in the complaint were fixed to the windscreens of said vehicles."

Objections to the relevancy of both the extortion and theft charges were taken on behalf of the appellant. The sheriff held that the extortion charges were relevant, but that the charges of theft were irrelevant. The appellant appealed against the sheriff's decision in respect of the extortion charges (as to which, see *infra*, p. 496) and the prosecutor appealed against the decision in respect of the theft charges. On appeal by the prosecutor:

THE LORD JUSTICE-GENERAL (HOPE): " ... It is common knowledge that the practice of wheel clamping has been introduced in order to deal with the ever increasing problem of illegally parked motor vehicles. The need to control parking has become a fact of everyday life. Parking restrictions are now almost universal in city and town centres throughout the country. And, as the available space for on street parking cannot provide spaces for everybody, and is frequently the subject of charges or other measures to restrict the time for which cars can be legally parked there, so the pressure grows for places to be found for off street parking in private or public car parks. The larger, supervised, car parks can be protected by devices which control entry and egress and by this means obtain payment for their use. But areas set aside for unsupervised private parking are vulnerable to abuse by persons who do not have permission to park there. Hence the attraction to the owners of these areas of a system to discourage illegal parking of this kind without restricting access to the car parking areas to an extent which would render their authorised use impracticable.

Wheel clamping has been approved by statute as one of the measures available to the police for dealing with vehicles which have been illegally, obstructively or dangerously parked or have been abandoned or broken down. Sections 99 to 106 of the Road Traffic Regulation Act 1984 contain a number of measures directed to that object, among which is section 105 which enables a constable who finds on a road a vehicle which has been permitted to remain at rest there in contravention of any prohibition or restriction imposed by or under any enactment to fix an immobilisation device to the vehicle while it remains in the place in which he finds it. Provision is made for the fixing of a notice to the vehicle indicating that a device has been fixed to it and specifying the steps to be taken to secure its release, which can be done only by or under the direction of a police constable. The charge which may be made for its release is prescribed by statutory instrument and the device or appliance which may be used to immobilise the vehicle must be of a type approved by the Secretary of State. Furthermore, the provisions relating to the immobilisation of vehicles by this means extend only to such areas as the Secretary of State may by order specify. The wheel clamping of vehicles by the police in accordance with these provisions is, of course, permitted by law so long as all the statutory requirements are complied with. This case is concerned with the quite different position of those who make use of this practice without the benefit of statutory powers.

[Having concluded that the sheriff was correct in rejecting the plea to the relevancy of the charges of extortion, the Lord Justice-General then considered the question of whether the complaints relevantly libelled charges of theft:]

I turn now to the appeals by the prosecutor against the sheriff's decision to sustain the pleas to the relevancy which were directed to the theft charges. The narrative in these charges is simply that the accused attached a device to the wheel of the motor car, thus depriving the person having charge of the car of the use of it. There is no averment that this was done for any particular purpose or for any particular period of time, such as until the sum demanded as a levy had been paid. Plainly the purpose of affixing the device was to immobilise the vehicle, but there was here no question of *amotio* in the ordinary sense of the word because the vehicle was not moved or taken away. The physical element which is said to amount to theft in this case is the attachment of the device to the vehicle, thus depriving the motorist of his use of the car by detaining it where it was found. The question is whether this action can properly be described as theft and whether, in the absence of any express indication in the libel of a dishonest purpose, the charge can be held to be relevant.

The typical example of theft is of theft by taking away. Hume, i, 57, regarded the fundamental circumstance of the crime of theft as the taking of the thing, 'in which it is implied, that the thing has not been previously in the possession of the thief, but in that of the owner, or some person for him, out of which the thief, without the consent of the owner, removes it'. The concept of taking away is to be seen also in Macdonald (5th ed.), at p. 16, where he defines the crime as the felonious taking and appropriation of property without the consent of the owner or custodier. His addition of the word 'appropriation' might seem to be mere surplusage, as the taking of the thing is the means by which it is appropriated. But it helps to show that the essential feature of the physical act necessary to constitute theft is the appropriation, by which control and possession of the thing are taken from its owner or custodier. In principle therefore the removal of the thing does not seem to be necessary, if the effect of the act which is done to it is its appropriation by the accused. . . .

It seems to me that the act of depriving the motorist of the use of his motor car by detaining it against his will can accurately be described as stealing something from him, and that on this basis the facts libelled are sufficient to constitute a charge of theft. The accused are said to have deliberately placed a wheel clamp on a wheel of the vehicle which they found in the car park, in order to detain it there and keep it under their control against the will of the motorist. There is no suggestion that it was intended by the motorist that they should have control over the car for any purpose, or that by parking the vehicle in the car park he intended that anyone else should have control over it. And the physical element of appropriation is clearly present, in my opinion, since the purpose and effect of the wheel clamp was to immobilise the vehicle and use of it as a motor car. . . .

I agree with the comment in Gordon's *Criminal Law* (2nd ed.), para. 14–63 that it is the owner's loss and not the other's gain which is important. Thus the deliberate nature of the act of appropriation in knowledge of its consequences is sufficient in this case to justify the inference of *mens rea*. I think that the necessary elements are all present in the libel and that the sheriff was wrong to hold that the alternative charges of theft were irrelevant.

It may seem unfortunate that actions designed to assist the landowner to preserve his land for his own use, or for use by others with his authority, should have this result. But in my opinion, an activity as sensitive to abuse as wheel clamping requires careful regulation under the law, and if it is to be continued this should only be done under the authority of Parliament—as it is already, in the case of the police.

For these reasons, while I would refuse the appeals in respect of the extortion charges, I would allow the appeals by the prosecutor against the sheriff's decision in respect of the theft charges. Accordingly I invite your Lordships to refuse the appeals which have been taken against the sheriff's decision as regards the first alternative charges in each complaint, to repel the pleas to the relevancy of the alternative charges of theft libelled in each complaint, and thereafter to remit these cases to the sheriff to proceed as accords."

Appeal refused.

NOTES

**11.09**    1. This case, perhaps more than any other, illustrates the extent to which the law of theft has changed radically since the time of Hume. There was clearly an interference with the owner's use of the property, but no taking possession of it by the alleged thief, and certainly no "carrying away" of the property. All that is required is "appropriation". Unfortunately, the meaning of this term has not been much explored by the courts, or commentators on the law. It is clear that appropriation does not require removal of the goods, but what does it require? Does it involve interference with the rights of *ownership*, or can theft be committed by interfering with rights of *possession*?

a. A drops his wallet while running to catch a bus. B sees this, picks it up and keeps it. This is a clear case of theft in modern practice, and involves a complete denial by B of A's rights as an owner. It involves, as it were an assumption of the rights of the owner by B.

b. A hires his car to B for two weeks. B sells the car to C. Again, B assumes the rights of the owner by alienating the property. There is no interference with A's possessory rights, since he has relinquished these to B for the duration of the loan.

c. A hires his car to B for two weeks. C steals the car from outside B's house. Here there is an assumption of A's rights as owner, and those of B as possessor. From whom has C stolen the car?

2. If appropriation involves interference with property rights, how much interference is required? In the English case of *R. v. Morris* [1984] A.C. 320, [1983] 3 All E.R. 288 the accused in two separate cases went to a supermarket and switched price labels on goods displayed on the shelves, replacing the labels with others showing a lower price than that attached by the supermarket. The goods were then presented at the check out. In one case the accused's stratagem was discovered before the false price was paid, but in the other it was not discovered until after the goods had been tendered and the substituted price paid. Both cases were eventually referred to the House of Lords for consideration of the question of whether switching the price labels in this way amounted to "appropriation" of the goods for the purpose of section 3(1) of the Theft Act 1968 Act which states that "[a]ny assumption by a person of the rights of an owner amounts to an appropriation ...". It was argued by counsel for the accused that section 3(1) should be construed as meaning that appropriation required the assumption of *all* of the rights of an owner, and that there had therefore been no appropriation by the accused when they switched the price labels on the goods. Since in neither case had the accused assumed all of the rights of the owner, there was no appropriation. The House of Lords disagreed. It was not necessary, in their Lordships' opinion for the thief to assume *all* of the rights of the owner; an assumption of *any* of the rights of the owner would suffice.

Would label switching of the kind encountered in *Morris* amount to appropriation in the law of Scotland? There has been an assumption of some of the rights of the owner, and *Black v. Carmichael* suggests that the assumption of *all* of the rights of the owner is not necessary for there to be an appropriation. But is an assumption of some of the rights of ownership in itself sufficient? The argument was raised in *Morris* that merely to remove the goods from the shelf would be an assumption of some of the rights of the owner, and that would mean, for example, that a customer who takes goods off the shelf to look at contents or to check the price would have "appropriated" those goods.

An alternative approach is that the mere assumption of some of the rights of ownership does not amount to appropriation unless it also amounts to a denial of those rights on the part of the owner. Suppose, for example, that A, visiting a friend's house, picks up a CD and puts it in the CD player to listen to it. That involves the assumption of some of the rights of ownership—the right to use and enjoy the property. But does it involve appropriation of the property? A is not denying to the owner any of his or her rights in respect of the property. If A's friend does not want her to play the CD she can assert her rights in respect of the property. There is nothing in A's actions which deprives the owner of any of her rights.

In all of these cases the question has been whether there has been an appropriation, not whether there has been theft. There are other reasons, discussed below, why actions which involve appropriation are nevertheless not to be regarded as theft—the requisite *mens rea* may not have been present. Another reason is that theft requires that the appropriation be done without the consent of the owner. So, in the case of a customer examining goods in the supermarket, even if there is appropriation, it is done with the consent of the owner. (The supermarket presumably consents to potential customers examining the goods before offering to buy them.)

3. In *Black v. Carmichael* it was accepted that there was appropriation where the accused interfered with the owner's right to use his property, albeit temporarily. No further interference with the owner's rights was involved—the owner's property was not damaged, and no attempt was made to deprive him of the property by transferring it to someone else. In the circumstances it was a substantial interference with the owner's right to use his property, but not much else. That being so, there is a very substantial overlap between theft and malicious mischief, as that offence has come to be understood, following the decision of the High Court in *H.M. Advocate v. Wilson*, 1984 S.L.T. 117. In that case it was held that the crime of malicious mischief could be committed where a person intentionally interfered with property belonging to another in such a way as to cause that "patrimonial" (*i.e.* economic) loss. Now, suppose that in the circumstances of a case such as this the immobilised vehicle had been, for example, a taxi, and that

the result of the immobilisation had been that the taxi-owner had not been able to use the taxi to carry on his or her business, with resulting loss of income. To make the example clearer. Suppose that the taxi-owner had been booked to pick up a fare at a particular time, and that as a result of immobilisation that had not been possible. What offence would have been committed? According to *Black v. Carmichael* the offence is theft. But is it not also malicious mischief within the meaning of *Wilson*?

4. A pays for the use of a reserved car-parking space in a car park. Frequently other car users occupy this space without her permission. Arriving at work one morning she finds a car in her space. The adjacent spaces are also occupied. She parks her car across the end of the parking space, thus preventing the other car from being moved until she leaves work at the end of the day. Is A guilty of theft?

## (b) Property that can be stolen

**11.10** Ideas about what could be stolen were originally closely linked to the manner in which theft could be committed. Since theft consisted in the taking and carrying away of the property, it followed that only property which could be taken and carried away could be stolen. As a general rule, then, only corporeal moveables could be stolen. Even in Hume's time, however, it was accepted that there could be exceptions to this rule. So, for example, land, or things forming part of the land, could be if they were severed from the land and physically removed. See, for example, the case of *James Miln,* Hume, i, 79, "who was transported for stealing shorn grain, shearing and carrying away grass, and puling up and carrying away growing pease, all which facts were libelled, and sent to the assize, under the name of theft only". Hume was also of the view that it was just as much theft to "come in the night and work coal in his neighbour's pit, or stone in his quarry, or fuel in his moss, and carry it away and hide it" as "cutting off the leaden spouts, or tearing up the iron spikes of his house and carrying them away". (Hume, i, 80.)

Whether restrictions linked to the requirement of a taking and carrying away are relevant to the modern concept of "appropriation" is quite a different question. Suppose, for example, that A shifts the boundary fence between his land and that of his neighbour, so as to increase his property, and diminish that of his neighbour. He has not severed the land, and this would not appear to be theft. However, is there today any convincing reason for saying that A has not "appropriated" the property?

The modern law has departed somewhat from the restriction of theft to the appropriation of corporeal moveable property. A clear example of this relates to electricity, which, as a form of energy, is neither corporeal nor moveable. Yet charges of theft of electricity are quite common, no doubt aided by the shift of emphasis in the law from "taking and carrying away" to "appropriation". It is worth contrasting this with English law which does not include the dishonest abstraction of electricity within the crime of theft. In *Low v. Blease* [1975] Crim. L.R. 513 it was held that since electricity was not property capable of being appropriated, it was not theft for a burglar to make an unauthorised telephone call from premises which he had entered as a trespasser. Section 13 of the Theft Act 1968 does, however, make it a separate offence to dishonestly abstract electricity. Similarly, in South African law, it has been held that electricity, as a form of energy, cannot be the subject of a charge of theft: *S v. Mintoor*, 1996 (1) S.AC.R. 514 (C). There too, special legislative provision is made for the unlawful use of electricity: Electricity Act 41 of 1987, s.27(2).

The situation regarding incorporeal property more generally is unclear. Again, the early restriction of theft to property which could be taken and carried away meant that incorporeal property could not be stolen, and it was Hume's opinion that the appropriation "only of a sort of incorporeal right or privilege ... is not the subject of theft": Hume, i, 75, Gordon takes the same view (p. 471). The shift of emphasis from taking and carrying away to appropriation does not yet seem to have affected the type of property which can be stolen, although one can figure many examples in which incorporeal rights could be "appropriated" dishonestly. Suppose, for example, that A copies confidential information belonging to B, and passes it on to C, a trade rival of B. Is A guilty of stealing the information? Or suppose that A gives B a quantity of share certificates for safe-keeping, and without A's knowledge or consent B transfers the shares to C. Is B guilty of stealing the shares (as opposed simply to the certificates)? Consider the following cases.

### H.M. Advocate v. Mackenzies
1913 S.C. (J.) 107

**11.11** (For the facts of the case, see *ante*, p. 191.) On the question whether the indictment disclosed a relevant charge of theft:

LORD JUSTICE-CLERK: "As regards the charge of theft, I cannot see any ground for holding it to be irrelevant. The charge is stealing a book, and that charge the prosecutor will have to prove by sufficient evidence. All defences, such as that there was only a trespass and not a theft, will be open to the accused. The indictment seems to hint at the book having been taken, not to appropriate the actual article itself, but in order to obtain the opportunity of copying part of its contents for an illegitimate purpose. That such a taking, although there is no intention to retain the article, may be theft is I think clear. The article is taken from its owner for the serious purpose of obtaining something of value through the possession of it. And that such an action may be theft is shown by the case of a person who desires to enter premises for a felonious purpose, and takes possession of the key by which the security of the premises is protected. Although he has no desire or intention to appropriate and keep the key he is held to have stolen the key, he having taken it in order to facilitate the carrying out of his criminal intention. In this case the prosecutor charging the accused with stealing a book described fulfils all the requirements of relevancy, and if he can make out by his evidence that the book was taken, and taken with a nefarious purpose, he may be able to obtain a direction in law from the Judge at the trial that what was done constituted a theft of the book. It is quite evident that a book of no real value in itself may be of great value because of what is written in it. I think, therefore, that the charge of theft against the male prisoner must be held to be relevant."

Charge of the theft held relevant.

NOTE

It is important to appreciate that in this case the charge of theft was held relevant with regard to the appropriation of the book containing the information. The indictment did not charge the accused with stealing the information. See also *Dewar* (1777) Burnett, 115; Hume, i. 75. In that case an apprentice took "certain valuable receipts" belonging to his employer, copied them and returned them. It appears that in that case the court did not regard what was done as amounting to theft. Can that case be distinguished from *Mackenzies*? **11.12**

**Grant v. Allan**
1988 S.L.T. 11

An employee was charged with clandestinely taking and detaining copies of computer print-outs containing lists of and other information about his employers' customers, all without lawful right or authority and with intent to dispose of the print-outs to trade rivals of his employers; and further, with offering to furnish that information to particular persons and attempting to induce them to pay for it. The sheriff rejected a preliminary plea that this was not a crime known to the law of Scotland. The accused appealed. **11.13**

LORD JUSTICE-CLERK (ROSS): "In opening the appeal, counsel for the appellant submitted first that where the word 'take' was used in the complaint in relation to copies of print-outs, it referred to the making of copies of computer print-outs, and was not used in the sense of appropriating copies of such print-outs. The advocate-depute conceded that this was so, and that in the context of this complaint the word 'take' was not used in the sense of 'appropriate'. Counsel for the appellant next submitted that what was libelled in this complaint did not disclose a crime known to the law of Scotland, there was no crime known to the law of Scotland, either nominate or innominate, into which the facts libelled could be fitted. Copies of computer print-outs were said to have been taken (or made) and thereafter detained, but if the taking of the copies was not criminal, the subsequent detention of the copies could not advance the position. Counsel for the appellant stated that information might be appropriated in a number of ways. For example, information might be committed to memory; that would not be criminal, nor would continuing to remember it. He next considered the position where information which had been memorised was written down later. Writing it down might be the equivalent of detention of the information, but detention of any kind would not render the act any more criminal than it was *ab initio*.

Counsel for the appellant pointed out that if an employee has taken notes of his employer's confidential information, that might be a breach of contract, in which event the employer might have a remedy in the civil court; the employee might be forced to surrender the notes, but that would be by virtue of his obligation under contract. In reaching his decision, the sheriff had considered a number of authorities, and counsel proceeded to subject these to a critical analysis. He submitted that on a true reading the authorities did not support the sheriff's conclusion. Counsel for the appellant accordingly submitted that what was libelled in the complaint did not constitute a crime under the law of Scotland. He recognised that this court has an inherent power to punish any act which is obviously of a criminal nature (Hume, i, 12; Macdonald (5th ed.), p. 193; *Sugden v. H.M. Advocate*). Counsel for the appellant, however, submitted that we should not exercise this declaratory power for a number of reasons.

The advocate-depute accepted that the charge in the complaint had not been laid as a charge of theft. He submitted that what was libelled in the complaint was a crime similar to that in the case of *Dewar*. It was an innominate crime, but it was a crime. He founded on *Dewar* and *H.M. Advocate v. Mackenzies*, and contended that the complaint did libel a crime recognised by the law; the crime was the dishonest exploitation of the confidential information of another person (in this case the accused's employer). The criminal element is the dishonesty. At the end of the day, he submitted that in the complaint what was libelled was a crime. Alternatively, if it was not a crime, it should be made a crime and the court should exercise its declaratory power to that effect.

Before determining this issue, which the advocate-depute correctly described as a nice point, it is necessary to examine the authorities. The starting point is *Dewar*. No full report of this case appears to exist, but it is referred to in a footnote by Burnett in his *Treatise on Criminal Law*, p. 115. The following appear to be the facts: 'The prisoner was an apprentice to a Printfield company, the proprietors of which were possessed of *receipts* for mixing and preparing their colours, and which being of great value to them they of course kept secret. These receipts were laid by in a pocket book belonging to one of the partners in a lock-fast room. The Prisoner, wishing to get possession of the receipts, in order to obtain a copy of them, and thereby gain the secret, broke open the room, and withdrew the pocket-book and receipts; and having carried them away, got them copied, and *afterwards replaced them in the situation from which they had been taken*.' He was indicted for theft and housebreaking, and following a debate on relevancy, the court pronounced an interlocutor finding the libel relevant to infer an arbitrary punishment. Burnett accordingly draws the inference that since the libel had not been restricted, the court did not hold this to be 'a proper theft, the paper having been fraudulently abstracted, with a view merely to take a copy of it, and then to return it'. The case is cited by Burnett as authority for the proposition that the mere taking of an article for use or for a temporary purpose is not theft, although it is a punishable act. (As the law has developed, temporary appropriation may be sufficient for theft—*Milne v. Tudhope.*) In the footnote, Burnett states that the jury found 'that the prisoner, by unlawful means got possession of the pocket-book, and receipt libelled, and was present at the receipt being copied, with copies he took with him, with the view of receiving benefit from them'. He further records that the prisoner was sentenced. It is not, however, entirely clear whether he was punished because he had unlawful possession of the book, or whether it was because of his dishonest retention and use of the copies.

The next case is the case of *John Deuchars*. Since this case proceeded on a plea of guilty, counsel were agreed that it could hardly be regarded as an authority.

Counsel next referred to *H.M. Advocate v. Mackenzies*. That case concerned an indictment against a husband and wife charging the husband (1) with stealing a book of recipes of chemical secrets belonging to his employers and (2) with making copies of the recipes with intent to dispose of them for profit in breach of an agreement of secrecy with his employers. The first charge was held to be relevant. With reference to the second charge, the report in 7 Adam contains the following passage from the opinion of the Lord Justice-Clerk: 'The second charge against the male prisoner is that he was bound by his agreement with his employers not to make known to others the secrets of their business, and that he did in breach of trust make copies of recipes, with intent to dispose of them for a valuable consideration to trade rivals. I am quite unable to hold that this is a relevant charge of crime, either completed crime or attempted crime. It is a charge covering a preparation for crime only—opining that the completed act or actual attempt would infer crime—but it is not a charge of anything done that can be called an overt act. The law does not strike at preparation to commit a crime, unless by special statutory enactment such preparation is placed in the category of crime' [at p. 195]. Counsel for the appellant drew attention to the fact that in the report of this case in 1913 S.C. at p. 111, the third sentence which I have quoted above reads: 'It is a charge covering a preparation for crime only—assuming that the completed act or actual attempt would infer crime—but it is not a charge of anything done that can be called an overt act.' Although it is not possible to know whether either of these reports was revised by the Lord Justice-Clerk in 1913, I am inclined to the view that the revised version is that which employs the word 'assuming'. In any event, in my opinion, it makes more sense to read the sentence in question with the word 'assuming' rather than the word 'opining'.

The ratio of that case was that the second charge was irrelevant because it merely charged the accused with the preparation for and not with the perpetration of a crime. I read the Lord Justice-Clerk as reserving his opinion upon the matter of whether in the circumstances of that case the completed act or an actual attempt would have constituted a crime. He neither says that it would have constituted a crime nor that it would not have constituted a crime. The advocate-depute drew attention to a passage from the opinion of Lord Salvesen (1913 S.C. at p. 113), where he said, under reference to the second charge: 'It may even be that the accused was demonstrably preparing himself to do his employer a wrong; but it is not a crime to make preparations with a view to committing some crime in the future.' In my opinion, however, Lord Salvesen is not in that passage expressing any concluded view that if the accused had completed the act or made an actual attempt, that would have been a crime according to the law of Scotland. So far as the issue raised in this appeal is concerned, I agree with counsel for the appellant that the case of *Mackenzies* is neutral.

Having considered the competing contentions of the appellant and the Crown, I have reached the conclusion that what is libelled in this complaint does not constitute a crime according to the law of Scotland. I do not regard the case of *Dewar* as authority for the proposition for which the advocate-depute has contended. It is significant that Burnett, Hume and Macdonald all treat the case of *Dewar* under the heading of theft; it is authority for the proposition that the taking of an article for use or for some temporary purpose and then to restore it is not theft. It is true that Burnett describes it none the less as 'an irregular and punishable act'. In the case of *Dewar* there was, however, an element of appropriation. The pocket-book was taken by the prisoner and was removed by him from his master's premises. Although that did not constitute theft, the fact that the prisoner had by unlawful means got possession of the pocket-book and receipts was a material part of the jury's verdict. The advocate depute described the crime as an innominate crime, and maintained that in the case of *Dewar* the taking away and retaining of the pocket-book and receipts constituted the mechanics of the crime rather than the essence of the crime. I am not, however, satisfied that that distinction can be drawn from the case of *Dewar*. The fact of the matter is that the advocate-depute was unable to point to any reported case or any statement of the institutional writers which supported his proposition that the law of Scotland recognises as a crime the dishonest exploitation of confidential information of another. In the absence of any reported case or statement of any of the institutional writers supporting the proposition that there is a crime of the character described by the advocate-depute, I am not prepared to hold that a crime of that character is recognised by the law of Scotland.

In *Mackenzies* under reference to the second charge, Lord Salvesen said (1913 S.C. at p. 113): 'It sets forth a breach of the accused's contract of service with his employers, but this is primarily a civil wrong.' In my opinion the same could properly be said here. What is described in the present complaint might well constitute a civil wrong for which the employers would have a remedy in the civil courts. For the appellant clandestinely to make copies of computer print-outs belonging to his employers may well have breached an express or implied obligation owed to his employers by him not to disclose confidential information obtained in his employment, but it is quite another thing to proceed to categorise such behaviour as criminal. If the advocate-depute were well founded in contending that it was a crime dishonestly to exploit confidential information of an employer, difficult questions might well arise as to whether that crime could be committed by an employee who did no more than memorise the information, and subsequently commit it to writing. Moreover if an employee during the course of his employment, memorised confidential information to assist him in his work, and subsequently left his employment by mutual agreement, would he be committing a crime if he proceeded to make use of that information while employed by another or while acting in a self-employed capacity? Clearly a question would arise in such circumstances as to whether the exploitation of the confidential information of his employer could be regarded as dishonest. However that may be, having regard to the authorities to which we were referred by both the appellant and the Crown, I am not prepared to hold that what is libelled in this complaint is a crime under the law of Scotland....

I should add that in moving us to refuse the appeal the advocate depute did not seek to support the reasoning of the sheriff in the present case, but confined himself to contending that the court should recognise that the dishonest exploitation of confidential information of another was a crime. That does not appear to have been an argument which was addressed to the sheriff. I should also add for the sake of completeness that the advocate-depute referred us to an English case and a Canadian case (*Oxford v. Moss* and *R. v. Stewart*). Since both these cases concerned the question of whether conduct constituted theft within the terms of statutes, I did not find these cases of assistance in determining the issue which arose in the present appeal. In all the circumstances, I would move your Lordships to sustain the appeal, to reverse the decision of the sheriff and remit the case to the sheriff with directions to him to dismiss the complaint."

Complaint dismissed.

NOTES

**11.14** 1. The Crown invited the Court to exercise its declaratory power and to declare criminal the dishonest appropriation of confidential information. In declining this invitation Lord Ross stated:

> "... Hume describes the declaratory power of the court as an inherent power to punish every act which is obviously of a criminal nature. Although there are circumstances where it will be appropriate for the court to exercise this power, I am of opinion that great care must be taken in the exercise of this power. Exercising the power may well conflict with the principle *nullum crimen sine lege*. The declaratory power has been considered in a number of cases over the last fifty years. I do not find it necessary to consider these cases because I am not satisfied that what is libelled in this complaint was so obviously of a criminal nature that it should be treated as a crime under the criminal law. No doubt what the appellant is alleged to have done was reprehensible and immoral, but as was recognised in *Mackenzies*, the fact that conduct is reprehensible or indicates moral delinquency is not sufficient to bring it within the scope of the criminal law. I recognise that there may be reasons for thinking that conduct of this kind ought to be regarded as criminal. However, if that is so, I am of opinion that it is for Parliament and not the courts to create any new crime in that regard."

2. In the area of misuse of confidential information (often linked to the problems of computer crime) the law has been slow to react. See, *e.g.* Scottish Law Commission Memorandum No. 40 on Confidential Information. Such protection as the criminal law affords to confidential information is indirect and can

be found, for example, in the Data Protection Acts 1984 and 1998 as well as the Interception of Communications Act 1985 and the Computer Misuse Act 1990.

3. Although Lord Ross did not think it appropriate to consider the cases of *Oxford v. Moss* (1978) 68 Cr. App. R., [1979] Crim. L.R. 119 and *Stewart v. The Queen* [1988] 1 S.C.R. 963, (1988) 50 D.L.R. (4th) 1, both support his view that the dishonest appropriation of information is not theft (under English or Canadian law respectively). In *R v. Cheeseborough*, 1948 (3) S.A. 756 (T) it was held that South African law did not recognise as theft the appropriation of "a design or idea" and in *S. v. Harper*, 1981 (2) S.A. 638 (D) the view was expressed that "[i]t is difficult to imagine the theft of an idea purely and simply".

4. The difficulties involved in holding that information can be stolen are considerable, and are not confined to the question of whether or not information is property. As the arguments in this case suggest, can it be said that the thief has "appropriated" the information merely by copying it? It might be possible to add that the thief "appropriates" the medium in which the information is contained, at least where that is in tangible form. But suppose that the thief merely memorised the information, or passed it on in electronic form (for example, by means of electronic mail). Would that amount to an appropriation? And in what sense has the owner been deprived of the "property" in the information? It can be said that the value of the information has been substantially impaired, but the owner is nonetheless still in a position to use it. If the thief destroys the owner's records of the information then charges of theft of the medium in which the information was stored (if corporeal) or malicious mischief. If the information is stored in electronic form there may be an offence under the Computer Misuse Act 1990.

5. At the same time, however, the realities of modern commercial transactions suggest that in certain circumstances the law ought to recognise theft of certain forms incorporeal property. Suppose, for example, that A and B both have current accounts with a bank. A has an overdraft of £250, while B has a credit balance in his account of £250. A, without authority, effects an electronic transfer of £350 from B's account into his own, thus extinguishing his own overdraft, creating a credit balance of £100 in his account, while at the same time creating an overdraft of £100 in B's account. At no time during or following this transaction does A take physical control of any cash from the bank.

What has happened here is that the debt which A owed the bank (his overdraft) has been replaced by an apparent debt owed to him by the bank (the credit balance), while at the same time, a debt owed by the bank to B (the credit balance) has been replaced by a debt owed to the bank by B. Why should this not be regarded as theft by B, simply because the property in question (the debts) is incorporeal?

## (c) *Belonging to another*

Theft requires that the property stolen belongs to someone other than the thief. It follows from this that **11.15** the property must be of a kind which is capable of being owned, that it is owned by someone, and that it is not owned, or at least entirely owned, by the thief.

## (i) Property which cannot be "owned"

Certain things are outside the scope of the law of theft because they cannot be owned. Examples are few **11.16** and far between. It is sometimes said that the clearest example of something which cannot be owned, and thus cannot be stolen, is a human being. But this general statement requires considerable qualification.

In the first place, there is a category of human beings which in the law of Scotland *can* be stolen: children below the legal age of puberty can be stolen. The crime is known as "*plagium*". In *Hamilton v. Wilson*, 1994 S.L.T. 431 *plagium* was described as "the deliberate taking of a child from the custody of a parent or other person who has for the time being the parental right of custody in terms of [the Children (Scotland) Act 1995] or under an order made by the court." Since the crime depends upon the interference with the parental right of custody, from which the natural parents of a child may be excluded, it follows that the crime can be committed by the child's parent (or parents). See generally, see *Downie v. H.M. Advocate*, 1984 S.C.C.R. 365, *Hamilton v. Mooney*, 1990 S.L.T. (Sh.Ct) 105, *Hamilton v. Wilson*, above. In *Hamilton v. Wilson* it was held that the Crown do not need to prove that that the accused intended to keep the child permanently.

Secondly, while it is clearly right that we do not consider living human beings, in general, to be "property", what about dead people, or parts of human beings? Again, while we might generally not wish to regard human remains as "property" would we always adopt this view? What, for example, of human remains such as those preserved in museums? Would it not be theft to appropriate such items? And what of human organs, or blood held by a hospital or blood transfusion service? Should it not be theft to take such property?

Scots law appears to draw a distinction according to whether or not the body has been interred. It is not theft to remove a body from a grave or tomb: "The raising of a dead body from the grave, cannot in any proper sense be regarded as a theft" (Hume, i, 85). To interfere with human remains which have been interred is, nevertheless "great indecency and a crime of its own sort" known as "violation of sepulchres" (Hume, i, 85). This crime cannot be committed until the body has been buried or placed in a tomb, and there comes a point at which, through decomposition, the body ceases to be an object of "reverential treatment" (Gordon, p. 999) and thus beyond the protection of the law. (See, generally, *Chas. Soutar*, (1882) 5 Couper 65, *H.M. Advocate v. Coutts* (1899) 3 Adam 50.

The position with regard to human remains which have not been interred is less clear. Hume (i, 85) Alison (i, 282) and Macdonald (p. 21) all cite the case of *McKenzie* (1733, Burnett, 124) as authority for the view that it is theft to carry off a dead body before it has been buried, but as is pointed out in *H.M. Advocate v. Coutts*, above, the charge in that case was not theft but "Ryot and Violence", so that case is not conclusive on the point. In *Dewar v. H.M. Advocate*, 1945 J.C. 5, *ante*, Chapter 2, the accused was charged with stealing coffin lids, and other property which had been consigned to him, as manager of a crematorium, for cremation. It appears to have been assumed by at least some members of the Court that human remains can be stolen before burial. (See, in particular, Lord Moncrieff, 1945 J.C. 5, at 14.) Gordon's conclusion (p. 479) is that a human body which has not been buried can be stolen, although this may be qualified by the examples of theft which he suggests, which are limited to cases of human remains which have been deliberately preserved through human skill.

This conclusion appears to be supported by English and other Commonwealth authority. (See *R. v. Kelly and Another* [1998] 3 All E.R. 741, *Doodeward v. Spence* (1908) 6 C.L.R. 406 (High Court of Australia) and *Dobson v. North Tyneside Health Authority* [1996] 4 All E.R. 474.)

## (ii) Property which is not owned

**11.17**  Property which is not already owned by anyone cannot be the subject of a charge of theft. There is probably only one instance in which property is outside the ownership of another and that is where it has not yet been the subject of ownership. One other possibility, namely, that the property, having been once owned, is no longer owned because it has been abandoned, does not arise in the law of Scotland since abandoned property belongs to the Crown. (See, on this, the case of *Lord Advocate v. University of Aberdeen and Budge*, 1963 S.C. 533.)

The clearest example of ownerless property is that of wild animals. Wild animals, native to Scotland, which have not been captured do not belong to anyone, even the owner of the land upon which they live. As a general rule, therefore, it is not theft to capture or kill such creatures. "It is established on the highest authority that, while animals such as deer and other game do not belong to anyone so long as they are at large, but are *res nullius*, they become the property of the captor or finder of them after they have been killed—see Stair, *Institutions*, II.i.33; Erskine, *Institute*, II.i.10; *Scott v. Everitt* (1853) 15 D. 288." (*Assessor for Argyll v. Broadlands Properties Ltd. and Others*, 1973 S.C. 152, *per* Lord Fraser.)

The same rule applies to salmon and other fish which are native to Scotland. In *Corbett v. Macnaughton*, 1985 S.L.T. 312 it was held that "because salmon is a *res nullius*, a dealer in poached salmon cannot be charged with reset". Similarly, "[f]ish such as trout which have not been confined are *res nullius* since they are in that state wild animals (*ferae naturae*); it is not therefore theft at common law to catch such unconfined trout even if in catching the trout a breach of the incorporeal rights of others results ...". (*Valentine v. Kennedy*, 1985 S.C.C.R. 90, *per* Sheriff Younger at p. 90.)

However, once a wild animal has been captured or otherwise reduced into possession by someone, it is theft for another to appropriate the creatures. "[T]rout may in my opinion lose their status as *res nullius* at common law if they are confined within an area such as a stank in the same way as other wild animals may lose that character by being enclosed .... There seems to me to be no difference in principle between an enclosure for wild animals such as deer and a water enclosure such as a stank for wild animals such as trout." (*Valentine v. Kennedy*, above, Sheriff Younger at pp. 90–91.)

Different considerations apply to creatures which are not native to Scotland. In *Valentine v. Kennedy* Sheriff Younger noted (at p. 91) that "when fish such as rainbow trout [which are not native to Scotland] have been bred in a fish farm and purchased therefrom, they have already lost their status as *res nullius* in my opinion, and in any event the inference that ownership of them has been retained by the purchaser if he releases them into his own enclosed water or stank, . . . seems to me to be very strong. Thereafter, if some of these rainbow trout escape occasionally in spite of proper precautions from that enclosed water or stank I consider that they as escapees remain the property of that purchaser in so far as they can be identified as his own property; accordingly, someone who catches trout which he knows to have escaped from a stank or enclosed water is guilty of theft if he does not return them to their rightful owner".

Despite the general rules of the common law, the taking of wild creatures is in practice subject to a range of criminal law restrictions. In the first place, the taking of certain wild creatures is treated as equivalent to theft. Thus the Act 1607, c.-3 of the Parliament of Scotland (now known as the Theft Act, 1607) provides, *inter alia*, that "whasoever . . . steals bees and fishes in proper stanks and lochs, shall be conveined and called therefore as an breaker of the law". In *Pollok v. McCabe and Another*, (1909) 4 Adam. 139 it was held that an artificial reservoir, created in order to provide supplies of drinking water, but which had been stocked with fish by the person having fishing rights in relation to the property was a "stank" for the purposes of the 1607 Act. See also *Valentine v. Kennedy* (above).

## (iii) Property in which the thief has an interest

The older authorities are all agreed that a person cannot be guilty of stealing his own property. Hume **11.18** states that he sees "no reason to believe that in our practice, a person shall in any case be held guilty of theft, though he may of some inferior wrong, for irregularly taking that which is his own" (Hume, i, 77). Alison (i, 277), Macdonald (p. 16) and modern texts all accept this statement of the law. This is an easily accepted proposition where the thief is the sole proprietor of the goods in question and where no other person has an interest. But since ownership is a collection of rights which may be shared by two or more people, the question arises as to whether there are cases in which a person may be guilty of stealing property in which he or she has an interest as an owner, but not the sole interest.

What is the situation where someone other than the owner has an interest in the property? Suppose, for example, that A takes his car to a garage for repair. The repairs are carried out according to his instructions. Instead of paying for the repairs, A surreptitiously removes the car from the garage. In these circumstances, the garage proprietor has a right to retain the vehicle, a "lien" by way of security for payment for the work carried out. Is the garage proprietor's interest in the vehicle sufficient to make A a thief? Again, the answer appears to be that he is not. Although Hume does suggest that in such circumstances the owner may be guilty of an offence (Hume, i, 59) he does not accept that an owner can steal his own goods, and that whatever offence the owner commits it is "some inferior wrong" rather than theft (Hume, i, 77). (*cf.* the definition of ownership in s.5(1) of the English Theft Act 1968, and the case of *R. v. Turner (No. 2)* [1971] 2 All E.R. 441, and also the South African cases of *R. v. Rudolph*, 1935 T.P.D. 79 and *R. v. Janoo*, 1959 (3) S.A. 107(A).)

## (d) *Without consent*

If the owner consents to the appropriation, there is no theft: Hume, i, 57–58, Alison, i, 250. In most cases **11.19** there will be no difficulty at all in holding that the appropriation took place without consent since most thieves appropriate the property without reference to the owner. Difficulties may, however, arise where the thief obtains the property with the agreement of the owner, but that agreement has been obtained by fraud. Two situations need to be distinguished here.

The first is where the thief induces the owner to part with the goods, but without there even being any question of the owner parting with ownership. Hume (i, 69) and Alison (1, 259) both refer to the case of *John Marshall* (April 26, 1792) as an illustration of this. In that case the accused hired a horse in Sanquhar, ostensibly to ride to Leadhills, a distance of about ten miles. He undertook to return the horse that same day. Instead, he rode the horse to Edinburgh where he sold it. The accused was charged with theft of the horse, or, alternatively, fraud. The court held that this was a case of theft. The conclusion would, indeed be the same, even in the absence of fraud, since the owner does not consent to the transfer of the property in either case.

Greater difficulties may, however, arise, where consent to transfer ownership has been obtained by fraud on the part of the transferee. Suppose, for example, that A steals a cheque book belonging to B.

He uses one of the cheques, forging B's signature on the cheque, to buy a second hand car from C. A then sells the car on to D. Is A guilty of theft of the car when he sells it to D, or merely of fraud when he obtains it from C? The answer to this question depends upon whether or not the fraud perpetrated by A prevents the title to the property passing to him. If the title to the property passes to A, then his appropriation of it (by selling it to D) cannot amount to theft, since the transaction makes him owner of the property. If, however, the fraud prevents title passing, then A is guilty of theft when he appropriates the goods. Consider, in this respect, the following case:

**Macleod v. Kerr and Another**
1965 S.C. 253

**11.20**     LORD PRESIDENT (CLYDE): "The issue in this case is whether a motor car at present in the custody of the procurator fiscal belongs in property now to Mr Kerr ... who at one time admittedly owned the car, or to Mr Gibson (the defender), who claims that it is now his. After a proof the sheriff-substitute decided the issue in favour of Mr Kerr and Mr Gibson has appealed to the Court of Session against this decision.

The facts are not essentially in dispute. Prior to February 12, 1964, the car was owned by Mr Kerr. He wished to dispose of it and advertised it for sale. On February 12, 1964 a man called on him in reply to the advertisement and after negotiations Mr Kerr agreed to take 375 pounds sterling for the car. This man purported to be named L Craig although his true name was Galloway. Galloway wrote out a cheque for 375 pounds sterling signing it L Craig. Mr Kerr gave him the registration book, and Galloway drove the car away. Next day Mr Kerr ascertained that the cheque book had been stolen and the cheque was dishonoured. Mr Kerr at once informed the police. On 14th February, Galloway, purporting to be Mr Kerr, called at Mr Gibson's garage with the car and sold it to Mr Gibson for 185 pounds sterling plus a small credit against the purchase of a new car. Mr Gibson purchased and paid for the car in good faith and without any knowledge of any defect in Galloway's title. Shortly thereafter the police took possession of the car. It was on these facts that the issue before us arises.

The sheriff-substitute decided the case upon the view that Galloway had stolen the car from Mr Kerr and he invoked the well-known principle that where goods are stolen the true owner has a right to recover them even against a third party who bona fide acquired them. In the view of the sheriff-substitute therefore Mr Kerr could now recover the car and Mr Gibson has no right to it. But the fallacy of this conclusion is that the car was not in fact stolen from Mr Kerr at all, he voluntarily agreed to transfer the car to the person who called in answer to the advertisement, and he did so transfer it. To constitute theft of the car from Mr Kerr there would have to be a taking away from Mr Kerr without any intention on his part to convey it and without his consent to the transfer. (Hume on *Crime* I, page 57: Alison on *Crime* I, page 259). On the facts in this case it is clear that Mr Kerr intended to transfer the car and did in fact voluntarily transfer it to the man who appeared in answer to the advertisement whom he honestly regarded as purchasing the car. The facts in the present case therefore exclude theft. It was consequently not open to the sheriff-substitute to hold that the car was stolen from Mr Kerr."

Appeal allowed.

NOTES

**11.21**     1. Lords Carmont and Guthrie agreed with Lord Clyde in holding that the nature of the fraud perpetrated by Galloway did not render the contract between him and Kerr void but merely voidable. *McLeod v. Kerr* was followed in *Young v. D.S. Dalgleish & Son (Hawick) Ltd*, 1994 S.C.L.R. 696. The case may, however, be different where the contract is not one of sale but of barter (exchange): *O'Neill v. Chief Constable, Strathclyde Police and Others*, 1994 S.C.L.R. 253. It may also be different where the deception creates an error as to some more fundamental question, such as the identity of the other party to the agreement: *Morrisson v. Robertson*, 1908 S.C. 332. But where the owner's intention is to transfer property in the goods, the fact that that consent has been obtained by fraud will not prevent property transferring. The contrary opinion adopted in *William Wilson* (1882) 5 Couper 48 is not supported by other authorities and is inconsistent with the civil law on the effect of fraud on the passing of property as determined in *McLeod v. Kerr*. Gordon notes (p. 494) that it is not followed in modern practice. It should be regarded as incorrectly decided.

## B. The *mens rea* of theft

### (a) The intention to deprive

This aspect of the law has undergone significant developments in the last 20 years. At one time it could **11.22** be stated that theft required an intention permanently to deprive the owner of the property. But it is clear that this statement now requires substantial qualification. There may, indeed, be four forms of intention to deprive in theft: (i) An intention permanently to deprive, (ii) an intention to deprive for a "nefarious" or "illegitimate" purpose, (iii) an intention to deprive indefinitely, or (iv) an intention to deprive temporarily.

### (i) Intention to deprive permanently

Gordon states (at p. 500) "it is clear that Scots law requires an intention to deprive the owner **11.23** permanently of his goods. In the absence of this intent, there can be no theft". He does not, however, provide any authority directly to support this opinion, and there is a dearth of authority on the question prior to the late 1970's. Hume's discussion of theftuous intent only briefly addresses this issue, although he does appear to take the view that an intention to appropriate implies an intention to deprive the owner of his goods, rather than the use of them:

> "The taking and carrying away must be with a felonious purpose; by one who knows that the thing belongs to another, and who means to deprive him of his property. Thus, on the one hand, it is not theft, to take away the property of another, though known to be his, if the taker's object is irregular only and improper, and not to appropriate the thing. Put the case, that a servant rides his master's horse in the night, on his own errand; or that finding his neighbour's plough lying in the field, a farmer openly uses it to till his own contiguous field; or that he drives his neighbour's cattle into his own inclosure in the night to poind them there, under the pretence of a trespass" (Hume, i, 73).

Alison (i, 270–271) reproduces the examples given by Hume, but also quotes the case of *Dewar* (1777, Hume, i, 75, Burnett 115) as an example of a case in which there was no theft but merely "an irregular and punishable act" of temporarily taking a book containing secret formulae and copying them. Macdonald (5th ed., pp. 19–20) is almost self-contradictory. Having stated that "[t]he taking must be with intent to appropriate and to deprive the owner of his property" he gives (without acknowledgment) Hume's example of A using B's plough which he has found and concludes that "this is only a trespass". He also states that "[i]f a person take a boat for a sail, or if a servant use a horse of his master's to go an errand of his own and return, there is no theft". However, he then proceeds to state that "[i]t is no defence to a charge of theft that the person charged had no intention of totally depriving the owner of the article. The crime is properly one of theft if the owner of property is clandestinely deprived of possession of it even although the deprivation be temporary". In support of this he refers to *Mackenzies* 1913 S.C. (J.) 107, *ante*, p. 450—in which the leading opinion was delivered by Macdonald himself.

Despite these ambiguities, Sheriff MacPhail had no hesitation in stating, in *Herron v. Best*, 1976 S.L.T. (Sh.Ct) 80 that "the essential feature of the *mens rea* of theft is an intention to appropriate, and that appropriation involves an intention to deprive the owner permanently of his goods". Furthermore, that an intention permanently to deprive was necessary for theft is the clear implication of the decision in *Strathern v. Seaforth*, 1926 J.C. 100, *post*, p. 483 in which it was held that it was a separate and distinct offence at common law clandestinely to take and use property belonging to another without that person's consent.

Establishing that the accused had this intention at the time of the appropriation may, however, be problematic. But this can be overcome by permitting inferences to be drawn from the way in which the accused deals with the property once it has come under his or her control:

### Kivlin v. Milne
1979 S.L.T. (Notes) 2

**11.24** An accused was charged with theft of a motor car, while acting along with another person. The vehicle was abandoned by the accused in a place where the owner was not liable to discover it. It was submitted to the sheriff that in order to establish the crime of theft it must be shown that there had been an intention to deprive the owner of permanent ownership or that the accused had quite recklessly taken away the property and had put it into such a situation that the owner was effectively prevented from getting it back. On appeal by stated case against conviction, the High Court stated:

OPINION OF THE COURT: "The argument advanced by learned counsel for the appellant was to the effect that the necessary conditions to constitute theft had not been established, in that the facts proved did not establish that there was present in the mind of the appellant, on each of the two occasions libelled, the intention permanently to deprive the owner of the motor car of the possession thereof. In the event counsel conceded that it was a matter of circumstances in each case, and having regard to the findings-in fact we are of the opinion that the learned sheriff in each of the two charges libelled was entitled to draw the inference that the appellant had the intention permanently to deprive the owner of the motor car of the possession thereof, in that he undoubtedly took possession of it without authority and left the car on each occasion in a place where the owner, by reason of his own investigations, was not liable to discover it. In that situation we are of the opinion that the question of law for the opinion of the court, falls to be answered in the affirmative and the appeal will accordingly be dismissed."

Appeal dismissed.

NOTE

**11.25** What sort of inquiries would it be reasonable for the owner to make in a case such as this? If the property is left in a place where the owner is likely to discover it, what is the appropriate charge? Where the property is a motor vehicle the prosecutor may have recourse to a charge of taking and driving away a motor vehicle, contrary to section 178 of the Road Traffic Act 1988, and alternative charges of theft and the statutory offence were sometimes encountered.

## (ii) Intention to deprive for a nefarious purpose

### Milne v. Tudhope
1981 J.C. 53

**11.26** Two accused persons were convicted of stealing certain articles which they had previously installed in a cottage which was under renovation. They did so after refusing to carry out remedial work on the cottage for the owner thereof, the latter having declined to make payment for such work. They subsequently offered to return the articles removed if the owner would pay additional remuneration. He refused and reported the matter to the police. Each accused appealed against conviction.

LORD JUSTICE-CLERK (WHEATLEY): "The submission by appellant's counsel on the other question which was whether the sheriff was entitled to convict the appellant of theft, was limited in scope. He did not attack the legal ground which was the basis of the sheriff's decision but maintained that the sheriff was not entitled to convict the appellant on the facts found when tested against that legal principle. The sheriff reviewed all the authorities at considerable length and in some detail. His final conclusion thereon was stated thus: 'It was primarily upon the view that a clandestine taking, aimed at achieving a nefarious purpose, constitutes theft, even if the taker intends all along to return the thing taken when his purpose has been achieved, that I decided to convict Mr Alistair Milne of theft as libelled.' In these circumstances it is unnecessary to repeat the authorities at length. All that is required is to see how far the findings justified the sheriff's conclusion on the view of the law which he took.

"Appellant's counsel made four submissions. They are all really interrelated. We propose to consider the first and second submissions together because they are, as counsel said, different ways of expressing the same point. The first submission was that on the facts found by the sheriff there was no basis for finding that *mens rea* was present in this crime and the second was that there was no basis in the facts for finding that the taking and holding of the articles in question was 'nefarious'. Reliance was placed on *Fraser v. Anderson* (1899) 1 F. (J.C.) 60; (1899) 2 Adam 705, where the majority of the court held, on the facts in that case, that there was no felonious intent. That case is clearly distinguishable on the facts. There the accused was in possession of the cattle which he had sold to another man and thought that he had a right to sell the cattle because the price had not reached him. In the present case the appellant took away articles which he knew belonged to Mr MacPhail. His reason for doing so was, as the sheriff said, that he was motivated 'partly by anger against Mr MacPhail, but principally by his anxiety lest he should not be allowed to complete the work at Biggar Cottage under the contract of July 5, 1978, by his desire to complete that work, and by his desire to obtain additional payment from Mr MacPhail for the additional work that would have to be done in order to bring the work already done up to the standard desired by Mr MacPhail. He was not prepared to do that additional work unless he received payment additional to the £13,000 he had already received, and he intended to retain the articles removed from Biggar Cottage on 19 December until he could force Mr MacPhail to agree to have a personal meeting with him, instead of dealing with him through Mr Barratt, and to get Mr MacPhail at that personal meeting to agree to allow him to complete the work under the contract of July 5, 1978 and to make him a further payment for bringing the work already done up to the desired standard'. It seems to us that the purpose was 'nefarious'. The appellant was trying to achieve something by a scheme which he must have known was unlawful. Whether 'nefarious' means 'criminal' in this context or unlawful does not matter for present purposes. The sheriff was entitled to reach the view which he did on the findings.

"The third submission was that there was nothing clandestine about the taking of the articles. Appellant's counsel appeared to suggest that something secret in the actual manner of taking was required before it could be said that it was 'clandestine'. This is to ignore the fact that the taking was secret so far as the owner of the articles was concerned and was without his authority. While this was done openly in one sense the facts show that it was done secretly so far as the owner of the articles was concerned.

"The fourth submission was that there was a conditional intention to return the articles and that elided the necessary criminal intent. This was said to be something different from the absence of *mens rea*, and some reliance was placed on a decision by Sheriff Macphail in *Herron v. Best*, 1976 S.L.T. (Sh. Ct.) 80. We have some difficulty in understanding this submission when the sheriff's view of the law was accepted and the argument was that the findings did not justify the application of that law to justify a conviction. We agree with the sheriff's statement of the law to the effect that 'in certain exceptional cases an intention to deprive temporarily will suffice' and disagree with Sheriff Macphail that 'an intention to deprive permanently' is essential."

Appeal refused.

## NOTES

1. Although it is not referred to in the opinion of the Lord Justice-Clerk, the seeds of this approach are **11.27** to be found in Lord Macdonald's opinion in *H.M. Advocate v. Mackenzies*, 1913 S.C. (J.) 107, *ante*, p. 450.

2. Although the court accepts that an intention to deprive, clandestinely and for a nefarious purpose, is sufficient for theft, it still treats this as an exception to a general rule that intention permanently to

deprive is required. Unfortunately, there is no discussion about how exceptional such circumstances have to be to bring into play a departure from the rule. In particular, there is no explanation of the content of what would count as a "nefarious purpose" sufficient to convert temporary deprivation into theft.

3. *Milne v. Tudhope* was followed in *Kidston v. Annan*, 1984 S.C.C.R. 20. In that case the accused was charged with theft of a television set. The owner claimed he had given it to the accused for a free estimate in respect of repairs. The accused repaired it without instructions and sought to retain it until the repair bill was paid. His conviction for theft was upheld by the High Court. The common feature of these two cases is that the accused was, as it were, holding the owner's property to ransom (a phrase which was, indeed, used by the High Court in *Kidston v. Annan*). It might therefore be argued that the "nefarious purpose" referred to in *Milne v. Tudhope* is confined to the case where the accused's conduct is directed towards compelling the owner of the goods to comply with the demands of the thief—effectively extortion.

4. That interpretation of the law does not, however, appear to have been accepted by the court in the cases of *Sandlan v. H.M. Advocate*, 1983 S.C.C.R. 71, *McGurk v. Donnelly*, High Court, May 28, 1999, unreported and *Carmichael v. Black; Black v. Carmichael*, 1992 S.L.T. 897.

In *Black v. Carmichael* the property was appropriated with a view to extorting money from the owner. However, the High Court did not rely on the "nefarious purpose" rule in order to hold that the accused were guilty of theft.

In *Sandlan* the "nefarious purpose" did not involve holding the property to ransom. In that case the appellant and another man, K, were charged with stealing jewellery, money and books containing sales records from a company of which the appellant was a director. The Crown's case was that the theft of the property was part of a plan by the appellant to falsely obtain insurance money by claiming that he had been robbed of the jewellery. K admitted arranging for the removal of the property, but claimed in his defence, *inter alia*, that the removal was only intended to be temporary, that the goods were to be returned, and were only removed to have them out of the way during the company's stocktaking to cover up alleged pilfering by the first accused. The trial judge, Lord Stewart, directed the jury as follows on the question of the intent necessary for theft:

> "If you accept King, the purpose for which the jewellery and books were removed was undoubtedly a nefarious one. Goods were removed in a clandestine fashion, that is to say, secretly. The law is that such a taking of the goods of another, aimed at achieving a nefarious purpose, constitutes theft even if the taker intends all along to return the thing taken when his purpose has been achieved . . ."

Lord Stewart appears to interpret "nefarious" as including any fraudulent purpose, although that could be qualified, in the light of the facts of *Sandlan* as being confined to a fraudulent purpose directed at the victim of the theft.

In *McGurk* the appellant was convicted, *inter alia*, of theft of a car number plate. He was observed by the police standing next to a parked car, looking through the passenger window. When the police approached him he ran away. The police found that the front number plate of an adjacent vehicle had been removed and was found forced between the window glass and the door frame of the car next to which the appellant had been seen. On appeal it was argued that the *mens rea* for theft had not been made out. The number plate had been taken only to be used as an implement with no intention of permanently depriving the owner of this property. In rejecting this argument Lord Sutherland stated that "when property is appropriated as this number plate was for an illegal use, that would constitute the crime of theft."

In this case, therefore, all that was required was appropriation of the property for use in the commission of a crime. Indeed, the term actually used by the court— "illegal use"—is capable of an even broader interpretation and in *Milne v. Tudhope* the court declined to state whether "nefarious purposes" were confined to crimes or included other "unlawful" acts. It should also be noted that in this case the owner of the property taken was not the intended of the victim for the commission of which the property was appropriated.

In this context it is also worth noting what, if any, meaning can be given to the term "clandestine". In *Sandlan* Lord Stewart said that this meant "secretly" (1983 S.C.C.R. 71, at p. 83). In *Milne v. Tudhope* it was objected that the property was taken openly. The court held that while this was true in one sense, it was taken without the knowledge or consent of the owner, and it was therefore taken "clandestinely".

5. In the light of the above, the conclusion appears to be that the appropriation of property without the knowledge and consent of the owner, for the purpose of committing an offence is theft, even if the person appropriating the property does not intend to deprive the owner permanently of the property.

6. But even in the absence of nefarious purposes and clandestine takings, it appears that the necessary theftuous intent may be present where the accused intends to deprive the owner of his property "indefinitely". See the following case.

## (iii) Intention to deprive indefinitely

### Fowler v. O'Brien
### 1994 S.C.C.R. 112

The appellant approached the complainer and asked him for a shot of his bicycle. The **11.28** complainer refused. The appellant took the bicycle anyway, without the complainer's consent. He was quite open about doing so. He did not make it clear if or when he would return the bicycle, or where he was going to leave it and took no steps to return it to the complainer. The complainer hunted for the bicycle but was unable to find it at first. He did, however, recover it several days later. The justice held that the actions of the appellant were "tantamount to being more than temporary deprivation". He also took the view that "the absence of any clandestine or nefarious purpose was immaterial because it was the intention of the appellant to deprive the owner of the bicycle more than just temporarily". The justice held that "this was an exceptional case in which an intention to deprive temporarily was sufficient to constitute theft" and convicted the appellant of theft of the bicycle. On appeal to the High Court:

Lord Justice-General (Hope): "The appellant is Robert Fowler, who went to trial in the district court of Cumnock and Doon Valley at Cumnock on a charge of stealing a pedal cycle and a separate charge of committing that offence while he was on bail. A motion was made at the end of the Crown case that there was no case to answer, but that motion was repelled. There was no defence evidence and the appellant was then found guilty as libelled.

He has applied, by way of stated case, for a review of the decision by the justice on grounds related to the sufficiency of the evidence that he was guilty of theft. The essential point in the application for a stated case is put in these terms.

'The matters which are desired to bring under review are . . . .

(b) in the absence of any clandestine taking or nefarious purpose, was the court entitled to take the view that this was an exceptional case in which a permanent intention to deprive was not essential to bring home the offence of theft?'

The reference to the question whether this was an exceptional case echoes a passage in *Milne v. Tudhope*, to which we shall refer later. . . .

Mr Muir submitted that the justice had reached an incorrect conclusion. He contended that on the findings there was no clandestine or nefarious purpose. He submitted that the taking of the bicycle was wholly a temporary taking and he pointed to the fact that in a proposed adjustment which the justice rejected the appellant had said that he would leave the bicycle at the swimming pool. He invited us to hold that, taking all the facts together, this was not such an exceptional case as would justify a conviction, bearing in mind that this really was a temporary taking of the bicycle. He reminded us that in *Milne v. Tudhope* a statement of the law by the sheriff was approved by the court to the effect that in certain exceptional cases intention to deprive temporarily would suffice and he submitted that this was not an exceptional case.

The learned advocate-depute submitted that, taking all the facts together, there was enough to show that this was a taking without consent, following which the bicycle was abandoned in a place where the owner was unlikely to find it, and that was sufficient to amount to theft. She referred to *Kivlin v. Milne*, where in similar circumstances the appellant was convicted of the theft of a motor-car. He had taken the car in the knowledge that the owner did not consent to this and had given no authority for it to be removed, and the vehicle was then abandoned in a place where the owner was not liable to discover it. In that use the court held that the sheriff was entitled to draw the inference that the appellant had the intention permanently to deprive the owner of the car of it.

The situation in this case on its facts must be taken to be as set out in the findings. The justice does not give a reason for rejecting the proposed adjustment that the appellant said to the complainer that he would leave the bicycle at the swimming pool. But we infer from the findings that he was not persuaded that the appellant made it clear to him when he took it away where he was going to leave the bicycle. Furthermore, the justice was satisfied on the evidence that he took no steps to return it to the complainer and that the complainer was able to find it after it had been taken away.

In our opinion, on a proper reading of the findings, the justice was not entitled to conclude that there was an intention to deprive the owner permanently of his bicycle, but he does not suggest that that was the view he took of the facts. Nor, in our view, was this an example, in the true sense, of a taking of an article temporarily from its owner, because it was at no point indicated to the complainer when or on what conditions the bicycle would be returned to him. It appears to us that it would be more accurate to say that the owner was deprived of his bicycle indefinitely, since it was not made clear to him whether and, if so, when it would ever be returned to him.

In these circumstances there was no need for any clandestine or nefarious purpose to be established. There was no need for any exceptional circumstance. The question simply is whether the necessary criminal intention was present for the taking away of the bicycle to amount to theft. We are persuaded, in the light of the findings, that the justice was entitled to reach that view and to regard this as an act of stealing the bicycle. For that reason we shall answer the first question in the affirmative. We do not find it necessary to answer the remaining questions and we shall refuse the appeal."

Appeal refused.

NOTE

**11.29** How does this case differ from *Kivlin v. Milne*?

## (iv) Intention to deprive temporarily

### Carmichael v. Black; Black v. Carmichael
1992 S.L.T. 897

**11.30** [For the fact of this case, see *ante*, p. 446.]

LORD JUSTICE-GENERAL (HOPE): [Having concluded that theft did not require a taking away of the property, his Lordship continued:] "Two further points should be noted at this stage. It has been held, in a case where there was undoubtedly *amotio*—goods had been taken away and were in effect being held to ransom—that an intention to deprive an owner permanently of his property is not essential to the crime, and accordingly that an intention to deprive temporarily will suffice: *Milne v. Tudhope*, per Lord Justice-Clerk Wheatley, 1981 S.L.T. (Notes) at p. 43. And the temporary appropriation of goods by retaining them to obtain payment for the cost of repairs which had not been instructed has also been held to be theft, on the view that the appellant was holding the goods to ransom within the meaning applied to the accused in *Milne v. Tudhope*: see *Kidston v. Annan*, per Lord Justice-General Emslie at 1984 S.L.T., p. 280. The appropriation in that case was for an unlawful purpose, which amounted in effect to extortion. But the libel of the charges in the present case does not state that it was the intention to hold the car to ransom for payment of a sum of money or for any other purpose whether temporary or otherwise. The proposition is simply that it was theft to detain the vehicle with the intention of depriving the motorist of the use of it, albeit temporarily, against his will.

The Lord Advocate submitted that there was no need to spell out in the charge what was the intention of the act. It was sufficient to state what the act was. The felonious intention could be left to inference. In the normal charge of theft, which describes the act of taking away or appropriation, the facts averred will invite the inference. So also in this case the intention necessary for *mens rea* could be inferred simply from the fact of depriving the motorist of the use of the car. Furthermore, by attaching the device to the wheel of the car, for whatever purpose, the accused were appropriating it because they were taking control of it away from the motorist. By asserting control over it for a different purpose, which was quite independent of the use of it by the motorist, they were in effect stealing it from him, and it was not necessary for there to be a relevant charge to say what the purpose was, let alone say that it was for use by the accused.... [I am of the view that] To deprive another of the possession and use of his property can only be described as theft if there is appropriation—whether by taking it away or doing something else to it to this effect—and this is done deliberately. As Hume, i, 75, puts it, 'the thing must be taken away with a purpose to detain it from the owner'. Leaving aside the suggestion that there must be a permanent intention to deprive, which in *Milne v. Tudhope* was held not to be necessary, Hume's discussion in this passage of the point that the intention of gain is not necessary seems to me to support the relevancy of the charges in this case."

LORD ALLANBRIDGE: [His Lordship agreed with Lord Hope that the charges of extortion and attempted extortion were relevant, and then considered the charges of theft]: "As the law has developed the nature of the *mens rea* involved can now properly be described as an intention to deprive the owner of his goods. I agree with para. 14–10 of Gordon, *supra*, where it is stated that this intention may be manifested in three different modes, namely, by taking, by conduct following on finding and by appropriating goods which have been neither taken from the owner without his consent nor found.

In this particular case I consider that the second of these modes could be said to apply. This was a case of conduct following on finding which manifested an intention to deprive the complainer of his motor car. I agree with your Lordship in the chair that it is the owner's loss and not the other's gain which is important, as stated at para. 14–63 of Gordon's *Criminal Law*. The next sentence in that paragraph states that the other person must intend to appropriate the goods, but this means only that he must intend to deprive the owner of them. By clamping the wheel of the car with a clamp which could no doubt be released later by the accused he had taken control of the car and deprived the owner of the use of it albeit on a temporary basis. In such a situation I am satisfied that by so clamping the car the accused had effectively stolen it."

LORD COWIE: "The crucial matter which the Crown must prove is that the accused intended to detain the cars from the owners (Hume, i, 75), and it is not necessary to prove that they intended to do so permanently (see *Milne v. Tudhope*).

I am satisfied that there are sufficient facts set out in the present charges from which such an inference of intention can be drawn, always bearing in mind that it is the owner's loss and not the accused's gain that is important: Gordon's *Criminal Law* (2nd ed.), para. 14–63."

Appeal refused.

NOTES

This case holds that it is theft to detain property with the intention of depriving the owner of the use of **11.31** it, albeit temporarily, against the owner's will. Would this not have been more than sufficient for the court in *Fowler v. O'Brien* to hold that the appellant was guilty of theft? Is there any need for a category of theft based on intention "indefinitely" to deprive? Is there any need for resort to notions of "nefarious purpose"?

## (b) Dishonesty

**11.32** Although theft is generally regarded as an offence of dishonesty, it is not clear whether "dishonesty" is required in addition to the intention to appropriate. The older authorities do not identify it as a distinct element of the offence, although notions of dishonesty might well be embraced by such terms as "theftuous intent" and "felonious purpose" (see Hume, i, 73). Macdonald makes no mention of it. Gordon describes theft as "the dishonest taking of the goods of another" but makes no further reference to dishonesty in his discussion of theft. McCall Smith and Sheldon make no reference to it as a distinct element in the definition of the crime, although they do use the term "wrongfully" to qualify appropriation which may embrace notions of dishonesty. Jones and Christie include theft in their discussion of "Crimes of Dishonesty" but acknowledge that "[n]o Scottish authority shows that any additional requirement of 'dishonesty' has to be shown or inferred" to establish theft. That view is, however, contrary to the opinion of Sheriff Scott Robinson in *Mackenzie v. Maclean*, 1981 S.L.T. (Sh.Ct) 40 in which he held that "dishonesty on the part of the accused ... is essential for a conviction of theft." That view is now, apparently, shared by the High Court:

### Kane v. Friel
### 1997 S.L.T. 1274

**11.33** LORD JUSTICE-GENERAL (RODGER): "The appellant was charged on a summary complaint in the following terms. 'On October 7, 1995 while acting along with a juvenile at Abercorn Street, Paisley, or elsewhere to the complainer unknown, having found a quantity of metal piping and a sink unit, you did without attempting to find the lawful owner thereof, appropriate same to your own use and did steal same.'

After trial the justice found the appellant guilty as libelled. He has appealed against the conviction by way of stated case. To judge by the terms of the charge, the appellant was found guilty of appropriating the metal piping and sink unit 'at Abercorn Street, Paisley, or elsewhere'. The fact that the appellant was convicted of a charge in these terms shows that the justice did not determine where the appellant appropriated the articles.

This is no mere technical detail, as becomes clear when the findings in fact are considered. They are to the following effect. On the day in question two police constables responded to an alarm at the sewerage works at Abercorn Street, Paisley. The time was about 12.45 p.m. While they were there, they noticed the appellant and his younger brother crossing waste ground towards Abercorn Street. They were watching the officers. The appellant was carrying a blue holdall full of neatly packed copper piping with a torch lying on top of it. His brother was carrying a sink. When questioned by the police officers, the appellant said that they had found the copper at the back of the 'poundy' apparently a reference to the local Poundstretcher premises. He said that they needed the torch because it was dark under the bridge and that they were going to the scrappies where they would get a tenner for 'this lot'. It appears from the justice's note that the appellant took the officers along a towpath to an area of waste ground where there was no trace of similar items. It also appears from the note that the copper piping was in lengths which fitted in the holdall. The police were unable to identify the origins of the copper piping or the sink—indeed in her note the justice records that no report of a theft was received. The justice concluded by finding that the appellant found the piping and sink with another and that they had appropriated the items for their own use.

The appeal was presented on the basis that the justice had been wrong to repel the submission of no case to answer in terms of section 160 of the Criminal Procedure (Scotland)

Act 1995, though in the end the discussion came to centre on the issues raised in question 2 (whether the justice had been entitled to infer that the goods belonged to another) and question 3 (whether she was entitled to draw the inference of evil intent).

As we have already noted, the justice makes no finding as to where the appropriation took place. More particularly perhaps, she does not make any finding as to where the appellant and his companion found the piping and sink. Nor was there any finding in fact as to the condition of the piping or the sink at the time when they were found. These are important matters. Had the articles been found, say, in the curtilage of a building or had they been in brand-new condition, it might have been easy for the justice to infer that their owners had intended to retain ownership of them. On the facts as found by the justice, however, the items could, for all we know, have been found on a heap of scrap and the sink in particular could have been in such a battered condition that the obvious inference would have been that its owner had decided to get rid of it. In other words, the findings of the justice are entirely consistent with the items having been abandoned by their owner. Putting the matter at its very lowest, there is nothing in those findings which would show that anyone, such as the appellant, coming across the piping and sink would have had reason to think that they had not been abandoned.

It is true that at common law most abandoned moveable property belongs to the Crown. The advocate-depute did not seek, however, to found on that somewhat technical doctrine when arguing that the appellant had had the necessary *mens rea* for conviction of the crime libelled. It should also be mentioned that neither the appellant's counsel nor the advocate-depute referred to Part VI of the Civic Government (Scotland) Act 1982. In terms of section 67 of that Act a person who finds property is under a duty to take care of it and to deliver it or report the matter to one of several people, including a police constable and the owner or occupier of the land where it was found. Under section 68 the chief constable may then take various steps, including offering the property to the finder after two months. These matters might have been of relevance to the argument—we express no view on that—but they were simply not raised.

The advocate-depute referred us to *Costello v. Macpherson*. In that case a railway employee was convicted of stealing coal from a coal bunker at Portobello Station. He had been found at five o'clock in the morning carrying a paper parcel near the bunker. When asked what was in the parcel, the appellant said 'old paper' but in fact it contained coal. At first the appellant said that he had got the coal from a miner, but subsequently admitted taking it from the bunker. In our view that case is clearly distinguishable. The appellant in Costello was spotted early in the morning. He lied about what was in the parcel. He then admitted taking the coal from the bunker near which he had been found. Since the coal was in the bunker, it would have been obvious that the company had not abandoned it. In these circumstances the necessary intent to steal the coal could be inferred. Here the circumstances are very different. . . .

The advocate-depute accepted that the Crown had to prove that the appropriation had been 'dishonest' and therefore that the intention must have been to appropriate the items dishonestly. He also accepted that there was nothing to show where the items had been found or what their condition was. Nor, he agreed, was there any indication of the worth of the items beyond the appellant's remark that they would 'get a tenner for this lot'. What was significant, he said, was that, although the appellant had just found the items, he was setting off to sell them. That showed that the appellant had the necessary dishonest intention.

As Macdonald remarks, 'Such cases must depend on special circumstances'. Were this a case where the appellant had found, say, a watch lying in the street and had immediately set off to sell it, then we have no doubt that it would be easy to infer the necessary dishonest intention. After all, if you see a watch lying in the street, the obvious inference is that someone has lost it. So if you pick it up and immediately go off to sell it, you are plainly appropriating the unknown person's watch dishonestly. But, as we have stressed, the Crown have not proved anything about the circumstances in which the piping or sink were found, about their condition or about their value—beyond the casual remark of the appellant. There is nothing in the case on these matters which would give the justice a basis for inferring that the appellant must have known that the items were property which someone intended to retain. For all we know, they may have been found in a situation or in a condition where the most obvious conclusion would have been that they had been thrown away—if anything, the value attributed to the items by the appellant might tend to suggest that this was so. It is relevant, moreover, to recall that no report was received that items of this kind had been stolen. In that situation we are satisfied that there was no sufficient basis on which the justice could infer that the appellant had the necessary dishonest intention to appropriate the copper and the sink. We refer to *Mackenzie v. Maclean*, where, in unusual circumstances, the sheriff acquitted the accused on the ground that the Crown had not proved the necessary dishonesty for theft.

For these reasons we shall answer the questions in the stated case in the negative and allow the appeal."

Appeal allowed.

NOTES

**11.34**    1. In *Mackenzie v. Maclean and Macpherson*, 1981 S.L.T. (Sh.Ct) 40, the accused were charged with theft of 275 cartons containing cans of beer belonging to Scottish and Newcastle Breweries Ltd. The cartons formed part of a larger consignment of beer which had fallen from a delivery lorry and which the consignee had refused to accept. Some of the consignment was accepted by an hotel at which the accused worked, and on the instruction of the Brewery, the manager of the hotel told the accused to dispose of the rest by throwing them into a skip. Members of the public approached the accused and offered money for some of the damaged cans, which the accused accepted. In view of the circumstances, and in particular the abandonment of the property by its owners (the Brewery) the sheriff held that there was no dishonesty in what the accused did, and therefore no theft.

2. A dishonesty requirement may serve a useful purpose in theft, especially when the requirement of an intention permanently to deprive has been abandoned. Suppose, for example, A's greenhouse is damaged by a ball kicked into her garden by the neighbour's children. On being asked to return the ball A refuses, saying that she will only return it once she has reported the matter to the children's parents, who are not due to return home until later that day. A has appropriated the property and (at least in terms of *Black v. Carmichael*) has the necessary theftuous intent. The children do not consent to her retaining the ball. But would it be appropriate to regard this as theft? Or suppose that B is caught listening to his Walkman in class. C, the teacher, confiscates the Walkman and tells C that he will not get it back until he accepts the discipline of the school. Again there is appropriation and intention to deprive indefinitely and, assuming B does not consent, this would appear to be theft. But do we want to make thieves of school teachers who are trying to enforce school discipline? Again, resort to notions of "dishonest" appropriation help to avoid what might be an inappropriate conclusion.

3. Section 1 of the English Theft Act 1968 includes a requirement of "dishonesty" which has proved problematic. See the cases of *Feely* [1973] Q.B. 530 and *Ghosh* [1982] Q.B. 1053 and the discussion of this issue in J. C. Smith, *The Law of Theft* (8th ed., 1997) at pp. 72–74.


# 2. HOUSEBREAKING, OPENING LOCKFAST PLACES AND PREPARATORY OR PREVENTIVE OFFENCES

**11.35**    "Housebreaking" and "opening lockfast places" are sometimes an aggravation of the crime of theft (as in cases of "theft by housebreaking" or "theft by opening lockfast places"). They may also be treated as "preparatory" offences, in the sense that they are committed in order to commit some other criminal act, such as housebreaking with intent to steal, or opening lockfast places with intent to steal. In the latter case, it is not necessary for the intended offence to be complete for the housebreaking or opening a lockfast place to be an offence. In either case, what constitutes housebreaking or opening a lockfast place remains the same. The closely related, statutory, offence of being found on premises in circumstances giving rise to a suspicion of some dishonest purpose is also discussed in this section.

## A. Housebreaking

### (a) What constitutes "housebreaking"

**11.36** Although at one time "housebreaking" may have required the "piercing or effraction" (Hume, i, 98) of a building, the essence of the modern concept is "overcoming the security" of the building. See Alison, i, 282 and the following case.

**Burns v. Allan**
1987 S.C.C.R. 449

**11.37** The steward of a private club locked up the club premises and activated a burglar alarm at about midnight. The appellant, along with another man, was seen by the bar steward standing in a doorway about fifty yards from the club premises at that time. About fifteen minutes later the control box of the alarm, which was on an external wall, was interfered with, activating the alarm which was directly linked to the police. Within a few moments the police arrived. The appellant was seen at the far end of a lane adjacent to the club premises apparently attempting to escape from the scene. He was apprehended by the police and on being searched was found to be in possession of various items including a large screwdriver, a small screwdriver and a pair of scissors. He had a plastic bin liner in the lining of his jacket.

The appellant and his companion were charged with attempted housebreaking with intent to steal by disconnecting the burglar alarm. An objection to the relevancy of the charge was repelled by the sheriff, who convicted both accused. The accused appealed by stated case to the High Court.

THE LORD JUSTICE-CLERK (ROSS): "The appellant and his co-accused intimated a plea to the relevancy of the complaint, and submitted that disconnecting a burglar alarm system was not an act which amounted to attempted housebreaking. It was contended that there could only be an attempted housebreaking if the security of the premises had been overcome, and it was submitted that if the burglar alarm system was not a part of the security of the premises. The sheriff repelled the pleas to relevancy, and the appellant and his co-accused then plead not guilty. After evidence had been led the sheriff found the appellant and his co-accused guilty as libelled. The appellant has now appealed against conviction by way of stated case.

The first question in the case raises the issue of whether the sheriff was entitled to repel the plea to relevancy of the complaint. On behalf of the appellant Mr Young submitted that the charge was a fundamental nullity since there was no link between the action which it was libelled he had taken and an intention to steal, that is to say it was not libelled that there had been any intention to enter. Mr Young referred to Macdonald on the Criminal Law of Scotland (5th ed.) at p. 50, and pointed out that for the offence of housebreaking there must be violation of the security of the building. He maintained that the burglar alarm was not part of the building. He further submitted that at best the charge libelled preparation, and not the perpetration of an overt act.

In our opinion, what was libelled in the complaint as amended was plainly an attempt to overcome the security of the building. Moreover, from what was libelled one can reasonably infer an intention to enter the building. In her note, the sheriff stated:

'I decided that to regard an alarm system as anything other than an integral part of the security of the building or the disconnection of it as other than an actual part of the act attempted housebreaking was to fly in the face of common sense.'

With that expression of opinion we find ourselves in complete agreement. In our opinion the sheriff was well founded in repelling the plea to the relevancy of the complaint. We shall accordingly answer the first question in the case in the affirmative . . . ."

Appeal refused.

NOTES

**11.38**    1. See also *Heywood v. Reid*, 1996 S.L.T. 378, in which it was held that smashing an external security light could constitute attempted housebreaking.

2. The security of a building can, of course, be achieved by force, but it may also be achieved by stealth—for example, by the use of a stolen key (*cf.* Hume, i, 99)—or by entering premises by an abnormal route. In *Rendal Courtney*, 1743, Hume, i, 99 the accused entered the building by means of the chimney. This was held to be housebreaking. Father Christmas beware!

3. It is not necessary, in order to establish housebreaking, that the accused has actually entered the premises, but in order to sustain a charge of theft by housebreaking it must be shown that the theft was achieved by that means.

4. There is very little modern discussion of what constitutes a "house" for these purposes. Housebreaking is not, however, confined to domestic premises. Virtually any building that has a roof and can be made secure will suffice. Hume states that "housebreaking" applies to "every edifice, to what use soever destined" provided that it "can properly be considered, and in common speech would be called, a house, or a shut and fast building, and not a mere open shed, booth or temporary place for lumber" (Hume, i, 103). In *John Fraser* (1831) Bell's Notes 41, the accused was sentenced to transportation for breaking into a henhouse. (Harsh as this may seem, it was an improvement on the earlier law which treated housebreaking as an aggravation of theft justifying the death penalty. See Hume, i, 102–103.)

5. It is not "housebreaking" to move from one part of a building to another by breaking into the latter. So, for example, where a guest in a hotel breaks into another guests room, that is not housebreaking, but it would be opening a lockfast place.

## (b)  The purpose of the housebreaking

**11.39**    It was established by the case of *Charles MacQueen and Alexander Baillie* (1810), Hume, i, 102, that housebreaking with intent to steal is a crime. But what is the situation where an accused breaks into premises with intent to commit some other offence? See the following case.

### H.M. Advocate v. Forbes
#### 1994 S.L.T. 861

**11.40**    The accused was charged with breaking into a flat, removing his clothing with the exception of a pair of boxer shorts, prowling around, removing articles from a chest of drawers, cutting holes in a shirt and fashioning it into a hood "all with intent to assault and rape" the complainer, a fourteen-year-old girl. The sheriff sustained an objection to the relevancy of the charge on the ground that it did not disclose a crime and dismissed the charge. On appeal by the Crown the following opinion was delivered by the Lord Justice-General (Hope):

OPINION OF THE COURT: "... The argument which was developed before us by the Solicitor General was that for a person to break into someone's house with intent to commit a crime there is itself a crime. He did not suggest that it was a crime for a person merely to enter someone else's premises, or that it was criminal for a person to form an intention to commit a crime. His point was that the putting together of these two things, by breaking into or entering the premises with the intention of committing a crime there, was sufficient for the activity as a whole to be treated as criminal. Where the intention was present the housebreaking was part of the criminal activity.

He pointed out that it has long been recognised that it is a crime for a person to break into a house with intent to steal. He referred us to two examples taken from the volumes of indictments kept in the Crown Office of persons being charged with housebreaking with intent to commit fireraising. *Margaret Morrison and Others* [Glasgow High Court, 1913, *unreported*] were charged with breaking into a dwellinghouse in Glasgow on July 23, 1913, conveying or causing to be conveyed there a quantity of firelighters and other materials, and placing them against a wooden door with intent to set fire to them and burn the house. *Frances*

*Gordon* [Glasgow High Court, 1914, *unreported*] was charged with breaking into a house in Rutherglen on April 2 or 3, 1914, conveying or causing to be conveyed there several packets of firelighters and other combustible materials, and depositing them or causing them to be deposited in the boot room of the house with intent to set fire to and burn the house. There is no record of there having been any challenge to the relevancy of these indictments, and the accused in each case were convicted as libelled. He referred also to *Khaliq v. H.M. Advocate*, 1983 S.C.C.R. at p. 492; 1984 S.L.T. at p. 143, where Lord Justice General Emslie said: "It is of course not an objection to the relevancy of a charge alleged to be one of criminal conduct merely to say that it is without precise precedent in previous decisions. The categories of criminal conduct are never to this extent closed. 'An old crime may certainly be committed in a new way; and a case, though never occurring before in its facts, may fall within the spirit of a previous decision, or within an established general principle'. So said Lord Cockburn in his dissenting judgment in the case of *Bernard Greenhuff* (1838) 2 Swin 236 at p. 274. In the case now before us it is to an established general principle that the Lord Advocate resorts in defence of the relevancy and sufficiency of the facts libelled to constitute an indictable crime, and that general principle is to be found in Hume, Vol. I (3rd ed.), p. 327 and, in particular, in the passage quoted by the trial judge in his opinion which I do not find it necessary to repeat. The general principle to be discovered from that passage is that within the category of conduct identified as criminal are acts, whatever their nature may be, which cause real injury to the person".

In the present case no injury to the person is alleged, but the Solicitor General submitted that the general principle was that it was a crime for someone to break into someone else's property with the intention to commit a crime there, and that on that general principle we should affirm the relevancy of the charge.

The Solicitor General indicated that he would be willing, if it was necessary for a *nomen iuris* to be supplied, to amend the charge to one of breach of the peace. The sheriff was advised by the respondent's counsel that he would have no objection if the procurator fiscal were to seek leave to amend the charge to one of breach of the peace, but the procurator fiscal depute declined to amend the charge to this effect. . . .

On the issue as to whether the act of breaking into a house with intent to commit a crime there was itself criminal, [counsel for the accused] submitted that this proposition was not supported by any authority. He accepted that housebreaking with intent to steal had been declared in 1810 to be a crime by the court: Hume, i, 102; Macdonald, pp. 24 and 50. But he submitted that this was not decided upon any principle but was simply a declaration of an ad hoc crime. He said that the two fireraising cases were distinguishable because the acts were said to have been carried out in the house preparatory to committing the crime of fireraising there, and the libel was in effect one of attempted fireraising.

We do not think that it can be asserted as a general proposition that it is a crime for someone to do something which is not in itself a crime with the intention to commit a crime. Unless what is done is itself a crime known to the law of Scotland, the libel will fall short of what is required to make the charge relevant.

The general principle upon which the relevancy of any charge must be determined is that only a completed crime or an attempted crime can be regarded as criminal. It is not a crime for a person to enter another man's house. If damage is done to the property that may be regarded as criminal, but the act of entering the house is not in itself a crime. Nor is it a crime for a person to form the intention of committing a crime. His action only becomes criminal when something is done by him with a view to committing it, in which event, if his action is interrupted at that stage, it may be regarded as an attempt to commit the crime which he intended to commit. The crime of housebreaking with intent to steal may be regarded as an exception to this principle. In *Charles McQueen and Alexander Baillie* [(1810) Hume, i, 102] it was held that a charge of breaking into a house or shop with intent to steal was a relevant charge. But as Gordon on *Criminal Law*, para. 6–08 points out, this is an example of the common law creation of a preventive crime to fill the gap created by the fact that at that time attempted theft was not indictable. There is no longer a need to fill that gap, as an attempt to commit any crime is itself criminal: see Criminal Procedure (Scotland) Act 1887, s.61, re-enacted as s.63 of the Criminal Procedure (Scotland) Act 1975. If new preventive crimes are needed, this is best left to the legislature, as Lord Justice-Clerk Aitchison indicated in *H.M. Advocate v. Semple,* at 1937 J.C., p. 46; 1937 S.L.T., p. 51. The question in that case was whether acts done with intent to procure an abortion of a woman who was not pregnant could be regarded as criminal.

As counsel for the respondent pointed out, with regard to the two charges of housebreaking with intent to commit fireraising, acts done with the intention to commit a crime may reach the stage when the crime of an attempt to commit a crime is being committed. We were not referred to any discussion of this matter in the authorities, and it may be open to question how far the accused must go in pursuance of his intention before he can be found guilty of an attempted crime. On one view the crime of attempted fireraising is not committed until the stage is reached of setting light to the materials which have been introduced to create the fire. That stage was not said to have been reached in either of these two cases, and it may be that it was for this reason that they were not charged as acts of attempted fireraising. But the acts libelled, which included the introduction of the combustible materials and placing them into position with a view to setting light to them, could be seen as having been done in order to give effect to the intention and not just to prepare for it. On that view, by breaking into the premises and doing these things there, the accused were attempting to commit the crime which they were said to have intended to commit, although the final stage of setting light to the material had not yet been reached.

In *Coventry v. Douglas,* [1944 J.C. 129, 1944 S.L.T. 137] the accused was charged with inserting her hand into a money box with intent to steal therefrom. An objection that this libelled an intention to steal merely, which was not a crime, was rejected on the ground that, although not in the statutory form, the charge set forth all matters which required to be proved in order to establish the charge of attempted theft. Lord Justice General Normand said this at 1944 J.C., p. 20; 1944 S.L.T., p. 132: "The mere presence of a person in a particular place may be only preparatory to the execution of the criminal intent, and not in itself an overt criminal act. But the insertion of the hand into a till or money receptacle is a further step which crosses the line separating preparation from perpetration, and it is an overt act although it never attains its purpose or goes beyond an attempt. The line of demarcation between preparation and perpetration cannot be defined in any general proposition, but here, I think, there is no doubt that the act described by the words used in the charge is clearly on the wrong side of the line. These words describe, not merely the act of one preparing to execute the intent, but an act in execution of the intent."

That case provides a simple example of an act done with the intent to commit a crime which amounted to an attempt to commit it. If such an act is to be treated as an attempt to commit the crime however, the proper course is for it to be libelled as such under the proper *nomen iuris* so as to make it clear that what is described in it is being charged as a crime known to the law of Scotland.

Since the fireraising cases are capable of being explained in this way, that is as examples of attempted fireraising, we do not think that they can with safety be relied upon as authority that housebreaking with intent to commit a crime other than theft is itself a crime. We note that Gordon, para. 15–59 states that there is no authority for treating housebreaking with intent to commit any crime other than theft as itself a substantive crime, and we are not aware of any authority to that effect. If the charge is to be held relevant therefore it cannot be on the ground submitted by the Solicitor General as his primary argument. He did not ask us to regard this as a case of attempted rape or offer to amend the charge to this effect. We can express no opinion one way or the other therefore as to whether the acts libelled in this charge, according to which the respondent entered the house and did various things there all with intent to assault and rape the complainer in the house, constituted an attempt to commit the crime of assault and rape."

Appeal allowed.

NOTES

1. The Court went on to hold that the indictment disclosed a relevant charge of breach of the **11.41** peace—but only subject to deletion of the allegations of an intent to assault and rape. Is this a satisfactory conclusion? Is breach of the peace, without any reference to the intent of the offender a proper solution in such a case? Surely the intent with which the accused allegedly entered the building was central to the threat which such behaviour presents.

2. Although it was no doubt correct for the court to decline to extend the law, the absence of an offence of housebreaking with intent to commit such a serious crime as rape is not easy to justify. Maintaining the security of persons in their home (and not just their property) is clearly a significant interest, and one for which an offence of the type attempted in this case would be valuable. Indeed, why is it not an offence to housebreak with intent to commit *any* serious offence in the premises? In English law, section 9 of the Theft Act 1968 includes within the definition of burglary, the situation where the accused enters a building as a trespasser with intent not only to steal, but also to inflict grievous bodily harm upon, or rape, any person in the building.

# B. Opening lockfast places

It is an aggravation of theft that it was committed by opening a lockfast place. Similarly, opening a **11.42** lockfast place with intent to steal is a recognised preventive offence. Again, this can be achieved by force, as when a safe is opened by means of explosives or the door to a room is broken down, or by stealth, where a lock is picked or opened by means of a stolen key.

In some cases of opening lockfast place with intent to steal it may be difficult for the Crown to establish what it is that the accused intended to steal. In particular, where the lockfast place is a motor vehicle, it may be an open question whether the accused intended to steal the vehicle, or something in the vehicle (or possibly both). What is the proper charge in such a case?

### McLeod v. Mason
#### 1981 S.L.T. (Notes) 109

Three accused persons were acquitted on charges of forcing open and attempting to force **11.43** open lockfast motor cars and that "they did attempt to steal". The Crown appealed by stated case.

OPINION OF THE COURT: "The first charge was a charge of opening a lockfast motor car in a particular location with intent to steal and the charge libels that they did attempt to steal. The second charge was a charge that at another locus the three respondents attempted to force open a lockfast motor car with intent to steal and that they did attempt to steal. No objection to the relevancy or specification of the complaint in these terms was tabled at any stage of the proceedings. Evidence was led and concluded and the sheriff *ex proprio motu* decided to question the specification of the two charges. He appeared to think that because the lockfast places were motor cars it was necessary for the Crown to libel and prove that the intention to steal was directed at the contents of the car or directed at the car itself or both. In the absence of such specification he took the view that it would be wrong to convict the respondents who had had no notice that the Crown might at the end of the day contend that it did not matter that they were unable to show that the intention was to steal the car or the contents or both. In effect, therefore, the sheriff held that the two charges were irrelevant for want of essential specification. In so holding he misdirected himself. As many decided cases show the charges as framed in this complaint were relevant in all essential respects. There was no need for the Crown in order to establish the commission of a completed crime to show that it was the intention of the respondents to steal the car or its contents or both. It is quite sufficient to libel the opening of a lockfast motor car with the criminal intent of theft and in many cases it will be impossible to prove more. Contrary to the sheriff's view we do not consider that a verdict of guilt upon a charge thus libelled presents any real difficulty in the matter of sentencing.

We now turn to the sheriff's second reason for holding the charges not proven. It was not established, he said, whether the illegitimate object of the respondents was theft or merely the statutory offence of contravention of s.175 of the Road Traffic Act 1972. That is no doubt a perfectly accurate observation, so far as it goes, but in the circumstances of this case it ought to have been presumed, in the absence of evidence that the illegitimate intention was merely contravention of a statute, that the intention was theft."

Appeal allowed.

NOTES

**11.44**     1. In spite of what the High Court says, an argument can be constructed to the effect that each charge here was in effect two bites at the one cherry. It would have been perfectly competent to charge either opening a lockfast motor car with intent to steal or attempted theft. In the former case the object of the theft is irrelevant. Whether it be the car, the contents or both. In the latter, it would probably be necessary (as a matter of relevancy) to identify in the charge the object of the theft and for that reason a prosecutor might select the former charge as preferable. But lumping the two together seems illogical and can indeed lead to difficulties in sentencing. See *McCormick v. Tudhope,* 1986 S.C.C.R. 620. In *Gillan v. Vannet,* 1997 S.L.T. 1299, the High Court was careful to reject an argument by the Crown which essentially suggested that there was no difference between forcing open a lockfast car with intent to steal it and attempting to steal it.

2. In England, section 9 of the Criminal Attempts Act 1981 provides for the offence of "vehicle interference" which is committed where a person interferes with a motor vehicle with the intention of stealing the vehicle, or anything carried in or on it, or taking the vehicle without the owner's consent (contrary to section 12 of the Theft Act 1968). Would a similar provision deal with the problem highlighted above?

## C. Other preparatory and preventive offences

### Civic Government (Scotland) Act 1982

**57.**—(1) Any person who, without lawful authority to be there, is found in or on a building or other premises, whether enclosed or not, or in its curtilage or in a vehicle or vessel so that, in all the circumstances, it may reasonably be inferred that he intended to commit theft there shall be guilty of an offence . . . .

(2) In this section "theft" includes any aggravation of theft including robbery.

NOTES

**11.45**     1. Can a person have lawful authority to be in a place notwithstanding an intention to commit theft there? Suppose, for example, that A goes into a supermarket intending to shoplift and is found there in circumstances which reveal his intentions. Can he claim that there is no offence under section 57(1) because, like customers in the shop, he has lawful authority (that of the shopkeeper who extends at least an implied invitation to persons to enter the premises)? In *Scott v. Friel,* 1999 S.L.T. 930 the appellant was found, along with four other youths, in an alcove between the public street and the main door leading into a shop. On either side of the alcove were window display areas, and goods on display there were visible from the alcove. There was no barrier to prevent the public walking into the alcove and no notice asking the public not to enter the alcove. When the police approached all of them ran away, and housebreaking tools were found in the alcove. The Crown argued that there was ample evidence of an intention to commit theft, and that in the circumstances the accused had no lawful authority to be there given his intentions. The accused was convicted and appealed. In delivering the opinion of the Court, Lord Prosser made the following observations:

"It was not disputed by the Crown that speaking generally, the locus was a place where members of the public had a right to be, and indeed that the display of goods could be seen as an invitation to the public to go into the alcove. In normal circumstances the appellant as a member of the public would have lawful authority to be in the alcove. The only evidence or facts which could be relied upon by the Crown in order to establish that he was there without lawful authority was the material which went to establish the other crucial element of the charge, namely, that it might reasonably be inferred that the appellant intended to commit theft there . . . .

There is some attraction in the argument that the owner of heritable subjects, even if permitting the general public to enter upon his premises, would not extend this permission to members of the public whose purpose in entering the subjects was to commit theft there. On the other hand, if there is general authority to enter, but the intention to commit theft is regarded as negating that authority, then lack of lawful authority and intention to commit theft would always go together, where the locus is on private property. On behalf of the appellant, it was submitted that this could not be the intention in relation to s.57(1): there were two separate requirements, and the words "without lawful authority to be there" would effectively be empty surplusage if the intention to commit theft entailed lack of lawful authority.

It does not appear to us that the construction adopted by the Solicitor General renders these crucial words entirely purposeless: so far as public places are concerned, or places where there is a positive right of presence, the Crown could not prove presence without lawful authority by an inference such as is said to be justified in a case such as the present. Nonetheless, it appears to us that the section draws a distinction between the first requirement, of being found in a particular place without lawful authority to be there, and the second requirement of a reasonable inference of intention to commit theft. Not merely are the two matters separately expressed, but in relation to the latter, and not the former, the words "in all the circumstances" are added. This does not appear to us to be a case in which we should attempt any general analysis or definition of the expression "without lawful authority to be there". No general legal argument was presented upon the matter; and it appears to us that there will be a very wide range of differing situations in which it can be argued that there was or was not lawful authority. If a person is found on private premises, where in general the public would have no express or implicit right of presence, lack of lawful authority, even if no barriers have been passed or overcome, may be quite easily inferred. But in a case such as the present, where the locus not merely gives on to a public street, but involves the element of invitation by the display of goods, the generally implied authority must in our opinion be taken as the starting point. In that context, and with the Crown requiring to prove an exception, we are not persuaded that the inference of a lack of lawful authority can properly be drawn, having regard to the terms and structure of the section, from the mere fact that an intention to commit theft can reasonably be inferred."

2. The inference of theft referred to in section 57 must be made by the Court before a conviction is justified. It is not sufficient for the court to hold that such an inference could reasonably be drawn from the circumstances of the case: in *Hamilton v. Donnelly*, 1994 S.L.T. 127.

3. On what evidence is needed to sustain a finding that an accused person was "found" in a place, compare *Marr v. Heywood*, 1993 S.L.T. 1254 and *Maclean v. Paterson*, 1968 S.L.T. 374.

4. Where a person is found in a place where he or she has no authority to be, and other circumstances (such as the time of night and the nature of the location) are such as to suggest an intention to commit theft, a great deal may turn on any explanation the accused offers for his or her presence. In *Gillies v. P.F. Glasgow*, January 26, 1999, *unreported*, Lord Prosser commented:

"If one is going to draw an inference of theft under this section absence of alternative explanations is plainly important. That would be particularly so in a case such as the present where there were no positive indications of intention such as the behaviour of the appellant, damage to the premises, tools or the like."

(The explanation offered by the accused was that he had entered an enclosed area behind a travel agents in order to urinate, and had then stopped to look at some travel brochures which had been discarded behind the travel agents' premises.)

### 2. Civic Government (Scotland) Act 1982

**58.**—(1) Any person who, being a person to whom this section applies—     **11.46**

    (a) has or has recently had in his possession any tool or other object from the possession of which it may reasonably be inferred that he intended to commit theft; and

    (b) is unable to demonstrate satisfactorily that his possession of such tool or other object is or was not for the purposes of committing theft,

shall be guilty of an offence ....

(2) For the purposes of subsection (1) above, a person shall have recently had possession of a tool or other object if he had possession of it within 14 days before the date of—

    (a) his arrest without warrant for the offence of having so possessed it in contravention of subsection (1) above; or

    (b) the issue of a warrant for his arrest for that offence; or

    (c) if earlier, the service upon him of the first complaint alleging that he has committed that offence.

(3) ...

(4) This section applies to a person who has two or more convictions for theft which are not, for the purposes of the Rehabilitation of Offenders Act 1974, spent convictions

(5) In this section "theft" includes any aggravation of theft including robbery.

NOTE

**11.47**    See *Docherty v. Normand*, 1996 S.L.T. 955.

## 3. EMBEZZLEMENT

### A. Embezzlement: what is it?

**11.48**    Many attempts have been made to define this crime, mostly with no success. Various suggested definitions are catalogued by Gordon, paras 17–01 to 17–04. None are particularly satisfactory, but the essence of the crime appears to be in the failure to account for goods or funds entrusted to the accused.

**Edgar v. Mackay**
1926 J.C. 94

**11.49**    A solicitor received instructions from clients to recover payment of a sum of money. Although the instructions had been given in August 1924, by November of that year nothing appeared to have been done and the clients cancelled the solicitor's mandate. In fact the solicitor had collected various sums of money but had not told the clients this. Meantime another solicitor was instructed who discovered what had happened. In November 1924 the clients wrote to the original solicitor saying that if they did not receive some sort of accounting from him, they would refer the matter to the Authorities. Subsequently repeated applications failed to produce any satisfaction and in September the following year the agent was arrested by the police. On the day of his arrest he finally accounted to his clients for the sums collected. He was convicted of embezzlement. On appeal against conviction:

LORD JUSTICE-CLERK (ALNESS): "The considerations which lead me to the Conclusion that the inference of dishonesty should receive effect are these. In the first place, there is the length of time which elapsed between the cancellation of the appellant's instructions and the demand for the money which he had collected, on the one hand, and, on the other, the date of his arrest in September of the following year when he sent the money. Many months had elapsed, and nothing was done by the appellant. In point of fact, to use a colloquial expression, he received a very large amount of rope before the drastic step of arrest was taken. Apart from the length of time, there is also what I regard as a crucial fact, to which I have already incidentally adverted, that no explanation consistent with honesty was at any time, so far as I know, tabled by the appellant to those who corresponded with him or who interviewed him. There is no suggestion in the letters which he wrote, no trace in the interviews which his brother solicitor had with him in Dumfries, of any reason assigned by him, consistent with honesty, why he delayed to forward the money which belonged to Campbell & Son and which, I take it, was then in his pocket. There had been a threat by them, as I read the correspondence, of civil and criminal proceedings, and yet no explanation was offered. A further consideration which weighs with me is that no payment was made by the appellant until after his arrest. To these facts I would add that the discovery that he had collected the money at all was made, not in consequence of anything which he communicated to Campbell & Son, but from the investigations of others. I confess that, for myself, I should like to have known what the appellant said in the witness-box. The case discloses that he was examined. I presume that he offered some explanation of his conduct. I think I am bound to assume, from the conclusion which the learned Sheriff reached, that he rejected any explanation which may have been given. If he had accepted it, it is inconceivable that the learned Sheriff could have reached the conclusion which he did. Therefore, I treat the case as if it contained the statement that any explanation, assuming it to have been given, was not accepted by the judge.

In these circumstances it appears to me that there is no competing theory in this case, as it comes before us, to displace what I regard as the inevitable conclusion from the facts found by the Sheriff that the money in question was fraudulently appropriated by the appellant. It may be impossible to state (indeed, it is generally impossible to state in such cases) the precise date at which that misappropriation took place. Nor is it necessary. It would be unfortunate in the interests of justice if the law were otherwise. Therefore, deciding the case, as we must do, on the facts before us, it appears to me that the only reasonable conclusion from these facts is that the appellant was guilty of the offence with which he was charged. In these circumstances, I am of opinion that the question of law stated by the learned Sheriff should be answered in the affirmative."

Appeal dismissed.

NOTE

This case highlights the problem of identifying whether the actings of the accused amount to dishonest **11.50** appropriation. For a more recent example of the same problem see *H.M. Advocate v. Wishart* (1975) S.C.C.R. Supp. 78.

## B. Distinguishing theft from embezzlement

This has never been an easy task for the Scots courts and still gives rise to problems today. Gordon at **11.51** paras 17–05 to 17–23 discusses the various criteria which have been used to distinguish the two crimes, some of which arise more as a matter of sociological "labelling" rather than as a matter of law. The subject is also made more difficult by the fact that Hume's ideas concerning custodiers and possessors persisted well into the nineteenth century.

### Cathrine Crossgrove or Bradley
(1850) J. Shaw 301

The accused was a pawnbroker charged with theft of articles pledged with her. **11.52**

LORD MONCREIFF: "There is no doubt that this case must turn on somewhat nice distinctions; and the cases which have been already decided, as to whether any particular *species facti* amount to embezzlement or theft, are sufficiently puzzling; but it appears to me that this case differs from that of the watchmaker, which has been cited in argument, and the analogous one of money being entrusted to a messenger, to be carried to the bank, and appropriated by the party on his way. In the present case, the party who pledged the property, by that act not merely gave a right of possession, but a title to the goods themselves, which, by lapse of time became absolute, and enabled the party to sell, and give a valid right to all the world."

LORD IVORY: "There is a great distinction between a lawful possession *de facto*, and a legal possession *proprio jure*. Here the latter was the right which the prisoner is alleged to have had, and it seems to me impossible to draw any distinction between the appropriation of the goods pledged, before the period when the sale might lawfully take place, or the proper title of the pawnbroker and his unlawful retention of any surplus pence which might be realised thereby, over and above the amount advanced, together with interest thereon, at proper rates; yet no one would undertake to say that the latter case would be one of theft."

LORD JUSTICE-CLERK (HOPE): "Looking to the legal import of the indictment, and the nature of the contract of pledge, I think embezzlement or breach of trust is the appropriate *nomen juris* in the circumstances. It is quite different from those former cases, where only a limited and temporary custody, unaccompanied with any title of property in the things themselves, had been given, for the purpose of having something done by the party who committed the offence. In this case a contract is set forth. It is for breach of that contract that the prisoner is charged; and I am of opinion that the criminal violation of a contract of trust constitutes the offence known by us as breach of trust or embezzlement, and not that of theft."

Charge held irrelevant.

NOTE

**11.53**    Despite these remarks by the judges, the charge of theft was almost certainly correct. For a critique of the decision, see Gordon, para. 17–08. Where someone has custody of an object for a limited time and purpose only there may be a choice of charges: but appropriation which has taken place after the accused has obtained the object for a short time or limited purpose may be theft, at least if this is libelled in the charge.

### William Taylor Keith
(1875) 3 Couper 125

**11.54**    The accused was an auctioneer who was instructed to sell a piano at a private house. If this was unsuccessful, he was entrusted with it to sell it at a public roup. He was charged that having failed to sell it at the house he took it to an auction room and "thus having obtained the temporary custody of it, he pawned it, appropriated the money thus realised and stole it".

LORD ARDMILLAN: "In order relevantly to have charged theft of the piano, the indictment would require to have set forth that the custody given was for some specific purpose, and for a short time. It is not sufficient to be able to gather that it was so, or may have been so, by implication from the terms of the charge. Where the custody is not for a short time and not for a specified purpose and the article is appropriated, a sort of trust is constituted, and the crime is breach of trust. But where the custody is for a short period and for a specified purpose, as, for example, to take a box to a railway station, the crime is theft: and so also where the purpose of the custody is such as to exclude all separate possession, such as a butler in charge of wine, or a shepherd of sheep, the appropriation is clearly theft. But in order to libel either crime relevantly, the prosecutor must set forth specifically the elements which go to constitute and to distinguish the crime. As these are not here stated, I think the objection to this charge of theft, as distinguished from the alternative charge of breach of trust, must be sustained."

Charge held irrelevant.

NOTE

**11.55**    This is a rather unsatisfactory case, especially since it is easy to argue that albeit the piano was "entrusted" to the accused, this was for the limited purpose of sale. In any event, the whole aura surrounding the distinction between the two crimes is pervaded by the consideration that one should not convict persons in responsible positions with the lowly crime of theft.

## H.M. Advocate v. Laing
### (1891) 2 White 572

The accused was a solicitor who received sums from a client for the purpose of discharging a **11.56** heritable security. He failed to carry out his instructions and paid some of the money into his own bank account. He was charged with theft.

Lord Kincairney (in charging the jury): "It was contended that an agent could not be said to steal or embezzle his client's money if he employed it in carrying on his business, as, for example, in making a payment to or on behalf of another client. I do not assent to that argument. There seems no doubt that if an agent receives money on behalf of a client, and uses it for his own purposes, he is guilty of theft or of embezzlement, whether he lodges it in his bank account, or employs it in his business, or pays it on account of other clients. But in any case there must be proof of his dishonest and felonious intention....

If one receives money merely to pass it on to another, his crime, if he feloniously appropriates the money, would be theft. If he gets it under an obligation to account for the like amount, the felonious appropriation would be embezzlement. The distinction nowadays is rather technical than substantial."

Accused convicted of embezzlement.

Note

But Laing did not even begin to carry out his instructions. Should not he have been convicted of theft **11.57** as libelled? If someone is given a power of administration over a fund or goods entrusted to him, then a misappropriation concomitant with the accused exceeding his mandate appears to be theft and not embezzlement.

## Kent v. H.M. Advocate
### 1950 J.C. 38

Lord Justice-General (Cooper): "The appellant was indicted before a Sheriff and Jury in **11.58** Glasgow on two charges, (1) of embezzlement and (2) of fraud. As the jury found him not guilty on the second charge, I make no further reference to it. The first charge related to a transaction (or series of transactions) too complicated for brief summary. It is significant to say that it was concerned with the disposal of a consignment of apple puree, valued at over £500, consigned to the Danish Bacon Company in Edinburgh by a firm in Northern Ireland and eventually sold by the appellant to a third party. The charge was brought when it later transpired that the price had neither been paid nor accounted for by the appellant....

I pass on to the point which was the subject of keen argument, and it has occasioned me much perplexity. In drafting the indictment the Procurator-fiscal, whose difficulties in disentangling an obscure series of business deals must have been grave, provided as a narrative to charge one a statement to the effect that the appellant had been authorised by the Danish Bacon Company and by the Northern Ireland firm to dispose of the consignment in question; and it was on the footing that he had been so authorised that the charge of embezzlement of the proceeds was then built up. It now appears—I shall not say by express concession from the Crown, but rather from an examination of the evidence—that no support, or no sufficient support, can be found for any inference that the appellant was ever authorised either by the one company or by the other or by anyone else to dispose of the consignment. Accordingly, since the indictment went to the jury in the form indicated, and as their attention was pointedly directed to this very matter in the course of the Sheriff-substitute's charge, the verdict as returned is not supported by the evidence.

But that is not necessarily the end of the matter in view of the duty laid upon us by section 3(2) of the Criminal Appeal (Scotland) Act 1926, and our over-riding obligation not to sustain appeals unless we are satisfied that there has been a substantial miscarriage of justice. It is at that stage of the matter that my difficulties have chiefly arisen. I am bound to say that from my reading of the evidence the impression conveyed is that the appellant is in a dilemma in this respect, that the facts proved mean either that he stole the consignment or that he embezzled its proceeds. But he was never charged with stealing the consignment. The Solicitor General maintained with force that from the verdict which they returned the jury must have been satisfied on four points: (first) that the consignment never at any time belonged to the appellant; (second) that he disposed of it; (third) that he was authorised to dispose of it; and (fourth) that he failed to account for the price; and he maintained that even on the assumption (which I have indicated is my own view) that the third of the propositions was not justified by the evidence, nevertheless, the remaining three propositions sufficed to satisfy the requirements of section 3(2) that the jury must have been satisfied of facts which led to the conclusion that the appellant was guilty of another offence, to wit, theft. He asked us therefore to substitute for the conviction of embezzlement of the proceeds a conviction of theft of the consignment."

LORD RUSSELL: "I am of the same opinion. In regard to the first ground of appeal I agree with the views expressed by your Lordship on the subject of the withdrawal of a case by a presiding Judge at the close of the Crown evidence. On the merits of the appeal I have found the case attended with difficulty. It is reasonably clear that the jury's verdict finding the appellant guilty of embezzlement cannot be supported owing to the absence of sufficient evidence to establish that the appellant had been "authorised" by the firms mentioned to dispose of the consignment of apple puree. It would have been open to the jury to return a verdict of guilty of theft if they believed that the evidence warranted such a verdict, but they were not so directed by the trial Judge. To give effect to the Crown's submission to apply the provisions of section 3(2) of the 1926 Act by substituting a verdict of guilty of theft, it is necessary for us to affirm now that the jury 'must have been satisfied of facts' which proved the appellant to be guilty of that offence. On a careful consideration of the whole relevant evidence I do not feel that I would be warranted in so affirming. That being so, it follows that the conviction appealed against must be quashed."

> Conviction for embezzlement quashed: motion to
> substitute verdict of guilty of theft refused, 'as
> unwarranted in the circumstances.'

NOTE

**11.59**  So embezzlement seems to be restricted to cases where the goods or money appropriated are in the accused's possession lawfully, where he has started upon a course of dealing with them and where he has carried out some unauthorised action with the goods or money; provided also there is some dishonest intention to appropriate.

### Guild v. Lees
1994 S.L.T. 68

**11.60**  An accused person was tried on summary complaint for embezzlement. The accused was secretary of a curling club which was responsible for his expenses while he was undertaking foreign visits on behalf of the club. He had exclusive charge of the club cheque book and drew a cheque to pay his private electricity bill. He was convicted and appealed, contending, *inter alia*, that the drawing of a cheque in favour of a third party could not in law amount to embezzlement as it was the transfer of incorporeal property. The appeal was refused. The opinion of the Court was delivered by the Lord Justice General (Hope).

OPINION OF THE COURT: "The final point which counsel for the appellant argued under reference to the grounds of application is that what was allegedly appropriated by the appellant was an item of incorporeal moveable property and therefore incapable in law of being embezzled. Counsel pointed to the terms of the charge, which as libelled states that what the appellant did was to embezzle £149.24 of money. He pointed out that in terms of section 312 (j) of the Criminal Procedure (Scotland) Act 1975 the word 'money' is defined as including all current coin of the realm, post office orders and postal orders and bank or banker's notes and other such items. There was, however, in this case no question of the appellant having handled items of that kind. He did not appropriate to his own use any items as listed in that definition. The question then was, what was it which formed the basis of the transaction which gave rise to the charge? The evidence revealed that what was done here was to transact on a bank account, and it was pointed out that the relationship between banker and customer is that of debtor and creditor. He submitted that what was done here was to enter into a transaction in relation to a part of the debt owed by The Royal Bank of Scotland to the federation. That debt was an item of incorporeal property and it was therefore incapable of being embezzled.

In support of his argument counsel for the appellant referred to *R. v. Kohn* (1979) 69 Cr.App.R. 395. That was a decision of the Court of Appeal in England which was concerned with charges brought under the Theft Act 1968. The question which arose in that case, having regard to the wording of the Theft Act, was whether what had been appropriated by the accused were things in action. We have read the various passages in the opinion of Geoffrey Lane L.J. to which our attention has been drawn, but it appears to us that that case is of no assistance whatever in regard to the approach which should be taken in a Scottish case as to the common law crimes either of theft or embezzlement. We have ample jurisprudence of our own which enables us to identify the way in which these crimes may be committed and what it is by way of property both corporeal and incorporeal that is capable of being embezzled.

As he developed the argument counsel for the appellant went on to say that he accepted that cash in hand could be embezzled. As we understood him, this was because the cash in hand was property which was of a corporeal nature which could be stolen. There was therefore a close analogy between the crime of theft, that being property which could be stolen, and what could be embezzled. On the other hand, he said, one cannot commit embezzlement by means of a cheque drawn in favour of a third party because there is no corporeal property which is in the hands of the alleged embezzler.

In our opinion that argument cannot succeed. The approach taken by the Crown is in accordance with normal practice in cases of this kind. The property which was the subject of the transaction was money held in a bank account and it was capable of being embezzled. The transaction described in the evidence was a typical example of a breach of trust giving rise to the allegation of embezzlement. The appellant appropriated the money held in the federation's bank account to his own use by means of the cheque book which had been entrusted to him. It was suggested that the crime ought to have been libelled as one of fraud, but in our opinion there was no fraud or misrepresentation either to the bank or to the payee. What was done was to obtain money which the appellant was not authorised to obtain, by means of the cheque drawn on an account on which, so far as the bank and the payee were concerned, he was perfectly entitled to draw cheques. It appears to us that the appellant's unauthorised actings in this case fall clearly within the scope of the crime of embezzlement as described by Macdonald on the Criminal Law of Scotland (5th ed.), at pp. 45–47. Accordingly that ground of appeal has no substance, in our opinion, and we are not prepared to accept the argument which was developed in support of it by counsel for the appellant."

Appeal refused.

NOTE

See *ante*, pp. 450–455 for a discussion of the question of theft of incorporeal property. The decision **11.61** illustrates a further difference between the crimes of theft and embezzlement, namely that incorporeal property cannot be stolen, but it can be embezzled.

## C. *Mens rea* of embezzlement

**11.62**  This is generally thought of as being the intention to appropriate money or goods due to another without his consent. The absence of proof of this will provide a defence.

**Allenby v. H.M. Advocate**
1938 J.C.55

**11.63**  LORD JUSTICE-CLERK (AITCHISON): "The appellant was tried and convicted in the Sheriff Court at Aberdeen on a charge of embezzlement. He was managing director of a company called Benjamin Allenby, Limited, and as such he acted as fish salesman for a number of trawl owners. It is common ground that he failed to account to four of these trawl owners in respect of sums amounting in all to upwards of £900. The practice of the appellant was to pay all the moneys he received from purchasers of fish into a common fund. I do not think that there was anything wrong in that, because, as was explained to us by Mr Burnet, a purchaser might on the same morning buy from half a dozen trawl owners, and make out one cheque to the appellant as fish salesman, and, therefore, the keeping of a common fund in the first instance was perfectly right and proper. The method of the appellant was then to pay out by means of his own cheques on the common fund to the different owners the sums due to them from time to time. It is in evidence that the books of the appellant were kept with scrupulous accuracy. Nothing was concealed. Not a single penny went into appellant's own pocket, except in the sense that he utilised the common fund for the purpose of making disbursements on behalf of all the trawl owners. It was part of his own business to make such disbursements. What happened was this (there is really no dispute about the facts) that he used some of the moneys that belonged to the four trawl owners in question to make advances to other trawl owners, whose moneys he applied when necessary in the same way. Now, there is little doubt that strictly speaking that was an irregular thing to do. It would have been better for the appellant to have kept separate accounts, and, although the moneys went into a common fund in the first instance, to have apportioned it and paid it over with the least possible delay, charging disbursements, when made, each against its own proper account. But while this would have been strictly the proper course to follow, I cannot find in what the appellant did any evidence of embezzlement; but, as we have not gone fully into the facts and as there is a clear ground of judgment in the terms of the charge, I say no more about that.

When the learned Sheriff came to charge the jury he said this (I read one passage only): 'If Mr Allenby did choose to act as fish salesman for those other ships, and if he did utilise moneys belonging to the four ships mentioned in the indictment for the purpose of meeting liabilities of those other ships, I must direct you that that in law amounts to embezzlement.' In my judgment, that was a misdirection. The passage I have read was calculated to convey to the minds of the jury that it was enough that the moneys had been used in the way they were by the appellant. I respectfully think that was a misdirection. Without laying down that a dishonest intention may not be inferred from an immixing of moneys, I think that this case was so exceptional that the jury should have been told explicitly that, unless they were satisfied that the appellant had acted dishonestly, they were bound in law to acquit him of the charge. No such direction was given. I think it was vitally important that it should have been given, having regard to two facts in the case (1) that there appears to have been some kind of practice prevailing in the fish business in Aberdeen not dissimilar to the practice followed by the appellant and (2) because the only accountant called in the case who had investigated the appellant's books said, not merely that they were kept with scrupulous accuracy and that nothing was concealed, but also that he could find no evidence of dishonest intention at all, and he had expressed that view to the proper authorities. When the leading witness for the Crown gives evidence of that kind one would require very clear and strong evidence before the Court would be justified in disregarding it; but, as I have already said the whole evidence is not before us, and it is enough for the disposal of this case that the direction given by the learned Sheriff was inadequate. On that ground I move your Lordships that the appeal be allowed, and the conviction and sentence set aside."

LORD WARK: "Speaking for myself, I do not think that there ever can be a conviction of embezzlement unless the jury find evidence of dishonest intention, although evidence of dishonest intention may be afforded either by acts which are deliberate or by acts which are reckless . . . .

I do not think it is necessary to make any reference to the authorities which were quoted to us except to say that the present case is one in which it was, in my opinion, much more necessary to direct the jury's attention to the question of honesty or dishonesty than either in the case of *Duncan* J. Shaw 270, or in the case of *Lee* 12 R.(J.) 2, 5 Coup. 492. In the case of Lee there was an admission that the accused had immixed funds of his client with his own and that he had used them for his own purposes, and in the case of Duncan there was a clear admission that the accused had used money with which he was entrusted for the purpose of paying his own private debts. And yet in both these cases it was thought necessary by the learned judge who presided at the trial to point out that it was a matter for the jury to consider whether the accused acted honestly or dishonestly. In this case I have no doubt, as I have said before, that that question should have been put. Towards the end of his charge the Sheriff came very near to putting it, because he said to the jury, 'You will consider whether or not the man did what he did, believing he was entitled to do it.' But then, that part of the charge is just as defective as the other to which your Lordship has referred, because the Sheriff did not go on to direct the jury, as he ought to have done, as to what the consequences would be of taking one view or the other of what the accused believed."

Conviction quashed.

NOTE

But was Allenby's defence a simple denial of dishonesty, or a specific claim that he was entitled to act **11.64** as he did? Perhaps both. Note that dishonesty has always been regarded as part of the definition of embezzlement.

## 4. OFFENCES OF TEMPORARY DEPRIVATION

Given the developments that have taken place in the law of theft over the last 20 years or so, with the **11.65** substantial dilution, or indeed removal, of the requirement of an intention permanently to deprive, the distinction between theft and the offences of temporary deprivation discussed below may well be redundant. However, for the time being at least, it is worth noting that there continue to be two offences, one common law and one statutory, of temporary deprivation which are different from theft.

## A. Clandestine taking and using

### Strathern v. Seaforth
1926 J.C. 100

The respondent was charged with clandestinely taking possession of a motor car, the property **11.66** of another, knowing that he had not received permission from the owner, and that he would not have obtained such permission to do so. An objection to the relevancy of the complaint, on the grounds that it did not disclose a crime known to the law of Scotland, was sustained by the sheriff substitute who, at the request of the prosecutor, stated a case to the High Court. The question of law for the High Court was whether the sheriff was right in sustaining the objection to the relevancy of the complaint.

LORD JUSTICE-CLERK (ALNESS): "Counsel for the Crown say that that complaint discloses a crime which the Court was bound to investigate, and that that crime consists in taking and using something clandestinely, without the permission of the owners having been given. It appears to me that the proposition for which the Crown contends is supported by the authorities which were cited. But, speaking for myself, I should not have required any authority to convince me that the circumstances set out in this complaint are sufficient, if proved and unexplained, to constitute an offence against the law of Scotland.

The matter may be tested by considering what the contention for the respondent involves. It plainly involves that a motor car, or for that matter any other article, may be taken from its owner, and may be retained for an indefinite time by the person who abstracts it and who may make a profit out of the adventure, but that, if he intends ultimately to return it, no offence against the law of Scotland has been committed. I venture to think that, if that were so, in these days when one is familiar with the circumstances in which motor cars are openly parked in the public street, the result would be not only lamentable but absurd. I am satisfied that our common law is not so powerless as to be unable to afford a remedy in circumstances such as these.

All that we are deciding, and I understand your Lordships agree, is that this is a relevant complaint. All defences will be open to the accused. We merely decide that the learned Sheriff-substitute has gone too fast is dismissing the complaint as irrelevant at this stage. It appears to me that investigation is necessary; and, in that view, I suggest to your Lordships that we should answer the question put to us in the negative."

LORD HUNTER: "I agree in thinking that the learned Sheriff substitute ought not to have thrown out this complaint without inquiry. It is, under section 5 of the Act of 1887 and also section 5 of the Summary Jurisdiction Act of 1908, not necessary in any indictment or complaint to specify by any *nomen juris* the crime which is charged; but it is sufficient if the indictment sets forth facts relevant to constitute an indictment of a crime.

As your Lordship has pointed out, it is not merely said that the respondent took the car without getting the owner's permission, but also that he did so clandestinely and knowing quite well that the owner would not have given permission. If the contention of the respondent is right, then no offence it committed under the criminal law of Scotland if anyone goes to a garage and takes a car and petrol clandestinely. It would be very unfortunate if that were the state of the law, when we know how so many cars are parked in cities like Glasgow and Edinburgh. I am satisfied, however, that the common law of Scotland does not consider that an act of that sort is not crime. It may turn out that the offence is more or less venial or more or less criminal, but it is not for us to speculate."

The court answered the question in the negative.

NOTE

**11.67**    "Joy-riding" of the above type is now dealt with under section 178 of the Road Traffic Act 1988, but the offence recognised in *Strathern v. Seaforth*, not being limited to road traffic offences, remains unaffected. (*Cf. Murray v. Robertson*, 1927 J.C. 1.) It may, however, be the case that the offence established in *Strathern v. Seaforth* is now embraced by the law of theft, or at least rendered irrelevant by developments in relation to the mental element in theft. See *ante*, pp. 459–466.

### Murray v. Robertson
1927 J.C. 1

**11.68**    LORD JUSTICE-CLERK (ALNESS): "This stated case relates to a complaint made by the respondent against the appellant, in which he is charged with clandestinely taking possession of twenty-four fish boxes, the property of certain people who are named, he well knowing that he had not received permission and would not have received permission from the owners, and with using these boxes by filling them with fish and dispatching them to Glasgow, or, alternatively, with the crime of theft. The Sheriff-substitute convicted the appellant on the first of these alternative charges, and the question which we have to decide is whether he was entitled to do so.

The facts in the case, which leave something to be desired in the matter of clarity, at least show this, that the appellant dispatched the fish in question from Ardrossan to Glasgow in boxes which lay in his yard, and which belonged to the persons whose names are mentioned in the complaint. Dealing with the two branches of the first alternative charge in the complaint, there was charged (first) clandestine possession obtained, and (second) use made of the boxes so obtained. I regard clandestine possession as an essential element in the charge which was made. If the charge sounds in crime at all, it is because possession was alleged to have been taken clandestinely. Now, there is not a vestige of evidence to the effect that possession in this case was so obtained. It is stated in the eleventh finding that it was not shown how—and the learned Sheriff might have added, or when—the boxes came into the appellant's yard, but that it was shown that they might have been deposited there by, or on behalf of, hawkers or owners of fish restaurants in order to get rid of them, or sent in as returned empties by fish merchants who had bought fish from the appellant in his own boxes. From the eleventh article it plainly appears that the possession obtained by the appellant, for aught that is found in this stated case, may have been, and probably was, entirely innocent and legitimate. That the use of the adverb 'clandestinely' was essential to the relevancy of the complaint I have no doubt at all. If that adverb were absent from the complaint, it would, on the face of it, be irrelevant. Accordingly, the appellant founds his appeal upon the fact that there is no finding which supports the view that the possession obtained by him was clandestinely obtained. With regard to the use to which the boxes were subsequently put, in my view, that use cannot, *per se*, be the foundation of a criminal charge. The facts stated disclose, it may be, a civil dispute, and may afford ground for a civil remedy; but I am quite unable to see that they point to any criminal act on the part of the appellant.

The case of *Strathern v. Seaforth*, 1926 J.C. 100, to which we were referred, has no application to the circumstances here. The opinions of the Judges who took part in that decision all found in the word 'clandestine'. Lord Hunter and Lord Anderson both regarded that as the foundation of the charge. For myself, I used the word 'abstracted', which I regarded, and still regard, as essential to the relevancy of that charge."

Appeal allowed: conviction quashed.

NOTE

If there is a difference between this crime and theft, then it may be worth noting that in relation to **11.69** "clandestine" taking and using the adverb "clandestine" appears to have a different meaning in the two offences. In relation to theft it appears to be enough for the property to have been taken without the knowledge or authority of the owner for it to be taken "clandestinely". For "clandestine taking and using" it seems to require that the property be taken secretly. Certainly the owner in *Murray v. Robertson* would have been unaware of the use to which the boxes were being put by the accused and had not authorised their use.


## B. Taking and driving away motor vehicles

### Road Traffic Act 1988

**178.**—(1) A person who in Scotland—                                                    **11.70**
   (a) takes and drives away a motor vehicle without having either the consent of the owner of the vehicle or other lawful authority, or
   (b) knowing that a motor vehicle has been so taken, drives it or allows himself to be driven in or on it without such consent or authority, is, subject to subsection (2) below, guilty of an offence.

(2) If—

(a) the jury, on proceedings under this section on indictment, or

(b) the court, on summary proceedings under this section,

is satisfied that the accused acted in the reasonable belief that the owner would, in the circumstances of the case, have given consent if he had been asked for it, the accused shall not be liable to be convicted of the offence.

NOTE

**11.71**   For a discussion of this offence, see Gordon (2nd ed.), pp. 531–533.

# Chapter 12

# ROBBERY AND EXTORTION

## 1. ROBBERY

Robbery is a "hybrid" offence, involving elements of interference with personal integrity and **12.01** interference with property interests. It is generally described as theft achieved by personal violence or the threat of violence. Hume, i, 104, describes it, generally, as "forcible theft"; Alison, i, 227, states that "robbery consists in the violent and forcible taking away the property of another"; Macdonald, 39, defines it as "the felonious taking and appropriation of property in opposition to the will of another under whose personal charge it is; and the force that need be used is a matter of degree"; Gordon, para. 16–01, states that "Robbery may be defined as theft accomplished by means of personal violence or intimidation", a definition which appears to have been adopted by Sheriff Pirie in *Cromar v. H.M. Advocate*, 1987 S.C.C.R. 635 (*infra*). See also, Jones and Christie, para. 10–47 and McCall Smith and Sheldon, p. 237.

Hume's discussion of robbery indicates that he regarded it as an aggravated form of theft, but it has long been accepted that robbery is a separate crime, rather than simply an aggravation of theft. (See *Ellen Falconer and Others* (1852) J. Shaw 546 and *Isabella Cowan and Others* (1845) 2 Broun 398.)

### A. Theft and robbery

Although robbery is recognised as a distinct crime, as opposed to an aggravated form of theft, there is a **12.02** clear link between the two crimes in that there can be no robbery unless there has been a theft. This means, broadly speaking, that all the elements of the crime of theft must be present before there can be a conviction for robbery. There are, however, some exceptions to this broad principle. Thus, so far as concerns the *actus reus* of theft, the shift from taking possession to "appropriation" is not reflected in the crime of robbery which still appears to require a "taking" of the property. Also, while it is clear that a claim of right on the part of the alleged thief will exclude liability for theft, the presence of such a claim is probably not a defence to a charge of robbery: *Harrison v. Jessop*, 1991 S.C.C.R. 329. However, the developments in relation to the intention to deprive in the law of theft may also apply in robbery. However, the developments in relation to the intention to deprive may also apply in robbery. In *Cameron v. H.M. Advocate*, 1971 J.C. 50, *post*, p. 490 it was accepted that an intention permanently to deprive was not required for piracy, which was regarded as a form of robbery.

### B. Robbery and violence

"It is another and indispensable circumstance that the thing be taken by violence; for herein lies the **12.03** distinctive character of the crime. But as to this article a great latitude of construction has been received. There may be a robbery without any wounding or beating of the person ... and without any forcible wrestling or tearing of the thing from the person; or even any sort of endeavour on the part of the sufferer to detain it. The law means only to oppose this sort of taking, as against the will of the owner, to that which happens privately, or by surprise, and without any application to his will or fears." (Hume, i, 106.)

The distinction between theft and robbery may in some cases be a fine one. Suppose, for example, that A snatches B's bag from under her arm, without any further force by A and without resistance by B. That would probably today qualify as theft. But if any further degree of force is used in order to effect the theft, then it may be robbery. In *Cromar v. H.M. Advocate*, 1987 S.C.C.R. 635 the appellant was charged with robbery. The evidence revealed that he had come up behind the complainer and pulled at a bag which the latter was holding. The complainer tried to hold on to it but its handles snapped and the appellant ran away with it. In his charge to the jury the sheriff stated, *inter alia*:

> "Now, ladies and gentlemen, robbery is [the] unlawful taking of property in opposition to the will of another in whose personal charge it is. There need not be violence applied to the person. It is sufficient if there is such conduct as causes reasonable fear of immediate bodily injury. It must be such as to overcome not merely passive but active and voluntary resistance. Violent conduct producing reasonable fear of coercion or bodily injury in consequence of which the owner or custodier submits to having the property taken from him is sufficient to constitute the crime. Robbery, accordingly, ladies and gentlemen, is theft accomplished by means of personal violence or intimidation and, accordingly, there can be no robbery unless there is a theft. Any violence used to effect the theft converts that theft into robbery and all that is necessary is that there should be sufficient force used to take the crime out of the category of a theft by surprise and so to distinguish it from theft by snatching or pickpocketing."

The jury convicted the accused who appealed on the ground that the degree of force used was not sufficient for robbery. The Lord Justice-Clerk, in delivering the opinion of the court stated that given the description of the way in which the bag was taken from the complainer, this was a case of robbery rather than theft. *Cf.* the South African cases of *S. v. Gqalowe*, 1992 (2) S.A.C.R. 172 (E), *S. v. Mogala*, 1978 (2) S.A. 412 (A) and *Sithole*, 1981 (1) S.A. 1186 (N) and the English cases of *Clouden* [1987] Crim. L.R. 56 and *Dawson and James* (1976) 64 Cr. App. R. 170.

## C. Assault and robbery

**12.04** Most modern charges of robbery allege that the accused "did assault X ... and rob him of ... ", which might seem to suggest that there are two crimes libelled. But provided there is violence or intimidation of any degree attached to the theft, then the crime is robbery, irrespective of whether there is evidence to prove the specific assault.

### O'Neill v. H.M. Advocate
1934 J.C. 98

**12.05** LORD JUSTICE-CLERK (AITCHISON): "The appellant was indicted on a charge of assault and robbery, the charge being that he assaulted the woman named in the indictment, 'and did knock her head and face against the wall of said close to the effusion of her blood and did rob her of a handbag' containing money and other articles. The case went to trial before a jury, and the jury found the charge of assault libelled in the indictment not proven, but found the appellant guilty of robbery.

The appellant was sentenced to three years' penal servitude, and he now appeals to this Court against the conviction, and also against the sentence.

As regards the conviction, the ground of appeal stated is that the verdict of guilty of robbery cannot be supported, having regard to the evidence. The case, as presented by Mr Prain, is that the jury having found assault not proven, the facts in the case, while habile to justify a conviction of theft, are not habile to justify a conviction of robbery.

The answer to the question thus raised depends upon what is the true legal definition of robbery. It is well settled that in robbery there must be violence. On the other hand, it is not necessary to robbery that there should be actual physical assault. It is enough if the degree of force used can reasonably be described as violence. I think the law upon this matter is as laid down by Baron Hume in his work on Crimes in words which have never been disputed. In Vol. i. (p. 106, para. 5), what Hume says is this: 'It is another and an indispensable circumstance that the thing be taken by violence, for herein lies the distinctive character of the crime. But as to this article a great latitude of construction has been received. There may be a robbery without any wounding or beating of the person (and when such violence is used, it may therefore be libelled as an aggravation, as it was in the case of James Andrew); and without any forcible wresting or tearing of the thing from the person; or even any sort of endeavour on the part of the sufferer to detain it. The law means only to oppose this sort of taking, as against the will of the owner; to that which happens privately, or by surprise, and without any application to his will or his fears; and it understood therefore to be violence, if the thing is taken by means of such behaviour, as justly alarms for the personal and immediate consequences of resistance or refusal.'

Now, that being the law, the distinction between theft and robbery may be very difficult of exact legal definition, and, in the particular case, it may not be easy to say whether the facts amount to robbery or amount to theft only. The question is really one of degree. But, in the present case, I think that there can be no doubt that this woman sustained an injury to her head and also suffered from concussion. We must, of course, take it that these were not the result of assault, because the jury has found assault not proven; but I think it is very clear upon the evidence that the injury which the woman sustained would not have been caused unless substantial force had been used in snatching her bag. Accordingly, I think it is plain that the injury which she suffered was the direct consequence of the snatching of her bag. That seems to me to indicate a degree of violence that places the crime here in the category rather of robbery than of theft.

The case seems to me to be substantially on all fours with the case of *H.M. Advocate v. Fegen*, (1838) 2 Swin. 25, to which we were referred. In that case, it appears from the report that the accused had come up to the complainer, seized his watch chain, and pulled his watch out of his pocket. The complainer fell, and then the report bears 'whether accidentally or from being tripped he could not say, but he stated that he would not have fallen if he had not been laid hold of'. The Court unanimously held that the degree of violence proved was sufficient to establish the charge of robbery, of which the jury, under the direction of the Lord Justice-General had found the panel guilty. I think exactly the same may be said in the present case. I think, therefore that the ground upon which this verdict is challenged fails, and that the verdict must stand in the form in which it was returned."

Appeal dismissed.

NOTE

For a discussion of the problems raised by this case, see Gordon (2nd ed.), paras 16–10 and 16–11.  **12.06**

# D. Threats

As indicated above, actual violence is not necessary for robbery. Threats of violence will suffice if they **12.07** are sufficiently serious and the violence threatened is immediate. "[I]t is understood to be violence if the thing is taken by such behaviour, as justly alarms for the personal and immediate consequences of resistance or refusal. The mere display of force, and preparation of mischief, whether these appear in the weapons shewn, in the number and combination of assailants, or in their words, gestures, and carriage, if in the whole circumstances of the situation they may reasonably intimidate and overawe, are therefore a proper description of violence, to found a charge of robbery." (Hume, i, 106–107)

It is not settled whether threats other than threats of personal violence will suffice for robbery. Hume leaves the question open (Hume, i, 108). Alison appears to suggest that a threat to burn down a person's house, or drag him off unlawfully to prison might suffice (Alison, i, 231). English law defines robbery in terms of theft by force (Theft Act 1968, s.8) which includes the case where the victim is put in fear of being then and there subjected to force, which appears to mean force applied to the person. See Smith, *op. cit.*, paras 3–04—3–05. Although there is no direct authority on the point, it is probably robbery where A threatens B in order to coerce C into relinquishing the property. So, for example, if A points a knife at B's child, C, and orders B to hand over her purse, that should be robbery.

The threat must be one of immediate violence. Where the threat is one of future violence, the crime is probably regarded as extortion rather than robbery. *Cf.* in this respect, the South African case of *S. v. Pachai*, 1962 (4) S.A. 246 (T).

## E. The timing and the purpose of the violence

**12.08**  For there to be robbery, the violence must precede the theft and must be used in order to commit the theft. It is not robbery, therefore if, having stolen property, the accused uses force in order to escape from the scene of the crime or to retain the property stolen.

In *H.M. Advocate v. Compton* (1871) 2 Coup. 140 the accused was charged with assault with intent to rape and robbing the victim of a sum of money. The accused was alleged to have assaulted the victim with intent to rape her. In an effort to get him to stop his attack upon her, the victim offered him a sum of money, which the accused then took. It was argued that the charge of robbery was irrelevant. The indictment did not charge the accused with having used any violence in order to obtain the money, but rather for the purpose of raping the victim. Furthermore, the victim was alleged to have offered him the money, but it was not said that the violence was used in order to compel or induce the victim to make that offer. The case is somewhat inconclusive, since the Crown, in view of the doubts about the relevancy of the robbery charge withdrew it, but in principle the accused's arguments would seem to be correct.

## F. Robbery of a ship: piracy

**12.09**  One special example of robbery is piracy which was described in the following case as robbery of a ship. There is only one case this century in Scotland where this has been charged.

### Cameron v. H.M. Advocate
### 1971 J.C. 50

**12.10**  Members of the crew of a British ship were charged on an indictment which set forth that, when the ship was about three miles off the Aberdeenshire coast, they threatened and robbed the master, put him and other members of the crew ashore and navigated the ship eastwards on to the high seas, and thus took masterful possession of the ship and appropriated it to their own use. The word "piracy" was not mentioned in the indictment. They all objected to the relevancy of the charge.

LORD CAMERON: "Piracy is a crime nowadays of rare occurrence, at least in the Courts of this country, and has over the years acquired certain picturesque and picaresque associations. But the crime itself, stripped of the highly coloured detail with which storybook romance has clothed the concept, is in essentials of sordid and squalid simplicity. Mr Douglas, in his careful address, complained that it was not possible to ascertain from the indictment whether the charge was piracy or theft or mutiny or just simply breach of the peace. If it were intended that it should be a charge of piracy, then the prosecutor should libel it as such. His argument ran that robbery was a necessary ingredient of piracy and that the possession obtained by the accused had to be against the will of the robbed and obtained forcibly and for the profit of the perpetrator. This, he said, was not relevantly averred in charge 1. His secondary contention was that, if the indictment did disclose any offence committed on the high seas, it was outside the jurisdiction of the Scottish Courts. I think that reference to section 686 of the Merchant Shipping Act, 1894, sufficiently answers that point, as it covers any offence committed by persons, British subjects or not, in or on board a British ship on the high seas. In any event, the offence itself, so far as the indictment discloses, at least began within territorial waters as appears from the words 'navigate said trawler on to the high seas'.

In support of his basic argument Mr Douglas cited passages from Hume, vol. i, pp. 480 and 482. He criticised the statement in Macdonald (5th ed.) p. 43, that 'taking possession of a vessel at sea, whether by those on board, or by others, or feloniously carrying off goods or persons from ships, are acts of piracy' as an inaccurate and incomplete statement of the law and not supported by the passages in Hume on which it is apparently based. What was lacking in this bald statement was any indication that robbery was a necessary ingredient of the crime. I agree with Mr Douglas to this extent, that I think that the statement, if taken by itself, and out of context, is less than accurate. In my opinion the 'taking possession' must itself be causally connected with actual violence employed to enable possession to be taken or with the threat of violence. And that this is so would appear to me to follow from the references to Hume on which the statement professes to be based, because, although the sentence in Macdonald is largely a repetition of language used by Hume on p. 482, yet I think that it is clear enough from what appears in the opening sentence of chapter XXIII on p. 480 that the element of violence and compulsion arising out of violence or the threat of it is of the essence of the crime.

Mr Fairbairn, for the accused Massie (in whose argument Mr Shaffer for Innes concurred), adopted Mr Douglas's arguments, but added a further submission that piracy was no more than robbery at sea of a particular kind, and that consequently there must be displayed an intention permanently to deprive the true owner of his property to the gain or profit of the robber. He cited in support of this contention the most recent authority on the matter, *In re Piracy Jure Gentium* [1934] A.C. 586. He maintained that the words 'appropriate to your own use' was not a phrase which was appropriate to a case of alleged piracy or robbery, however proper to a charge of embezzlement. The distinction between embezzlement and robbery was that in the latter the intention must be to deprive the true owner permanently of his property, while in the former even replacement of the funds embezzled or a proved intention to replace after use by the criminal was no answer to the charge of embezzlement. No doubt the crime of embezzlement is complete even though the money is subsequently repaid or returned in full, but on the particular point raised by Mr Fairbairn, that an intention to deprive permanently is of the essence of theft and robbery and that a gain to the accused must also arise, I am against his contentions. In the first place, the indictment does no more than allege appropriation to the use of the accused: this, I should think, is on the face of it indicative of an intent to dispossess permanently or at least for such indefinite period as to be of permanent character. But, apart from this, Mr Fairbairn could cite no authority for his proposition, which would seem at least to conflict radically with the considerable authority of Hume. At p. 79 in vol. i. Baron Hume wrote: 'When once contracted by a proper taking and carrying away, the guilt cannot afterwards be effaced by any course of conduct, not even by an early and spontaneous restitution of the spoil, and much less by payment of the value, or any other atonement or amends.' Whether the intent be permanent or only temporary appropriation, the clandestine or felonious taking of the article constitutes the crime. On the question of profit Hume had this to say (vol. i, p. 76): '... it is certain, that in the ordinary case the *animus lucri* is to be presumed from the act itself of taking away the thing .... It is also to be remembered, that if the thing is kept, it signifies not for what purpose ... every object is lucre in the estimation of law ....' Now, of course, in these passages Hume was dealing with theft, but I see no possible ground for holding that different principles apply to robbery, which itself is forcible theft. And here I may pause to refer to a later passage in the same chapter, when Hume points out that the display or use of arms or weapons is not a necessary ingredient of robbery. 'Any reasonable fear of danger, arising from a constructive violence, which is gathered from the mode and circumstances of the demand, being such as are attended with awe and alarm, and may naturally induce a man to surrender his property for the safety of his person, is sufficient to make a taking against the will of the sufferer; which is the essence of a robbery. Thus it is a robbery to break into a house, and openly to take away effects in the presence of the owner, who, out of terror, makes no resistance, or perhaps, on demand, himself produces the effects or delivers the keys of his repositories, though situated even in another apartment.' (Hume, vol. i, p. 107.)

The matter is put more briefly in Macdonald (5th ed.) p. 39: 'Robbery is the felonious taking and appropriation of property in opposition to the will of another under whose personal charge it is; and the force that need be used is a matter of degree.' The force referred to is violence or the threat of violence. It will be noted that nothing is said by Hume or Macdonald about the violence or threat of it being such as would be likely to overcome the will of a reasonable man—a point which Mr Fairbairn endeavoured to make and for which he could find no support in authority or text-writer.

If, then, piracy, as Hume would suggest, includes not only privateering without a commission or letters of marque, but also robbery of a ship or of the effects in it, then it may not be necessary to go further than to consider whether what is set out in charge 1, if proved, would constitute robbery of the trawler *Mary Craig*. The question thus is whether there is anything in recent authority to prohibit that course. In the case of *In re Piracy Jure Gentium*, [1934] A.C. 586, the Privy Council were asked to give an answer to one simple question: 'Whether actual robbery is an essential element of the crime of piracy *jure gentium*, or whether a frustrated attempt to commit a piratical robbery is not equally piracy *jure gentium*.' I pause to note that the question itself somewhat confuses the issue by the use of the words 'piratical robbery'. However this may be, the Judicial Committee of the Privy Council, after a full consideration of the authorities, national and international, including our own Baron Hume, returned this answer: 'Actual robbery is not an essential element in the crime of piracy *jure gentium*. A frustrated attempt to commit a piratical robbery is equally piracy *jure gentium*.' After their very full consideration of the law as developed in the jurisprudence of maritime nations, their Lordships (at p. 600) quoted the language of one of Napoleon's commissioners, who said: 'We have guarded against the dangerous ambition of wishing to regulate and to foresee everything.... A new question springs up. Then how is it to be decided? To this question it is replied that the office of the law is to fix by enlarged rules the general maxims of right and wrong, to establish firm principles fruitful in consequences, and not to descend to the detail of all the questions which may arise upon each particular topic.' Their Lordships also made this observation: 'A careful examination of the subject shows a gradual widening of the earlier definition of piracy to bring it from time to time more in consonance with situations either not thought of or not in existence when the older jurisconsults were expressing their opinions.' Hall, writing in 1924 (International Law (8th ed.) p. 314), said: 'The various acts which are recognised or alleged to be piratical may be classed as follows: robbery or attempt at robbery of a vessel, by force or intimidation, either by way of attack from without, or by way of revolt of the crew and conversion of the vessel and cargo to their own use.' While it is true that it is said in *In re Piracy Jure Gentium* that a definition of piracy as sea robbery 'is both too narrow and too wide', the statement I have cited from Hall was quoted without criticism or disapproval. In the case of *In re Piracy Jure Gentium* the Privy Council in the course of their opinion said this (at p. 600): '... their Lordships do not themselves propose to hazard a definition of piracy' an observation which precedes the quotation from M Portalis, Napoleon's commissioner, which I have just cited. I also would decline to incur the navigational hazard of attempting by definition to mark out a safe course among so many expressions of view and opinion as are collected and set out in the opinion of the Privy Council. It would be both unprofitable, and I think in this case unnecessary, to attempt to do so. There is enough, however, in the authorities to make it possible to say that, when a ship is feloniously taken out of the possession of the owner or those in whose charge the vessel has been placed, against their will and by means of violence or threats of violence and, so taken, thereafter appropriated to the use of those who have done so, the crime so committed is piracy *jure gentium*. The essential elements of this crime are no more and no less than those which are requisite to a relevant charge of robbery where the crime is committed in respect of property on land and within the ordinary jurisdiction of the High Court. I therefore conclude that, where the facts set out in an indictment relevantly allege robbery of a ship by members of her crew, that will constitute a relevant charge of piracy, whatever may be the future ambit of the crime of piracy *jure gentium*."

Objection to relevancy repelled.

NOTE

All the accused in this case were convicted of piracy. Their appeals against conviction were all **12.11** dismissed; the High Court on appeal approved of Lord Cameron's decision on what constituted piracy in Scots law. On the argument that an intention permanently to deprive the owner of his property is of the essence of theft (and robbery), see *ante*, Chapter 9.

## 2. EXTORTION

Extortion is a rather curious crime. It consists in the conjunction of acts and statements which, when **12.12** separated, the accused may be perfectly entitled to carry out. Suppose, for example, A discovers that B, a local councillor, is guilty of corruption. He goes to B and tells him to resign from the council. There is nothing criminal in that. Suppose, again, that instead of confronting B he goes to the local newspaper and reveals everything to them. Again, there is nothing criminal in doing so. Suppose finally that, A goes to B and tells him to resign, and also says that if B does not do so, he will reveal all to the local press. That, it would seem, is a crime, the crime of extortion.

The rather surprising nature of the crime is further highlighted when one considers that extortion may be committed where the accused is merely trying to secure compliance by the other party with an obligation which the latter owes to the accused. Suppose, for example, that A, a small business woman, is owed a substantial sum of money by one of her clients, B. B regularly withholds payment, and on more than one occasion A has been put to the expense of pursuing legal action for the recovery of the sums owed to her. On this occasion, exasperated by B's intransigence, she tells B that if he does not pay the sum owed within seven days she will expose his sharp business practice to the local Chamber of Commerce. A is guilty of extortion. If, however, A merely threatened to sue B, then she would not be guilty of any offence. Wherein lies the difference, and what is the justification for treating such demands as extortionate? See, in this respect, the case of *Black v. Carmichael*, below. For a general discussion of the paradoxes of extortion, see Leo Katz, *Ill-Gotten Gains: Evasion, Blackmail, Fraud, and Kindred Puzzles of the Law*, University of Chicago Press, 1996, Part Two.

In *H.M. Advocate v. Crawford* (1850) J. Shaw 309 the Lord Justice-Clerk (Hope) described the crime of extortion in the following way (at p. 322):

'The crime consists in using [a] threat to concuss a person into paying a demand which he intends to resist; and the crime, the use of the threat for that purpose, is the same, whether the party using the threats thinks his demand good or bad.'

### Silverstein v. H.M. Advocate
#### 1949 S.L.T. 386

The appellant was the managing director of a company which owned premises occupied by **12.13** tenants on a yearly basis. He was charged with extorting and attempting to extort payments from the tenants by threatening to arrange that his company would take the appropriate steps to dispossess them of the premises. An objection to the relevancy of the indictment was repelled by the sheriff and he was convicted. He appealed to the High Court of Justiciary on the ground, *inter alia*, that the indictment did not set out any facts from which criminal conduct could be inferred.

LORD JUSTICE-CLERK (THOMSON): "The appellant is charged with three charges." [His Lordship narrated the charges, and proceeded:]

"Broadly, the crime charged is that he, with the object of putting money in his own pocket, threatened that he would use his influence as managing director of Lions Ltd to induce that company to terminate the shop tenancies of two tenants of the company. The ambit of the debate was limited by the Solicitor-General's concession that had the appellant been the landlord he would not have been liable to criminal prosecution if he had threatened to terminate the tenancies unless the tenants paid the sums demanded. This concession was based on the view that a landlord is free to make what bargain he can with his tenant and that in putting pressure on his tenant to pay an increased sum of money a landlord is doing no more than asserting a right which the law gives him. We have therefore simply to deal with the case of a man charged with employing threats that he will use his influence to terminate the benefits enjoyed by his victims unless they buy him off, he having no legal right to demand payment.

The first point taken was that the indictment was irrelevant and that the *species facti* narrated in it did not constitute a crime by the law of Scotland. It was pointed out by Lord Justice-Clerk Inglis in *H.M. Advocate v. Miller*, 1862, 4 Irv. 238, that there are certain threats the uttering of which constitute crimes *per se*, while there are other threats which are not *per se* obnoxious to the criminal law but become so if they are coupled with demands for money to which the person making the demand has no legal right. His Lordship does not attempt to lay down any principles for the determining into which category any particular threat falls and it is unnecessary to do so here as the Solicitor said that he did not maintain that the threats here fall into the first of the Lord Justice-Clerk's categories. Accordingly, we must approach this indictment on the footing that the demand for money to buy off the threatened action is of the essence of the charge.

I have no doubt at all that the indictment is relevant and that it falls into the second of Lord Justice-Clerk Inglis's categories. Money is demanded not as of legal right but as the price of the appellant's forbearance in using his influence to dispossess Weatherston and Arcari of their tenancies. This threat to use his influence to their hurt to his own personal advantage is a crime. The extraction of money from people by certain means is criminal. Fraud is the obvious example. There the perpetrator induces the victim to part with his money by deception. In the case of threats the inducement is some form of pressure. Where the pressure consists in creating in the victim fear that, unless he yields, his position will be altered for the worse, it is criminal unless the pressure sought to be exerted is recognised by the law as legitimate. Legal process is such a form of pressure. So too in the light of the Solicitor's concession is the pressure exerted by one contracting party on another contracting party. I need not consider whether these are exhaustive of legitimate forms of pressure, but I am quite satisfied that the threat to use one's own position and influence as a lever to alter the position of another to his detriment unless that other buys immunity is a relevant ground of charge. What brings about this result is that the payment demanded is not a payment to which the claimant has any right arising out of his legal relationship to the victim.

The crime being relevantly averred, the next question is whether there was evidence put before the jury on which it was entitled to convict."

[Having considered the evidence, and the sheriff's charge to the jury, his Lordship concluded:] "On the whole matter, I am of opinion that the charge was relevant, the evidence sufficient to entitle the jury to convict and that the jury were adequately directed. I suggest to your Lordships that we refuse the appeal."

LORD MACKAY: [After dealing with other matters:] "Turning from that aspect to the other interesting propositions argued, the first was by way of an attack on the relevancy of the three charges in the indictment. To me this attempted disposal of the whole case will be found in the end of the day to go deeply into all the grounds of appeal. It took the main form of saying that at the basis of any charge was the word, and the conception, of 'extortion'. The challenge was that by the use of that word (in its setting at least) no crime known to the law of Scotland was set forth: and the submission was constantly focused in the phrase 'Extortion, whatever that may mean'. The Solicitor-General in reply brought two cases to our notice: *H.M. Advocate v. Crawford*, 1850, Shaw 309, and *H.M. Advocate v. Miller*, 1862, 4 Irv. 238 at p. 244. While these two cases are helpful, I prefer to put my answer on a wider basis. If extortion be fully understood, in the two sides which it must necessarily present, and if such a dangerous social evil be not cognisable by the criminal law, then I think a very serious gap would exist in our

Scots law. Extortion has been spoken of as crime or as punishable in all countries for centuries bypast. In Rome, a *lex* was passed by the Comitia Tributa in 149 B.C. against extortion, *eo nomine* (Cowell's "Cicero", p. 158). The passage in our Hume (vol. I, pp. 135, 439) is one implying that all form of extortion by threat is punishable. Thus I need quote no more than the sidenote at p. 439: 'Extorting of money by a letter is not robbery'; and at p. 441 we find this relative to a case of *James Gray v. H.M. Advocate*: 'The truth is that we have little reason to regret the want of these Statutes [certain English Acts] because our common law has native vigour to punish these enormities in a manner which the common law of England would not have authorised'. The said case of *James Gray*, as also another of *John Fraser* immediately thereafter mentioned, was the case of threatening all sorts of violence if a purse of money were not paid to him and in a certain place. And so again of Macdonald's well-known textbook (Criminal Law). In the third edition (at p. 175) and fifth edition (at pp. 128–129) there is a clear reference to extortion both under the general head 'Oppression' and under the head 'Threats'. Thus (to take a single instance) the author says: 'In another case the charge was combined with one of obtaining of goods and money by extortion and oppression ... without legal warrant ... in defraud of public justice.' And so again, a mere reference to the imagined case of the threats used by Front-de-Boeuf to Isaac of York, in 'Ivanhoe', may suffice to shew what lengths are involved in the contrary submission. I cannot imagine anyone saying that such treatment is not a crime, and one known to every system of law. Further, I do not think any good answer was afforded to the suggestion that the well-known and now everyday crime of blackmail is just a special case of the Roman 'extortion'. It has both sides, the threat of consequences or violence, and the overcoming of the will in order to obtain money. I therefore find no principle for the view that Scots law does not afford a criminal remedy for all such acts. The two sides to which I have referred should not be mixed up and confused. There is the element of force or fear applied—that is, the 'threat'; there is the element of intention (for all extortion effected or attempted), the intention being to overcome the reluctance of the victim; and there is the element of so 'extorting'—forcing out a benefit to oneself which the will of the victim would otherwise have refused to afford or to pay. The simplest case is extortion of money by fear induced by a threat that some disaster will be brought on the victim *unless* the sum is paid. I think the simplest way to put the matter is that that conjunction 'unless' is what couples up the two sides of the criminal transaction, and is enough to infer an illegality.

This leads to my last remark. The further argumentative attack was that to make out any sort of case, the compulsitor used must be that of an 'illegal' threat. This was much insisted in. I am of the opposite opinion. Macdonald says: 'It is no defence that the demand made was for something justly due, no one being entitled to concuss another's will.' So, he says, 'the procurator need not disprove accusations made by the offender nor is it competent to prove their truth.' The notion that one can talk of the substance of the threat as being 'illegal', *i.e.*, as I understand, that the instrument of the 'fear' induced might be something forbidden by the law, received a measure of assent for a time, but I have been, and remain, of opinion, whether on the authority of Lord Justice-Clerk Hope in *Crawford* (*supra*) or that of Lord Justice-Clerk Inglis in *Miller* (*supra*), or just upon plain principle, that such a proposition has no substance.

In other words, the illegality of the whole thing consists in the apposition of threats with the forcing of the unwilling will, the collocation of the two sides being the conjunction which I have placed as the necessary link: 'unless'.

Now, as to the three charges, that being the law, in this present sample they are, to my thinking, not very strongly fortified in the essential matter of specification; but that line was not definitely pursued. They all do sufficiently indicate the purpose of the threat and the overpowering of the will." [His Lordship then dealt with other matters.]

Appeal refused.

### Carmichael v. Black; Black v. Carmichael
1992 S.L.T. 897

**12.14** [For the facts of this case, see Chap. 11, *ante*.]

LORD JUSTICE-GENERAL (HOPE): "The primary argument for the Crown is that private wheel clamping—that is, the wheel clamping of a vehicle until it is released on payment of a charge which is not done under the authority of a statute—amounts to extortion and as such is accordingly criminal. In order to deal with this argument it is necessary to go back to first principles. No one can be allowed to take the law into his own hands. A person who robs another to give to charity is nevertheless guilty of a crime. The result or motive cannot justify the means, if what is done constitutes an offence. What then is the essence of the crime of extortion? In my opinion this was explained with sufficient clarity by Lord Justice-Clerk Hope in *Crawford* [*Crawford (Alex. F.)* (1850) J. Shaw 309] at p. 322 in these terms: 'The act of sending a threatening letter, for the purpose of getting money, instead of resorting to due form of law in order to its recovery, is the crime .... The crime consists in using the threat to concuss a person into paying a demand which he intends to resist; and the crime, the use of threat for that purpose, is the same, whether the party using the threat thinks his demand good or bad.'

At p. 324 he went on to say this: 'Every man has a right to dispute the demand of his creditor in a court of justice, and it is no answer to a charge of threatening to burn his house, to say that the debt which the party sought by that threat to recover was really due. Now, there can be no difference as to the nature and essence of the crime from the character of the threat: the crime is the same, whether the threat is of personal violence or of the character of those contained in the present case.'

That was a case where the writer of a letter sought to obtain payment of a sum which he claimed was due to him as a debt by threatening to make allegations of shameful conduct. It was held that it was not necessary for the prosecutor to allege either that the debt demanded was not due or that the accusations by means of which it was attempted to be enforced were untrue. Lord Moncreiff summed the matter up precisely at p. 329 when he said: 'It seems to me that the offence is complete so soon as the party attempts to enforce either legal or illegal demands by illegal means.'

There is a more recent discussion of the crime of extortion in *Silverstein v. H.M. Advocate* where the extortion was said to consist of a threat made by the director of a landlord company to the tenants of the property that he would get them evicted unless they paid money to him personally. The payment which he sought was not a payment which he had any right to demand from his victim, and it was this feature of the case which was said by Lord Justice-Clerk Thomson, 1949 J.C. at p. 163 to lead to the result that the charge was relevant. I do not agree with some of the comments elsewhere in his opinion which might suggest that the use of threats is legitimate if there is a right to demand payment. This argument was rejected by Lord Mackay, 1949 J.C. at p. 165 under reference to *Crawford* and to the comment in Macdonald on the *Criminal Law of Scotland* (5th ed., p. 128), that: 'It is no defence that the threat was made in order to compel performance of something justly due, no one being entitled to concuss another.' In my opinion it is extortion to seek to enforce a legitimate debt by means which the law regards as illegitimate, just as it is extortion to seek by such means to obtain money or some other advantage to which the accused has no right at all. Furthermore, the only means which the law regards as legitimate to force a debtor to make payment of his debt are those provided by due legal process. To use due legal process, such as an action in a court of law or a right of lien or retention available under contract, or to threaten to do so, is no doubt legitimate. It is not extortion if the debtor pays up as a result. But it is illegitimate to use other means, such as threats which are not related to the use of legal process, or the unauthorised detention of the debtor's person or his property, and it is extortion if the purpose in doing so is to obtain payment of the debt.

Counsel's argument that the extortion charges in these cases were irrelevant can be summarised in this way. He submitted that the complaints did not disclose a direct threat by either of the accused, nor was it suggested that their purpose was to seek to gain a personal advantage of any kind. It was not said that the accused were the people who demanded or were to receive the money. All they were said to have done was to fix the clamp and put the notice on the windscreen, and on these facts they were merely the employees or agents of someone else. What was really in issue here was the legality of the action taken by the owner of the private property. Notice had been given to those who had parked in the car park without authority that there would be a levy if their vehicles were immobilised. The notice made it clear that this was private property and that vehicles left there would be regarded as unauthorised and unlawfully parked. What the landowner was doing in these circumstances was enforcing his right to the exclusive possession of his own property, and the demand for payment was a legitimate demand in these circumstances. He had acted within his rights in instructing the use of the wheel clamping, just as he would have been entitled if he wished to enclose vehicles within the car park by means of a fence or by a locked gate.

I have every sympathy with landowners who find it intolerable that others should park their motor vehicles without permission on their private property. But I am not persuaded that the means which have been selected in this case to deter that activity can be regarded as legitimate. On the contrary it seems to me that they fall plainly within the proper limits of the crime of extortion, since the whole purpose of the wheel clamping as described in each charge was to obtain money as a condition of the release of the vehicle. It is no answer to the charge to say that the driver of the vehicle had no right to park it where it was clamped, or that the landowner was entitled to exclude it from his property. Nor would it matter for this purpose if the landowner had been entitled to be paid a parking charge—although it should be made clear that counsel did not contend that in this case that was the position. There was no offer and acceptance here, since it is not being suggested that the landowner had invited the motorists to use his ground on payment as a car park. As it happens there can be no suggestion in this case that there was a debt due or a right to obtain payment which could be enforced by means of an action in the court. But that point is not, I think, decisive in this case, nor does it matter that the recipients of the levy, if paid, were to be persons other than the accused. As the Lord Advocate pointed out, it would be quite irrelevant as a defence to the charge of extortion to show that the sum sought to be recovered by the wheel clamping was a legitimate charge for parking the car, and I agree with him that the accused must be taken to have been involved at least art and part in the charge of extortion since they are said to have affixed the clamp and put the notice on the windscreen. It is not a necessary element in the crime of extortion that the person who makes the threat or issues the demand should be alleged to have been seeking an advantage for himself. As I said earlier, he who robs another in order to give to charity is guilty of the crime of robbery, and so it is with extortion.

The essential step in the argument, which makes the practice of wheel clamping illegal on the ground of extortion unless authorised by statute, is that it amounts to a demand for payment accompanied by the threat that until payment the vehicle will not be released. I do not accept counsel's argument that there was here no threat. It seems to me that the placing of the notice on the windscreen stating the terms for release was a clear threat that the vehicle would remain immobilised until the levy was paid. Furthermore, I derive no assistance from the analogy which was suggested by counsel of the landowner enclosing his land by a fence or by a locked gate for his own purposes. No doubt persons who park their vehicles without permission on private land run the risk that their vehicles will be detained there if the landowner, for a legitimate purpose such as his own security, decides to close the entrance and in consequence makes it impossible for the vehicles for the time being to be driven away. But that is an entirely different matter from the taking of unauthorised action to detain vehicles on his own land for no purpose other than to enforce a demand for payment for parking there. It is not suggested that the landowner in this case had any lien or other right implied by law to detain the vehicles. There was no statutory authority for what was done, in contrast to that which is available, in the case of a straying animal, to detain it for the limited purpose of preventing injury or damage by it, in terms of section 3 of the Animals (Scotland) Act 1987. In short, it is illegal for vehicles to be held to ransom in the manner described in these charges, and those who are proved to have done so, whether by the fixing of the wheel clamps or by the placing of the notice on the windscreen or otherwise, are guilty of attempted extortion or, if the levy has been paid, of the completed crime of extortion.

For these reasons I consider that the sheriff was right to repel the pleas to the relevancy of the charges of extortion and attempted extortion, and I would refuse the appeals which have been taken against his decision in that regard."

Appeal refused.

### H.M. Advocate v. Donoghue and Another
#### 1971 S.L.T. 2

**12.15** Michael Donoghue and Edward Stuart Burns were charged on indictment that "you did (1) on September 12, 1969 in the premises owned by Raymond Bamford at 23 Regent Terrace, Edinburgh, force open a lockfast storeroom, steal a key therefrom and by means of said key open a lockfast room in said premises and steal therefrom five paintings, a clock and two candelabra; and (2) on various occasions between November 12 and 22, 1969, both dates inclusive, at the house occupied by you, Edward Stuart Burns, at 5/2 Burnhead Loan, Edinburgh, in the Captain's Cabin public house at Captain's Road, Edinburgh, and in the house occupied by Peter London, at 12 Grosvenor Crescent, Edinburgh, inform said Peter London, who was the agent for the owner of said stolen paintings, that you were in a position to secure the return of said stolen paintings to said Peter London if he handed to you £1,200 of money and you did attempt to extort from said Peter London £1,200 of money for the return of said stolen paintings."

It was argued for the panels that the second charge was irrelevant in that it did not constitute a crime. There were no relevant averments of attempted extortion. In a charge of attempted extortion there must be some element of threat and an element of obtaining money or some other advantage by threat. The Crown conceded that an element of threat was required, but argued that there was here an implied or tacit threat that if the money were not paid the paintings would not be returned.

The Lord Justice-Clerk (Grant) held that the second charge was irrelevant. Without giving an opinion, he indicated that the words libelled, in the absence of averments of specific threats and words importing a tacit or implied threat, did not constitute a crime.

Plea to the relevancy of Charge 2 upheld.

### Rae v. Donnelly
#### 1982 S.C.C.R. 148

**12.16** The appellant ran a garage business. Two of his employees D, a woman, and L, a married man had an affair. D became pregnant. D identified L as the father of her child. When the appellant learned of this he sacked her. D raised an action for unfair dismissal. The appellant later met with D and asked her to withdraw her claim for unfair dismissal. He also stated that if she did so he was prepared to keep quiet about the affair. However, he also stated that he would tell what he knew to D's parents and to L's wife. Neither D's parents nor L's wife knew who it was that D claimed was the father of her child. The accused was convicted of extortion and appealed.

LORD JUSTICE-CLERK (WHEATLEY): "This is an appeal against conviction by John Rae who was charged with an attempt to extort from one of his employees, Susan Douglas, the withdrawal of her complaint of unfair dismissal by threats which the appellant had uttered towards her. I do not require to recite the facts of the case as they are fully set out in the findings. At the end of the day the issue turned on whether on findings 20, 21, and 22 it was legitimate for the sheriff to read out of these findings that what the appellant had threatened to disclose to the parents of Miss Douglas and to the wife of Mr Lowrie was the affair between these two which had resulted in the procreation of the child to Miss Douglas. It was strenuously argued by Mr Kerrigan that that interpretation could not be taken out of these findings when read against the other findings in the case, and particularly finding 19. I cannot sustain that argument. In my view the inference from the evidence is clearly that what was threatened was not simply a disclosure of the association in relation to the dismissal but was a disclosure in relation to the association of the sexual nature between Miss Douglas and Mr Lowrie. That was clearly brought out in the note by the sheriff when he said that the only meaning which can be attributed to the words which the appellant said he uttered is that he would tell her parents and Mrs Lowrie that Mr Lowrie was the father of Miss Douglas's child. In the context of the other facts in the case the purpose underlying that threat is obvious. Once that was established then by concession the charge was established. As I am of the view that it was established for the reasons which I have given I would move your Lordships to answer the question of law in the affirmative and to refuse the appeal."

Appeal refused.

NOTES

In *Hill v. McGrogan*, 1945 S.L.T. (Sh.Ct) 18 the accused was charged with sending a letter to the **12.17** complainer demanding that she resign from her job as a cleaner in a local authority school. The letter stated that if she did not do so he would report her to the Ministry of Education and have her charged with theft of government property. The complaint also narrated that all of this was done for the purpose of forcing the complainer to leave her job. The sheriff found that the letter was not written for the purpose of extorting money, and there was no averment of malice. An objection to the relevancy of the complaint was therefore upheld by the sheriff since the threat was neither criminal in itself nor done for an improper purpose.

It is clear today that extortion can be committed without any attempt by the accused to obtain money from the victim.

# Chapter 13

# Fraud, Forgery and Uttering

## 1. Fraud

**13.01** The crime of fraud in Scotland is very broadly defined. All that is required is that the accused, by a false pretence, induces the victim to do something which he or she would not otherwise have done. Unlike other systems, there is no requirement that fraud have any economic element, or any requirement that the victim has been induced to act to his or her detriment (although the typical cause of fraud will involve some loss to the victim).

### A. The *actus reus* of fraud

### (a) The false pretence

#### Tapsell v. Prentice
(1910) 6 Adam 354

**13.02** A hawker was convicted on a complaint which set forth that "within the shop at . . . occupied by J. McB., you did assume the name of Mrs G. and did pretend that you were manageress of a company of travelling gipsies who were about to encamp in the neighbourhood for several weeks, and that you intended to purchase provisions for said gipsies from the said J. McB. to the value of £30 sterling or thereby, and relying solely on the truth of said representation did thus induce him to purchase from you a rug in excess of its proper value, and you did thus defraud the said J. McB. "She appealed to the High Court by bill of suspension.

LORD JUSTICE-CLERK (MACDONALD): "I am quite clear that the bill of suspension must be sustained without making any comment on, or proposing to detract from the authority of, any case that has been quoted to us. I do not think these cases have any bearing upon the present case. The act that is charged here is selling a rug in excess of its value, which is a thing that is done any day, and is not a criminal offence. Then it is a curious form of charge to say 'in excess of its value', when we are not told what the prosecutor thought was the true value of the rug, nor what was the price paid. I think the charge is hopelessly irrelevant, and that is really sufficient to dispose of the case.

But further, it is said that this person is a fraudulent person and assumed a false name and represented that she was manageress of a company of travelling gipsies who were about to encamp in the neighbourhood, and that she intended to purchase provisions from the complainer, and did thus induce him to purchase the rug. Now, the person who bought the rug is presumably as capable of estimating its value as anyone else, and though, no doubt, the suggestion is that the object of his purchasing it was to keep the gipsies, as it were, thirled to his shop, yet misstatements of that kind do not amount to falsehood, fraud, and wilful imposition in the criminal sense. The cases cited to us were all cases of misrepresentation about the article sold. In the horse case, *Turnbull v. Stuart*, 25 R. (J.) 78, the purpose was to get a better price for the horse by representing that it had been hunted by Mr and Mrs Younger, well-known people. There is nothing said here to suggest that this woman made any misrepresentations about the rug or its value. I therefore think that on this ground also the conviction must be quashed."

LORD ARDWALL: "Two obvious criticisms can be made on this complaint. In the first place, there is no statement that any money passed, and so far as the complaint goes the rug said to have been sold may never have been paid for to this day. Secondly, we are not told what the proper value of the rug was, nor how much in excess of that was the price agreed upon. That, again, seems to me to be a defect in this complaint, apart from other things. But the most serious defect is the want of any statement that there was any fraudulent misrepresentation regarding the article sold. It is said that the accused made certain representations about herself and a gang of gipsies which she was taking about the country. These are just the ordinary lies which people tell when they want to induce credulous members of the public to purchase goods, or to do something for them. But these representations are not directly connected with the rug, which may have been a perfectly good one. Now, there can be no crime in such a sale as is here alleged unless the fraudulent misrepresentations relate directly to the articles to be sold. I am therefore of opinion that all the allegations of misrepresentation made in this complaint are irrelevant, and that the conviction must be set aside."

LORD SALVESEN: "I am very far from commending the conduct of this accused, but I agree that there is no relevant charge. The complaint should at least have contained a statement that the complainer not merely purchased the rug but paid the accused for it. If there was only a purchase without payment, it could never be said that this accused got any advantage, or that the purchaser suffered any injury by her false pretences."

Conviction quashed.

NOTE

This case (although trivial in monetary terms) illustrates the difficulties facing the common law in **13.03** relation to business dealings, where the spectre of criminality is hard to find. With regard to advertisements in the normal course of business, dealers are far more likely to fall foul of the Trade Descriptions Acts than the common law of fraud, unless there is some clear element of dishonesty. So far as concerns the more complicated business frauds, these are of course notoriously difficult to detect and prove. In England there has been so much concern about frauds in the City of London that investigation thereof is now to be carried out by the Serious Fraud Office established under the Criminal Justice Act 1987. For Scotland, see the Criminal Justice (Scotland) Act 1987, ss.51 to 55.

### Strathern v. Fogal
### 1922 J.C. 73

A father and his sons were charged with (1) having entered into a fraudulent scheme for **13.04** obtaining from the tenants of shops owned by the father payments for a continuation of their tenancy, by falsely representing that the shops had been let to the sons, and that, unless the payments were made, the tenants would be ejected; and (2) having made returns to the City Assessor which did not include grassums received from the tenants of the shops, intending that the figures thus returned should enter the valuation roll, as they did; and with thus having defrauded the rating authorities of the rates and taxes assessable in respect of the grassums. The Sheriff-substitute dismissed the complaint as irrelevant. On appeal by the procurator-fiscal:

LORD HUNTER: "I have formed a clear opinion, agreeing in this with the Sheriff-substitute, that the complaint sets forth no specific and relevant averments of criminal fraud committed against the tenants of the accused Myer Fogal. According to the complaint, the accused and three of his sons, two of whom are also charged with the offence, 'having entered into a scheme to fraudulently obtain from the tenants of said shops payments of money in respect of said tenants being permitted to continue in the tenancy of the shops already occupied by them, or to obtain a grant of new lets of such shops, by pretending to them that a *bona fide* let of said respective shops had been entered into between you Myer Fogal, as proprietor, and you Harris Fogal, Lion Fogal, presently of Bleicherweg, Zurich, Switzerland, and you Joseph Fogal, as tenants, and that unless said payments were made said tenants would be ejected, ... did ... fraudulently obtain from the respective tenants specified in the second column, in respect of the lets of the shops specified in the third column, the amounts respectively specified in the fourth column, all of the first schedule hereto annexed, which sums you forthwith appropriated to your own uses.' As I read the complaint at first, I thought the suggestion was that the accused Myer Fogal was not entitled to exact any premium for the renewal of the leases or the grant of new leases. Some, if not all, of the members of the jury might think that was a natural meaning to attach to the words. But it was admitted that the accused Myer Fogal was quite entitled to bargain with his tenants for the payment of a sum of money as a condition of their being allowed to remain in occupation, or to get from new tenants a higher rent than he had obtained from old tenants, and to obtain that increase by receiving payment of a grassum. Nor do I see that it would have been any crime on the part of Myer Fogal and his sons to arrange that the sons should be put in possession, if the tenants refused to agree to the landlord's terms. Apart from any specific arrangement, what crime would have been committed by threat to dispossess? It was contended that the crime was committed by pretending that a *bona fide* let of the shops had been entered into between the parties. There is no specification of the language employed to create a belief in the minds of the intending tenants of the existence of, or terms of, the lease. I do not, however, think that a false statement by the parties accused upon this matter renders them liable to be prosecuted for the crime of defrauding the tenants, whatever the civil rights might thereby be conferred upon the latter for reduction of the leases or damages. The misrepresentation, if made, did not in any real sense affect the subject of the bargain, but was essentially collateral, though it might be material and induce the contract.

The appellant relied upon the authority of *Hood v. Young*, 1 Irv. 236, and *Turnbull v. Stuart*, 25 R. (J.) 78, 2 Adam 536. In the former of these cases Hood and another were charged with fraud 'in so far as they fraudulently and feloniously formed the design to expose two unsound horses or mares belonging to them, or one or other of them, to public sale, and, with a view to obtain higher prices for them, fraudulently to represent that they were the property of a farmer, who had worked them for a year bygone or thereby, and that they were sound and good workers, and only parted with because the owner was about to emigrate'. These statements were repeated by the auctioneer to intending purchasers who attended the sale. The accused was convicted and a note of suspension refused. This case was followed in the later case of *Turnbull*, where a false and fraudulent description of horses had been made to an auctioneer which was inserted in the sale catalogue. Both these cases were before the Court in *Tapsell v. Prentice*, 1911 S.C. (J.) 67, 6 Adam 354 [noted *supra*] .... That case appears to me to be authority for our holding that the complaint, so far as it charges the accused with defrauding the tenants, is irrelevant. As regards the alternative charge, I am unable to agree with the Sheriff-substitute. The alleged offence is that the accused defrauded the rating authorities of a large sum of money by supplying false information to the Assessor as to the return from the property. It is also said that the false information was supplied with the intention that it should be inserted in the Valuation-roll; and that it was so inserted, with the result that the accused escaped payment of rates for which they were, or at all events the accused Myer Fogal was, liable. I am of opinion that the facts averred in the complaint, if proved, establish a common law offence."

First charge held irrelevant;
Second charge relevant.

Note

The first charge in *Strathern v. Fogal* really concerned an objectionable but non-criminal course of **13.05** action, while the second charge was clearly fraud. But the finding of Lord Hunter that the statements made by the accused in the first charge were merely collateral has been criticised: see Gordon, para. 18–28. There was still a pretence which was false; and it still had a practical result. On the question of collateral statements, see also *Richards v. H.M. Advocate, infra.*

### Richards v. H.M. Advocate
1971 S.L.T. 115

The accused was convicted of fraud on an indictment which charged: "that having formed a **13.06** fraudulent scheme to induce the Corporation of the City of Edinburgh to dispone in feu the property known as Hillwood House and policies in Corstorphine, Edinburgh, by means of false pretences as to the party desirous of obtaining such feu and the purposes for which it was desired you did in pursuance of said scheme (1) between February 1, 1968 and February 1, 1969, both dates inclusive, in Edinburgh, cause Walter Erfyl Burns, [and others] to pretend to the said Corporation in verbal and written communications that said Walter Erfyl Burns desired to purchase for the private residential use of himself and his family the foresaid property ... and did thereby induce the said Corporation on January 8, 1969 to make an offer to feu the said subjects to the said Walter Erfyl Burns for a price of £4,000 which offer was accepted on behalf of the said Walter Erfyl Burns on January 21, 1969, the truth being that the said Walter Erfyl Burns had no intention that the said subjects should be used for the private residence of himself and his family and that you intended to acquire the said subjects for your own purposes and you did fraudulently induce the said Corporation to do an act which they would not otherwise have done, namely to accept the said Walter Erfyl Burns as the genuine offerer to purchase in feu said subjects for the private residential use of himself and his family and to enter into missives with him thereanent."

The accused sought leave to appeal against his conviction on the ground, *inter alia*, that the indictment was irrelevant in that: (i) the facts set forth in support of the first charge did not constitute a crime known to the law; (ii) the said misrepresentation did not relate to a past or present fact but to future intention; (iii) the alleged misrepresentation set forth in the first charge related to a matter collateral to the contract alleged to have been induced.

Lord Justice-Clerk (Grant): "The substance of [the first] two reasons is that, as the misrepresentation libelled relates not to a past or present fact but to a future intention, the charge discloses no crime known to the law of Scotland. It seems to me that 'future intention' is an elliptical and somewhat ambiguous phrase. Assuming, for the moment, that the misrepresentation libelled is of intention only (and the Crown do not concede this), it is one of present intention as to future conduct. This, I think, was how [counsel for the appellant] treated the matter and I shall do likewise. I shall also proceed meantime on the basis (which again is disputed by the Crown) that there is no difference in principle between a misrepresentation by A of his own intention and the causing by A of a misrepresentation to be made as to the intention of a third party.

So far as I can trace, the appellant's argument on this branch of the case derives no support from Hume or Alison, neither of whom appears to draw a distinction between misrepresentation of a 'fact' and misrepresentation of 'intention'. It is a distinction, however, which was made in *Hall* (1881) 4 Couper 438, where Lord Young held an indictment libelling fraud irrelevant because the misrepresentations averred related not to past or present facts but to intention as to future conduct. A new indictment, framed to meet this objection, later came before the High Court on a different point, but at that stage no comment was made on Lord Young's ruling on the earlier indictment. [See *Hall* at p. 500.] Then we come to an *obiter dictum* of Lord Ashmore in *Strathern v. Fogal*, 1922 J.C. 73, at p. 82, to the effect that the complaint (which had been held to be irrelevant for another reason) was also irrelevant because the false pretences alleged related to future conduct. Finally, the appellant relied strongly on the case of *Regina v. Dent* [1955] 2 Q.B. 590, which, if it represents the law of Scotland, is directly in point here.

In my opinion, however, it does not and, despite the reasoning of Devlin, J. (as he then was), I can see no reason in principle why it should: for it seems to me that a man's present intention is just as much a fact as his name or his occupation or the size of his bank balance. Quite apart from general principle, however, we find as far back as 1849 the case of *Chisholm*, J. Shaw 241, in which Lord Justice-Clerk Hope sat with Lords Wood and Ivory. The main question in that case related to the relevancy of a cumulative charge of fraud and theft on the same *species facti*. There was a further question, however, as to the relevancy of the fraud charge *per se*. The misrepresentation libelled was that the accused had promised to pay the price of certain goods at specified places at a future time. On the amendment of the libel (at the suggestion of the Court) by the insertion of a statement that the accused had entered upon the transactions with the intention of not paying for the goods, the libel was held relevant. This decision seems to me to be directly in point here as does that in the later case of *Macleod v. Mactavish* (1897) 2 Adam 354, (1897) 5 S.L.T. 150. There the sole misrepresentation was that the accused intended to remain in his employer's service for another half year. On a bill of suspension being taken the complaint was held to be relevant and the conviction upheld. One may also take into account the 'board and lodging' cases (*cf.* Macdonald, at p. 56) and the specimen form of complaint set out in the Summary Jurisdiction (Scotland) Act, 1908, and repeated with one small amendment in the Second Schedule to the consolidating Act of 1954 thus: 'You did obtain from C.D. board and lodgings to the value of 12s. without paying and intending not to pay therefor.' (The phrase 'and intending not' was originally 'or intending'.) If the appellant is right, it is difficult to see how such a complaint could be relevant. We were also referred to Gordon on Criminal Law (1st ed.), in which the authorities are reviewed at pp. 546 to 548. His conclusion that 'a statement of present intention as to future conduct can ground a charge of fraud' is, in my opinion, fully justified by authority.

For these reasons I am of opinion that subheads (i) and (ii) of the first ground of appeal must fail.

In his argument on subhead (iii) [counsel for the appellant] relied mainly on the cases of *Tapsell v. Prentice*, (1911) 6 Adam 354 and *Strathern v. Fogal*. On their facts, however, these cases are clearly distinguishable from the present. No doubt there are many cases where the future use of heritable subjects is of no moment to the seller and may be a matter extraneous to the actual contract for the sale of those subjects. Here, however, on the face of the indictment (and I am not, of course, concerned at this stage with what may or may not have been established in evidence) the future use of the subjects was of crucial importance and was an essential governing factor in the completion of the contract for the sale of those same subjects. It cannot, in my opinion, be treated merely as a matter collateral to the contract."

The indictment was held relevant and grounds of appeal (i)–(iii) were rejected, but conviction quashed on other grounds.

NOTE

**13.07**   Richards illustrates just how wide the Scots law of fraud has become and how it compares to the convoluted statutory provisions contained in the Theft Acts of 1968 and 1978 in England. The common law in Scotland is certainly flexible enough to deal with the fraudulent use of cheque cards and credit cards, a matter which has perplexed the English courts. See, for example, *R. v. Kovacs* [1974] 1 W.L.R. 370 where an accused had presented to various suppliers her cheque card along with cheques which she knew would not be honoured. She was convicted under the then existing s.16(1) of the Theft Act 1968 of obtaining a pecuniary advantage by deception. It was argued that she had deceived not the bank, but the person to whom she had presented the cheques. However, the Court of Appeal held that she had obtained the pecuniary advantage for herself from the bank in increasing her overdraft by inducing the suppliers to believe she was entitled to use the cheque card when she was not. In *R. v. Charles* [1977] A.C. 177 the House of Lords held that when the drawer of a cheque accepted in exchange for goods, services or cash used a cheque card, he made to the payee a representation that he had the actual authority of the bank to enter on its behalf into the contract expressed on the card that it would honour the cheque on presentment for payment. In *R. v. Lambie* [1982] A.C. 449 the same reasoning was applied to a credit card.

## McKenzie v. H.M. Advocate
### 1988 S.C.C.R. 153

Three accused were charged with forming a fraudulent scheme to obtain money from Caley **13.08** Fisheries (Partnerships) Ltd, and that in pursuance of this scheme they induced separate solicitors by false representations to raise two actions for payment against the company, and so attempted to obtain sums of money by fraud. The sheriff rejected preliminary pleas to the relevancy of the indictment. The accused appealed to the High Court.

OPINION OF THE COURT: "On behalf of the first two appellants Mr Bell submitted that the indictment did not disclose a crime known to the law of Scotland; the stage had not been reached when an attempted fraud had taken place. He contended that the raising of the two actions without any foundation could not constitute fraud or attempted fraud. He submitted that before there could be fraud there required to be false pretences which brought about a practical result: Here it was libelled that the appellants had consulted solicitors and induced them to raise proceedings, but no irrevocable step had been taken. The raising of the action could be stopped. Mr Bell submitted that the critical question was whether the raising of an action was sufficient to amount to attempted fraud. He founded upon *H.M. Advocate v. Tannahill and Neilson*, 1943 J.C. 150 at p. 153 where Lord Wark in charging the jury said:

'I have to direct you that there is no evidence on this part of the charge which would entitle you to bring in a verdict of an attempt to defraud, because in order to get as far as that I think you would require to have some overt act, the consequences of which cannot be recalled by the accused, which goes towards the commission of the crime, before you can convict even of attempt.'

Mr Bell contended that the raising of an action was something which could be recalled, and that accordingly it did not constitute the sort of overt act which was necessary to constitute an attempt to defraud.

In our opinion, the raising of an action in court is an overt act, and moreover once the action has been raised it cannot be recalled. No doubt the action can be abandoned, but it cannot be expunged or blotted out. Moreover, the present case is different on its facts from *H.M. Advocate v. Tannahill and Neilson*. In the latter case, all that was done was that the appellants suggested in a conversation that false and fabricated accounts might be put forward, but that was as far as matters went. In the present case, on the other hand, solicitors were induced by false statements to raise actions which were without any foundation. In our opinion, the advocate-depute was well-founded when he contended that what was libelled in the present indictment was the making of false representations to solicitors which were acted on by them with the consequence that actions were raised; there were thus dishonest representations which had a practical effect. That was sufficient to make a relevant case of attempted fraud.

On behalf of the third appellant Mr Campbell contended that what was libelled could not amount to fraud because the critical facts must have been in the knowledge of the defenders in the two actions. In our opinion, however, that submission by Mr Campbell is not necessarily well-founded. The critical facts may not have been within the knowledge of the defenders; unless they had full and accurate records Caley Fisheries (Partnerships) Ltd might have been deceived by the actions which were raised.

Mr Campbell also contended that the charges in the indictment were misconceived because inducing someone by false pretence to invoke the judicial process was deceiving the court and not the party against whom the judicial process was directed. In our opinion, that submission is unsound. An action for payment is a petitory action, that is one in which a demand is made upon the defender; it is a demand for payment against the defenders.

Mr Campbell presented an alternative argument to the effect that the fraudulent scheme had not progressed far enough to amount to a criminal attempt. He submitted that the situation might have been different if the action had proceeded to the stage of evidence being given during a proof or of the pursuer moving for decree. With that proposition we do not agree. Mr Campbell's argument was somewhat undermined when he conceded that sending a letter of claim could amount to an attempt to defraud. If the sending of such a letter would be sufficient to amount to attempted fraud, then in our opinion taking the matter further and raising an action would *a fortiori* be sufficient to amount to attempted fraud. It might be different if all that had occurred was that the raising of an action was discussed or contemplated but was never raised. Here however positive and overt steps were taken, namely the raising of the actions, and in our opinion what is averred in this indictment amounts to two separate attempts to obtain money by fraud. The indictment is therefore relevant."

Appeal dismissed.

NOTE

**13.09** Although this is as much a case on the law of attempted crime as it is on the law of fraud, it is included here because of the novel implication in the decision that if the scheme had been successful a completed fraud would have been committed through the medium of the solicitors concerned. It is a sad fact that the instructions given by many clients to their solicitors are less than truthful; a solicitor will quite often be induced to take some step which he would not otherwise have taken had he been told a more accurate version of events. A solicitor is not bound to judge the veracity of what he is told, for that is not his function; and while he is bound to give proper professional advice, it will often be through his innocent hands that, *e.g.* a false defence is stated in a criminal court; an unmerited remedy pursued; or a course of dealing carried on which is based on entirely false premises.

This case appears to decide that (a) the solicitors were induced to do something they otherwise would not have done (raise the actions) by means of the pretences, which would appear to be a completed fraud on them; and (b) there was an attempted fraud on Caley Fisheries (Partnerships) Ltd who, assuming they did not know the critical facts, might have paid the moneys to the accused. Proposition (a) raises problems for solicitors, for on one view it forces them to judge the instructions given to them by clients with more than one eye on the criminal law and may put them under additional professional responsibilities. It is easy to say that a solicitor should be able to spot a phoney client with a phoney case, but the situation is rarely clear-cut. Proposition (b) is probably the ratio of this case, but it is worth stressing that the scheme was a long way from completion. On the law of attempts generally, see Chap. 6, *ante*.

## (b) The practical result

### Adcock v. Archibald
### 1925 J.C. 58

**13.10** A coal miner was convicted of fraud in that he induced his employers to do something they would otherwise not have done, namely, crediting him with a bonus payment to which he was not entitled. Adcock had tampered with the "pin" on a fellow miner's hutch of coal so as fraudulently to represent that he was responsible for mining that particular coal. He appealed by bill of suspension on the broad ground that his pretence had not actually caused any loss to his employers.

LORD JUSTICE-GENERAL (CLYDE): "The grounds of suspension are to be found in the circumstance that, while in this as in other pits the miners are paid on the amount of the coal gotten by them, there is in force a minimum rate of wage per shift; and, if the wage of any particular miner, earned on the coal gotten by him falls short of the minimum shift-wage, he receives a 'make-up' representing the difference. The suspender's point is that the increase in the amount of wage (calculated on the coal gotten by him)—which was paid to him in consequence of his having tampered with the pins—did not equal, still less exceed, the difference between the wage to which he was entitled in respect of the coal gotten and the minimum shift-wage. He did not, in short, actually succeed in getting anything more out of his employers than the minimum shift-wage, to which he was in any case entitled. On this he argues that, at most, he was guilty of no more than attempted fraud.

It is, however, a mistake to suppose that to the commission of a fraud it is necessary to prove an actual gain by the accused, or an actual loss on the part of the person alleged to be defrauded. Any definite practical result achieved by fraud is enough. In the present case, the employers were undoubtedly induced, by the fraudulent tampering with the pins, to credit the accused with wages, for coal gotten by him, to an extent to which they would not otherwise have done so. They were also induced to credit his fellow-miner with wages for coal gotten by him to a less extent than they would otherwise have done. This was the definite practical result of the accused's fraud. It is not, in my opinion, any answer to say that such result did not involve the employers in paying more than the minimum shift-wage.

I think, accordingly, that the bill of suspension should be refused."

LORD HUNTER: "I agree. A fraud may be committed, although in the result the person defrauded may not have suffered any pecuniary loss. The essence of the offence consists in inducing the person who is defrauded either to take some article he would not otherwise have taken, or to do some act he would not otherwise have done, or to become the medium of some unlawful act. In the present case I think it was relevant to aver that a wrongful act had been done by the accused, with the result that the company were induced to do something they would not otherwise have done. That being so, it is of no account to consider whether in the result the colliery company have not in fact been out of pocket."

Appeal dismissed.

NOTES

1. For a trenchant critique of the decision in *Adcock*, see Gordon, para. 18–16. The only "practical" **13.11** result was the making of the entry in the books, the triviality of which is in stark contrast to the practical results commonly encountered as giving rise to charges of fraud, such as obtaining property by deception. See also *William Fraser* (1847) Ark. 280 (*ante*) where Lord Cockburn at p. 312 remarked that any deceit that injures and violates the rights of another is punishable.

2. What kind of "practical result" will suffice for fraud? The history of the crime of fraud shows that it at one time had an "economic" element. It was an offence "committed by some false assumption of name, character, commission or errand for the purpose of obtaining goods or money, or other valuable thing, to the offender's profit". (See Hume, i, 172.) Authority for the view that fraud was a crime involving economic or patrimonial advantage and disadvantage can be found well into the nineteenth century (see, *e.g.*, *H.M. Advocate v. Livingstone* (1888) 15 R. (J.) 48 and *H.M. Advocate v. Witherington* (1881) 4 Coup. 475). But the possibility of non-economic frauds was recognised as early as the middle of the nineteenth century in the case of *William Fraser* (1847) Ark. 280, *ante*, Chap. 7. Nevertheless, even if it was accepted that fraud no longer required financial prejudice, some element of prejudice to the victim appears to have been present in all cases prior to *Adcock v. Archibald*. The argument that fraud required proof of some economic or financial prejudice was again raised in *H.M. Advocate v. Wishart* (1975) S.C.C.R. Supp. 78, but the court, following *Adcock v. Archibald* rejected the argument. But the notion of prejudice is surely still important otherwise it would be a criminal offence to induce someone to act to their advantage by deception.

3. Is it enough that a practical result is achieved as a result of the deception, or must it be shown that the practical result involves some act or omission on the part of the person deceived? Suppose, for example, that A, playing a malicious practical joke, telephones B to tell him, falsely, that his wife has been injured in an accident. B is so upset by this that he has a heart attack and dies. Is that fraud or some form of homicide?

4. The breadth of the Scottish offence can be illustrated by comparing it with the commonly encountered frauds under the English Theft Acts 1968 and 1978. The Scottish offence of fraud is capable of covering the conduct presently dealt with in English law by section 15 of the Theft Act 1968 (obtaining property by deception), section 15A (as inserted by the Theft (Amendment) Act 1996—obtaining a

money transfer by deception), section 16 of the 1968 Act (obtaining a pecuniary advantage by deception), section 20(2) of the 1968 Act (procuring the execution of a valuable security by deception), section 1 of the Theft Act 1978 (obtaining services by deception), and section 2 of the 1978 Act (evasion of liability by deception).

Certain other forms of dishonest and fraudulent behaviour, which are only with difficulty dealt with in English law, are readily brought within common law fraud in Scotland. Obtaining the hire of a motor vehicle by means of a deception which does not relate to the question of payment (as, for example, where a false driving licence is tendered in support of a false identity) is one example. It is unlikely that this could be charged as obtaining property by deception contrary to section 15 of the Theft Act 1968, since that requires proof of an intention permanently to deprive, which would in many cases be difficult to establish. It seems, further, that this would not constitute taking the vehicle without consent, contrary to section 12 of the 1968 Act. (See, in this regard, *Whittaker v. Campbell* [1983] Crim. L.R. 812.) It is only with some explanation that this transaction can be fitted into the crime of obtaining services by deception. (See Smith, *The Law of Theft* (8th ed.) para. 4–76.) But a simple fraud of this kind would present no difficulties in current Scottish practice.

5. A more significant illustration of the advantages of simplicity is to be found in a consideration of the case of *Preddy and Others* [1996] 3 All E.R. 481. The fraud involved here was a very common type of mortgage fraud. The appellants obtained a large number of mortgage advances from banks and building societies by means of fraudulent statements on the mortgage application forms. They were eventually charged with, and convicted of, obtaining property belonging to another by deception, contrary to section 15(1) of the Theft Act 1968. Their convictions were eventually quashed by the House of Lords. Their Lordships held that when funds were transferred from the lender's bank to the borrower's bank the lender's bank account was debited and the borrower's credited with the relevant sums. However, the transaction properly described did not involve the transfer of property from one bank to the other. When the money was transferred, the property of the lender (a debt owed to him by his bank) was extinguished. A new item of incorporeal property (a debt owed by the borrower's bank to the borrower) was at the same time brought into existence in the defendant's bank. The appellants were not, therefore, guilty of obtaining property *of another* by deception.

Not surprisingly, the decision was not well received and was effectively reversed by the Theft (Amendment) Act 1996, which creates the new offence of obtaining a money transfer by deception, contrary to section 15A of the 1968 Act. Such problems would not arise in Scotland. If the borrower makes fraudulent statements in a mortgage application (or any other such application) and thereby induces the lender to bring about a transfer of funds which would not otherwise have been provided, then the offence of fraud is made out, without any need to determine the legal effect of the transaction with regard to the passing of property.

## (c) *The causal connection*

The accused's deception must bring about the practical result.

### Mather v. H.M. Advocate
(1914) 7 Adam 525

**13.12** The accused was charged that "on June 7, 1913, having purchased and obtained delivery of nine cattle through the Farmers' Mart Limited, Brechin, within their premises at Park Road, Brechin aforesaid, you did on said date and within said premises fraudulently tender to John William Henderson, Cashier of the said premises Farmers' Mart Limited, a cheque for £189. 2s. 6d. in payment of the price of said cattle, which amounted to £183. 12s. 6d., and of a balance of £5. 10s., due by you on a former transaction, the said cheque being drawn by you on the West End Perth Branch of the British Linen Bank, you having no funds in said Bank to meet said cheque and well knowing that said cheque would not be honoured, and you did thus defraud the said Farmers' Mart Limited, of the sum of £183. 12s. 6d." An objection to the relevancy of the charge was repelled and the accused was convicted after trial. On appeal to the High Court:

LORD JUSTICE-GENERAL (STRATHCLYDE): "I think this indictment relevantly charged the accused with telling a falsehood, but telling a falsehood simpliciter is not a crime by the law of Scotland. I think it is equally clear that it does not charge the complainer with fraud according to the law of Scotland; because it appears that he actually had purchased and obtained delivery of the nine cattle and had obtained credit for the former debt of £5. 10s., before granting the cheque in question in this case. It is not a relevant statement of a crime to say, as the indictment does, that when the accused granted the cheque he knew that he had no funds at the bank to meet the cheque. Is it then relevant to infer fraud to add that he well knew that the cheque would not be honoured? I think not.

In plain language what he did was this. Having obtained delivery of the cattle—I know not how long before the cheque was granted—he said to the seller of the cattle: 'Here is a written order upon A.B., who will pay you the money,' well knowing that A.B. would not pay the money. That was a falsehood, but it was not the means by which he either secured delivery of these cattle or obtained credit for £5. 10s. I do not for a moment doubt that the law is as stated in the cases to which we were referred, *viz.*, that if a person obtains goods or money by issuing a cheque he having no funds in bank and knowing the cheque will not be honoured, he commits a fraud. The essence of that statement lies in the little preposition 'by', which is lacking in this indictment. That, I think, is a fatal flaw.

Therefore I am of opinion that the conviction ought to be suspended and liberation granted."

Appeal allowed.

NOTE

So *Mather* seems to be authority for the proposition that a successful defence to fraud may be run if **13.13** the pretence was not the cause of the actings of the dupe. What is the situation where the accused's actings bring about the result, in combination with other factors? Suppose, for example, that A wants to buy a yellow Beetle motor car. He finds one at a garage which he likes and which is within his price range. The garage proprietor falsely tells him that it has only had one owner when in fact it has had three. A is already very keen to buy the car and when he hears this statement he is convinced that this is the car for him. Is this a case of fraud?

In the English case of *Miller* (1992) 95 Cr. App. R. 421 the accused induced the victim to enter his car by representing to him that it was a taxi. At the end of the journey the accused demanded a grossly inflated fare. The victim paid because he was afraid, although by this time he was probably aware that the vehicle was not a taxi. The court held that provided the deception was a cause of payment it was not necessary that it should be the sole cause of payment. In this case the victim would not have entered the car, and therefore not have faced the demand for payment, had it not been for the deception practiced by the accused, and that was sufficient causal link.

## B. The *mens rea* of fraud

There is very little discussion of the *mens rea* of fraud in modern Scots law. So far as concerns the **13.14** practical result, it is said that fraud is a "crime of intent" so that "A cannot be guilty of fraudulently inducing B to do x unless he intended to produce such a result by his falsehood" (Gordon, para. 18–32). So far as concerns the truth or otherwise of the representation, it is clear that if a person knows the representation to be false he can be convicted of fraud. But what if that person does not know it to be false, but is reckless as to its truth. Suppose, for example, that A tells B that a car that he, A, is trying to sell to B "has never had a serious breakdown". A does not know that for a fact, and realises that it may have had such a breakdown at some time in the past. If, in fact, the car has broken down in the past, is A's reckless statement sufficient for fraud? And what would be the case if A genuinely believed that the car was free from a history of breakdowns, but had reached that view without making any serious inquiry into its history?

There is some authority for the view that where A makes a statement, believing it to be true, there is no fraud, even if A was grossly careless in reaching that conclusion: *Brander v. Buttercup Dairy Co*, 1920 2 S.L.T. 381, but this is a case decided under the curious provisions of section 430 of the Burgh Police (Scotland) Act 1892, and there is very little discussion of the issue.

If the approach of the High Court in the case of *Jamieson v. H.M. Advocate*, 1994 S.L.T. 537 (see, *ante*, Chapter 9) were to be followed, it might be argued that where a person honestly (albeit carelessly) believes that what he is saying is true, there is no fraud. If, however, the accused has never turned his or her mind to the truth or otherwise of the statement, then to make the statement in question would be fraudulent.

In principle, however, there seems to be no reason for holding that where a person is reckless as to the truth of any representation that he or she makes, and intends the person to whom it is made to accept it as true and to act upon it, that should be sufficient for a charge of fraud at common law.

## 2. Forgery and uttering

**13.15** At common law forgery is not itself a crime. If A chooses to pass the time by copying the signatures of his friends and neighbours there is nothing criminal in that. It is only when the forgery is "uttered" that a crime is committed:

### 1. Hume, i, 148–149

**13.16** "Our description of this sort of falsehood lead [*sic*] us to remark in the next place, ... that the crime is not complete by the fabrication of the writing, unless it is also uttered, or put to use. If when fabricated it is kept lying with the artist, unemployed, and is only brought to light by some accident (in the course, perhaps, of a search for some other writing), the evidence is wanting, though such discovery must excite suspicion, of the fraudulent and felonious purpose of their fabrication; wherein lies the essence of the crime. Or grant that evidence were even recovered to that effect, as by the pannel's own letters, bearing his intention to utter the false writing at such a time and place; still it is no more than a bare purpose, just as in the case of a libel composed, but not published, or an incendiary letter written but not dispatched; and of which it is not yet too late to repent, while no attempt has followed on it, to the prejudice of a neighbour. It is the act of uttering which first brings the crime to such a shape and consummation, as give the magistrate a title to inquire into it: Till then it is a mere wickedness of the heart, for which the offender answers not in any human tribunal."

Passing off an article (usually a document) as genuine will normally found a charge of uttering, provided it is towards the prejudice of another. But what about "false documents"?

### 2. Simon Fraser
#### (1859) 3 Irv. 467

**13.17** Lord Inglis: "The second charge of this indictment is in a different position; it is libelled in the major proposition as forgery, and the uttering, *as genuine*, of a forged execution. The *species facti* libelled in the minor, to support this charge, is, that the panel, being a sheriff-officer, procured one John Forrest, to *subscribe* his own name on a blank piece of paper, adding thereto the word 'witness', that he then wrote or procured to be written above the said subscription, an execution of citation, and then subscribed the writing with his own name, as the officer making the service, 'you the said Simon Fraser intending said execution of citation to pass for, and be received as, a genuine execution of the service of the said criminal libel, certifying that a copy thereof had been delivered by you to the said John Cunningham personally'. And further, it is libelled, that the panel 'did use and utter, *as genuine*', this forged execution of citation, knowing the same to be forged, by delivering the same, '*as genuine*, to the said Donald Macbean', &c.

There is here, unquestionably a charge of falsehood; and the falsehood consists in knowingly making and uttering a formal writing containing a false statement. It is stated that John Forrest subscribed the paper, adding the word witness to his name, and it is obvious, therefore, on the face of the indictment, that John Forrest wrote his name there, intending that it should be used as a *subscription* to some writing to be afterwards written above it. It is not alleged or suggested that John Forrest intended his subscription to be used for any other purpose than that to which it was applied by the panel, or that the panel, having obtained this subscription for one purpose, used it for another and unauthorised purpose. The fair construction of the libel therefore is, that John Forrest put his subscription on the blank sheet of paper, for the purpose of its being used as that of witness to the execution. The case, therefore, is the same in effect as if John Forrest had subscribed after the execution was written out. And the charge thus resolves into an allegation, that the panel and Forrest wrote and subscribed a document, which falsely stated that they, as officer and witness respectively, had made a service which never was made, and uttered that document as a true execution.

This statement constitutes a serious charge of falsehood against both the panel and Forrest, and such a charge is, beyond doubt, a relevant point of dittay. But, in my opinion, it is not a relevant charge of forgery.

Forgery, at least as it is understood in modern times, consists in making and uttering a writing, falsely intended to represent and pass for the genuine writing of another person. And, accordingly, the charge of uttering, which is generally the most important part of the indictment for forgery, is invariably libelled as 'the using and uttering, *as genuine*', that which is not genuine, but forged. The ordinary style of our indictments thus shows, that *forged* and *genuine* are precisely opposite and contradictory terms; and, consequently, that which is forged cannot be genuine, and that which is genuine cannot be forged.

But, if the panel and John Forrest were to be tried for writing and subscribing a writing, containing a false statement, that they made a service which they never made, the first fact to be proved by the prosecutor would be, that the writing was made and subscribed by them, or, in other words, that it is their *genuine writ*. In a merely colloquial sense, the term 'genuine' is sometimes loosely enough employed, but when applied to a writing, its only proper sense is, that the writing is the act or deed of the person whose act or deed it professes to be. In the scientific study of the evidences of Christianity, one becomes familiar with the distinction between the genuineness and the authenticity of the books of the New Testament—the term 'genuineness', as applied to them, expressing merely the fact that they were written by the persons whose names they bear, apart altogether from any question as to the truth or credibility of their contents. For a writing, though genuine, may contain nothing but falsehoods. A genuine letter, containing a false and scandalous libel, is a good ground for prosecuting the writer for libel, because it is his genuine production, and the first step towards making him answerable for writing it, is to prove that it is genuine. And so here, supposing the panel and Forrest were both charged in terms of the minor proposition of this indictment, they must be proved to be the authors of the false execution, before they could be made responsible for it; or, in other words, it would be indispensable as the foundation of the charge against them, as laid, that the execution should be proved to be their genuine production. The offence, therefore, which they have committed, is not the using and uttering as genuine that which is not genuine; and yet that is the charge in the major proposition of this indictment.

I am quite aware that, in our earlier practice, the distinction between forgery, properly so called, and other species of the *crimen falsi*, was not much observed or acted on, the more ordinary classification, as given by Sir G. Mackenzie, being falsehood committed *by means of writing*, falsehood by witness, falsification of the coin of the realm, and the using of false weights and measures. But it is quite impossible to read that learned author's enumeration of the various kinds of falsehood, committed by means of writing, without being satisfied that falsehood by means of writing, and forgery, can never be convertible or commensurate terms. Indeed, it is historically true, as stated by the counsel for the panel, that forgery is not a *nomen juris* in our older law; nor is it until modern times, that the name has been distinctively applied to one particular kind of the falsehoods committed by means of writing. But that it is now used only in this definite and restricted meaning, I hold to be proved by the invariable style of our indictments, and by the fact that the Crown counsel, with all their sources of information, have not been able to produce to us a single example of an indictment for forgery, which, in its minor proposition, libelled anything short of the making and uttering, by the accused, of a writing falsely intended to represent and pass for the genuine writing of another person.

I am therefore of opinion, that the second charge of forgery and uttering is irrelevant."

Lord Neaves: "The forgery of a writing may be committed in two ways; either by the person signing the name of some one else to a writ, or by bringing a false writ to a true signature. As there were two ways in which Mahomet and the mountain might be brought together, so there are two ways in which a forged bond may be made, either by signing a false name below the bond, or by writing the bond above the genuine signature without permission, and in that way fabricating the thing as a whole, it not being the genuine instrument of the party. But the falsehood must be in the external execution of the writing, and not in the signification or narrative of the deed. A man who signs his own writing, and tells a lie in it, is not guilty of forgery. There is a plain distinction between the fabrication of the *corpus* of the writing, and the falsehood of the allegations contained in it."

Charge of uttering held irrelevant.

Note

**13.18**   On this case, see Gordon (2nd ed.), paras 18–45—18–48. On the question of whether articles other than documents can be uttered, see *Bannatyne* (1847) Ark. 361.

It is clear that uttering does not require that *actual* prejudice be caused to the victim, provided that the presentation of the forgery is *towards* his prejudice.

**3. Macdonald v. Tudhope**
1984 S.L.T. 23

**13.19**   The treasurer of a club was convicted of uttering as genuine to the club secretary certain certificates as to the balance of moneys withdrawn from gaming machines for which the treasurer was responsible. Each certificate purported to have been checked and signed by a third party, when in fact it had not. He appealed against conviction.

Opinion of the Court: "Counsel for the appellant conceded that it would be incompetent for him at this stage to attack the relevancy of the charge, but sought to maintain, as a preliminary point, that he was entitled to attack the complaint as being a fundamental nullity, as libelling no offence known to the criminal law of this country.

All that the complaint libelled was presentation of a document with false signatures. At best this could not constitute the crime of uttering. Uttering required not only presentation of a forged document but one which was to the prejudice of the party to whom it was uttered. Counsel for the appellant referred to and founded upon the recent case of *H.M. Advocate v. Arthur*, 1982 (Crown Office Circular A50/82). In this case there could be no prejudice to the recipient who was merely the secretary of the club referred to. The complaint did not libel that any sums had been taken from the machine or any moneys wrongly disposed of. It was not alleged that the certificates were not a true record of what sums had been extracted or what had been left in the machine. In any case counsel for the appellant pointed to the fact that after investigation it appeared no gain had accrued to the appellant. Thus no offence appeared on the face of this libel, which was therefore a fundamental nullity and could be attacked at any stage even though no question was raised in the case.

For the Crown the learned advocate-depute submitted that the complaint properly set out the essentials of the crime of uttering—the presentation of forged documents to deceive the recipient and towards his prejudice—that the forged certificates should be accepted as genuine and as vouching the movements of moneys for which the appellant was responsible. Such presentation to an officer of the club concerned was clearly designed towards the prejudice of the recipient. It was not necessary that actual prejudice should ensue: what was essential was that uttering should be towards prejudice of the intended recipient. There was no substance in the appellant's argument on this point.

In our opinion the preliminary point taken by counsel for the appellant is unsound. Here there is plainly libelled the presentation of forged documents for a particular and prejudicial purpose. That is enough, if established, to constitute the crime of uttering. As it is put in Macdonald (5th ed.) at p. 59: 'The crime is complete when the writing is dishonestly used towards the prejudice of some person, but it is not necessary that any person should actually have been injured, or that any definite practical result should have been attained by the use'. Presentation of forged vouchers of expenditure is in our view clearly intended towards prejudice of a recipient, who is intended to accept them as genuine documents of account and make use of them accordingly."

Appeal dismissed.

NOTE

"Uttering" requires that the document or article concerned is uttered as genuine, and the uttering **13.20** must be towards the prejudice of someone. It is not necessary for the Crown to show that actual prejudice resulted from the uttering, merely that the uttering is calculated, in an objective sense, to lead prejudice. See Gordon, pp. 624–625. A document or thing is "uttered" when it is presented to a third party or where it is placed beyond the control of the forger. The most common example of uttering is where a forged document is put in the post. (See *William Harvey* (1833) Bell's Notes 57.)

# Chapter 14

# RESET

**14.01** As described by Hume (i, 113) reset "is the receiving and keeping of stolen goods, knowing them to be such, and with an intention to conceal and withhold them from the owner". The crime of reset exists because thieves need to convert the property they have stolen into cash or other goods, or to divest themselves of the primary evidence of theft. The crime of reset operates as a disincentive to theft by ensuring that those who receive stolen property in the knowledge that it has been dishonestly come by will themselves be guilty of an offence.

Although originally limited to reset of theft, reset was extended to include the retention of goods obtained by robbery and other offences. Section 51 of the Criminal Law (Consolidation) (Scotland) Act 1995 now provides that "Criminal resetting of property shall not be limited to the receiving of property taken by theft or robbery, but shall extend to the receiving of property appropriated by breach of trust and embezzlement and by falsehood, fraud and wilful imposition."

## 1. THE *ACTUS REUS* of reset

**14.02** According to Hume (i, 113), "It is the fundamental circumstance is the description of this crime, that the stolen goods are received into the offender's possession". It does not matter on what basis the resetter takes possession of the goods. Thus, assuming the necessary guilty knowledge, it is reset where the accused buys the goods (whether cheaply or for a fair price), or stores them for the thief. (Again it does not matter whether this is done as a commercial transaction or as a favour.) (See, in this respect, Hume, i, 113). This relatively simple idea has, however, been extended and made more complex by the introduction into the law of the proposition that an accused can be guilty of reset by being "privy to the retention" of goods dishonestly acquired.

### A. The concept of being "privy to the retention" of property dishonestly acquired

#### H.M. Advocate v. Browne
(1903) 6 F. (J.) 24

**14.03** The accused was charged along with others with stealing a sum of money in banknotes, some for large amounts. The evidence showed that on the day of their arrest and for some days previously, the accused had been in possession of similar notes. The numbers of the stolen notes were not proved. In the course of charging the Jury:

LORD JUSTICE-CLERK (MACDONALD): "Now, gentlemen, supposing you feel yourselves not able to come to the conclusion that the prisoners at the bar were the thieves—that is to say, were privy to the theft at the time it took place, you then need to consider the further question, whether or not they, being in possession of money that you are satisfied was stolen money, were guiltily in possession of that stolen money—in other words, whether they can be found guilty of receiving stolen property knowing it to be stolen. Now, as regards that, I must tell you that it is not necessary according to law that the actual property which is said to have been received guiltily has ever passed into the personal possession of the receiver at all. If a man steals a bundle of notes out of a man's pocket, and after that informs another man that he has got these notes, that he has stolen them, or if the other man saw him stealing them and knew that they were stolen, then if the other man connived at it remaining in the possession of the thief or being put in any place for safe custody, such as hiding it in a cupboard, he is guilty of receiving feloniously even although he never puts his fingers on the notes at all. Reset consists of being privy to the retaining of property that has been dishonestly come by.

Now, assuming that you do not think that the theft is made out, the question comes to be whether you are not satisfied that all these three men knew that this large amount of property which was between them was stolen property, and were doing their best to dispose of it by arrangements which were made in opening accounts with banks, and so on, and whether, whichever of them had the money in his possession at the time they were apprehended, they were all privy to that money dishonestly come by being in the possession of the individual who happened to have it in his pocket or bag—if you are satisfied of these facts you would be quite entitled to find that they were all guilty of reset."

The accused was convicted of reset.

NOTE

1. The idea that reset may be committed by being "privy to the retention" of stolen property is quite **14.04** unsupported by authority. It makes an appearance, however, in the first edition of Macdonald's textbook. Hume makes reference to a householder's "privity and connivance" when stolen property is found in his house. But that passage is as much to do with the *mens rea* of the offence as anything else, and in any case still makes it clear that the accused must have physical control of the property. It seems impossible to reconcile what is said by Macdonald with Hume. See, in this respect, the observations of the court in the case of *Clark v. H.M. Advocate*, 1965 S.L.T. 250, below, and Gordon's critique, at pp. 692–693 (2nd ed.).

**Clark v. H.M. Advocate**
1965 S.L.T. 250

An accused was charged along with a man Mackenzie with theft of 38,800 cigarettes, 12 lbs of **14.05** tobacco and a sum of money. He was convicted of reset of 13,000 cigarettes. He appealed against conviction on grounds of insufficiency of evidence and on alleged misdirection by the sheriff on the material elements necessary to constitute the crime of reset.

LORD JUSTICE-CLERK (GRANT): "The main evidence against the appellant was as follows. His fingerprints were found on a package of 100 of the stolen cigarettes. He had seen these and the other stolen cigarettes in Mackenzie's house shortly after the housebreaking, he had handled some of them and it is a fair inference from the evidence that he knew they were stolen. He then accompanied Mackenzie to a bus depot where they both sat down at a table in the canteen with the witness Walkinshaw. Mackenzie handed over a parcel containing 1,000 cigarettes to Walkinshaw who agreed to try to sell the cigarettes on Mackenzie's behalf at 30s. [£1.50] per 200 package to his fellow employees. No payment was then made but it was arranged that Walkinshaw should meet Mackenzie in the Kenmore public house that evening and hand over the proceeds. All this happened in the presence and hearing of the appellant though there is no evidence that he took part in the conversation. The appellant was again with Mackenzie in the Kenmore that evening, but was not present in the lavatory when payment was made there by Walkinshaw to Mackenzie.

In these rather unusual circumstances the learned sheriff charged the jury to the effect that reset 'consists in knowingly receiving articles taken by theft, robbery, embezzlement or fraud and feloniously retaining them, or being privy to the retaining of property that has been dishonestly come by. It is reset for a person to connive at a third party possessing or retaining the stolen goods, even if the person charged never laid a finger on the stolen property.' This passage comes from Macdonald on *Criminal Law*, 5th edition, page 67 and goes back to at least the second edition of that work published in 1877. The learned sheriff then quoted to the jury a passage from Lord Justice-Clerk Macdonald's charge in *H.M. Advocate v. Browne* (1903) 6 F. (J.) 24, at page 26 (11 S.L.T. 353) to the following effect:—'I must tell you that it is not necessary according to law that the actual property which is said to have been received guiltily has ever passed into the personal possession of the receiver at all. If a man steals a bundle of notes out of a man's pocket, and after that informs another man that he has got these notes, that he has stolen them, or if the other man saw him stealing them and knew that they were stolen, then if the other man connived at it remaining in the possession of the thief or being put in any place for safe custody, such as hiding it in a cupboard, he is guilty of receiving feloniously even although he never puts his fingers on the notes at all. Reset consists of being privy to the retaining of property that has been dishonestly come by.' The learned sheriff then went on to warn the jury that merely knowing that the thief has stolen property is not enough—there must be connivance. He then reviewed the evidence and left it to the jury to decide whether, on that evidence, connivance had been established.

Some time after retiring, the jury returned for further directions as to what was meant by connivance. In the course of his further direction the learned sheriff stated, *inter alia*: 'I think that you would be entitled to draw an inference from the fact that he did nothing whatever to inform the police or anyone of that sort that stolen property was being disposed of, and that might raise an inference of connivance, but you have got to find this thing called connivance or whatever it is first of all, the mere fact that the accused was in company with the thief is not by itself sufficient.'

It was on this direction by the learned sheriff that counsel for the appellant launched his main attack. He did not attack the passages from Macdonald, *Criminal Law*, 5th edition, page 67 and from the charge in *H.M. Advocate v. Browne* (*supra*) to which I have referred as being unsound in law, but said that they must be read on the basis that connivance involved some overt act, something on the accused's part of an active character. With this the learned Solicitor-General appeared to agree and such an interpretation would be in line with that placed on connivance in the consistorial sphere. (*Cf. Thomson v. Thomson*, 1908 S.C. 179, *per* Lord President Dunedin, at page 185.)

On that basis, the passage which I have just quoted from the learned sheriff's charge was, in my opinion, a misdirection in law. It was a direction that connivance could be inferred from mere inactivity and I do not think, nor did the Crown argue, that in a case such as this, it properly can. The Crown argument appeared to be that the charge, read as a whole, was adequate and sound in law. This direction, however, was given at a time when the jury were clearly puzzled as to what connivance involved and it was the last direction they received on that matter before finally retiring to consider their verdict. In those circumstances it is impossible to say, in a narrow case such as this, that the jury, if properly directed would still have convicted the appellant. I would, accordingly, allow the appeal and quash the conviction.

I may say that I have considerable sympathy with the learned sheriff in the difficult task which he had in charging the jury in this case. He had to rely on *dicta* in Macdonald and in *Browne* which, I confess, I do not fully understand, and which I have some difficulty in reconciling with the principle laid down both in Hume on *Crimes* (volume I, page 113) and Alison on *Criminal Law* (volume I, page 328) to the effect that it is fundamental to the crime of reset that the stolen goods be received into the accused's possession. It may be noted that when Hume ((*supra*), page 114) refers to 'privity and connivance' in a case of reset, he is dealing (as appears from the example which he cites in the passage immediately following) with the type of case where the stolen goods are found in the accused's premises. That is a very different type of case from the present and I would think that, in the type of case with which Hume was dealing, 'privity and connivance' are relevant, not so much to the question of possession, as to the question of intention to retain the goods as against the true owner. (I am not, of course, concerned here with the case where an accused, though not in actual possession, may be found guilty art and part. That was not an issue in the present case.) Furthermore, the facts in the present case appear to be far removed from those in *Browne*. These, however, are issues which go much wider than those argued in the present case and I express no concluded opinion upon them."

LORD STRACHAN: I confess that I have some difficulty in reconciling the directions of the Lord Justice-Clerk in *Browne* with the statement in Hume on *Crimes* (volume I, page 113) that: 'It is the fundamental circumstance in the description of this crime that the stolen goods are received into the offender's possession' and the similar statement in Alison on *Criminal Law* (volume I, page 328) that: 'It is indispensable to this crime that the goods are received into the prisoner's keeping'. In the present appeal, however, counsel for the appellant did not maintain that the directions in *Browne* were wrong, and the Solicitor-General seemed to concede that when Lord Justice-Clerk Macdonald spoke of the 'other man' conniving at the stolen goods remaining in the possession of the thief, he meant connivance which involved some positive act. In these circumstances this is not an appropriate case in which to question the soundness of the directions in *Browne*. Those directions and the corresponding statements in Macdonald on *Criminal Law*, appear to have remained unquestioned for more than sixty years and they could not be overruled without hearing adequate argument on both sides. I content myself therefore with the observation that in an appropriate case they may have to be reconsidered.

Conviction quashed.

### McNeil v. H.M. Advocate
1968 J.C. 29

A person was convicted of reset after being found in a car carrying stolen goods. The accused **14.06** had introduced the thief of the articles to another person who was to reset them. He appealed against conviction on the grounds of alleged misdirection by the sheriff.

LORD JUSTICE-GENERAL (CLYDE): "As regards the first ground of appeal the Sheriff-substitute in the course of his charge to the jury defined reset as including, *inter alia*, a situation where the accused, although not in actual possession of stolen property, was privy to its retention from the owner. This direction was challenged as unsound.

It is, however, in conformity with the direction to the jury given by the presiding judge in the case of *H.M. Advocate v. Browne*, 6 F. (J.) 24, at p. 26. (Compare Macdonald on Criminal Law (5th ed.) p. 67.) The argument for the applicant was that the soundness of this direction had been doubted in the case of *Clark v. H.M. Advocate*, 1965 S.L.T. 250. But in the first place the observations as to the soundness of the direction made by the Lord Justice Clerk and Lord Strachan in the latter case were obiter in that case. In the second place the Court in *Clark's* case was not referred to the unreported decision in 1959 by the High Court in *H.M. Advocate v. McCawley*, July 23, 1959. In *McCawley's* case objection was taken to a direction that the crime of reset consists in knowingly receiving articles taken by theft or being privy to the retaining of property which had been dishonestly come by .... The Court held that this direction was sound in law and affirmed the correctness of the direction in *Browne's* case. (Compare Hume on *Crimes*, Vol. i, p. 114.)

In my opinion, therefore, the direction of the Sheriff-substitute in the present case was correct, and if an accused is privy to the retention of property dishonestly come by, he may be guilty of reset, although he is not in actual possession of the goods."

Appeal dismissed.

NOTES

1. So Macdonald's view in *Browne* correctly represents the law. But what is connivance? In *Clark* all **14.07** that really happened was that the High Court held that the sheriff's definition was wrong; nowhere does the court say what "connivance" really means.

2. On this question, see *McCawley v. H.M. Advocate* (1959) S.C.C.R. Supp. 3, discussed in Wallace,

"Reset without Possession" (1960) 5 J.L.S. 55, a case which suggests that it is reset to ride in a car which one knows to be stolen. Compare that case with *Hipson v. Tudhope*, 1983 S.L.T. 659, in which it was held that the appellant should not have been convicted of reset when he allowed himself to be driven around in a stolen car, which had failed to stop when pursued by the police. The Crown had argued that in view of the manner in which the car was being driven when it was being chased by the police, and the failure by the driver of the car to obey the police signals to stop, it was reasonable to infer that the appellant must have known or had reasonable cause to know that the car was stolen. The Crown had also argued that the appellant did not dissociate himself from the stealing of the car when questioned by the police, but merely stated "not guilty". The accused gave evidence that he did not know the vehicle was stolen, and that he had innocently accepted an offer of a "run" in the car. But leaving aside the question of knowledge, what is it that the passenger does which amounts to "connivance" in this context? Presumably a person who becomes aware of the fact the vehicle in which he or she is being driven is stolen can ask to get out, but what if the driver refuses to stop? Is there "connivance" then?

3. In *Girdwood v. Houston*, 1989 S.C.C.R. 578, the police were informed that some fishing rods had gone missing from a house. The appellant was questioned, and at first denied all knowledge of the theft or the whereabouts of the rods. On receiving information that the appellant was responsible for the theft, the police questioned him again. He again denied all knowledge, but then admitted that he knew where the rods were, and who had taken them, but refused to identify the thief because, he said, he would get his legs broken if he did. He then took the police to a place where the rods were found, carefully concealed. The appellant's conviction for reset was upheld by the High Court on the basis that he had been privy to the retention of stolen property. What was it that he had *done* that made him privy to this?

## B. Theft and reset mutually exclusive

**14.08**  An accused cannot be guilty of theft and reset of the same property. In *Druce v. Friel*, 1994 S.L.T. 1209, for example, an accused was charged on summary complaint which contained three charges. The first of these contained an allegation of theft by breaking into a house and stealing various items of property, including a cheque book and cheque card. The second was a charge of fraud involving the use of the cheque book and cheque card, and the third was a charge of resetting the cheque book and cheque card. The accused pleaded guilty to the theft and fraud charges. The sheriff convicted the accused of resetting the cheque book and cheque card. On appeal it was argued on behalf of the appellant that the conviction for reset could not stand along with the conviction for theft. This submission was accepted by the Crown and the appeal court. The cheque book and cheque card referred to in charges 1 and 3 were the same property and, the appellant could not be found guilty of both theft and reset of the same property.

## C. What can be reset?

**14.09**  Any property which can be the subject of theft or robbery, or which can be obtained by fraud, can be reset. This includes, apparently, a child under the age of puberty: *H.M. Advocate v. Cairney or Cook and another*, (1897) 5 S.L.T. 254. It may not be possible to have reset of embezzlement, since there is no property to reset, at least where the embezzlement consists in appropriating funds where there is a duty to account but no duty to deliver specific property to the owner.

What is the situation where the thief or resetter realises the stolen property and converts it into cash or other goods? Can these proceeds be reset? Suppose, for example, that A steals property, sells it to B for cash, and hands the cash to C for safekeeping. If C knows the provenance of the cash, is she guilty of reset? Or suppose that A uses the cash to buy a present for C. If C knows how A came by the money to buy the present, is C guilty of reset?

Anderson (p. 187) states that "Reset only applies to specific articles dishonestly obtained. If stolen property has been sold or pledged, it is not reset to receive the proceeds". Macdonald expresses a similar opinion: "It is not reset to receive the produce of the sale or pledging of property dishonestly obtained." (Macdonald, p. 68.) In *Helen Blair* (1848) Ark 459 the accused was charged with resetting a sum of money (£32) in one pound notes. These were alleged to be the change from two £20 notes which had been stolen. An objection was raised that the accused was not guilty of reset, because the one pound notes in question were not stolen, but the issue was not resolved.

Gordon's view is that "No *vitium reale* attaches to the surrogate of stolen goods, and ... reset should be restricted to those cases in which the owner would have a real action against the resetter for his property" (para. 20–07). (It is worth noting, in passing, that a resetter is liable in reparation to the owner of the property to the extent of the value of the goods not recovered by the owner: *Dalhanna Knitwear Co. Ltd v. Mohammed Ali*, 1967 S.L.T. (Sh.Ct) 74.)

English law takes a different view. Section 24(2) of the Theft Act provides that for the purpose of section 22 (handling stolen goods), references to stolen goods include the goods originally stolen and goods which, directly or indirectly represent the stolen goods.

## D. The wife's privilege

The traditional approach of Scots law was generally to exempt a wife from criminal responsibility for resetting goods stolen by her husband, unless she took an active part in the disposal of the goods. This tradition was examined in the following case. **14.10**

**Smith v. Watson**
1982 S.L.T. 359

A wife was acquitted of resetting money stolen by her husband. The procurator fiscal appealed. **14.11**

OPINION OF THE COURT: "This appeal is concerned with a doctrine in the law of reset which developed under a social and legal order substantially different from that which prevails at the present day. However, the doctrine appears to be firmly rooted in our law and it is therefore necessary to consider its ambit. The doctrine is summarised in Macdonald, *Criminal Law of Scotland* (5th ed.), p. 68 as follows: 'A wife is not in the ordinary case held guilty of reset if she conceal property to screen her husband, without proof of active participation.' This summary may, in my opinion, be taken as setting the limits for application of the doctrine, and I do not consider that the doctrine is one which should now be extended in its scope beyond the limits established by the leading authorities to which we were referred: Alison, i, 338–339; *John Hamilton and Mary Hamilton* (1849) J. Shaw 149; Macdonald, *Criminal Law of Scotland*, (*cit. supra*). Alison considered that the privilege did not extend in similar circumstances to a husband, which perhaps suggests that the doctrine is a relic of an age when wives were expected as a matter of course to submit to their husbands and could therefore be presumed to have done wrong *ex reverentia mariti*.

According to Alison the justification for the doctrine is 'that the wife is considered as bound, by the humanity of the law, to cherish and protect her husband, and, so far from informing against him, to conceal his delinquencies, and protect him from punishment'. The idea that the wife has handled or concealed the goods in an attempt to screen her husband and to protect him from detection and punishment is in my opinion central to the application of the doctrine. Moreover, if the wife is to enjoy the advantage of a privilege which is intended to be merciful it is of importance, as appears from the passage in Alison to which reference has been made, to show that the stolen property was brought into the matrimonial home by the husband.

Examining the findings in the present case in the light of the foregoing principles, I am clearly of opinion that the doctrine does not apply in this case and that in the circumstances the learned sheriff was not entitled to acquit the respondent of the reset with which she was charged. The findings make it clear that the money which was the subject-matter of the charge against the respondent, namely £350 in notes stained with a red dye, was not brought into the matrimonial home by the respondent's husband. On the contrary it is plain that the notes were put through the respondent's letter-box about December 12, 1980 by someone other than her husband, the latter having on September 25, 1980 been convicted of the robbery and sentenced to five years' imprisonment. Moreover, the effect of the findings is that the respondent kept and concealed the money for a purpose and with an object other than the screening or protection from detection or punishment of her husband. The findings, as explained in the note by the sheriff which follows them, demonstrate that the respondent was simply retaining part of the proceeds of the crime until such time as her husband should be released from prison. She was not, and it may be added could not, have been screening or protecting him at the material time as he had already been convicted of the robbery and received his sentence some 21 months before the money came into the possession of the respondent."

Appeal allowed.

NOTE

**14.12** Alison qualifies the wife's privilege by stating that "A wife cannot be charged with reset for receiving or concealing the stolen goods brought in by her husband, unless she make a trade of the crime, and has taken a part in disposing of the stolen goods" (Alison, i, 338). In *Clark v. Mone*, 1950 S.L.T. (Sh.Ct) 69 a man was convicted of stealing a woman's suit. Six months later his wife was found wearing the suit. She admitted that she knew that her husband had stolen the property, and had concealed it, along with other stolen property, in their house. The wife was charged with reset, but acquitted on the ground that she had not forfeited her privilege as a wife. In order to forfeit her privilege, she would have to have embarked upon a "new course of guilt for herself in which she took a principal share—as by selling the stolen goods or carrying on the infamous traffic of a resetter". The sheriff found that there was no evidence of this in the instant case.

The doctrine laid down by Alison therefore still stands, but clearly will not be applied beyond strict limits. It is to be noted that a husband does not enjoy the privilege of avoiding prosecution for reset in respect of his wife's thefts, and presumably cohabitees (of both sexes) are struck at with the full vigour of the criminal law.

Whether the discriminatory nature of the privilege would withstand a challenge under the European Convention on Human Rights is uncertain. Could a man, charged with resetting property stolen by his wife, or a female cohabitee charged with resetting property stolen by her male partner claim that they were the victims of discrimination?

## E. When does property cease to be stolen?

**14.13** If goods which have been stolen, or otherwise dishonestly acquired, are returned to their owner or other lawful custody, do they cease to be stolen for the purpose of reset? Suppose, for example, that the police become aware that stolen goods are stored in a particular place, and they maintain a watch on the goods in order to catch the thieves or resetters. Are the goods still "stolen"?

The question has not been settled in Scots law. The only case in which it appears to have been discussed is *Alexander Hamilton* (1833) Bell's Notes, 46. There the accused was charged with resetting two silver forks which had been stolen from an hotel. The goods had been seized from the thief, and returned to him by the police, so that he might take them to sell to the accused (who was clearly under suspicion) which he duly did. The police then went and recovered the forks from the accused. It was objected that this was not reset because the property was, when received by the accused, no longer under the control of the thief, but under the control of the owner. The court, given that the point "had occurred on a sudden and was one certainly of novelty" and was one about which there was considerable doubt, expressed the view that the charge of reset should not go to the jury and it was not proceeded with.

In English law, section 24(3) of the Theft Act 1968 provides that "no goods shall be regarded as having continued to be stolen goods after they have been restored to the person from whom they were stolen or to other lawful possession or custody ...". In *Haughton v. Smith* [1973] 3 All E.R. 1109; [1974] 2 WLR 1, a lorry load of stolen goods was intercepted by the police on the way from Liverpool to London. Police officers were placed in the lorry, and when the vehicle reached its destination, the trap was sprung and those dealing with the goods were arrested. Were the goods still "stolen"? It was assumed in that case that the goods had ceased to be stolen, although the correctness of that assumption was not tested.

The issue was more fully explored in *Re Attorney-General's Reference (No. 1 of 1974)*, [1974] 2 All E.R. 899. There it was held that where stolen goods are discovered by the police, the question whether they have been restored to lawful possession or custody within the meaning of section 24(3) of the 1968 Act depends primarily on the intentions of the police.

## 2. THE *MENS REA* OF RESET

There are two elements to the *mens rea* of reset—knowledge about the provenance of the goods, and the **14.14** intention to keep the goods from the owner.

## A. Guilty knowledge

Reset requires proof that the accused knew that the goods were stolen. It is not enough that he or she **14.15** suspected as much: "Bare suspicion ... or reasons of hesitation and conjecture on the subject, are no sufficient grounds of conviction" (Hume, i, 114). But such knowledge would in practice be difficult to establish, and so the law moderates this requirement, first of all by recognising "wilful blindness" to the origins of the goods as sufficient, and secondly, by the evidential rule that if the accused is found in possession of recently stolen property in suspicious or "criminative" circumstances, an inference of guilt, which he or she must displace. On the latter, evidential question, see, *inter alia, Fox v. Patterson*, 1948 S.L.T. 547; *Druce v. Friel, supra*; *Young v. Webster*, 1993 S.L.T. 349; *Steele v. H.M. Advocate*, 1992 S.L.T. 847 and *Craigie v. H.M. Advocate*, 1989 S.L.T. 631.

### Latta v. Herron
(1967) S.C.C.R. Sup. 18

The appellant was convicted of the reset of two guns, and appealed by stated case to the High **14.16** Court. The circumstances of the appeal are set out in the opinion of the court.

OPINION OF THE COURT: This is a stated case in which the appellant was charged and found guilty of reset of a revolver and a shotgun, the same having been dishonestly appropriated by theft. The sheriff substitute, after the evidence had been led, found the charge of reset proved and the question argued before us is whether on the facts admitted or proved the sheriff substitute was entitled to find the appellant guilty of reset of the firearms.

The only issue argued before us was whether the sheriff substitute was entitled to hold on these facts that the appellant knew that the goods had been stolen. According to Alison on *Criminal Law*, Vol. 1, p. 330, it is stated that 'it is sufficient if circumstances are proved which to persons of ordinary understanding and situated as the panel was must have led to the conclusion that they were theftuously acquired'. In the present case I find it unnecessary to examine the facts in any detail as in the case the learned sheriff substitute states 'I was inclined to believe that when the appellant purchased the firearms he was not conscious of the fact that they had been stolen, but, it seems to me that if this were so he had wilfully blinded himself to the obvious and that the inescapable inference from the circumstances in which the transaction was carried out, the price paid, and the fact that the appellant knew the character of the persons with whom he was dealing was that, after a reasonable time for reflection and certainly before the firearms were seised by the police on 24 November, he must have come to realise that they were dishonestly obtained.'

It appears to me that this view of the evidence, which the facts narrated in the case seem to me ample to warrant, does more than satisfy the criterion set out in the passage from Alison to which I referred. The matter is essentially one of fact for the sheriff substitute and the facts led him to an inescapable inference which those facts certainly warranted, and with which this court cannot possibly interfere. In my view, accordingly, the question falls to be answered in the affirmative."

Appeal dismissed.

Notes

**14.17**     *Cf. Knox v. Boyd*, 1941 J.C. 82, and *Mackay Bros. v. Gibb*, 1969 S.L.T. 216, and Gordon's comments, paras 7–72—7–74 and *Friel v. Docherty*, 1990 S.C.C.R. 351.

## B. Intention to keep from the owner

**14.18**     A person who receives stolen goods, knowing them to be stolen is not necessarily guilty of reset if, in taking possession of the goods, he does not intend to detain them from the owner (see Hume, 1, 113). So, for example, if A is gives stolen goods to B, and B puts them in the bottom of his wardrobe, intended to notify the police, or to return the goods to their owner, he is not guilty of reset.

# Chapter 15

# DAMAGING AND DESTROYING PROPERTY

This chapter discusses the offences of malicious mischief, fire-raising and vandalism. The common **15.01** theme to all of these is that they involve damage to, or destruction of, property belonging to another.

## 1. MALICIOUS MISCHIEF

Despite its rather archaic name, the general parameters of malicious mischief are well understood. In its **15.02** typical form it consists in intentional or reckless damage to, or destruction of, the corporeal property of another person. As such, malicious mischief is sufficiently broad to embrace the closely related statutory crime of "vandalism"—an offence which was introduced into the law by section 78 of the Criminal Justice (Scotland) Act 1980. The creation of this offence owes more to political opportunism than any real (or even perceived) gap in the criminal law. Nevertheless, it has become established as an offence in its own right, and the courts have determined that it is not merely a statutory reproduction of the common law. (See *post*, pp. 551–552.) Malicious mischief is also broad enough to include fire-raising, which could be regarded merely as an aggravated form of causing damage. However, the offence has existed as a distinct crime for centuries, and, even today there are arguments in favour of retaining a separate crime of fire-raising, to mark it out as an especially dangerous form of criminal damage.

Prior to the decision of the High Court in *H.M. Advocate v. Wilson*, 1984 S.L.T. 117, it was accepted that the crime of malicious mischief required damage to, or destruction of, corporeal property. That decision, however, challenged the traditional view of the law, and extended malicious mischief to include causing "patrimonial loss" to a third party by "interfering" with his or her property. Although at the time this was a radical departure from accepted ideas about the limits of that offence, in practice "*Wilson* malicious mischief" has not been heavily relied upon.

### A. The *actus reus* of malicious mischief

#### Hume, i, 122–124
#### "OF WILFUL FIRE RAISING AND MALICIOUS MISCHIEF.

Next after theft, housebreaking, and stouthrief, the principal ways of taking property from **15.03** the owner, we shall attend to those offences, by which it may be wilfully damaged or destroyed.

I. It may be affirmed generally, with respect to every act of great and wilful damage done to the property of another, and whether done from malice, or misapprehension of right, that it is cognisable with us as a crime at common law; if it is done, as ordinarily happens, with circumstances of tumult and disorder, and of contempt and indignity to the owner. For instance, to enter a neighbour's lands with a convocation of servants and dependants, and cast down the houses, or root out or spoil the woods, or throw open and deface the inclosures; to break down, in the like fashion, the sluices and aqueducts of a mill; to break or burn the boats and nets at a fishery; to tear and destroy the peats, turf, and fuel, in a heath or moss: All these are competent articles of dittay. The same is true even of the bare usurpation of possession, though without any great damage done to the property, if it is accomplished with the show of a masterful force, so as to have a mixture of *riot*, as well as *molestation* or intrusion. . . .

In the case of Mungo Grant and others, it was found relevant, that, with an armed force, he had intruded himself into the possession of the house of Castlegrant, and excluded the lawful possessor. And the like judgment was given on the libel at instance of Glass of Sauchie, against Monro of Auchinbowie and others, his baron-officer and tenants, for pulling down a dam-dike, of which the pursuer had been in possession, and thereby *setting or stopping his mill*. The libel in this case was laid on possession rather than right: And the jury having found, that, though the pursuer had for some years been in possession of the dam-dike, yet the pannel had formerly been in the practice of opening a breach in it, and *setting the mill at pleasure*; the issue was only a sentence to repair the dike, and abstain from pulling it down for the future, without the order of law. [Hume refers to a number of other cases, and continues:]

Upon the whole series of them, these things seem to be observable: 1. It does not serve to acquit the pannel, that there is a controversy between him and the prosecutor concerning the matter of patrimonial right (as in the several instances above mentioned); and that he proceeded in the belief of a civil wrong, previously committed by the pursuer against him. He is not excusable when he forgets that the courts of law are open to his complaint. 2. It is grounded in the same reason, namely, the due regard to the order and tranquillity of society, that the pannel shall equally be convicted, whether he interfere with the property of another, or with his state only of peaceable and lawful possession: For neither is this to be disturbed but by the order of law. This rule is plainly implied in the terms of the interlocutor in the case of Munro. 3. That which the law chiefly regards in such debates, is not so much the patrimonial damage, which in most of those instances was but trifling, as the insult to the public and the individual, by the violence and tumult attending the execution.

This limitation is, however, applicable only to the case of inconsiderable injuries to property, or to such as the pannel may have done under a misapprehension of right. For if any one go and poison his neighbour's dogs, sheep, or cattle, or mangle them by cutting out their tongues, breaking their limbs, or the like, certainly this is a crime, and severely punishable, though he proceed ever so covertly in the execution of his malicious purpose. Nay, I find that for poisoning poultry, Thomas Bellie, burgess of Brechin, came in the King's will, and was banished under pain of death; having mixed arsenic with dough, and thrown it into the court-yard of his neighbour, Janet Clerk, to poison her fowls; some of which accordingly died."

## NOTE

**15.04**  Much of Hume's discussion of malicious mischief is of historical interest only. It is clear that for Hume the offence was rooted not so much in the protection of property as in the preservation of the public peace. While this association of criminal damage and public disorder is still present in early editions of Macdonald, by the end of the nineteenth century it was established that "tumult and riot . . . do not form essential elements of the crime of malicious mischief" (*Forbes v. Ross* (1898) 2 Adam 513, 518), and prior to the case of *H.M. Advocate v. Wilson*, 1984 S.L.T. 117, it was generally accepted that the modern offence consisted simply in the destruction or damage of the property of another (see Gordon (2nd ed.), para. 22–01).

The decision in *H.M. Advocate v. Wilson* (*post*, p. 525) was reached after an examination of, and in ostensible reliance upon, the foregoing passages from Hume. These have been set out at length so that the court's analysis and interpretation of Hume can be properly assessed.

### H.M. Advocate v. Wilson
#### 1984 S.L.T. 117

The respondent was charged with "wilfully, recklessly and maliciously" activating an **15.05** emergency stop button on a generator at a power station, as a result of which electricity generation to the value of £147,000 was lost and had to be replaced from other sources. It was accepted by the prosecutor that this was intended as a charge of malicious mischief. A plea to the relevancy on the ground that malicious mischief required damage to property and that this was not specified in the indictment was upheld by the sheriff. The Crown appealed to the High Court.

LORD JUSTICE-CLERK: "... The question for this court is not whether the act complained of here should be held to be an offence when previously it was not, but is whether it constitutes an offence in the law as it stands. The Crown are not seeking to create a new offence—the Crown are seeking to bring within the ambit of the existing offence of malicious mischief the facts set out in the libel.

What then constitutes the crime of malicious mischief in the law of Scotland? Hume on *Crimes* (3rd ed., 1829), i, 122 *et seq.* deals with the offences of wilful fire-raising and malicious mischief. Speaking generally he says: 'It may be affirmed generally, with respect to every act of great and wilful damage done to the property of another, and whether done from malice, or misapprehension of right, that is cognisable with us as a crime at common law; if it is done, as ordinarily happens, with circumstances of tumult and disorder, and of contempt and indignity to the owner.' The cases cited by Hume in relation to this exposition of the law involved physical damage to property, and these are cited as specimens of the offence. At p. 124 Hume tabulates certain things which 'seem to be observable' from the series of cases he has referred to. The second of these is: 'It is grounded in the same reason, namely, the due regard to the order and tranquillity of society, that the pannel shall equally be convicted, whether he interfere with the property of another, or with his state only of peaceable and lawful possession: For neither is this to be disturbed but by the order of law.' In dealing with wilful fire-raising, which he classifies as the most important type of this form of offence, Hume says [at p. 125]: 'to this I have assigned a place in the present chapter, because the act is ordinarily intended to do a patrimonial injury, though it may be, and sometimes, but more rarely, has been directed against life and person'. The third thing stated by Hume is [at p. 124]: 'That which the law chiefly regards in such debates, is not so much the patrimonial damage, which in most of these cases was but trifling, as the insult to the public and the individual, by the violence and tumult attending the execution.' Alison's *Criminal Law*, vol. 1 at p. 448, simply states that: 'At common law, every act of serious and wilful damage done to the property of another, whether from malice or gross misapprehension of legal right, is an indictable offence.' He then examines some of the old cases. Macdonald's *Criminal Law* (5th ed.) at p. 84, refers to malicious mischief as applying to 'injuries to, or destruction of property, where there is no taking, but only the indulgence of cruelty or malice'.

As the cases to which we were referred did not deal directly with the point at issue here, I deem it desirable to consider the matter from the point of view of principle and apply what I consider to be the principle to the facts of the case. Thereafter I shall consider whether such an approach and result offend against the learned writers or the cases cited.

What are the basic constituents involved in the crime of malicious mischief relevant to circumstances which are libelled here? It has to be a deliberate and malicious act to damage another's property, or to interfere with it to the detriment of the owner or lawful possessor. The Crown properly conceded that consequential injury has to be intended by the initial act. And damage has to result. So far as terminology is concerned in the name given to the crime, the following definitions seem apposite. Malice connotes the evil intent deliberately to do injury or damage to the property. In the *Shorter Oxford English Dictionary* 'mischief' is given a variety of meanings, but the appropriate one in the present context is: 'Harm or evil as wrought by a person.' In the same dictionary damage is, *inter alia*, defined as: (1) 'loss or detriment caused by hurt or injury affecting the estate, condition, or circumstances)' and (2) 'injury, harm'.

It is clear from the words used in the libel that the Crown seek to establish that the act of the respondent founded upon was deliberate and malicious. The Crown further seek to prove that this act resulted in a generating turbine being brought to a halt for an extended period of time with a consequential loss of generated electricity. In terms of Hume's second ground, *supra*, this would be an interference with the employer's property and the wording of the libel is such as to be habile to carry the inference that the initial positive wilful, reckless and malicious act was intended to harm the employer by causing patrimonial injury.

This leaves for consideration only the question whether what resulted from this initial act was 'damage' or 'patrimonial injury'. There is no doubt that as a result of the respondent's act the employers suffered patrimonial loss. What occasioned that was the stopping of the generating turbine and so the stopping of production. It was not suggested, nor could it be, that if the turbine had been stopped not by pressing the emergency stop button by hand but by hitting the button with a hammer in such a way as to stop the turbine, the crime of malicious mischief would not have been committed. In my opinion, the occurrence has to be looked at as a whole. If the malicious intention improperly to stop the production of electricity is established, and the achievement of that had the effect of rendering inoperative a machine which should have been operating productively and profitably, then in my view that is just as much damage to the employer's property as would be the case in any of the more physical acts of sabotage. To interfere deliberately with the plant so as to sterilise its functioning with resultant financial loss such as is libelled here is in my view a clear case of interference with another's property which falls within Hume's classification of malicious mischief, and consists with the words in the phrase.

As previously indicated, the main thrust of the respondent's argument was that the actings of the respondent had not resulted in any physical damage to the turbine, and the infliction of physical damage was essential to the commission of the offence. If my reasoning *supra* is correct, then this argument has no effect. I must, however, deal with the submission that physical injury to the property is a *sine qua non* of the commission of the offence. The logic of that is that no matter how deliberate and malicious the invasion of and interference with the other's property may be, if the positive act which sets in train the real injury to the other's property does not involve physical injury to the property, then irrespective of what the consequences of the invasion and interference of other's peaceable possession may be, the act is not one of malicious mischief. That to me is unsupportable. The main support advanced for that proposition was the submission that in all the cases cited there had in fact been some physical damage. Physical damage was involved in the cases canvassed by Hume and Alison, and in the case of *Murdoch* (1849) J. Shaw 229. In the case of *Miller* (1848) Ark. 525, however, a stone was placed on a railway line but was removed by a third party before the train arrived at the spot and no damage was incurred. Further support was sought from the opinion of Lord Neaves in *Speid v. Whyte* (1864) 4 Irv. 584 where his Lordship said at p. 586 in delivering the judgment of the court in relation to a charge of malicious mischief: 'the circumstances disclosed did not warrant the judgment, because they do not amount to that reckless and wilful destruction of property which is essential to the constitution of the crime of malicious mischief'. That, however, leaves unanswered the question of what is involved in 'damage' or 'patrimonial injury' to property. Reference was also made to what was said by Lord Justice-Clerk Aitchison in *Ward v. Robertson*, 1938 J.C. 32 and approved of by Lord Justice-Clerk Clyde in *Clark v. Syme,* 1957 J.C. 1, but as this related to the extension of malicious mischief to a wilful disregard of or indifference to the rights of others it may be of little or no relevance in a case which is simply based on the original ground of a wicked and deliberate intent to injure. On the other hand, it does suggest that there is a wider cover to be given to the earlier view of the nature of the offence.

I do not consider that the fact that since in the cases relied upon by the respondent there was an element of physical damage to the property, there requires to be such an element in the narrower sense which counsel for the respondent maintained. Normally there may well be such an element, but in my view that does not exclude cases where the element of damage or patrimonial injury is of the broader nature which is present in this case. Each case will require to be considered on its own facts, and for that reason I do not consider it necessary to consider in this case what the position might be in a case where the initial act was of a negative and not a positive nature.

It follows from what I have said that I regard the facts libelled as constituting a relevant charge of malicious mischief. In doing so I do not consider that this is in effect introducing a new crime into the law of Scotland. The view which I have taken seems to me to fall within the considerations and desiderata of Hume, and is simply fitting the facts into the principles and considerations of the traditional law. I would accordingly allow the appeal, hold the libel relevant, and remit the case back to the sheriff to proceed as accords."

Lord Stewart (*dissenting*): "It was argued by the advocate-depute that this was a relevant charge of malicious mischief. It was submitted that in principle any act with malicious intent which brings about injury by interference with possession or with another's property may be relevant to infer the crime of malicious mischief. It is noticeable, as the sheriff points out in his report to this court, that it is not libelled that the accused person did any more than activate a button which was meant to stop, and did stop, an electricity generator. The Crown argument was that such damage was unnecessary. If the machine did not continue to operate and the owner thereby suffered loss, his peaceful and lawful possession had been interfered with. The touchstone was the intention on the part of the accused to do patrimonial injury. However, in his helpful review of the authorities it is noteworthy that the advocate depute was unable to cite any case where there was neither physical damage caused to property nor was such damage the probable result of the offender's malicious act. I cannot accept that the concept of the causation of physical damage or the prospect of such causation can be extended to include the causation of economic loss so that the crime known as malicious mischief would be committed whenever a malicious act caused loss. The advocate depute sought to found on the old case of *Glass of Sauchie* (Hume on Crimes, i, 122) as an indicator of principle. While it was there libelled that the operation of a mill had been stopped by the offender's actings I regard that element as simply having been libelled as an aggravation of a crime already constituted by the physical damage done to the dam-dike.

It can be argued that insistence on the element of physical damage (or the prospect thereof) to constitute the crime creates an artificial distinction excluding from criminality certain circumstances where serious loss may have been suffered as the result of malice. To this it can be answered that if the infliction of damage is an essential element of the crime then the absence of such damage takes the actings, however reprehensible, out of the category of criminality. It was argued that if the respondent here had used a hammer to operate the button and had thus damaged the button that would undoubtedly have been malicious mischief. Why, then, should he not be guilty of the same crime if he simply used his finger to operate the button and thus achieved the same result in stopping the generator? On the hammer hypothesis the accused causes damage to the machine while on the finger hypothesis he does not; that is, in my view, where the dividing line lies. The distinction may seem narrow and artificial but it is nevertheless a distinction which in my opinion the law has made. The advocate-depute conceded in his argument that an omission could never be an act of malicious mischief. Yet it is obvious that if a person, charged with the task of operating a button to activate a generator, maliciously failed to switch the generator on, then he could cause exactly the same 'damage' as a person who maliciously switched it off once it was operating.

I accept as accurate the definition of the crime of malicious mischief as set out in Gordon's *Criminal Law* (2nd ed.), p. 711: '[T]he modern crime consists simply in the destruction or damage of the property of another whether by destroying crops, killing or injuring animals, knocking down walls or fences, or in any other way.' This statement of the law is in line with that formulated by earlier textbook writers. Alison (*Criminal Law*, vol. 1, p. 448) writes: 'At common law, every act of serious and wilful damage done to the property of another, whether from malice or gross misapprehension of legal right, is an indictable offence.' Anderson's *Criminal Law* (2nd ed.) at p. 214, states that the term malicious mischief is used to describe the felonious destruction of or injury done to property, such as breaking fences, burning stacked wood, smashing windows, etc., Macdonald's *Criminal Law* (5th ed.) at p. 84, makes clear that the term mischief applies to injuries to, or destruction of, property, and gives various examples. The term also includes maliciously placing any obstruction on a railway or wilfully and recklessly doing so in a manner calculated to obstruct (see *Miller* and *Murdoch, supra*). Actual damage to property may not be necessary if the malicious act is clearly intended to cause such damage.

I do not take from the cases of *Ward v. Robertson, supra* and *Clark v. Syme, supra*, that there has been any change in recent years in what has always been regarded as an essential of the crime, namely the presence or prospect of damage to property. These cases were concerned with other matters. In both cases there were findings of actual damage to property, although in the case of Ward that damage was perhaps not great. In *Ward*, which was concerned mainly with *mens rea*, Lord Justice-Clerk Aitchison said (1938 S.L.T. at p. 167): 'I am prepared to take the case upon the footing, although it may involve some departure from the law as laid down by Hume, that it is enough if the damage is done by a person who shows a deliberate disregard of, or even indifference to, the property or possessory rights of others.' In the context of the facts of that case, which included a finding that growing grass had been trampled down and destroyed to an extent which rendered it useless or unsuitable for grazing purposes, I cannot read that passage as giving support to the proposition that the word 'damage' can be construed as going beyond physical damage.

The present indictment does not in my opinion include the essential constituent of the crime which is the libelling of an act causing or likely to cause physical damage. As was said by Lord Neaves in *Speid v. Whyte* (1864) 4 Irv. 584 at p. 586, reckless and wilful destruction of property is essential to the constitution of the crime of malicious mischief. What is libelled here is the loss of production. There are certain statutory offences in connection with the interruption of electricity supplies but these do not appear to be applicable to the circumstances set out in the indictment. The libel in the indictment is in my view an unwarranted extension of the crime as hitherto known. What is said to have happened here is a wilful, reckless and malicious stopping of a turbine. It is not libelled that this caused damage to the turbine or to any related piece of machinery or that it was likely to cause such damage. This is not, in my view, merely a case where the modus of an established crime may change with changing circumstances. Rather is it a case where an essential constituent of the crime is seen to be missing from the libel. I do not consider that the failure of a machine to operate through being switched off can be equated to the failure of a machine to be able to operate through being destroyed or damaged. Subject to the modification already noted, whereby the likelihood of damage to property may be sufficient to justify a charge of malicious mischief, I consider that actual destruction or damage is an essential of the crime.

I would therefore be in favour of disposing of the Lord Advocate's note of appeal by a finding that the indictment discloses no crime known to the law of Scotland."

Appeal allowed; case remitted to the sheriff to<br>proceed as accords.

NOTES

**15.06** 1. Lord McDonald agreed with the Lord Justice-Clerk.

## (1) The court's use of Hume, i, 122–124

Hume's introductory paragraph leaves little room for doubt as to how he viewed the offences of malicious mischief and wilful fire-raising. His description of them as offences "by which [property] may be wilfully damaged or destroyed" plainly suggests physical damage to corporeal property. This is reflected in the contrast which he draws between theft, housebreaking and stouthrief on the one hand, and criminal damage on the other. Hume is talking about ways in which a person may be deprived of his or her property; he is not talking about the loss which is consequential upon such deprivation.

Physical damage is central to the examples cited and discussed by Hume. In none of the cases considered could it be said that the offence consisted in mere "interference" with the property in question. This much is recognised by the court in *Wilson*. Lord McDonald, however, thought it "significant" that the word "physical" does not appear in Hume's statement that "every act of great and wilful damage done to the property of another . . . is cognisable with us a crime at common law". It may be, however, that the emphasis on the type of *harm* is misplaced. What is more significant is the type of *property* under consideration. It is clear from Hume's discussion, and the examples given, that he was discussing corporeal property, and it is difficult to see how such property can suffer damage or destruction that is other than "physical". No doubt the owner or possessor of property may suffer loss from its damage or destruction (or even through "interference" with it) but that, as is suggested above, is clearly distinguishable from the notion of "damaging" the property.

How do the majority overcome the clear emphasis on physical damage in the language ("cast down", "root out" "break down", etc.) and examples used by Hume? Essentially this is done by emphasising two aspects of Hume's discussion:

(a) The use of the word "interfere" in the second of his general observations from the cases: Both the Lord Justice-Clerk and Lord McDonald rely on this as supporting the view that mere interference with the property of another, resulting in "patrimonial loss" may be sufficient for malicious mischief. This does seem, however, to be a misreading of the passage in question. Hume is not here drawing a distinction between "interference" and "damage". Rather he is making the point that malicious mischief may be committed against the *possessor* of property as well as against the owner. This, it is submitted, is clear from the terms of the libel in the case of *Monro of Auchinbowie* which, as Hume is at pains to point out, was based on the possessory rights of the owner and which plainly involved physical damage to a dam. To contend that the word "interfere" means "mere" interference without damage ignores the whole context in which the word is used. Why, after all, should it be assumed that "interference" does not imply damage? The word can quite well imply damage.

(b) The use of the word "patrimonial" as in "patrimonial damage": The majority of the court treat this as synonymous with "economic" as in "economic loss." Again, this is open to question. Hume appears to use the terms "patrimonial damage" and "patrimonial injury" to describe damage to property and to distinguish such damage from injury to the person or other interests. Thus in the third of his general observations from the cases he draws a distinction between the "patrimonial damage" involved and the "insult to the public and the individual". Similarly, when introducing his discussion of wilful fire-raising (i, 125) he states that he has placed that topic in the same chapter as malicious mischief "because the act is ordinarily intended to do a patrimonial injury, though it may be, and sometimes, but more rarely, has been directed against life and person too". Again the contrast is clear: on the one hand injury to property, on the other, injury to the person.

## *(2) The case-law*

**15.07** Apart from the cases mentioned by Hume, very few of the authorities discussed by the court are relevant to the point raised in *Wilson*. As Gordon suggests (1983 S.C.C.R. 420 at p. 429) the cases of *David Miller* (1848) and *John Murdoch* (1849) seem more like examples of the crime of endangering the lives or safety of the lieges than cases of malicious mischief. This seems to be confirmed by what is said by the Lord Justice-Clerk in the case of *Miller*. In that case (as in *Murdoch*) the accused was charged with a violation of section 15 of the Railway Regulation Act 1840, and also with "wilfully, maliciously and unlawfully" placing a stone on a railway line "in a manner calculated and intended to obstruct such trains or carriages, and to endanger the lives or safety of the passengers". An objection was taken to the relevancy of the statutory offence, on the ground that it did not allege that any passenger was actually endangered (the obstruction having been removed before any train passed along the line) as was required by the statute. According to the report ((1848) Arkley 525 at p. 527) the Lord Justice-Clerk "thought that there might be a difference in what was necessary to complete the offence of obstruction under the state, and what would be required to render the panel liable to the charge of *having endangered the safety of persons conveyed along the line*" (emphasis added).

The cases of *Speid v. Whyte*, *Ward v. Robertson* and *Clark v. Syme* would seem to be equally irrelevant. *Ward v. Robertson* deals with the *mens rea* of malicious mischief while the other two cases deal with claims of right in malicious mischief. If, as the Lord Justice-Clerk observed, *Ward v. Robertson* suggests "that there is a wider cover to be given to the earlier view of the nature of the offence" then, it is submitted, that relates to the question of non-wilful damage, *i.e.* the mental element.

One case which receives very scant attention, and which may well be relevant is the case of *David Monro* (High Court, July 12 and 16, 1831, *unreported*; Alison, *Principles*, 451, Macdonald (5th ed.), p. 84). This is the case referred to by Lord McDonald, involving the malicious removal of a bung from an oil barrel, causing the oil to escape. The case was not fully explored by the court, but an examination of the Books of Adjournal (March 13, 1831 to December 29, 1831) reveals the following indictment: "Albeit by the laws of this and every other well governed realm, Malicious Mischief, particularly the maliciously, wantonly and feloniously injuring, wasting and rendering useless, or otherwise destroying the property of any of the lieges to their great loss and damage, especially when committed by means of Housebreaking, and more especially still when committed by a servant upon the property of a person in whose employment he has recently before been, is a crime of an heinous nature and severely punishable ... Yet, [etc.] ... you either thus or by some other means to the prosecutor unknown, obtained an entrance into said oil cellar, or warehouse, and having so obtained admittance thereto, you did then and there wickedly and wilfuly, maliciously and wantonly and feloniously, open the cocks or cranes of five cisterns or reservoirs containing oil, or at least one or more cisterns containing oil, situated in the said cellar or warehouse, which cisterns were previously shut and tight, whereby the whole or a great part of the contents of the said cisterns, amounting to upwards of two thousand three hundred gallons of oil or thereby, were run out, wasted and lost or otherwise destroyed, and which oil was then the property or in the lawful possession of the said Alexander Miller." The pannel was convicted on this indictment and sentenced to 18 months imprisonment with hard labour (Books of Adjournal, July 16, 1831).

At first sight the case seems very similar to that of *Wilson*. There is "interference" with the cisterns which causes the oil to escape, causing loss to the owner. But is the analogy exact? Surely in this case it was alleged that the oil was "wasted and lost or otherwise destroyed". In other words, this is not a case of "pure economic loss". The opening of the taps resulted in the loss of the oil just as surely as if, for example, it had been consumed by fire. This may be contrasted with the situation in *Wilson* where, if anything, the accused's actions prevented the creation of a commodity, rather than brought about its loss.

There are some cases to which the court does not seem to have been referred, which might have been considered relevant to the question of whether malicious mischief requires proof of physical damage. In *Cameron v. H.M. Advocate*, 1971 J.C. 50 (*ante*, p. 574) the accused were charged, *inter alia*, with navigating a ship on a course intending to cause a collision with another ship, and attempting to ram it and a life-raft alongside it, to the danger of the lives of the crew of the ship and the occupants of the life-raft. Objection was taken to the relevancy of these charges on the ground that no indictable offence was disclosed, and in particular, if the charges were to be read as allegations of malicious mischief, they were irrelevant as not narrating that actual damage was caused. It was argued by the Crown, and accepted by the court (Lord Cameron) that the charges relevantly libelled *attempted* malicious mischief.

The case of *Skeen v. Peacock*, 1970 S.L.T. (Sh.Ct) 66 also appears to have been overlooked. In that case the accused was originally charged with wilfully and maliciously driving a car in front of a bus, causing its driver to brake sharply to avoid a collision. This complaint was amended to include an allegation of endangering the safety of the driver of the bus and of the passengers. A plea to the relevancy of this complaint was taken on two grounds: (i) if it was a charge of malicious mischief it lacked the necessary allegation of damage to property, and (ii) even if it were possible to commit malicious mischief without physical damage, the complaint was lacking in specification. After a consideration of various authorities, including *David Miller*, the Sheriff held that the complaint did not disclose a criminal offence. In view of the authorities on endangering public safety this may be open to question, but it is clear that the court did not think that a relevant charge of malicious mischief could be laid without an allegation of physical damage to property.

## (3) The implications of Wilson

**15.08**  (a) It appears that there are two kinds of malicious mischief: (i) the "traditional" form which requires physical damage to corporeal property, and (ii) the "Wilson" form which does not require physical damage but which does require economic loss. Of course most cases of malicious mischief will result in loss, but it is possible to envisage cases in which there is no loss, or at least where the issue of loss is questionable. In such cases it will be important to determine whether or not there has been "damage" or merely "interference," since merely to interfere with the property of another, without causing any consequential loss is not (yet) malicious mischief. The question of what constitutes "damage" in the context of offences of malicious mischief does not seem to have been considered in any reported Scottish case, but it has been considered in a number of English and Commonwealth cases in connection with offences of criminal damage. The general conclusion which may be drawn from these authorities appears to be that whether or not the accused's conduct has resulted in "damage" is a question of fact and circumstance.

In *Samuels v. Stubbs* (1972) 4 S.A.S.R. 200 it was held that the "temporary functional derangement" of a police officer's hat, caused by the defendant stamping on it could amount to "damage". The fact that the property was fairly easily restored to its original condition, and at no financial cost to the owner, was immaterial. In *Hardman v. Chief Constable of Avon and Somerset Constabulary* [1986] Crim.L.R. 330 the defendants, as part of a demonstration marking the fortieth anniversary of the bombing of Hiroshima, painted human silhouettes on an asphalt pavement. The medium employed was an unstable, water-soluble whitewash which it was expected would be washed away by rain. The silhouettes were in fact removed by council employees using high pressure water jets. The Crown Court held that the accused had caused "damage" within the meaning of section 1 of the Criminal Damage Act 1971. The following passage from the judgment of Walters J. in *Samuels v. Stubbs* was approved by the court: "It seems ... that it is difficult to lay down any very general and, at the same time? precise and absolute rule as to what constitutes 'damage.' One must be guided in a great degree by the circumstances of each case, the nature of the article, and the mode in which it is affected or treated. Moreover, the meaning of the word 'damage' must, ... be controlled by its context. The word may be used in the sense of 'mischief done to property'."

The importance of the particular circumstances of any case is illustrated by the case of *"A."* *(a juvenile) v. R.* [1978] Crim.L.R. 689. The appellant was convicted of criminal damage to a police officer's service raincoat by spitting on it. No attempt was made to clean the coat, other than by wiping it with a paper tissue. On appeal to the Crown Court it was held that while spitting on a garment could amount to criminal damage, it was important to consider the specific garment which has allegedly been damaged. Thus spitting on a satin wedding-dress would almost inevitably cause damage since any attempt to remove the spittle might itself leave a mark or stain, whereas spitting on a police officer's coat, which is designed to be robust, might not necessarily amount to damaging it.

Given the reluctance of the High Court to attempt to provide generally applicable guidelines, it is likely that if the question of whether or not the accused had "damaged" property came before the Scottish courts, a similar approach, *i.e.* that it is a question of fact and circumstance, would be adopted.

(b) Throughout their judgments the Lord Justice-Clerk and Lord McDonald refer to the requirement of "interference" with the property of another. If interference is a necessary element of *Wilson* malicious mischief, then there ought to be no liability for this form of malicious mischief based on a failure to act (unless, of course, it is possible to "interfere" by omission). But it is difficult to see why, in principle, this should be so. Once a duty to act is established, a malicious refusal to carry out that duty, resulting in economic loss to the party to whom the duty is owned ought arguably to be malicious mischief. It might be suggested that in general the offence of malicious mischief cannot be committed by omission, but while examples might be rare, it is possible to envisage cases of damage by omission in which charges of malicious mischief would be appropriate. In the English case of *Miller* [1983] 2 A.C. 161 the accused, who had been drinking, lay down to sleep on a mattress in a house in which he was squatting. He lit a cigarette, but fell asleep before it was finished. He awoke to find the mattress smouldering, but did nothing to put out the fire which subsequently did £800 worth of damage to the house. His conviction for arson contrary to sections 1(1) and 1(3) of the Criminal Damage Act 1971 was upheld on appeal to the House of Lords. Their Lordships held that the appellant's liability was based on his reckless failure to take steps to prevent the spread of the fire once he had discovered that the mattress was on fire. Given that Scots law also recognises that a person is under a duty to remove a danger which he or she has, by their non-criminal conduct, created (see *MacPhail v. Clark*, 1982 S.C.C.R. 395, *ante*, p. 52), it is difficult to see how a Scottish court could come to a different conclusion in similar circumstances.

If the above argument is correct, then it appears that malicious mischief may now be committed by any act or omission which causes economic loss to a third party (provided, of course, that it is "malicious"). *Wilson* may, therefore, represent a much greater extension of the offence than merely dispensing with the requirement of physical damage. Suppose, for example, that an accused who is under a contractual duty to operate a machine wilfully and maliciously refuses to do so, thereby causing loss to the owner of the machine (for example through lost production). Would that person be guilty of malicious mischief? If the answer to that question is "yes" (and on the above argument it is difficult to see how it could be otherwise), then it seems that strikes and other forms of industrial action which involve non-performance of duties and which result in economic loss are criminal offences in Scotland. By the same token, an employer's lock-out might also result in criminal liability.

It is true that the Lord Justice-Clerk reserved his opinion on the question of omission, so that the question remains open. It might have been better, however, for the issue to have been settled so as to exclude any such inappropriate use of the criminal law.

(c) Even if *Wilson* is understood as relating only to positive acts, it is clear that malicious mischief as re-interpreted in that case is capable of supplanting other offences in certain circumstances, or indeed extending the criminal law into areas not presently thought to be covered by the criminal law. Thus, for example, an accused who tampers with an electricity supply meter, so as to obtain electricity without charge, is now clearly guilty of malicious mischief (whereas hitherto only theft charges have been available).

In *Grant v. Allan*, 1988 S.L.T. 11, 1987 S.C.C.R. 402 (*ante*, p. 451) it was held that it was not a crime dishonestly to exploit the confidential information of another person. Where such exploitation has involved "interference" with the property of another, and has caused him loss, then, it is submitted, a charge of malicious mischief ought to be relevant. (*Cf. Oxford v. Moss* [1979] Crim.L.R. 119 in which a student "borrowed" the proof of an exam which he was due to sit. It was held that he was not guilty of the theft of the information, nor of the proof (which he had always intended to return.) A similar result would probably be reached in Scotland. But if the examination body discovered what had happened, and was forced to prepare new exam papers, then surely there has been interference with another's property resulting in economic loss?)

In *Carmichael v. Black; Black v. Carmichael*, 1992 S.L.T. 897 (*ante*, Chapters 11 and 12), Black was convicted of stealing two cars by attaching wheel clamps to them so that they could not be driven away by their owners. (The cars had been parked in a private car park, without permission.) There was clearly here an "interference" with the property. If, in such a case, the clamping has caused the owners patrimonial loss, then it is difficult to see why the accused was not also guilty of malicious mischief.

## *(4) Wilson and human rights*

**15.09** Article 7 of the European Convention on Human Rights was discussed in Chapter 1. Article 7(1) is intended to ensure that acts which were not previously punishable should not be held by the courts to involve criminal liability, and that existing offences should not be extended to cover facts which previously "did not clearly constitute a criminal offence": Application No. 8710/79, DR 28, at p. 77; *S.W. and C.R. v. United Kingdom*, Commission Report at paras 47 and 48. The constituent elements of an offence may not be "essentially changed to the detriment of an accused" and any "progressive development by way of interpretation" must satisfy the test of reasonable foreseeability. 8710/79; 10505/83; 13079; *SW and CR v. United Kingdom*, Commission Report at paras 48 and 49. Judicial development of the law is not forbidden by the Convention—in practical terms it simply could not be—but judicial development of the criminal law is permissible only provided that such developments can reasonably be brought under the original concept of the offence: *SW and CR v. United Kingdom*, above. The resultant development must be "consistent with the essence of the offence" (and could reasonably be foreseen): *S.W. v. United Kingdom*, (Court) above, at para. 36; *C.R. v. United Kingdom*, (Court) *supra*, at para. 34.

Applying those statement to what happened in *Wilson* it would seem that that decision was a violation of the accused's right not to be prosecuted for an act which was not, at the time he committed it, a criminal offence. Of course, now that the High Court has established that this form of malicious mischief does exist future prosecutions for "*Wilson* malicious mischief" could not be challenged as a violation of Article 7.

## (5) Developments since Wilson

An unsuccessful attempt was made in *Bett v. Brown,* 1997 S.L.T. 1310 to apply *Wilson* to a case in which the accused, using a pole or some other device, allegedly moved a security camera placed by a bank outside one of its premises, so that the camera was no longer covering the front of the building, thus exposing the bank to greater risk of loss or damage to its property. The complaint narrated that the funds invested by the bank in installing and running the camera had thus been wasted. The Court held that this did not amount to an offence, since there was not, in the view of the court, any patrimonial loss.

## B. The *mens rea* of malicious mischief

### Ward v. Robertson
1938 J.C. 32

Lord Justice-Clerk (Aitchison): "This case raises a short but not unimportant point. The **15.10** appellant was tried and convicted in the Burgh Court at Hamilton on a summary complaint which charged him with the common law offence of malicious mischief. The question which is put to us in the case is whether, on the facts stated by the magistrate, he was entitled to find the appellant guilty of the charge libelled. The appellant was charged along with two other persons who were also convicted.

The evidence before the magistrate shows that, on the date libelled, the appellant with two companions walked across a field which was in the tenancy of a cattle dealer who was a grazing tenant. It is found that, in consequence of the appellant walking across the field, growing grass was trampled down and destroyed to an extent which rendered it useless or unsuitable for grazing purposes. Some criticism was directed to that finding, and it may seem an astounding finding, but it is there as a finding of fact and we must so take it. It appears also that the appellant in crossing the field was a trespasser. He was not there in the assertion of any right, whether of way, or of access, or of property, or of possession. He was admittedly a trespasser. The case accordingly stands in this position, that a trespass was clearly proved before the magistrate, as was also damage to the permanent grass which was growing in the field.

The question we have to consider is whether that is enough to justify a conviction of malicious mischief. I confess I have not found the question free from difficulty, but the conclusion to which I have come is that this conviction cannot stand. It is not essential to the offence of malicious mischief that there should be a deliberate wicked intent to injure another in his property. I am prepared to take the case upon the footing, although it may involve some departure from the law as laid down by Hume, that it is enough if the damage is done by a person who shows a deliberate disregard of, or even indifference to, the property or possessory rights of others. But the difficulty which arises in this case is in saying there was any fact from which the magistrate could draw an inference that the appellant acted with such indifference or disregard. If this had been a case of a person crossing over an ordinary growing crop, I should have taken the view that the magistrate was entitled to infer that the appellant must have had knowledge that what he was doing was something that was calculated to cause damage to the growing crop, and, if in fact damage resulted, and if the person accused was not there in virtue of any right or permission, then I think that would have been enough.

The whole difficulty here is to say that the appellant had knowledge, or should have had knowledge, that by crossing this field he was doing, or even was likely to do, any damage to the permanent grass with which the field was laid down. Upon that ground and that very limited ground I am in favour of allowing this appeal. If the magistrate had found in fact that the appellant knew he was doing something likely to cause damage, or had even found in fact that the appellant knew that other people doing the same thing were causing damage to this field, as may very well have been the case, I should have been against allowing the appeal. But, if the element of indifference is entirely absent, then it cannot be said that the appellant acted maliciously in what he did. I have great sympathy with a person in the position of this grazing tenant who finds his ground invaded by people who show no regard as to whether the ground is private or public, and it may be extremely hard if there is no remedy other than the civil remedy of interdict; but, however that may be, we are not justified in re-defining malicious mischief so as to eliminate from it the element of malice or what in law may be the equivalent of malice. I regret that the appeal must be allowed. Question 3 will be answered in the negative."

LORD MACKAY: "I concur. I propose to add a few perhaps disjointed remarks, but I think perhaps these few remarks will tend to clarify the position as we leave it. In the first place I feel that, in the case of a stroller or walker who is not said to have done anything more than walk across a patch of permanent grass, the law of malicious trespass and the law of malicious mischief should not be extended rashly. And without full inquiry we ought not to stretch the law of Scotland beyond what was laid down by Professor Rankine in his book as late as 1909 [Rankine on *Landownership* (4th ed.), p. 140]. I shall read three passages. 'As the law of Scotland never recognised the infliction of imprisonment for debt so it knows of no penalty for a simple act of trespass; but in the same way as a debtor was imprisoned, as a rebel, for allowing himself to be put to the horn, the trespasser may be severely dealt with, as in contempt of Court. He may indeed jeer at the time-honoured placard which threatens him with rigorous prosecution, as *brulum fulmen*.' But then that is qualified in the subsequent passages, showing that it is not to be read too absolutely. I read this passage: 'If the trespass be accompanied with destruction of property—such as woods, fences, and the like—the common law of malicious mischief is comprehensive enough to reach, and adequate to punish, such offences without calling in the assistance of a series of old statutes which are practically in abeyance.' [*Ibid.*] And then lastly, 'But in cases of simple trespass the only remedy at law is the purely civil preventive process of interdict' [at p. 141].

Now, it is quite clear that the learned Professor leaves room in a proper case for the rules as to malicious mischief to remedy what might in England be regarded as a defect, in that the criminal law does not make trespass a crime but only a civil wrong; and it is for that reason that we have to be careful in a case which seems to be very near the margin line between malicious damage and mere trespass.

Now that that is said, the elements which I find to be notably absent in the findings in the present case are these: (1) There is no assertion in any of the statements of fact of malice in the mind of the walker, of *mens rea* on his part, of an intention to do damage. That differentiates it very clearly from the most recent unreported case, [*Findlay v. Macgregor*, High Court of Justiciary, November 20, 1922] which otherwise is a little difficult to distinguish, but where there was a definite finding that the person did the thing maliciously. Here I think the magistrate intends to leave it to us as if it should be an inference in law from the facts actually found by him, facts which he carefully states without the inclusion of any such phrase as wrongful intention, *mens rea*, or even the general word 'maliciously'. (2) There is an absence of any statement as to boundaries, fences, or the like as enclosing the plot of land in question, which is called rather significantly the 'Cricket Green'. If the walker here had been proved, as in one of the other cases cited to us, to have necessarily got there by breaking down a gate, and if he had made his exit from the field by climbing a boundary fence, that might have sufficed to have taken the matter into another category altogether. (3) There is no suggestion that any gesture or use of his feet or other part of his body was made by this walker otherwise than in the ordinary act of walking. If I had thought the magistrate meant that there was a deliberate attempt to trample down grass, as by going round and round in circles or deliberately taking a great many more steps than were necessary, it might have been different; we might have sustained the conviction. (4) There is no question here at all that the proprietor took any exception to this or other persons making a short cut home. After all, trespass is a matter with the owner. We are here dealing with an injured person complaining of the cumulative damage done him by many walkers, and he is merely a person having the right to graze his sheep upon what I must assume to be permanent pasture. It seems clear enough to common sense by many familiar examples that sheep successfully graze where the feet of passers by are to be found concurrently. As to the assumption of grass laid down as permanent, although 'crop' is a word used by the magistrate, he does not give us any facts to infer that it was a specially sown grass crop between two green or other crops. It seems to me to be a case of permanent grass—a view which is again corroborated by the name of the place, 'Cricket Green'.

These various absences are, in my opinion, notable, and, therefore, being left, as I think we are, to draw an inference from the proved facts as to whether malice in the sense of *mens rea* can legitimately be deduced as an inference in law, and ought to be so deduced, I think the only safe course is to say it cannot. I therefore agree with your Lordship. I desire to leave open the matter of the general questions debated before us, as to the general apprehension said to be common to the public that they may go through any permanent grass anywhere, if not appreciating any substantial damage, without offence to the law in its criminal aspect. There is room for further and fuller argument should a further case be brought.

I desire that my opinion should be understood as definitely proceeding on this footing, that to carry the view of malicious mischief, in the case of pure walking as a trespasser, the length to which we are asked to carry it would, firstly, be going beyond any case hitherto decided, and would, secondly, be leaving behind us many of the older cases and dicta of weight in which deliberate violence or the like was held to be a necessary element in the crime. There remains a difference in Scotland between the civil wrong to the proprietor or tenant of trespassing (even with damage), and the crime of doing that maliciously, with malicious intent; and I think that this case, though narrow, just falls on the wrong side, for the prosecution, of that distinction."

Lord Pitman: "I concur. In my opinion no question of general importance as to the liability of trespassers, who in fact do damage through trespassing, to be prosecuted for malicious mischief arises in this case. The accused is charged with trampling down the grass and doing damage maliciously. There is no finding in fact that he trampled at all. The only finding against him is that he walked so many yards across a grass park where sheep happened to be grazing; that is all. When challenged for having done it, he and the two other men replied, 'We did not think we were doing any harm'. Now, if that is true, how can they possibly be prosecuted for doing damage maliciously? A person who thinks he is doing no harm cannot rightly be convicted of doing something maliciously. The two things are incompatible. And, when I look at the facts, I find nothing to show that that statement in answer to the charge is not an absolutely true statement. The mere fact that a man walks across a grass field, and in fact does some damage to the grass, is not sufficient in my opinion to warrant a conviction for malicious mischief."

Appeal allowed.

## Notes

Some older cases of malicious mischief suggest that malice, in the sense of spite or ill-will against the **15.11** owner or possessor of property, was necessary for this offence (see *William Reid* (1833) Bell's *Notes*, p. 47, and Gordon para. 22–04). It is clear that this is no longer the case. Provided that the accused deliberately damages the property, or shows that "indifference" to the rights of others mentioned in *Ward v. Robertson* the presence or absence of spite is irrelevant to the question of guilt.

In certain circumstances an accused may deliberately destroy property belonging to another and yet not be guilty of malicious mischief. So, for example, where the accused damages property in the belief that it is his own he will not be guilty of malicious mischief because he has no intention of damaging property belonging to another (*cf. R. v. Smith* [1974] 1 Q.B. 354). If, however, his belief is a reckless one, he may be guilty since his state of mind would display "indifference" to the rights of the owner.

The belief that the property in question is one's own to dispose of, which may have the effect of excluding the *mens rea*, should be contrasted with the belief that one is entitled to damage or destroy the property of another in order to vindicate one's own property rights—as in the following case.

### Clark v. Syme
### 1957 J.C. 32

**15.12** The respondent was charged with maliciously shooting and killing a sheep belonging to a neighbour. The latter had received complaints from the respondent about damage to his crops from trespassing sheep, and the respondent had delivered an ultimatum warning the neighbour that he would shoot sheep which wandered on to his land in the future. The Sheriff-substitute found the respondent not guilty, on the view that any inference of malice in the respondent's actions was displaced by the respondent's genuine misconceptions as to his legal rights in such cases. The prosecutor appealed by stated case to the High Court.

LORD JUSTICE-GENERAL (CLYDE): "The Sheriff-substitute ground for holding the respondent 'not guilty' is stated by him in the following terms: 'The presumption of malice which is essential and is normally inferred in such cases was adequately displaced by the respondent's explanation (which I accepted) that in the circumstances he genuinely misconceived his legal rights in the matter, and further that his desire to vindicate his own property for the future in the face of such persistent provocation was excusable.'

I am quite unable to accept either of these grounds as justifying the Sheriff-substitute in finding the respondent not guilty. A misconception of legal rights, however gross, will never justify the substitution of the law of the jungle for rules of civilised behaviour or even of common sense. The Sheriff-substitute indeed appears to have misunderstood the nature of the facts which require to be proved to establish the crime charged in this case. No question of a presumption of malice is involved in this crime at all. Malicious mischief either involves a deliberate and wicked intent to injure, or it may equally be established by proof of a wilful disregard of or indifference to the rights of others (see the opinion of the Lord Justice-Clerk (Aitchison) in the case of *Ward v. Robertson.* I accept this statement of the law as sound. If, as in the case of *Ward v. Robertson,* it was not clear whether the appellant knew that by doing what he did he was doing or was likely to do damage, the Crown might fail; for the necessary wilfulness might not then be present. But in this case no such doubt could possibly arise. The respondent in this case acted deliberately. He knew what he was doing and he displayed in his actings a complete disregard of the rights of others. The mere fact that his criminal act was performed under a misconception of what legal remedies he might otherwise have had does not make it any the less criminal. So far, therefore, as concerns the first of the two grounds for his conclusion set out by the Sheriff-substitute, it appears to me quite unfounded in law.

As regards his second reason for finding the respondent 'not guilty' (namely, that the respondent's desire to vindicate his own property for the future in the face of persistent provocation was excusable), I have found in the case no facts which would warrant any such conclusion. A desire to vindicate his own rights of property is all very well in its proper place, but, when that involves the deliberate destruction of the property and the invasion of the rights of others, it ceases, in my view, to be excusable.

We were referred to two other authorities on the question of malicious mischief. The first of these was *Black v. Laing* [1938 J.C. 32]. But in that case, which was concerned with the destruction of a fence across an access to the appellants' garden, the Court held that the conviction should be quashed upon the ground that the appellants were on the whole justified in removing the fence, since the only access to their garden was through the gap where that fence had been erected. This case affords no analogy nor assistance in the circumstances before us to-day. The other case referred to was a case of *Speid v. Whyte* (1864) 4 Irv. 584. It was concerned with a relatively trivial injury to part of the harness attached to a vehicle, and here again the Court held that the circumstances did not warrant the conviction. But the ground upon which that conclusion was reached was that there was not in that case, in view of the trivial nature of the injury done, that degree of recklessness and wilful destruction of property which is essential to the constitution of the crime of malicious mischief. The killing of the sheep in the present case affords just that link which was missing in *Speid v. Whyte*.

In the whole circumstances, accordingly, in my view, the question put to us in this case should be answered in the negative, and I so move your Lordships."

Appeal allowed.

NOTE

**15.13**

Lord Carmont and Lord Sorn delivered concurring opinions.

The Lord Justice-General does not fully deal with the circumstances of *Speid v. Whyte* or with the opinion of the court as delivered by Lord Neaves. In that case Speid was charged with maliciously cutting part of a horse harness. His defence was that he had done so in order to prevent the owner of the horse carting off timber which was the subject of a contract between the parties, but which was still the property of Speid. In delivering the judgment of the court, Lord Neaves stated that the circumstances of the case did not disclose that "reckless and wilful destruction of property which is essential to the constitution of the crime of malicious mischief. Mr Speid was undoubtedly the proprietor of the wood until the conditions of sale were implemented, which they had not been; and although he may not have acted judiciously, or even legally, in the course he adopted to vindicate his property, still he did act in vindication of his supposed rights, and not merely from a desire to injure or destroy the property of another".

In view of this passage the Lord Justice-General's attempts to distinguish the case seem unconvincing since it is clear that the true ground of the decision in *Speid v. Whyte* was the supposed vindication of property rights. *Speid v. Whyte* must, therefore, be treated as effectively overruled by *Clark v. Syme*. To the extent that it suggests that one may damage another's property in order to exercise one's own property rights. *Black v. Laing* must also be regarded as a suspect decision. It is true that it that case the court stated that the accused acted because otherwise they would not have access to their own property, which suggests some kind of necessity, but given that other avenues were open to the accused to have the fence removed, it could hardly be argued that their actions were in a real sense necessary. There may, of course, be circumstances in which a person could claim legitimately to have destroyed someone else's property in order to protect his own. Suppose, for example, that a farmer sees a dog worrying his sheep and shoots the dog in order to protect the sheep. In such circumstances it is arguable that a defence of necessity should be available, provided that his property was in imminent danger and that there was no other practicable lawful way of preventing the harm. (*Cf. Farrell v. Marshall*, 1962 S.L.T. (Sh.Ct) 65—a prosecution under section 1 of the Protection of Animals (Scotland) Act 1912; *Mitchell v. Duncan* (1953) 69 Sh. Ct Rep. 182; *Workman v. Cowper* [1961] 1 All E.R. 683.) In *Lord Advocate's Reference (No. 1 of 2000)* High Court, March 30, 2001, *unreported, ante*, the Court appears to accept that necessity (as explained in that case and *Moss v. Howdle, ante*, Chap. 7, could provide a defence to a charge of malicious mischief.

## 2. FIRE-RAISING

Setting fire to another's property has long been regarded as the most serious form of criminal damage. **15.14** Several old Scots statutes provided that certain instances of fire-raising were to be punished with death (see, for examples, Acts 1525 c. 10, 1526 c. 10; 1540 c. 38) and the distinction between capital and non-capital fire raising is central to Hume's discussion of the topic. The distinction between capital and non-capital fire-raising depended upon the type of property involved. The burning of "houses, corn, coal heughs, woods and under-woods" was capital (Hume, i, 131). The burning of other types of property, while criminal, was not capital. During the nineteenth century capital fire-raising came to be known as "wilful" fire-raising, while the burning of other types of property came to be known as "culpable and reckless" fire-raising. The terminology was not, however, consistently applied. In the case of *Geo. Macbean* (1847) Ark. 262, for example, the accused was convicted of the culpable and reckless burning of a house, thus demonstrating that it was not only the "wilful" burning of houses, etc., that was criminal. Similarly, it appears that there was some recognition that the "wilful" burning of property other than houses, etc., was a recognised offence, different from the culpable and reckless burning of such property.

As the law developed during the last century it became clear that it was in an unsatisfactory state. Matters were taken in hand by the High Court in the following case, which came before the court initially as an appeal against sentence following conviction in the sheriff court. The case was continued to allow the accused the opportunity of appealing against conviction. When the appeal against conviction was heard, the court decided that the issues should be remitted to a court of five judges. The opinions reproduced below deal with the appeal against conviction.

## Byrne v. H.M. Advocate
### 2000 S.C.C.R. 77

**15.15**  OPINION OF THE COURT (LORD COULSFIELD): "The appellant was charged with wilful fire raising and was eventually convicted, by the verdict of a jury, on August 29, 1997 and, after reports had been obtained, was sentenced on September 26, 1997 to 12 months detention. He appealed against sentence only but when the appeal came before the court it emerged that there might be reason to question the conviction and leave to lodge grounds of appeal against conviction late was granted.

The original indictment alleged that the appellant did, on May 26, 1997, set fire to the premises at 133 Broughty Ferry Road, Dundee known as Carolina House occupied by Hillcrest Housing Association whereby the fire took effect on said premises and that he did this wilfully. After evidence had been led, the indictment was amended and the terms of the indictment which went before the jury were as follows:

"You Joseph Byrne did, on May 26, 1997 at the premises at 133 Broughty Ferry Road, Dundee ... set fire to paper or similar material and a bed and mattress on the floor of said premises whereby the fire took effect on the said paper, bed and mattress and said floor and took effect on said premises whereby the said paper, bed, mattress, floor and premises were damaged and this you did wilfully."

In their verdict the jury deleted the references to the bed and mattress, so that the appellant was convicted of setting fire to paper or similar material on the floor of the premises, "whereby the fire took effect on said paper and said floor and took effect on said premises, whereby the said paper, floor and premises were damaged and that you did wilfully".

To understand the significance of the amendments made by the Crown and the jury it is necessary to have regard to the evidence. The sheriff's account of the evidence is brief, but the appellant's counsel and the advocate depute were able to supplement it in some respects. The premises in question were a large house in the neighbourhood of Broughty Ferry which was unoccupied and to which groups of boys had from time to time resorted. The appellant and four or five other boys went to the house on the occasion libelled, apparently to smoke. The appellant and another boy went to an upper floor in the premises while the remainder of the group stayed on the ground floor. On the upper floor, the appellant, as he admitted to the police shortly afterwards, obtained some crumpled paper, probably wallpaper, and set fire to that paper. The appellant's account, both in his statement to the police and in his evidence, was that he dropped the paper on the floor and that the other boy, Jones, then threw a mattress and the base of a bed on top of the burning paper. The mattress, according to the appellant, began to smoke and he and Jones ran out of the building. They found some of the other boys and indicated that there was a fire whereupon two of the other boys went to the room and saw the mattress flaring. One of those boys, we were informed, said that he threw an old wardrobe onto the burning mattress and that that in turn caught fire. The appellant lodged a special defence, incriminating Jones. In his evidence, Jones accepted that he had pushed a mattress onto the burning paper but said that he had done this in order to put the fire out. The advocate depute informed us that there was further evidence from the other three boys in the house who said that the appellant and Jones had gone upstairs and come back, Jones shouting that the appellant had set the building on fire, and that at least one of them described the appellant as laughing when he came down. The advocate depute also informed us that in the course of his statement to the police the appellant had said "I thought we'd hae a wee fire" as well as giving his account of the incriminee pushing the mattress onto the fire.

The sheriff observes that he found the jury's verdict somewhat curious, in so far as it deleted the reference to the bed and mattress and he also states that it was his own personal view that the appellant did not intend to set fire to the whole building but only the paper and probably the bedding and mattress, but he expresses the view that there was sufficient evidence on which the jury were entitled to convict the appellant of setting fire to the building. There is no ground of appeal relating to sufficiency of evidence so that that issue does not properly arise for us. We agree, however, with the sheriff in his view that there was a sufficient evidence.

When the sheriff came to direct the jury as to the crime of wilful fireraising, he said:

"The requirement for an offence of wilful fireraising is to deliberately set fire to the property of another, the property in this case refers to paper or similar material, the floor and bed and mattress, and the said premises as detailed in the narrative. And I would emphasise to you the word 'wilful'. A crime of wilful fireraising cannot be committed accidentally, carelessly or even recklessly, it can only be committed intentionally, that is deliberately. Therefore the Crown must establish firstly that the fire was set or kindled deliberately by the accused. So you have to decide how far, from the evidence you have heard, what the accused's intentions were and whether they extended up to and including the whole building or only the lesser items.

Now this intention can be implied from conduct which indicates an utter disregard of the likelihood of the fire spreading. In the present case it would appear that the defence accepts that the accused set fire to the paper, and possibly the flooring, that this was deliberate, but so far as the rest is concerned the defence do not accept that it came into the category of wilful. Accordingly, it may be or will be for you to decide whether you return a verdict in respect of the whole charge or you may if you do not consider that the accused's actings were wilful in respect of all of the items in the charge delete various items from the charge if you consider that the Crown has not proved the reckless intention so far as these are concerned. So that you are entitled to delete, for example, the building or bed or mattress or whatever, that is a matter for you at the end of the day."

Later, having referred to the evidence, the sheriff said:

"At the end of the day it comes down to you having to decide whether or not the accused is guilty either of the minimal charge of wilful fireraising in respect of the paper, secondly somewhere in between, having in the floor and the bed or mattress and/or mattress, as detailed in the narrative of the charge or the other extreme whether he is guilty of the whole charge, including the building. And I would remind you and emphasise to you what I said about the definition of wilful fireraising and the importance in it of the question of deliberate intention and its implications."

After retiring, the jury returned and asked for repetition of what they described as "the two meanings of wilful you gave us". The sheriff reminded them that the crime could only be committed intentionally and added:

"But what you have to decide is how far the intention went, whether the intention was confined to the first item set on fire or whether the intention went on to include the others, going as far as the whole building. Now this intention can be implied from the conduct of the accused person, which may indicate a total disregard of what the consequences are likely to be but if you take the view that he did not have the intention of what eventually happened then you cannot convict him of the whole."

The grounds of appeal against conviction were that the sheriff had given inadequate directions to the jury by failing to direct them that they had to consider whether the Crown had proved that the spreading of the fire to the building was a foreseeable and intended consequence of the appellant's initial deliberate act; that the jury's deletion of the words "bed and mattress" indicated that they had at least a reasonable doubt whether the appellant had set fire to the bed and mattress; and that given that doubt no reasonable jury could have found the appellant guilty of setting fire to the building. Reference was made to the decisions in *Blane v. H.M. Advocate,* 1991 S.C.C.R. 576 and *McKelvie v. H.M. Advocate,* 1997 S.L.T. 758 and, as the argument developed, it became apparent that the appeal touches on questions about the nature and standing in modern times of the crime of wilful fireraising which are not easy to answer.

The discussion of wilful fireraising in Hume (I. 125) begins by stressing that the crime had always been regarded as one of a high degree and therefore as a capital crime and proceeds to narrate the various statutes which have dealt with wilful fireraising in Scotland. At p. 126 Hume discusses the requirement that the fire must "take effect" and, at 128, deals with the requirement that the fire must be raised wilfully. He says:

> "The only other, but an indispensable quality of the act, is, that the fire be raised wilfully—with a purpose to destroy the thing to which it is applied. If it be kindled *recklessly*, or from *misgovernance*, as it is called in our old statute 1426 c 75 the consequence cannot well be deeper than a fine or short imprisonment, joined to the reparation of the damage, sustained by the private party."

Hume then discusses the method of proof of the wilful character of the fireraising and, at 131, says:

> "It remains to enquire concerning the things or subjects on which the capital crime of fireraising may be committed. There can be no question with respect to those subjects, namely, houses, corn, coal-heughs, woods and underwoods, which are specially mentioned in the old statutes .... And these, for obvious reasons, are certainly the possessions which most require to be defended from this sort of violence. Nor have I observed that any judgment has extended the construction of this crime any further, so as to punish with death for the burning of furze, heaths, mosses, stacks of fuel or in general any sort of moveable effects."

The crime described by Hume therefore was one of a special character, defined in a strict, and possibly in some respects arbitrary, fashion, in view of its status as a capital crime. The law did, however, also recognise the crime of culpable and reckless fireraising, which was not capital but subject to an arbitrary penalty. Both types of crime were considered by the court in *Angus v. H.M. Advocate,* 1905 8 F. (J) 10. That was a case in which a person had been indicted on a charge of wilfully setting fire to a screw or stack of hay. The accused objected to the relevancy of the indictment on the ground that the crime of wilful fireraising was restricted to the specific forms of property, which did not include stacks of hay; it was held that the indictment set out a crime known to the law although not the specific crime "wilful fireraising". At p. 13, the Lord Justice General described the capital crime of wilful fireraising as it had been defined and then said:

> "That being so, and the crime being of so serious a nature, and visited by the heaviest sentence known to the law, it is easy to see why care was taken that the subject-matter of the crime should not be unduly extended. And so it was that the crime, which would be charged in the major as 'wilful fireraising', could only be committed by setting fire to heritable property or to certain special forms of moveable property. But there was always another crime known to the law—an innominate crime and visited by an arbitrary

penalty—which consisted in setting fire, or attempting to set fire, to anything. It is true that the epithet in that case was not 'wilful', the words used being 'culpably and recklessly'; but I think that this is of no moment, for I do not doubt that the element of wilfulness was always present, *i.e.* that no conviction could have followed if it were shown that the fireraising had been caused by mere accident, and in entire absence of set intention."

The Lord Justice General went on to say that in modern times the materiality of the distinction had been swept away, in view of the abolition of the death penalty for wilful fireraising, and that the indictment set out a charge known to the law. He continued:

"As I have already pointed out, it is no longer necessary to specify a major, so all we have to consider is whether the facts set forth in the indictment—that the accused set fire to a stack of hay; that the fire took effect; and that he did it wilfully—amount to a crime. I think that they do. It seems that in drawing this indictment the word 'wilfully' has been used instead of the words 'culpably and recklessly', and that is perhaps unfortunate, as it seems to have given rise to some confusion. But it would really be absurd to say that what would amount to a crime if it were done culpably and recklessly is not a crime if it is done wilfully. I therefore think that the facts set forth in this indictment amount to a relevant description of a crime, and a crime known to the law of Scotland."

Lord Adam and Lord McLaren agreed, Lord Adam observing:

"I do not know if in old days the offence hear charged would not have been libelled as having been done culpably and recklessly, but I am quite clear that as it stands it is a perfectly good charge of the innominate crime of fireraising. I do not know that wilful fireraising and culpable and reckless fireraising are quite the same, but I have no doubt that the setting fire to a stack of hay wilfully is in Scotland a crime, and that the crime has been relevantly libelled here."

In *Blane*, the appellant had set fire to some bedding with, according to himself, the intention of choking himself with the smoke. The sheriff directed the jury that it was not necessary for the Crown to prove that the fire was set directly to the premises provided that the burning of any part of the premises resulted from the act of the appellant deliberately setting fire to some article such as the bedding. It was held that that was a misdirection. There was then a problem as to how to dispose of the case, and the solution adopted by the court was to hold that it was clear that the appellant had deliberately set fire to the bedding, that that was a criminal act and that a verdict of wilfully setting fire to the bedding should be substituted. The ground on which the court proceeded, as appears from the opinion of the Lord Justice General (at p. 583 and 584) was that there had ceased to be any material distinction between wilful fireraising and culpable and reckless fireraising and that, since it was not necessary to specify a *nomen juris* under the modern procedure, it was sufficient that the actings specified in the indictment should amount to a crime. At p. 584, the Lord Justice General said:

"The terms 'culpably and recklessly' and 'wilfully' have different meanings since an action cannot be said to be wilful if it was not intentional or deliberate. But a wilful action can also be described as culpable and reckless, so these expressions are both apt to describe the essential nature of the criminal activity which occurred in this case when the appellant deliberate set fire to the quilt."

It is easy to see that the distinction between wilful fireraising, as defined by Hume, and other criminal fireraising was based on the fact that wilful fireraising was a capital crime and that the distinction is outmoded. However, the way in which the decisions in *Angus* and *Blane* are expressed is not without problems. Logically, it might have been sufficient for the decision in both cases simply to say that deliberately setting fire to moveable property counted as an innominate crime. On that approach, it might have been said that there were, in effect, three species of crime, namely (1) wilful fireraising committed intentionally in respect of property of the specified kinds; (2) deliberate setting of fire to property other than property in the specified classes; and (3) culpable and reckless fireraising. However in *Angus* the court clearly linked the crime in class (2) above with that in class (3): that is to say it appeared to treat deliberately setting fire to moveable property as a species of culpable and reckless fireraising. Lord Adam's opinion in *Angus* perhaps indicates some reservation as to whether that link need be made, but it is clearly made in the opinion of the Lord Justice General and is taken up in the opinion of the Lord Justice General in *Blane*. That has the somewhat curious consequence that it would appear to be possible for a jury dealing with an indictment alleging wilful fireraising to return a verdict of guilty in relation to the setting on fire of moveable objects, a verdict which then falls to be treated as if it were a verdict of guilty of culpable and reckless fireraising. There is an additional difficulty in that there is authority that actual intention must be proved in a charge of wilful fireraising and that even gross recklessness is not sufficient (*H.M.A. v. Macbean* (1847) Ark. 262; *H.M.A.* v. *Smillie* (1883) 5 Cooper 287). Presumably, however, the ordinary rule that a person's intention can be inferred from his action applies in a charge of wilful fireraising. In applying that rule, and in giving directions to a jury, care may be necessary to distinguish between apparent gross indifference to the consequences of an action as a ground for inferring that the actor intended those consequences, on the one hand, and as a ground for holding that the actor acted recklessly on the other, and the approach taken in *Blane* may not make it any easier to do so.

*McKelvie* was a case in which, according to the verdict, the accused had set fire to some clothing in a house and the fire had spread and taken effect on the house and adjoining property. The sheriff had directed the jury that if the accused had intentionally set fire to the clothing it was irrelevant that his intention was simply to burn the clothing and that if the fire was deliberately started and spread to take effect on heritable property, that was a case of wilful fireraising. It was held that that was a misdirection. What the court then did was to give effect to the motion which had been made to the court on behalf of the appellant by substituting for the jury's verdict of guilty of wilful fireraising a verdict of guilty of culpable and reckless fireraising. It may be that some further consideration should have been given to the question whether that was the appropriate way to dispose of the appeal, since the amendment made to the verdict involved either writing words into the indictment which were not there or treating culpable and reckless fireraising as a potential alternative verdict on an indictment alleging wilful fireraising, both of which would be difficult to justify technically, however much the outcome of the case may have appeared sensible. In any case, the decision in *McKelvie* does not assist in resolving any of the difficulties in the law, and the court in that case did suggest that it would be desirable that the law should be re-examined.

No review of the law has been put in hand to our knowledge. There have been relatively few reported decisions in regard to wilful fireraising, but fireraisings do occur from time to time, and can be matters of the utmost gravity. We have therefore come to the conclusion that it is unsatisfactory to have the law in its present state, and that this case should be remitted to a court of five judges to reconsider the authorities to which reference has been made."

The case was then remitted to a court of five judges which allowed the accused's appeal against conviction. The opinion of the court was again delivered by Lord Coulsfield.

OPINION OF THE COURT: "The circumstances of this case and the history of the proceedings are set out in the opinion of the Court of three judges issued on May 5, 1999 and it is not necessary to repeat them. We merely recall that the terms of the indictment which went before the jury were:

"You JOSEPH BYRNE did, on May 26, 1997, at the premises at 133 Broughty Ferry Road, Dundee, known as Carolina House, owned by Hillcrest Housing Association, 4 South Ward Road, Dundee, set fire to paper or similar material and a bed and mattress on the floor of said premises whereby the fire took effect on the said paper, bed and mattress and said floor and took effect on said premises whereby the said paper, bed, mattress, floor and premises were damaged and this you did wilfully".

In their verdict the jury deleted the references to the bed and mattress, so that the appellant was convicted of setting fire to paper or similar material on the floor of the premises, "whereby the fire took effect on said paper and said floor and took effect on said premises, whereby the said paper, floor and premises were damaged and that you did wilfully."

As is explained in the opinion, the case was remitted to a court of five judges in order to allow some apparent difficulties and inconsistencies in the authorities relating to the crime of wilful fireraising and, in particular, some observations in the cases of *Angus v. H.M. Advocate* (1905) 8 F. (J.) 10 and *Blane v. H.M. Advocate* 1991 S.C.C.R. 576 to be reconsidered. When the case was heard before five judges on October 18, 1999, Miss Dorrian, Q.C., who appeared for the appellant, and the Lord Advocate analysed the earlier authorities in detail in order to show how the crime of wilful fireraising was understood prior to the decision in *Angus supra* and to compare that understanding with the observations in *Angus* and in *Blane*. In the result, there was little or no difference between the conclusions which Miss Dorrian and the Lord Advocate drew from the authorities. It was also, in the end, not disputed that, if the law was correctly understood, there had been a misdirection in the present case and accordingly that the conviction should be quashed.

In these circumstances, it is not necessary to examine all the earlier authorities in great detail. It is, however, necessary to look closely at Hume's explanation of the crime. His treatment is found in chapter 4 of volume 1 which is headed "Of wilful fireraising and malicious mischief". Early in that chapter (at p. 122) Hume says:

"It may be affirmed generally, with respect to every act of great and wilful damage done to the property of another, and whether done from malice, or misapprehension of right, that it is cognisable with us as a crime at common law; if it is done, as ordinarily happens, with circumstances of tumult and disorder, and of contempt and indignity to the owner."

Hume then treats of crimes of invasion of property and casting down of houses and other similar matters and comes to deal with wilful fireraising at page 125. He explains that wilful fireraising has always been treated as a crime of very high degree and refers to the statutes which made wilful fireraising in relation to certain types of property capital. At p. 128 he says:

"The only other, but an indispensable quality of the act, is, that the fire be raised wilfully—with a purpose to destroy the thing to which it is applied. If it be kindled *recklessly*, or from *misgovernance*, as it is called in our old statute 1426 c.75, the consequence cannot well be deeper than a fine or short imprisonment, joined to the reparation of the damage sustained by the private party."

After some further discussion of the intent necessary to constitute the crime Hume returns to the question of the subjects in relation to which the crime of wilful fireraising is capital and says (at p. 131):

"It remains to inquire concerning the things or subjects, on which the capital crime of fire-raising may be committed. There can be no question with respect to those subjects, namely, houses, corn, coal-heughs, woods and under-woods, which are specially mentioned in the old statutes, 1525, 1526, 1540, 1592, and that of the 1st of George I. c. 48. And these, for obvious reasons, are certainly the possessions which most require to be defended from this sort of violence. Nor have I observed, that any judgment has extended the construction of this crime any farther, so as to punish with death for the burning of furze, heaths, mosses, stacks of fuel, or in general any sort of moveable effects. Whatever may be true as to other modes of charge, it does not therefore seem to be capital as a fire-raising that a mob, after rifling a house, collect the effects and burn them in the street; or even that within the house, they burn the owner's title-deeds, bank-notes and bonds, or other goods, however valuable, gathered into a heap in the fire-place, or upon the hearth."

Later again, at p. 135, after some further discussion of the subjects on which the capital crime may be committed and of the position where a person sets fire to his own property, Hume says:

"Thus much may suffice as to the capital crime of fire-raising, which can only be committed upon property of certain sorts. But our view of this part of the law will be incomplete, unless we attend also to the following particulars.

1. To destroy by fire any of the other sorts of property, moveable or immoveable, is always a heinous crime and punishable in every instance, at common law, with the highest arbitrary pains."

If we put aside what has been said in later authorities and look only at what Hume said, it seems to us to be abundantly clear that he recognised a crime of wilful fireraising in relation to certain subjects, which was capital under statute, and a crime of wilful fireraising in relation to any other subjects which was a heinous crime punishable with the highest arbitrary penalty. Equally, it is clear that Hume also recognised that kindling a fire, "*recklessly* or from *misgovernance*" was a crime punishable by a lesser penalty of a short period of imprisonment or a fine. Statements of the law to exactly the same effect are found in Alison. In chapter 16 of volume I, he explains, at p. 429, the capital crime of wilful fireraising; at p. 442 he explains that "the wilful burning ... of any sort of moveables, though not by law capital, is an indictable offence, punishable" with arbitrary penalties. At p. 433 he says that, if fire is kindled recklessly or from misgovernment, "the crime is not wilful fireraising, but an inferior delinquence, punishable by fine or imprisonment". Burnett in his *Treatise* begins (at p. 213) by examining the statutory offence relating to the burning of houses, etc., but adds (at p. 215) that the malicious destruction by burning or setting fire to moveable property may infer a high punishment. It may be added that both Hume (i.128) and Alison (i.442) indicate no distinction between the intention which has to be proved in the case of wilful fireraising as a capital crime and that which requires to be proved in relation to wilful fireraising as a crime punishable by an arbitrary penalty.

Section 56 of the Criminal Procedure (Scotland) Act 1887 abolished capital punishment for wilful fireraising, among other crimes, and the need for a distinction based upon the existence of a capital penalty therefore ceased. In addition, section 5 of the 1887 Act provided that it was not necessary in any indictment to specify the crime charged by any *nomen juris* but that it should be sufficient that the indictment set out facts relevant and sufficient to constitute an indictable crime. Further, section 8 made it unnecessary to include words such as "wilfully" or "knowingly" in an indictment. Nevertheless, the distinction between wilful fireraising and culpable and reckless fireraising was recognised in the examples of indictments given in Schedule A to the 1887 Act. The relevant form of indictment is in the following terms:

"... you did set fire to a warehouse occupied by Peter Cranston in Holly Lane, Greenock, and the fire took effect on said warehouse and this you did wilfully (*or* culpably and recklessly) ...."

The effect of the 1887 Act was discussed by a Full Bench in *H.M. Advocate v. Swan* (1882) 2 White 137. The charge in that case was a charge of fraud but in the course of his opinion Lord Justice Clerk Macdonald referred to charges of fireraising. He said:

"But the Act by its clauses and the illustrations in the schedule indicates that in the ordinary case the statement by the prosecutor is to be limited practically to acts done. The only cases in which anything further is required, are, first, those in which the acts done must be followed by special consequences in order to constitute the crime charged; and second, those cases in which the nature of the crime may vary according to the state of mind of the perpetrator being either a directly malicious state, or one culpable in a minor degree only. An instance of the first is the case of crime by bodily violence. The consequence in a case of violent assault might be death or injury. It is necessary in such a case to state whether death or only injury resulted. An instance of the second class of cases is the crime of fire-raising, where there may be a criminal intent or only a culpable fault. The prisoner, therefore, in cases of fire-raising, is entitled to have information whether his offence is alleged to have been done by him 'wilfully' or only 'culpably and recklessly'. With the exception of these two classes of cases, I know of no class of crimes in reference to which it is necessary under this statute and its schedule to do more than to state the acts which are alleged to have been done."

As was noted in the previous opinion, the later case of *Angus* was one in which a person had been indicted on a charge of wilfully setting fire to a stack of hay. It was objected that the indictment was irrelevant because the crime of wilful fireraising was restricted to specific forms of property which did not include stacks of hay. The argument for the panel included reference to Schedule A to the 1887 Act and to the alternatives of wilful and culpable and reckless fireraising and it was submitted, as the argument is recorded, that the alternatives set forth in the Schedule embodied the distinction known to the old law; that a charge of setting fire wilfully was applicable only to the crime formerly known as "wilful fireraising"; and that that form of charge was therefore not relevant to a case of setting fire to stacks of hay. The argument for the Crown is recorded as follows:

> "It was always a crime in Scotland to set fire wilfully to any kind of property, and though setting fire to certain special kinds of property was a special crime, visited with capital punishment, and known by the *nomen juris* of 'wilful fire-raising', that punishment was now abolished, and the distinction between the two crimes no longer obtained. The words of the charge here sufficiently described a crime well known to the law of Scotland."

That statement of the position by the Crown appears to be precisely in accordance with the law as laid down in the authorities to which we have referred. In his opinion, the Lord Justice General (Dunedin) referred to the statutes which had made wilful fireraising a capital crime and continued (at p. 13):

> "And so it was that the crime, which would be charged in the major as 'wilful fire-raising,' could only be committed by setting fire to heritable property or to certain special forms of moveable property. But there was always another crime known to the law—an innominate crime and visited by an arbitrary penalty—which consisted in setting fire, or attempting to set fire, to anything. It is true that the epithet in that case was not 'wilful', the words used being 'culpably and recklessly'; but I think that this is of no moment, for I do not doubt that the element of wilfulness was always present, *i.e.*, that no conviction could have followed if it were shewn that the fire-raising had been caused by mere accident and in entire absence of set intention."

The Lord Justice General then referred to the abolition of capital punishment for fireraising and the abolition of the requirement to specify a *nomen juris*, and indicated that he would be reluctant to quash a conviction for a serious matter such as setting fire to anything deliberately on a technicality and continued (at p. 13):

"The crime charged is the crime of setting on fire wilfully—a very serious crime, and one which deserves a heavy punishment—and I should have been reluctant to have quashed a conviction for such a crime on a technical point based on a mere matter of form. But I do not think we are driven to such a course. As I have already pointed out, it is no longer necessary to specify a major, so all we have to consider is whether the facts set forth in the indictment—that the accused set fire to a stack of hay; that the fire took effect; and that he did it wilfully—amount to a crime. I think that they do."

So far, the opinion of the Lord Justice General could be taken as being in accordance with the law as explained by Hume. The reference to the wording of an indictment for the innominate crime, in the earlier passage quoted, was not correct, but that error might not, in itself, have given rise to much confusion. However, the Lord Justice General continued:

"It seems that in drawing this indictment the word 'wilfully' has been used instead of the words 'culpably and recklessly', and that is perhaps unfortunate, as it seems to have given rise to some confusion. But it would really be absurd to say that what would amount to a crime if it were done culpably and recklessly is not a crime if it is done wilfully. I therefore think that the facts set forth in this indictment amount to a relevant description of a crime, and a crime known to the law of Scotland."

Lord Adam said (at p. 14) he was quite clear that

"as it stands it is a perfectly good charge of the innominate crime of fire-raising. I do not know that wilful fire-raising and culpable and reckless fire-raising are quite the same, but I have no doubt that the setting fire to a stack of hay wilfully is in Scotland a crime . . .".

Lord McLaren said (at p. 14):

"The difficulty which seems to have arisen in this case largely disappears when we consider that the malicious setting fire to a stack of hay has always been treated as an offence punishable in this Court or by the Sheriff, although it did not come within the technical category of wilful fire-raising. Under our present code of procedure it is not necessary to specify the category of crime with which the accused is charged. It suffices that the description of the acts alleged to be done amounts to the statement of a crime. I agree with your Lordships that we have in this complaint a relevant description of the crime of maliciously setting fire to moveable property."

It appears that the Lord Justice General accepted the argument for the panel to the extent of regarding the crime of wilfully setting fire to moveable property as properly falling under the alternative form of charge ("culpably and recklessly") set out in the Schedule to the 1887 Act, rather than as falling under wilful fireraising. On the other hand, the opinions of the other two members of the court can be seen simply as an application of the law as previously explained by Hume and the other authorities to the facts of the particular case. There can, in any event, be no doubt that the actual decision in *Angus* was correct and in accordance with the law as explained by Hume.

The observations of the Lord Justice General in relation to what might be comprised in "culpable and reckless fireraising" were neither necessary to the decision nor in accordance with the law as it had previously been stated. They have, however, become a source of confusion in subsequent cases and are the ultimate source of the muddled account of the law to be found in the fifth (but not any earlier) edition of Macdonald's *Criminal Law*, pp. 79–82, especially at p. 81. It does not appear that in any of the decisions which have followed *Angus* has the court had the benefit of the full analysis of the law before *Angus* which has been provided to us in the present case. The result has been that attempts to explain the observations of Lord Justice General Dunedin have not resolved the difficulty and may, indeed, have made the position more obscure. In the light of the full discussion of the authorities which we have heard, we are satisfied that the observations of the Lord Justice General were incorrect and should not now be followed.

As was mentioned in the previous opinion, *Blane* was a case in which the accused was charged with wilful fireraising in that he set fire to bedding in his room in a hostel and the fire took effect on the premises. The sheriff directed the jury that the Crown did not require to prove that the accused had set fire directly to the premises provided that the burning of any part of the premises resulted from the act of the accused in deliberately setting fire to some article, such as the bedding. It was held that that was a misdirection. We shall return to the reasons for that view. It was, however, clear on the evidence that the accused had set fire to the quilt deliberately and, as the Lord Justice General (Hope) observed at page 583, since that was a wilful act on his part in regard to something which was not his own property, he was guilty of a criminal act. That view, as so far set out, was in accordance with the law as it was before the decision in *Angus*. However, the court clearly felt constrained by the observations of Lord Dunedin in *Angus*. The Lord Justice General in *Blane*, therefore, referred to the observations in *Angus* and to section 44 of the Criminal Procedure (Scotland) Act 1975 (which replaced section 5 of the 1887 Act) and went on to say:

> "In these circumstances, I do not think that we need be troubled by the distinction which has continued, for what seems to me to be no very good reason, to exist between culpable and reckless fireraising and wilful fireraising as separate species of crime. The terms 'culpably and recklessly' and 'wilfully' have separate meanings since an action cannot be said to be wilful if it was not intentional or deliberate. But a wilful action can also be described as culpable and reckless, so these expressions are both apt to describe the essential nature of the criminal activity which occurred in this case when the appellant deliberately set fire to the quilt."

In our view, once the proper state of the law before the decision in *Angus* is appreciated, these observations, like the observations in *Angus*, can be seen to be unnecessary to the decision and as really conflating two distinct crimes. It is only necessary to add that the same confusion was carried forward into the decision in *McKelvie* v. *H.M. Advocate* 1997 S.L.T. 758, with the result that the court in that case erred by substituting a verdict of guilty of culpable and reckless fireraising for one of guilty of wilful fireraising, a course which was not open because culpable and reckless fireraising is not an implied alternative to a charge of wilful fireraising. See section 64(6) of, and Schedule 3 to, the 1995 Act.

As we have observed earlier, the authorities are clear to the effect that, to establish wilful fireraising, it is necessary for the Crown to prove an actual intention on the part of the accused to set fire to the subjects which are libelled as the subject of fireraising in the charge. We have also noted that there is nothing in the earlier authorities to suggest that there is, or was, any distinction in this respect between the crime of wilful fireraising in relation to the specified subjects, the capital crime, and that of wilful fireraising in relation to any other subjects. One of the features of fireraising as a crime, however, is that it is notoriously difficult to predict what the spread of a fire will be once it has been kindled. It may be as a consequence of that characteristic of fire that some of the statements about fireraising in the earlier authorities are capable of being interpreted as involving the application of some doctrine of "transferred intent": that is to say, as suggesting that if the Crown prove that an accused person deliberately set fire to *something* and that the fire then spread to other subjects, then this may be sufficient to make him guilty of wilful fireraising in relation to all the subjects. That was the view on which the sheriff directed the jury in the case of *Blane*. However, the court in *Blane* discussed the relevant passages in the authorities fully and came to the conclusion that there was no room for a doctrine of transferred intent. The Lord Justice General said, at page 581:

"Since wilful fire-raising is a common law crime it requires *mens rea*, and this must extend to all the material circumstances of the offence. There may be room for argument as to whether the *mens rea* in the case of this crime is confined to intention, so that the actus reus extends only to the intended consequences of the acts of the accused, or whether it may consist also of recklessness. I prefer Gordon's view that the crime of wilful fire-raising can be committed only intentionally, since this is in accordance with the ordinary meaning of the word 'wilful'. Hume volume i, p. 128 states that it is an indispensable quality of the act that the fire be raised wilfully, 'with a purpose to destroy the thing to which it is applied'."

We respectfully agree with those observations. The Lord Justice General then cited *George Macbean* (1847) Ark. 262 at p. 263 in which Lord Justice Clerk Hope said that for a person to commit wilful fireraising he must designedly and in cold blood set fire to the subjects "well knowing what he was about, and intending to do so" and continued (at pages 581–582):

"Of course, proof of intention may present difficulties, especially in regard to the consequences of the initial deliberate act. But since the matter must be approached objectively I think that it is open to inference, where the accused is shown to have acted with a reckless disregard for the likely consequences of what he does, that he intended those consequences to occur. Lord Kincraig's charge in *H.M. Advocate v. Boyd*, to which Gordon refers in paragraph 22–26, note 72, makes this point in terms which I think we can and should approve:

'Charge (2) sets forth the crime of wilful fire-raising, and that crime consists in setting fire to certain property including a house wilfully, that is to say not accidentally or carelessly—deliberately; and if the fire is applied deliberately to any of the contents of the house which will be likely to spread and set fire to the house itself, the crime is wilful fire-raising. Thus here if the house was burned down because fire was deliberately applied to any of its contents—for example, the bedclothes—and if that act would have, as a likely consequence, the burning of the house, and did indeed lead to the burning of the house, the crime is wilful fire-raising. In short, if fire is applied so as to manifest an intention that it shall spread to the house and it does so spread the crime is complete, and the intention to set fire to the house will be implied from such conduct as indicates utter disregard of the likelihood of the fire spreading'.

The last sentence of this passage makes the essential point that the mental element which is required is the intention to set fire to the property described in the charge. It is the absence of any direction to the jury to consider the likely consequences of the appellant's action in setting fire to the quilt, and whether these displayed at least an utter indifference to the likelihood that the fire would spread to other articles in his room and to the building itself if he sets fire to it, that gives rise to the defect in this case."

In our respectful view Lord Kincraig's charge in *Boyd* in fact embodied a misdirection and the passage in the opinion of the court in *Blane* approving that misdirection must be overruled. As we have explained, if the Crown are to secure a conviction of wilful fireraising in respect of any subjects, they must satisfy the jury that the accused actually intended to set fire to those subjects. In this, as in any other area of the law, proof of intention will usually depend on the jury being able to draw the necessary inference from all the circumstances, including the accused's conduct. If the evidence would not permit the jury to infer that the accused had intended to set fire to the subjects in question, then the judge must sustain a no case to answer submission. But in other cases the evidence may be capable of one of three constructions: either that the accused intended to set fire to the subjects or that he was reckless, showing an utter disregard for the likelihood of the fire spreading to the subjects, or that he was simply careless. It is for the jury to determine, as a matter of fact, which inference they draw. If they conclude that the accused actually intended to set fire to the subjects, then they will convict him of wilful fireraising. If they find that the accused was merely careless, then obviously they will acquit him. If, however, the jury conclude that he was reckless, showing an utter disregard for the likelihood of the fire spreading to the subjects, then in that situation also they must acquit him of the charge of wilful fireraising in respect of those subjects. They could, of course, convict him of a charge of culpable and reckless fireraising in respect of the subjects, if the Crown had expressly libelled such an alternative.

The misdirection by Lord Kincraig in *Boyd* lay in his telling the jury that the necessary intention to set fire to the subjects could be *implied* from conduct indicating an utter disregard of the likelihood of the fire spreading to the subjects in question. It may be that his Lordship had in mind the familiar position in murder where the jury can convict if they are satisfied either that the accused intended to kill the victim or that he displayed a wicked recklessness as to whether the victim lived or died. The crime of murder, however, can be committed by someone having one of two states of mind, either the intention to kill or wicked recklessness. The crime of wilful fireraising is different: the only *mens rea* is intention. Before they can convict, the jury must therefore be satisfied that the accused actually intended to set fire to the subjects. If all that they infer from the evidence is that the accused was reckless, even if to a very high degree, that does not entitle them to convict him of wilful fireraising. They can do so only if they go further and infer from the evidence that the accused was not merely reckless but actually intended to set fire to the subjects. In directing a jury it is therefore vital for a judge to keep the concepts of intention and recklessness distinct.

Unfortunately in his charge to the jury in this case the sheriff did not keep the concepts distinct. It is obvious indeed that he was led into confusion by trying to follow the guidance provided by *Boyd* and *Blane*. At one point he directed the jury that the crime could "only be committed intentionally, that is deliberately" but shortly afterwards he said that the accused's intention could "be implied from conduct which indicates an utter disregard of the likelihood of the fire spreading". Later still, he spoke of the jury considering the accused's conduct for its implication, "if you consider the accused's conduct to have shown an utter disregard of the likelihood of the fire starting, or spreading rather". Perhaps most clearly, in certain supplementary directions he spoke of the intention being "implied from the conduct of the accused person, which may indicate a total disregard of what the consequences are likely to be, but if you take the view that he did not have the intention of what eventually happened then you cannot convict him of the whole". The Lord Advocate acknowledged that these directions were confusing and erroneous. He therefore did not seek to support the conviction.

We recapitulate our conclusions on the law.

There are two distinct crimes of fireraising: wilful fireraising and culpable and reckless fireraising.

The crime of wilful fireraising may be committed in respect of any form of property. Before an accused can be convicted of wilful fireraising in respect of any particular item of property in the charge, the Crown must establish beyond reasonable doubt that he intended to set fire to that item of property. Where the jury are not so satisfied in respect of any of several items averred in the charge, they should delete it. The jury may infer the necessary intention from all the relevant circumstances, but there is no room for any doctrine of transferred intent. Nor can any form of recklessness be treated as equivalent to intent.

The crime of culpable and reckless fireraising can also be committed in respect of any form of property. In that respect it is similar to wilful fireraising. The difference from wilful fireraising lies in the *mens rea*. Mere negligence is not enough: the property must have been set on fire due to an act of the accused displaying a reckless disregard as to what the result of his act would be.

Contrary to what has sometimes been suggested, the distinction between the crimes remains important since the degree of blameworthiness will be relevant to penalty. A charge of wilful fireraising does not contain an implied alternative charge of culpable and reckless fireraising. So, where the only charge is one of wilful fireraising, the judge may not direct the jury that they can return a verdict of culpable and reckless fireraising. Nor may this court substitute a verdict of culpable and reckless fireraising in an appeal against a conviction of wilful fireraising.

On the other hand it is open to the Crown to aver wilful fireraising and, in the alternative, culpable and reckless fireraising. On an indictment so framed, it will, of course, be open to the jury either to convict of wilful fireraising or to convict of culpable and reckless fireraising. We note that the alternatives were averred in short compass in the minor premise in the indictments in *Macbean* and *H.M. Advocate v. Smillie* (1883) 5 Coup. 521. In neither case do the trial judges seem to have had undue difficulty in charging the jury. Of course, there may be cases in which an accused deliberately sets fire to paper, rubbish or discarded property of no value, but the fire spreads and burns down premises and their contents. In such cases, the lighting of the paper or rubbish may really only be the source of the fire which constitutes the substance of the charge. In such cases, care may be required in framing the indictment to avoid the unwelcome complexity which might arise if the indictment were so framed that, for instance, a jury might have to convict the accused of wilful fireraising in respect of the rubbish but of the alternative of culpable and reckless fireraising in respect of the premises and contents. The Lord Advocate indicated that, in the light of our decision, Crown counsel would reflect on how indictments might be framed in future.

For these reasons, in view of the misdirection which we have identified, we allow the appeal and quash the conviction.

Appeal allowed.

NOTES

**15.16**     1. The decision of the Court in this case brings much needed clarity to the law, and dispenses with the need to consider, and to try to reconcile, the conflicts and confusions in the cases which precede it. The exclusion of transferred intent in fire-raising dispenses with the decision of the High Court in *Blane*. The rejection of extreme recklessness as evidence of intent likewise dispenses with *Carr v. H.M. Advocate*, 1995 S.L.T. 800.

2. For a detailed evaluation of the court's opinion, see J. Chalmers, "From the Ashes", 1999 S.L.T. (News) 1.

3. Gordon regrets (commentary to *Byrne*, 2000 S.C.C.R. 92) that the court did not go the whole way and abolish fire-raising altogether as a separate crime, "and simply leave arsonists to be dealt with for malicious mischief". What reasons are there for retaining the separate offence of fire-raising? (When Parliament reformed this area of the law in England and Wales it too determined that it was appropriate to retain a nominate offence of fire-raising to mark the especial dangers of fire as an instrument for damaging or destroying property. See the Criminal Damage Act 1971. That act does not, however, maintain a distinction between intentional and reckless conduct, but treats these as alternative forms of the same crime.)

4. Given that the court insists that reckless fire-raising is not an alternative verdict that can be brought in on a charge of wilful fire-raising, it is likely that many indictments will contain alternative charges.

5. The decision of the court in *Byrne* is, of course, concerned with the *mens rea* of the offence of fire-raising. The *actus reus* of the two types of fire-raising is the same, and consists in setting fire to corporeal property. An issue which remains unclear in Scots law is whether it is possible to commit fire-raising (of either variety) by means of an omission. See, in this respect, the English case of *Miller* [1983] 2 A.C. 161. The accused in that case fell asleep on a mattress while smoking. He awoke a little while later to find that the mattress was smouldering. Instead of taking steps to put out the fire he went to sleep in another room. The fire spread from the mattress and eventually the building was destroyed by fire. Could such a case be prosecuted as fire-raising? And would it be wilful or reckless?

6. Is it possible to commit fire-raising by setting fire to something other than inanimate property? Would it be fire-raising to set fire, for example, to an animal? In *Wither v. Adie*, 1986 S.L.T. (Sh.Ct) 32 the accused was charged that he set fire to shoelaces worn by another person "to his danger as he was dozing, and the fire took effect thereon and on his trousers to the injury of his leg". It was objected that the offence of fire-raising could not be committed when the object set alight was a person. The sheriff repelled the objection, holding that the charge libelled setting fire to inanimate objects, with the aggravation that a person had thereby been injured.

7. Generally speaking it is not an offence to destroy or damage one's own property. It is, however, an offence to damage or destroy one's own property by fire with intent to defraud insurers. See *Alexander*

*Pollock* (1869) 1 Couper 257; *McTamney* (1867) 5 Irvie 363; *William McCreeadie* (1862) 4 Irvine, 214. *Cf. Sutherland v. H.M. Advocate,* 1994 S.L.T. 634.

## 3. VANDALISM

### Criminal Law (Consolidation) (Scotland) Act 1995

**52.**—(1) Subject to subsection (2) below, any person who, without reasonable excuse, wilfully **15.17** or recklessly destroys or damages any property belonging to another shall be guilty of the offence of vandalism.

(2) It shall not be competent to charge acts which constitute the offence of wilful fire-raising as vandalism under this section.

(3) Any person convicted of the offence of vandalism shall be liable on summary conviction—

    (a) in the district court, to imprisonment for a term not exceeding 60 days, or to a fine not exceeding level 3 on the standard scale, or to both;

    (b) in the sheriff court—

        (i) for a first such offence, to imprisonment for a term not exceeding 3 months or to a fine not exceeding the prescribed sum (within the meaning of section 225(8) of the Criminal Procedure (Scotland) Act 1995), or to both; and

        (ii) for any subsequent such offence, to imprisonment for a term not exceeding 6 months, or to the fine mentioned in sub-paragraph (i) above, or to both.

NOTES

The question which immediately arises is the relationship of this offence to the crime of malicious **15.18** mischief. The statutory offence of vandalism was introduced by section 78 of the Criminal Justice (Scotland) Act 1980. During the debates on the Criminal Justice (Scotland) Bill some members opposed this provision on the grounds that it was a "facade", that it was unnecessary in view of the common law, and that it would have no impact on the prevalence of criminal damage.

Section 78 was, however, defended by supporters of the Government. Mr Peter Fraser had this to say: "In its substance, of course it [the new offence] adds nothing new to the law of Scotland. However, it serves two useful purposes. First, the general public do not understand what the offences are of which people might otherwise be convicted when, for example, a window is broken or a wall sprayed upon. The fact that it now has a modern name which is understandable and acceptable to people seems to me to make up part of the public duty of this House to ensure that people understand what is put forward as an offence. That seems to me to be one acceptable objective.

The second acceptable objective of the clause is to ensure that, when an offender comes up on a future occasion charged with the same offence, on his list of previous convictions the offence appears as vandalism. Although that is a limited objective, I see it as both necessary and desirable." (First Scottish Standing Committee, June 19, 1980, cols. 469 *et seq.*) The view that section 78 merely reproduces the common law in a statutory form was, however, rejected in the following case.

### Black v. Allan
### 1985 S.C.C.R. 11

LORD JUSTICE-GENERAL: "The appellants are James Black, John George Black and Keith **15.19** William McLauchlan who went to trial in the district court on summary complaint upon a charge that on a named date, at the Clydesdale Bank, 28 High Street, Penicuik, Midlothian, without reasonable excuse, they wilfully and recklessly destroyed property, namely, a window belonging to another and did cause one of them to fall against the window and break it. After trial the justice found all three appellants guilty, and this appeal is brought to challenge the conviction. At the outset, let it be said that the Crown interest in this appeal is simply to guard against the risk that any support should be given for the view that the offence created by section 78(1) of the Criminal Justice (Scotland) Act 1980 is simply an echo of the common law crime of malicious mischief. If anyone thought that it was such an echo, then the sooner they disabuse themselves of that notion the better. The statutory offence is an offence standing on its own language and it is committed if the conduct in question resulting in damage to property is wilful or if the conduct in question causing damage to property is reckless.

Having got out of the way the particular problem which concerned the Crown in this case, our task is a relatively easy one because it simply comes down to this. Was the justice in the circumstances of this case entitled to conclude that these three people recklessly destroyed the window of the bank in the proved circumstances. The answer to that question is very simple. The justice was not so entitled, and it seems clear to us that he did not ask himself the right questions and did not address himself to what is necessary in order to attach the label reckless to particular conduct. What is necessary to attach the label reckless to particular conduct is sufficiently demonstrated in the case of *Allan v. Patterson*, 1980 J.C. 57. What the justice did was to look at what the three young men were engaged in and this is what he found. Outside the Clydesdale Bank the appellant Keith McLauchlan jumped on the back of the appellant James Black and was shrugged off and pushed all in one movement so that he went into one of the bank's front windows. Now that is the conduct and it will be observed that it involved only two of the appellants and it is not surprising, therefore, that the Crown conceded that they could not support the conviction of John Black who was not involved in the incident at all. Having made that finding as to the conduct the justice went on to say this: 'The damage was not caused wilfully. However, the window was broken as a direct result of the reckless horseplay of all three appellants acting together, there being always some danger of plate-glass windows being smashed if people push, shove and jump on each other on the pavement'. Now what the justice did not do, as we understand it, was to ask himself if in the circumstances of this case the conduct described ... created an obvious and material risk of damage to the window, and having failed to ask himself that question he was unable to ask himself the important question whether in this case these appellants, or two of them, recklessly destroyed the property by breaking the window. In all the circumstances we find little difficulty in allowing the appeal of each of the appellants, and in doing so we are conscious that we do no injury to the offences under section 78(1) without fear of being confronted with any mistaken view about the purpose of that section."

Convictions quashed.

NOTES

**15.20**   1. Unfortunately, the court did not trouble to explain the difference between vandalism and malicious mischief. One obvious difference, in the light of *H.M Advocate v. Wilson* (*ante*, p. 525) is that vandalism requires proof of physical damage whereas malicious mischief does not (provided that there is proof of "patrimonial loss"). But in the ordinary case of physical damage to property there does not seem to be any obvious reason for characterising the conduct as "vandalism" rather than "malicious mischief" and vice versa. Nor is it easy to distinguish the offences by reference to the mental element. A person who deliberately damages someone else's property could be charged with either offence. The only possible ground of distinction, therefore, relates to the idea of "recklessness". It is clear from this case that something more than mere carelessness is required for a conviction under section 52, and that recklessness of the *Allan v. Patterson* (*ante*, p. 46) variety is required. According to the High Court in *Ward v. Robertson* (*ante*, p. 533) "it is not essential to the offence of malicious mischief that there should be a deliberate wicked intent to injure another in his property ... it is enough if the damage is done by a person who shows a deliberate disregard of, or even indifference to, the property or possessory rights of others". It remains to be seen what, if any, difference there is between such "indifference" to the rights of others and *Allan v. Patterson* recklessness. If there is a difference, then it is submitted that the common law offence should require proof of a greater degree of culpability. It would certainly seem odd if a summary statutory offence which carries a maximum penalty of six months' imprisonment were to require a greater degree of culpability than the common law offence.

2. Since vandalism can only be committed in respect of property belonging to another, it should be a defence to a charge under section 52 that the accused believed that the property was his. A person who destroys property in the belief that it is his own cannot be said to have "wilfully" destroyed property belonging to another. And if his belief has not been reached recklessly, then he cannot be held responsible on that ground either. If this argument is not correct, then it may still be open to the accused to claim that he had a "reasonable excuse" for destroying the property, under section 52(1).

3. Where the defence of reasonable excuse is raised, it is for the prosecutor to prove that the accused did not have such an excuse: *MacDougall v. Ho*, 1985 S.C.C.R. 199. In that case the accused smashed the windscreen of a taxi. His explanation for this was that he was trying to prevent the escape in the vehicle of persons whom, wrongly as it turned out, he suspected of having committed vandalism (or malicious mischief) against his property. It was held that in the circumstances he had a "reasonable excuse" for acting as he did. In *Murray v. O'Brien*, 1994 S.L.T. 1051 the accused was charged with vandalism, by damaging a car headlamp. She claimed that she had a reasonable excuse for doing this, because she was attempting to prevent the driver of the vehicle leaving the locus where, she believed he had stabbed her husband. The justices held that she did not have a reasonable excuse. The High Court held that whether or not there is a reasonable excuse for damaging property is a matter to be determined by the court of first instance, depending upon all the facts and circumstances of the case.

4. In this connection, compare *Ho* with *Clark v. Syme* (*ante*, p. 536). Suppose that the accused in *Ho* had been charged with malicious mischief. Would his explanation have provided him with a defence to the common law charge?

# Chapter 16

## Offences Against Public Order and Decency

### 1. Breach of the Peace

**16.01** The breadth of this offence is notorious and an enormous range of conduct has been held to constitute a breach of the peace, or at least capable in law of amounting to a breach of the peace. Conduct which has been held to amount to a breach of the peace includes:

Playing football in the street at night (*Cameron v. Normand*, 1992 S.C.C.R. 866; *cf.* the old case of *John Meekison and Tutor v. Mackay* (1848) Arkley 503 which concerned playing marbles in the street on a Sunday afternoon); "peeping" into houses at night (*Raffaeli v. Heatly*, 1949 J.C. 101, see *infra*); secretly observing women using a sunbed (*MacDougall v. Dochree*, 1992 S.C.C.R. 531); shouting political slogans in support, *inter alia*, of the IRA outside a football ground (*Duffield v. Skeen*, 1981 S.C.C.R. 66); causing offence by selling National Front newspapers outside a football ground (*Alexander v. Smith*, 1984 S.L.T. 176); distributing pamphlets seeking support for pupil power and sexual freedom to young girls to the annoyance of their parents (*Turner v. Kennedy* (1972) S.C.C.R. Supp. 30); cross-dressing in Perth (*Robert Fraser, The Scotsman*, March 23, 1978 (Perth Sheriff Court)); cross-dressing in red-light area of Aberdeen (*Stewart v. Lockhart*, 1990 S.C.C.R. 390); swearing at the police (*Logan v. Jessop*, 1988 S.C.C.R. 604; *Boyle v. Wilson*, 1988 S.C.C.R. 485; *Stewart v. Jessop*, 1988 S.C.C.R. 492; *McGivern v. Jessop*, 1988 S.C.C.R. 511; *Norris v. McLeod*, 1988 S.C.C.R. 572; *Saltman v. Allan*, 1988 S.C.C.R. 640; *McMillan v. Normand*, 1989 S.C.C.R. 269; *Cavanagh v. Wilson*, 1995 S.C.C.R. 693; but see *Kinnaird v. Higson*, High Court, April 24, 2001, *unreported*); "kerb-crawling" by males seeking the services of prostitutes (*Lauder v. Heatly*, High Court, 1962, *unreported*. See M. Christie, *Breach of the Peace*, Butterworths, 1990, at p. 98); threatening to commit suicide in a public place (*John MacLean, The Scotsman*, October 30, 1979 (Inverness Sheriff Court)); swearing by the police (*Elliot v. Tudhope*, 1987 S.C.C.R. 492); begging in an aggressive manner (*Wyness v. Lockhart,* 1992 S.C.C.R. 809. Begging *per se* is not breach of the peace: *Donaldson v. Vannet*, 1998 S.L.T. 957); sitting on a felled tree as a protest at its destruction and obstructing its being cut up (*Colhoun v. Friel*, 1996 S.C.C.R. 497); loitering in and about a liquor store in a suspicious manner (*McKenzie v. Normand*, 1992 S.C.C.R. 14; *cf. Glancy v. McFadyen*), High Court, June 10, 1999, *unreported*); injecting one's self in a locked toilet cubicle (*Thompson v. MacPhail*, 1989 S.C.C.R. 266); ordering an Orange Order band to play as it passed a Catholic church as the congregation were going in to mass (*McAvoy v. Jessop*, 1989 S.C.C.R. 301); alarming a third party by glue-sniffing in her presence (*Taylor v. Hamilton*, 1984 S.C.C.R. 393. In the earlier case of *Fisher v. Keane*, 1981 J.C. 50 it had been held that glue-sniffing was not, *per se*, a breach of the peace); repeatedly executing handbrake turns and causing a car to skid in a public car park (*Horsburgh v. Russell*, 1994 S.L.T. 942); causing alarm by inviting a young girl to come to up to a flat (*Biggins v. Stott*, 1999 S.L.T. 1037); making threatening telephone calls (*Robertson v. Vannet*, 1999 S.L.T. 1081); driving a motor vehicle in a threatening and inconsiderate manner (*Austin v. Fraser*, 1998 S.L.T. 106); making indecent remarks to women (*Sinclair v. Annan*, 1980 S.L.T. 55. *Cf. Gibson v. Heywood*, 1997 S.L.T. 101 and *Farrell v. Normand*, 1993 S.L.T. 793); persistently making advances to a young woman, watching her at her place of work and offering unwanted gifts (*Elliott v. P.F. (Glasgow)*, High Court, May 12, 1999, *unreported*); repeatedly driving past a group of young women and staring at them (*Faroux v. Brown*, 1997 S.L.T. 988); clandestinely taking pictures of children in a school playground (*H.M. Advocate v. Carson*, 1997 S.L.T. 1119); secretly video-recording a young girl, from the street, as she is undressing prior to going to bed (*Bryce v. Normand*, 1997 S.L.T. 1351); walking purposefully towards a place where trouble might be anticipated, carrying a potential weapon (*Chittick v. Fraser*, 1997 S.L.T. 1300); following a person travelling on a bus and stopping behind the bus when it came to a halt at bus stops (*Lees v. Greer*, 1996 S.L.T. 1096); breaking into a house and prowling around (*H.M. Advocate v. Forbes*, 1994 S.L.T. 861); making racist comments (*Harrier v. P.F. Perth*, High Court, May 12, 1999, *unreported*).

## A. The *actus reus* of breach of the peace

### Raffaelli v. Heatly
1949 J.C. 101

An accused person was convicted on a charge that he conducted himself in a disorderly **16.02** manner, peered in at a lighted window of a dwelling-house in a street about 11.50 p.m., put residents in the street in a state of fear and alarm and committed a breach of the peace. He appealed to the High Court.

Lord Justice-Clerk (Thomson): "Mr Thomson [counsel for the appellant] has argued to us with his usual persuasiveness that there were no sufficient facts found to justify the conclusion reached. Mr Thomson says that the facts as found are no more than that the accused walked down the street and stopped on a public pavement and stared through a chink of some curtains into the room of a dwelling-house in which there was a light and that he did so on two occasions. Mr Thomson says that there was no evidence that anybody was alarmed or disturbed. None of the three women who gave evidence said that they were upset. There was no evidence as to what was going on in the house into which the appellant looked, and Mr Thomson says that there was really no evidence at all that there was anybody alarmed or that anything took place that might be reasonably expected to alarm anybody.

It is usual to charge this offence as a breach of the peace, because it is a species of disorderly conduct; where something is done in breach of public order or decorum which might reasonably be expected to lead to the lieges being alarmed or upset or tempted to make reprisals at their own hand, the circumstances are such as to amount to breach of the peace.

It seems to me in the present case there are sufficient facts to entitle a judge to draw the inference of disorderly conduct in that sense. It was argued that the earlier findings related to an earlier date, but the fact remains that on the very night when the offence took place this Mrs Price was keeping watch and she had been so upset about the matter that she informed the police, but she was afraid to inform her own husband as to the situation in case he would through distaste be tempted into a breach of the peace. All that, taken in conjunction with other facts found, in particular with the fact that the accused returned to this particular window and again looked into this window, seems to me thoroughly to warrant the conclusion which was reached."

Appeal dismissed.

Note

See also *MacDougall v. Dochree*, 1992 S.C.C.R. 531 in which the accused was convicted of breach of **16.03** the peace by watching women using a sunbed by peeping through a hole in a partition separating a toilet cubicle and the solarium where the sunbed was located.

### Young v. Heatly
1959 J.C. 66

A schoolmaster was convicted of breach of the peace. He appealed by stated case. **16.04**

Lord Justice-General (Clyde): "This is a stated case from the Burgh Court of

Edinburgh, arising out of a complaint in which a depute headmaster at a technical school in Edinburgh was charged with four breaches of the peace, or alternatively with four contraventions of a subsection of the Edinburgh Corporation Order, 1933. The charges arose out of four separate interviews which the depute headmaster had in his room at the school, at each of which he and a pupil alone were present, and at each of which he was alleged to have made grossly improper remarks and suggestions to a pupil aged sixteen or seventeen. After hearing the evidence, the police judge found the appellant guilty of each of the four charges subject to certain very minor modifications, and he sentenced him to sixty days' imprisonment . . . .

It is said that to establish breach of the peace the acts in question must take place in public and produce alarm in the minds of the lieges and offence to public decorum. Here it is said that the incidents referred to in the complaint each took place in the master's private room at the school, and on each occasion only the appellant and one youth were present. There is no finding of alarm being created to spectators or to the public, none of whom either saw or heard what took place, nor is there any finding of alarm to the boys themselves. In these circumstances it is said that the facts do not establish a breach of the peace.

Breach of the peace, however is an offence the limits of which have never been sharply defined. It is so largely in each case a question of circumstances and of degree. It is well settled that it can take place in a private house—*Matthews & Rodden v. Linton*, 3 Irv. 570. Moreover, although normally evidence of alarm on the part of third persons is produced in cases of this sort, such evidence is not essential. As Lord McLaren said in the case of *Ferguson v. Carnochan*, 2 White 278 (at p. 282): 'It is enough if the conduct of those who are found brawling and using the offensive language is such as to excite reasonable apprehension that mischief may ensue to the persons who are misconducting themselves, or to others.' In the later case of *Raffaelli v. Heatly*, 1949 J.C. 101, there 'was really no evidence at all that there was anybody alarmed or that anything took place that might be reasonably expected to alarm anybody'—see Lord Justice-Clerk at p. 104. Yet the conviction was sustained. As the Lord Justice-Clerk said, 'It is usual to charge this offence as a breach of the peace, because it is a species of disorderly conduct; where something is done in breach of public order or decorum which might reasonably be expected to lead to the lieges being alarmed or upset or tempted to make reprisals at their own hand, the circumstances are such as to amount to breach of the peace.' Lord Mackay (at p. 105) referred to the argument that it was essential that the witnesses should say that they personally were alarmed or that they were annoyed, and he then observed: 'I do not think the definition allows that. If acts are repeated and are calculated to cause alarm and annoyance and are indecorous, I think that is enough.' It follows therefore that it is not essential for the constitution of this crime that witnesses should be produced who speak to being alarmed or annoyed. At the same time, however, I consider that a very special case requires to be made out by the prosecution if a conviction for breach of the peace is to follow in the absence of such evidence of alarm or annoyance. For then the nature of the conduct giving rise to the offence must be so flagrant as to entitle the Court to draw the necessary inference from the conduct itself.

The present case, in my opinion, does fall within this special category. The disgusting nature of the suggestions made, the fact that they took place within a matter of hours with a series of adolescent boys, and the fact that they were made to pupils by a depute headmaster to whom they would normally have looked for help and guidance—all these facts would in the special circumstances of this case justify the inference which the judge clearly drew, and would entitle him to hold a breach of the peace proved. But such a result could not have followed apart from these special circumstances. In my opinion, therefore, the first question and the second question should be answered in the affirmative. So far as the third question is concerned (namely; Was the sentence harsh and oppressive?) the revolting conduct established in this case appears to me amply to warrant the sentence which the Court thought fit to impose."

Appeal dismissed.

**Donaldson v. Vannet**
1998 S.L.T. 957

The appellant was seen to approach and stop a number of people, almost all of them women, **16.05** in a busy street and ask them for money. There was no physical contact made between the appellant and the people he approached. He was not abusive, but there was evidence that some of them had been alarmed by his conduct. He was convicted of breach of the peace and appealed. The opinion of the court was delivered by Lord Johnston.

OPINION OF THE COURT: "... On the part of the appellant the contention was short and sharp, namely, that on the findings of fact made by the magistrate the essential ingredients of the crime of breach of the peace were not made out. While examples of conduct, capable of being categorised as breach of the peace, were extremely variable, the essential element, to be assessed objectively, was that the conduct complained of must be likely to alarm or cause fear to the lieges. While in this case there was a finding that certain of the persons were placed in a state of alarm, the magistrate, it was submitted, had not directed herself by reference to the essential objective test.

The advocate depute submitted that the findings were sufficient to sustain the conviction, particularly upon the basis that the approaches made were to different people as part of a continuing course of conduct in the street. In particular the absence of physical contact did not preclude the conclusion that the conduct was likely to cause alarm to the lieges—indeed it had actually caused alarm. He relied particularly on *Wyness v. Lockhart*, 1992 S.C.C.R. 808, a case, he submitted, which was almost on all fours with the present one.

The locus classicus of the definition of the crime of breach of the peace is to be found in the opinion of the Lord Justice Clerk in *Raffaelli v. Heatly*, 1949 J.C. p. 104; 1949 S.L.T., p. 285 where his Lordship states: "Where something is done in breach of public order or decorum which might reasonably be expected to lead to the lieges being alarmed or upset or tempted to make reprisals at their own hand the circumstances are such as to amount to breach of the peace."

What that passage essentially states is that in assessing whether conduct is capable of being classified as breach of the peace the court must apply an objective test to determine whether, upon the facts, the conduct was likely to cause alarm or fear. Of course, if such alarm or fear is actually caused, that may be strong evidence that the conduct meets the test but it cannot be conclusive, since the subjective reactions of the alleged victims may vary according to their temperament and are thus merely indicators. In the present case the appellant was begging, but on the findings he did not have physical contact with any of the people whom he approached. The high point of the Crown's case in this respect was the fact that he apparently walked alongside some of the people he was approaching for a distance on the pavement.

Against that background we have come to the conclusion, with some hesitation, that since begging in itself cannot be classified as breach of the peace, each case of this type must depend upon the way in which the begging operation is being conducted. One can envisage many examples where begging, in particular when accompanied by menaces or by menacing conduct, could amount to breach of the peace. In this respect we think the *Wyness* case is distinguishable because there was physical contact with the potential victims. While we recognise in this case that the magistrate has found it proved that some of the persons approached were placed in a state of alarm, we do not consider that the findings are sufficient to show that the objective test has been met. We have a suspicion that there may have been further aspects to the conduct of the appellant which first of all brought him to the attention of the police and later encouraged them to make the arrest but we cannot speculate upon that matter nor draw any inference as to what those aspects were.

For these reasons, and in the particular circumstances of this case, we consider that this appeal succeeds and we shall quash the conviction.

Appeal allowed.

NOTES

**16.06**    1. *Raffaelli v. Heatly* and *Young v. Heatly* confirm that proof of actual alarm or fear is unnecessary to support a charge of breach of the peace, provided that the conduct in question is, objectively speaking, likely to cause alarm or fear. *Donaldson v. Vannet* confirms that the question whether the accused's conduct was capable of producing that effect is an objective one. The fact that actual alarm was caused is not conclusive of the question whether there is a breach of the peace. It might be that in the circumstances of a case the accused's conduct, while actually causing alarm to a third party, was not such as would, objectively speaking, be likely to do so. The victim might have been abnormally sensitive.

2. In this connection the question has arisen as to whether or not it is possible to commit a breach of the peace when the only other persons present are the police. The decision in *Logan v. Jessop*, 1987 S.C.C.R. 604 appeared to suggest that police officers could be regarded so sufficiently "battle-hardened" that in the absence of alarm or annoyance to other persons, shouting and swearing at the police might not constitute a breach of the peace.

In that case two brothers were charged with shouting and swearing and committing a breach of the peace. The shouting and swearing was directed at two police officers, and who appeared to be the only other persons present at the time. The district court justice convicted them. On appeal it was held that the convictions should be quashed. In delivering the opinion of the court, Lord Ross stated:

> "No doubt the appellants used thoroughly offensive language to the police but, having regard to the findings which the justice has made, we are of opinion that he was not entitled to conclude that the uttering of these words in the circumstances might reasonably be expected to cause any person to be alarmed, upset or annoyed. The situation might well have been different if there had been a finding to the effect that these words had been uttered in the presence of other members of the public who might have been expected to react to them in one way or another, but in the absence of any such finding we have come to the conclusion that the findings made by the justice are insufficient to justify a finding of guilty of breach of the peace."

It has since been held that *Logan v. Jessop* is a decision confined to its own particular facts: *Saltman v. Allan*, 1989 S.L.T. 262; 1988 S.C.C.R. 640; *McMillan v. Normand*, 1989 J.C. 95; 1989 S.C.C.R. 269.

There is, therefore, no rule that breach of the peace cannot be committed when only the police are present. In *Saltman v. Allan*, Lord Emslie stated: "It is not the law that if upon the evidence it appears that the only persons present at the immediate scene were police officers, there can be no breach of the peace, nor is it the law that a police officer is not to be regarded as a person liable to be affected by disorderly conduct."

*Logan v. Jessop* has frequently been distinguished (see, for examples, *Saltman v. Allan, supra*, and *Boyle v. Wilson*, 1988 S.C.C.R. 485). It has also been held that it is sufficient to sustain a conviction for breach of the peace if there is a finding to the effect that the police were "concerned" about the accused's conduct or language (*McMillan v. Normand*, 1989 J.C. 95; 1989 S.C.C.R. 269).

However, where the facts are on all fours with *Logan v. Jessop*, and there is no finding that the police were in fact upset or alarmed, or even "concerned" by the accused's conduct, then a conviction for breach of the peace cannot be sustained. In *Cavanagh v. Wilson*, 1995 S.C.C.R. 693, the appellant was convicted of breach of the peace by swearing at the police in her own home. No one else was present in the house at the time, and there was no finding that the police were alarmed, upset or annoyed. Nor was there any finding to the effect that there was reasonable cause to apprehend that the police would be so upset, alarmed or annoyed. On appeal the High Court held that the decision in *Logan v. Jessop* should be followed in this case, and that the conviction should be quashed.

### Sinclair v. Annan
#### 1980 S.L.T. 55

**16.07**   An accused was convicted of breach of the peace in that he conducted himself in a disorderly manner and made indecent remarks to ladies. There was no evidence that either lady was alarmed or annoyed, but that only one of them was embarrassed. The accused appealed.

OPINION OF THE COURT: "This appeal is brought to challenge conviction and the short point taken was that on the findings—in fact the necessary elements were not proved so as to entitle the sheriff to conclude that the offence of breach of the peace had been made out. We do not propose to rehearse the precise nature of the offensive remarks which the sheriff has found were made. Under reference to the law laid down in the case of *Raffaelli v. Heatly*, 1949 S.L.T. 284; 1949 J.C. 101, especially in the opinion of the Lord Justice-Clerk at 1949 J.C. 104, and in the more recent case of *Young v. Heatly*, 1959 S.L.T. 250; 1959 J.C. 66, especially in the opinion of the Lord Justice-General at 1959 J.C. 70, it was argued that since in this case there was no finding that either of the ladies was annoyed or alarmed, the conduct of the appellant had to be examined closely because it had to be of a flagrant nature to entitle the court to draw the necessary inference from the conduct itself. The submission was that it was not enough for the sheriff to proceed upon the basis that Miss Mackay was embarrassed. More was required, and, in short, the circumstances found in fact did not justify the sheriff's conclusion that a breach of the peace had taken place at all. We do not agree. The sheriff addressed himself quite correctly to the case of *Young v. Heatly*. He was very conscious of the points which had been taken on behalf of the appellant today and he reached his conclusion, in our judgment, by applying the law correctly as he understood it. It was open to him in the circumstances disclosed in the findings to reach the conclusion that he did. The remarks in the context in which they were uttered were of a particularly offensive character and there is an express finding of embarrassment on the part of Miss Mackay. In our judgment that was enough, if the sheriff so chose to deal with it, to justify the conclusion that all the necessary ingredients of the offence of breach of the peace had been made out. For these reasons the appeal will be refused and we shall formally answer the only question in the case in the affirmative."

Appeal dismissed.

NOTE

Making indecent remarks to others, who find these remarks upsetting or even embarrassing, has been **16.08** held to constitute a breach of the peace. See, in addition to *Sinclair v. Annan*, *Gibson v. Heywood*, 1997 S.L.T. 101 and *Farrell v. Normand*, 1993 S.L.T. 793.

This type of case is rather different from *Young v. Heatly*, 1959 J.C. 66, *supra*, in which there was no evidence to suggest that the persons to whom the teachers comments were addressed had been upset or embarrassed by what was said.

### Duffield and Crosbie v. Skeen
1981 S.C.C.R. 66

The appellants were charged with committing a breach of the peace by conducting themselves **16.09** in a disorderly manner and shouting "inflammatory" slogans. The appellants stood outside Celtic football ground while people were entering the ground to watch a football game. They were holding copies of a newspaper entitled "Fight Racism. Fight Imperialism", and copies of a magazine entitled "Hands off Ireland". They were also shouting "Support your IRA", "Hands off Ireland", and "Brits out of Ireland". The police told them to stop but they did not do so, but continued to shout various slogans, even when arrested. There was evidence that some members of the crowd supported them. The sheriff found that many members of the crowd, would, however, have found the slogans highly provocative and inflammatory, and convicted them. Their convictions were upheld by the High Court.

OPINION OF THE COURT: When charged on summary complaint both appellants tendered pleas of not guilty to the charge in the following terms: 'On August 9, 1980 in Janefield Street, Glasgow, near Holywell Street, you did conduct yourselves in a disorderly manner, shout inflammatory slogans likely to occasion a breach of the peace and did thereby commit a breach of the peace.' About that charge two things require to be said. In the first place it is not suggested and it cannot be suggested that that is not a perfectly relevant libel of the common law crime or offence of breach of the peace. The second thing to be observed is that the charge is concerned with conduct likely to occasion a breach of the peace and does not libel that a particular disturbance was in the event the result of that conduct. After trial both appellants were convicted and in these stated cases both challenged conviction by inviting us to answer one question in the negative. The question is in these terms: 'On the facts stated, was I entitled to convict the appellant?' There is no need in 1981 to explain again the nature and the ingredients of the offence of breach of the peace in the law of Scotland. The only question for us is whether upon the facts found the sheriff was entitled to hold that the crime libelled had been made out. The answer to that question, on a reading of the facts found, is inevitable and is in the affirmative. Having described the circumstances which, of course, are highly relevant in any consideration of what conduct may or may not be likely to produce a disturbance of the peace, the sheriff tells us that in the described circumstances each of the appellants was shouting in a loud voice three so-called slogans: 'Support your IRA', 'Hands off Ireland', 'Brits out of Ireland'. These then were the slogans, but note what follows.

In finding 10 the sheriff records as a fact that a small section of Celtic supporters are sympathetic with the sentiments of the slogans shouted by the appellants. He then goes on to add that a large section are disgusted with such slogans. To finding 10 one must add the contents of finding 12: "In the circumstances above set forth the slogans shouted by each of the appellants were inflammatory and likely to occasion a breach of the peace." We have not the slightest doubt that it was within the sheriff's power to treat the facts found by him as a sufficient basis for a finding that the charge libelled in the complaint against each appellant had been made out. He was accordingly entitled on these facts to convict and the appeal on the merits is therefore refused in the case of both appellants.

NOTES

**16.10**     1. Sheriff found as "facts" that "A small section of Celtic supporters are sympathetic with the sentiments of the slogans shouted by the appellants. A large section are disgusted with such slogans." How were these facts established? Or were these more in the nature of assumptions by the court? (Establishing that large numbers of the crown would object to what the accused were saying is important, since it is only on that assumption that the court would be justified in holding that their actions were likely to provoke a breach of the peace.)

2. This is an example of breach of the peace being used where the accused's actions in themselves would not necessarily amount to a breach of the peace but are likely to lead to a breach of the peace by those who take exception to the accused's words or actions. Other examples can be found in *Alexander v. Smith*, 1984 S.L.T. 176 and in *Turner v. Kennedy* (1972) S.C.C.R. Supplement 30. In the former the appellant was convicted of breach of the peace by selling a National Front newspaper outside Tynecastle football ground. In that case there was direct evidence that persons entering the football ground were annoyed by the appellant's conduct. In *Turner v. Kennedy* the accused was convicted of breach of the peace by distributing pamphlets seeking support for "pupil power" and sexual freedom to young girls to the annoyance of their parents.

In such cases the arrest and prosecution of the accused constitutes an interference with their right to freedom of expression under article 10(1) of the European Convention on Human Rights. As such, such action must now be justified in terms of article 10(2). This is true even though, as in the cases of *Duffield* and *Alexander* the accused's actions may not be entirely peaceable, and may, indeed, interfere with the lawful activities of others. In *Steel and Others v. United Kingdom*, R.J.D. 1998-VI, the applicants included a number of people who had been involved in demonstrations which took the form of physically impeding the activities of which the applicants disapproved. The United Kingdom argued that such actions were not protected by article 10(1) at all. That view, however, was rejected by the Court. Despite the interference with the actions of others, the actions of the applicants did constitute the expression of opinion within the meaning of article 10(1). Their arrest by the police therefore constituted an interference with their rights under that provision.

In *Handyside v. United Kingdom* (1976) 1 E.H.R.R. 737, the applicant published a book called "The Little Red Schoolbook". The book, which was directed at young people contained, amongst other things, a chapter on sexual matters. The applicant was convicted of publishing an obscene work, contrary to the Obscene Publications Act 1959, and the book's destruction was ordered by the court.

The European Court of Human Rights held that the applicant's prosecution, and the subsequent seizure and destruction of the book all constituted an interference with the applicant's freedom of expression. The Court, however, went on to hold that the United Kingdom was entitled to interfere with the applicant's freedom of expression in order to protect the morals of the young persons at whom the book was mainly directed. While public attitudes may well have become rather more liberal since the decision in *Handyside*, it would probably not be difficult, even today, to justify the action taken in *Turner v. Kennedy* in terms of article 10(2).

Measures of the kind taken in the cases of *Duffield* and *Alexander* may also be justifiable in terms of article 10(2).

The European Court of Human Rights places a substantial premium on freedom of political expression.

> "As the Court has often observed, freedom of expression constitutes an essential foundation of democratic society and one of the basic conditions for its progress and for each individual's self-fulfilment." (See *Steel and Others v. United Kingdom*, *supra*, para. 101.) States do, however, enjoy "a certain margin of appreciation in assessing whether and to what extent any interference with the exercise of freedom of expression is necessary, particularly as regards the choice of reasonable and appropriate means to be used to ensure that, and on freedom of the press."

Recognising this margin of appreciation, the Court has shown itself to be largely unwilling to interfere with decisions of the kind taken in *Duffield* and *Alexander*—that is, where the action taken is to prevent potential breaches of the peace. In *Chorherr v. Austria* (1993) 17 E.H.R.R. 358, the applicant distributed leaflets calling for a referendum on the purchase of a fighter aircraft by the Austrian armed forces at a military ceremony held to mark 30 years of Austrian neutrality and the 40th anniversary of the end of World War II. The police told him to stop as he was causing a commotion in the crowd, some of whom objected to their view of the proceedings being obstructed. He refused to do so, despite further warnings from the police and increasingly loud protests from the crowd. He was eventually arrested for causing a breach of the peace by conduct likely to cause annoyance. Before the European Court of Human Rights, he claimed, *inter alia*, that the action taken against him interfered with his right to freedom of expression. The Court accepted that there had been an interference with the applicant's rights under article 10, but went on to hold that the Austrian authorities had been entitled to take the action that they did, the applicant's arrest having been necessary in order to prevent a breach of the peace.

Where, however, a protestor's actions are entirely peaceful, and where there is no indication of substantial obstruction of the freedom of others to go about their business, or action likely to provoke others to violence, an arrest or charge of breach of the peace will not be "lawful" in terms of article 10(2), and there not justifiable under that provision. See *Steel and Others v. United Kingdom*, *supra*.

## Stewart v. Lockhart
### 1990 S.C.C.R. 390

OPINION OF THE COURT: "The appellant is Joseph Hendry Stewart. He went to trial in the **16.11** district court in Aberdeen on a complaint libelling a charge of breach of the peace. The particular charge was that he had conducted himself in a disorderly manner by dressing in female clothing whereby a breach of peace was likely to be occasioned and that he thereby created a breach of the peace. He was found guilty and against his conviction he has now appealed by means of stated case.

Today counsel on his behalf has drawn attention to the findings in fact which the justice made. The appellant is a male aged 33. On October 15, 1988, at about 10.20 p.m., he was seen by police witnesses to be walking along Virginia Street, Aberdeen, into Mearns Street and thereafter into James Street. It is found in fact that these streets are not residential and form part of the red light district of Aberdeen, being an area known to be frequented by prostitutes. When the appellant saw the police officers he moved away quickly and walked off into another street. The justice has further found that the appellant at the time was dressed in a female trouser suit and high heeled sandals. His hair was permed, he was wearing rouge, eye shadow and lipstick and was carrying a ladies' umbrella and handbag. He was wearing a brassiere padded out with cotton wool. There then follow findings 5 and 6 which are in the following terms: "(5) That the appellant's intention was to appear to be female. (6) That the appellant's conduct was likely to occasion a breach of the peace."

Counsel has maintained that on these findings the justice was not entitled to find the appellant guilty of breach of the peace. She contended that before there could be breach of the peace there would require to have been some flagrant conduct on the part of the appellant. The justice, in his note, makes it plain that he quite recognised that a man might go to a fancy dress party, for example, dressed in women's clothing and in such a situation there would be no question of a breach of the peace being committed. The justice observed that in almost any other place the appellant appearing dressed as a female would cause no concern or annoyance. The justice, however, took the view that the important factor here was the area in which the appellant was when seen by the police. It was an area frequented by female prostitutes and accordingly would be frequented by men seeking the services of female prostitutes. In these circumstances the justice formed the following view: "There was a very real possibility that the appellant would be approached by a man or even by several men looking for the services of a female prostitute who would be annoyed to discover a male in such circumstances and might cause a disturbance." Counsel maintained that there was no finding to the effect that the appellant was loitering or that he was going to any particular place, nor indeed that he knew that it was a red light district where he was. In that context however we regard it as of significance that when the appellant saw the police officers he moved off quickly and walked on into another street.

The test of what constitutes breach of the peace is well recognised. In *Raffaelli v. Heatly,* Lord Justice-Clerk Thomson said at 1949 S.L.T., p. 285:

> "where something is done in breach of public order or decorum which might reasonably be expected to lead to the lieges being alarmed or upset, or tempted to make reprisals at their own hand, the circumstances are such as to amount to breach of the peace". In *Wilson v. Brown* Lord Dunpark said at 1982 S.L.T., p. 362: "It is well settled that a test which may be applied in charges of breach of the peace is whether the proved conduct may reasonably be expected to cause any person to be alarmed, upset or annoyed or to provoke a disturbance of the peace. Positive evidence of actual alarm, upset, annoyance or disturbance created by reprisal is not a prerequisite of conviction."

In the present case counsel has pointed out that there is no finding that anyone else was present at the time, but, in our opinion, the conduct of the appellant clearly falls within the two definitions to which we have referred. The justice formed the view that in the circumstances there was a real possibility that members of the public might cause a disturbance having regard to the way in which the appellant was conducting himself at the material time. In finding 6 the justice states that the appellant's conduct was likely to occasion a breach of the peace. Counsel sought to argue that that finding was wrong, but the finding has not been challenged in this case and there is no question addressed to us asking whether the justice was entitled to make such a finding. Having regard to that finding it appears plain to us that the appellant's conduct was of such a kind that it constituted breach of the peace. It follows that counsel has failed to satisfy us that there is any reason for doubting the soundness of the justice's conclusion that the appellant was guilty of this charge. Accordingly we answer the question in the case in the affirmative and the appeal is refused.

Appeal refused.

NOTES

**16.12** 1. In *Kara v. United Kingdom*, Application No. 36528/97, October 22, 1998, the European Commission on Human Rights found that "constraints imposed on a person's mode of dress" constitute an interference with private life under Art. 8 of the Convention. (The applicant in that case was a male bisexual transvestite.) That being so, the arrest and conviction of the accused in *Stewart v. Lockhart* would appear to have been an interference with his rights under article 10(1), which would require to be justified in terms of Art. 8. Given that the manner in which he was behaving was entirely peaceful and that he did not obstruct anyone else going about their business, it could only be justified on the ground that others were likely to be provoked to violence by what he did. But given that there was no imminent risk of that (or at least no finding to that effect) can the arrest and conviction of the accused be regarded as "necessary" in the circumstances?

2. The decision is based on the supposition that a man, looking for a female prostitute, might, on discovering that the accused in this case was a man, have committed an offence. Suppose that A, who is a lesbian, goes into a bar. She gets into a conversation with a man, B, who invites her to come back to his flat. A declines, explaining that she is a lesbian. B gets very angry and begins to shout at A. Is A guilty of a breach of the peace?

### Biggins v. Stott
### 1999 S.L.T. 1037

The appellant was convicted of a breach of the peace by inviting a 13-year-old girl, on two **16.13** occasions, to come up to his flat. He offered her money. The girl was put in a state of fear as a result of the appellant's approaches to her.

OPINION OF THE COURT: "... Counsel for the appellant submitted that there had not been sufficient evidence to entitle the sheriff to convict the appellant. In particular, the Crown had not proved that a breach of the peace had been committed. At the outset it was important to note that what was alleged to constitute a breach of the peace was what the appellant had said, not any aggressive or abusive conduct on his part. Counsel accepted that there was corroboration of the appellant's initial invitation to the complainer to come up to his flat but submitted that that invitation on its own had not been capable of constituting a breach of the peace. Counsel referred to *Reynolds v. Normand*, 1992 S.C.C.R. 859 and *Donaldson v. Vannet*, 1998 S.C.C.R. 422. On the basis that such an invitation had been made, the fact that the complainer was upset by it could not turn what the appellant had said into a breach of the peace. The gravamen of the Crown case was that the appellant was alleged to have invited the complainer to his flat on two occasions, within a few minutes of each other. However, there was no corroboration of the fact that the second invitation had been made as no one had heard what the appellant had said to the complainer. The evidence that the appellant had been seen speaking to her and that she was distressed afterwards was not capable of providing corroboration of what he had actually said to her. All that the distress showed was that something distressing to her had taken place. There was certainly no corroboration of her evidence that he had offered her money to induce her to go to his flat and such corroboration was essential to the Crown case. In the circumstances the Crown had not proved that the appellant had repeatedly invited the complainer to go to his flat. Even if it was established that the appellant had repeated the invitation to come up to his flat, the two invitations taken together would not have been capable of constituting a breach of the peace. If there had been proof of threats or violent conduct the position might have been different. On the evidence all that the Crown could found upon in this case was the appellant's invitation to the complainer which was made from the window of his flat and was corroborated but that could not, in law, constitute a breach of the peace as it could not reasonably have been expected to cause fear or alarm.

In reply, the advocate depute submitted that, applying the test set out in *Raffaelli v. Heatly* 1949 J.C. 101 (at page 104), the action of the appellant in shouting down to a 13-year-old girl in the street an invitation to come up to his flat was in itself capable of constituting a breach of the peace in that such conduct was likely to lead to the girl being alarmed or upset, and there was evidence that the invitation had, in fact, upset the complainer. The complainer gave evidence of the second invitation which the appellant had made to her in the street and in that connection it was important to note that it had taken place only a few minutes after the first invitation, so that the two invitations taken together could be regarded as one course of conduct. The advocate depute accepted that, if the complainer's evidence about what the appellant had said to her in the street was taken on its own, the evidence of the complainer's distress could not corroborate her account of what the appellant had said to her. But her evidence that, when the appellant spoke to her in the street, he had repeated his invitation to go up to his flat could be sufficiently corroborated by her distress taken along with the evidence that the appellant had extended the same invitation to her a few minutes earlier and that she had been upset by it. There was thus corroborated evidence of the two invitations made a few minutes apart, and these two invitations, taken together, were clearly capable of constituting a breach of the peace. In these circumstances, on the authority of *Yates v. H.M. Advocate,* 1972 S.L.T. (Notes) 42, the complainer's evidence that the appellant had offered her money did not require to be corroborated. The sheriff had been entitled to find the appellant guilty as libelled.

In our opinion the submissions made by the advocate depute were well-founded. It was common ground that there was corroborated evidence of the invitation which the appellant made to the complainer when he shouted down from the window of his flat and she was playing in the street. At that time he invited the complainer, who was 13 years of age, to come up to his flat and there was evidence that she was upset by the unexpected invitation. The complainer also spoke to a second invitation to his flat which the appellant made to her when she was playing further down the street only minutes later. No-one else heard what the appellant said to her on the second occasion but there was supporting evidence that he had been seen speaking to her, after having apparently singled her out, and that when she left the appellant she was in a distressed condition. Counsel for the appellant submitted that there was no corroboration of the second invitation but in our opinion the complainer's evidence that the appellant had again invited her up to his flat a few minutes after the first invitation had been made was corroborated by the evidence that the earlier invitation had been made and her distress after the appellant had spoken to her in the street. The sheriff accepted the evidence of the complainer and the other witnesses led by the Crown and in our opinion the conduct of the appellant in twice, within the space of a few minutes, inviting a 13-year-old girl playing in the street to come up to his nearby flat was conduct which might reasonably be expected to lead to the complainer being alarmed or upset and constituted a breach of the peace. In the circumstances we do not require to deal with the advocate depute's submission that the appellant's first invitation to the complainer, taken on its own, could have constituted a breach of the peace. We are further of the opinion that in the circumstances of this case the complainer's evidence that the appellant, when he spoke to her on the second occasion, offered her money did not require to be corroborated (*Yates v. H.M. Advocate, supra*). On the whole matter we are satisfied that the sheriff was entitled to find the appellant guilty as libelled.

Appeal refused.

NOTES

**16.14**   1. Breach of the peace may thus be used to deal with persons who may be contemplating engaging in unlawful sexual acts without the necessity of waiting until such an act takes place. See also, in this respect, *Farrell v. Normand*, 1993 S.L.T. 793, and *Faroux v. Brown*, 1997 S.L.T. 988.

2. Charges of breach of the peace may also be led where the accused has engaged in more overly sexual behaviour. Thus in *Taylor v. Lees*, High Court, January 22, 1999, *unreported*, the High Court upheld that convictions of two men for breach of the peace by handling and exposing their private parts and buttocks at a window overlooking a primary school playground.

3. In *H.M. Advocate v. Carson*, 1997 S.L.T. 119, it was held that clandestinely taking pictures of children in a school playground could constitute a breach of the peace. In *Bryce v. Normand*, 1997 S.L.T. 1351, it was held that to video-record a young woman while she was undressing for bed, from outside her

home, the recording showing her wearing nothing but her underwear could constitute a breach of the peace. It is interesting to note, in this respect, that there would, apparently be no civil action against the accused in such circumstances. In other words, certain forms of invasion of privacy may be a criminal offence, even though there is no right of privacy, as such, recognised by the civil law.

## B. The *mens rea* of breach of the peace

The mental element required for breach of the peace has only rarely been considered, and at times the offence appears to be almost one of strict liability. The question received attention in the following two cases. **16.15**

### Butcher v. Jessop
1989 S.L.T. 593

The appellant and three other accused were charged with conducting themselves in a disorderly manner and committing a breach of the peace during a match between Glasgow Rangers and Celtic football teams. The charges arose out of incidents during which the Rangers goalkeeper, Woods, struck a Celtic player, McAvennie, with his elbow, grabbed him by the throat and pushed him to the ground. The appellant, who was the Rangers captain, also pushed the Celtic player. The incident provoked a strong reaction from the crowd, and it looked at one point as if there might be an invasion of the pitch. Following conviction by the sheriff, two of the accused, Wood and Butcher appealed to the High Court. The following is an excerpt from the opinion of the Lord Justice-Clerk in Butcher's appeal. **16.16**

THE LORD JUSTICE-CLERK (ROSS): "... Counsel's next submission ... was that football was a game which was played under rules, and was a contact sport where it was inevitable that from time to time players would come into contact with one another. This was recognised by the laws of the game which dealt *inter alia* with fouls and misconduct on the pitch. That being so he submitted that before conduct on the field could constitute a breach of the peace it must be shown that it had gone beyond what one might expect to happen in the environment of a sporting contest. He submitted that if what had occurred on this occasion constituted a breach of the peace, there would be few incidents upon a football pitch which could not be capable of being regarded as a breach of the peace. His submission was that before conduct in a football match could be regarded as breach of the peace, it would have to be extreme conduct which went beyond what one might expect to happen in the context of a football game. He also stressed that the referee was in charge of the match and that it was significant that at the end of the day, although he had sent off Woods and McAvennie, he had merely cautioned the first appellant.

Counsel also submitted that the sheriff had clearly misdirected himself in that he had in reality convicted the first appellant of assault. He also submitted that there had been no material before the sheriff entitling him to infer *mens rea* on the part of the first appellant.

The advocate-depute on the other hand submitted that there was no question of the first appellant having been convicted of assault. He also stressed that so far as *mens rea* was concerned the position in relation to breach of the peace was different from the position in relation to assault. In the case of assault the actings of the accused must have been intended to cause some harm to the victim, and this matter fell to be considered subjectively. On the other hand in the case of breach of the peace no such intent is necessary; there was no need to infer that an accused intended to commit a breach of the peace; it was enough that his actings were such that the court of first instance was entitled to regard them objectively as constituting a breach of the peace.

In my opinion the argument of the advocate-depute on this matter is to be preferred. As already observed it was quite unnecessary for the sheriff to reach the conclusion which he did to the effect that the actings of the first appellant were an assault. It was no part of the Crown's case that the first appellant had been guilty of assault. In my opinion the sheriff displayed a correct approach to this question when he expressed the view that breach of the peace was constituted by the actings of the first appellant detailed in finding in fact 17. In my opinion the law is correctly stated by Sheriff Gordon in his *Criminal Law* (2nd ed.), para. 41–09: "It is clear from the above cases that it is not necessary to show that the accused intended to provoke a disturbance, it is enough that his conduct was such that the court regarded it as objectively calculated to do so."

That the test is an objective one is plain from *Ferguson v. Carnochan* [(1889) 16 R. (J.) 93]. At p. 94 the Lord Justice-Clerk said: "Breach of the peace consists in such acts as will reasonably produce alarm in the minds of the lieges, not necessarily alarm in the sense of personal fear, but alarm lest if what is going on is allowed to continue it will lead to the breaking up of the social peace." I agree with the advocate-depute that the use of the word "reasonably" shows that the test is an objective one. Where breach of the peace is concerned, it has been held that it is no answer to submit that the first accused had a good motive for what he did (*Palazzo v. Copeland*) [1976 J.C. 72, *infra*].

So far as counsel for Butcher's earlier submission is concerned, the advocate-depute stated that he would not disagree with the proposition that for conduct to constitute breach of the peace in circumstances such as arose in the present case, the conduct would have to be outwith the normal scope of the sport. He submitted however that it was truly a question of fact and degree, and that that was a question for the court of first instance to determine.

In my opinion the advocate-depute's approach to this problem is the correct one. Whether or not particular conduct amounts to breach of the peace depends upon the place where and the context in which the conduct took place. In *Raffaeli v. Heatly*, 1949 S.L.T. 284, the Lord Justice-Clerk said (at p. 285): "where something is done in breach of public order or decorum which might reasonably be expected to lead to the lieges being alarmed or upset, or tempted to make reprisals at their own hand, the circumstances are such as to amount to breach of the peace". Applying that test, what the sheriff had to do in the present case was to determine whether the actings complained of were deliberate, and, if so, whether they amounted to breach of the peace as so defined.

In my opinion the conduct of the first appellant as described in finding 17 [Finding (17) was to the effect that "The appellant rushed in shouting, stretched both his arms out in front of him and pushed McAvennie who was then standing about 6 ft from the goalkeeper, violently in the chest with the palms of his extended hands so that he stumbled back. McAvennie brought both his hands up to grasp the appellant's forearms."] was capable of constituting breach of the peace particularly having regard to the fact that he behaved in this way at this particular football match where there was known to be intense rivalry between supporters which included an element of animosity, and where it was known that there was always considerable excitement and tension on the part of the spectators. In finding 24 the sheriff has described the effect which this incident had upon the spectators, and, in my opinion, he was clearly entitled to conclude that what was done by the first appellant might reasonably be expected to lead to spectators being alarmed or upset or resorting to violent behaviour. The sheriff clearly had regard to the fact that this incident took place in the context of a game of football which is a contact sport in which members of opposing teams may come into contact with one another. Bearing that in mind the sheriff took the view that the actings of the first appellant could not be justified or excused as being a normal incident in a game of football. In his so called finding in fact and law the sheriff held (and this must be regarded as a finding in fact): "that these actings were unjustified by the rules of the game, his duties as captain, the heat of the contest in the course of a vigorous contact sport or any other factors."

In these circumstances I am satisfied that on the findings in this case the sheriff was entitled to hold that the conduct of the first appellant constituted a breach of the peace. I am also satisfied that he was entitled to hold that although the first appellant's conduct took place in the context of a football match, there was no justification in the circumstances for what he did. . . .

Appeal refused.

**Hughes v. Crowe**
1993 S.C.C.R. 320

An accused was charged with breach of the peace by playing loud music, and making loud **16.17**
banging noises in his flat between 7.15 a.m. and 8.15 a.m. on a Saturday morning. The
occupants of the flat below were disturbed by the noise to the extent that they eventually
called the police. The accused was convicted. The question of what mental element was
required arose during consideration of the appeal.

THE LORD JUSTICE-GENERAL (HOPE): "... The second point relates to the facts and
circumstances of the case as described in the evidence. Mr Ogg [counsel for the appellant]
developed this argument on one particular issue only, which was whether on the facts found
the justice was entitled to hold that there was a breach of the peace. He did not seek to argue
that the justice was not entitled to hold that the appellant had committed the breach of the
peace, if indeed a breach of the peace was being committed. In developing his argument he
pointed out that there was no finding that the various acts which gave rise to the noises were
calculated to create a nuisance. They were, as he correctly said, noises which emanated from
inside a flat and the acts which created them were not done in public. He then said that the acts
were not so flagrant as to amount to a breach of the peace. There were no findings that the
person who created the noises was aware that there were residents in the flat below, or that
they could hear the noise or that the noises caused them upset, nor was there anything in the
evidence to show that he had been asked to stop making the noise. What the justice should
have done was to ask himself whether, on the facts which he was disposed to accept as proved
in the evidence, these activities were such as might reasonably be expected to cause alarm and
upset to members of the public. *Mens rea* was required, the conduct had to be flagrant, and on
the whole chapter of evidence that necessary standard had not been achieved.

The learned Solicitor-General submitted that it was a proper inference from all the facts
and circumstances that the noise which was the subject of this charge could amount to a
breach of the peace, this being a question of fact for the justice. He pointed to the degree of
noise which is described by witnesses as having been extreme or very loud, to the duration of
the noise which continued for up to sixty minutes, to the time when the noise occurred which
was between 7.15 and 8.15 on a Saturday morning when people might be expected to be still in
their houses, and the location of the noise, which was in a part of an old stable block which had
been divided into at least four flats. It might have been expected that other people would be
affected by noise of that quality, and that was sufficient to amount to a breach of the peace.

In our opinion this was a matter of fact and degree for the justice. We accept Mr Ogg's point
that the actings complained of had to be of a sufficient quality to enable the inference to be
drawn of *mens rea*. That is an inference to be drawn from the nature and quality of the acts
complained of, and in this case it can reasonably be said that the evidence described a course
of conduct persisted in for a substantial period of time which indicated a gross lack of
consideration for others who might be present in the other flats in the block at the time. The
time of day, the nature of the accommodation, the degree of noise and its duration all fall to be
taken together in considering the essential question whether acts of the necessary nature and
quality to establish a breach of the peace had been established. Treating this as a question of
fact and degree primarily for the justice to decide, we cannot say that the decision which he
reached was one which he was not entitled to reach on the evidence."

Appeal refused.

NOTES

1. So what *mens rea* is required for breach of the peace? It is clear that it is not necessary for the **16.18**
prosecutor to show that the accused intended to commit a breach of the peace, or that he was reckless as
to that outcome. Both cases suggest, however, that some degree of knowledge on the part of the accused
of the circumstances which might render his conduct a breach of the peace.

In *Hughes v. Crowe*, the accused must at least have known that he lived in a flat, in close proximity to other flats that might be occupied. That being so, the court could infer that he was guilty of a breach of the peace by engaging in conduct that was likely to annoy his neighbours, if any there were. So far as can be ascertained, the accused took no steps to ensure that his conduct would not adversely affect his neighbours, and overall it looks almost as if negligence as to the affect on others is sufficient.

In *Butcher's* case the circumstances in which the pushing of the opposing player—including the general context of an Old Firm game would have been apparent to the accused.

2. For a detailed consideration of the *mens rea* in breach of the peace see M. Christie, *op. cit.*, pp. 30–34.


## 2. MOBBING

**16.19**    Although this is still thought of in conjunction with the old crime of rioting, the *nomen juris* "mobbing and rioting" is inapplicable today since the abolition of the Riot Act 1714. Modern indictments for the crime still however refer commonly to the accused "forming part of a riotous mob".


### H.M. Advocate v. Robertson and Others
(1842) 1 Broun 152

**16.20**    A number of persons were charged with mobbing. In his charge to the jury the Lord Justice-Clerk (Hope) provided the following definition of a mob:

THE LORD JUSTICE-CLERK (HOPE): "... An illegal mob is any assemblage of people, acting together for a common and illegal purpose, effecting, or attempting to effect their purpose, either by violence, or by demonstration of force or numbers, or by a species of intimidation, impediment, or obstruction, calculated to effect their object.... It is not necessary that the purpose or object of the mob should have been previously concerted, or that they should be brought together and congregated with the view previously formed of effecting the object subsequently attempted. It is enough, that after they have been so assembled and brought together, finding their numbers, and ascertaining a common feeling, they then act in concert, and take up and resolve to effect a common purpose. There must, however, be a common purpose and object, for which they are combined and acting in concert, after they are congregated and operating as such throughout the acts alleged to be acts of mobbing.... Presence in a mob, if such presence is in order to countenance what is done, will be a fact sufficient to establish a party's guilt of all that is done by the mob, of all which arises, as might be anticipated, out of the acts and excesses of a mob, once set in motion, and acting in order to accomplish a particular end."

NOTES

**16.21**    1. The above statement of the law was approved by the High Court in *Hancock and Others v. H.M. Advocate*, 1981 J.C. 74. In that case the Lord Justice-General (Emslie) remarked (at p. 86):

"A mob is essentially a combination of persons, sharing a common criminal purpose, which proceeds to carry out that purpose by violence, or by intimidation by sheer force of numbers. A mob has, therefore, a will and a purpose of its own, and all members of the mob contribute by their presence to the achievement of the mob's purpose, and to the terror of its victims, even where only a few directly engage in the commission of the specific unlawful acts which it is the mob's common purpose to commit. Where there has assembled a mob which proceeds to behave as a mob a question may arise whether all those present when it acts to achieve its common purpose are truly members of the mob or mere spectators. Membership of a mob is not to be inferred from proof of mere presence at the scene of its activities. The inference of membership is, however, legitimate if there is evidence that an individual's presence is a 'countenancing' or contributory presence, *i.e.*, if his presence is for the purpose of countenancing or contributing to the achievement of the mob's unlawful objectives."

2. In *Hancock,* the Crown were strongly criticised by the High Court for "overcharging", *i.e.* overloading an indictment with a number of sub-heads following a general charge of mobbing. The jury convicted every accused of the latter, but acquitted of some of the sub-heads. On appeal, all convictions were quashed since there was no evidence of any antecedent concerted criminal enterprise. The Court's criticisms in this case were directed at the unnecessary use of mobbing charges.

3. While there must be cases where a charge of mobbing is appropriate, this can only rarely be the case. The use of such charges in *Hancock* proved to be both unworkable and, arguably, contrary to the interests of justice, both from the point of view fairness to the accused, and the public interest in ensuring that those who commit offences while acting together are properly convicted when the evidence warrants this result. Reliance upon charges of mobbing may unnecessarily complicate cases which could, in most instances, be dealt with by the application of the ordinary principles of art and part responsibility. The difficulties associated with the use of charges of mobbing, and in particular the problems in allocating individual responsibility for the acts of the mob, were highlighted by Lord Coulsfield in *Coleman and Others v. H.M. Advocate*, 1999 S.L.T. 1261:

"... the rule imposing responsibility for what the mob does derived from supporting presence is easy enough, perhaps, to apply where the purpose of the mob is explicit ... The position is considerably more difficult when the purpose of the mob has to be gathered from its actings, and more difficult still where the purpose is, or may have been, one which evolves or develops as the incident goes on. That is especially so when it is necessary to decide whether a murder has been committed and the murderous quality of the assault has to be derived, not from expressions of intention or other evidence of direct intent to kill, but from actions which display wicked recklessness. Further, I think that it is possible to detect in the authorities some tension between the general statements of what might be called the strong view, on which mere presence is sufficient to infer responsibility for a wide range of actions of the mob, and the weaker view which requires evidence of actual participation. As a result, in my view, it becomes difficult to see what real difference there is between the evidence required to hold a person guilty of murder as a member of a mob acting with gross and wicked recklessness and what is necessary to hold a person guilty on the more normal basis of art and part participation in a concerted attack. It might be added that it is perhaps possible to see that there is justification for extending responsibility beyond the normal limits of the law of concert when the event in question is of the character of the Porteous riot, the Reform Bill agitation, or the public disturbances which arose from the controversies over lay patronage: it is much less easy to see in the case of a gang fight or family feud.

In my view, therefore, far from providing a simple means of dealing with cases of group violence, a charge of mobbing and rioting involves embarking on an area of law which is full of uncertainties and narrow distinctions. The result is that the jury in a case of mobbing and rioting have to be directed very precisely indeed if they are to approach the matter properly. The need for such precision, and the risk that the jury will run into confusion, were clear as a result of the case of *Hancock* and it is, to my mind, somewhat surprising, in view of the disaster which overtook the prosecution in that case, that the Crown should resort to a charge of mobbing and rioting in a case such as the present in which there was no necessity to do so and in which, as the event shows, to do so risked nothing but an increase in confusion and possible prejudice to the outcome of a trial."

3. There is, with respect, much to be said for the view that reliance on the general doctrine of art and part taken in conjunction with any substantive offences will in most cases satisfy the interests of justice, without reliance upon the objectionable doctrine of the common purpose of the mob.

### Sloan v. Macmillan
1922 J.C. 1

Three coal miners, who were on strike from their colliery, were convicted of forming part of a **16.22** riotous mob, which, acting of a common purpose with a view to unlawfully compelling a number of persons who were then working at the colliery to abstain from working, and, in breach of the public peace and to the alarm of the lieges, invading the colliery at 2.30 a.m., demanding that the said workmen abstain from work, threatening them with violence if they did not so abstain, unlawfully compelling them to abstain from working and stopping the carrying on of work at said colliery. They appealed to the High Court.

LORD JUSTICE-CLERK (SCOTT DICKSON): "What they did was to set out from a place some distance from this pit for the purpose of stopping the voluntary workers, who were at the pit to preserve the works so that, when the strike was over, the miners might at once get access to the workings and carry on their employment. It is found as a fact that seventeen people went to this pit for the purpose of ordering the fires to be drawn so that the workings should be drowned out, and of enforcing their orders. That was obviously an illegal purpose, and the suggestion, which is made in article 16 of the stated case, that Alexander Sloan and his associates did no more than use peaceful persuasion to the voluntary workers, is simply nonsense. Sloan went there with several of his associates and, for the purpose of intimidating the workers there, persistently lied—as he now represents in the argument to us—to the police and to some of the voluntary workers by stating that he was backed up by hundreds of desperate men. In point of fact he did intimidate the workers there, and the fear which Sloan and his associates engendered was a perfectly justifiable fear that, if the voluntary workers did not do what they were asked to do, grievous bodily harm would happen to them. By what is now said on his behalf to be his lying representations Sloan succeeded in getting the men in the pithead to cease stoking the fires and to raise the men in the pit up to the pithead. I think it is impossible to hold that there was anything of the nature of peaceful picketing on this occasion, and, if it is the belief that this was peaceful picketing the sooner that belief is dispelled the better. It was not peaceful picketing; it was riotous conduct which is liable to punishment. The result was that five men, three of whom are the appellants, and twelve or thirteen others who were personally present at the pithead, succeeded by threats of what would happen to the voluntary workers, if not by actual violence, in carrying out the illegal purpose which they had set out to achieve; and so terrified the voluntary workers—who are quite entitled to work at this pithead if they pleased—that they gave up their work so that the workings were liable to be destroyed....

The charge is that the appellants formed part of a riotous mob which, acting of common purpose with a view unlawfully to compel certain people who were then working at the colliery to abstain from doing what they were quite entitled to do, carried out their purpose. There is no rule of law apart from the Riot Act and the decision to which Mr Sandeman referred, *Gollan* (1883) 5 Couper 317, which says anything about the number of persons required to constitute a mob. But I think the law is that the number of people required to constitute a mob depends on what these people do, the violence they show, the threats they use. In this case the three appellants through their spokesman, Sloan, lied persistently to the police and to the workmen in order to produce terror on the part of the workmen, and did produce terror by saying that there were hundreds of desperate men outside. That seems to me to be enough to make the appellants constitute part of a riotous mob, when one considers the threats, their character, the time when they were uttered, and the result they produced, for they succeeded, by these illegal threats, in frightening the men who were working to do what the mob desired. That to my mind was quite sufficient to justify the Sheriff in coming to the conclusion in fact that there was here a riotous mob assembled for the illegal purpose of compelling the voluntary workers to abstain from doing the work they were doing."

LORD SALVESEN: "It is not necessary that any actual violence shall be used in order that a mob may be deemed riotous; it is sufficient if the mob assembles for the purpose of intimidating people in the lawful performance of their duties. If no resistance is made to the intimidation, perhaps violence will never be used. But the very object of intimidation, if it is to be effective, is to induce the belief in the minds of those intimidated that, unless they submit, worse things will happen and the thing will be done forcibly.

Accordingly I see no ground in law—and our province is limited to reviewing the Sheriff upon points of law—for holding that this conviction was otherwise than perfectly justified by the facts which the Sheriff has found proved.

I express no opinion as to whether a riotous mob may not consist of no more than five persons."

Appeal dismissed.

NOTE

Lord Salvesen's doubt as to how many persons constitute a "mob" has never been resolved. **16.23**

## 3. PUBLIC INDECENCY

Public indecency is generally prosecuted as shameless indecency, which in this context may take two **16.24** forms. Following the case of *Watt v. Annan*, *infra*, charges of shameless indecency were used to control access to indecent material such as films, books and magazines, and to control indecent displays (such as sexually explicit public performances). Charges of shameless indecency are also used in the context of indecent exposure.

## A. Indecent material and indecent displays

**Watt v. Annan**
1978 S.L.T. 198

An accused was charged on summary complaint with shamelessly indecent conduct in that he **16.25** showed an obscene film to a number of persons in a hotel. The complaint also narrated that the film: "was liable to create depraved, inordinate and lustful desires in those watching said film and to corrupt the morals of the lieges". An objection to the relevancy of the complaint on the grounds that it did not disclose a crime at Scots law was repelled and the accused went to trial. The evidence disclosed that the film had been shown to members of a private club and that the showing had taken place in private in the lounge bar of the hotel, the door of which had been locked by the accused to keep out the public and non-subscribing members of the club. The accused was convicted and appealed by stated case.

LORD CAMERON: "The statement that 'all shamelessly indecent conduct is criminal' makes its first appearance in the first edition of Macdonald's Criminal Law and is repeated in all subsequent editions without comment or criticism in any decided case. It was approved by Lord Clyde in *McLaughlan v. Boyd*, 1933 S.L.T. at p. 631 when he declared it to be sound and correctly expressing the law of Scotland. It is true that this observation was obiter but it was concurred in by the other members of the court and has not been since subjected to criticism or doubt. It is clear however that, as the Crown maintained, it is not the indecency of the conduct itself which makes it criminal but it is the quality of 'shamelessness', and the question is what is the content of this qualification? It was accepted, and rightly so, in the submission for the Crown that the conduct to be criminal, in such circumstances as the facts in the present case disclose, must be directed towards some person or persons with an intention or knowledge that it should corrupt or be calculated or liable to corrupt or deprave those towards whom the indecent or obscene conduct was directed. Whether or not conduct which is admittedly indecent or obscene is to be held criminal will depend on proof of the necessary *mens rea* and upon the facts and circumstances of the particular case. It would be impracticable as well as undesirable to attempt to define precisely the limits and ambit of this particular offence, far less to decide that the nature of the premises or place in which the conduct charged has occurred should alone be decisive in transforming conduct which would otherwise be proper subject of prosecution into conduct which may do no more than offend the canons of personal propriety or standards of contemporary morals. If it were considered desirable or necessary that this was a chapter of the criminal law in which precise boundaries or limits were to be set then it might be thought that the task is one which is more appropriate for the hand of the legislator.

In the present case there is no dispute that the film displayed amply deserved the description of indecent or obscene or that its display was calculated or liable to corrupt or deprave the morals of those who viewed it, whether they were consenters or otherwise. The question is then narrowed to this, whether the circumstances of the display as found by the sheriff in this case were such as to render the conduct of the appellant shamelessly indecent. It was strongly urged for the appellant that the circumstances here lack that necessary element of publicity or affront to public morals which is essential to commission of the offence. The argument derived its force from the citation of opinions in the context of obscene publication cases ranging from *Robinson* (1843) 1 Broun 590 to the more recent decisions already cited in *McGowan v. Langmuir*, 1931 J.C. 10 and *Galletly v. Laird*, 1953 J.C. 16. These decisions however and the judgments pronounced in them must be considered in light of their own facts. In particular, they arose out of admitted publication in respect that the books or prints were offered for sale to members of the public and were on public display. Nothing which is said in them therefore casts directly or by implication any doubt on the soundness of that broad general statement of the law founded upon by the Crown which has stood unchallenged for over a century. Neither the publicity nor the privacy of the locus of the conduct charged necessarily affects far less determines the criminal quality of indecent conduct libelled as shameless. That this is so can be readily inferred from the context in which this statement of the law appears, particularly in Macdonald's first edition and in those subsequent editions which were revised by the Lord Justice-Clerk himself. In my opinion therefore it is not essential to relevancy of a charge of shamelessly indecent conduct that it must be libelled that the conduct in question occurred in a public place or was a matter of public exhibition. The case of *Mackenzie v. Whyte* ((1864) 4 Irv. 570) makes it clear that the offence of indecent exposure, an offence against public morals, 'consists of a person exposing himself in a state of nudity in a public place or where he can be seen by a multitude of persons' (see per Lord Justice-Clerk at p. 577). It is therefore no more essential than an offence of shamelessly indecent conduct, within which category indecent exposure falls, should be libelled as having been committed in a public place than it is in a charge of lewd and libidinous practices, which is an offence whether committed in domestic privacy and secrecy or in a place of public resort (see *McLaughlan v. Boyd*).

The criminal character of the act of indecency must therefore depend on proof of the necessary criminal intent as well as proof of the nature of the conduct itself and of the circumstances in which it takes place. Conduct that may be legitimate and innocent in the laboratory of the anthropologist may well be shamelessly indecent if carried on or exhibited in other places or circumstances, and whether these can be characterised as private or public may be no matter. In any event, it may well be asked what should be the criterion of 'publicity' as opposed to 'privacy' which is to determine the critical issue of deciding that conduct which might otherwise be regarded only as in conflict with accepted morals becomes in breach of the criminal law. To this question the submissions for the appellant provide no answer and the obscene publication cases are no guide. In these circumstances and for these reasons I am of opinion that the appellant's attack on the relevancy of this complaint fails and the first question should be answered in the affirmative. The answer to the second question posed in the case is to be found in the facts found by the sheriff. Prior notice of the display of this film had been given not only by members of the club but by others, presumably not members of the club. Membership of the club was based upon no special qualification nor subject to a period of application or probation. Membership was enjoyed on a weekly basis and on payment of a modest weekly subscription. Prima facie any person could apply for and, so far as the rules disclose, in fact receive the privilege of membership on tendering to an appropriate official at any time or place the modest sum of 10p for which he could enjoy the privileges of the club for a period of three weeks without further payment. It is significant that while the club has a treasurer it has, again so far as the rules disclose, neither secretary nor time or place of meeting, nor any regular mechanism for intimation of meetings. Further, as appears from finding, the door of the room in which the club meeting was held was only locked by the chairman after the display of the film of the club outing and before the showing of the film in question. It is found by the sheriff that the locking of the door was to keep out the public during the showing of the film libelled and also to keep 'non-subscribing members' out; that is, those in arrears with their subscriptions. There is nothing therefore in this finding to negative the idea that any person could be enrolled there and then as a subscribing member of the club on payment of 10p and thus enjoy the benefit of viewing this admittedly obscene film.

In light of these undisputed facts it appears to me idle to maintain that this was a performance in circumstances which were inconsistent with affront to public decency or morals. Even if it were to be argued that a mere domestic and gratuitous entertainment of family and friends by a display of such a film would not attract penal consequences the facts found in the present case bear no resemblance to any such situation. So far as the findings-in-fact disclose there was little, if any, control over indiscriminate access in premises to which the public had a right of entry to an exhibition, the character of which it is not in dispute, was accurately described in the complaint and in the sheriff's finding-in-fact. The appellant's conduct was intentionally directed towards whoever could avail himself of the opportunity to be present and it was conduct which the sheriff, in my opinion, was entitled to find was calculated or liable to deprave or to corrupt in light of the admitted nature of the film. Having regard to these findings, to the whole circumstances in which the film came to be exhibited, the audience to which it was displayed and the admitted purpose for which the audience had been gathered together, I am of opinion that the sheriff was entitled to reach the conclusion at which he arrived and that the second question should also be answered in the affirmative."

Appeal dismissed.

## NOTES

1. For a general discussion of the development of shameless indecency, see: G. H. Gordon, **16.26** "Shameless Indecency and Obscenity" 25 J.L.S. 262, S. L. Stuart, "The Case of the Shameless Company" (1981) 26 J.L.S. 176, 222; G. Maher, "The Enforcement of Morals Continued", 1978 S.L.T. (News) 28; I. D. Willock "Shameless Indecency—How far has the Crown Office Reached?" (1981) 52 SCOLAG Bul. 199; Christopher Gane, *Sexual Offences*, Butterworths, 1992, Chapter 8.

2. The success for the Crown in *Watt v. Annan* provoked a spate of prosecutions for shamelessly indecent conduct in connection with the sale and supply of allegedly obscene literature. This form of the offence consists in selling or exposing for sale material which is "indecent and obscene" and which is "likely to deprave and corrupt the morals of the lieges". In *Robertson v. Smith*, 1979 S.L.T. (Notes) 51, it was held that the offence could be committed in respect of articles which were not exposed for sale, but which were kept to hand to replace articles which were sold. In *Tudhope v. Somerville*, 1981 J.C. 58, however, it was held that a wholesaler who "warehoused" obscene articles did not commit an offence, since his premises were not premises to which the public resorted so that there was no affront to public decency and no conduct which in itself was designed or calculated to corrupt the morals of the lieges.

3. It was at one time general practice for complaints of shameless indecency of this sort to libel that the articles in question were not only likely to deprave and corrupt the morals of the lieges, but that they were likely to "create in their minds inordinate and lustful desires" (and for an erudite examination of these terms see *Tudhope v. Barlow*, 1981 S.L.T. (Sh.Ct) 94). In *Ingram v. Macari*, 1981 S.C.C.R. 184, however, it was held that a complaint which charged the accused with selling an "indecent and obscene magazine" without the further explanation relating to its potential effects was relevant. According to the court, the omission of these additional words was irrelevant because the words "indecent or

obscene" were to be understood as meaning that the publication in question was liable to deprave and corrupt those to whom it was sold or exposed. It follows from this view that where articles were found to be indecent and obscene "in normal parlance", it was not open to the accused to lead evidence designed to show that the material had no tendency to deprave or corrupt: *Ingram v. Macari*, 1982 S.C.C.R. 372.

4. Material which is merely offensive, vulgar or in bad taste does not satisfy the requirement of being liable to deprave or corrupt. In *Lockhart v. Stephen*, 1987 S.C.C.R. 642 (Sh.Ct) the accused was charged with conducting himself in a shamelessly indecent manner by hiring performers to give a series of indecent performances in premises of which he was the licensee. The performances (by both men and women) included strip-tease acts, representations of sexual acts and physical contact between naked performers and members of the audience. Sheriff Stewart declined to convict:

> "I have come to the conclusion that the activities carried out in the carious performances were not liable to deprave and corrupt any person who was likely to see them. Vulgar and in bad taste they almost certainly were. Many people have been disgusted by them. They may well also have been such as to cause offence to certain persons, for example feminists, who resent the exploitation of the female body. But the causing of offence or disgust and being vulgar or in bad taste are not the same as being liable to deprave or corrupt. If it were, then it might well be that many of today's newspaper editors, television producers and advertisers would be guilty of the offence of shameless and indecent conduct."

5. It is probably the case that material which does no more than stimulate a "normal" sexual response in adults would not be regarded as being liable to deprave and corrupt. In *Lockhart v. Stephen, ante,* Sheriff Stewart held that for material or a performance to satisfy that test, "There must, for example, be something to encourage perverted or violent conduct". The sheriff also noted that sexual attitudes and tastes change, and that conduct which some years ago might have been regarded as "perverted" might today be considered acceptable. He did suggest, however, that "current public opinion would still take the view that any sexual activity involving children would be perverted."

6. It is necessary for a conviction for the Crown to show that the accused was aware of the obscene nature of the articles in question. And it is also necessary to show that the accused's conduct was directed at some member of the public with the intention of corrupting them, or at least in the knowledge that the material was calculated to corrupt. Where a shopkeeper attempted to restrict access to materials to adults, this could be taken as evidence of the accused's awareness of the obscene character of the material: *Robertson v. Smith, ante.*

7. The development of this area of the law was slowed, although not halted, by the decision of the High Court in *Dean v. John Menzies (Holdings) Ltd*, 1981 J.C. 23, *ante*, Chap. 3. Prior to this decision it was not clear whether or not a limited company could conduct itself in a shamelessly indecent manner. The significance of this was that many of the shameless indecency cases involved sales from outlets owned and managed by large companies. Once it was held that the company could not be found guilty of this offence there was a clear inequity in prosecuting the shop manager who sold or exposed indecent and obscene articles when the company whose policy it was to stock and sell such material was immune from prosecution.

8. The most recent decisions of the High Court concerning shameless indecency suggest an ambivalence about this offence on the part of the courts. On the one hand, there is unease about the developments which took place during the 1980's, and a reluctance to allow the offence to be extended beyond its existing parameters. See, for example, *H.M. Advocate v. Roose*, 1999 S.C.C.R. 259 (*ante*, Chap. 9) and the following case. On the other hand, there remains a willingness to allow development of the offence within existing categories—as in the case of *Usai v. Russell*, 2000 S.C.C.R. 57, discussed *infra*, pp. 579–580.

### Paterson v. Lees
#### 1999 S.C.C.R. 231

**16.27** The appellant was charged with conducting himself in a shamelessly indecent manner towards an 11-year-old boy and a 9-year-old girl by showing them a film of an obscene nature which depicted acts of human sexual intercourse. At the close of the Crown case the complaint was amended to one of allowing the children to watch the film, rather than showing it to them. The sheriff convicted the appellant on the amended charge. On appeal to the High Court:

THE LORD JUSTICE-GENERAL (LORD RODGER OF EARLSFERRY): "The evidence upon which the Crown relied, both in the court below and in this court, was fairly circumscribed. It showed that the appellant had been left in charge of his neighbours' children, including the two complainers, in their house, while the neighbours went out for a drink. The male complainer and his younger brother wanted to watch a video and the appellant told them that there were videos in a bag behind the sofa. There was nothing in the evidence to suggest that the videos belonged to the appellant. The male complainer selected one and put it into the video recorder. The video in question contained a variety of material, a considerable amount of it obscene, including pictures of human sexual intercourse. The appellant was present when the tape was put into the recorder and while it was playing. The two complainers watched the video, including the scenes of intercourse, in the presence of the appellant. The female complainer did not want to watch the video because it was "dirty".

The evidence was sufficient to entitle the Sheriff to hold that the Crown had proved the averment that the appellant "did permit [the complainers] to see a film of an obscene and indecent nature which depicted acts of human sexual intercourse". The argument for the appellant, both in this court and in the court below, was, however, that proof of these facts was not relevant to establish guilt of the crime libelled, shameless and indecent conduct.

In rejecting the submission of no case to answer, the Sheriff took the view that the Crown amendment made no difference and that it did not matter that, instead of putting the video into the recorder himself and showing it to the children, the appellant had simply allowed the children to watch the video. The Sheriff emphasised the fact that, even though the appellant could see the nature of the film, he did not turn it off. He said that what the appellant did could be described as

> "passive action by allowing the tape to continue playing knowing that it contained sexual explicit material. I was entitled to conclude that, by not turning the video off in these circumstances, the appellant was then intending that the children watch it."

The Sheriff accordingly rejected the defence submission and in due course convicted the appellant of the libel as amended.

I have no doubt that, in a similar situation, an adult who deliberately showed a video tape containing a film of an obscene and indecent nature, with scenes of human sexual intercourse, to children of nine and eleven would commit an offence at common law. Indeed the Crown originally set out to prove that the appellant had done just that, but on the evidence they failed. The present question therefore arises only because of the Crown's failure to prove the actual case which they brought against the appellant. Doubtless, developments in our law often occur as a result of such accidents, but none the less in these circumstances the court should look with considerable care at any novel interpretation which the Crown proffer to support the conviction.

We are, of course, concerned only with questions of criminal law. The fact that the appellant sat back and allowed the children to watch an obscene and indecent film is deplorable and no right-thinking adult would have done what he did. Saying that does not, however, answer the question before the court since we have to consider, not whether the appellant behaved anti-socially or immorally, but whether he behaved criminally.

The Crown averred that the appellant conducted himself in a shameless and indecent manner towards the complainers. In *McLaughlan v. Boyd*, 1934 J.C. 19, at p. 23, Lord Justice-General Clyde affirmed the general proposition that "All shamelessly indecent conduct is criminal" (Macdonald's *Criminal Law* (5th ed.), 150). This court accepted that proposition as a sound statement of the law in *Watt v. Annan*, 1978 J.C. 84, 88–89 when Lord Cameron explained that conduct is criminal not because it is indecent, but because it is "*shamelessly* indecent". In some of the cases, however, the term "shamelessly" has been glossed in ways which take it beyond its normal meaning and hence beyond the meaning which, one might suppose, Macdonald would have intended it to bear when he framed his proposition in 1866. As a result, the crime which the adverb is meant to define has become amorphous, with any limits being hard to discern. For present purposes, this makes it all the more important to identify those aspects of the crime which are common to the examples identified by this court. One such aspect is that the accused has done a positive act—whether exhibiting a pornographic film to an audience of adult males or engaging in some form of sexual activity. Here, by contrast, the Sheriff was faced with a situation where, on the evidence upon which the Crown relied in support of this charge, the appellant actually did nothing at all: at most he failed to switch the film off and so permitted the children to watch it. So, by convicting the appellant of shamelessly indecent behaviour in these circumstances, the Sheriff went further than judges in previous cases.

The Sheriff held that the appellant could properly be said to have conducted himself in a shameless and indecent manner towards the children merely by reason of his passive behaviour of sitting back and permitting the children to see the film. If the only point at issue were the interpretation of the word "conduct", the Sheriff's, conclusion would appear to me to be, at best, doubtful. But, of course, the real question is one of substance. The Sheriff took what may, in his view, have been one small step for him, but it was one giant leap for the law. By holding that it was criminal for the appellant to do nothing and so to permit the children to view the film, the Sheriff was in effect affirming that our criminal law imposes upon a person in the appellant's position a positive duty to prevent children from seeing obscene and indecent material. Even on the assumption that the appellant was *in loco parentis,* the advocate-depute could cite no authority for the existence of such a duty in Scottish criminal law. This is hardly surprising since, for very good reasons, it is only in a limited range of situations that the common law regards a failure to act, even on the part of a parent, as criminal. See the discussion in Gordon's *Criminal Law* (2nd ed.), especially paragraph 3–34.

The potentially far-reaching implications of the common law duty for which the Crown contend in this case are obvious, especially in a world where more and more television channels reach into people's homes and where there is widespread access to the internet. If, in the light of these developments, the criminal law is to impose on parents and others new duties to prevent children from seeing indecent or obscene material and to decree the appropriate punishments for failures to observe those duties, the formulation of those duties and the determination of those punishments are tasks for Parliament rather than for the courts.

For these reasons I am satisfied that the charge in its amended form was irrelevant and that, on the facts proved, the appellant was not guilty of any crime known to the common law of Scotland. I therefore move your Lordships to answer Question 1 in the negative and to allow the appeal.

LORD SUTHERLAND: "... Counsel for the appellant raised two issues. In the first place he submitted that there was insufficient material before the sheriff to entitle him to come to the conclusion that this was shamelessly indecent conduct. Secondly he submitted that in any event the worst that could be said about the appellant's conduct was that it was an omission and while an omission may be criminal in certain circumstances it cannot be criminal in circumstances such as the present. The fact that the appellant might have a moral duty towards the children does not mean that by failing in that duty he is committing a criminal act.

In *Watt v. Annan*, 1978 J.C. 84, where the charge was one of exhibiting a film of an indecent or obscene nature which was liable to corrupt the morals of the lieges, it was said that it is not the indecency of the conduct itself which makes it criminal but it is the quality of shamelessness. The view of the court was that in such circumstances as the facts of that case the conduct in order to be criminal must be directed towards some person or persons with an intention or knowledge that it should corrupt or be calculated or liable to corrupt or deprave those towards whom the indecent or obscene conduct was directed. It was also said that it would be impracticable as well as undesirable to attempt to define precisely the limits and ambit of this particular offence.

It is in my view impossible to produce a definition of shamelessly indecent conduct which encompasses all forms of such conduct. Indeed one of the criticisms of the whole concept of shameless indecency is that it is an amorphous offence which can gradually extend its boundaries and thus become an offence which can only be defined by reference to what the court may class at any time as being shameless. The advocate depute for his part accepted that in all cases of shameless indecency the *Watt* test falls to be applied and accepted that it would accordingly be necessary for the Crown to prove that the conduct was liable to deprave or corrupt. Whether particular conduct falls into that category will depend on the facts of each case but factors of importance are the age of the persons liable to be corrupted, and in the case of children, whether or not the accused is in some position of trust (see *H.M. Advocate v. Batty,* 1995 S.C.C.R. 525). For my part I am not convinced that in all cases it is necessary that there should be the element of liability to deprave or corrupt. There may be cases where the conduct is of such a nature as to offend against any reasonable standard of public decency or morals and can thus be described as shamelessly indecent. For example, if two people stripped naked in full view in a public park and commenced having sexual intercourse the necessary criteria would appear to be present for shameless indecency, although perhaps it would be more appropriate to categorise such conduct as being included in the equally amorphous offence of breach of the peace. However, in cases such as the present involving the demonstration of pornographic material to young children I have no doubt that the advocate depute is correct in saying that the *Watt* test has to be applied. What also has to be borne in mind, however, is that shamelessly indecent conduct is an offence at common law and thus involves the element of *mens rea.* There must accordingly be shown an intention to commit the offence which in turn involves an intention to show the material either intending to corrupt or deprave or at least in the knowledge that the material is of such a nature that it is liable to corrupt or deprave. In my view, therefore, if the book, magazine, video film or other material is of an indecent and obscene nature and that material is deliberately shown to a young child or children the inference can readily be drawn that the person showing the material is guilty of the offence of shameless indecency in that he must have known that the showing of such material would be liable to corrupt or deprave the child, and it is difficult to see what other intention he might have had.

The present case, however, is complicated by the fact that while the original charge alleged that the appellant showed this video to the children, the amended version reduced the charge to being one of permitting the children to watch the video. There is no doubt in the present case that the appellant took no part in the selection of the video and, indeed, as it was not his house, he may well not have known what the video contained before it was inserted into the machine. It is, of course, quite clear from the findings in fact that the appellant would soon become aware that indecent material was being shown on this video and equally it is clear that he took no steps to stop the children watching this material by switching the video off. The question then becomes whether his passivity constituted the criminal offence of shamelessly indecent conduct. In my opinion the circumstances of the present case do not disclose conduct of such a nature. It may be that any adult person would have a moral duty to shield young children from material of this nature, although it should be pointed out that the activities shown on this video were apparently of what might be described as normal sexual activity as opposed to any particularly degrading form of sexual activity. The fact that someone may fail in a moral duty, however, does not automatically mean that his conduct can be categorised as criminal. I do not find in the evidence in this case anything which would indicate that the appellant intended that the children should be corrupted or depraved or, indeed, that he took any active steps at all. The high water mark of the Crown case is that the appellant, in the knowledge that the video was of an indecent nature, took no steps to stop the children from viewing it. In my view, despite the amorphous nature of a charge of this kind, limits have to be drawn somewhere and I consider that this case falls outwith the acceptable limits. For these reasons I would allow this appeal.

LORD COULSFIELD: "The decisions in *McLaughlin v. Boyd,* 1934 J.C. 19 and *Watt v. Annan,* 1978 J.C. 84, established that the proposition "all shameless indecent conduct is criminal", found in *Macdonald's Criminal Law* (5th ed.) 150, is a correct general statement of a rule of law. The proposition occurs in a section headed "Indecent Practices" which begins by setting out firstly that it is a crime wilfully and indecently to expose the male private parts in view of women in public places and secondly that lewd, indecent and libidinous practices towards children, tending to corrupt the morals of the young, are criminal, although there be no assault. Macdonald gives wilful and indecent exposure of the private parts before young children as an instance of this offence and continues,

> "The essence of indecent exposure is, in the case of children, that it is calculated to corrupt their morals; and, in the case of adults, that it is an offence against public decency".

Macdonald then instances indecent handling of children as another example of a similar offence and he, or the editor of the 1948 edition of his works, goes on to deal with exposure to and practices upon females both at common law and under the Criminal Law Amendment Act 1922. He then deals with the statutory offence of gross indecency between males, also under the 1885 Act, and proceeds,

> "All shamelessly indecent conduct is criminal. A charge of 'indecent exposure' without further specification is not relevant; but the form of charge authorised by the Act (the Summary Jurisdiction Act 1908) will generally be sufficient. The question whether the acts done constitute the offence depends on two elements—the impropriety itself and its effect on the person to whom the exposure is made."

In the absence of other authority, I might have been inclined to the view that Macdonald was concerned only with a limited crime, namely indecent exposure or lewd and libidinous practices involving indecent handling of children. In its context, the sentence on which so much attention has been fixed might have meant no more than that it was not necessary to define what forms of indecent exposure or indecent conduct in the presence of other persons was criminal. The word "shameless" in its context would appear appropriate in relation to public conduct causing offence.

However, the decisions in *McLaughlin v. Boyd* and *Watt v. Annan* have taken Macdonald's proposition as a free-standing definition of a crime. The nature of that crime was explained in *Watt v. Annan*, which was a case of an obscene film shown behind locked doors in private to a selected and consenting audience. In his opinion at page 88, Lord Cameron noted the statement from Macdonald and its approval by the court *in McLaughlin v. Boyd*, although he appreciated that the observations in that case were *obiter*. He went on to say,

> "It is clear however that, as the Crown maintained, it is not the indecency of the conduct itself which makes it criminal but it is the quality of 'shamelessness', and the question is what is the content of this qualification? It was accepted, and rightly so, in the submission for the Crown that the conduct to be criminal, in such circumstances as the facts in the present case disclose, must be directed towards some person or persons with an intention or knowledge that it should corrupt or be calculated to liable to corrupt or deprave those towards whom the indecent or obscene conduct was directed. Whether or not conduct which is admittedly indecent or obscene is to be held criminal will depend on proof of the necessary *mens rea* and upon the facts and circumstances of the particular case. It would be impracticable as well as undesirable to attempt to define precisely and limits and ambit

of this particular offence, far less to decide that the nature of the premises or place in which the conduct charged has occurred should alone be decisive in transforming conduct which would otherwise be a proper subject of prosecution into conduct which may do no more than offend the canons of personal propriety or standards of contemporary morals. If it were considered desirable or necessary that this was a chapter of the criminal law in which precise boundaries or limits were to be set then the task is one which is more appropriate for the hand of the legislator."

It is of course true that it is very difficult to define what sort of conduct is indecent or obscene, a matter which in any event may be affected by social changes. What is difficult to follow in *Watt v. Annan* is how the addition of the qualification that the conduct must be shameless, in the broader sense which the court apparently gave it, advances the matter at all. On that ground, forceful criticisms have been expressed of the development of the crime of shameless indecency, both as unwarranted by previous authority and as lacking proper determination. Those are criticisms with which I have a great deal of sympathy. The correctness of the decision in *Watt v. Annan* is not a matter with which this court could deal, but I think that the fact that there is doubt about the definition of the crime can legitimately be borne in mind when considering the particular problem which arises in this case. In many contexts, I would be inclined to regard a distinction between doing something and allowing it to happen as a somewhat thin one, particularly in a context in which the responsibility of an adult for the welfare of children was in issue. However, in the case of this particular crime it seems to me that a limit to its amorphous extension must be placed somewhere. I note also that Lord Cameron in *Watt v. Annan* did stress the importance of *mens rea* and emphasised the Crown's acceptance that there must be conduct directed towards some person or persons. That being so, it seems to me that, once it had been decided that the appellant had not taken any positive step to show the indecent film to the children, there was no relevant charge left. I therefore agree that the appeal should be allowed.

Appeal allowed.

## B. Indecent exposure

A very common form of shamelessly indecent conduct is "indecent exposure". In *Lees, Petitioner*, 1999 **16.28** S.L.T. 405, the High Court confirmed that to expose one's self publicly, in a shameless and indecent manner is not a separate offence in its own right, but a form of shameless indecency. There is a difference between this kind of indecency and "*Watt v. Annan*" shameless indecency in that it does not require proof of an intention to deprave or corrupt. (*Cf.* the observations of Lord Sutherland, *supra*.)

## C. The *mens rea* of shameless indecency

Where shameless indecency is of the *Watt v. Annan* type it requires proof of an intention on the part of **16.29** the accused to deprave and corrupt those to whom the material is exposed or made available, or at least knowledge on the part of the accused that the material is of a kind liable to deprave and corrupt. Where shameless indecency takes the form of public indecency—such as indecent exposure—it does not require such an intention, but it does require knowledge of the accused of the circumstances which make his or her conduct shamelessly indecent.

In *Usai v. Russell*, 2000 S.C.C.R. 57 the accused was charged with conducting himself in a shamelessly indecent manner by exposing himself towards various people. The accused was inside his own home at the time, standing naked at or near his living room window, where he was seen to handle his penis. It was argued that he could not be guilty of the offence unless he was directing his conduct at other persons, and that this was not possible in this case since, owing to weak eyesight he would not have been able to see any of the persons who observed his conduct. The sheriff convicted. On appeal the High Court upheld the conviction. In doing so Lord McCluskey, delivering the opinion of the court, stated:

"We are satisfied that proof of actual knowledge that some other person is in fact witnessing the indecent exposure is not an essential ingredient in a charge of this kind. If it were, a person who donned a blindfold and put thick wax into his ears would be able to claim that he was in fact ignorant as to whether or not there were any to witness his sexual displays on to the street from his illuminated windows. In our view, the *mens rea* necessary for committing the crime of shameless indecency can be properly inferred in circumstances where the accused person was in fact observed behaving as the appellant did behave, where the likelihood was that there would be persons who would observe what was being done and that the appellant was recklessly indifferent as to whether or not he was observed. In the present case, on the facts found, the appellant must, at least, have chosen to stand in a clearly visible place at the window without his contact lenses, and thus unable to see more than a few yards, and paraded his nakedness and played with his genitals in close proximity to places and houses from which he could readily be observed and at times when there were likely to be persons in such places and houses. In the circumstances, we consider that there was ample material to warrant the conclusion which the sheriff drew from the facts."

It appears to have been conceded by the solicitor-advocate for the appellant that recklessness was a sufficient *mens rea* for *all* forms of shameless indecency. This, however, is not supported by the authorities.

# Chapter 17

# OFFENCES AGAINST THE ADMINISTRATION OF JUSTICE

There exists in Scottish criminal law a range of offences directed towards protecting the course of **17.01** justice. Offences of this kind are encountered at all stages of the criminal process, from the point at which an investigation is begun by the police into what may—or may not—be a crime, to the point at which an offender undergoes the punishment imposed by the court. It is, thus, an offence to set in motion a police investigation by deliberately giving false information to the police, to pervert or attempt to pervert the course of justice once police inquiries have begun, to give false evidence in judicial proceedings, or to induce another to do so and it is an offence to escape from lawful custody once a sentence has been imposed. In addition to these offences (all of which are based on the common law) the courts enjoy a comprehensive power to punish for contempt of court those who by their conduct manifest disrespect for the court and its proceedings, or who put at risk the right of an accused person to a fair trial. The offences which are discussed below are set out in broadly this chronological order. Contempt of court, which is not a crime as such, is discussed at the end of this chapter.

## 1. WASTING POLICE TIME BY GIVING FALSE INFORMATION

### Kerr v. Hill
1936 J.C. 71

LORD JUSTICE-GENERAL (NORMAND): "In this case the appellant appeals against conviction **17.02** and against sentence. He was charged in the Sheriff Court at Paisley with falsely representing to the police that he had seen a pedal cyclist struck by a motor omnibus belonging to Young's Bus Services, as a result of which the pedal cyclist was thrown on to the pavement. The results of this representation to the police are set forth in the charge. It is said that he caused the officers of the Renfrewshire Constabulary, maintained at the public expense for the public benefit, to devote their time and service to the investigation of the false story told by him, and did temporarily deprive the lieges of the services of the officers, and rendered the lieges, and particularly drivers of motor omnibuses belonging to Young's Bus Services, liable to suspicion and accusations of driving recklessly.

The appeal is by way of a bill of suspension and liberation, and the ground of the appeal against conviction is that the charge is funditus null, because it discloses nothing that is a crime according to the law of Scotland. It was admitted, and rightly admitted, by counsel that it is a crime to give information falsely of a crime against a named individual; but it was contended that, unless some individual is named, no crime is committed. It was further maintained that, unless information given to the police was not merely, as in this case, that somebody was knocked over by a motor omnibus, but also that the motor omnibus driver was guilty of criminal negligence or the like in driving the omnibus at the time, the giving of that information, although it was false, was not criminal.

I do not agree with the contentions put forward on behalf of the appellant. The story which the appellant told to the police was an invented story, it was told to the police with the intention that they should commence criminal investigations, and it had in fact that result. In my opinion, the giving to the police of information known to be false, for the purpose of causing them to institute an investigation with a view to criminal proceedings, is in itself a crime.

Great injury and damage may be caused to the public interest which is mainly to be regarded, by a false accusation, although no individual is named or pointed at by the informer. A charge which is perfectly general, and leaves the public at large open to suspicion, does nevertheless constitute a crime if it is falsely made. That the appellant when he gave the information to the police did not actually charge a particular crime, but left open the possibility that the knocking over of the pedal cyclist might have been the result of an innocent accident, is also, in my opinion, immaterial. The point is that the criminal authorities were deliberately set in motion by a malicious person by means of an invented story. That is the essence of the crime, and, when these essentials are present, I think that a crime is committed. Accordingly, I am of the opinion that the appeal against conviction fails."

Appeal dismissed.

NOTE

**17.03** *Kerr v. Hill* was the first case of its type and is now used as the standard authority for this type of charge. While it is clearly not in the public interest that the time of the police should be wasted in this way, there is also a danger in holding it to be a crime to give false information to the police. Members of the public might be discouraged from giving information to the police if they thought that giving information, albeit in good faith, might lead to criminal charges if it turns out that the information is untrue. This point was emphasised by the Lord Justice-General (Cooper) in the case of *Gray v. Morrison*, 1954 J.C. 31. In that case his Lordship made the following observation: "I should be very sorry to think that any deterrent were placed against the public communicating to the police in good faith information which they thought ought to be in the possession of the police, and that any ideas should get abroad that, if the information is not found on investigation to be exactly accurate, the informant is liable to prosecution and possibly imprisonment. It therefore appears to me that ... it would be a wise and proper step in the public interest that there should be inserted in such complaints some such words as 'knowing the same to be false', so as to indicate that the gravamen of the charge is not the giving of incorrect information but the deliberate setting in motion of the police authorities by an invented story."

The ambit of the offence first recognised in *Kerr v. Hill* was discussed in *Bowers v. Tudhope*, 1987 S.C.C.R. 77. The question which was explored in that case is whether or not the offence of wasting police time by giving false information is limited to a false report that a crime has been committed, or whether it is sufficient that a police investigation is set in motion by a false report. The Court in that case, referring both to *Kerr v. Hill* and *Gray v. Morrison*, confirmed that the essence of the offence was, as Lord Cooper stated in the latter case, that the criminal authorities were deliberately set in motion by a malicious person by means of an invented story. In *Bowers v. Tudhope* the charge against the accused was that he had falsely reported to the police that he had lost a giro cheque, thereby causing the officers to waste their time investigating that report, which the accused knew to be false. For a critique of this case see (1987) 32 J.L.S. 354, where it is argued that the decision is based on a misunderstanding of *Kerr v. Hill.*

Cases of this type could quite easily be regarded also as fraud, but this is not an approach which has found favour with the High Court, as the following case indicates.

### Robertson v. Hamilton
1987 S.C.C.R. 477

**17.04** Two accused persons challenged the relevancy of a complaint served on them. Their preliminary pleas were repelled and they appealed to the High Court.

OPINION OF THE COURT: "The appellants were charged on a summary complaint before the sheriff court at Dunfermline. The charge was in the following terms:

'The charge against you is that (a) on January 21, 1986 by a letter written on your behalf by

Catherine-Anne Petrie, solicitor, from her office at 8 Abbey Park Place, Dunfermline, to the Chief Constable, Fife Constabulary, Wemyss Road, Dysart, you both did falsely represent to said Chief Constable that when you were arrested in the Railway Workshops Repair Yard, Kingseat Road, Halbeath a police dog attacked you Norman Shanley Robertson biting you on the head, requiring you to receive treatment of Dunfermline and West Fife Hospital, that said dog then attacked you William George McLennan, biting you on the shoulders, that said dog did not respond to command and that said dog was outwith control; (b) on February 19, 1986 at Dunfermline Police Station, Holyrood Place, Dunfermline you Norman Shanley Robertson did falsely represent to James Hepburn, Inspector and Stanley Lazmirski, Sergeant, both Fife Constabulary, that said dog had on the occasion of your said arrest, bitten you on the neck; (c) you William George McLennan did, date and place last libelled, falsely represent to said James Hepburn and Stanley Lazmirski that said dog had bitten you on the back; and by said false representations you both did cause officers of said Fife Constabulary, maintained at the public expense for the public benefit, to devote their time and service in the investigation of said representations made by you and which you knew to be false and did temporarily deprive the public of the services of said officers and did render David Ewan Ramsay, Constable, Fife Constabulary, the handler of said dog, liable to suspicion and accusation of wilfully or recklessly allowing said dog to bite you and to police disciplinary action for failing to keep his police dog under proper control.'

On the appellants' behalf objection was taken to the relevancy of the complaint on the ground that it did not disclose a crime known to the law of Scotland. After hearing the solicitor for the appellants and procurator fiscal depute, the sheriff on March 31, 1987 repelled the plea taken to the relevancy by the appellants and held that the complaint disclosed a crime being a species of fraud. The appellants were thereafter called upon to plead to the complaint and severally pled not guilty and a diet of trial was fixed for September 16, 1987. Thereafter the present appeal was taken. In seeking to support the appeal, Mr McEachran for the appellants maintained that the complaint to the chief constable was made to the police as being responsible for the dog and was not made to the chief constable as criminal investigative authority. He further submitted that it was not a crime to make a false report where there was no intention to institute investigation with a view to criminal proceedings.

Before the sheriff the contention of the procurator fiscal depute was that the libel of the complaint read fairly amounted to a charge of fraud. Reference was made to Macdonald on the *Criminal Law of Scotland* (5th ed.), at p. 52: 'Fraud involves a false pretence made dishonestly in order to bring about some definite practical result .... Where the practical result is achieved the fraud is complete.' The submission was that the essential practical result here was the taking up of police time. Reference was also made to Macdonald at p. 55, where the author gives as an example of fraud: 'The making of false representations to the police and causing investigation to be made although no individual is accused.'

Although the sheriff reached the conclusion that the complaint relevantly libelled a species of fraud, we are not satisfied that his approach was the correct one. It is significant that in *Kerr v. Hill*, 1936 J.C. 71, the Crown contended that the offence of giving false information to the police with the object of inducing investigation was a type of fraud, but the court made no mention of this submission in delivering their opinions. It follows that the passage in Macdonald at p. 55 quoted above is not in fact justified by the case of *Kerr v. Hill* which is cited in the footnote. In all the circumstances, however, we do not find it necessary to express any concluded opinion on the issue of whether the present complaint discloses a type of fraud.

In our opinion, the complaint is relevant on the authority of *Kerr v. Hill* and subsequent cases. In *Kerr v. Hill*, at p. 75, the Lord Justice-General said: 'In my opinion, the giving to the police of information known to be false, for the purpose of causing them to institute an investigation with a view to criminal proceedings, is in itself a crime.' Subsequently he added: 'The point is that the criminal authorities were deliberately set in motion by a malicious person by means of an invented story. That is the essence of the crime, and when these essentials are present, I think that a crime is committed.'

The matter was stated more widely by Lord Fleming at p. 76: 'The *nomen juris* of a charge is, however, immaterial. I am prepared to hold that, if a person maliciously makes a statement, known to be false, to the police authorities, with the intention and effect of causing them to make inquiries into it, he commits a criminal offence.'

Mr McEachran maintained that the making of a false report was only criminal if there was an intention to institute investigation with a view to criminal proceedings, but it is clear from the opinion of Lord Fleming that his view was that it was sufficient if the intention was to cause the authorities to make enquiries into the matter reported. In the subsequent case of *Gray v. Morrison*, 1954 J.C. 31 at p. 34, the Lord Justice-General indicated that it would be a wise and proper step that there should be inserted in complaints of this kind some such words as: 'knowing the same to be false' so as 'to indicate that the gravamen of the charge is not the giving of incorrect information but the deliberate setting in motion of the police authorities by an invented story.'

It is thus clear that it is sufficient for a charge to be relevant if the allegation is that the false report was made with the intention of causing the police authorities to investigate the matter reported. In *Bowers v. Tudhope*, 1987 S.C.C.R. 77, the view was expressed that the essence of a crime of this kind was causing the police to devote their time to investigating a false representation. That case concerned a false representation to the police by an accused that he had lost a giro cheque. The point was made that the representation had not been that the cheque had been stolen but merely that it had been lost. After referring to the cases of *Kerr v. Hill* and *Gray v. Morrison* the court said this:

'When one has regard to the terms of this charge it appears to us that that is indeed just what this charge libels. It is said that the appellant reported or falsely represented to the police that he had lost a giro cheque and that he caused the officers to devote their time and service in the investigation of that representation made by him which he knew to be false. It appears to us that a charge in these terms falls clearly within the description of the offence which was given in both *Kerr v. Hill* and *Gray v. Morrison*.'

The point was also made in that case that it would be a matter for proof at the trial as to whether the Crown were able to establish all the parts of the libel. With regard to the point taken that the representation had not been that the cheque had been stolen but merely that it had been lost, it was observed that the evidence would show whether steps of an investigative nature had been taken by the police involved.

In our opinion the present complaint is similar to the complaint which was considered in the case of *Bowers v. Tudhope*. The essence of this complaint is that false representations were made in the knowledge that they were false and that these caused police officers to devote their time and service to the investigation of these representations and thus temporarily deprived the public of the services of these officers. Just as the complaint in *Bowers v. Tudhope* was held to be relevant, so the complaint here should also be held to be relevant.

For the sake of completeness, it should be noted that before the sheriff, the procurator fiscal depute maintained that the last four lines of the complaint could be read *pro non scripto* without affecting the issue. Before this court neither Mr McEachran nor the advocate-depute sought to suggest that the last four lines were material from the point of view of determining the relevancy of the complaint.

It follows that the sheriff was well-founded in concluding that the complaint was relevant although not for the reasons which the sheriff stated in support of his conclusion. We shall accordingly affirm the decision of the sheriff and remit the case to him to proceed as accords."

Appeal dismissed.

## 2. PERVERTING OR ATTEMPTING TO PERVERT THE COURSE OF JUSTICE

This is an offence which is capable of covering a wide range of conduct. Amongst the commonest **17.05** examples of this offence are cases in which the accused is alleged to have given false information to police officers investigating an offence in order to avoid detection and prosecution. For examples of cases of this kind see *Dean v. Stewart*, 1980 S.L.T. 85, *H.M. Advocate v. Davies*, 1993 S.L.T. 296, *Russell v. H.M. Advocate*, 1993 S.L.T. 358, *H.M. Advocate v. Keegan*, 1980 S.L.T. 35, *H.M. Advocate v. Davies*, 1993 S.L.T. 296. Charges of this type may also be linked to the crime of wasting police time by giving them false information (see *Elder v. H.M. Advocate*, 1994 S.L.T. 579).

In *Dean v. Stewart*, above, it was held that when "the course of justice" begins depends upon the circumstances, but that at the very least it will have begun once it is established that a crime has been committed and the police have embarked upon the investigation of that crime. In *Watson v. H.M. Advocate*, 1993 S.C.C.R 875, however, it was held that there could be an attempt to defeat the ends of justice by knowingly making a false statement to the police even though the incident under investigation was not libelled to be a crime. Indeed, at the time the accused made the statement to the police it was not clear that an offence had been committed, let alone who might have been the perpetrator.

Another commonly encountered type of charge is that the accused has intimidated, or attempted to intimidate, witnesses likely to be called to give evidence against the accused or another person. For examples of charges of this type see *Kenny v. H.M. Advocate*, 1951 S.L.T. 363, *S. v. H.M. Advocate*, 1989 S.L.T. 469, *Fyfe v. H.M. Advocate*, 1989 S.L.T. 50, *Brown v. H.M. Advocate*, 1991 S.L.T. 272, *Darroch v. H.M. Advocate*, 1979 S.L.T. 33. Conduct on the part of the accused which has the effect of intimidating a witness will not amount to an attempt to defeat the ends of justice unless it is proved that the accused deliberately behaved in a way designed to intimidate the witness and so pervert the course of justice: *Carney v. H.M. Advocate*, 1994 S.L.T. 1208.

While this is generally encountered in relation to criminal proceedings, it is clear that it is also a crime to intimidate witnesses in other types of proceedings: *McGregor v. D.*, 1977 S.L.T. 182 (children's hearings). There is authority for the view that to interfere with potential witnesses in a civil action may be punished as a contempt of court: *Forkes v. Weir*, 1897 S.L.T. 194.

It is apparently also an offence to induce or to attempt to induce a potential witness to falsely fail to identify a suspect: *Dalton v. H.M. Advocate*, 1951 S.L.T. 294. See also, *Scott v. H.M. Advocate*, 1946 J.C. 90

Knowingly to bring false criminal charges against an individual would amount to perverting the course of justice, even if those charges did not result in criminal prosecution. For examples of a charge of this type, see *McFarlane v. Jessop*, 1988 S.L.T. 596 and falsely to accuse another person of a crime is itself an offence. In *Lieper v. McGlennan*, 1995 S.C.C.R. 465, for example, the accused was convicted of accusing her husband of threatening her with a gun. In fact she knew that the gun was a toy, but did not reveal this to the police. As a result of this accusation, the husband was charged on petition, remanded in custody for three weeks, and indicted on a charge of assaulting the appellant by placing a gun at her head and threatening to shoot her. On the day of his trial the indictment was amended to a charge of assault by slapping.

In a number of cases the courts have held it to be a criminal offence for a person to attempt to mislead the police in relation to his own involvement in an offence, or to cover up his involvement in an offence.

### Johnstone v. Lees
#### 1995 S.L.T. 1174

The appellant received a summary complaint charging him with driving while uninsured. In **17.06** returning the reply form in response to this charge the appellant stated that he knew nothing about the offence. Based on this response he was subsequently charged with an attempt to pervert the course of justice by falsely stating that he knew nothing about the offence with intent to induce the prosecutor to discontinue criminal proceedings against him in relation to the original charge and with intent to avoid conviction for that offence. A plea to the relevancy of the charge, on the ground that it did not disclose a crime, was repelled by the sheriff. The appellant appealed to the High Court.

LORD JUSTICE-GENERAL (HOPE): "Charge (2) is concerned of course with the procedure by which a person who is accused on summary complaint may state his plea by letter in reply to the complaint. The terms of the letter are set out in Form 49 in the Act of Adjournal (Consolidation) 1988. It provides the accused person with the alternative either of pleading not guilty or of pleading guilty and sending a written explanation. What charge (2) alleges is that this form was filled in by the appellant in such a way as to amount to a statement by him that he knew nothing about the offence and that he did this with the intention which is set out in the charge. A plea was taken to the effect that charge (2) was not a relevant charge, in that the facts to which it referred did not give rise to an allegation of a crime known to the law of Scotland. When that matter was debated before him, the sheriff reached the view that, while an accused person was entitled to put the Crown to the test by tendering a plea of not guilty, he could not go further than that and intimate, for example, a false alibi. He held that in this case the appellant had gone further than simply stating a plea of not guilty. He accepted the argument for the procurator fiscal depute and found the charge to be competent.

Mr McVicar submitted today that the sheriff had reached the wrong decision on this point and he invited us to allow the appeal. He did not dispute that to attempt to pervert the course of justice was a crime known to the law of Scotland. Indeed he referred us to two examples in the decided cases where facts and circumstances were held to constitute that crime. One of these was *Dalton v. H.M. Advocate* [above], where the allegation was that steps had been taken to destroy evidence. The other was *Waddell v. MacPhail* [above], in which false information had been given to a police officer. In this case, however, according to Mr McVicar's argument, all the appellant had done was to fill in a form to indicate that he wished to plead not guilty. He was in effect doing no more than stating that he was not guilty of this offence. Mr McVicar submitted that it would be going too far to accuse somebody who filled in a form in the way described in this case of an attempt to pervert the course of justice. None of the cases had gone as far as that and there would be a risk of injustice if such facts were held to constitute that offence.

The charge with which we are concerned in this case is certainly unusual and no doubt some latitude must be given to people who complete these forms, no doubt without legal advice, in the use of language which they may adopt. On the other hand, the assertion that somebody who puts information on the form with the intention of dissuading the prosecutor from taking further proceedings against him cannot be held to be guilty of the crime of attempting to pervert the course of justice seems to us to be untenable. It all depends on the intention with which the misleading information was put on the form. This is a matter which has to be determined accordingly to precisely what was said, how it was said and in what circumstances and what implication or meaning the prosecutor was entitled to take from it. For these reasons we consider that it would be premature at this stage to say that what is libelled in this complaint cannot constitute a crime according to the law of Scotland. The facts will no doubt have to be looked at very carefully once the evidence is out. For the present all we can say, however, is that the libel set out in charge (2) appears to us to be capable, when read fully and according to its terms, of amounting to the crime of attempting to pervert the course of justice. As was pointed out in the course of the argument, it all depends what the intention was with which the form was completed and that in the end depends upon the inferences which can properly be drawn in the light of the evidence.

For these reasons we consider that the sheriff was entitled to repel the plea, and we shall refuse this appeal."

Appeal refused.

NOTES

**17.07**    1. How far is one entitled to go in denying one's guilt? The accused in this case was not charged with attempting to mislead the prosecutor, but merely with making a false statement with intent to dissuade the prosecutor from proceeding. How close does this come to making it an offence falsely to deny guilt, without any further elaboration?

2. Persons who commit crimes and then take positive steps to conceal their guilt may be convicted of attempting to defeat the ends of justice. Thus in *Mack v. H.M. Advocate*, 1999 S.L.T. 1163 the appellant was convicted of murdering a woman. The indictment contained a further charge that he had wrapped the deceased's body in black plastic bags, transported it to a field and abandoned it there within a growing crop of barley and so had attempted to defeat the ends of justice.

3. In *Mellors v. Normand*, 1996 S.L.T. 704 it was held that an accused, who refused to cooperate in the execution of warrants authorising the taking of dental impressions and saliva samples from him could be convicted of an attempt to defeat the ends of justice.

4. In *Waddell v. MacPhail*, 1986 S.C.C.R. 593, a conviction at common law for attempting to pervert the course of justice was upheld in a situation where the accused had given a false reply to a police request as to the identity of a driver of a car in terms of section 168 of the Road Traffic Act 1972.

5. Persons who deliberately take steps to avoid giving evidence when required to do so may likewise be convicted of attempting to defeat the ends of justice. See the following case.

### H.M. Advocate v. Mannion
### 1961 J.C. 79

Hugh Kelly Mannion and Frances Egan or Mannion were charged on the following **17.08** indictment:—"That between August 17 and September 7, 1960, both dates inclusive, in the house occupied by you at 22/7 Muirhouse Medway, Edinburgh, or elsewhere in Scotland to the Prosecutor unknown, you did form a criminal purpose to hinder and frustrate the course of justice, in pursuance of which you, knowing that you were required to give evidence for the prosecution in the trial of Samuel McKay, now a prisoner in the Prison of Aberdeen, at a sitting of the High Court of Justiciary, Glasgow, commencing on September 13, 1960, on charges of attempting to open a lockfast place and theft by opening a lockfast place, did leave your said house and go into hiding somewhere to the Prosecutor unknown for the purpose of avoiding giving evidence as aforesaid, and the diet of said trial having been deserted *pro loco et tempore*, and a new diet appointed for trial in said High Court on November 7, 1960, you, again knowing that you were required to give evidence as aforesaid, continued to hide for the purpose aforesaid until said Samuel McKay had been tried in said High Court, all with intent that your evidence would not be available to the prosecution and with intent to hinder and frustrate the course of justice, and you remained in hiding until December 6, 1960, when you were apprehended by officers of police, and you did attempt to defeat the ends of justice." The accused pled to the relevancy of the indictment.

LORD JUSTICE-CLERK (THOMSON): "I have listened very carefully to the ingenious argument which Mr Stewart has presented in support of this motion. Mr Stewart's argument really comes to this, in the end of the day:—That until a man has actually received a citation to come to a criminal court, it is open to him to take any steps he likes to remove himself from the possibility of being called upon to give evidence, and that, while this may be socially reprehensible, it is not criminal. I find myself unable to agree with this proposition, and I do not think that I am doing anything revolutionary in failing to agree with it. It seems to me to be clear that if a man, with the evil intention of defeating the ends of justice, takes steps to prevent evidence being available, that is a crime by the law of Scotland. Evil intention, of course, is of the essence of the matter and must be established. This indictment clearly narrates the evil intention of the accused to avoid being called upon to give evidence, and that is sufficient to make the indictment relevant. Accordingly I refuse the motion."

Objection to relevancy repelled.

NOTE

For a comment on the case of *Mannion*, see Gordon, para. 48–41. Attempting to defeat the ends of **17.09** justice, or perverting its course, can take many forms. For a recent example of this type of charge, see *Mack v. H.M. Advocate*, 1999 S.L.T. 1163.

## 3. PERJURY

**17.10** Perjury is the wilful giving of false evidence in any judicial proceeding. For there to be a conviction on a charge of perjury it must, of course, be proved that the evidence given was false, and that it was given on oath or affirmation (as to which, see *Davidson v. McFadyen*, 1942 S.L.T. 37). It is well established that the evidence given should have been competent and relevant at the earlier trial, either in proof of the libel or in relation to the credibility of the witness. (See Hume, i, 369, Alison, i, 469, *H.M. Advocate v. Smith*, 1934 S.L.T. 485, *Angus v. H.M. Advocate*, 1934 S.L.T. 501, *Graham v. H.M. Advocate*, 1969 S.L.T. 166, *Aitchison v. Simon*, 1975 S.L.T. 73.) The issue of the "materiality" of the evidence is, however, a matter upon which, until recently, there was less agreement. The following case, however, makes it clear that the materiality of the evidence is not something which need concern the jury in a trial for perjury.

### Lord Advocate's Reference (No. 1 of 1985)
1987 S.L.T. 187

**17.11** An accused person was acquitted of perjury. The Lord Advocate subsequently referred two questions to the High Court under the provisions of s.263A of the Criminal Procedure (Scotland) Act 1975, namely (1) whether, in a trial for perjury where the accused was not an accused in the previous trial, it is of any relevance that a statement made by him and falsely denied under oath was allegedly obtained by means described as unfair; and (2) whether in a trial for perjury the "materiality" of the false evidence to the issue in the earlier trial is (a) a prerequisite to conviction and in any event (b) a matter of fact to be left to the jury.

In answer to the first question, the High Court held that the law relating to the admissibility of evidence of alleged confessions by an accused person had no part to play in the matter of admissibility of evidence in a perjury trial that a statement, denied on oath, was in fact made. In answer to the second question, the High Court had this to say:

LORD JUSTICE-GENERAL (EMSLIE): "The background to this question is that in his charge to the jury the learned trial judge, in explaining the essential ingredients of the crime of perjury, said this: 'Thirdly, the falsehood must be material and relevant to the issue in the proceedings in which the statement was made—that is, to the original trial. A false statement which is unimportant and trivial and has no bearing on the result of the proceedings in which it is made will not found a charge of perjury. Whether a false statement is material and relevant to the issue in the proceedings in which it is made is a question of fact to be decided by you with reference to the circumstances of the case, but it is well settled that facts affecting the credibility of a witness in the original trial may found a charge of perjury.'

It is common ground that the learned trial judge was in error in that passage in asking the jury to decide on the relevance of the false testimony at the earlier trial, for that is a question of law. The question for us is whether false testimony which was not only competent and relevant in proof of the substantial facts at the trial (*i.e.* whether the crime libelled was committed and if so whether the accused are identified as the perpetrators) must also, in order to amount to perjury, have had a 'material' bearing on the result of the trial, and if so, whether 'materiality' in that sense is a question of fact for the jury at the trial for perjury. If 'materiality' in that sense is a proper issue for a jury in a perjury trial as an ingredient of the crime itself those who prosecute at the trial in which the alleged false testimony was given may increasingly become involved as witnesses at the perjury trial, and in a wide ranging investigation of issues at the earlier trial, which must inevitably provide the jury with less than a complete picture of all that was there involved. The problem for decision by the jury at the perjury trial, if 'materiality' is their province, will almost certainly have to be resolved upon incomplete information and there will clearly be logical difficulties when the evidence is directed solely to the credibility of a witness who may in the end give no useful evidence against the accused.

As the debate to which we listened demonstrated it has undoubtedly been said or written on several occasions that, in order to constitute perjury, the evidence which is challenged as false must have been 'material' to the matters in issue at the trial and the question comes to be whether there is any warrant in binding authority or principle for the view that the word 'material' ought to mean something different from 'relevant', and involve decisions upon a question of fact. For our assistance the literature of the law from Hume onwards was examined by counsel on both sides of the bar, and my own consideration of it persuades me that until 1935 at least there is no support in the authorities for the proposition that 'material' means anything other than 'relevant' or 'pertinent'.

I begin with the third edition of Hume, i, 368–369 which, it was suggested, might be understood to provide a foundation for the proposition that the false testimony must, in order to constitute perjury, have had a bearing on the outcome of the particular trial, and that it is for the jury at the perjury trial to decide if it did have such a bearing. In this passage Hume writes: 'The falsehood must be *wilfully* affirmed; by one who knows the truth, and out of malice, or for some corrupt and sinister purpose, resolves to conceal it.' He then goes on to say this: 'It is another consequence of the same principle, that the oath, in that part of it which is challenged as false, must be pertinent to the point at issue. It must relate to some of those substantial facts, which may have an influence in the decision of the interest that is at stake, in the proceeding where the oath is made. As for minute or insignificant particulars, such as could not be supposed to draw the attention of the person swearing, or to affect the opinion of those who had to judge of his oath; any error in these shall not be deemed malicious, but rather be excused on the ground of inadvertency, or want of recollection. Certainly, however, it is not meant to be said, that a charge of perjury may not lie against a witness who is false in initialibus, equally as against one who is so in causa. It is material to the issue, if he swear falsely that he has not been bribed or instructed, or that he is nowise related to the party who cites him, and if he is in consequence received as a good witness in his behalf.' In spite of the side note which says 'Oath must be material to the matter at issue', I construe this passage to mean no more than that the oath which is challenged as false must be pertinent, *i.e.* relevant, to the point at issue in the sense that it relates to some of the substantial facts which may have an influence in the decision (or to the credibility of the witness). The sentence which begins 'As for minute or insignificant particulars' is, in my opinion, to be understood as referable to the jury's right to decide whether the falsehood was wilful and corrupt, or as an illustration of circumstances in which a prosecution for perjury would not be instituted by the Lord Advocate. The soundness of this construction of the foregoing passage in Hume appears to me to be amply confirmed by reference to Burnett, *Criminal Law*, p. 206 where, having discussed circumstances in which a charge of perjury may lie, the author says this: 'It may be different, however, with respect to an oath regarding a fact not pertinent or relevant to the issue. In such case, the oath being irregular and incompetent, ought not, any more than an oath *coram non judice*, to be the ground of a prosecution for perjury. This seemed to be the ground why the trial did not proceed against *McCurley* (November 27, 1777), who was accused of perjury, by swearing falsely that he had not given a different account of the matter in his declaration, when precognised. Such a question was irregular and incompetent.' Alison, in his *Criminal Law of Scotland*, at p. 469 in Vol. 1, puts the matter beyond doubt in these words: 'The falsehood must be in a matter pertinent to the issue, and competent to be asked of the witness; but if this be the case, it matters not in how trivial a matter the falsehood may consist, or how far from the original relevant matter the witness may have been led before he makes the false affirmation.' Macdonald in the third edition of the *Criminal Law of Scotland* (1894) at p. 216 is equally clear: 'Sixth, the statements must be material; being statements of fact either pertinent to the matter in issue, or pertinent to the question of the party's own qualification to make the oath, or credibility in making it.' Although there was a change of language in the fifth edition where it is stated that the alleged false testimony 'must be competent evidence and also be material', it is perfectly clear from the passage read as a whole that the word 'material' is there being used a synonym for 'pertinent' or 'relevant'.

For the moment I shall leave for later consideration the remaining textbook writer, Dr Gordon, and look briefly at the reported cases which it was thought might be of assistance in finding the correct answer to question 2 in this reference. The first is *Brown v. H.M.*

*Advocate* in which the court repelled an objection to the relevancy of a libel of perjury based upon the proposition that the falsehoods alleged to have been sworn (at the particular trial) were 'not material to the issues of that trial'. This case provides a very clear indication that the true meaning of 'material' as it has been used in discussions of the crime of perjury, involves the issue of relevancy or pertinency and nothing more. An even clearer indication is to be found in *Strathern v. Burns* where the issue was as to the relevancy of the libel. The Lord Justice-General (Clyde) at p. 94 said this: 'It is quite true that the pertinence or relevancy of the false testimony is necessary to a conviction; but the only matter of fact on which the pertinence or relevancy of the false testimony turns is that it was given in evidence in the course of proceedings in a cause which is sufficiently described in the complaint. Once that fact is established, all that remains is a question of law, *viz.*, whether the false statements made were pertinent and relevant to the issue presented by the cause in question.' The origin of the heresy, if I may so call it, that there is a separate issue of 'materiality' for decision by the jury may be found, I think, in an observation of Lord Morison in *Angus v. H.M. Advocate*, at p. 6, to the following effect: 'The law relating to perjury is, I think, this—that, if any person wilfully gives false evidence on oath in any judicial proceeding, he is liable to be indicted for perjury, and, if the jury who try the case are of opinion that the false evidence is material to an issue in the trial, they are entitled to convict.'

It will be observed that he had earlier in his opinion used the word 'material' in the sense of 'relevant', and I am bound to say that his concluding observation is neither founded upon authority nor principle.

So much for judicial pronouncements. All that I need now do is to consider two sentences in the work of Dr Gordon which, I suspect, may provide the explanation for the learned judge's direction to the jury in the trial of "A".

In the first edition of his *Criminal Law* Dr Gordon declares at p. 995, under the heading 'Materiality': 'A false statement which is unimportant and trivial, and has no bearing on the result of the process in which it is made, does not constitute perjury.' In the relevant footnote the author cites: 'Hume, i, 369, Macdonald, 165; but see Alison, i, 469.' With respect to Dr Gordon there is no warrant in these sources when they are properly understood, for the proposition in the terms in which I have just recorded it, and there is no authority whatever for the second sentence which reads as follows: 'Materiality is a question of fact to be decided by reference to the circumstances of each case.' As the footnote shows the author does not rely for this assertion on Lord Morison. The footnote merely says: '*Cf. Strathern v. Burns*, 1921 J.C. 92' which, as has been shown, lends no support for the assertion at all. Events since the publication of the first edition of Dr Gordon's work do nothing to take the matter further. As it happens the Lord Justice-Clerk (Grant) in charging a jury in the trial of *Wilson, Latta and Rooney* for subornation of perjury on February 14, 1968, had the first edition of Dr Gordon's work before him. He directed them that if they were 'of opinion that the false evidence given at the earlier trial was material to an issue at that trial' they would be entitled to convict. Although the particular direction does not wholly echo Dr Gordon's assertions on the matter, it is reasonable to suppose that the Lord Justice-Clerk left 'materiality' to the jury under their influence. Be that as it may, the only alteration in the second edition of Dr Gordon's work under the heading of 'Materiality' is that in the footnote to the second sentence, Lord Grant's charge in the case of *Wilson, Latta and Rooney* is also cited.

Upon the whole matter, so far as question 2 is concerned, I am in no doubt that it should be answered as follows: Question (2)(a) should be answered in the affirmative insofar only as 'materiality' is understood to mean 'relevancy'. Question 2(b) should, in my opinion, be answered in the negative. I have only to add that in light of all that has been said in my review of the law of perjury since the time of Hume it would be well if the word 'material' ceased to be employed in describing the crime. All that is required is that it should be clearly understood that a charge of perjury will not lie unless the evidence alleged to be false was both competent and relevant at the earlier trial, either in proof of the libel or in relation to the credibility of the witness."

NOTES

1. This case is also reported at 1986 S.C.C.R. 329. In his commentary on that report Sheriff Gordon **17.12** sets out the passage on "materiality" from the opinion of the appeal court in the appeal against his conviction by "A" on other charges of perjury in the same case. In that passage the Lord Justice-Clerk (with whom Lords Hunter and Robertson concurred) expressed satisfaction with the trial judges' directions on the question of materiality, which was apparently the same on all the charges, whether followed by conviction or by the acquittal which led to this Reference.

2. Where an accused person has given evidence at his own trial, and it subsequently appears that he has given false evidence at that trial, is there any objection to his being tried for perjury? Can it be argued, for example, that to do so is tantamount to retrying him for the offence of which he was acquitted at the earlier trial? This issue was raised in the following case.

### H.M. Advocate v. Cairns
1967 J.C. 37

The accused was charged with perjury in that when giving evidence at his own trial for the **17.13** murder in Barlinnie Prison of a man Malcolmson of which he was acquitted he gave evidence that he did not assault and stab Malcolmson, the truth being as he well knew that he did assault and stab him.

He pled to the relevancy of the indictment on the grounds that it was incompetent, irrelevant and contrary to natural justice and criminal practice in Scotland. His arguments were heard by a bench of three judges in the High Court.

LORD JUSTICE-CLERK (GRANT): "The plea in bar of trial and the objections to competency and relevancy are three different facets of what is basically the same point. The question raised in each case is whether, if an accused person is acquitted at his trial, having given evidence on oath denying the crime charged, the Crown is entitled thereafter to charge him with perjury in respect of that evidence. In seeking to persuade us to answer that question in the negative Mr Bennett based his argument on the maxim that no man can be made to thole an assize twice for the same matter (Hume, Vol. ii, pp. 465–467) and on considerations of practice and natural Justice.

As Hume points out (at p. 466), the prosecutor cannot evade the maxim by altering the shape of the former charge and laying the second libel 'for the same facts, under a new denomination of the crime,' *e.g.* by charging fraud instead of forgery. On the other hand, for the maxim to apply, the previous trial 'must have been for the same crime, depending upon the same evidence, and not for what is truly another crime.' [Macdonald on the Criminal Law of Scotland (5th ed.) p. 272]. Thus it is well settled that a person who has been tried and acquitted, or tried and convicted, on a charge of assault may subsequently be tried on a charge of murder if, after the first trial, the victim dies (*Cobb or Fairweather*, 1 Swin. 354; *Stewart*, 5 Irv. 310). That is so notwithstanding the fact that the Crown will seek to establish at the second trial the assault which was the sole de quo at the first. The supervening event changes the character of the offence and the second charge is one which could not possibly have been made at the earlier trial.

In the present case the Crown are, in my opinion, in an even stronger position than in the cases to which I have just referred. The perjury charged in the present indictment is alleged to have occurred in the course of the earlier trial. Not only could it not have been the subject of a charge at that trial, but it is a crime wholly different and it is libelled as having taken place at a different place and on a different date. In *Fraser*, 1 Irv. 66, Lord Justice General McNeill points out (at p. 73) that a person may be tried if he has never been in jeopardy for the offence with which he is charged; and in *Dorward v. Mackay*, 1 Coup. 392, Lord Neaves refers (at p. 397) to the 'plain identity' of charges which is needed if the maxim is to apply. The panel here has never been in jeopardy for any offence libelled as having been committed in the High Court at Glasgow on March 1, 1966 and I can find no identity between the present charge and the charge of murder of which he was acquitted. Evidence will no doubt be led tending to show that, as is set out in the indictment, he did in fact assault and stab Malcolmson, but that seems to me to be of no more avail to the panel than it was in *Cobb or Fairweather* and *Stewart*. It is identity of the charges and not of the evidence that is the crucial factor. In my opinion, the plea that the panel has tholed his assize clearly fails."

LORD WHEATLEY: "I now turn to examine Mr Bennett's argument that what the Crown proposed to do in this case, namely lead evidence of the assault on Malcolmson by the panel, was contrary to equity, natural justice and criminal practice in Scotland.

In the first place he argued that humane considerations should preclude the panel from being exposed to the de facto ordeal of having to undergo what was tantamount to a second trial of having assaulted and stabbed Malcolmson. A corollary of this was that if he was convicted of the present charge, he would suffer the de facto guilt of the original charge of which he had already been acquitted. Yet the second trial, which brought about this unfortunate result, would take place at a later date, when the dice might be more heavily loaded against the panel. The original jury would have had the advantage of evidence which was fresher in the minds of witnesses; evidence vital for the defence might not be available at the second trial; real evidence might be lost or destroyed; the Crown might have obtained further evidence in the interval which strengthened the Crown case; and the second jury might have read the previous case in the press, to the detriment of the panel.

Once again Mr Bennett's argument proceeds on a misconception. The points which he made might have had validity if what was being considered was whether the panel should be charged again with the crime of assaulting and stabbing Malcolmson. What in fact will be investigated at the trial on the present indictment is whether the panel committed perjury at his original trial. If in the establishment of an essential part of that charge the Crown are in a better position—or a worse position—than in a previous trial when an entirely different charge was being investigated, that seems to me to be a matter of no relevance so far as the competency of the second charge is concerned, or of the evidence adduced in support of it. The issue in the present case is the truth or otherwise of the allegation that the panel committed perjury on the occasion libelled, and I do not see why the evidence on that issue should be circumscribed because some of the facts relevant to the charge were the subject matter of a jury's verdict on a previous occasion in relation to an entirely different charge.

So far as criminal practice in Scotland is concerned, this can only date back in this context to 1898, when the Criminal Evidence Act of that year came into operation. As far as I know, Mr Bennett was correct in saying that this was the first time within that period that an accused person has been charged with perjury in relation to his denial on oath in the witness box that he had committed the offence with which he was charged. If it has been a practice in the past not to charge an accused with perjury in such circumstances, this is not a practice which has been hallowed by our criminal courts. The Lord Advocate is master of the instance in criminal proceedings and if such a practice has existed, it is a practice of Lord Advocates and not of the Court. With the discretion which is vested in him in these matters, there is no reason why a Lord Advocate should not decide in a particular case to depart from a practice which his predecessors have observed, and indeed circumstances may arise when he may feel that in the public interest it is his duty to do so. The Court cannot interfere with that discretion—it can only hold that a particular charge libelled is incompetent or irrelevant on some legal ground. If the charge is competent and relevant, as I consider the present one to be, it is not in my opinion open to the Court to refuse to entertain it because the Lord Advocate has in his discretion departed from the practice of his predecessors. I accordingly do not consider that this point has any substance.

Mr Bennett in his final submission seemed to accept that his argument on practice had little validity and switched his argument from practice to equity. If the Crown were right, he argued, then every accused person who gave evidence to the effect that he did not commit the offence libelled against him was liable to be charged with perjury at the discretion of the Lord Advocate, irrespective of whether he was convicted or acquitted of the original offence. One result of this would be that every innocent accused would have to decide whether he dared go into the witness box to deny the offence with which he was charged, because, if the prosecution witnesses were believed, he was liable to find himself charged with perjury. This seemed to me to be an unrealistic plea to extremities, and to ignore the whole basis of our system of public prosecution in Scotland, which has its ultimate foundation in the person, in the impartiality and in the discretion of the Lord Advocate. This system has stood the test of time and, while it remains, there is no reason to suppose that the standards of fairness, impartiality and equity will be relaxed. Extreme cases may be conjured up, but the proper exercise of his discretion by Her Majesty's Advocate in Scotland is the guarantee against excesses and abuses or unfairness, injustice or inequity in bringing prosecutions. I do not consider that the fears expressed by Mr Bennett have any foundation in the normal case. On the other hand, if his argument is sound to the extent that no such prosecution could be taken for perjury irrespective of the circumstances, however blatant they may be, then the administration of justice could easily fall into disrepute. Considerations of equity operate in different ways, and while our Courts have always been jealous to protect the legitimate rights of individuals and to see that the individual is not exposed to injustices, they have a duty towards the general public and the maintenance of a proper standard of justice. To give a general immunity to accused persons to commit perjury, however blatant, and perhaps even publicly boast of its success, would only bring the law into disrepute. To fetter the Lord Advocate in his right to prosecute for perjury in what he conceives to be appropriate circumstances would in my view be doing something contrary to the public interest. If it were otherwise, and by Mr Bennett's submission was well-founded, there would be a bonus for successful perjury or subornation of perjury, and the administration of justice might be openly flouted without redress. I do not consider that the decision which I have reached or my reasons therefor will lead to the wholesale prosecutions for perjury which Mr Bennett envisaged, or place an accused person in the normal case in the dilemma which he postulated. In my opinion the discretion of the Lord Advocate will confine such charges to those cases where the public interest seems to require that a prosecution should proceed.

In the whole circumstances, therefore, I would repel the objections tabled on behalf of the panel and pass the indictment for trial."

Objections to competency and relevancy repelled.

NOTE

Individuals such as Cairns are rarely prosecuted for perjury, but in this case there would have been **17.14** good evidence that the denial of murder was false, had the perjury trial proceeded. In fact the accused died before the trial diet. A similar conclusion on the point raised in this case has been reached by the English courts: *D.P.P. v. Humphrys* [1977] A.C. 1, HL. For a highly unusual case where a man charged with driving while disqualified and without insurance changed his plea to guilty after cross-examination and was later charged with (and convicted of) perjury in his own defence, see *Milne v. H.M. Advocate*, 1995 S.L.T. 775. (The report of this case at 1995 S.C.C.R. 751 contains a useful extract from the sheriff's remarks at the sentencing stage.)

# 4. Offences involving convicted persons

## A. Harbouring or concealing a convicted person

### Miln v. Stirton
### 1982 S.L.T. (Sh.Ct) 11

The accused was charged that she did harbouring and concealing her husband at the **17.15** matrimonial home, "knowing that there was an extract conviction warrant outstanding for his apprehension, and this she did in an attempt to defeat the ends of justice". The accused took pleas to the relevancy and competency of the complaint, arguing in relation to the latter that the libel did not set forth an offence known to the law of Scotland.

SHERIFF ISOBEL POOLE: "... It was contended for the accused that the libel did not set forth facts which constituted a crime at common law or a contravention of an Act of Parliament applicable to Scotland, and *esto* that if it did, it lacked specification and was irrelevant. In short, it was no crime in the law of Scotland for a wife to harbour her husband and thus attempt to defeat the ends of justice. In support of that proposition solicitor for the accused cited Alison, I, 669; Hume, I, 46, 47; *Encyclopaedia of the Laws of Scotland,* VII, 697; Clive and Wilson, *Husband and Wife*, p. 376; Gordon, *Criminal Law* (2nd ed.), p. 685. For the Crown, the procurator fiscal disputed that proposition and contended that since the days of Hume and Alison the status of a wife had changed. In this case the prosecution was based on an extract warrant for payment of a fine and did not result from hot pursuit, where a man runs to his house after committing a crime of the nature discussed in the authorities. He also referred to the case of *John and Mary Hamilton* (1849) J. Shaw 149. The solicitor for the accused in reply, referred to the case of the *Hamiltons* as supporting his contention.

I took the case to avizandum in order to consult the authorities cited to me and to consider the question further.

The Scottish authorities in my view showed that, whereas being a married woman in itself did not alter the capacity of a person to commit a crime, in certain cases the law recognised that, in relation to her husband, a married woman's responsibility was different from that of other persons. The question of a married woman in relation to her husband seems to have been considered, firstly, where she harboured her husband, secondly, in prosecutions for reset or theft where the stolen goods were found in the matrimonial home and, thirdly, in the law of evidence as to whether she could be a competent or compellable witness.

The earliest Scottish reference I traced was to the *Regiam Majestatem* and *Quoniam Attachiamenta* (1609 ed.), where it is stated, referring to the statute of King William c. 19, that: 'the wyfe is nocht oblisched to accuse hir husband; nor to disclose his thift or felonie; because scho hes na power of hir selfe'. Had that remained the sole reason for a wife's special position in relation to her husband's crimes I might well have been persuaded that the Crown's contention was well founded.

However, Sir George Mackenzie, in *The Laws and Customs of Scotland in Matters Criminal* (1678 ed.), at XX.II.2., stated when discussing reset: 'It may be inferred that the lodging a kinsman, a wife or husband's entertaining one another, will not infer recept, because that is presumed to be done rather, out of love, than avarice or dole ... which was extended ... to a Mistris concealing her sweet-heart; In all such cases the receptors are only to be excused, if they communicat not in the Theft, for else they are to be punished as Thieves, for that is not the effect of love, but of fraud.' Later, when in discussing prison breaking in chap. XXII he stated: 'But I have seen that sisters have assisted their brothers, and wives their husbands, to escape, even for crimes, without being punished ... the receptors of such near relations are conniv'd at so gently is the law, and so much it both follows and pardons nature'.

Turning to Hume and the passages relied on by the solicitor for the accused, Hume fully discussed the question of the capacity of a wife, while discussing other defences such as minority—as did Mackenzie. He pointed out that, unlike the law of England, there was no presumption that the wife committed crimes out of dread of her husband and said: 'And truly, for my own part, I see nothing exceptionable in this disposition of our practice: because it will ordinarily happen, that the spouses mutually confirm each other in their profligacy; or if there is seduction in the case, it may as well be on the part of the woman as the man. The utmost lenity, therefore, to which our Judges might incline, would be to excuse the wife for venial trespasses or petty crimes, to which her obedience of his orders may have constrained her; and to mitigate her sentence for the more grave offences, if, in the circumstances of the case, it is presumable that she is the less guilty of the two .... Last of all, it is not to be imagined, that the wife shall in any case be held guilty, or be implicated as art and part of the husband's crime, by affording him that harbourage or concealment and comfort after the fact, which the feelings of nature and duty require of her at that season of terror and distress, when her fidelity has become his only refuge. And indeed, it is not to be presumed that she has it in her power, if she were so disposed, to refuse him this assistance' (Hume on *Crimes* (Bell's ed.), I, 49). I considered that it was significant that Hume, having effectively rejected the view that a wife had no criminal capacity of her own, made an exception where she was merely harbouring or concealing her husband.

Further, in Alison's *Criminal Law* (I, 668), it is stated: 'Nothing is better established in our practice, than that the authority or coercion of the husband is no palliation for the commission of crimes by the wife, who is presumed to have at least such freedom of action left as to be capable of resisting the temptations to crime, of whatever sort they may be.' And at p. 669: 'A wife shall not be held answerable for harbouring, concealing or comforting, her husband, even after the commission of the greatest crimes; and if any crime with which she is charged appears to have flowed from such a motive, she shall be absolved for its commission. By the first principles of Nature, a wife is bound to protect, defend, and cherish her husband in all circumstances, and not the less so because he has been involved in crime and has no refuge but in her affection and fidelity'.

From the passages cited it can be seen that Mackenzie, Hume and Alison were not saying that a wife had no criminal capacity, because of a husband's potestas, but that, for reasons of the law of nature, she was in a different position quoad her husband than were other persons.

Given that a distinction was drawn between English and Scottish criminal law on the subject of a wife's capacity, I referred to English criminal law for comparative purposes. In Hale's *Historia Placitorum Coronae* (1736 ed.) at VII.3.6 it is stated: 'If the husband commit a felony or treason and the wife knowingly receive him, she shall neither be accessory after as to the felony, nor principal as to the treason, for such bare reception of her husband for she is *sub potestate viri,* and she is bound to receive her husband; but otherwise it is, of the husband's receiving a wife knowingly after an offence of this nature committed by her.' Further, Blackstone, in his *Commentaries on the Laws of England* (10th ed.), vol. IV, chap. 2, said: 'The principal case where the constraint of a superior is allowed as an excuse for criminal misconduct, is the subjection of the wife to her husband ... in some cases the command or authority of the husband, either express or implied, will privilege the wife from punishment, even for capital offences. And other civil offences against the laws of society by the coercion of her husband; or even in his company, which the law construes a coercion; she is not guilty of any crime; being considered as acting by compulsion and not of her own will, which doctrine is at least a thousand years old in this kingdom, being to be found among the laws of King Ina the West Saxon.' Chapter 57 of the laws of King Ina in its Latin translation in the *Leges Anglo-Saxonicae* (1721 ed.) stated: 'Si maritus aliquid depraedetur, & persuadeat ad id uxorem suam, & deprehensus fit in eo vir, tunc suam partem compenset ille, excepta uxore, quoniam ipsa superiori suo obedire debet.' Vide, also, Russell on *Crime* (12th ed.), vol. 1, pp. 94–95 and the reversal of that presumption, by s.47 of the Criminal Justice Act 1925. That appeared indeed to be a different approach from that followed in Scotland.

I was unable to trace recent reported decisions where the law has been judicially considered in Scotland. Clive and Wilson in their *Husband and Wife* (1974) at pp. 376–377 considered the effect of marriage on the law of reset and harbouring in the criminal law and concluded that: 'the essence of the rule is simply that in a conflict between conjugal and public obligations the law in this case, as in certain of the rules on evidence, allows the conjugal obligations to prevail. The family is *pro tanto* preferred to the state'. See also Gordon's *Criminal Law* (2nd ed.) at p. 1685.

There have been reported decisions in the last two centuries over the question of reset. In *Clark v. Mone,* 1950 S.L.T. (Sh.Ct) 69 the sheriff-substitute (Cullen) held that a wife was protected even where, as in that case, she was wearing a suit in the street, which she knew her husband had been convicted for stealing six months previously. The sheriff-substitute apparently believed that he was following the passages in Alison cited *supra*, although, with respect to that decision, I would suggest that what Alison and the other writers were concerned to show was that: 'A wife is not in the ordinary case held guilty of reset if she conceal property to screen her husband, without proof of active participation.' In the case of the *Hamiltons* already referred to, Lord Justice-Clerk Hope directed a jury, in a case where a wife was found with part of the stolen proceeds on her:

'that it would not be enough, to infer that she was guilty, if after the offence had been committed, she endeavoured to assist her husband in avoiding detection by concealing the article.' She was in fact assoilzied simpliciter. In *Harris Rosenberg and Alithia Barnett or Rosenberg,* Brown 367, a case of wilful fire-raising, the jury apparently took the view that Mrs Rosenberg had been acting under her husband's influence, but found that to be mitigatory rather than exculpatory. That decision clearly followed the Scottish rather than the English approach to a woman's criminal capacity. For completeness, I also referred to the obiter dicta of Lord Dunedin in the case of *H.M. Advocate v. Camerons* (1911) 6 Adam 456 at pp. 487–488. Lord Dunedin, during his direction to the jury on the question of concert added; 'If what he [the husband] really did was that at a late period—that is to say, after the simulated theft—he only learned of the scheme then, and did what he did do after that time to screen his wife, then no doubt he has been guilty of an offence against the law, for it is an offence against the law to screen the guilty'. Lord Dunedin's remarks were obiter, and one does not know whether he had applied his mind fully to the subject. In any event, that was not the question I had to decide here.

The third area where the position of a spouse has, at common law, been different from that of other persons was that the spouse of an accused person was not a competent witness. That has been eroded by statute, particularly for the protection of the family as against an accused spouse (Walkers on *Evidence,* pp. 376, 377).

The Thomson Committee's very recent report, and the Scottish Law Commission's Memorandum on Evidence (September, 1980) were available to me for a clearer statement of the law and the issues involved behind that law. In particular both bodies would have in mind that a wife's position in law as a persona had changed. Both agreed that, although the balance was now in favour of the spouse being a competent witness, he or she should not be compellable in all cases: 'We think that social considerations should remain paramount.' That view has been enacted by s.29 of the Criminal Justice (Scotland) Act 1980.

I considered, but rejected, the procurator fiscal's second contention that *esto* harbouring and concealing a husband *per se* was not a crime known to the law of Scotland, the present circumstances libelled were distinguishable. I was persuaded that the principles laid down by the authorities that I have referred to applied to the present case. Having further considered, therefore, the argument to the competency of the libel of the complaint before me, I rejected the Crown's contention as ill-founded in law and upheld the accused's plea to the competency."

## B. Escaping from lawful custody

**17.16**  Quite apart from the crime of prison breaking, there are situations where escaping from custody will itself be criminal.

### H.M. Advocate v. Martin and Others
1956 J.C. 1

**17.17**  A prisoner escaped from a working party outside the prison. He and two others who assisted him were charged with attempts to defeat the ends of justice. All three objected to the relevancy of the indictment.

LORD CAMERON: "It was admitted by Mr Elliott that a criminal libel, to be relevant, does not require to name a specific crime or be stamped with any particular *nomen juris*.

Nevertheless he maintained that the facts set out must be such that, if proved, they would infer the commission of what is already recognised as a crime by the law of Scotland. Much of Mr Elliott's very careful argument was devoted to demonstrating what he maintained to be the limits of the well-recognised offence of prison-breaking, but the accused in this indictment are not charged with prison-breaking, nor are they charged with assisting or being art and part in the crime of prison-breaking. I was referred to the closing passages in Baron Hume's work on Crimes and Alison's Principles and Practice of the Criminal Law, dealing with the offence of prison-breaking. It is significant that both those writers were writing at a time when modern ideas of places of confinement for persons under sentence had not been developed and when prisons, in the words of Alison, were in the main 'gloomy abodes'. Further, it must be borne in mind that the chapter in Hume (vol. i, p. 401) which deals with breaking prison comes in that section of his work which relates to the category or the genus of offences against the course of justice of which the offence of prison-breaking is itself a species or illustration, and the chapter in Alison's Principles (vol. i, p. 555) which deals with the same matter begins with the significant opening paragraph which I quote: 'The act of prison-breaking, however natural to the inmates of those gloomy abodes, cannot be overlooked by the law, as being a violation of the order and course of justice, and a direct infringement of regulations essential to the peace and well-being of society.' So it is quite plain that the writer of those words regarded the act of breaking the type of prison in use when he wrote as being an act in violation of the order and course of justice, and an act in direct infringement of regulations essential to the peace and well-being of society. In an authority which is familiar, to which Mr Elliott drew attention, the case of *Bernard Greenhuff* in 1838, 2 Swin. 236, Lord Cockburn in his dissenting judgment, upon which Mr Elliott laid much reliance, said this (at p. 274): 'I may only say at present, that I am far from holding that the Court can never deal with any thing as a crime, unless there be a fixed nomen juris for the specific act, or unless there be a direct precedent. An old crime may certainly be committed in a new way; and a case, though never occurring before in its facts, may fall within the spirit of a previous decision, or within an established general principle. And such is the comprehensiveness of our common law, that it is no easy matter for any newly invented guilt to escape it.'

In my opinion, the offence of escaping from lawful custody, as lawful custody is nowadays defined in section 12 of the Prisons (Scotland) Act of 1952, is an offence which falls within an established general principle, even although there might not be a precise precedent directly in point. However that may be, I do find that in the recent case of *Turnbull*, 1953 J.C. 59, an indictment libelled that an accused person formed a criminal purpose to hinder the course of justice by effecting the escape from lawful custody of Hugh Kelly Mannion, then a prisoner in the prison of Edinburgh, by fraud and the uttering of forged documents. The relevancy of that indictment was challenged, and was sustained by the Lord Justice-Clerk, and therefore it seems to me that, even if a precise precedent were required for the form of indictment which appears in this case, the case of Turnbull does provide such a precedent. But, in my opinion, there can be no doubt that to form a criminal purpose to hinder the course of justice by effecting escape of a prisoner from lawful custody, or by taking other steps to frustrate the ends of criminal justice, is and always has been a crime by the common law of Scotland, and that those who aid the escape are equally guilty with the prisoner who by their aid escapes from lawful custody. What is libelled in this indictment is very plainly an attempt to hinder the course of justice and frustrate its ends by seeking to assist a sentenced criminal to escape or evade the penalty of his crime. That is an offence against public order and against the course of justice. If I am correct in that view—and if I am wrong, I can be corrected—then that is the end of the matter, because what is libelled here is but one species of a well recognised and undoubted genus of crime.

Mr Elliott, however, argued strongly that to hold the facts in this libel relevant would be to designate a new crime in the law of Scotland and that, because nowadays the High Court has no power to declare new crimes, his plea to the relevancy must be sustained. I express no view upon the very careful and interesting argument which Mr Elliott submitted on the extent to which the power to declare new crimes still remains with the Courts to-day, or, if it does, in what circumstances it could or should be exercised, because I do not find it necessary to invoke that power in determining the relevancy of this indictment."

Objections to relevancy repelled.

## 5. CONTEMPT OF COURT

**17.18** Contempt of court in Scotland can arise either at common law or under the Contempt of Court Act 1981. The 1981 Act is primarily concerned with the circumstances under which an individual or organisation may be found to have committed a contempt by publishing material likely to prejudice the course of justice in 'active' proceedings (whether civil or criminal). While it also makes some changes to the common law regarding contempt "in the face" of the court by restricting the powers of punishment by the courts to a maximum of two years' imprisonment, such contempts are otherwise unaffected by the 1981 Act. Indeed, although proceedings for contempt in relation to publications are generally brought under the Act, the common law in this area has not been entirely superseded by the legislative provisions.

Contempt of court, whether at common law or under the 1981 Act is not a criminal offence in the sense that that term is ordinarily understood. Rather it is an offence *sui generis*.

It would not, therefore, be correct to bring a summary criminal complaint (or, presumably an indictment) against an offender alleging that he or she has committed a contempt of court. On this, see *Dyce v. Aitchison*, 1985 S.L.T. 512.

All courts, both civil and criminal have an inherent common law power to punish for contempt, whether in the face of the court. The High Court has no jurisdiction in relation to contempt of the Court of Session: *Cordiner, Petr*, 1973 S.L.T. 125. A finding of contempt in the High Court may be appealed against by an application to the *nobile officium* of that Court: *Wylie and Another v. H.M. Advocate*, 1966 S.L.T. 149. A finding of contempt in the sheriff or district courts may be suspended by the High Court: *Butterworth v. Herron*, 1975 S.L.T. 56.

## A. Contempt in the face of the court

**17.19** This may arise in a number of ways. The following—showing disrespect for the court by misconduct in court, failing to appear, prevarication—are all examples of this type of contempt.

### (a) Misconduct in court

**Dawes v. Cardle**
1987 S.C.C.R. 135

**17.20** An accused was convicted of contempt of court. She appealed by bill of suspension.

LORD JUSTICE-GENERAL (EMSLIE): In this bill of suspension the complainer is Ruth Dawes and we have before us the bill and answers for the Crown and, surprisingly enough, we have a luxury which we don't usually enjoy, namely, a report from the sheriff. The bill is brought to challenge a finding that Miss Dawes was in contempt of court and also a sentence of imprisonment which was imposed upon her in the circumstances set out in the bill. It seems that there was a demonstration at an establishment in the district of the particular court and the result of that was that thirty-eight people including the complainer were charged and were brought to court. From the various papers which are in front of us we are told that Miss Dawes and two others were the first to arrive at the court but the last to enter it and it appears from what the sheriff tells us, and this is supported by the answers for the Crown, that the appellant and her friends declined to leave the cells until the sheriff himself convened the court in the cell area and persuaded them to stop what they had been doing and to come into the courtroom to allow matters to proceed. It is said, and this of course is said in the report by the sheriff, that during the day they had been singing in the cells to his annoyance. In any event, when Miss Dawes was brought into court and was faced with a particular charge she was asked to plead guilty or not guilty, and she did neither. What she did do was to make a statement accepting that she had been on the land in question and that she did not move on when told. At this point, to return to the sheriff's report, he took the view that that explanation was neither plea of guilty nor a plea of not guilty and he attempted to explain to her that that attitude was not acceptable. At this point, according to the sheriff, Miss Dawes raised her voice, eventually shouting at him and making it impossible for him to take any kind of plea from her. We are told that she was clearly not prepared to listen to any advice the sheriff could give her and that her attitude was one of open defiance and disrespect to the bench, and here comes the reason for a finding of contempt which is the subject of this bill:

'I regarded her behaviour then, coming on top of her earlier behaviour, as the last straw. If I had not taken a firm step at that stage it would have been an indication to the many protesters who were in the public benches that they could defy the court with impunity.'

The sheriff then went on to explain why he selected an immediate sentence of detention.

In support of the bill, counsel has addressed us upon a number of matters which are neither supported by averments in the bill nor included in the plea. So far as the bill is concerned the only averment which appears to be critical of the conduct of proceedings in the court is that the sheriff continued the case without plea and that he should have afforded to the complainer the opportunity of legal advice if he had doubts about the plea being offered by her. Upon these scanty averments the submission was that the sheriff's behaviour in general was oppressive, constituting injustice, and that his prejudice was demonstrated by his visit to the cells. By that time he had formed an attitude which showed that he was prejudiced against this particular complainer. There were difficulties, it was said, in taking pleas from other accused and in some cases the sheriff had given advice about the way to tender a plea to competency and relevancy based upon an attack on the *vires* of certain byelaws. In this case, said counsel, the sheriff did not offer the same advice to this complainer and what is more, other accused, particularly the two accused who had remained with the complainer in the cells, had not been found in contempt whereas this particular complainer had been singled out for that particular treatment. On the whole the case was presented as one redolent of oppression and prejudice.

We have no hesitation in saying that these submissions, which have no foundation in the averments of the bill, have not persuaded us that the finding of contempt should be disturbed. On the account given by the Crown of the events of that day, supplemented by the account given by the sheriff himself, we are not in the least surprised that he decided to make the finding of contempt which he did. It is nothing to the point that he might also have found others in contempt. We are satisfied that the finding of contempt in the case of this complainer was properly made, at least it was a finding the sheriff was well entitled to make and that is as far as we need to go. Let us for the avoidance of doubt say this. It is true that the sheriff does not appear to have given advice about the possibility of tendering a plea to the competency and relevancy to this complainer. The fact that he did so in other cases, of course, is readily to be explained by the fact that they had made it clear that they were objecting to the *vires* of the byelaws. This complainer said nothing to suggest that that was her attitude, and as we have already explained her only response to a request to state her position in the matter of plea was to make the statement which is recorded in statement 2 of the bill.

On the whole matter, accordingly, we shall refuse to pass the bill on the merits and in the matter of sentence we shall quash the sentence of twenty days' imprisonment which was in any event incompetent and in the events which have happened substitute an admonition."

Conviction upheld, but sentence quashed as
incompetent.

Notes

**17.21**  1. The sentence of 20 days' imprisonment was incompetent because Miss Dawes was under 21 and the sheriff had not obtained the necessary pre-sentencing information required by section 207 of the Criminal Procedure (Scotland) Act 1995, as applied to sentences for contempt by section 15(3) of the Contempt of Court Act 1981. See also *Dyce v. Aitchison*, 1985 S.L.T. 512, s*upra*.

2. In *Wilson v. John Angus & Sons*, 1921 S.L.T. 139 a person summoned for jury duty in a civil case arrived in court in an intoxicated condition and allowed himself to be empanelled as one of the jury. After he had sat on the jury for several hours, during which time his behaviour was such as to demonstrate that he was not in a fit state to act as a juror, and that he made it difficult for his fellow jurors to give proper attention to the case the Lord Ordinary dismissed him from the jury, and subsequently found him to be in contempt of court and fined him £25. See also, in this respect, the case of *H.M. Advocate v. Yates* (1847) Arkley 238.

3. In any case of contempt, before making a finding of contempt or imposing any punishment, it is essential that the court should give the individual in question an opportunity to explain his or her conduct. In *Royle v. Gray*, 1972 S.L.T. 31 the Lord Justice-General (Emslie) made the following observations on this issue:

> "The complainer in this bill was held to be in contempt of court by the police judge at Dundee and was fined the sum of £10. The alleged contempt is said to have consisted of the complainer shaking his head while sitting in the public benches during the course of the address of the procurator-fiscal to the Bench at the conclusion of the evidence. We have not the slightest hesitation in finding that, on no reasonable view could the conduct of the complainer have constituted contempt of court and for that reason alone we are for passing the bill. But the matter does not end there. Having decided that what the complainer did probably constituted a contempt of his court, the magistrate failed to afford to the complainer any opportunity to explain what he had done and for that reason also, since it militates against fairness and justice, we would have been for passing the bill.
>
> This is the latest of a number of instances drawn to our attention recently in which magistrates in burgh courts have purported to exercise the court's power to punish contempt in circumstances which do not amount to contempt at all. It appears to be necessary, therefore, to emphasise once again that the court's undoubted power, and a necessary power at that, to punish contempt should be exercised with the greatest of care and the wisest discretion. Having said that, it is desirable to draw once again to the attention of those who may be in doubt about the position, what was said by Lord President Normand in the case of *Milburn*, 1946 S.C. 301 (1946 S.L.T. 219), in that passage of his opinion which appears on p. 315 of the report. The quotation which should be remembered is this:—'It has been said over and over again that the greatest restraint and discretion should be used by the court in dealing with contempt of court, lest a process, the purpose of which is to prevent interference with the administration of justice, should degenerate into an oppressive or vindictive abuse of the court's powers.'"

See also in this respect, *Morrison v. Jessop*, 1988 S.L.T. 86, *Caldwell v. Normand*, 1993 S.L.T. 489 and *Macara v. Macfarlane*, 1979 S.L.T. 26.

## (b) Failure by witnesses, parties or legal representatives to appear

**17.22**  A not uncommon practical difficulty faced by the courts is that of cases which cannot proceed because one of the central 'actors' in the proceedings has not appeared before the court. This may arise where the accused, or a witness, or even one of the legal representatives is not present. The power to punish for contempt in such circumstances is clearly seen as being a useful tool to be used by the court in an appropriate case. However, some important questions must be determined before the court adopts the fairly drastic measure of punishing for contempt. In what circumstances will failure to appear amount to contempt? Suppose, for example, that the failure to appear is due to circumstances beyond the control of the individual? And even if this is not the case, is a distinction to be drawn between those who fail to appear in wilful defiance of the court, and those who fail to appear through carelessness, inadvertence or even simple fecklessness?

## Pirie v. Hawthorn
### 1962 S.L.T. 291

An accused person was found to be in contempt for failing to appear before the court when his **17.23** case was called, although he had been properly cited to appear. He appealed by bill of suspension against the finding of contempt.

LORD JUSTICE-GENERAL (CLYDE): "This is a somewhat unusual case. It comes before us under a bill of suspension following upon a complaint charging the complainer Pirie with using a motor vehicle without "L" plates displayed, the complainer being the holder only of a provisional licence and not yet having passed his driving test.

The case was called in the Sheriff Court in Stirling on May 2. The complainer did not appear when the case was called at the Court in the morning. The case was consequently and quite properly continued till 2.15 p.m. that day and the police got in touch with the complainer's home by telephone. The complainer was seventeen years of age. He works on a farm with his father. When he had received the complaint originally he handed it to his father. He did not read the details requiring him to appear on the morning of May 2 in the Sheriff Court in Stirling. On that particular morning his father and he were engaged in a difficult calving at the farm and we are informed that in the anxiety and worry connected with that operation the father omitted to inform his son of the time when he had to be in the Sheriff Court. When the police telephoned, the father promised that his son would be in Court at 2.15 p.m. His son duly appeared in Court then when the case was called. He pled guilty and was fined £4. No question arises in regard to that matter. The acting sheriff-substitute, however, then proceeded to find the complainer guilty of contempt of court and to impose a penalty of £15 or sixty days. It is quite clear from the statement in the bill and the answers by the procurator-fiscal that no question of any defiance of the authority of the Court was involved in the failure to turn up in the morning or in the conduct of the complainer in the afternoon and, it is, moreover, clear that there was no wilful failure on the complainer's part to attend at the proper time. For that failure was obviously attributable to the understandable forgetfulness on his father's part because of the calving operations at the farm that day.

Two highly technical arguments were advanced to us in regard to the conviction for contempt. [His Lordship discounted these and continued:]

Apart from the technical contentions, however, that were put forward the question still remains whether contempt of court was made out. In the circumstances, as I have narrated them, it appears to me that there was no justification at all for holding contempt to be established in the present case. There was no wilful defiance of the Court at any stage and no wilful failure to appear at the proper time or to explain why appearance was not made in the morning. The essential element in contempt of court is thus absent.

In these circumstances, in my view this conviction cannot stand and I move your Lordships that we grant the bill."

Bill of Suspension passed; finding of contempt quashed.

## NOTES

See also *Morrison v. Jessop*, 1988 S.L.T. 86.          **17.24**

This decision appears to suggest that that wilful defiance of the authority of the court is an essential aspect of contempt of court, and it has been said explicitly elsewhere that this is an essential element of contempt of court (*McMillan v. Carmichael*, 1994 S.L.T. 510, at 511). See, however, *Caldwell v. Normand*, 1993 S.L.T. 489, where C had slept in and missed a deferred sentence hearing at the district court. The High Court suspended the finding of contempt on the basis that the justice had followed the wrong procedure in making an immediate finding of contempt and immediately sentencing C, but did not appear prepared to say that oversleeping and inadvertently missing a court hearing could not amount to contempt. See also the following case concerning contempt by legal representatives who have failed to appear before the court to represent their clients, and which holds that contempt of this sort may be committed recklessly, or even carelessly.

Muirhead v. Douglas<br>1979 S.L.T. (Notes) 17

**17.25** A solicitor was convicted of contempt of court. He appealed by bill of suspension.

LORD CAMERON: "The matter arose out of a summary criminal proceeding in which the complainer had been instructed on behalf of one accused of a contravention of section 3 of the Road Traffic Act 1972. A plea of not guilty had been tendered on the client's behalf and trial fixed for September 7, 1978 on which date the complainer attended and, on his client's behalf, adhered to the plea of not guilty. The trial was one of three listed for that day's sitting of the court and was second on the list. The time the plea was tendered was approximately 11.15. Thereafter the complainer left the court and proceeded to his office, which is said to be only 100 yards or thereby from the court buildings. According to the complainer's own statement in the bill he asked the agent instructed in the first trial for its likely duration, and was given an estimate of two hours. In point of fact the trial came to a premature conclusion by the tender of a plea of guilty after the evidence of only two of the Crown witnesses. The complainer alleges that he left 'instructions' that he was to be 'contacted on the conclusion of the first trial'. It appeared that the 'instructions' related to a private arrangement with the court officer. It was said in the bill, but not admitted by the respondent, that this is in accordance with 'normal procedure at Dunfermline Sheriff Court'—though nothing is said as to the proximity of other solicitors' offices to the court buildings.

Shortly after his return to his office the complainer narrates that, as he was going on holiday the next day, he would take the opportunity of conducting some other outstanding professional business. This was the making of an adoption report to the court in his capacity as *curator ad litem*. To do this he required to visit the proposed adopters who (it is said) 'lived close to his office' and obtain the information he required for his report. The complainer does not say for what length of time he expected to be absent on this inquiry, but does state he informed his receptionist he was leaving the office. He does not however state that he informed her where he was going, how long he would be absent, or what to do if a message came from the sheriff court intimating that the first trial was concluded. The complainer goes on to aver that he returned shortly after noon but 'due to an oversight' did not inform his receptionist of the fact. Having dictated his report the complainer avers that he returned to court at about 12.25 and then learned that the first trial had come to a premature conclusion at about 12.05. During the complainer's absence a message was received by the receptionist, who merely noted that the complainer was to 'contact the Respondent's office on his return'. She did nothing more as, according to the complainer, she had not been informed that there was any urgency in the matter.

The complainer avers that when he appeared before the sheriff at approximately 12.30 he informed him of what had occurred and made full apology. After hearing explanation and apology the sheriff found that the complainer's absence was 'in itself contempt of court' and convicted him of that offence and imposed a fine of £25. According to the complainer's statement in the bill: 'the sheriff indicated that in his opinion the Complainer should not have absented himself from his office while there was a possibility that he might be recalled to court'. The complainer's version of the events of that morning so far as his own actions are concerned is not admitted by the Crown, but its general accuracy was not challenged.

On that assumption of fact the complainer pleads that his actings did not amount in law to a contempt of court and that in any event the sentence was harsh and oppressive.

In moving that the bill be passed and the conviction quashed, counsel for the complainer submitted that, while his conduct might call for a measure of censure, it did not fall within the category of contempt of court. For conduct to be held as contempt it was necessary that there should be an element of deliberation, of wilful disobedience of an order of court or non-compliance with its requirements or a deliberate intention to interfere with or obstruct the course of justice. In the circumstances disclosed in the bill and not challenged or contradicted by the Crown, this was no more than a case of carelessness and a series of unfortunate mistakes in which the element of intent or wilful disregard of the interests of the court was absent. Such a failure as was here disclosed could therefore not be characterised as 'contempt of court'. Carelessness as disclosed here, while deserving of censure, was not contempt in the absence of any fact indicative of an intention to ignore or flout an order of court or hinder the due administration of justice. In support of this wide proposition, counsel relied on the case of *Pirie v. Hawthorn*, 1962 S.L.T. 291; 1962 J.C. 69 and the judgment of Lord Clyde. That was a case in which a youth of 17 was charged on summary complaint. He failed to appear at the trial diet when his case was called, and in respect of that failure was held as in contempt in spite of the explanation tendered for his initial failure. This was to the effect that the complaint had been handed over to the accused's father, who forgot to inform the accused of his obligation to appear on the date and at the time stated in the complaint. The reason for the omission was said to be pressure of urgent farming duties. The Lord Justice-General said (1962 S.L.T. at p. 293): 'There was no wilful defiance of the Court at any stage and no wilful failure to appear at the proper time or to explain why appearance was not made in the morning. The essential element in contempt of court it thus absent.' On this statement two comments may be made. First, the sole allegation against the complainer was of wilful disobedience to the order of the court. When this was shown to be erroneous there was no alternative allegation against him of carelessness or reckless disregard of the citation and it was in these particular circumstances that Lord Clyde made these observations. In the second place, as Lord Clyde had only recently given judgment in the case of *Stirling v. Associated Newspapers Ltd*, 1960 S.L.T. 5; 1960 J.C. 5, in which no issue of wilful or deliberate attempts to interfere with or pervert the course of justice was raised, it is clear that in the case of *Pirie* the court was not limiting and was not intending to limit the boundaries of contempt in the way for which counsel contended. Further, recent decisions such as that in *Hall v. Associated Newspapers Ltd and Others*, 1978 S.L.T. 241, make it abundantly clear that the element of deliberate intent to cause prejudice to the administration of justice is not an essential element in contempt. Indeed, counsel was constrained to concede that there could be such a degree of carelessness or disregard of obligation leading to interference with or material disruption in the course of the administration of justice as to be equiparated with wilful or deliberate disobedience or interference. I therefore think that the complainer's argument so far as based on the judgment in the particular circumstances of *Pirie v. Hawthorn* is unsound.

It would be undesirable in this case to endeavour to define the limits of conduct which may be held to constitute contempt of court. The variety and quality of the acts or omissions which in particular cases may fall within that description are not capable of precise delimitation or formulation. On the other hand it may be said that where there has been in fact a failure to obey or obtemper an order or requirement of a court such a failure demands satisfactory explanation and excuse, and in the absence of such may be held to constitute a contempt of court of varying degree of gravity. I can see no reason in principle and there is certainly none in authority, for an assertion that failure due to carelessness alone may in no circumstances constitute contempt of court. The question in my opinion is essentially one of fact and circumstances in which the position and duties of the party alleged to be in contempt are necessarily material considerations. . . .

In my opinion the bill should be refused.

NOTE

Since *Muirhead*, there have been several other instances in which a solicitor has been made the **17.26** subject of contempt proceedings: see *Macara v. Macfarlane*, 1980 S.L.T. (Notes) 26 and *McKinnon v.*

*Douglas*, 1982 S.C.C.R. 80, in both of which the solicitors concerned successfully appealed by bill of suspension against their respective "convictions". In *Blair-Wilson, Petr*, 1997 S.L.T. 621 a solicitor was held in contempt by a sheriff on the ground that he had refused to comply with a ruling made by the sheriff. The High Court held that while "there is no doubt that a sheriff is entitled to find a solicitor in contempt of court if he makes a ruling in clear terms which the solicitor then refuses to comply with or obey" the sheriff had not, in this instance, made a clear ruling with which it was the solicitor's duty to comply. In failing to comply with the views expressed by the sheriff, which related largely to how the solicitor should conduct the case for the defence, the solicitor was not in contempt. In reaching this conclusion the court, under reference to *McMillan v. Carmichael*, 1997 S.L.T. 511 and *Ferguson v. Normand*, 1994 S.L.T. 1356, confirmed that "an intention to challenge or affront the authority of the court or to defy its order is a necessary element without which it cannot be held that a contempt of court has been committed .... The question of law which is raised in all cases of alleged contempt is whether the conduct in question amount to wilfully defying the court or intending disrespect to the court or acting in any way against the court."

## (c) Prevarication by witnesses

**17.27** Prevarication by a witness is another common basis of an allegation of contempt of court. Prevarication arises where the witness refuses to answer (or demonstrates an obvious unwillingness to answer) questions put by prosecution, defence or the court.

In *McLeod v. Speirs* (1884) 5 Couper 387 Lord Young described prevarication in the following way (at page 405): "It is a loose and indefinite term, which may mean many different things short of perjury; the general idea which it conveys is manifest unwillingness candidly to tell the whole truth, fencing with questions in such manner as to show reluctance to disclose the truth, and a disposition to conceal or withhold it."

Hume (i, 380) describes it in the following terms:

"Before I close this chapter, it will not be amiss to add a word or two concerning prevarication upon oath, or the wilful concealment of the truth; which is next in degree to perjury, and seems chiefly to differ from it in the inferior boldness of the culprit; who though desirous to mislead the Judge, and make a false impression, has rather chosen to compass this object in the way of an artful and tricking oath, than by the direct averment of utter falsehoods; or if he has ventured on any such, has not persisted in them till the close of his oath. This sort of guilt is chiefly to be gathered from the evasive and equivocal answers of the witness, the inconsistency of the different parts of his oath, and his affected ignorance and want of memory, with respect to things which he cannot but know; more especially if he is at last driven from all these shifts, and is constrained to emit a true, though, taken on the whole, an incoherent and a contradictory deposition."

The above passage was accepted by the court in *Childs v. McLeod*, 1980 S.L.T. 27 as setting out the elements of prevarication. See also Alison, 1, 485.

It is important that the court (and the prosecutor) in dealing with a case of prevarication (or perjury) should avoid taking steps which might prejudice the right of the accused during whose trial the alleged prevarication or perjury occurs to a fair trial. A finding that witnesses for the defence have prevaricated, or committed perjury, if it becomes known to the jury, has the capacity to prejudice the jury who may reach the conclusion that because certain witnesses are lying, or deliberately refusing to testify, the accused are guilty of the offences with which they are charged. On this problem, see *Hutchison v. H.M. Advocate*, 1983 S.L.T. 233.

Section 155(1) of the Criminal Procedure (Scotland) Act 1995 provides that if a witness in a summary prosecution—(a) wilfully fails to attend after being duly cited; or (b) unlawfully refuses to be sworn; or (c) after the oath has been administered to him refuses to answer any question which the court may allow; or (d) prevaricates in his evidence, he shall be deemed guilty of contempt of court "and be liable to be summarily punished forwith for such contempt of court". In *Grundy v. Procurator Fiscal, Airdrie*, April 11, 2001, *unreported*, it was argued that the power of summary punishment was incompatible with the witness's right to a fair trial under Article 6(1) of the European Convention on Human Rights. A person allegedly guilty of contempt ought not to be dealt with summarily by the court in which he or she was allegedly in contempt since that court would not be an impartial tribunal as required by Article 6(1). Sheriff I. C. Simpson ruled that contempt proceedings were "criminal" for the purpose of Article 6(1), but went on to hold that proceedings under section 155 would not be incompatible with Article 6(1) "provided that the action taken is immediately necessary to enforce the authority of the court or to secure the proper running of the trial in progress". In the absence of such circumstances, however, the Sheriff thought that the section should not be invoked since, "[t]aken at face value it offends against the principles of having an independent and impartial tribunal, the ability to call witnesses and cross-examine contrary evidence, and the presumption of innocence" [para. 20]. See also, in this connection, *R. v. MacLeod*, Court of Appeal (Criminal Division) November 29, 2000.

The special case of a journalist who refuses to answer questions on the basis that he or she wishes to protect his sources was considered in *H.M. Advocate v. Airs*, 1975 S.L.T. 177. In that case, two persons were charged with conspiracy to further the aims of the Scottish Army of the Provisional Government by criminal means. A was a Daily Record reporter who had made contact with extremist Scottish nationalist organisations as part of his job. At one point, he arranged to meet a member of the group. When asked in court to identify the man whom he had spoken to, he refused on the basis that he had given an undertaking not to reveal whom he was meeting. Proceedings were subsequently brought against A for contempt. The High Court found that he had been in contempt of court, observing (at p. 180) that:

> "In our opinion there is a legal duty to answer any question which is both competent and relevant. A relevant question is one the answer to which a judge or jury is entitled to hear in reaching the decision upon the facts, although the precise weight and bearing which ought to be attached to the answer can never be determined until all the evidence has been led. Indeed it is hard to figure any circumstances in which a relevant question could, in course of a trial or proof, be judged unnecessary or not useful but, if such circumstances were ever to arise, and they could only be quite exceptional circumstances, there remains a residual discretion in the court to excuse a witness, who seeks to be excused upon a group of conscience, from answering a relevant question in accordance with his legal duty."

This decision must be read subject to section 10 of the Contempt of Court Act 1981, which gives some **17.28** protection to editors and publishers. The section provides: "No court may require a person to disclose, nor is any person guilty of contempt of court for refusing to disclose, the source of information contained in a publication for which he is responsible, unless it be established to the satisfaction of the court that disclosure is necessary in the interests of justice or national security or for the prevention of disorder or crime." So Mr Airs would still be guilty of contempt at common law today in the same circumstances, for the section has no applicability to the situation in which he found himself, there having been no prior publication of the information he sought to conceal. But the section does introduce the "necessity" test into Scots law.

2. Section 10 has relevance beyond criminal proceedings, and may be invoked in the context of civil proceedings where a party wishes to protect the confidentiality of his or her sources of information. In *X. Ltd v. Morgan-Grampian Ltd* [1991] 1 A.C. 1, Lord Bridge commented (at p. 195):

> "It will not be sufficient, *per se*, for a party seeking disclosure of a source protected by section 10 to show merely that he will be unable without disclosure to exercise the legal right or to avert the threatened legal wrong on which he bases his claim in order to establish the necessity of disclosure. The judge's task will always be to weigh in the scales the importance of enabling the ends of justice to be attained in the circumstances of the particular case on the one hand against the importance of protecting the source on the other hand. In this balancing exercise it is only if the judge is satisfied that disclosure in the interests of justice is of such preponderating importance as to override the statutory privilege against disclosure that the threshold of necessity will be reached."

In *Pearson v. Educational Institute of Scotland*, 1998 S.L.T 189 the Inner House expressed the view that in terms of section 10, "the public interest is limited to the communication of information in good faith and not maliciously. There is no good reason to confer public interest protection on an anonymous informer who is actuated by malice." (*Per* Lord Nimmo Smith at p. 195.)

Where a person is required to make disclosure of his or her sources, and in particular where a journalist is required to do so, there will be an interference with that person's freedom of expression in terms of Article 10(1) of the Convention, which must be justified in terms of Article 10(2). If it is not so justified, then there will be a violation of Article 10. See, in this respect, *Goodwin v. United Kingdom*,

European Court of Human Rights (1996) 22 E.H.R.R. 123, R.J.D. 1996-II, No. 7 (a sequel to *X. Ltd v. Morgan-Grampian Ltd*, *supra*).

For further discussion of section 10, see, *inter alia*, *John v. Express Newspapers* [2000] 3 All E.R. 257; *Saunders v. Punch Ltd (Trading as Liberty Press)* [1998] 1 W.L.R. 986; [1998] 1 All E.R. 234.

A witness is of course entitled to the privilege against self-incrimination and will not be guilty of contempt in refusing to answer a question the answer to which is privileged: *Bacon, Petr*, 1986 S.C.C.R. 265.

## (B) Protection from prejudicial pre-trial publicity

**17.29**      The Scottish courts have traditionally taken a strict line on publications which are considered to be likely to prejudice the right of an accused to a fair trial, and, indeed, the rights of parties to civil litigation. The extent to which those responsible for the publication of an article which it is alleged has the capacity to prejudice the impartial administration of justice was at one time determined by the common law. See, for example, *Stirling v. Associated Newspapers Ltd and Another*, 1960 S.L.T. 5, *Atkins v. London Weekend Television Ltd*, 1978 J.C. 48, *Hall v. Associated Newspapers Ltd and Others*, 1978 S.L.T. 241, *H.M. Advocate v. Stuurman and Other*, 1980 S.L.T. 182, *H.M. Advocate v. George Outram & Co. Ltd*, 1979 S.L.T. 13.

This issue is now largely, but not exclusively, dealt with under the Contempt of Court Act 1981.

A detailed exposition of the provisions of the 1981 Act is beyond the scope of this work. In outline, however, section 1 of the Act sets out the "strict liability" rule in relation to publications whereby conduct may be treated as a contempt of court as tending to interfere with the course of justice in particular legal proceedings regardless of intent to do so.

The rule is limited in scope. Under section 2 it applies only to "publications" and only to publications which create "a substantial risk that the course of justice in the proceedings in question will be seriously impeded or prejudiced": section 2(2). For these purposes a "publication" includes any speech, writing, broadcast or other communication in whatever form, which is addressed to the public at large or any section of the public: section 2(1). Furthermore, it only applies to proceedings which are "active" at the time of the publication: section 2(3). For these purposes criminal proceedings, in general become "active" when the subject of the proceedings has been arrested without warrant, where a warrant for his arrest has been granted, when a warrant to cite has been granted, or on the service of a complaint or indictment. Such proceedings remain active until they are concluded by acquittal or by sentence, or by any other verdict, order or decision putting an end to the proceedings, or where the proceedings are discontinued by operation of law: Schedule 1. There are analogous provisions for appellate proceedings.

It is a defence under section 3 if the person publishing a publication covered by the strict liability rule, having taken all reasonable care, did not know, and had no reason to suspect that the relevant proceedings were active. It is a defence under section 3 for the distributor of a publication to which the strict liability rule applies if, having taken all reasonable care, he did not know, at the time of distribution that it contained matter of the kind struck at by the strict liability rule. A person is not guilty of contempt of court under the strict liability rule in respect of a fair and accurate report of legal proceedings held in public, published contemporaneously and in good faith: section 4.

A publication made as or as part of a discussion in good faith of public affairs or other matters of general public interest is not to be treated as a contempt of court under the strict liability rule if the risk of impediment or prejudice to particular legal proceedings is merely incidental to the discussion: section 5. (*Cf. Atkins v. London Weekend Television Ltd*, 1978 J.C. 48.)

The Act has been discussed in the following Scottish authorities: *H.M. Advocate v. Scotsman Publications Limited and Others*, 1999 S.L.T. 466; 1999 S.C.C.R. 163; *H.M. Advocate v. Newsgroup Newspapers Limited*, 1989 S.C.C.R. 156; *H.M. Advocate v. Caledonian Newspapers Limited*, 1995 S.L.T. 926; *H.M. Advocate v. Scottish Media Newspapers Limited & Others*, 2000 S.L.T. 331; *Abdelbasset Ali Mohamed Al Megrahi and Al Amin Khalifa Fhima v. Times Newspapers Limited and Others*, 2000 J.C. 22; *H.M. Advocate v. Caledonian Newspapers Limited*, 1995 S.L.T. 926; *Robb v. Caledonian Newspapers Ltd*, 1994 S.L.T. 631; *Muir and Others v. British Broadcasting Corporation*, 1997 S.L.T. 425.

# INDEX

Location references are to page numbers. References to Hume are to principle extracts.